CLIMATE OF THE ARCTIC

Edited by:

Gunter Weller and Sue Ann Bowling

Published by the Geophysical Institute
University of Alaska, Fairbanks, Alaska.

Twenty-Fourth Alaska Science Conference

Fairbanks, Alaska

August 15 to 17, 1973

Sponsored by the American Association for the Advancement of Science

and the American Meteorological Society

FOREWORD

The climate is a unifying theme of interest and concern to all who live and work in the Arctic, and especially for scientists. This concern may be expressed in the study of climate in its own right—how the Arctic gains and loses heat through the year, the role of the polar region as a "heat sink" in the general circulation of the atmosphere, the causes and effects of sea ice, the past, present and future glaciation of this polar region, etc. It may focus on the impact of man upon climate—deliberate experiments in weather modification or the inadvertent effects of cities and industries. Or it may lead to studies of the effects of climate upon man—how he designs cities, runs a railroad, raises crops and manages wildlife, maintains radio and other communications, provides health care, obtains recreation and develops natural resources in an environment of low temperature and perennial snow cover. Or scientists may study how other species have responded to climate—the gradual adaptations of plants and animals, their mutual relationships and relation to the surroundings, the seasonal biological cycle of growth and decay, and the naturalization of native man to the Arctic. The common links is climate. Some study it. Some study its effects. We all live with its consequences.

It is particularly appropriate that the *Climate of the Arctic* conference should have been held in the arctic (more precisely, the sub-arctic) locale of Fairbanks. Moreover, the Geophysical Institute has maintained an active and increasing interest in climate research over the years. For these reasons, and for the reward that such a meeting always brings in fresh contacts with interstate and overseas visitors, it was a pleasure to host the conference and see its proceedings brought to publication.

KEITH B. MATHER
Director

Geophysical Institute
University of Alaska, Fairbanks

PREFACE

The Alaska Science Conference is held annually under the auspices of the American Association for the Advancement of Science. In 1973, the 24th Alaska Science Conference took place from August 15 to 17 on the campus of the University of Alaska, in Fairbanks. It was sponsored by both the American Association for the Advancement of Science and the American Meteorological Society. The theme of the conference was the Climate of the Arctic, its physical causes, biological effects and consequences to man. Of the more than 100 papers presented in three simultaneous sessions, 56 have been selected for publication in this volume. Although most of these papers deal with the climate of the Arctic and its hemispherical or global implications, four papers deal specifically with the Southern Hemisphere and Antarctica. These latter papers were included in this volume because of the interest in comparing climates in both polar regions, but did not justify adopting the title "Climate of the Polar Regions" for the volume.

Financial support for the conference was provided by the University of Alaska, the Rockefeller Foundation and the National Science Foundation. The conference was organized by staff members of the Geophysical Institute of the University of Alaska; particular thanks are due to Mr. Daniel C. Crevensten, Mrs. Ann Shilling and Miss Karen Brown.

Publication of this volume was possible through financial assistance from the Office of Climate Dynamics of the National Science Foundation.

GUNTER WELLER
SUE ANN BOWLING

November, 1974

The Poles: A Key to Climate Change

I want to start by saying that it is really very exciting for me to come back here to College, Alaska and the University of Alaska after more than 10 years, to see the natural beauty of the place and, perhaps more striking, the changes that have taken place in such a short time here at the University of Alaska. I have always been strongly drawn to the Arctic and I am very glad that in the new field in which I have become deeply involved, namely climate theory, it is entirely legitimate to be interested in the polar regions. So this combination of climate theory and polar research is going to be an important theme of my talk today.

Actually, the title of the present conference is "Climate of the Arctic." I have had some difficulty explaining just what we are going to be talking about here. For instance, there was a young lady sitting next to me on the plane last Sunday, and when I told her I was going to go spend some time at the University of Alaska talking about the climate of the Arctic; she said, "Well, climate of the arctic—so what's new? It's cold in winter, isn't it? and there arc mosquitos in summer, right? So, what are you going to spend three days talking about?"

I think that this audience hardly needs to be told what we are going to be talking about—climatic theory, climatic change, and the polar regions. And of course when we say "climatic theory," we are going far beyond the subject that we used to talk about in our high school geography classes, where we memorized the climate of various regions of the world. We see the atmosphere, the oceans, the ice masses, and the land as an interacting, dynamic system; it is sensitive to changes, it has instabilities built into it that we do not understand very well, and yet in spite of these instabilities that we know must exist (and we will hear a lot about them in the next three days) there has been a sort of uneasy equilibrium which we would dearly like to understand. If there had not been such an equilibrium during the last 4 billion years while life was spawning on this earth, we would not be here. If somehow this equilibrium had been pushed too far, we might have been pushed, as was our sister planet Venus, into something called a "runaway greenhouse effect," which would have left our planet much too hot to live on; and if we had lost the water vapor, as Mars has done, we would have a sort of wall-to-wall desert on the earth.

Obviously, neither of these has happened; we are very fortunate. We would like to know why the earth's climate has remained as almost-steady as it has, and of course we would also like to know why it varies within certain ranges which are big enough to cause very large changes on the face of the earth.

In addition to this growing interest in climatic theory as a fascinating subject scientifically, we're aware of the fact that man is now beginning to play a role in determining climate. Some of his activities are on a large enough scale so that we can no longer neglect him in the climate equation. If we look to the future (and we do not have to look too far) we can see that he will soon be a very large factor in modifying the earth's climate. This, too, is cause for a growing interest in the subject. If we find that he is going too far too fast, maybe we can do something about it, *if* we can understand what the factors are.

This new interest in climate is the reason that when the Global Atmospheric Research Program (or GARP, as it is called for short) was conceived there were two objectives: One objective was to make better forecasts of the weather on a timescale of a week or so, and the second objective of GARP was to understand the physical and dynamical basis of climatic change. Another evidence of this concern was the fact that the Study of Critical Environmental Problems (SCEP) of 1970 and its sequel, the Study of Man's Impact on the Climate (SMIC) of 1971, which some of the people in this room took part in, attracted so much attention—not just among scientists, but among the lay public. In fact, the "SMIC Report," as it was called, was distributed to all the attendees at the U. N. Conference on the Environment in Stockholm the following year.

We saw climatic theory featured at the last AGU meeting in Washington, where a great deal of attention was given by several of the sections to climatic theory. We note that the subject of a recent National Academy of Science's Report is Weather and Climate Modification. We note also that the Joint Organizing Committee of GARP has in its wisdom decided that the second objective of GARP is so important that it is going to have another major international meeting next summer, held at the same place, Skeparholmen, where the first meeting on GARP took place, devoted *entirely* to the second objective of GARP. We've been focusing on better weather prediction, and now we are going to start focusing on better climate prediction, although we know that it's a very remote goal.

Now, the other subject of this Conference is, of course, polar or arctic research. Climatic research is bringing the polar regions into a new perspective, because they are not only sensitive indicators of climatic change, with temperature fluctuations three to five times larger than the temperature fluctuations of the hemisphere as a whole, but because they also have large masses to ice in them that respond to temperature changes in a special way. They have what you might call "flip-flops" in the climate circuit. It has been noted for a long time that in geological history we seem either to have frozen poles or not to have frozen poles, and there does not seem to be any condition in between that was stable. When one pole freezes the other pole seems to freeze shortly thereafter. (I am now speaking on a geological time-scale of millions of years.) Ninety per cent of the time in the earth's history the planet has apparently had unfrozen poles, and, as we know, they are frozen now, so you could say that we are in an anomalous condition as seen in the geological record of the earth. So the polar regions, because of their sensitivity and their control of the climate are a very important aspect of climate research.

Of course even before this particular point was appreciated the poles had attracted scientists. The International Polar Years are probably well known to all of you, even those who are not necessarily experts in polar research. The First International Polar Year was 1882–83 and the second polar year was 1932–33, and they were extraordinary examples of international collaboration in geophysical research. They were mostly inspired by people who were interested in the earth's magnetic field and the upper atmosphere, but we learned a great deal generally about the poles in addition to aeronomy. Then there was the International Geophysical Year, or IGY, which came 25 years after the Second Polar Year and further extended the concept of international collaboration in geophysical research to include the whole world and, as we remember, the space around it.

Perhaps of even more importance to the meteorology and climatology of the arctic were not these international polar years but the extraordinary and daring voyages of a few explorers who went into the Arctic and into the Antarctic and made observations there. One of the most notable is the voyage of the Fram, organized by F. Nansen, and of the Maud, when H. Sverdrup, whom many of us remember well, spent two years making classical studies of the boundary layer of the Arctic Ocean, and of the interactions between the atmosphere, the ice and the water, while the Maud drifted half-way across the Arctic Ocean.

More recently, starting in the 1930's, the Soviet Union began putting manned stations out on the Arctic icepack, and this adventurous and important program is continuing to this day. It's interesting that the present head of the Soviet Hydrometeorological Service, Academician Feodorov, did his first research out on the arctic icepack. And many of you will remember as an exciting adventure story the

time the Russian ice station drifted all the way across the Arctic Ocean and came out into the Atlantic, the crew of this station being rescued as their ice floe was drifting out into the warmer waters and melting away. I think this must go down as one of the more exciting adventures in the annals of science.

In late 1940's a young Lt. Colonel in the U. S. Air Force, Joseph Fletcher, as commander of the weather reconnaissance squadron based at Eielson Air Force Base, just next door here, noticed that on a radar scope there were large patches in the vast ice pack of the Arctic Ocean over which the weather reconnaissance flights were made that seemed to have a different character and were recognizable flight after flight as they flew over them. He was able to persuade his bosses in the Air Force to organize a small expedition to go out and land on one of these large patches, and the one that he chose and landed on turned out to be the largest that we have found so far. Now it's called T-3, although many of us still like to call it Fletcher's Island. It is a major geophysical and biological observing station, and it drifts 'round and 'round in the Arctic Ocean making a circuit every few years. It is right now north of Ellesmere Island, I believe, and stalled on its circuit, but it has houses and laboratories and will undoubtedly be reoccupied from time to time as a major meteorological and oceanographic observing station.

I had the privilege of visiting T-3 more than 10 years ago, when it was a few hundred miles from Point Barrow, and I was impressed by the fact that there were so many different kinds of scientist on it. There was a Japanese oceanographer and a German biologist that I remember particularly, and this leads me to the subject of the interdisciplinary nature of polar and climate research. It is not only international, but interdisciplinary.

The mix of scientists which has to deal with the Arctic is a very large mix, and I will mention just a few of the aspects of it that I happen to know about: For instance there is the Tundra Biome Project, which is supported largely by NSF and with Canadian participation, and in which the ecology of a large area of the Alaskan North Slope is being studied before man has a chance to muck it up. (There is much more that can be said about this man-in-the-Arctic question, but that's not the subject of my talk.)

Another aspect of the biology of the Arctic, which I think is more well-known to those of us who have gotten into the question of climate, is the study of past climates. From studies of glacial moraines and tills, from the studies of the pollen found in lake sediments, and from the studies of the cores that are brought up from the ocean bottom, biologists have been able to determine past temperatures. The distribution of ancient pollen tells what kind of trees were there, from which we can deduce something about temperatures; the distribution of foraminifera or "forams" for short, tells something about the climate that was over the ocean when these little creatures died and sank to the bottom. In addition to these biological studies, there are more subtle evidences from which past climates can be deduced, and I was thinking here, for example, of the paper that will be given on ancient tree lines in northern Canada and Alaska. The ancient tree lines obviously give an idea of the past climates.

Now, how do we date these things? Here another group of scientists comes in—the radioisotope people, who look at the isotope ratios of samples and can determine from the concentration ratios of various natural radioactive isotopes how old the sample is. Another powerful isotopic technique is measuring the ratio of certain stable isotopes, especially oxygen-18 and oxygen-16. It turns out that the temperature at which a rain drop was formed and fell to the ground will be reflected in this ratio. So this way we can get another handle on the past temperatures.

I wouldn't dwell so long on this matter of paleoclimatology if it weren't for the fact that it demonstrates that this subject needs scientists of many disciplines learning to talk together; they all have to be in the same business. I was impressed by how many biologists and ecologists attended the last American Geophysical Union Meeting in Washington D. C. for instance, since they knew that climate would be a matter of considerable interest at that meeting.

We have taken a step recently to formalize the international mechanisms that are responsible for coordinating polar research. In 1972 the Soviet Union proposed to the GARP Joint Organizing Committee that GARP include a sub-program of intensive study of the polar regions called "POLEX." The Soviet proposal stressed the heat balance of the poles, since this is in fact the key role that the poles play in determining climate. They proposed that emphasis be on the arctic as far as POLEX was concerned. They also proposed in their initial proposal some other things which are of more practical long-term interest, such as trying to figure out what the effect would be of diverting some of the rivers that flow northward into the Arctic Ocean. Now POLEX is under active discussion; here in the U. S. there is a committee of the National Academy of Sciences chaired by

Professor Richard Goody of Harvard, which is working to prepare the U. S. plan for participation in POLEX. Several members of the U. S. POLEX Committee, including myself, are here, and we are planning to talk this week with Professor Borisenkov, Director of the Main Geophysical Observatory in Leningrad, who is trying to prepare the Soviet plan for POLEX in conjunction with us. We are also working very closely with our Canadian colleagues in planning the POLEX program.

One of the key aspects of our plan for POLEX is bound to be our ice-dynamics program which is already underway, sponsored by the Office of Polar Programs of the National Science Foundation, a program that is known as AIDJEX; you will hear more about it, I am sure, in the course of this meeting. It is a joint U. S.-Canadian program which will be an important part of POLEX.

I feel that one of the things that we have to study in connection with the U. S. contribution to polar research and POLEX is better use of meteorological and earth resources satellites for polar regions research. Here again you will hear about some of the new advances in satellite observations of the polar regions at this meeting. I think we have only just scratched the surface and we have a ways to go before we can really get good polar observations.

Another aspect of POLEX that we will have to work on very hard is the boundary layer, the atmosphere-ocean-ice and snow interface in the polar regions. We need to know more about this in order to put this aspect of the atmospheric heat engine into our general circulation models, the models that we use to make weather predictions as well as climate predictions. So all of these things will be part of the POLEX program, and we are trying to put these together. Hopefully there will be an official plan for the international program of POLEX by some time next spring.

At this meeting, I think, we are taking part in an historic occasion; one that history will note as a junction between a long and distinguished tradition of polar research and a new thrust, a new direction of scientific endeavor in which the polar regions play their role as both indicator and controller of the world's climate.

William W. Kellogg
President, American Meteorological Society

CONTENTS

PART I: THE CHANGING CLIMATE

Late Quaternary Climatic Changes in the Norwegian and Greenland Seas*

THOMAS B. KELLOGG

*CLIMAP, Lamont-Doherty Geological Observatory, Palisades, New York 10964***

Abstract

Analyses of total carbonate and coarse fraction content in 29 deep-sea cores and faunal analyses of plank-tonic foraminifera in 7 cores provide climatic data for the past 150,000 years. These data show that tem-peratures have been much colder than at present for most of the past 150,000 years in the Norwegian and Greenland Seas. Only during the Eemian interglacial did temperatures moderate to about present levels. Quantitative paleo-temperature estimates, derived by applying the Imbrie & Kipp (1971) technique to seven cores, show that except for the Eemian and Recent interglacials, temperatures less than 0C in winter and 5C in summer prevailed throughout the region. This temperature regime is identical to that of the northwestern Greenland Sea today, where sea-ice is present during the winters. For about 100,000 of the past 127,000 years, therefore, ice has probably covered most or all of the Norwegian and Greenland Seas, at least during the winters.

The Norwegian Current, a branch of the Gulf Stream, is responsible for the relatively warm climate of Scandinavia at the same latitude where Greenland supports an ice cap. In addition, the Norwegian Current controls the present distributions of planktonic and benthonic foraminifera and the present extent of sea-ice cover. Based on faunal and sedimentary changes in the deep-sea cores, most of the past 150,000 years (at least) was characterized by a surface water circulation pattern in which the Norwegian Current was either much weaker or absent, thus allowing sea-ice formation throughout the region. The only exception to this observation occurs during the Eemian interglacial when conditions were comparable to those of the present.

---

1. Introduction

The Norwegian and Greenland Seas (referred to collectively in this paper as the "Norwegian Sea"), are bounded on the north by the Arctic Ocean, on the east by Spitsbergen, Norway and the Barents Sea, on the south by the Denmark Strait, Iceland, and the Iceland-Faeroe Ridge, and on the west by Greenland. Both Greenland and the Arctic currently experience climates that support ice.

The climatic history of the Norwegian Sea is im-portant for a number of reasons. 1) The present climate of Scandinavia depends on the transport of heat from the subtropic regions by the Gulf Stream and Norwegian Current. This pumping of heat toward the polar regions makes possible the temperate climate of Scandinavia at the same latitude where Greenland supports an ice cap. 2) The bottom water of the North Atlantic basin currently forms in the Norwegian Sea as warm saline Norwegian Current water cools and becomes more dense by evaporation. This extremely dense water overflows the Denmark Strait and Iceland-Faeroe Ridge to form Lower North Atlantic Deep Water (Dietrich, 1956a, 1956b) or Norwegian Sea Overflow Water (Worthington, 1970). 3) The region is an im-portant link between climatic studies in the Arctic Ocean (Bé, 1960; Clark, 1969, 1970; Darby, 1971; Ericson, *et al.*, 1964a; Mullen, *et al.*, 1972; Steuerwald, *et al.*, 1968; Steuerwald and Clark, 1972; and others), the North Atlantic (Bramlette and Bradley, 1941; Ericson, *et al.*, 1964b; McIntyre, 1967; Ruddiman, *et al.*, 1970; Sancetta, *et al.*, 1972; McIntyre, *et al.*, 1972; and many others), and climatic studies on the surrounding continents: Greenland (Dansgaard, *et al.*, 1971), Northern Europe (van der Hammen, *et al.*, 1971) and Scandinavia.

Norwegian Sea deep-sea sediments are relatively un-studied. A number of workers have dealt with the description of a fossil assemblage retrieved from one to several cores (Saito, *et al.*, 1967; Stadum and Ling, 1969; Bjørklund and Kellogg, 1972). Other workers have studied limited numbers of cores covering only small portions of the region (Böggild, 1907; Holtedahl, 1959; Ericson, *et al.*, 1964a; Olausson, 1972; Schreiber, 1967). The most comprehensive of these studies is the work of Ericson, *et al.*, 1964a. In 26 cores from the Norwegian and Greenland Seas, they noted the pre-dominance of "glacial-marine sediment" and suggested, on the basis of frequencies of foraminiferal species in six cores, that the last ice age ended 11,000 years ago in this region. Kellogg (*in press*) analyzed 34 surface-sediment samples and 6 cores spanning the past 150,000 years and made climatic interpretations based on fre-

* Lamont-Doherty Geological Observatory contribution #2172.
** Present address: Department of Geological Sciences, Brown University, Providence, Rhode Island 02912.

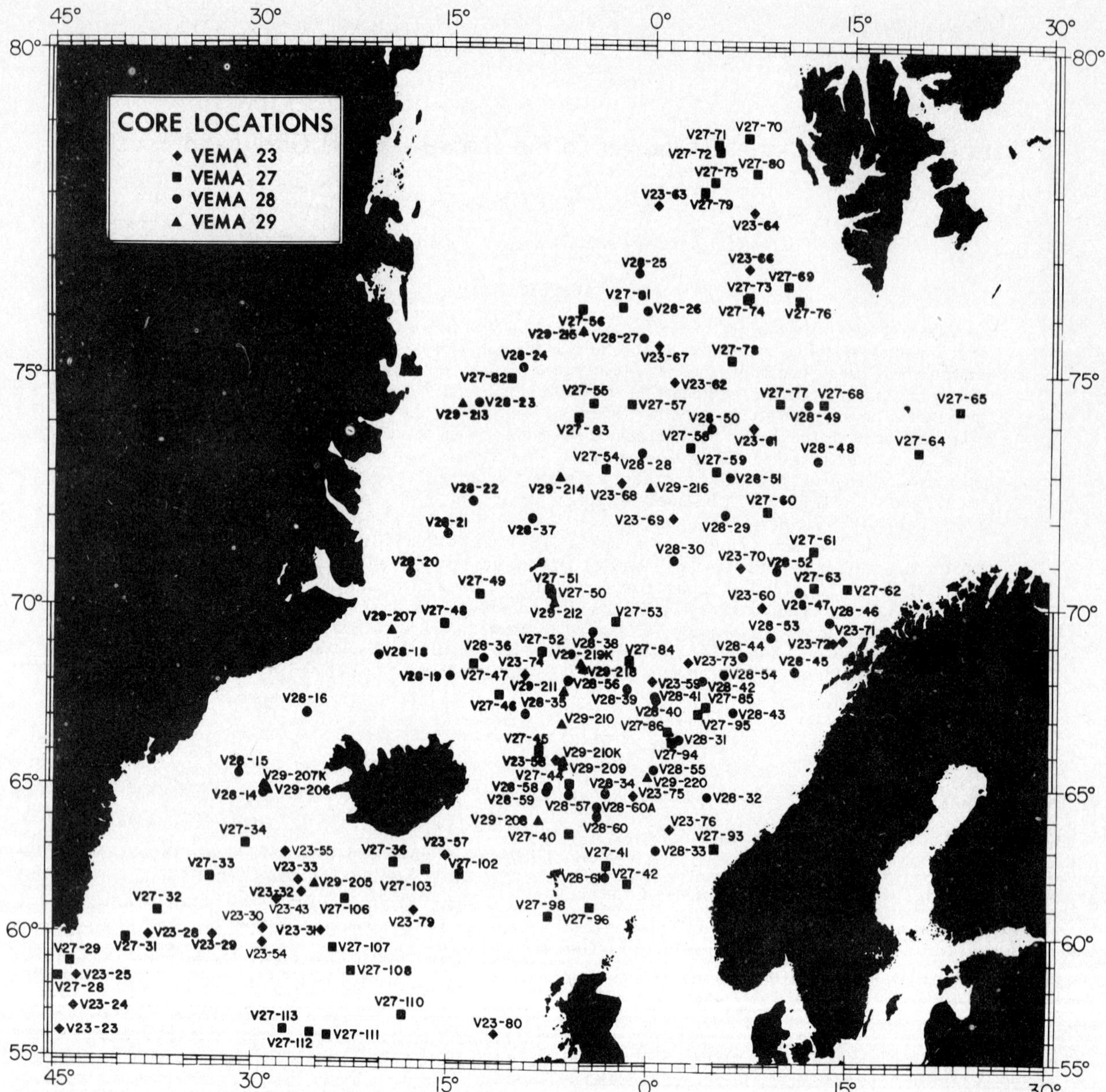

FIG. 1. Locations of cores taken in the Norwegian and Greenland Seas by R. V. Vema.

quencies of foraminiferal species. The present paper is a continuation of the work reported by Kellogg (*in press*). Many of the same samples are analyzed using different techniques.

The purpose of this work is to demonstrate the importance of the Norwegian Current for the present distribution of sedimentary types and faunal elements by study of surface sediments. Sedimentary and faunal parameters are then analyzed in the same six cores studied by Kellogg (*in press*) to show how climate has changed in the past. Quantitative estimates of the magnitude of the observed changes are made using the Imbrie and Kipp (1971) technique.

2. Surface sediments

Cores used for this study were taken by the Lamont-Doherty Geological Observatory research vessel Vema on cruises 23, 27, 28 and 29 during 1966, 1969, 1970 and 1972. Short gravity or trigger-weight cores (TW) obtained from the tripping mechanism of the longer piston cores were sampled in order to study the surface sediment, because the sediment-water interface in the tops of piston cores is commonly badly disturbed or lost during coring. These TW tops represent at most no more than the last 2000 to 4000 years of sedimentation (Imbrie and Kipp, 1971). 169 TW tops were analyzed for carbonate- and coarse-fraction contents. These

TABLE 1. Position and water depth (meters) for cores discussed in this paper.

Core No.	Latitude	Longitude	Depth (m)	Core No.	Latitude	Longitude	Depth (m)
V23 23	56 04.5N	44 33.0W	3292	V27 70	78 54.1N	7 03.2E	1300
V23 24	57 05.0N	43 26.0W	3475	V27 71	78 49.9N	4 37.9E	2439
V23 25	58 16.0N	43 10.0W	2958	V27 72	78 44.2N	4 38.1E	2343
V23 27	59 46.0N	39 25.0W	2774	V27 73	76 29.9N	7 02.8E	3089
V23 28	59 48.5N	37.52.0W	3102	V27 74	76 27.9N	6 54.5E	2778
V23 29	59 57.0N	32 51.0W	2186	V27 75	78 16.4N	4 26.4E	2412
V23 30	60 07.0N	29 09.0W	1139	V27 76	76 25.4N	10 48.0E	2113
V23 31	60 10.5N	24 37.0W	2178	V27 77	74 29.2N	9 30.6E	2395
V23 32	61 24.5N	26 01.0W	1329	V27 78	75 17.7N	5 56.5E	2765
V23 33	61 53.0N	26 23.0W	873	V27 79	78 07.1N	3 37.4E	2308
V23 36	63 13.1N	28 24.5W	1624	V27 80	78 23.5N	7 25.4E	2915
V23 43	61 23.1N	28 03.3W	1362	V27 81	76 14.8N	2 23.6E	3709
V23 54	59 49.7N	29 16.3W	1291	V27 82	74 59.6N	10 48.4E	2895
V23 55	62 51.8N	27 13.5W	1364	V27 83	74 11.6N	5 42.9W	3416
V23 57	62 47.0N	15 08.0W	1873	V27 84	68 37.7N	1 35.7W	3404
V23 58	65 46.0N	7 07.0W	1796	V27 85	67 21.7N	4 01.6E	1247
V23 59	68 02.0N	0 01.0E	3083	V27 86	66 36.4N	1 07.1E	2900
V23 60	70 03.0N	8 19.0E	2974	V27 88	60 24.0N	6 25.0E	845
V23 61	74 01.5N	7 23.8E	1928	V27 89	60 08.2N	6 05.5E	662
V23 62	74 54.0N	1 36.5E	3713	V27 90	59 54.7N	5 45.0E	499
V23 63	77 57.4N	0 12.2E	3050	V27 91	59 44.9N	5 31.4E	340
V23 64	77 51.7N	7 16.2E	2529	V27 92	59 54.7N	5 31.2E	342
V23 65	78 20.1N	15 12.0E	249	V27 93	62 56.1N	4 16.8E	786
V23 66	76 59.3N	7 04.9E	2941	V27 94	66 17.3N	1 29.5E	2781
V23 67	75 36.2N	0 17.0E	2511	V27 95	67 08.1N	3 28.8E	1250
V23 68	72 51.9N	2 29.9W	2450	V27 96	61 00.6N	4 20.3W	1138
V23 69	72 04.3N	1 24.0E	2246	V27 98	60 39.2N	7 25.5W	980
V23 70	70 59.1N	6 41.4E	3047	V27 102	62 07.7N	14 12.3W	1641
V23 71	69 15.7N	14 23.9E	1011	V27 103	62 21.6N	16 28.0W	2103
V23 72	69 14.4N	13 51.8E	2332	V27 106	61 13.7N	22 51.5W	1900
V23 73	68 32.8N	2 43.0E	2970	V27 107	59 27.4N	23 57.5W	2492
V23 74	68 11.2N	9 36.0W	1926	V27 108	58 32.8N	22 12.3W	2933
V23 75	64 48.0N	1 19.0W	2930	V27 110	56 53.6N	18 29.6W	1264
V23 76	63 39.0N	1 22.0E	1734	V27 111	56 03.9N	24 05.2W	2809
V23 79	60 56.0N	17 34.0W	2478	V27 112	56 07.6N	25 30.9W	3217
V23 80	56 09.7N	11 18.9W	2597	V27 113	56 09.8N	27 37.4W	2622
V27 28	58 11.2N	44 36.8W	2308	V28 14	64 47.0N	29 34.0W	1855
V27 29	58 54.1N	43 49.8W	1604	V28 15	65 17.0N	31 20.0W	1174
V27 31	59 40.7N	39 47.9W	2765	V28 16	67 06.0N	25 37.0W	955
V27 32	60 42.2N	37 16.5W	2953	V28 18	68 47.0N	20 46.0W	1326
V27 33	61 56.0N	33 16.3W	2946	V28 19	68 13.0N	15 16.0W	1374
V27 34	63 01.2N	30 57.3W	2283	V28 20	71 46.0N	15 30.0W	971
V27 36	62 26.9N	19 06.2W	1359	V28 21	71 46.0N	15 30.0W	971
V27 40	63 26.9N	6 07.8W	1652	V28 22	72 26.0N	13 39.0W	1284
V27 41	62 29.5N	3 15.8W	635	V28 23	74 31.0N	13 07.0W	2325
V27 42	61 50.5N	1 27.8W	954	V28 24	75 10.0N	10 52.0W	2459
V27 44	65 01.3N	6 13.2W	2772	V28 25	76 49.0N	1 20.0W	3136
V27 45	66 02.9N	8 35.5W	1038	V28 26	76 13.0N	0 42.0W	2089
V27 46	67 35.2N	11 31.2W	1728	V28 27	75 45.0N	0 53.0W	3700
V27 47	68 27.7N	13 32.5W	1717	V28 28	73 29.0N	0 50.0W	2288
V27 48	69 26.3N	15 53.9W	1017	V28 29	72 11.0N	5 16.0E	2547
V27 49	70 14.9N	13 04.0W	1392	V28 30	71 10.0N	1 37.0E	2915
V27 50	70 23.3N	7 45.3W	1076	V28 31	66 27.0N	2 10.0E	1679
V27 51	70 23.6N	7 47.1W	950	V28 32	64 47.0N	4 18.0E	929
V27 52	68 49.1N	9 19.6W	1624	V28 33	62 54.0N	0 35.0E	1170
V27 53	69 32.7N	2 49.1W	3124	V28 34	64 50.0N	3 35.0W	3217
V27 54	73 06.5N	3 42.7W	2834	V28 35	67 07.0N	9 34.0W	1376
V27 55	74 29.7N	4 39.4W	3519	V28 36	68 43.0N	12 43.0W	1816
V27 56	76 09.5N	5 23.9W	2736	V28 37	72 04.0N	9 04.0W	2395
V27 57	74 27.9N	1 11.4W	3605	V28 38	69 23.0N	4 24.0W	3411
V27 58	73 32.4N	2 39.8W	2745	V28 39	67 53.0N	1 56.0W	3374
V27 59	73 04.2N	4 49.2E	2299	V28 40	67 38.0N	0 15.0E	3517
V27 60	72 11.0N	8 34.8E	2525	V28 41	67 41.0N	0 14.0E	3545
V27 61	71 19.2N	12 04.1E	2299	V28 42	68 05.0N	3 51.0E	1515
V27 62	70 24.3N	14 47.2E	2428	V28 43	67 12.0N	6 10.0E	1259
V27 63	70 25.4N	12 04.6E	2725	V28 44	68 40.0N	6 37.0E	3032
V27 64	73 30.9N	19 59.9E	479	V28 45	68 20.0N	10 44.0E	914
V27 65	74 22.8N	22 58.5E	170	V28 46	69 42.0N	13 20.0E	2739
V27 66	71 59.8N	30 24.5E	336	V28 47	70 22.0N	16 00.0E	2088
V27 67	72 29.8N	36 59.9E	227	V28 48	73 20.0N	12 29.0E	1668
V27 68	74 30.0N	12 39.4E	2265	V28 49	74 29.0N	11 40.0E	2327
V27 69	76 41.9N	10 00.7E	2237	V28 50	74 00.0N	4 14.0E	3200

TABLE 1 (*continued*)

Core No.	Latitude	Longitude	Depth (m)	Core No.	Latitude	Longitude	Depth (m)
V28 51	73 03.0N	5 49.0E	3180	A152 84+	44 21.0N	30 16.0W	2750
V28 52	70 56.0N	9 23.0E	2714	A157 3+	50 56.0N	41 45.0W	4025
V28 53	69 17.0N	8 59.0E	3027	R9 7+	59 39.2N	22 46.2W	2770
V28 54	68 15.0N	5 22.0E	1825	RC9 225+	54 58.6N	15 23.5W	2334
V28 55	65 31.0N	0 12.0E	2886	SP9 3+	53 52.5N	21 06.0W	2743
V28 56	68 02.0N	6 07.0W	2941	SP10 5+	63 28.5N	0 04.0W	2012
V28 57	64 38.0N	11 09.0W	430	V16 227+	60 02.0N	50 50.0W	3305
V28 58	65 00.0N	7 49.0W	1360	V23 22+	54 12.0N	45 58.0W	3669
V28 59	64 52.0N	7 52.0W	2622	V23 81+	54 15.0N	16 50.0W	2393
V28 60	64 05.0N	4 02.0W	3244	V23 82+	52 35.1N	21 56.0W	3974
V28 60A	64 25.0N	4 02.0W	3231	V23 83+	49 52.3N	24 15.0W	3871
V29 206	64 54.3N	29 17.4W	1608	V23 84+	46 00.3N	16 55.0W	4513
V29 207	69 15.7N	19 30.5W	1461	V27 20+	54 00.0N	46 12.0W	3510
V29 207K	64 55.6N	29 20.1W	1686	V27 122+	48 17.7N	16 58.4W	4696
V29 208	63 58.0N	8 12.0W	1149	V29 178+	42 50.9N	25 09.3W	3362
V29 209	65 34.4N	6 29.2W	2688	V29 179+	44 00.6N	24 32.4W	3248
V29 210	66 43.5N	6 43.5W	2454	V29 180+	45 18.2N	23 52.4W	3102
V29 210K	65 36.6N	6 29.0W	2737	V29 183K+	49 08.3N	25 30.1W	3539
V29 211	67 47.4N	6 40.8W	2547	V29 184+	49 08.3N	25 30.1W	3556
V29 212	70 09.0N	7 20.7W	1447	V29 189+	52 22.0N	17 32.0W	3981
V29 213	74 21.2N	14 22.1W	466	V29 190+	52 40.0N	15 10.0W	1428
V29 214	72 58.1N	6 59.4W	2600	V29 193+	55 24.0N	18 44.0W	1300
V29 215	75 55.5N	5 07.0W	3118	V29 194+	57 00.2N	21 19.3W	2052
V29 216	73 48.5N	0 05.7W	2961	V29 198+	58 43.5N	15 33.8W	1122
V29 218	68 23.4N	5 25.6W	3351	V29 202+	60 23.0N	20 58.0W	2615
V29 219K	68 23.1N	5 27.6W	3325	V29 203+	60 48.4N	22 26.5W	2060
V29 220	65 10.5N	0 04.8W	2833	V29 205+	61 33.1N	25 07.2W	1368

cores provide excellent geographic coverage of the region (Fig. 1, Table 1).

Techniques

Samples were taken from the top centimeter of each trigger core. About 0.5 gram was set aside for carbonate analysis, the remainder was dried, weighed and then soaked in water containing a small amount of Calgon (sodium hexametaphosphate) to disaggregate the material. The sample was agitated sonically and washed on a 62 μm sieve. Both coarse and fine fractions were saved, and the coarse fraction was dried and weighed.

Carbonate analyses were made by the gasometric technique with an apparatus similar to that described by Hülsemann (1966). The accuracy of this technique is $\pm 3\%$ for samples containing more than 50% $CaCO_3$; for samples with less than 50% $CaCO_3$, uncertainty is probably about $\pm 5\%$ or greater because of the small volume of CO_2 generated (Siesser and Rogers, 1971).

All foraminifera were picked from an aliquot of the fraction of sample greater than 149 μm (obtained by dry-sieving the greater than 62 μm fraction). The aliquot was obtained by splitting the sample repeatedly until 300 to 500 planktonic foraminifera remained. All specimens were identified and mounted by species on a cardboard microslide. Each species was counted and the number recorded. Benthonic foraminifera were separated and their total number determined but species were not identified.

Surface Sediment

Excluding volcanic ash, which is only locally important, sediments from the Norwegian Sea result from a three-component sedimentary system in which the prevailing climatic regime is reflected in the relative proportions of the components. These are "glacial-marine" detritus (Philippi, 1912), clay-sized material derived from erosion on land, and biogenic material, mostly in the form of planktonic foraminiferal shells composed of $CaCO_3$.

The distribution of coarse material (larger than 62 μm) in the Norwegian Sea is shown in Fig. 2. This coarse material is composed of both glacial-marine detritus and foraminiferal shells. Because neither of these components is entirely contained in the larger than 62 μm fraction, their quantitative separation is difficult.

The distribution of sediment types in Norwegian Sea surface sediments is shown in Fig. 3. Sediments are classified as clay if less than 10% $CaCO_3$ is present, as foraminiferal clay if $CaCO_3$ is between 10 and 30%, as foraminiferal marl if $CaCO_3$ is between 30 and 60%, and as foraminiferal ooze if more than 60% $CaCO_3$ is present (see Fig. 7). A brief microscopic examination was made of each TW top to estimate the proportion of coarse noncarbonate material (largely ice-rafted detritus). Samples containing 10 to 40% terrigenous sand were termed "sandy" clay, marl or ooze depending on the carbonate content. No evidence of turbidity current deposition was found in any of the TW tops.

Most of the Norwegian Sea floor is covered by sandy clays, marls and oozes except in the southeast portion of the region (Fig. 3). The sandy material is largely attributed to ice-rafting. Under the Norwegian Current, foraminiferal clays, marls and oozes occur with little or no terrigenous sandy material. Two areas have surface sediments with low carbonate contents and little or no ice-rafted material. These are to the west of Spitsbergen and in a band trending toward Spitsbergen from Greenland. In both these areas, winter ice cover

is often present today. As I have sampled an ice floe carrying rafted detritus in the region off Greenland during the summer of 1970, I am surprised to find so little evidence of ice rafting in the underlying sediment.

Terrigenous sands found in sediments off the coast of Norway and on the Iceland-Faeroe Ridge are probably relict Pleistocene deposits similar to those found along the continental margin off eastern North America (Stetson, 1939) caused by bottom scour. Elsewhere in the Norwegian Sea, sandy material is attributed to ice-rafting. The distribution of ice-rafted detritus fits closely with our knowledge of ice cover (Figs. 4–6).

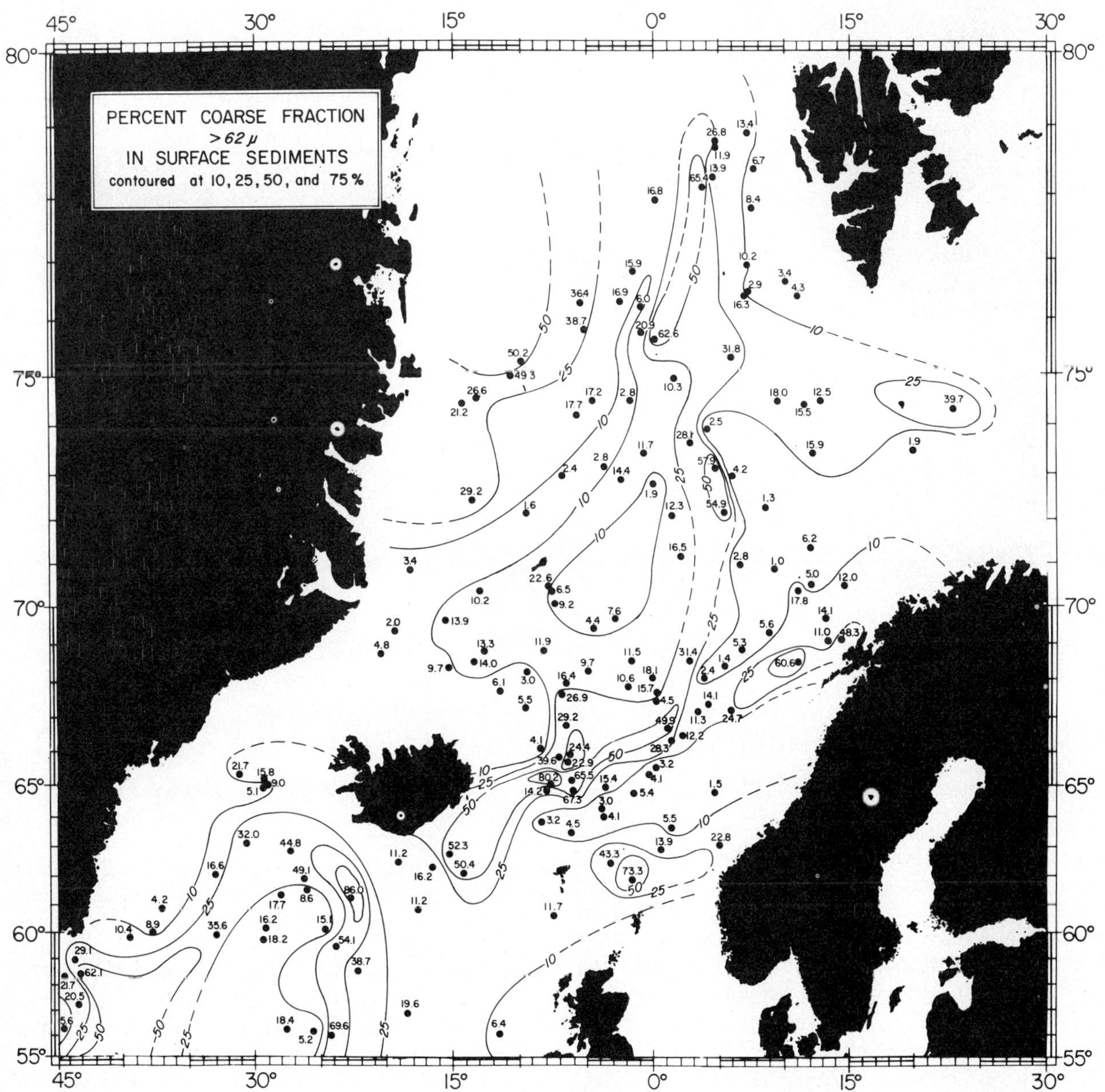

FIG. 2. Distribution of coarse material (larger than 62 μm) in Norwegian Sea TW tops.

FIG. 3. Distribution of sediment types in Norwegian Sea surface sediments.

Surface Sediment Distribution of CaCO₃

Analyses of calcium-carbonate content in Norwegian Sea surface sediments should measure both total biogenic input and, more specifically, foraminiferal productivity in surface waters, because foraminiferal shells ($CaCO_3$) are by far the most abundant biogenic component of the sediments. Other sources of $CaCO_3$ are usually not significant. Benthonic foraminifera are usually present, but at levels about two orders of magnitude less than that of the planktonic species. Coccoliths are not found in surface waters north of the 2.0C (35.6F) isotherm at present (McIntyre and Bé, 1967).

Coccoliths should not be an important source of $CaCO_3$ in the Norwegian Sea because most of the region is north of this isotherm for at least part of the year. Detrital material derived from the surrounding lands is another possible source of carbonate. Dolomite and calcite are present in Paleozoic rocks in Greenland (Raasch, 1961). Glacial scour might transport this material to the sea. Kellogg (*in press*) showed by X-ray diffraction analyses of Norwegian Sea sediments that most of the carbonate present is in the form of calcite. Dolomite occurs only in trace amounts, suggesting that deposition of detrital carbonate is not significant in this region.

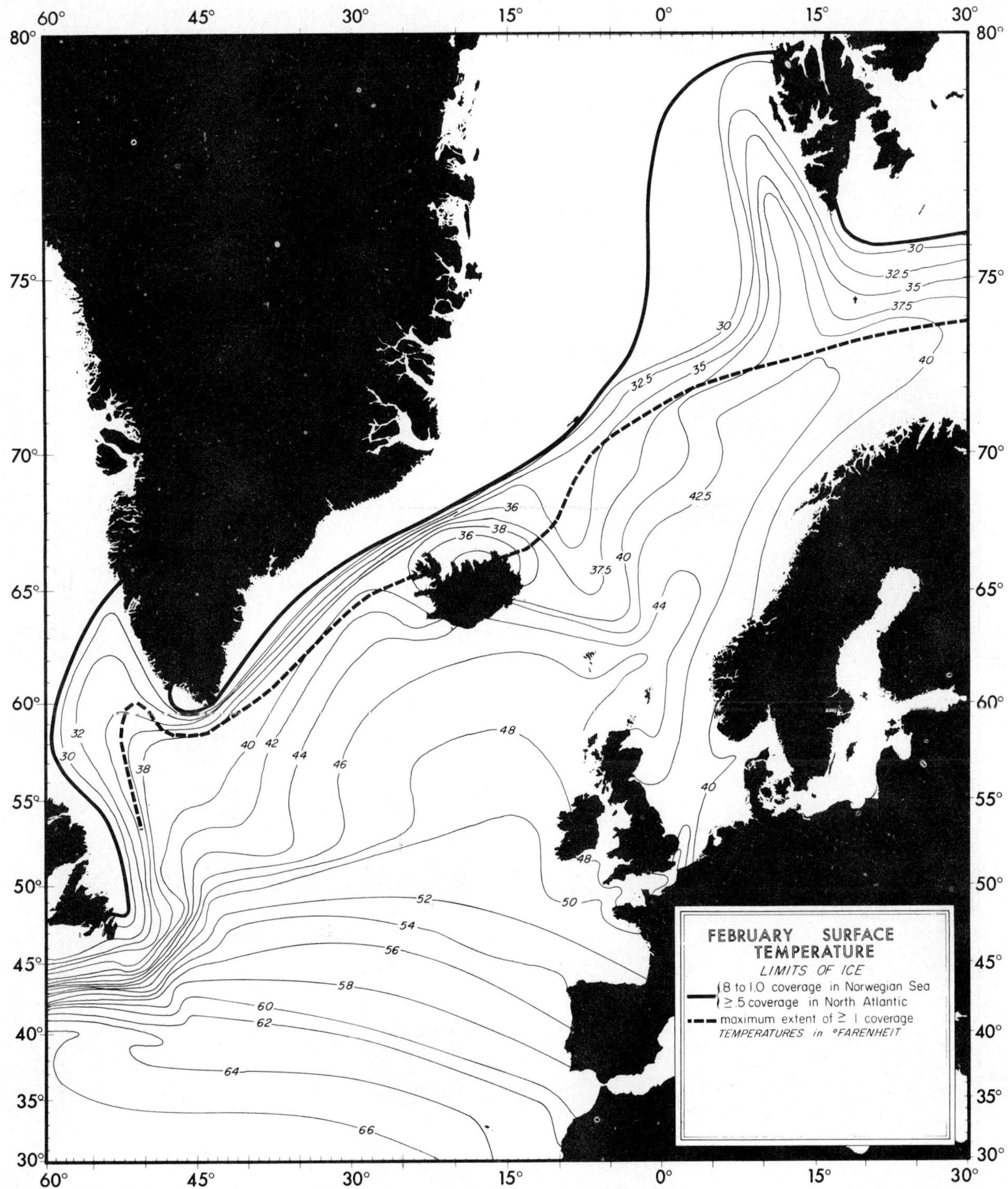

FIG. 4. February sea-surface temperature and ice limits. Compiled from: *Oceanographic Atlas of the North Atlantic Ocean, Sect. 2, Physical Properties*, U. S. Naval Oceanographic Office, 1967; and *Oceanographic Atlas of the Polar Seas, Part II, Arctic*, U. S. Navy Hydrographic Office, 1958.

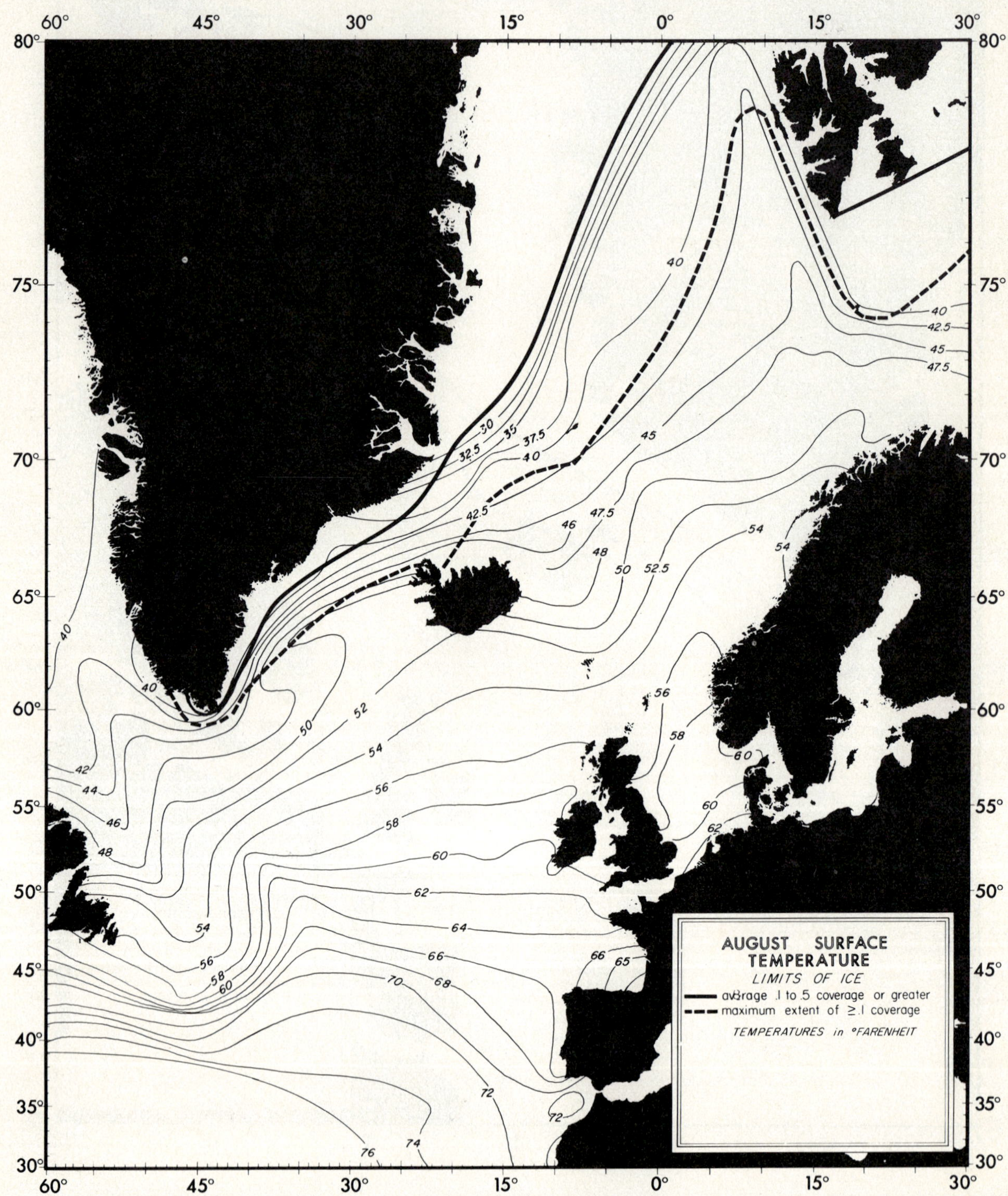

Fig. 5. August sea-surface temperature and ice limits. Sources as for Fig. 4.

The surface-sediment distribution of CaCO₃ is shown in Fig. 7. This distribution reflects the present surface-circulation pattern (Fig. 8) with high carbonate values underlying warm surface currents, especially the Norwegian Current. High carbonate values tend to cut across topographic barriers, suggesting that carbonate dissolution is not a major factor in this region. The same conclusion was reached by Kellogg (*in press*) on the basis of foraminiferal studies of 34 Norwegian Sea trigger-weight tops. Most of the Norwegian Sea floor lies above 4000 meters, and most of the cores studied were taken from depths of less than 3000 meters. Li, *et al.* (1969) report that the carbonate compensation depth in the North Atlantic lies at 4500 meters. Thus the Norwegian Sea should not suffer from carbonate dissolution to any great extent. Planktonic foraminiferal specimens studied showed little or no evidence of dissolution. In a few cores taken from the deeper parts of the Greenland Basin, benthonic foraminiferal specimens are considerably more abundant than elsewhere in the Norwegian Sea (up to 50% of the total foraminiferal fauna) and have a chalky texture suggestive of dissolution (Streeter, personal communication). Thus dissolution appears to be insignificant in the Norwegian Basin. In the slightly deeper Greenland Basin, dissolution may be locally important.

Because the carbonate in surface sediments from the Norwegian Sea is largely in the form of foraminiferal shells, and because dissolution is not significant in this region, the surface sediment distribution of CaCO₃ is a measure of surface-water productivity. Productivity is in turn associated with warm surface-water circulation (compare Figs. 7 and 8).

Planktonic Foraminifera

The taxonomy used follows that of Bé (1967) with one important exception. *Globigerina pachyderma* (dextral) shows an apparent tendency to intergrade with *Globoquadrina dutertrei*. These intermediate forms were counted separately as follows. Specimens having five or more chambers in the final whorl and having an apertural tooth were considered *G. dutertrei*. Specimens with four or less chambers lacking a tooth were counted as *G. pachyderma* (dextral). Those specimens having between four and five chambers in the final whorl and lacking an apertural tooth were counted as "P-D Intergrade."

In most Norwegian Sea samples, planktonic foraminiferal faunas are dominated by *Globigerina pachyderma*. Ericson (1959) showed that this species coils dextrally in relatively warm waters and sinistrally in cold polar waters. Other species present include *G. bulloides, G. Quinqueloba, Globorotalia inflata, Globigerinita glutinata* and a number of rare species. Kellogg (in press) showed that dextral *G. pachyderma* and the "warm species" (all species except *G. pachyderma* lumped together) have distribution patterns with

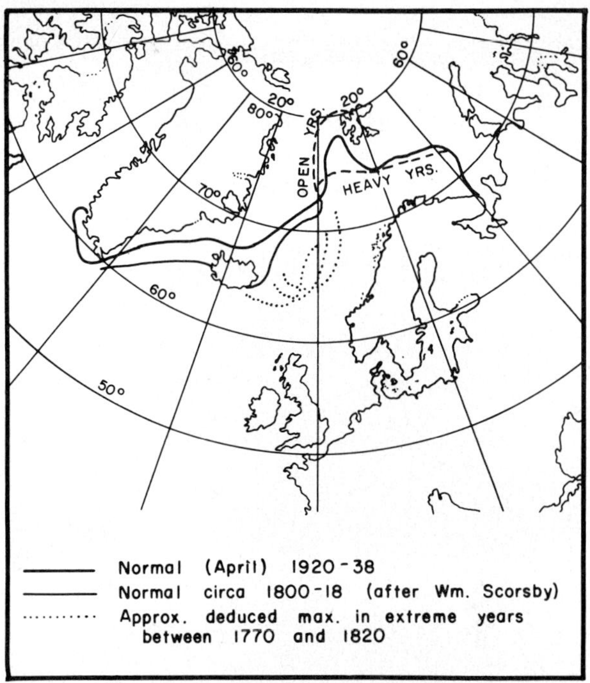

FIG. 6. Maximum extent of spring pack-ice— 18th to 20th centuries (after Lamb, 1963).

highest values under the axis of the Norwegian Current (Figs. 9 and 10). He also showed that large percentages of sinistral *G. pachyderma* in planktonic foraminiferal assemblages indicate present surface ice-cover or proximity to ice cover.

Two separate sets of results based on a varimax solution of Q-Mode factor analysis of planktonic foraminiferal assemblages in Norwegian Sea core-tops are presented below. In the first (Equation 1), 25 samples containing 11 species from the Norwegian Sea are analyzed. A separate analysis is based on core tops from the Norwegian Sea and adjacent northern North Atlantic (Equation 2). These contain 25 species (data supplied by Kipp, personal communication). In all samples used, a census of all planktonic foraminiferal specimens larger than 149 μm in an aliquot consisting of between 300 and 500 specimens was made. These raw counts were converted to percent of total sample and factored using the FORTRAN program CABFAC (Klovan and Imbrie, 1971) according to the method developed by Imbrie and Kipp (1971). The reader is referred to these papers for details on the method. Raw data, factor matrices and tables of regression coefficients may be found in Kellogg (1973). The factor analysis technique establishes the present ecological distribution of the foraminiferal species in order that these distributions may be related to known environmental parameters (in this case, surface-water temperatures) by transfer functions. The transfer functions are then used to make paleoenvironmental estimates in the latter part of this paper.

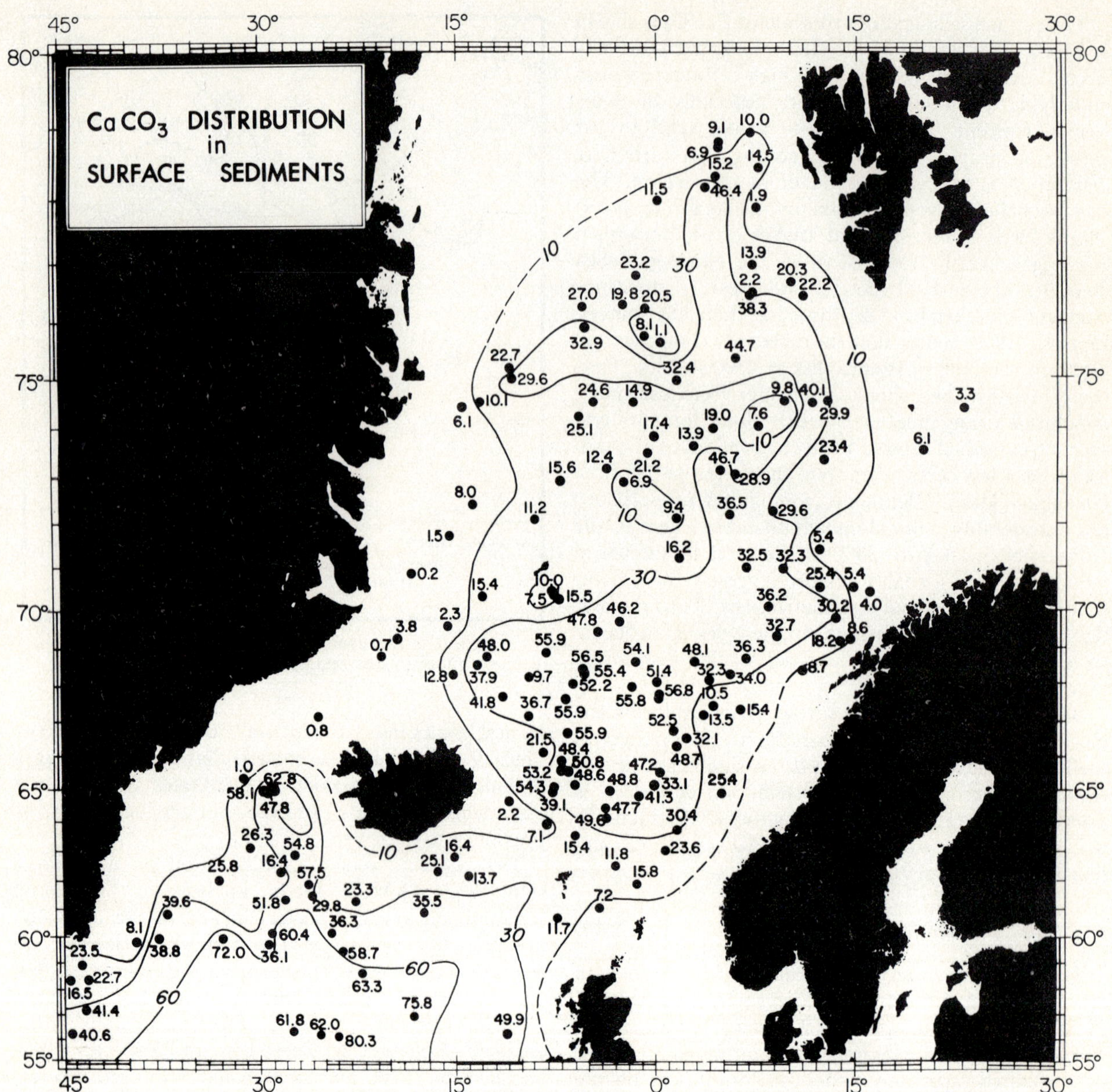

FIG. 7. Distribution of calcium carbonate in Norwegian Sea surface sediments (weight percent).

Equation 1 Results on Surface Sediments

Locations of the core tops used in Equation 1 are shown in Fig. 11. The cores provide good geographic coverage of the region. Three assemblage factors were found to explain 98.56% of the total sum of squares of the raw data. For each factor, values of the varimax matrix for each core location are plotted on maps (Figs. 12–14). Factor 1, a polar assemblage dominated by *G. pachyderma* (sinistral) and having a sum of squares of 71.85, is by far the strongest of the three factors (Fig. 12). Factor 2 is a subpolar assemblage with a sum of squares of 15.38 consisting of, in order of importance,

G. pachyderma (dextral), *G. glutinata* and the P-D intergrade (Fig. 13). Factor 3, the weakest with a sum of squares of only 11.33, consists almost entirely of *G. quinqueloba*. Factor 3 was judged significant because values of the varimax matrix for each core plotted on Fig. 14 in a pattern that showed both a regional gradient and a relationship with a known oceanographic parameter (the Norwegian Current).

Maps of factors 1 and 2 confirm the results reported by Kellogg (*in press*) shown in Figs. 9 and 10. Factor 3 is weak but tends to show high values in the region under the western boundary of the Norwegian Current where the "warm species" (Fig. 10) also have high values. Thus the factor analysis presents reasonable results for this region.

Equation 2 Results on Surface Sediments

Locations of the 52 trigger-core tops used in Equation 2 are shown in Fig. 15. Three assemblage factors were found to explain 94.54% of the total sum of squares of the data. For each assemblage factor, values of the varimax matrix for each core location are plotted on maps in Figs. 16–18.

Factor 1 is again a polar assemblage having almost the same geographic distribution as factor 1 from Equation 1. The geographic coverage provided by the additional 27 core tops permits the extension of the contours outside the Norwegian Sea. Factor 1 consists of *G. pachyderma*, (sinistral) and has a sum of squares of 47.76. Factor 2 is a sub-polar assemblage showing much the same distribution as factor 2 from Equation 1 and consisting of *G. pachyderma* (dextral), *G. bulloides*, *G. glutinata* and the P-D intergrade (Fig. 17). The sum of squares of factor 2 is 43.30. Factor 3 is a complex assemblage with a sum of squares of only 3.49. Species present in factor 3 include (+)*G. bulloides*, (−)*G. pachyderma* (dextral), (−)*G. glutinata*, (+)*G. inflata*, (+)*G. falconensis* and (−)P-D intergrade in order of importance and where (+) indicates presence and (−) indicates absence. Although this factor has a small sum of squares, definite regional patterns are observed (Fig. 18) and the assemblage is judged significant.

Surface Sediments—Summary

The single most important agent influencing the distribution of sediments and plankton in the Norwegian

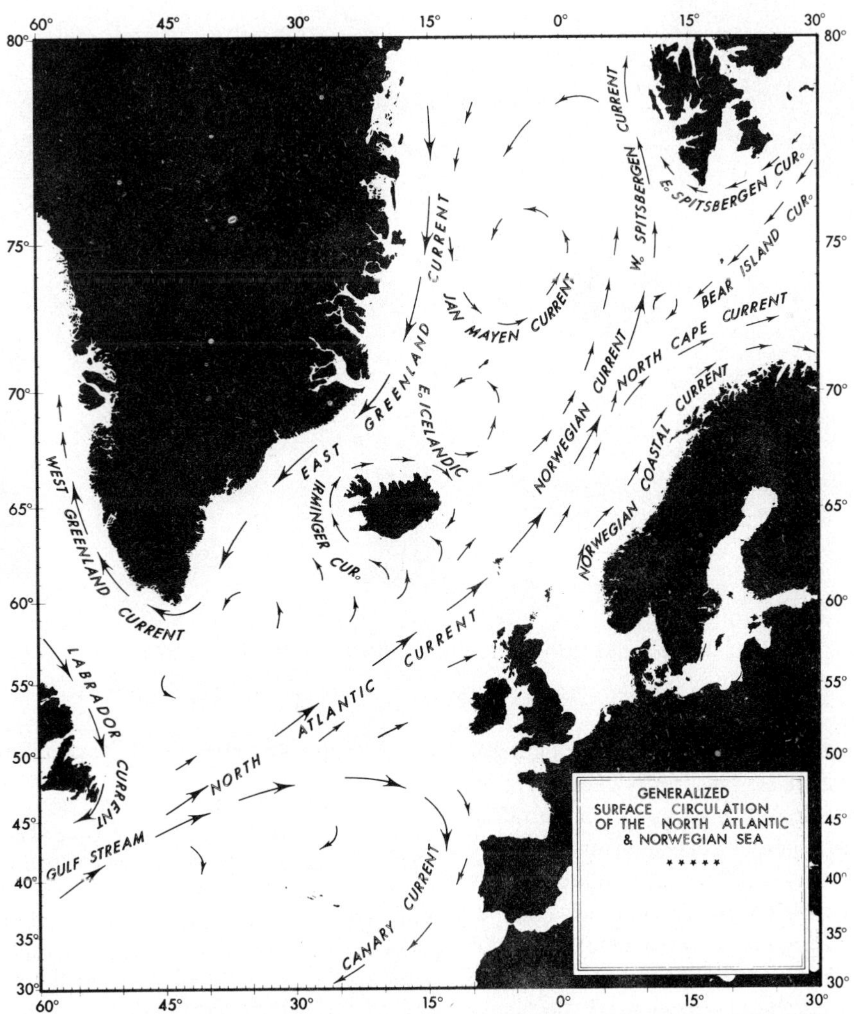

FIG. 8. Generalized surface circulation of the North Atlantic and Norwegian Sea. Compiled from: *Oceanographic Atlas of the North Atlantic Ocean, Sect. 1, Tides and Currents,* U. S. Naval Oceanographic Office, 1965; and *Oceanographic Atlas of the Polar Seas, Part II, Arctic,* U. S. Navy Hydrographic Office, 1958.

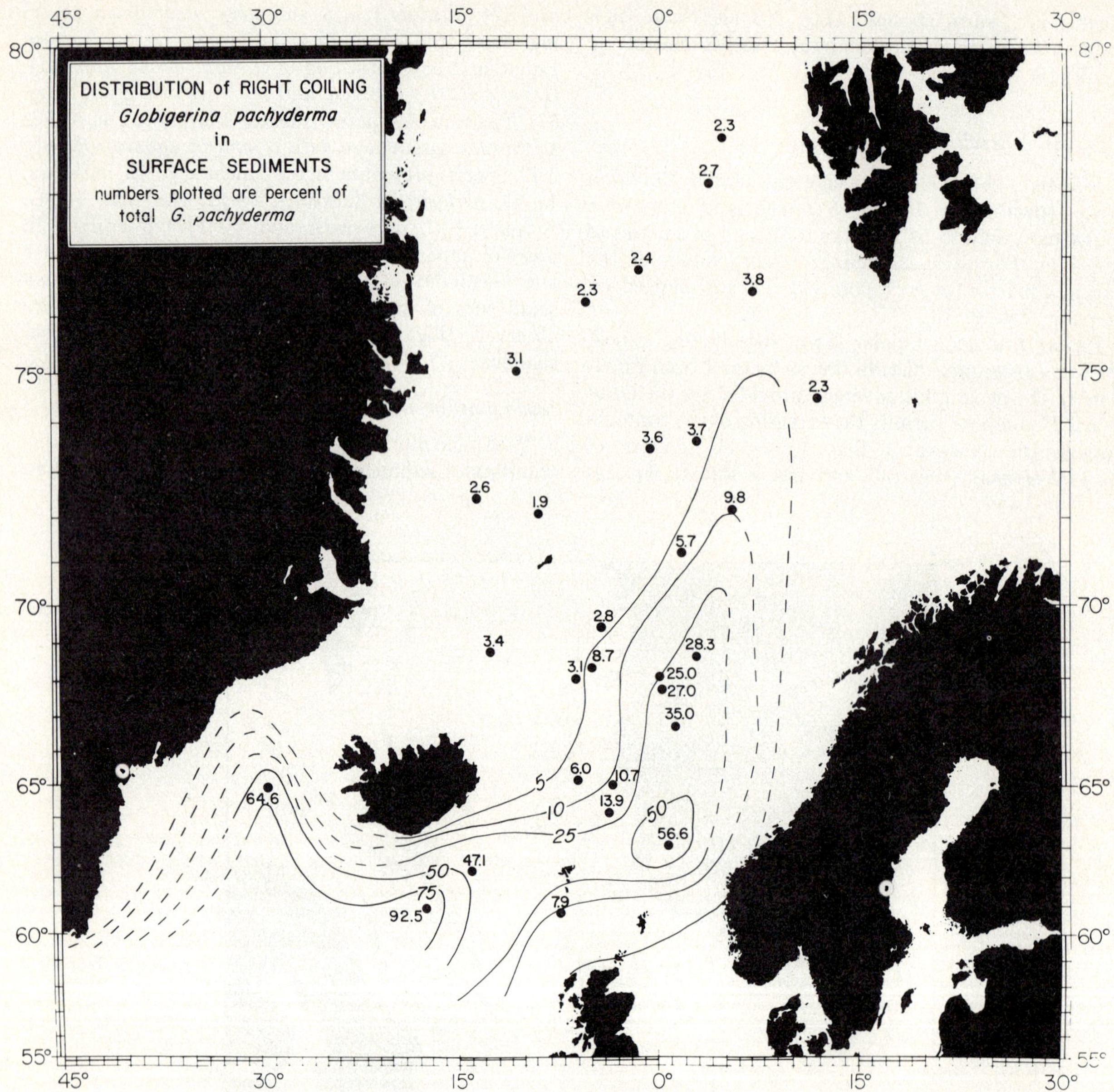

FIG. 9. Distribution of dextral *Globigerina pachyderma* in surface sediments of the Norwegian Sea (after Kellogg, in press).

Sea is the warm Norwegian Current. This warm current exists as a limiting factor to the spread of sea-ice cover and thus controls the present distribution of ice-rafted detritus. The carbonate content of sediments under the Norwegian Current is high because productivity is highest in the warm surface waters and because dissolution does not remove significant amounts of material in the relatively shallow Norwegian Sea. Warm surface circulation also controls the distributions of the planktonic foraminiferal species as shown by Kellogg (*in press*) and confirmed by the distributions of the assemblage factors described by Q-mode factor analysis.

3. Stratigraphic studies of Norwegian Sea cores

29 Norwegian Sea cores were analyzed at close intervals for carbonate content (Fig. 19). The resulting curves were initially used to pick cores for more detailed study, and later, as a stratigraphic tool. Six of the cores were chosen to form a warm water—cold water traverse of the region (Fig. 20). Quantitative paleotemperature estimates, based on application of the Imbrie and Kipp (1971) method to foraminiferal data, were made for each core. In addition, quantitative estimates of glacial-marine input were made using the FORTRAN program *RAFT* as described below.

FIG. 10. Percentage of "warm" planktonic foraminifera in Norwegian Sea surface-sediment samples as percent of the total planktonic foraminiferal fauna (after Kellogg, in press).

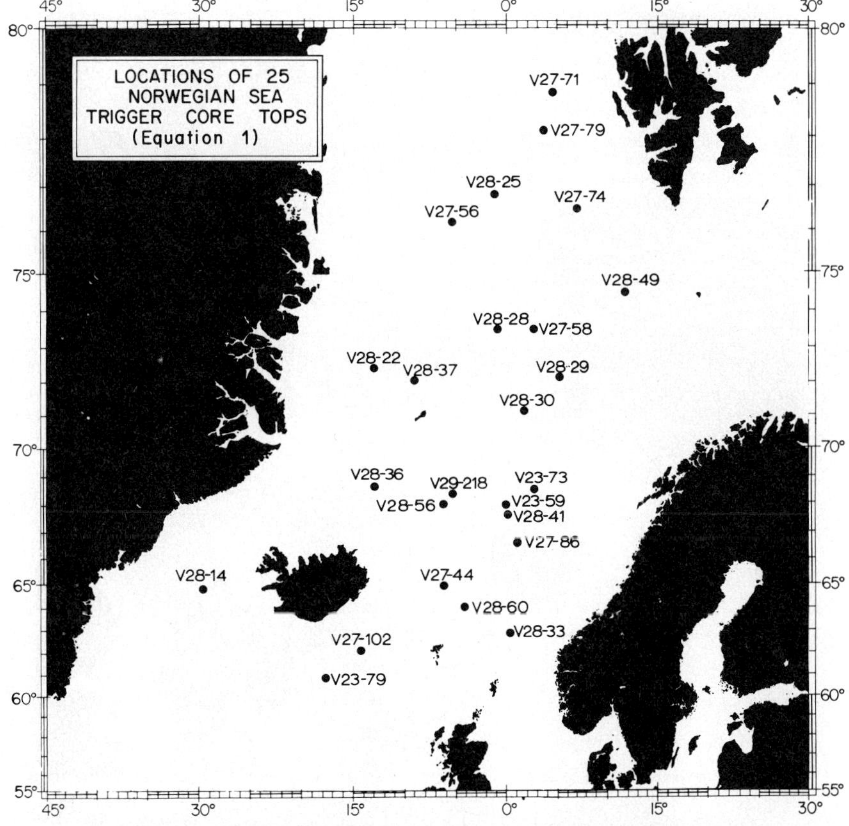

FIG. 11. Locations of 25 Norwegian Sea TW tops used in Equation 1.

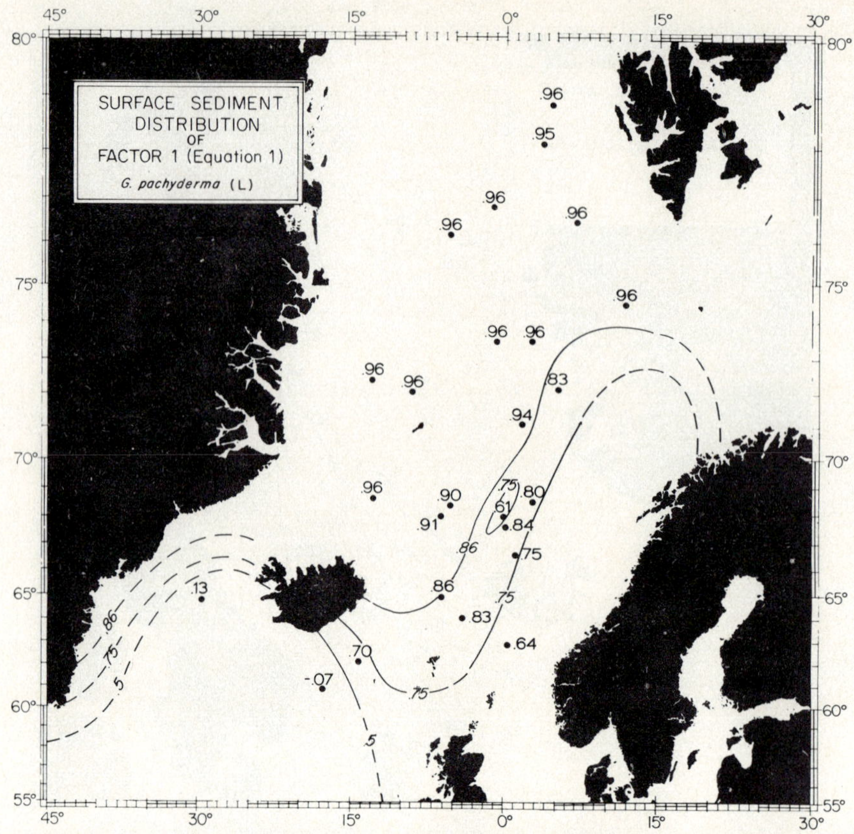

FIG. 12. Varimax factor-loadings for the polar assemblage (Equation 1). Contoured at 0.5, 0.75 and 0.86 (corresponding to 25, 50 and 75%).

FIG. 13. Varimax factor-loading for the subpolar assemblage (Equation 1). Contoured as in Fig. 12.

FIG. 14. Varimax factor-loadings for assemblage factor 3 (Equation 1).
Contoured as in Fig. 12.

The sediments at the tops of the 6 cores reflect the diverse sedimentary conditions present in the Norwegian Sea today. These conditions constitute a complete gradation from sediments with polar faunas being deposited under essentially glacial conditions in the northern and western Greenland Sea (V28-25) to sediments with sub-polar faunas deposited under nonglacial conditions at present in the southern portion of the region (V28-14 and V27-86).

Techniques

Each core was sampled at ten centimeter intervals from top to bottom. The rind of contaminated material formed during coring was removed leaving samples averaging 4 to 5 grams. Carbonate, coarse-fraction, and faunal analyses were made as described for the trigger-core tops.

The FORTRAN program *RAFT* was written to quantify the input of ice-rafted detritus in the six cores chosen for the north-south traverse. The coarse fraction (larger than 62 μm) contains both ice-rafted debris and the shells of planktonic foraminifera. This biogenic component could easily have been removed by treatment with hydrochloric acid but, because foraminiferal studies were being made, a different approach was necessary. Each sediment sample was treated as a four-component sedimentary system: coarse carbonate (foraminiferal shells), coarse noncarbonate (ice-rafted debris), fine carbonate (broken foraminiferal shells and some coccoliths in southern cores) and fine noncarbonate (clay-sized terrigenous material and fine ice-rafted detritus). Because the total coarse-fraction and carbonate contents were already known, measurement of any one of the four components would make possible calculation of the other three. Analyses of the carbonate content of the less than 62 μm fraction were made for each sample. The basic input to *RAFT* were: original sample weight (before washing), total carbonate, total coarse fraction, and fine-fraction carbonate. All percents were first converted to weights. Because the coarse fraction was measured, the fine fraction must equal:

Fine Fract. Wt.

$$= \text{Original Samp. Wt.} - \text{Coarse Fract. Wt.}$$

Fine fraction carbonate was actually measured as percent of the fine fraction and not as percent of the total sample. Because the weight of the fine fraction is known:

$$\text{Fine } CaCO_3 \text{ Wt.} = \text{Fine } CaCO_3\% \times \text{Fine Fract. Wt.}$$

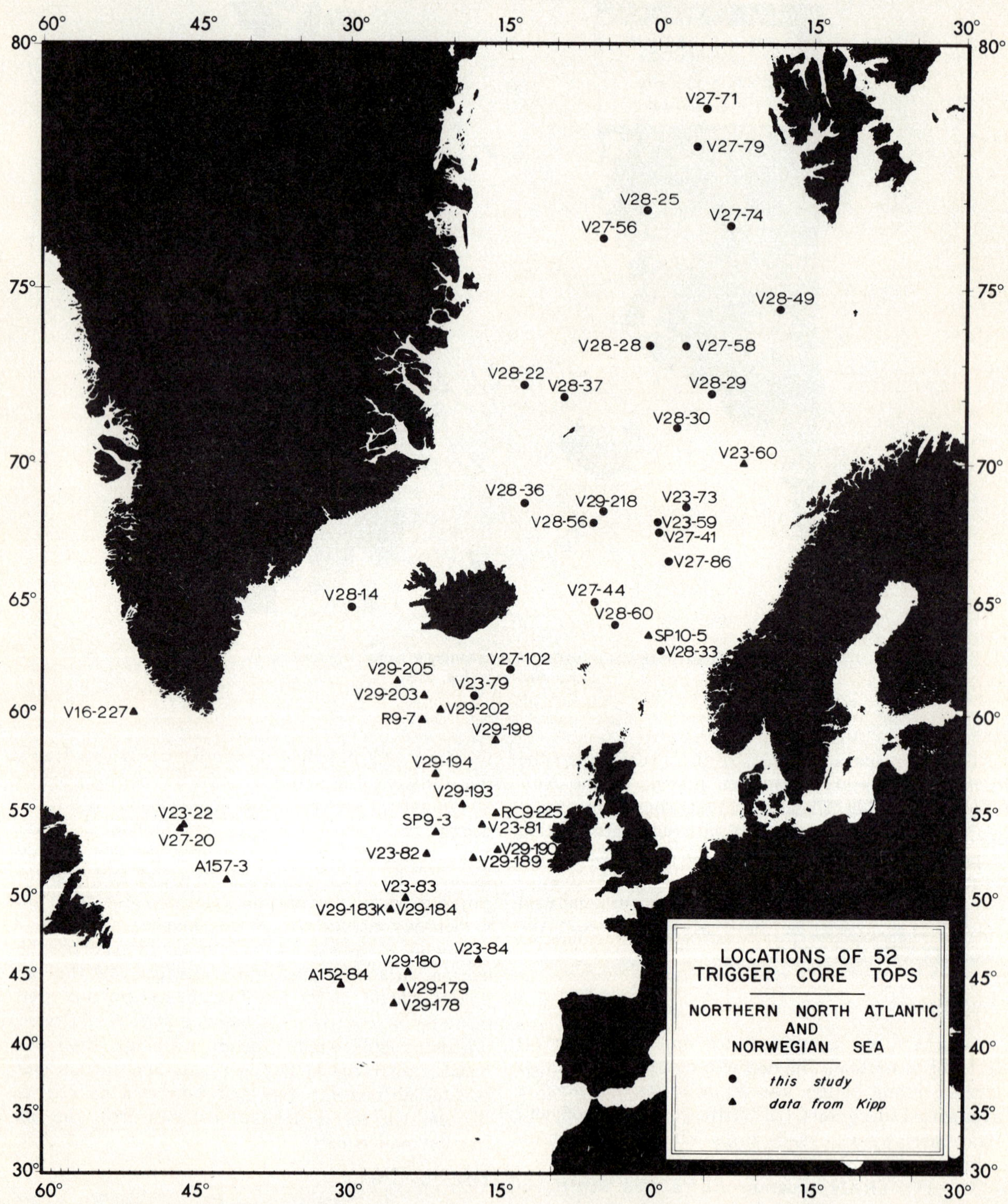

FIG. 15. Locations of 52 Norwegian Sea and northern North Atlantic TW tops used in Equation 2.
North Atlantic data was supplied by Kipp (personal communication).

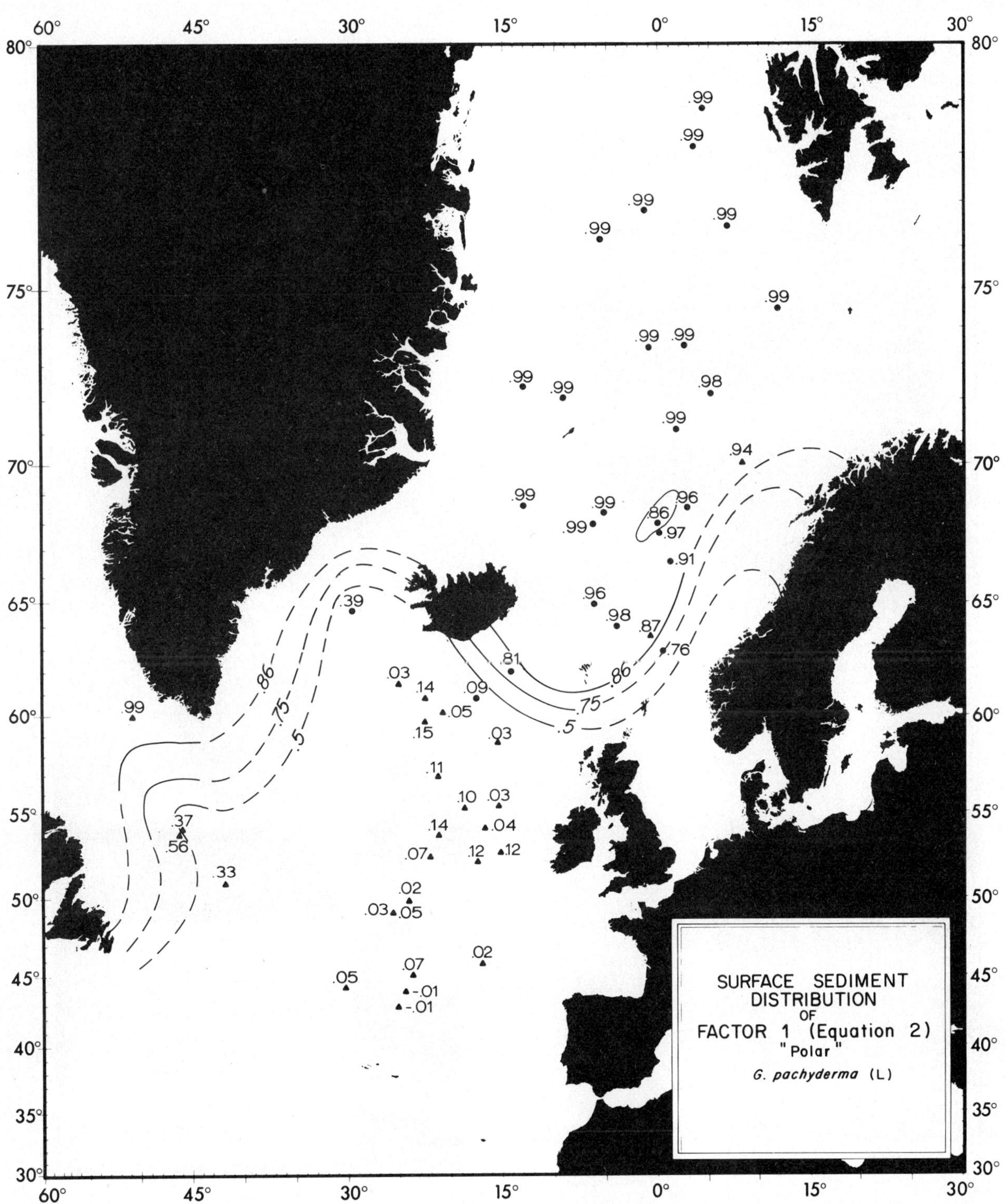

FIG. 16. Varimax factor-loadings for the polar assemblage (Equation 2). Contoured as in Fig. 12.

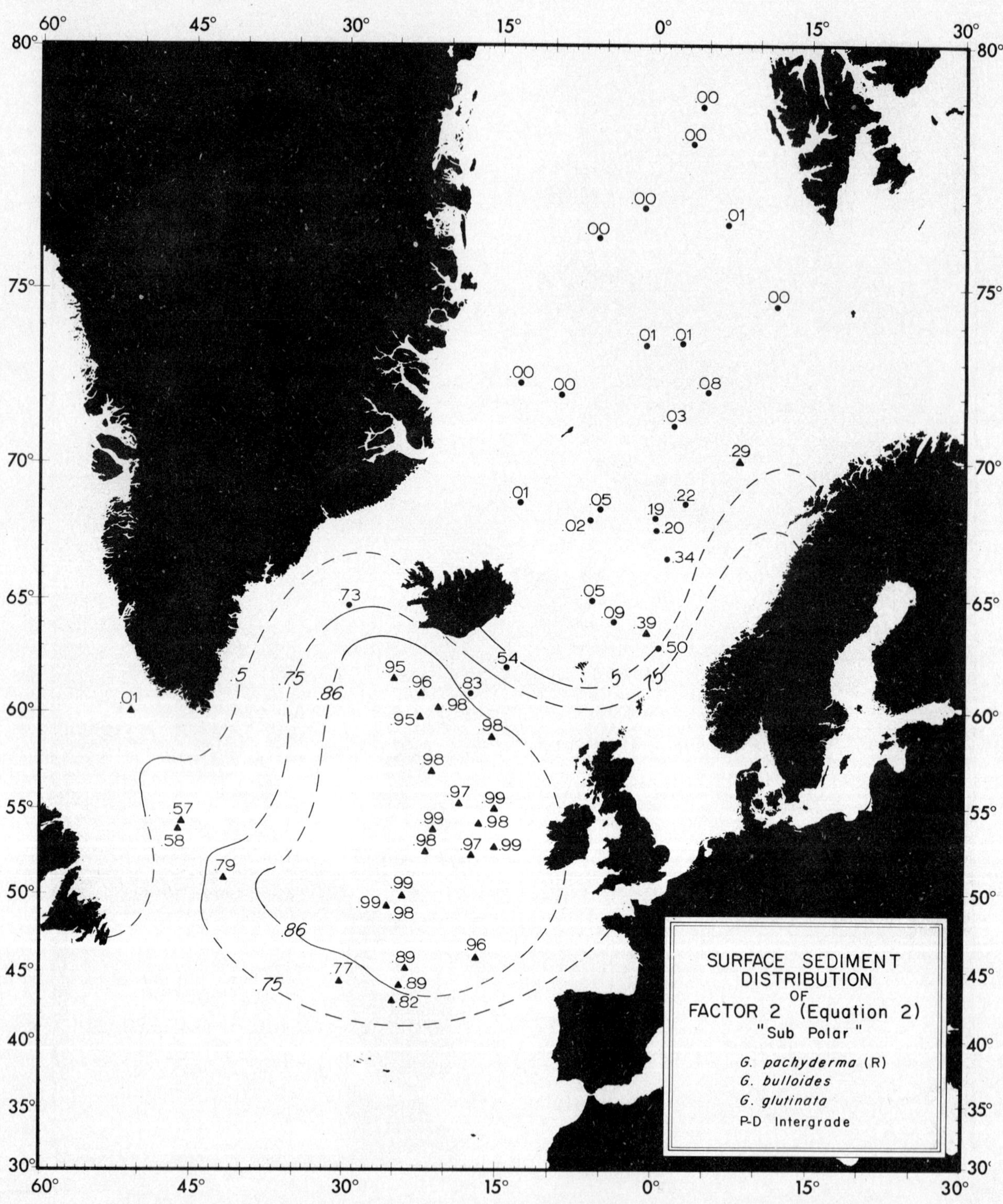

FIG. 17. Varimax factor-loadings for the subpolar assemblage (Equation 2). Contoured as in Fig. 12.

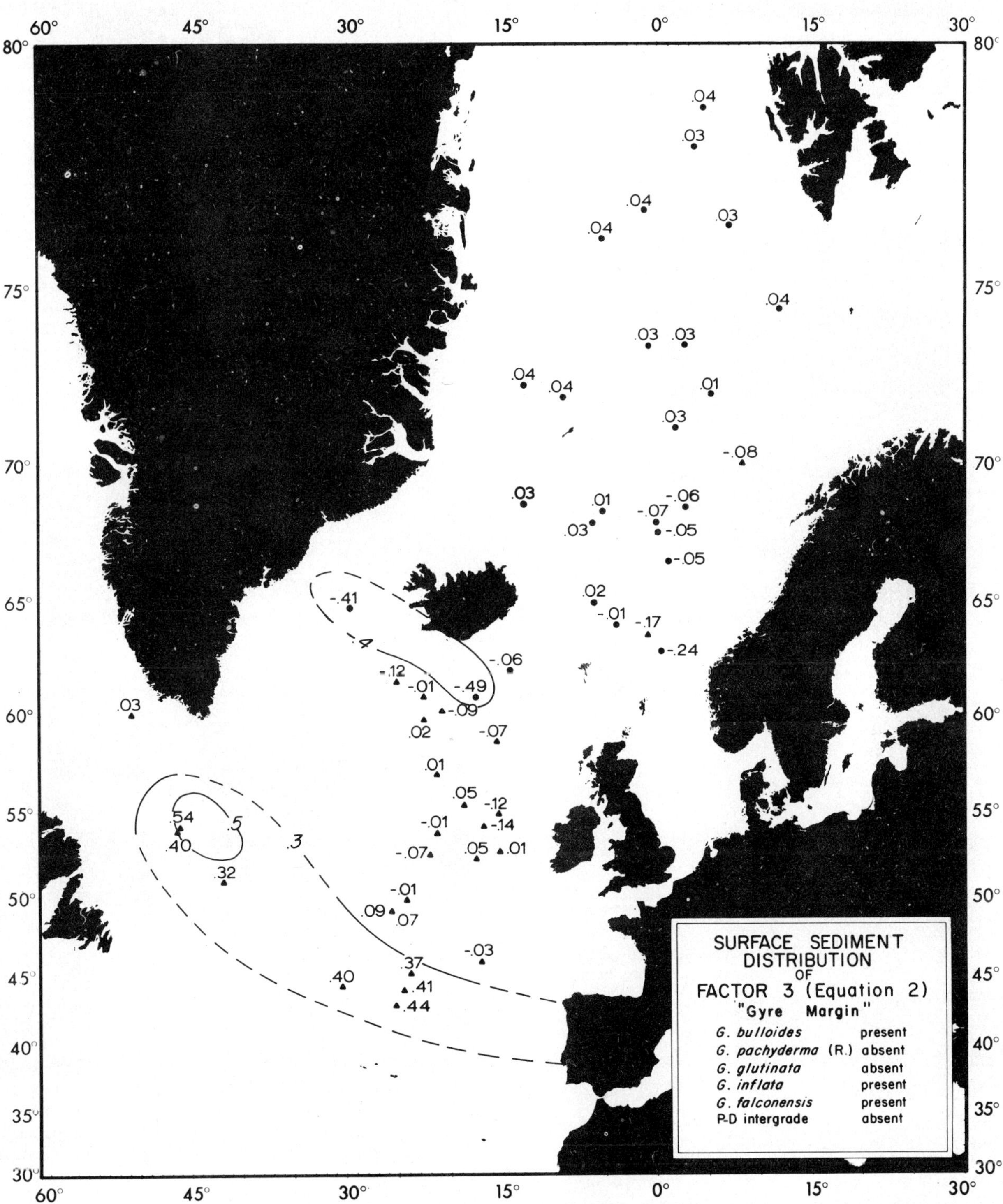

FIG. 18. Varimax factor loadings for assemblage factor 3 (Equation 2). Contoured at 0.3, 0.4 and 0.5
(corresponding to 9, 16 and 25%).

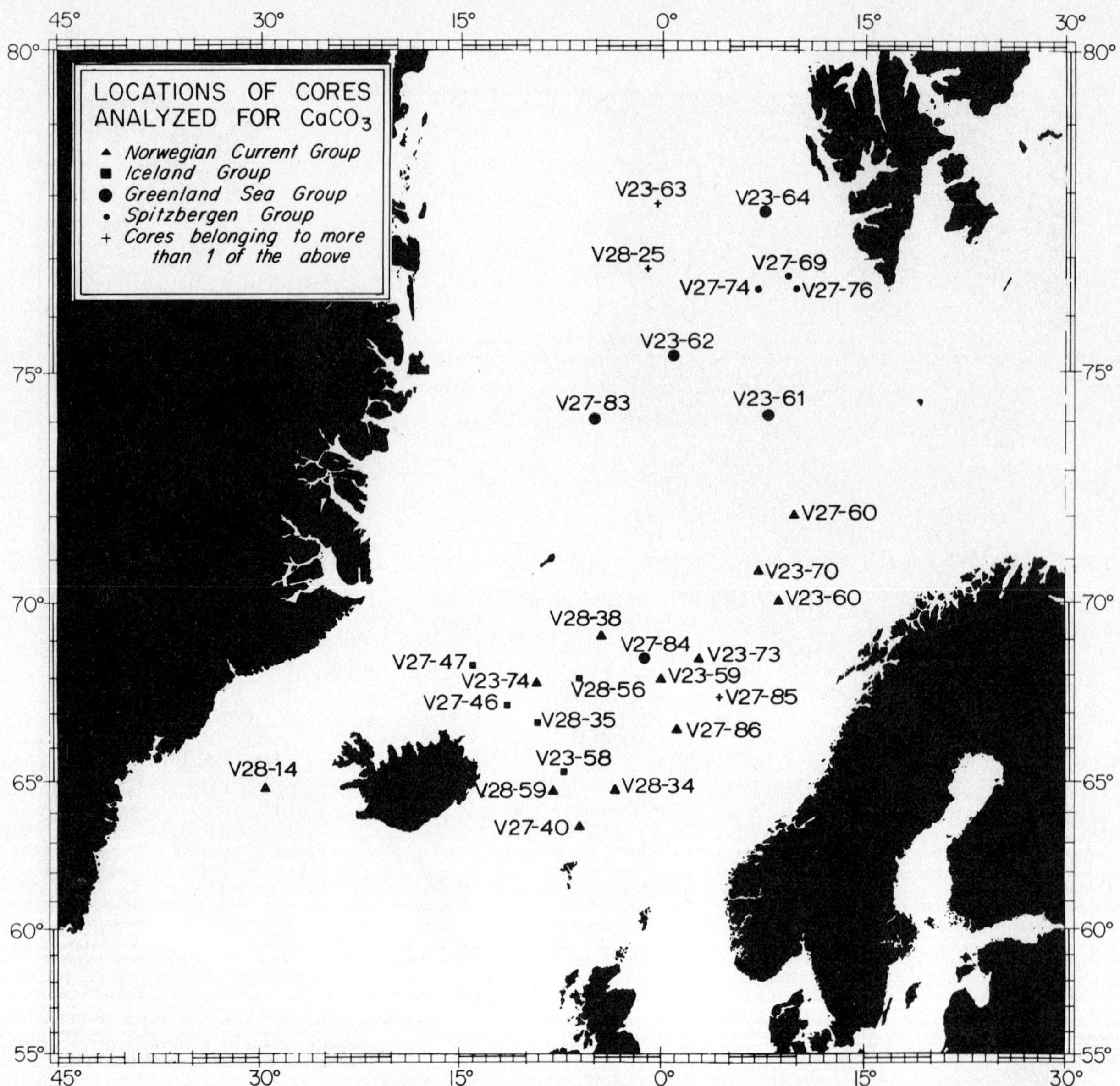

FIG. 19. Locations of cores analyzed for calcium carbonate content. Cores having similar patterns
of carbonate fluctuation are indicated by various symbols.

and:

Coarse CaCO₃ Wt.

$$= \text{Total CaCO}_3 \text{ Wt.} - \text{Fine CaCO}_3 \text{ Wt.}$$

Once the weights of coarse- and fine-fraction carbonate are known, it follows that the weights of coarse- and fine-fraction *non*carbonate are also known. *RAFT*, after completing these calculations for each sample, converts all weights to percent of total sample, lists all weights and percents, and plots coarse-fraction carbonate, coarse-fraction noncarbonate and fine-fraction noncarbonate versus depth in core.

Quantitative paleotemperature estimates were made using the method of Imbrie and Kipp (1971). Varimax factor matrices developed for the trigger-core tops were linked by curvilinear regression with observed winter (February) and summer (August) sea-surface temperature data (Figs. 4 and 5) obtained from the *Oceanographic Atlas of the North Atlantic Ocean*, Sect. 2, *Physical Properties* (U. S. Naval Oceanographic Office, 1967) and the *Oceanographic Atlas of the Polar Seas*, Part II, *Arctic* (U. S. Navy Hydrographic Office, 1958), The resulting paleotemperature equations were applied to planktonic foraminiferal populations picked from the cores using the technique applied to the trigger-core tops.

Carbonate Curves

Numerous workers including Arrhenius (1952), Hays, *et al.* (1969), Olausson (1967), McIntyre, *et al.* (1972), Oba (1969) and Broecker, *et al.* (1968) have made calcium-carbonate analyses on deep-sea sediments. Equatorial Pacific cores generally have a cyclic pattern of highs and lows starting with low values at the top. Atlantic cores show similar cyclic patterns but have high values at their tops. Interpretation of carbonate curves is usually on a climatic basis although carbonate deposition is a complicated process with many controlling factors (Broecker, 1971).

High carbonate values in Atlantic cores are correlated with warm climate. Schott (1935) attributed the correspondence of high carbonate values with warm periods to higher input of terrigenous material during cold periods, thus masking the carbonate. Broecker, *et al.* (1958) showed that net carbonate input increased during the glacial in one North Atlantic core, but was masked or diluted by an even larger increase in terrigenous lutite. Ruddiman and McIntyre (*in press*), in a number of North Atlantic cores, find higher absolute rates of biogenous input during interglacial climates but greater delivery of terrigenous sediments during glacial climates. They explain the constancy of sedimentation

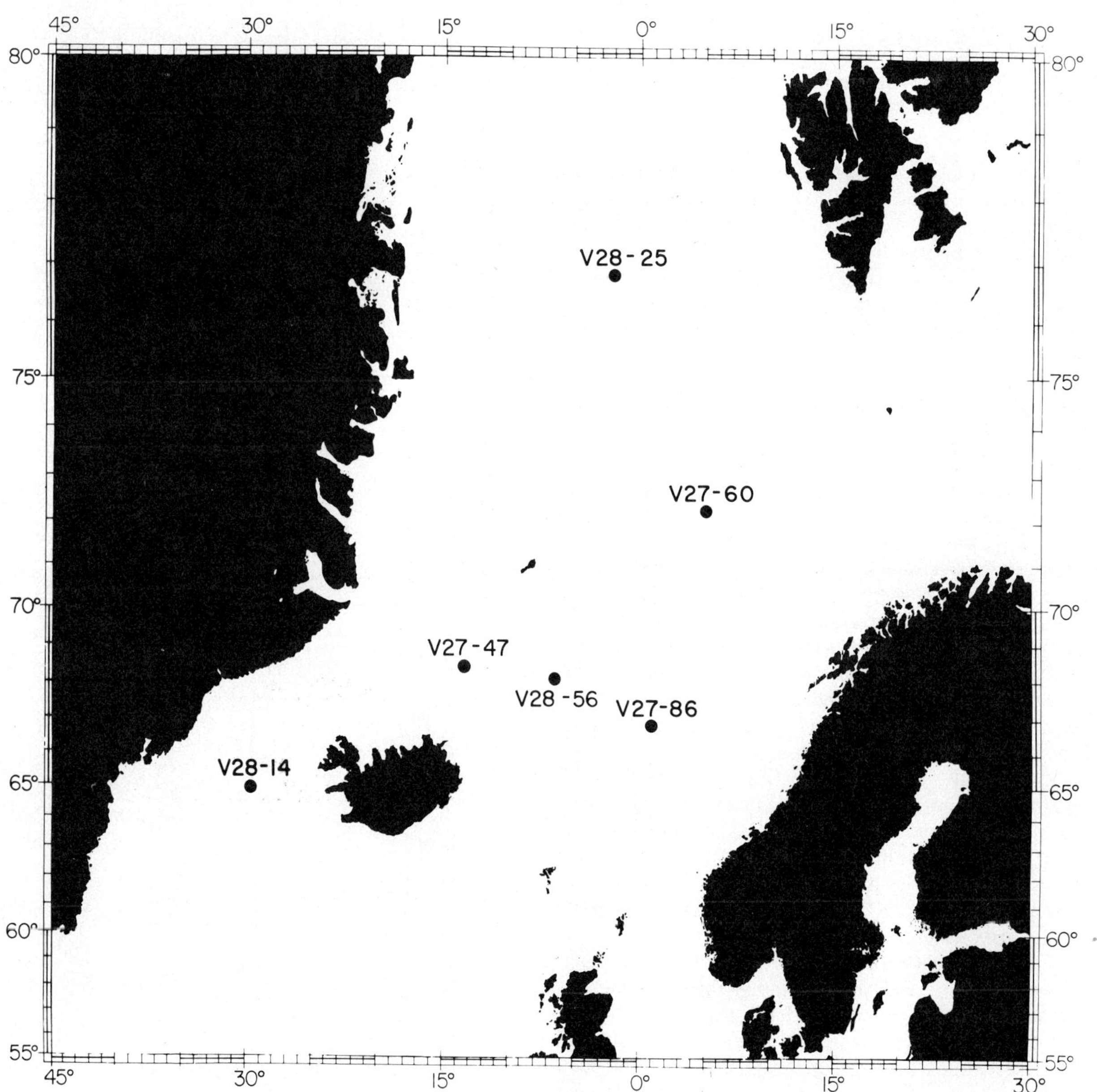

Fig. 20. Locations of six piston cores for which faunal and sedimentary studies were made.

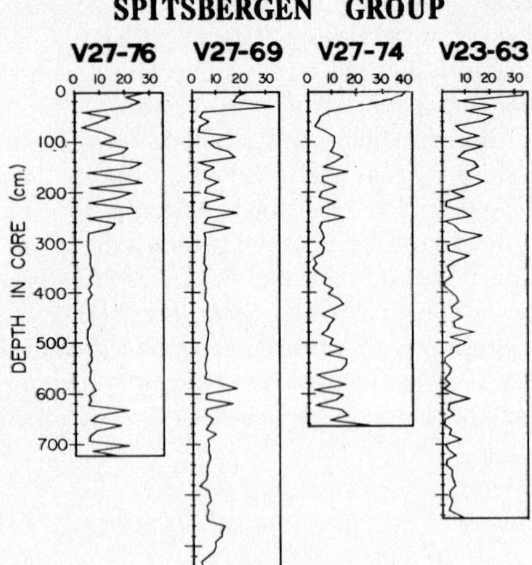

FIG. 21. Weight-percent carbonate curves
for Spitsbergen Group cores.

rate which they observe between glacial and interglacial
climates by a coincidental balancing of the oceanically
produced biogenous input and the continentally derived
terrigenous input.

The 29 Norwegian Sea cores analyzed for carbonate
content show four distinct patterns of fluctuation. Each
pattern is restricted to a particular area within the
region.

Cores of the Spitsbergen Group (Fig. 21) are characterized by the presence of numerous low-amplitude
peaks in the top three meters above a zone of almost
constant carbonate (about 5%). These characteristics
are best expressed in V27-69 and V27-76. V27-74 and
V23-63 are included in the Spitsbergen Group, though
they lack the constant carbonate zone, because they
share the upper zone and because of their locations.

Cores of the Norwegian Current Group (Fig. 22) are
located in the Norwegian Basin roughly along the
path of the Norwegian Current. The carbonate curves,
which show cyclic fluctuations, may be correlated with
North Atlantic curves mentioned above. These cores
usually penetrate through sediments deposited during
one complete climatic cycle.

Cores of the Iceland Group (Fig. 23), like the Norwegian Current Group cores, have a cyclic pattern of
carbonate fluctuation similar to that of cores from the
North Atlantic. Sedimentation rates in Iceland Group
cores appear to be much slower than in Norwegian
Current Group cores, because three or more climatic
cycles are commonly recorded.

Cores of the Greenland Sea Group (Fig. 24) commonly have high carbonate values at their tops but low
values throughout the remainder of the core.

Carbonate curves of the Norwegian Current and
Iceland Groups are interpreted as follows. The high
carbonate zone at the top, termed here the "Recent
high-carbonate zone" is preceeded by a low carbonate

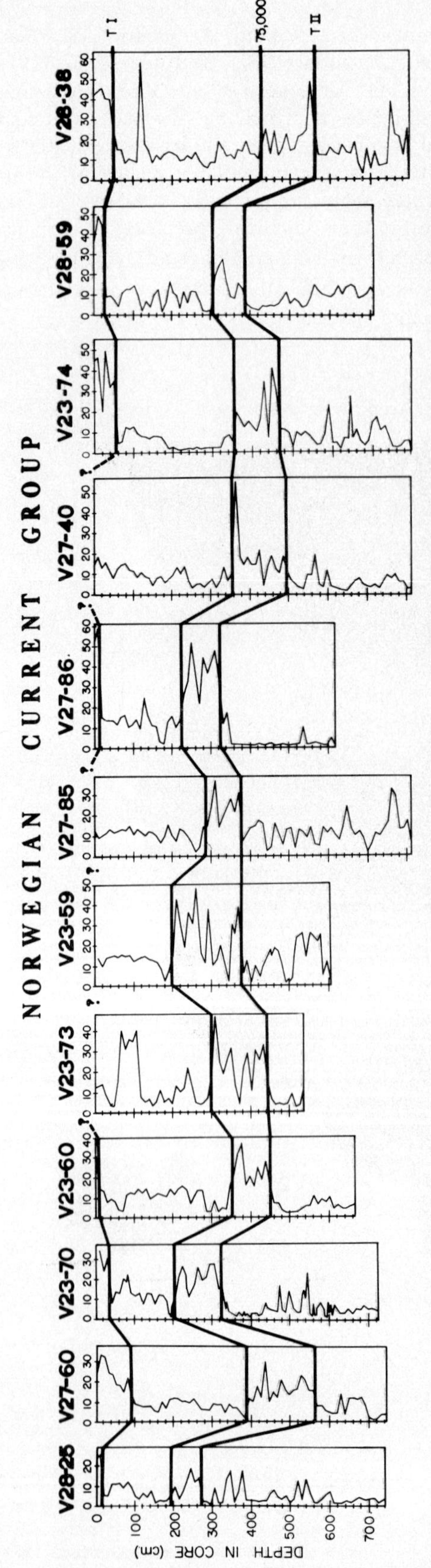

FIG. 22. Weight-percent carbonate curves for Norwegian Current Group cores. Curves are correlated at carbonate terminations I and II and at the 75,000 YBP isochron (Broecker, 1971), on the basis of radiometric dating of core V28-14 (Fig. 25).

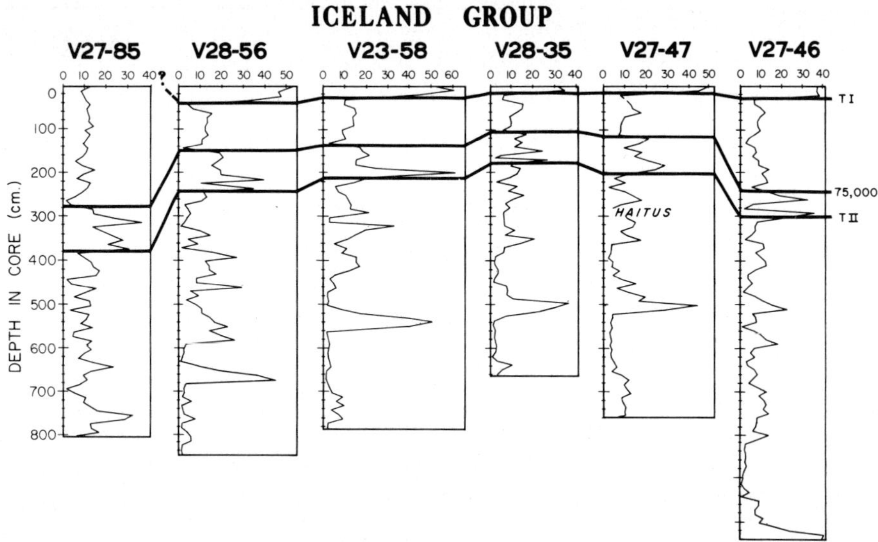

FIG. 23. Weight-percent carbonate curves for Iceland Group cores.
Curves are correlated as in Fig. 22.

zone, the "last glacial." The last glacial is in turn preceeded by the "penultimate high-carbonate zone"
(PCH) which is in part correlated with the Eemian
interglacial as described below. The zones are separated
by carbonate terminations I (about 11,000 YBP), II
(about 127,000 YBP) and the 75,000 YBP isochron
(Figs. 22 and 23). These dates are based on radiocarbon and ionium measurements made on V28-14
from the Denmark Strait (Fig. 25) by Kellogg (*in press*).

This interpretation and the dates used (after Kellogg,
in press) are consistent with the typical Atlantic pattern
of carbonate fluctuation and with the present distribution of calcium carbonate in the Norwegian Sea. Carbonate values at the tops of the piston cores are usually
almost identical with values in the tops of the corresponding TW cores. High carbonate values in the piston

cores are thus indicative of relatively warm surface
water and high productivity, because high values in
the trigger cores are directly related to these parameters.

Carbonate curves of the Spitsbergen and Greenland
Sea Groups have not yet been interpreted.

Glacial-Marine Sediment

For each of the cores in the north-south traverse,
curves from the *RAFT* program are shown along with
total coarse-fraction and total carbonate curves and a
sedimentary section in Figs. 26 to 31 (shown in order
of increasing latitude from south to north).

Total coarse-fraction curves shown in Figs. 26–31
tend to show highly variable patterns of fluctuation or
patterns related to sedimentary changes, such as from

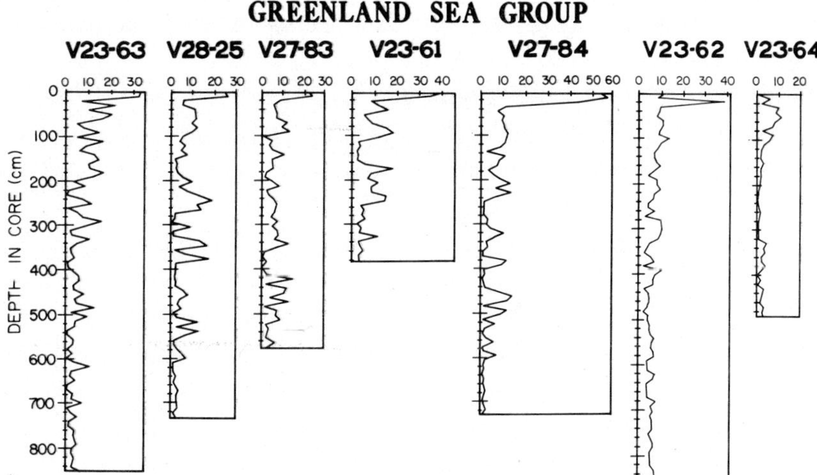

FIG. 24. Weight-percent carbonate curves for Greenland Sea Group cores.

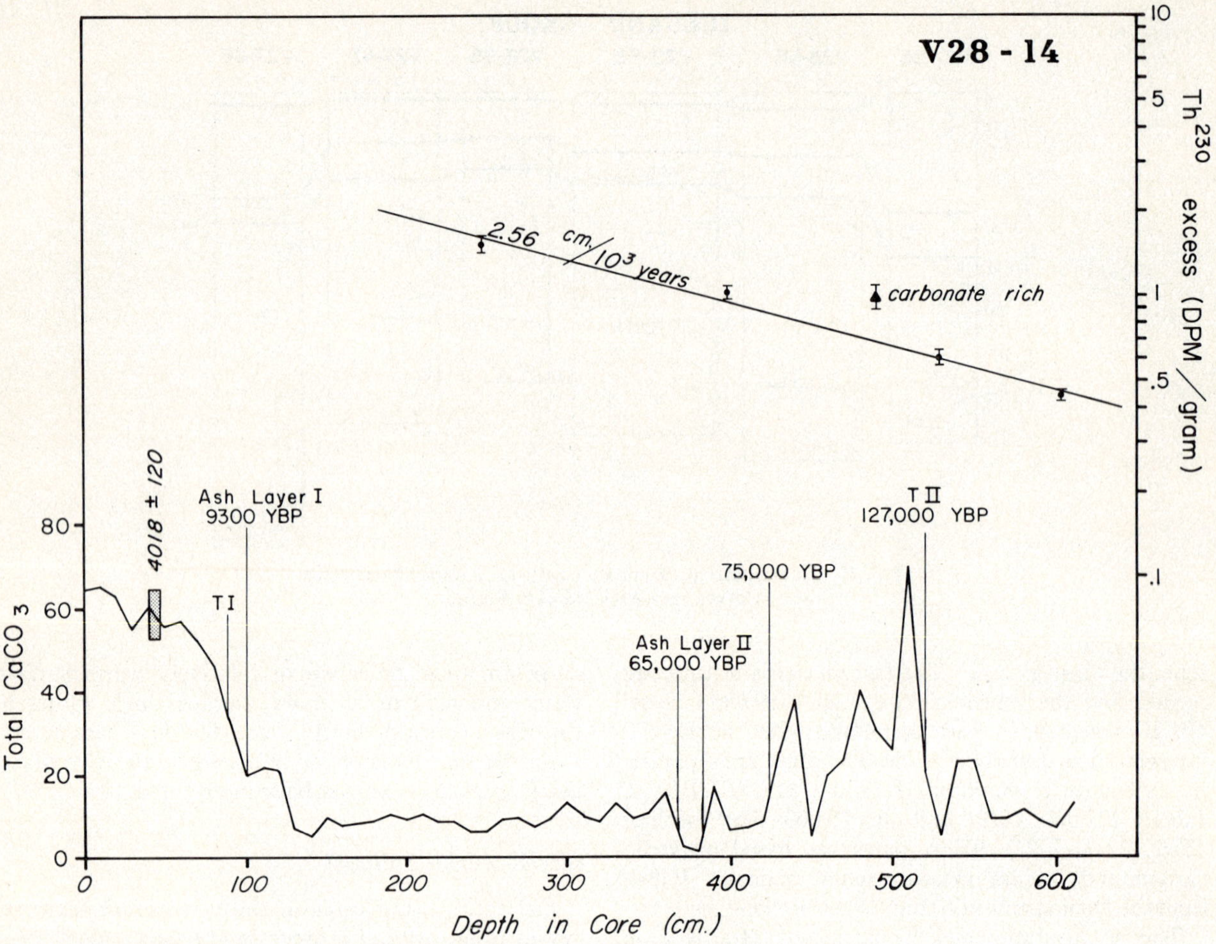

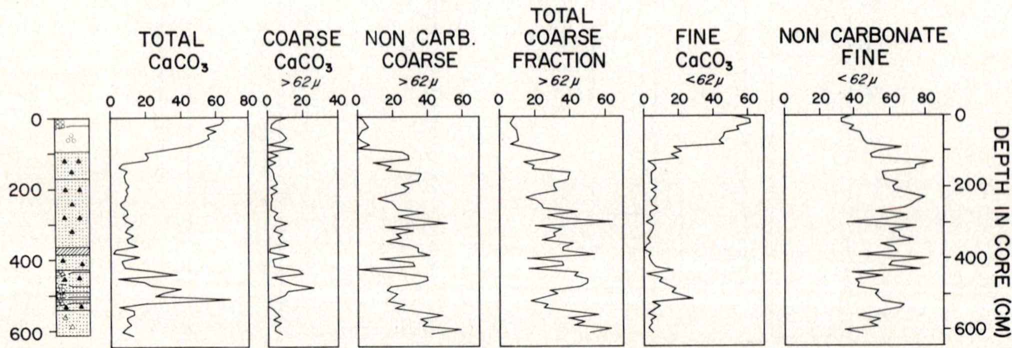

FIG. 25. Total-carbonate curve for V28-14 showing locations of carbonate terminations I and II, Ash Layers 1 and 2 and the radiocarbon dated sample at 40 to 47 centimeters. Excess Th²³⁰ values are plotted versus depth (right hand scale) above the carbonate curve to show where samples were taken for Ionium measurement (after Kellogg, in press, Fig. 20).

low carbonate to high or to ash layers and layers deposited by turbidity currents. Removal of the carbonate by the *RAFT* calculations does not remove this noise to the extent that a clear picture of glacial-marine input emerges. In this sense, the *RAFT* calculations are a failure. However, study of the fine-noncarbonate curves (clay-sized terrigenous material and fine glacial-marine detritus) shows that high values are recorded at times of low carbonate input (glacial conditions) and low values are found at times of high carbonate

FIG. 26. Sedimentary section and *RAFT* curves for V28-14. All scales are weight percent.

V 27-86

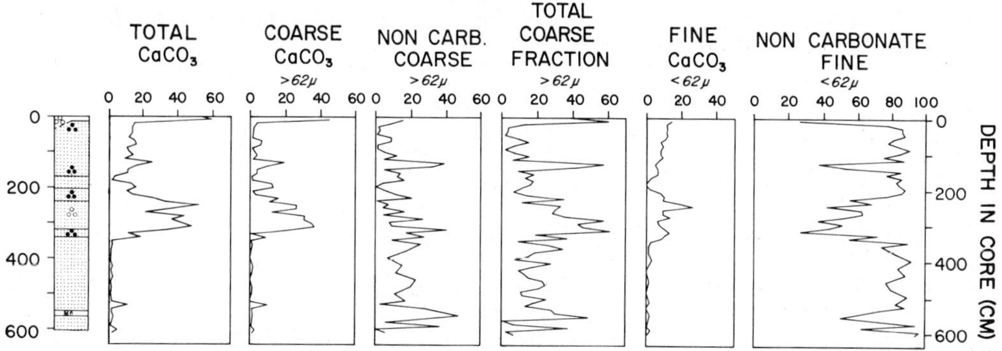

FIG. 27. Sedimentary section and *RAFT* curves for V27-86.

V 28-56

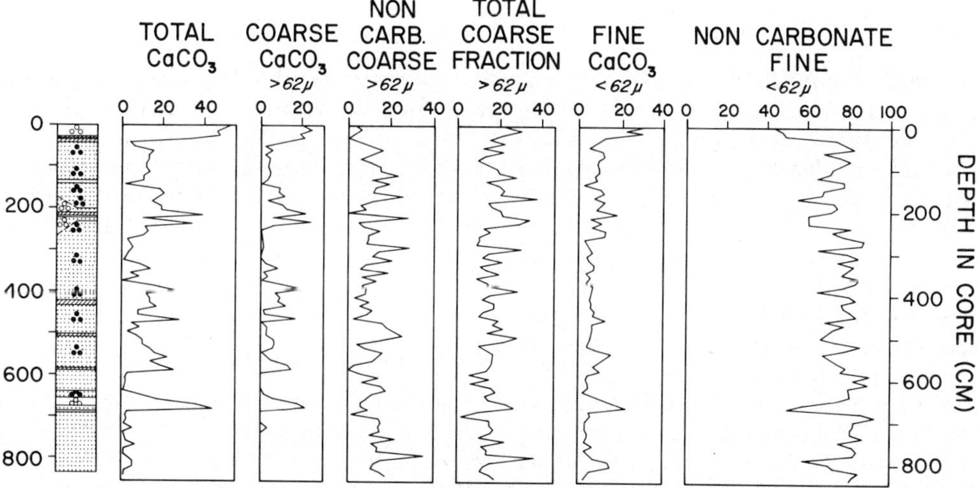

FIG. 28. Sedimentary section and *RAFT* curves for V28-56.

V 27-60

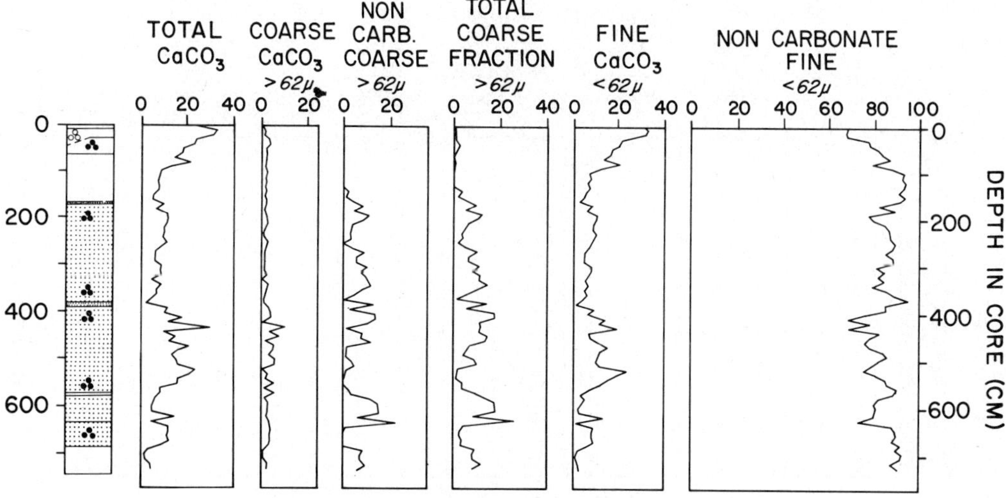

FIG. 29. Sedimentary section and *RAFT* curves for V27-60.

V27-47

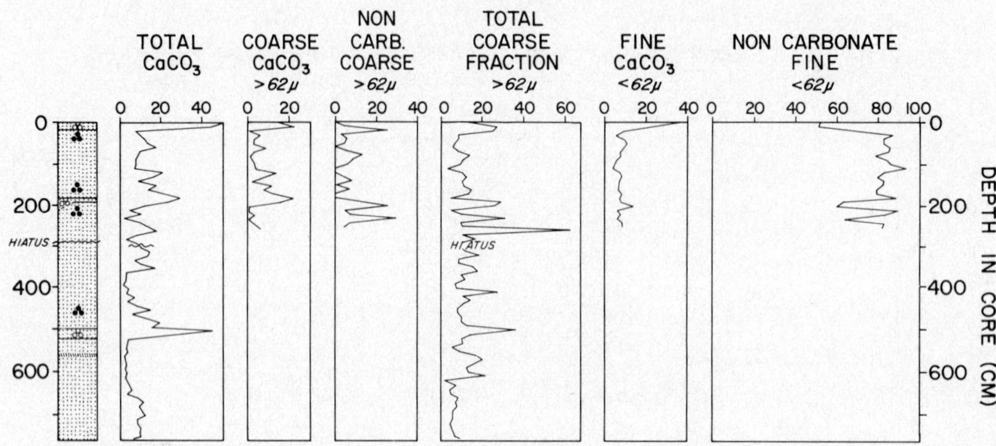

FIG. 30. Sedimentary section and *RAFT* curves for V27-47. The hiatus marked at 292 centimeters results from the loss of 180 centimeters of core during transportation from the ship to the laboratory.

input ("interglacial" conditions). This result is not surprising when the chancy nature of the ice-rafting mechanism is considered. Statistically, ice rafting should form a uniform blanket of material covering the ocean floor wherever ice cover was present. When the 2½ inch diameter circle represented by a piston core is considered in the context of the entire Norwegian Sea floor, it seems unlikely that there would not be large variations in contained glacial-marine detritus frome one place to another. The fine material dropped by the ice is subject to the action of currents as is the clay-sized terrigenous material which blankets most of the ocean floors in the form of red clay. This smoothing effect apparently causes the fine-noncarbonate fraction to be a reliable indicator of glacial-marine input.

Separation of the clay-sized terrigenous material from the clay-sized glacial-marine sediment will probably never be possible for Norwegian Sea sediments, because most of both these components are derived from the same sources on the lands surrounding the region. Separation of the silt-sized glacial-marine material is possible using standard sedimentologic techniques but was not made here.

Paleotemperature Estimates

Paleotemperature estimates were made for samples taken at ten centimeter intervals in the six cores (Fig. 20) using the method developed by Imbrie and Kipp (1971). Two separate sets of winter and summer esti-

V28-25

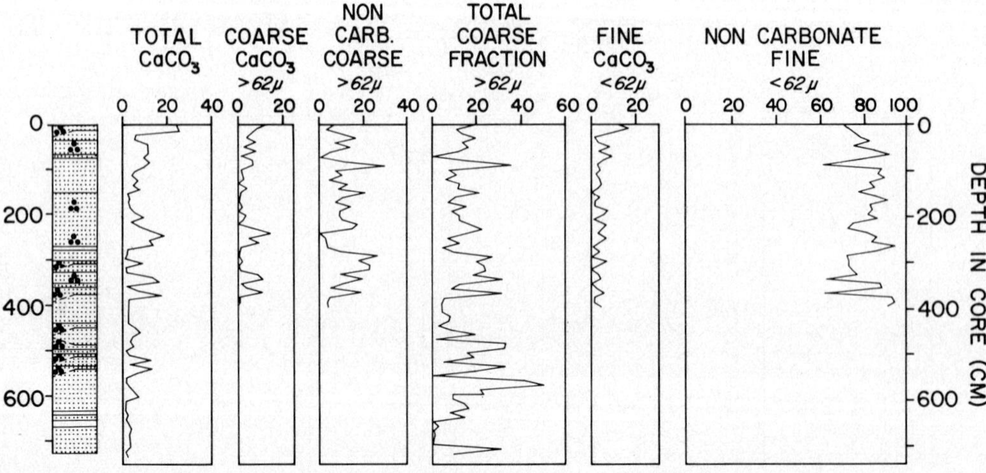

FIG. 31. Sedimentary section and *RAFT* curves for V28-25.

mates were made using as a base the factor analysis of the 25 TW tops from the Norwegian Sea and the 52 TW tops from the Norwegian Sea and northern North Atlantic. Varimax factor matrices from these two studies were related by curvilinear regression to known sea-surface temperature data. Statistics for the paleo-temperature equations are given in Table 2. Note that Equation 2 is based on a considerably larger tempera-ture range than Equation 1. Equation 1, however, should make more reliable estimates in the temperature range between −1.7C and 12.8C.

A number of cores contain barren zones and zones in which planktonic foraminifera are rare. More than 300 specimens were counted wherever possible. Where this was not possible, estimates are based on the ob-served population. Samples containing less than 25 specimens were considered barren and not plotted on Figs. 32 to 37. Samples with between 25 and 200 speci-mens are shown by small dots and are connected by dashed lines to indicate their statistical uncertainty. Samples with more than 200 specimens are indicated with large dots and are connected by solid lines.

Equation 1 paleotemperature estimates, based on the 25 Norwegian Sea TW tops, are shown in Figs. 32 to

TABLE 2. Temperature ranges and statistics for Equations 1 and 2.

Statistic	Equation 1		Equation 2	
	Winter	Summer	Winter	Summer
Temperature Range*				
Minimum	−1.7	1.1	−1.7	1.1
Maximum	8.3	12.8	13.9	20.6
Standard error of estimate*	1.2	1.97	1.53	2.19
Multiple correlation coefficient	0.95	0.895	0.955	0.913

* (°C).

37 (in order of increasing latitude). In all six cores, winter temperatures between −2.0C and 0.0C and summer temperatures between 3.0C and 6.0C are recorded in the low carbonate (glacial) intervals.

In the Recent high-carbonate zone, southern cores show high temperatures which decrease from core to core northward along the traverse until, in the two northernmost cores (V27-47 and V28-25), temperatures are indistinguishable from glacial values. V28-14, the

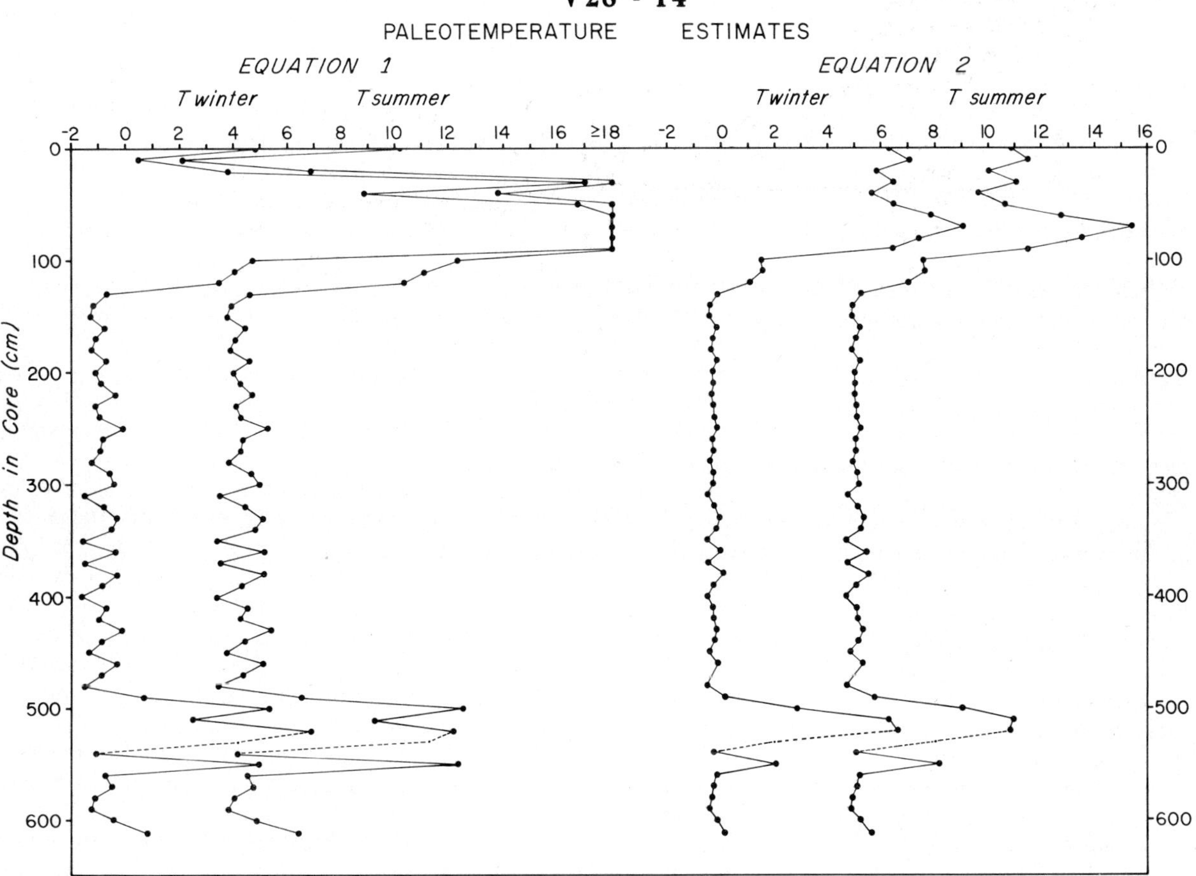

FIG. 32. Equation 1 and 2 paleotemperature estimates (°C) for V28-14.

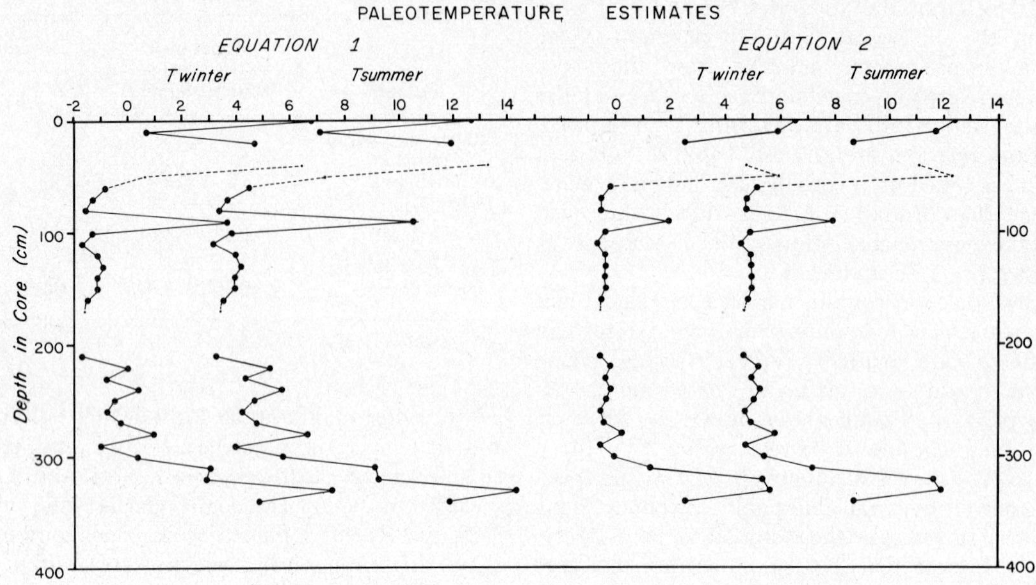

FIG. 33. Equation 1 and 2 paleotemperature estimates (°C) for V27-86.

southernmost core, shows temperatures greater than 18.0C in the Recent high-carbonate zone (Fig. 32). The values estimated reach 76C, an impossibly high value. This estimate results from the limiting effect of using an equation based on only a local region. The samples for which the impossible values were estimated contain foraminiferal populations characteristic of conditions warmer than were found in any of the 25 TW tops. Thus the estimates were computed by extrapolating from the observed data base and are obviously invalid. (See Webb and Bryan, 1972 for a discussion of how to choose core tops).

High temperatures are recorded only in the basal portion of the penultimate high-carbonate zone. They appear as a short sharp pulse of warm conditions which dies out in both intensity and duration from core to core moving northward along the traverse. Temperatures estimated for the PCH in V28-25, the northernmost core, are indistinguishable from glacial values (Fig. 37).

Equation 2 paleotemperature estimates, based on the 52 Norwegian Sea and northern North Atlantic TW tops, are shown in Figs. 32 to 37 to the right of the Equation 1 estimates. In all six cores, winter temperatures between −1.0C and 0.0C and summer temperatures between 4.0C and 6.0C are recorded in the low-carbonate (glacial) intervals.

In the Recent and penultimate high-carbonate zones, the same pattern observed with Equation 1 estimates is seen. High values in southern cores decrease to the north and become indistinguishable from glacial values at the northern end of the traverse. The major difference between estimates based on Equations 1 and 2 is that Equation 2 estimates are lower (in both winter and summer) for each sample. Curves of Equation 2 estimates also appear smoother than Equation 1 curves.

V28-14, for which Equation 1 estimated temperatures of up to 76C in summer, has a maximum temperature estimate of 15.4C using Equation 2. This result is considered reasonable because of the larger data base (52 TW tops representing a range of sea-surface temperatures between −1.7C and 20.6C). Thus the estimates were based on interpolation instead of extrapolation as was the case with Equation 1.

Discussion of Paleotemperature estimates

The prevailing climatic message presented by the paleotemperature estimates shown in Figs. 32 to 37 is one of extreme cold. Results from both equations suggest winter temperatures between −2.0C and 0.0C and summer temperatures between 3.0C and 6.0C prevailed throughout the Norwegian Sea for most of the time represented by the sediments, not only during low-carbonate (glacial) intervals, but also during the majority of the penultimate high-carbonate zone ("inter-glacial"). The only exceptions to these cold conditions are the warm pulses which occurred during the Recent high-carbonate zone and in the basal portion of the PCH. In each core, the pulses are usually of about equal magnitude but are strongest and last longest in the southernmost cores and gradually become shorter (in time and magnitude) toward the north. V28-25, the northernmost core, shows no indication of any warming in either the Recent or penultimate high-carbonate zones (Fig. 37) even though high-carbonate values are recorded. This result suggests that productivity of *G. pachyderma* (sinistral), the dominant species in this core, is more sensitive to climatic changes involving small changes in temperature near the freezing point of sea water than are the ecological responses of the remaining species.

This last observation points out one of the major problems involved with using the Imbrie and Kipp (1971) technique in the Norwegian Sea. For most of the time represented by these cores (low-carbonate zones), the planktonic foraminiferal assemblage is essentially monospecific (*G. pachyderma*, sinistral). Other species usually comprise less than 3% of the total planktonic foraminiferal assemblage. Ideally the Imbrie and Kipp (1971) technique should be used where one must extract information from a large data matrix consisting of numerous samples containing many species. This limitation might be partially overcome in the Norwegian Sea if a way could be found to split the admittedly highly variable morphology of sinistral *G. pachyderma* in some ecologically significant manner.

Most studies employing the Imbrie and Kipp (1971) method to date (Sancetta, *et al.*, 1972; Imbrie, *et al.*, 1973; Luz, 1973; Sachs, 1973a and 1973b; Sancetta, *et al.*, 1973) have dealt with fossil populations living in surface waters with environmental parameters which are not close to extreme maxima or minima (for example, water at its freezing and boiling points or with a salinity of 0.0‰). This study pushes the temperature scale to the freezing point (-1.7C for water with a salinity of about 34.0‰). For much of the lower portion of this range (-1.7 to about 4.0C) only one assemblage (Factor 1—*G. pachyderma* sinistral) dominates. Thus the equations are incapable of distinguishing between these temperatures and no real meaning

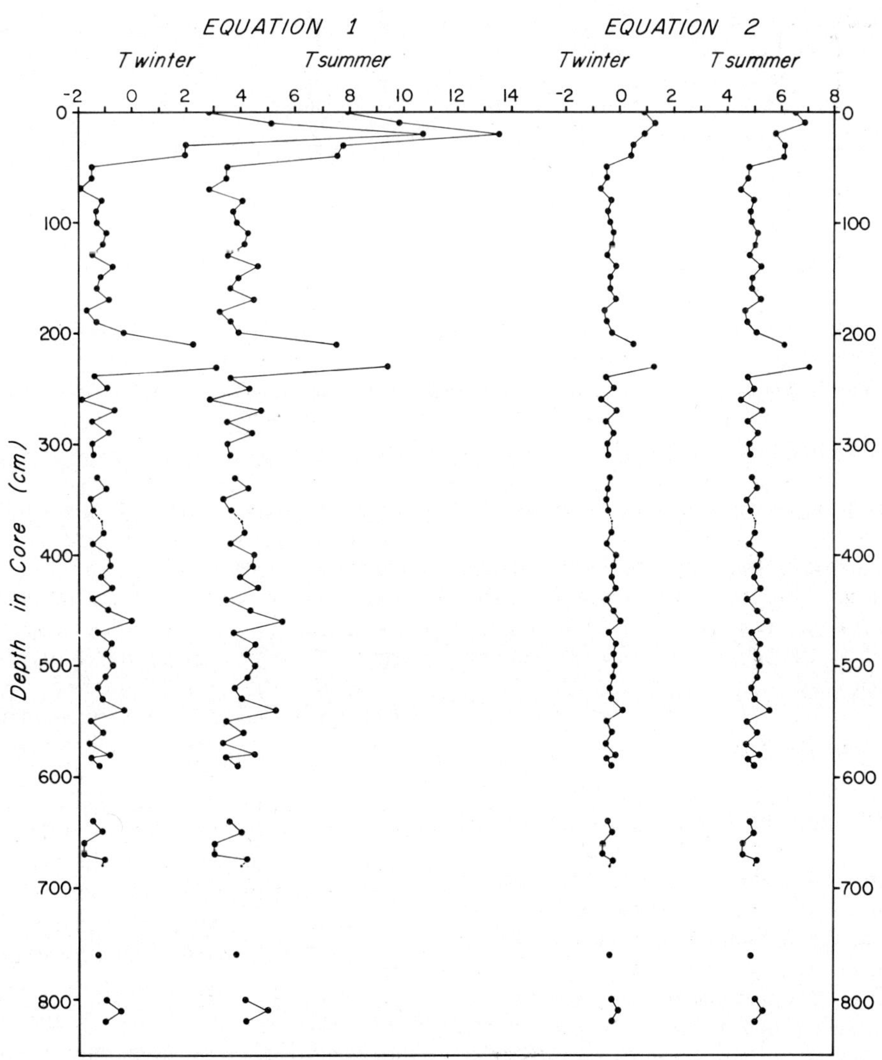

FIG. 34. Equation 1 and 2 paleotemperature estimated (°C) for V28-56.

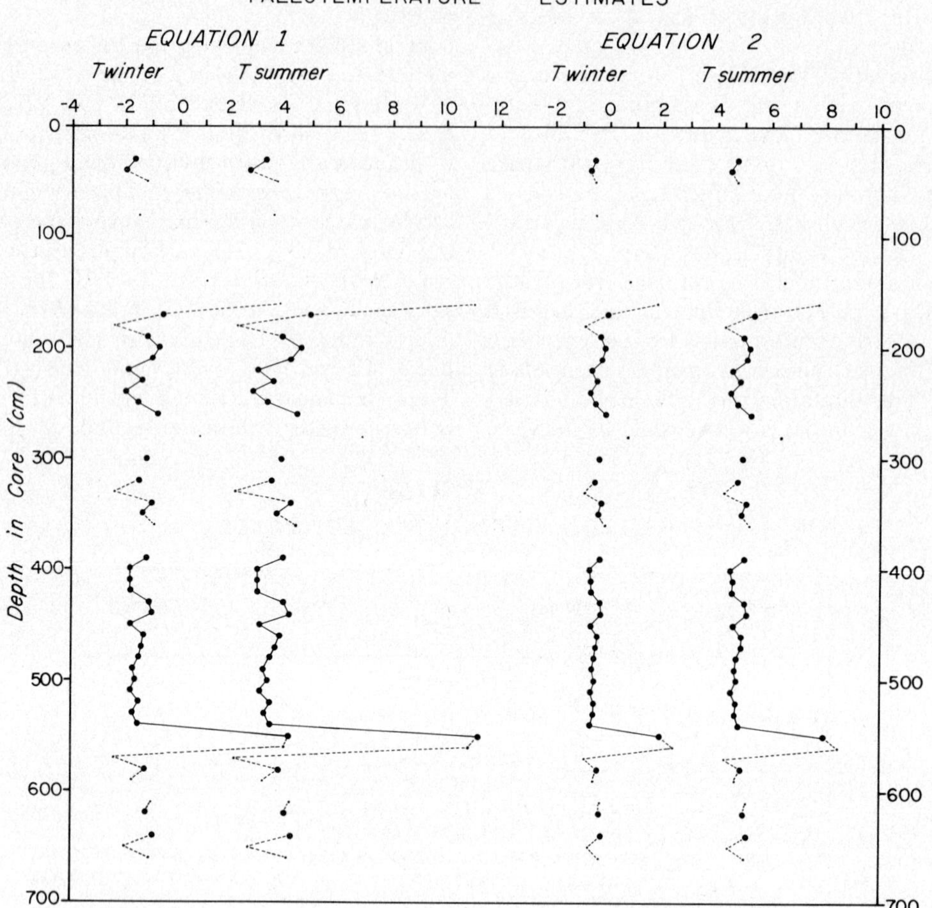

FIG. 35. Equation 1 and 2 paleotemperature estimates (°C) for V27-60. The top 150 centimeters of this core is largely barren of planktonic foraminifera.

should be assigned to variations estimated within this range.

In summary, although there is considerable doubt concerning the accuracy of paleotemperature estimates for temperatures less than about 4.0C, the basic climatic picture presented by the estimates for Norwegian Sea cores is considered valid.

4. Discussion and conclusions

The prevailing climatic message presented by the paleotemperature estimates is one of extreme cold. Warm water entered the region in two short pulses during the Recent and during the basal portion of the penultimate high-carbonate zone. These relationships are summarized in Fig. 38. The dating scheme used in Fig. 38 is based on work by Kellogg (*in press*). He showed that pulses of warm water, indicated by the presence of high percentages of dextral *G. pachyderma* in the same six Norwegian Sea cores, occurred in the Recent and in the basal portion of the PCH. The warm pulse at the base of the PCH was correlated with the Eemian interglacial event in western Europe (about 110,000 to 127,000 YBP).

The Eemian was the last interglacial period in western Europe. It was immediately followed by an intense but short cold period (Matthews, 1972; Sancetta, *et al.*, 1972; Kukla and Koči, 1972 and others) and in turn by a return to warmer conditions (but not as warm as during the Eemian) termed Early Glacial (van der Hammen, *et al.*, 1971, Fig. 2). In Norwegian Sea cores, the Early Glacial is represented by the upper portion of the PCH. This was a time with low temperature estimates when productivity, measured by carbonate content, remained high.

This observation suggests that four climatic regimes may be differentiated in the Norwegian Sea. 1) Interglacial conditions are characterized by high productivity (carbonate) and warm temperature estimates. These conditions occurred on only two occasions in the past 150,000 years: during the Recent and penultimate high-carbonate pulses. 2) Intermediate conditions are characterized by high productivity and low temperature estimates. This regime occurred during the majority of the PCH excepting only the basal warm pulse. The Intermediate climatic regime is encountered in the northern and western Greenland Sea today (V28-25) and is accompanied by partial ice cover. 3) Glacial conditions are characterized by low carbonate values and low temperature estimates. This regime is found in the low-carbonate zones and is apparently characterized by conditions more severe than those present today at the locations of V28-25 and V27-47. Since these locations presently experience sea-ice cover for part of the year, glacial conditions in the Norwegian Sea are inferred to have included complete ice cover, probably on a year around basis. 4) Barren zones, when present in the cores, coincide with ultra-low carbonate values and low temperature estimates. They are usually found at three distinct times, with respect to the carbonate curves, in the cores, These are, the top and bottom of the last glacial sequence and just below the base of the PCH. The first two barren zones are probably correlative with the early and late Wisconsin ice advances and the last zone probably corresponds to the pre-Sangamon or pre-Eemian ice maximum.

In the first section of this paper, the Norwegian Current was shown to exert an extremely important influence on both sedimentary and faunal distributions in the Norwegian Sea today. The data presented above suggest that only during the Recent and Eemian was the current active in its present location. For the remainder of the time (100,000 or more of the past 127,000 years), the Norwegian Current was either much weaker, or completely absent from the region. The change in surface circulation probably permitted year-around ice cover of the entire region. It certainly permitted sea-

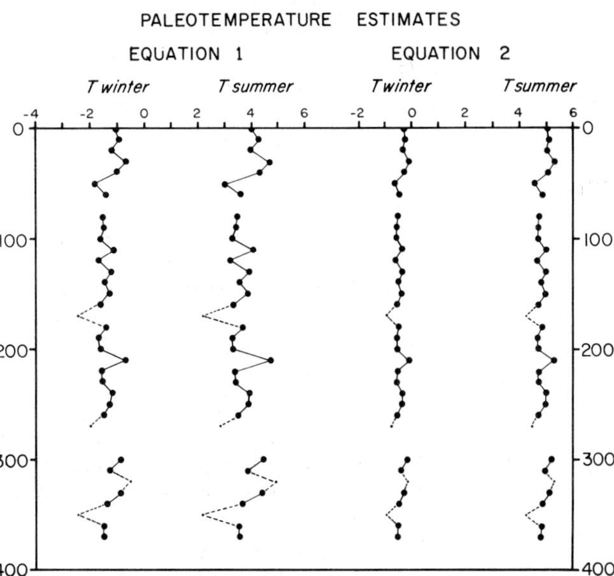

Fig. 37. Equation 1 and 2 paleotemperature estimates (°C) for V28-25.

sonal ice cover of the entire region, as evidenced by the influx of glacial-marine detritus in low-carbonate zones.

The absence of the Norwegian Current suggests that a major source of heat for the surrounding landmasses at present was absent for most of the past 127,000 years. The changing climate probably caused this change in circulation, which probably represents a feedback mechanism that helped to accentuate the effects of worldwide cooling in Scandinavia and northern Europe.

The exodus of the Norwegian Current permitted the spread of polar waters into presently subpolar regions, thus enhancing sea-ice formation throughout the Norwegian Sea. Both faunal and sedimentary evidence show that during the last glacial, ice covered the entire region, at least on a seasonal basis. This observation is important for the deep-water circulation of the North Atlantic. If the Norwegian Current, the source of saline water which presently becomes denser by evaporation to form Norwegian Sea Overflow Water, were absent and ice covered the region effectively prohibiting evaporation, Norwegian Sea Overflow Water would not have formed in the Norwegian Sea. This appears to have been the case during the majority of the past 127,000 years. This idea is supported by Streeter's (1973) work with North Atlantic benthonic foraminifera which suggests that glacial bottom water in the North Atlantic had considerably different temperature and salinity characteristics than presently forming Norwegian Sea Overflow Water.

In conclusion it should be noted that the data presented here directly refute the assertion by Olausson (1972) that the Arctic Ocean and Norwegian Sea were

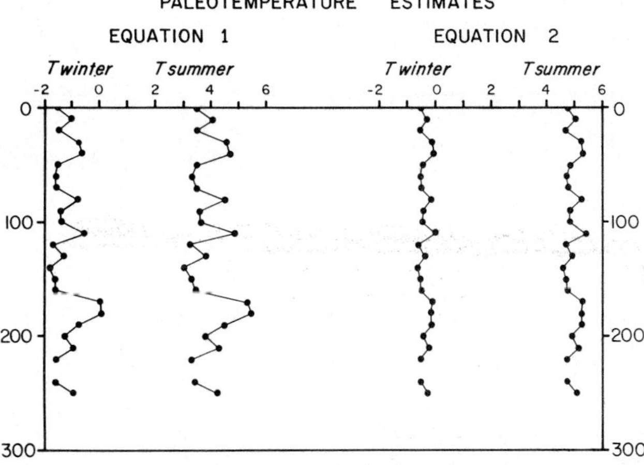

Fig. 36. Equation 1 and 2 paleotemperature estimates (°C) for V27-47.

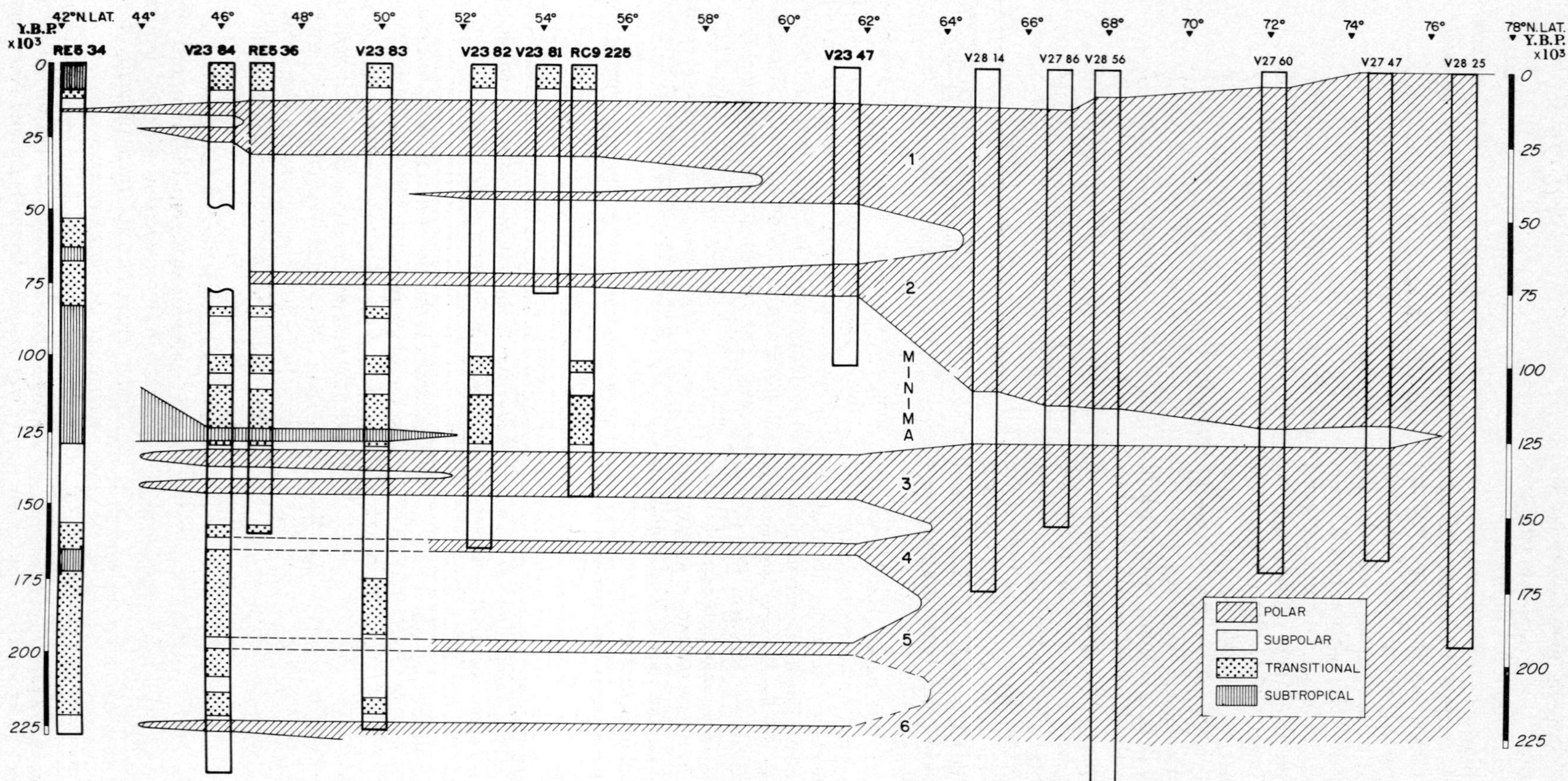

Fig. 38. Variations in the faunal and floral composition in the Norwegian Sea and northern North Atlantic. Climatic zones south of 62°N are based on coccoliths (McIntyre, *et al.* 1972). Note that subpolar faunas have been present in the Norwegian Sea only twice in the last 150,000 years: at present and about 120,000 years BP., corresponding to the Recent and Eemian (after Kellogg, *in press*, Fig. 23).

ice free during the Würm or Wisconsin glacial and served as a source of moisture for the great northern ice caps.

Acknowledgments. I wish to thank Drs. Thompson Webb, Robley Matthews, James Hays and Andrew McIntyre for critical review of the manuscript. Discussions with Drs. Lloyd Burckle, George Kukla, Tsunemasa Saito, Allan Bé, Dennis Darby, Warren Prell, Kenneth King, James Gardner and John Damuth and members of the IDOE CLIMAP group were very helpful. Dr. John Imbrie provided much needed encouragement. Mary Matthews assisted with the drafting, and Rosalind Mellor typed the final manuscript. Thanks are due to Captain Kohler and the chief scientists and crews on Vema cruises 23, 27, 28 and 29, and to Roy Capo, curator of the Lamont-Doherty core library. Special thanks go to Rose Marie Cline for cutting red tape on a number of occasions. Most important, I thank Dr. Davida Kellogg for inspiration and encouragement. Financial support was provided by Office of Naval Research grant N00014-67-A—1-8-0004 and National Science Foundation grants GX 28671, GA 35454, GA 29460 and GA 19690. This work is part of a Ph.D. thesis prepared under the helpful supervision of Dr. James Hays submitted to Columbia University.

REFERENCES

Arrhenius, G., 1952: Properties of the sediment and their distribution, Part 1. *Reports of the Swedish Deep-Sea Expedition,* **5**, Sediment cores from the east Pacific, 89 p.

Bé, A. W. H., 1960: Some observations on Arctic planktonic foraminifera. *Contrib. Cushman Found. Foram. Res.,* **6**, Pt. 2, 64–68.

Bé, A. W. H., 1967: Foraminiferal families *Globigerinidae* and *Globorotaliidae. Fiches d'identification du zooplankton, Conseil Permanent International pour L'exploration de la Mer,* Charlottenlund Slot, Denmark.

Bjørklund, K. R., and D. E. Kellogg, 1972: Five new Eocene radiolarian species from the Norwegian Sea. *Micropaleo.,* **18**, 386–396.

Böggild, O. B., 1907: Sediments sous-marine requeilles dans la mer du Grönland. p. 85–98 *in* Duc d'Orleans, ed., *Croisiere Oceanographique accomplie a brod de la Belgica dans la Mer du Grönland,* 1905.

Bramlette, M. N., and W. H. Bradley, 1941: *Geology and biology of North Atlantic deep-sea cores between Newfoundland and Ireland; I. Lithology and geologic interpretation.* U. S. Geol. Survey Prof. Paper 196A, 1–34.

Broecker, W. S., 1971: Calcite accumulation rates and glacial to interglacial changes in oceanic mixing. p. 239–265 *in* Turekian, K. ed., *Late Cenozoic Glacial Ages,* Yale Univ. Press, New Haven.

Broecker, W. S., K. K. Turekian and B. C. Heezen, 1958: The relation of deep-sea sedimentation rates to variations in climate. *Am. Jour. Sci.,* **256**, 503–517.

Broecker, W. S., D. L. Thurber, J. Goddard, T-L. Ku, R. K. Matthews and K. J. Mesolella, 1968: Milankovitch hypothesis supported by precise dating of coral reefs and deep-sea sediments. *Science,* **159**, 297–300.

Clark, D. L., 1969: Paleoecology and sedimentation in part of the Arctic basin. *Arctic,* **22**, 233–245.

Clark, D. L., 1970: Magnetic reversals and sedimentation rates in the Arctic Ocean. *Geol. Soc. Am. Bull.,* **81**, 3129–3134.

Dansgaard, W., S. J. Johnsen, H. B. Clausen and C. C. Langway, 1971: Climatic record revealed by the Camp Century ice core. p. 37–56. *In, Late Cenozoic Glacial Ages,* K. Turekian, Ed., Yale Univ. Press, New Haven.

Darby, D. A., 1971: Carbonate cycles and clay mineralogy of Arctic Ocean sediment cores. PhD thesis, Univ. of Wisconsin.

Dietrich, G., 1956a: Uberströmung des Island-Färoër-Rückens in Bodennähe nach Beobachtungen mit dem Forschungschiff "Anton Dohrn", 1955/56. *Deut. Hydrogr. Zeit.,* **9** (2) 78–89.

Dietrich, G., 1956b: Schichtung und Zirkulation der Irminger See im Juni 1955. *Ber. d. Deut. Wiss. Komm. f. Meeresforschung,* **15**(4), 255–312 (Berlin).

Ericson, D. B., 1959: Coiling direction of *Globigerina pachyderma* as a climatic index. *Science,* **130**, 219–220.

Ericson, D. B., M. Ewing and G. Wollin, 1964a: Sediment cores from the Arctic and subarctic seas. *Science,* **144**, 1183–1192.

Ericson, D. B., M. Ewing and G. Wollin, 1964b: The Pleistocene epoch in deep-sea sediments. *Science,* **146**, 723–732.

van der Hammen, T., T. A. Wijmstra and W. H. Zagwijn, 1971: The floral record of the late Cenozoic of Europe. p. 391–424. *In, Late Cenozoic Glacial Ages,* K. K. Turekian, Ed., Yale Univ. Press, New Haven.

Hays, J. D., T. Saito, N. D. Opdyke and L. H. Burckle, 1969: Pliocene-Pleistocene sediments of the equatorial Pacific: Their paleomagnetic, biostratigraphic, and climatic record. *Geol. Soc. Am. Bull.,* **80**, 1481–1514.

Holtedahl, H., 1959: Geology and paleontology of Norwegian Sea bottom cores. *Jour. Sediment. Petrology,* **29**, 16–29.

Hülsemann, J., 1966: On the routine analysis of carbonates in unconsolidated sediments. *Jour. Sediment. Petrology,* **36**, 622–625.

Imbrie, J., and N. G. Kipp, 1971: A new micropaleontologic method for quantitative paleoclimatology: Application to a late Pleistocene Caribbean core. p. 71–191. *In Late Cenozoic Glacial Ages,* K. K. Turekian, Ed., Yale Univ. Press, New Haven.

Imbrie, J. I., J. van Donk and N. G. Kipp, 1973: Paleoclimatic investigation of a late Pleistocene Caribbean deep-sea core: Comparison of isotopic and faunal methods. *Quaternary Research,* 3(1), 10–38.

Kellogg, T. B., 1973. Late Pleistocene climatic record in Norwegian and Greenland Sea deep-sea cores. Doctoral Dissertation, Columbia University, New York, New York.

Kellogg, T. B., (in press): Late Quaternary climatic changes: Evidence from Norwegian and Greenland Sea deep-sea cores. G. S. A. Special Paper.

Klovan, J. E., and J. Imbrie, 1971: An algorithm and FORTRAN IV program for large scale Q-mode factor analysis and calculation of factor scores. *Mathematical Geology,* **3**, 61–77.

Kukla, G. J., and A. Koči, 1972: End of the last interglacial in the loess record. *Quaternary Research,* **2**, 347–383.

Lamb, H. H., 1963: Mapping methods applied to the study of climatic variations and vicissitudes. Chapter 4 *in The Changing Climate, Selected papers by H. H. Lamb,* Methuen & Co. Ltd., London, 1968.

Li, Yuan-Hui, T. Takahashi and W. S. Broecker, 1969: Degree of saturation of $CaCO_3$ in the oceans. *Jour. Geophys. Research,* **74**, 5507–5525.

Luz, B., 1973: Stratigraphic and paleoclimatic analysis of late Pleistocene tropical southeast Pacific cores. *Quaternary Research,* 3(1), 56–72.

Matthews, R. K., 1972: Dynamics of ocean-cryosphere system: Barbados data. *Quaternary Research,* **2**, 368–373.

Mullen, R. E., D. Darby and D. L. Clark, 1972: Significance of atmospheric dust and ice rafting for Arctic Ocean sediment. *Geol. Soc. Am. Bull.,* **83**, 205–212.

McIntyre, A., 1967: Coccoliths as paleoclimatic indicators of Pleistocene glaciation. *Science,* **158**, 1314–1317.

McIntyre, A., and A. W. H. Bé, 1967: Modern Coccolithophoridae of the Atlantic Ocean—I; Placoliths and Cyrtoliths. *Deep Sea Research*, 14, 561–597.

McIntyre, A., W. F. Ruddiman and R. Jantzen, 1972: Southward penetrations of the North Atlantic polar front: Faunal and floral evidence of large-scale surface water mass movements over the last 225,000 years. *Deep Sea Research*, 19, 61–77.

Oba, T., 1969: Biostratigraphy and isotopic paleotemperature of some deep-sea cores from the Indian Ocean. Sci. *Repts. Tohoku Univ.*, Sendai, 2nd Series (Geol.), 41(2), 129–195.

Olausson, E., 1967: Climatological, geochemical and paleooceanographical aspects of carbonate deposition. *Progress in Oceanography*, 5, 245–265.

Olausson, E. 1972: Norwegian Sea in an ice age model. *Ambio Special Report No. 2*, 13–17.

Philippi, E., 1912: Die Grundproben der deutschen Südpolar expedition. p. 431–434. *In, Deutsche Sudpolar Expedition*, E. von Drygalski, Ed., 1901–1903, 2.

Raasch, G. O. (editor), 1961: *Geology of the Arctic*. Univ. of Toronto Press, Toronto, Canada, 1196p.

Ruddiman, W. F., D. S. Tolderlund and A. W. H. Bé, 1970: Foraminiferal evidence of a modern warming of the North Atlantic Ocean. *Deep Sea Research*, 17, 141–155.

Ruddiman, W. F., and A. McIntyre, (*in press*): Northeast Atlantic paleoclimatic changes over the last 600,000 years. *Geol. Soc. Am. Special Paper*.

Sachs, H. M., 1973a: North Pacific Radiolarian assemblages and their relationship to oceanographic parameters. *Quaternary Research*, 3(1), 73–88.

Sachs, H. M., 1973b: Late Pleistocene history of the North Pacific: Evidence from a quantitative study of Radiolaria in core V21-173. *Quaternary Research*, 3(1), 89–98.

Saito, T., L. H. Burckle and D. R. Horn, 1967: Paleocene core from the Norwegian basin. *Nature*, 216, 357–359.

Sancetta, C., J. Imbrie, N. G. Kipp, A. McIntyre and W. F. Ruddiman, 1972: Climatic record in North Atlantic core V23-82: Comparison of the last and present interglacials based on quantitative time series. *Quaternary Research*, 2, 363–367.

Sancetta, C., J. Imbrie and N. G. Kipp, 1973: Climatic record of the past 130,000 years in North Atlantic deep-sea core V23-82: Correlation with the terrestrial record. *Quaternary Research*, 3(1), 110–116.

Schott, W., 1935: Die Foraminiferen in dem aequatorialen Teil des Atlantischen Ozeans. p. 43–134 *in Wissenschaftliche Ergebnisse Deutschen Atlantik Expedition Meteor*, 1925–1927, 3.

Schreiber, B. C., 1967: Area SF, Volume 8, Core, sound velocimeter, hydrographic, and bottom photographic stations—cores. Marine Geophysical Survey Program 65–67 Western North Atlantic and Eastern and Central North Pacific Oceans, Alpine Geophysical Associates, Inc. for U. S. Naval Oceanographic Office.

Siesser, W. G., and J. Rogers, 1971: An investigation of the suitability of four methods used in routine carbonate analysis of marine sediments. *Deep Sea Research*, 18, 135–139.

Stadum, C. J., and H.-Y. Ling, 1969: Tripylean radiolaria in deepsea sediments of the Norwegian Sea. *Micropaleo.*, 15, 481–489.

Stetson, H. C., 1939: Summary of sedimentary conditions on the continental shelf off the east coast of the United States. p. 230–244. *In, Recent Marine Sediments*, P. Trask, Ed., Am. Assoc. Petroleum Geol., Tulsa, Oklahoma.

Steuerwald, B. A., D. L. Clark and J. A. Andrew, 1968: Magnetic stratigraphy and faunal patterns in Arctic Ocean sediments. *Earth and Planetary Sci. Letters*, 5, 79–85.

Steuerwald, B. A. and D. L. Clark, 1972: *Globigerina pachyderma* in Pleistocene and Recent Arctic Ocean sediments. *Jour. Paleo.*, 46, 573–580.

Streeter, S. S., 1973: Bottom water and benthonic foraminifera in the North Atlantic—glacial-interglacial contrasts. *Quaternary Research*, 3, 131–141.

U. S. Naval Oceanographic Office, 1965: Oceanographic Atlas of the North Atlantic Ocean, Sect. 1, Tides and Currents. Washington, D. C., publication no. 700.

U. S. Naval Oceanographic Office, 1967: Oceanographic Atlas of the North Atlantic Ocean, Sect. 2, Physical Properties. Washington, D. C., publication no. 700.

U. S. Navy Hydrographic Office, 1958: Oceanographic Atlas of the Polar Seas, Pt. II, Arctic. Washington, D. C., publication no. 705.

Webb, T., and R. A. Bryson, 1972: Late- and Postglacial climatic change in the northern midwest, USA: Quantitative estimates derived from fossil pollen spectra by multivariate statistical analysis. *Quaternary Research*, 2(2), 70–115.

Worthington, L. V., 1970: The Norwegian Sea as a mediterranean basin. *Deep Sea Research*, 17, 77–84.

Radiolarian-Based Estimate of North Pacific Summer Sea-Surface Temperature Regime During the Latest Glacial Maximum

HARVEY MAURICE SACHS, CLIMAP

School of Oceanography, Oregon State University, Corvallis, Oregon 97331

Abstract

Objective quantitative estimates of paleo-oceanographic conditions in the Subarctic Pacific can be made by analyses of radiolarian assemblages. By appropriate computations, transfer functions developed in a study of surface sediments can be used to estimate oceanographic conditions in deep-sea cores containing late Pleistocene faunas. For this study, two core traverses (at about 166°E and 165°W, between 35° and 50°N) were examined. Glacial maximum conditions were taken as the most recent temperature minima encountered. (More precise age control is not yet feasible in these slow deposition-rate, carbonate-free, cores). The results indicate that parts of the North Pacific were significantly colder than today (by about 4–5 C at 45°N), and can be used to reconstruct oceanographic conditions during this time interval.

1. Introduction

Recent methodological advances in paleo-ecology have made it possible to derive objective quantitative estimates of past oceanographic conditions by the study of fossils of plankton. The transfer function techniques developed by Imbrie and Kipp (1971) for planktonic foraminifera cannot be applied in most of the Pacific, since the carbonate tests of this group are dissolved at great depths. Consequently, Sachs (1973a, b) adapted and applied the transfer function method to the study of the (opaline silica) skeletons of Radiolaria, which are present in most Pacific sediments North of about 30°N.

The flow chart (Fig. 1) illustrates the algebraic basis of the approach developed by Imbrie and Kipp, and now widely used by the CLIMAP group. In the first stage, the planktonic fauna (e g., radiolarians) in deep-sea core tops from the region of interest is analyzed. In general, these samples contain the faunal elements now living in the vicinity of the sample location, and may be considered to represent average population on a long-term basis (several hundred to thousand years). Relict samples usually can be identified (Sachs, 1973a). Since there may be over 100 species present in a region, a "pretreatment" step is utilized to eliminate species which never attain significant abundance, and Q-mode factor analysis is used to determine assemblages (or factors) of organisms which occur in the same samples. Regression analysis is utilized to determine the relationship between the faunal assemblages at each sample location and the value of oceanographic parameters (such as surface temperature) at these locations.

In the next step, the faunas preserved at each level in deep-sea cores are used to obtain estimates of past oceanographic conditions at these levels by estimating the values of the surface assemblage factors for each level and then using the regression equations previously computed.

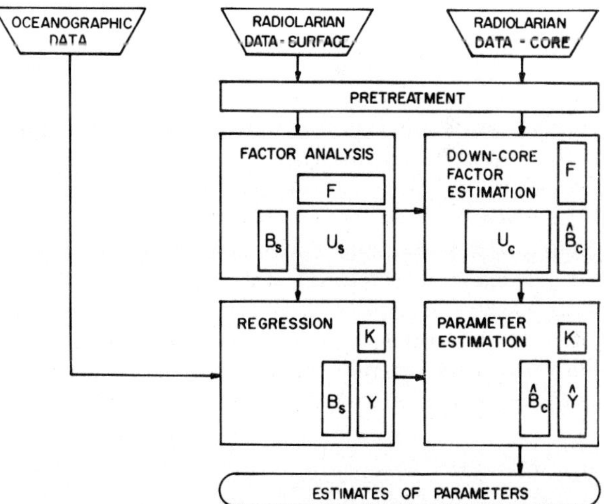

FIG. 1. Flow chart illustrating the algebraic basis of the paleo-oceanographic method employed. The notation is that of Imbrie and Kipp (1971). U_s = pretreated matrix of surface data, of size N samples by n important species. B_s = matrix of factor values on samples, of size N samples by m factors by n species. Y = the values of oceanographic parameters of interest at sample locations, of size N samples by j parameters, where $j+1$ is no greater than m. Then k is the set of regression equations mapping the factor values onto the parameter values. U_c = the pretreated core data, and is strictly analogous to U_s. $\hat{B}_c$ = the set of estimated factor loadings determined by postmultiplying U_c by the transposed matrix of factor loadings on species, F'. Then $\hat{Y}$ = the set of parameter estimates for the given down-core samples. The assumptions involved are treated by Imbrie and Kipp (1971) and Sachs (1973a).

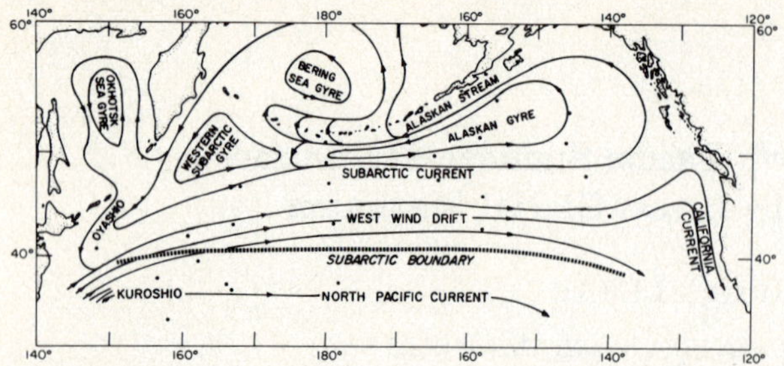

Fig. 2. Subarctic circulation, surface relative to 1000 decibars. Dashed line indicates Subarctic Boundary. Dots indicate many of the surface sample locations used in this study. From Sachs, 1973a, redrawn from Dodimead and others, 1963, Fig. 109.

Such estimates have been used in the study of the sequence of temporal change at particular locations (Imbrie and Kipp, 1971; Sachs, 1973b). A second application is the production of CLIMAPs: If a time-plane of interest can be recognized in a region for which transfer functions have been developed, and if objective estimates of paleo-oceanographic conditions are made at these levels, then a map of the parameter value on that surface can be drawn. This paper comprises the first results of an ongoing study of conditions in the North Pacific during the latest glacial maximum, and is part of a cooperative effort to generate such maps for the World Ocean on this datum.

2. The subarctic Pacific

The oceanography of the North Pacific has been reviewed by Dodimead *et al* (1963). The circulation of the region is dominated by the major clockwise gyre whose northern arm is the West Wind Drift–North Pacific Current sytem (Fig. 2). In the Subarctic region, a series of counterclockwise gyres is developed, and upwelling is associated with the divergence of these features. Salinities are very low in the upper waters of this region, and there is a permanent halocline. In general, meridional gradients in near-surface parameter distributions are much larger than East-

West variations (Fig. 3). In previous work, Sachs (1973b) established that one site (core V21-173, at 44°N, 164°W) was about 7 C colder during the latest glacial maximum than today or in earlier (interglacial) times. The present study has been designed to investigate whether this temperature minimum extended throughout the region, and, if so, what the oceanographic concomitants of this condition were

3. Methods

Radiolaria are planktonic protists, two large orders of which secrete ornate opaline silica tests, of size about 50–1000 μm. These tests are preserved in sediments in the North Pacific, and the assemblages present in surface sediments vary regionally, in a manner generally corresponding with Recent Pacific oceanographic conditions (Sachs, 1973a).

For this study, about 300 or 500 Radiolaria were counted in each of 57 samples from 42 core tops. The data set is largely that of Sachs (1973a) with some additional samples (Table 1). The sample grid was biased by the distribution of available core top samples, and by the desire to increase sample density along the dominant North-South parameter gradients. Duplicate samples at some sites were included to examine within-location variability. Species were assigned to one of about 120 taxonomic categories ("species"); unidentified specimens almost always accounted for less than 10% of the total population.

A four-factor Q-mode solution of these data gave optimal results. The factors and the proportion of the total variance accounted for by each are:

Factor	Variance
1	34.9%
2	29.2
3	17.6
4	9.2
—	—
Total	91.0 (rounded)

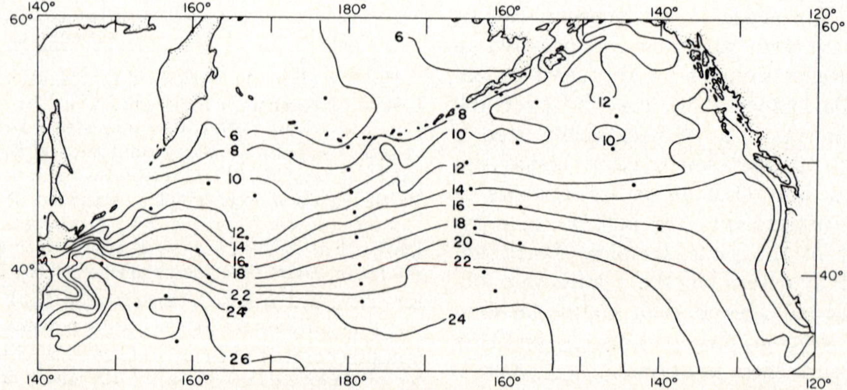

Fig. 3. Temperature (°C) at 10m depth, Summer 1955. From Sachs, 1973a, redrawn from NORPAC Atlas, 1960, Plate 13.

The most important factor for each core-top location is sketched in Fig. 4. Detailed examination of maps of individual factor loadings indicates that the distribution patterns of factors 1, 2, and 4 reflect near-surface oceanographic conditions, but that factor 3 is independent of these conditions. This assemblage comprises a suite of unusually robust forms, and may reflect solution or winnowing on the sea bottom, as discussed elsewhere (Sachs, 1973a).

A stepwise regression procedure was used to determine the coefficients of the equation relating the values of the three correlated factors to sea surface data for 48 surface sample locations. Appropriate control samples were withheld from the computation for later testing as "unknowns." To allow for possible nonlinearities in the relationship, not only the three factors (1, 2, and 4), but also their second order and cross product terms were included.

Naval Oceanographic Office (1969) monthly sea-surface charts for maximum August temperature (°F) were used as the oceanographic data source. Possible systematic errors in using ship inlet temperature data are considered unimportant, as the regional field in this source closely resembles that of others, and in this study regional changes with time are considered more important than exact modern values. Values used in the regression computation were determined by visual interpolation from atlas contours, using a sample location overlay map. Scale conversion to °C was done at the conclusion of the study. The observed temperature range in the study area was 14.6 C, and the average (absolute) residual between the temperature observed and that computed by the regression equation for each location was 1.48 C, indicating that the system is sufficiently accurate. Temperatures estimated for the control samples used as unknowns were within 2 C of observed temperatures.

4. Down-core temperature estimates

In order to map Glacial Maximum sea-surface temperatures, we need both a method of estimating tem-

TABLE 1. Core top samples used to augment set given in Sachs, 1973a, Table 1.

Latitude (N)	Longitude	Core	Type*	Sample Depth (cm)	Sample Code
50°19′	165°25′E	RC 14-113	TW	0	204
50°21′	172°43′E	V20-118	TW	1–3	211
47°24′	167°45′E	V20-120	TW	0–2	215
43°17′	166°54′E	RC12-413	TW	0–2	213
40°41′	166°59′E	RC12-412	TW	0–2	218
54°39′	177°00′E	V21-157	TW	0–3	212
51°01′	179°58′W	V20-111	TW	0–2	209
49°14′	180°00′W	V20-110	TW	3–4	210
47°19′	180°00′W	V20-109	TW	1–3	214
43°24′	178°52′W	V20-107	TW	0–2	208
40°52′	178°28′W	V20-106	TW	3	216
39°00′	178°17′W	V20-105	TW	10	220
37°18′	178°10′W	V20-104	TW	4	219
51°15′	164°53′W	RC11-172	TW	1	203
44°55.9′	165°1.0′W	Y70-1.15	MG	0–1	205
38°51′	164°02′W	RC12-432	TW	0	201
36°13′	162°40′W	RC12-433	TW	0	202
50°57′	146°05′W	RC10-217	TW	0–2	200
50°57′	146°05′W	RC10-217	TW	2–3	217
45°00′	142°35′W	Y70-1.6	PC	0–12	206
45°00′	140°00′W	Y70-1.5P	PC	0–1	207

* MG: Multiple Gravity; PC: Piston Core; TW: Trigger Weight.

perature from the faunas contained in deep-sea cores, and a method of recognizing the time-plane of interest in each core. Pelagic sedimentation in the North Pacific is slow, ranging from about 0.3–3.0 cm/1000 years (Hays and Ninkovich, 1970). Because of mixing and burrowing on the sea bottom and the sample thickness required, the uncertainty of chronological resolution in cores from much of the region is several thousand years. In addition, good dating or correlation techniques for recognizing the time of the latest glacial maximum in this region are not yet available. Given these limitations, in this study the time of the latest glacial maximum is considered to be the time of the most recent down-core temperature minimum.

To find the minimum temperature levels for the 11 cores utilized for this report, 500 Radiolaria were counted in each of 97 samples (3–12 per core). The cores studied lie in the two meridional traverses at

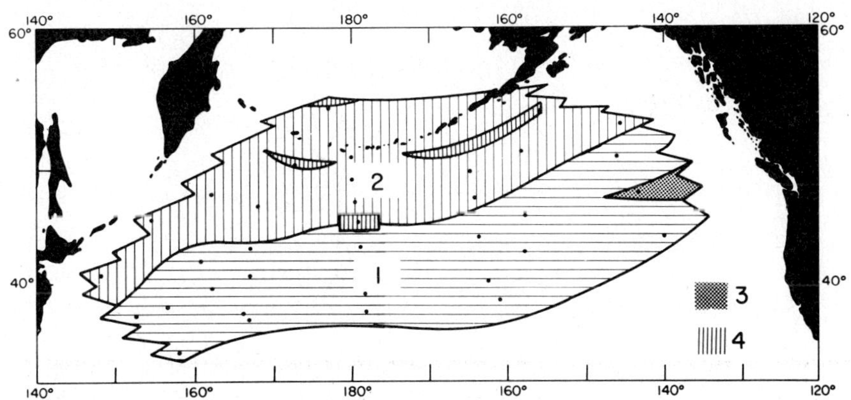

FIG. 4. Dominant factor distribution. The most important factor at each surface sample location is indicated.

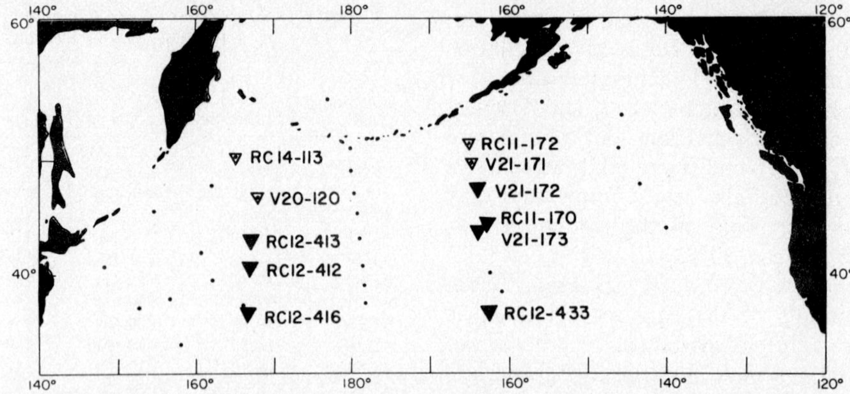

Fig. 5. Locations of Lamont-Doherty cores studied. Open triangles indicate cores which probably did not penetrate to the level of the latest glacial maximum (see text and Fig. 6).

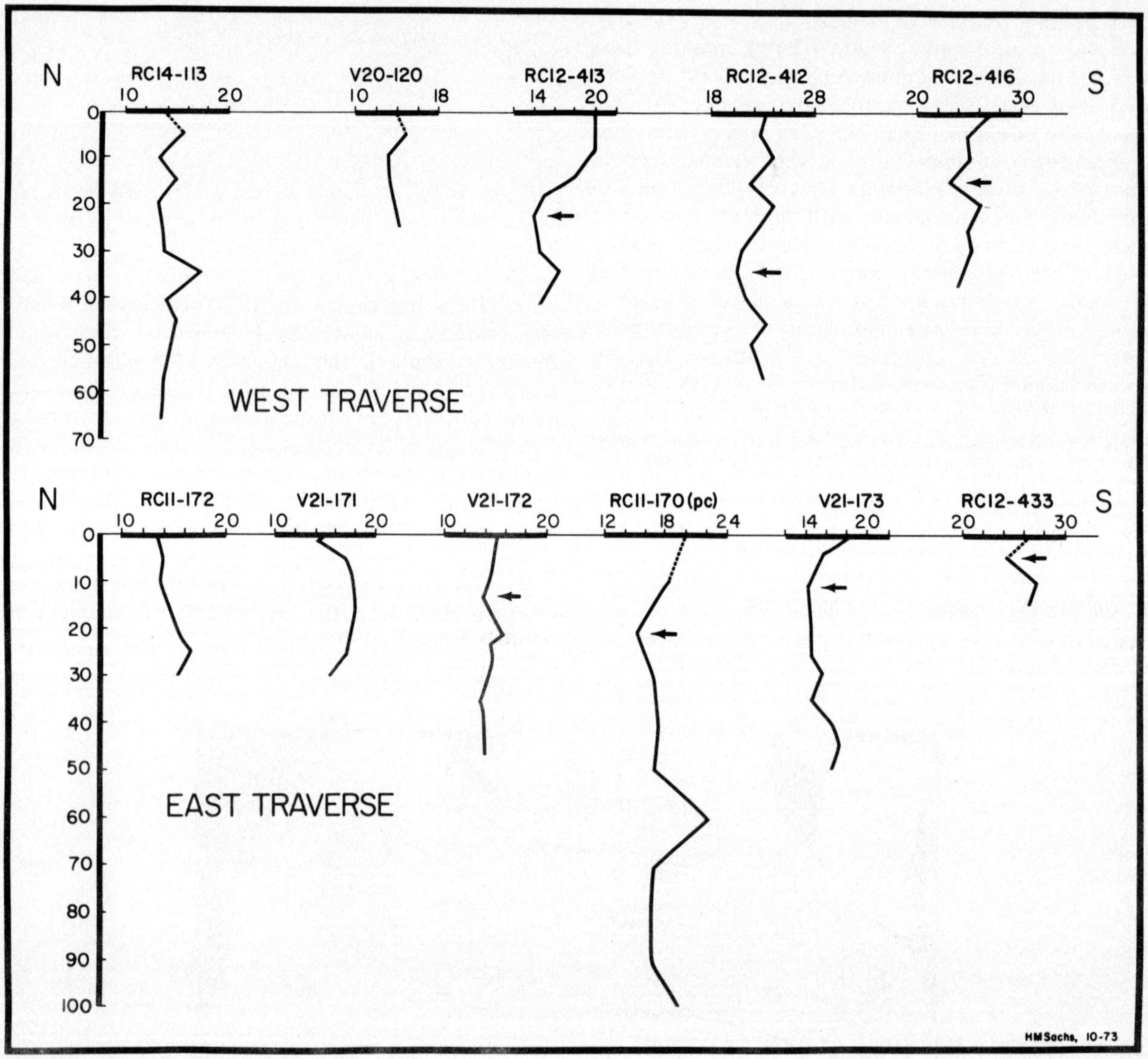

Fig. 6. Radiolarian-based sea-surface temperature estimates (°C) as functions of depth in core (cm) for the 11 cores located in Fig. 5. "pc" indicates piston core; all others are trigger weight (gravity) cores. Arrowheads locate values chosen as representing glacial maximum conditions.

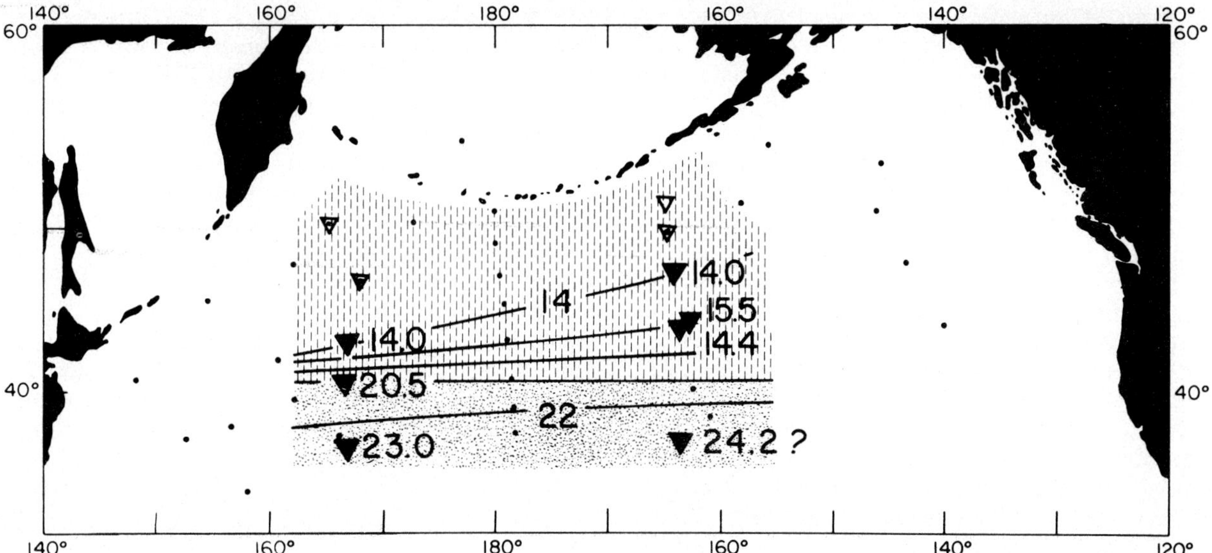

FIG. 7. Estimated values of maximum August sea-surface temperature (°C) during the most recent glacial maximum. Values taken from the cores plotted in Fig. 6.

about 166°E and 165°W (Fig. 5). In general, gravity cores were selected in preference to piston cores, as their upper portions are less likely to be disturbed.

Downcore temperature estimates for each core are plotted in Fig. 6. Because of the generally higher sedimentation rates in the North, it is felt that the four northernmost cores did not reach the time of the latest Glacial Maximum (RC14-113, V20-120, RC11-172, and V21-171). Work continues on piston core samples from these sites. (Piston cores are typically about 10 m long; gravity cores about 50 cm, so the piston cores include much longer records.) In the southern part of the area core RC12-433 is also suspect because of radiolarian solution. Work continues on other cores from this region as well

5. Results

The resolution of maps based on less than a dozen points is not great, but basic trends can be discerned. Fig. 7 shows the Glacial Maximum map based on the best estimates of the time plane and temperature for the cores in Fig. 6. For comparison, Fig. 8 suggests the modern August maximum temperature map that could

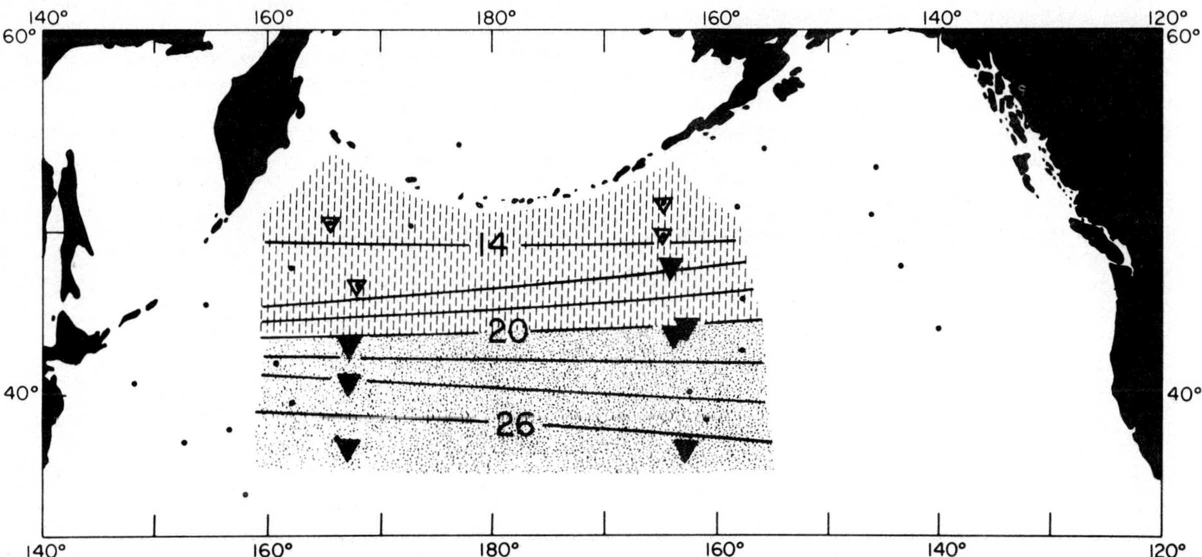

FIG. 8. Maximum August sea-surface temperature map (°C), based on Naval Oceanographic Office (1969) data. Contours are drawn on the basis of data for the locations of Fig. 5, in order to give the figure the limited resolution of the paleotemperature reconstruction of Fig. 7.

be drawn if data were only available for locations corresponding to the available core sites.

Comparison of Figs. 7 and 8 clearly implies that the North Pacific sea-surface was about 5 C cooler than at present during the Summer. Since the cores generally showed distinct temperature minima at appropriate levels, this conclusion is considered valid and not an artifact of the method. From the present data set, it is not clear whether this reflects worldwide cooling, or more immediate regional oceanographic changes. Comparison of Figs. 2 and 7 shows that the present data set is inadequate to resolve this question. For example, it is possible that mean storm tracks were displaced during Glacial times (Sellers, 1965, p. 204) and that the Subarctic Boundary and northern regional features, including the Alaskan Gyre, were displaced as a response. It is not clear at present whether this would result in a broadened Alaskan Stream South of the Aleutians (Fig. 2), or an expansion of the Alaskan Gyre, or both. If the relatively small (ca. 2 C) Glacial/Recent contrast in notheastern core V21-172 is verified by ongoing work, it would indicate that the core of the gyre was displaced. In this case, sites further South became the mean loci of the upwelling which now seems to occur in the vicinity of this core.

6. Conclusions

1) North Pacific surface temperatures during the latest Glacial were about 5 C cooler than at present. The extent of this deterioration can be objectively estimated by analysis of radiolarian assemblages.

2) Despite the limitations of presently used stratigraphic techniques, the time of this change can be located in deep-sea cores with sufficient precision to allow the temperature minimum surface to be considered as a time-plane.

3) Inferences from objective estimates of past conditions may have value in determining the nature of past changes in regional circulation patterns; work continues on this aspect of the problem.

Acknowledgments. This work is one aspect of CLIMAP, a multi-institutional effort in paleo-oceanographic studies funded through the International Decade of Ocean Exploration program. Work at OSU is supported by NSF/IDOE Grant GX 28673. Core samples were made available through the courtesy of Mr. Roy R. Capo and Ms. Dorothy Cook from the Lamont-Doherty Geological Observatory collection, supported by ONR (00014-67-A-0108-0004) and NSF (GA 29460). I have received invaluable stimulation and encouragement from my host at OSU, T. C. Moore, Jr., who also read this paper. The computer programs utilized were assembled at OSU by N. G. Pisias; J. Imbrie, N. G. Kipp and W. H. Hutson wrote most of the programs. S. Hee, L. Lee and D. Ericson prepared samples, and C. Yamashiro determined atlas values of oceanographic parameters. Linda Wille typed the manuscript.

REFERENCES

Dodimead, A. J., F. Favorite and T. Hirano, 1963: Review of Oceanography of the Subarctic Pacific Region. International North Pacific Fisheries Commission Bulletin Number 13.

Hays, J. D., and D. Ninkovich, 1970: North Pacific deep-sea ash chronology and age of present Aleutian underthrusting. In: "Geological Investigations of the North Pacific" (J. D. Hays, Ed.), 263–290, Geological Society of America Memoir 126, Geological Society of America, New York.

Imbrie, J., and N. G. Kipp, 1971: A new micropaleontological method for quantitative paleoclimatology: application to a late Pleistocene Caribbean core. In: "The Late Cenozoic Glacial Ages" (K. K. Turekian, Ed.), 71–181. Yale University Press, New Haven.

Naval Oceanographic Office, 1969: Monthly Charts of Mean, Minimum, and Maximum Sea Surface Temperature of the North Pacific Ocean. Naval Oceanographic Office Special Publication SP-123, 58 p.

NORPAC Committee, 1960: "Oceanic observations of the Pacific: 1955. The NORPAC Atlas." 123 maps. University of California Press and University of Tokyo Press, Berkeley and Tokyo.

Sachs, H. M., 1973a: North Pacific radiolarian assemblages and relationship to oceanographic parameters. *Quarternary Research*, **3**, 73–88.

Sachs, H. M., 1973b: Late Pleistocene history of the North Pacific: Evidence from a quantitative study of Radiolaria in core V21–173. *Quarternary Research*, **3**, 89–98.

Sellers, W. D., 1965: "Physical Climatology." University of Chicago Press. Chicago.

A Palynological Study of Late Holocene Vegetation and Climate in the Healy Lake Area, Alaska

J. H. ANDERSON

Institute of Arctic Biology, University of Alaska, Fairbanks, Alaska 99701

Abstract

A preliminary palynological study of the Healy Lake area in southeastern interior Alaska is reported. With the minor exception of pine, pollen profiles show no important trends for the past 4600 radiocarbon years, percentages at depth being similar to surface samples. Therefore it is tentatively concluded that late Thermal Maximum and Neoglacial vegetation changes, if any, were slight. There is some evidence that lodgepole pine has migrated toward the area from the southeast during the Holocene.

1. Introduction

The Healy Lake area, in the upper mid-Tanana River valley in southeastern interior Alaska (Fig. 1), was studied archaeologically by Cook (1969) and Cook and McKennan (1970a, b), and geomorphologically by Ager (1972) and Hamilton (1973). Principal findings included (a) a human population has lived in the area at least intermittently for approximately 11,000 years, (b) the geologic component of the landscape has changed significantly during this time as a result of late- and postglacial fluvial, eolian and cryopedologic processes, (c) the present Healy Lake probably is young, with an age of only some 4000 years, and (d) macroclimatic changes associated with the Thermal Maximum and Neoglaciation have occurred.

In conjunction with this research a palynologically based attempt was begun in 1970 to determine something of the vegetation history of the area and more of the climatic history as related to vegetation. Specific objectives are (a) further information on the environment in which early human activity took place, (b) geobotanical information to complement geomorphologic studies and (c) new paleophytogeographic and paleophytocenologic knowledge of the interior Alaska boreal forest. Analysis of some of the palynological samples resulted in minor progress toward meeting these objectives. A preliminary view was achieved and initial interpretations made of the record for possibly the past 4600 radiocarbon years, less than half the span of the geomorphologic and archeological interpretations. In view of the importance of the area for studies of the past, particularly with respect to the human population of the Americas, more could profitably be done toward extending and refining knowledge of the geobotanical record.

Healy Lake lies at 64°00′N latitude and 144°45′W longitude, at an elevation of 343 m (Fig. 1). Aspects of the geology, climate and vegetation of the area were described and referenced by the investigators cited above, and information on regional vegetation was published by Lutz (1956), Spetzman (1963), Matthews (1970) and Viereck (1973).

Ordinarily the character of only the upland vegetation may be identified with some degree of reliability in the palynological record, as plants of lowland habitats such as bogs tend to be poorly represented. In the Healy Lake area the upland vegetation comprises white and black spruce (*Picea glauca* and *P. mariana*), paper birch (*Betula papyrifera*), aspen (*Populus tremuloides*), balsam poplar (*P. balsamifera*), willows (*Salix* spp.), shrub birch (*Betula glandulosa*), and a number of other woody plants, plus numerous herb and cryptogam species. The species listed contribute most to the physiognomy, plant biomass and pollen rain of the upland vegetation from the lowest elevations to treeline at around 900 m. Mixtures of two or more dominant species are most widespread, but among forest communities stands dominated by one species are common. The vegetation is overall a mosaic of stands, often intergrading, of forest, scrub and other communities. It would not be possible to sort out, in the palynological record, the stands constituting past plant communities with respect to diversity, relative abundance and distribution, except perhaps by detailed studies of samples from many sites throughout the area. Instead, a composite picture has to do for any one point in time.

Non-quantitative field observations indicate that among the most conspicuous species, birch is most important areally, followed in order by aspen, white spruce, black spruce and balsam poplar. Alders and willows are less important in forest communities but are common in upland scrub and in scrub vegetation types along streams and lake margins. Willows and

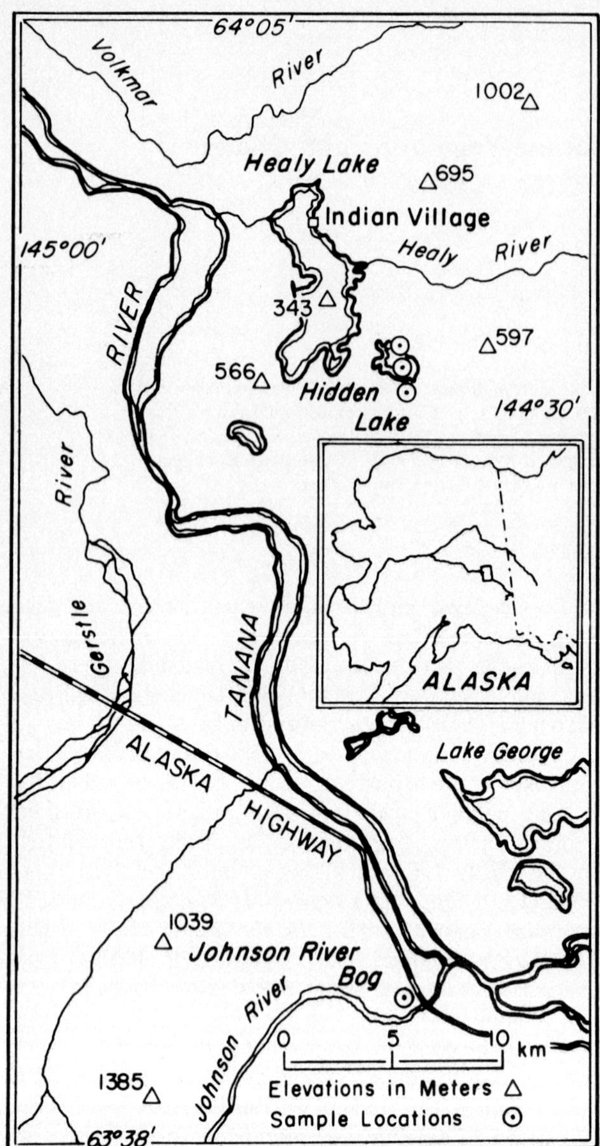

Fig. 1. Map of the Healy Lake area.

shrub birch are important in non-forest bog vegetation. An Earth Resources Technology Satellite image, scene 1029-20383, was interpreted as showing forest and scrub over an estimated 60 per cent of the Healy Lake area. The rest of the area appeared covered by non- and sparsely forested bogs and, above timberline, by various alpine tundra communities. Ager (1972: 7 ff) presented good illustrations of the distribution of vegetation types according to elevation, slope, aspect, soil type and permafrost.

The vegetation is related to a boreal continental macroclimate. Characteristically summers are short, warm, moderately dry and occasionally breezy. Frontal storm systems prevail perhaps 25 per cent of the time, keeping temperatures in the 10 to 15 C range and providing the bulk of precipitation. During clear weather daytime temperatures commonly are 20 to 25 C, and a substantial amount of rain may fall locally in short-duration convection storms. Summer insolation is high, and this combined with warmth and adequate moisture promotes rapid plant growth.

Winters are long, cold and dry, and the winter landscape features a continuous, moderately thick snow cover. Wind is insignificant except during infrequent frontal storms entering from the north Pacific, which are the primary winter precipitation source. Mid-winter insolation is very low.

Winter and summer are separated by a short spring and fall. Plant growth begins in mid-May and ends in early September. Permafrost is of consequence to plant growth in the low lying, poorly drained bogs and on north slopes. Permafrost terrain occupies perhaps 40 per cent of the Healy Lake area.

Johnson and Hartman (1969) published maps from which values of several climatic variables in the Healy Lake area were approximated. These are presented in Table 1.

2. Methods

Sample locations are shown in Figure 1. Hidden Lake was chosen for sampling instead of Healy Lake because of the possibility that the sedimentary, erosional and thermokarst processes proposed by Ager (1972) as preceding and active in the evolution of Healy Lake have been less intense here. This is indicated by the fact that Hidden Lake is, in fact, somewhat hidden physiographically from these processes. It was judged that only nearby, in the lower Healy River valley on the north and in the main Healy Lake basin, has physiographic instability, including sediment mixing, been significant. It was assumed that the Hidden Lake basin has been stable enough for palynological purposes.

The Johnson River bog, probably evolving from a glacial kettle pond, is located 22 km south of Healy Lake. It was selected for sampling because probing

TABLE 1. Mean values of selected macroclimatic variables in the Healy Lake area, approximated from maps published by Johnson and Hartman (1969).

Temperature (°C)		Precipitation	
Annual	−4.4	Annual	280 mm
January, min.	−26.7	Snowfall	1270 mm
January, max.	−17.8	Wet day probability	
		at Big Delta, c 55 km NW:	
January	−22.2		
July, min.	10.0	June–August	0.18
July, max.	21.2	Sept–Oct	0.10
July	15.5	Nov–March	0.13
Seasonal variation	18.8*	April–May	0.05

Light
Hours sunlight: Late June—22; late December—4.

* This is about mid-way in the range given for a continental climate.

indicated a thick sedimentary sequence and because the bog is easily accessible.

A square-rod Livingstone sampler was used. In Hidden Lake the depth of penetration, hence the time spans of the several cores, was determined by the moderately heavy consistency of the mucky sediments and the physical limitations of three persons working over the side of a light boat. The average length of the three cores selected for analysis was 58 cm. Water depths at coring locations were 79 to 183 cm. In the Johnson River bog, where a lack of machinery for driving and extracting the sampler again was limiting, a 287 cm core was obtained. Subsequently T. A. Ager (pers. comm. 1972) obtained longer cores here, analysis and dating of which are under way.

Extra material was obtained near the lowest core levels for radiocarbon dating at the Institute of Marine Science, University of Alaska.

Palynological preparations were made according to standard procedures (Faegri and Iversen 1964: 66 ff). Most pollen identifications were made, and counting done, under 100 power magnification. A minimum of 200 grains were counted on most slides for calculating percentage occurrences of the nine taxa judged numerically and ecologically important. Fewer were counted on some slides where grains were scarce. The percentages were plotted against depth to produce standard palynological diagrams.

3. Results and discussion

The palynological diagrams (Fig. 2) show relative percentages of pollen grains at each sample depth and radiocarbon dates. As no date was obtained for the Johnson River bog, an estimate for the bottom level was made from peat accumulation rates in similar environments given by Hansen (1953: 538) and Anderson (1970: 189). Whereas the cores when removed from the sampler were compressed, the sample depths shown are adjusted to original levels assuming a linear compaction rate.

Radiocarbon dating revealed the part of the palynological record brought to light extends from around 4600 years BP possibly to the present. The pollen profiles show no important trends during this time interval, the percentages at most depths being approximately the same as those of surface samples. These percentages are more or less the same as those of surface samples elsewhere in the boreal forest of interior Alaska as determined by Matthews (1970). Therefore it appears that the composition of the vegetation of the Healy Lake area, to the extent that it is reflected here, has been constant for at least the past 4600 years. This would seem to indicate that the macroclimate has not changed during this time.

Geologists, however, have found evidence for a regional Neoglaciation, with an accompanying Neoglacial climate, beginning approximately 3000 years

BP and lasting to within the past few decades (Ager 1972; Hamilton 1973). In addition, geobotanical evidence of a preceding Thermal Maximum, ending between 3000 and 4000 years BP, has been found in nearby areas (Heusser 1960; Anderson 1970; Rampton 1971). Therefore it is concluded that late Thermal Maximum and Neoglacial vegetation changes, if any, in the Healy Lake area were slight. This supports Ager's (1972: 96) conjecture: "Cooler Neoglacial temperatures may have slightly reduced the elevation of timberline, but vegetation in general probably was not affected." A more intensive palynological study might reveal some vegetation changes.

In interpreting percentage-based palynological diagrams it normally is necessary to apply the modern analogs technique or the technique of determining correction factors relating pollen percentages with vegetation composition. There seems no need to consider either of these here because the fluctuations in pollen percentages (Fig. 2) are within the margins of error of the sampling and analysis procedure. It could be said, however, that the modern analogs technique was applied, in that the present vegetation serves as an analog of that of the past.

Heusser (1967) and Anderson (1970, 1971) treated a hypothesis that the present northwestern Canada population of lodgepole pine, *Pinus contorta* ssp. *latifolia*, the inland subspecies, derives from a Wisconsin Age population in a glacial refugium in northeastern British Columbia and northwestern Alberta. Anderson presented palynological information from northwestern British Columbia and south-central Yukon Territory consonant with a slow migration from the southeast during the Holocene.

A refugium probably did not exist here during the Wisconsin glacial maximum, and pine probably persisted only south of the continental ice sheet at this time. It appears, however, that a corridor between the Cordilleran and Laurentide ice sheets opened northward early in deglaciation, allowing migration of pine, and no doubt other species, to the northeastern British Columbia area, possibly by the close of the Wisconsin. From this area Holocene migration northwestward could have continued. The current northwestern limit of lodgepole pine is southwestern Yukon Territory. It is possible that the species is still slowly migrating, as it grows well and sets seed when planted in interior Alaska much farther to the northwest, although seedling establishment under natural conditions has not been observed (L. A. Viereck, pers. comm. 1974).

Minor occurrences of pine pollen in the upper Johnson River bog sediments and in one of the Hidden Lake cores (Fig. 2) are further evidence for this pine migration pattern, assuming that the few grains found would not have been transported to these sites until the species had migrated as close to them as it has.

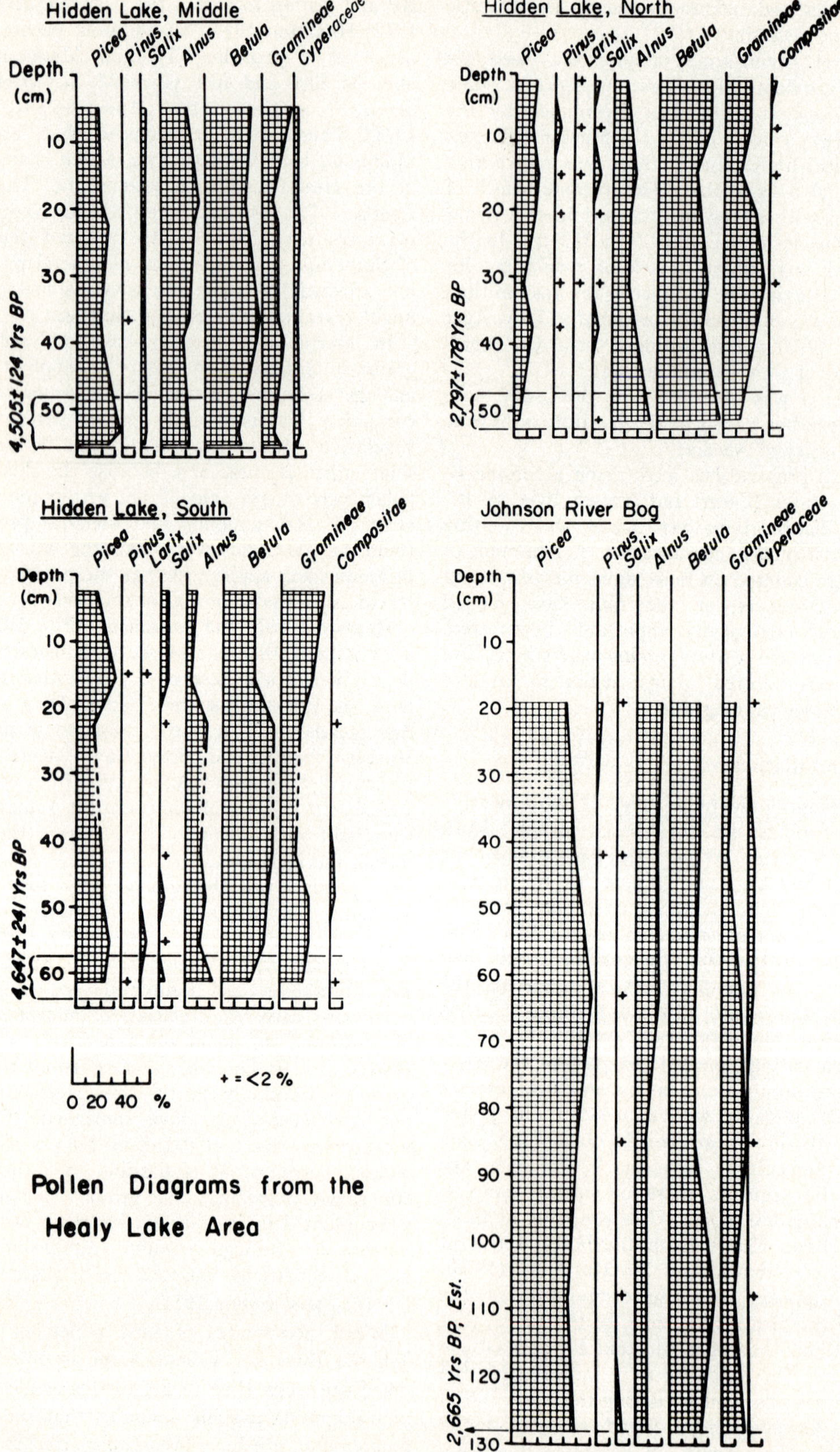

FIG. 2. Pollen diagrams from the Healy Lake area.

Acknowledgments. The study was assisted by B. K. Bright, K. P. Gormley and J. T. Kline. Support was from the National Science Foundation through Grant No. GS-2584.

REFERENCES

Ager, T. A., 1972: Surficial geology and Quaternary history of the Healy Lake area, Alaska. M.S. thesis, Department of Geology, University of Alaska, Fairbanks. 128 p.

Anderson, J. H., 1970: A geobotanical study in the Atlin region in northwestern British Columbia and south-central Yukon Territory. Ph.D. thesis, Department of Botany and Plant Pathology, Michigan State University, East Lansing. 380 p.

Anderson, J. H., 1971: A note on the roles of white spruce and lodgepole pine in the late Pleistocene phytogeography of northwestern Canada, p. 33. *In* F. A. Milan, Ed., Proceedings of the 22nd Alaska Science Conference. 163 p. Abstract.

Cook, J. P., 1969: The early prehistory of Healy Lake, Alaska. Ph.D. thesis, University of Wisconsin, Madison. 352 p.

Cook, J. P., and R. A. McKennan, 1970a: The Athapaskan tradition: A view from Healy Lake in the Yukon-Tanana Upland. Paper presented at the 10th annual meeting of the Northeastern Anthropological Association, Ottawa, May 7–9, 1970. 9 p. Mimeo. Department of Anthropology, University of Alaska, Fairbanks.

Cook, J. P., and R. A. McKennan, 1970b: The village site at Healy Lake, Alaska: an interim report. Paper presented at the 35th Annual Meeting of the Society for American Archaeology, Mexico City, April 30–May 2, 1970. 5 p. Mimeo. Department of Anthropology, University of Alaska, Fairbanks.

Faegri, K., and J. Iversen, 1964: *Textbook of pollen analysis.* Hafner Publishing Co., New York. 237 p.

Hamilton, T. D., 1973: Late Quaternary glacial history, Delta-Johnson Rivers region, northeastern Alaska Range. Unpublished Report. Geology Department, University of Alaska, Fairbanks. 43 p.

Hansen, H. P., 1953: Postglacial forests in the Yukon Territory and Alaska. *American Journal of Science,* 251, 505–542.

Heusser, C. J., 1960: Late-Pleistocene environments of North Pacific North America. American Geographical Society Special Publication 35. 308 p.

Heusser, C. J., 1967: Pleistocene and postglacial vegetation of Alaska and the Yukon Territory, p. 131–151. *In* Arctic Biology, H. P. Hansen, Ed., Oregon State University Press, Corvallis. 2nd Edition. 318 p.

Johnson, P. R., and C. W. Hartman, 1969: Environmental atlas of Alaska. Institute of Arctic Environmental Engineering, University of Alaska, Fairbanks, 111 p.

Lutz, H. J., 1956: Ecological effects of forest fires in the interior of Alaska. U. S. Department of Agriculture Technical Bulletin No. 1133. 121 p.

Matthews, J. V., Jr., 1970: Quarternary environmental history of interior Alaska: Pollen samples from organic colluvium and peats. *Arctic and Alpine Research,* 2, 241–251.

Rampton, V. N., 1971: Late Quaternary vegetational and climatic history of the Snag-Klutlan area, southwestern Yukon Territory, Canada. *Geological Society of American Bulletin,* 82, 959–978.

Viereck, L. A., 1973: Wildfire in the taiga of Alaska. *Quaternary Research,* 3, 465–495.

Past Climate of Alaska and Northwestern Canada as Reconstructed from Tree Rings

T. J. BLASING AND H. C. FRITTS

Laboratory of Tree-Ring Research, University of Arizona, Tucson, Arizona 85721

Abstract

Spatial anomaly patterns of sea-level pressures over North America, the North Pacific, and eastern Asia in the 20th century can be statistically calibrated with spatial anomaly pattern of tree growth in semi-arid western North America. Growth anomalies prior to 1900 were substituted into the calibration equations to reconstruct past circulation features for the 18th and 19th centuries. The success of the reconstructions for the Arctic was tested against climatic data where possible and against the variations in growth of Arctic trees which respond to variations in climate. Ten different types of tree-growth anomaly pattern were identified in the Arctic between 1800 and 1939. Climatic conditions inferred from the growth anomalies of Arctic trees were compared to circulation anomalies over the Arctic as reconstructed from the arid-site trees to the south. Both of these sources of information were used to infer climatic conditions for the period 1800–1939. Tentative inferences are presented as to climatic conditions for each of five regions in Alaska and northwestern Canada in hope that they may be tested against other lines of evidence.

1. Introduction

Variations of ring-widths in trees from certain sites reflect information about variations in climatic parameters such as temperature and precipitation. This occurs because such climatic variables often limit certain biological processes which determine ring-width (Fritts, 1971). Therefore, ring-width variations can be calibrated with recent climatic anomalies, and ring-width data from the past, when substituted into the calibration equations, can then provide estimates of past climatic variation.

Ring-width growth in arid regions is most often limited by drought resulting from periods of low precipitation and high temperature, but there are sites where growth is limited by high precipitation and low temperature, especially when these conditions occur during the cooler months of the year (Fritts, *in press*). The growth of trees in Arctic regions is often limited by low temperatures (and possibly by conditions associated with low temperatures) occurring during the summer months (Eklund, 1956; Hustich, 1956; Slastad, 1957).

2. Analysis of data from arid site trees

The ring-width variations as expressed in the chronologies derived from arid-site trees can be calibrated directly with anomalies of sea-level pressure (computed from measured surface pressure) over a large geographic region (Fritts *et al.*, 1971). This is possible because pressure anomalies reflect the large scale atmospheric circulation anomalies that produce anomalous temperatures and precipitation amounts on the specific tree sites

Different trees integrate the annual climate into their growth response in different ways depending on site characteristics, species, etc. This variation in climatic response as expressed by differences in chronologies from neighboring sites can be used to obtain information on intra-annual (seasonal) climatic variations. Also, there may be a time lag between the climatic input and the growth effect so that several rings in succession may each contain some information about the climate of any one year. Climatic anomalies for seasons prior to as well as concurrent with ring formation have been successfully calibrated with spatial anomaly patterns of ring-width in which several chronologies of varying climatic response were included (Fritts *et al.*, 1971).

Multivariate statistical techniques have been used to calibrate an array of 49 site chronologies from southern Canada, the western United States, and northern Mexico with seasonally averaged sea-level pressure anomaly patterns over large areas of the Northern Hemisphere (Fritts *et al.*, 1971). Research along this line has continued (Blasing, 1973; Fritts and Blasing, 1971) to the extent that ring-width variations now account for 55% of the pressure variance for summer (July–August) over an area extending from 80°W westward across the Pacific to 100°E and from 20°N to 70°N, thus extending into the Arctic. For the ten gridpoints included north of the Arctic Circle the reduced variance is 60.7%, as arid-site trees appear to be sensitive to circulation changes involving the polar anticyclone. The period of calibration is 1899–1962. Each of the ring-width chronologies used extends back to at least 1700 A.D. so that once the calibration was made it was immediately usable to estimate sea-level pressure patterns for the period 1700–1898. In this paper we examine the reconstructions of Arctic climate derived from the multivariate climatic calibration of the 49 arid tree sites. We then attempt to use climatic and tree-ring data from the Arctic to test the validity of the estimates and to make tentative inferences on past variations of Arctic climate.

3. Analysis and verification of reconstructed summer circulation using climatic data

Is it possible to use independent data to verify our reconstructions of Arctic climate prior to 1899 which were made from arid-site trees? At lower latitudes where climatic data are relatively abundant, verification has been successfully carried out (Blasing, 1973; Fritts and Blasing, 1973). For Alaska and northwestern Canada very little climatic data are available for such purposes.

However, temperature data taken at a Russian fort at Illoolook, Unalaska from 1829–1833, inclusive, were provided by Kutzbach and Wendland (1973). Monthly mean temperatures were estimated from the average of the daily maxima and minima for each month. If it is assumed that anomalous geostrophic northerly wind leads to cool conditions and anomalous southerly geostrophic wind leads to warm conditions at that station, then the temperature data can be used to test the reconstructed pressure anomaly patterns since anomalous geostrophic wind is taken directly from the isolines of estimated pressure anomaly. The direction of the estimated anomalous geostrophic wind, along with the observed summer (mean of July and August) temperatures are presented as Table 1. For those years when the estimated anomalous geostrophic wind was from the west-northwest (1829 and 1831) the observed temperatures are seen to be several degrees lower than during the years when the estimated geostrophic wind anomaly was from the southwest or west-southwest. Precipitation at Sitka, which was far south of our study area, also provided some encouraging, but inconclusive, verification. Other records from early settlements are sought for further testing of these reconstructions.

4. Analysis and verification using tree-rings as proxies of climate

The ring-widths of Arctic and sub-Arctic trees have been shown to respond to climate and in particular to summer temperature (Eklund, 1956; Hustich, 1956;

TABLE 1. Reconstructed anomalous geostrophic wind direction and observed mean summer (July–August) temperatures for Illoolook, Unalaska from 1829–1833.

Year	Reconstructed direction of anomalous geostrophic wind	Mean summer temperature
1829	West–northwest	53.5F
1830	Southwest	58.6F
1831	West–northwest	51.4F
1832	West–southwest	58.1F
1833	West–southwest	58.2F

Slastad, 1957). If Arctic and sub-Arctic trees respond to temperature they must, in some way, reflect circulation anomalies that produce the variations in temperature. Hence, it should be possible to use the ring-widths from these trees as indicators of past summer climate. Since ring-widths from Arctic and sub-Arctic trees are independent of the data from the arid-site trees, the Arctic and sub-Arctic tree-rings can serve as an indirect but independent check of the climatic reconstructions based on growth anomalies in the arid sites. Our first step in this analysis is to find relationships between some of the reconstructed pressure anomaly patterns and patterns of growth response of the Arctic and sub-Arctic trees.

The actual and reconstructed spatial anomaly patterns of pressure can be interpreted more easily if they are first reduced to a smaller set of "characteristic" anomaly patterns defined in such a way that several summers are representative of each "characteristic" pattern. A classification scheme to accomplish this was developed by Lund (1963) and refined by the first author who incorporated many suggestions of Wahl (1971). A more detailed discussion of the technique used here is given by Blasing (1973). Essentially, this scheme first finds that departure pattern which is highly correlated with the greatest number of other departure patterns. The average of that pattern and the five other departure patterns with which it is most highly correlated are then averaged to determine the characteristic anomaly features of the first pressure type. This average anomaly pattern (type 1) is then re-correlated with every departure pattern included in the analysis. Those departure patterns having a high correlation with the type 1 pattern are classified as being of type 1 and are removed from the data set whereupon the analysis is repeated to find additional types. Eventually a group of summers is left which are unclassifiable. That is, they are not well correlated with any type or with each other.

This sort of analysis was applied to actual pressure data over our area of study in western North America and the North Pacific sector from 1899 to 1966. Five pressure types were found. These are presented as Fig. 1.

Type 1 summers are characterized by high pressures in the central Pacific and low pressures in Arctic

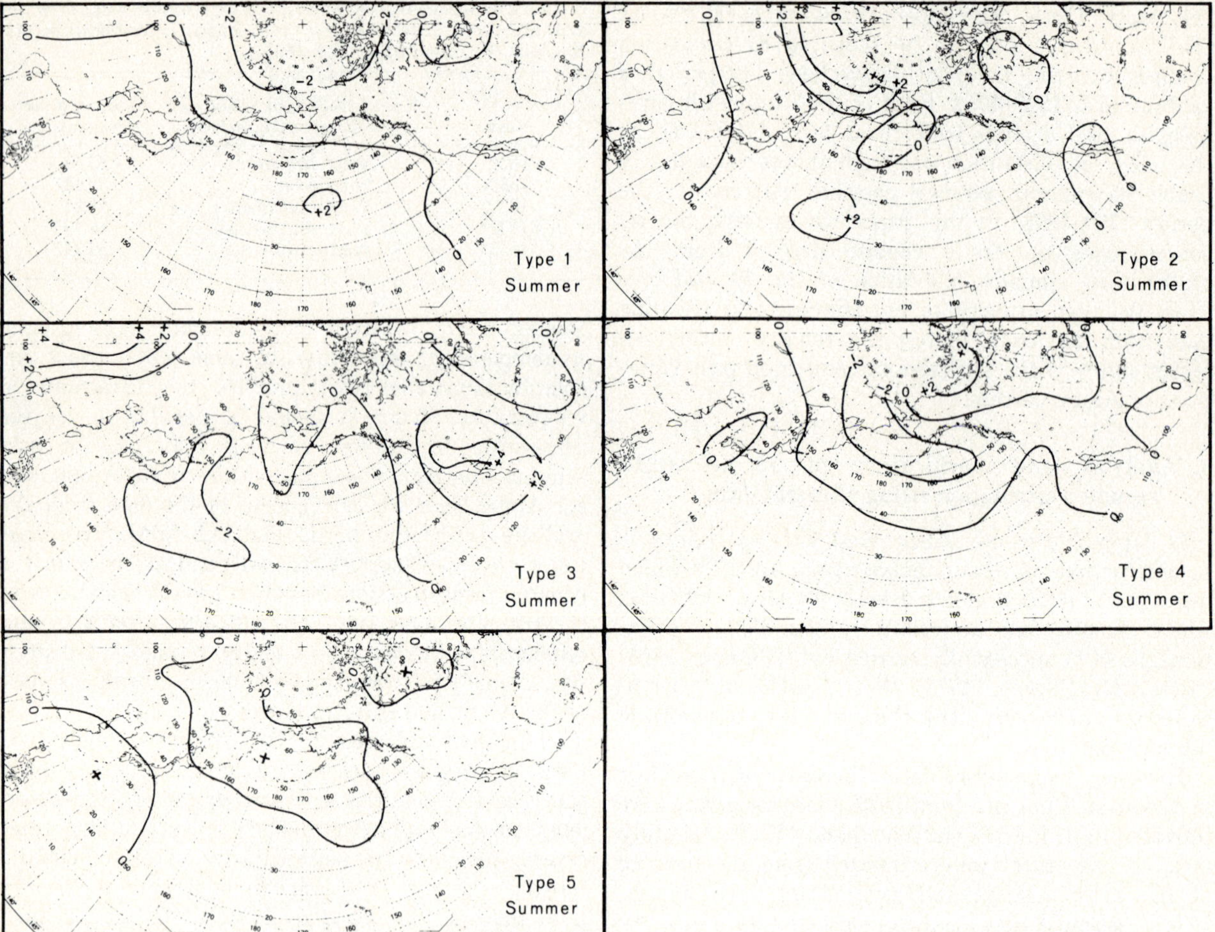

FIG. 1. Pressure anomaly types in the North Pacific sector and western North America for summer. Isolines of pressure anomaly are drawn for every two millibars.

regions. This anomaly pattern reflects a northward displacement of the summer storm track at all longitudes included and a well developed subtropical high over most of the central Pacific. During type 2 summers high pressure anomalies in Siberia reflect the frequent presence of the polar high there. Type 3 summers show anomalously high pressures over the Bering Strait, in southeast Asia, and in the western United States while low pressures are found over the west Pacific. The Pacific subtropical high is displaced eastward and is not as strong in the Gulf of Alaska as normally. The pressure anomalies of type 4 summers are seen to resemble certain features of the mean winter circulation including low pressure in the Aleutian region and high pressure extending from the Arctic over much of Canada. Type 5 summers are characterized by small pressure anomalies which reflect a slight northward displacement of the Pacific subtropical high.

The pressure anomalies estimated from arid site trees for each year in the 18th and 19th centuries often resembled one of the five above types for the 20th century. The resemblance was measured by correlating the spatial pattern of each reconstructed summer pressure anomaly for 1700–1898 with each of the 20th century spatial anomaly types (Fig. 1).

If the correlation properly identifies the years in the past for which circulation was similar to each 20th century type, then the tree-growth patterns for such years should resemble the growth patterns associated with the corresponding 20th century type.

FIG. 2. Locations of the 21 chronologies used in this study.

A test was made using 21 available ring-width chronologies for Alaska and northwestern Canada (Fig. 2, Table 2). The tree-ring data selected include stations from near the tree line with growth values for 1800–1939. Difficulties were encountered when some of the years representative of a given type occurred after 1939 or when the years of best correlation of the types with reconstructed pressure patterns occurred before 1800. Whenever a tree-ring chronology did not cover all years reconstructed to be of a given type, it was not included in the particular analysis.

From the pressure anomalies of the 20th century types in the region of northwestern North America (Fig. 1), it was expected that types 3 and 4 would be associated with the most conspicuous and distinct anomaly patterns of tree-growth in that region. The mean growth in Alaska and northwestern Canada for type 3 and type 4 years in the 20th century were mapped along with the mean growth for years in the past reconstructed to be of each of those types (Fig. 3) Tree-growth corresponding to pressure type 3 in the 20th century record exhibits anomalously high values in the Seward Peninsula area, in northeast Alaska, and the Mackenzie Delta area, while growth is less to the south The growth anomalies in the past are similar with the exception of one chronology in northeastern Alaska and the two chronologies in the eastern part of the District of Mackenzie. The growth anomalies corresponding to type 4 in both the modern and the past (reconstructed) record exhibit higher than normal growth along the south slope of the Brooks

TABLE 2. Locations and citations for ring-width chronologies used in this study.

1. 67°15′N:162°48′W (Giddings, 1941)
2. 67°04′N:159°44′W (Ibid.)
3. 66°46′N:155°10′W (Ibid.)
4. 64°55′N:160°48′W (Ibid.)
5. 64°27′N:162°39′W (Giddings, 1951)
6. 63°58′N:147°16′W (Giddings, 1941)
7. 63°45′N:148°56′W (Oswalt, 1958)
8. 62°40′N:143°55′W (Oswalt, 1952)
9. 61°38′N:144°31′W (Ibid.)
10. 67°40′N:142°40′W (Haugen, 1973)
11. 65°20′N:146°00′W (Ibid.)
12. 64°50′N:144°15′W (Ibid.)
13. 64°10′N:141°45′W (Ibid.)
14. 63°45′N:142°00′W (Ibid.)
15. 67°20′N:148°20′W (Ibid.)
16. 65°25′N:147°30′W (Ibid.)
17. 68°N:135°W (Giddings, 1953)
18. 63°50′N:103°15′W (Fritts, 1973)
19. 63°30′N:112°17′W (Ibid.)
20. 61°01′N:138°37′W (Fritts and Parker, 1973)
21. 64°08′N:140°10′W (Ibid.)

Range, but lower than normal growth to the north and south. The Mackenzie Delta chronology represents the only major difference between the two maps.

Considering the fact that growth responds to climate in June as well as July and that the pressure anomalies were typed over our entire pressure study grid rather than only over the Arctic, the agreement appears sufficient to encourage further investigation as to whether summer temperature anomalies reconstructed from Arctic growth data are in accord with the anomalies

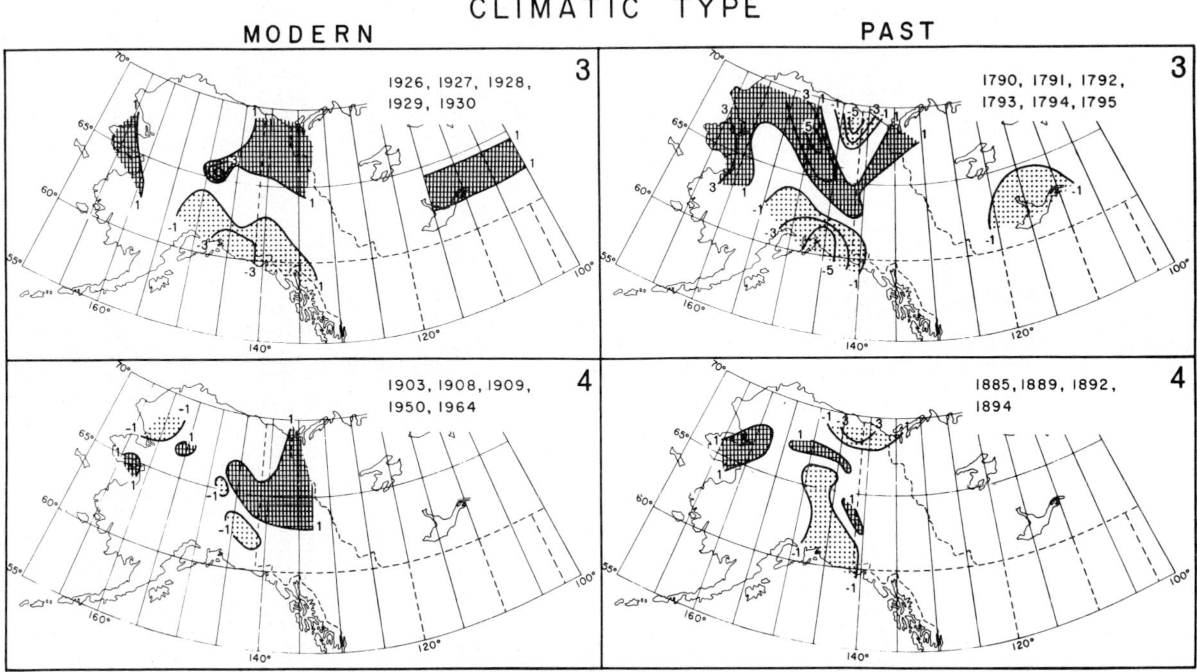

FIG. 3. Average ring width index anomaly pattern corresponding to pressure anomaly types 3 and 4 in the modern record (left) and in the reconstruction prior to 1900 (right). The years included are listed above the figure.

TABLE 3. Climatic estimates for selected areas of Alaska and northern Canada inferred from tree growth in the Arctic and circulation in the Arctic estimated from the growth of arid-site trees. Compass directions are abbreviated. Other abbreviations: fropa—frontal passage; H—high; PSH—Pacific subtropical high; G of A—Gulf of Alaska; H.B.—Hudson Bay; mT, mP—maritime tropical, polar.

Type	1	2	3	4	5
Years	1804–1811	1812, 14–16, 18, 22, 23, 28	1824, 26, 27, 29, 31–36	1837–41, 43, 51	1845, 47–50, 52–57, 60, 63
General Circulation	PSH strong in G of A, high over H.B., storms N of Alaska move S, path W of Great Bear Lake and Great Slave Lake	PSH moves W, merges with polar H W of Bering Strait, storm track as before, increased cold fropa NW Alaska	PSH strong in G of A, storms still N of Alaska and Mackenzie Dist., more zonal track across N. Canada, polar H strong	Polar H, PSH merged in Bering Strait; PSH strong S of Alaska Peninsula; increasing pressure over American Arctic	Similar to Type 1 but PSH stronger; no H over H.B.; mT replaces mP; summers earlier?
Seward Peninsula					
Anomalies: growth; wind flow; pressure Comments	average from NW; average to low	decreases to low from NW; average increased cold fropa	increases, average to high from NNW; average to low cold fropa but sunny	decreases, average to low from NW; high cold but sunny, more intense polar outbreaks	increases to high from W; low
Inferred temperature	cool	cool	average to cool	cool	average to warm
Northeast Alaska					
Anomalies: growth;	low	still low	increases slightly but still low	remains slightly low	increases slightly to high
wind flow; pressure	from WNW; low	from WNW; low	from WNW; low	from NW (weak); slightly low	from NW; low
Comments	frequent cyclones	frequent cyclones	cyclones still frequent, but less than previous; still cloudy		more cyclones
Inferred temperature	cool	cool	cool to average	cool	average
Interior Alaska					
Anomalies: growth;	high	decreases to low	decreases, now quite low	increases slightly, still quite low	increases, average to high
wind flow; pressure Comments	from W; low cyclones far to north; frequent fropa	from NW; low increased cold fropa	from WNW; low cloudy, frequent frop; cause of extremely low growth not certain	from NW; average some cold fropa	from W; average to low fropa about average to a little more frequent, esp. cold in N, average-cool N, average-warm S
Inferred temperature	uncertain	cool	cool	cool	
Southeast Alaska					
Anomalies: growth; wind flow; pressure Comments	low from W; low to average some anomalous cool fropa	increases to slightly high from NW; average few clouds; wind from interior	increases, now quite high from WNW; low fewer fropa; clear	high, still increasing from NW; high flow from interior; sunny	increases, all-time high from WSW; average more air from PSH
Inferred temperature	cool	average	warm	warm	warm
N. W. Territories					
Anomalies: growth;	high	decreases to average	variable	decreases to low	increases, still average to slightly low
wind flow; pressure	from S; high	from SW; average	from W; low	from W (weak); average to low	from S; slightly low
Comments	sunny, clear		some cold fropa	storms to south and southwest; few warm fropa	cloudy
Infrerred temperature	warm	average to below average	average	cool	average to low

TABLE 3.—(*Continued*)

Type	6	7	8	9	10
Years	1858, 73, 74, 76–78, 81, 94	1879, 80, 82–86, 88–91, 93 95, 96	1901, 03, 04, 06–11, 14	1916, 17, 19–24, 38	1925–32
General Circulation	PSH strong S of Alaska peninsula, less strong in G of A; polar H cannot be found	PSH strong in G of A; cannot find polar H; storms over Alaska farther south than before	Polar H over Canada & Siberia (somewhat); storm tracks farther south; PSH weaker	Polar H only over Siberia; more storms in modern normal storm track over Canada	PSH displaced eastward; increased cyclone activity SE of Alaska Peninsula; H over western N. America
Seward Peninsula					
Anomalies: growth; wind flow; pressure Comments	remains high from WNW; slightly low storms far N; strong flow from PSH	decreases, average to high from SW; slightly low frequent warm fropa, but cloudy	variable from SE; slightly high clear	low from NE; average to low average conditions, weak flow	variable weak; average
Inferred temperature	warm	average to warm	warm in south	average to cool	average
Northeast Alaska					
Anomalies: growth; wind flow; pressure Comments	decreases to average from NW; low more wind from Arctic Ocean	increases, now above average weak; average to low less northerly flow	above average from SE; high warm continental air	variable weak; average	high to east weak; average clear
Inferred temperature	cool	average to warm	warm	average	warm
Interior Alaska					
Anomalies: growth; wind flow; pressure Comments	remains average to high from NW; slightly low	variable weak; average to low	variable from ESE; high	variable from SE; average	high weak; average
Inferred temperature	average	average	variable	average	warm
Southeast Alaska					
Anomalies: growth; wind flow; pressure Comments	decreases, average to low from NW; slightly low	decreases, low from SW; low cool, cloudy, more storms	low from SE; average SE flow from G of A	low from ESE; average to low cool air from G of A; more storms; cloudy	low from SSE; low storms in G of A; cloudy
Inferred temperature	average to cool	cool	cool	cool	cool
N. W. Territories					
Anomalies: growth;	remains average to slightly low	high in east	low in east; high in west	high in east	high in east; low in west
wind flow; pressure Comments	from S; low cloudy	from SE; low warm fropa	from E; high cold air from north of H.B.	from SE; low cloudy, warm fropa	from NW; about average
Inferred temperature	average to cool	average to warm	cool in east; warm in west	average to warm	average to warm

GROWTH TYPES

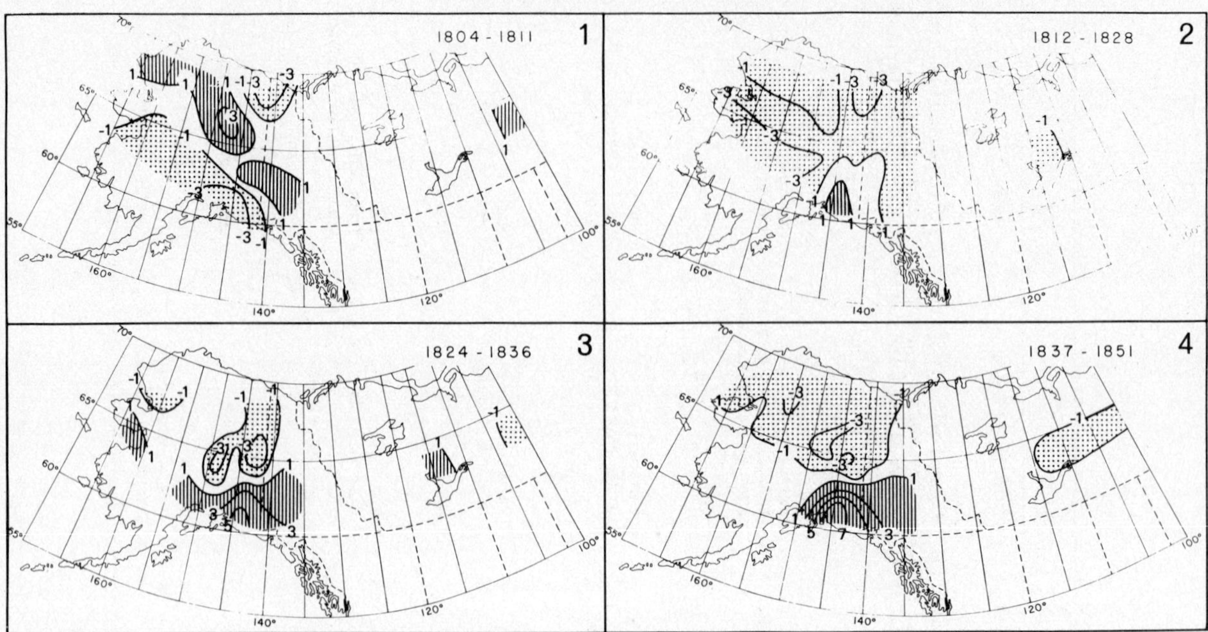

FIG. 4. Growth types 1–4 for ring widths from Alaskan and north Canadian trees 1800 to 1939. The first and last years of each type are listed on each corresponding map.

of pressure reconstructed from ring-width variations in arid-site trees.

5. Growth types of Alaskan and north Canadian trees 1800–1939

Tree-growth departure patterns, like pressure anomaly patterns, can often be more easily interpreted if they are first reduced to a smaller set of "characteristic" anomaly types. The same statistical technique that was used to identify anomaly types of pressure was used to identify spatial anomaly types of ring-width index for trees in Alaska and northwestern Canada. Ring-width index data were available for all chronologies for the period 1800–1939.

Ten tree-growth patterns were found to occur during that period. Due to the high serial correlation generally present in these Arctic and sub-Arctic tree-ring data, the growth types, unlike the pressure types, were generally confined to distinct periods of time. That is, one growth type would occur more or less exclusively for a definite period of time to be succeeded by another growth type during the following period. The individual years during which each growth type occurred are listed in Table 3. For the years of each growth type, the reconstructed pressure anomaly patterns were averaged to display circulation anomalies, estimated from the arid-site trees, associated with that type. Table 3 summarizes the growth types and associated pressure anomalies, along with a summary of climatic conditions inferred from these two inde-

pendent sources, for each of five regions in Alaska and northwestern Canada.

6. Discussion of the reconstructed climatic anomalies

The following paragraphs include a discussion of the more general aspects of the inferred climatic variations in Alaska and northwestern Canada for each of the ten periods of tree-growth. The first tree-growth anomaly pattern (chronologically ordered) occurs during the first decade of the 19th century. This pattern (Fig. 4) shows low growth in southern and northeastern Alaska with a band of above normal growth in between. Above normal growth also occurs in the eastern part of the District of Mackenzie. From this we might infer increased storminess and cool weather in northeastern Alaska and mild conditions to the south. Sunny and mild conditions would be expected for the eastern District of Mackenzie. Increased storminess and/or increased southeasterly onshore winds might be expected to account for low growth in southern Alaska. The reconstructed pressure anomalies associated with growth type 1 (Fig. 5) suggest that the Pacific subtropical high and the summer storm track were both displaced northward of their present normal positions in the Alaska area so that the storm track was in the vicinity of the Arctic Coast. The storm track then appears to turn southward, between two areas of high pressure anomaly, just west of the Great Bear and Great Slave

Lakes. These climatic anomalies are in agreement with the inferences made from the growth pattern in northeastern Alaska and in the eastern District of Mackenzie However, for northwestern and southern Alaska the reconstructed pressure maps do not appear to be in accord with the climatic anomalies inferred from Alaskan tree-rings. A likely explanation for these discrepancies results from the way the grwoth types were derived and the "chronological boundary effects" resulting from serial correlation. In this case the first tree-growth type (chronologically speaking) may not really be a distinct type, but rather a transition pattern between two types, one occurring primarily before 1800 and the other beginning about 1812 (the second type presented in Fig. 4). If this is the case, tree-growth type 1 should bear conclusive resemblance to a distinct tree-growth pattern which dominated the period shortly before 1800. From Fig. 3 it is seen that modern pressure anomaly type 3 was reconstructed for most of the 1790's and its associated tree-growth pattern closely resembles tree-growth type 1. From this it may be inferred that the period around 1800 was a transition period from anomalies similar to those of modern pressure type 3 to those associated with growth type 1.

For the following three types (or periods) of tree-growth, the growth anomalies are in general accord with the reconstructed pressure anomalies throughout the region of study. These periods extend roughly from 1812 to 1850 (Fig. 4). All show similar patterns of low growth in northern regions associated with reconstructed pressure anomalies (Fig. 5) suggestive of a northerly displaced storm track and associated cool, cloudy conditions in northern Alaska. In the southern portions of Alaska and the Yukon Territory, higher than normal growth is associated with pressure anomalies suggestive of a northerly displaced Pacific subtropical high and associated sunny and mild weather.

These conditions of a northerly displaced storm track and mild weather in the southern Alaska area appear to dominate the first half of the 19th century. However, slight variations of this general climatic pattern are evident such as the variability of pressure anomalies in the Hudson Bay area and the westward, as well as northward displacement of the Pacific subtropical high which occurred during period 2 (Fig. 5). High values of ring-width index appear to be associated with fewer than normal storms while below average growth in northern Alaska appears to be associated with frequent storms and anomalous northerly wind.

Starting in the late 1840's tree-growth anomalies tend to become positive over northern, as well as southern Alaska though they remain negative over northwestern Canada (Fig. 6). The reconstructed circulation (pressure) anomalies (Fig. 7) are similar to those of earlier in the century, but with the apparently important difference that the anomalous reconstructed wind in Alaska had shifted from a northerly direction to a more westerly one, bringing warmer air into the northern portion of the state and conditions more favorable for tree-growth.

The last 40 years of the 19th century are dominated by growth types 6 and 7 (Fig. 6) in which growth for the northern and western portions of Alaska is higher

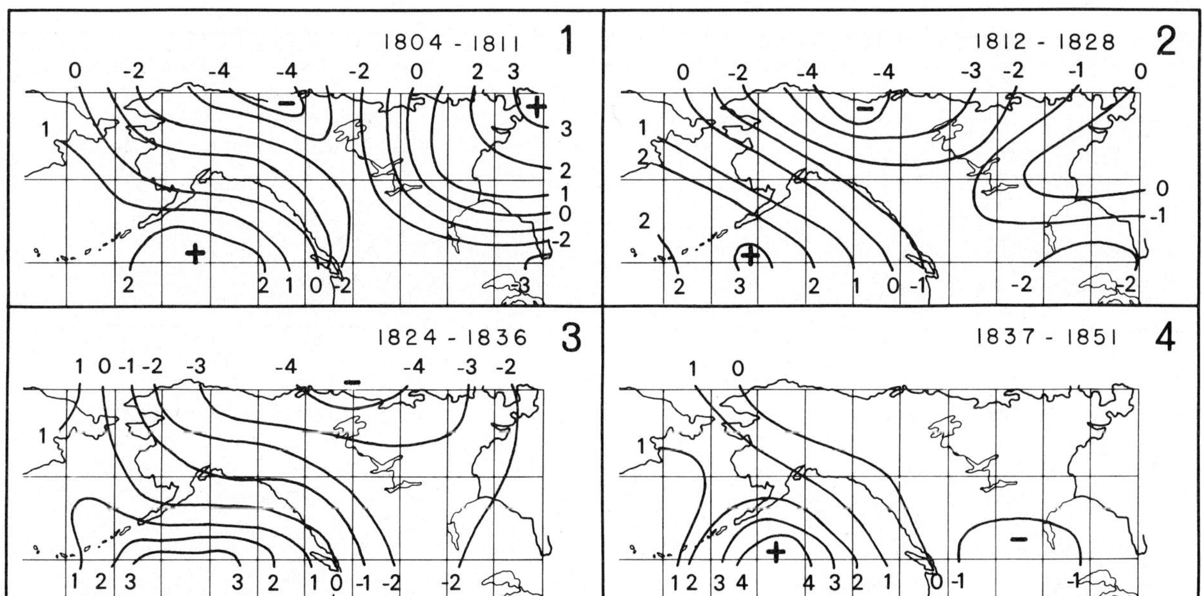

FIG. 5. Pressure anomalies, reconstructed from arid-site trees, averaged over all years corresponding to each of tree growth types 1–4. First and last years of each tree growth type are listed with each corresponding pressure anomaly map.

GROWTH TYPES

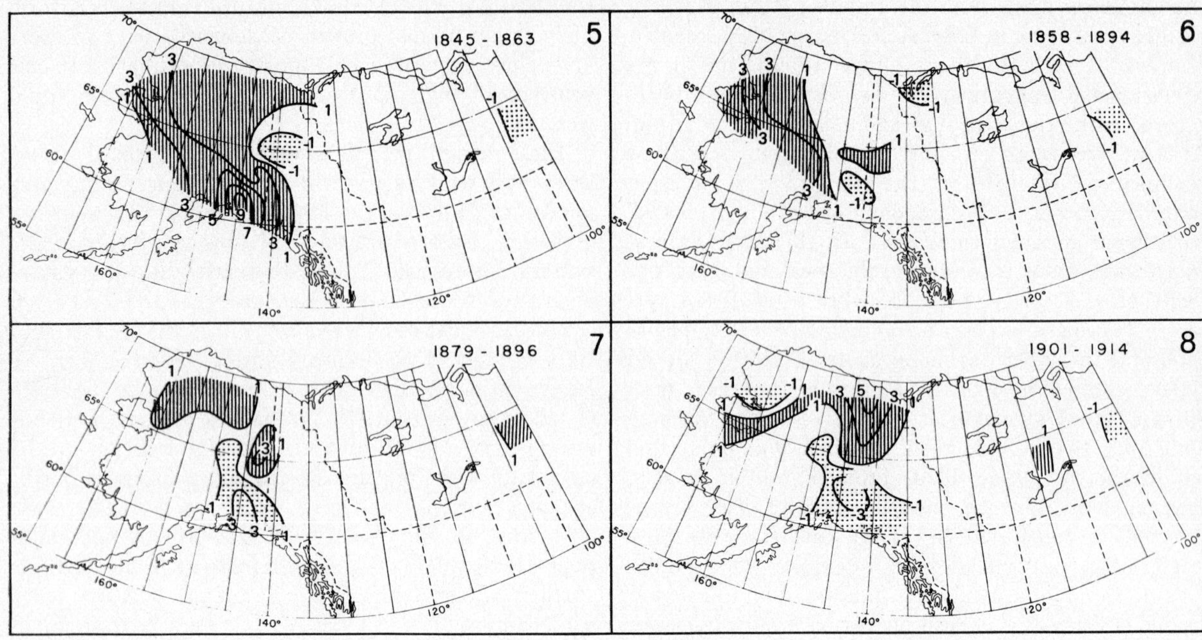

FIG. 6. Same as Fig. 4 for growth types 5–8.

than normal while growth in the southeastern portion of the state and adjacent areas of the Yukon Territory is below normal. The reconstructed pressure anomalies for the same periods (Fig. 7) show continued westerly flow along the Alaskan west coast but above normal cyclonic activity in the Mackenzie District associated with below normal growth there as well as in the southeastern Alaska area. The last two decades of the 19th century are dominated by growth type 7 and are characterized by high growth in northern Alaska but low growth centered north of Prince William Sound. The reconstructed pressure (Fig. 7) is near normal in northern Alaska though more northerly winds in the eastern part of the state and in the Yukon Territory are reconstructed in association with lower than normal pressure, and probably frequent cyclones, in western Canada. The major area of low pressure anomaly has now moved southeast-

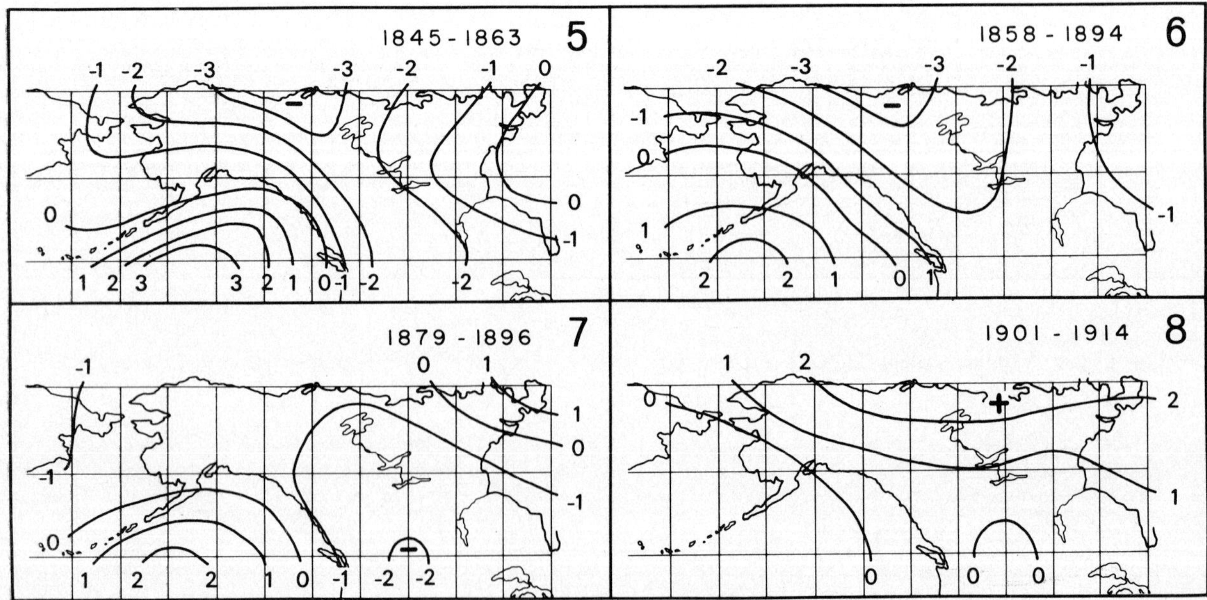

FIG. 7. Same as Fig. 5 for growth types 5–8.

GROWTH TYPES

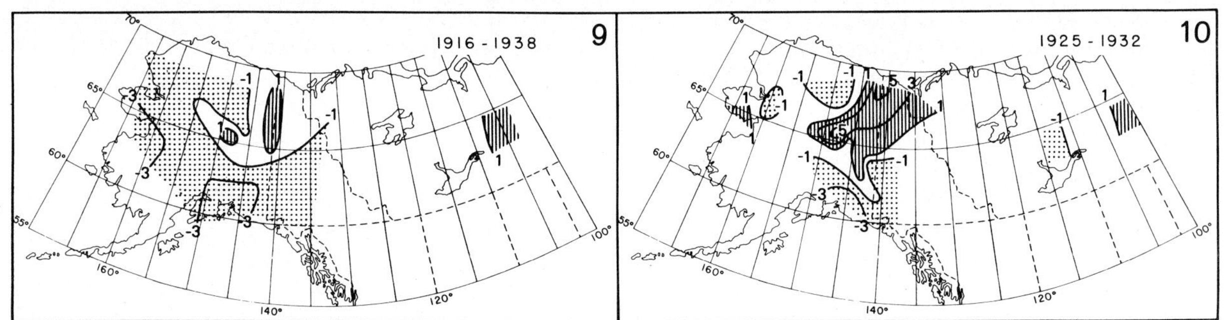

Fig. 8. Same as Fig. 4 for growth types 9–10.

ward from the northeastern Alaska area to the Prairie Provinces and this shift may be related to the decreased growth in southeastern Alaska during period 7.

The growth patterns for the first fifteen years of the 20th century (Fig. 6) indicate continued low growth in southeastern Alaska but some reduction in growth from the previous period in the extreme northwest. The reconstructed pressure anomalies (Fig. 7) characteristic of the preceding century tend to disappear, or in some cases reverse slightly, in the beginning of the 20th century. Average to low pressures are reconstructed in the Gulf of Alaska. This could be the result of a southward shift of the storm track to its present, or 20th century normal, position. Temperatures were favorable for growth in central Alaska and the Mackenzie District because of the decrease, from the preceding period, of anomalous northerly wind and an associated decrease in the number of storms probably moving through that region.

Two growth types were common between 1916 and 1938 (Fig. 8). Type 9 is characterized by low growth except for the northeastern part of Alaska and one chronology in the eastern part of the District of Mackenzie. Type 10 exhibits a larger area of high growth centered in northeastern Alaska but average to low growth elsewhere. Fig. 9 shows that for type 9 there appeared to be anomalously low pressures centered over the eastern part of the Mackenzie District, but pressures are near normal elsewhere. The below

normal growth in western and southern Alaska could be due to a slight increase in cyclonic activity suggested by lower than normal reconstructed pressures there. In the case of type 10, pressures were below normal in the Gulf of Alaska (Fig. 9), a feature which is the reverse of that indicated for the early and mid-19th century. This pattern of lower than normal pressure over the Gulf of Alaska likely reflects an increase of summer storms, cloudy weather, and southeasterly onshore winds bringing low temperatures and poor growing conditions along the eastern part of the Alaskan south coast.

These inferences should be regarded only as tentative, or first approximations to the reconstruction of climate. We expect that considerably improved estimates can be obtained with the development of new calibrations using more tree sites, including updated chronologies from the Arctic.

7. Concluding remarks

It is inferred from the coincidence of growth anomalies in Arctic and sub-Arctic regions with certain anomalies in the reconstructed pressure patterns that the pressure reconstructions do provide some valid information on past climate in those regions. Both types of data suggest that during the 19th century the summer storm track in the region of Alaska was displaced north of its present day "normal" position and that the Pacific subtropical high was also dis-

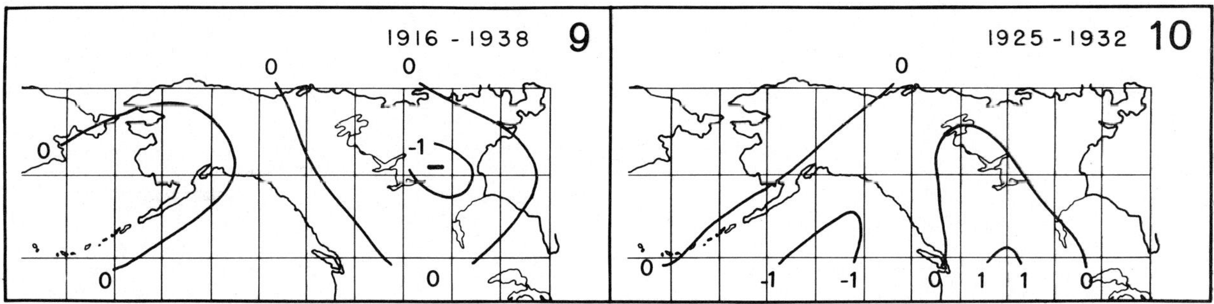

Fig. 9. Same as Fig. 5 for growth types 9–10.

placed northward so as to be particularly strong in the Gulf of Alaska. We have also reconstructed pressure anomaly patterns for North America west of 80°W (not discussed in this paper) and inferred from them that in the central and eastern parts of the continent the summer storm track during the 19th century was displaced south of its 20th century normal position. The overall reconstructions imply a more meridional circulation in the 19th century than in the first half of the 20th. This pattern should not be confused with pressure type 1 (Fig. 1) in which the northward displacement of the storm track is suggested at all longitudes over North America, the Pacific subtropical high is not particularly strong in the Gulf of Alaska, and the anomalous circulation is relatively zonal (Blasing, 1973).

It should be recognized that tree-growth in the Arctic is affected by June conditions as well as those of July and August. The anomalies of pressure used here represented only the July–August period. Some inconsistencies can result between these pressure anomalies and those of growth whenever conditions in June become limiting to growth. If some attention is given to the timing of the movement of the Pacific subtropical high into its "summer" position, which usually takes place during the latter third of June, it might be possible to find a sufficient relationship with the tree-growth anomaly patterns to be able to identify those years when the timing of that event was anomalously early or late. It should also be possible to calibrate the Arctic and sub-Arctic tree-ring data directly with pressure as was done for the arid-site trees to the south. As more tree-ring data are added to the set of predictor variables, the resulting reconstructions of past climate should become even more precise.

Acknowledgments. The authors wish to express appreciation to John Kutzbach and Wayne Wendland, University of Wisconsin, Center for Climatic Research, for supplying us with meteorological data taken at Russian forts in Alaska during the early 19th Century, Appreciation is also extended to Val LaMarche. Laboratory of Tree-Ring Research, for his comments on the preliminary manuscript. This research was supported by NSF Grant GA-26581 and Advanced Research Projects Administration Grant AFOSR-72-2406.

REFERENCES

Blasing, T. J., 1973: Methods for analyzing climatic variations in the North Pacific sector and western North America for the last 500 years. Ph.D. thesis, Department of Meteorology, University of Wisconsin. (In review.)

Fritts, H. C., 1971: Dendroclimatology and dendroecology. *Quaternary Research*, **1**, 419–449.

Fritts, H. C., T. J. Blasing, B. P. Hayden, and J. E. Kutzbach, 1971: Multivariate techniques for specifying tree-growth and climate relationships and for reconstructing anomalies in paleoclimate. *Journal of Applied Meteorology*, **10**, 845–864.

Fritts, H. C., 1973: Unpublished data, University of Arizona.

Fritts, H. C., and T. J. Blasing, 1973: Progress report on grant GA-26581 entitled Tree-ring analysis of environmental variability. Laboratory of Tree-Ring Research, University of Arizona, 35 pp.

Fritts, H. C., and M. Parker, 1973: Unpublished data, University of Arizona.

Fritts, H. C., *in press:* Relations of ring-widths in arid-site conifers to variations in monthly temperature and precipitation. (Submitted for publication).

Eklund, B., 1956: The annual ring variations in spruce in the centre of northern Sweden and their relation to the climatic conditions. *Meddelanden Fran Statens Skogforskningsinstitut*, **47**, 2–63.

Giddings, J. L., Jr., 1941: Dendrochronology in northern Alaska. University of Arizona Bulletin XII, No 4/Laboratory of Tree-Ring Research Bulletin No. 1, Published jointly by the University of Arizona and the University of Alaska, 107 pp.

Giddings, J. L. Jr., 1951: The forest edge at Norton Bay, Alaska. *Tree Ring Bulletin*, **18**, 2–6.

Giddings, J. L. Jr., 1953: Yukon River spruce growth. *Tree Ring Bulletin*, **20**, 2–5.

Haugen, R., 1973: Personal communication.

Hustich, I., 1956: Notes on the growth of Scotch Pine in Utsjoki in northernmost Finland. *Acta Botanica Fennica*, **56**, 3–13.

Kutzbach, J. E., and W. Wendland, 1973: Personal communication.

Lund, I. A., 1963: Map pattern classification by statistical methods. *Journal of Applied Meteorology*, **2**, 56–65.

Oswalt, W., 1952: Spruce samples from the Copper River drainage, Alaska. *Tree Ring Bulletin*, **19**, 5–10.

Oswalt, W., 1958: Tree-ring chronologies in south central Alaska. *Tree Ring Bulletin*, **22**, 16–22.

Slastad, T., 1957: Tree-ring analyses in Gudbrandsdalen. *Meddelelser fra Det Norske Skogforsoksvesen*, **48**, 577–620.

Wahl, E. W., 1971: Personal communication.

Clay Mineralogy and Geochemistry of Some Arctic Ocean Sediments: Significance on Paleoclimate Interpretation

A. S. NAIDU,[1] T. C. MOWATT,[2] D. B. HAWKINS[3] AND D. W. HOOD[1]

University of Alaska and Alaska State Geological Survey

Abstract

Clay mineral and chemical compositions of contemporary marine sediments of the Arctic were analyzed by X-ray diffraction and atomic absorption spectrophotometry, respectively. The clay mineral assemblage of the Arctic Ocean sediments do not substantiate the scheme of latitudinal variations of clay minerals in world ocean sediments as suggested by some authors. Thus, interpretation of paleoclimate on the basis of clay mineral assemblages in ancient marine sediments must be made with extreme caution.

The Arctic Ocean deep-sea clays have a significant deficiency of Mn, Ca, Mg, Na, K, Rb, Co, Cu, Zn and Ni, as compared with nonpolar deep-sea clays. In view of the possibility that the differences in polar and nonpolar sediment chemistries may be related to regional differences in several nonclimatic factors as well as to regional climate, geochemical criteria have limited applicability as a paleoclimatic indicator. In the Asian–American Basin of the Arctic Ocean, where the sedimentation rate and source apparently have remained unchanged and the tectonic history has been stable over the Quaternary, it is tempting to surmise that in that region the post-Tertiary stratigraphic differences in sediment chemistries do reflect climatic variations.

1. Introduction

The potential use of some physicochemical and paleontological attributes of marine and nonmarine sediments in the inference of paleogeography and paleoclimate has been recognized for a long time. The commonly cited criteria for the deciphering of paleoclimate relate to palynological studies of sediments (refer to a special section on this subject in Marine Geology, V. 4, 1966), the nature of shell coiling—dextral or sinistral—of the planktonic foraminifer *Globigerina pachyderma* (EHRENBERG) (Bandy, 1960), and the abundance of another foraminifer *Globorotalia menardi* (Turekian, 1968). Other potentially useful indicators of paleoclimate are the sediment chemistry (Belov and Lapina, 1970), the O^{18}/O^{16} isotopic ratios of carbonate fossil shells (Emiliani, 1955), clay minerals (Turekian, 1968; Belov and Lapina, 1970), sediment texture (Belov and Lapina, 1970; Kent *et al.*, 1971; and Lisitzin, 1972), the distribution of plagioclase-quartz ratios (Goldberg and Griffin, 1964), and racemization studies on amino acids in sediments (Schroeder and Bada, 1973).

The purpose of this paper is to present clay mineral and chemical compositions of some contemporary marine sediments of the Arctic Ocean, and to discuss the possible significance of the data in paleoclimatic studies.

2. Area of study and sampling

Traditionally, the Arctic Ocean has been arbitrarily delineated into two geographic units—the east and

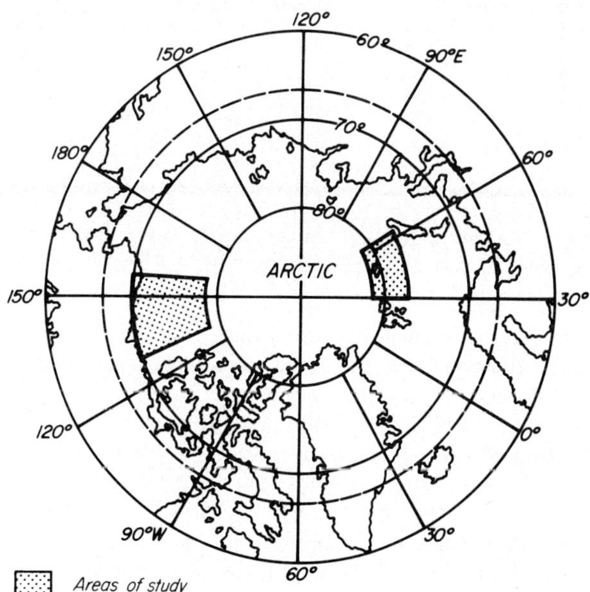

FIG. 1. Map of the Arctic Ocean, showing the areas of study.

---

[1] Institute of Marine Science, University of Alaska, Fairbanks, Ak 99701.

[2] Alaska State Geological Survey, and Institute of Marine Science, University of Alaska, Fairbanks, Ak 99701.

[3] Department of Geology, and Institute of Marine Science, University of Alaska, Fairbanks, Ak 99701.

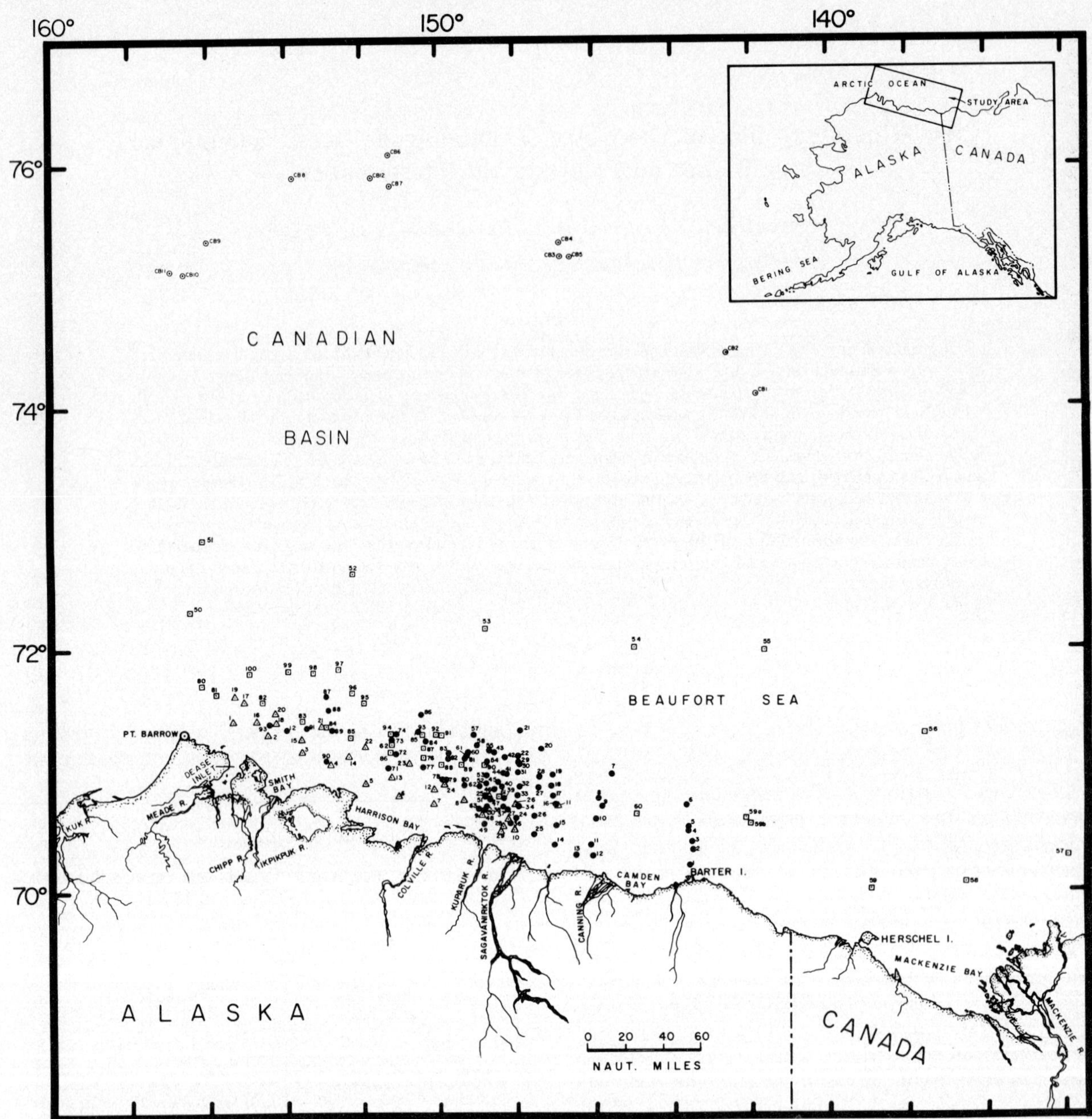

Fig. 2. Map of the Beaufort Sea and Canada Basin, showing the locations of sediment samples. Locations depicted by squares have a prefix BBS, whereas those by open circles have T-3.

west Arctic Oceans—by the Prime Meridian dispositions. However, on the basis of observed differences in sediment depositional regimes it appears, at least from the standpoint of the present study, that the division of the Arctic Ocean into three broad units is more logical. In the present investigation, the Arctic Ocean area included by the 75°W and 70°E meridians has been considered as one unit (henceforth called the "Greenland–European Basin"), the area between 70°E and 125°W as the second unit ("Asian–American Basin") and the small remaining region of the Arctic Ocean as the third unit ("Canadian Archipelago Basin"). The Greenland–European Basin, unlike the other two units, is exposed to slightly warmer oceanic currents and locally to volcanic activity, has higher biological productivity and is relatively free from polar pack ice cover. Further, the terrigenous source of the Greenland–European Basin consists predominantly of high-grade metamorphic, plutonic, and volcanic rocks, whereas that of the Asian–American Basin consists predominantly of sedimentary rocks. The Canadian Archipelago Basin has a complex hydrography as well as depositional pattern. Because of the relatively enclosed nature of this basin sediment dispersal is restricted and the nature of the sediment is quite different from those of the two open marine regimes of the Arctic. Consequently, sediments from the Canadian Archipelago Basin have not been considered in the present study. Because of the large area and logistic problems involved it was not feasible to obtain sediment samples from all the areas of the Arctic Ocean. Therefore, we chose two type areas representing the two major oceanic provinces of the Arctic (Fig. 1). Sediment samples typifying Greenland–European Basin deposits were gathered from the north Barents and Kara Seas, whereas sediments of the continental margin of north Arctic Alaska, Mackenzie Delta, Beaufort Sea and the Canada Basin represent samples from the Asian–American Basin (Figs. 2 and 3).

Sediment samples from north Arctic Alaska and Mackenzie Delta were collected from the R/V NATCHIK and the H. M. S. RICHARDSON, respectively. The sediments from the relatively ice free areas of the Beaufort Sea, the Barents Sea and the Kara Sea were obtained from U. S. Coast Guard ice-breakers (Fig. 4). Samples from the Canada Basin were collected from Fletcher's ice island, T-3. Only surficial bottom sediments from either short-trigger core or grab samples have been considered in this study.

The unique climatic setting of the Arctic Ocean is quite in contrast with those prevailing in the middle and low latitudes. Nine to eleven months of the year most of the Arctic Ocean is covered by either heavy pack ice or broken sea ice, the annual mean temperature is around $-12C$, and the annual mean precipitation of 11.6 cm is comparable to that of arid and semi-arid regions.

3. Analytical techniques

The elemental and clay mineral analyses of sediments were accomplished by atomic absorption spectrophotometry and X-ray diffraction, respectively. The sediment carbonate contents were manometrically

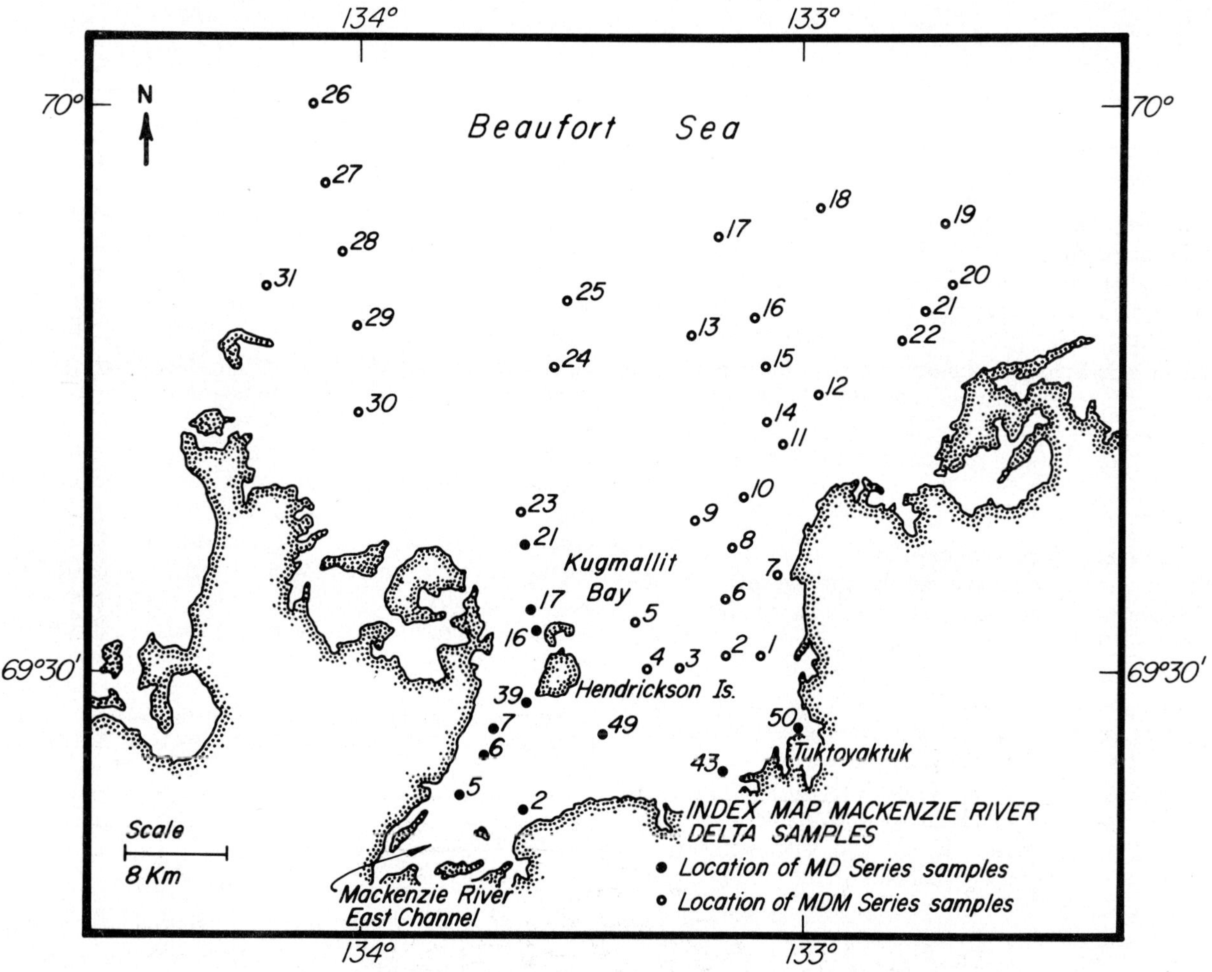

FIG. 3. Map of the Mackenzie Delta, showing locations of sediment samples.

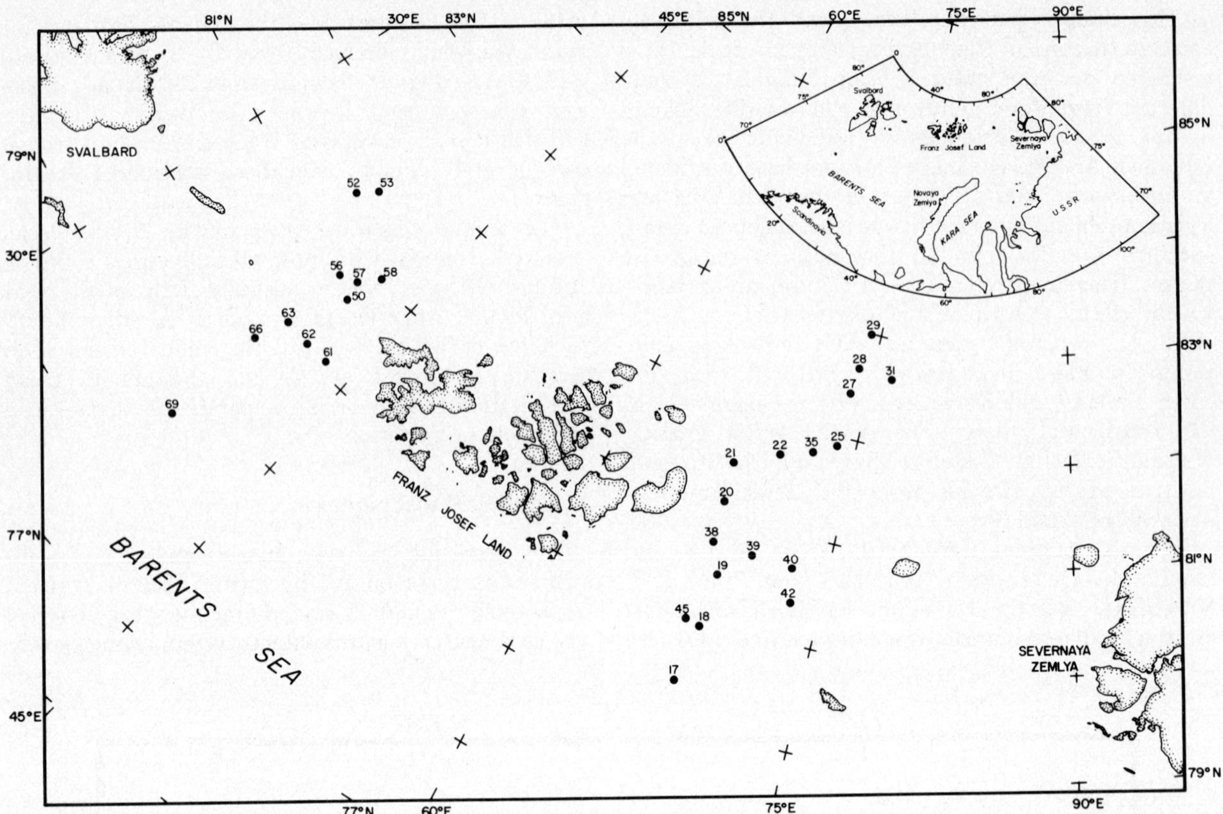

FIG. 4. Map of the North Barents Sea and Kara Sea, showing location of sediment samples. Each of the sample locations should have a prefix BRT, (refer to Table 3).

analyzed, and the contents of organic carbon were determined by using a double beam infrared analyzer. Details of the analytical methods have been summarized in earlier papers (Naidu *et al.*, 1972; Naidu and Hood, 1972; and Naidu and Mowatt, 1973a).

The significance in the differences of average abundances of elements between the deep-sea sediments of the Arctic Ocean and tropical-temperature ocean were statistically checked by the student-*t* or Z tests.

4. Results

The clay mineral compositions of the $< 2\,\mu$m fraction of recent sediments of the marine facies of the Mackenzie Delta, and those of the Canada Basin are given in Table 1 and 2, respectively. Earlier Naidu *et al.* (1971) and Naidu and Mowatt (1973a and 1973b) presented the clay mineral compositions of the western Beaufort Sea and the continental margin sediments of the north Arctic Alaska. It is quite evident from all the data available to date that the predominant clay mineral in the above mentioned marine areas is illite; chlorite and kaolinite occur in significant but lesser amounts, and smectite and mixed-layer phases are usually the least abundant. The kaolinite/chlorite ratios that are of particular interest to this study range from 0.4 to 1.3. However, except for three, all samples have kaolinite/chlorite ratios of 0.6 or higher.

The abundances of some alkaline, alkaline-earth and transition metals in recent deep-sea sediments of the Beaufort Sea and Canada Basin are included in Table 2. In Table 3, results of a similar chemical analysis of sediments from the north Barents Sea and Kara Sea are presented. From the basic data in the above two tables, average abundances of some common elements in deep-sea sediments of the Arctic Ocean were calculated, and are compared with the average elemental abundances of deep-sea sediments from tropical-temperature oceans (Table 4). It is observed that with the exception of Fe all the elements analyzed so far are deficient in the Arctic sediments relative to the tropical-temperate sediments, at the 90% confidence level. The differences between the Fe contents of the two different groups of clays are statistically insignificant. The student-*t* test calculation was not undertaken in the case of Li because of an insufficient number of nonpolar samples (two) analyzed.

5. Discussion

Use of Clay Minerals as a Paleoclimatic Indicator

On the basis of clay mineral analyses of marine clays of the tropical and temperate oceanic regimes, Biscaye (1965), Giffin *et al.* (1968) and Rateev *et al.* (1969) have independently suggested that there are latitudinal variations in clay mineral assemblages. It has been shown that there is a progressive decrease in kaolinite with an attendant increase in chlorite from the equatorial zone to the subpolar regions. This latitudinal variation in clay mineral assemblages in the ocean has been ascribed to latitudinal differences in climate prevailing in the adjacent continents that form source areas for the marine sediments. Under the more intense chemical weathering conditions of the tropical and humid regions, kaolinite is generally the more abundant clay mineral in the subaerial weathering residue In the frigid and subfrigid areas of the earth where chemical weathering of rocks is less intense, the soils derived from primary rocks are generally enriched in chlorite. In light of the regional clay mineral variations that have been observed, a concept has developed over the years among paleo-ecologists that kaolinite is a typical low-latitude clay mineral whereas chlorite is a typical high-latitude clay mineral. On the basis of this concept and using strati-graphic variations in clay mineral assemblages in marine sediment cores, several interpretations have been made of the fluctuation of climate over con-tinents that are situated adjacent to major oceanic belts.

Results of our clay mineral studies on contemporary sediments of the Beaufort Sea and Canada Basin (Tables 1 and 2) do not substantiate the scheme of latitudinal variations of clay minerals as suggested by some authors. This is quite evident from the sig-nificantly high contents of kaolinite and kaolinite/chlorite ratios encountered in the polar sediments. As mentioned earlier, we have noted an average of 13% kaolinite. Kaolinite/chlorite ratios were invari-ably greater than 0.6, and in some samples were as

TABLE 1. Weighted peak area percentages (after Biscaye, 1965) of clay minerals in 2 micron fraction of Mackenzie deltaic sediments.

Station Number	Smec-tite	Illite	Kaolin-ite	Chlo-rite	Kaolinite / Chlorite
MDM 1	5	68	9	18	0.5
MDM 2	4	66	10	16	0.6
MDM 3	6	67	9	18	0.5
MDM 4	4	64	18	14	1.3
MDM 5	4	70	10	16	0.6
MDM 6	12	63	12	13	0.9
MDM 8	10	63	13	14	0.9
MDM 9	4	68	11	17	0.7
MDM 10	5	66	11	18	0.6
MDM 11	3	72	12	13	0.9
MDM 12	2	70	18	20	0.9
MDM 13	6	64	12	18	0.7
MDM 14	8	63	12	17	0.7
MDM 15	5	68	11	16	0.7
MDM 16	9	68	9	14	0.6
MDM 17	3	69	11	17	0.7
MDM 18	5	65	10	20	0.5
MDM 19	3	68	12	17	0.7
MDM 20	6	66	13	15	0.9
MDM 21	9	63	12	16	0.8
MDM 22	6	65	10	19	0.5
MDM 23	5	66	10	19	0.5
MDM 24	4	71	12	13	0.9
MDM 25	4	68	12	16	0.8
MDM 26	5	69	11	15	0.7
MDM 27	2	71	12	15	0.8
MDM 28	4	69	11	16	0.7
MDM 29	3	51	25	21	1.2
MDM 30	5	67	10	18	0.6
MDM 31	4	66	11	19	0.6
MD 2	6	69	11	14	0.8
MD 5	8	62	13	17	0.8
MD 6	6	68	11	14	0.8
MD 7	7	65	10	18	0.6
MD 16	8	51	19	22	0.9
MD 17	2	67	11	19	0.6
MD 21	3	69	11	16	0.7
MD 39	6	66	12	16	0.8
MD 43	4	67	15	14	1.1
MD 49	6	63	17	14	1.2

TABLE 2. Chemical and clay mineral compositions of deep-sea sediments, Beaufort Sea–Canada Basin, West Arctic Ocean. Chemical abundances are in wt. percents. The clay mineral abundances are expressed as weighted peak area percentages (Biscaye, 1965).

Sample No.	Water Depth (m)	C_{org}	$CO_3^=$	Fe	Mn	Na	K	Ca	Mg	Li	Rb	Cu	SMT	ILT	KLT	CLT	KLT/ CLT
T3-1	3637	0.74	4.2	5.15	0.48	2.03	2.37	1.99	1.38	0.0065	.0090	.0060	11	62	12	15	0.8
T3-2	3650	0.71	3.1	4.90	0.40	2.59	2.19	1.68	1.52	0.0063	0.0083	0.0052	7	57	13	23	0.6
T3-3	3795	0.73	0.6	5.45	0.32	2.84	2.12	0.96	1.57	0.0073	0.0115	0.0125	14	57	11	18	0.6
T3-4	3792	0.74	2.9	5.25	0.48	4.13	2.39	1.29	1.57	0.0070	0.0100	0.0082	13	56	13	18	0.7
T3-5	3761	0.75	1.2	5.20	0.36	2.74	2.26	0.94	1.41	0.0068	0.0112	0.0052	14	57	13	16	0.8
T3-6	3827	0.79	1.1	5.40	0.33	3.46	2.25	0.82	1.65	0.0073	0.0112	0.0055	8	62	12	18	0.7
T3-7	3830	0.77	0.9	5.25	0.38	3.74	2.49	0.88	1.68	0.0068	0.0098	0.0050	15	55	13	17	0.8
T3-8	3833	1.16	1.2	5.10	0.49	3.43	2.27	1.11	1.66	0.0073	0.0112	0.0049	12	52	20	16	1.3
T3-9	2860	0.39	5.3	6.05	0.58	4.32	2.87	6.52	4.72	0.0074	0.0125	0.0085	6	58	14	22	0.6
T3-10	1705	0.39	8.0	5.10	0.37	2.97	1.82	5.92	2.16	0.0050	0.0075	0.0048	3	65	16	16	1.0
T3-11	1160	0.47	4.1	4.60	0.50	3.82	1.97	5.12	2.14	0.0055	0.0085	0.0046	6	64	11	19	0.6
T3-12	3835	0.79	0.8	5.10	0.50	3.27	2.27	1.14	1.57	0.0075	0.0110	0.0052	5	62	16	17	0.9
BSS 51	2477	0.91	1.25	4.55	0.86	2.85	2.38	0.03	4.33	0.0047	0.0083	0.0080	7	64	11	18	0.6
BSS 54	3458	0.88	2.65	4.88	0.33	2.56	2.54	0.08	2.67	0.0053	0.0063	0.0061	4	59	16	21	0.8
BSS 97	1500	1.34	3.15	4.06	0.03	3.04	2.27	0.71	5.49	0.0052	0.0160	0.0060	11	55	11	23	0.5
BSS 92	1600	1.11	1.75	3.65	0.03	1.74	2.38	0.02	1.15	0.0063	0.0092	0.0092	5	60	10	25	0.4
BSS 91	1800	1.41	0.15	4.06	0.08	2.38	2.22	0.07	1.48	0.0042	0.0089	0.0053	5	60	10	25	0.4
Averages of 17 Samples		0.82	2.49	4.92	0.38	3.11	2.30	1.72	2.24	0.0063	0.0100	0.0065					

Note. SMT: Smectite; ILT: Illite; KLT: Kaolinite; CLT: Chlorite.

TABLE 3. Chemical composition of bottom sediments of the North Kara and Barents seas. Please refer to Figure 4 for sample locations. Elemental abundances are in wt. percents.

Sample No.	Depth (m)	Fe	Mn	Ca	Mg	Na	K	Rb	Li	Cu	Mn/Fe	Na/K	Ca/Mg
BRT—17	530	5.35	0.37	0.68	1.14	2.52	1.96	0.0075	0.0053	0.0174	0.069	1.29	0.60
BRT—18	550	5.00	0.41	0.58	1.13	2.75	1.97	0.0072	0.0053	0.0184	0.082	1.40	0.51
BRT—19	585	6.40	0.48	0.50	1.32	4.09	2.16	0.0083	0.0066	0.0307	0.075	1.89	0.38
BRT—20	545	5.35	0.31	0.64	1.24	2.29	1.88	0.0075	0.0056	0.0142	0.058	1.22	0.52
BRT—21	585	5.40	0.41	0.64	1.38	2.52	2.06	0.0083	0.0060	0.0087	0.076	1.22	0.46
BRT—22	645	6.25	0.39	0.50	1.32	4.39	2.05	0.0078	0.0063	0.0285	0.062	2.14	0.38
BRT—25	605	4.85	0.10	0.58	1.23	2.42	2.05	0.0076	0.0053	0.0050	0.021	1.18	0.47
BRT—27	1150	4.35	0.34	1.00	1.11	2.30	2.85	0.0072	0.0049	0.0192	0.078	0.81	0.90
BRT—28	1900	5.45	0.33	2.54	1.48	2.64	2.47	0.0078	0.0067	0.0210	0.061	1.07	1.72
BRT—29	2560	5.20	0.21	0.71	1.26	2.59	2.11	0.0065	0.0058	0.0235	0.040	1.23	0.56
BRT—31	2287	5.60	0.33	2.07	1.52	2.72	2.32	0.0092	0.0063	0.0072	0.059	1.17	1.36
BRT—35	640	8.90	0.24	0.54	1.29	2.29	1.88	0.0077	0.0053	0.0043	0.027	1.22	0.42
BRT—38	567	7.60	0.52	0.59	1.57	2.52	2.36	0.0092	0.0063	0.0300	0.068	1.07	0.38
BRT—39	585	6.50	0.70	0.45	1.38	2.52	1.99	0.0073	0.0046	0.0212	0.108	1.27	0.33
BRT—40	507	3.30	0.04	0.54	0.73	2.07	1.90	0.0065	0.0037	0.0433	0.012	1.09	0.74
BRT—42	439	2.55	0.19	0.59	0.52	2.34	1.92	0.0055	0.0020	0.0050	0.075	1.22	1.13
BRT—45	542	5.95	0.38	0.48	1.40	2.59	1.90	0.0065	0.0062	0.0215	0.064	1.36	0.34
BRT—50	366	4.45	0.30	1.10	1.29	2.37	1.90	0.0072	0.0053	0.0533	0.067	1.25	0.85
BRT—52	350	4.00	0.14	1.36	1.29	2.19	1.96	0.0085	0.0053	0.0416	0.035	1.12	1.05
BRT—53	430	5.80	0.36	0.67	1.34	2.32	2.01	0.0085	0.0060	0.0218	0.062	1.15	0.50
BRT—56	347	3.10	0.12	1.36	1.10	2.10	1.59	0.0058	0.0038	0.0113	0.038	1.32	1.24
BRT—57	549	6.75	0.47	1.00	1.44	2.54	2.15	0.0092	0.0070	0.0200	0.070	1.18	0.69
BRT—58	485	7.30	0.70	0.76	1.54	2.74	1.97	0.0033	0.0070	0.0132	0.095	1.39	0.49
BRT—61	384	5.60	0.09	0.54	1.42	2.31	2.28	0.0099	0.0080	0.0050	0.016	1.01	0.38
BRT—62	377	6.55	0.11	0.69	1.33	2.08	1.27	0.0092	0.0073	0.0050	0.017	1.50	0.52
BRT—66	320	5.10	0.07	1.63	1.32	2.42	1.40	0.0095	0.0070	0.0040	0.014	1.73	0.48
BRT—69	315	6.40	0.05	0.58	0.64	2.52	2.31	0.0094	0.0075	0.0042	0.008	1.09	0.91
Average of 27 samples		5.52	0.30	0.83	1.25	2.56	2.03	0.0079	0.0058	0.0186	0.054	1.28	0.68

high as 1.3. It appears that notable amounts of kaolinite are quite widespread in contemporary Arctic Ocean sediments, as documented by Mullen *et al.* (1972) and Andrew (1973). In sediments of the North Kara Sea, adjacent to Franz Joseph Land, Andrew (1973) observed about 14% kaolinite, and kaolinite/chlorite ratios that ranged from 2 to 3. These values

TABLE 4. Differences in the average abundances of some elements in the deep-sea clays of the Arctic and Tropical-Temperate Oceans, The abundances are in weight percents.

Element	Beaufort Sea (Continental Rise & Slope)	Canada Basin	Kara-Barent Sea	Arctic Ocean	Tropical-Temperate Ocean	't' test Result
Fe	3.22	4.92	5.52	4.85	5.22[b,c,e]	insignificant
Mn	0.03	0.38	0.30	0.27	0.66[b,c,e]	significant*
Ca	0.24	1.72	0.83	0.97	2.97[c]	significant*
Mg	1.20	2.24	1.25	1.54	1.81[c]	significant**
Na	1.80	3.11	2.56	2.56	3.50[c]	significant*
K	1.90	2.30	2.03	2.16	2.48[c]	significant**
Rb	0.0078	0.1000	0.0079	0.0085	0.0119[d,e]	significant*
Li	0.0039	0.0063	0.0058	0.0058	0.0057[d]	
Co	0.0025	0.0036		0.0028	0.0104[b,c,e]	significant*
Cu	0.0049	0.0065	0.0186	0.0121	0.0348[b,c,e]	significant*
Zn	0.0077	0.0091		0.0081	0.0125[e]	significant*
Ni	0.0056	0.0056		0.0056	0.0205[b,c,e]	significant*

[a] This study.
[b] Cronan (1969).
[c] Goldberg and Arrhenius (1958).
[d] Horstman (1957).
[e] Wedepohl (1960).
* Differences significant at 99% confidence level.
** Differences significant at 90% confidence level.

and those reported by us (Tables 1 and 2) are compareable to kaolinite and kaolinite/chlorite ratios commonly encountered in marine sediments of temperature and subtropical climatic belts (Biscaye, 1965; Griffin *et al.*, 1968; Rateev *et al.*, 1969; Goldberg and Griffin, 1970; and Venkatarathnam and Biscaye, 1973). Thus extreme caution must be exercised in the interpretation of paleoclimate on the basis of clay mineral assemblages in ancient sediments. Similar conclusions made earlier by Naidu *et al.* (1971) are reinforced by this study. The presence of notable amounts of kaolinite in the north polar marine sediments has very little bearing on the contemporary climate of the hinterland; the relative abundance rather is to be ascribed to the kaolinite-bearing sedimentary source rocks (Naidu *et al.*, 1971; Naidu and Mowatt, 1973; and Andrew, 1973).

Interpretation of Paleoclimate from Sediment Geochemistry

The chemical data summarized in Table 4 show that there is a significant deficiency in Mn, Ca, Mg, Na, K, Rb, Co, Cu, Zn and Ni in deep-sea clays of the arctic as compared to those of the tropical-temperate regions. Substantiating this observation, Belov and Lapina (1970) and Belov *et al.* (1970) have indicated that, except in areas influenced by warm Atlantic water masses, there are relatively low contents of Fe, Mn and carbonate in deep-sea clays of the Arctic Ocean as compared to tropical-temperature regions. If the observed differences in element contents have a geologically meaningful base, then we may speculate that paleosediments deposited under polar and nonpolar climatic conditions can be effectively distinguished from one another chemically, and that such geochemical criteria may be useful in the interpretation of paleoclimate. However, such a conclusion is merited only if subject to the rather obvious conditions that the regional differences in the sediment chemistries are basically a reflection of regional differences in the prevailing climate. Some of the possible direct effects of polar climate in bringing about paucity of some alkaline, alkaline earth and transition metals have been discussed by Belov *et al.* (1970) and Naidu and Hood (1972). Notwithstanding the effects of climate, there are several other factors which could significantly contribute to the observed differences in the sediment chemistries of polar and nonpolar regions. Differences in sampling, sample handling, and analytical techniques among the various samples compared could conceivably cause the observed differences in element content. We have attempted to minimize the analytical variability in our data by using frequent check analyses of U. S. Geological Survey standard rock samples G-1 and AGV-1.

Other factors that merit particular consideration are: the regional differences in marine sedimentation rates, the possible regional differences in the volume of volcanogenic components incorporated in sediments—during or subsequent to the sediment deposition—and the possible differences in post-depositional regimes of sediment chemistry in the polar and nonpolar oceanic areas.

Higher sedimentation rates in the ocean, resulting chiefly from accelerated microfaunal shell and/or terrigenous detrital deposition, tend to dilute the concentrations of the chemogeneous and adsorbed components in the bulk sediment. The rate of sedimentation in the pelagic area of the Arctic is in the order of 1.5 to 3 mm/1000 yrs. (Hunkins and Kutschale, 1967; Ku and Broecker, 1967; Clark, 1970; Gakkel *et al.*, 1970). This rate is either comparable to or lower than that generally observed in nonpolar deep-sea regions. It would therefore appear that a difference in sedimentation rates is probably not a significant factor in bringing about the relative paucity of the elements analyzed by us in the Arctic sediments (Table 4).

The contribution of volcanogenic components to the gross chemistry of recent deep-sea sediments of various world oceans has not been quantitatively assessed on a regional basis. However, it may reasonably be assumed that the volume of this component in any region will be closely related to the intensity of contemporary submarine tectonism and the associated

sea floor spreading. The geophysical data summarized by Ostenso and Wold (1973), and as well by Hall (1973) strongly indicate that at the present time the Arctic Ocean as a whole is relatively less active tectonically than other oceanic regimes. In the light of this observation the differences between the polar and nonpolar sediment chemistries (Table 4) may be related to regional differences in marine tectonics as well as to regional climate. If this is true then our initial suggestion regarding the application of geochemical criteria relative to the recognition of paleoclimate of marine depositional basins patently becomes invalid. Obviously, application of such an approach will then be limited to marine areas such as the Asian–American Basin of the Arctic Ocean that have had a demonstrably stable tectonic history over a protracted period of geologic time. The Asian–American Basin was apparently active as a tectonic plate only during limited portions of the early Paleozoic and late Mesozoic–early Tertiary (Hall, 1973). Since the early Tertiary, the focus of sea-floor spreading in the Arctic Ocean has shifted to the Greenland–European Basin in the area now dominated by Gakkel (or Nansen) Ridge and the adjacent deeps (Churkin, 1973; Ostenso and Wold, 1973). Concurrent with this tectonic activity the Greenland–European Basin has also been volcanically active (Churkin, 1973). As a result of this it might be expected that at least some of the chemical components of the Greenland–European Basin sediments would have volcanogeneous derivatives. In the Greenland–European Basin, therefore, sediment geochemical criteria can not effectively be applied in attempts to decipher variation in paleoclimate. From the foregoing discussion it would appear that if the sedimentation rates have been fairly uniform,* the stratigraphic variations in sediment chemistry of the Asian–American Basin, at least during the Quaternary period, must reflect variations in paleoclimate in that area. This contention is strongly substantiated by the work of Belov and Lapina (1970), through their studies of several long sediment cores (200 to 400 cm lengths) from the deep water troughs of the Arctic Basin. On the basis of combined investigations on the chemical, mineralogical, granulometric and microfaunal compositions of sediments that were deposited within the time span of the last 200,000 yrs, Belov and Lapina (1970) detected several alternate periods of climatic cooling and warming over the Arctic. Further, they were able to correlate the chemical data on Arctic Ocean sediments with glacial and interglacial epochs that have been established in the stratigraphy of Siberia and Alaska (Belov and Lapina, 1970, p. 30) by more standard methods.

---

* The average rates of sedimentation over much longer time spans than the past 70,000 years—presumably encompassing the entire Quaternary period—appear to have been similar, as suggested by paleomagnetic dating methods (Hunkins *et al.*, 1971, p. 216).

In summary, it seems implicit from data obtained during the present study, combined with the various factors discussed regarding sedimentologic, geochemical, and tectonic aspects of the problem, that any attempts to elucidate paleoclimatic regimen in a given region, based upon geochemical relationships in sediments is likely to be of restricted value. Although this approach may well be useful in certain areas in which the interrelationships of the several variables are deemed well understood, any interpretations should be viewed with reservations, given the complexities of the general case. The method has a certain appeal, but seems fraught with perils which may be difficult, at best, to resolve in any given instance.

Acknowledgments. The authors wish to acknowledge with grateful thanks the help of several persons and agencies in the collection and supply of sediment samples. The Canada Basin sediments were collected from the ice–island T-3, by Dr. K. Hunkins of the Lamont–Doherty Geological Observatory of Columbia University, with support of the Office of Naval Research under contract N00014-67-A-0108-0016. The Mackenzie deltaic sediments were kindly provided by Drs. A. A. Levinson and B. R. Pelletier of the University of Calgary and the Bedford Institute (Nova Scotia), respectively. These deltaic sediments were collected by the crew of H. M. S. Richardson with support from the Department of Energy, Mines and Resources, Government of Canada. The Barents Sea–Kara Sea sediments were made available by Dr. D. C. Burrell of the University of Alaska.

Ice-breaker ship support was provided by the U. S. Coast Guard. The help of Drs. Peter Barnes and Erk Reimnitz and Jim Trumbull of the U. S. Geological Survey, Joe Dygas, Bob Tucker and Terry Hall of the Institute of Marine Science, University of Alaska, Tom Furgatsch, Dave Mountain, and officers and crew of the U. S. C. G. C. GLACIER and STATEN ISLAND, in the collection of samples is gratefully acknowledged. The X-ray analysis was conducted by Mrs. Namok C. Veach.

This work was supported by the Office of Marine Geology, U. S. Geological Survey (Contract 14-09-001-12559), NOAA Office of Sea Grant, Department of Commerce (Contract 04-3-158-41), U. S. Environmental Protection Agency (Contract R-801124), Prudhoe Bay Environmental Subcommittee and by the State of Alaska.

Contribution No. 205 of the Institute of Marine Science, University of Alaska.

REFERENCES

Andrew, J., 1973: Sediment distribution in deep areas of the Northern Kara Sea. Ph.D. thesis, Univ. of Wisconsin, 34 p. (Unpublished.)

Bandy, O. L., 1960: The geological significance of coiling ratios in the foraminifer *Globigerina pachyderma* (Ehrenberg). *Jour. Paleontology*, **34**, 671–681.

Belov, N. A., and N. N. Lapina, 1970: Climatic variations of the Arctic in the light of analysis of bottom depositions. *In:* The Arctic Ocean and its shores during the Cenozoic, Hydrometeorological Publishers, Leningrad, (English Trans. by L. A. Hutchinson, UCSD, La Jolla, Calif.), 27–33.

Belov, N. A., N. N. Kulikov, N. N. Lapina and Y. P. Semenov, 1970: Distribution of iron, manganese, and carbonates in Arctic Ocean sediments. *In:* Problems of Polar Geography (Transl. from Russian), M. I. Belov, Editor, Natn'l. Sci., Foundation, Washington, D. C., 71–77.

Biscaye, P. E., 1965: Mineralogy and sedimentation of recent deep-sea clays in the Atlantic Ocean and adjacent seas and oceans. *Geol. Soc. Amer. Bull.*, **76**, 803–832.

Churkin, Jr., M., 1973: Geologic concepts of Arctic Ocean Basin. *In:* Arctic Geology, Max G. Pitcher, Editor, Amer. Assoc. Petroleum Geologists, Tulsa, Oklahoma, 485–499.

Clark, D. L., 1970: Magnetic reversals and sedimentation rates in the Arctic Ocean. *Geol. Soc. Amer.*, **81**, 3129–3134.

Cronan, D. S., 1969: Average abundances of Mn, Fe, Ni, Co, Cu, Pb, Mo, V, Cr, Ti and P in Pacific pelagic clays. *Geochim. Cosmochim. Acta*, **33**, 1562–1565.

Emiliani, C., 1955: Pleistocene temperatures. *Jour. Geol.*, **63**, 538–578.

Gakkel, Y. Y., N. A. Belov, V. D. Dibner and N. N. Lapina, 1970: The morphostructure and benthic sediments of the Arctic Basin. *In:* Problems of Polar Geography, M. I. Belov, Editor, Natn'l. Sci. Foundation, Washington, D. C. (Trans. from Russian), 13–27.

Griffin, J. J., H. Windom and E. D. Goldberg, 1968: The distribution of clay minerals in the world ocean. *Deep-sea Research*, **15**, 433–59.

Goldberg, E. D., and G. O. S. Arrhenius, 1958: Chemistry of Pacific pelagic sediments. *Geochim. Cosmochim. Acta*, **13**, 153–212.

Goldberg, E. D., and J. J. Griffin, 1964: Sedimentation rates and mineralogy in the South Atlantic. *Jour. Geophys. Res.*, **69**, 4293–4309.

Goldberg, E. D., and J. J. Griffin, 1970: The sediments of the northern Indian Ocean. *Deep-Sea Research*, **17**, 513–537.

Hall, J. K., 1973: Geophysical evidence for ancient sea-floor spreading from Alpha Cordillera and Mendeleyev Ridge. *In:* Arctic Geology, Max G. Pitcher, Editor, Amer. Assoc. Petroleum Geologists, Tulsa, Oklahoma, 542–561.

Horstman, E. L., 1957: The distribution of lithium, rubidium and cesium in igneous and sedimentary rocks. *Geochim. Cosmochim. Acta*, **12**, 1–28.

Hunkins, K., and H. Kutschale, 1967: Quaternary sedimentation in the Arctic Ocean. *In:* Progress in Oceanography, 4, M. Sears, Editor, Pergamon Press, London, 89–94.

Hunkins, K., A. W. H. Be', N. D. Opdyke and G. Mathieu, 1971: The late Cenozoic history of the Arctic Ocean. *In:* The Late Cenozoic Glacial Ages, K. K. Turekian, Editor, Yale Univ. Press, New Haven, 215–237.

Kent, D., N. D. Opdyke, and M. Ewing, 1970: Climate change in the North Pacific using ice-rafted detritus as a climatic indicator. *Geol. Soc. America Bull.*, **82**, 2741–2754.

Ku, T. L. and W. S. Broecker, 1967: Rates of sedimentation in the Arctic Ocean. *In:* Progress in Oceanography, 4, M. Sears, Editor, Pergamon Press, London, 95–104.

Lisitzin, A. P., 1972: Sedimentation in the world ocean. Soc. Econ. Paleont. Minierlg, Special Pub. 17, Tulsa, Oklahoma, 218 p.

Marine Geology, 4, 1966: Marine Palynology. A. A. Manten, Editor, 385–574.

Mullen, R. E., D. A. Darby and D. L. Clark, 1972: Significance of atmospheric dust and ice rafting for Arctic Ocean sediment. *Geol. Soc. America Bull.*, **83**, 205–212.

Naidu, A. S., D. C. Burrell and D. W. Hood, 1971: Clay mineral composition and geological significance of some Beaufort Sea sediments. *Jour. Sedimentary Petrology*, **41**, 691–94.

Naidu, A. S., and D. W. Hood, 1972: Chemical composition of bottom sediments of the Beaufort Sea, Arctic Ocean. Proc. 24th International Geological Congress, Montreal, Canada, 1972, Section 10, 307–317.

Naidu, A. S., and T. C. Mowatt, 1973: Aspects of size distributions, mineralogy and geochemistry of deltaic and adjacent shallow marine sediments, north arctic Alaska. U. S. Coast Guard Oceanographic Report, CGS Srs. (In press.)

Ostenso, N. A., and R. J. Wold, 1973: Aeromagnetic evidence for origin of Arctic Ocean Basin. *In:* Arctic Geology, Max G. Pitcher, Editor, Amer. Assoc. Petroleum Geologists, Tulsa, Oklahoma, 506–516.

Rateev, M. A., Z. N. Gorbunova, A. P. Lisitzyn and G. L. Nosov, 1969: The distribution of clay minerals in the oceans. *Sedimentology*, **13**, 21–43.

Schroeder, R. A., and J. L. Bada, 1973: Glacial-postglacial temperature difference deduced from aspartic acid racemization in fossil bones. *Science*, **182**, 479–482.

Turekian, K. K., 1968: Oceans, Prentice-Hall, Inc., New Jersey, 120 p.

Venkatarathnam, K., and P. E. Biscaye, 1973: Clay mineralogy and sedimentation in the eastern Indian Ocean. *Deep-Sea Research*, **20**, 727–738.

Wedepohl, K. H., 1956: Spurenanalytische Untersuchungen an Tiefseetonen aus dem Atlantik. *Geochim. Cosmochim. Acta*, **18**, 200–231.

Year-to-Year Variations in the Energy Balance of the Arctic Atmosphere*

ABRAHAM H. OORT

Geophysical Fluid Dynamics Laboratory/NOAA, Princeton University, Princeton, New Jersey 08540

Abstract

In order to better understand the processes responsible for maintaining the arctic climate, a study has been made of the energy budget at high latitudes. For simplicity this study is restricted to budget calculations for a polar cap that contains almost the entire atmospheric mass north of a latitude of 60°N. The computations are based on five years of daily upper air observations of wind, temperature, geopotential height and specific humidity for the period May 1958 through April 1963, contained in the so-called MIT General Circulation Library. Of the hemispheric network of radiosonde stations available in the Library more than 200 stations are located north of 50°N. All these stations were used in the analyses to define the meteorological parameters in the Arctic.

Averaged over the year about 75% of the energy needed to balance radiative cooling in the polar cap is found to be transported by atmospheric processes across the southern boundary. The remaining 25% is probably supplied through a direct exchange of sensible and latent heat at the earth's surface in the polar cap.

Throughout the year the influx of sensible heat plus potential energy dominates over that of latent heat. A further breakdown according to the mechanism of transfer shows that at 60°N transient and stationary disturbances are far more effective than the mean meridional circulation in transporting energy poleward. Using Budyko's values for the surface energy flux, indirect estimates could be made of the radiative heat loss in the polar cap that are in good agreement with earlier, direct estimates. The computed cooling curve has an interesting asymmetry; it shows a rapid decrease of cooling from about -1.4 C day^{-1} in winter to about -0.6 C day^{-1} in May followed by a slow increase throughout the summer and fall.

The year-to-year variability in inflow of energy from middle latitudes seems to be large, especially during the winter half year. Since observed temperature deviations in the polar cap appear to be on the average a factor of five smaller than the variations in inflow, these deviations must be largely compensated for by variations in radiative cooling or in heat supply from the earth's surface. The present evidence tends to underline the complexity of the mechanisms responsible for climatic anomalies in the Arctic.

---

1. Introduction

The recent development of numerical models for weather and climate predictions on a global scale has

ENERGY BUDGET FOR POLAR CAP

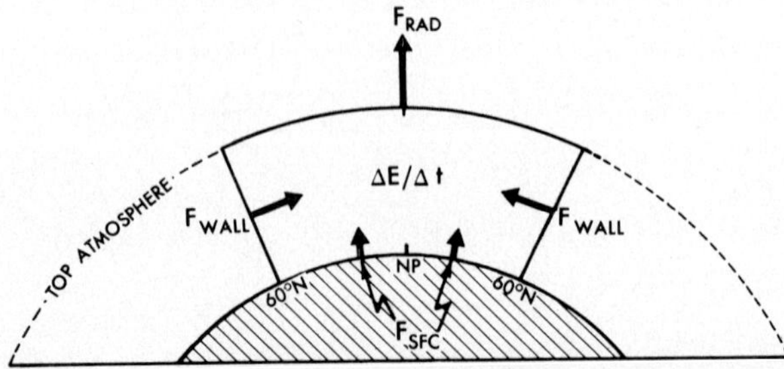

FIG. 1. Schematic diagram of energy budget for a polar cap (note that F_{rad} includes net radiative flux from atmosphere to earth's surface).

---

* Reprinted with kind permission from the Journal of Geophysical Research, Volume 79, No. 9, pp. 1253–1260, March 20, 1974 (in a slightly modified form).

spurred a renewed interest in the polar regions as heat sinks for the general circulation. Ambitious observational programs such as the Polar Experiment (POLEX) have been initiated to extend our knowledge of the polar regions (see Weller and Bierly, 1973). The present study is an example of what can be done with the routinely available atmospheric data. One of the more direct aims of the study has been to clarify the role of atmospheric energy advection from middle latitudes in the arctic heat balance.

Most earlier studies of the arctic heat balance have been largely limited to calculations at the earth's surface (see, e.g., Fletcher, 1965, and Vowinckel and Orvig, 1970). Although such studies are, of course, of great practical importance, there may also be some interest in finding out what happens away from the surface in the arctic atmosphere.

In the present paper the heat balance is studied in a polar cap that is rather arbitrarily chosen to contain the entire atmospheric mass between the surface and about 18 km height north of the latitude of 60°N. A drawback of this approach is that regions

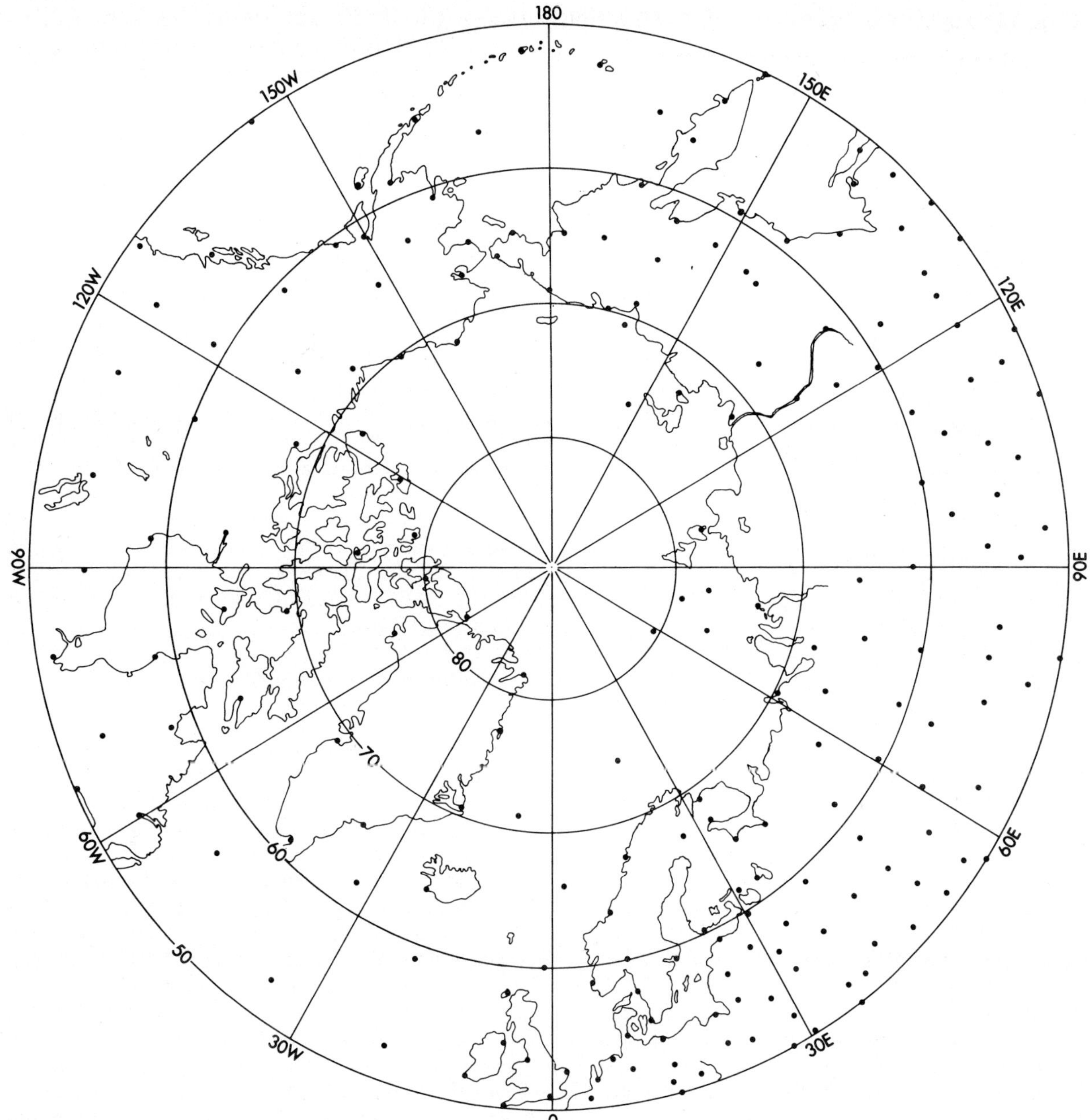

FIG. 2. Distribution of upper air stations north of 50°N used in the present analysis.

of different climatic character such as the Arctic Ocean area and the Greenland and Norwegian Sea areas are lumped together. On the other hand, there are obvious conceptional and computational advantages in chosing a symmetrical polar cap limited by an imaginary wall at a fixed latitude.

The energy budget for a polar cap north of 60°N is shown schematically in Fig. 1. The budget can be written in the form

$$\Delta E/\Delta t = F_{\mathrm{wall}} + F_{\mathrm{sfc}} - F_{\mathrm{rad}} \qquad (1)$$

where

$\Delta E/\Delta t =$ rate of change with time of energy in polar cap,

$F_{\mathrm{wall}} =$ flux of energy into polar cap across wall at 60°N,

$F_{\mathrm{sfc}} =$ flux of energy into polar cap across earth's surface,

and

$F_{\mathrm{rad}} =$ net cooling rate of arctic atmosphere due to radiative effects alone.

ANNUAL MEAN ENERGY FLUX ACROSS 60°N

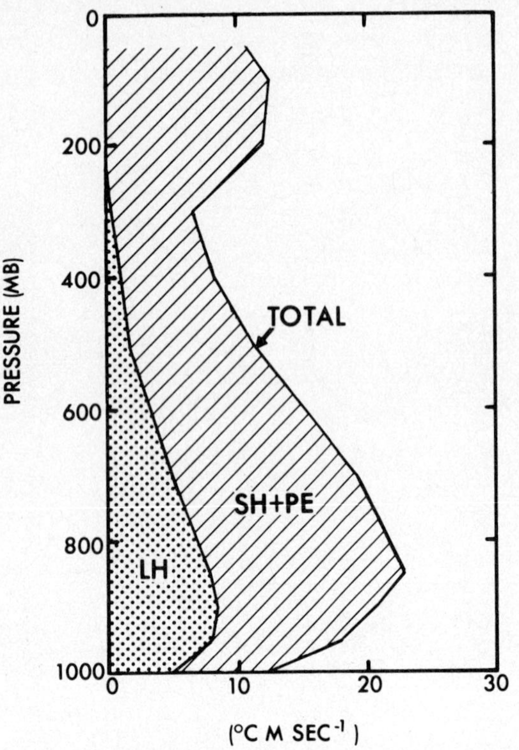

FIG. 3. Annual-mean poleward flux of energy across 60°N in the form of sensible heat plus potential energy and latent heat (note that the flux of kinetic energy can be neglected). Units are in °C m sec⁻¹ (multiply numbers by 0.0506 or 0.0084 to find average heating rate in polar cap in °C day⁻¹ or ly min⁻¹, resp.).

The station distribution used in the present study is shown in Figure 2. Of the more than 200 reporting stations north of 50°N, about 90 are located in the polar cap north of 60°N. The stations in the 50°–60°N latitude belt are important because through the objective analysis method used they may contribute to the value of the fluxes at 60°N itself and to a lesser degree also to the value of the parameters inside the polar cap.

Because of this dense network of upper air stations in the vicinity of the 60°N parallel, one can make a fairly reliable evaluation of the horizontal influx of energy, F_{wall}. Further, the station distribution inside the polar cap seems sufficient to estimate the rate of change of energy, $\Delta E/\Delta t$. However, the other two terms in the energy budget equation, i.e., F_{sfc} and F_{rad}, cannot be readily obtained from radiosonde observations.

The data source for the present estimates is a five-year sample of carefully checked, daily radiosonde observations contained in the MIT General Circulation Library. The period covers May 1958 through April 1963. Actual observed horizontal wind components were used in conjunction with temperature, geopotential height and specific humidity data to compute the different components of the energy budget. In studies of atmospheric energetics the use of actual winds is generally preferable to the use of winds derived from geostrophic or other balance relations because of the inherent approximations in these last quantities.

The data handling and analysis proceeded as follows. For each station and each month the necessary statistics were computed separately at 11 levels between the surface and 50 mb (about 20 km in height). The levels selected were the 1000, 950, 900, 850, 700, 500, 400, 300, 200, 100 and 50 mb pressure surfaces. Next an objective analysis method was used to interpolate the statistics at each level to a regular grid. Integration in the vertical was carried out from the ground up to about 75 mb (18 km). The final integrals are thus representative for about 92% of the atmosphere in the polar cap. A smoothed topography consistent with the resolution of the analysis grid (about 500×500 km² near 60°N) was taken into account. For further details concerning the data reduction and analysis one is referred to a publication by Oort and Rasmusson (1971).

2. Annual-mean conditions

The long-term mean inflow of energy into the Arctic is shown in Figure 3. This graph represents average conditions for the entire five-year period. It shows that the largest influx takes place in the lower troposphere around 850 mb with a secondary maximum between 200 and 100 mb in the lower stratosphere. The bulk of the computed transport occurs in the form of sensible heat (72%) and latent heat (21%), while only a small fraction is in the form of potential energy (7%) and kinetic energy (less than 1%) Throughout the year the influx of kinetic energy is more than two orders of magnitude smaller than the total energy flux (Oort, 1971).

For some purposes it may be of interest to consider separately the contribution of transient eddies, stationary eddies and the mean meridional circulation. This breakdown according to mechanism is given in Fig. 4. It should be mentioned that in the annual mean case all eddies with a time-scale less than a year are included in the transient eddies. Apparently for the year as a whole, the transient processes account for most of the energy transfer. Traveling cyclones and anticyclones are examples of these transient waves At the latitude of 60°N the zonal-mean overturning seems to be of little importance except possibly in winter, as we shall see later.

Averaged over the year the present transport calculations, combined with Budyko's (1963) surface flux estimates, suggest that 73% of the energy needed to balance radiational cooling is supplied through atmospheric transport from middle latitudes and that

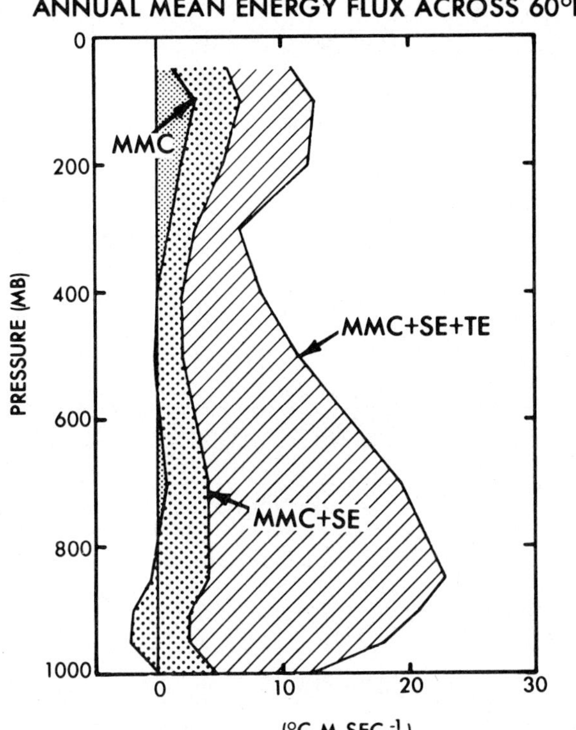

Fig. 4. Annual-mean poleward flux of energy across 60°N broken down into three components associated with transient eddies, stationary eddies and the mean meridional circulation. Units are in °C m sec⁻¹.

the remaining 27% is supplied by the exchange of sensible and latent heat from the underlying surface (see line labelled "annual" in Table 1). This question will be further discussed later in the paper.

3. Annual cycle in the energy balance

The computed annual variation of energy in the Arctic is shown in Fig. 5 as a plot of the vertical-

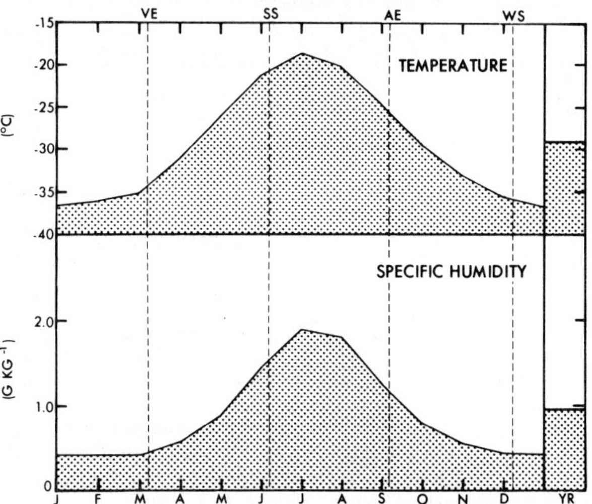

Fig. 5. Annual cycle of vertical mean temperature (°C) and specific humidity (g kg⁻¹) for polar cap. VE=vernal equinox, SS=summer solstice, AE=autumnal equinox and WS=winter solstice. For a direct comparison of temperature and humidity as components of the total energy one should multiply the values on the lower scale by a factor of 2.5.

mean temperature and specific humidity averaged horizontally over the polar cap. A rather sharp maximum is reached by the end of July, while there is a flat minimum in winter during the polar night. The derived month-to-month changes are given in Table 1.

The influx of energy across 60°N is the most important process that protects the arctic climate from even more extreme seasonal variations than are observed now. According to the estimates in Figs. 6 and 7 the total inflow is almost a factor of four larger in winter than in summer Further, the breakdown according to the particular transport mechanism in operation suggests that in winter stationary eddies are slightly more important than transient eddies In

TABLE 1. Monthly energy blance estimates for a polar cap north of 60°N (units °C day⁻¹).

| | $\Delta E/\Delta t$ | | | F_{wall} | | | F_{sfc} | | | |
	IE + PE	LH	Total	SH+PE	LH	Total	SH	LH	Total	F_{rad}
Jan	−0.01	0.00	−0.01	0.99	0.13	1.12	0.10	0.16	0.26	1.39
Feb	0.02	0.00	0.02	1.00	0.16	1.16	0.09	0.17	0.26	1.40
Mar	0.08	0.01	0.09	0.82	0.14	0.96	0.06	0.16	0.22	1.09
Apr	0.15	0.02	0.17	0.61	0.14	0.75	0.03	0.15	0.18	0.76
May	0.16	0.04	0.20	0.37	0.13	0.50	0.05	0.20	0.25	0.55
Jun	0.12	0.04	0.16	0.22	0.15	0.37	0.12	0.29	0.41	0.62
Jul	0.01	0.02	0.03	0.15	0.19	0.34	0.12	0.31	0.43	0.74
Aug	0.09	−0.03	−0.12	0.23	0.18	0.41	0.06	0.25	0.31	0.84
Sep	−0.16	−0.04	−0.20	0.36	0.21	0.57	0.06	0.20	0.26	1.03
Oct	−0.14	−0.03	−0.17	0.65	0.20	0.85	0.04	0.19	0.23	1.25
Nov	−0.11	−0.01	−0.12	0.81	0.20	1.01	0.05	0.17	0.22	1.35
Dec	−0.06	−0.00	−0.06	0.90	0.16	1.06	0.09	0.19	0.28	1.40
Annual	0.00	0.00	0.00	0.59	0.15	0.74	0.07	0.20	0.27	1.01
Data source	present study			present study			Budyko (1963)			residual

Note. The monthly fluxes for, e.g., January were calculated as the average of the fluxes for the five individual January months from the period May 1958 through April 1963. IE = internal energy, PE = potential energy, LH = latent heat and SH = sensible heat.

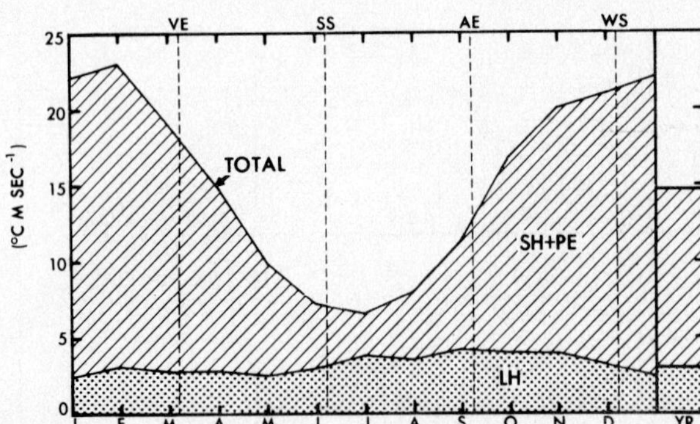

FIG. 6. Annual cycle of poleward flux of energy across 60°N in the form of sensible heat plus potential energy and of latent heat. Units are in °C m sec⁻¹ (multiply flux values by 0.0506 or 1.54 to convert to °C day⁻¹ or °C month⁻¹, resp.).

summer on the other hand, practically the entire transport appears to occur by transient eddies. The transport by the mean meridional circulation can be neglected except during winter.

As a summary, the rate of change of the various energy components and the values of the energy fluxes across 60°N are shown in Fig. 8 and also given in Table 1. It is clear from the tabulated values that the transport of sensible heat plus potential energy dominates over that of latent heat except during the summer when they contribute equally. Also tabulated are the fluxes of sensible and latent heat across the earth's surface as taken from Budyko's (1963) heat atlas. Finally, the last column in Table 1 shows the radiational cooling rates calculated as a residual in equation (1) to balance the other contributions. Even if one allows for possible errors or unrepresentativeness

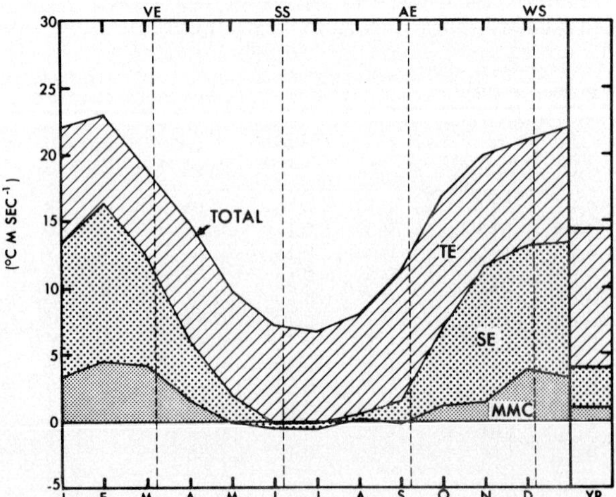

FIG. 7. Annual cycle of poleward flux of energy across 60°N broken down into three components associated with transient eddies, stationary eddies and the mean meridional circulation. Units are in °C m sec⁻¹.

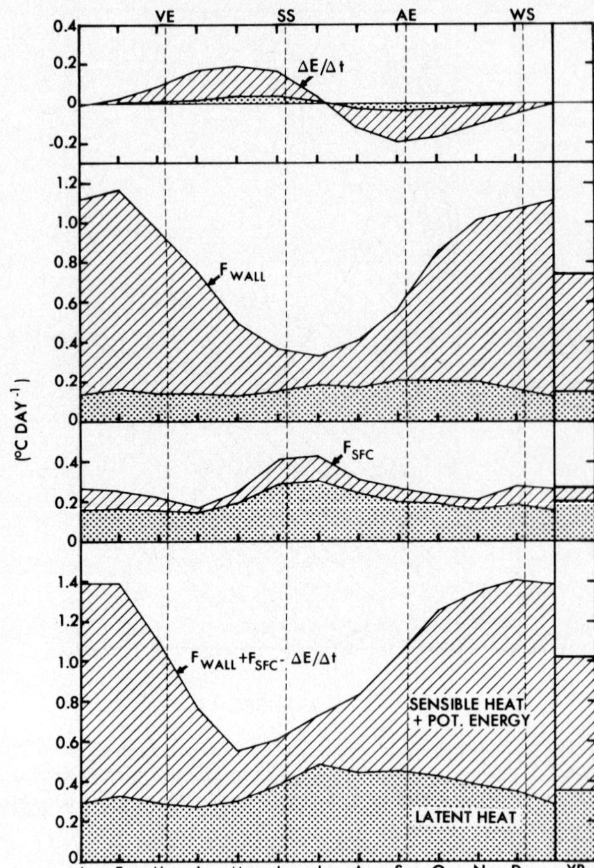

FIG. 8. Annual cycle of different energy budget terms for the polar cap. Units are in °C day⁻¹ (multiply numbers by 0.166 to convert to ly min⁻¹).

of the estimates involved it is clear that the atmospheric heat flow into the polar cap must be the dominant term that balances the extreme radiative heat losses in the Arctic. The residual radiative cooling rates are also shown graphically in Fig. 9 together with rough estimates of the spread to be expected between values for individual years. The spread was evaluated from residual calculations for the same calendar month from different years. For comparison mid-season cooling rates from Rodgers (1967) are inserted in Fig. 9; his values are based purely on radiation data. There appears to be reasonably good agreement between the two independent evaluations.[1]

---

[1] Recently Dopplick (1970) has reevaluated Rodgers' estimates with, among other differences, a modified treatment of clouds. In the Arctic, the new radiative cooling estimates are much smaller than those of Rodgers (1967). For example, Dopplick's values lead to average cooling rates for the year, January and July of −0.55, −0.82 and −0.22 C day⁻¹, resp., while Rodgers' cooling rates are −1.03, −1.20 and −0.81 C day⁻¹. The present indirect estimates could not, in the author's opinion, be in error by more than a few tenths of a degree centigrade, and thus tend to support the earlier values of Rodgers.

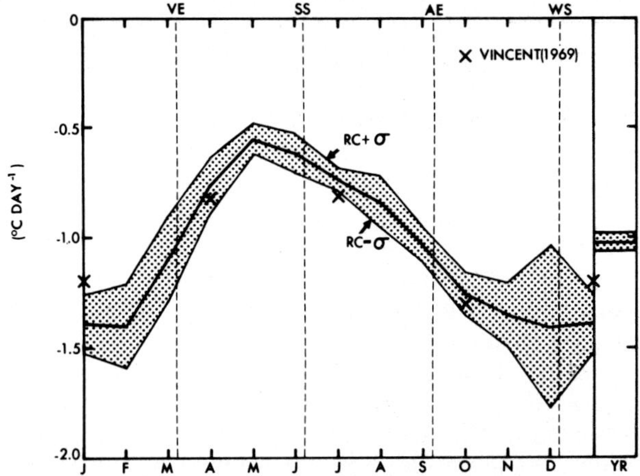

FIG. 9. Annual cycle of inferred radiative cooling rates ($\pm$ standard deviation computed from five individual years) for the atmosphere in the polar cap. Crosses indicate Rodgers' (1967) directly computed radiative cooling rates for the mid-season months. Units are in °C day^{-1} (multiply numbers by 0.166 to convert to ly min^{-1}).

The asymmetry in the cooling rate curve as shown by a rapid decrease in radiative cooling in the spring and a slow increase from early summer to midwinter seems intriguing. It can probably be explained in part by the occurrence of relatively warm temperatures in fall compared to spring (due to heat storage), that would result in stronger radiative cooling in the fall. Although this effect is probably the primary factor, the net cooling will be also affected by the observed increase in cloudiness and albedo during the fall.

4. Year-to-year variations in the energy balance

Mean monthly temperature and specific humidity values for the five-year period studied are presented in Tables 2 and 3. The entries in the tables represent mean values averaged over practically the entire atmospheric mass north of 60°N. A closer look at the

different values and their deviations from the five-year normal indicates that changes in the arctic energy content are dominated by changes in temperature, and not by changes in humidity. The last variations contribute only between 10 and 20% to the total energy change.

It seems of considerable interest to investigate which term or which combination of terms in budget equation (1) could be the cause of the observed temperature anomalies. The three possible effects are (1) an abnormal influx of energy from middle latitudes, (2) an abnormal exchange of heat at the ocean or ground surface north of 60°N, and (3) an abnormal radiative cooling in the polar cap. The present data set only enables us to evaluate the first effect. The computed values of the influx of sensible plus latent heat by eddies are given in Table 4 and as deviations from normal in Fig. 10. The contribution by mean meridional circulations has not been included in the table since this term is virtually impossible to determine with any degree of confidence on the basis of one month of data alone. Furthermore, the results for the five-year mean as shown in Fig. 7 suggest that inclusion of the mean meridional circulations

TABLE 2. Mean monthly mass-average temperature (°C) in arctic.

	1958–59	1959–60	1960–61	1961–62	1962–63	1958–63
May	−26.8	−26.1	−25.4	−25.8	−27.2	−26.3
Jun	−21.5	−21.4	−21.4	−21.0	−22.0	−21.5
Jul	−19.0	−18.9	−18.7	−18.4	−19.4	−18.9
Aug	−20.6	−20.1	19.8	20.5	20.9	−20.4
Sep	−25.1	−24.2	−24.6	−24.4	−25.4	−24.7
Oct	−29.6	−29.6	−29.8	−29.3	−29.8	−29.6
Nov	−33.8	−32.6	−33.6	−33.6	−33.1	−33.3
Dec	−35.9	−35.8	−33.8	−37.1	−36.4	−35.8
Jan	−36.3	−35.8	−36.0	−37.8	−37.5	−36.7
Feb	−36.8	−36.2	−36.9	−36.9	−35.8	−36.5
Mar	−34.7	−35.5	−35.9	−35.1	−36.2	−35.5
Apr	−31.0	−31.2	−31.1	−31.9	−31.3	−31.3
Year	−29.3	−29.0	−28.9	−29.3	−29.6	−29.2

TABLE 3. Mean monthly mass-average specific humidity (g kg^{-1}) in arctic.

	1958–59	1959–60	1960–61	1961–62	1962–63	1958–63
May	0.89	0.91	0.97	0.91	0.85	0.91
Jun	1.45	1.45	1.48	1.48	1.40	1.45
Jul	1.90	1.94	1.98	1.90	1.86	1.92
Aug	1.80	1.80	1.80	1.74	1.78	1.78
Sep	1.25	1.30	1.25	1.23	1.15	1.24
Oct	0.85	0.84	0.71	0.84	0.79	0.81
Nov	0.57	0.63	0.56	0.54	0.58	0.58
Dec	0.43	0.46	0.53	0.40	0.43	0.45
Jan	0.43	0.43	0.43	0.43	0.43	0.43
Feb	0.46	0.64	0.40	0.43	0.35	0.46
Mar	0.51	0.50	0.44	0.40	0.34	0.44
Apr	0.59	0.63	0.49	0.57	0.57	0.57
Year	0.93	0.96	0.92	0.91	0.88	0.918

TABLE 4. Mean monthly energy flux (°C m sec^{-1}) across 60°N by transient plus stationary eddies.

	1958–59	1959–60	1960–61	1961–62	1962–63	1958–63
May	10.2	10.2	10.2	10.8	10.4	10.3
Jun	7.1	8.0	6.3	8.2	9.4	7.8
Jul	6.4	7.0	6.5	8.8	7.5	7.2
Aug	7.4	8.9	6.8	7.6	7.4	7.6
Sep	11.5	12.3	10.9	12.2	12.2	11.8
Oct	14.4	14.3	13.2	19.6	15.6	15.4
Nov	22.4	17.1	16.9	16.9	18.2	18.3
Dec	11.2	19.4	22.3	12.2	19.6	16.9
Jan	14.8	15.8	19.8	22.8	23.4	19.3
Feb	22.8	14.2	17.9	22.3	14.3	18.3
Mar	17.8	13.4	17.3	11.4	12.6	14.5
Apr	11.2	12.4	12.4	14.5	16.0	13.3
Ave.	13.1	12.7	13.4	13.9	13.9	13.4

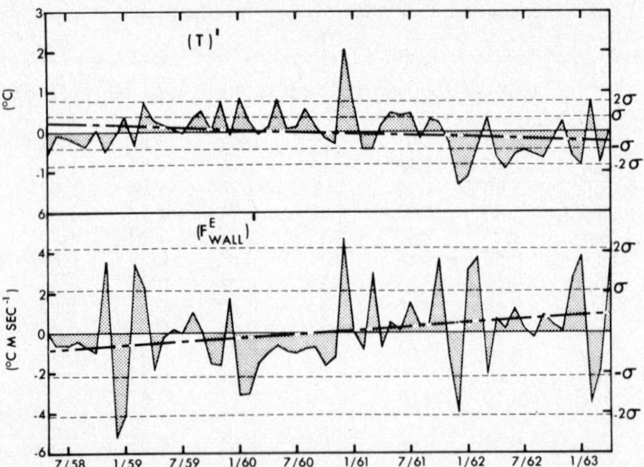

Fɪɢ. 10. Deviations from normal of average temperature (°C) in polar cap and of poleward eddy flux of energy (°C m sec⁻¹) across 60°N for the period May 1958 through April 1963. The normal annual cycle as computed from the 5-year sample has been subtracted out. The standard deviation and the linear trend computed for the 60-month samples are also shown as dashed and dash-dot lines, resp., (multiply flux values by 0.0506 or 1.54 to convert to °C day⁻¹ or °C month⁻¹, resp.).

would not greatly affect the transport values as shown here. Thus, in the further discussion the values in Table 4 are assumed to be representative of the total energy influx through the wall.

The interannual variations in F_{wall} reflect besides true variations also variations due to errors or unrepresentativeness of the data. Although the data coverage as exhibited in Fig. 2 seems very good, it is difficult to prove through standard error analysis that the computed variations are indeed significant and real.[2]

Returning to the question of the importance of the abnormal atmospheric influx of energy to the Arctic, one can compare these values directly with the computed temperature anomalies within the arctic cap. This comparison is shown in Fig. 10. First of all, the two series are only weakly correlated (correlation coefficient=0.15). Further the variations in temperature are about a factor of five smaller than one would expect on the basis of advection alone. Thus if one accepts the reliability of the data one has to conclude that the variations in atmospheric inflow must be largely compensated for by similar variations in radiational cooling or—perhaps less likely—by variations in the exchange of heat with the underlying earth's surface. This sequence of events does not seem improbable because it is also typical for the variation during the normal annual cycle where the net change tends to be small compared with the other terms (compare Table 1).

Let us also mention the possible significance of anomalies in exchange of heat with the ocean and

ground surface in the Arctic. Many authors have stressed the possible importance of fluctuations in the extent of ice and snow cover in the Arctic (see for example, Fletcher, 1965; Budyko, 1969; and the recent numerical model experiment by Wetherald and Manabe, 1972). Such fluctuations would affect not only the direct heat exchange between ocean and atmosphere but also the arctic radiation balance through changes in the surface albedo. The anomalies in oceanic conditions would in this case have to be supported by abnormal influxes of heat across 60°N carried by ocean currents instead of by atmospheric currents as discussed earlier in the paper.

Finally, radiational cooling seems an unlikely candidate to initiate climatic anomalies such as those presented in Fig. 10. Nevertheless, radiational cooling could certainly have a secondary influence as a modifier of the temperature anomalies brought about by an abnormal energy influx from middle latitudes or from the earth's surface.

It is also of interest to note the slow net cooling of −0.46 C/5 year in the polar cap during the period May 1958 through April 1963. This cooling is in agreement with the hemispheric cooling trend of −0.60 C/5 year during that period reported by Starr and Oort (1973). However, the arctic temperature is certainly not monotonically decreasing. The trend seems rather to consist of a slight warming before the year 1960 followed by a cooling since that time.

In summary, the present study suggests that observed climatic anomalies cannot be explained by one factor alone such as, for example, the abnormal atmospheric inflow of energy from middle latitudes. Although these last deviations are found to be large they must be compensated by almost equally large deviations in atmospheric cooling or in heat exchange with the arctic surface. Climatic anomalies probably come about by a complex chain of events that may prove difficult to unravel.

Acknowledgments. The author wishes to thank Dr. Syukuro Manabe and the reviewer of this paper in the Journal of Geophysical Research for their critical comments and suggestions, Mr. Melvin Rosenstein for drafting the figures, Mr. Harold D. Bowman II for help in the calculations and Mrs. Elaine D'Amico for typing the manuscript.

---

² For a further discussion of these questions, see the original version of this paper in the Journal of Geophysical Research.

REFERENCES

Budyko, M. I., 1963: Atlas of the heat balance of the globe (in Russian). Moscow, Hydrometeorological Service, 69 pp.
Budyko, M. I., 1969: The effect of solar radiation variations on the climate of the earth. *Tellus*, **21**, 611–619.
Dopplick, Th. G., 1970: Global radiative heating of the earth's atmosphere. Rept. 24, 128 pp., Mass. Inst. of Technol., Dept. of Meteorol., Planetary Circulations Project.
Fletcher, J. O., 1965: The heat budget of the arctic basin and its relation to climate. Report R-444-PR, 179 pp., The Rand Corporation.

Oort, A. H., 1971: The observed annual cycle in the meridional transport of atmospheric energy. *J. Atmos. Sci.*, 28, 325–339.

Oort, A. H., and Rasmusson, E. M., 1971: Atmospheric circulation statistics. NOAA Professional Paper No. 5, U. S. Government Printing Office, Washington, D. C., 323 pp.

Rodgers, C. D., 1967: The radiative heat budget of the troposphere and lower stratosphere. Rep. A2, 99 pp., Mass. Inst. of Technol., Dept. of Meteorol., Planetary Circulations Project.

Starr, V. P., and Oort, A. H., 1973: Five-year climatic trend for the Northern Hemisphere. *Nature*, Vol. 242, No. 5396, 310–313.

Vowinckel, E., and Orvig, S., 1970: The climate of the North Polar Basin. In Climates of the Polar Regions, S. Orvig (ed.), World Survey of Climatology, Volume 14, Elsevier Publishing Company, Amsterdam, 370 pp.

Weller, G., and Bierly, E. W., 1973: The Polar Experiment (POLEX). *Bull. Amer. Meteorol. Soc.*, 54, 212–218.

Wetherald, R. T., and Manabe, S., 1972: Response of the joint ocean-atmosphere model to the seasonal variation of the solar radiation. *Mon. Weather Rev.*, 100, 42–59.

Recent Climatic Changes in the Eastern North American Sub-Arctic

I. I. Schell, D. A. Corkum, and E. N. Sabbagh

Ocean-Atmosphere Research Institute, Cambridge, Massachusetts 02138

Abstract

An analysis of the iceberg count, mainly April–June months, off Newfoundland during the period 1921–1970 showed a sharp decrease in the number of bergs crossing 48°N, from an average of 435 bergs per year in the 1921–50 period (470, 419, 418 respectively in the first, second, and third decades) to 240 in the 1951–60 and to 150 in the 1961–70 decades. The decrease was associated with a decrease in the strength of the December–February northwesterly winds along the Labrador and Newfoundland coasts as measured by the pressure differences between 50°N, 60°W and 60°N, 50°W (from 10.8 mb in the December–February 1920/1–1949/0 period to 8.0 mb in the 1950/1–1959/0 and to 5.0 mb in the 1960/1–1969/0 decades), and also a decrease in the winds farther north, causing fewer bergs to drift southward with the Labrador Current. It was also associated with a more northeasterly direction of the April winds in the 1961–70 decade than in the preceding 1951–60 decade and with a still greater northeasterly direction than in the 1921–50 period, allowing for a greater proportion of the reduced numbers of bergs to drift southwestward, there to be grounded in the bays and shallows along the coasts. The decrease in bergs was further associated with an increase in the December–February air temperatures at St. John's (Torbay), Newfoundland from −3.6 C to −2.1 C between the 1920/1–1949/0 and 1950/1–1959/0 periods, and a further increase of 0.2 C in the 1960/1–1969/0 decade over the 1950/1–1959/0 decade. The low berg count in the 1961–70 decade was followed in 1972 by the heaviest count on record (1590 bergs) and by another heavy count in excess of 800, or more than twice the long-term average, in 1973.

Also, the sharp decrease in icebergs in the 1961–70 decade was associated with a marked increase in the ice off Iceland and a somewhat longer ice season extending into September in Baffin Bay, showing that the climatic elements in this decade underwent different changes in each of the regions in accordance with Faegri's law: the shorter the period of climatic change, the smaller the area similarly affected.

---

1. Introduction

In studying climatic changes, there appear to be three factors that need to be considered: (1) the region of the climatic change, (2) the period, or length of years, and (3) the climatic element. In accordance with Faegri's law (1950)—the longer the period of climatic change, the wider the area similarly affected— we can expect that for a longer period, say an Ice Age, the reduction in temperature would encompass the entire globe, yet other climatic elements would respond differently from each other according to the region, or, more explicitly, according to the circulation over it. Thus, during an Ice Age and a widespread lowering of temperature, regions under the influence of increased storminess would be receiving greatly increased precipitation. This has led to an Ice Age being sometimes called a Pluvial. Other regions under the influence of a greatly expanded anticyclonic circulation, which in effect would block storms from penetrating the region, would receive very little precipitation and lead an Ice Age there to be called an Anti-Pluvial. Over shorter periods of time, of the order of decades only, the climatic change over a region could differ even more from that of another. Thus the climatic record must be studied region by

region to establish the different characteristics of the change in each region, both for the proper input in models and for establishing an orderly sequence of past climatic changes as a basis for their possible prediction. Here we shall concern ourselves with the climatic changes during the last 50 years, 1921–70, in the eastern North American Sub-Arctic (broadly speaking, the region of Davis Strait, the Labrador Sea, and the lands bordering these waters).

By far the longest observational record of a climatic element made by actual observers in the eastern North American Sub-Arctic is the severity of the iceberg season or the count of icebergs off Newfoundland. This record goes back in some detail to 1900 and in less detail to 1881. Understandably, the threat to shipping by the icebergs (which in some years may drift south as far as latitude 40°N or even lower) made many report their presence. This soon led to their study, notably by Schott (1903, 1904), Meinardus (1904), and Mecking (1906, 1907). The establishment of the International Ice Patrol and Observational Service soon after the *Titanic* sinking in 1912 led to their further study by Smith (1931), Soule and Challender (1949), Soule *et al.* (1950), Lenczyk (1965), Morgan (1970), and others, as well as to attempts at

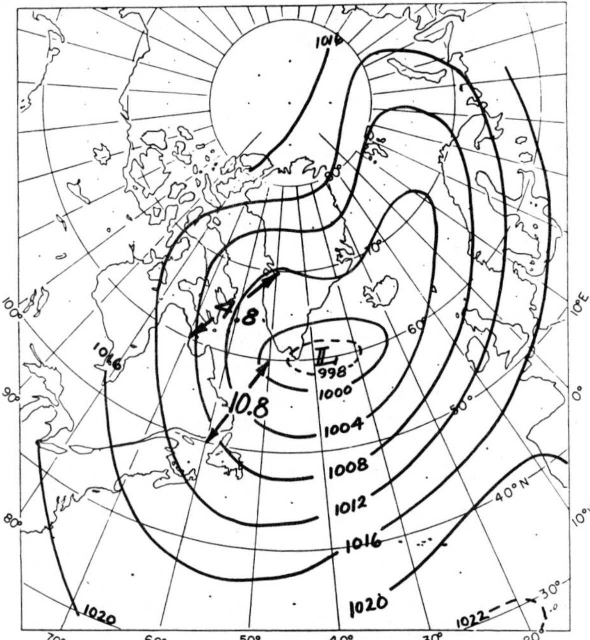

FIG. 1. December–February 1920/1–49/0 pressure (mb). Average number of icebergs drifting south of 48°N a year, 436.

their prediction (Smith, 1931; Groissmayr, 1939; Schell, 1953, 1962; see also Corkum, 1971).

Along with nearly 100 years of records of icebergs crossing 48°N, tabulations of pressure at standard intersections (grid-points) were developed from daily synoptic charts that were augmented by mean monthly tabulations from stations in the general area. This provided data for the computation of pressure gradients as a measure of the strength of the winds as far back as 1880, while observations of air temperatures at St. John's begun in 1872 (Smithsonian Institution, 1944, 1947; U. S. Weather Bureau, 1959, 1965) gave an equally long record of temperature changes. Finally, measurements of the Labrador Current, unfortunately limited to but a few times a year and at first to only once a year, that were instituted in the 1920's, gave the volume transport and temperature (Dinsmore and Moynihan, 1972).

2. Frequency of icebergs

Few surveys of the iceberg population in Baffin Bay and Davis Strait have been made, so there is little reliable information about the supply of bergs available each year for transport southward to the Grand Banks region (see Feazel and Kollmeyer, 1972). The production of bergs, primarily from the glaciers on the west coast of Greenland, is such that large numbers are always present along this coast. How many are actually transported each year across Baffin Bay and Davis Strait to the Canadian side, thence to drift to the Grand Banks region, appears to be unknown. Counts of bergs drifting down each year to the Grand

Banks region were compiled by Mecking (1907), Smith (1931), and since then annually by various members of the International Ice Patrol (see International Ice Patrol and Observational Service in the North Atlantic Ocean, U. S. Coast Guard Bulletins).

Although the iceberg record prior to 1950 shows extremes for individual years (as when, for example only two icebergs were counted crossing 48°N in 1941 and 1942, and over 1000 in 1912), the yearly count averaged over a decade beginning with the 1900's, some 450 bergs, was fairly constant until the 1950's. A sharp drop occurred in the 1950's and another in the 1960's when decadal averages of only 241 and 151 bergs a year, respectively, were observed. This indicated a basic change in the circulation and other climatic elements over that general area.

The frequency of icebergs crossing latitude 48°N off Newfoundland on their way southward may be said to be a function of several variables: (1) supply, which is determined primarily by the calving of glaciers along the west coast of Greenland (see also below), (2) transport by the winds and the West Greenland and Labrador Currents which are affected by the winds, (3) mortality due to melting, as the bergs move southward to the Grand Banks, especially as they near the less cold waters in spring and summer, and finally (4) the pack ice which acts to "preserve" icebergs within the pack thus allowing them to drift southward or, when the pack along the Labrador and Newfoundland coasts is less extensive, to drift into the bays and shallows where they are grounded

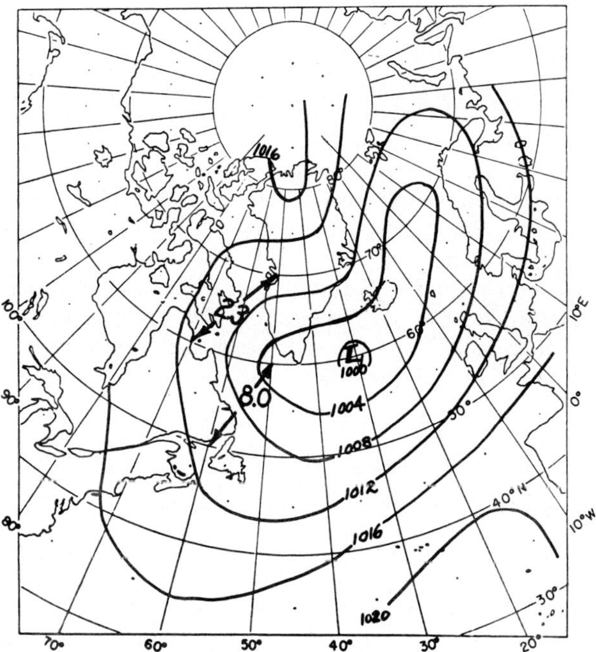

FIG. 2. December–February 1950/1–59/0 pressure (mb). Average number of icebergs drifting south of 48°N a year, 241.

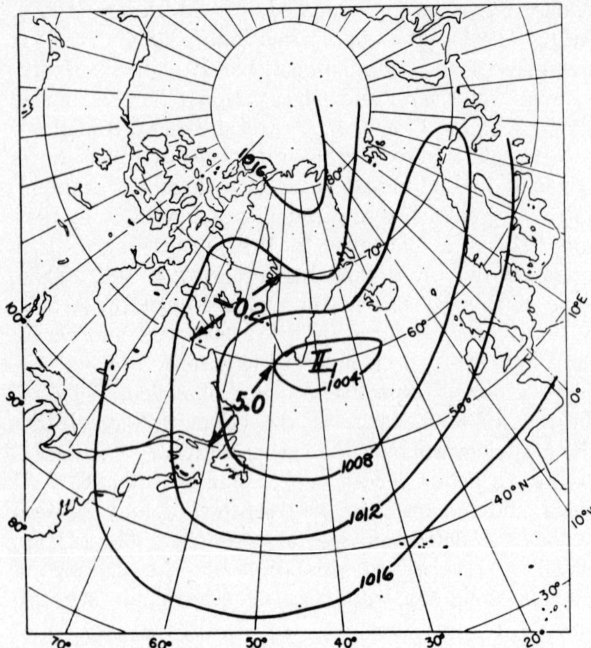

FIG. 3. December–February 1960/1–69/0 pressure (mb). Average number of icebergs drifting south of 48°N a year, 151.

and thus prevented from drifting to the Grand Banks region.

3. Winter winds and temperatures

Of the different factors which play a part in the frequency of bergs crossing latitude 48°N on their way southward, the strength of the northwesterly winds in winter along the Labrador and Newfoundland coasts has been variously emphasized. The strength of these northwesterly winds may be estimated by taking the difference between the mean December–February pressures at 50°N, 60°W and 60°N, 50°W. This difference, which was 10.5 mb in the 1920/1–1949/0 period, decreased to 8.0 mb in 1950/1–1959/0, and then dropped to 5.0 mb in 1960/1–1969/0, as shown in Figs. 1–3 and Table 1. The pressure gradient between 60°N, 70°W and 70°N, 50°W also decreased. Associated with the decrease in the strength of the northwesterly winds were rising air temperatures (Table 1), and, we may assume, a diminution of

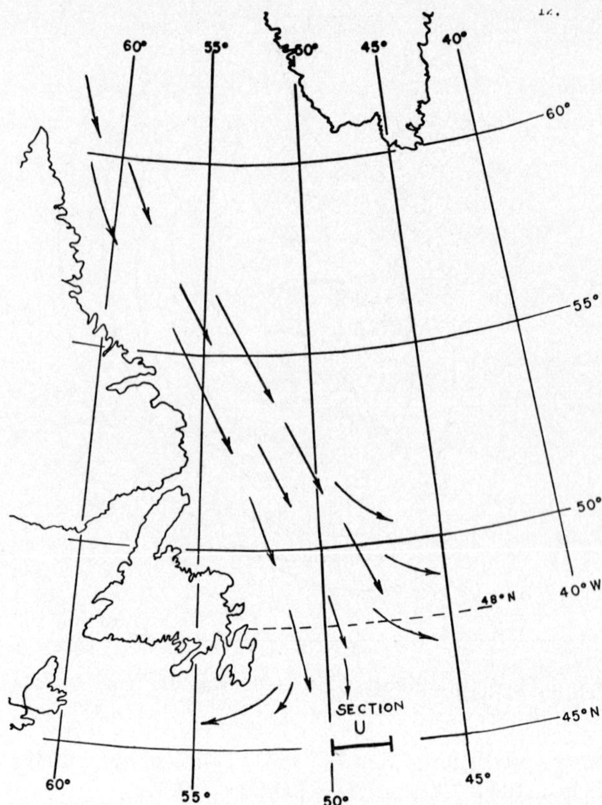

FIG. 4. Location of Section U (volume transport of Labrador current).

pack ice along the coast (see also below), thus allowing bergs to drift to the right of the Labrador Current and into the bays and shallows under the influence of Coriolis acceleration.

4. Labrador current

The Labrador Current (Fig. 4) originates as cold water flowing southward along the coast of Baffin Land with an admixture of cold water from Hudson Bay. Farther south, this cold current is joined by relatively warm West Greenland Current water. Thus, the extent to which West Greenland Current water is added to the Labrador Current will affect the latter's coldness. A greater volume transport of the Labrador Current would indicate higher rather than lower temperatures, if the increased volume is due to an above-average contribution from the W. Green-

TABLE 1. Mean Dec.–Feb. pressure differences: 50°N, 60°W, minus 60°N, 50°W (P.D.₁) and 60°N, 70°W minus 70°N, 50°W (P.D.₂), and St. John's (Torbay) temperatures 1920/1–1969/0, and iceberg count mainly April–June 1921–1970.

Period	P.D.$_1$ in mb	P.D.$_2$ in mb	St. John's T. in °C	Berg count at 48°N
1920/1–49/0	10.8	4.8	−3.6	436
1950/1–59/0	8.0	2.3	−2.1	241
1960/1–69/0	5.0	−0.2	−1.9	151

TABLE 2. April volume transport and sea temperature, Section U, Labrador current and iceberg count.

Period	Vol. Transp., 10^6 m³ sec⁻¹	Temp., °C	Berg count at 48°N
1931–40	6.1	1.9	419
1951–60	4.6	1.5	241
1961–65	4.3	1.9	141

TABLE 3. Mean April pressure differences: 50°N, 60°W minus 60°N, 50°W, and iceberg count, mainly April–June, 1921–1970.

Period	Pressure diff. in mb	Berg count at 48°N
1920/1–49/0	3.4	436
1950/1–59/0	3.2	241
1960/1–69/0	2.1	151

land Current. A strengthened Labrador Current may then be associated with faster melting of icebergs as well as a stronger drift of bergs southward.

The volume transport of the Labrador Current southeast of Newfoundland (Section U, see Fig. 4), computed usually for April, showed lower values in the 1950's than in the 1930's (there were too few values in the 1920's and, because of World War II, also in the 1940's for consideration) and a further decrease from the 1950's to the first five years of the 1960's—the only part of the decade for which observations were available (Table 2). The corresponding iceberg count decreased from an average of 430 in the 1930's to 241 in the 1951–60 decade, and again to an average of 151 in the 1961–65 period. Actually, computations of the volume transport of the Labrador Current are to a depth of 50 m or so from the bottom, and since icebergs extend downward only a few hundred feet on the average, the available measurements cannot be regarded as a true measure of the transport affecting the icebergs drifting with the current.

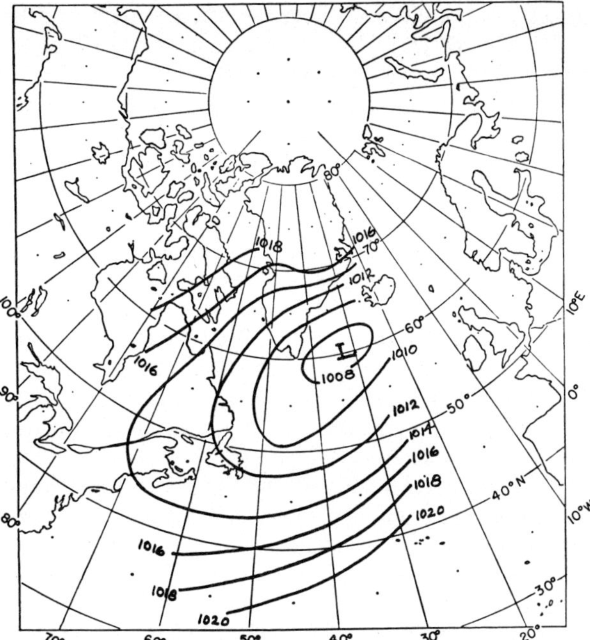

FIG. 6. April pressure 1951–60 (mb).

5. April winds

As April is the month during which the greatest percentage of bergs are counted crossing 48°N, the April winds are of special interest. We may expect that the last decade (1961–70) with the lowest berg count, would show a weaker northwesterly component than in the preceding decade and a still weaker component than in the 1921–50 period. Table 3 giving the

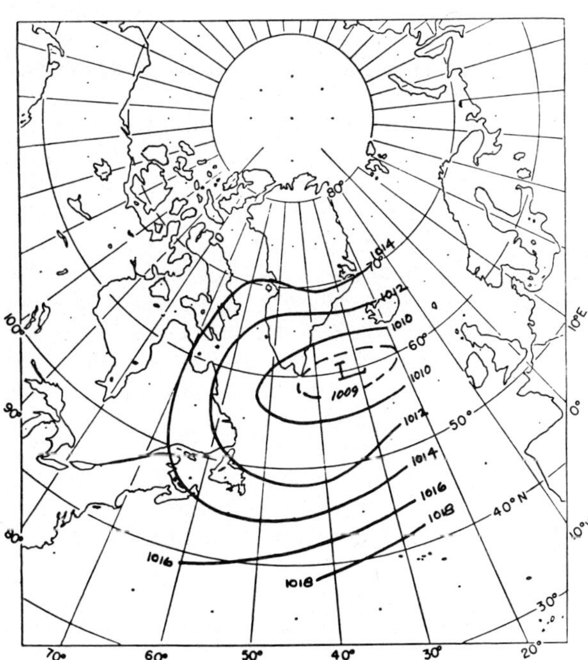

FIG. 5. April pressure 1921–50 (mb).

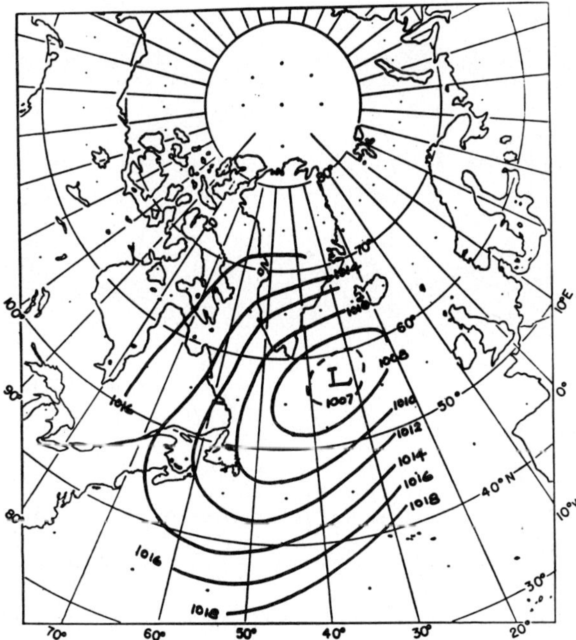

FIG. 7. April pressure 1961–70 (mb).

April pressure differences between the grid-points 60°W, 50°N and 50°W, 60°N shows a sharp decrease in the pressure difference from the 1951–60 to the 1961–70 decades when the berg count dropped from an average of 241 to 151 bergs, but little change in the pressure differences between the 1921–50 and the 1951–60 periods when the number of bergs showed an even greater decrease.

Actually, Figs. 5–7 giving the average April pressure distribution for the 1921–50, 1951–60, and 1961–70 periods show considerable differences in the direction of the mean air flow or the winds over the region. Thus, while the April winds along the Labrador–Newfoundland coasts in the 1921–50 period are predominantly from the northwest in continuation of the strong northwesterlies the winter before, those in the 1951–60 decade reveal a veering to the north-northeast with the mean air flow directed appreciably towards the Labrador–Newfoundland coasts rather than along them; and an even sharper veering of the winds from the northwest to the northeast in the 1961–70 decade, as seen also from the differences in pressures between the 1951–60 and 1961–70 decades respectively and the pressures in the 1921–50 period (Figs. 8 and 9).

Thus, while the northwesterly winds in winter figure in the initiation of a lesser or greater transport of bergs southward—the weaker the northwesterly winds the smaller the count of bergs drifting southward—equally, the greater the northeasterly component of the winds in April, the fewer will reach the

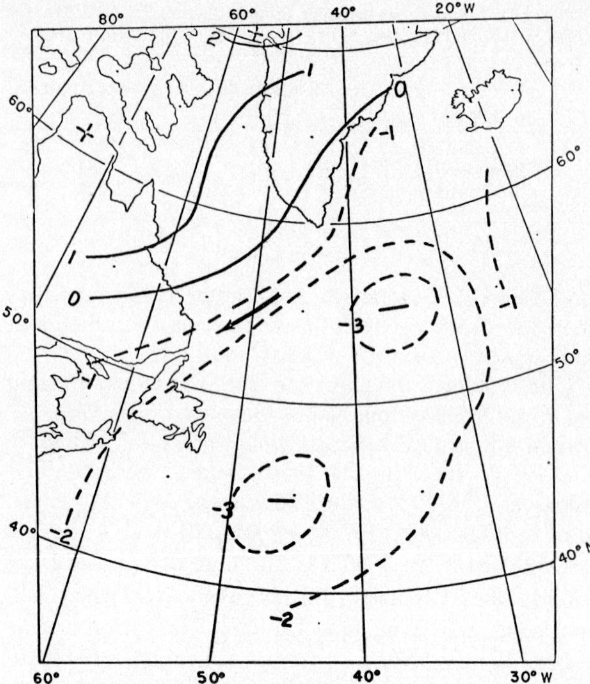

FIG. 9. April pressure difference: 1961–1970 minus 1921–1950 (mb). Arrow indicates change in mean wind direction from that in the 1921–50 period.

Grand Banks regions as a greater proportion of their reduced number drifts toward the coasts.

6. Summary and conclusion

The results obtained from the comparisons made between the 1921–50 and 1951–60 and 1961–70 periods show a distinct climatic change of that region as reflected in the diminished iceberg count in the last two decades and in the strength of the northwesterly winds in winter and their veering towards the northeast in April when the biggest percentage of bergs of the season drift southward across 48°N. The results show also agreement with the air temperature.

There is too little information about the Labrador Current (volume transport and temperature) to allow conclusions about its possible contribution to the icebergs' transport and their "mortality" due to melting. This could be due to a lack of measurements of the first few hundred feet below the surface and to the uncertainty about the contribution of West Greenland Current water.

A recent investigation of a possible relationship between the masses of several icebergs and the sea subsurface and air temperatures, wind velocity, and height and direction of waves showed little agreement (Wolford, 1973).

It needs to be pointed out that the sharp decrease in the number of icebergs in the 1961–70 decade was associated with a marked increase in the ice off Iceland (Schell, 1973) and also with a somewhat longer

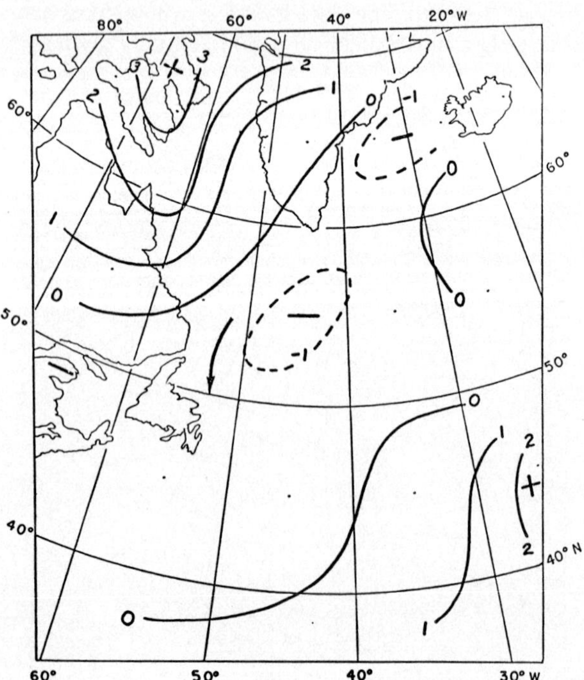

FIG. 8. April pressure difference: 1951–1960 minus 1921–1950 (mb). Arrow indicates change in mean wind direction from that in the 1921–50 period.

ice season, extending into September, in Baffin Bay (Dunbar, 1972), showing that for climatic changes over periods as long as a decade, different regions can undergo opposite changes in their climatic elements in accordance with Faegri's law: the shorter the period of a climatic change, the smaller the area similarly affected.

It may be added that the low count of icebergs in the 1961–70 decade was followed by the heaviest iceberg season on record, 1590 bergs in 1972, and another heavy iceberg count in 1973, with over 800 bergs—more than twice the long-term average.

Acknowledgments. This research was supported by the Advanced Research Projects Agency of the Department of Defense and was monitored by the Air Force Office of Scientific Research under Contract No. F44620-72-C-0040.

REFERENCES

Corkum, D. A., 1971: Performance of Formula for Predicting the Iceberg Count off Newfoundland. *J. Appl. Meteorol.* **10**(3), 605–7.

Dinsmore, R., and M. J. Moynihan, 1972: On the Interchange of Labrador Sea and North Atlantic Ocean Waters. Symp. on Physical Variability in the North Atlantic. *Rap. Process Verb., Reun. Cons. Intern. l'Explor. Mer.* **162**, 206–12. Copenhagen.

Dunbar, M. 1972: Increasing severity of ice conditions in Baffin Bay and Davis Strait and its effect on the extreme limits of ice. *In* "Sea Ice," *Proc. Intern. Conf., Reykjavik, Iceland, 1971.* Natl. Res. Counc., pp. 87–93.

Faegri, K., 1950: On the value of palaeoclimatological evidence. *R. Meteor. Soc., Centenary Proc.,* pp. 188–95.

Feazel, C. T., and R. C. Kollmyer, 1972: Major iceberg producing glaciers of West Greenland. *In* "Sea Ice," *Proc. Int. Conf., Reykjavik, Iceland, 1971,* Natl. Res. Counc., pp. 140–5.

Groissmayr, F., 1939: Schwere und leichte Eisjahre bei Neufundland und Vorwetter. *Ann. Hydr. Mar. Meteorol.* **67**(1), 26–30.

Lebedev, A. A., 1965: Variations of Ice conditions in the Northwestern North Atlantic. Trans. (Trudy) State Oceanogr. Instit., **87**, 32–50. (Translated from the Russian, *U. S. Naval Oceanogr. Office,* Transl. No. 382, 1968).

Lenczyk, R. E., 1965: "The effect of monthly mean sea level atmospheric pressure distribution on the Grand Banks ice season." *In* Rept. Intern. Ice Patrol and Observ. Serv. in the No. Atlantic Ocean. *U. S. Coast Guard Bull.* No. 50, 46–68.

Mecking, L., 1906: Die Eisdrift aus den Bereich der Baffin Bay beherscht von Strom und Wetter. *Veröf. Instit. Meeresk.* **7**, 1–132.

Mecking, L., 1907: Die Treibeiserscheinungen bei Neufundland in ihrer Abhangigkeit von Witterungsverhältnissen. *Ann. Hydr. Mar. Meteorol.* **35**, 348–555, 396–409.

Meinardus, W., 1904: Ueber Schwannkungen der nordatlandtischen Zirculation und ihre Folgen. *Ann. Hydr. Mar. Meteorol.* **32**, 353–62.

Morgan, C. W., 1970: Decreased Iceberg Threat in the Northwest Atlantic Ocean. Unpubl. MS., 15 pp., 4 figs.

Schell, I. I., 1952: Stability and Mutual Compensation of Relationships with the Iceberg Severity off Newfoundland. *Trans. Am. Geophys. Un.* **33**(1), 27–30.

Schell, I. I., 1962: On the Iceberg Severity off Newfoundland and Its Prediction. *J. Glaciol.* **4**(32), 161–72.

Schell, I. I., 1973: On the Thermal Lag in the Ocean during a Period of Climatic Change. Unpubl. MS., *Ocean-Atmosphere Research Instit.,* OARI-1-73, 22 pp., 9 figs. Cambridge, Mass. 02138.

Schott, G. 1903: Die Jahrige grosse Eisdrift an der Ostkante der Neufundlandbank. *Ann. Hydr. Mar. Meteorol.* **31**, 204.

Schott, G., 1904: Über die Grenzen der Treibeises bei der Neufundlandbank sowie über eine Beziehung zwischen neufundlandischen und ostgronlandischen Triebeises. *Ann. Hydr. Mar. Meteorol.* **32**, 305–9.

Smith, E. G., 1931: The Marion Expedition to Davis Straight and Baffin Bay, 1928. *U. S. Coast Guard Bull.,* **19**(3), 221 pp.

Smithsonian Institution, 1944: World Weather Records, 1921–1930. *Smiths. Misc. Coll.,* **90**, Washington, D. C.

Smithsonian Institution, 1947: World Weather Records, 1931–1940. *Smiths. Misc. Coll.,* **105**, Washington, D. C.

Soule, F. M., and E. R. Challender, 1949: "Discussion of Some of the Effects of Winds on Ice Distribution in the Vicinity of the Grand Banks and the Labrador Shelf." *In* Rept. Intern. Ice Patrol and Observ. Serv. in the No. Atlantic Ocean, *U. S. Coast Guard Bull.,* **33**, 58–61.

Soule, F. M. et al., 1950: "Oceanography of the Grand Banks Regions and the Labrador Sea." *In* Rept. Intern. Ice Patrol and Observ. Serv. in the No. Atlantic Ocean, *U. S. Coast Guard Bull.* **34**, 67–98.

U. S. Coast Guard Bull. (annually): International Ice Patrol and Observ. Serv. in the No. Atlantic Ocean, Dept. of Commerce, Wash., D. C.

U. S. Weather Bureau, 1959: World Weather Records, 1941–50. Dept. of Commerce, Wash., D. C.

U. S. Weather Bureau, 1965: World Weather Records, 1951–60, **1**, Dept. of Commerce. Wash., D. C.

Wolford, T. C., 1973: Observed Iceberg Masses (Abstract). *Trans. Am. Geophys. Un.* EOS, **54**(4), 319.

Synoptic Climatological Studies of the Baffin Island Area

R. G. Barry, R. S. Bradley,* and J. D. Jacobs

Institute of Arctic and Alpine Research

and

Department of Geography, University of Colorado, Boulder, Colorado

Abstract

Using a classification of MSL pressure map patterns for the area 55°–80°N, 50°–100°W, a daily catalog of synoptic regimes has been developed for July–August 1961–1972 and for other seasons for a shorter period. Temperature and precipitation conditions relating to the classification categories have been determined for several stations in eastern Baffin Island. The precipitation characteristics are of primary interest here. At Broughton Island there is a clear dominance of summer precipitation totals by the occurrence of lows centered over Baffin Island while in autumn and mid-winter this control is less pronounced. In autumn, patterns with lows in Davis Strait–Baffin Bay, or over Baffin Island, are the major contributors to precipitation. Examination of the vertically-integrated horizontal vapor flux for the central low type indicates strong flux convergence over the southeastern part of the island.

Apart from providing a useful basis for analysis of local and regional climatic characteristics, the classification and catalog are being applied in energy budget investigations. The basis has been laid for a synoptic climatology of energy budgets using satellite data (visual and IR imagery, and SIRS-B profiles) supplemented by synoptic weather observations.

Studies of the response of fast ice in Home Bay and of the Boas Glacier (naer Broughton Island) to climatic conditions show the importance of individual synoptic events. A preliminary characterization can be made of the synoptic types in relation to glacier and fast ice processes.

Examination of present and past glacierization of eastern Baffin Island in relation to climate suggests that a decline in summer temperatures in the area during the 1960's, and perhaps also the concomitant marked increase in persistence of sea ice in Baffin Bay, is related to a higher frequency of easterly and northeasterly airflow. Apart from the summer cooling, winters in eastern Baffin Island were milder and more snowy in the 1960's. Such anomalies are associated with a westward displacement of the mean 700 mb trough over eastern North America which encourages northward movement of cyclones into Baffin Bay. The evident sensitivity of this area to climatic fluctuations on both short and long time scales makes it a rewarding area for interdisciplinary environmental studies.

---

1. Introduction

This work began as an exploratory study of the synoptic conditions influencing the climate of Baffin Island, particularly with respect to its glacierization. First, the seasonal climatic characteristics were examined in terms of a classification of the MSL pressure field. Subsequently, the synoptic climatological results have been used as a basis for interpreting present climatic fluctuations and for estimating paleoclimatic conditions. This paper presents some of the general results derived from a number of specific studies.

2. Characteristics of the synoptic types

Classification categories. The MSL pressure field over the sector 55°–80°N, 50° 100°W (Fig. 1) has been

---

* Present address: Department of Geography, University of Massachusetts, Amherst.

classified on a daily basis for January, February, April, September, and October, 1961–5, July and August, 1961–70. A subjective scheme of 40 ("static") types was initially used (Barry, 1973); in order to simplify the classification scheme for present purposes, and to increase the sample sizes in each category, 12 type-groups are identified—six cyclonic and six anticyclonic (Figs. 2a and b). The frequency of these groups is shown in Table 1. Apart from April when anticyclonic patterns are dominant, reflecting the mean pressure field at this season over the Canadian Arctic Archipelago, the other seasons have a nearly equal frequency of cyclonic and anticyclonic patterns.

Precipitation. Before discussing the climatic characteristics of the type-groups, it is worth noting that September–October received 22–40% of the annual precipitation total for 1961–65 at the four stations on the east coast of Baffin Island (Cape Dyer, Broughton Island, Cape Hooper and Clyde). The next largest proportion, for the months considered, was in July–

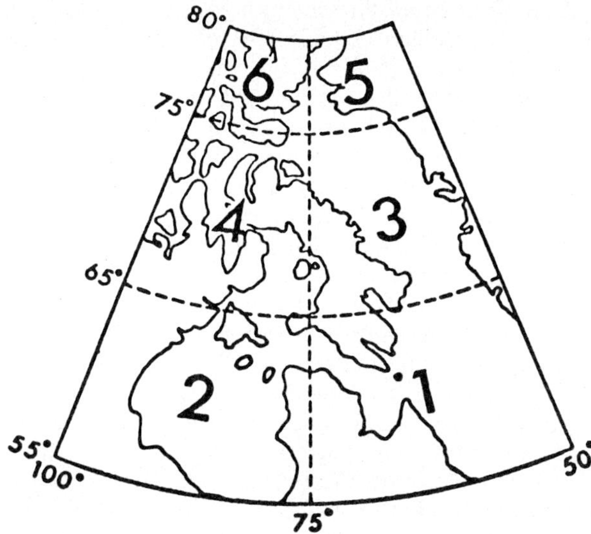

FIG. 1. Outline map of the area to which the MSL pressure field classification refers. Particular attention is given in the classification to sector 3.

August with 12–16% for 1961–70, except at Clyde where the figure rose to 25% (Table 2).

The precipitation characteristics of the type-groups are summarized in Figs. 3 and 4. In mid-winter the central low/trough group is a major contributor to the total although at Broughton Island 31% occurred

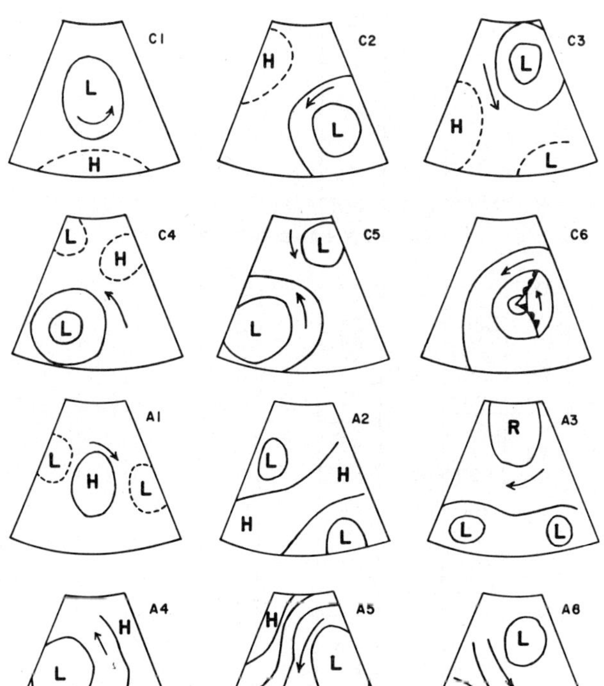

FIG. 2. Schematic maps of MSL pressure-type groups for the area shown in Fig. 1: (a) cyclonic groups; and (b) anticyclonic groups.

TABLE 1. Frequency of type-groups (percent) 1961–65.

Type-Group	Jan–Feb	April	July–Aug (1961–70)	Sep–Oct
Cyclonic				
C1. Central low	11	7	16	15
C2. Davis St. low	10	4	9	14
C3. Baffin Bay low	19	9	5	13
C4. SW low	4	6	10	6
C5. SW low & others	5	2	9	9
C6. Inverted low	4	—	—	—
	53	28	49	57
Anticyclonic				
A1. Anticyclone	7	17	10	8
A2. Ridge	10	5	8	6
A3. Ridge, low to S.	2	7	10	3
A4. High in E, low to W.	3	5	10	7
A5. Ridge, Baffin Bay low (NE flow)	11	11	4	5
A6. Ridge, Baffin Bay low (N–NW flow)	14	27	9	14
	47	72	51	43

with the infrequent "inverted low" pattern and at Cape Hooper lows to the southwest or south were the most important. Clyde is different again in receiving 25% of its mid-winter precipitation from southerly flow patterns with a high or ridge over Baffin Bay–West Greenland.

April accounts for only 4% of the annual precipitation as an average for the four stations and, as a result, the importance of any one type-group to the monthly total varies widely between stations. The anticyclonic patterns are the principal contributors, reflecting the high frequency of these types in spring.

In July–August the central low and the Davis Strait low groups account for 45–50% of the totals for 1961–70 at all four stations. The "raininess" of a particular pattern is indicated by the expression[1]:

$$\frac{P_A}{P} \frac{N}{N_A}(\times 100)$$

where

P = total seasonal precipitation over the period;

TABLE 2. Precipitation as percentage of the annual total (1961–65).

	Clyde	Cape Hooper	Broughton Island	Cape Dyer
Jan.–Feb.	7.3	3.5	6.4	10.8
April	1.9	7.2	3.8	3.8
July–Aug. (1961–70)	24.9	15.5	12.5	12.4
Sep.–Oct.	39.7	31.3	39.5	22.4
	73.8	57.5	62.2	49.4

[1] This is similar to the "specific precipitation density" (Maede, 1951), except that the latter refers to the frequency of days with precipitation, not all days.

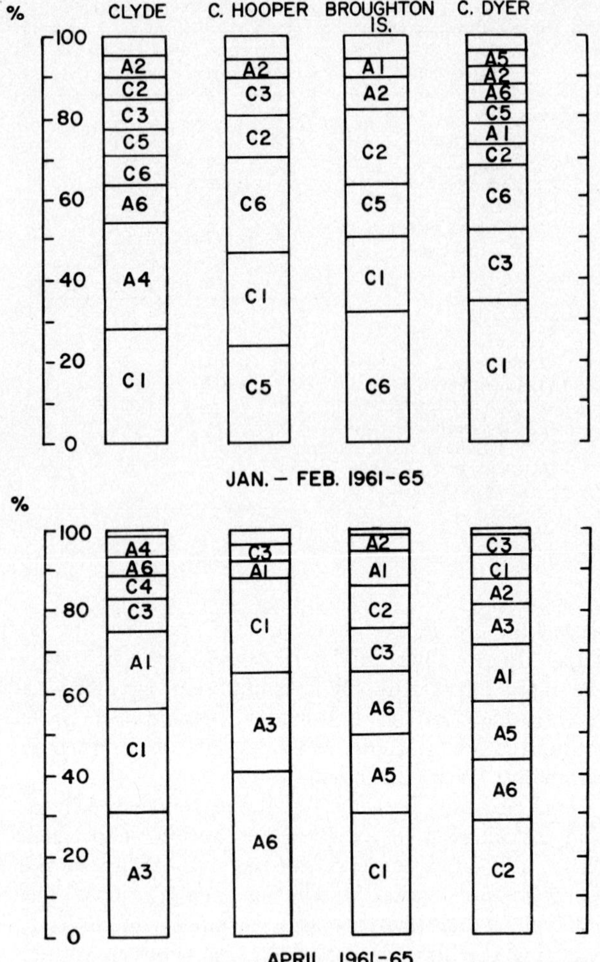

FIG. 3. The contribution of the different synoptic type groups to total precipitation January–February and April 1961–65 at Clyde, Cape Hooper, Broughton Island and Cape Dyer.

P_A = seasonal precipitation with group A over the period;

N = total number of days;

N_A = frequency of group A.

Table 3 shows that groups 1 and 2 are the most effective precipitation bearers in July–August. With the Davis Strait low (Group 2) there is a marked decrease in effectiveness northward. Ridge and anticyclone patterns have efficiencies of less than 50–60% in most cases.

In September–October, patterns with a low in Davis Strait–Baffin Bay, or a central low, contribute most of the precipitation although these are also the most frequent patterns. Ridge patterns with northerly flow are also important at Broughton Island. Table 3 shows a less consistent pattern of precipitation efficiency than in summer. This is especially the case at Broughton Island with anticyclonic patterns. In part the data reflect the inadequacy of a five-year data sample for such an analysis.

Analysis of vapor flux-divergence for the central low type in September–October 1961–65 (Fig. 5) shows large convergence (5–8 cm) over the Davis Strait and southeastern Baffin Island. This flux convergence represents 23 days of central low type (subtype 100) which gave a total of 6 cm precipitation at Broughton Island and 5 cm at Cape Dyer. Neglecting atmospheric storage changes and evaporation, these magnitudes agree well with the map values. A similar analysis for the Davis Strait low cases showed zero convergence over the area, however. It is probable that in this case, effects of orography in the onshore flow must be taken into account (Fogarasi, 1972).

Temperature. The temperature characteristics of the types will be only briefly considered. In July–August the Davis Strait low pattern gives the lowest mean daily temperature at all stations with values of only 0.5 C at Cape Hooper and 1.6 C at Broughton Island (Table 4). In view of the precipitation characteristics

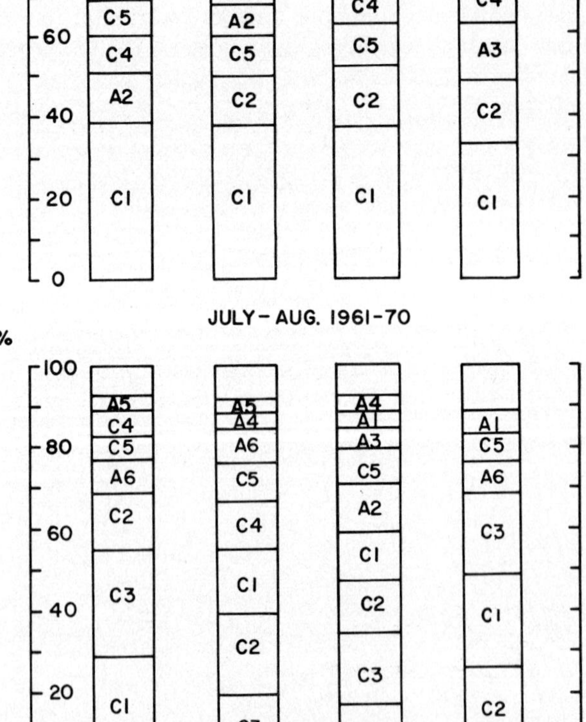

FIG. 4. The contribution of the different synoptic type groups to total precipitation July–August 1961–70 and September–October 1961–65 at Clyde, Cape Hooper, Broughton Island and Cape Dyer.

TABLE 3. Precipitation-effectiveness of the type-groups (percent).

Type-Group	Clyde	Cape Hooper	Broughton Is.	Cape Dyer
(a) July–Aug. (1961–70)				
Central low	249	244	238	213
Davis St. low	66	126	156	163
Baffin Bay low	108	78	123	38
SW low	92	60	100	125
SW low & others	96	108	114	94
Anticyclone	20	89	48	39
Ridge	138	41	62	27
Ridge, low to S	25	49	63	138
Ridge to E, low to W	75	73	16	25
Ridge (NE flow)	40	86	35	29
Ridge (N–NW flow)	68	35	24	53
(b) Sep.–Oct. (1961–65)				
Central low	196	108	82	156
Davis St. low	100	146	94	214
Baffin Bay low	193	149	126	149
SW low	95	189	47	28
SW low & others	76	110	103	76
Anticyclone	7	36	52	76
Ridge	43	33	188	24
Ridge, low to S	43	73	177	30
High to E, low to W	21	57	54	23
Ridge (NE flow)	81	71	51	32
Ridge (N–NW flow)	60	57	130	55

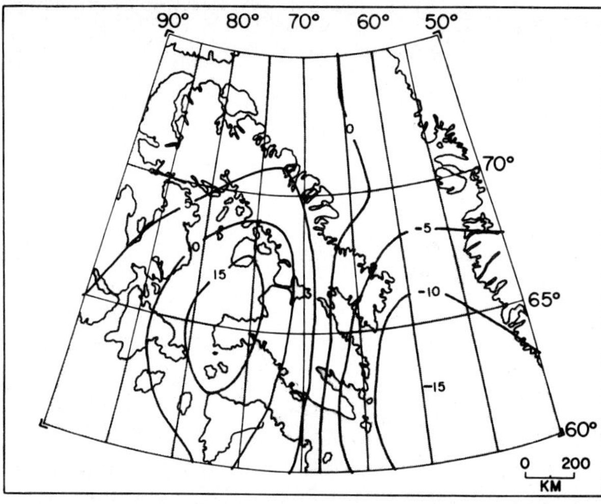

FIG. 5. Vapor-flux divergence (vertically integrated) for 23 days of central low synoptic type, September–October 1961–65 (cm).

of the Labrador Sea there are clear skies and warm air giving rise to a large positive energy flux to the surface. There is also substantial heat gain in the North Water of northern Baffin Bay due to its low albedo, in spite of air temperatures around −2 C. In general, albedo proves to be a key factor in determining surface energy fluxes in anticyclonic situations, while for cyclonic regimes the effect of cloud cover is at least as critical.

This work indicates the feasibility of determining regional energy budgets in the Arctic from a combination of satellite and conventional data. Such material will provide a vital input to the adequate determination of glacio-climatic interactions in the Arctic.

4. Climate-ice interaction studies

Glaciological studies on the Boas Glacier (55 km W.N.W. of Broughton Island) since 1969 show marked

of this pattern, its frequency is clearly of glaciological significance It may be noted that approximately 38% of the July–August precipitation (w.e.) at Broughton Island (elevation 581 m) falls as snow. The warmest type in July–August at all stations is with an anticyclone to the east and southerly airflow. Mean daily temperatures are close to 7 C (6 C at Clyde) and this pattern has a particularly low precipitation effectiveness (≤25%) over the Cumberland Peninsula.

3. Synoptic energy budgets

The pressure field classification provides a useful basis for stratifying the synoptic regimes in terms of conventional climatic parameters, but it is clearly vital for glaciological and sea ice studies to determine synoptic energy budget climatologies. A basis has been laid for this using satellite data supplemented by conventional synoptic weather observations for summer 1970 (Jacobs et al., 1972).

Computations were made of the individual energy budget components and of net radiation using appropriate parameters estimated from a variety of data sources. These are summarized in Table 5. Figs. 6–8 show selected maps illustrating the type of product for conditions at local noon on 26 June 1970. There was a low centered in Davis Strait and a trough extending northward. The effects of cloud cover, high albedo and northerly airflow combine to give negative net fluxes over the western Davis Strait area, while in the warm sector of the system over the open water

TABLE 4. Temperature characteristics of the type-groups (°C).

	Clyde (3 m)	Cape Hooper (401 m)	Broughton Is. (581 m)	Cape Dyer (376 m)
(a) July–Aug. (1961–70)				
Warmest (High to E, low to W)	5.9	7.1	7.1	6.8
Mean daily	4.1	3.7	4.0	4.8
Coldest (Davis St. low)	2.7	0.5	1.6	3.6
(b) Sep.–Oct. (1961–65)				
Warmest (Central low)	−1.6	−3.1	−2.8	−2.5
Mean daily	−3.5	−4.7	−5.0	−4.5
Coldest (Ridge, N–NW flow)	−7.4	−8.4	−8.5	−7.2

TABLE 5. Data sources for energy budget terms.

Energy budget component	Parameter	Data source
Solar radiation absorbed at surface.	Surface albedo; cloud cover	Visual imagery (AVCS, APT, IDCS, Minimum brightness)
I-R flux from surface	Surface temperature	THIR temperature maps
Atmospheric I-R flux to surface	Temperature and optical thickness; Sasamori (1968) model with single cloud layer	SIRS-B temperature and humidity profile data
Sensible heat flux	Wind speed, temperature	Synoptic data
Latent heat flux	Wind speed, temperature, pressure, vapor pressure	Synoptic data

inter-annual fluctuations in glacier mass budget which can be correlated with the synoptic characteristics of the accumulation and ablation seasons (Andrews, Barry *et al.*, 1972). The month of June is apparently critical in terms of synoptic conditions and, therefore, radiation receipts and the surface albedo of the glacier. For example, the snowpack of 0.25 m was entirely removed in summer 1971. A major factor seems to have been 18 days of anticyclonic patterns in June, in spite of near-normal cyclonic activity in July–August (Table 6). In contrast, only 0.15 m of the 0.4 m snowpack was removed in 1970 following a June with 19 cyclonic days, many of them of the central low type and with cyclonic activity in July–August

1970 also near normal for the 1961–1970 decade. Although no detailed measurements were made the 1969 summer net budget was apparently similar to 1971; in this case the synoptic data suggest that the frequent anticyclones in July–August account for the observed condition on the glacier.

Investigations on the fast ice and pack ice in Home Bay (Jacobs, 1973) also demonstrate the significant impact of individual synoptic events on the ice growth and break-up processes. Warm, rainy cyclonic situations and warm, clear anticyclonic situations will both accelerate ablation through reduced albedo and increased net radiation. On the basis of these studies, a preliminary characterization of the synoptic types in relation to glacier and sea ice processes can be made. For the summer season, where there is good agreement between effects inferred from climatic data and those actually observed, the relationships are summarized in Table 7. This approach provides a basis for inferring glacial response from synoptic data,

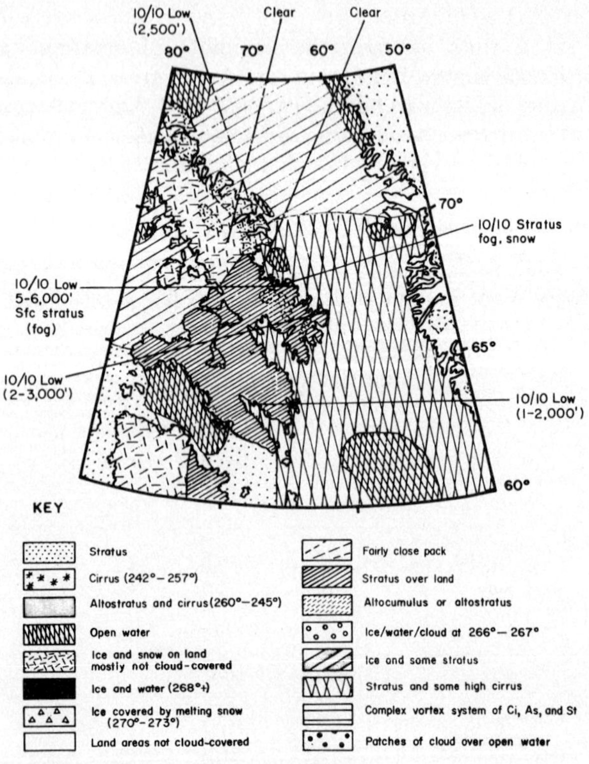

FIG. 6. An example of a cloud cover and ice cover analysis for the Baffin Island region, 26 June 1970, determined from visual and infrared imagery.

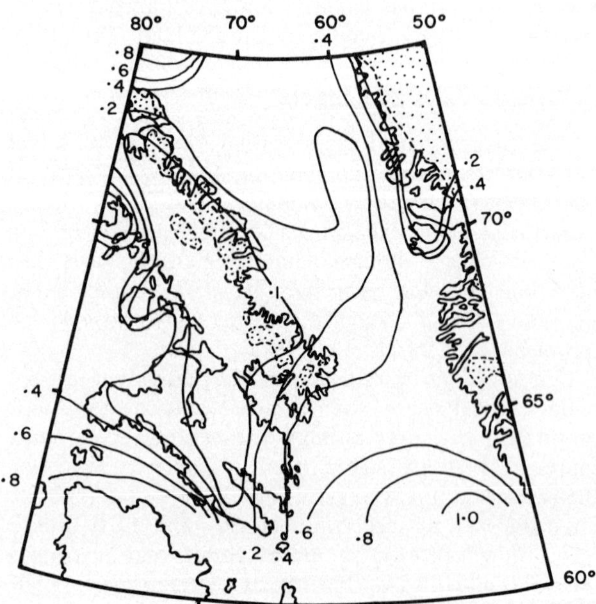

FIG. 7. Analysis of absorbed solar radiation at the surface, mid-day 26 June 1970 (cal cm⁻² min⁻¹).

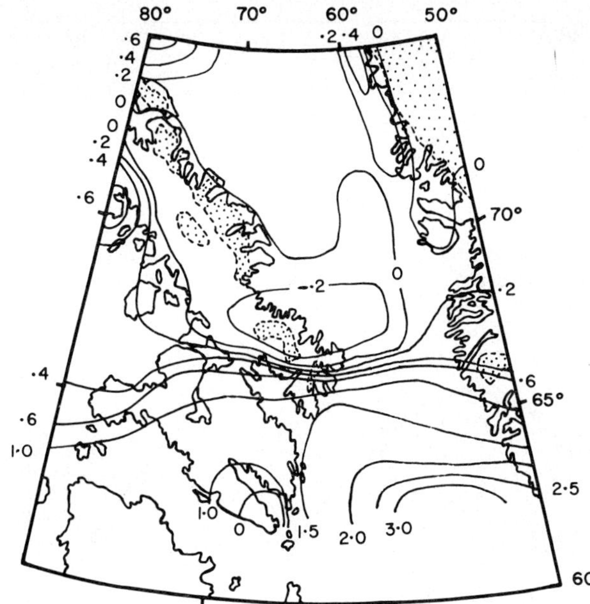

FIG. 8. Analysis of regional energy budget estimates, mid-day 26 June 1970 (cal cm^{-2} min^{-1}).

TABLE 6. Comparison of circulation regimes, summers 1969–71.

		July–Aug. Difference from 1961–70 (%)			June Frequency (days)		
		1969	1970	1971	1969	1970	1971
C1.	Central low	−12.4	+0.5	+3.8	2	10	1
C2.	Davis St. low	−2.9	+1.9	+0.3	7	4	3
C3.	Baffin Bay low	+0.1	−1.5	+3.4	4	3	0
C4.	SW low	+1.1	−5.4	−5.4	0	0	2
C5.	SW low & others	−2.7	+0.5	−4.4	6	2	6
	Cyclonic control	−16.8	−4.0	−2.3	19	19	12
A1.	Anticyclone	+22.3	+7.7	−3.5	1	3	8
A2.	Ridge	−5.2	−1.9	+1.3	3	3	1
A3.	Ridge, low to S	−0.6	+1.0	+5.8	3	1	6
A4.	High to E, low to W	−0.1	+1.5	−0.1	0	3	0
A5.	Ridge (NE flow)	+6.0	−0.5	−3.7	2	0	1
A6.	Ridge (N–NW flow)	−5.5	−3.9	+2.6	2	1	2
	Anticyclonic control	+16.9	+3.9	+2.4	11	11	18

or for inferring synoptic conditions from glaciological evidence. Both cases are pertinent in palaeoclimatic reconstruction and climatic modeling.

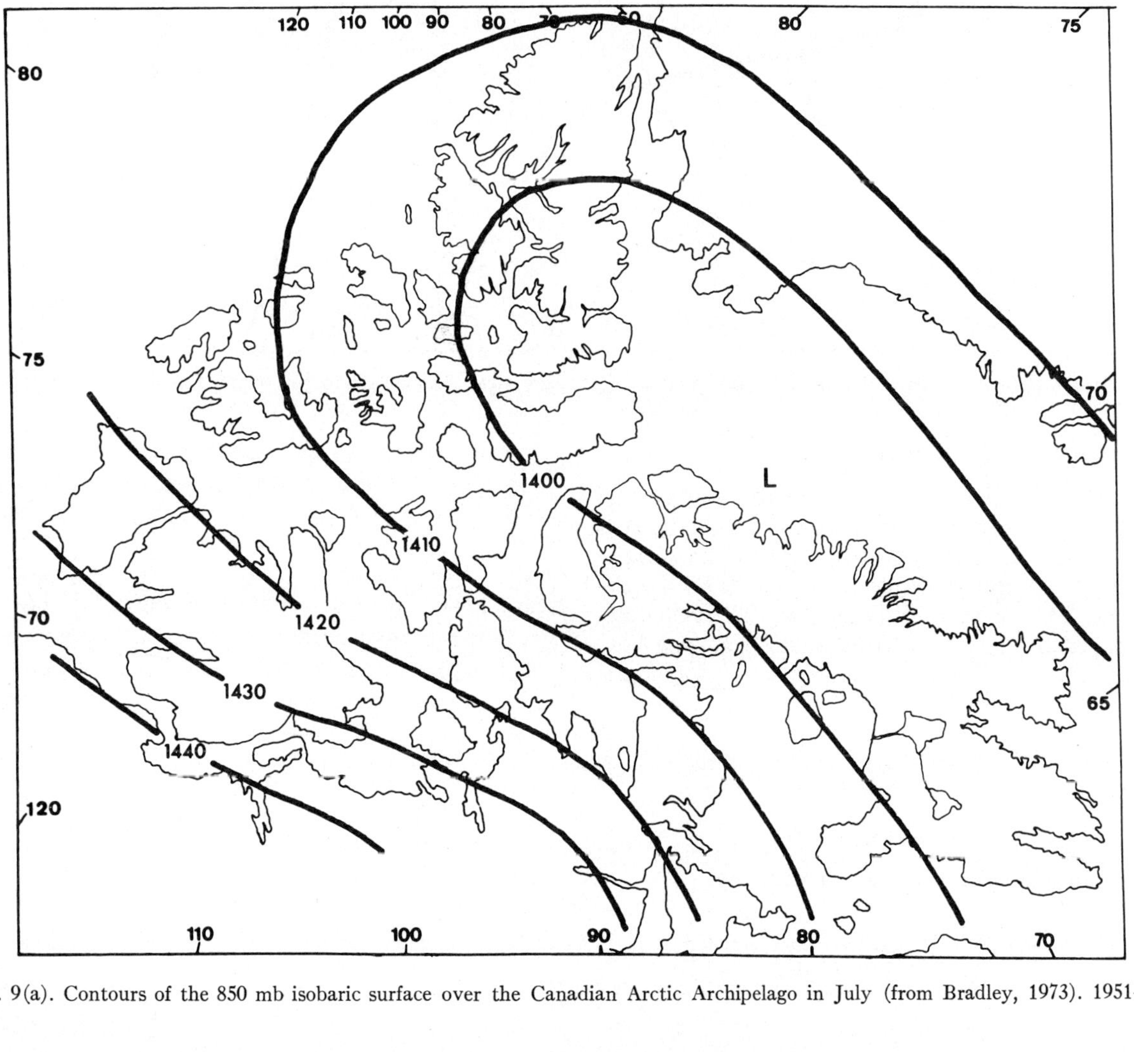

FIG. 9(a). Contours of the 850 mb isobaric surface over the Canadian Arctic Archipelago in July (from Bradley, 1973). 1951–60.

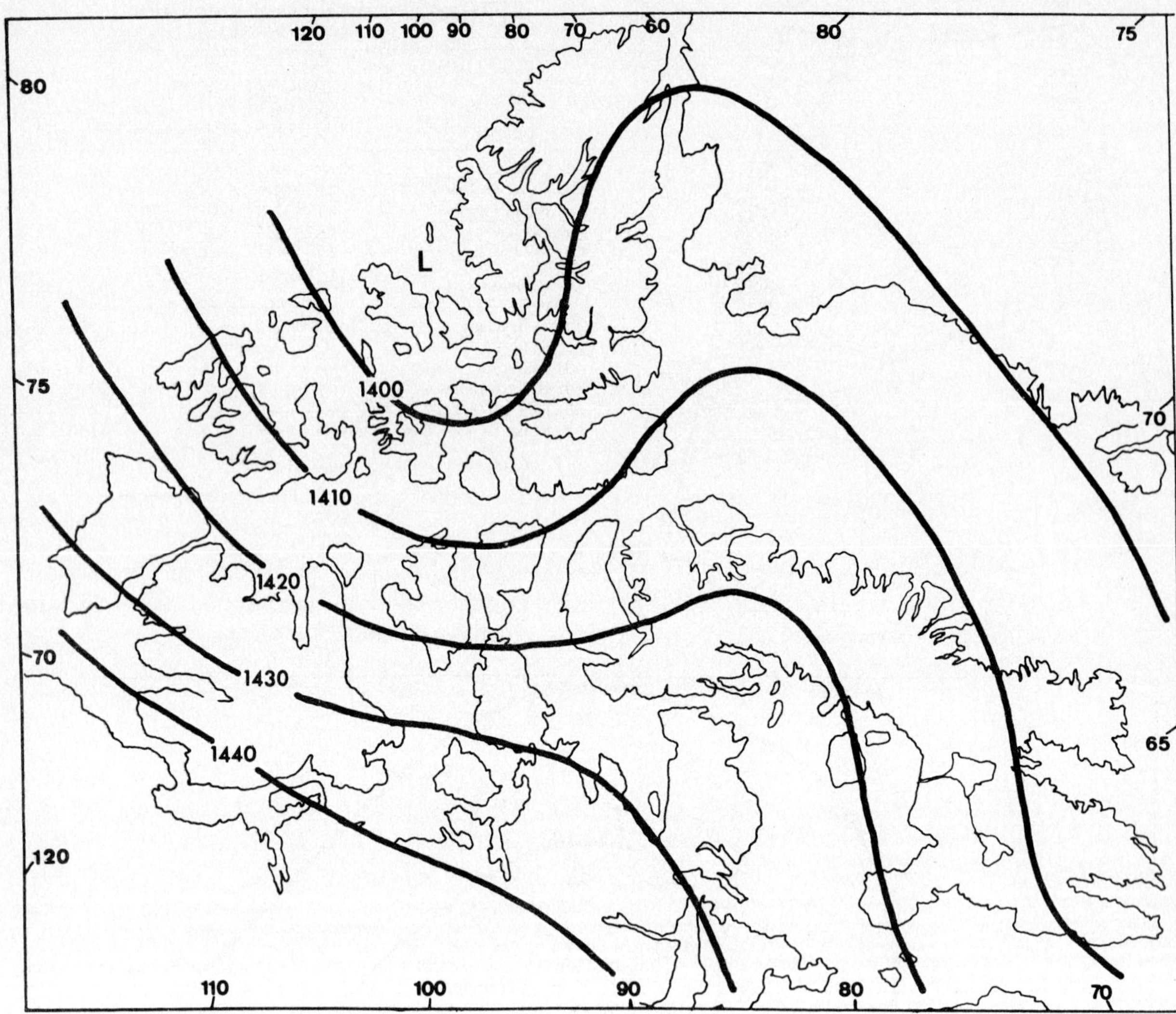

FIG. 9(b). Contours of the 850 mb isobaric surface over the Canadian Arctic Archipelago in July (from Bradley, 1973). 1961–70.

5. Climatic change studies

A major objective of our work is the assessment of decadal and longer term trends in glacio-climatic conditions in the eastern Canadian Arctic. Our premise is that on the regional scale these conditions are determined by the synoptic climatological events, although caution is needed in ascribing changing conditions solely to changes in the frequency of synoptic types (*cf.* Perry and Barry, 1973).

For the decade so far examined in detail through the synoptic catalog, there has been a marked increase in anticyclonic patterns at 850 mb over Baffin Island in July compared with the 1950's (Figs. 9a and b). Also, as shown in Table 8, the frequency of anticyclonic patterns increased in the latter half of the 1960's. Paradoxically, in terms of the generally higher temperatures for the anticyclonic type-groups, summer temperatures in the area *declined* in the 1960's

TABLE 7. Synoptic types in relation to processes on glaciers and fast ice in the summer season.

| State | Favorable Weather | Favorable Synoptic Patterns | |
		Glacier	Fast Ice
Advanced ice wastage	Clear; warm and windy; rainfall	*Central low*, low to SW, *ridge*, high, high in E	Central low, low to SW, high, high in E, central ridge
Retarded ice wastage	High overcast; snowfall; cold and calm	*Davis Strait low*, Baffin Bay low, *ridge over Baffin with NE flow*	

(Bradley, 1973b). Dunbar (1972) reports a marked increase in the late summer persistence of pack ice in western Baffin Bay since 1963 which may be related in part to more frequent easterly and northeasterly airflow (cf. Figs. 9a and b). Patterns of this type increased by 39% in 1966–70 compared with 1961–65, with a corresponding reduction in westerly and southwesterly patterns. However, the summer cooling is apparently widespread throughout the Canadian Arctic (Bradley, 1973a) so that a larger scale control must be sought. As far as Baffin Island is concerned, the recent climatic trend to cooler summers and, for the east coast, milder, more snowy winters, tends to be associated in both seasons with a westward displacement of the mean 700 mb trough over eastern North America, and this favors the northward movement of cyclones into Baffin Bay (Brinkmann and Barry, 1972). The fact that snow banks in the Cumberland Peninsula of Baffin Island and small glaciers and ice fields in the Queen Elizabeth Islands appear to be responding to the cooler summers and more snowy winters (Bradley and Miller, 1972; Hattersley-Smith and Serson, 1972) indicates the sensitivity of this sector of the Arctic to climatic fluctuations. Clearly it is a key area for interdisciplinary studies of the Arctic environment and its stability.

6. Further work

Our ongoing field program in eastern Baffin Island on the fast ice and on the Boas Glacier aims to provide a firmer basis for the synoptic energy budget studies in relation to ice mass balance, and to document a wide range of interannual fluctuations for analysis. It is planned to extend the synoptic catalog and to evaluate it more fully by comparison with objective schemes such as that of Fogarasi (1972). A classification of 700 mb height departures from normal for the area has already been prepared for July–August 1966–70 using the Lund (1963) correlation method, for example. Assessment of the effectiveness of these different approaches in discriminating between weather characteristics will be carried out in the near future.

Acknowledgments. The climatological research program has been supported primarily by the National Science Foundation, Office of Polar Programs through grants GV 28218 and GV 28220. Additional support from the Glaciology Division, Inland Waters Directorate, Environment, Canada, is also acknowledged. The authors are indebted to Dr. E. P. McClain and Mr. H. M. Woolf of the National Environmental Satellite Service, NOAA, the Nimbus Applications Group, Allied Research Associates Goddard, and the Climatology Division, Atmospheric Environment Service, Downsview, Ontario, for the provision of data; also to Margaret Eccles and Larry Williams, Lois Perkins, and Jill Williams, INSTAAR, for assistance with programming, drafting, and map analyses, respectively.

TABLE 8. Changes in frequency of type-groups in July–August.

Type-Group	1961–65	1966–70	Difference (% of total)
Central low	59	38	−7.0
Davis St. low	35	23	−4.0
Baffin Bay low	14	15	+0.3
SW low	33	30	−1.0
SW low & others	24	33	+3.0
Total cyclonic	165	139	−8.7
Anticyclone	19	43	+8.0
Ridge situations	24	28	+1.3
Ridge, low to S	25	39	+4.7
High in E, low to W	25	36	+3.7
Ridge (NE flow)	14	9	−1.7
Ridge (N–NW flow)	38	16	−7.3
Total anticyclonic	145	171	+8.7

REFERENCES

Andrews, J. T., R. G. Barry, *et al.*, 1973: Present and paleoclimatic influences on the glacierization and deglacierization of Cumberland Peninsula, N.W.T., Canada. *Institute of Arctic and Alpine Research, Occasional Paper No. 2*, University of Colorado, Boulder, 220 pp.

Barry, R. G., 1973: Further climatological studies of Baffin Island, N.W.T., *Inland Waters Directorate, Technical Report Series*, No. 65, Environment Canada, Ottawa (in press).

Bradley, R. S., 1973a: Recent freezing level changes and climatic deterioration in the Canadian Arctic Archipelago. *Nature*, **243**, 398–400.

Bradley, R. S., 1973b: Seasonal climatic fluctuations on Baffin Island, N.W.T., during the period of instrumental records. *Arctic* (in press).

Bradley, R. S., and G. H. Miller, 1972: Recent climatic change and increased glacierization in the eastern Canadian Arctic. *Nature*, **237**, 385–387.

Brinkmann, W. A. R., and R. G. Barry, 1972: Paleoclimatological aspects of the synoptic climatology of Keewatin, Northwest Territories, Canada. *Palaeogeography, Palaeoclimatology, Palaeoecology*, **11**, 77–91.

Dunbar, Moira, 1972: Increased severity of ice conditions in Baffin Bay and Davis Strait and its effect on the extreme limits of ice. In: *Sea Ice Conference Proceedings, Reykjavik*, 87–93.

Fogarasi, S., 1972: Weather systems and precipitation characteristics over the Arctic Archipelago in the summer of 1968. *Inland Waters Directorate, Water Resources Branch, Scientific Series No. 16*, Environment Canada, Ottawa, 116 pp.

Hattersley-Smith, G. and H. Serson, 1972: Reconnaissance of a small ice-cap near St. Patrick Bay, Robeson Channel, Northern Ellesmere Island. *Technical Note No. 72–32*. Defence Research Establishment, Ottawa, Canada, 4 pp.

Jacobs, J. D., 1973: Synoptic energy budget studies in the eastern Baffin Island–Davis Strait region. Unpub. Ph.D. thesis, University of Colorado, Boulder, 218 pp.

Jacobs, J. D., R. G. Barry, B. Stankov and J. Williams, 1972: Short-term air-sea interactions and surface effects in the Baffin Bay–Davis Strait region from satellite observations. *Institute of Arctic and Alpine Research, Occasional Paper No. 4*, University of Colorado, Boulder, 80 pp.

Lund, I. I., 1963: Map-pattern classification by statistical methods. *Journal of Applied Meteorology, 2*, 56–65.

Maede, H., 1951: Zur Frage der Abgrenzung des Witterungs bereiches einer Wetterlage. *Zeitschrift für Meteorologie, 5*, 268–273.

Perry, A. H., and R. G. Barry, 1973: Recent temperature changes due to changes in the frequency and average temperature of weather types over the British Isles. *Meteorological Magazine, 102*, 73–82.

Sasamori, T., 1968: The radiative cooling calculation for application to general circulation experiments. *Journal of Applied Meteorology, 7*, 721–729.

Possible Significance of Recent Weather and Circulation Anomalies in Northeastern Canada for the Initiation of Continental Glaciation

S. A. BOWLING

Geophysical Institute, University of Alaska, Fairbanks, Alaska

Abstract

The basic causes of climatic fluctuation between glacial and interglacial conditions remain debatable. On a purely phenomenological basis, though, deep-sea cores and ice-sheet cores strongly suggest the following: (i) Uninterrupted periods of temperatures near or above present levels have rarely exceeded 10,000–20,000 years in length. The Holocene has already lasted around 10,000 years. (ii) Interglacials such as the present tend to be interrupted by extremely rapid drops to near-glacial conditions. Suggested time scales are less than 100 years for cooling, 1000 years or more for recovery. In addition to the direct effects of a cold pulse, major redistribution of precipitation would occur, which could have drastic effects on agriculture.

Most theories are in agreement that the first observable signs of reformation of continental ice sheets would be an increase in the perennial snow cover in northeastern Canada and/or Scandinavia. Widespread perennial snow cover would affect the general circulation of the atmosphere in much the same way as would a major ice sheet, with two exceptions. The orographic effect of an ice sheet would not be present, which could lead to even colder conditions in surrounding areas than would a true ice sheet. Also, a perennial snow cover which had not yet reached the ice sheet stage would be considerably less stable than a true ice sheet. Such a perennial snow cover could explain the observed brief cold pulses observed towards the end of previous interglacials. In terms of a human life span, of course, the distinction between a 1000-year cold pulse and the beginning of a major ice sheet would be unnoticeable.

In the process of examining available climatological data for Labrador–Ungava, Keewatin and the northeastern Canadian islands, we found that monthly mean temperatures in these areas were not above normal (and were at time as much as 8C below normal) from November, 1971 to February 1973. Investigation of 700 mb monthly mean maps since 1949 indicated that the 700 mb height at 65°N, 75°W was not significantly above normal for at least 18 months. Since the position 65°N, 75°W is approximately the center of the 700 mb low that has been proposed as part of an early glacial-age circulation, the recent weather anomalies in the United States and elsewhere may serve as a useful analogue to the climatic anomalies which could be expected in the early stages of a cold pulse.

---

1. Introduction

The classical time scale for the Pleistocene involved four major ice advances, each of which lasted roughly 100,000 years, comfortably separated by interglacials lasting from 125,000 to 250,000 years (Emiliani, 1972). In such a context, the possibility of a future ice age made for interesting speculations, but appeared to have little practical significance. But with the advent of improved methods both of dating ancient deposits and of inferring the temperatures at which they were formed, a totally different picture has emerged. While there is still controversy over the exact length of glacials and interglacials, and over the criteria used to define the end of an interglacial (Kukla *et al.*, 1972), there is a general consensus of opinion that a complete glacial/interglacial cycle occurred in little more than 100,000 years, that *uninterrupted* periods with temperatures comparable to the present have rarely exceeded 10,000–15,000 years in length, and that the present interglacial has already lasted some

10 to 12 thousand years. Furthermore, there is evidence that the "interruptions" represented climatic shifts far more extreme than anything that has occurred in the Holocene, and that these shifts occurred on time scales comparable to that of a human lifetime. There are also indications that considerable drops in sea level occurred during these "short" cold spells (Kennett and Huddleston, 1972), which suggests considerable ice accumulation on land. The climatic shifts involved were probably quite similar to those initiating a pleniglacial period On the basis of what we now know, such a shift to a glacial climate could occur at any time. As Flohn (this volume) has pointed out, it would make little difference to the human population of our planet whether such a climatic change lasted 1000 or 90,000 years.

It is not the purpose of this paper to examine the possible causes of such a change in climate. Rather, the intension is to consider the nature of the kinds of climatic changes which might be expected in other

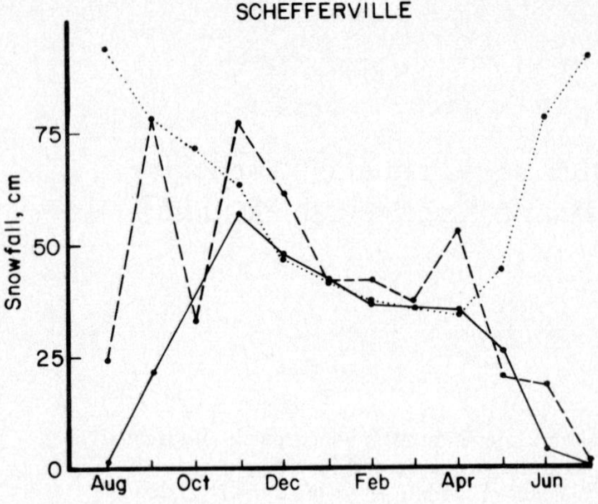

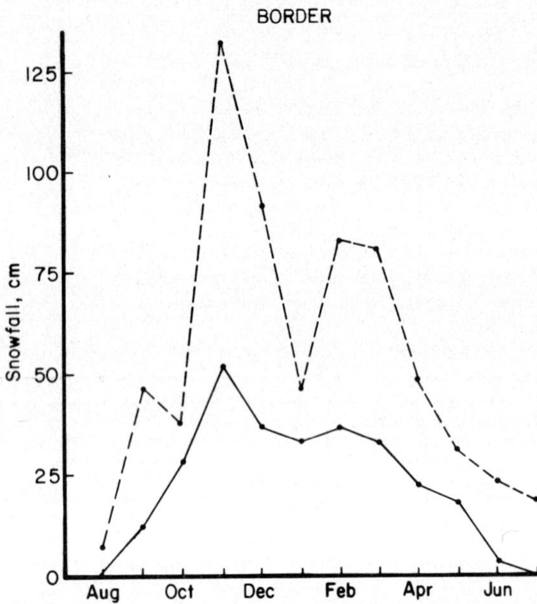

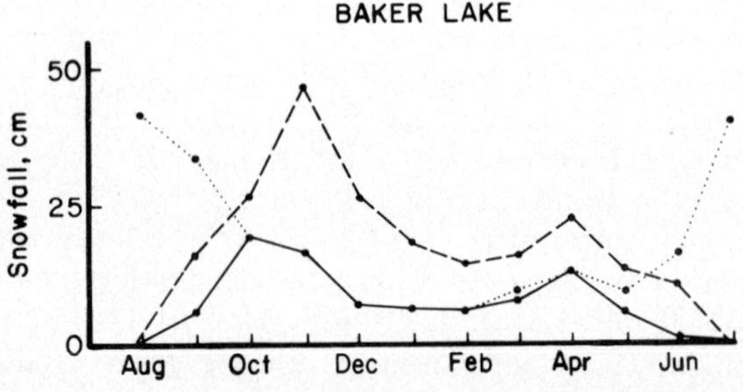

Fig. 1. Monthly snowfall at three inland stations in north-eastern Canada. Solid line—1953-1954—1972-73 mean; dashed line—difference between record and mean snowfalls, dotted line—mean monthly precipitation multiplied by 10 (to approximate snow with the same water content).

regions, given conditions favorable for glaciation. Specifically, an increase is assumed in the area of perennial snow cover over part of northeastern Canada: Labrador-Ungava, Keewatin and the northeastern islands. The snow/ice thickness is assumed to be small enough so that no topographic changes need to be considered, and the initial accumulation is assumed to occur north of the tree line. We will conclude by examining a recent example of potentially glaciogenic conditions.

2. Local meteorological considerations

During the winter months, the early glacial state hypothesized above would be essentially identical to present winter conditions, at least insofar as surface conditions in the glaciating area were concerned. Patterns of sea ice extent, early snow cover, and sea surface temperature inherited from the fall months would be expected to influence the general circulation during at least the early winter, and the possibility of some direct "memory" of the fall circulation must also be considered. However, it is difficult to predict how such inherited influences would actually be expressed.

Winter is also the most nearly neutral season in terms of the effect of the general circulation on glaciation. Weather records north of 55°N are mainly from coastal locations, and are likely to be unrepresentative of inland snowfall. Baker Lake (Keewatin) and Border/Indian House Lake and Schefferville/Knob Lake (Quebec) records for the last twenty years agree in showing late fall snowfall maxima, with a secondary spring maximum at Baker Lake (see Fig. 1). The dashed line is the difference between the twenty-year record and the twenty-year mean; it supplies some measure of the potential for increasing the snowfall from November (October at Baker Lake) though April. It is apparent that winter—especially January—is not the period with the greatest potential for increased snowfall. Another important point is that fresh snow over a perennial snowbank in spring or fall may reduce ablation as well as increasing accumulation.

Finally, the results of Brinkmann and Barry (1972) indicate that monthly mean flow is not early so important in precipitation as are a few days with strong southerly to southeasterly flow. This suggests an extremely high amplitude wave pattern on a daily basis, with the monthly pattern depending primarily on chance fluctuations in the day-to-day position of troughs and ridges.

In summary, it appears that the main constraints on the evolution of the monthly mean circulations from December through February would be that the December circulation must evolve from a glaciogenic fall pattern, and that the February circulation must evolve into a glaciogenic spring pattern. Within these constraints, patterns favoring heavy snowfall (e.g., the cyclonic southerly mean flow suggested by Lamb and Woodroffe or the fluctuating pattern suggested in the previous paragraph) are the most favorable for glacier growth.

Snow cover north of the treeline is normally present, although it may be melting, through late May and into June with the present climate. The atmosphere in spring (March–May) will again be responding to essentially the present surface conditions, with feedback confined to currently unpredictable oceanic temperature and sea ice perturbations. In early spring, the incoming solar radiation is low enough that melting of the snowpack will occur only under exceptional conditions of warm air advection. Potential snowfall is greater than in winter, and a glaciogenic circulation might include brief periods of southerly to southeasterly flow aloft, with possible thawing at the surface followed and counteracted by the presence of a fresh snow cover and cold air advection. *Mean* southerly flow would be of doubtful effectiveness as a glaciogenic factor by late March, and by April in the south and May farther north the incoming solar radiation has increased to the point that the reduction of ablation becomes the most important consideration.

Fresh snow absorbs only about 20% of the incident solar radiation, compared with around 50% for melting snow. Frequent fresh snow is obviously of tremendous importance not only in adding to the total accumulation, but also in delaying ablation of the entire snowpack. Clouds reduce the amount of shortwave radiation, but under conditions of high albedo this reduction is relatively small, and may be more than counteracted by the increase in incoming longwave radiation which they provide. The ideal situation would have thick clouds with cold lower surfaces, but only during the hours around noon. This is probably impossible. There is some possibility, at least, that advection of very cold, dry air over a snowpack approaching the melting point due to solar radiation would result in daytime convective cloudiness (probably low cumulus or stratocumulus, the moisture being supplied by the snow surface). Advection of cold, dry air at low levels would also allow part of the net radiation gain by the snow surface to be offset by evaporation. High, cold clouds above a layer of cold air advection would also help delay melting.

In spring the Arctic Ocean provides an essentially cold continental air source to the north, while the high efficiency of low-albedo trees in transferring solar energy to the atmosphere as heat makes the tree line a warm air boundary to the south. The cold air advection required by all of the considerations above would thus come from (preferably convergent) flow from the Arctic Ocean towards the tree line. The result would be an amplification of the present late spring longwave pattern, with a deepened trough along the Labrador coast and possibly a stronger ridge over the Mackenzie area. There is no obvious way in which feedback effects would maintain such a pattern, but the late spring season is extremely critical for ablation. This could be an excellent point of action for an external triggering mechanism.

The ideal summer climate for the initiation of glaciation would be similar, but a diurnal convective regime over snow is probably no longer possible. The Arctic Ocean is rapidly becoming an oceanic region, and there is no source area for significantly subfreezing air. On the other hand, the feedback effect of a perennial snow cover on the circulation of the atmosphere should peak in summer. Thermally, a perennial snow cover over Keewatin, Labrador-Ungava and/or the northeastern islands should behave as an extension of the Arctic Ocean. This implies probably an Arctic-stratus type cloud cover, with precipitation mainly in the form of drizzle or light snow. Currently, the region has a late summer maximum in liquid (and total) precipitation. To the extent that the existing precipitation is linked to the zone of thermal contrast along the Arctic Coast, summer rains should be concentrated more along the tree line, while an Arctic regime, with some orographic effects, would dominate over the snow cover. Low temperatures would still be highly beneficial for glaciogenesis, and would probably occur if the east coast trough were deepened to correspond with the effective southward extension of the Arctic Ocean surface conditions (Brinkmann and Barry, 1972).

At the present time, total precipitation in northeastern Canada decreases rather slowly from the summer peak through the following spring, while the snowfall fraction increases from traces in August to essentially all of the precipitation received in November (see Fig. 1). August and September snow rarely remains on the ground. Precipitation which leaves a cloud base as snow, however, will very likely reach the ground as snow if it falls on extensive residual snow areas and as rain if it falls on bare ground still warm from summer. Also, snow will be less likely to melt after it has fallen on an old snowpack. Direct microclimatic effects should thus lead to earlier establishment of a high-albedo winter snow cover (probably by early September) over a perennial snow cover, even assuming some initial discontinuities. Since the Arctic Ocean is at its most open condition in September, with Hudson Bay, at least, remaining partially open into December, northerly flow in early fall will be relatively wet. Heavy September snow occurs at Baker Lake with strong northerly mean flow in the present era, and early development of a cold wedge over the continent might enhance this tendency. As the season advances and new ice forms in the Archipelago, flow from Hudson Bay becomes important on a daily basis for snowfalls in Keewatin. None of the inland stations in Labrador–Ungava are well situated to observe any direct influence of Hudson Bay— Schefferville and Border are both almost on the Atlantic–Hudson Strait divide, and Nitchequan is too far south. The November peak in snowfall at both stations does suggest the possibility of some effect. Certainly the presence of local open water in fall would be expected to influence snowfall, just as a late ice cover in summer (due to the same factors which act to delay snowmelt) would affect summer temperatures. It is possible that reduced summer runoff as more winter snow was retained would affect the salinity structure of the water so as to delay fall cooling and freezeup.

The discussion above was presented as if only local feedback was involved, but external forcing, whether terrestrial or extraterrestrial, should not greatly change the arguments. The basic requirement is for a highly meridional circulation which is stabilized longitudinally by feedback from the surface in summer and early fall. It may fluctuate longitudinally in late fall, winter, and early spring but must restabilize to give northerly flow over the developing snow pack by late spring, *before* surface feedback becomes effective. Proposed external triggers for an ice age should thus produce a meridional general circulation throughout the year and a locking in place of the east coast trough during the late spring–early summer season. The two phenomena could, of course, be caused by totally different mechanisms.

3. Evidence from past glaciations

The most important climatic changes outside the glaciated regions are likely to be those involving the water balance. Decreased precipitation due only to decreased mixing ratios at lower temperatures would be very nearly balanced by decreased evaporation. Since it is the local balance of precipitation to evaporation which is recorded by most palaeoclimatic indicators, major recorded changes in humidity must be attributed to changes in precipitation mechanisms. This includes both the general circulation and processes dependent on absolute temperature through, for instance, freezing level height or the difference between adiabatic and pseudoadiabatic lapse rates.

The available evidence from early stages of past glaciations outside the ultimately glaciated areas generally suggests increasing drought in subtropical and tropical latitudes (Fairbridge, 1972; Hays and Perruzza, 1972; Flohn, this volume). Fairbridge's suggestion that subtropical drought was caused by decreased evaporation over tropical oceans which remained warm as air temperature decreased (due to cooler land areas?) is meteorologically unsound. The warm ocean–cooling land situation would tend to decrease precipitation on land by weakening the monsoon circulation. (Evaporation and precipitation over the tropical oceans would most likely increase in this case.) If the oceans cooled first (Flohn, this volume), the monsoon circulation would tend to be stronger but drier.

An expanded and highly meridional westerly circulation would also reduce subtropical precipitation, as has in fact been observed for the least few years (Winstanley, 1973).

Flohn (this volume) reviews evidence for oceanic temperature decreases during "short" coolings. In some cases the observed decreases are probably due to displaced current systems (e.g., the results of McIntyre and Ruddiman, 1972, which imply a more southerly course for a warmer North Atlantic Drift). If the ocean surface temperatures south of about 30°N were substantially decreased, tropical storm formation would be inhibited or even completely suppressed. Areas currently subject to hurricane/typhoon influence would show a decrease in precipitation due to this factor. It is interesting to note that ponds in central Florida and southern Georgia were apparently dry during much of the Wisconsin (Wright, 1971). This was attributed to a ground water table tied to a lower sea level, but it is not inconsistent with a decrease in precipitation.

North of about 30°N, most of the available evidence is for increased humidity on the basis both of lake levels and of vegetation; where detailed records are available, oscillation between cool-wet and warm-dry conditions occurs between interglacial and full glacial conditions (Farrand, 1971). Exceptionally detailed records from Czechoslovakia (Kukla and Kôĉi, 1972) and Macedonia (Van der Hammen *et al.*, 1971), however, show early glacial conditions to be drought-ridden, with occasional torrential rains in Czechoslovakia. To some extent this could be due to cooler temperatures in the northeast Atlantic as the North Atlantic Drift shifted southward, although in Czechoslovakia, at least, drought appeared to precede cooling. Orientation of mountain ranges could also have an effect. In the Americas, north-south ranges produce rain shadows under westerly flow, while meridional flow, especially from the south, may bring moisture around the end of the barrier mountains. In Europe, east-west mountain chains provide little barrier to westerly flow, but could produce major rain shadow effects with a meridional circulation—especially one in which the ridge and trough positions were stable during the summer months. It is interesting to note that inland Alaska, where the major ranges do run east-west, apparently was drier than at present during cold episodes, although the effect of changing sea level may also have been important there (Hopkins, 1967).

Pleistocene faunas in the southern plains of the United States are remarkable for the simultaneous occurrence of forms limited by cold winters and hot summers (Hibbard *et al.*, 1965). A well-developed ice

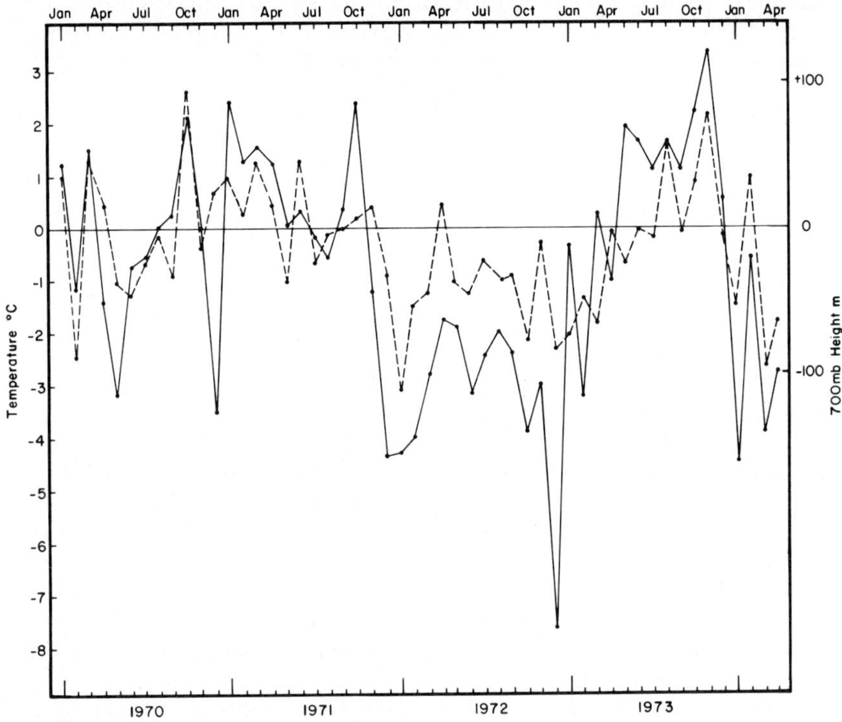

FIG. 2. Solid line—monthly mean temperature anomalies averaged over Keewatin, Franklin East, and Hudson Bay/Hudson Strait districts, Canada. Dashed line—700 mb height anomaly, 65°N 75°W.

sheet in Canada, acting as an orographic barrier against cold air in winter and as a source of cold air in summer, would be the most likely geographical cause of such an equable climate (Terasmae, 1973). The highly meridional circulations postulated earlier for the "glacial" spells in the late interglacial–early glacial period of climatic oscillations would be expected to produce an unstable climate on a year-to-year basis, with a probable increase in violent storms (cumulonimbus), and possibly more temperature extremes in both directions. (Troughs at 60°N and 40°N need not be in phase.) A thousand years or so of such a regime need not have left any recognizable impact on the sedimentation record unless drought was sufficient to disrupt the vegetation cover, as occurred in Czechoslovakia.

In the desert southwest of the United States, there is strong evidence that high lake levels and increased availability of moisture for plant growth accompany worldwide glaciation on time scales of several millenia (Morrison, 1965; Martin and Mehrinyer, 1965; Eardley et al., 1973). The last major interpluvial in northern Nevada appears to have ended with increased moisture, high temperatures, and a probable increase in windstorms, especially those with southwesterly winds (Morrison, 1964). Farther south, summer rainfall is more important, but there is no good paleoclimatic evidence for earliest glacial times. Droughts or floods are both possibilities.

4. The weather of November 1971–March 1973

Present-day weather sequences which deviate from "normal" in the same direction as early glacial climates apparently did may help to provide additional insight into likely climatic shifts in areas for which direct paleoclimatic evidence is not available. One period of interest centers around 1972.

Temperatures in the Canadian Archipelago, western Canada north of 55°N, and most of Quebec dropped below normal in November 1971, and by December Ontario was the only province with any significant area of above normal temperature. Western Canada warmed in March 1972 and remained warm through August, but the northeastern third of the country was subject to temperatures as much as 11 C below normal continuously through February 1973. The critical areas around Hudson Bay north of the treeline did not recover normal temperatures until May. Snowfall at the three inland stations mentioned earlier did not drop with temperature; Baker Lake was slightly above the twenty-year normal in both 1971–72 and 1972–73, Border was definitely above normal, and Scheffervill/Knob Lake and its greatest nsowfall in twenty years in 1971–72 and exceeded it in 1972–73. Fig. 2 shows the temperature anomalies, averaged over the Franklin East (archipelago) and Keewatin districts of the Northwest Territories and the Hudson Bay/Hudson Strait drainages of Quebec, from 1970 through April 1974.

Fig. 2 also gives the 700 mb height anomaly at 65°N 75°W (southwestern Baffin Island). The actual anomaly center ranged from 60° to 75°N and from 60° to 95°W, with heights as much as 142 m below normal (Wagner, 1972). The actual monthly mean circulation centers were generally between 70° and 75°N at all seasons, with winter longitudes generally 70°–80°W and summer longitudes 60°–70°W (Wagner, 1973).

Since conditions in northeastern Canada appeared to be shifted rather strongly towards those likely to be associated with the early stages of ice sheet growth, it seems reasonable to assume that conditions elsewhere might also display similarities to those typical of the late interglacial/early glacial oscillations of the past.

Details of the circulation outside of northeastern Canada varied considerably from month to month, with troughs in the United States at a wide variety of longitudes. Heights were generally above normal over the Atlantic, leading to a very fast (but still generally meridional—see Wahl, 1972) flow from New England to Europe, and blocking over Europe was common.

The general pattern of weather anomalies was reasonably consistent with available evidence for early-glacial climates of the east. Central Europe was droughty, but with some local severe flooding from thunderstorms. The Mediterranean area was wet, with considerable snowfall and some severe frosts. In Africa, the Sahelian drought was well underway (WMO, 1973; Winstanley, 1973).

In the western hemisphere, Atlantic hurricanes were relatively scarce due to subnormal sea-surface temperatures in their normal breeding grounds. Strong 200 mb westerlies at relatively low latitudes were also in existence (Simpson and Hebert, 1973). The only fully tropical storm, Agnes, obtained its initial energy from warm waters in the Caribbean and possibly even in the equatorial Pacific (Namias, 1973a); its formation and subsequent path can further be linked to the east coast extension of the deep Canadian low (Namias, 1973b).

Aside from Agnes, major flooding in the spring and summer was due to violent convective storms. The total number of tornadoes in the United States was large but not overwhelmingly so. The distribution of tornadoes was unusual, however, in that the "corners" of the United States were so strongly affected. Arizona had 17 tornadoes, breaking a previous record of 7; Washington, Georgia and the New England states were also well above their usual numbers and above the numbers recorded in the record year of 1973 (Poultney, 1973).

In the desert southwest, record drought from January to May of 1972 was followed by record-breaking wet weather in June and October to give yearly precipitation totals which were generally above normal. It would be interesting and possibly informative to compare how the year affected tree rings, alluviation, and lake levels.

Autumn was cold and wet over much of the United States, leading to delays in harvesting. Finally, a full-latitude trough extending south from the Canadian low in early 1973 was partly responsible for record snowfall in the southeast.

Asia, Australia and South America had similar types of anomalous weather patterns—droughts broken in places by torrential rains, weakening or failure of monsoon rains, and snow, frost, and heavy winter precipitation in the poleward fringes of the major climatic desert belts. Kukla and Kukla (1974) have also pointed out that the northern hemisphere snow cover apparently increased temporarily in spring of 1971 and more permanently in the fall of the same year, shortly before the Canadian anomaly became established.

In general, the weather of 1972 and early 1973 was fairly close to that recorded by the few available paleoclimatic indicators for early glacial periods. If the 1972 data is used to extend the spatial coverage of the paleoclimatic data, the picture which emerges is similar to that drawn up by Fairbridge (1972) for the tropics and subtropics. In middle latitudes the initial stages of an early-glacial cold pulse would probably bring an increase in the variability of precipitation and an increase in violent storms, with absolute increases in precipitation confined mainly to the present winter-rain belt and to areas currently in the rain shadows of north-south oriented mountain ranges. Even in these areas the initial increase is likely to be sporadic, with seasons and years of severe drought when mid-latitude trough positions (which fluctuate considerably from the high latitude trough longitudes) are unfavorably located. Even assuming that good 50-year climatic predictions were available and that the best crops for each area were actually grown by the farmers of that area, the global potential food production would probably drop.

The predictions above should be checked by additional continental paleoclimatic data. Correlation of vegetation—especially of genera intolerant of drought—with lake levels and alluviation in the American southwest could provide information on whether the initial rise in lake levels was due to an increase in reliable precipitation or to torrential rains. The possibility of obtaining soil-stratigraphic records like those of Czechoslovakia should be investigated in the central Great Plains and in other present agricultural areas. The effect of years such as 1972 on erosional and sedimentary features, and on plant communities, should be investigated as well.

Acknowledgments: The author thanks the Long Range Prediction Group of the National Weather Service for supplying 700 mb monthly data, and also the Atmospheric Environment Service, Environment Canada, for Canadian weather and sea ice data. This research was supported by State of Alaska funds.

REFERENCES

Brinkman, W. A. R., and R. G. Barry, 1972: Palaeoclimatological aspects of the synoptic climatology of Keewatin, Northwest Territories, Canada. *Palaeogeography, Palaeoclimatology, Palaeoecology,* **11**, 77–91.

Eardley, A. J., R. T. Shuey, V. Gvosdetsky, W. P. Nash, M. Dane Picard, D. C. Grey and G. J. Kukla, 1973: Lake cycles in the Bonneville Basin, Utah. *Geological Soc. of American Bull.,* **84**, 211–216.

Emiliani, Cesare, 1972: Quaternary hypsithermals. *Quaternary Research,* **2**, 270–273.

Fairbridge, Rhodes W., 1972: Climatology of a glacial cycle. *Quaternary Research,* **2**, 283–302.

Farrand, William R., 1971: Late quaternary palaeoclimates of the eastern Mediterranean area. *Late Cenozoic Glacial Ages,* K. K. Turekian, Ed., New Haven, Yale University Press, 529–564.

Flohn, Hermann, 1975: Background of a geophysical model of the initiation of the next glaciation. This volume, 98–110

Hays, James D., and Albert Perruzza, 1972: The significance of calcium carbonate oscillations in eastern equatorial Atlantic deep-sea sediments for the end of the Holocene warm interval. *Quaternary Research,* **2**, 355–362.

Hibbard, C. W., D. E. Ray, D. E. Savage, D. W. Taylor and J. E. Guilday, 1965: Quaternary mammals of North America. *The Quaternary of the United States,* H. E. Wright and D. G. Frey, Eds., Princeton, Princeton University Press, 509–525.

Hopkins, David M., 1967: The Cenozoic history of Beringia— a synthesis. *The Bering Land Bridge,* D. M. Hopkins, Ed., Stanford, Stanford University Press, 451–484.

Kennett, James P., and Paul Huddleston, 1972: Abrupt climatic change at 90,000 yr. BP: faunal evidence from Gulf of Mexico cores. *Quaternary Research,* **2**, 384–395.

Kukla, George J., and Alois Koĉi, 1972: End of the last interglacial in the loess record. *Quaternary Research,* **2**, 374–383.

Kukla, George J., and Helena J. Kukla, 1974: Increased surface albedo in the northern hemisphere. *Science,* **183**, 709–714.

Kukla, George J., R. K. Matthews and J. M. Mitchell, Jr., 1972: The end of the present interglacial. *Quaternary Research,* **2**, 261–269.

Lamb, H. H., and A. Woodroffe, 1970: Atmospheric circulation during the last ice age. *Quaternary Research,* **1**, 29–58.

McIntyre, A., and W. F. Ruddiman, 1972: Northeast Atlantic post-Eemian paleooceanography: a predictive analog of the future. *Quaternary Research,* **2**, 350–354.

Martin, P. S., and P. J. Mehringer, Jr., 1965: Pleistocene pollen analysis and biogeography of the Southwest. *The Quaternary of the United States,* H. E. Wright and D. G. Frey, Eds., Princeton, Princeton University Press, 433–451.

Morrison, R. B., 1964: Lake Lahontan: geology of southern Carson Desert, Nevada. Geological Survey Professional Paper 401, Washington, Govt. Printing Office, 156 pp.

Morrison, Roger B., 1965: Quaternary geology of the Great Basin. *The Quaternary of the United States,* H. E. Wright, Jr. and D. G. Frey, Eds., Princeton, Princeton University Press, 265–285.

Namias, Jerome, 1973a: Birth of Hurricane Agnes—triggered by the transequatorial movement of a mesoscale system into a favorable large-scale environment. *Monthly Weather Review,* **101**, 177–179.

Namias, Jerome, 1973b: Hurricane Agnes—an event shaped by large scale air-sea systems generated during antecedent months. *Quart. Journ. Roy. Met. Soc.,* **99**, 506–519.

Poultney, Norman E., 1973: The tornado season of 1972. *Weatherwise,* **26**, 22–27.

Simpson, R. H., and Paul J. Hebert, 1973: Atlantic hurricane season of 1972. *Monthly Weather Review,* **101**, 323–333.

Terasmae, J., 1973: Notes on late Wisconsin and early Holocene history of vegetation in Canada. *Arctic and Alpine Research,* **5**, 201–222.

Van der Hammen, T., T. A. Wijmstra and W. H. Zagwijn, 1971: The floral record of the late Cenozoic of Europe. *Late Cenozoic Glacial Ages,* Karl K. Turekian, Ed., New Haven, Yale University Press, 391–424.

Wagner, A. James, 1972: Weather and circulation of January 1972—a month with record strong midlatitude westerlies. *Monthly Weather Review,* **100**, 322–328.

Wagner, A. James, 1973: The circulation and weather of 1972. *Weatherwise,* **26**, 4–13, 21.

Wahl, Eberhard W., 1972: Climatological studies of the large-scale circulation in the northern hemisphere I. zonal and meridional indices at the 700-millibar level. *Monthly Weather Review,* **100**, 553–564.

Winstanley, Derek, 1973: Rainfall patterns and general atmospheric circulation. *Nature,* **245**, 190–194.

World Meteorological Organization, 1973: Significant weather in 1972. *WMO Bulletin,* XXII, 99–107.

World Meteorological Organization, 1974: Significant weather in 1973. *WMO Bulletin,* XXIII, 82–93.

Background of a Geophysical Model of the Initiation of the Next Glaciation

HERMANN FLOHN

Meteorologisches Institut der Universität, 53 Bonn/Rhein, Federal Republic of Germany

Abstract

During the last 10^5 years, at least five coolings of a hemispheric or global scale have been revealed, with a sudden temperature drop of 4–6 C, in a time span in the order of 10^2 years, as examples for the intransitivity of climate at a large time-scale. Based on the equilibrium between surface albedo and average surface temperature according to the model of Manabe–Wetherald, large-scale Antarctic surges—as suggested by Wilson (1964), with some modifications—are assumed to initiate remarkable changes in the atmospheric and oceanic heat budget.

The advection of cool Antarctic water in the Atlantic may then produce, by air-sea interaction, marked anomalies of the atmospheric circulation, enhancing snowfall together with low summer temperatures in the centers of the two last glaciations, allowing the snow-cover to survive during summer.

Some other prerequisites given, subsequent spreading—caused by synoptic-physical feedback—may lead to the formation of the nucleus of a continental glaciation during a remarkably short time-span.

1. Introduction

In a recent symposium (Kukla *et al.*, 1972; Kukla and Matthews, 1972), several well-known Pleistocene specialists discussed the question: When will the present Interglacial end? A few results will be considered here from a meteorological viewpoint.

a) Since about 1945 global cooling, on a scale of $\sim$0.01 C/year, has reversed the warming trend of the first decades of our century. The bulk of these changes is most probably not man-made, but of natural origin. Evidence exists for several short cool periods during the last 5000 years, as well as for catastrophic dry periods in subtropical areas lasting a few decades. None of these variations is comparable in scale with the Allerod fluctuations (Chapter IV).

b) The climatic optimum of the present interglacial was reached 6–7000 years ago. Evidence from Northern Germany and England shows that the last interglacial (Eem=Sangamon) lasted little more than 10,000 years; it was slightly warmer and wetter than the present interglacial, with a quite similar climatic time sequence.

c) Based on more than 800 measurements of the O^{18}/O^{16} ratio from fossil foraminifera, it has been concluded (Emiliani, 1972) that the tropical ocean surface temperatures were as high as or higher than today for only 10 percent of the last 400,000 years. Considering the length of a glacial-interglacial cycle to be nearly 10^5 years (Broecker and van Donk, 1970) the average duration of a warm epoch cannot have been longer than 10^4 years.

d) A large majority of the participants concluded that the present warm epoch has reached its final phase, and that—disregarding possible man-made effects—the natural end of this interglacial epoch is "Undoubtedly near." The time-scale of this transition may be a few millenia, perhaps only centuries.

If this is correct, earth scientists are confronted with a hitherto neglected question: What are the initial stages of a glaciation? How can we imagine the triggering of the formation of ice-sheets on the northern continents eventually covering about 17×10^6 km² in North America and nearly 11×10^6 km² in Eurasia, with ice domes up to 3 or 4 km in height, thus reducing the ocean volume by about 4 percent, with a eustatic sinking of the sea-level to -100 m, sometimes to -130 m? This question is not only of academic interest: its immediacy will be demonstrated in the following chapters.

2. Stability or instability of climate?

E. Lorenz (1968) has recently raised a quite deep-rooted question: How stable is our climate? Considering a complete set of basic equations with fixed external parameters—such as the solar "constant," the rotation rate and radius of the earth, and the chemical composition of the atmosphere—as a base for simulating the climate defined as a time-averaged state of the atmosphere, he discusses the number of possible solutions. Climate is defined as *transitive* if only one solution exists. One may also perceive several more or less quasi-stationary different solutions, which may transform from one state into another by a sort of flip-flop-mechanism ("vacillation"): this situation is defined as *intransitive*. Without discussing at length

TABLE 1. Surface Albedo (a_s) and equilibrium temperature (T) deviations.
(Areas in 10^6 km²)

| Albedo | Oceans | | Continents | | | Average albedo a_s | Deviation T (°K) | Remarks |
	Open 0.05	Ice 0.70	Open 0.12	Ice 0.75	Snow 0.30			
N. Hemisphere	145	10	70	3	27	0.1294	—	Actual (1901–50)
S. Hemisphere	190	16	33	13	3	0.1384	—	
Earth (E)	335	26	103	16	30	0.1339	—	
Model NH 0	142	13	70	3	27	0.1373	−0.95	N. Hemis. 1890
Model SH 0	188	18	33	13	3	0.1434	−0.60	S. Hemis. 1850
Model E 4	317	30	108	49	6	0.1731	−4.6	Ice age
Model E 5	307	40				0.1860	−6.2	(sea level −100 m)
Model SH 3	165	41	33	13	3	0.2022	−7.6	Wilson surge

evidence for and against, Lorenz considers our climate as *semi-intransitive*.

If this is true, we cannot expect to obtain from mathematical modelling unambiguous forecasts of climatic patterns. Simplified models with a crude parameterization of synoptic-scale meridional exchange processes—such as the models developed by Budyko (1969) and Sellers (1969, 1973)—showed either a great sensitivity to comparatively small changes of external conditions or (worse than that) distinct intransitivity under exactly the same conditions. In contrast to this, Washington (1972) demonstrated on the base of the much more advanced NCAR circulation model that the response of the model to different and even contrasting externally induced disturbances was nearly identical. This state of affairs—incomplete as it stands now—is seriously disquieting. Therefore, one of the most urgent tasks is a careful and critical search for evidence of climatic instability on a hemispheric or, better, global scale.

Examples of partial (regional) instability have been given elsewhere (Flohn, 1973). The best example is known from the equatorial Pacific, where the oceanic Ekman drift causes either equatorial upwelling or downwelling, depending on the surface wind distribution, and causing in the atmosphere either a stable, cloudless and dry equatorial zone or instability near the equator with high convective activity. Apart from short transition periods, any intermediate state cannot remain stable. Because of the large differences in oceanic evaporation and precipitation, these contrasting patterns are correlated with many teleconnections over wide areas of the globe (Bjerknes, 1969; Flohn, 1972; and Rowntree, 1972).

3. The role of surface albedo

Within the heat budget of the earth's surface, the high albedo of ice and snow (0.70–0.80) in contrast to all other surfaces (except clouds) (0.05–0.35) dominates most other terms. During winter the tropospheric baroclinic zones have a tendency to follow the margins of the seasonal continental snow-cover. In spite of all

vegaries of weather, such a pattern remains superimposed in a statistical sense.

There exists (Manabe and Wetherald, 1967) a direct relation between surface albedo and an equilibrium temperature (Table 1), assuming constant relative humidity and an average cloud distribution. This relation can be checked against data on the varying extent of the Arctic and Antarctic sea-ice during the 19th and 20th centuries (Flohn, 1973). The observed decrease of the Arctic sea-ice from about 1880 to 1940 and the estimated increase of the Antarctic sea-ice during the 19th century (Lamb, 1967), both of the order of nearly 2 or 3×10^6 km², should correlate with changes in the hemispheric equilibrium temperature of the order of 0.6–0.9 C, in good agreement with the observed data (Table 1, Models SH 0 and NH 0).

A further check can be derived from the last glaciation, with a glaciated continental area of 49×10^6 km², accompanied by a eustatic drop of the sea-level to −100 m, increasing the land area of the earth from 149 to about 163×10^6 km². In this case (Model E 4) the equilibrium temperature of the whole earth should be 4–5 C lower than today, once more in agreement with the observed data. There is sufficient evidence that the Atlantic sea-ice reached, during the maximum of the last glaciation, an average latitude of about 43°N (McIntyre *et al.*, 1972). Its extension into the Bay of Biscay must also be assumed when interpreting the exceptional cooling of the adjacent territories (from northern Spain to southern Ireland) by about 12 C, compared with only 5 C at the same latitudes at the Pacific coast of North America (Flohn, 1969). In this case the area covered by sea-ice increases to about 40×10^6 km² with a simultaneous global temperature drop of 6 C (Model E 5).

The good agreement between the predicted and observed equilibrium temperatures convinces us that the role of the albedo in the long-term climatic oscillations during the Pleistocene is certainly greater than that of variations of solar radiation due to the earth's orbital elements (Hoinkes, 1971). It should be remembered that this point was raised as early as 1938

(Wundt, 1938); numerical model computations of the climatic effects of the Milankovich mechanism neglecting the positive feedback effect of albedo changes are incomplete. The role of surface albedo has also been demonstrated (Kukla and Kukla, 1972) from seasonal and interannual changes of the snow-cover. The existence of a quasi-equilibrium between area-surface temperature and area-averaged surface albedo (Flohn, 1969, 1973) leads to a serious consequence: if a climate-independent mechanism producing variations of the extension of ice exists—as suggested by A. T. Wilson (1964)—the usual chain of cause and effect may be reversed: large-scale Antarctic surges will produce immediate hemispheric cooling (Model SH 3). This necessitates a critical investigation of the real time-scale of Pleistocene coolings, which appears to be inconsistent with the Milankovich time-scale.

4. Time-scale of global coolings

Based on investigations of ice cores, ocean bottom cores and fossil peats bogs, several drastic coolings during the last 10^5 years have recently been revealed. Some of these, with multiple evidence, will be reviewed in stratigraphic sequence, ignoring some inevitable minor differences of time and time sequence interpretation in the literature.

1) During the recession of the last glaciation, the well-known sequence Bølling Interstadial (warm)— Older Dryas (cold)—Allerød Interstadial (warm)— Younger Dryas (cold) covered less than 2000 years, with variation in the annual temperature of up to 6 C (Mercer, 1969). In the Mediterranean and at other subtropical and tropical sites only the second half of the sequence was marked, and the Older Dryas period was insignificant (van der Hammen et al., 1971, Fig. 2). The Allerød warming period coincides with the abrupt global environmental change after the Würm-Wisconsin Glaciation, occurring at about 11,000 BP in the space of a few centuries, while the melting of the ice domes—reflected in the global eustatic sea-level rise— lasted some 8000 years.

This time sequence has been derived mainly from palynological evidence, hampered by the limited migration speed of biotopes. On the other hand, the isotopic changes preserved in the Greenland ice-cap represent largely—disregarding here some systematic sources of error (Johnson et al., 1972; Dansgaard et al., 1971)—the temperature of formation of precipitation particles in clouds, i.e., the regional climate. Here (Johnson et al., 1972, Fig. 6) the cooling prior to the younger Dryas lasted less than 350 years; the following warming, 300 years. Simultaneity of the climatic changes on both sides of the Atlantic has been doubted (Mercer, 1969). However, the hypothesis of grounded ice shelves in the Arctic (Mercer, 1970) is in contradiction with the idea of an open Arctic Ocean (Olaussen et al., 1971); it would require the freezing

of a further 13×10^6 km³ of water in addition to that in the continental ice sheets, but would have no significant effect on the sea level.

2) Before the last long warm Interstadial within the Würm-Wisconsin Glaciation (Fliri, 1970)—known as Stillfried B or Plum Point—a marked cold period of not more than about 2000 years duration occurred at about 38,000 BP. It has been found in the Greenland ice-core (Johnson et al., 1972) as well as in Southern Chile (Mercer and Laugenie, 1973) and in the Indian Ocean off the Somali Coast (4–8°N) (Olaussen et al., 1971); here the time between the beginning of the event and the temperature minimum is estimated to be not more than about 500 years.

3) Another cold period of this magnitude is also found in the Somali Current Area, interpreted as the beginning of the Würm I Glaciation at about 55,000 BP. It coincides well with the marked cooling in the Greenland core after the Odderade Interstadial and in Macedonia (van der Hammen, 1971) around 59,000 BP.

4) The short cooling between the Brørup and Odderade Interstadials, near 70,000 BP, is quite dramatic: In Macedonia the vegetation changed from oak forest into steppe in much less than 1000 years. It coincides with a marked cold period in the Greenland area, while in the Indian Ocean (Olaussen et al., 1971) only a hint has been found. At the same time, a short intense cooling has been observed (Sancetta et al., 1972) in an Atlantic deep-sea core at 52°N, 22°W

5) The most dramatic short-lived cooling event was observed (Fig. 1) in the Greenland ice at about 89,000 BP (all Greenland dates before 12,000 BP are slightly uncertain). Here the climate changed within 100 years ("almost instantaneously") from warmer than today into full glacial severity (Dansgaard et al., 1972). This event has also been found in a stalagmite in a French cave (Duplessy et al., 1971) at 97,000 BP with a cooling of the cave (!) by 3 C in a few centuries and an extremely rapid cooling (in less than 350 years) has been described in many cores from the Gulf of Mexico at 90,000 BP (Kennett and Huddleston, 1972). At the same time the first strong cooling after the Eem Interglacial was observed in Macedonia and in the Netherlands (van der Hammen, 1971); and multiple evidence exists for a sudden sea-level rise at the eastern coast of North America and at Bermuda, possibly caused by an Antarctic surge (Hollin, 1972).

These five events show coolings of the order of up to 5 C century^{-1} in contrast to not more than 1 C century^{-1} in recent fluctuations. This rate is in fact a minimum value because of the smoothing role of molecular diffusion processes (Johnson et al., 1972). Of particular interest are the events in the area of the Somali Current (Olaussen et al., 1971) which are far too short-lived to be interpreted as caused by orbital changes. Some other peaks, especially in the

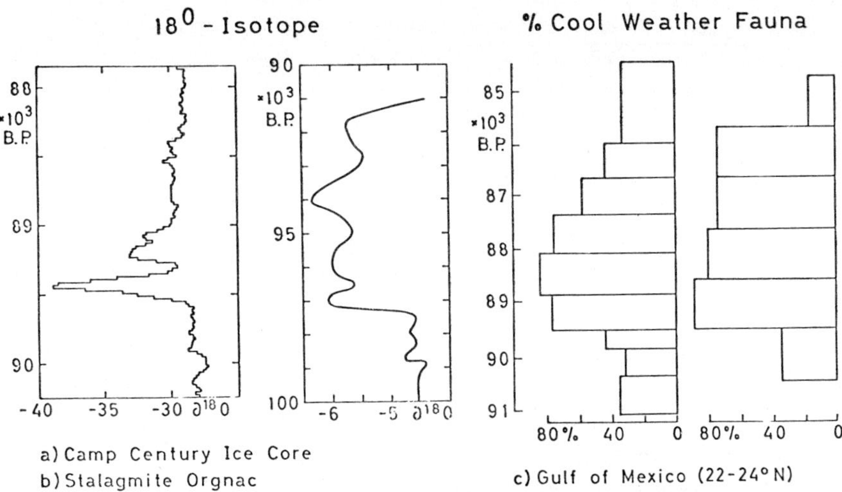

Fig. 1. Temperature variations at about 90,000 B.P. (see text). a) O^{18}/O^{16} ratio in Greenland ice core (76°N), b) the same in a cave near Orgnac (S. France), c) percentage of cool weather foraminifera from the Gulf of Mexico.

Greenland ice core (Fig. 2), may be added to this list, but (up to now) without supporting evidence from other sites.

Only one of these selected cases initiated, in the northern hemisphere, a continental glaciation: this is the beginning of Würm I (case 3). If we assume a maximum glaciation of the northern continents (with a volume of 47.4×10^6 km^3 and an area of 29.5×10^6 km^2, i.e., with an average thickness of 1610 m) as resulting from an average annual accumulation of 40 cm, the growth period lasts about 4000 years, and the minimum duration of a full glaciation is still of the order of 10,000 years (Lamb and Woodroffe, 1970). During that time the local increase of albedo favours the persistence of glaciogenic conditions. The other four cases represent only short-lived events, with a glaciogenic anomaly of the atmospheric and/or oceanic circulation lasting "only" a few centuries (case 5), certainly less than 2–3000 years. From the view-point of a meteorologist, these incomplete or "abortive glaciations" are by no means less interesting: they reveal a very remarkable instability of the atmosphere-ocean-ice system repeating non-periodically over a time-scale of the order of 2×10^4 years.

In view of the rapidity of development the initial stages must have lasted less than a century, probably only a few decades. What kind of atmosphere/ocean circulation anomalies are able to produce such catastrophic events?

5. Climatic conditions of the initial stages of a glaciation

The evidence of such dramatic global coolings with a quite short time-scale is of high importance when discussing the initiation of the glaciations of the northern continents, i.e., of the Laurentide and Scandinavian ice-sheets. This initiation is in any case a problem: while in Scandinavia a spreading of the existing mountain glaciers (Svartisen, Jötunheimen) could be caused by a temperature drop of 5–6 C, without any necessity for a substantial increase of precipitation, this is not the case in North America. Here the Rocky Mountain Ice, which expanded from the (at present heavily glaciated) high mountains in western Canada and southern Alaska, remained of medium size and never did extend far to the east. The major glaciation of North America was due to the Laurentide ice sheet, which formed on the presently unglaciated Ungava Plateau of Labrador and Quebec (now at an altitude of 600–800 m, between 53° and 60°N latitude) and even on the low-lying Keewatin country west of Hudson Bay, between 58° and 65°N. Only during the maximum phase of the last glaciation were the two ice sheets joined.

Loewe (1971) has discussed the climatic conditions in Ungava and Keewatin, and concluded that a 6 C temperature drop alone would be insufficient to cause a permanent snow-cover without an increase in total precipitation (snowfall). Because of the large extent of the Laurentian ice-dome (which contained more than 62% of the total increase in ice volume during a glaciation), its formation must have a key position in the sequence of events.

The recent climate in Labrador–Ungava and Keewatin is characterized by summer temperatures (June–August) of 11–12 C and by annual precipitation near 75–80 cm in Ungava but only about 35 cm in Keewatin.

Barry et al. (1959) and Brinkmann and Barry (1972) have investigated, by the methods of synoptic climatology, the meteorological conditions associated with high precipitation in the Labrador–Ungava area as well as in the Keewatin area, with different results.

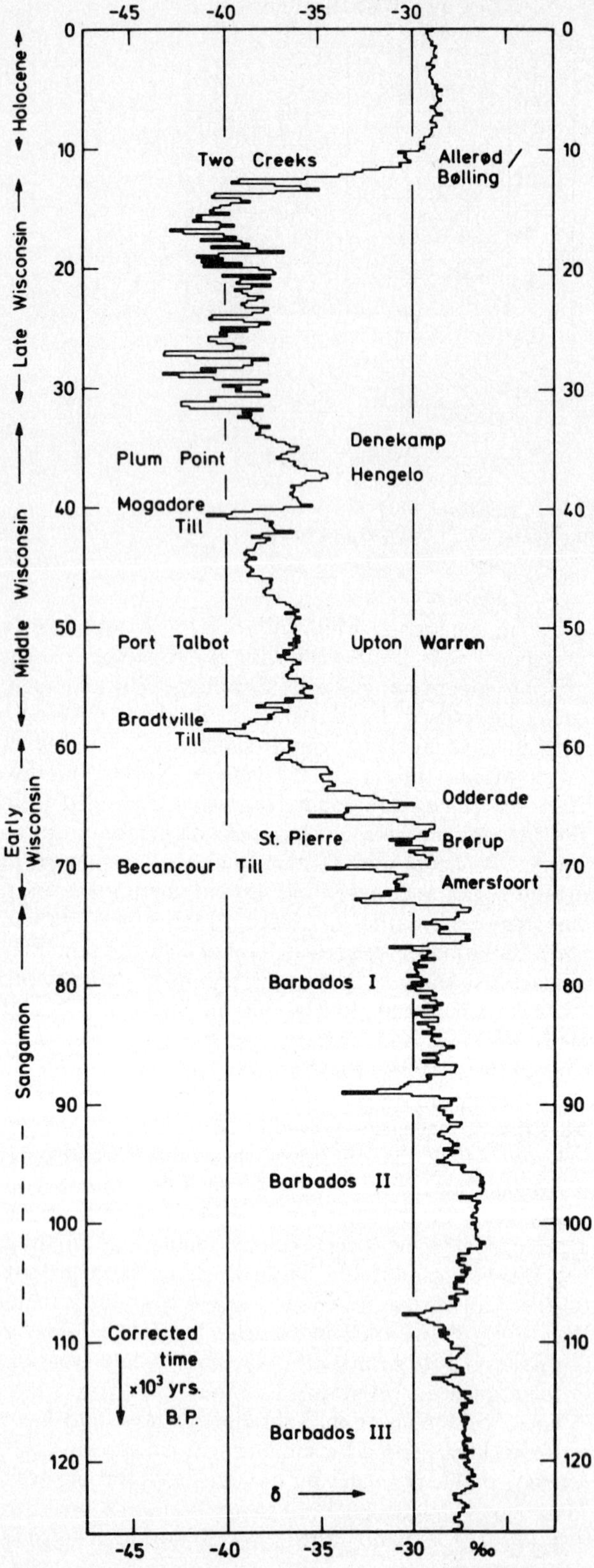

Fig. 2. Greenland ice core versus corrected time scale (Dansgaard *et al.*, 1971), plotted in 200-year intervals, with tentative interpretation in European (right) and American (left) terminology.

The formation of a nucleus of the ice-dome on the Labrador highlands, with a temperature drop of about 6 C together with an increase of precipitation, is only possible for a semi-permanent upper cold cyclone centered near 55°N, 72°W or a deep upper trough extending from Baffin Bay or Ellesmere Island into the area near Boston. In this situation low-level flow from N or NW would permanently cool the area, between about Long. 85° and 70°W, on the southern flank of low-level cyclones which themselves extended even farther east. Above 700 mb, however, relatively warm and moist air from the south would flow northward above the Labrador Peninsula, forced to ascend along a more or less stationary frontal surface and causing abundant precipitation, most frequently as snow.

In a boreal subpolar climate, the snow-melting process is not finished before late May or early June, and the first snowfall may occur as early as the end of August or early September. Each glaciation must start with a permanent snow-cover lasting during the summer; its high albedo (even in a half-melted stage) prevents the soil from storing heat. If a snow-cover can survive one summer with its high sunshine duration, the probability of a much higher snow-cover in the next year rises substantially; this is the beginning of a positive feedback process. A few consecutive years of this type would be sufficient to build up a snow-cover of several meters over the whole Ungava plateau with an area of about 60,000 km² above 600 m: then the high surface albedo during summer will prevent easy destruction, even if the large-scale flow-type changes.

Let us assume a 20 percent increase of precipitation to 90 cm year⁻¹, a (high) snow-cover density of 0.3 and a snowfall fraction of 80 percent of precipitation, we obtain an annual growth rate of the snow-cover of 240 cm. Assuming an increase of snow density to 0.5–0.6 (firn), a 15 m tall forest would be covered after 10–12 years, producing a further rise in albedo. Cold air will then be permanently produced near the surface, due to the combined effects of high albedo and longwave radiation from the snow-cover. This will lead, once a synoptic-scale diameter (300–500 km) is reached, to the formation of a superimposed cold low, which will force the upper flow to curve cyclonically and will further enhance snowfall. Such a powerful positive feedback mechanism is well known to the experienced meteorologist; it was discussed half a century ago by C. E. P. Brooks (1926). It can be qualitatively interpreted with the aid of the heat balance equation for an atmospheric column:

$$H + LP - \operatorname{div} \mathbf{Q}{\downarrow} - \operatorname{div} \mathbf{A}_h - \Delta T = 0$$

(H = flux of sensible heat into air, LP = release of latent heat by precipitation, div $Q{\downarrow}$ = divergence of radiative fluxes, div $\mathbf{A}_h$ = divergence of advective heat transport, $\Delta T =$ heat storage in the column). In high latitudes LP is not as predominant as in the tropics; above a snow-cover H is usually negative (from air to surface) and div $Q\downarrow$ is strongly negative, thus ΔT is likely to represent a heat sink.

The geophysical causes of this initial anomaly of the atmospheric circulation will be discussed in Section VI. Here it may be useful to outline the large-scale pattern connected with a deep semipermanent trough along 70°W, with a cold cyclonic center above western Labrador. This causes a meridionalization of the upper tropospheric flow, with anticyclonic ridges (and frequent blocking highs) near 125°W (Canadian NW Territories) and 20°W (Iceland) (Flohn, 1969; Lamb and Woodroffe, 1970). A secondary trough over Scandinavia and Central Europe will develop near 15°E, together with a warm ridge in 50–70°E, including the mountains of Central Asia. The occurrence of a blocking high just east of Alaska leads to southerly flow over Alaska itself, locally reducing the rate of cooling. The frequent occurrence of a blocking high between Iceland and Scotland causes northerly flow over Scandinavia and Central Europe, increasing snowfall and cooling This in turn causes a quasi-stationary pattern above Eastern Europe (25–40°E) corresponding to that above Labrador, with similar consequences, starting on the eastern flank of the Scandinavian mountains and in Finland. Such a pattern is nowadays frequent in cold winters and springs; here it is visualized—quite differently from today—as existing during the climax of the warm season.

6. Antarctic surges and their geophysical consequences

Since the observed short time-scale of global cooling events (cf. Section 4) is inconsistent with orbital effects, we ought to consider quite seriously the unorthodox Antarctic Surge hypothesis of A. T. Wilson (1964, 1966, 1969), based on the idea of a large-scale instability of the Antarctic ice-dome. Since many recent examples of mountain glacier surges are known, particularly in the Alaskan mountains, and since some physical properties of glacier ice are subject to marked changes in the vicinity of the melting-point, this hypothesis appears to be generally consistent with glaciological knowledge. Budd *et al.*, (1970) have developed a geophysical model of the Antarctic ice, mapping such quantities as ice cap streamlines, balance flow velocities, strain and basal heating rates, temperatures and melt rates. One of the prerequisites of a surge is basal melting, which has been found at Byrd Station, 80°S, 120°W, at a depth of 2164 m (Gow *et al.*, 1968). However, according to this model less than 10 percent of the recent Antarctic ice-cap is now subject to melting processes near the ground. According to Oswald and Robin (1973) 17 sub-ice lakes have been discovered in East Antarctica by radio-echo sounding flights, in regions of high ice thickness (2800–4200 m) and minimum velocity. Because of their small size (diameter along flight path between 2 and 15 km only), they cover, in the area of maximum frequency (around 75°S, 125°E), only 0.5 percent of the surface.

Wilson's hypothesis of simultaneous circumpolar Antarctic surges in its original form is hardly consistent with the roughness of the subglacial topography and with the results of this model. We should expect surges—not necessarily simultaneous—concentrated around the present ice shelves: the Weddell and Ross Ice shelves, and, to a lesser degree, the Amery Ice shelf (near 70°E). In analogy to present conditions the Weddell area should always have been the most productive. From the viewpoint of the heat budget and of the weather conditions in southern oceans, Wilson's assumption of a continuous quasipermanent ice-shelf around Antarctica with a size of 20 to 30 $\times 16^6$ km² is unrealistic and unnecessary.

However, a surge spreading one fourth or one third of the present mass of the Antarctic ice-dome—that means a volume of 6 to 10×10^6 km³—more or less distintegrated from the existing shelf zones into the ocean, during a time-span of a few decades or even centuries, does not seem too unrealistic. Assuming an average thickness of 200 m for tabular icebergs, a nearly simultaneous outbreak of 6×10^6 km³ would produce an ice-covered ocean area of 30×10^6 km² (Table 1, model SII 3). One of the prerequisites of such an event should be that the height of the ice-dome approaches the highest mark on the ice-free mountains (Hoinkes, 1961), which indicates a further growth of 2–300 m is required before the next surge. (If the average positive mass budget is assumed to be—at a maximum!—4 cm year^{-1} (Schwerdtfeger, 1970) a growth of 200 m would need another 5000 years; both figures, however, are crude estimates).

Independently of the duration of the surge, each outbreak of continental ice into the ocean must lead to a significant rise of the sea-level; some evidence for such glacio-eustatic rises has been found (Hollen, 1972). Assuming a mean density of 0.88 g cm^{-3}, each surging volume of 10^6 km³ should produce a eustatic rise of 2.44 m. Then the first serious consequence of a surge of the size assumed by Wilson (1964) and Hollin (1972) would be a sea-level rise of the order of 15 to 25 m, most probably spread over several decades; at any rate, it would be catastrophic for the densely populated coastal area, including all seaports. Denton *et al.*, (1971) have given a critical survey of the climatic and glaciological history of the Antarctic ice-sheets. Evidence for and against the former occurrence of large-scale surges is presented; no really conclusive proof exists at this time. Several height fluctuations of the ice of East Antarctica are quite conspicuous; they do not coincide with the northern

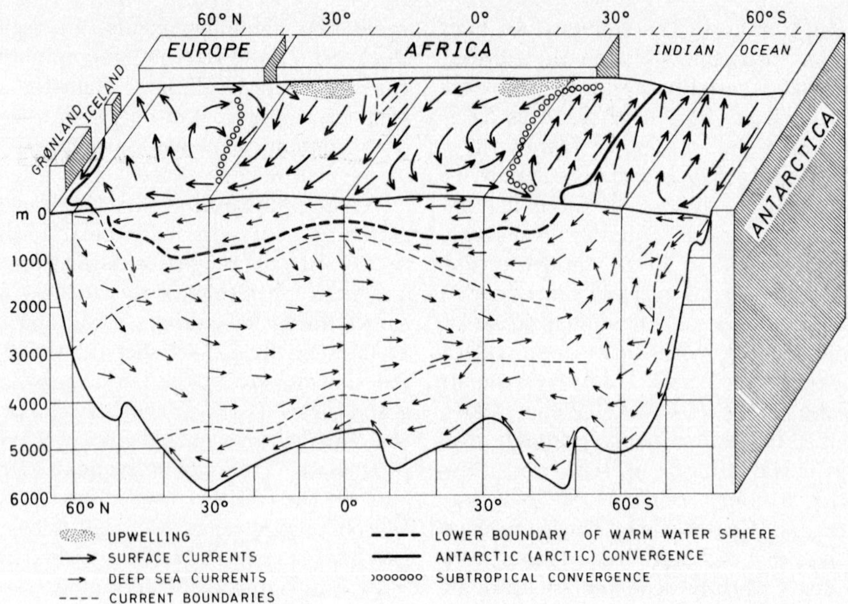

FIG. 3. Meridional cross section of abyssal circulation and surface currents of the Atlantic Ocean. Heavy dashed line: boundary between warm and cold layers, light dashed line: layer of zero current.

hemisphere glaciation, in spite of the nearly parallel trend of temperature in both hemispheres. If this is real, it can be taken as a suggestion that short-lived large surges generally produce brief coolings, while the large-scale climatic fluctuations are controlled by the long-lasting glaciations of the northern hemisphere and their role in the atmosphere-ocean heat budget.

The effect of an Antarctic surge of this size on the oceanic heat budget depends mainly on ice volume and temperature. Even more important is the effect on surface albedo and thus on the atmospheric heat budget: this depends on the albedo of and the area covered by ice, regardless of the degree of its disintegration. From the Manabe–Wetherald Model (1967) it can be concluded that a surge of the size indicated by Wilson's hypothesis, with a sea-ice area increase of 30×10^6 km², is equivalent to a southern hemisphere temperature drop of 7–8 C (model SH 3).

South of the oceanic Antarctic Convergence—now situated at Lat. 49–50°S in the Atlantic and in the adjacent Indian Ocean, and near 60°S in the Pacific—melting of the surged ice will be quite slow, due to the low surface temperatures of the subantarctic ocean (between 0 and +3 C). Here the latent heat of melting plays only an insignificant role; antarctic cold water is permanently sinking and disappearing at the Antarctic Convergence, feeding the subantarctic intermediate water at a depth of 500–2000 meters (Fig. 3). Let us assume that 40 percent of the injected ice (10^{22} g water equivalent) melts in this belt, consuming 32 $\times 10^{22}$ gcal in latent heat distributed over a 1000 m deep ocean layer ($\sim 3 \times 10^{22}$ cm³) during a period of 100 years. If all other terms of the heat budget remain

constant (which is certainly unrealistic), this melting would produce an annual cooling of about 0.1 C. Thus the regional effect of an ice surge on the heat budget of the subantarctic ocean is only small and short-lived.

The other 60 percent of the injected ice is assumed to be driven across the Antarctic Convergence into the warmer water on its northern flank. Here it will be disintegrated and melted much faster than before. Because of the position of the Weddell Sea—and in agreement with observations during the 19th century (Lamb, 1967; Schott, 1942) we may assume that 35 percent of the total ice volume penetrates into the narrow Atlantic sector (Fig. 4) (i.e., between Long. 20°E and the Drake Passage), and the remaining 25 percent into the vast areas of the Indian Ocean and of the Pacific, covering three fourths of the eath's circumference.

Over the Atlantic sector the drop of the equilibrium temperature according to the Manabe–Wetherald model (1967) will then extend much farther north than over the Pacific and Indian sectors. One may therefore expect a broad, more or less permanent upper tropospheric trough extending to (and partly across) the equatorial region, thus disturbing the subtropical anticyclonic ridge and displacing the ITC region even more to the northern hemisphere than at present, especially during the southern summer. Under present conditions a similar (but weaker) pattern is frequent only during the southern winter. The annual distribution of winds and water temperature anomalies in the equatorial region will then resenble the present northern summer situation: e.g., a southerly flow across the equator and, consequently, prevalence of equatorial upwelling (cf. the results obtained by Henning for July–September, see Flohn, 1972, Figs. 3 and 4).

While the ice floating into the Indo-Pacific section is of lesser, only regional importance—e.g., in the narrow belt along the eastern coast of Africa (Olaussen *et al.*, 1971)—the ice transported into the Atlantic sector plays a key role. As a basis for discussion we may use the heat balance equation for an upper mixed oceanic layer with constant depth, above the thermocline, in the following form:

$$Q_{sf} - (H_a + LE) - H_m - \operatorname{div} \mathbf{A}_t - \Delta T = 0.$$

Here Q_{sf} is the net radiation at the surface, $H_a + LE$ is the turbulent flux of sensible and latent heat from sea into air, H_m is the heat used for melting of ice, div $\mathbf{A}_t$ = divergence of advective heat flux of the ocean layer.

For a first-order estimate of the heat budget changes within the Atlantic current system (Table 2), let us assume that the ice floating across the Antarctic Convergence Zone melts in a short period (of a few decades or centuries) in the south Atlantic between Lat. 25° and 50°S ($\sim 18.6 \times 10^{16}$ cm²). In this area, just in front of the main surge region of the Weddell Sea, the ice coverage must be assumed to rise to 0.50; then, with an ice albedo of 0.8, the average albedo is 0.40. With a global radiation of about 118 kLy year⁻¹ (Sellers, 1965) and an atmospheric counter-radiation of 63 kLy year⁻¹ (after Brunt's formula with $T = 273$K), Q_{sf} will be drastically reduced from its present value of 74 kLy year⁻¹ 9 kLy year⁻¹ for a total energy loss of 16.7×10^{20} gcal year⁻¹. The average water temperature of about 14 C should drop to 0 C: this is equivalent—assuming a mixing layer of 100 m—to $\Delta T = 260 \times 10^{20}$ gcal. The melting of 35×10^{20} g ice (water equivalent) needs 28×10^{22} gcal or the equivalent of 168 years' net radiation. During the melting period, the fluxes of H_a and LE will be small and are thus neglected, as a first-order approximation. Assuming durations of the melting period in this zone A of 50 or 100 years, the estimated annual heat budgets of the mixing layer are given in Table 2

(T_{exit} is the temperature of the resulting mixing layer at the northern boundary of the zone).

In the following and in Table 2 we consider only this oceanic current system: Benguela current—South Equatorial current and its branch north of the South American continent (Guayana Current)—Gulf Stream. It must be assumed that during the melting period many icebergs reach Lat. 25°S—even in the 19th century some reached Lat. 35°S; the intensity of the cold Benguela Current is therefore assumed to increase from 6 to 8×10^6 m³/s (disregarding the contribution of layers below 100 m). In the zones B, C and D (Table 2) it is assumed that the extremely cold water increases atmospheric stability, and that the turbulent fluxes $H_a + LE$ are reduced by 40 percent. If we select a reduction rate of 30 percent or less (Flohn, 1969) the water temperature (T_{exit}) remains too low; this supports the idea of a drastic reduction of the oceanic evaporation and therefore of tropical rainfall (cf. Section 7).

A crucial point is the crossing of the equator: here we may assume that under nearly constant southerly winds (triggered by the difference of ocean temperatures in the two hemispheres) constant upwelling occurs. Its order of magnitude may be estimated by the use of Stommel's (1964) figures: he obtains, averaged between 5°N and 5°S, an upward velocity of 4×10^{-4} cm s⁻¹ (about 35 cm d⁻¹). According to Henning's data (Flohn, 1972) we restrict upwelling to the latitudinal belt 5°S to 1°N; then the upward flow reaches, above an area of 4.3×10^6 km², a value of about 17×10^6 m³ s⁻¹. This value is of the same order as the mass transport of the powerful South Equatorial Current of the Atlantic. In calculating the heat budget, we assume a temperature of 14 C for the ascending flow—i.e., the permanent upwelling is assumed to have the minimum temperature observed near the Galapagos. The assumption of a higher ascending mass transport would lead to unreasonably low temperatures (which should have destroyed the coral reefs in the Carribean). It should also be mentioned that, due to the semipermanent trough situation above the South Atlantic, the splitting of the

TABLE 2. Estimated heat budget: mixing layer during surge melting $Q_{sf} - (H_a + LE) - H_m + \operatorname{div} \mathbf{A}_t - \Delta T = 0$.

Atlantic zone	Area 10^6 km²	Transport 10^6 m³/s	Q_{sf}	$H_a + LE$	H_m	div $\mathbf{A}_t$	ΔT 10^{20} cal/a	T_{exit} °C
A. 25–50°S, 50 yrs.	18.6	8	16.7	0	56	−34	+ 5.4	0
25–50°S, 100 yrs.	18.6	8	16.7	0	28	−8.6	+ 2.7	0
B. 5–25°S (E only) Benguela current	6.0	8	66	38	0	−28	+28	11.2
C. 5°S-Carib Isl. Guayana current	4.3	$\overrightarrow{8}$ $17\!\uparrow$ } 25	51	31	0	$\overrightarrow{-20}$ $-22\!\uparrow$ }	+42	15.8
D. Caribbean + Gulf of Mexico	4.2	25	50	31	0	−28	+28	18.2

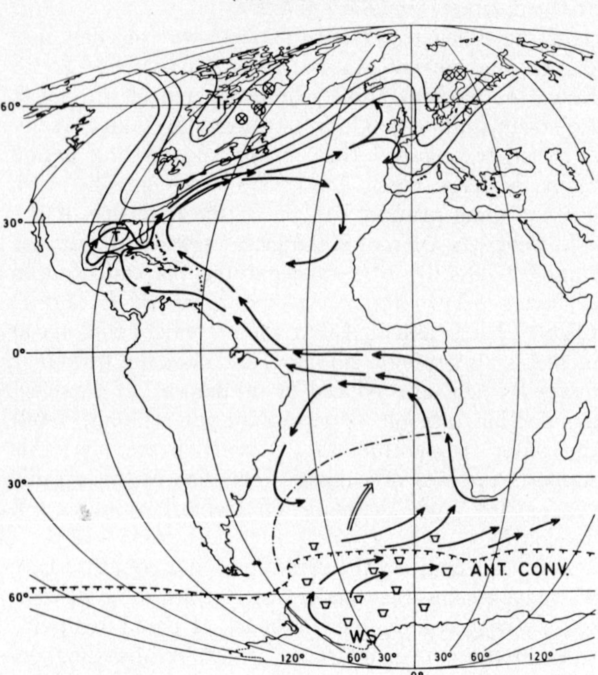

Fig. 4. Initiation of a glacial period (proposed scheme). Southern hemisphere: Wilson surge (double arrow) across Antarctic Convergence (actual position) up to about Lat. 25°S (dash-dot line). Ocean currents actual situation. Northern hemisphere: during melting period: cold pool in Gulf of Mexico, upper troughs along Long. 80°W and W Europe, centers of early continental glaciation.

South Equatorial Current should be displaced to the north, leading to a higher mass transport along the northern coast of South America and reducing the southward Falkland current.

A final value of T_{exit} as low as 18 C in the Gulf of Mexico is not presently supported by any evidence. However, if we take into account that the branch of the North Equatorial Current entering the area as the Caribbean Current, with a similar transport of 26×10^6 km³ s⁻¹ and a temperature of 26 C, flows in a baroclinic pattern parallel to the course of the chilled waters from the Southern hemisphere, we come to the result that the observed surface temperature of 21–22 C during the ice-ages (Emiliani, 1970) (i.e., averaged over a much longer period of some 10^4 years) are consistent with an area—averaged value near 22 C.

It would go beyond the purpose of this article to estimate the heat budget of the Gulf Stream during the melting period. It is sufficient to mention that its temperature at Florida Strait should be perhaps 5 C lower than today.

Such an—admittedly crude—consideration of the oceanic heat budget is necessary since the heat capacity of a 3 m water column is the same as that of the whole atmospheric column. If the ocean maintained its temperature and the cooling of the atmosphere above the greatest part of the globe occurred only due to advective processes in the air, the global climatic effect of an Antarctic ice outbreak would be rather insignificant. In this case it would be impossible to understand in what way the albedo-produced cooling of the subantarctic atmosphere could expand into the northern hemisphere, across the vast area of the warm tropical oceans covering—between Lat. 30°S and 15°N—about 78 percent of the surface.

It has been shown in Section 5 that the key to the initiation of a northern glaciation (either complete or incomplete) is the summer climate of Labrador–Ungava, including Keewatin and probably Baffin Island. A quasipermanent pattern of low level polar air advection together with upgliding warm moist air can only be conceived together with a quasipermanent east-coast trough reaching from Labrador to Florida (Fig. 4) Such a situation must be produced, sustained and fixed by a pool of cold water in the Gulf of Mexico and Caribbean, with surface temperatures around 22 C instead of 27–28 C The effect of this situation in summer (with the strongly heated continent in the north) is much stronger than in winter; during the warm season a permanent high-tropospheric vortex will be maintained, and an upper trough will be fixed along the east coast by a slightly cooler Gulf Stream.

The geophysical model which has been outlined here has one advantage over others: it needs only a quite short time-span of 50 or 100 years to produce a nucleus for glaciation growing by positive feedback, and is therefore apparently consistent with the evidence presented in Section 4. A crucial test of this model, however, lies in the magnitude of the un-avoidable sea-level rise (Hollin, 1972). The evidence presented to date is hardly sufficiently conclusive; however, it is certainly difficult to find convincing traces of a marine transgression with a lifetime of the order of only 10^3 years. Immediately after the establishment of this circulation anomaly, the storage of water in the form of ice above the northern continents begins and increases rapidly by the above-mentioned feedback process.

7. Time and space correlations

Interpreting global coolings as caused by large-scale surges of the Antarctic Ice, concentrated mainly in the Weddell Sea-Atlantic section, we may also comprehend some correlations with other evidence which remained hitherto hardly understandable.

a) In all tropical continents, definite signs of a marked desiccation simultaneously with the northern glaciations have been found (Fairbridge, 1972). This is even true for the equatorial rain-forests in Central Africa and South America (Vuilleumier, 1972; van

Zinderen Bakker and Coetzee, 1972); in both areas semi-arid dry forest prevailed, with only a few islands of humid forest. If under the present radiation regime the oceans are advectively cooled, the evaporation from the tropical oceans as the main source of the global hydrological cycle (68 percent) must have been substantially lower; a rough estimate based on advective processes alone (Flohn, 1969) gave a decrease of about 30 percent. Under such conditions the intensity and extension of the tropical Hadley cell must have decreased in comparison with present conditions.

b) In several parts of the Atlantic sector the lowering of the snow-line and vegetation limits during glacials was much greater than usual (equatorial zone some 800 m, mid-latitudes about 1200 m). Here we mention the Itatiaya near Rio de Janeiro (Mortensen, 1957), the Costa Rica Volcanoes (Weyl, 1956) and, at least in some times, the Sabana of Bogota (van der Kammen *et al.*, 1971), each with a glacial cooling of up to 8 C (in earlier glaciations even 11 C) instead of 5 C in other areas (East Africa, Indonesia, New Guinea). Similar data have been collected from the humid Andes mountains of Colombia and Venezuela (Wilhelmy, 1957. Of special interest is the somewhat controversial evidence for a wide-spread low-land glaciation of Eastern Patagonia (Czajka, 1957). At the South African coast, Butzer (1973) estimates a drop in winter temperatures of about 10 C.

c) According to new data collected in an interdisciplinary German-Mexican Project (Heine, 1973a and 1973b), the C¹⁴ time-scale of climatic events in the last 40,000 years in the high volcanoes in Central Mexico deviates in a characteristic way from the usual sequence; the greatest glacial advances occurred at about 32,000 and (during 4–500 years only) 12,000 BP, i.e., within the Allerod oscillation.

d) The striking contrast between the glacial temperature anomalies in the area around the Bay of Biscay, from Ireland to Northern Spain (−12 C or even more), and at the same latitude at the Pacific coast of North and South America (about −5 C) has been stressed earlier (Flohn, 1969); it is consistent with abrupt progressions of polar water masses to Lat. 42°N in the Atlantic (McIntyre *et al.*, 1972), i.e., more than 20° south of their present position. From a comparison between micropaleontological evidence and isotopic temperatures, Emiliani (1971) concludes that glacial surface temperatures were about 7–8 C lower in the Caribbean, 5–6 C in the equatorial Atlantic, but only 3–4 C in the equatorial Pacific. The contrast of the large extension of ice sheets on both sides of the Atlantic with the comparatively small glaciation on both sides of the Pacific requires also a geophysical interpretation (Flohn, 1969). According to this version of the Antarctic Surge model, cooling of the Pacific may have occurred only as a secondary effect.

After the revised calculation of the solar radiation fluctuations due to orbital variations (Vernekar, 1972) the equal severity of the most recent and earlier glaciations is difficult to understand. In contrast to the solar variations, the glacial and climatic history of at least the last 20,000 years shows a clear coincidence at both hemispheres, instead of a time-lag of the order of 10,000 years. Together with the discrepancies in the time-scale involved, this seems to be one of the strongest arguments against a primary role of the extraterrestrial "Milankovich effect," which appears to have mesmerized nearly two generations of earth scientists, in spite of many sober and critical voices.

According to heat transport considerations (Newell, 1973) the initiation of a glaciation needs a heat deficit of 1 to 3×10^{19} gcal d^{-1}. A Wilson surge (Model SH 3) yields, with an average global radiation of 350 Ly d^{-1}, a heat deficit of about 9×10^{19} gcal d^{-1} or about 4500 terawatt lasting about a century. If the melting process of the ice lasts the same period, an additional loss of nearly 2×10^{19} gcal d^{-1} is to be added.

In contrast to this, the peak-to-peak variation of summer insolation due to the Milankovich effect— i.e., spread over a period of several 10^4 years!—is 35×10^{20} gcal (Broecker, 1968) or little less than 2×10^{19} gcal d^{-1}, equivalent to 3.8 W/m² or 970 terawatt.

The mass of new evidence, consisting of quantitative determinations of temperature and age (certainly not without sources of systematic error!) has shown that the time-scale of the glacial-interglacial sequence is much more complex than the classical one (Emiliani, 1972). Obviously a series of hemispheric-scale coolings occurred, some followed by a glaciation on the northern continents, others not. Such "abortive" coolings, with a time-scale of a few centuries, are of vital interest to the meteorologist: in the human time-scale they are "irreversible," i.e., from the view-point of living mankind, of the economist and the politician. They indicate that Lorenz's (1968) unorthodox suggestion of a potential instability of our climate is quite realistic and must be taken as a serious challenge of utmost significance.

In the Ross Ice Shelf portion of West Antarctica the ice profile obviously has not yet reached the equilibrium stage (Hughes, 1973); similar studies on the much larger East Antarctic ice-dome are necessary.

The powerful feedback between the strong albedo gradient on the outer boundary of the snow- and ice-covered region and the baroclinic frontal zones (acting as cyclone tracks) contributes strongly to the development and maintenance of continental glaciations in the northern hemisphere. It is much more difficult to understand the total interruption of this process, which leads to disintegration and finally to deglaciation. In other words: what physical causes are responsible for the transition from an ice-accumulating to an ice-destroying pattern of the atmospheric circulation, right at the culmination of each glacial? It has been argued (Hoinkes, 1961; Boch, 1964), that the aridity of northern continents causes Loess dust from the barren fluvioglacial deposists around the ice (with most particles well below 2 μm) to be blown onto the ice, resulting in a lowering of the surface albedo. However, the role of a dust-laden atmosphere—as it can be observed now during summer above Pakistan, Turkestan and Sinkiang—is more complex: Low-level dust absorbs solar and long-wave radiation and heats the atmosphere and the surface substantially. A most remarkable example of this effect has been observed recently in the Martian atmosphere (Gierash and Goody, 1972). Direct heating and atmospheric infrared radiation (at high temperatures) are more powerful melting agents than the decrease of the albedo alone. Time variations of the Ca content of the Greenland ice (Hamilton and Seligo, 1972) are apparently consistent with this hypothesis; the occurrence of Ca maxima after the beginning of cooling supports our view.

8. Summary

In a time-scale of 10^4–10^6 years the climate of the earth-atmosphere-hydrosphere-cryosphere system is in fact unstable. This complex, self-regulating system—with nearly constant energy input—is in a delicate state of equilibrium, with its energy budget depending on the variable area of its subsystems. During the last 10^5 years, evidence of at least 5 rapid hemispheric or global coolings has been found with temperature changes of about 5 C (i.e., the full difference between present and ice-age climate), occurring during a time-span of the order of a century. Only some of them led to a complete glaciation of the northern continents, others ended after a few centuries with a sudden warming. These facts are not compatible with the widely accepted orbital variations with a time-scale of some 10^4 years ("Milankovich effect").

Starting from a modified version of A. T. Wilson's hypothesis of large-scale surges of the Antarctic ice-dome, a purely geophysical model of such rapid coolings can be outlined:

1) After a period of slow accumulation, the Antarctic ice-dome surges—not necessarily simultaneously—mainly in the existing shelf areas, especially in the Weddell Sea. The amount of ice calving into the ocean is estimated to be 6 to 10×10^6 km³, causing a eustatic sea-level rise of 15 to 25 m, spread over several decades or centuries.

2) The disintegrated ice spreads, in enormous tabular ice-bergs, over an area of 20 to 30×10^6 km²; due to the increase of the surface albedo the average temperature of the southern hemisphere drops about 7 C.

Since the tropical zone is, at the very beginning, only weakly affected, the mid-latitude circulation intensifies significantly.

3) During the melting period, a considerable part of the ice crosses the oceanic Antarctic Convergence, notably in the Weddell Sea-Atlantic sector. According to an estimate of the heat budget of the upper mixed layer, the melting process causes advective cooling of the system Benguela-Current—South Equatorial Current—Gulf Stream of the order of at least 6 to 8 C during a time-span of about 50 to 100 years, in addition to the albedo-produced cooling. This cooling should be accompanied by a broad upper trough in the South Atlantic and a marked cold-arid phase in the neighbouring continents.

4) Advective cooling of the surface of the Caribbean and the Gulf of Mexico, together with the Gulf Stream, causes, during the warm season, a permanent high-tropospheric vortex together with a deep trough along the eastern coast of North America. This circulation anomaly produces cooling and increased snowfall in the Labrador–Ungava region and enables a survival of the snow-cover during summer, as a potential nucleus of a continental glaciation.

5) When the permanent snow-cover has reached a diameter of several hundred kms, a positive feedback mechanism (snow surface with high albedo-tropospheric cooling—cold upper vortex—enhanced snowfall) leads to a fast-growing ice-sheet. This localized heat sink maintains a quasipermanent trough-ridge pattern with blocking highs east of Alaska and east of Iceland, the latter producing a second ice center in the mountains of Fennoscania.

6) Further development of these ice-centers either to a complete glaciation or to a reversal may perhaps be controlled by the actual state of the orbital elements; further studies are needed. From the meteorological point of view, an incomplete ("abortive") glaciation with a duration of only a few centuries is as important as a complete glaciation with a period of 10,000 years.

7) The final disintegration of the ice-domes of the northern continents—in spite of the powerful feedback referred to under 5—can be understood as caused by frequent dust-storms, lowering the surface albedo of the glacier and heating the lower atmosphere through absorption of solar and long-wave radiation.

Such a geophysical model may serve as a background for a complete physico-mathematical model of the complex multi-phase system designed to simulate these most dramatic events in the climatic history of the earth. Admittedly, our knowledge of the complex interaction of processes in our geophysical system is at this time rather inadequate Several highly interesting model experiments try to simulate the climate of a fully developed glacial epoch (Alyea, 1972; Williams et al., 1973). Here we propose a much more difficult, but also more rewarding future task: the simulation of the initiation of a new glaciation. If—as stated in the introduction—a new glaciation should be expected to begin during the next, say, 5000 years, one should expect, perhaps, a probability near one percent, that this may happen during the next 50 years.

Man can hardly interfere with the mass budget and the intensity of the Antarctic ice. Denton *et al.* (1971), have pointed out that a minor increase of temperature—as we expect as a result of man-made effects—may lead to disintegration of the smaller West Antarctic ice-sheet; both effects should rise the accumulation rate in East Antarctica. At any rate, this problem is not only of pure academic interest: it refers to our own planet Earth, to our habitat now and in the future. Within the life-time of our generation, it deserves a much higher priority.

Acknowledgments. The author wishes to express his gratitude to many colleagues, with whom he had the privilege to discuss some of the ideas presented here: M. R. Bloch (Beer-Sheba), K. Brunnacker (Koln), M. I. Budyko (Leningrad), H. Hoinkes (Innsbruck), F. Loewe (Melbourne), U. Radok (Melbourne), M. Schwarzback (Koln), C Troll (Bonn), A. T. Wilson (Wairakei, N. Z.), E. M. van Zinderen Bakker (Bloemfontein). A preliminary draft of this paper was first presented in a lecture at the University of Melbourne, August 1972.

REFERENCES

Alyea, J., 1972: Numerical simulation of an ice age paleoclimate. Atm. Sci. Pap. No. 193, Dept. Atm. Sci., Colorado State Univ., Fort Collins, 120 pp.

Barry, R. G., 1959: A synoptic climatology for Labrador-Ungava. Publ. in Meteor. No. 17, Arct. Meteor. Res. Group, McGill Univ., Montreal, 168 pp., Append.

Barry, R. G., 1966: Meteorological aspects of the glacial history of Labrador-Ungava with special reference to atmospheric vapour transport. *Geogr. Bull.*, **8**, 319–340.

Bjerknes, J., 1969: Atmospheric teleconnections from the equatorial Pacific. *Mo. Wea. Rev.*, **97**, 163–172.

Bloch, M. R., 1964: Die Beeinflussung der Albedo von Eisflächen durch Staub und ihre Wirkung auf Ozeanhöhe und Klima. *Geol. Rdsch.*, **54**, 515–522.

Brinkmann, R., and R. C. Barry, 1972: Paleoclimatological aspects of the synoptic climatology of Keewatin, Northwest territories, Canada. *Palaeogeography, Palaeoclimatology, Palaeoceology*, **11**, 77–91.

Broecker, W. S., 1968: In defense of the astronomical theory of glaciation. *Amer. Meteor. Soc., Meteor. Monogr.*, **8**, No. 30, 139–141.

Broecker, W. S., and J. Van Donk, 1970: Insolation changes, ice volumes and the O^{18} record in deep-sea cores. *Rev. Geophys. Space Physics*, **8**, 169–198.

Brooks, C. E. P., (1926), 1949: Climate through the ages. 2nd ed. London.

Budd, M., D. Jenssen and U. Radok, 1970: The extent of basal melting in Antarctica. *Polarforschung*, **6**, 293–306.

Budyko, M., 1969: The effect of solar radiation variations on the climate of the earth. *Tellus*, **21**, 611–619.

Budyko, M., 1972: The future climate, *Transact. Amer. Geophys. Union (Eos)*, **53**, 868–874.

Bull, C., and P. N. Webb, 1973: Some recent developments in the investigation of the glacial history and glaciology of Antartica. In: *Palaeoecology of Africa*, E. M. Van Zinderen Bakker, Ed., 8, Cape Town, Balkema, 55–84.

Butzer, K. W., 1973: Pleistocene "periglacial" phenomena in southern Africa. *Boreas*, **2**, 1–11.

Czajka, W., 1957: Die Reichweite der pleistozänen Vereisung Patagoniens. *Geol. Rdsch.*, **45**, 634–686.

Dansgaard, W., S. J. Johnsen, H. B. Clausen and C. C. Langway Jr., 1971: Climatic record revealed by the camp century ice core. In: *Late Cenozoic Glacial Ages*, K. Turekian, Ed., 37–56.

Dansgaard, W., S. J. Johnson, H. B. Clausen and C. C. Langway Jr., 1972: Speculations about the next glaciation. *Quatern. Res.*, **2**, 396–398.

Denton, G. H., R. L. Armstrong and M. Stuiver, 1971: The late cenocoic glacial history of Antarctica. In: *Late cenozoic glacial ages*, K. Turekian, Ed., 267–306.

Duplessy, J. C., J. Labeyrie, C. Lalou and H. V. Nguyen, 1971: La mesure des variation climatiques continentales. Application à la période comprise entre 130.000 et 90.000 ans B. P. *Quaternary Research*, **1**, 162–174.

Emiliani, C., 1970: Pleistocene paleotemperatures. *Science*, **168**, 822–825.

Emiliani, C., 1971: The amplitude of pleistocene climatic cycles at low latitudes and the isotopic composition of glacial ice. In: *Late Cenozoic Glacial Ages*, K. Turekian, Ed., 183–197.

Emiliani, C., 1972: Quaternary paleotemperatures and the duration of the high-temperature intervals. *Science*, **178**, 398–401.

Fairbridge, R. W., 1972: Climatology of a glacial cycle. *Quaternary Research*, **2**, 283–302.

Fliri, F., S. Bortenschlager and H. Felber (u. a.), 1970: Der Bänderton von Baumkirchen (Inntal, Tirol). Eine neue Schlüsselstellung zur Kenntnis der Würmvereisung der Alpen. *Z. Gletscherkunde u. Glazialgeol.*, **6**, 5–35.

Fliri, F., H. Hilscher und V. Markgraf, 1971: Weitere Untersuchungen zur Chronologie der alpinen Vereisung (Bänderton von Baumkirchen, Inntal, Nordtirol). *Z. Gletscherk. u. Glazialgeol.*, **7**, 5–24.

Flohn, H., 1969: Ein geophysikalisches Eiszeit-Modell. *Eiszeitalter u. Gegenwart*, **20**, 204–231.

Flohn, H., 1972: Investigation of equatorial upwelling and its climatic role. In: *Studies in Physical Oceanography*, A. H. Gordon, Ed., Vol. 1. A Tribute to Georg Wüst on his eightieth Birthday. New York, London, Gordon & Breach, 93–102.

Flohn, H., 1973: Globale Energiebilanz und Klimaschwankungen. *Vorträge Rhein.-Westf. Akad. Wiss.*, N 234, 75–117.

Flohn, H., 1973b: Antarctica and the global cenozoic evolution: A geophysical model. In: *Palaeoecology of Africa*, E. M. Van Zinderen Bakker, Ed., 8, Cape Town, Balkema, 37–53.

Gierasch, P. J., and R. M. Goody, 1972: The effect of dust on the temperature of the Martian atmosphere. *J. Atmos. Sci.*, **29**, 400–402.

Gow, A. J., H. T. Ueda and D. E. Garfield, 1968: Antarctic ice sheet: Preliminary results of first core hole to Bedrock. *Science*, **161**, 1011–1013.

Hamilton, W. L., and Th. A. Seliga, 1972: Atmospheric turbidity and surface temperature on the polar ice sheets. *Nature*, **235**, 320–322.

Heine, K., 1973a: Die jungpleistozänen und holozänen Gletschervorstöße am Malinche-Vulkan, Mexiko. *Eiszeitalter u. Gegenwart*, **23**, 46–62.

Heine, K., 1973b: Variaciones más importantes del clima durante los ultimos 40.000 años en México. *Comunicationes Puebla, Mex.*, **7**, 51–58.

Hoinkes, H., 1961: Die Antarktis und die geophysikalische Erforschung der Erde. *Naturwissensch.*, **48**, 354–374.

Hoinkes, H., 1971: Neue Ergebnisse und Gedanken zur Eiszeitforschung. *Jahrb. Akad. Wiss. Lit. Mainz*, 102–103.

Hollin, J. T., 1972: Interglacial climate and Antarctic ice surges. *Quaternary Res.*, **2**, 401–408.

Hughes, T., 1973: Is the West Antarctic Ice Sheet Disintegrating? *Journ. Geophys. Res.*, **78**, 7884–7910.

Johnsen, S. J., W. Dangsgaard, H. B. Clausen and C. C. Langway, Jr., 1972: Oxygen isotope profiles through the Antarctic and Greenland ice sheets. *Nature*, **235**, 429–434.

Kennett, J. P., and P. Huddlestun, 1972: Abrupt climatic change at 90.000 yr BP: Faunal evidence from Gulf of Mexico cores. *Quaternary Res.*, **2**, 384–395.

Kukla, G. J., R. K. Matthews and J. M. Mitchell, Jr., 1972a: The end of the present interglacial. *Quaternary Res.*, **2**, 261–269.

Kukla, G. J., and R. K. Matthews, 1972b: When will the present interglacial end? *Science*, **178**, 190–191.

Kukla, G. J., and H. J. Kukla, 1972c: Insolation regime of interglacials. *Quatern. Res.*, **2**, 412–424.

Lamb, H. H., 1967: On climatic variations affecting the Far South. World Meteor. Organ. Techn. Note No. 87, 428–453.

Lamb, H. H., and A. Woodroffe, 1970: Atmospheric circulation during the last ice-age. *Quatern. Res.*, **1**, 29–58.

Loewe, F., 1971: Considerations on the origin of the quaternary ice sheet of North America. *Arct. and Alpine Res.*, **3**, 331–344.

Lorenz, E. N., 1968: Climatic determinism. *Meteor. Monogr.*, **8**, No. 30, Amer. Meteor. Soc., 1–3.

Lorenz, E. N., 1970: Climatic change as a mathematical problem. *J. Appl. Meteor.*, **9**, 325–329.

McIntyre, A., W. F. Ruddiman and R. Jantzen, 1972: Southward penetration of the North Atlantic polar front: Faunal and floral evidence of the large-scale surface movements over the last 225,000 years. *Deep-Sea Res.*, **19**, 61–77.

Manabe, S., and R. T. Wetherald, 1967: Thermal equilibrium of the atmosphere with a given distribution of relative humidity. *J. Atm. Sci.*, **24**, 241–259.

Mercer, J. H., 1969: The Allerød oscillation: a European climatic anomaly? *Arct. and Alpine Res.*, **1**, 227–234.

Mercer, J. H., 1970: A former ice sheet in the Arctic Ocean? *Palaeogeogr., Palaeoclim., Palaeoecol.*, **8**, 19–27.

Mercer, J. H., and C. A. Laugenie, 1973: Glacier in Chile ended a major readvance about 36,000 years ago: some global comparisons. *Science*, **182**, 1017–1019.

Mitchell, J. M., Jr., 1972: The natural break-down of the present interglacial and its possible intervention by human activities. *Quatern. Res.*, **2**, 436–445.

Mortensen, H., 1957: Temperaturgradient und Eiszeitklima am Beispiel der pleistozänen Schneegrenzdepression in den Rand- und Subtropen. *Z. Geomorph.*, N. F., **1**, 44–56.

Newell, R., 1973: Abstract. In: *BAMS*, **54**, 428.

Olaussen, E., U. I. Bilal Ul Haq, G. B. Karlson and J. N. Olsson, 1971: Evidence in Indian Ocean cores of late pleistocene changes in oceanic and atmospheric circulation. *Geol. För. Förh.*, **93**, Stockholm, 51–84.

Oswald, G. K. A., and G. de Q. Robin, 1973: Lakes beneath the Antarctic ice sheet. *Nature*, **245**, 251–254.

Rowntree, P. R., 1972: The influence of tropical East Pacific Ocean temperatures on the atmosphere. *Quart. J. Roy. Meteor. Soc.*, **98**, 290–321.

Sancetta, C., J. Imbrie, N. G. Kipp, A. McIntyre and W. F. Ruddiman, 1972: Climatic record in North Atlantic deep-sea cores V 23–82: Comparison of the last and present interglacials based on quantitative time series. *Quatern. Res.*, **2**, 363–367.

Schott, G., 1944: Geographie des Atlantischen Ozeans. 3. Aufl. Hamburg, Boysen, 438 S.

Schwerdtfeger, W., 1970: The Climate of the Antarctic. In: *World Survey of Climatology*, **14**, Amsterdam, London, New York, Elsevier, 253–355.

Sellers, W. D., 1965: Physical Climatology. Chicago, Univ. of Chicago Pr., 272 S.

Sellers, W. D., 1969: A global climatic model based on the energy balance of the earth-atmosphere system. *J. Appl. Meteor.*, **8**, 392–400.

Sellers, W. D., 1973: A new global climatic model. *J. Appl. Meteor.*, **12**, 241–254.

Stommel, H., 1964: Summary charts of the mean dynamic topography and current field at the surface of the ocean, and related fields of the mean wind-stress. In: *Studies on Oceanography*, K. Yoshida, Ed., Tokyo, Univ. of Tokyo Pr., 53–58.

Van Der Hammen, T., T. A. Wijmstra and W. H. Zagwijn, 1971: Floral record of the late cenozoic of Europe. In: *Late Cenozoic Glacial Ages*, K. Turekian, Ed., New Haven, Yale Univ. Pr., 391–424.

Van Zinderen Bakker, and J. A. Coetzee, 1972: A re-appraisal of late-quaternary climatic evidence from tropical Africa. In: *Palaeoecology of Africa*, E. M. Van Zinderen Bakker, Ed., Cape Town, Balkema, **7**, 151–181.

Vernekar, A. D., 1972: Long-period global variations of incoming solar radiation. *Amer. Meteor. Soc., Meteor. Monogr.*, **12**, No. 34.

Vuilleumier, B. S., 1971: Pleistocene changes in the flora and fauna of South America. *Science*, **173**, 771–780.

Washington, W. W., 1972: Numerical climatic-change experiments: The effect of man's production of thermal energy. *J. Appl. Meteor.*, **11**, 768–772.

Weyl, R., 1956: Spuren eiszeitlicher Vergletscherung in der Cordillera de Calamanca Costa Rica (Mittelamerika). *N. Jahrb. Geol. Paläont. Abh.*, **102**, 283–294.

Wilhelmy, H., 1957: Eiszeit und Eiszeitklima in den feuchttropischen Anden. Petermanns Geogr. Mitt. Ergänz. Heft No. 262, 281–310.

Williams, J., R. G. Barry and W. W. Washington, 1973: Simulation of the climate at the last glacial maximum using the NCAR global circulation model. Occas. Pap. No. 5, Inst. of Alpine and Arctic Res., Univ. of Colorado, Blouder, Colo.

Wilson, A. T., 1964: Origin of ice ages: An ice shelf theory for pleistocene glaciation. *Nature*, **201**, 147–149.

Wilson, A. T., 1966: Variation in solar insolation to the south polar region as a trigger which induces instability in the Antarctic ice-sheet. *Nature*, **210**, 477–478.

Wilson, A. T., 1969: The climatic effects of large-scale surges of ice sheets. *Canad. J. Earth Sci.*, **6**, 911–918.

Wundt, W., 1938: Das Reflexionsvermögen der Erde zur Eiszeit. *Meteor. Z.*, **55**, 81–87.

Climatic Feedback Mechanisms Involving the Polar Regions

WILLIAM W. KELLOGG

National Center for Atmospheric Research[1], Boulder, Colorado

Abstract

The climate is largely determined by complex interactions within the total system made up of the atmosphere, the oceans, the solid earth, and the cryosphere. Since no complete model of this total system has been constructed so far, it has been useful to investigate certain sets of interactions more or less by themselves, and these have been referred to as "feedback loops," where the response of some part of the system to a change is influenced by the response of other parts. Some feedback mechanisms that involve the cryosphere and the polar regions are apparently very powerful, and there are others which are probably less important or still to be evaluated. A partial list of such feedback mechanisms that deserve to be studied further is as follows:

Albedo-polar ice cover-temperature
Albedo-polar cloud cover-temperature.
Sea ice-ocean circulation-winds
Sea ice-air/sea exchange-surface layer mixing
Snowfall-ice cap height-mass of ice cap
Mass of continental ice-sea level height-Arctic sea ice
Continental ice extent-winds-dust-albedo of ice
Sea ice extent-low level cooling-katabatic wind

Each of these will be briefly discussed and its overall importance assessed.

---

1. Climate models and climate change

While there is some controversy about the exact definition of "the climate" and the time period over which it is supposed to apply, we can take it to mean generally the set of conditions that describe the *mean* state of the atmosphere-ocean-cryosphere-earth system, together with the *season-to-season changes* in this state. The fact that the climate changes from year to year, from decade to decade, from century to century, from millenium to millenium, and so forth on up to periods of millions of years, can be taken as an indication that there is no single equilibrium state for this system. Something in it, it seems, is always changing or is due to change.

The objective of "climate theory" then, is to develop a model that will simulate this system and its search for an equilibrium, and more particularly will describe the *changes* of the climate as the system moves from one state to the next. The fact that we do not have such a model of the system, or "climate model," should not discourage us from the effort to work toward one, and in the process we can study the various system interactions individually. There are still too many physical processes, too many inter-

actions, for even the cleverest modelers working with the fastest computers available to combine into one model.

It is useful therefore to pull the system apart, as it were, and study these interactions, or "feedback loops" (to be explained in the next section), by themselves (SMIC, 1971; Schneider and Kellogg, 1973). By doing this one can gain a sense of how each one operates, specifically:

o The *direction* of its influence on a change in the state of the system, whether it is a reinforcing (amplifying) loop or a damping loop,
o Its *relative* influence, compared with other loops.

The latter is generally much harder to assess.

It will be clear at the outset, as we have said, that no feedback loop exists in isolation, but that they are in fact interconnected in a kind of network. Often a feedback system of two or more connected loops must be considered, where it would not be useful to consider each loop by itself.

In the following sections we will discuss the concept of simple feedback loops and explain a symbolism that has proved useful in discussing them—a kind of shorthand to represent a complex set of ideas. Then we will briefly describe some specific examples of feedback loops that involve the polar regions.

---

[1] The National Center for Atmospheric Research is sponsored by the National Science Foundation.

ALBEDO - POLAR ICE COVER - TEMPERATURE

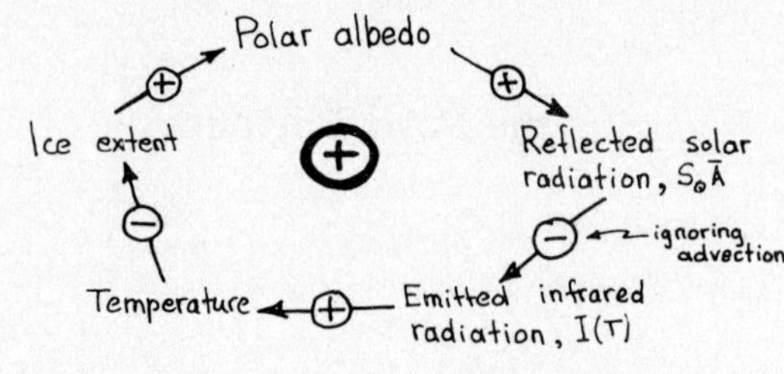

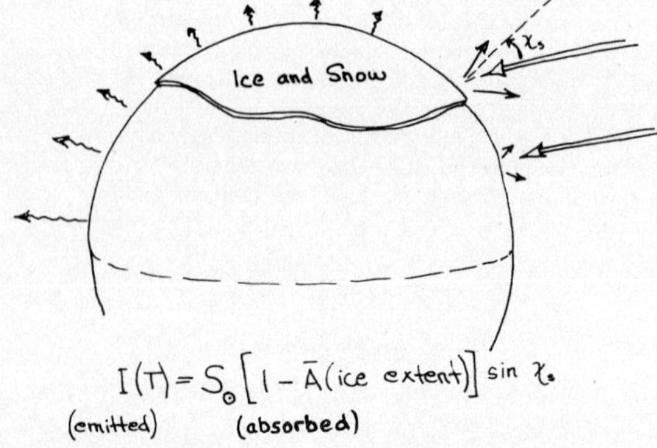

$$I(T) = S_0 \left[1 - \bar{A}(\text{ice extent}) \right] \sin \chi_0$$
$$\text{(emitted)} \qquad \text{(absorbed)}$$

Fig. 1. The albedo-polar ice cover-temperature feedback loop. At the top is the description, in symbolic form, of the various processes involved in the loop together with the sign of the action of each process with the next process in the sequence. The overall sign of the loop is indicated in the center. At the bottom is a highly stylized sketch that illustrates the various factors involved in the system. See text for discussion.

2. Introduction to simple feedback loops

Consider three parameters that influence each other through a sequence of physical processes, so that the sequence is closed in a loop. We can represent such a loop as follows:

where

$$B \sim K_B A^{n_B},$$
$$C \sim K_C B^{n_C},$$
$$A \sim K_A C^{n_A}.$$

These proportional relationships, or "links," are generally not reversible, since they represent cause-and-effect in the physical world. It follows that a proportional change in one parameter causes a proportional change in the next parameter as follows:

$$\frac{\Delta B}{B} \sim n_B \frac{\Delta A}{A},$$
$$\frac{\Delta C}{C} \sim n_C \frac{\Delta B}{B},$$
$$\frac{\Delta A}{A} \sim n_A \frac{\Delta C}{C},$$

and we say that a link is positive when $n > 0$, negative when $n < 0$, and represent such links by the symbols

$$—\oplus\rightarrow$$
$$—\ominus\rightarrow$$

Now consider what happens when we perturb parameter A by an amount $\Delta A/A$. By simply substituting in the set of equations it can be seen that the resulting proportional change $(\Delta A'/A')$ after the perturbation has traveled around the loop is

$$\frac{\Delta A'}{A'} \sim n_A \cdot n_B \cdot n_C \frac{\Delta A}{A}.$$

Thus, whether $\Delta A'$ has the same or different sign compared with ΔA depends on the product of the n's. If

$$n_A \cdot n_B \cdot n_C > 1$$

the loop is an amplifying, or strongly positive loop. If

$$n_A \cdot n_B \cdot n_C < 0$$

it is a reversing or negative loop, and in the absence of other strong damping factors a perturbation results in an occillation of the loop with a characteristic frequency. If

$$0 \leqslant n_A \cdot n_B \cdot n_C < 1$$

the loop is one that eventually damps out a perturbation, but does not reverse it—it is weakly positive.

In the examples that will be discussed in the next

ALBEDO - POLAR CLOUD COVER - TEMPERATURE

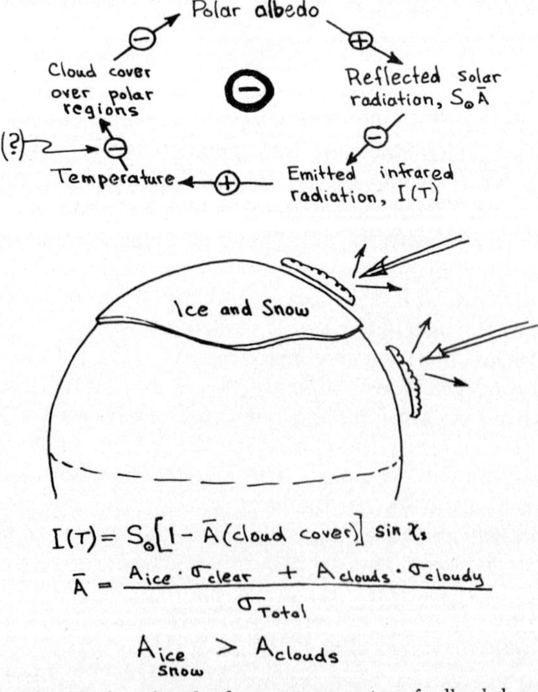

$$I(T) = S_0 \left[1 - \bar{A}(\text{cloud cover}) \right] \sin \chi_s$$
$$\bar{A} = \frac{A_{ice} \cdot \sigma_{clear} + A_{clouds} \cdot \sigma_{cloudy}}{\sigma_{Total}}$$
$$A_{\substack{ice \\ snow}} > A_{clouds}$$

Fig. 2. The albedo-polar cloud cover-temperature feedback loop. See Fig. 1 for explanation.

SEA ICE - OCEAN CIRCULATIONS - WINDS

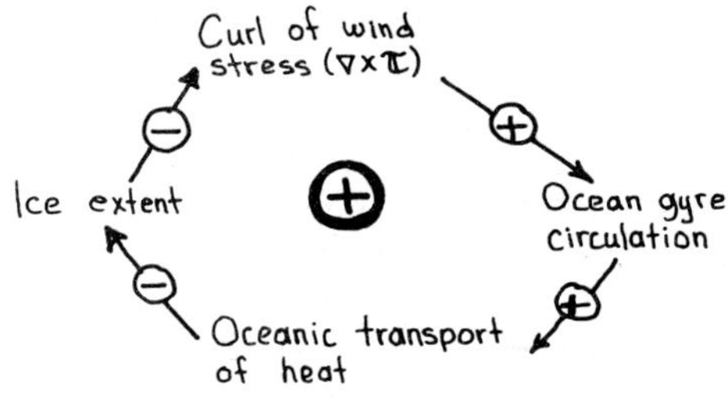

FIG. 3. The sea ice-ocean circulations-winds feedback loop.

section we will be able to distinguish between positive and negative loops by simply counting the number of negative links. An odd number of negative links, no matter how many links there are in the loop, will result in a negative loop, while an even number means that the loop is positive. We will not usually be able to distinguish between weakly positive (slightly damping) and strongly positive (amplifying) loops.

The student of feedback loops will recognize that this is a very simplified approach to the subject, and we intended it that way. The purpose is merely to distinguish positive and negative feedback loops in the climate system, even though most cannot yet be quantified. When we can quantify them better it should be possible to apply well known mathematical techniques, such as matrix algebra, to their evaluation.

3. Examples of polar feedback loops

Here we will resort to the shorthand symbolism described above, and the parameters and connecting processes in each loop will be presented in diagram form, along with a sketch that should convey the general idea of what is involved physically. (We have left the diagrams and sketches in the original home-made form to emphasize the tentative and somewhat intuitive nature of this approach.) It will be impossible to discuss each in detail, but the general message should be clear from the sketches.

None of these is truly original, since there are references in the literature to all of them. Some are well known to even the most casual student of climate theory (e.g., the polar ice-temperature-albedo effect)

while others have received little attention—and may, indeed, turn out to be relatively unimportant or even downright wrong. It is fair to say, though, that we cannot dismiss any of them at this time.

The albedo-polar ice cover-temperature loop (Fig. 1) is treated explicitly in all climate models that make any pretense to being complete, notably those of Sellers (1969; 1973) and Budyko (1969; 1972). It is generally considered to be *strongly* positive, and it is largely responsible for the sensitivity of these models to a "runaway polar cap," or an ice age induced by as little as a 1.5 to 2% decrease in solar input. Schneider and Gal-Chen (1973) have discussed the possible fallacy in this approach, and Schneider (1975) summarizes these points in a companion paper at this conference.

The albedo-cloud cover-temperature loop (Fig. 2) is negative in polar regions, where the albedo of the clouds is generally less than that of the underlying ice and snow, assuming that there are more clouds when the temperature falls (Schneider, 1972). In the case of air mass clouds (low stratus and stratocumulus) this negative temperature dependence of cloud cover may be reasonable, and recent tests at NCAR by Schneider and Washington (1972), using the NCAR general circulation model, show that this also appears to be the case at low and middle latitudes where

SEA ICE - AIR/SEA EXCHANGE - SURFACE LAYER

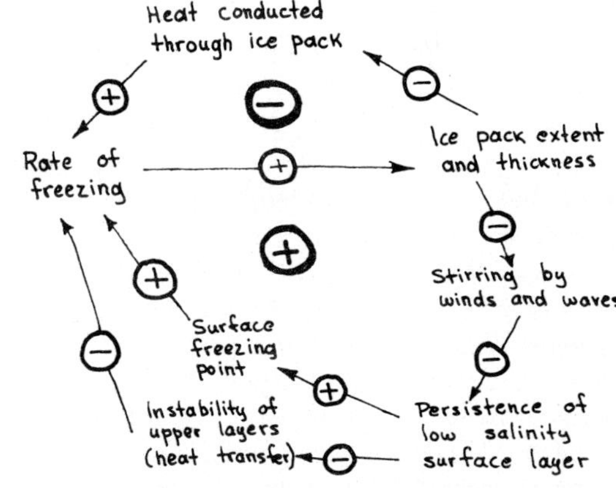

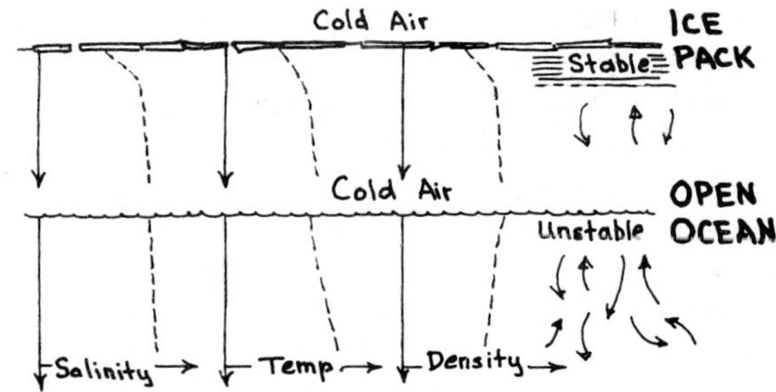

FIG. 4. The sea ice-air/sea exchange-surface layer of the water feedback loop.

Snowfall – Ice Cap Height

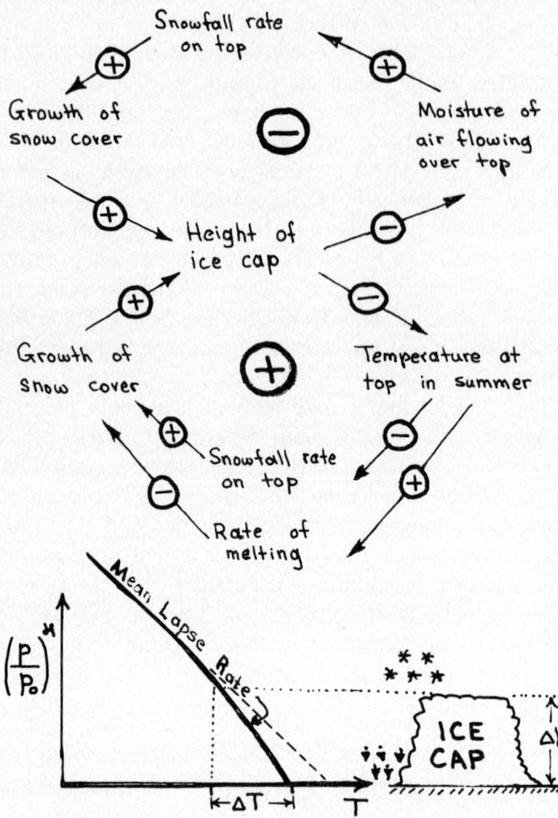

Fig. 5. The snowfall-ice cap height feedback loop

large-scale vertical motion or convection over the open ocean is the dominant cloud forming process. The net effect of this loop, *away from the poles* where the surface albedo is less than that of clouds, therefore appears to be positive and amplifying.

The sea ice-ocean circulation-winds loop (Fig. 3) depends on the inhibiting effect of ocean pack ice on the wind-driven ocean circulations, and this in turn reduces the meridional transport of heat by the major oceanic gyres. It is positive, but we cannot now say how strong it is.

Another point about ocean pack ice is that it tends to maintain itself in the face of fluctuations in mean temperature due to the layer of stable low-salinity water that it protects (a positive feedback), but also, as shown in Fig. 4, it has a self-limiting effect as it grows thicker due to the poor thermal conductivity of ice (Untersteiner and Maykut, 1971). The positive loop in this case predicts that sea ice will tend to persist, but once removed it will not reform until temperatures fall very low. This can be thought of as a "polar ice flip-flop" in the climate system, in analogy to a switch that is either on or off with no in-between position.

Fig. 5 is another case of a double loop, with a tendency to grow or disappear once perturbed past a certain point, and a self-limiting or stabilizing mechanism that comes into play as the altitude of the ice cap (Δh) gets several kilometers high. It is the positive, or reinforcing, aspect to the great ice caps of Greenland and the Antarctic that make off-hand statements about their rapid melting in the face of a global warming somewhat irresponsible. We need to know what the turn-over point is, at which the ice cap will disappear instead of grow.

A variation of this feedback loop (not reproduced here) contains the *area* of the ice-cover on land as well as its altitude, and has been referenced in connection with relatively short-term climatic anomalies and the growth of the ice caps on such "sensitive" areas as Baffin Island (Bradley and Miller, 1972). However, as Namias (1970) has pointed out, such anomalies are probably connected with larger-scale interactions (such as ocean surface temperature), and a relatively small region can only provide an additional push to a climatic perturbation that is initiated elsewhere.

We now come to one of the more celebrated and controversial of the polar feedback mechanisms, first proposed by Ewing and Donn (1956). The hypothesis,

Ewing–Donn Hypothesis

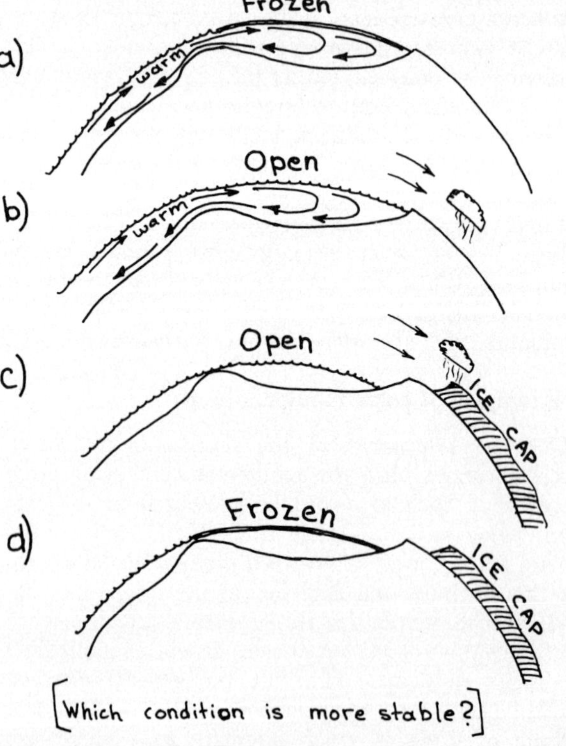

Fig. 6. A sketch of the main factors involved in the Ewing-Donn hypothesis.

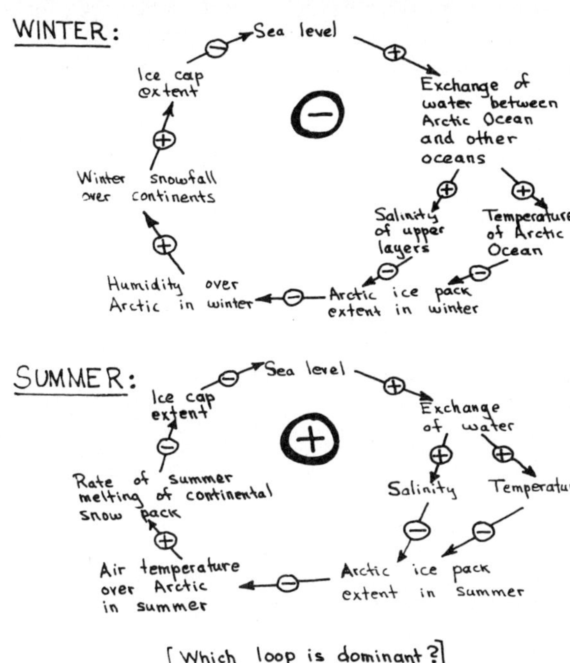

FIG. 7. The feedback loops for winter and summer that pertain to the Ewing-Donn hypothesis. The question is: Which loop is dominant?

outlined in Fig. 6, is that an open Arctic Ocean free of ice will cause more snowfall (in winter) around the ocean and begin to build up even larger permanent ice caps on the surrounding continents. The previous mechanism (Fig. 5) would come into play after a certain amount of continental ice accretion, and these ice caps once formed would grow until the ocean level fell by many hundreds of meters. This would cut off the warm Atlantic water that now enters the Arctic Ocean, through shallow passages, lowering the Arctic Ocean temperature until it froze over again. This would reduce the snowfall and the ice caps would start to shrink again. The feedback mechanisms involved are shown in schematic form in Fig. 7. The dominant loop for the oscillation to occur is the one that operates in winter; but in summer the extra warmth would work the other way and tend to reduce snow cover when the Arctic Ocean was ice free—and there are reasons to believe that it is the summer conditions that determine whether an ice cap will form and grow.

The Ewing-Donn hypothesis has been criticized on theoretical grounds and on the basis that there is counter evidence for there having been an open Arctic Ocean at any time during the last glaciation cycle, following the Eemian interglacial of about 100 to 200 thousand years before the present. Nevertheless, it is a hypothesis that continues to have great appeal and certainly cannot yet be dismissed.

The fact that the great ice caps of North America and northern Europe disappeared so rapidly about 10,000 years ago has led to considerable speculation about some mechanism that would come into play and drive them rapidly back once the ice caps reached a certain size. One hypothesis is shown in Fig. 8, and needs little further explanation. While it seems to have the right sign (negative) it is exceedingly hard to quantify, since we are just beginning to learn about the mechanisms of dust storms and dust transport, and how dust deposited on snow would affect its heat balance. The weakest link in the loop is probably the assumption that there will be a dry region at the equatorward edge of the ice cap, since one could argue that the storm track would pass along this zone and bring plenty of precipitation to maintain vegetation. Obviously this "weakest link" must be studied further.

Fig. 9 is a relatively straightforward mechanism, cited, for example, by Fletcher (1969), that contributes to the dramatic growth of the sea ice around the Antarctic each winter. The cooling of the low level air over the continent in winter results in a strong outward flow in the lower troposphere (katabatic winds), and this cold air flowing out over the marginal

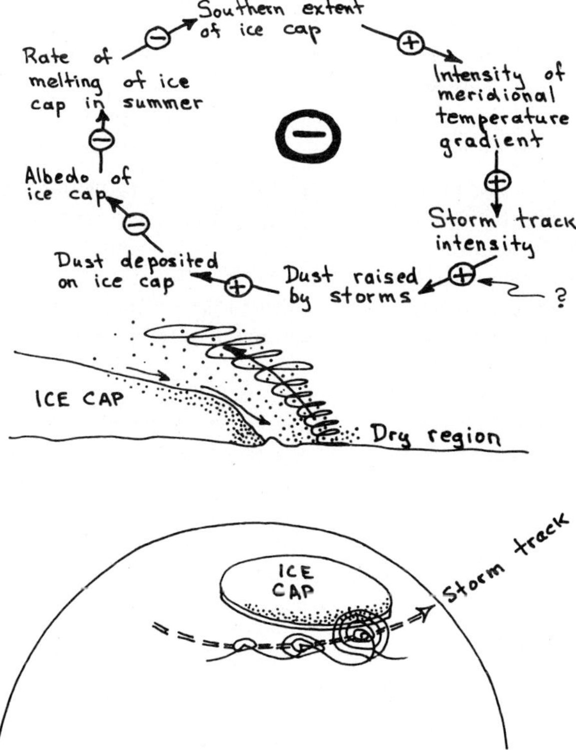

FIG. 8. The winds-dust-albedo of ice cap feedback loop. As explained in the text, there seem to be troubles with this one.

SEA ICE EXTENT-KATABATICS

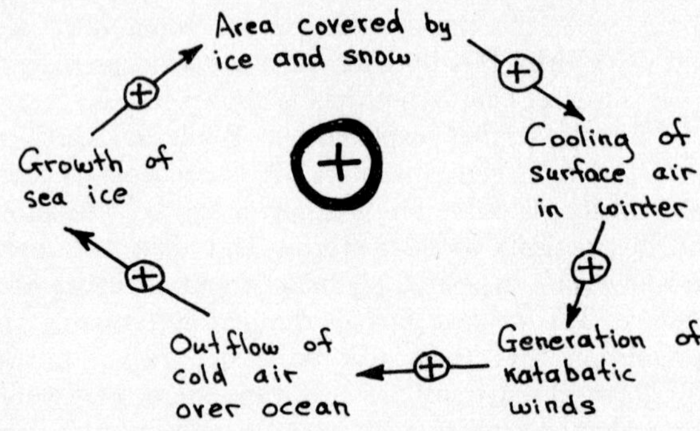

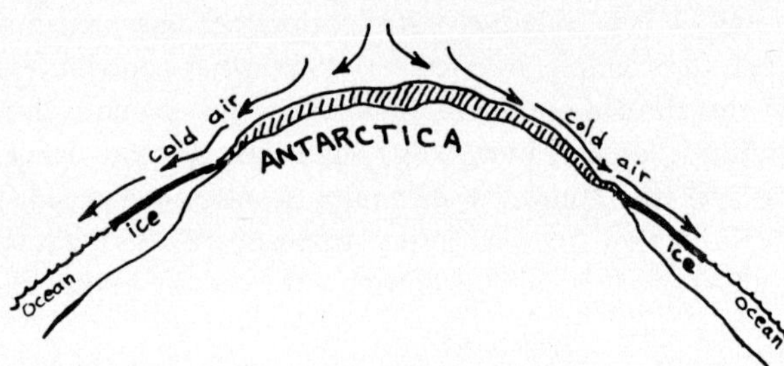

FIG. 9. The sea ice extent-katabatic wind feedback loop. This applies best to the Antarctic continent.

sea ice cools the surrounding ocean water and extends that sea ice still further.

4. Conclusions

The above has been a review of a collection of feedback mechanisms or "loops" that play some role in the climate system—or may have at some time in the past. We cannot be very precise about any of them at this time, yet it is clear that we cannot create adequate climate models without taking some of them into account quantitatively. Furthermore, one does not need to go far into the subject to see that these loops are by no means isolated, as we have shown them here, but linked with other loops to form a complex network. Indeed, we can safely predict that one climate model of the future will be in effect just such a network of feedback loops.

REFERENCES

Bradley, R. S., and G. H. Miller, 1972: Recent climatic change and increased glacierization in the eastern Canadian Arctic, *Nature*, **237**, 385–387.

Budyko, M. I., 1969: The effect of solar radiation variation on the climate of the earth, *Tellus*, **21**, 611–619.

Budyko, M. I., 1972: The future climate, *EOS*, **53**, 868–874.

Ewing, M., and W. L. Donn, 1956: A theory of ice ages, *Science*, **123**, 1061–1066; ibid., 1958: *Science*, **127**, 1159–1162.

Fletcher, J. O., 1969: Ice extent on the Southern Ocean and its relation to world climate, Rand Corp. RM-5793-NSF, Santa Monica, California.

Namias, J., 1970: Climatic anomaly over the United States during the 1960's, *Science*, **170**, 741–743.

Schneider, S. H., 1972: Cloudiness as a global climatic feedback mechanism: The effects on the radiation balance and surface temperature of variations in cloudiness, *J. Atmos. Sci.*, **29**, 1413–1422.

Schneider, S. H., 1975: Surface temperature-albedo coupling: Implications for climate stability, *Proc. 24th Alaskan Science Conference*, Fairbanks, Alaska.

Schneider, S. H., and T. Gal-Chen, 1973: Numerical experiments in climate stability, *J. Geophys. Res.*, **78**, 6182–6194.

Schneider, S. H., and W. W. Washington, 1973: Personal communication.

Schneider, S. H., and W. W. Kellogg, 1973: The chemical basis for climatic change, in *Chemistry of the Lower Atmosphere*, ed. by S. I. Rasool, Chapter 5, pp. 203–249, Plenum Press, N. Y. C.

Sellers, W. D., 1969: A global climatic model based on the energy balance of the earth-atmosphere system. *J. Appl. Met.*, **8**, 392–400.

Sellers, W. D., 1973: A new global climatic model, *J. Appl. Met.*, **12**, 241–254.

Study of Man's Impact on Climate (SMIC), 1971: *Inadvertent Climate Modification*, MIT Press, Cambridge, Mass.

Untersteiner, N., and G. A. Maykut, 1971: Some results from a time dependent, thermodynamic model of sea ice, *J. Geophys. Res.*, **76**, 1550–1575.

Ice Ages and Northern Forests

W. R. Schmitt, C. K. Stidd, and J. D. Isaacs

University of California, San Diego, California

Abstract

Some investigators see the world's climate as being in precarious balance between powerful cooling and warming trends. Large deviations from local conditions, natural or artificial, probably will be considered undesirable. Thus large-scale climate management soon may be taken under consideration.

One mechanism by which climate may be modified is the albedo change occasioned by changes in vegetation cover. This paper examines the climatic effectiveness of forest removal. Worldwide cooling resulting from this alone apparently is insufficient for ice age causation, now and in the past, but possibly is sufficient to modulate climatic changes originating from other sources.

1. Introduction

Students of climatic change are predicting an end to the present interglacial (Kukla *et al.*, 1972). They describe the similarities of present conditions to those of the last interglacial, and they discuss a number of mechanisms for change. The available evidence does not permit a firm ranking of the importance of these mechanisms, but there is majority agreement on: the uniqueness and precariousness of the climate of the last several millenia; the environmental hazards posed by man's quest to utilize global resources in industry and food production; and the desirability of organizing interdisciplinary research and international programs on these climatological problems. It is in this context that we offer the following considerations for discussion.

2. The mechanism

Kukla and Kukla (1972) point out the possibility that interannual changes in snow and pack-ice cover alter the earth's energy budget more powefully than could any expected extraterrestrial mechanism by virtue of the following feedback: as ice and snow advance, Earth's albedo increases, with a resulting decrease in solar heat absorption and an ever more favorable condition for continued ice and snow advance.

This feedback cycle could perhaps be set in motion by a transient albedo increase, as for example by the removal of northern evergreen forests which would lead to a sharp reflectivity increase in winter and a moderate one in summer. Removal could either be advertent, as in the clearing for cultivation or logging, or it could be inadvertent, as in natural and accidental forest fires. How strongly could such changes influence the global heat budget?

3. Calculation of effect

Budyko (1969) estimates that a 1.6% reduction in solar radiation would suffice to trigger an ice advance to a mean latitude of 50°N, when it would approach the equator through self-development without further radiation decrease. This estimate is independently confirmed by Sellers (1969) using a climatic model based on energy balance and exchange. We are inclined to the opinion that the globe's climate is not that unstable, rather that a steeper temperature gradient equator-to-pole would accelerate the general circulation of the atmosphere *and oceans* with consequent greater mixing and greater heat transfer. Although the effects of the oceans may exacerbate the formation of glaciers through increased high-latitude cloud cover and precipitation, they probably also limit the glaciers' low-latitude advance.

While heat transfer by the oceans was neglected by Budyko and Sellers, it would be instructive to see by how much, in comparison to the 1.6% critical level, absorbed radiation would be lessened if all evergreen and mixed mid-latitude forests were removed in some manner and replaced by grass or crop land.

This effect would be stronger in the northern hemisphere than in the southern since 57% of the snow belt area (40°–65° of latitude) are land in the northern versus only 1.8% in the southern hemisphere (Kukla and Kukla, 1972). Thermally the hemispheres are relatively independent, and since we are estimating a radiation reduction that can be compared to Budyko's limiting value, we will follow his procedure and restrict our computation to the northern half of the globe.

For convenience we take the snow belt as 40–70°N and divide it into 10° latitude zones. Column 4 in Table 1 gives the extent of evergreen and mixed forests

TABLE 1. Solar radiation incident on Northern Hemisphere evergreen mid-latitude forests.

1 Zone latitude ϕ	2 Proportional area	3 Forested portion	4 Proportion in forest $A_f(\phi)$	5 Summer rad. share $r_s(\phi)$	6 Proportion summer rad. $R_s(\phi)$	7 Winter rad. share $r_w(\phi)$	8 Proportion winter rad. $R_w(\phi)$
60–70	0.072	0.200	0.0144	0.928	0.0137	0.127	0.00183
50–60	0.100	0.328	0.0328	0.996	0.0327	0.403	0.0132
40–50	0.124	0.161	0.0200	1.030	0.0206	0.658	0.0132
Totals					0.0670		0.0282
Hemispheric average radiation Ly/day				883		471	

Column 2 is the proportion of the total area of the Northern Hemisphere which lies in the indicated 10° zone of latitude.
Column 3 is the forested protion of the total area of each zone (from Goode's World Atlas).
Column 4 (product of columns 2 and 3) is the forested portion of the Northern Hemisphere.
Column 5 is the summer radiation in the zone divided by the hemispheric summer average.
Column 6 (product of columns 4 and 5) is the proportion of the total hemispheric summer radiation falling on the forest.
Co.umn 7 is the winter radiation in the zone divided by the hemispheric winter average.
Column 8 (product of columns 4 and 7) is the proportion of the total hemispheric winter radiation falling on the forest.

within these zones (from Goode's World Atlas). Columns 5 through 8 determine the proportion of the hemisphere's insolation that these forests receive in summer and in winter, using the relationship

$$R_{s/w}(\phi) = r_{s/w}(\phi) A_f(\phi)$$

$$= A_f(\phi) Q_e(\phi) \sum_{5°}^{85°} \cos(\phi) / \sum_{5°}^{85°} Q_e(\phi) \cos(\phi)$$

where

$R_{s/w}(\phi)$ is the zonal forest's proportion of the full hemispheric radiation in summer or winter;

$r_{s/w}(\phi)$ is a zone's share of the hemisphere's solar radiation (outside the atmosphere) in summer or winter;

$A_f(\phi)$ is the areal portion of the northern hemisphere in evergreen and mixed forest; and

$Q_e(\phi)$ is the solar radiation (outside the atmosphere) on a horizontal surface at latitude ϕ (Fritz, 1951). May 10 and Nov. 10 are taken to represent summer and winter average intensities.

We assume that no change in the radiative properties of the atmosphere accompany the surface change, although albedo may influence moisture levels and cloudiness. Hence, the sums of columns 6 and 8 are multiplied only by the relative decrease in absorption due to surface albedo increase. In summer, these forests absorb about 85% of incident radiation compared to 75% for grass or crops (and less for bare soil); in winter an 80% forest absorptivity would be cut at least in half, to 40%, by tree removal and resulting snow fields.

We obtain a decrease of radiation absorption in summer of

$$0.0670 \times \frac{0.85 - 0.75}{0.85} = 0.8\%,$$

and a decrease in winter of

$$0.0282 \times \frac{0.8 - 0.4}{0.8} = 1.4\%,$$

yielding a weighted annual average of 1.0%.

This magnitude of the effect of total forest removal thus appears to be of the same order as Budyko's 1.6% critical level of radiation reduction. Both our calculations and Budyko's model are however only rough approximations of nature's complex reactions to some powerful transient event. If we, for instance, included the secondary effect of the lingering spring snow cover on the resultant open areas, the agreement would be even closer. Also, subtle climate-dependent changes like deciduous trees succeeding coniferous ones, causing similar absorptivity reduction, cannot *a priori* be ignored.

4. Past and present implications

The calculation, though, does not clearly support the possibility that forest destruction may have been the primary cause of ice age initiation. It is unlikely that a total burn-off of the mid-latitude forests could occur. Droughts that might promote this are limited in extent and duration and could not simultaneously or within a few years envelop all of the areas in question. Forest removal through man's intervention, either by active clearing for timber and crops or by passive disappearance from overgrazing, affects only a relatively small proportion of these forests; man-made removal, also, has occurred during the warmer period of the present interglacial and no record of parallel cooling has been revealed.

The possibility remains, however, that forest removal might modulate more powerful climatic agents or trends. Kukla and Kukla (1972) have introduced an insolation chronology based on astronomic factors and the Milankovitch theory. In it, positive insolation regimes, PIR, (progressively increasing winter insolation in the northern hemisphere) alternate, in variable cycles averaging approximately 21,000 years in length, with negative insolation regimes, NIR, (progressively decreasing winter insolation). For the past 150,000 years no NIR phase corresponds to a generally warm period. These authors state that Earth in 1950 entered an NIR phase that will last 8,000 years. What we do with our snow-belt forests during this period of cooling might have important climatic consequences.

Other trends of climatological significance are apparent. Carbon dioxide is entering the atmosphere at an increasing rate, as are aerosols; these agents tend to counteract each other in influencing the globe's thermal budget. However, by the burning of fossil fuels and now by the use of atomic energy, man is producing increasing total amounts of heat. In terms of the sun's absorbed heat of 1.3×10^{17} watts, present world heat production is a negligible 7×10^{12} watts (Roberts, 1973, assuming a world: US ratio of 3:1); it may, however, rise to one percent or more of the sun's absorbed heat within one hundred years, given growth rates of power production that could gradually recede from the present 8% per annum (Cook, 1973). This can be compared with Budyko's 1.6% freeze limit, and Budyko (1972) in fact predicts that by 2050 AD man-made heat will have melted the north polar ice pack.

5. Conclusions

It would seem that artificial warming might soon override any cooling that could be generated by forest removal. Yet long-range projections have always been risky and are particularly risky now that environmental and resource limitations can no longer be ignored. Also, though weather and climate may leave much to be desired in many parts of the world, natural and/or willful changes are likely to be resisted since they often are accompanied by unpredictable and undesirable changes elsewhere. We may thus see the gradual development of climate modification techniques for the purpose of fine-tuning world climate to a narrow range of fluctuation. Manipulating the globe's albedo by control of forests could be one of the tools.

REFERENCES

Budyko, M. I., 1969: The effect of solar radiation variations on the climate of the earth. *Tellus*, **31**(5), 611–617.

Budyko, M. I., 1972: The future climate. *EOS*, **53**(10), 868–874.

Cook, C. S., 1973: Energy: planning for the future. *Amer. Sci.*, **61**, 61–65.

Fritz, S., 1951: Solar radiant energy and its modification by earth and its atmosphere, in *Compendium of Meteorology*. (T. F. Malone, Ed.), Am. Meteor. Soc.

Goode's World Atlas. 1964. Rand McNally.

Kukla, G. J., and H. J. Kukla, 1972: Insolation regime of interglacials. *Quaternary Research*, **2**, 412–424.

Kukla, G. J., R. K. Matthews and J. M. Mitchell, 1972: The end of the present interglacial. *Quaternary Research*, **2**, 261–269.

Roberts, R., 1973: Energy sources and conversion techniques. *Amer. Sci.*, **61**, 66–67.

Sellers, W. D., 1969: A global climatic model based on the energy balance of the earth atmosphere system. *J. Applied Meteorol.*, **8**(3), 392–400.

On Climatic Control by the Waters of the Gulf of Alaska

THOMAS C. ROYER

Institute of Marine Science, University of Alaska

Abstract

Semipermanent centers of action in the atmosphere exert considerable influence over the total atmospheric circulation pattern. Processes altering these centers will therefore affect general atmospheric circulation. Since strong correlations exist between large scale positive sea surface temperature anomalies and negative anomalies in atmospheric pressure above the sea surface, relatively warm ocean temperatures will increase the intensity and alter the position of the overlying low pressure system. The response of the Aleutian Low to the positive sea surface temperature anomaly in the Gulf of Alaska during the 1957–1958 winter with accompanying large scale atmospheric changes is an example of this interrelationship. From seasonal oceanographic data for the Gulf of Alaska during 1970–1972, it was found that the shorter term, seasonal variations in sea surface temperature do not have a significant influence on the seasonal atmospheric circulation. There is, however, significant effect by the seasonal atmospheric circulation on the water temperature structure in the Gulf of Alaska. Winter low pressure systems cause coastal convergence of surface waters with downwelling near the coast and upwelling in the Alaskan Gyre. The opposite effects occur in summer. Local temperature inversions in the water column, in concert with the upwelling, can maintain or increase the air-sea temperature difference, though the influence is believed to be small.

1. Introduction

Changes in atmospheric circulation in the region of the Gulf of Alaska have been shown to have far reaching atmospheric effects via teleconnections. In a discussion of the semipermanent centers of action in the atmosphere and their control of total atmospheric circulation, Rossby (1939) cited the Aleutian Low as one of these semipermanent centers of atmospheric action. It was established that the position of the Aleutian Low was well correlated with the intensity of the zonal circulation at that latitude over the entire hemisphere. In a more recent work, Bjerknes (1966) found that during the 1956–7 winter, weaker than usual westerlies were present over the eastern Pacific corresponding to a positive surface pressure anomaly in an area south of Alaska. He postulated that the moderately negative anomaly over Hudson Bay and the strongly negative anomaly in the Icelandic Low that year were related to the previously mentioned positive anomaly via teleconnections. In the following winter (1957–8) a strong negative surface pressure anomaly persisted over the entire quadrant of the hemisphere from 180°W to 90°W. The usual downstream short wave system was replaced by a long wave system with a length of about 180°. The Icelandic Low was weakened via teleconnections and occupied a position east of Iceland rather than its typical position southwest of the island. This change in the position of the low pressure system resulted in a greater advection of arctic air over the European continent, and consequently a more severe winter.

Correlations have been established between changes in this large scale atmospheric circulation and variations in sea surface temperature beneath the atmospheric system. Both Bjerknes (1966) and Namias (1959) have linked large scale positive anomalies in sea surface temperature with negative sea level pressure anomalies. These deviations are based on deviations from long term monthly means. The negative pressure anomalies are created by greater than normal atmospheric warming, causing a surface atmospheric convergence. The atmospheric warming is caused by the high sensible heat transfer due to the anomalously warm sea surface temperatures. Bjerknes (1966) reported that the strong negative surface pressure during the 1957–58 winter was accompanied by anomalous warming of the North Pacific surface waters. Conversely, negative anomalies in sea surface temperature, indicating cold water, are well correlated with positive anomalies in sea level pressure (Namias, 1969).

Using the above results concerning large scale ocean-atmosphere processes, we wish now to examine the shorter term, seasonal changes in these systems. Examination of these seasonal processes is now possible with the acquisition of the first seasonal hydrographic data for the Gulf of Alaska. Specifically, can variations in the sea level pressure be related to changes in sea surface temperature on a seasonal basis? Such a comparison is analogous to the large scale correlation between sea surface temperature and sea level pressure anomalies on an annual basis. In each of these situ-

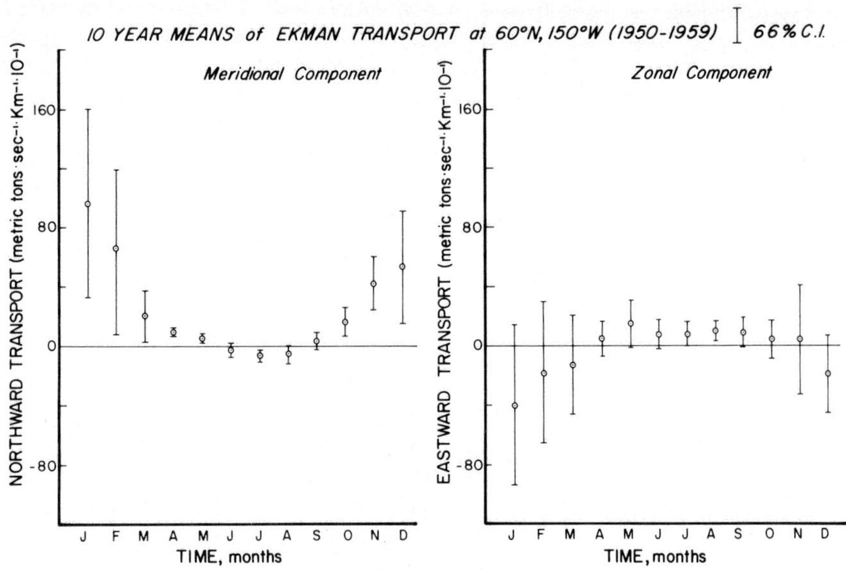

FIG. 1. Monthly mean Ekman transport at 60°N, 150°W (1950–1959) as determined
from the Fofonoff computations (Fofonoff and Dobson, 1963).

ations the control of the atmospheric circulation is dependent upon the ability of the ocean to supply energy to the atmosphere. This energy transfer is dependent on the sea surface temperature along with other factors.

2. Seasonal variations

The seasonal variation in atmospheric pressure over the Gulf of Alaska results in a change of the surface winds on a seasonal basis. These winds cause the Ekman transport to change seasonally. Since the atmospheric and ocean surface circulation are linked through the Ekman transport, it is this quantity that will be used to describe the seasonal circulation patterns. The Ekman transports have been calculated by Fofonoff and Dobson (1963) for the period 1950–1959 and monthly mean values have been established on 5° grid squares. These transports were obtained from

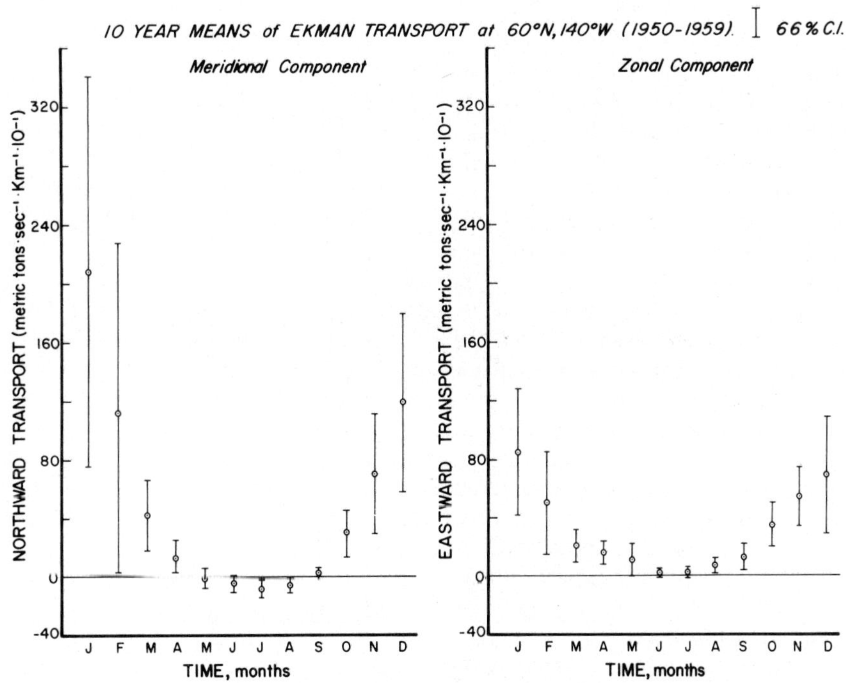

FIG. 2. Monthly mean Ekman transport at 60°N, 140°W (1950–1959) as determined
from the Fofonoff computations (Fofonoff and Dobson, 1963).

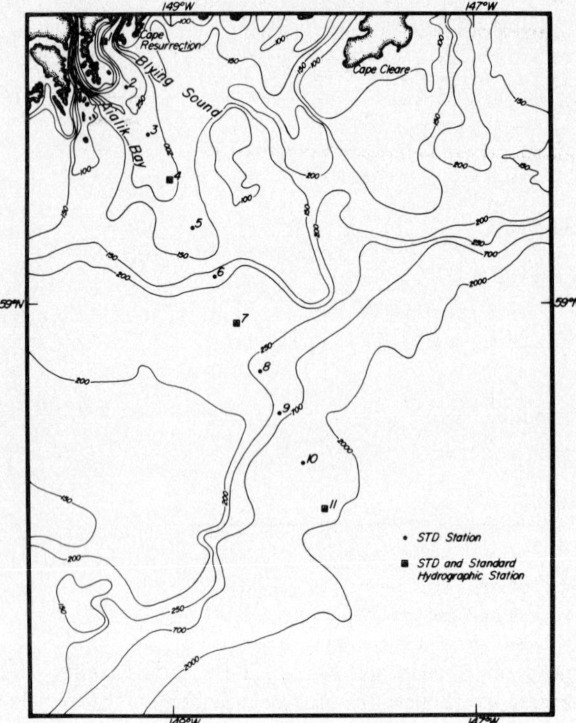

FIG. 3. Station positions for the series of R/V ACONA cruises—December 1970 through October 1972. (Depths in meters)

wind stress data calculated from the geostrophic winds, which were determined from monthly averaged sea level pressures. The mean monthly Ekman transports for 1950–1959 and their 66% confidence intervals are illustrated in Figs. 1 and 2. Fig. 1 represents conditions at the northwest corner of the Gulf of Alaska (60°N, 150°W) and Fig. 2 represents conditions at the northeast corner of the Gulf of Alaska (60°N, 140°W). Intense northward meridional Ekman transport from strong easterly winds occurs throughout the winter months. This transport shifts to weak, occasionally southward transport in the summer as a consequence of the light, variable summer winds. The zonal Ekman transports display a similar seasonal reversal with westward winter transports at 60°N, 150°W and eastward winter transports at 60°N, 140°W. This shift in wind regime over the Gulf of Alaska is a consequence of the change in the atmospheric pressure system from intense low pressure activity in winter to a weak high pressure system in summer.

Does this variability in the atmospheric circulation depend in large measure on the seasonal variations in the sea surface temperatures? Ideally, to answer this question the records of the seasonal variations in sea surface temperature in the Gulf of Alaska from 1950–1959 should be examined. Unfortunately, though that period of time contains the majority of oceanographic data for the Gulf of Alaska, there are not enough measurements to establish seasonal variations. Instead,

attention will be directed to some recent, closely sampled data gathered on the northern shelf of the Gulf from December 1970 through October 1972. During this period, a series of eight oceanographic cruises were conducted by the Institute of Marine Science, University of Alaska for the purpose of gathering the first seasonal hydrographic data for this region. The locations of the station positions are shown in Fig. 3. The sampling time intervals were irregular due to weather and ship scheduling, and not all stations were occupied on each cruise as a result of high sea states. Complete hydrographic data consisting of temperature, salinity and dissolved oxygen were taken. The time distribution of water temperature at station 1 (nearest to the coastline) are presented in Fig. 4 for the period December 1970–October 1972. The maximum sea surface temperatures at this location were found in mid to late summer and the temperature was greatest (>12 C) in July 1971. The minimum sea surface temperatures occurred in spring (March–April) with a value of less than 2 C. Therefore, the maximum sea surface temperature is not in phase with the maximum low pressure atmospheric activity but is instead 5–6 months in advance. The meridional and zonal Ekman transports for this region during the period of investigation are displayed in Figs. 5 and 6.

Apparently, the local sea surface temperature alone does not exhibit extensive control over the seasonal atmospheric circulation in the Gulf of Alaska. Other factors must be of greater importance in the control

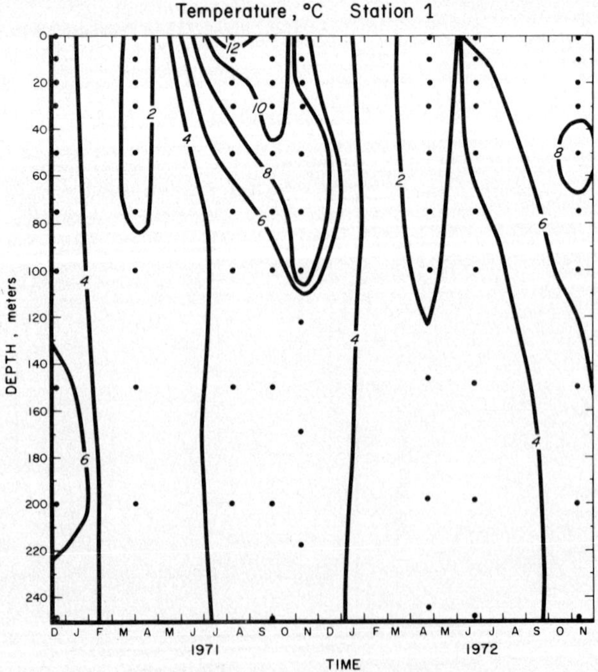

FIG. 4. Temperature vs. depth time series for station 1 from December 1970 to October 1972.

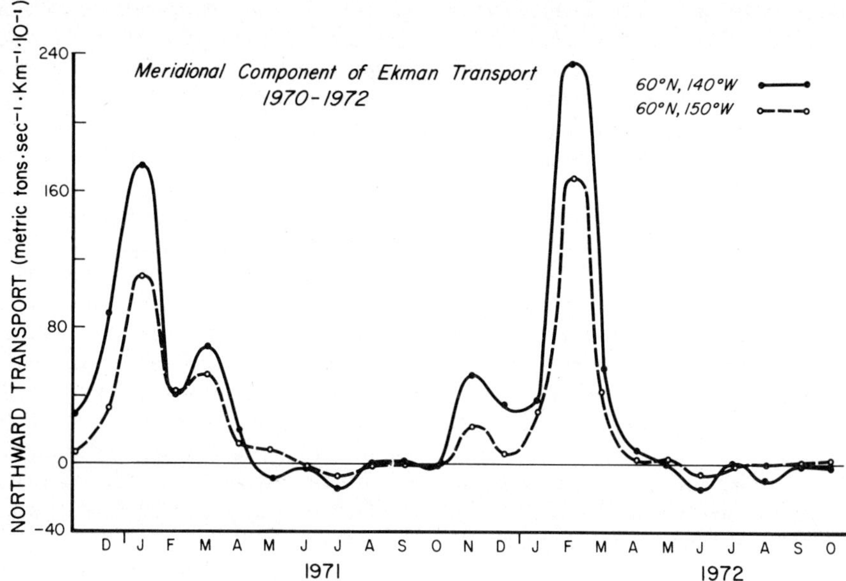

FIG. 5. Meridional component of Ekman transport as determined from the Fofonoff computations for December 1970–October 1972 at 60°N, 140°W and 60°N, 150°W. (Wickett and Thomson, 1971; Wickett, 1972a, 1972b).

of the seasonal energy transfer from ocean to atmosphere. Those factors affecting this transfer are air-sea temperature differences, relative humidity of the air and the wind speed. It is beyond the scope of this paper to evaluate these other influences, however, Winston (1955) has found that the flow of cold, dry arctic air over the waters of the Gulf of Alaska can cause heat transfers of up to 2000 langleys/day. Since the seasonal variations in air temperature are more than twice the same variations in water temperature, it is reasonable to assume that the air-sea temperature difference is more highly dependent on air properties then local water properties.

Though the seasonal atmospheric changes cannot be attributed to the seasonal variation in water temperature in the Gulf of Alaska, some changes in the water temperature structure are the result of changes in the atmospheric circulation. The seasonal changes in the Ekman transport cause changes in the water structure on the shelf region. This is the direct result of advection of surface waters either toward or away from the coastline, depending on the time of year. In winter, the dominance of low pressure systems over the Gulf of Alaska causes northward surface transport and a convergence at the coastline. This, in effect, cools the entire water column at station 1 in the winter. Clearly, convective processes could not account for a decrease in temperature of the entire water column since the column retains some temperature structure below the isothermal mixed layer. The surface convergence causes downwelling which forces the bottom water off the shelf and thus winter-cooled surface water covers the

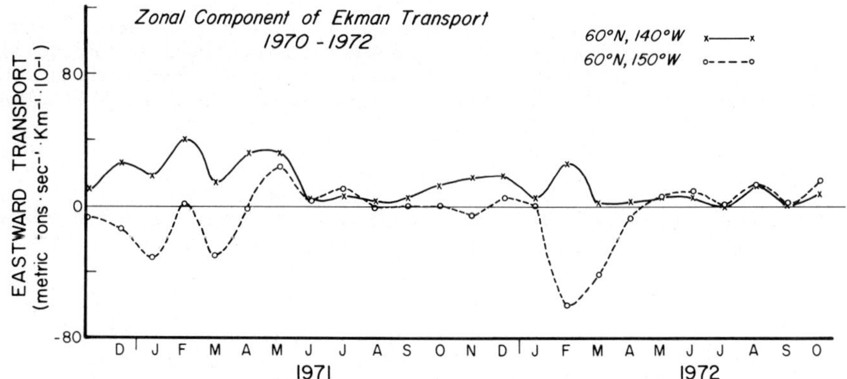

FIG. 6. Zonal component of Ekman transport as determined from the Fofonoff computations for December 1970–October 1972 at 60°N, 140°W and 60°N, 150°W. (Wickett and Thomson, 1971; Wickett, 1972a, 1972b).

entire shelf. Simultaneously, a surface divergence is created in the central part of the Gulf of Alaska gyre, causing upwelling there. Under summer conditions, the slight reversal in the atmospheric conditions will cause a reversal in the water circulation, that is, summer coastal upwelling and deep water downwelling.

The winter downwelling can be observed in Figure 4. Comparing the calculated meridional Ekman transport with oceanographic data, one can see that the increased Ekman transport in February 1972 was accompanied by an increased depth penetration of the 2 C isotherm relative to the previous year. This may simply be a fortuitous circumstance. A longer time series is required before definite conclusions can be drawn on the dependence of temperature structure on atmospheric circulation.

It is of interest to consider the consequences of the temperature structure in the North Pacific on the seasonal circulation in the surface waters. Throughout most of the world's oceans, the water temperature decreases with increasing depth. In the Gulf of Alaska, however, temperature inversions are common in fall and winter. Without a temperature inversion, the surface water divergence would cause colder water to upwell in the region of the divergence. This colder water would decrease the air-sea temperature difference, reducing the energy transfer which was originally supplying energy to the cyclonic activity. Therefore without a temperature inversion, cyclogenesis is self limiting. The same atmospheric situation with a temperature inversion in the water column is no longer self limiting It is possible actually to increase the air-sea temperature difference and increase the rate of energy transfer to the atmosphere with upwelling. Such conditions could exist in the Gulf of Alaska in fall and winter. Our data do not allow us to examine seasonal changes in the horizontal patterns of sea-surface temperature on a spatial scale comparable with that of the major atmospheric features, so we cannot state whether the situation described above leads to a local warm pool in the Gulf of Alaska during the winter.

3. Conclusion

The low pressure atmospheric system located over the Gulf of Alaska during much of the winter is known to influence weather patterns over the entire hemisphere via teleconnections. On a large scale, anomalies in sea surface temperature cause anomalies in sea level pressure of the atmosphere above, with warm sea surface temperatures causing negative pressure anomalies and the reverse for cold sea surfaces. It appears that on a smaller scale, seasonal basis, the seasonal variations in sea surface temperatures in the Gulf of Alaska do not have a significant influence on the atmospheric circulation. The Ekman transports in the region do alter the water temperature structure on a seasonal scale, with coastal winter convergences and slight summer divergences. The central portion of the Alaskan Gyre will experience the opposite effects. These seasonal effects coupled with a temperature inversion can lead to a situation where a surface divergence and accompanying upwelling can maintain or increase the sea surface temperature. The parameters of air temperature and humidity and wind speed need to be evaluated more carefully before the relative importance of all the air-sea parameters over the Gulf of Alaska can be determined.

Acknowledgments. Appreciation is extended to all those persons assisting in the data gathering phase of this study, especially Captain K. Turner and the crew of the R/V ACONA. This work was supported by the Office of Naval Research under contract N00014-67-A-0314-0002.

REFERENCES

Bjerknes, J. 1966. A possible response of the atmospheric Hadley circulation to the equatorial anomalies of ocean temperature. *Tellus*, **18**, 4, 820–829.

Fofonoff, N. P., and F. W. Dobson. 1963. Transport computations for the North Pacific Ocean 1950–1959, 10 year means and standard deviations by months, wind stress and vertical velocity annual means 1955–1960. *Fisheries Res. Bd. Canada.* Manuscript Report Series No. 166. 179 pp.

Namias, J. 1959. Recent seasonal interactions between North Pacific waters and the overlaying atmospheric circulation. *J. Geop. Res.*, **64**, 631–646.

Namias, J. 1969. Seasonal interactions between the North Pacific Ocean and the atmosphere during the 1960's. *Monthly Wea. Rev.*, **97**, 3, 1973–92.

Rossby, C. G. 1939. Relation between variations in the intensity of the zonal circulation of the atmosphere and the displacements of the semipermanent centers of action. *J. Mar. Res.*, **2**, 1, 38–55.

Wickett, W. P. 1972a. North Pacific Transport 1971. *Fisheries Res. Bd. Canada.* Unpublished manuscript.

Wickett, W. P. 1972b. Meridional and zonal components of Ekman transport, Jan.–Oct. 1972. *Fisheries Res. Bd. Canada.* Unpublished manuscript.

Wickett, W. P., and J. A. Thomson. 1971. Transport computations for the North Pacific Ocean, 1970. *Fisheries Res. Bd. Canada.* Tech. Report 238. 104 pp.

Winston, J. 1955. Physical aspects of rapid cyclogenesis in the Gulf of Alaska. *Tellus*, **1**, 4, 481–500.

Atmospheric Variability and Climatic Modelling

ELMAR R. REITER

Dept. of Atmospheric Science, Colorado State University, Ft. Collins, Colorado 80521

Abstract

Some of the economic effects of interannual atmospheric variability are pointed out. Examples of parameters that vary interannually on a hemispheric basis are given in the form of cold-air extent over the north polar region during winter, the stratospheric polar vortex of March at the 10-mb surface, and monthly mean vorticity and standard deviations of vorticity at 300 mb.

1. Introduction

Experience tells us that the atmosphere possesses a large degree of variability at all scales up to several years of "periodicity." This is demonstrated in Fig. 1 which contains the kinetic energy spectrum of E–W wind component observations in the free atmosphere and in an Eulerian reference frame according to Vinnichenko and Dutton (1969). As we can see from this diagram, there is an energy peak at frequencies corresponding to the seasonal variability of the atmosphere (one year periodicity). Beyond this point the energy spectrum falls off, reaching a minimum near two years. (The biennial wind oscillation of the tropics was not considered in this diagram. If it had been, it would have had a strong effect on the shape of the spectrum curve.) We do know, however, that, at least on a regional basis, the behavior of the atmosphere varies considerably from one season in one year to the same season in another year. We experience, for instance, cold or warm winters, wet or dry summers, early or late springs, etc. None of the present climatic "models" are fine-tuned to a degree that elevates this natural variability of the atmosphere on time scales slightly beyond the seasonal forcing cycle above the noise level of the model. With this deficiency in mind we are raising the following questions:

(1) Are there atmospheric parameters which vary *significantly* on a *hemispheric* rather than on a *regional* basis, so that fine-tuning of climatic models to accomodate such variability is warranted?

(2) If such hemispheric interannual changes are detected, can they be traced to "forcing functions" or "forcing fields" in the earth-ocean-cryosphere-atmosphere system?

(3) What is the economic impact of atmospheric variability?

This paper presents a very preliminary survey of possible answers to these questions. For a proper motivation of this investigation we will reverse the logical order of these three questions.

2. Economic impact of atmospheric variability

In Fig. 1 we have indicated dollar values of certain "disasters." (Values were taken from Maunder, 1970. They constitute extreme rather than average values.) We detect from the few data points supplied here a more or less exponential increase in the potential loss factor with the time and/or space scale of the phenomenon. The "spectrum of potential economic loss" shows a gap between tornadoes and hail storms. Since we have chosen to attribute the phenomena of

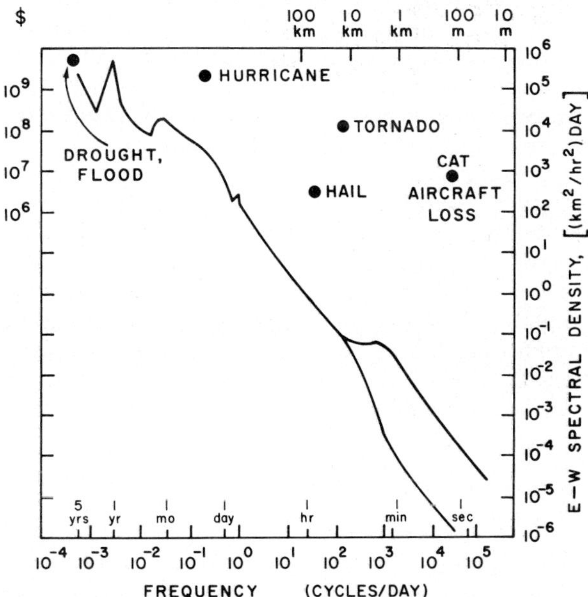

FIG. 1. Spectrum of the kinetic energy of the W-E wind component (after Vinnichenko and Dutton, 1969), units of (Km²/hr²) Day labelled on the right side of diagram, and approximate dollar values of weather-related disasters (after Maunder, 1970), labelled on left side of diagram.

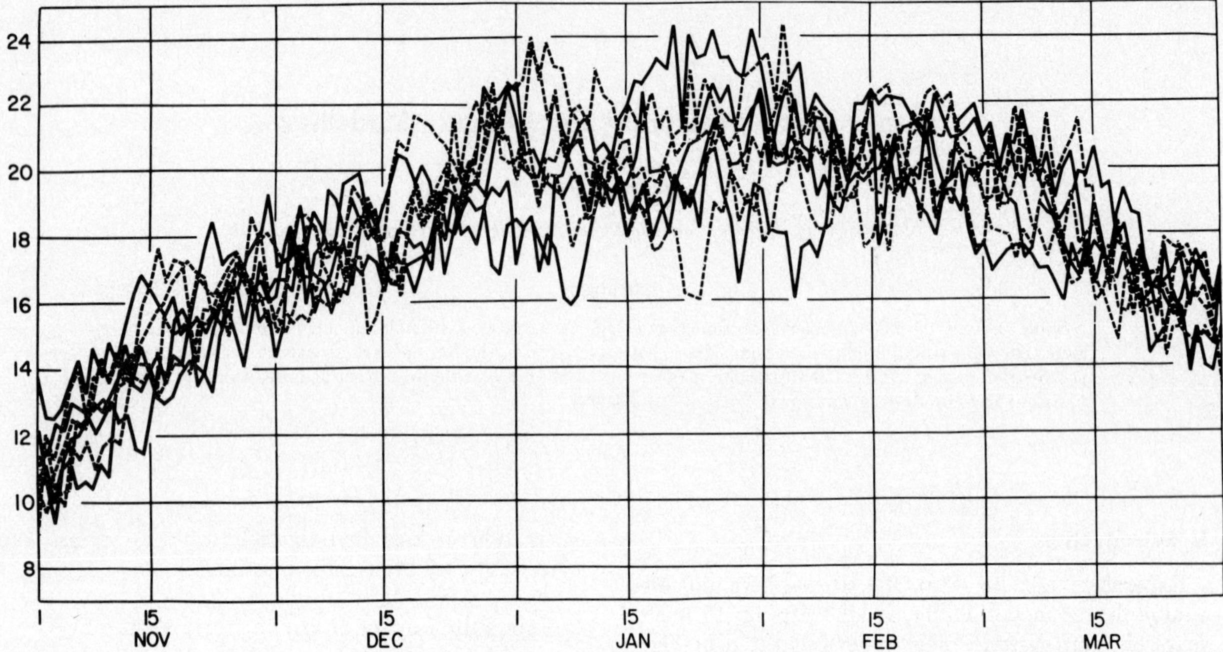

FIG. 2. Areal extent of cold polar air inside the −30°C isotherm at the 500-mb surface as a function of time, for the cold seasons between 1 November 1953 and 31 March 1961. (From Reiter and Macdonald, *Archives of Meteor. Geophys., Bioclim., Ser. A*, **22**: 147, 1973).

droughts and floods to scales beyond the seasonal cycle, there also is a gap in the "economic loss spectrum" at scales of one year. We can justify this as follows: "Normal" seasonal behavior is the fundamental basis of economic planning: Winters in middle and high latitudes require heating fuel, springs bring on the planting season, etc. It is the *abnormality* of certain seasons that spell disaster: above-normal thaw or large-scale precipitation yield brings about widespread floods; below-normal winter temperatures over a large region may cause fuel oil shortages, etc. Abnormal seasonal behavior, however, is measured in terms of *interannual variability* when it comes to estimating its economic effects, rather than in terms of the few weeks or months of duration (time scale ≪1 year) of the disastrous phenomenon. We may, thus, conclude that the interannual variability of the atmosphere has an economic impact that exceeds by far the impact of the "normal," hence planned-for, seasonal variability. The economic impact is accentuated if certain trends in weather patterns of one season extend over more than just one "abnormal" year. As examples we may quote the dust-bowl years in the American West, or the recent drought in a wide belt extending along the southern border of the Sahara. Such "disasters" easily escalate into sizeable percentages of the Gross National Product of the afflicted country.

From the foregoing discussion it appears that the economic impact of interannual atmospheric variability justifies a major effort in increasing our understanding of this variability.

3. Cause-effect relationships through forcing functions

According to Lorenz (1968) we do not know at this point whether the atmosphere—at time scales of more than one year—behaves as a "transitive" system that arrives at a certain state *without* "remembering" the initial conditions, or whether it is an "intransitive" system whose state is determined by the initial conditions. Chances are, that within the time scales in question the atmosphere is "almost-intransitive." This would mean that at the scale of interannual variability there still are certain effects of initial conditions, or forcing functions, but these effects are buried under a layer of "transitive" noise which is independent of these functions. It will take a major research effort to determine the extent of "intransitivity" in the atmosphere at scales of two or more years. If a certain amount of "memory" for initial forcing functions can be detected at all in the atmosphere, seasonal weather-trend prediction may receive a new impetus.

4. Interannual variability of the atmosphere on a hemispheric scale

Fig. 2 shows on an arbitrary scale (ordinate) the areal extent of polar cold air inside the −30 C isotherm

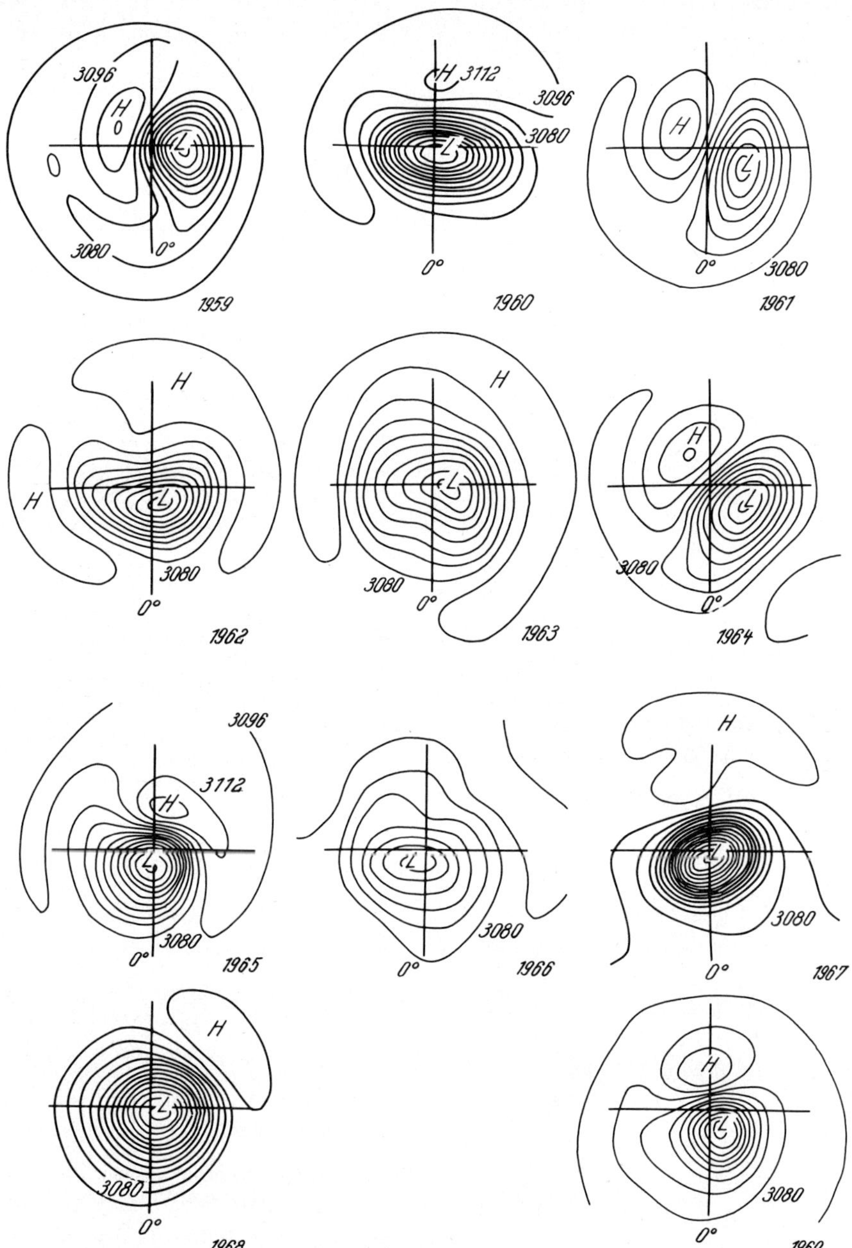

FIG. 3. Mean contour heights (dynamic decameters) of the 10-mb surface during March of the years indicated (From Reiter and Macdonald, *Archives of Meteor., Geophys., Bioclim.*, Ser. A, **22**: 153–154, 1973).

at the 500-mb level as a function of time. Eight years of data are plotted on this diagram. This particular isotherm was chosen because it describes fairly well the position of the polar front at 500 mb (Reiter and Macdonald, 1973). Two astounding facts become evident from Fig. 2:

(1) The range of interannual variability of the extent of the northern hemispheric cold air supply during the height of winter is ±20 percent of the mean value. This 40 percent variability, measured on a *hemispheric*, not a regional, basis most certainly has a profound effect on the character of the winter season in those regions which lie in the latitude belt over which the polar front normally meanders

(2) Abnormally large or abnormally small supplies of polar cold air persist over periods in excess of one month The period of abnormality, thus, is long enough to impress its character upon the whole winter season

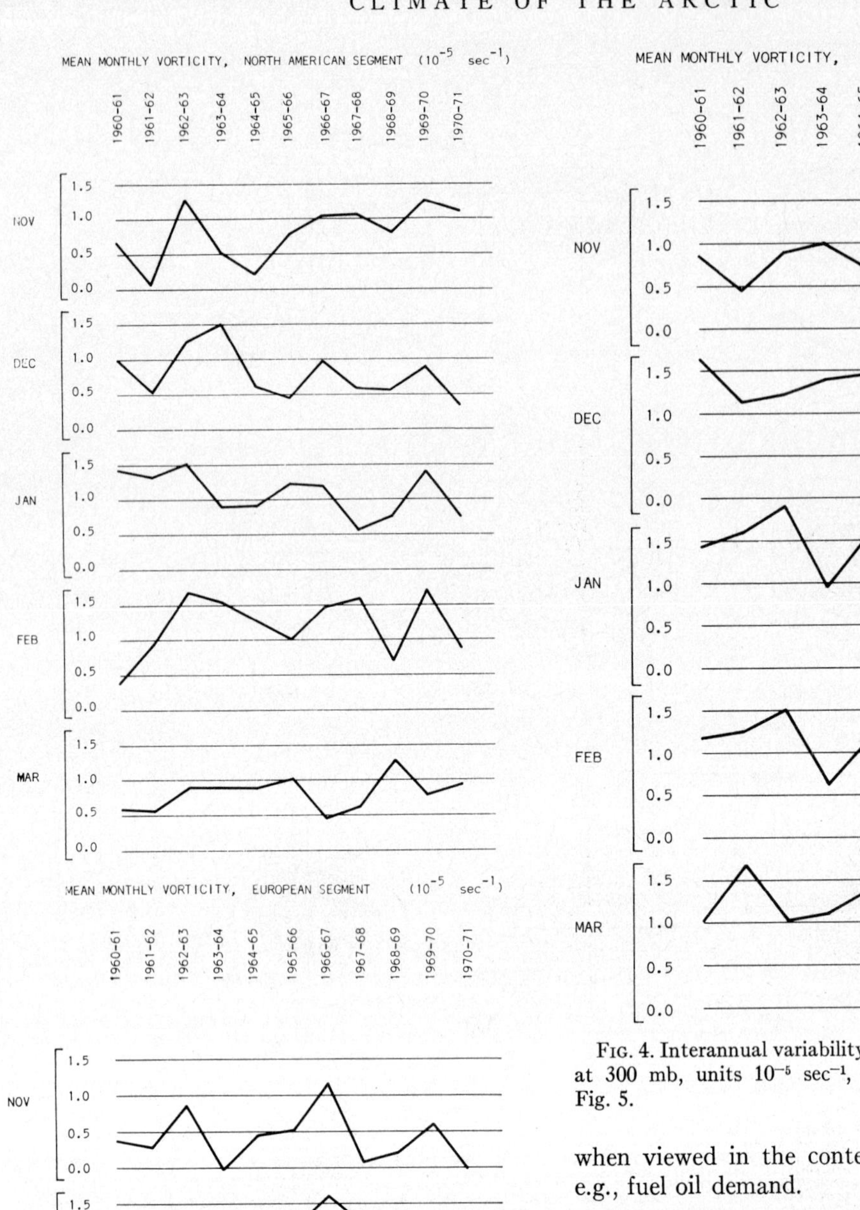

FIG. 4. Interannual variability of monthly mean vorticity values at 300 mb, units 10^{-5} sec^{-1}, averaged over sectors shown in Fig. 5.

when viewed in the context of economic parameters, e.g., fuel oil demand.

What are the possible causes for such a large interannual variability? Most likely the major blame can be laid on the doorstep of interannual variability of quasi-horizontal transports of sensible and latent heat by the atmosphere (see e.g., Oort, 1975). But variations in hemispheric cloud cover, surface albedo, heat exchange through the earth and ocean surfaces, latent heat release within the polar regions and quasi-adiabatic large-scale vertical motions will have to be considered critically in terms of their possible effects on the heat balance of the polar atmosphere.

As a second example we may quote the interannual variability of the stratospheric polar vortex. Fig. 3 demonstrates this variability through the mean 10-mb contour patterns of the months of March in 11 sequential years. It is difficult to visualize that this variability is caused by variations in the stratospheric "heat engine." More likely, interaction with the tropo-

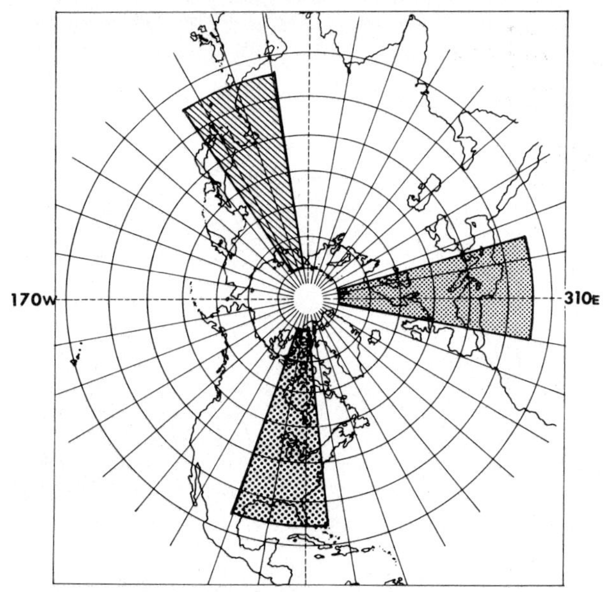

FIG. 5. Geographic sectors used for mean vorticity calculations.

sphere and its variability—demonstrated in Fig. 2—
play a major role in forcing stratospheric variability.
There exists, however, an intricate feedback mecha-

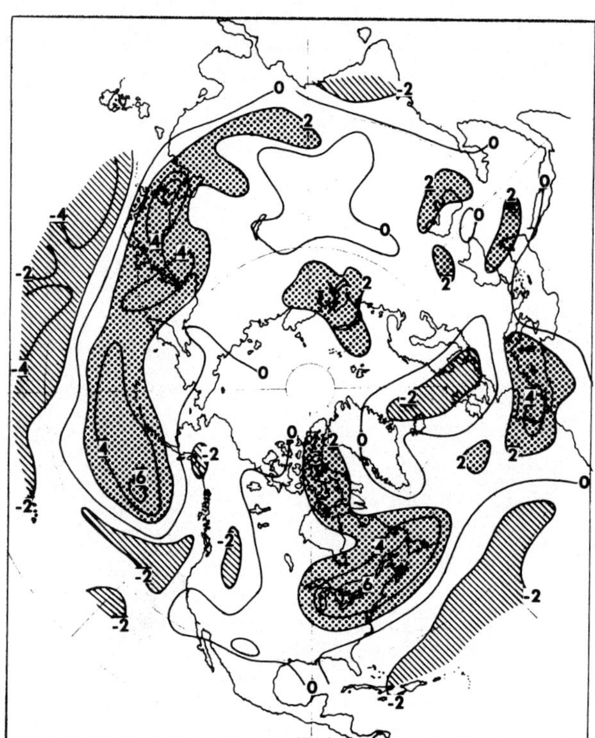

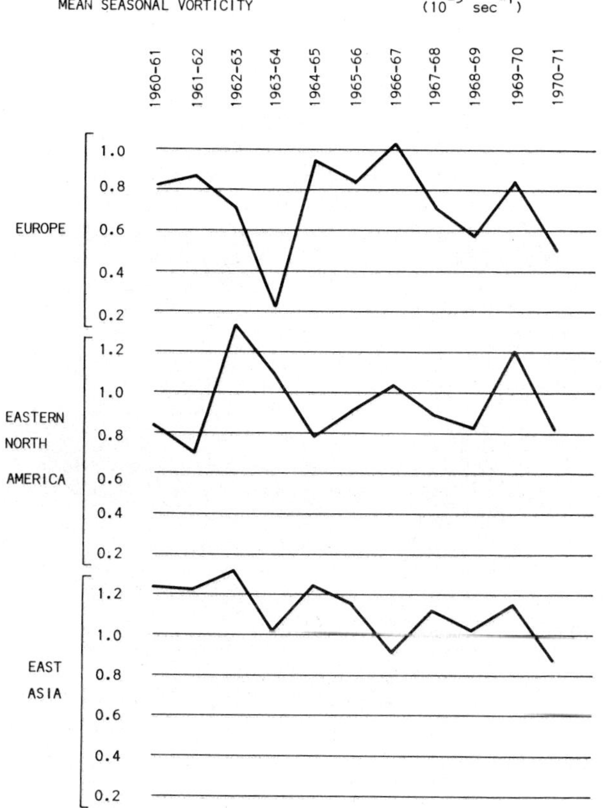

FIG. 6. "Cold-season" average (November to March) vorticity,
units 10^{-5} sec^{-1}, for sectors as indicated.

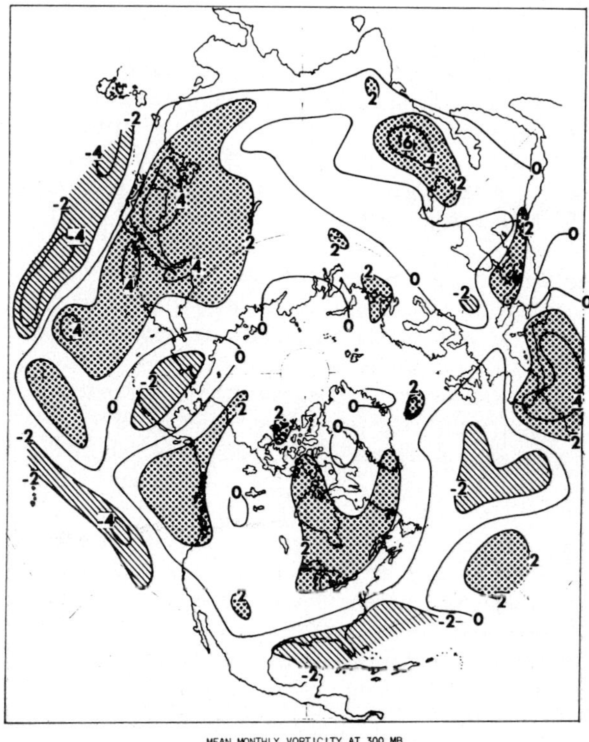

FIG. 7. Mean vorticity values (units 10^{-5} sec^{-1}) for
(a) December 1963, and (b) December 1964.

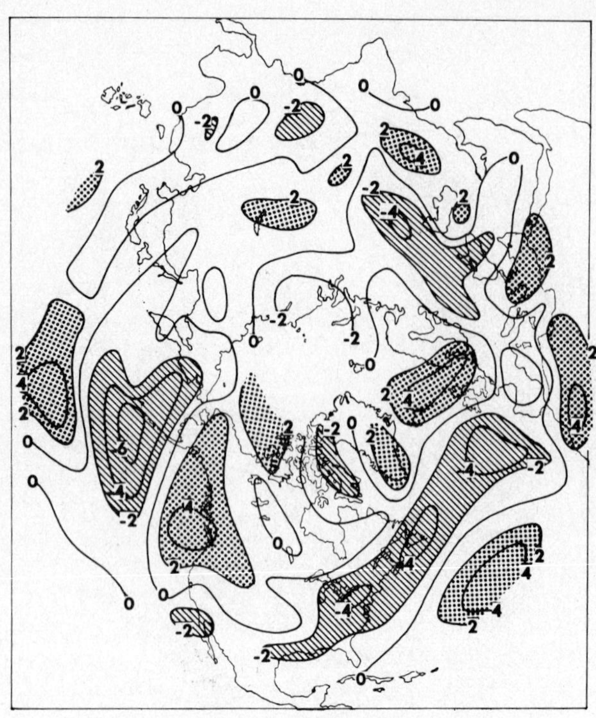

FIG. 8. Differences between mean vorticity values of December 1964—December 1963. (units 10^{-5} sec^{-1}).

nism between stratosphere and troposphere which works in both directions (see Reiter and Macdonald, 1973).

We have also made a preliminary study of the interannual variability of northern hemisphere vorticity patterns. Fig. 4, prepared by Mr. Bruce C. Macdonald, shows the interannual variability of monthly mean vorticity values at 300 mb computed over three sectors, each extending from 25°N to 80°N and measuring 25° longitude in width (Fig 5). In each sector this mean vorticity, which essentially measures the shift in planetary long-wave patterns, reveals an interannual variability that amounts to about 100 percent (±50% about the mean value). Even a combination of all five months from November to March into "cold season" average values of vorticity shows a dramatic interannual variability of approximately ±30 percent about the mean value, especially in the European and North American sectors (Fig. 6). Such shifts in long-wave pattern intensities and positions are expected to leave a pronounced imprint on the characteristics of the winter seasons in these geographic regions.

The geographic distribution of monthly mean vorticity values at longitude-latitude grid points was tested for the two months of December 1963 and December 1964 which, in Fig. 5, have revealed marked interannual variability. Such variability, again, is clearly marked in the two charts shown in Fig. 7,

and in the difference values analyzed with only a slight touch of smoothing in Fig. 8. At this point we cannot offer any reasonable speculations as to the

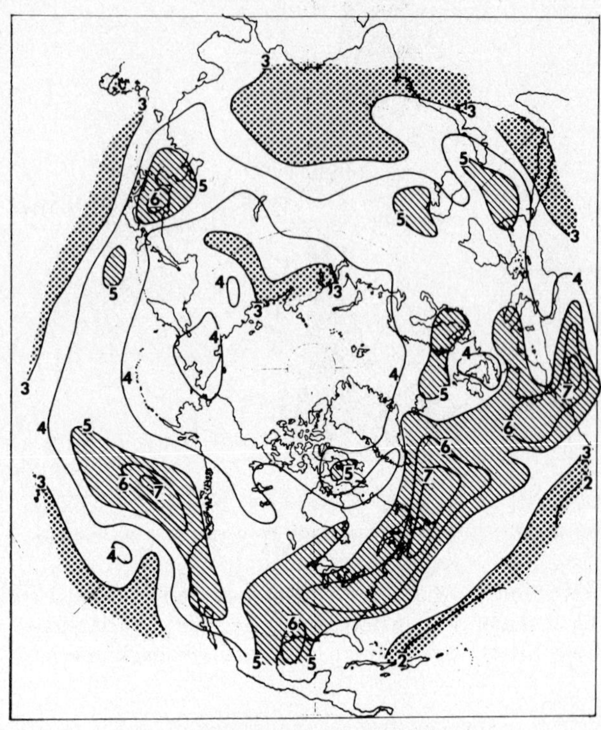

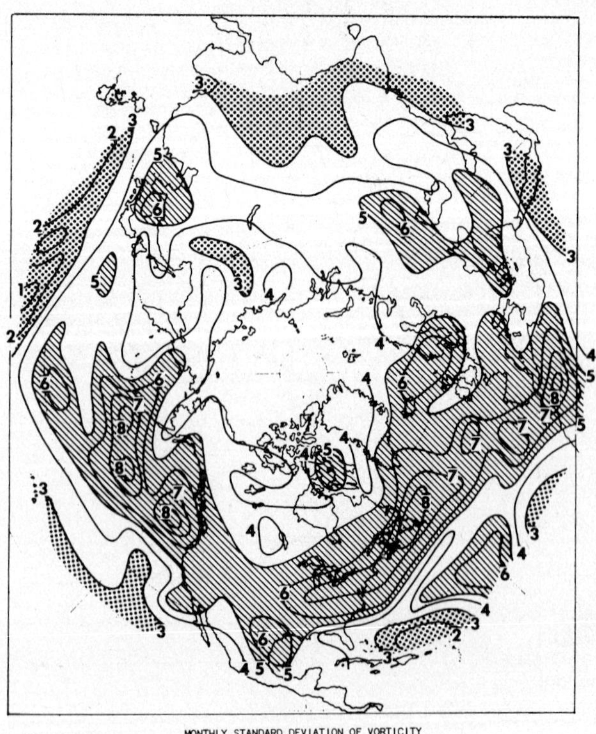

FIG. 9. Standard deviations of daily vorticity values (units 10^{-5} sec^{-1} for (a) December 1963, (b) December 1964.

possible causes of the observed shifts in vorticity patterns. We cannot even tell whether these shifts were produced by (perhaps recognizable) changes in forcing functions as behooves an "intransitive" atmosphere, or whether they were caused by internal instabilities in a "transitive" atmosphere.

The standard deviations of daily vorticity values for the same two December months are shown in Fig. 9 These values give a combined measure of the intensity of, and of the frequency of change between, cyclonic and anticyclonic traveling disturbances. Again, the interannual variability of this parameter is astounding. The change from December 1963 to December 1964 seems to result in a *hemispheric increase* of cyclonic and anticyclonic activity (Fig. 10). The effect of such changes in the activity of traveling wave disturbances is open to conjecture. It most likely has a significant impact on stratospheric-tropospheric mass exchange which depends strongly on cyclone activity (for references see Reiter, 1972). It may also have an impact on mean monthly precipitation values in middle and high latitudes, hence on the latent-heat release in a broad latitude belt. This possibility deserves further investigation.

5. Conclusions

The few examples of atmospheric interannual variability on a hemispheric basis presented in this paper, together with the demonstrated economic impact of such variability, suggest a major expenditure of time and effort to explore the possible causes and effects of interannual variability. We know next to nothing about the variety of mechanisms that may effect the atmosphere on this time scale. Most likely the strong *annual* variability of the atmosphere, shown in Fig. 1, will "swamp" many signals that might suggest an *interannual* variability of the atmosphere. A search for the causes of interannual variability, therefore, is by no means viewed as an easy task.

As an incentive to venture onto such a path of inquiry we can list the economic impact of interannual variability in the fields of agriculture, fuel industry, and many other branches of enterprising business. We should also consider, however, that interannual variability is a basic characteristic of our atmosphere, and thus becomes a significant part of our climate. Before we can truly begin to understand the causes for climatic change we have to come to a full recognition of those factors which help on the one hand to determine the variability of the atmosphere, especially on time scales from one to several years, and on the other hand prevent under present conditions the same variability either to become catastrophically large or to become persistent with the same sign of anomaly

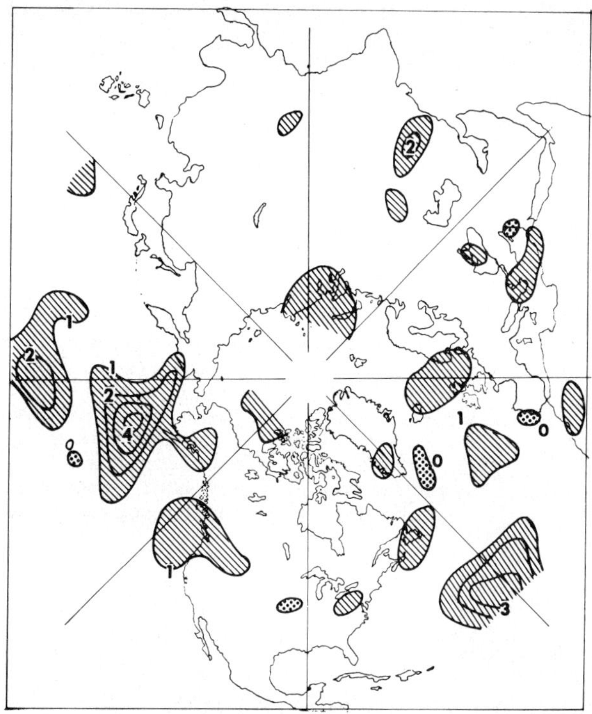

FIG. 10. Differences between standard deviations of daily vorticity values of December 1964—December 1963 (units 10^{-5} sec^{-1}).

over long time periods. Such an understanding would then help us to isolate those parameters and their variabilities that *have* during past geological history resulted in upsets of climatic conditions.

Acknowledgments. The research reported in this paper was sponsored by the U. S. Atomic Energy Commission under Contract AT (11-1)1340. The author is indebted to Mr. Bruce C. Macdonald for preparing the statistical data on hemispheric vorticity behavior as part of his M.S. thesis research.

REFERENCES

Maunder, W. J., 1970: *The value of the weather.* Methuen & Co. Ltd., London, 388 pp.

Oort, A., 1975: Year-to-year variations in climate. *Proceedings, AAAS-AMS Conference, Climate of the Arctic,* Fairbanks, Alaska, 15–17 August 1963.

Reiter, E. R., 1972: Atmospheric transport processes, Part 3: Hydrodynamic tracers. *U. S. Atomic Energy Commission, AEC Critical Review Series,* TID-25731, 212 pp.

Reiter, E. R., and B. C. Macdonald, 1973: Quasi-biennial variations in the winter-time circulation of high latitudes. *Archiv f. Meteorol. Geophys. Bioklim.,* Ser. A, **22,** 145–167.

Vinnichenko, N. K., and J. A. Dutton, 1969: Empirical studies of atmospheric structure and spectra in the free atmosphere. *Radio Science,* **4,** 1115–1126.

The Simulation of Arctic Climate with a Global General Circulation Model

W. Lawrence Gates

The Rand Corporation, Santa Monica, California

Abstract

A two-level global circulation model is used to simulate the Arctic climate for both January and July. From separate month-long simulations, the summer and winter distributions of pressure, surface air temperature, precipitation and cloudiness north of 50N are compared with the corresponding observed fields. While the model's results bear an overall resemblance to observation, a number of errors are noted: the model's January surface air temperatures are too high, the summer rainfall is too low over the North Atlantic and North Pacific oceans, and the cloudiness is much too low over the entire region. These are attributed primarily to the model's inadequate treatment of the surface boundary layer and low-level marine convection. The need for further climatological observations in the Arctic is also recognized.

1. Introduction

The atmospheric general circulation is driven by differential heating, principally composed of the radiation imbalance between high and low latitudes, by the sensible heating over land and ocean, and by the release of latent heat of condensation, primarily in the low and middle latitudes. Each part of the global system therefore plays a role in the thermal forcing of the atmospheric general circulation, and participates in the transport of heat, momentum and moisture which results from that circulation. The Arctic plays a special role, however, since it is the principal region of radiative energy deficit, and maintains its climatic equilibrium by the receipt of energy transported from lower latitudes. Variations in the Arctic thermal equilibrium may therefore be expected to affect the character of the global circulation, and it is for this reason difficult to separate the Arctic from the remainder of the atmosphere in an analysis of the large-scale circulation and climate.

To study such a problem, the numerical general circulation models would appear to be an ideal tool. Their global coverage is an essential feature, and their flexibility permits the introduction of a wide range of physical processes. Of the many effects represented in the more general atmospheric models (see, for example, Holloway and Manabe, 1971, or Kasahara and Washington, 1971), one is of particular importance to the Arctic region: the *surface heat balance*. Each of its component processes, such as net radiation, surface sensible heat flux, and cloudiness, plays an important role in Arctic climate, and should be given careful consideration. The purpose of the present paper is to initiate such an analysis of simulated Arctic climate, so that the adequacy of both the numerical models and of the data base in this region can be assessed. This in turn should lead to the design and evaluation of new numerical simulations in which the physical processes important in the Arctic are more accurately described, and to the assembly of a more complete Arctic climatological data base.

2. Model summary and review

The model used here is a version of the two-level Mintz-Arakawa general circulation model, for which a comprehensive documentation has been prepared by Gates *et al.* (1971) and to which reference may be made for further detail of the model's formulation and numerical solution. In broad outline, this model predicts the distribution of the horizontal wind velocity (V), the temperature (T) and the pressure (p) or geopotential (ϕ) at two tropospheric levels surrounding the globe. These levels approximate the

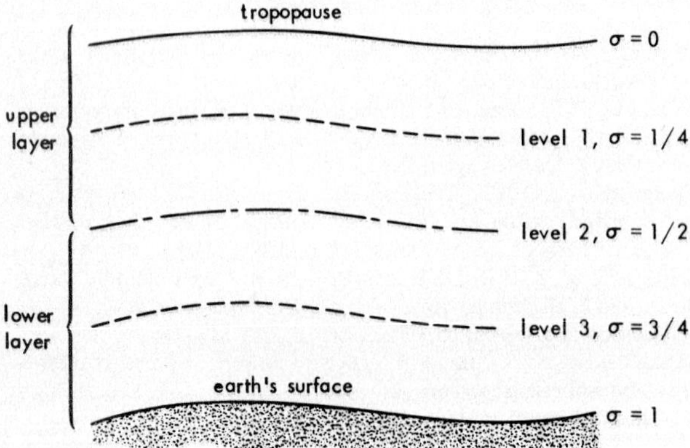

Fig. 1. The vertical structure of the two-level circulation model (after Gates, 1972).

400 mb and 800 mb surfaces and are designated $\sigma=\frac{1}{4}$ and $\sigma=\frac{3}{4}$ in the sigma (σ) coordinate system (see Fig. 1), wherein $\sigma=1$ corresponds to the earth's surface and $\sigma=0$ is the top of the model atmosphere. In addition the model determines the vertical velocity $(\dot\sigma_2)$ at a mid-level $(\sigma=\frac{1}{2})$, and carries the atmospheric moisture or mixing ratio (q_3) only at the lower level (near 800 mb).

The model's governing equations of motion and thermodynamic energy may be written

$$\frac{\partial}{\partial t}(\pi\mathbf{V})+\mathbf{V}(\nabla\cdot\pi\mathbf{V})+(\pi\mathbf{V}\cdot\nabla)\mathbf{V}\pm\pi\dot\sigma_2\mathbf{V}_2$$

$$+\pi f\mathbf{k}\times\mathbf{V}+\pi\nabla\phi+\sigma\pi\alpha\nabla\pi=\pi\mathbf{F} \quad (1)$$

$$\frac{\partial}{\partial t}(\pi T)+\nabla\cdot\pi T\mathbf{V}-\frac{\sigma\pi\alpha}{c_p}\dot\pi\pm\pi\dot\sigma_2 T_2=\pi\dot H/c_p \quad (2)$$

where $\pi=p_s-p_T$, with p_s the (variable) surface pressure and $p_T(=200\text{ mb})$ an assumed tropopause pressure, f the Coriolis parameter, α the specific volume, and ∇ is the horizontal gradient operator. Here $\mathbf{F}$ and $\dot H$ are the frictional force and diabatic heating rate, respectively, per unit mass. The upper sign in the fourth terms of (1) and (2) applies when the equations are applied at the upper level $(\sigma=\sigma_1=\frac{1}{4})$, with the lower sign applying at the lower level $(\sigma=\sigma_3=\frac{3}{4})$; at these levels the variables $\mathbf{V}$, ϕ, α, T, p, $\mathbf{F}$ and $\dot H$ assume the subscripts 1 and 3, respectively.

In (1) and (2) the coordinate σ is given by

$$\sigma=(p-p_T)/\pi \quad (3)$$

and the velocity $\mathbf{V}_2$ and temperature T_2 are the averages of the values at levels 1 and 3. The geopotential ϕ is found from the hydrostatic equation $\partial\phi/\partial\sigma=-\pi\alpha$, with the assumption that the potential temperature $\theta=T(p_0/p)^\kappa$ is linear in p^κ-space, where $\kappa=0.286$ and $p_0=1000$ mb.

At the lower model level the water vapor continuity equation is applied in the form

$$\frac{\partial}{\partial t}(\pi q_3)+\nabla\cdot\pi q_3\mathbf{V}_{3.5}=2g(E-C) \quad (4)$$

where $\mathbf{V}_{3.5}$ is the wind velocity extrapolated to the (fictitious) level 3.5 $(\sigma=7/8)$, g is gravity, and $E-P$ is the difference between the surface evaporation rate E and the condensation rate C. The precipitation rate P is assumed to be equal to the condensation rate C, with no allowance for either the liquid water content of clouds or for evaporation from falling precipitation.

At the earth's surface $(\sigma=1)$ the rate of change of the surface pressure is found from the continuity

equation in the form

$$\frac{\partial\pi}{\partial t}=-\nabla\cdot\pi\mathbf{V}_2 \quad (5)$$

while at the level 2 the vertical velocity is given by

$$\dot\sigma_2=-\frac{1}{4\pi}\nabla\cdot\pi(\mathbf{V}_1-\mathbf{V}_3) \quad (6)$$

The frictional force $\mathbf{F}$ in (1) consists of an internal stress (proportional to the vertical wind shear between the levels 1 and 3) serving to transfer momentum between the model's layers, and a surface stress or drag (dependent upon the surface wind) serving to transfer momentum to the earth. Of more interest here, however, is the heating rate $\dot H$ in (2). At the upper level, this consists of the absorption rate of solar radiation in the upper model layer, the rate of long-wave radiation loss, the heat transferred by convection, and the possible release of latent heat during (convective) condensation. At the lower level, the heating rate consists of corresponding energy sources, plus the warming of the lower layer by the release of latent heat accompanying large-scale condensation and the sensible heat flux from the earth's surface (dependent upon the surface—air temperature difference and the surface wind). Further details of these parameterizations and those for the evaporation, condensation, and cloudiness are given below in connection with the surface heat balance, and have been described in complete detail elsewhere (Gates et al., 1971).

Boundary conditions

Accompanying the model's equations (1)–(6) are the dynamical boundary conditions that $\dot\sigma=0$ at $\sigma=0$ (where $p=p_T=200$ mb) and $\dot\sigma=0$ at $\sigma=1$ (where $p=p_s$, the earth's surface, thereby including the effect of orography). In addition, there is a thermal boundary condition at the surface: over land and ice a zero net surface heat balance is assumed, with the resulting diagnostic equation used to determine the surface temperature; over the oceans the surface water temperature is fixed at the appropriate seasonal climatological values. Neither the sea-surface temperature nor the assigned locations of ice are allowed to change during the course of the present integrations, although the sun's declination is changed daily. At all locations the surface albedo has been taken from the seasonal tabulations of Posey and Clapp (1964), as summarized by Schutz and Gates (1971, 1972).

Sensible heat flux

The vertical turbulent flux of sensible heat, Γ, is modeled according to the bulk transfer formula

$$\Gamma=\rho_s c_p c_D|\mathbf{V}_s|(T_s-T_a), \quad (7)$$

where ρ_s is the surface air density, c_p the air's specific heat at constant pressure, c_D the drag coefficient[1], $\mathbf{V}_s$ the surface wind speed (taken as 0.7 of the value extrapolated to the surface from levels 1 and 3), and T_a the air temperature near the surface (at anemometer level).

Evaporation

The vertical moisture flux or evaporation rate E is similarly modeled by the formula

$$E = \rho_s c_D |\mathbf{V}_s| (q_s - q_a) \tag{8}$$

where q_s is the mixing ratio at the surface itself, and q_a is that in the overlying air (at anemometer level). Over water, q_s is taken as the saturation value at T_s; over ice it assumes the saturation value at the surface temperature; over land it is a fraction of the T_s-saturation value, depending on the ground wetness determined by the local rainfall.

Cloudiness

Clouds are produced in the model in response to simulated condensation, that is, when saturation is achieved as a result of either large-scale moisture flux convergence or vertical convective adjustment. The type of cloud depends upon the condensation process: large-scale cloudiness accompanies large-scale condensation (that induced by $\dot{\sigma}_2$) and extends between levels 2 and 3; convective cloudiness generally accompanies any condensation as a result of vertical convection (lapse-rate adjustments made to maintain static stability), and extends between levels 1 and 3 (penetrating convection) or is confined to level 3 itself (low-level, non-raining convection). The amount of cloud cover at a point is the sum of that for all three cloud types (but limited to 10/10 cover); the convective cloudiness depends upon the relative humidity at level 3 (RH_3) according to $-0.25+1.25\ RH_3$, whereas a complete overcast is assumed for large-scale clouds.

Although cloudiness in the model modifies the fluxes of both short- and long-wave radiation through reflection and absorption, no provision is made for the clouds' liquid water content (all of the condensed water falling as rain), and the clouds themselves are not advected horizontally with the wind. Of particular importance in the Arctic, moreover, is the fact that no provision is made in the present model for the occurrence of large-scale non-precipitating clouds, particularly of the stratus variety.

---

[1] The drag coefficient is itself given by $c_D = 0.002 + 0.009$ $(z/5000\ \mathrm{m})$ over land, ice and snow, and by $c_D = \min\ [0.0025,$ $1.0 + 0.07\,|\mathbf{V}_s|10^{-3}]$ over the ocean, where z is the local terrain height.

Surface heat balance

We may write the heat balance equation at the surface for the present model in the form

$$(1-\alpha)S - R - \Gamma - LE = C_g \tag{9}$$

where α is the surface albedo; S, the short-wave radiation incident at the surface; R, the net long-wave radiation flux leaving the surface; Γ, the sensible heat flux; C_g, the conduction of heat from beneath the surface, and E is the surface evaporation rate with L the latent heat. Over bare land, and over ice- and snow-covered land surfaces, this equation serves to determine the surface temperature T_s through the temperature dependence of the terms R and Γ, with C_g assumed zero; over sea-ice, the term $C_g = K(T_s - T_f)$, where $K = 1.4$ ly day^{-1} deg^{-1} (corresponding to an ice thermal conductivity of 0.005 ly cm sec^{-1} deg^{-1} and an assumed ice thickness of 3 m), and T_f is the freezing point of sea water beneath the ice. The surface temperature of sea ice, however, is not allowed to rise above the melting point.

Numerical solution method

The numerical methods used in the solution of the model's governing equations are due to Arakawa, and are described in detail elsewhere (Gates *et al.*, 1971). The general computational philosophy is to write finite-difference equations for the system (1)–(6) in such a way that the solutions will remain stable while resolving the important features of the circulation with reasonable accuracy. This is achieved by using numerical methods which very nearly preserve (in the absence of sources and sinks) the model's total mass, momentum and energy, along with the mean vorticity and the mean square of the potential temperature.

The computational net consists of two global interlocking grids with points spaced 4 degrees latitude and 5 degrees longitude apart. One grid, on which the temperature, pressure and moisture are determined, includes points at 90N, 86N, ..., 2N, ... and 0, 5W, 10W, ...; the other grid, on which the wind velocity is determined, includes points at 88N, 84N, ..., 0, ... and 2.5W, 7.5W, ... The time integration proceeds in steps of 6 minutes each using a version of a scheme due to Matsuno, which introduces a damping of the higher-frequency solutions.

The source terms or forcing functions $\mathbf{F}$, $\dot{H}$ and $(E-C)$ in (1), (2) and (4) are calculated every fifth time step, along with the introduction of a limited amount of smoothing. The calculations require about 15 min on an IBM 360-91 computer to simulate one model day.

Performance review

Summaries of the overall global performance of the basic two-level model in the simulation of January

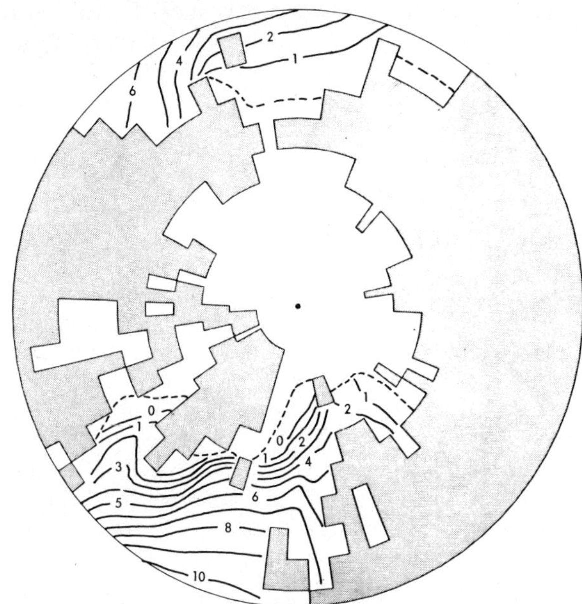

FIG. 2. The average sea-surface temperature (°C) and ice limit (shown by the dashed line) for January, from data of Washington and Thiel (1970) as summarized by Schutz and Gates (1971). On this and subsequent figures the land as resolved by the 4-deg latitude, 5-deg longitude numerical grid is shaded north of 50N.

climate have been given by Gates (1972, 1973). Considering the relative simplicity of the model, the simulated climate may be considered generally satisfactory. The large-scale features of the general circulation are reasonably well portrayed, including the location and strength of the average pressure and wind systems, the free-air temperature distribution, and the broad-scale distribution of the precipitation and evaporation.

Closer examination, however, reveals a number of systematic errors: the mid-latitude transient cyclones are generally too few and too weak (while the longer quasi-stationary cyclones are too intense); the air at 400 mb over the tropics is some 6 deg C too warm, and as a consequence the mid-latitude zonal westerlies are too strong (by nearly 60 percent); the surface air over the tropical oceans and continental interior is too warm (by several deg C); and the evaporation and precipitation rates are generally too large (by nearly 100 percent), particularly in the lower latitudes where the convective processes are evidently oversimulated.

Perhaps the most striking error, however, is in the cloudiness, which in the simulation is everywhere too low by about a factor of two. This error has undoubtedly affected the model's heat balance and permitted excessive solar radiation to reach the surface, especially in the higher latitudes of the Southern Hemisphere. Since most of this radiation falls into the sea and is thereby lost (in the model), the surface heat balance is not markedly distorted. The simulated surface sensible heat flux, however, is negative at low latitudes whereas the observed flux is everywhere positive.

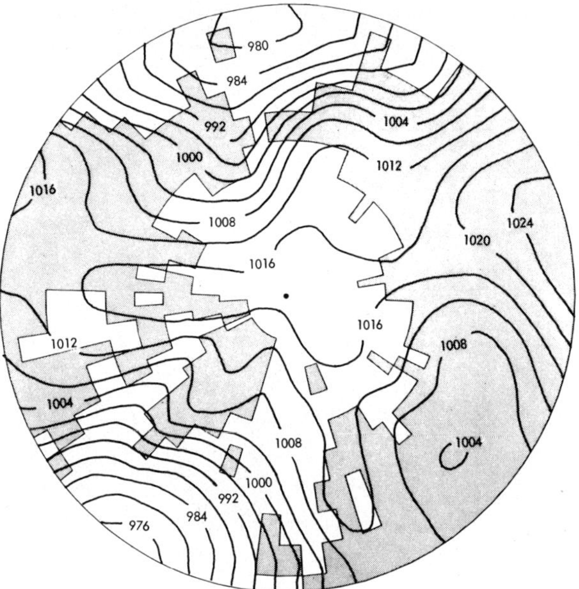

FIG. 3a. The simulated January sea-level pressure (mb).

The global January and July climate simulated by a newly revised version[2] of the two-level model has been described by Gates (1974b), and it is from this version that the present Arctic simulations have been drawn. In general, the overall quality of the solutions is similar

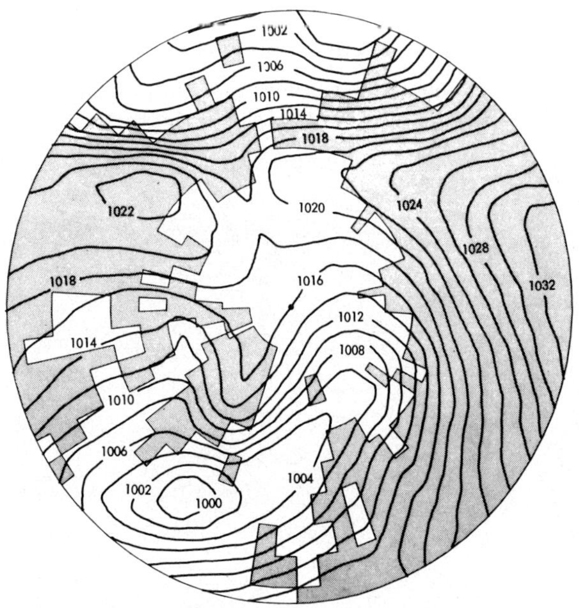

FIG. 3b. The observed January sea-level pressure (mb), from data of Crutcher and Meserve (1970) as summarized by Schutz and Gates (1971).

---

[2] The principal changes were minor revisions of the convective cloudiness criteria, provision for large-scale cloudiness at 90 percent relative humidity, and use of empirical grid-point surface albedos (replacing the three constants previously used for all land, ice and ocean).

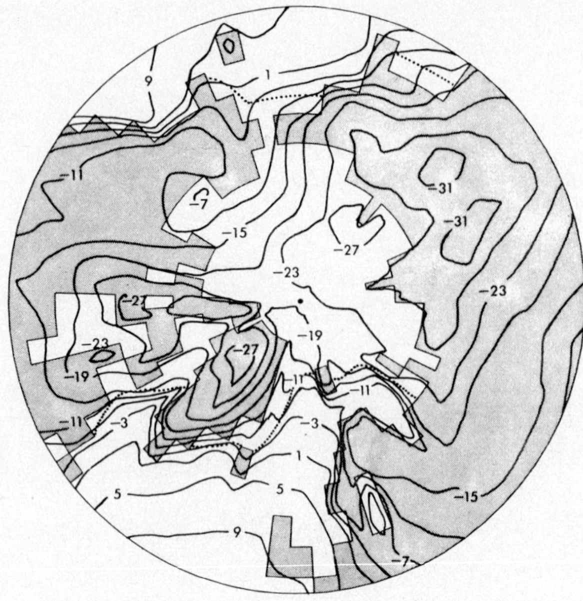

Fig. 4a. The simulated January surface air temperature (°C),
with the dotted line denoting the pack ice limit.

to that discussed above, with the same characteristic
errors. The simulated cloudiness, in particular, is now
in better agreement with observation in the tropics,
but continues to be systematically too low in the middle
and high latitudes of both the summer and winter
hemispheres.

3. The simulated arctic January climate

From the month-long numerical solutions intended
to simulate elements of the global January climate

Fig. 4b. The observed January surface air temperature (°C),
from data of Crutcher and Meserve (1970) as summarized by
Schutz and Gates (1971).

(Gates, 1974b), the portions north of 50N have been
extracted and are displayed in polar projection in
Figs. 2–6. A similar procedure was followed for the July
simulations which are discussed below and shown in
Figs. 7–11. The corresponding observed data are also
displayed in the same format in order to facilitate
comparsion in the Arctic region.

Sea-surface temperature and ice

The distribution of sea-surface temperature and the
sea-ice limit for January is shown in Fig. 2. This analysis
is based on the data of Washington and Thiel (1970) and
Navy Hydrographic Office sources as summarized by
Schutz and Gates (1971), and the corresponding grid-
point data were used as surface boundary conditions
in the model. The ice pack is assumed to be continuous
north of the dashed line in the model, which corresponds
to the observed position of 50 percent ice cover. The
surface albedo (not shown) was interpolated from the
seasonal distributions given by Posey and Clapp (1964).
Fig. 2 also serves to display the continental outlines
as resolved by the 4-deg latitude, 5-deg longitude grid.

Sea-level pressure

The simulated January distribution of sea-level
pressure is shown in Fig. 3a, and the observed distribution from Crutcher and Meserve (1970) as summarized by Schutz and Gates (1971) is shown in Fig.
3b. Both patterns are dominated by a high-pressure
ridge across the polar basin between Siberia and Northern Canada, and by low pressure centers in the North
Atlantic and North Pacific oceans. The model, however,
gives too low a pressure for all of these features, while
correctly simulating the polar pressure itself. Perhaps
the greatest discrepancy is the model's failure to repro-
duce the broad region of southwesterly flow over Europe
and the associated low pressure in the Norwegian sea.
This is caused by the simulation of too few migratory
cyclones, especially across Northern Europe, and is a
characteristic deficiency of the model.

Surface air temperature

The simulated and observed January distributions of
surface air temperature are shown in Figs. 4a and 4b,
respectively. The simulation clearly shows the cold
air pools observed over Siberia, Northeast Canada,
and over the Greenland ice cap (Crutcher and Meserve,
1970; Schutz and Gates, 1971). The simulated temperature is seen to be rather accurate over the North
Atlantic and Europe (in spite of the surface pressure
errors noted above); this is likely due to the model's
use of observed sea-surface temperatures which control
to some extent the surface air temperatures over the
sea and surrounding regions. The model's greatest
error is seen to be a systematic underestimate of the
intensity of the low-level inversion over the snow-

FIG. 5a. The simulated January precipitation rate (mm day⁻¹).
Note that the full isolines are drawn at 0.2 mm day⁻¹ intervals,
while the dashed isolines are drawn at 1.0 mm day⁻¹ intervals.

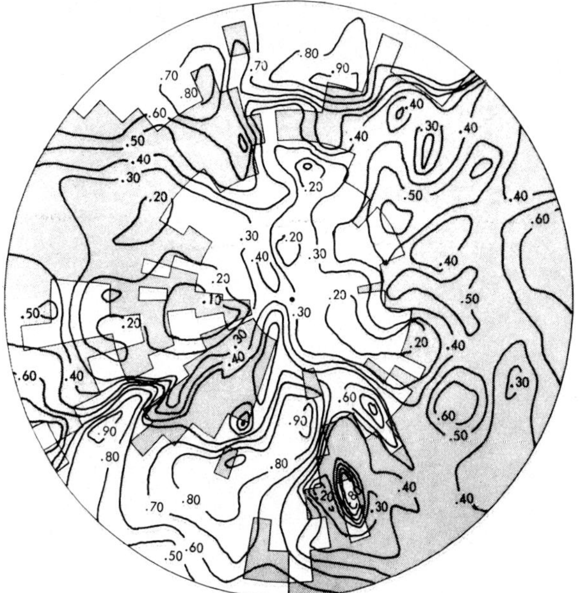

FIG. 6a. The simulated January cloudiness
(in fractions of sky cover).

covered land and over the Arctic pack ice; here the
simulated air temperatures are some 10 to 20 C too
high. This is doubtless related to the two-level model's
inability to correctly treat the surface boundary layer.

Precipitation

The simulated distribution of total January precipitation is shown in Fig. 5a, and the observed dis-

tribution from Möller (1951) as summarized by Schutz
and Gates (1971) is shown in Fig. 5b. We at once see
that the heavier January precipitation rates are confined to the waters of the North Atlantic and North
Pacific, and the adjacent coastal regions of Alaska
and Western Europe, in both observation and simulation. Generally light precipitation occurs in the continental interiors and over the Arctic polar ice. We may
note that the model's precipitation has a somewhat more
cellular structure than does the observed precipitation;

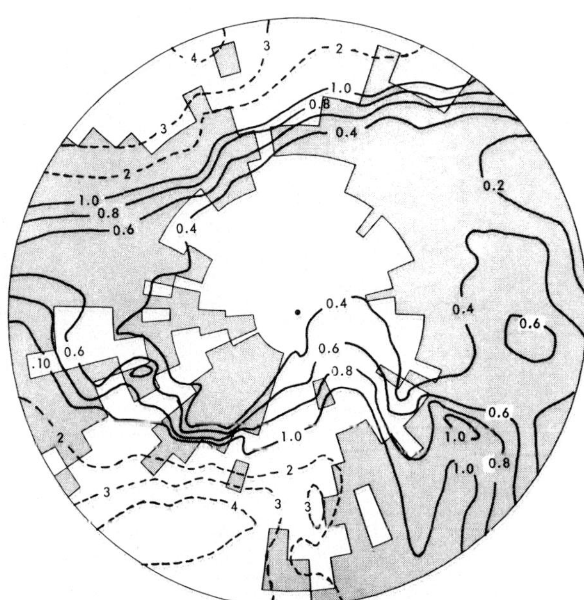

FIG. 5b. The observed January precipitation rate (mm day⁻¹),
from data of Möller (1951) as summarized by Schutz and Gates
(1971). See also Fig. 5a.

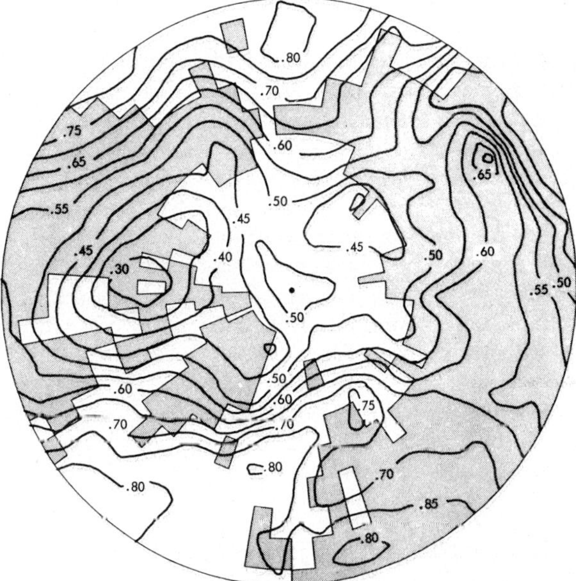

FIG. 6b. The observed January cloudiness (in fractions of sky
cover), from data of ETAC (1971) as summarized by Schutz and
Gates (1971).

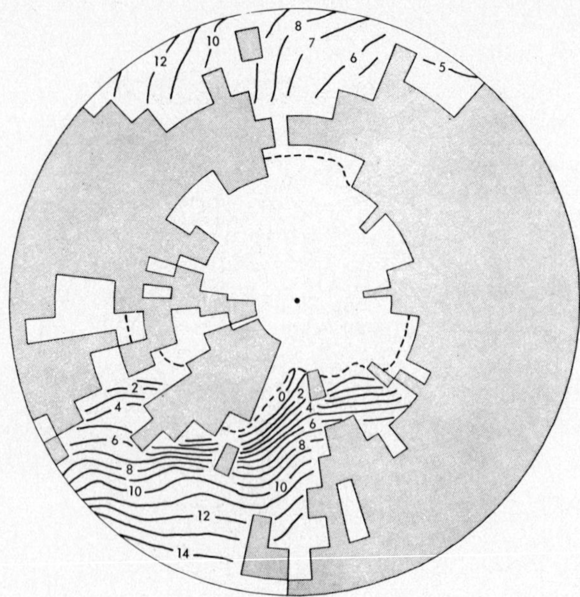

FIG. 7. The average sea-surface temperature (°C) and ice limit (shown by the dashed line) for July, from data of Washington and Thiel (1970) as summarized by Schutz and Gates (1972).

this is probably caused by the use of only a single month's simulation. We should also recognize that the accurate observation of January precipitation in the Arctic is difficult, and that there are few reliable climatological observations over the pack ice. Since almost all of the Arctic January precipitation falls in association with cyclonic vertical motion, the overall agreement in Figs. 5a and 5b may be considered an encouraging verification of the model's ability to depict these large-scale processes.

Cloudiness

The simulated and observed distributions of total January cloudiness are shown in Figs. 6a and 6b. The highest amounts of both simulated and observed cloud are found over the relatively warm waters of the North Atlantic and North Pacific (as was the precipitation), with the lowest cloud amounts found to the north of Hudson's Bay. The observed cloudiness (ETAC, 1971) is at a secondary minimum of about 50 percent over the Arctic ice, where the simulated cloud amounts are systematically lower, averaging only about 35 percent. Considering the model's crudity of cloud parameterization and the scarcity of polar cloud observations, this may be considered a reasonably good comparison; the simulation's agreement with the mean January cloud amounts given by Vowinckel and Orvig (1970) is even more satisfactory.

4. The simulated arctic July climate

Sea-surface temperature and ice

The distribution of mean sea-surface temperature and the sea-ice limit for July is shown in Fig. 7, given

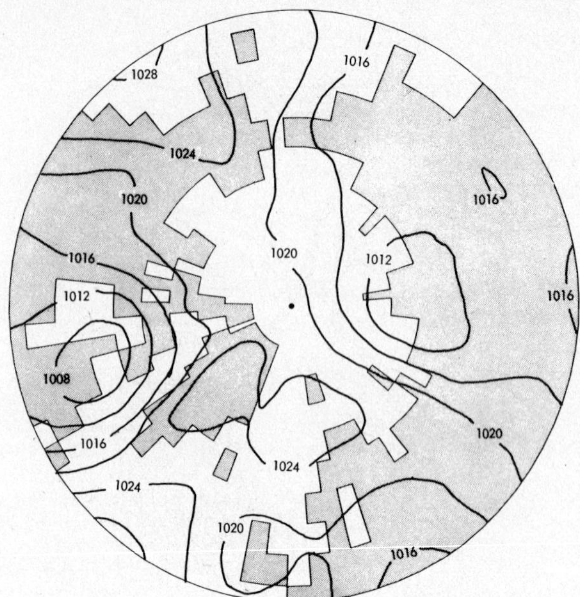

FIG. 8a. The simulated July sea-level pressure (mb).

by the data of Washington and Thiel (1970) as summarized by Schutz and Gates (1972). A general warming and a retreat of the ice limit is evident upon comparison with January (Fig. 2). We may also note that no open water is modeled north of Canada, Alaska, Spitzbergen or central Siberia.

Sea-level pressure

The simulated and observed distributions of sea-level pressure for July are shown in Figs. 8a and 8b.

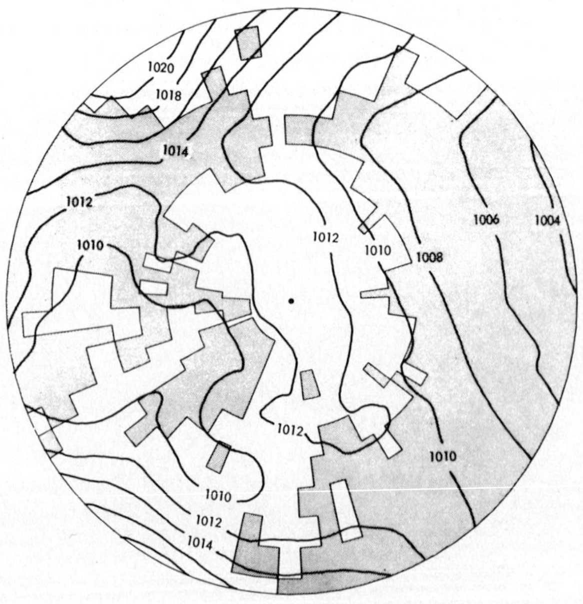

FIG. 8b. The observed July sea-level pressure (mb), from data of Crutcher and Meserve (1970) as summarized by Schutz and Gates (1972).

In contrast to January (Fig. 3), the simulated sea-level pressure is generally too high, although the pattern bears some resemblance to that observed. The greatest discrepancy occurs over western Europe, where the westerly flow from the Atlantic is poorly simulated, although the observed anticyclonic pattern over northern Scandinavia is reproduced.

Surface-air temperature

The simulated and observed distributions of July surface air temperatures are shown in Figs. 9a and 9b. Both maps show temperatures between 0 and 3C over the Arctic ice, although the model's temperatures are slightly too warm. At this season the ice is melting at the surface, and provides a strong control on the air temperature just above the ice. Aside from Greenland (where the model's surface temperatures are too warm, as they were in January), the strongest temperature gradients occur around the edge of the ice in both Figs. 9a and 9b. In general the model also shows temperatures close to those observed over the now largely bare land surrounding the Arctic. As in January, the simulated patterns over the North Atlantic and North Pacific oceans are largely controlled by the model's use of observed sea-surface temperatures (Fig. 7).

Precipitation

The simulated and observed distribution of total July precipitation are shown in Figs. 10a and 10b. In contrast to January, there is now considerable rainfall observed over both the ocean and land areas surrounding the Arctic between 50N and 70N, especially in Europe and Asia. The model's rainfall, on the other

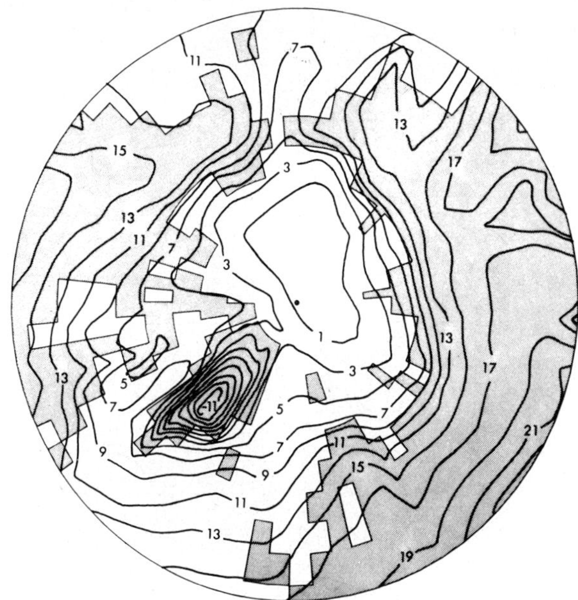

Fig. 9b. The observed July surface air temperature (°C), from data of Crutcher and Meserve (1970) as summarized by Schutz and Gates (1972).

hand, is almost exclusively over the land. This asymmetry in the model's precipitation is due to its apparently successful simulation of deep convection over the land, and its almost complete failure to simulate the extensive rainfall over the oceans. This is clear evidence of the need for improved parameterization of summer marine convection. Relatively light precipitation is given by both the model and by observation over the central Arctic, although the observed data base is relatively poor.

Cloudiness

The modeled and observed distributions of July cloud cover are shown in Figs. 11a and 11b. While this comparison has not been deliberately saved for last, it is unquestionably the model's poorest simulation. In July the Arctic is characterized by extensive and persistent cloud cover (Vowinckel and Orvig, 1970), principally of the low stratus type. The Arctic, together with the adjacent North Pacific and North Atlantic oceans, forms a continuous region with over 80 percent cloud cover. The least observed July cloudiness is found over the continental interiors, in spite of the presence of extensive rainfall (Fig. 10b). The model, by comparison, simulates too little cloudiness everywhere north of 50N, and fails completely to represent the high cloud cover amounts over the Arctic basin; here the computed pattern is rather cellular and averages less than half that observed. In some locations in the Arctic, the simulated cloudiness is seen to be as low as 10 percent. Over the land, the model's cloudiness is similarly only a fraction of that observed.

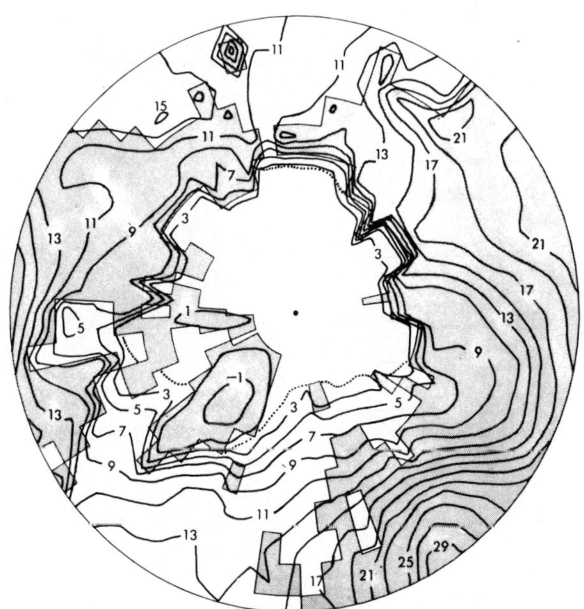

Fig. 9a. The simulated July surface air temperature (°C), with the dotted line denoting the pack ice limit.

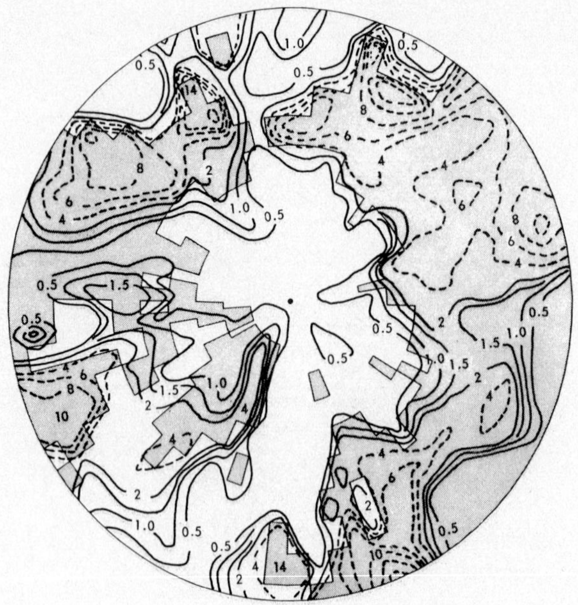

FIG. 10a. The simulated July precipitation rate (mm day⁻¹).
Note that the full isolines are drawn at 0.5 mm day⁻¹ intervals,
while the dashed isolines are drawn at 2.0 mm day⁻¹ intervals.

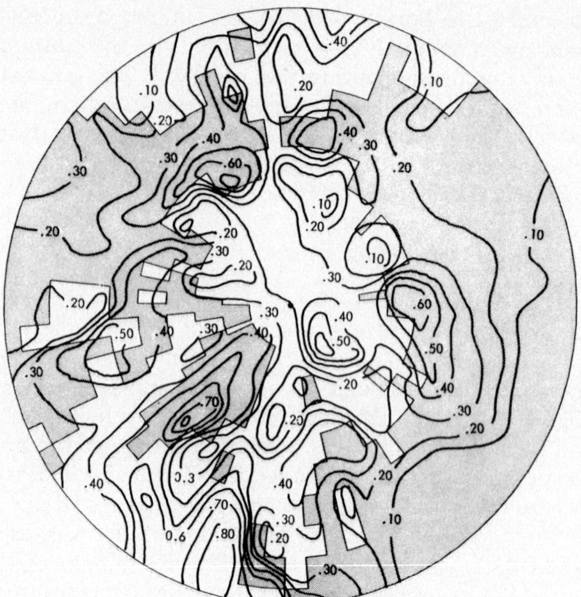

FIG. 11a. The simulated July cloudiness
(in fractions of sky cover).

From a diagnosis of the model's total cloudiness it is
found that most of the cloud cover in Fig. 11a is associated with either large-scale condensation or with penetrating (deep) convection. While these processes contribute to the precipitation (Fig. 10a), they are evidently not responsible for much of the cloudiness. The
model simulates virtually no low clouds (at level 3) in
July, and Fig. 11a shows the consequences. Clearly, the
treatment of low-level convection and stratiform clouds
must be improved in the model if the simulations of
summer cloudiness are to be useful.

5. Summary and further research

Although there is significant geographic structure to
most of the simulations as noted above, we may form
an overview of the model's Arctic performance by
averaging the results in the region between 70N and

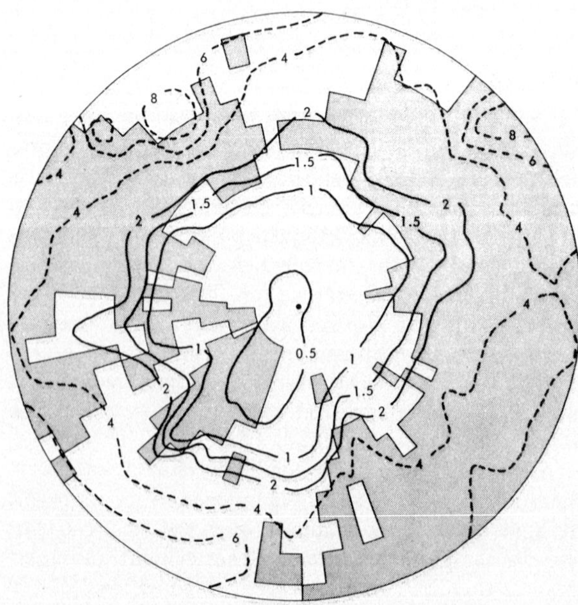

FIG. 10b. The observed July precipitation rate (mm day⁻¹),
from data of Möller (1951) as summarized by Schutz and Gates
(1972). See also Fig. 10a.

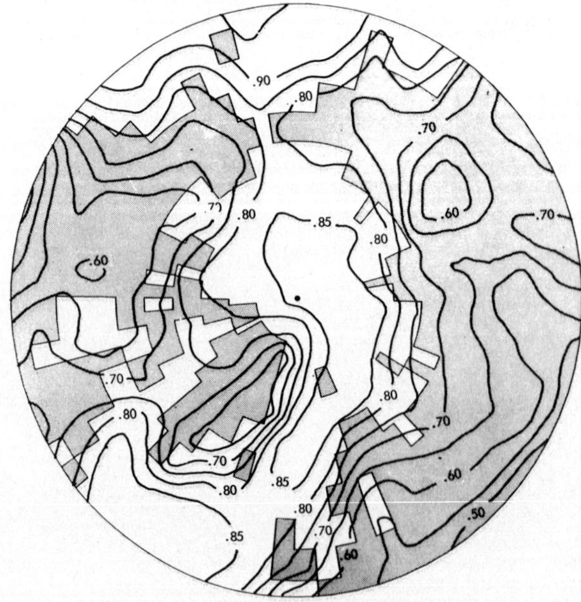

FIG. 11b. The observed July cloudiness (in fractions of sky
cover), from data of ETAC (1971) as summarized by Schutz and
Gates (1972).

90N. Such data are presented in Table 1 for the climatic variables just discussed, together with corresponding data for the free air and for selected elements of the surface heat balance. In this table the model's major characteristic errors in the Arctic may be clearly seen: in winter, prediction of surface temperatures which are too high and cloudiness which is too low over land and ice and, in summer, prediction of too little precipitation over water and insufficient cloudiness over the entire region.

In spite of these errors, the simulated evaporation rate (8) of about 0.5 mm day^{-1} is evidently reasonable, although the observed evaporation over the Arctic ice is not well known (Budyko, 1963). The model's simulated sensible heat flux (7) is negative over the Arctic in both winter and summer, indicating a heat flow from the air to the surface. Again the available observations (Budyko, 1963) are insufficient to determine a climatological mean, although the observed sensible heat flux appears to be positive at least in winter (when the influence of open water would be most significant; see Vowinckel and Orvig, 1970).

The model's surface heat balance (9) is dominated in January by the sensible heat flux and the outgoing long-wave radiation; the residual of about -50 ly day^{-1} shown in Table 1 represents the average conduction of heat toward the surface through the sea ice itself. The presence of even 10 percent open water might be sufficient to reserve the sign of this balance through the sensible heat flux and evaporation (Vowinckel and Orvig, 1970), but is an effect not presently in the model. In July the surface heat balance is positive, largely through the contributions of the absorbed solar radiation (which the model underestimates), and the evaporation from the wet ice surface.

The present comparison suggests the need for a number of improvements in the circulation model on the one hand, and of extension of the Arctic data base on the other. Most important is perhaps the model's treatment of cloudiness, which should be improved to represent stratus clouds and the rainfall from low-level marine convection. An improved parameterization of the surface boundary layer which recognizes the presence of shallow surface inversions is likewise needed. Over the ice pack itself it would also be desirable to introduce some parameterization of the effects of open water on the surface heat balance as just discussed.

There is also a need for further observations in order to establish the seasonal regimes of the important climatic elements in the Arctic. The present data bank is probably not sufficient for even the conventional variables of pressure, temperature and wind (Hastings, 1971), and is completely inadequate for those variables related to the climatically important surface thermal forcing functions: the net exchanges of heat and moisture with the underlying surface. There is a particular need for more adequate observations of the Arctic seasonal regimes of cloudiness, precipitation, evapora-

TABLE 1. Average climatic elements over the arctic basin (70N–90N).

Element	January		July	
	Simulated	Observed	Simulated	Observed
Surface air temperature (°C)	-20	-28	1	1
800 mb temperature (°C)	-26	-23	-6	-3
400 mb temperature (°C)	-49	-49	-33	-33
800 mb relative humidity (%)	70	60	75	65
Precipitation (mm/day)	1.0	0.5 (?)	0.5	1.0 (?)
Cloudiness (%)	40	50	35	85
Evaporation (mm/day)	0.5	0.2 (?)	0.5	0.3 (?)
Sensible heat flux (ly/day)	-70	50 (?)	-50	0 (?)
Surface heat balance (ly/day)	-50	0 (?)	300	400 (?)

tion, and the surface sensible heat flux. It may be hoped that such observations will result from the new polar research envisaged as part of the international POLEX program (Weller and Bierly, 1973; Gates, 1974a).

In the meantime, it is worthwhile to systematically evaluate the Arctic performance of present circulation models. In this way results such as those shown here can serve as a guide for both model improvement and data acquisition.

Acknowledgments. This research was performed as part of the RAND Climate Dynamics Project, which is supported by the Defense Advanced Research Projects Agency under contract DAHC15-73-C-0181. Thanks are due my colleagues A. B. Nelson and L. Bregman for their assistance in preparing the figures.

REFERENCES

Budyko, M. I., 1963: *Atlas of the Heat Balance of the Earth,* Gidrometeorizdat, Moscow, USSR.

Crutcher, H. L., and J. M. Merserve, 1970: *Selected Level Heights, Temperatures and Dew Points for the Northern Hemisphere,* NAVAIR 50-IC-52, Naval Weather Service Command, Washington, D. C.

Environmental Technical Applications Center (ETAC), 1971: *Northern Hemisphere Cloud Cover,* Project No. 6168, Department of the Air Force, Washington, D. C.

Gates, W. L., *et al.*, 1971: "A documentation of the Mintz-Arakawa two-level atmospheric general circulation model," R-877-ARPA, The Rand Corporation, Santa Monica, California, 408 pp. (to be published in *J. Atmos. Sci.,* **32,** 1975).

Gates, W. L., 1972: "The January global climate simulated by the two-level Mintz-Arakawa model: a comparison with observation," R-1005-ARPA, The Rand Corporation, Santa Monica, California, 106 pp.

Gates, W. L., 1973: "Analysis of the mean forcing fields simulated by the two-level Mintz-Arakawa atmospheric model," *Mon. Wea. Rev.,* **101:** 412–425.

Gates, W. L., 1974a: "Numerical modeling experiments," in U. S. Contribution to the Polar Experiment (POLEX), Draft Report of the Joint U. S. POLEX Panel, National Academy of Sciences, Appendix D, 19 pp.

Gates, W. L., 1974b: "The January and July climates simulated by a global two-level general circulation model: a new comparison with observation," The Rand Corporation, Santa Monica, California (in preparation).

Hastings, A. D., Jr., 1971: "Surface Climate of the Arctic Basin," Report ETL-TR-71-5, U. S. Army Engineer Topographic Laboratories, Ft. Belvoir, Va., 98 pp.

Holloway, J. L., Jr., and S. Manabe, 1971: "Simulation of climate by a global general circulation model," *Mon. Wea. Rev.*, **99**: 335–370.

Kasahara, A., and W. M. Washington, 1971: "General circulation experiments with a six-layer NCAR model, including orography, cloudiness and surface temperature calculations," *J. Atmos. Sci.*, **28**: 657–701.

Möller, F., 1951: "Vierteljahrskarten des Niederschlags für die ganze Erde," *Pettermanns Geogr. Mitteil.*, Justus Perthes, Gotha, pp. 1–7.

Posey, J. W., and P. F. Clapp, 1964: "Global distribution of normal surface albedo," *Geofisica Internacional*, **4(1)**: 33–48.

Schutz, C., and W. L. Gates, 1971: "Global climatic data for surface, 800 mb, 400 mb: January," R-915-ARPA, The Rand Corporation, Santa Monica, California, 173 pp. (and as supplemented in R-915/1-ARPA, 1972).

Schutz, C., and W. L. Gates, 1972: "Global climatic data for surface, 800 mb, 400 mb: July," R-1029-ARPA, The Rand Corporation, Santa Monica, California, 180 pp. (and as supplemented in R-1029/1-ARPA, 1973).

Vowinckel, E., and S. Orvig, 1970: "The climate of the North Polar Basin," in *Climates of the Polar Regions* (World Survey of Climatology, Vol. 14), Elsevier, New York, N. Y., pp. 129–252.

Washington, W. M., and L. G. Thiel, 1970: "Digitized global monthly mean ocean surface temperatures," NCAR-TN-54, National Center for Atmospheric Research, Boulder, Colorado.

Weller, G., and E. W. Bierly, 1973: "The polar experiment (POLEX)," *Bull. Amer. Meteor. Soc.*, **54**, 212–218.

Ice Age Experiments with the NCAR General Circulation Model: Conditions in the Vicinity of the Northern Continental Ice Sheets

JILL WILLIAMS[1] AND R. G. BARRY

Institute of Arctic and Alpine Research, University of Colorado, Boulder

Abstract

Global conditions for January and July have been simulated using the NCAR atmospheric circulation model in the vicinity of the North American and European ice sheets with boundary conditions corresponding to the present day and the last glacial maximum. Results from the simulations are discussed on the basis of 30 day means of the meteorological fields (days 51 to 80). The principal features observed at the present day are well-represented in the control cases, and the major differences between these and the ice age cases indicate the probable directions of change under ice age conditions.

Ground temperatures in North America and Europe are between 5C to 40C lower in January and July ice age cases than in the control cases and the meridional temperature gradients over the continents are greatly increased in January and July for the ice age cases. Changes in the zonal winds vary markedly according to season and longitude, and the jet stream does not move southward to skirt the ice sheets in the ice age cases. Precipitation amounts for the ice age cases are reduced in January and especially in July over North America and Europe, compared with the control cases.

In spite of its present limitations the NCAR model represents a valuable new tool for paleoclimatic studies.

---

1. Introduction

Global climatic conditions for January and July have been simulated using the atmospheric circulation model of the National Center for Atmospheric Research with boundary conditions corresponding to the present day and the last glacial maximum (*ca.* 20,000 BP). Details of the model are given by Kasahara and Washington (1971). A discussion of the input data and some results of the modeling are given in Williams, Barry and Washington (1973). For the control cases, which simulated modern January and July conditions, the input boundary conditions (orography, albedos, ocean surface temperatures) were based on present day information. For the ice age cases, the input boundary conditions were derived from a wide variety of geological and paleobiological sources. Results from the simulations are discussed on the basis of 30 day means of the meteorological fields (days 51 to 80) for each case. The present paper reports comparisons of ground temperature, zonal wind and precipitation distributions in the vicinity of the Laurentian and Scandinavian ice sheets, using January and July control and ice age cases and observed data.

2. Ground temperature

In the model, ocean surface temperatures are specified as input boundary conditions and are not recalculated during the simulation; surface temperature is computed over land and snow-ice areas based on the condition that there is no net heat flux through the atmosphere-ground interface. Over snow-ice regions an upper limit of 0C is assumed (Kasahara and Washington, 1971). Figures 1a and 1b show the simulated ground temperatures in the northern hemisphere for the January control case and ice age case respectively. Attention will be focused here on the temperatures in the vicinity of the ice sheets.

The January control case shows that the observed ocean-continent contrast is simulated, with North America and Asia significantly colder than the oceans. Europe is only slightly colder than the Atlantic as a result of strong maritime influences. Comparison of Fig. 1 with the map of surface mean ambient temperature for January, produced by Crutcher and Meserve (1970), shows that the January control case has simulated temperature distribution very well. Surface ambient temperature and ground temperature in the model usually differ by only a few degrees (Kasahara and Washington, 1971).

The January ice age ground temperatures (Fig. 1b) are much lower than those in the control case. The coldest area is still the Greenland ice cap, but the temperature has been reduced from −40C in the control case to −75C in the ice age case. The North American Arctic coast has temperatures from −10C to −30C in the control case and these fall to −30C to −60C in the ice age case. There is a stronger equator to pole temperature gradient over the North America continent in the ice age simulation. The presence of snow cover and an ice sheet in the ice age case has displaced th 0C isotherm only 4° latitude southward of its position over

---

[1] Present affiliation National Center for Atmospheric Research, Boulder, Colorado.

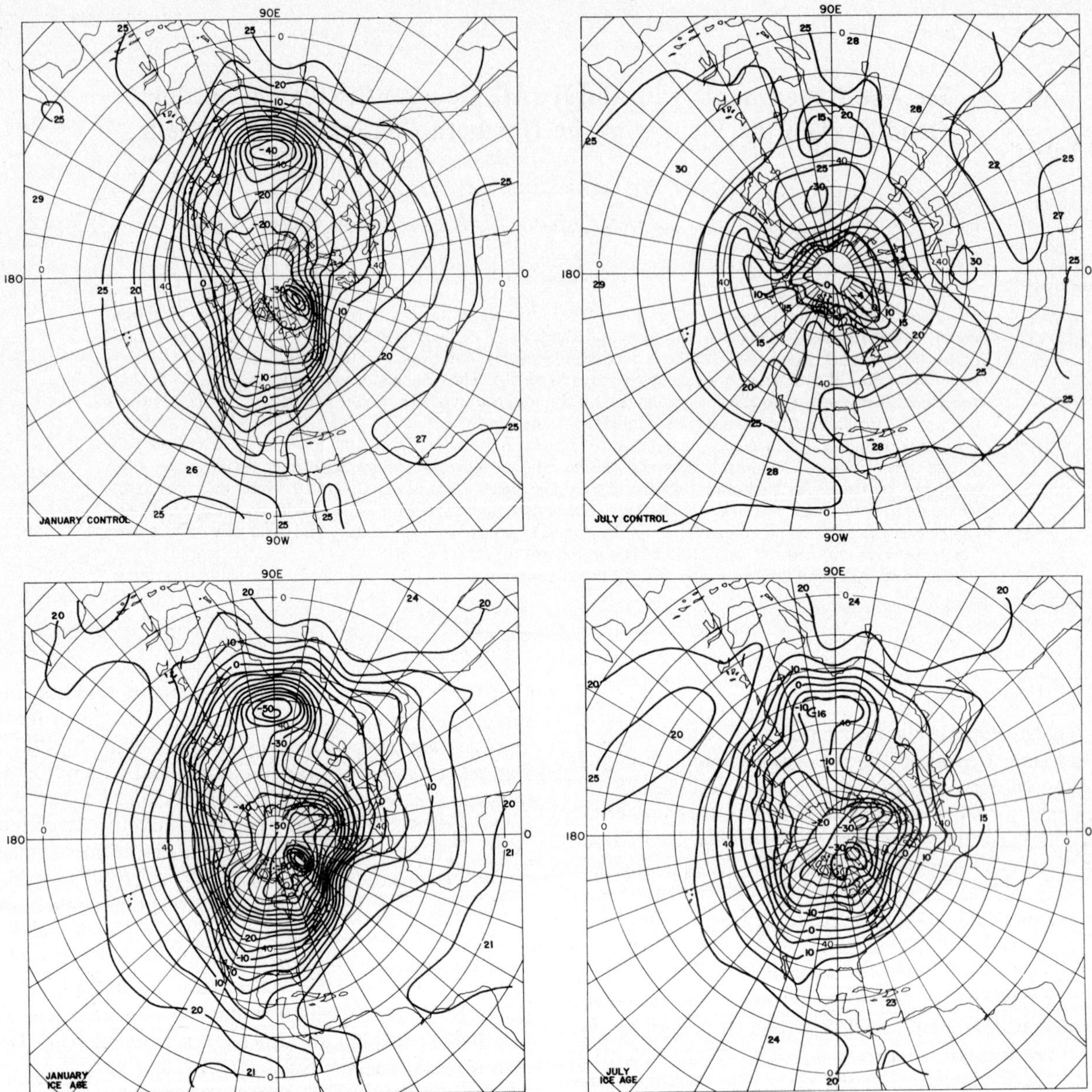

FIG. 1. 30-day mean ground temperature (°C); contour interval is 5C; 0C isotherm marked. a) January control case
(northern hemisphere); b) January ice age case; c) July control case; d) July ice age case.

North America in the control case. Thus, the temperature change between the equator and 30°N is at most only 5C from the control case to the ice age case, whereas the temperature change north of 30° latitude is at maximum about 30C. The major temperature change between the two cases is therefore in the vicinity of the Laurentide ice sheet in the North American sector.

Over northern Europe, there is a pronounced change in ground temperature between the control case and ice age case in January. In the control case, northern Norway is crossed by the 15C isotherm, in the ice age case it is crossed by the −55C isotherm. The 0C iso-

therm is shifted in the ice age case to 40°N; in the control case it occurs at between 60°N and 50°N over northwestern Europe. The maritime influence of the Atlantic Ocean upon northwestern Europe has been eliminated and a very strong temperature gradient occurs north of 50°N over the continent in the ice age case, in sharp contrast to the control case conditions.

Figs. 1c and 1d show the temperature distribution in the July control case and ice age case respectively. Again the control case data compare favorably with the observed data of Crutcher and Meserve. The continents are warmer than the oceans in the control case and the greatest temperature gradient occurs along the Arctic coast. The 0C isotherm occurs poleward of 80° latitude except in the vicinity of Greenland where it extends southward to about 65°N. However, the few grid points poleward of latitude 75°N causes uncertainty in the interpolated positions of the isotherms.

The July ice age ground temperature distribution strongly resembles that of the January control case. The 0C isotherm over North America is between 40°N and 45°N in the ice age case and the present-day continent-ocean thermal contrast is reversed so that the continents are colder than the oceans. The temperature of the North American Arctic coast is approximately

10C in the control case and from −30C to −15C in the ice age case. Over Europe the ground temperatures are much lower in the ice age case, with the meridional temperature gradient much increased. The inclusion of age boundary conditions in the general circulation model (GCM) has concentrated temperature gradients, caused strong cooling north of 40°N and much lower continental temperatures.

It has been pointed out to the authors, since this paper was written, that the parameterization of diffuse radiation in the GCM is not wholly realistic (Washington, pers. commun., 1974). The discrepancy causes

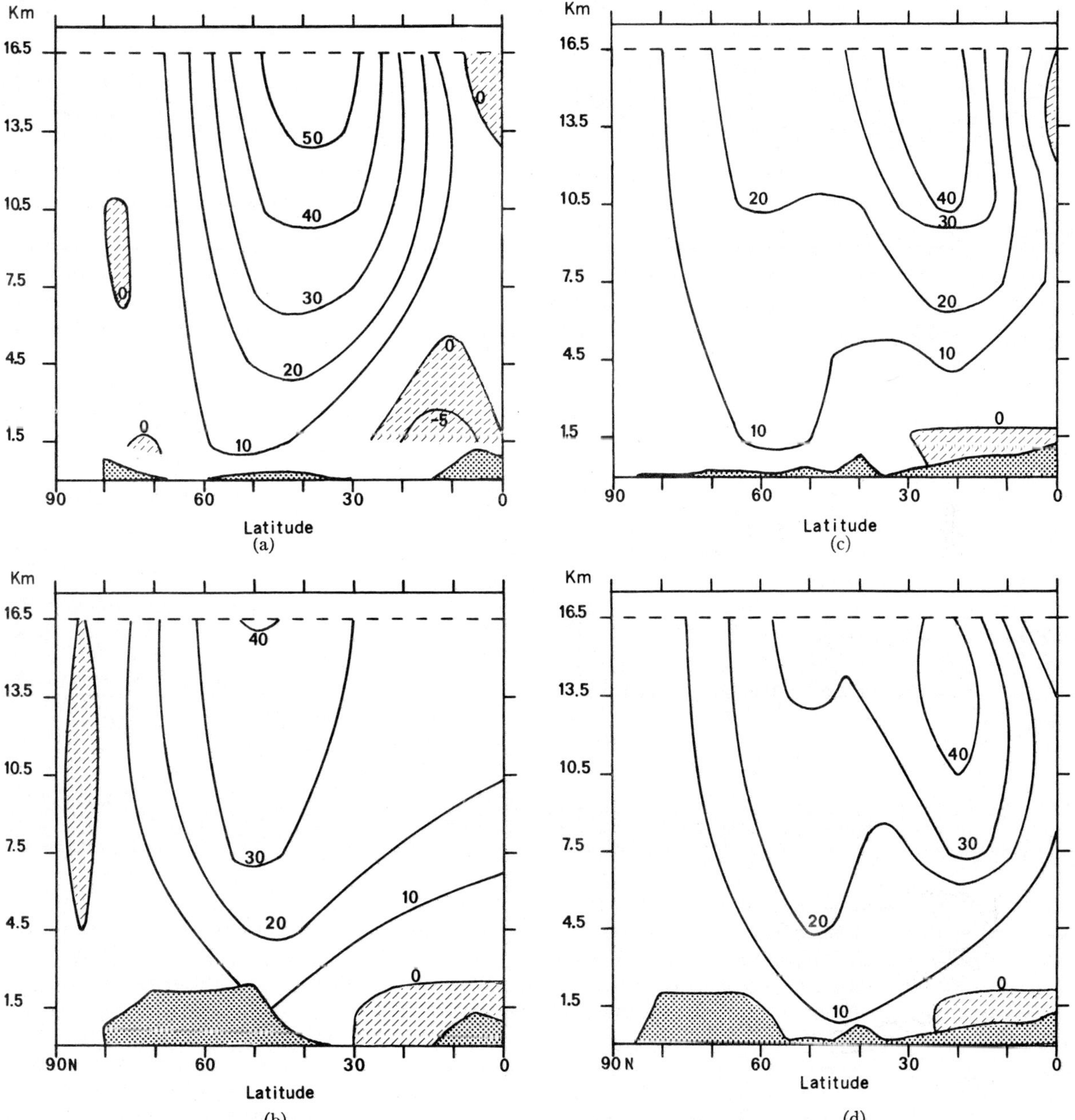

FIG. 2. Latitude-height distribution of 30-day mean zonal wind component (m sec⁻¹). a) January control case at 75°W; b) January ice age case at 75°W; c) January control case at 30°E; d) January ice age case at 30°E.

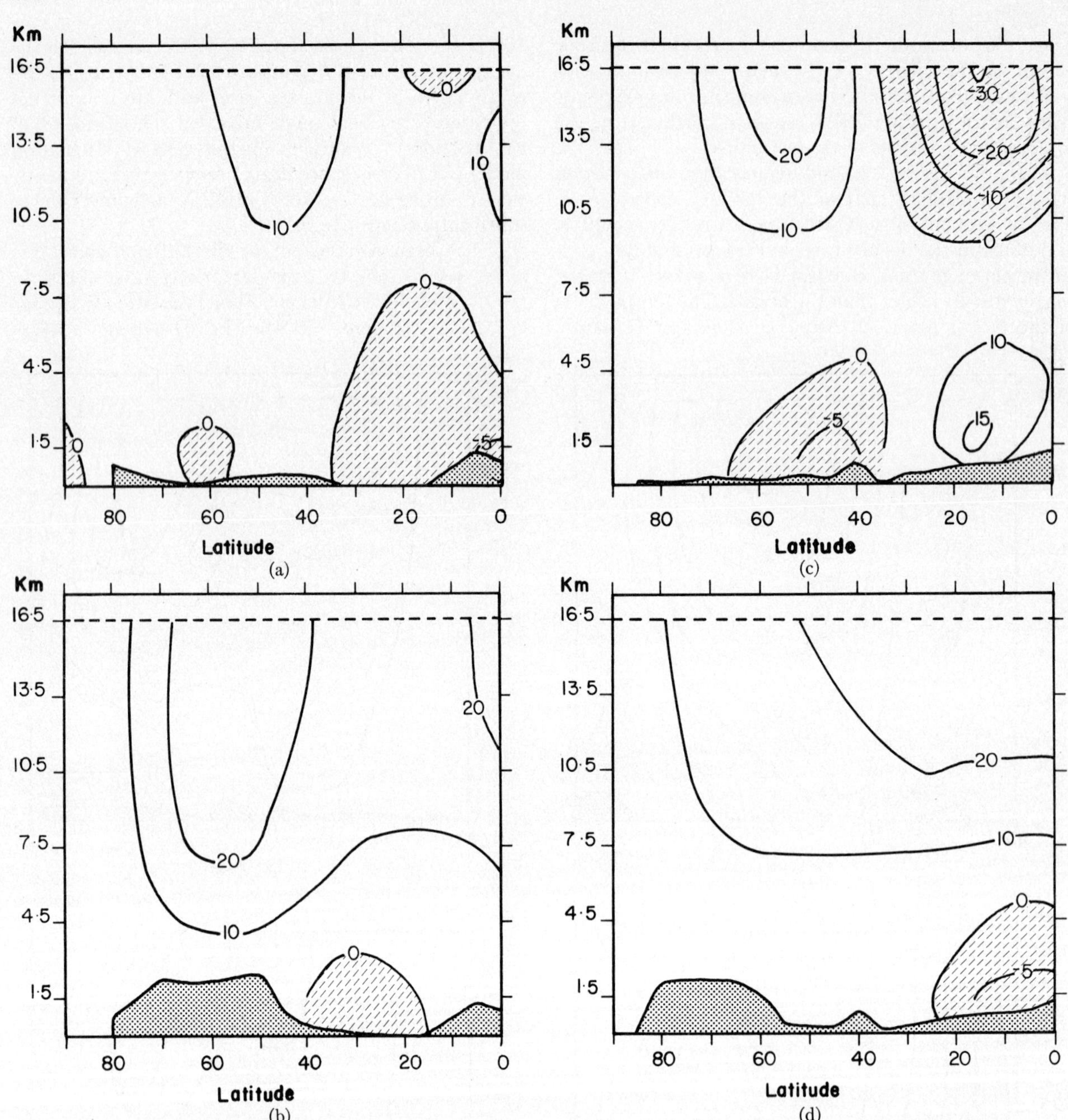

FIG. 3. Latitude-height distribution of 30-day mean zonal wind component (m sec⁻¹). a) July control case at 75°W; b) July ice age case at 75°W; c) July control case at 30°E; d) July ice age case at 30°E.

3. Zonal winds

surface temperatures to be underestimated when there is a high percentage of cloudiness. This will result in particularly low ground temperatures in the July ice age case, in which zonally averaged cloudiness was increased at nearly all latitudes compared with the control case.

The zonal wind structure at 75°W (over the Laurentide ice sheet) and at 30°E (over the European ice sheet) is shown in Figs. 2a–d for the January control cases and ice age cases and Figs. 3a–d for the July control cases and ice age cases. Cross sections for the January and July cases will be discussed. The control case meridional cross sections have been compared with a number of observed meridional sections at the same longitudes and no major discrepancies between observed and control case zonal wind structures have been observed.

At 75°W in January the ice age jet stream is weaker than in the control case, the upper tropical easterlies are missing and the polar easterlies are less extensive. In July, the jet stream in the ice age case is stronger (ice age case, 20 ms⁻¹, control case, 10 ms⁻¹) in response to

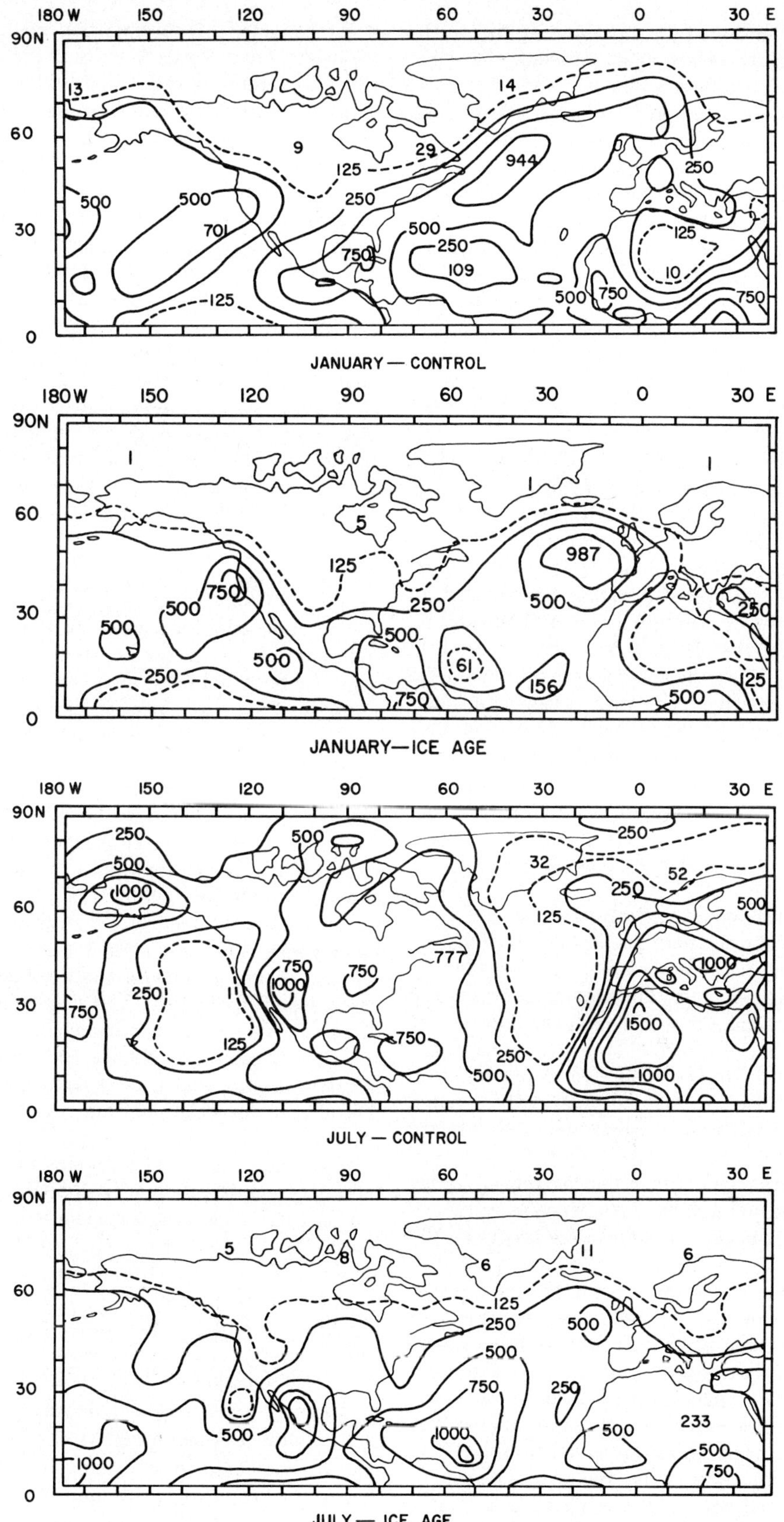

FIG. 4. 30-day mean precipitation (mm/90 days). Contour interval 250 mm. Dashed line marks 125 mm/90 days contour. a) January control case; b) January ice age case; c) July control case; d) July ice age case.

the intensified meridional temperature gradient, the upper tropical easterlies are again missing, the lower tropical easterlies are less extensive and the polar easterlies are missing, compared with the control case.

At 30°E in January the ice age case jet stream has the same strength as that in the control case and the only significant difference between the two cases is in the absence of upper tropical easterlies in the ice age case. In the July ice age case there is no pronounced jet stream but rather a belt of westerlies of 20 ms^{-1} extending from 50°N to the equator above 10.5 km. The July tropical easterly jet, situated between 35°N and 10°S in the control case, is not found in the ice age case nor are surface westerlies in the tropics. Surface easterlies in the control case between 30°N and 70°N are not found in the ice age case.

Meridional cross sections of the wind field show that the response of the zonal winds to inclusion of ice age boundary conditions in the NCAR GCM was not identical in the vicinity of the two major northern hemisphere ice sheets. There is no evidence to support the suggestion that the jet stream was forced south to skirt the ice sheets (for example, Lamb and Woodroffe, 1970). The ice age case jet stream is not consistently stronger or weaker than the control case jet stream, its strength and its location vary with season and longitude. The elimination of the tropical easterly jet over Africa in July suggests a weakening of the summer monsoon; the letter has indeed been proposed for India at the maximum of the last ice age by Joshi (1969).

4. Precipitation

Figs. 4a and 4b show the distribution of precipitation over the sector of the northern hemisphere in which the two major ice sheets were situated, for the January control case and ice age case. The major features of the observed distributions shown by Möller (1951) are depicted in the control case and it is clear that in the ice age simulation there is a reduction of precipitation in the vicinity of the ice sheets. Over North America the reduction is small since precipitation amounts are already low in the control case. Over northwestern Europe, precipitation amounts in the control case range from about 100 to 400 mm/90 days, whereas in the ice age case the precipitation is everywhere less than 100 mm/90 days.

The precipitation distributions over the same sector for the July control and ice age cases are shown in Figs. 4c and 4d. The control case compares less favorably with observed patterns for July, in particular, over the Sahara Desert. Experiments have shown that this type of anomaly is a result of the assumption in the model of a Bowen ratio uniformly equal to unity. The pattern of the changes between the two cases must, therefore, be treated with caution. There is a greater difference between the control and ice age cases than for the January cases and again the obvious difference

is the reduction of precipitation in the vicinity of the ice sheets. Over North America in the control case, precipitation amounts range from 300 to 900 mm/90 days, while in the ice age case there is a large reduction of precipitation, especially along the Arctic coast where there is less than 10 mm/90 days. Over northern Europe, control case precipitation amounts range from 50 to 600 mm/90 days. Again, the amounts along the Arctic coast are reduced greatly during the ice age simulation and are also reduced in the vicinity of the ice sheet.

Simulation of the atmospheric circulation using ice age boundary conditions has suggested that there was less precipitation in January and July especially in the vicinity of the Laurentian and Scandinavian ice sheets. It is interesting to note that several authors, often basing their ideas on geological evidence, have suggested that the maximum of the last ice age was drier than at present by *ca.* 20–30% (for example, Galloway, 1965, Flohn, 1964, Bonatti, 1966).

5. Conclusions

The simulation results show that there are major differences between the control cases and the ice age cases in both January and July. The significance of these differences will be evaluated in the near future by sensitivity tests on the model but it seems probable that at least the major features can be safely accepted.

The ground temperatures in North America and Europe are, as expected, much lower in the ice age case. The equator to pole temperature gradient over the continents is greatly increased in the ice age case and the continents are colder than the oceans even in summer. The temperature reduction in Arctic areas amounted to 40C in places. Precipitation amounts are reduced in the vicinity of the ice sheets in the ice age cases, especially in July. The zonal wind in the vicinity of the ice sheets did not change consistently between the control cases and the ice age cases; the difference between ice age and control varied with location and season and the jet stream did not move south to skirt the ice sheets.

This study shows what effects inclusion of ice age boundary conditions in the NCAR circulation model has on certain climatic elements in the vicinity of the ice sheets. While it is not claimed that the conditions simulated for the maximum of the last ice age represent in detail those prevailing at 20,000 BP, at least the direction of most of the major changes between the control cases and ice age cases should be valid. Meteorological inferences of this type can be tested with field evidence by geologists, palynologists, glaciologists and others, once it is confirmed that none of the primary features indicated in the ice age experiments is model dependent. Key areas needing improvement for such investigations relate to the terrestrial hydrological cycle and to ocean dynamics and thermodynamics.

Acknowledgments. We would like to thank Dr. Warren Washington of NCAR for his encouragement and assistance, Gloria Williamson of NCAR for supervising the running of the model and the NCAR computing facility for their support. The National Center for Atmospheric Research, Boulder, is supported by the National Science Foundation. Jill Williams is supported by a fellowship from the University of Colorado.

REFERENCES

Bonatti, E., 1966: North Mediterranean climate during the last Würm glaciation. *Nature*, **209**, 984–985.

Crutcher, H. L., and J. M. Meserve, 1970: Selected level heights, temperatures and dew points for the Northern Hemisphere, NAVAIR 50-1C-52. Revised Nav. Weather Serv. Command, Washington, D. C., 1970.

Flohn, H., 1964: Grundfragen der Palaoklimatologie im Lichte einer theoretischen Klimatologie. *Geologische Rundschau*, **54**, 504–575.

Galloway, R. W., 1965: Late Quaternary climates in Australia. *Journal of Geology*, **73**, 603–618.

Joshi, R., 1969: The characteristics of the Pleistocene climatic events of the Indian sub-continent. A land of monsoon climate. Études sur le Quaternaire dans le monde, VIII Congrès INQUA, Paris 1969, 493–500.

Kasahara, A., and W. M. Washington, 1971: General circulation experiments with a six layer NCAR model, including orography and cloudiness and surface temperature calculations. *Journal of Atmospheric Science*, **28**, 657–701.

Lamb, H. H., and A. Woodroffe, 1970: Atmospheric circulation during the last ice age. *Quaternary Research*, **1**, 29–58.

Möller, F., 1951: Vierteljahrskarten des Niederschlags für die ganze Erde. *Petermann's Geographische Mitteilungen*, **9**, 1–7.

Williams, Jill, R. G. Barry and W. M. Washington, 1973: Simulation of the climate at the last glacial maximum using the NCAR global circulational model. *Institute of Arctic and Alpine Research Occasional Paper* No. 5, University of Colorado, Boulder, 23 pp.

The Atmospheric Response to a Stratospheric Dust Cloud as Simulated by a General Circulation Model

E. S. Batten

The RAND Corporation, Santa Monica, California 90406

Abstract

The Rand version of the Mintz-Arakawa General Circulation model has been used to investigate the initial atmospheric response to a stratospheric dust cloud spread uniformly in a zone between 25°N and 75°N. In the experiment to be discussed, the dust cloud is assumed to consist of particles $2\,\mu$ in diameter or smaller, totaling 4×10^{-2} km³. This volume of dust is equal to the estimated volume ejected into the stratosphere by the 1883 eruption of Krakatoa. The stratospheric dust cloud is assumed to perturb the atmosphere by attenuating the solar radiation and by stimulating the precipitation process.

The model was integrated for a simulated period of 60 days corresponding to the months of January and February. The results were compared with a control experiment starting from the same initial conditions and simulating the same period. The following anomalies in temperature, precipitation, and atmospheric circulation were noted. In the atmosphere and at the surface beneath the dust cloud, the temperature decreased 2 to 3C and the normal wintertime land/ocean temperature contrasts were increased. Despite the specification of a 20-percent increase, the total precipitation at latitudes affected by the cloud did not change significantly. However, the latitudinal distribution of precipitation was modified. The precipitation at high latitudes (46°N to 74°N) actually decreased by about 20 percent, while at low latitudes (26°N to 46°N) the precipitation increased by about 23 percent. Although some of the anomalous precipitation patterns can be explained by anomalies in the evaporation, most are a direct result of changes in the circulation and moisture flux. The joint effects of decreasing the solar radiation and increasing the precipitation resulted in a weakening of the midlatitude Ferrel circulations, a decrease in the baroclinicity (and therefore in northward eddy transports of moisture) at high latitudes and an increase in the baroclinicity (and therefore northward eddy transports) at low latitudes.

---

1. Introduction

Man has become increasingly concerned with possible climatic changes produced by natural causes or inadvertently caused by human activities (SCEP, 1970; SMIC, 1971). With the present state of the art in general circulation models (GCMs), one has a tool with which to begin a more systematic evaluation of man's influence on his environment. To be sure, none of the atmospheric simulations produced by GCMs available today can be considered as totally accurate representations of the real atmosphere. The GCMs are, however, capable of simulating many of the important interactions taking place in the real atmosphere and capable of duplicating many details of the general circulation. It seems appropriate, then, to begin testing the GCMs' usefulness as a tool in climate studies. By comparing atmospheric simulations containing hypothetical anomalies with a control simulation that starts from identical initial conditions, perhaps one can gain both a better appreciation for the sensitivity of the model and some understanding of the perturbations produced by the anomalies. Several such experiments have already appeared in the literature (Washington, 1971 and 1972; Spar, 1973; Warshaw and Rapp, 1973; Kahle and Deirmendjian, 1973).

One of the above studies, *The Black Cloud Experiment* (Kahle and Deirmendjian, 1973), simulated a global reduction of solar radiation which, under some conditions, could be attributed to a turbid layer above the top of the model atmosphere. A turbid stratosphere has frequently been invoked to explain variations in the transmission and absorption of solar radiation leading to long-term changes in climate. Some proposed sources of the turbidity are volcanic eruptions (Humphreys, 1940, and Wexler, 1956), nuclear explosions (Stonier, 1963), and recently, particulate matter produced by supersonic transports (SCEP, 1970). It is possible that, under some conditions, the stratospheric turbidity layer would be confined primarily to one hemisphere either as a result of the location of the injection or by redistribution by the stratospheric circulation. As an interesting departure from the global nature of the Black Cloud Experiment, the experiment discussed here will investigate the effects of a stratospheric dust layer confined to the northern hemisphere.

It has also been suggested that particulate matter falling from the stratosphere to the troposphere might influence the precipitation process (Wexler, 1953 and 1956; Menzel, 1953, and Batten, 1966). Thus, in addition to attenuating the solar radiation, this experiment assumes that the dust cloud will act to stimulate the precipitation process.

The Mintz-Arakawa GCM described by Gates, *et al.* (1971) was used to perform the integration. As the results of the experiment are presented, we will be concerned not only with their interpretation as an anomalous event but also with how specifications of future models might improve interpretations of future experiments.

2. Design of the experiment

In addition to asking how human activities might produce climatic changes, one might ask how climatic changes influence human activities. When evaluating this inverse question, it would be helpful to have some estimates of the upper limits of climatic change. Accordingly, this experiment will employ a "worst case" strategy. That is, extreme values of stratospheric dust loading and upper limit estimates of cloud seeding effects will be assumed.

It has been estimated that the 1883 eruption of Krakatoa produced a volume of dust totaling about 4×10^{-2} km³ and consisting of particles $2\,\mu$ in diameter or smaller. However, the Krakatoa dust was confined to the zone between 30°S and 30°N. We are assuming in this experiment that the dust will be confined to a latitude belt of 25°N to 75°N, approximately half the area covered by the Krakatoa cloud.

Attenuation of solar radiation

Deirmendjian (1971) evaluated the role of the volcanic dust in increasing atmospheric particulate turbidity. On the basis of his conclusions he also provided a "dirty cloud" model for use in a "worst case" experiment. The rationale for the "dirty cloud" model can be found in the above-mentioned report. Here I will only discuss the changes to the Mintz-Arakawa model.

The solar radiation simulated in the Mintz-Arakawa model is divided into two parts (see Gates, *et al.*, 1971, Chapter II, Section G). The radiation of wavelength $\lambda < 0.9\,\mu$ is assumed to be subject to Rayleigh scattering only; that of wavelength $\lambda > 0.9\,\mu$ is assumed to be subject to absorportion only in a clear atmosphere. The part subject to scattering is given by $0.651\,S_0$ where S_0 is the solar constant. Only the part subject to scattering is assumed to be affected in this experiment. Deirmendjian's dirty cloud then consists in assigning the following optical thicknesses over the short-wave range:

$$\tau_D = 1.05 \quad \text{"blue sun" stage,}$$

$$\tau_D = 0.92 \quad \text{"Bishop's ring" stage,}$$

where the first is representative of the initial few weeks after the Krakatoa eruption, and the second to the more stable stage. In this experiment the Bishop's ring mean optical thickness is used. Thus the solar radiation subject to scattering is reduced by a factor

$$e^{-\tau_D} = 0.4, \tag{1}$$

amounting to a loss of total incoming radiation under the dust cloud given by

$$0.651(1 - e^{-\tau_D})S_0 = 0.39\,S_0 \tag{2}$$

This amount of attenuation represents a decrease in the globally averaged incoming radiation of about 5 percent, if the dust cloud is in the winter hemisphere, and of about 15 percent if it is in the summer hemisphere. Since the experiment discussed here is simulating northern winter conditions, the net attenuation is comparable to that assumed in the Black Cloud experiment (Kahle and Deirmendjian, 1973). However, in that experiment, the solar radiation was attenuated globally, whereas in this one, the attenuation is confined to a broad belt in the northern hemisphere.

Modification of precipitation

The Bergeron ice-crystal process is one mechanism by which cloud droplets grow to sizes large enough to fall as some form of precipitation. Briefly, the ice-crystal theory states that ice crystals, when surrounded by supercooled water droplets, will grow at the expense of the water droplets, since vapor pressure is less over ice than over water. In other words, when the air is saturated with respect to water it is supersaturated with respect to ice, and condensation on the ice crystal will result. Water droplets are observed in clouds often at temperatures as low as $-20C$ and sometimes $-35C$; hence if ice crystals are introduced into the cloud, the stage is set for creation of precipitation. As in the case of condensation, the initiation of freezing requires a suitable nucleus. The most active ice nuclei are non-soluble, wettable particles of dust and soil about $1\,\mu$ in radius. The prevalence of liquid-water clouds down to $-15C$ suggests that efficient ice nuclei are rare, at least at the altitudes where ice crystals "seed" the supercooled clouds. It is not unreasonable to suspect that the efficiency of the Bergeron process might increase as the stratospheric dust slowly falls into the upper troposphere. It is also possible that the dust may inhibit precipitation by "over-seeding" the clouds. In this experiment we assume that the precipitation will increase by approximately 20 percent in the zone between 25°N and 75°N.

The Mintz-Arakawa model simulates three types of precipitation. Large-scale precipitation occurs when the relative humidity at a point exceeds 100 percent. The amount of large-scale precipitation is equal to the amount of moisture that must be removed to reduce the relative humidity to 100 percent. In this experiment, the increased precipitation is simulated by lowering the threshold for rain to 99.675 percent relative humidity. In a separate study it was determined

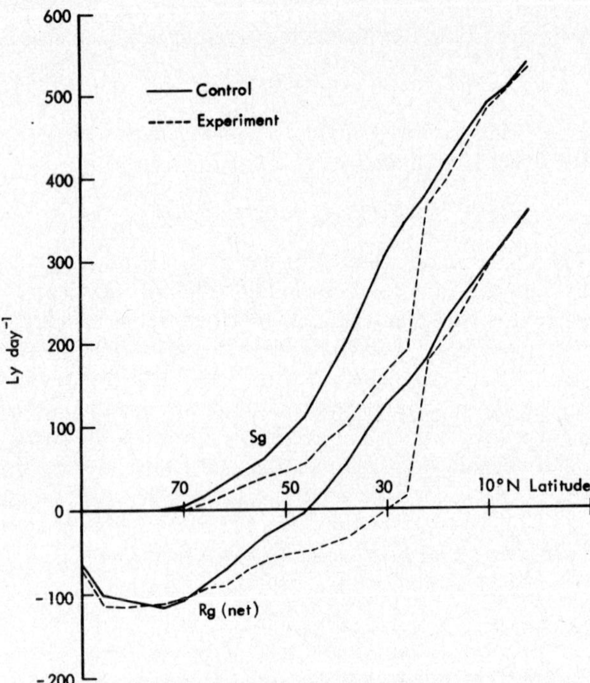

FIG. 1. Radiation budget at the ground. S_g is the solar radiation absorbed at the ground, R_g (net) is the net radiation at the ground (solar long wave).

that lowering the threshold to this value was equivalent to an increase in precipitation of 20 percent.

The other two types of precipitation, middle-level and penetrating convective rain, are similar in that they both require regions of moist convective instabilities in the atmosphere (Gates, *et al.*, 1971, Chapter II, Section F). The amount of convective precipitation is determined by the amount of condensation required to relieve the instability through the release of latent heat. Not all of the instability is removed at once, the rate being controlled by a time constant determined by the parameterized amount of convective activity occurring in each grid cell. In this experiment, the convective precipitation is assumed to increase by 20 percent, which is equivalent to decreasing the *e*-folding time for the decay of the moist convective instability. In other words, we have made the convective activity more vigorous.

3. Results

The data used in this Report are from Control III and the Stratospheric Dust Cloud experiment (experiment 17). The Control III was integrated for a 90-day period that corresponds to the months of December, January, and February. After the changes to the model outlined in Section II were made, experiment 17 was integrated for a 60-day period. This period corresponds to 31 December through 28 February. The results of experiment 17 at best represent the model's initial responses to the simulated stratospheric dust cloud.

The period chosen for analysis was a 25-day period

(21 January through 14 February). The choice of this period was dictated by the occurrence of unusually high and unrealistic rates of precipitation in both Control III and experiment 17. In Control III extremely high rates of precipitation were encountered in a small area on the northwest coast of South America. In experiment 17 similar conditions occurred over the Amazon Basin. To exclude these anomalous events, only a 25-day average was analyzed to eliminate as much as possible their influence on the interpretation of the results. The cause of the events will be the subject of a future investigation.

Changes in the radiation budget

Since we have assumed that the dust cloud affects only the radiation subject to scattering by the atmosphere, the initial effect of the cloud will be to decrease the radiation absorbed at the ground. The imposed anomaly in the solar radiation absorbed at the ground (S_g) is shown by the upper pair of curves in Fig. 1. The solid line gives S_g for the control run, and the dashed line gives S_g for this experiment. The difference between these two curves essentially reflects the attenuation indicated by Eq. (2).

The lower pair of curves in Fig. 1 gives the net radiation gained at the ground (solar radiation absorbed less the long-wave radiation lost by the ground). The normal winter pattern for the net radiation gained at the ground is demonstrated by the R_g (net) curve for the control; the ground in polar regions cools radiatively in winter while the ground in lower latitudes is warmed radiatively. The effect of the anomaly produced in the radiation budget by the dust cloud is to extend the region of radiative cooling southward to 30°N. The difference between R_g (net) curves represent the radiation anomaly imposed on the earth-atmosphere system by the dust cloud.

The way in which the radiation anomaly is communicated to the more tangible meteorological variables of the lower boundary, and then to the atmosphere, is partially restricted by assumptions made in formulating the numerical model. In the Mintz-Arakawa model, ocean temperatures are assumed to be constant in time. In effect, we are assuming an infinite heat capacity for the ocean. On the other hand, over the land, zero heat capacity is assumed, and the ground temperatures there are determined from a balance between net radiation at the surface, the heat loss by evaporation, and the sensible heat flux from the surface. Thus ground temperatures over land are permitted to cool in response to the imposed radiation anomaly, whereas ocean temperatures remain fixed.

The anomalies of the zonal average ground temperature over land are shown in Fig. 2. The ground temperatures over land beneath most of the dust cloud have been decreased by 2 to 4 degrees. The large anomaly near the North Pole is probably due to the normal

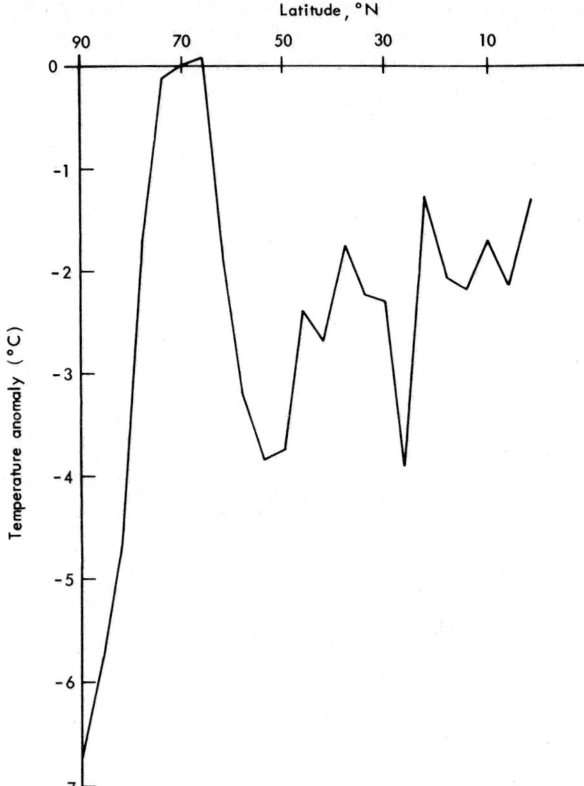

Fig. 2. Zonal average ground temperature anomaly (°C).

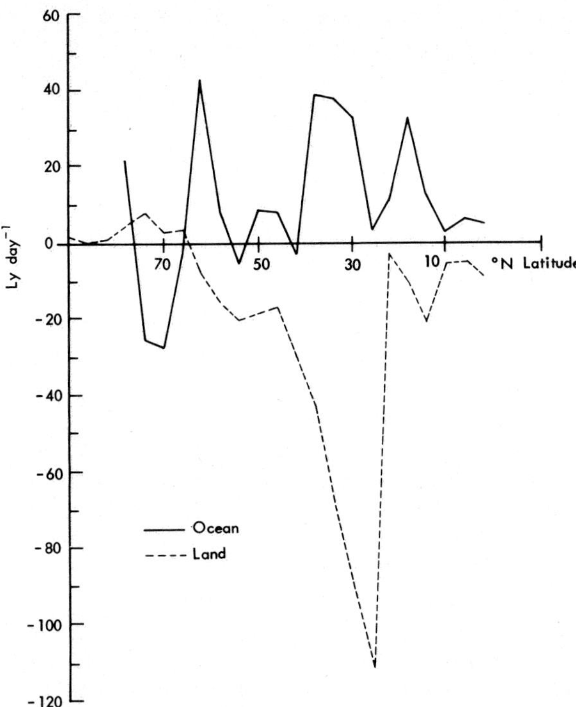

Fig. 3. Zonal average sensible heat flux anomaly (ly day⁻¹). Positive values represent an increased flux to the atmosphere.

variability of the atmosphere and not a result of the experiment. Similar large fluctuations of ground temperature have been observed in data from earlier model experiments.*

Although the zonal average ground temperature of the land masses as a general rule has decreased, local exceptions to this rule can be found in areas of increased cloudiness. In areas of a positive cloudiness anomaly, the amount of long-wave radiation trapped in the lowest layer and returned to the surface has increased (the "greenhouse" effect), thus counteracting some of the cooling due to the loss of solar radiation at the surface. The zero ground temperature anomaly at 70 degrees latitude and the minimum anomaly near 40 degrees latitude, shown in Fig. 2, result from belts of increased cloudiness. As we shall see later, the southern belt of increased cloudiness is associated with a region of increased precipitation.

The anomalies in the ground temperature produced by the dust cloud are communicated to the atmosphere principally through the flux of sensible heat from the ground. On a long-term average, the net loss of radiation in the atmosphere is balanced by the transfer of the excess energy received at the surface through the processes of sensible and latent heat flux to the atmo-

sphere. During winter, air passing over the land masses is cooled from below and that passing over the oceans is warmed from below. During summer the roles are reversed; the ocean acts as a heat sink and the land as

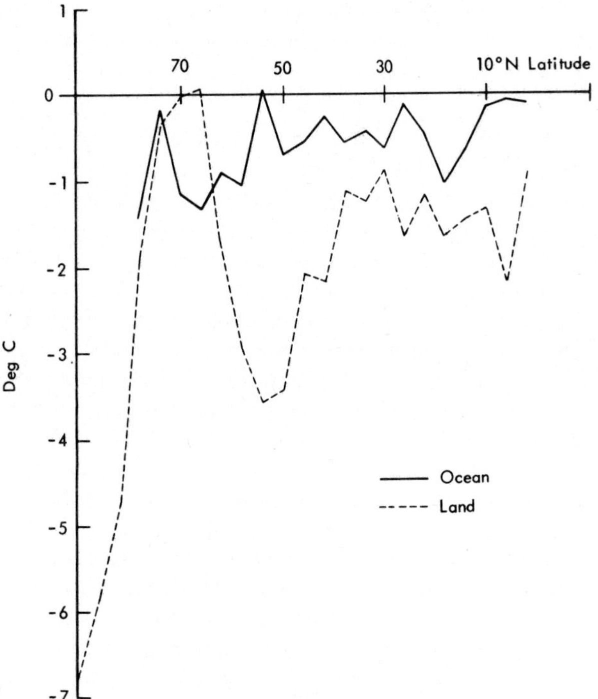

Fig. 4. Zonal average surface air temperature anomaly (°C).

---

* See, for example, Warshaw and Rapp (1973) and Kahle and Diermendjian (1973).

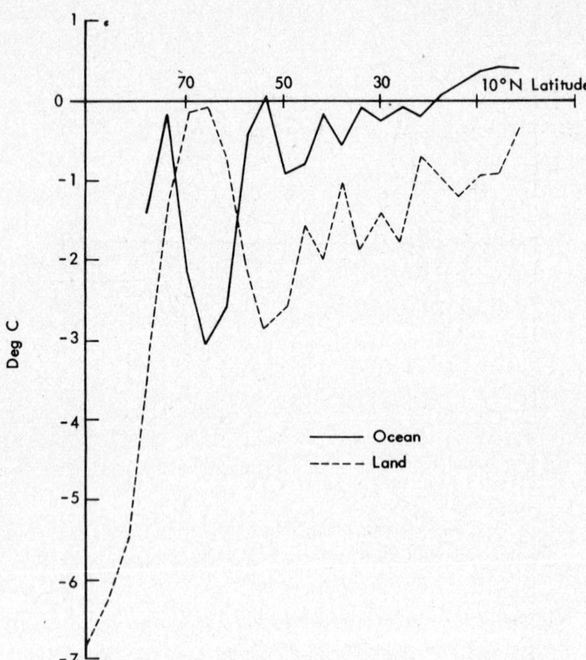

Fig. 5. Zonal average 800 mb temperature anomaly (°C).

a source. The sensible heat flux anomaly given in Fig. 3 shows that the dust cloud has magnified the normal winter role of the ocean as an atmospheric heat source and the land as a heat sink.

The effect of these anomalous sources and sinks on atmospheric temperature is shown in Fig. 4 for the surface air temperature anomaly and Fig. 5 for the 800 mb temperature anomaly. At both the surface and 800 mb the air over the land has cooled relative to the air over the ocean. This magnified land-ocean temperature contrast is not evident at the 400 mb level.

Moisture balance anomalies

This experiment postulates a 20 percent increase of precipitation in the region beneath the dust cloud (25°N to 74°N). In nature precipitation normally exceeds evaporation in the region north of 35°N. This deficit of moisture in the midlatitude storm belt is made up by a net northward flux of water vapor from the subtropical region where evaporation exceeds precipitation. The latitude of zero northward flux of water vapor lies near 25°N. Hence, north of 25°N, precipitation is in balance with evaporation. For the 20 percent increase of precipitation in the experiment to be maintained for any extended period of time, either the evaporation must increase, the moisture flux patterns must change, or both must change to accommodate the increase.

Figure 6 gives the precipitation, evaporation, and moisture flux-convergence anomalies produced by the dust cloud. We note that the precipitation (Fig. 6a) has increased between 26°N and 46°N. But, despite the conditions specified in the experiment, the precipi-

tation has decreased in the latitude belt between 46°N and 74°N. The anomaly at low latitudes (26°N–46°N) beneath the dust cloud represent a 22.8-percent increase and that at high latitudes (47°N–74°N) a 19.5-percent decrease in precipitation. The total precipitation beneath the dust cloud has increased slightly. The slight increase in precipitation at latitudes affected by the cloud is not statistically significant. However, the decrease at high latitudes is significant at the 5-percent level and the low-latitude increase is significant at the 1-percent level.

Some of the moisture (39 percent) for the increase in precipitation at low latitudes is supplied by an increase in evaporation (Fig. 6b). At higher latitudes the evaporation is substantially unchanged. The remainder of the precipitation increase at low latitudes (61 percent) and the decrease in precipitation at high latitudes must, therefore, result from changes in the pattern of moisture flux.

Figure 6c gives the moisture flux-convergence anomaly. At high latitudes almost all of the decrease in precipitation results from a decreased convergence of moisture into the region. The moisture balance for the southern and northern regions beneath the dust cloud are summarized in Table 1.

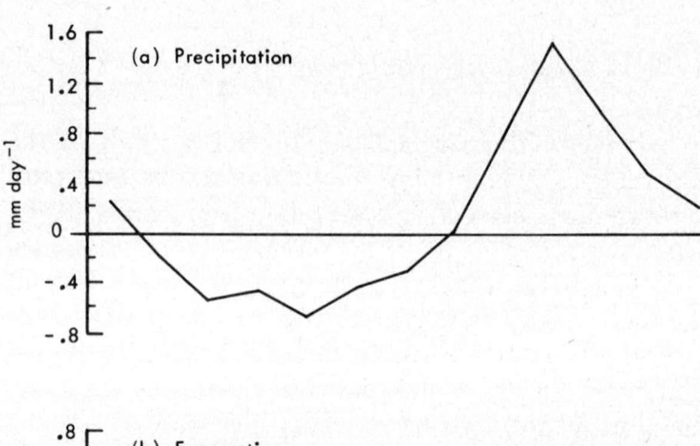

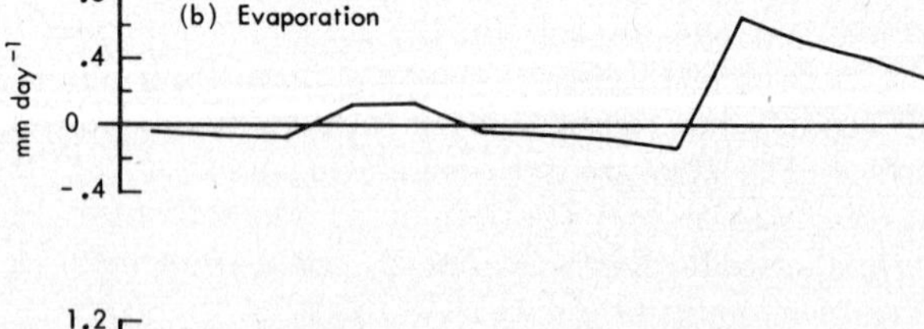

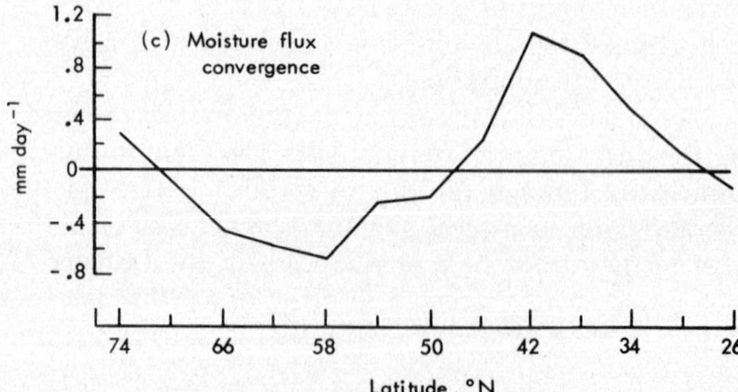

Fig. 6. Moisture balance anomalies.

TABLE 1. Moisture balance beneath the cloud.
(all units in mm day^{-1})

		26°N to 46°N	50°N to 74°N
Precipitation	Control	17.536	11.628
	Experiment 17	21.472	9.361
	Anomaly	+3.936	−2.267
Evaporation	Control	24.820	4.840
	Experiment 17	26.357	4.863
	Anomaly	+1.536	+0.023
Moisture convergence	Control	−7.429	6.620
	Experiment 17	−4.800	4.641
	Anomaly	+2.629	−1.979

The net effect of the dust cloud has been to produce a low-latitude belt of increased precipitation and a high-latitude belt of decreased precipitation. Most of the change in the precipitation pattern has been a result of changes in the moisture flux and thus of changes in the circulation. To explore the nature of the changes in the circulation patterns, the moisture flux for the control and the experiment are shown in Fig. 7. While the moisture flux given in Fig. 7 is about a factor of 2 larger than is observed in nature, the latitude distribution is reproduced fairly well. The important features of Fig. 7 are the increased northward flux south of about 40°N and the decreased northward flux north of 40°N. These two regions correspond to the regions of convergence and divergence shown in Fig. 6c. The net moisture flux can be considered to be the sum of the flux due to the mean meridional circulation and the flux due to eddies both standing and transient. This division is shown in Fig. 8 displayed as an anomaly (experiment minus control).

The solid curve in Fig. 8 is the total moisture-flux anomaly and is the difference between the two curves in Fig. 7. The dashed curve is the moisture flux anomaly due to the mean meridional circulation. As can be seen, the mean meridional circulation increases the southward flux of moisture from beneath the dust cloud. Exceptions are found near 70°N and 30°N, where small positive values are shown (northward flux). Thus the mean meridional circulation does not supply the moisture for the southern rain belt. The convergence of moisture there is provided by an increase in the eddy flux of moisture (dot and dash curve of Fig. 8). The mean meridional circulation and a southward eddy flux contribute equally to the northern region of moisture divergence.

Circulation anomalies

The anomalies in the mean meridional circulation and the eddy activity suggested by Fig. 8 can be seen more clearly in Figs. 9–11. Figure 9 shows the zonally averaged mass flux for the control. A strong Hadley cell is evident at low latitudes and a weak Ferrel cell at

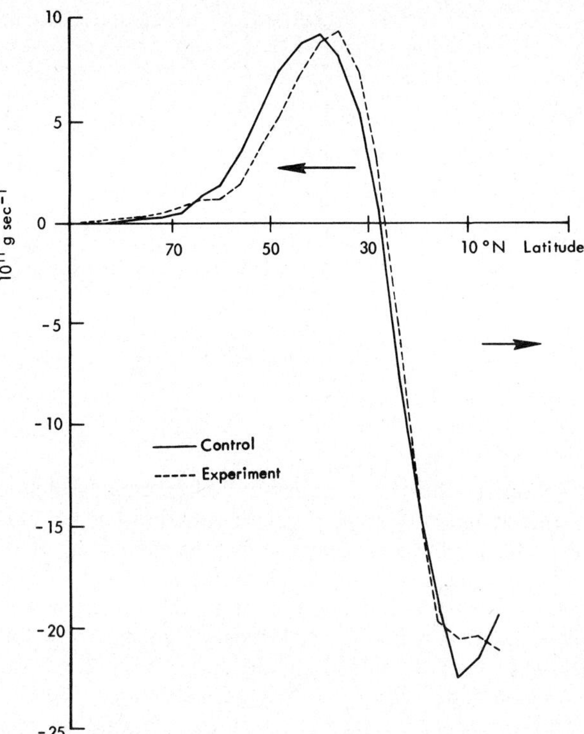

FIG. 7. Moisture flux 10^{11} g sec^{-1}: Positive values represent a northward flux. Negative values represent a southward flux.

midlatitudes. Figure 9 is similar to the results from an earlier control discussed by Gates (1972). Figure 10 gives the zonally averaged mass-flux anomaly produced by the experiment. Near the center of the region beneath the dust cloud, the anomaly shows that a strong direct-circulation cell (Hadley type) has been produced with weak indirect cells (Ferrel type) near the northern and

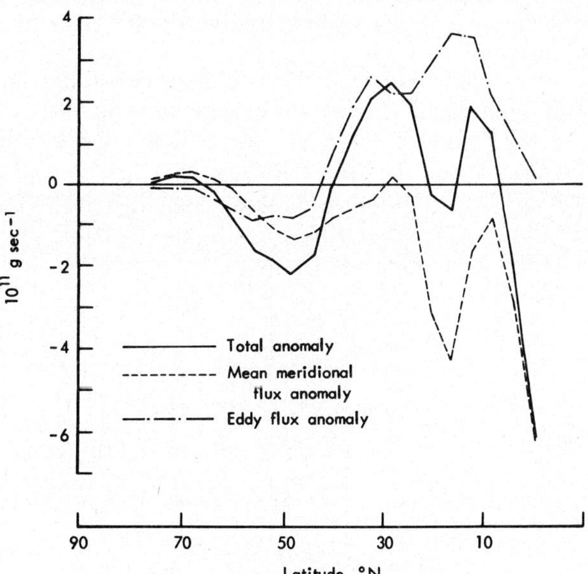

FIG. 8. Moisture flux anomaly (10^{11} gm sec^{-1}).

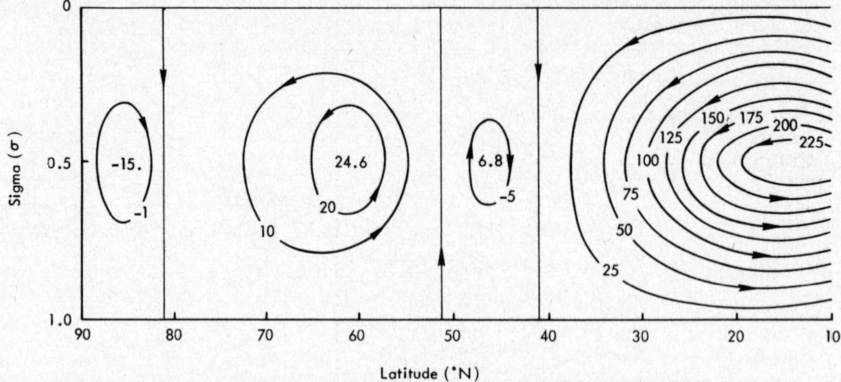

FIG. 9. Zonally averaged mass flux (10^{12} g sec^{-1}) for the control.

southern boundaries. The rising and sinking branches of this anomalous circulation correspond exactly to the wet and dry belts as shown in Fig. 6a suggesting that the maintenance of this circulation is to a large extent due to the release of latent heat in the southern wet zone. As shown in Fig. 8, however, the moisture for the wet zone is supplied by an increased eddy flux. The increased eddy activity accompanies an increase in the baroclinicity produced by latent heat release in the ascending branch of the circulation, coupled with cooling at higher latitudes induced by the surface heat sink discussed in the section on the radiation budget. The stronger north–south temperature gradients at 800 mb can be inferred from Fig. 5. Other measures of the changing patterns of baroclinicity, shown in Fig. 11, are the anomaly in the vertical wind shear and eddy kinetic-energy anomaly. Both the wind shear and the eddy kinetic energy show a decrease in the same high latitude belt where a decrease in northward eddy flux of moisture was observed (Fig. 8). At lower latitudes, the increased wind shear and eddy kinetic energy corresponds to the region of increased northward eddy flux of moisture.

In summary, the joint effects of decreasing the solar radiation and increasing the precipitation has led to the weakening of the Ferrel circulation cell beneath the dust cloud. The baroclinicity has decreased beneath the northern portion of the dust cloud and increased beneath the southern portion. The baroclinic zone is thus moved to a position near the southern boundary of the dust cloud, where the associated eddies provide the transport mechanism that feeds moisture to a belt of increased precipitation.

4. Discussion

The results presented in the previous section raise some interesting questions that cannot be answered by a short 60-day simulation using a model with the present formulation. The results of the Black Cloud experiment (Kahle and Deirmendjian, 1973) suggest that the atmosphere has not yet reached a winter equilibrium state at the end of a 60-day simulation. There is no reason to believe that this experiment differs from the Black Cloud in that respect. Perhaps more significant to this experiment, which purports to represent conditions following a cataclysmic event, is the question of the model's ability to respond to events created by the perturbing influence and its ability to propagate these responses through the annual cycle and to other latitudes. The restrictions placed in the present model on the lower boundary conditions over both ocean and land surfaces represent a serious impediment to the model's ability to respond. Even by relaxing the restrictions on the lower boundary by specifying seasonally varying surface conditions, the model at best would be asked to respond to a previous

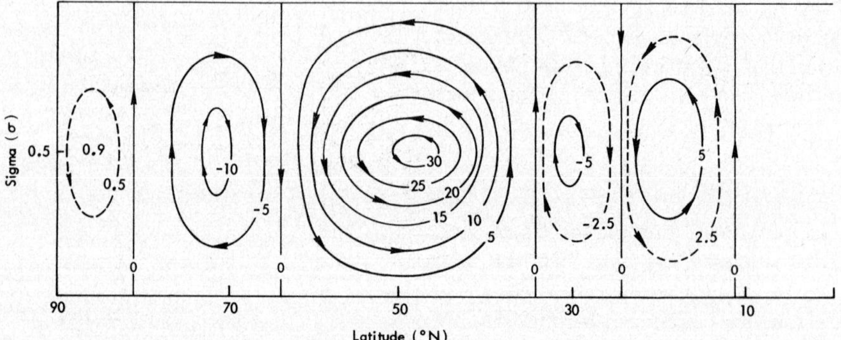

FIG. 10. Zonally averaged mass flux anomaly (10^{12} g sec^{-1}).

"climate" not necessarily similar to the one the experiment attempts to produce. This experiment is a good example of some of these problems.

The presence of the dust cloud has resulted in decreasing temperatures over the land. One can reasonably assume that this would result in a southward extension of the snow field. The increase in the surface albedo produced by the snow covering would further reduce the solar radiation absorbed at the ground. At the present time the surface albedo is specified for each grid point and held constant in time. Clearly, a variable surface condition must be permitted in the basic model in order to realize the full impact on the atmosphere of perturbations like the stratospheric dust cloud.

Once having produced an abnormal southward extension of the snow field, it may be maintained for a longer period of time through spring and perhaps summer. Normally the surface near 45° latitude receives about 300 ly day^{-1} in spring and 500 ly day^{-1} in summer. A debris cloud persistent through the spring and summer seasons would reduce these amounts to approximately 180 ly day^{-1} and 300 ly day^{-1}; a substantial loss of energy normally available to be used to melt snow and thaw the ground.

While the 39 percent loss of radiation to the atmosphere due to the dust cloud is in itself significant, the longer lasting high albedo of the persistent snow cover, a delayed snow melt, and a delayed thawing of the ground represent an additional loss of energy to the spring and summer atmosphere. For example, the albedo of old snow is 50 percent (Houghton, 1958) reducing the already depleted radiation absorbed by the ground into 90 ly day^{-1}. Again, according to Houghton (1958), the loss of energy to the atmosphere in melting 5 cm of snow is 40 ly day^{-1} and thawing the ground in cloudy conditions is 80 ly day^{-1}. One must anticipate a greatly modified spring and summer followed by a winter with anomalous conditions substantially different from those shown by the present data.

In summary, the interesting results produced by this experiment suggest that further experimentation with perturbations of a similar nature is warranted. However, future experiments should be performed with a model capable of simulating the important feedback mechanisms, since we are looking for quasi-permanent changes that can be propagated in time and that are not diminished or removed as the dust cloud is removed. Some of the feedback mechanisms that the model should be able to simulate have been enumerated in the preceding paragraphs. One that has not been listed and that should not be overlooked is the need to include a truly interactive ocean. As the land cools in response to the decreased solar radiation so should the ocean. Plans to include an ocean model are currently underway.

Finally, in addition to the improved model but equally important, is the need to improve our understanding of the physical processes that are ultimately

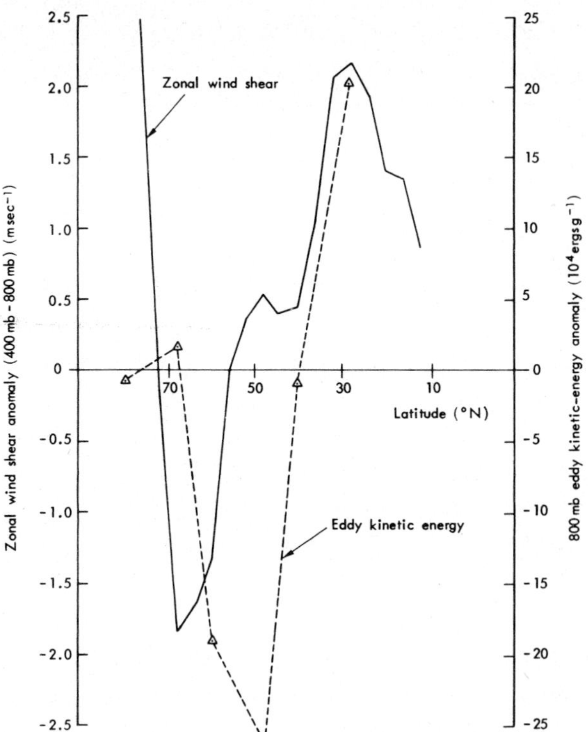

FIG. 11. Measures of baroclinic instability anomalies.

responsible for the attenuation of the solar radiation and modification of the precipitation. The effects of aerosols on solar radiation need further research if we are to improve the first-order estimates of the attenuation used in this experiment. Similarly, the effect of an increase of ice nuclei needs to be clarified. Regardless of the quality of the model and its integration, if we are not confident in our understanding of these processes, the interpretation of the results of any experiment will remain "in doubt."

Acknowledgments. The author would like to thank Dr. D. Deirmendjian and A. B. Kahle for helpful suggestions, and for carefully reviewing and commenting on the manuscript.

REFERENCES

Batten, E. S., 1966: *The Effects of Nuclear War on the Weather and Climate.* The Rand Corporation, RM-4989-TAB.

Deirmendjian, D., 1971: *Global Turbidity Studies: I. Volcanic Dust Effects—A Critical Survey.* The Rand Corporation, R-886-ARPA. See also "On Volcanic and Other Turbidity Anomalies," *Adv. Geoph.,* 16, 267–296 (1973).

Gates, W. L., E. S. Batten, A. B. Kahle and A. B. Nelson, 1971: *A Documentation of the Mintz-Arakawa Two-Level Atmospheric General Circulation Model.* The Rand Corporation, R-877-ARPA.

Gates, W. L., 1972: *The January Global Climate Simulated by the Two-Level Mintz-Arakawa Model: A Comparison with Observation.* The Rand Corporation, R-1005-ARPA.

Houghton, D. M., 1958: Heat Sources and Sinks at the Earth's Surface. *Meteorol. Mag.,* 87, 132–143.

Humphreys, W. J., 1940: *Physics of the Air*, New York and London, McGraw-Hill.

Kahle, A. B., and D. Deirmendjian, 1973: *The Black Cloud Experiment*. The Rand Corporation, R-1263-ARPA.

Menzel, Donald H., 1953: On the Causes of the Ice Ages, Chapter 7, *Climatic Change*. Harlow Shapley (Ed.), Harvard University Press, Cambridge, Mass.

SCEP, 1970: *Man's Impact on the Environment. Report of the Study of Critical Environmental Problems*. MIT Press, Cambridge, 319 pp.

SMIC, 1971. *Inadvertent Climate Modification. Report of the Study of Man's Impact on the Environment (SMIC)*. MIT Press, 308 pp.

Spar, Jerome, 1973: Some Effects of Surface Anomalies in a Global General Circulation Model. *Monthly Weather Rev.*, **101**, 2, 91–100.

Stonier, T., 1963: *Nuclear Disaster*. Meridian Books (M154), The World Publishing Company, Cleveland and New York.

Warshaw, M., and R. R. Rapp, 1973: An Experiment on the Sensitivity of a Global Circulation Model. *J. Appl. Meteorol.*, **12**, 1, 43–49.

Washington, Warren M., 1971: On the Possible Use of Global Atmospheric Models for the Study of Air and Thermal Pollution. *Man's Impact on the Climate*, W. H. Matthews, *et al.* (Eds.), Cambridge, Mass., The MIT Press, 265–276.

Washington, Warren M., 1972: Numerical Climatic-Change Experiments: The Effect of Man's Production of Thermal Energy. *J. Appl. Meteorol.*, **11**, 5, 768–771.

Wexler, H., 1953: *Radiation Balance of the Earth as a Factor in Climatic Change*, Chapter 5, *Climatic Change*, Harlow Shapley (Ed.), Harvard University Press, Cambridge, Mass.

Wexler, H., 1956: Variations in Insolation, General Circulation and Climate. *Tellus*, **8**, 4, 480–494.

Man-Made Aerosols and the Heating of the Atmosphere over Polar Regions

PETR CHÝLEK* AND JAMES A. COAKLEY, JR.

*Advanced Study Program, National Center for Atmospheric Research,** Boulder, Colorado 80302*

Abstract

The heating of the earth-atmosphere system caused by an aerosol layer has been analyzed using the two stream-approximation for the equation of radiative transfer. Two models using this approximation have been developed—one is applicable to global average conditions, while the second model includes the dependence of the heating on the solar zenith angle and thus is applicable to regional conditions. For the global average model the sign of the heating is independent of the optical depth of the layer, and it is determined by the ratio of the absorption cross section to average backscattering cross section of the aerosol and the albedo of the underlying earth-atmosphere system. The results of the zenith angle model imply that it is likely that an aerosol layer will cause cooling in the polar regions due to the large zenith angles found there. However, if the albedos of the polar regions are sufficiently large, it may be possible for an aerosol layer to cause heating there. Owing to the low albedos found in the lower latitudes, aerosol layers are likely to cool the lower latitudes. Since the heating of the polar regions is significantly affected by the energy transported from lower latitudes by the circulation of the atmosphere and oceans, the presence of aerosol layers in the lower latitudes may play a prominent role in determining the climatic trends of the polar regions.

---

1. Introduction

The effect of aerosols on the global climate has been the subject of numerous investigations in recent years. These investigations have been motivated by the possibility that the observed cooling of the northern hemisphere (Budyko, 1969 and Starr and Oort, 1973) is directly related to an increase in the abundance of atmospheric aerosols. Evidently, this increase is the result of human activity. Urban environments have substantially higher numbers of aerosols than non-urban environments (Ludwig, Morgan and McMullin, 1970). Furthermore, measurements of the sea-level electrical conductivity of the atmosphere reveal that the amount of aerosols has been increasing since the start of this century over vast portions of the northern hemisphere but has remained constant over the southern hemisphere (Cobb and Wells, 1970 and Cobb, 1973). With our present technology it is likely that the aerosol loading of the atmosphere will continue to increase for decades. Consequently, it is important for us to assess the possible influence of aerosols on the climate.

An aerosol layer above the earth-atmosphere system may heat or cool the resulting combined system depending on the fractions of the incident solar radiation it backscatters and absorbs. Backscattering leads to cooling while absorption leads to heating. To determine the net effect of these two competing factors for an arbitrary aerosol layer the approximate equation of radiative transfer must be solved. We present two approximate solutions for the equation of transfer—both of which rely on the two-stream approximation. The first model is for the case of globally averaged conditions. From this model the relative importance of the aerosol absorption and backscattering cross sections as well as the reflectivity of the underlying system may be examined. The second model includes the influence of the solar zenith angle on the heating caused by the aerosol layer. The influence of the zenith angle is particularly important in the polar regions where the zenith angle of the sun is always large. The results of both models are compared with those of numerical solutions to the equation of radiative transfer. It is seen from these comparisons that both approximations are sufficiently accurate for studies of the effect of aerosols on the climate.

2. Global average model

The equation of radiative transfer for a plane-parallel, purely scattering aerosol layer is

$$\mu \frac{dI(\tau,\mu)}{d\tau} = I(\tau,\mu) - \frac{1}{2} \int_{-1}^{1} d\mu' \, p(\mu,\mu') I(\tau,\mu') \qquad (1)$$

where $I(\tau,\mu)$ is the specific intensity at the optical depth τ within the layer and in the direction specified by μ, the direction cosine with respect to the normal of

---

* Present address: Department of Atmospheric Science, State University of New York, Albany, New York 12222.

** The National Center for Atmospheric Research is sponsored by the National Science Foundation.

the surface of the aerosol layer; and $p(\mu, \mu')$ is the scattering phase function of the aerosol. The phase function is normalized so that

$$\frac{1}{2} \int_{-1}^{1} d\mu'\, p(\mu,\mu') = \tilde{\omega}_0,$$

the single scattering albedo. The single scattering albedo is the fraction of radiation which the aerosol scatters at each scattering. Consequently, $1-\tilde{\omega}_0$ is the fraction of radiation which is absorbed by the aerosol at each scattering.

The equation of radiative transfer is an integro-differential equation which has been solved analytically only for a few simple cases. In practice either numerical techniques or approximate analytic methods are used to obtain solutions to the equation. Approximate analytic solutions, provided that they are accurate, have the advantages of revealing the relative importance of the physical processes which are sometimes obscured in the numerical solutions, and of providing a relatively simple procedure for obtaining quantitative results for a given situation. Here we use the two-stream approximation to the equation of radiative transfer.

In the two-stream approximation the specific intensities $I(\tau, \mu) = I^+(\tau)$ and $I(\tau, -\mu) = I^-(\tau)$ are isotropic over the upper and lower hemispheres respectively. Therefore, integrating (1) over μ yields the following pair of coupled linear differential equations

$$\frac{1}{2} \frac{dI^+(\tau)}{d\tau} = I^+(\tau) - I^+(\tau)\tilde{\omega}_0(1-\beta) - I^-(\tau)\tilde{\omega}_0\beta \quad (2)$$

$$-\frac{1}{2} \frac{dI^-}{d\tau} = I^-(\tau) - I^-(\tau)\tilde{\omega}_0(1-\beta) - I^+(\tau)\tilde{\omega}_0\beta \quad (3)$$

with

$$\tilde{\omega}_0\beta = \frac{1}{2} \int_0^1 d\mu \int_0^1 d\mu'\, p(\mu, -\mu')$$

which is proportional to the average backscattering cross section of the aerosol. Equations (2) and (3) are similar to the two-stream equations of Sagan and Pollack (1967). The important difference is the definition of $\tilde{\omega}_0\beta$. Their definition was designed to make the two-stream applicable to the optically thick atmosphere of Venus, whereas we are interested in applying it to an optically thin aerosol layer above the earth-atmosphere system.

Equations (2) and (3) are readily solved with the boundary conditions that at the top of an aerosol layer of optical depth τ_1, $I^-(0) = I_0$, which is isotropic over the downward hemisphere, and at the bottom of the layer there is no incident radiation, $I^+(\tau_1) = 0$. The solutions have the form

$$I^+(0) = RI_0 \quad \text{and} \quad I^-(\tau_1) = TI_0$$

where

$$R = \frac{(U+1)(U-1)(e^{2\alpha\tau_1} - e^{-2\alpha\tau_1})}{(U+1)^2 e^{2\alpha\tau_1} - (U-1)^2 e^{-2\alpha\tau_1}} \quad (4)$$

$$T = \frac{4U}{(U+1)^2 e^{2\alpha\tau_1} - (U-1)^2 e^{-2\alpha\tau_1}} \quad (5)$$

with

$$\alpha = \sqrt{(1-\tilde{\omega}_0)(1-\tilde{\omega}_0+2\tilde{\omega}_0\beta)} \quad (6)$$

and

$$U = \sqrt{\frac{(1-\tilde{\omega}_0+2\tilde{\omega}_0\beta)}{(1-\tilde{\omega}_0)}}. \quad (7)$$

Since I_0 is isotropic over the downward hemisphere, R may be interpreted as the ratio of the flux of radiation reflected by the layer to the average flux normally incident on the layer where the direction of the incident beam has been averaged over the entire downward hemisphere. Consequently, R represents the spherical albedo of the aerosol layer.

Since for the present and for the forseeable future, the optical depth of a global aerosol layer will be small (Rasool and Schneider, 1971) it is important that the two-stream approximation reduces to the single scattering approximation which becomes accurate in the limit of very small optical depths. In the limit $\tau_1 \to 0$

$$R \to \alpha\tau_1(U^2-1)/U = 2\tilde{\omega}_0\beta\tau_1$$

and

$$T \to 1 - \alpha\tau_1(U^2+1)/U = 1 - 2(1-\tilde{\omega}_0+\tilde{\omega}_0\beta)\tau_1$$

which are identical to the results obtained from the single scattering approximation as will be seen later. Of course, the two-stream approximation is better than the single scattering approximation because it correctly predicts the deviations from the linear dependence of R and T on τ_1 which occur even at very small optical depths.

When the aerosol layer is placed over a reflecting system such as the earth-atmosphere system, the contribution to the intensities due to the multiple reflections between the aerosol layer and the underlying system must be included. Thus the radiation reflected by the combined aerosol-earth-atmosphere system is $I^+(0) = R'I_0$ where R' includes the multiple reflections. With the albedo of the underlying system represented by a

$$R' = R + TaT + TaRaT + TaRaRaT + \cdots$$

$$= R + \frac{aT^2}{1-aR}. \quad (8)$$

The amount of heating caused by the presence of the aerosol layer is simply $a - R'$. If $a - R' > 0$, then the

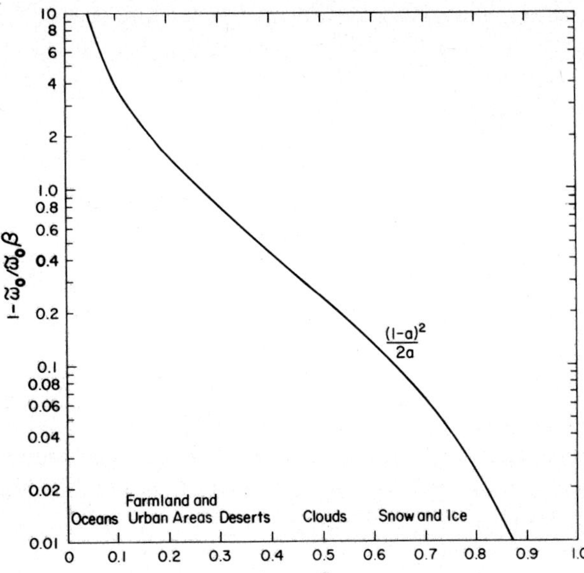

FIG. 1. The critical ratio of the absorption cross section to the average backscattering cross section of the aerosol, $(1-\tilde{\omega}_0)/\tilde{\omega}_0\beta = (1-a)^2/2a$, where a is the albedo of the underlying earth-atmosphere system.

unmodified earth-atmosphere system reflected more of the incoming solar radiation than it does with the aerosol layer present. Thus the effect of the aerosol layer is to heat the combined system. From (4)–(8)

$$a-R' = \frac{2a(1-\tilde{\omega}_0)-(1-a)^2\tilde{\omega}_0\beta}{1-\tilde{\omega}_0+(1-a)\tilde{\omega}_0\beta+\alpha/\tanh(2\alpha\tau_1)}. \qquad (9)$$

Since the denominator is always positive, the sign of the heating is completely determined by the numerator.

$$\frac{(1-\tilde{\omega}_0)}{\tilde{\omega}_0\beta}-\frac{(1-a)^2}{2a}\begin{cases} >0 & \text{heating} \\ =0 & \text{no change} \\ <0 & \text{cooling.} \end{cases} \qquad (10)$$

Thus, in the globally averaged two-stream approximation the sign of the heating is independent of the optical depth, and therefore, it is independent of the thickness of the aerosol layer. It depends only on the ratio of the absorption to the average backscattering cross sections of the aerosol and the albedo of the underlying system.

Fig. 1 shows the critical ratio of the absorption to average backscattering cross sections as a function of the albedo of the underlying system. It is seen from this figure that heating is favored by large ratios of the absorption to average backscattering cross sections of the aerosol and high albedos while cooling is favored by the opposite conditions.

Several previous attempts have been made by other investigators to obtain heating conditions similar to (10) for the case of an optically thin layer. Mitchell (1971) obtained an identical heating condition using

the single scattering approximation to the radiative transfer processes. On the other hand, Ensor *et al.* (1971) and Atwater (1970) obtained heating conditions for optically thin layers entirely different from our results due to their neglect of some of the scattering terms which are important in the limit of thin aerosol layers.

In Fig. 2 the amount of heating obtained using (9) is compared with the results of numerical solutions to the equation of transfer. The comparison was made for the case of spherical aerosol particles with radii which were small compared to the wavelength of the incident solar radiation. The resulting phase function, which was derived from Mie's theory (van de Hulst, 1957), is

$$P(\mu)=a(1+\mu^2)+b\mu$$

with

$$a=\tfrac{3}{4}\tilde{\omega}_0$$

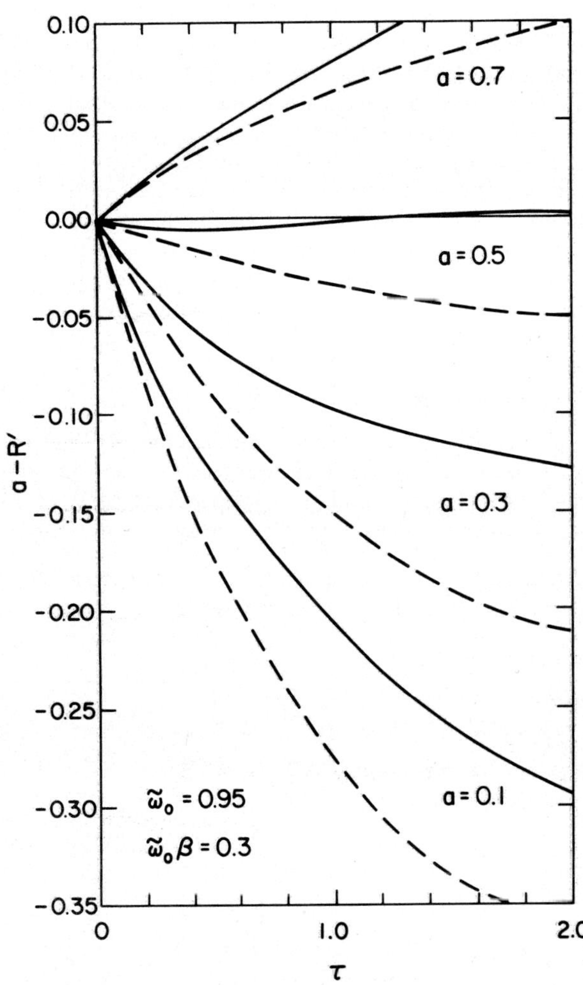

FIG. 2. The amount of heating $a-R'$, as a function of the optical depth of the aerosol layer, τ. The dashed lines are the results for the two-stream approximation, and the solid lines are the results for the numerical solutions to the equation of radiative transfer. The albedo of the underlying system is represented by a.

and

$$b = 4\tilde{\omega}_0 - 8\tilde{\omega}_0\beta$$

where μ is the cosine of the scattering angle. It is seen from Fig. 2 that, as expected, the two-stream results are accurate for thin layers where single scattering dominates. On the other hand, as the optical depth increases, the accuracy of the two-stream approximation rapidly diminishes. In practice this is not a serious limitation because, as shown by Budyko (1969) and Sellers (1969 and 1973), dramatic climatic changes may occur even for a 2% change in the solar constant. An equivalent change in the planetary albedo of the earth is readily achieved by a very thin aerosol layer. Also, from Fig. 2 it is evident that the prediction of the two-stream approximation that the sign of the heating is independent of the optical depth of the aerosol layer is not correct. Nevertheless, the sign of the heating is correctly predicted by the two-stream approximation for optically thin layers.

Thus the global average model has demonstrated the relative importance of the absorption and backscattering of the aerosols as well as the albedo of the underlying system. It has also demonstrated that the two-stream approximation is useful for the study of the effects of a global aerosol layer on the global climate. On the other hand, it does not include the influence of the solar zenith angle on the heating which should be important for the polar regions. Therefore, it is necessary to develop a model which includes this effect in order to study the possible heating of the polar regions caused by an aerosol layer.

3. Zenith angle model

To obtain the zenith angle dependent model we return to the equation of radiative transfer (1) and apply the two-stream approximation. As before $I^+(\tau)$ and $I^-(\tau)$ are isotropic over their respective hemisphere. We obtain

$$\mu\frac{dI^+(\tau)}{d\tau} = I^+(\tau) - I^+(\tau)\tilde{\omega}_0[1-\beta'(\mu)]$$

$$-I^-(\tau)\tilde{\omega}_0\beta'(\mu) \quad (11)$$

and

$$-\mu\frac{dI^-(\tau)}{d\tau} = I^-(\tau) - I^-(\tau)\tilde{\omega}_0[1-\beta'(\mu)]$$

$$-I^+(\tau)\tilde{\omega}_0\beta'(\mu) \quad (12)$$

with

$$\tilde{\omega}_0\beta'(\mu) = \frac{1}{2}\int_0^1 d\mu' p(\mu, -\mu').$$

Equations (11) and (12) are similar to the two-stream equations of Chu and Churchill (1955) which were also used by Irvine (1968). Again, the important difference is the definition of $\tilde{\omega}_0\beta'(\mu)$.

Equations (11) and (12) are readily solved with the previously used boundary conditions. The resulting solutions have the form $I^+(0,\mu) = R(\mu)I_0$ and $I^-(\tau_1,\mu) = T(\mu)I_0$ with

$$R(\mu) = \frac{(U'+1)(U'-1)(e^{\alpha'\tau_1/\mu} - e^{-\alpha'\tau_1/\mu})}{(U'+1)^2 e^{\alpha'\tau_1/\mu} - (U'-1)^2 e^{-\alpha'\tau_1/\mu}}$$

and

$$T(\mu) = \frac{4U'}{(U'+1)^2 e^{\alpha'\tau_1/\mu} - (U'-1)^2 e^{-\alpha'\tau_1/\mu}} \quad (13)$$

where $\beta'(\mu)$ has been substituted for β in the expressions for α and U to obtain α' and U'. $I^+(0, \mu)$ may be interpreted as the intensity along the direction specified by μ due to the reflection of the incident intensity I_0 which is isotropic over the downward hemisphere. On the other hand, for a sufficiently thin aerosol layer it may also be interpreted as the flux of radiation reflected by the layer due to an incident beam of intensity I_0 along the direction specified by μ. Therefore, since we are primarily interested in a thin aerosol layer, $R(\mu)$ is equivalent to the planar or local albedo; and $\mu = \mu_0$ is the zenith angle of the incident beam.

Again, since we wish to apply this two-stream approximation to an aerosol layer which is probably optically thin it is necessary for the approximation to reduce to the single scattering approximation in the limit of small optical depth. As before, in the limit that $\tau_1 \to 0$

$$R(\mu_0) \to \tilde{\omega}_0\beta(\mu_0)\tau_1/\mu_0 = \frac{1}{2\mu_0}\int_0^1 d\mu\, p(\mu_0, -\mu)\tau_1$$

and

$$T(\mu_0) \to 1 - [1-\tilde{\omega}_0 + \tilde{\omega}_0\beta(\mu_0)]\tau_1/\mu_0 = 1$$

$$-\left[1-\tilde{\omega}_0 + \frac{1}{2}\int_0^1 d\mu\, p(\mu_0, -\mu)\right]\tau_1/\mu_0.$$

These results are identical to those obtained using the single scattering approximation, as will be demonstrated below. Finally, this two-stream model is also better than the single scattering approximation for the previously stated reasons.

4. Single scattering approximation

From the principle of invariance the intensity of radiation reflected by an aerosol layer of optical depth τ_1 due to an incident beam with flux πF per unit area normal to the direction of propagation specified by μ_0 and ϕ_0 is given by (Chandrasekhar, p. 161, 1960)

$$I^+(0;\mu,\phi) = \frac{F}{4\mu}S(\tau_1;\mu,\phi;\mu_0,\phi_0)$$

where ϕ specifies the azimuthal direction. Similarly, the diffusely transmitted radiation is given by

$$I^-(\tau_1;\mu,\phi)=\frac{F}{4\mu}T(\tau_1;\mu,\phi;\mu_0,\phi_0).$$

The flux of radiation reflected by the layer is

$$\pi F^+=\int_0^{2\pi}d\phi\int_0^1 d\mu\,\mu I^+(0,\mu,\phi)=\frac{\pi F}{2}\int_0^1 d\mu\,S(\mu,\mu_0)$$

where

$$S(\mu,\mu_0)=\frac{1}{2\pi}\int_0^{2\pi}d\phi\,S(\tau;\mu,\phi;\mu_0,\phi_0).$$

Thus

$$\frac{\pi F^+}{\mu_0\pi F}=R(\mu_0)=\frac{1}{2\mu_0}\int_0^1 d\mu\,S(\mu,\mu_0).$$

In the limit $\tau_1\to 0$ (Chandrasekhar, p. 172, 1970)

$$S(\mu,\mu_0)\to\tau_1 p(\mu,-\mu_0)$$

where

$$p(\mu,-\mu_0)=\frac{1}{2\pi}\int_0^{2\pi}d\phi\,p(\mu,\phi;-\mu_0,\phi_0).$$

Consequently,

$$R(\mu_0)\to\frac{1}{2\mu_0}\int_0^1 d\mu\,p(\mu_0,-\mu)\tau_1,$$

since $p(\mu,-\mu_0)=p(-\mu_0,\mu)=p(\mu_0,-\mu)$. For the flux transmitted through the aerosol layer

$$\pi F^-=\int_0^{2\pi}d\phi\int_0^1 d\mu\,\mu I^-(\tau_1;\mu,\phi)+\mu_0\pi Fe^{-\tau_1/\mu_0}$$

$$=\frac{\pi F}{2}\int_0^1 d\mu\,T(\mu,\mu_0)+\mu_0\pi Fe^{-\tau_1/\mu_0}$$

where the second term is the contribution to πF^- due to the unscattered part of the incident direct beam. Thus,

$$\frac{\pi F^-}{\mu_0\pi F}=T(\mu_0)=\frac{1}{2\mu_0}\int_0^1 d\mu\,T(\mu,\mu_0)+e^{-\tau_1/\mu_0}.$$

In the limit $\tau_1\to 0\ T(\mu,\mu_0)\to p(\mu,\mu_0)\tau_1$. Consequently,

$$T(\mu_0)\to 1-\left[1-\tilde\omega_0+\frac{1}{2}\int_0^1 d\mu\,p(\mu_0,-\mu)\right]\tau_1/\mu_0.$$

So the expressions for $R(\mu_0)$ and $T(\mu_0)$ given by the two-stream approximation reduce to those of the single scattering approximation in the limit of an optically thin aerosol layer.

Finally, the spherical albedo is given by

$$R=2\int_0^1 d\mu_0\mu_0 R(\mu_0) \tag{14}$$

and similarly the corresponding transmission is given by

$$T=2\int_0^1 d\mu_0\mu_0 T(\mu_0). \tag{15}$$

In the limit $\tau_1\to 0$

$$R\to\int_0^1 d\mu\int_0^1 d\mu'\,p(\mu-\mu')\tau_1=2\tilde\omega\beta\tau_1$$

and

$$T\to 1-2(1-\tilde\omega_0+\tilde\omega\beta)\tau_1.$$

Thus, the results of the global average two-stream also reduce to the single scattering results for an optically thin layer.

5. Zenith angle model with underlying reflecting system

Again, when the aerosol layer is placed over a reflecting earth-atmosphere system, the multiple reflections which occur between the layer and the underlying system must be included. As a result of these reflections, $R'(\mu_0)$ for the combined system is given by (Chandrasekhar, p. 273, 1960).

$$R'(\mu_0)=R(\mu_0)+\frac{aT\,T(\mu_0)}{1-aR}. \tag{16}$$

To obtain R and T for the zenith angle model the expressions for $R(\mu_0)$ and $T(\mu_0)$ should be substituted into (14) and (15). However, since we are primarily interested in the heating caused by an optically thin layer, adequate results should be obtained when the expressions for R and T given by (4) and (5) are used instead. In this manner the complicated integrals of (14) and (15) are avoided.

The amount of heating caused by the presence of an aerosol layer is given by $a-R'(\mu_0)$. If we investigate the sign of the heating in the limit of the single scattering approximation, we find that

$$\frac{1-\tilde\omega_0}{\tilde\omega_0\beta}-\left(\frac{2\mu_0}{1+2\mu_0}\right)\left[a-1+\frac{(1-a)}{a}\frac{1}{2\mu_0}\frac{1}{\tilde\omega_0\beta}\right.$$

$$\left.\times\frac{1}{2}\int_0^1 d\mu\,p(\mu_0,-\mu)\right]\begin{cases}>0\text{ heating}\\=0\text{ no change}\\<0\text{ cooling}.\end{cases} \tag{17}$$

Consequently, the sign of the heating depends not only on the ratio of the absorption to average back-scattering cross sections of the aerosol and the albedo of the underlying system, but it also depends on the zenith angle μ_0 and the explicit expression for the phase function $p(\mu, \mu_0)$.

There are two interesting limits of (17)—normal incidence, $\mu_0 = 1$, and large zenith angles, $\mu_0 \to 0$. For large zenith angles the condition which the aerosol must satisfy to cause heating is

$$\frac{1-\tilde{\omega}_0}{\tilde{\omega}_0\beta} - \frac{(1-a)}{a}\frac{1}{\tilde{\omega}_0\beta}\frac{1}{2}\int_0^1 d\mu\, p(\mu_0, -\mu) > 0. \quad (18)$$

For the case of a symmetric phase function, $p(\mu, \mu_0) = p(\mu, -\mu_0)$,

$$\frac{1}{2}\int_0^1 d\mu\, p(\mu_0, -\mu) = \tilde{\omega}_0\beta.$$

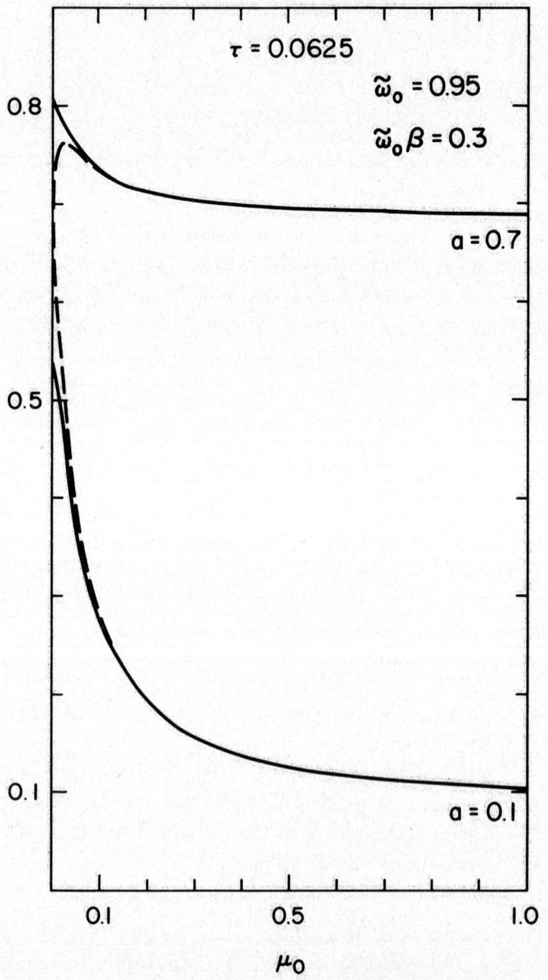

This gives for the heating condition

$$\frac{1-\tilde{\omega}_0}{\tilde{\omega}_0\beta} - \frac{(1-a)}{a} > 0. \quad (19)$$

Similarly, for normal incidence we obtain

$$\frac{1-\tilde{\omega}_0}{\tilde{\omega}_0\beta} - \frac{2}{3}\left[a-1+\frac{(1-a)}{2a}\frac{1}{\tilde{\omega}_0\beta}\frac{1}{2}\int_0^1 d\mu\, p(\mu_0-\mu)\right] > 0. \quad (20)$$

Again, for a symmetric phase function we obtain

$$\frac{1-\tilde{\omega}_0}{\tilde{\omega}_0\beta} - \frac{(1-a)(1-2a)}{3a} > 0. \quad (21)$$

Therefore, it appears that for thin layers the possibility of cooling is enhanced by large zenith angles while heating is enhanced by normal incidence. It is also interesting to note that the inequality suggests that a nonabsorbing aerosol may cause heating provided the sun is near the zenith and the albedo of the underlying system is large. This is due to an increase in the downward flux of radiation beneath the layer and thus an increase of absorption by the underlying system caused by the multiple reflections between the layer and the underlying system. Of course, this effect occurs only for a thin aerosol layer. As the optical depth of a nonabsorbing aerosol layer becomes moderately large, the layer causes cooling as would normally be expected.

Incidentally, another interesting property of (17) is that it reduces to (10) when $\mu_0 = 0.5$ for a symmetric phase function.

The results for $R'(\mu_0)$ obtained using the two-stream approximation are compared with those obtained from numerical solutions to the equation of radiative transfer. Again, the comparisons were made for the case of an aerosol having a small particle phase function. It is seen that except for very large zenith angles, $\mu_0 < 0.1$, even for moderately thick aerosol layers, $\tau = 0.25$, the two-stream approximation yields quantitatively good results. Of course, the results are accurate in the limit that the effective optical depth, τ_1/μ_0, becomes very small and the single scattering approximation is realized. The accuracy of the approximation decreases as the effective optical depth increases. Nevertheless, since it is unlikely for the optical depth of an aerosol layer which covers a vast region of the globe to become much larger than a few tenths, the zenith angle dependent model should be useful in determining the regional heating caused by the existence of an aerosol layer.

FIG. 3. The reflectivity of the combined aerosol-earth-atmosphere system $R'(\mu_0)$, as a function of solar zenith angle μ_0. The dashed lines are the results for the two-stream approximation, and the solid lines are the results for the numerical solutions to the equation of radiative transfer. The albedo of the underlying system is represented by a. The optical depth of the aerosol layer is 0.0625.

6. Discussion

We see from Figs. 3 and 4 that for large zenith angles $R' > a$ and the effect of an aerosol layer is likely to be one of cooling. On the other hand, we also see that if the albedo of the underlying system is sufficiently large,

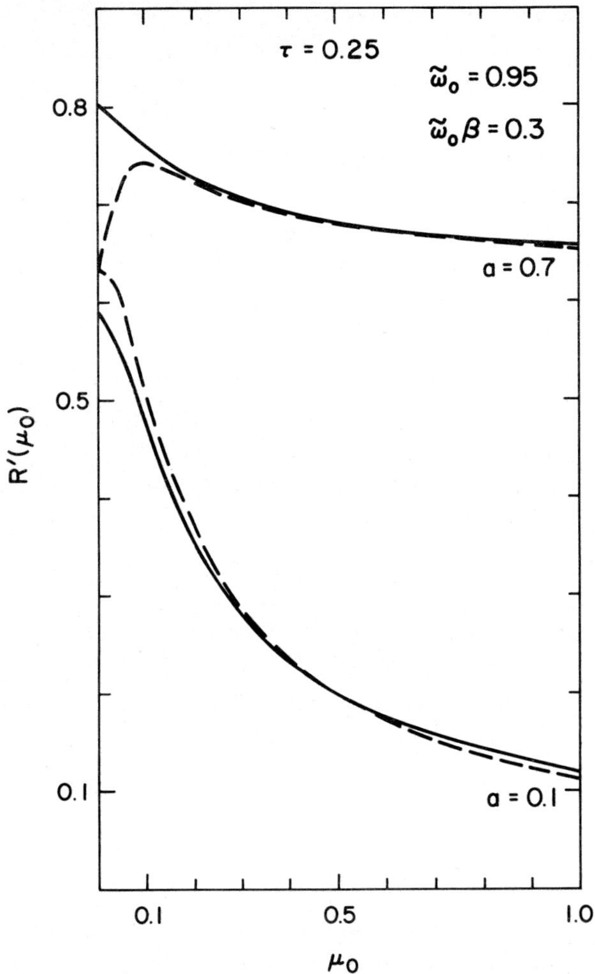

FIG. 4. Same as Fig. 3. The optical depth of the aerosol layer is 0.25.

we can expect heating to occur due to the presence of a weakly absorbing aerosol even at moderately large zenith angles. Thus, we suspect that it may be possible for a regional aerosol to heat the polar regions. However, due to the low albedos in the lower latitudes the effect of an aerosol layer in those regions will likely be one of cooling. In fact, since most of the energy in the polar regions is imported from the lower latitudes through the circulation of the atmosphere and oceans (London and Sasamori, 1971), the cooling of the lower latitudes by an aerosol layer may be sufficient to diminish the energy available to the polar regions and thus cause a cooling in the polar regions despite the possible heating effect of a polar aerosol layer. In fact, such a result has been obtained by Sellers (1973) with his new climatic model.

Unfortunately, measurements of the aerosol parameters required to estimate the effect of aerosols on the climate are not available on a global scale. Furthermore, the climatic data presently available does not give any definite clues to the role aerosols may play in determining the global climate. Consequently, it is not possible to draw any conclusions concerning the impact of aerosols on the climate. We can only guess that since the smallest particles survive the longest in the atmosphere and assuming that these particles are only weakly absorbing, small ratios of the absorption to average backscattering cross sections are favored and thus cooling may be the generally expected effect. However, such speculation may not survive once the measurements of the aerosol characteristics have been made.

REFERENCES

Atwater, M. A., 1970: Planetary albedo changes due to aerosols. *Science*, **170**, 64–66.

Budyko, M. I., 1969: The effect of solar radiation variations on the climate of the Earth, *Tellus*, **21**, 611–619.

Chandrasekhar, S., 1960: *Radiative Transfer*. Dover, N. Y.

Chu, C. M., and Churchill, W., 1955: Numerical solution of problems in multiple scattering of electromagnetic radiation. *J. Phys. Chem.*, **59**, 855–863.

Cobb, W. E., and Wells, H. J., 1970: The electrical conductivity of oceanic air and its correlation to global atmospheric pollution. *J. Atmos. Sci.*, **27**, 814–819.

Cobb, W. E., 1973: Oceanic aerosol levels deduced from measurements of the electrical conductivity of the atmosphere. *J. Atmos. Sci.*, **30**, 101–106.

Ensor, D. S., Porch, W. M., Pilat, M. J. and Charlson, R. J., 1971: Influence of the atmospheric aerosol on albedo. *J. Appl. Meteor.*, **10**, 1303–1306.

Irvine, W. H., 1968: Multiple scattering by large particles II. Optically thick layers. *Astrophys. J.*, **152**, 823–834.

London, J., and Sasamori, T., 1971: Radiative energy budget of the atmosphere. *Space Research XI—Akad. Verlag, Berlin*, 639–649.

Ludwig, J. H., Morgan, G. B. and McMullen, T. B., 1970: Trends in urban air quality. *Trans. Amer. Geophys. Union*, **51**, 468–475.

Mitchell, J. M., Jr., 1971: The effect of atmospheric aerosols on climate with special reference to temperature near the Earth's surface. *J. Appl. Meteor.*, **10**, 703–714.

Rasool, S. I., and Schneider, S. H., 1971: Atmospheric carbon dioxide and aerosols: effects of large increases on global climate. *Science*, **173**, 138–141.

Sagan, C., and Pollack, J. B., 1967: Anisotropic nonconservative scattering and the clouds of Venus. *J. Geophys. Res.*, **72**, 469–477.

Sellers, W. D., 1969: A global climatic model based on the energy balance of the earth-atmosphere system. *J. Appl. Meteor.*, **8**, 392–400.

——, 1973: A new global climatic model. *J. Appl. Meteor.*, **12**, 241–254.

Starr, V. P., and Oort, A. H., 1973: Five-year climatic trend for the northern hemisphere, *Nature*, **242**, 310–313.

van de Hulst, H. C., 1957: *Light Scattering by Small Particles*, Wiley & Sons, N. Y.

Surface Temperature—Albedo Coupling : Implications for Climate Stability

STEPHEN H. SCHNEIDER

National Center for Atmospheric Research, Boulder, Colorado*

Abstract

The semi-empirical climate models of Budyko (1969) and Sellers (1969) are formulated as time-dependent problems in order to study the stability of their asymptotic steady-state equilibrium solutions to perturbations in *internal* (in this case, initial) conditions. Whereas these models have shown dramatic sensitivity to slight changes in *external* parameters (e.g., solar constant), here they are found to be relatively stable to perturbations in initial conditions. For fixed external conditions our time-dependent versions of these models exhibit fully transitive behavior to positive perturbations in initial conditions, slight intransivity to negative perturbations up to -18 K, and an ice-covered earth regime is obtained for extremely large negative perturbations in initial temperatures (below -18 K). The parameterization that is found to be most critical in these models is the albedo-temperature coupling, especially in tropical regions. Numerical experimentation with these semi-empirical models shows the important role of the tropics in maintaining the equilibrium climate, and suggests that the radiation balance in equatorial latitudes might have a controlling influence on the equatorward extent of the polar ice cap. This is because the large radiation deficit in polar regions is balanced by horizontal transports of energy whose energy source is located in low latitudes. The major assumptions and approximations of semi-empirical climate models are discussed critically.

---

1. Introduction

It is clear that the climate of the earth has undergone dramatic fluctuations in the past (e.g., Dansgaard, *et al.*, 1971) and there is every reason to suspect that it will undergo similarly severe changes in the future. Up until now most changes in climate could hardly be attributed to man's activities, however, man is now altering the face of the earth and the chemical composition of the atmosphere and inputting energy on a sufficiently large basis that his influence may already be or may soon become comparable to nature's in affecting climate change. This realization had led to many studies of inadvertent climate change (SMIC, 1971; SCEP, 1970, among others).

In the light of the past record of large climatic fluctuations, one of the major concerns of climatologists studying the possible impact on the climate of man's activities has been the question of the *stability* of the global climate. This question led Budyko (1969) and Sellers (1969) to develop (independently) semi-empirical models of the earth's climate based on the equations of the zonally-averaged heat balance of the earth-atmosphere system for the purpose of testing the sensitivity of the equilibrium state of the climate to changes in external conditions (such as the solar constant or the amount of fixed constituents in the earth's atmosphere).

One important parameteric relationship common to their models is the coupling between the planetary albedo and the temperature of the atmosphere near the earth's surface. This coupling leads to a strong positive feedback link between a change in surface temperature and a corresponding variation in albedo (e.g., a decrease in temperature would correspond to an increase in albedo—presumably due to expanded snow and ice cover). [For a more detailed discussion of climatic feedback mechanisms see Kellogg, 1975, Chapter 6 of SMIC, 1971, Schneider and Kellogg, 1973 or Schneider, 1972.] Thus, Budyko and Sellers found that, because of the positive feedback albedo-temperature effect included in their models, changes in the global energy budget on the order of one percent could result in extensive changes to the equilibrium climate (e.g., a near melting of the ice caps or a significant expansion of glaciation). The dramatic results of these models, although they are based only on simplified parameterizations of most atmospheric transport processes, are, nevertheless, sufficiently compelling to indicate the need for further study of climatic stability so that it can be determined just how large a perturbation in the environment would be required, in view of the various climatic feedback processes, to significantly alter our climatic regime (see also, Budyko, 1972).

The object of this study is to explore the sensitivity of *time-dependent* versions of some of Budyko (1969) and Sellers (1969) originally time-independent param-

* The National Center for Atmospheric Research is sponsored by the National Science Foundation.

eterizations to changes in *internal* as well as external conditions. That is, since the models of Budyko or Sellers are time-independent formulations (the solutions of which are automatically equilibrium "climatic" statistics) the stability of their models' equilibrium climates can be tested only by variations in external or environmental parameters—such as the solar input, amount of atmospheric turbidity, boundary conditions, etc. However, in this work the problem is formulated as an initial value problem in which the basic equations (which are close in many respects to those of Budyko and Sellers) are integrated from a given initial state until a final asymptotic equilibrium state (i.e., climate) is (hopefully) obtained. Thus, we are able to test the sensitivity of the asymptotic steady-state equilibrium climate to changes in internal (in this case initial) conditions, while leaving all external or environmental parameters fixed. The rationale for such an approach has been articulated in the well-known works of E. Lorenz (1968, 1970).

As discussed in the last section, experiments with these energy balance models show that temperature-albedo coupling has important implications for climate stability.

This paper is an offshoot of the more detailed work Schneider and Gal-Chen (1973).

2. Modeling assumptions

A time-dependent version of the zonally-averaged, vertically-integrated equation of the heat balance of the earth-atmosphere system is,

$$R\frac{\partial T}{\partial t}=R_e+\mathrm{div}(\mathbf{F}),\qquad(1)$$

where R is the mass-specific heat product (thermal inertia coefficient) for a zonal column through the land/ocean/atmosphere system (its value was chosen following Sellers, 1965, p. 242) based on 25 meter mixed layer in the oceans and linearly varying temperature profile down to zero degree Celsius at a depth of 125 meters. The value of thermal inertia, R, could also be interpreted as a scaling factor for the time scale, t, if R were to be changed by the same factor at all latitudes, ϕ. In these computations $R(\phi)$ is also made proportional to the fraction of the area of the zone covered by oceans. However, the effect of variations in the latitudinal distribution of R on the equilibrium solution is not considered here. t is time, T is the zonally-averaged 1000 mb temperature, R_e is the radiation balance terms for a zonal column through the earth-atmosphere system:

$$R_e=Q_{SC}(1-\alpha)-F_{IR},\qquad(2)$$

where $Q_{SC}(\phi)$ is the yearly-average, zonally-averaged value of solar energy input at latitude ϕ; α is the planetary albedo at latitude ϕ, F_{IR} is the outgoing infrared radiation flux to space:

$$F_{IR}=c(\phi)\sigma T^4[1-m\tanh(19T^6\times10^{-16})]\qquad(3)$$

where $c(\phi)$ is a consistency factor described in Schneider and Gal-Chen. When $c(\phi)=1$, Equation (3) is identical to the infrared flux formulation of Sellers (1969); and in all cases computed here $c(\phi)$ was found empirically to be in the range:

$$0.92\le c(\phi)\le1.04$$

$\mathrm{div}(\mathbf{F})$ is the net energy flux transport for latitude ϕ and is parameterized differently for the various models used.

Two are considered. The first one, labelled (S) is:

$$(S)\quad\mathrm{div}(\mathbf{F})=\frac{1}{\sin\theta}\frac{\partial}{\partial y}\sin\theta(F_0+F_A+F_q)$$

where

$y=a\theta$
$a=$ radius of earth

$$\theta=\frac{\pi}{2}-\phi$$

$\phi=$ latitude belt
$F_0=$ sensible heat transport due to ocean currents
$F_A=$ sensible heat transport due to atmospheric motion
$F_q=$ transport of latent heat energy.
The dynamical parameterization for (S) is:

$$F_0\propto K_0\frac{\partial T}{\partial y}$$

$$F_A\propto K_A\frac{\partial T}{\partial y}-\bar{v}T\qquad(S)$$

$$F_q\propto K_q\frac{\partial q(T)}{\partial y}-\bar{v}q(T)$$

where $q(T)$ is proportional to the water vapor mixing ratio, $\bar{v}$ is some vertical integrated mean meridional velocity and is parameterized as a function of latitudinal temperature gradient. The K's are eddy diffusion coefficients. They are evaluated from empirical data for temperature and transport distributions (see Fig. 2). The albedo is:

$$\alpha=\begin{cases}b(\phi)-0.009\,T & T<283.16\text{ K}\\ b(\phi)-0.009(283.16) & T>283.16\text{ K}\end{cases}$$

$$(0.25\le\alpha\le0.85,\text{ all }T).\qquad(4)$$

However, if $\alpha(T)$ turns out to be greater than 0.85, then α is set equal to 0.85, and if α turns out to be less than 0.25, α is set equal to 0.25. Formulation (S) is based

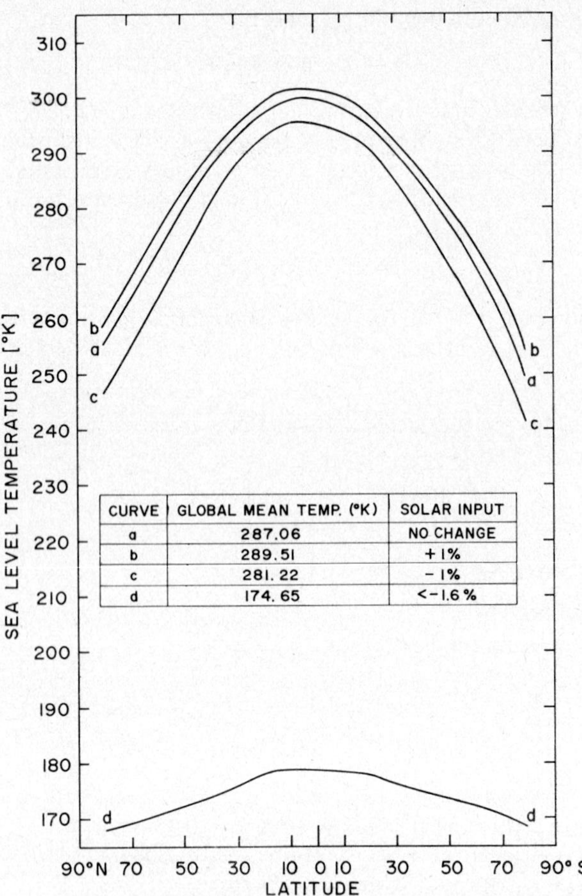

CURVE	GLOBAL MEAN TEMP. (°K)	SOLAR INPUT
a	287.06	NO CHANGE
b	289.51	+ 1%
c	281.22	− 1%
d	174. 65	< −1.6 %

FIG. 1. Asymptotic, steady-state, equilibrium, sea level (1000 mb) temperature distributions computed for parameterizations like Sellers (1969), as a function of solar input.

on Sellers (1969), from which further details can be obtained.

The second formulation, labelled (B), is:

$$(B) \qquad \mathrm{div}(\mathbf{F}) = -\beta(T - \bar{T}_p)$$

where β is an empirically determined coefficient given by Budyko (1969) as $\beta = 0.235$ [kcal cm^{-2} month^{-1} deg K^{-1}], and $\bar{T}_p$ is the mean (global average) planetary temperature (at 1000 mb). Formulation (B) is based on the dynamical parameterization from the model of Budyko (1969).

The boundary conditions applied at the poles are that the horizontal gradients of temperature vanish at the poles. This condition is equivalent to the statement that no heat is transferred across the poles. For a linear "diffusion equation" these boundary conditions are sufficient to assure that the mathematical problem is well-posed (that is, a unique solution for a particular choice of initial conditions that depends continuously on the initial conditions can be obtained).

3. Discussion of results

The heat balance equation, (1), together with the boundary conditions are solved by numerical integra-

tion with the use of the fully (time and space) centered implicit finite difference scheme of Crank and Nicholson. The non-linear coefficients in the finite difference formulation are treated by iterating the solution so that the non-linear coefficients can also be treated implicitly.

In the introduction it was mentioned that dramatic instability of the climate was found in the steady-state model of Sellers (and Budyko) as a result of small changes in the value of the solar constant. We felt that our time-dependent version of Sellers model should be able to recover his results. That is, the asymptotic equilibrium climate from our model should exhibit similar sensitivity to changes in the value of the solar constant as the Sellers (and Budyko) model, provided that our model is internally consistent (see Schneider and Gal-Chen, 1973) and that our initial state is near to the present-day equilibrium or control climate. This agreement of our asymptotic state with the Sellers steady-state is found, as can be seen on Fig. 1, which is computed for the Sellers dynamical parameterization (S). Curve a on Fig. 1 is the asymptotic (after about 10 years of $2\frac{1}{2}$ day time steps) equilibrium climate, with a mean 1000 mb temperature of 287.06 K, which will be referred to from now on as the *control climate*. The initial temperature distribution used to produce the control distribution had a mean temperature of 287.30 K, which is quite close to the final steady-state value of 287.06 K. The closeness in value between the initial and final state mean temperatures is a result of a satisfactory degree of interval consistency built into the model. Curves b and c result from a one percent increase or decrease, respecitvely, in the value of the solar constant. We see that a 1% increase in solar input causes an increase in mean global temperature to 289.51 K (shown by curve b on Fig. 1) which is significantly larger than a $\sim$1.5 K increase, that would be obtained if there were no positive feedback between the albedo and temperature. On the other hand, a 1% decrease in solar constant shown in curve c yields a mean global temperature of 281.22 K—a significant decrease in temperature due to the increased planetary albedo arising from the decreased surface temperature—and shows very strong positive feedback. For a decrease in solar constant of more than 1.6%, we obtain a planetary mean temperature of 174.65 K, which corresponds to an entirely ice-covered earth. It is results such as these, which are in agreement with the works of Budyko and Sellers, which have led many climatologists to be concerned with the stability of the present climate. Very similar general results are obtained using the Budyko (B) dynamical parameterization instead of (S).

Now, experiments are performed with the time dependent models described in Section 2. A perturbation is added to the initial temperature distribution while all other parameters in the models are held fixed. It is found in both Sellers and Budyko dynamical parameterization cases, as summarized in Table 1, that the steady-state control climate, $T = 287.06$ in the Sellers case (S), and $T = 287.09$ in the Budyko case (B), can be recovered exactly if the perturbation added to the initial temperature is greater than 0. Perturbations of $+2$ K and $+16$ K are tried, and in both cases (which would imply a melting of the polar ice caps) energy balance dictates alone produce a return to the control climate. That is, fully unique, fully stable, transitive (i.e., unique equilibrium state independent of the initial state; see Lorenz, 1970) control climates, with mean temperatures of 287.06 and 287.09 for Sellers and Budyko dynamical formulations, respectively, are recovered. However, for an initial temperature decrease less than 18.3 K (i.e., $-18.3 < $ perturbation $ < 0$) the equilibrium climate is slightly intransitive (i.e., different equilibrium states can be obtained from different initial states). That is, the final equilibrium climate is 286.67 K and 286.87 K for Sellers and Budyko respectively, which are a few tenths of a degree lower than the control climates, but are still very close to the present day control equilibrium statistics. The latitudinal distributions of temperature are also very similar, and thus the global average values are representative of the particular climatic states. It is possible that there might also exist other intransitive climates for initial perturbations between -2 and 0, or for some particular initial perturbation in the latitudinal distribution of initial temperature. However, no additional states were found, even after considerable numerical experimentation. Thus the asymptotic equilibrium climate is found to be extremely insensitive to changes in *initial conditions*. A 17 K perturbation in initial temperature is an incredibly large decrease, yet the asymptotic solution was able to return very near to the present equilibrium state.

Most interestingly, however, for initial temperature perturbations less than -18.3 K in both Sellers and Budyko dynamical parameterization cases, we obtain the ice-covered earth solution corresponding to curve d of Fig. 1 (which was for a 1.6% decrease in solar constant, an *external* parameter). Of course, in these initial temperature perturbation experiments the solar constant is held fixed. Thus, it takes an extremely large, greater in magnitude than 18.3 K, negative initial temperature perturbation to lead into a highly intransitive alternative climatic regime for these models, namely an ice-covered earth. At first this result was quite puzzling. However, if one looks carefully at the control temperature distribution, given by curve a in Fig. 1, one can see that in the equatorial latitudes the surface temperature is about 300 K. If we now look at Eq. (4) for the albedo formulation, we note that only when the mean zonal temperature is *less than 283 K* does the albedo become temperature dependent. Now if we subtract 18 from 300 we get 282, and thus it appears that the reason the model is relatively insensitive to decreases in initial conditions of less than 18 K is that

TABLE 1. Asymptotic steady-state global-average temperatures resulting from various perturbations to the initial temperature distribution for the parameterization (see text for explanation of parameterizations used here) of Sellers (1969) and the dynamical parameterization of Budyko (1969).

Initial temperature perturbation P		Mean planetary temperature [K]	
		Sellers (S)	Budyko (B)
0		287.06	287.09
$0 < P < 16$	all ϕ	287.06	287.09
$-18.3 < P \leq 0$	all ϕ	286.67	286.87
$P < -18.3$	all ϕ	175.58	175.44
-22 0	$\|\phi\| \geq 20°$ $\|\phi\| < 20°$	286.67	286.87
-32 0	$\|\phi\| \geq 20°$ $\|\phi\| < 20°$	175.58	175.49
-32 0	$\|\phi\| \geq 30°$ $\|\phi\| < 30°$	286.67	175.49
-32 0	$\|\phi\| \geq 40°$ $\|\phi\| < 40°$	286.67	286.87

the albedo of the equatorial region has not been changed by the perturbation. But in these experiments the solar input has been held constant, and even though the temperature and polar latitudes could be ice covered by virtue of the large negative initial temperature perturbation there is still enough energy available to the tropics (with unaltered albedo since $T > 283$) to transport sufficient heat poleward to "melt the ice" and restore the equilibrium climate to the near present day value. However, if the equatorial temperature is decreased sufficiently, that is by more than 18.3 K, by the initial temperature perturbation so as to lower it into the range of the positive feedback temperature-albedo coupling implicit in equation (4), then climatic instability is evidenced and the ice-covered earth regime results. Thus, the ice-covered earth solutions of both the Budyko (1969) and Sellers (1969) models that were obtained by a decrease in the solar constant of more than 1.6% were a result of the fact that the solar constant was decreased *everywhere*, and thus the energy available to the tropics was also reduced. Therefore, the tropics were no longer able to export the energy necessary to prevent the positive feedback albedo-temperature coupling in the temperate and polar latitudes (where $T < 283$) from causing a run-away ice age. To test further this hypothesis we take a very large negative perturbation in initial temperature, namely -22 K, and apply it to all latitudes poleward of $20°$ while leaving the initial temperature at the equator and at latitude zones $10°$N and $10°$S fixed. In both Sellers and Budyko parameterization cases (as can be seen in Table 1) the result is a return to the near present day climate. Thus, an extreme initial ice age in temperate and polar latitudes is unable to cause a run-away ice-covered earth because the energy input to the tropics

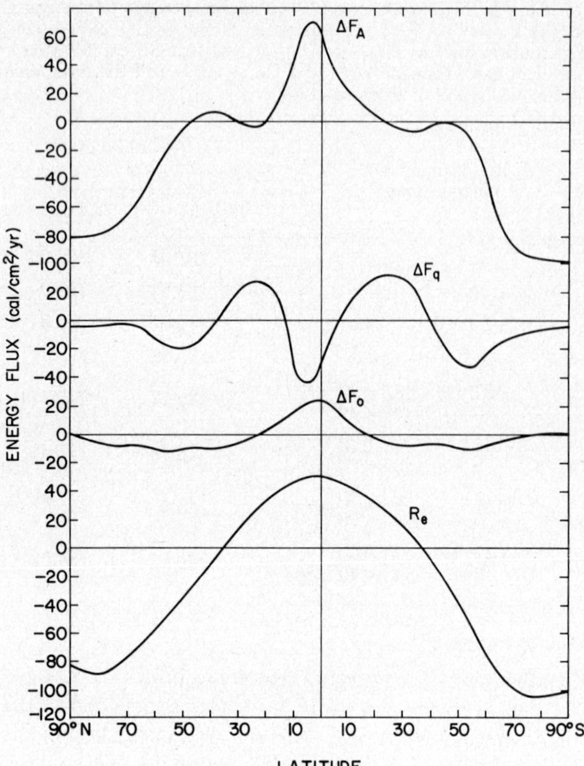

FIG. 2. Radiation balance of the earth atmosphere system, R_e, which is balanced by horizontal energy flux transports of atmospheric sensible heat, ΔF_A, latent heat, ΔF_q and oceanic heat transport ΔF_0. Curves are from empirical data for the present climate compiled by Sellers (1969).

has been maintained. Furthermore, the dynamical parameterization coefficients (e.g., K_0, K_A, ...) remain unaltered by the change in climate. Thus, a very strong negative feedback is inherent in the dynamical parameterization of both Budyko and Sellers, since these parameterizations [(S) and (B)] transport increased energy poleward if the equator-to-pole temperature contrast is increased (this is a sort of parameterized mimic of the baroclinic instability mechanism which has been parameterized more realistically by Stone 1973, e.g.). Thus, for the -22 K non-equatorial perturbation case, where the energy input available to the tropics is the same initially as in the control case, the model was able to restore the equilibrium climate to the near present day climate. This is even more amply demonstrated in the lowest 3 rows on Table 1 where a -32 K temperature perturbation is added for latitudes greater than or equal to 30° and no perturbation is applied for equatorial and tropical regions inside of 30°. In the Sellers formulation even this extremely large 32 K perturbation is still insufficient to cause an ice-covered earth. However, in the Budyko formulation, Table 1 shows that an ice-covered earth was possible at this amount of initial perturbation. For both Sellers and Budyko parameterization cases, however, if this

large negative perturbation of -32 K is applied as far equatorward as the 20° latitude, then an ice-covered earth is the asymptotic solution. Finally, for the Budyko case if the -32 K perturbation is confined to latitudes 40° and poleward (which would correspond to an absurdly severe ice age in temperate and polar latitudes) then Table 1 indicates that even this initial ice age is unable to "feed on itself" and grow to the ice-covered earth regime. Again, this is a direct consequence of an unaltered radiation input in the tropical latitudes.

4. Concluding remarks

One conclusion of this study is that the transitivity and stability of a climatic model, and possibly the transitivity of the earth's climate, is very much dependent on the functional relationship between the albedo and the surface temperature.

Another conclusion that seems to be consistently obtained from these experiments is that if the energy input to the tropics is left nearly constant then large changes in the temperature and albedo of middle and polar latitudes can eventually be ameliorated by the exporting of sufficient energy from the tropics. This suggests that one possible reason that ice sheets never have proceeded equatorward much below the middle latitudes is that the energy input to the tropics was large enough to sustain poleward energy fluxes that prevented the further expansion of the ice sheets, and in fact eventually led to their recession—possibly accelerated by the positive feedback albedo-temperature coupling.

Thus, the apparently sensitive nature of the climatic state in polar regions may be traceable to very small changes in the energy budget in tropical and temperate latitudes, which in turn could lead to significant modifications to the amount of energy flux originating in tropical regions that is subsequently transported horizontally into polar regions. Figure 2 (from Sellers, 1969), which is empirical data for the present climate, shows that the large radiation deficit in polar regions (i.e., negative values of R_e) is balanced by the horizontal convergence of energy flux. The transport of atmospheric sensible heat, ΔF_A, latent heat, ΔF_q, and energy by ocean currents, ΔF_0, into polar regions depends upon both atmospheric and oceanic motions. More important, perhaps, the horizontal flux transport derives its source from the energy surplus in lower latitudes. Since half the earth's surface area and most of the solar input is contained in latitudes between 30°N and 30°S, relatively small changes in the radiation balance in this zone could affect the horizontal fluxes ΔF_A, ΔF_q and ΔF_0 by an amount that might not be relatively small in polar regions. Thus, although the simple parameterized energy balance models we have used here cannot accurately predict this dependence, they do show the importance of temperature-albedo coupling in the tropics on the export of energy to higher latitudes.

However, it must again be repeated that the albedo-temperature formulation used in these models does not explicitly include coupling to the hydrological cycle, nor do the dynamical parameterizations used in these models make provisions for a change in the values of effective eddy diffusion coefficients with changes in climate, which undoubtably would occur should the climate change as drastically as we have been experimenting with in these runs (Stone, 1973). It must be born in mind that the results obtained with simplified empirical parameterizations used here should, by no means, be generalized to explain phenomena observed on earth. Nevertheless, these models do satisfy the energy balance of the earth-atmosphere system, and in the long term it is the energy balance which must determine the surface temperature. Thus these models are, at the very least, a very valuable "educational toy," as they have been described by G. D. Robinson, and their results suggest that climate stability and transitivity experiments should be attempted with much more sophisticated models (atmospheric, oceanic and joint atmosphere/ocean) that explicitly include detailed hydrological cycle and dynamical calculations.

REFERENCES

Budyko, M. I., 1972: The future climate. *Trans. Am. Geophys. Union*, **53**, 868–874.

Budyko, M. I., 1969: The effect of solar radiation variations on the climate of the earth. *Tellus*, **21**, 611–619.

Dansgaard, W., S. J. Johnsen, H. B. Clausen and C. C. Langway, 1971: *The Late Cenozoic Glacial Ages*, symposium edited by K. K. Turkekian (Yale Univ. Press, New Haven, Conn.).

Kellogg, W. W., 1975: Climatic feedback mechanisms involving the polar regions. *Proc. 24th Alaskan Science Conf.*, Fairbanks.

Lorenz, E. N., 1970: Climatic change as a mathematical problem. *J. Appl. Met.*, **9**, 325–329.

Lorenz, E. N., 1968: Climatic determinism. *Meteorological Monographs*, **5**, 1–3.

Schneider, S. H., and Gal-Chen, T., 1973: Numerical experiments in climate stability, *J. Geophys. Res.*, **78**, 6182–6194.

Schneider, S. H., and W. W. Kellogg, 1973: The chemical basis for climatic change, *Chemistry of the Lower Atmosphere*, edited by S. I. Rasool, Chap. 5, Plenum Press, N. Y., 203–249.

Sellers, W. D., 1969: A global climatic model based on the energy balance of the earth-atmosphere system. *J. Appl. Met.*, **8**, 392–400.

Sellers, W. D., 1965: *Physical Climatology*, The University of Chicago Press, Chicago.

Stone, P. H., 1973: The effect of large-scale eddies on climatic change. *J. Atmos. Sci.*, **30**, 521–529.

Study of Critical Environmental Problems (SCEP), 1970: *Man's Impact on the Global Environment*, MIT Press, Cambridge, Mass.

Study of Man's Impact on Climate (SMIC), 1971: *Inadvertent Climate Modification*, MIT Press, Cambridge, Mass.

PART II: THE CURRENT CLIMATE

Long Waves in the Polar Atmosphere

BERNHARD HAURWITZ

National Center for Atmospheric Research, Boulder, Colorado*

and

Geophysical Institute, University of Alaska, College, Alaska

Abstract

The polar regions differ from the lower-latitude zones by the much smaller meridional variation of the Coriolis parameter and by the singularities at the poles. Assuming an atmosphere at rest, apart from the wave motions, one finds as an approximate formula for the period T of the Rossby waves, in sidereal days, the formula (16) where the bracket may in general be put equal to one.

The case of non-divergent horizontal motion is obtained by letting the depth H tend to infinity in (16). For realistic values of the parameters the resulting periods are then of the order of one month for oscillations extending from the pole to 60° latitude, and about half a month for oscillations extending to 50° latitude. For tropical zones of similar latitudinal extent the periods are only about one half to one fourth of these values. The presence of a basic zonal wind may shorten these periods considerably and change the direction of wave propagation from westward to eastward. If the divergence is not zero (H finite) the period may be longer or shorter than in the nondivergent case depending on the sign of H, which may be interpreted as the equivalent depth of atmospheric tidal theory. The case of negative H is of significance in connection with forced oscillations when the period is given and H is to be determined. Empirical data need to be obtained for the identification of possible mechanisms causing these waves, and for the characterization of different atmospheric conditions by dynamic considerations.

---

1. Non-divergent motion

In contrast to middle and tropical latitudes, little or no attention has been given to long waves in the polar regions, although the polar atmosphere plays an important part in atmospheric dynamics containing the atmospheric heat sinks and large regions with variable ice cover. A complete study of these long waves is best conducted for the whole earth, with the aid of spherical harmonic analysis. But there are some advantages for both the theoretical and the empirical analysis if a preliminary investigation is concentrated on a smaller, meteorologically distinctive area such as the polar regions.

Among the differences between the polar regions and the lower latitudes are the different rates of latitude variation of the Coriolis parameter and the singularities at the poles. Because of the latter it is convenient to approximate the earth's spherical shape, by a plane tangential to the pole and a plane polar coordinate system with r as the linear distance from the pole, λ the geographic longitude so that

$$r = E \cdot \theta$$

where E is the earth's radius, θ the colatitude.

<hr>

* The National Center for Atmospheric Research is sponsored by the National Science Foundation.

The simplest case is that of a barotropic atmosphere in horizontal, non-divergent motion. Such a model shows, despite the unrealistic assumptions, the essential behavior of the long waves, especially the effect of the variation of the Coriolis parameter with latitude, as first elucidated by Rossby (1939). In the present case the total absolute vorticity must remain constant,

$$\frac{D}{Dt}(\zeta + Z + f) = 0. \tag{1}$$

Here

$$f = 2\omega[1 - r^2/(2E^2)] \tag{2}$$

is the Coriolis parameter, ζ is the perturbation vorticity and Z, the relative vorticity due to the undisturbed motion, which may be a zonal current V_λ depending on r only. It will be assumed that

$$V_\lambda = \alpha r \tag{3}$$

this being the simplest case. With this assumption

$$Z = 2\alpha$$

which is constant, in contrast to the expression (2) for f, the vorticity due to the earth's rotation. In order to have formal similarity between Z and f and with the analogous case of long waves on a sphere (Haurwitz,

TABLE I. Period in days, no zonal motion, for plane polar (P), spherical (S), and rectangular (R) coordinates.

Longitudinal wave number k	$d/E=\frac{1}{2},\ \theta=28.6°$			$d/E=\frac{2}{3},\ \theta=38.2°$		
	P	S	R	P	S	R
1	29.2	28.0	28.0	16.4	15.0	14.5
2	26.2	27.5	26.3	14.7	14.0	13.8
3	27.0	26.0	31.2	15.2	15.0	17.3
4	28.7	30.0	37.8	16.1	16.5	21.1
5	30.7	30.6	45.0	17.2	18.2	25.3

1940), we shall use for Z the value given by a zonal velocity distribution of the form $V_\lambda = \alpha E \sin\theta$ so that

$$Z = \frac{1}{E \sin\theta}\frac{\partial}{E\partial\theta}(\alpha E^2 \sin^2\theta) = 2\alpha\cos\theta = 2\alpha[1 - r^2/(2E^2)] \quad (4)$$

Because of the non-divergence of the motion a perturbation stream function ψ exists, and the radial and longitudinal perturbation velocities v_r and v_λ are

$$v_r = -\partial\psi/r\partial\lambda, \quad v_\lambda = \partial\psi/\partial r$$

and the perturbation vorticity is

$$\zeta = \nabla^2\psi = \frac{1}{r}\frac{\partial}{\partial r}\left(r\frac{\partial\psi}{\partial r}\right) + \frac{1}{r^2}\frac{\partial^2\psi}{\partial\lambda^2}. \quad (5)$$

Then from (1) because of the perturbation assumption

$$\left(\frac{\partial}{\partial t} + \alpha\frac{\partial}{\partial\lambda}\right)\nabla^2\psi + 2(\omega+\alpha)\frac{1}{E^2}\frac{\partial\psi}{\partial\lambda} = 0. \quad (6)$$

The dependence of ψ on t, λ, and r is assumed to be of the form

$$\psi = \varphi(r)\exp i(\sigma t + k\lambda) \quad (7)$$

representing a wave with the frequency σ and longitudinal wave number k (positive for westward propagation). Then from (6)

$$\frac{d^2\varphi}{dr^2} + \frac{1}{r}\frac{d\varphi}{dr} + \left(\frac{1}{b^2} - \frac{k^2}{r^2}\right)\varphi = 0 \quad (8)$$

with

$$b = E\left[\frac{\sigma+k\alpha}{2(\omega+\alpha)k}\right]^{\frac{1}{2}} \quad (9)$$

It will be noted from (9) that with (3) for V_λ the undisturbed zonal current produces merely a Doppler shift of the frequency.

The stream function, and hence φ, must be bounded at the pole. Further we require that the radial velocity v_r vanish at a distance $r=d$ from the pole. This distance may be regarded as the equatorward extent of the wave motion. Then

$$\varphi(r) = CJ_k\left(\frac{r}{b}\right)$$

where C is an arbitrary constant and J_k a Bessel function of order k.

If $b^2 < 0$ the solution of (8) would be a modified Bessel function which has a zero at the pole only so that the boundary condition at $r=d$ cannot be satisfied. Therefore, $b^2 > 0$, always. Consequently, in the absence of a mean zonal current $k > 0$, and according to (7) the waves move westward. This is to be expected in analogy to the solutions for the rectangular β plane and the sphere.

From the boundary condition that $v_r = 0$ at $r = d$, it follows with (10) that

$$d/b = j_{k,s}$$

where $j_{k,s}$ is the s'th root of J_k. Hence with (9)

$$\frac{E^2}{b^2} = \frac{2(\omega+\alpha)k}{\sigma+k\alpha} = (E/d)^2 j_{k,s}{}^2. \quad (11)$$

When $\alpha = 0$

$$T = \omega/\sigma = (E/d)^2 j_{k,s}{}^2/(2k). \quad (12)$$

Here T is a non-dimensional number giving the period in sidereal days. This formula corresponds to

$$T = \frac{n(n+1)}{2k}$$

for the spherical case where n is the degree of the appropriate associate Legendre function. In Table I values of T are given for various wave numbers k if the first nodal parallel of v_r is at $d/E = \frac{1}{2}$ or $\frac{2}{3}$, corresponding to colatitudes 28.6° and 38.2°, respectively. The columns headed P show the periods computed from (12). These periods are considerably longer than those for waves at tropical latitudes of similar meridional extent because of the smaller latitudinal variation of the Coriolis parameter at high than at low latitudes. The period decreases rapidly with increasing meridional extent of the disturbance so that its velocity increases. This would be expected since a wider disturbance extends into regions of greater change of the Coriolis parameter.

The columns marked S in Table I give the periods computed by the foregoing formula for a spherical geometry. The degree n of the Legendre function $P_n{}^k$ has here been chosen so that the lowest zero of $P_n{}^k$ is as close as possible to the assumed value of d. The agreement between columns P and S is quite satisfactory. It is also of some interest to compare the values of T in Table I with those obtained for the case of a rectangular coordinate system. In this case one has for the period

$$T = 4\pi^2(1 + L^2/D^2)/(\beta \cdot L)$$

where β is the meridional variation of the Coriolis parameter, $L =$ the wavelength, D twice the width of

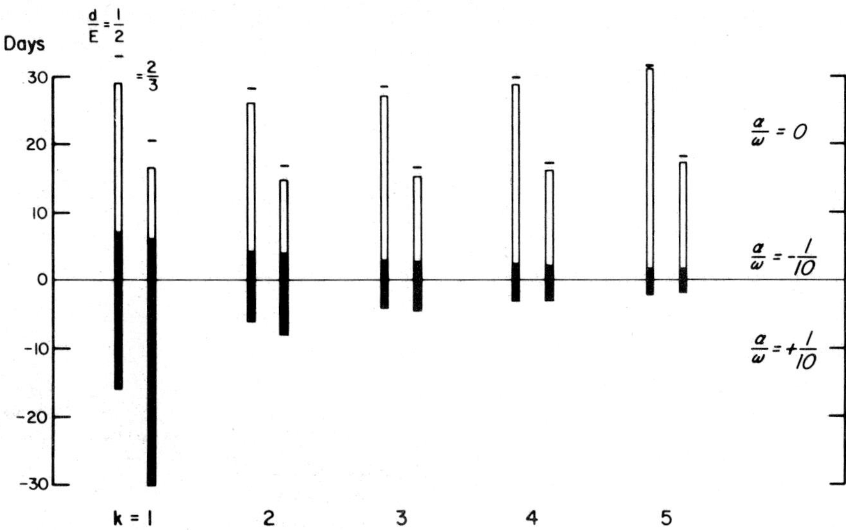

FIG. 1. Periods of long waves in a very deep atmosphere at high latidues for wave numbers $k=1$ to 5; perturbations extending to horizontal distances of $\frac{1}{2}$ and $\frac{2}{3}$ of an earth radius from the pole. The unshaded rectangles show the periods if there is no mean zonal current. The shaded rectangles show the period if the mean zonal current has an angular velocity equal to one tenth of the earth's rotation; the values above the abscissa apply to a westerly flow, those below to an easterly flow. The short horizontal lines give the periods, in the absence of a mean flow, if the depth of the atmosphere is 10 km.

the disturbance. If one uses for the colatitude the central value for the region the values in columns R of Table I are obtained. For large wave numbers the rectangular formula does not represent a good approximation.

If the zonal current is not zero it follows from (11) that the period

$$T = T_0\left[1 - \frac{\alpha}{\omega}(kT_0 - 1)\right]^{-1} \qquad (13)$$

where T_0 denotes now the period when $\alpha = 0$, given by (12). Figure 1 shows the effect of zonal currents towards east, $\alpha/\omega = 0.1$, and towards west, $\alpha/\omega = -0.1$ for the two cases, considered in Table I, where the equatorward boundary, d, of the wave motion is $\frac{1}{2}$ or $\frac{2}{3}$ of the Earth's radius, E. The total, shaded plus unshaded, rectangle above the abscissa gives again the period without a zonal current, the shaded part above the abscissa is the period for an easterly current, the shaded part below for a westerly current. In the latter case the waves move eastward because of the effect of the zonal current. This direction of propagation is indicated in Fig. 1 by a negative T rather than a negative k.

In the numerical examples given here the equatorward limit is the only nodal parallel of the stream function and of v_r. Therefore, the lowest root $j_{k,1}$ is used. If the area studied contains more nodal parallels appropriate higher roots must be used.

In general, it will not be possible to represent the observed flow pattern for a given wave number k by a single Bessel function, but then the latitude dependence

of the flow pattern can be expressed by a series of the form

$$\sum_s a_s J_k\left(\frac{r}{d}j_{k,s}\right)$$

whose terms move, of course, with different speeds.

The velocity components v_r and v_λ can be easily determined from the stream function ψ, and the perturbation pressure is found from one of the momentum equations.

2. Divergent motion

We shall here only briefly describe the derivation of the relevant equations for an incompressible and homogeneous fluid and discuss applications to a compressible atmosphere by making reference to the pertinent results obtained in the theory of the atmospheric tides (see Chapman-Lindzen 1970, e.g.).

If the assumption of non-divergence is dropped let the mean depth of the fluid be H and its perturbation due to the wave motion be η. Since the quasistatic assumption holds for long waves, the perturbation pressure p is given by

$$p = gQ\eta,$$

where Q is the undisturbed density, g, the acceleration of gravity.

As in the preceding section the dependence of the

perturbation variables η, v_r, v_λ on t and λ may be

$$\exp i(\sigma t + k\lambda).$$

If it is further assumed that the undisturbed atmosphere is at rest, the equations of motion and continuity are

$$i\sigma v_r - f v_\lambda = -g\partial\eta/\partial r$$
$$i\sigma v_\lambda + f v_r = -ikg\eta/r$$
$$i\sigma\eta/H + (1/r)\partial(rv_r)/\partial r + ikv_\lambda/r = 0$$

By eliminating here v_λ and η and by introducing

$$U = r \cdot v_r$$

one finds that

$$\frac{d^2U}{dr^2} + \frac{1}{r}\frac{1+\epsilon^2 r^2}{1-\epsilon^2 r^2}\frac{dU}{dr}$$

$$+ \left[\frac{2\omega k}{\sigma E^2} - \frac{2f\sigma}{gkH}\frac{1}{1-\epsilon^2 r^2} - \frac{f^2-\sigma^2}{gH} - \frac{k^2}{r^2}\right]U = 0 \quad (14)$$

where

$$\epsilon^2 = \sigma^2/(k^2 gH)$$

As H tends to infinity the divergence tends to zero, and (14) becomes identical with (8), as expected.

Equation (14) may be simplified for the discussion of waves in the polar cap with periods longer than a day—which are considered here—because in general

$$\epsilon^2 r^2 \ll 1$$

Since the disturbance will be required to terminate at $r=d$, only the maximum value $\epsilon^2 d^2$ needs to be considered. It may be written, in order to estimate its magnitude,

$$\epsilon^2 d^2 = \frac{\omega^2 E^2}{gH}\left(\frac{d}{E}\right)^2\frac{1}{k^2 T^2}$$

where T is, as before, the period in days.

In the case of an incompressible fluid considered here, H is the mean fluid depth. In order to make a realistic numerical choice of H applicable to a compressible atmosphere reference may be made to the theory of atmospheric tides where it is found that H is replaced in (14) by a separation constant, usually denoted by h_n, the "equivalent depth." In the case of free oscillations h_n depends on the structure of the atmosphere and can be computed from the theory. It can also be estimated from the observed propagation velocity of long waves, in particular those observed with Krakatoa explosion (Taylor, 1936). Both methods lead to a value of about 10 km which will be used here. With $d/E=\frac{2}{3}$, $k=2$, $T=3$ days, it follows that $\epsilon^2 d^2=0.03$. Hence the terms with ϵ in (14) may be neglected compared to one. Further, the variable Coriolis parameter f in the factor of U in (14) may be replaced by a suitable mean value $\bar{f}$ for the region. This procedure is cus-

tomary in the study of these long waves where f is regarded as constant except when it is differentiated with regard to latitude (the first term in the bracket). Equation (14) becomes then a Bessel equation for U whose solution is

$$U = CJ_k(mr)$$

which satisfies the condition that v_r be bounded at the pole, and where

$$m^2 = \frac{2\omega k}{\sigma E^2} - \frac{2\bar{f}\sigma}{kgH} - \frac{\bar{f}^2-\sigma^2}{gH} \quad (15)$$

The other boundary condition that $v_r=0$ at $r=d$ requires that $md=j_{k,s}$ where $j_{k,s}$ is again the s'th zero of the Bessel function of order k. Thus the period, in sidereal days, is approximately

$$T = (E/d)^2 j_{k,s}^2/(2k) + 2\omega^2 E^2\cos^2\bar{\theta}/(gkH)$$
$$\times[1 + 1/(kT\cos\bar{\theta}) - 1/(4T^2\cos^2\bar{\theta})] \quad (16)$$

For sufficiently long periods the parenthesis is nearly one; otherwise, the value for T obtained by assuming the parenthesis to be one may be substituted into the parenthesis to determine a better approximation for T. This formula has been used to compute the periods for the cases shown in Fig. 1 if $H=10$ km rather than infinite. The periods corrected for finite depth are indicated in the figure by short horizontal lines above the corresponding vertical bars for infinite depth. The corrections are only small and increase the period lengths.

Equation (16) is cubic in T. Thus three values of T belong to each value of H. The one in which we are interested here, and which is approximated by (16), is large. The two other periods are much shorter. They belong to oscillations which are gravity waves.

As discussed before, from the theory of the atmospheric tides it is known that in the case of a compressible atmosphere H is replaced by the equivalent depth h_n which, in the case of free oscillations, can be determined from the theory so that the period of the free oscillations is given. On the other hand, if an oscillation is excited by a forcing function with a given period T, Eq. (16) becomes an equation for the determination of the equivalent depth h_n, and the value of h_n determines how the atmosphere responds to the excitation, and whether the oscillation is confined to the layer of excitation or is propagating vertically. Since the equivalent depth h_n is a separation constant, not an actual depth, it may be negative as well as positive, and shorter periods than those for $h_n=\infty$ may occur when h_n is negative. As an example, Fig. 2 shows for long-period oscillations the equivalent depths as functions of T computed with (16) when $d/E=\frac{2}{3}$, corresponding to a boundary colatitude of 38.2°, and for wave numbers $k=2$ and 4. The periods for infinite equivalent depths are marked on the abscissa by $T_{2,\infty}$ and $T_{4,\infty}$. The broken parts of the curves indicate that

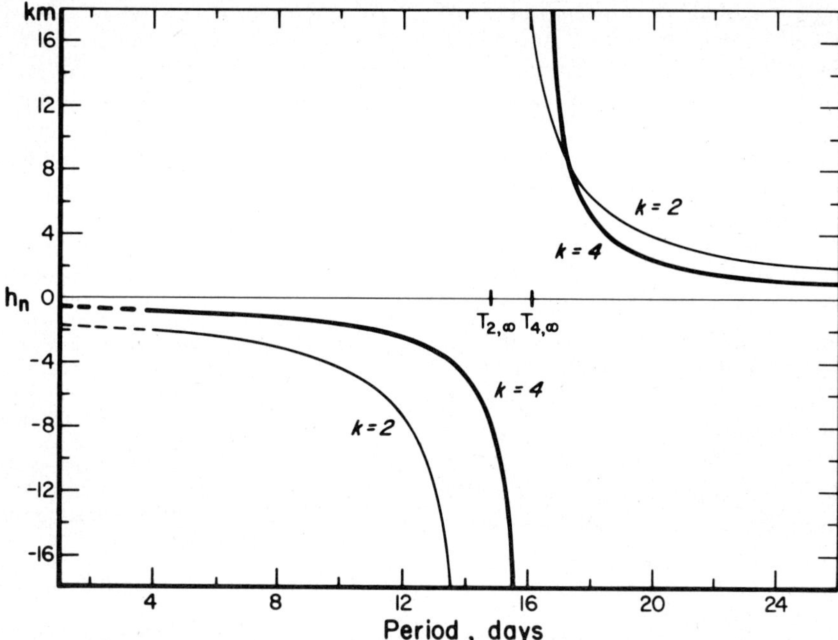

FIG. 2. Relation between period and equivalent depth for wave numbers $k=2, 4$ when the perturbation extends to a horizontal distance of $\frac{2}{3}$ of an earth radius from the pole. Periods for infinite depth indicated by $T_{k,\infty}$ on the abscissa.

for periods shorter than 4 days the approximations become poor. It may be recalled from tidal theory that for negative equivalent depths the waves will not propagate vertically.

3. Concluding remarks

Only very few data are available at present to check the deductions of the preceding sections. Eliasen and Machenhauer (1968), among others, have made spherical and hemispherical harmonic analyses of the atmospheric pressure-height fields during some periods of the International Geophysical Year 1957/58 for the 500 mb and 1000 mb levels. One of their results (their Table II) is reproduced here as Table II. It gives the contribution to the total height variance of various groups of terms in the harmonic representation of the pressure field, characterized by the longitudinal wave numbers k and meridional wave numbers $n-k$. This table is based on analyses of the northern hemisphere for January 1958. With particular reference to wave motions in the polar regions, it is pertinent to note that the harmonics with larger meridional wave numbers, $n-k=8$ to 15, which have zeros at high latitudes, contain a substantial amount of variance.

In the same paper the 24-hourly phase-angle changes have been determined for the various terms in the harmonic series for the time interval from 1 October 1957 through 31 January 1958. The vector means of these changes for each mode may be regarded as average velocities of the modes. For values of n equal to 5 or larger there is reasonable agreement of these velocities

with those given by the simple formula for barotropic, non-divergent waves, but the scatter of the observed velocities around their means is large according to the authors.

For a more thorough quantitative investigation of the flow and pressure patterns of the atmosphere it will be necessary to have available a much longer series of harmonically analysed flow and pressure patterns. Such data will show the relative importance of the various spectral modes during different years and different seasons. They will further enable quantitative characterizations to be made of mean (annual, seasonal, monthly), as well as of daily patterns by means of the predominating spectral modes.

Some of the modes of the flow and pressure fields are presumably due to geographic features, such as water and land distribution and mountain barriers and are more or less stationary. But the majority must be due to variable forcing functions, especially to time-and space-dependent heating. To the extent that it may be possible to attribute such modes to forcing functions—and to the varying atmospheric responses—such a study can be expected to contribute to the quantitative

TABLE II. Variance of horizontal gradient of 500 mb level (m²). Spectral distribution. After Eliasen and Machenbauer (1969).

		k		
$n-k$	0	1–4	5–8	9–12
0–7	469	307	139	41
8–15	47	146	59	20
16–23	5	24	12	6

explanation of the great variability of the atmosphere from year to year and over longer times. As of now there are only a few types of oscillations for which the forcing functions have been identified, in particular the gravitational and thermal tides. For other types of oscillations the forcing functions may be what is loosely called, of a random nature; that is, they may consist of impulses which are irregularly distributed in space and time, to which the atmosphere responds according to its stratification and velocity distribution. Since the atmospheric response itself will modify this distribution, especially in the case of larger, non-linear responses, this feedback can lead to substantial changes. Such changes may be further magnified when extraneous conditions, for instance ocean temperatures, ice conditions, and surface albedo are also affected. Reference must also be made in this connection to the possible effects of the baroclinicity of the atmospheric mean state which allows the development of unstable waves, as discussed by Charney (1947) and others.

All these factors contribute to atmospheric variability and may even produce variations of sufficient magnitude and persistence to appear as climatic variations. This applies especially to high latitudes where relatively small changes in temperature and precipitation can produce significant changes in the distribution of the ice cover over both land and water.

REFERENCES

Chapman, S., and R. S. Lindzen, 1970: *Atmospheric Tides*, 200 pp., D. Reidel, Dordrecht-Holland.

Charney, J. G., 1947: The dynamics of long waves in a baroclinic westerly current. *Journ. of Meteorology*, 4, 135–162.

Eliasen, E., and B. Machenhauer, 1969: On the observed large-scale atmospheric wave motions. *Tellus*, 21, 149–166.

Haurwitz, B., 1940: The motion of atmospheric disturbances on the spherical earth. *Journ. of Marine Research*, 3, 254–267.

Rossby, C. G., and collab., 1939: Relations between variations in the intensity of the zonal circulation of the atmosphere and the displacements of the semipermanent centers of action. *Journ. of Marine Research*, 2, 38–55.

Taylor, G. I., 1936: The oscillations of the atmosphere. *Proceedings Royal Society, London, A*, **156**, 318–326.

Satellite Studies of the Atmospheric Circulation
of the Southern Hemisphere

N. A. STRETEN*

Geophysical Institute, University of Alaska, Fairbanks, Alaska 99701

Abstract

Aspects of the climate of the oceanic regions of the Southern Hemisphere have been studied in three separate projects utilizing satellite-derived information:

(i) Sequences of daily satellite mosaics have been employed to derive information on the distribution, structure, and life history of mid-latitude depressions.
(ii) Sequences of 5-day averaged brightness maps have been used to investigate the behaviour of the extensive cloud bands over the hemisphere and their relation to the long wave pattern.
(iii) 5 day minimum brightness maps have been studied to examine the gross extent of the Antarctic sea ice and its summer decay, and to compare the strength of the southern westerlies for two years at the time of maximum ice extent.

These projects are briefly reviewed.

1. Introduction

Meteorological satellites have now been providing data since April 1960 when TIROS 1 was launched. However, it would be fair to say that the technical developments in photographic and radiometric instrumentation, in the timely computer processing of global mosaics, and in the development of entirely new techniques (e.g., SIRS measurements of temperature profiles on a global basis) have far outstripped the detailed analysis of the vast mass of derived data to study the various scales of atmospheric motion. The great utility of satellite derived data in dynamic climatology has recently been pointed out by Bugaev (1973), and broad scale global climatology of cloudiness is becoming a reality (Miller and Feddes 1971). Satellite technology is now in sight of the goal of providing a global network of quantitative observations which will permit a sound base for day to day analysis and for longer term general circulation modelling experiments. Despite this, however, the synthesis of the presently existing series of pictorial satellite observations is a task to which, perhaps, more effort might be devoted.

In some regions (in particular, the Southern Hemisphere) it has been necessary to utilize this satellite data to a greater extent for operational purposes than in regions with high observation density such as North America and western Europe where the data are often merely supplementary. Over most of the southern oceans pictorial satellite data has been the primary tool in synoptic analysis, and its interpretation has become a more prominent problem since the introduction of hemispheric analysis and prognosis (Gauntlett and Hincksman 1971). Attempts over the past four years to obtain more quantitative methods of using pictorial data have led to associated studies of the synoptic meteorology of the hemisphere—an important area of investigation which has depended largely, until recently, on the detailed and painstaking (though subjective) analysis of a number of chart series—notably that for the I.G.Y. (Taljaard 1972).

In Australia a number of such investigations have been carried out at the Commonwealth Meteorology Research Centre in Melbourne. The data so far used have been exclusively the daily computer-mapped hemispheric mosaics (e.g., Fig. 1) based on the ESSA series of satellites dating from late 1966 (Bristor *et al.*, 1966), and the derived multi-day imagery (principally 5-day averaged and minimum brightness mosaics—Booth *et al.*, 1969). Various periods from 1967 to 1971 have been examined covering all months, but largely excluding those of the southern winter (June to September) when the solar elevation is too low to permit production of high quality photographic mosaics at high latitudes.

The present review is designed to describe briefly the principal results of these projects, which are individually reported on more fully elsewhere, and to emphasize the future use of satellite data (in particular the newer HRIR and VHRR information) for

* Present address: Commonwealth Meteorology Research Center, Melbourne, Australia.

FIG. 1. Southern hemisphere computer generated mosaic (South American sector).

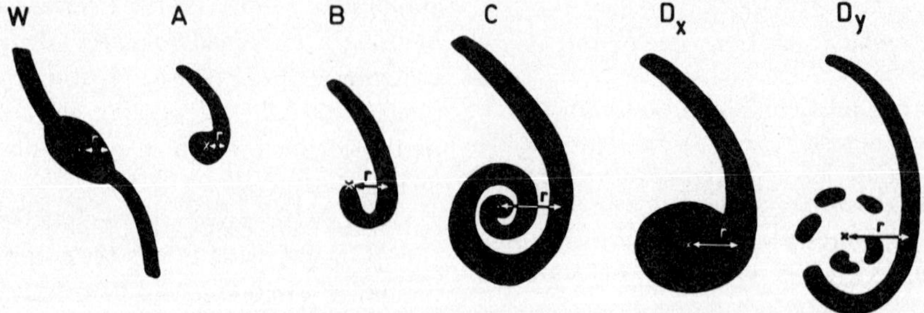

FIG. 2. Schematic diagram of the primary classification of extratropical vortex evolutionary patterns. The distance taken as the vortex radius in each case is shown by r.

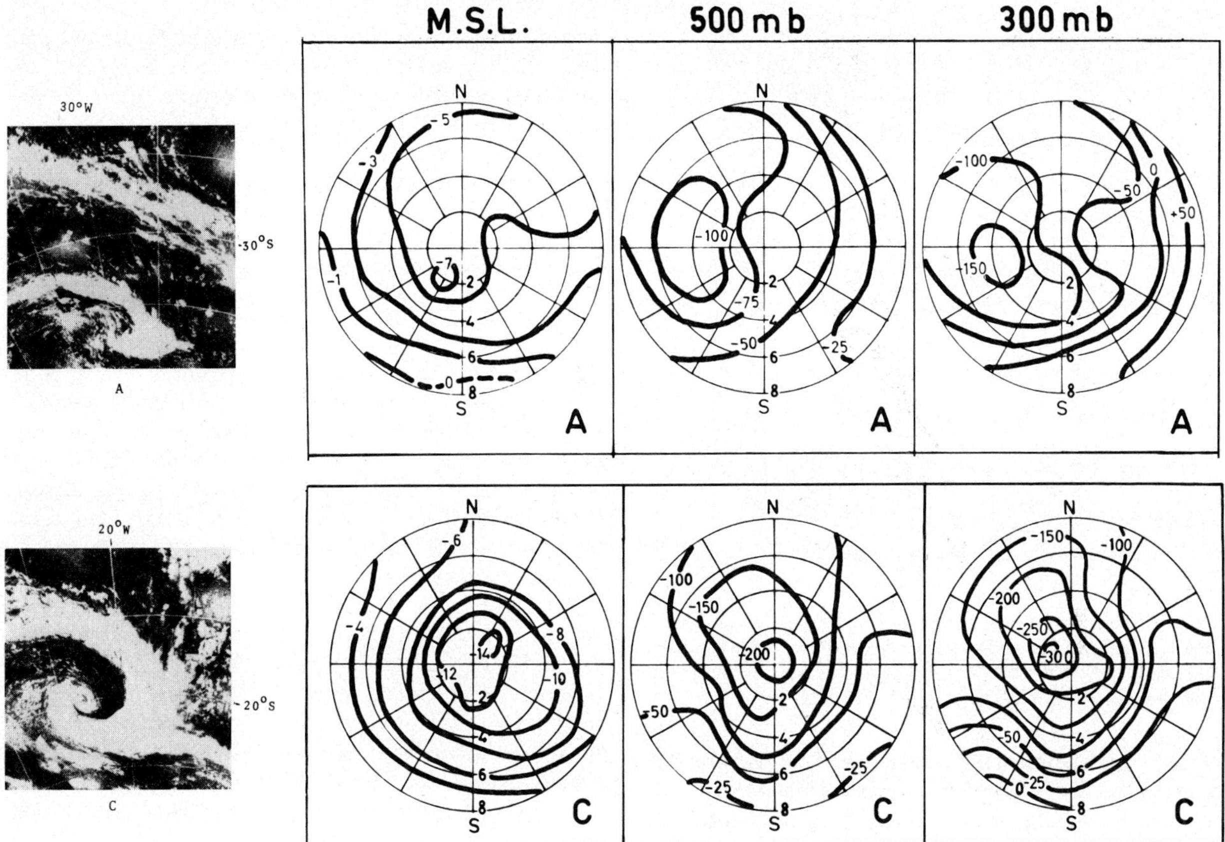

FIG. 3. Examples of vortex types A and C, and model anomaly patterns of M.S.L. pressure (mb) and 500 and 300 mb geopotential (m) for these types. The anomaly patterns are shown on a grid with 2° latitude circles and 30° longitude intervals centered on the vortex center.

similar but more detailed studies over regions of poor conventional data—notably the Arctic Basin.

2. Satellite observed cloud vortices

Satellites provide a unique method of observing the development and life history of synoptic-scale cloud vortices. This is true particularly over the Southern Hemisphere where a depression may encounter no substantial land mass during its life, and may be viewed against a uniform sea surface background. A classification scheme for cloud vortices observed on hemispheric digital mosaics southward of 20°S was employed to construct statistical models of the associated atmospheric structure. This classification of signatures identified, for example, 5 principal stages of development of extratropical depressions (A or W to D), shown schematically in Fig. 2, which could be regularly observed on the mosaics. Some 4600 conventional surface observations and 1600 upper air soundings quasi-coincident in time and space with the observed cloud vortices, and derived principally from island stations, ships, and exposed coastal continental stations, were used to obtain patterns of observations for each vortex type. Such patterns were expressed in terms of departure of surface pressure and 500 and 300 mb geopotential from the monthly mean data of the Southern Hemisphere Altas (Taljaard et al., 1969). An example of such anomaly patterns for A-type vortices (comma clouds) and C-types (mature depressions with a spiral cloud vortex) is shown in Fig. 3. The patterns were further refined by calculating statistical variations in intensity associated with different latitude and size, (as measured by the radii of Fig. 2) the latter correction being rather small. The decay stage (D) proved to require further subclassification to reveal its main features. Despite a fairly large standard deviation in the anomaly values, the patterns appear to be, in general, physically and numerically realistic in depicting stages of cyclonic development, and have been used, with other methods, as an aid in numerical hemispheric analysis in the World Meteorological Centre in Melbourne. This work is described more fully by Troup and Streten (1972) and Streten and Kellas (1973).

The sequence of vortex tracks and development may also be used to derive synoptic climatological information about the hemispheric circulation—e.g., Fig. 4 depicts the axes of the zone of highest frequency

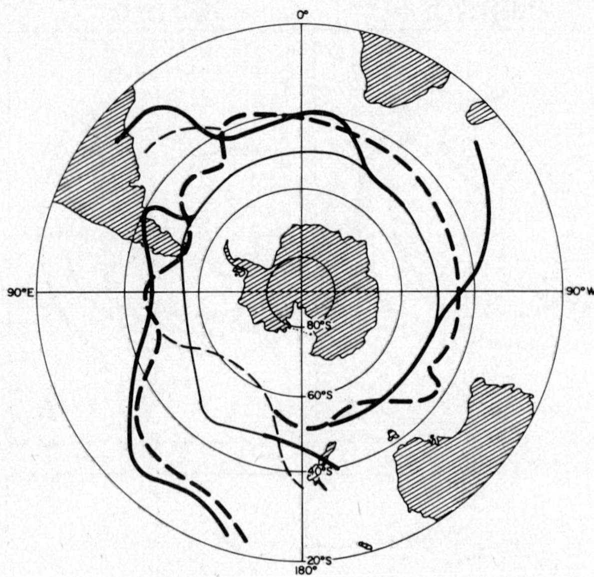

FIG. 4. Axes of the zone of highest frequency of early development (A and W) for summer (dashed) and Intermediate season (full line). Where a secondary maximum occurs it is shown in a finer line.

of early development (W and A types) of extratropical depressions for Summer (December to March) and the "Intermediate Season" (April, May, October and November) based on over 500 observations of these types of development. The axes delineate the principal frontal zones of the hemisphere and agree well with IGY studies. The frequency with which depressions develop in the absence of previously observed cloud bands is observed to be some 55 to 60% of the total, and the frequency of such "non-frontal" development increases towards higher latitudes but remains numerically similar in both seasons. With advancing stage of development the median latitude of highest frequency is located further poleward—e.g., for types A and W the median latitude in summer is 44°S and for type D the corresponding latitude is 57°S. Further analysis of the sequences of evolution provide data such as

(a) The distribution of vortex lifetime for particular signature states.
(b) The percentage frequency with which one vortex type is succeeded by another on the next daily mosaic (i.e., in approximately 24 hours).
(c) The geographical distribution of location of vortex formation, tracks, and decay.
(d) The distribution of vortex speeds in relation to the strength of the zonal westerly circulation.

It is found that the pattern of cyclonic formation and decay and the tracks of the systems tend to point to a high frequency of a basic pattern of 3 long waves around the hemisphere, particularly in summer. Such a pattern displays cyclogenesis east of South

America associated with cyclolysis near Enderby Land and further east; cyclogenesis from Kerguelen to southern Australia with cyclolysis near Terre Adelie and the Ross Sea; and cyclogenesis in the central Pacific with cyclolysis in the Bellinghausen Sea. The synoptic climatology of the vortices is described more fully by Streten and Troup (1973).

3. Satellite-observed zones of persistent cloudiness

Multi-day averages of brightness (cloudiness) over the Southern Hemisphere depict some interesting features—e.g., the extensive bands lying over a wide latitude zone and often remaining quasi-conservative in position from one 5-day averaging period to the next. The band over the South Pacific (Fig. 5) is particularly prominent and is found to be closely coincident in location with maxima in the long term observations of rainfall distribution over the South Pacific (Streten 1970).

The long-wave pattern over the Southern Hemisphere is not well defined by conventional observations. However, for the period when the best data coverage is available (e.g., that of the first GARP period in November 1969) a high quality analysis may be obtained and subjected to a scale separation technique due to Holl (1968). Such an experiment yields an approximation to the long-wave field which may be compared with the location of the cloud bands over the hemisphere (Fig. 6). It is found that the cloud bands lie, in general, somewhat eastward of the long wave troughs. As the bands appear to be principally associated with depression tracks and with

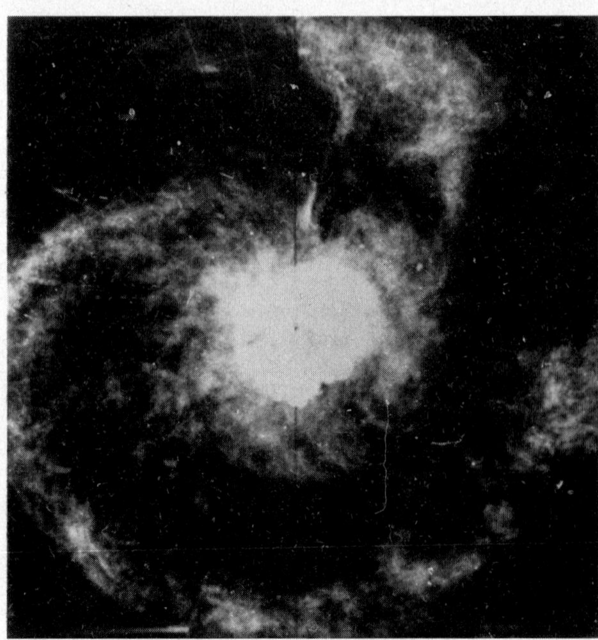

FIG. 5. Multiple image mosaic showing averaged cloud for December 1967. (Picture produced by J. Kornfield at University of Wisconsin.)

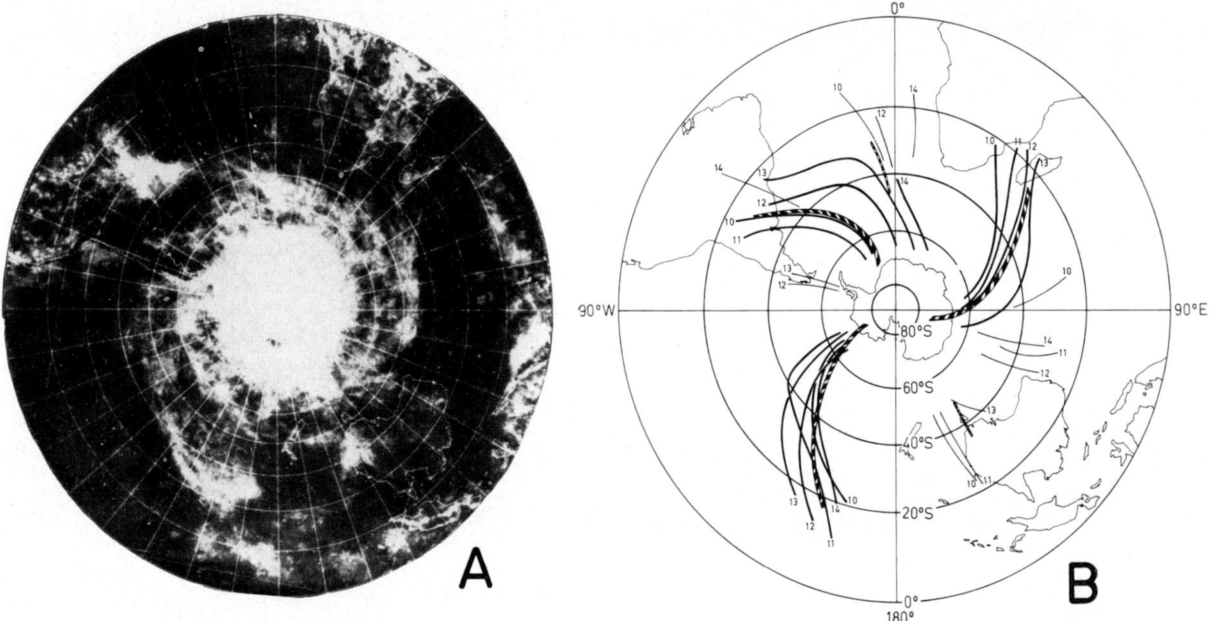

FIG. 6. (A) 5-day averaged mosaic November 10–14, 1969. (B) Location of 700 mb troughs in the long wave scale separated components (see text) for corresponding indicated dates. Full lines—well defined troughs; fine lines—minor troughs. Striped lines, troughs in mean 5 day field.

lines of low level convergence such a result is consistent with synoptic experience.

Further statistical analysis of the location of the large scale bands (which are defined as extending through at least 20 parallels of latitude and as being at least 5° of latitude in width) yields an annual distribution shown in Fig. 7. The number of bands on an individual 5-day averaged mosaic (the "band number") varies from 0 to 7 (Fig. 8). However, a predominance of band numbers 3 and 4 exists between 20°S and 50°S. If the band number represents

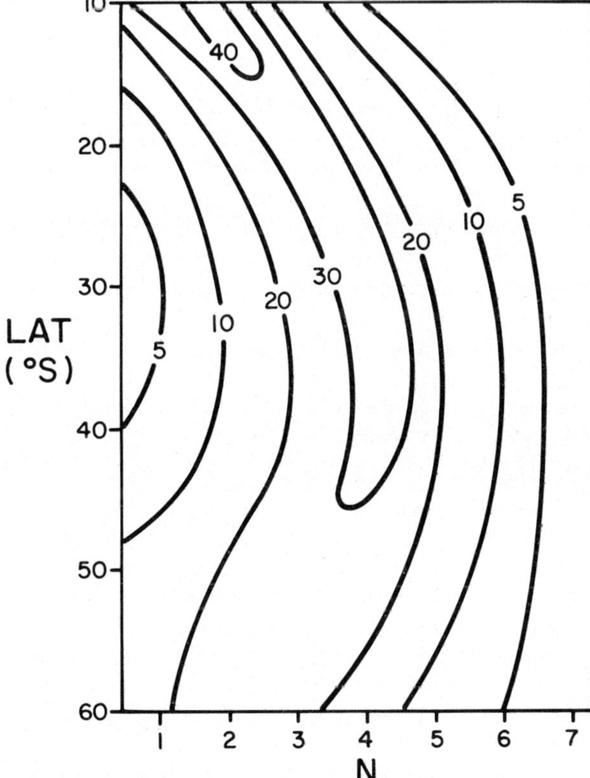

FIG. 7. Annual percentage frequency of 5-day averaged mosaics having axes of major cloud bands within 5° Latitude by 10° Longitude square (based on period of November 1968–October 1971).

FIG. 8. Percentage frequency of the number of cloud bands on individual mosaics (band number N) at particular latitudes.

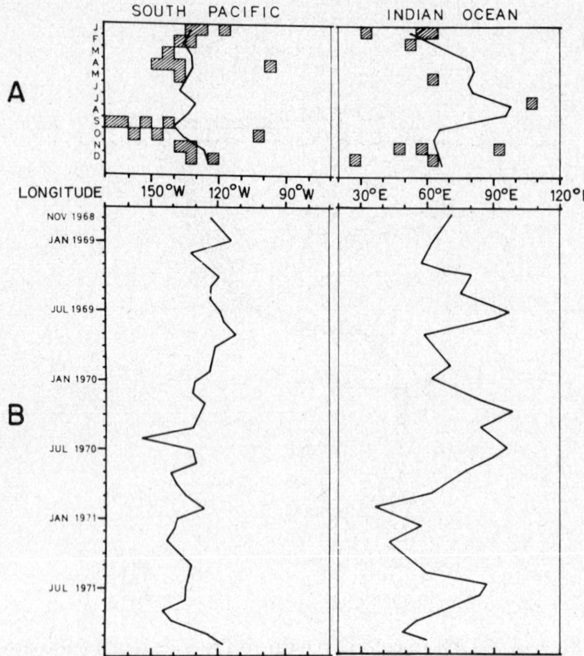

FIG. 9. Monthly mean longitude of 5 day averaged bands for 2 geographical sectors averaged between 30°S and 40°S. (A)—averaged over 3 years: (B) in time section. Shaded squares in (A) indicate months and regions with band frequency ≥1 per month at either 30°S or 40°S.

an approximation to the wave number these results are, in general, consistent with the analysis of the zonal harmonic standing waves over the hemisphere (Van Loon and Jenne, 1972) and with inferences from 5-day means of pressure and geopotential (Noar, 1973). The average band number is found to be highest in late winter and spring, and lowest in mid-summer and early autumn when the three-wave pattern previously inferred from the movement of depressions over the hemisphere again appears to predominate.

Interesting variations occur in the locations of the cloudiness bands over the period of observation. Examples are shown in Fig. 9 for the Pacific and Indian Ocean sectors.

(a) *The South Pacific Zone:* The median location of the Pacific band axes at mid-latitudes moves little from month to month (Fig. 7 and Fig. 9A) and the permanence of this broadscale feature is reflected in the limited longer term climatological data that is available (Streten 1970). However Fig. 9B appears to indicate a slow trend in the band axis towards the west from the spring of 1969 to that of 1971, the movement being some 10° to 20° of longitude during this period. There is some evidence for this movement in rainfall data for two island stations—Rapa (Lat. 27°S Long. 144°W) and Pitcairn Is. (Lat. 25°S Long. 130°W) which are given in Table 1. The

rainfall at Rapa is slightly above the long term average during the period, but as the band position tends to lie increasingly west of Pitcairn Island this station records many very dry months with a large overall rainfall deficit. This situation is probably associated at least in part with the westward displacement of highest band frequency.

(b) *The Indian Ocean Zone:* This sector displays a substantial (30°–40° longitude) seasonal variation in the median location of the band from the western part of the ocean in January eastward to the vicinity of 90°E in late winter (Fig. 9A) with a transition occurring, in the mean, quite rapidly in spring. Despite some difficulty in assessing the cloud band data in this area due to the "daybreak" in satellite mosaics, the displacement was similar in all 3 years (Fig. 9B) and the pattern appears to be real.

Van Loon (1971) indicates a mid-latitude association between the location of the speed maximum in the sea surface current and that of the center of the mean sub-tropical High over the Indian Ocean—both being further east in summer and west in winter. The variation in the location of the anticyclone is further confirmed by the total cloudiness pattern revealed in the four year data of Miller and Feddes (1971).

The band location is in opposite phase to that of the anticyclone. In summer, the band most frequently extends from tropical Africa and Madagascar SE into the ocean to the west of the High. In winter, when the anticyclone is located further west, the median position of the cloud bands is to the west of Australia in longitudes 85° to 95°E. In the latter season a further band is often located to the west of the High, but with lower frequency than that near 90°E.

The westward location of the median position of the band in summer is consistent with the analysis of Lamb (1959), who concluded that the summer movement of the broad trough in the Indian Ocean westward to about 60°E was the only recognizable seasonal shift in the trough-ridge pattern that could be inferred from conventional observations for the entire hemisphere. However other investigations (see e.g., the discussion by Noar 1973) have found evidence for a westward displacement in winter. The present data appears to imply substantial frequencies of troughs in both the eastern and western parts of

TABLE 1. Rainfall data—South Pacific Islands.
(October 1969 to September 1971)

P —Percentage departure of rainfall total from long term mean p (mm).
N_1—Number of months with rainfall ≥ 50% above normal.
N_2—Number of months with rainfall ≤ 50% below normal.

Station	$P(p)$	N_1	N_2
Rapa	+ 6 (2893)	6	4
Pitcairn Is.	−18 (1830)	2	9

the ocean in winter, but with those in the east predominating.

It may be significant that, in summer, frequent advection of moist air is occurring from tropical Africa southeastward along the longitudes of the prominent band. In winter, to the east of the ocean, advection of tropical maritime air frequently occurs to the west of large detached High pressure systems centered over Australia. However, at this time drier air from continental southern Africa may be advected over southern waters westward of the principal oceanic anticyclone, resulting in less prominent cloud band development. The striking differences in the cloud cover statistics from summer to winter over southern Africa are evident in the seasonal data of Miller and Feddes (1971).

The nature of the mid-latitude band structures is still uncertain. However, the evidence suggests that their location is, in general, related closely to that of the long wave hemispheric pattern. It is notable that the three more distinct low latitude termini of high band frequency are located over Africa, South America, and in particular the eastern tip of New Guinea—the eastern extremity of the so called "maritime continent." The bands may thus visually represent the mean channels wherein energy flow occurs into the mid latitude westerlies from these tropical continental areas of most active convection. It is interesting that ATS 3 pictures for the South American region give a distinct impression of the movement of cloud features from the tropical Amazon region southeastward into the persistent cloud band over the South Atlantic. The mean bands may thus be climatologically analogous to the bands connected with particular tropical cyclones, studied by Erickson and Winston (1972), as channels of poleward energy transfer.

It may be possible for the satellite-observed features of the circulation described here to be tested and numerically reproduced by general circulation models of the Southern Hemisphere currently being developed in Australia.

A more detailed account of the investigation of the cloud bands over the hemisphere is given elsewhere (Streten 1973b in press).

4. Satellite observations of the antarctic sea ice

Sequences of hemispheric 5-day minimum brightness mosaics (e.g., Fig. 10) (Booth *et al.*, 1969) have been used to plot the decay of Antarctic pack ice over three summer seasons and to locate extremes at particular dates. This technique helps to filter out more transitory features such as cloud, and reveal more clearly the sea ice edge which changes only slightly. The comparison of successive 5-day minimum brightness imagery enables the major features of the progression and fluctuation in the decay of the ice extent

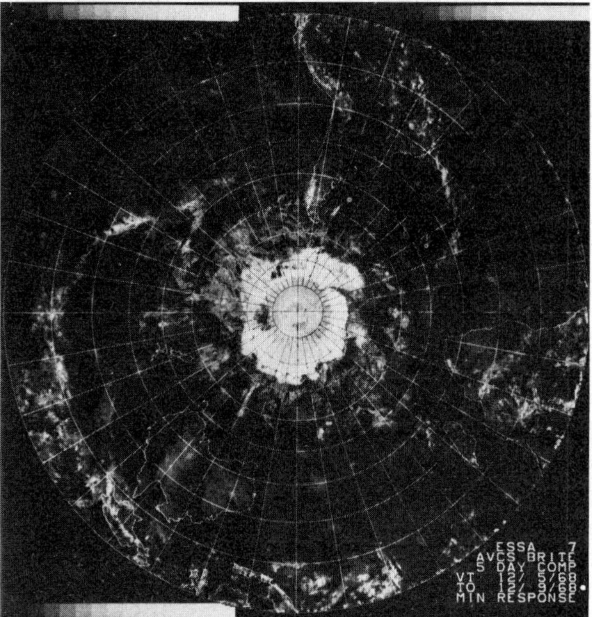

FIG. 10. Typical 5 day minimum brightness mosaic for 5th–9th December 1968.

around the entire continent to be recorded as a function of time for the greater part of the summer season.

The geographical distribution of the major polynyas was plotted, and found to support the general theory (e.g., as discussed by Knapp 1969) that these features tend to form westward of north-south trending coastlines or substantial iceberg or iceshelf tongues extending northward from the Antarctic coast. The progression of ice decay in the large embayments of the Ross and Weddell Seas and in Prydz Bay was found to show considerable similarities in each of the three seasons.

Information of the extent and variation of the sea ice cover is of obvious importance to navigation in polar waters. However, it has more far-reaching significance in the study of the large scale climate of the earth. A change of one degree of latitude in the Antarctic pack ice limit represents a change of about 15 percent in the total coverage of hemispheric sea ice at a particular date (Lamb 1961). Such changes in the ice cover of the hemisphere represent a considerable change in the components of the energy balance of the earth, and may cause marked changes in the atmospheric circulation pattern.

Increased ice cover of the ocean results in a cutting off or a substantial reduction in air-sea interaction, and if this exists over a large area it may lead to an intensification of the atmospheric circulation. Fletcher (1969) shows that this effect is of greatest importance in winter with extensive sea ice rather than in the summer decay period. In the present observations, the extent on 1 October, 1969 appeared to be considerably greater over the southeast Pacific and South

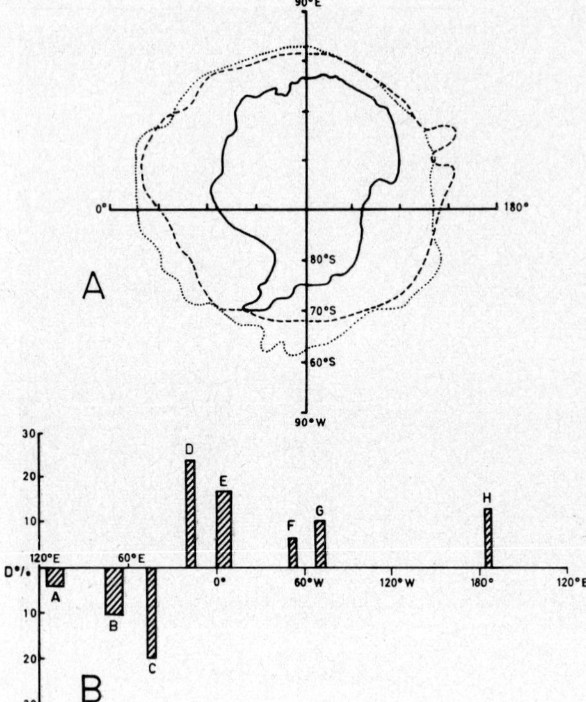

Fig. 11. (A) Ice extent on October 1st 1969 (dotted) and 1970 (dashed). (B) Percentage departure of the 1969 Zonal Index D (difference in mean monthly October MSL pressure between the following pairs of stations) from that of 1970: A. Perth-Mirny, B. New Amsterdam-Mawson, C. Marion Is.-Molodezhnaya, D. Capetown-Novolazarevskaya, E. Gough Is.-SANAE, F. Montevideo-O'Higgins, G. Puerto Montt-Adelaide Is., H. Wellington-McMurdo Sound.

Atlantic sector than for the corresponding date of 1970 (Fig. 11a). The total extent at the beginning of October was measured as being some 19 percent higher in 1969 than in 1970. Fig. 11b shows some indices of the strength of the southern westerlies between approximately 40°S and Antarctica in terms of mean monthly pressure difference between pairs of stations at different longitudes for the month of October in 1969 and 1970. The difference between the months is indicated by showing the index value for 1969 in terms of a percentage departure from the corresponding figure in 1970. The departures are positive over the greater part of the South Pacific and South Atlantic sectors (the region of more extensive sea ice in 1969), and small and negative in the Australian and Indian Ocean sectors where the ice was similar in both years. Even such short term observations are interesting in the light of Fletcher's (1969) analysis of similarities in long term variation in the strength of the westerly circulation over southern New Zealand in July, and the single long-term index of southern ice extent (i.e., the date of closing of Scotia Bay in the South Orkneys by ice).

Such multi-day mosaics, particularly if they are derived from the newer infrared data for winter,

should enable better records of the ice extent at all seasons to be obtained from year to year. These data will permit associated studies of hypothetical variations in the southern hemisphere and even global circulation, related to variations in Antarctic ice extent, to be undertaken on a more quantitative basis. The analysis of the sea ice measurements is reported in more detail by Streten (1973a).

5. Concluding remarks

The utility of satellite pictorial data observed in long sequences has been demonstrated in investigations into the climatology of the Southern Hemisphere. Further studies using the expanding range of satellite-derived information may be expected to yield new and more detailed results for this and other regions of the world where meteorological station networks are poor.

REFERENCES

Booth, A. L., and V. R. Taylor, 1969, Meso-scale archive and computer products of digitized video data from ESSA satellites. *Bull. Meteor. Soc.*, **50**, 431–438.

Bristor, C. L., W. M. Callicot and R. E. Bradford, 1966, Operational processing of satellite cloud pictures by computer. *Mon. Wea. Review*, **94**, 515–527.

Bugaev, V. A., 1973, Dynamic climatology in the light of satellite information. *Bull. Amer. Meteor. Soc.*, **54**, 394–418.

Erickson, C. O., and J. S. Winston, 1972, Tropical storm, mid-latitude cloud band connections, and the autumnal buildup of the planetary circulation. *J. Appl. Meteor.*, **11**, 23–36.

Fletcher, J. O., 1969, Ice extent on the southern ocean and its relation to world climate, Memorandum RM-5793-NSF: The Rand Corporation, Santa Monica, California.

Gauntlett, D. J., and D. R. Hincksman, 1971, A six-level primitive equation model suitable for extended operational prediction in the southern hemisphere. *J. Appl. Meteor.*, **10**, 613–625.

Holl, M. M., 1963, Scale and pattern spectra and decompositions, Technical Memorandum No. 3 Contract N228-(62271), 60550 Meteorology International Inc., Monterey, California.

Knapp, W. W., 1969, A satellite study of large stationary polynyas in Antarctic coastal waters. Ph.D. thesis, University of Wisconsin.

Lamb, H. H., 1959, The southern westerlies: a preliminary survey; main characteristics and apparent associations. *Quarterly Journal of the Royal Meteorological Society*, **85**, 1–23.

Lamb, H. H., 1961, Fundamentals of climate in "Descriptive Paleoclimatology," A. E. M. Nairn, Ed., Interscience Publishers Inc., New York.

Miller, D. B., and R. G. Feddes, 1971, Global atlas of relative cloud cover 1967–70 based on photographic signals from meteorological satellites, NOAA (NESS)/USAF (Air Weather Service—MAC) Joint Production, Washington, D. C.

Noar, P. F., 1973, Energy dispersion and other features of the middle latitude circulation of the Australian region, Meteorological Study No. 24, Bureau of Meteorology, Melbourne.

Streten, N. A., 1970, A note on the climatology of the satellite observed zone of high cloudiness in the central south Pacific. *Australian Meteorological Magazine*, **18**, 31–38.

Streten, N. A., 1973a, Satellite Observations of the summer decay of the Antarctic sea ice. *Arch. Met. Geoph. Biokl. Series A.*, **22**, 119–134.

Streten, N. A., 1973b, Some characteristics of satellite observed bands of persistent cloudiness over the southern hemisphere. *Mon. Wea. Review* **101**, 486–495.

Streten, N. A., and A. J. Troup, 1973, A synoptic climatology of satellite observed cloud vortices over the southern hemisphere. *Quarterly Journal of the Royal Meteorological Society*, **99**, 56–72.

Streten, N. A., and W. R. Kellas, 1973, Aspects of cloud pattern signatures of depressions in maturity and decay. *J. Appl. Meteor.*, **12**, 23–27.

Taljaard, J. J., 1972, Synoptic Meteorology of the southern hemisphere in "Meteorology of the Southern Hemisphere," Chester W. Newton, Ed., Amer. Meteor. Soc., Boston.

Taljaard, J. J., H. Van Loon, H. L. Crutcher and R. L. Jenne, 1969, Climate of the upper air. Part 1—Southern hemisphere, Vol. 1, U. S. Navy NAVAIR 50-1C-55, Washington, D. C.

Troup, A. J., and N. A. Streten, 1972. Satellite observed southern hemisphere cloud vortices in relation to conventional observations. *J. Appl. Meteor.* 909–917.

Van Loon, H., 1971, A half yearly variation of the circumpolar surface drift in the southern hemisphere. *Tellus*, **23**, 511–516.

Van Loon, H., and R. L. Jenne, 1972, The zonal harmonic standing waves in the southern hemisphere. *J. Geophys. Res.*, **77**, 992–1003.

Aspects of the Climate of the Southern Hemisphere: Preliminary Interpretations of the "EOLE" Experiment

PETER J. WEBSTER

Department of Meteorology, University of California, Los Angeles*

Abstract

The EOLE satellite-balloon system provided a dense Lagrangian data set of the Southern Hemisphere upper troposphere in the vicinity of the 200 mb surface between August 1971 and July 1972. The data is treated and analysed to provide a picture of the hemispheric dynamic climatology. Arrays of various mean measured and derived quantities for periods varying from one year to several days are presented and are discussed in their relation to the large scale structure of the Southern Hemisphere. These estimates are compared with earlier estimates made using conventional data and the similarity and differences are explained. The momentum flux due to standing and transient eddies is discussed as a function of both time and space scales and their relevance in the maintenance of the general circulation of the Southern Hemisphere.

Time spectra of the various quantities show statistically significant peaks. These indicate strong 20 and 30-day rhythms and it is speculated that they may be representative of barotropic and baroclinic vacillations of the hemispheric energy balance. Spectra of total ozone at certain Southern Hemisphere stations show a similar variability suggesting that the tropospheric fluctuation may be an important energy source for the stratosphere.

1. Introduction

The recent EOLE satellite-balloon atmospheric sensing experiment, conducted in the Southern Hemisphere between August 1971 and July 1972, provided large quantities of upper tropospheric data in a hitherto near-dataless region. Besides measurements of ambient temperature and pressure reported directly from the balloon to the satellite, the experiment allowed the calculation of series of highly accurate Lagrangian velocities by the positioning of the balloon between successive satellite orbits. The number of balloons in operation at any one time and the resultant latitudinal distribution of the number of velocity observations per month for the constant density surface near 200 mb

are shown in Figs. 1 and 2. A complete description of the experiment is given in Morel and Bandeen (1973), Webster (1973) and Webster *et al.* (1973a, b).

The EOLE data was received in the form of lists of balloon positions as sensed by the satellite in a particular orbit. After obviously erroneous data were eliminated, the position of a particular balloon was matched to its position as sensed by the next satellite orbit. This resulted in a 2-hour average Lagrangian velocity determination. If the balloon was sensed by the satellite during the next orbit, another 2-hour average velocity was determined, and so on. In this way, 2 to 3 consecutive determinations could usually

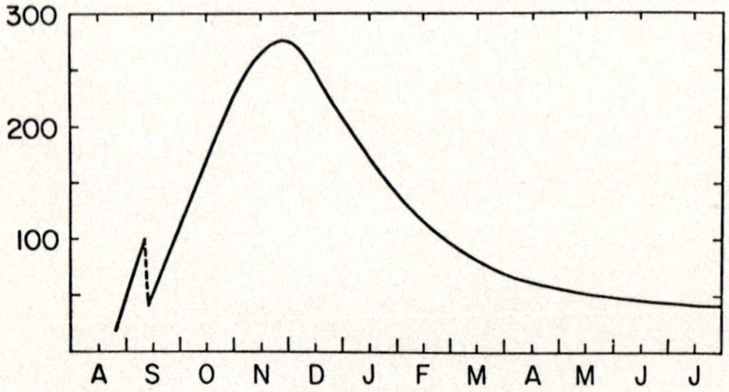

FIG. 1. Number of balloons in operation.

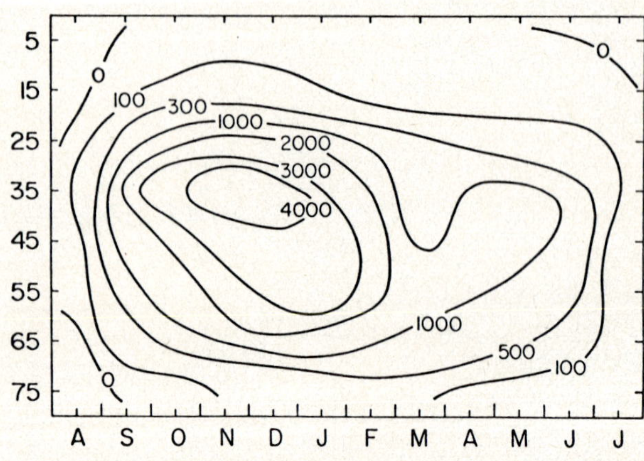

FIG. 2. Distribution of observations per month in 10° latitude bands.

* Present affiliation: Department of Atmospheric Sciences, University of Washington, Seattle, Washington, 98195.

be made for each balloon before the satellite precessed beyond the balloon horizon. With the return of the satellite some 20 hours later another cluster of velocities could be determined.

Examples of the 24-hour velocity vector distribution will be shown in Fig. 20. With each of these diagrams there exists a 24-hour discontinuity in the velocity field due to the motion of the satellite. In this sense, the charts are not synoptic, and a great deal more effort is required to produce synoptic variable distributions.

Because of the near randomness in space of the balloon (and therefore velocity) distribution, the data are not particularly useful for the compilation of Eulerian statistics. Two problems are immediately apparent. First is the reduction of Lagrangian data to an approximation of Eulerian data. This is discussed by both Dyer (1973) and Webster *et al.* (1973a). Second is the logistical problem of the randomness in space and, at any one point, in time of the data. The determination of a suitable averaging scheme is discussed in detail by Webster *et al.* (1973a), but may be briefly described as follows. The daily average of a particular quantity was calculated for each 10° latitude by 30° longitude area. Using these daily averages as the basis, mean quantities for time scales of months, seasons and one year were calculated.

2. Southern hemisphere climatology

Within the confines and restrictions pertaining to the data from the EOLE experiment, we will now discuss inferences that may be made regarding the average circulation in the upper troposphere of the Southern Hemisphere.

(i) *Temporal Variations:* Time sections of the zonal averages of several quantities as a function of time and latitude are shown in Figs. 3 through 6. In all the diagrams the dashed isopleths denote interpolation in regions of poor data, and all fields represent a constant density surface near 200 mb.

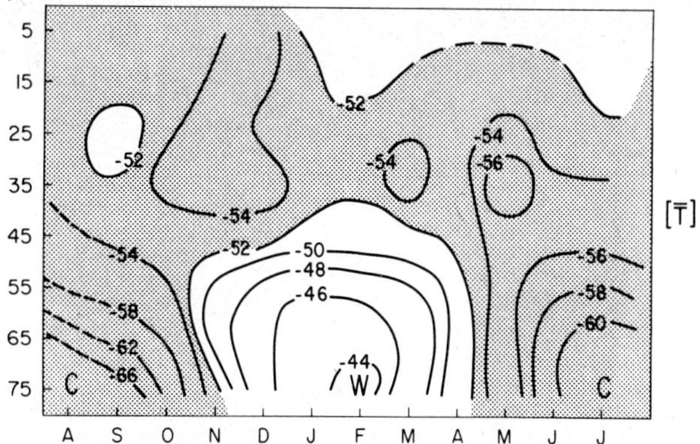

Fig. 4. Same as Fig. 3 except for the zonally averaged temperature. Units °C.

The time-section of the zonal average of the eastward velocity component (Fig. 3) shows the characteristic diminution of the strength of the westerlies in the summer time. Besides the decrease in the magnitude of the velocities, the latitude of maximum westerlies tends to move poleward during summer. Most interesting is the absence of the southern hemisphere double jet maximum noted by earlier workers [e.g., Obasi (1963)]. Most likely this is a function of the geographic locations of the Eulerian sensors which produce statistics giving the illusion of a double jet. We will discuss this point later.

Fig. 4 shows the time-section for the temperature of the constant density surface in the upper troposphere. The most notable features are the small latitudinal temperature gradient in the middle-low latitude region and the strong temperature change between summer and winter. A warming of over 22 C occurs near 70°S in the spring and changes the coolest region of the upper troposphere near 200 mb to the warmest. This reverses the hemispheric temperature gradient. Despite the intensity of the change, the warming appears to be somewhat weaker than in the northern hemisphere.

The time sections of the momentum and heat fluxes are given in Figs. 5 and 6. The notation is described

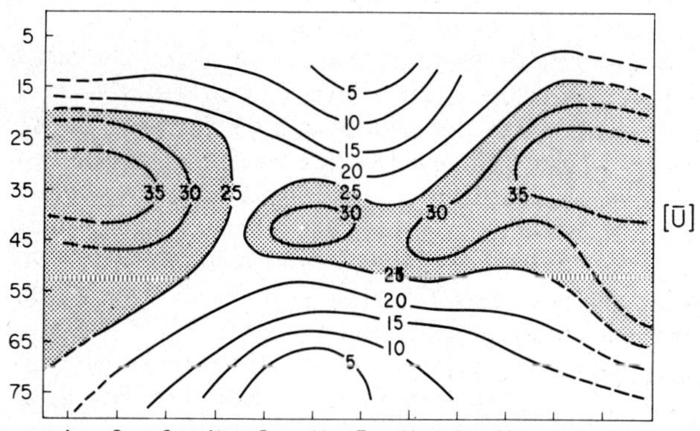

Fig. 3. Variation through the EOLE period of the zonally averaged zonal velocity component ($[u]$) near 200 mb. Units are m s⁻¹.

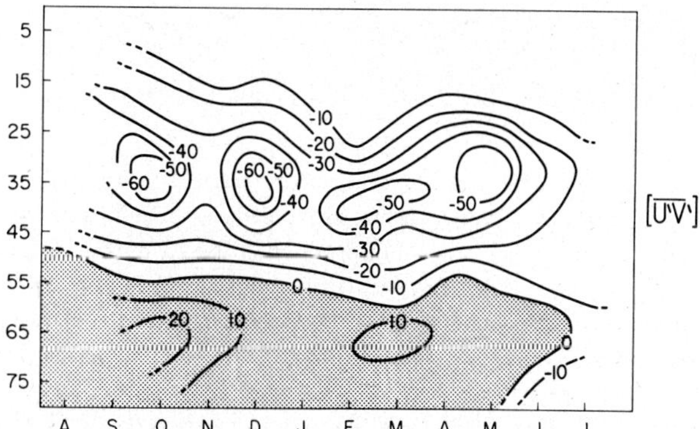

Fig. 5. Same as Fig. 3 except for the zonally averaged northward momentum flux due to the transient eddies, ($[u'v']$). Units m² s⁻².

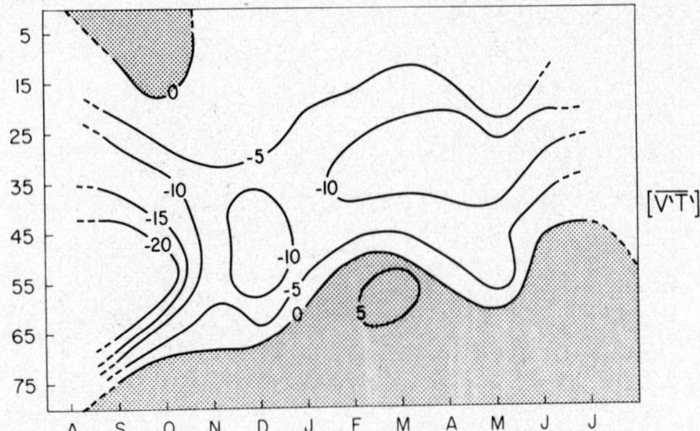

FIG. 6. Same as Fig. 3 except for the zonally averaged northward flux of sensible heat by the eddies. ($[v'T']$). Units °K m s^{-1}.

below. If we have two quantities X and Y that may be expressed as time and space means and deviations from these means, i.e.,

$$X(x,y,t)=\bar{X}(x,y)+X'(x,y,t) \qquad (1)$$

and

$$X(x,y,t)=[X(y,t)]+X^*(x,y,t),$$

where the overbar denotes a temporal mean and the square brackets, a spatial mean, it is easy to show

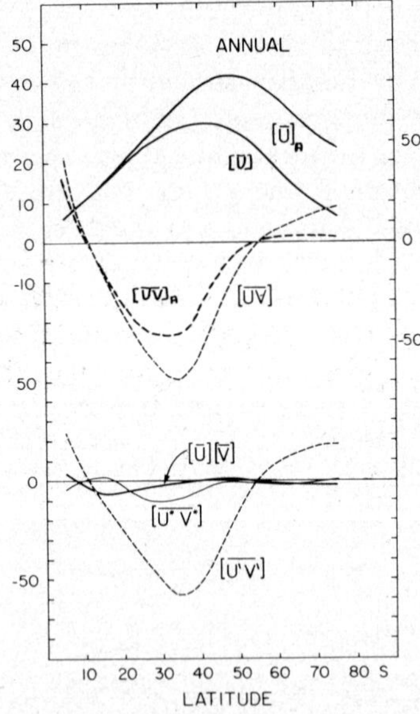

FIG. 7. Hemispheric momentum budget for entire EOLE period. Upper section of diagram shows the zonally averaged eastward wind component $[\bar{u}]$ in m s^{-1} (scale of left). The total momentum flux $[\overline{uv}]$ is shown by the dashed curve and is referred to the right hand scale (units m^2 s^{-2}). Quantities proportional to angular counterparts of $[\bar{u}]$ and $[\overline{uv}]$ are also shown with subscript A. Their units are m s^{-1} and m^2 s^{-2} respectively. The lower diagram shows the three components of the total momentum flux, $[\bar{u}][\bar{v}]$, $[\overline{u'v'}]$ and $[\overline{u^*v^*}]$ which represent, respectively, the flux due to the mean motion, the transient eddies and the standing eddies. Units are m^2 s^{-2}. Shaded area denotes region of poor data coverage.

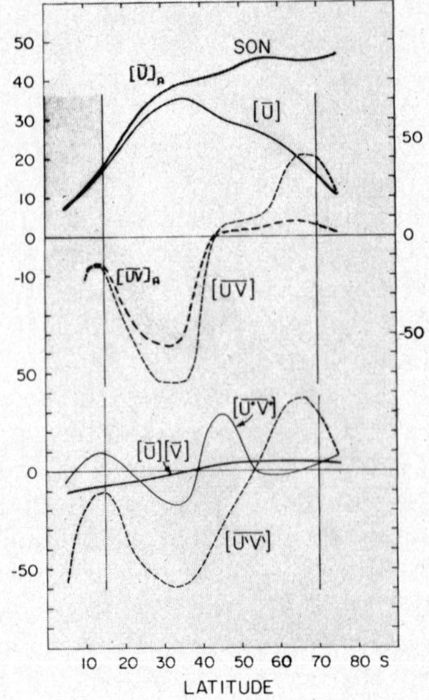

FIG. 8. Same as Fig. 7 except for spring season.

that:

$$[\overline{XY}]=[\bar{X}][\bar{Y}]+[\overline{X^*Y^*}]+[\overline{X'Y'}] \qquad (2)$$

The product $[\overline{XY}]$ is made up of contributions due to the mean zonally averaged flow, to the stationary or time-independent eddies (time-independent on the time scale defined by the time-averaging period) and to the transient eddies, respectively.

Fig. 5 indicates that there are two major regimes in the momentum flux. North of about 45°S the flux is negative (to the south), while poleward of this latitude it is northward. Viewing the $[\bar{u}]$ distribution simultaneously, we can see that the maximum southward transport, in all months, is equatorward of the maximum $[\bar{u}]$. This signifies a convergence of momentum into the jet stream, lending credence to the theory that the mean zonal flow is maintained principally by the "up-the-gradient" flux of momentum, i.e., at the expense of the eddies.

Fig. 6 shows the northward heat flux. The most important feature is the extremely strong flux of heat to the south into the cold polar night in winter. With the coming of summer, the flux weakens and the belt of negative contributions is displaced equatorward. Most importantly, the heat flux changes sign in high latitudes signifying the flux of warm air from the polar regions, reflecting the change of sign of the temperature gradient in Fig. 4.

In summary, Figs. 5 and 6 illustrate clearly the mean effect of the transient eddies. Besides maintaining the mean flow, the time-dependent eddies also tend to reduce the gradients of the mean temperature field. This of course presents the anomaly, in one case, of tending to provide a momentum flux against the

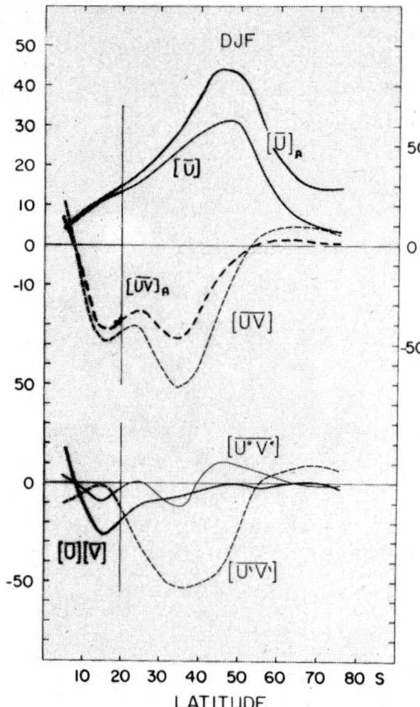

FIG. 9. Same as FIG. 8 except for summer season.

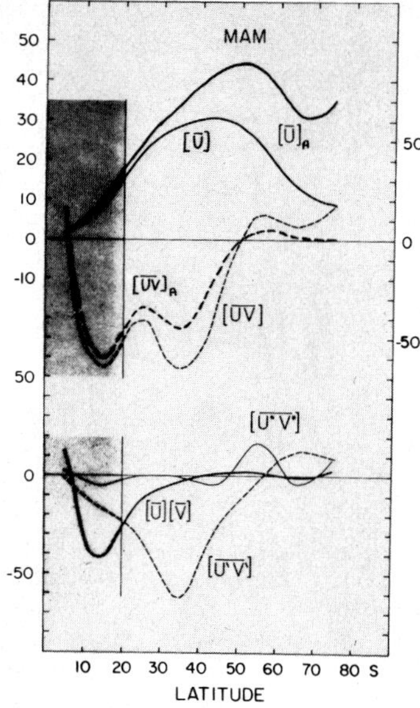

FIG. 10. Same as FIG. 9 except for fall season.

gradient of the momentum itself, but in the other allowing a thermal flux down-the-gradient of the mean temperature. This means that the transient eddies seem to increase the basic momentum gradient but tend to destroy the basic temperature gradient.

(ii) *Hemispheric Momentum Budget:* The momentum budget for the Southern Hemisphere is shown in Figs. 7 through 11, with the notation matching that of (1) and (2). In the upper portion of each diagram is the total zonally averaged northward momentum flux, $[\overline{uv}]$, plotted on the same curve as the zonally averaged zonal velocity component. A breakdown of the total momentum is shown on the lower diagrams. The period of the time average is indicated on each diagram and the shaded regions poleward and equatorward of the vertical lines denote regions of insufficient data to produce meaningful statistics. The budget for winter (June through August) (Fig. 11) is doubtful in all regions.

The following features appear common for all seasons and the annual budget. First, the largest contributor to the momentum flux is due to the transient eddies, with the contributions of the standing eddies and the mean motions small in comparison. This illustrates a major difference between the two hemispheres, as similar budgets for the Northern Hemisphere suggest parity between these two flux forms. This is obviously a reflection on the physical make-up of the Southern Hemisphere which, except for the Andes, lacks large longitudinally-dependent physical features or sea-surface temperature variations that may prompt the excitation of intense stationary modes. The second feature may be seen by comparing the $[\bar{u}]$ and $[\overline{uv}]$ profiles, or the angular counterparts shown in the same diagram. These are defined by the following proportionalities:

Total angular momentum is proportional to $[\overline{uv}]\cos^2\phi \equiv [\overline{uv}]_A$.

Angular velocity is proportional to $[\bar{u}]/\cos\phi \equiv [\bar{u}]_A$.

In all seasons, except for the data-deficient winter season, the maximum southward momentum flux is equatorward of the zonal velocity, signifying once again a convergence of momentum into the westerly jet-stream. The different character of the winter profiles is probably due to the lack of data rather than to a physical difference. Finally, all budgets are similar in that there is a convergence of momentum on the southern side of the jet, signifying that transient eddies in high latitudes tend to act in the same manner and support the energetics of the mean flow.

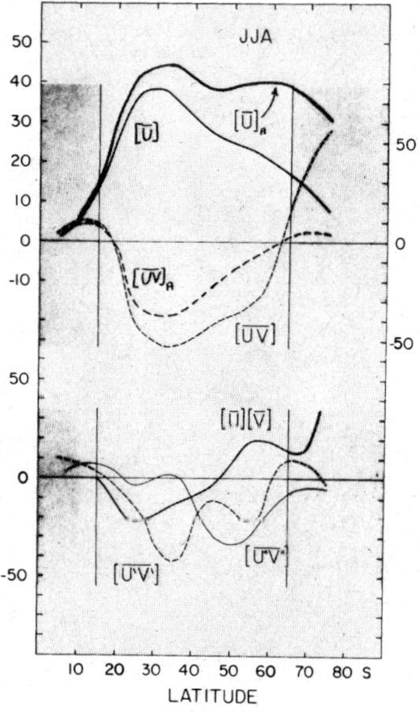

FIG. 11. Same as FIG. 10 except for winter season.

Detailed energetics and conversions from one form to another have been calculated and will appear in Webster and Curtin (1973a).

(iii) *Longitudinal Structure of the Averaged Quantities:* Use of a conventional network of land based radiosonde stations has the distinct disadvantage of not allowing the accurate description of the longitudinal structure of the time-averaged fields. The longitudinal

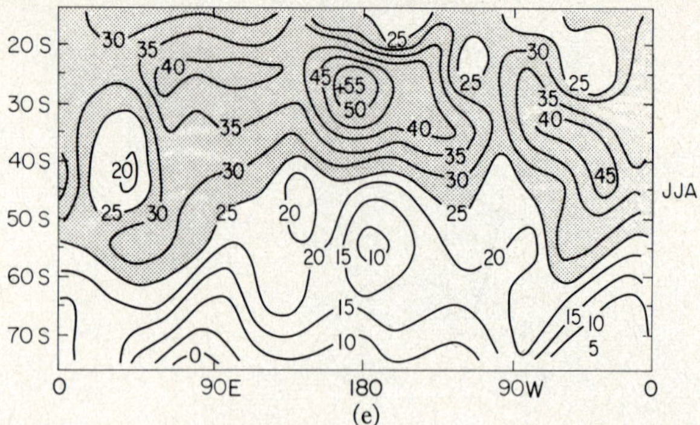

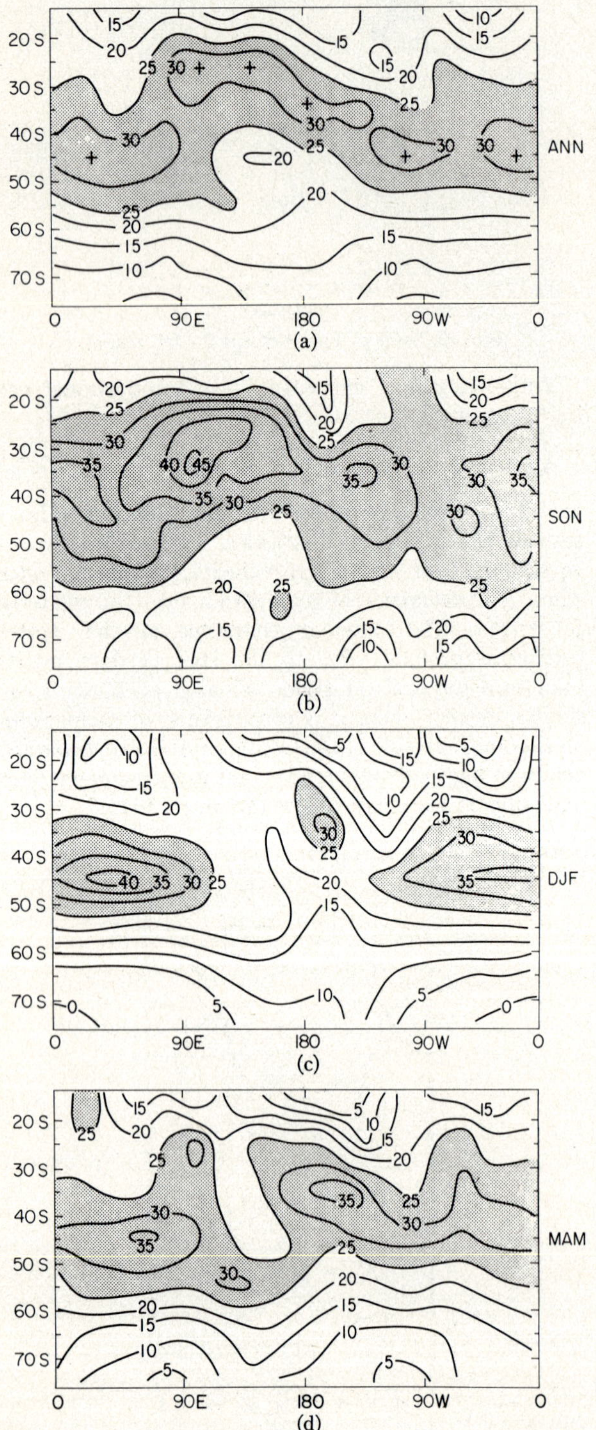

FIG. 12. The longitude-latitude distribution of the zonal velocity component $\bar{u}$. Shaded areas denote speeds in excess of 25 m s^{-1}. Diagrams labelled (a) through (e) refer to the time averages annual, spring, summer, fall, and winter, respectively. Units m s^{-1}.

density of the observations from the EOLE system are particularly suitable for this type of study. In this section the longitudinal structure of some of the fields are briefly discussed.

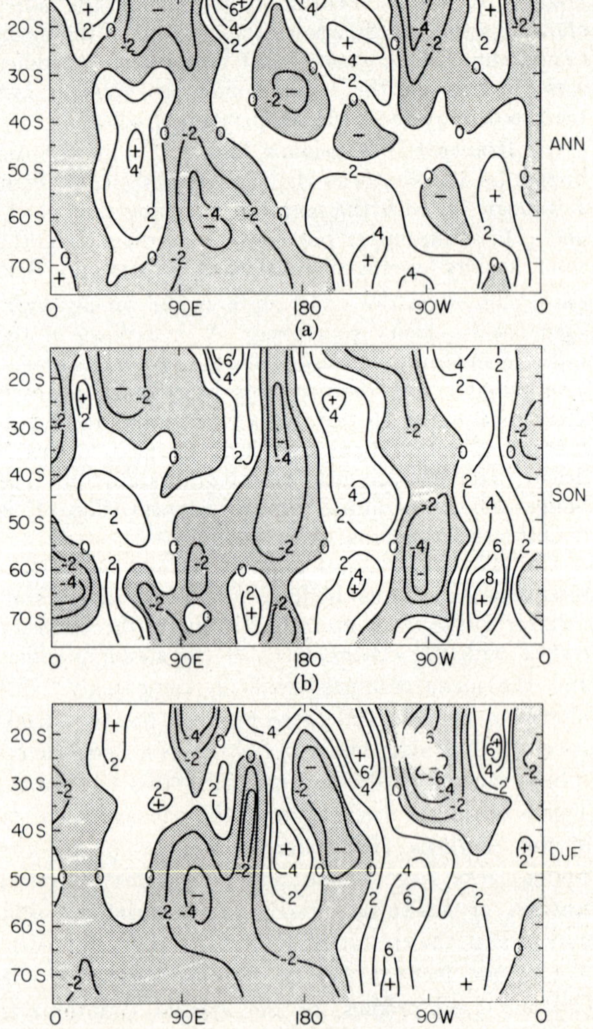

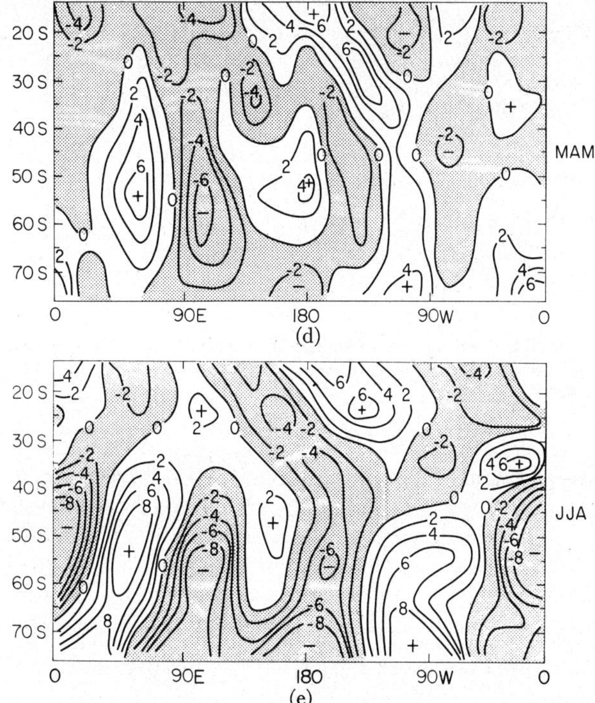

FIG. 13. Same as Fig. 12 except for the time-averaged meridional velocity component [∇]. Shaded region represents southward component. Units m s⁻¹.

Just as Figs. 3 and 7 through 11 showed large variations in the latitude and time structure of the zonal velocity component, Figs. 12a through e illustrate an equally large longitudinal variation. In each diagram, the shaded area denotes speed in excess of 25 m s⁻¹. Also, because of the variation of data with latitude and time, Figs. 7 through 11 should be examined in conjunction with Fig. 2 in order to identify the regions of poor data. It is worth reiterating that the data for winter are highly suspect due to the very few balloons reporting during this time.

All seasons show a broad "jet" meandering through mid-latitudes, tending to move equatorward in the spring and autumn. On each diagram this band of maximum winds is seen to shift towards the equator between 90E and 180E with the effect of producing strong westerlies over the Australian region and weak westerlies in the ocean regions to the south. This maximum over the Australian sector is referred to as the Sub Tropical Jet stream. However, we find it to be a meander of the westerly maximum and not an entity girdling the subtropics as it is often described as in the literature.

Figs. 13a through e show the longitudinal variation of the $\bar{v}$-components. All charts are seen to possess regions of alternating northward winds ($\bar{v} > 0$) and southward winds ($\bar{v} < 0$), with maximum amplitudes of 5–6 m s⁻¹. The dominent feature in the annual field is the high latitude variation where a strong longitudinal wave number 1 is evident. This varies in strength and position throughout the year. Moving equatorward, the structure exhibits a strong wave number 2 power. This will be discussed later.

A detailed study of the zonal average of the meridional velocity component is not presented in this report. This is because of the closeness of the zonal average to zero and the possibility of the errors being sufficiently large as not to exclude zero in the estimate. Because of this only a first estimate of the average is shown in Table 1. This is the mean of the daily means as discussed in preceding sections.

The temperature distribution shown in Figs. 14 tends to follow the time-sections of the zonally averaged temperature (Fig. 4). This suggests that the time-variation through the year is much larger than the longitudinal variation in magnitude in any one season. Longitudinal variations in midlatitudes are of the order of 2 to 3C and are much the same nearer the equator. The variations in high latitudes are somewhat larger but still far smaller than the corresponding variations in the Northern Hemisphere.

Compared to the relatively small longitudinal variation in the $\bar{T}$-fields, the distributions of the northward momentum flux shown in Figs. 15 suggest a strong longitudinal preference. This means that, on the average, the transient eddies tend to contribute to the zonally averaged northward momentum flux more in some geographic locations than in others. For example, a "preferred" region of positive flux exists in the high latitudes of the Pacific Ocean, whereas centers of negative flux occur near South America and south of South Africa. Note that the regions of intense negative flux appear to the north of the westerly maximum.

The reason for this spatial preference of the transient eddies is puzzling. It is easy to understand the spatial preference of the standing eddy momentum flux (not shown here) as this is tied to the positions of the standing eddies themselves. Also the standing eddies only contribute some 10% of the total momentum flux and the longitudinal variation is less important. Most probably such areas are preferred regions of transient wave development or regions in which the transient eddies most often acquire the phasal orientation that maximizes the cross-latitude flux. The reason why eddies are in such a state in these locations is of great importance as these may be regions

TABLE 1. Zonally-averaged meridional velocity (m s⁻¹) computed from the daily values averaged in a 10° latitude by 30° longitude grid.

Latitude (°S)	5	15	25	35	45	55	65	75
Annual	−0.3	+0.2	−0.2	−0.3	+0.2	+0.0	−0.2	+0.0
Spring	−1.0	+0.3	−0.6	−0.3	+0.4	−0.3	−0.4	+0.2
Summer	+1.0	−0.8	+0.1	−0.5	±0.4	+0.3	−0.0	−0.2
Fall	+1.5	−0.7	−0.0	−0.0	−0.1	+0.7	−0.3	+0.9
Winter	+1.5	+0.5	−0.1	+0.0	−1.1	−1.3	−0.5	−0.9

where the production of mean zonal kinetic energy is a maximum also.

Figs. 16 show the northward heat flux due to the transient waves. Besides reflecting the basic latitudinal variation over the year, as seen in Fig. 6, there is also a strong spatial preference with longitude, although not proportionally as strong as with the momentum flux.

(iv) *Sensible Heat Flux:* The latitudinal average of the sensible heat flux is shown in Fig. 17 for each season and for the entire year. Two main features

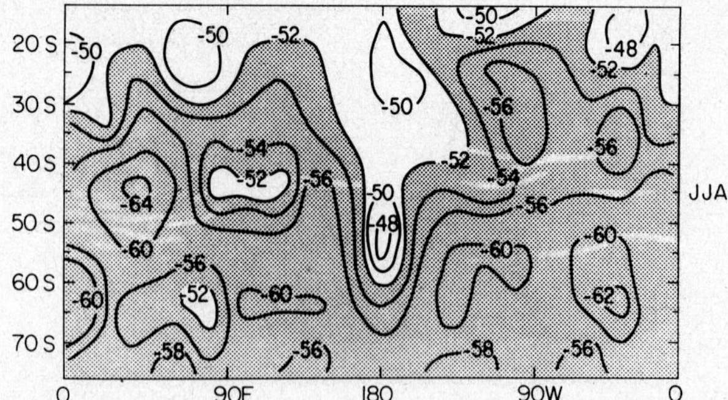

Fig. 14. Same as Fig. 12 except for the time-averaged temperature field $\bar{T}$. Shaded region represents temperatures cooler than -52C. Units °C.

are apparent. First, the net sensible heat transport to the north by the standing eddies (dashed line) is generally much smaller than that due to the transient eddies in regions of good data coverage (the unshaded area). Except for winter, there appears to be an order of magnitude difference between the two fluxes. This

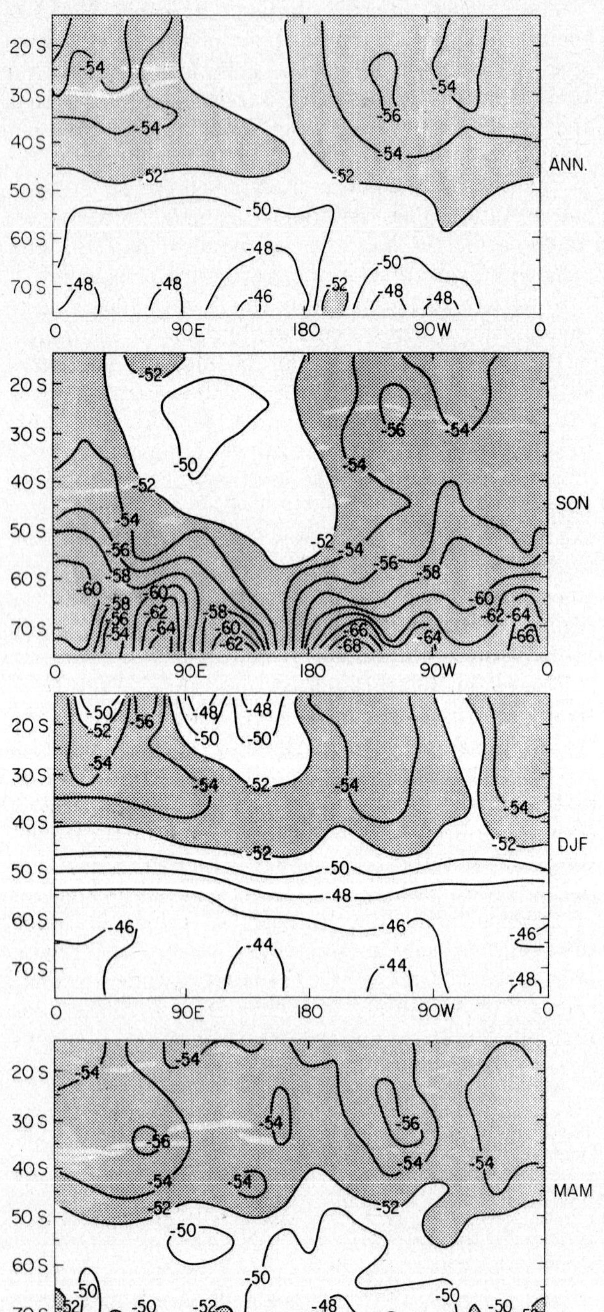

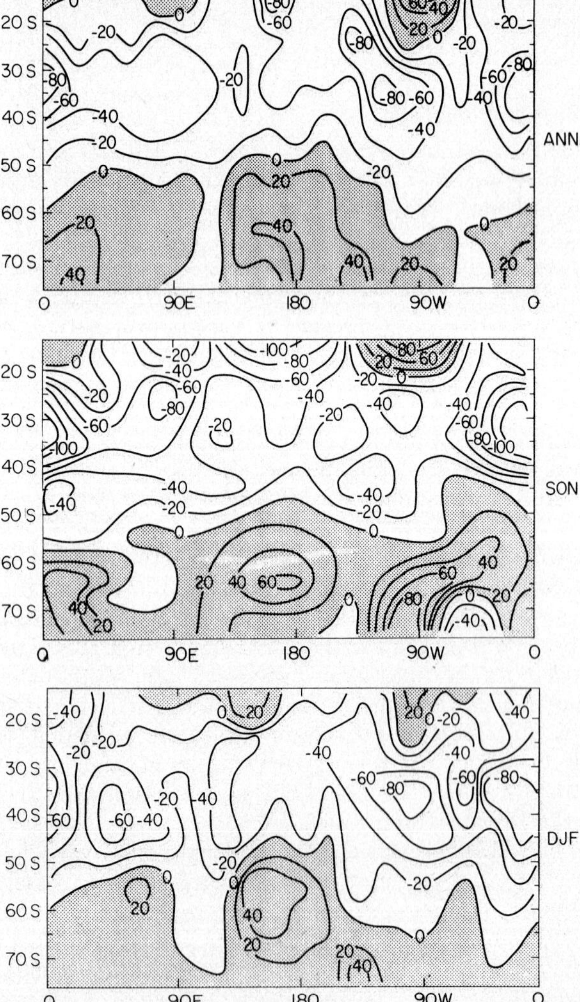

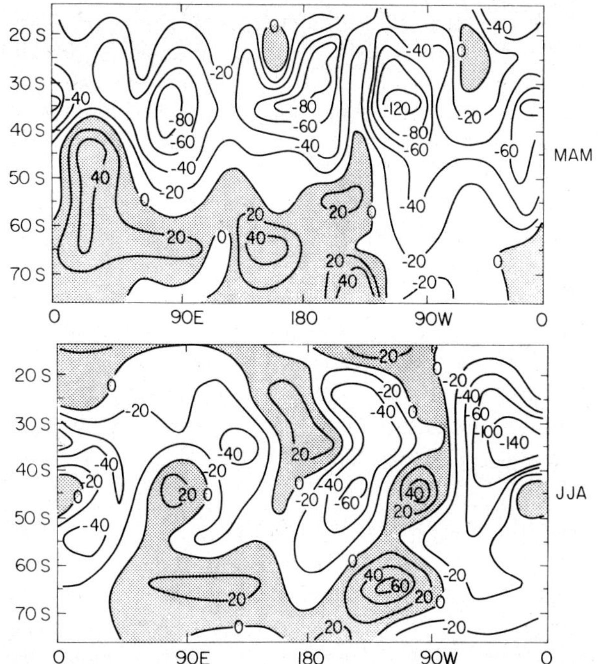

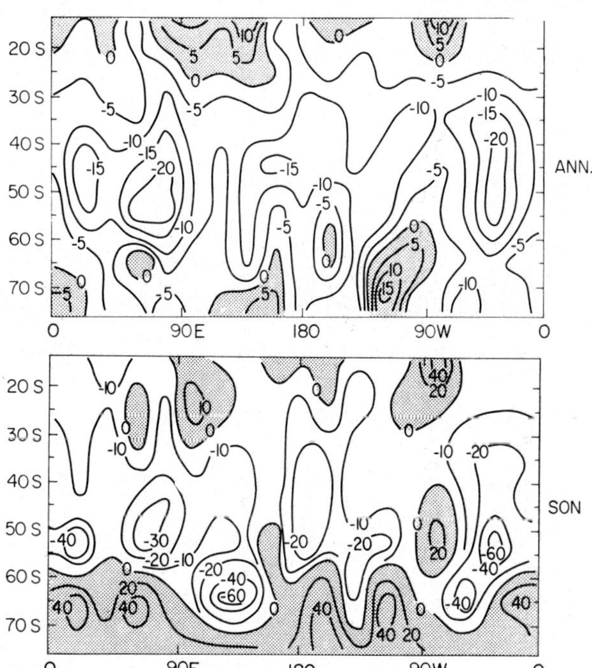

Fig. 15. Same as Fig. 12 except for the time averaged northerly flux of momentum due to the transient eddies. Shaded region represents northward flux. Units m² s⁻².

again is in contrast to the northern hemisphere where they are of near equal importance.

In general, all profiles tend to show a strong negative flux in midlatitudes (the advection of warm air southward or cool air northward by the transient eddies) and in summer and fall, a counter flux near Antarctica.

(v) *Spatial Variation:* In preceding paragraphs, the

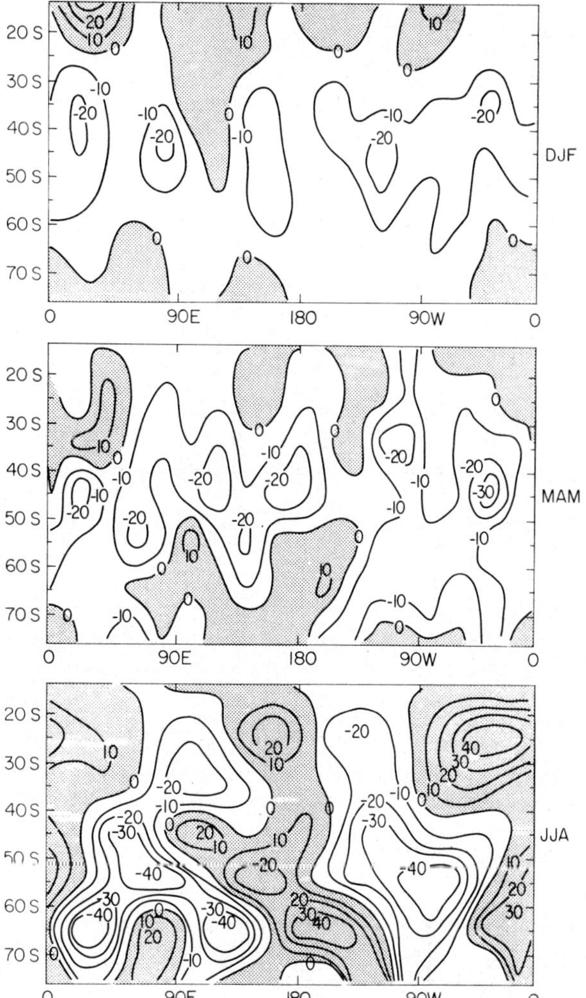

Fig. 16: Same as Fig. 12 except for the time averaged northerly flux of sensible heat due to the transient eddies. Shaded region represents northward flux. Units °K m s⁻¹.

variety of spatial variations exhibited by the various variables measured and derived by the EOLE satellite-balloon system has been pointed out. Examples of this variation are shown in Table 2 where the power spectra as a function of latitude are tabulated for the annual averages of u, v, T, $u'v'$ and u^*v^*.

The spectral structure of u and T are similar in that the majority of the power of the variables resides in the $s=0$ wave (or the zonal mean). In the wave structure, most of the power of u is in the very long waves, especially at high latitudes. Towards the equator a reversal takes place, and the energy is spread through the first 5 or 6 waves. This is also reflected in the T structure. A possible reason for this difference in wave structure with latitude is that the density surface upon which the balloons reside is possibly in the lower stratosphere in the higher latitudes, especially, in the early fall, spring and winter periods.

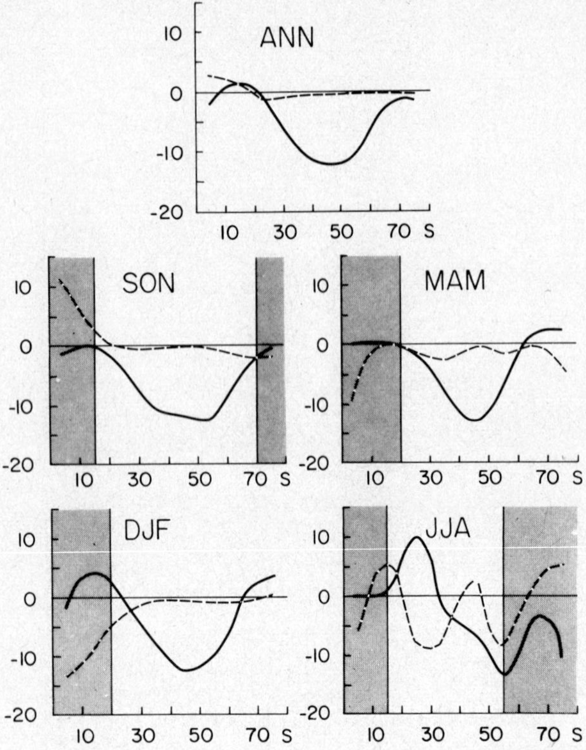

Fig. 17. Latitudinal variation of the northward sensible heat flux by the transient eddies (solid curves) and the standing eddies (dashed curves) for the time periods indicated. Shaded areas denote poor data regions.

The structure of v differs in that the zonal mean ($s=0$) is smaller than the energy residing in the shorter length scales. This has been noted before in studying the longitudinal structure of the meridional velocity component (Figs. 13). Except for this, the structure is similar to u for $s>0$.

The momentum fluxes, (standing and transient), however, differ markedly in that there is a spread of energy through the entire wave spectrum. One must be careful in this interpretation. It does not mean that wave number s contributes the particular momentum flux denoted on Table 2, but illustrates only the spread in scale of the flux. The role of each wave must be calculated from the structure of each wave individually, or more formally:

$$\overline{u_s' v_s'} \neq \overline{(u'v')}_s \qquad (3)$$

The role of particular waves in transportation of momentum over latitude circles is currently being studied. However it is very interesting to note that there resides a large amount of energy in the momentum flux at smaller space scales than there exists in either u, v and T. Probably the smaller length scales may be more efficient at transportation of momentum, or the quadratic aspect of the momentum formulation, as seen in (2), may be evident. For

TABLE 2. Distribution of the latitudinal spectra, $s=0.9$ of various annually averaged quantities for latitudes 25° to 65°S. Sign in parenthesis indicates sign of the $s=0$ or latitudinal average of the quantity.

	Lat°	$s=0$	1	2	3	4	5	6	7	8	9
$\bar{u}$	25	(+) 22.9	5.1	4.5	1.7	2.5	0.4	1.2	0.4	0.5	0.3
	35	(+) 28.3	0.8	1.7	1.8	2.0	0.4	0.3	0.3	0.1	0.5
	45	(+) 29.5	5.8	3.2	0.8	0.6	0.8	0.2	0.3	0.1	0.2
	55	(+) 22.8	2.3	1.0	1.0	1.1	0.4	0.4	0.2	0.1	0.2
	65	(+) 11.6	2.7	1.5	0.7	0.4	0.3	0.2	0.4	0.8	0.5
v	25	(−) 0.2	1.1	0.9	1.4	2.5	1.1	0.3	0.4	0.4	0.5
	35	(−) 0.3	0.3	0.8	0.5	0.9	0.3	0.5	0.4	0.1	0.6
	45	(+) 0.2	0.3	0.3	1.0	1.1	0.4	0.5	0.5	0.3	0.3
	55	(+) 0.0	1.3	1.2	1.6	1.3	0.2	0.6	0.1	0.3	0.3
	65	(−) 0.2	1.9	1.2	1.0	0.7	0.3	0.3	0.2	0.3	0.2
T	25	(−) 53.3	1.5	1.2	0.7	0.6	0.3	0.3	0.3	0.1	0.1
	35	(−) 54.0	1.2	0.9	0.5	0.4	0.2	0.1	0.1	0.2	0.1
	45	(−) 52.8	0.4	0.2	0.2	0.3	0.1	0.4	0.1	0.1	0.1
	55	(−) 50.0	1.0	0.2	0.4	0.2	0.2	0.2	0.1	0.1	0.5
	65	(−) 49.0	1.1	0.3	0.3	0.4	0.4	0.0	0.1	0.3	0.0
$\overline{u'v'}$	25	(−) 38.1	2.6	10.5	15.6	3.5	7.2	8.2	4.8	10.4	4.3
	35	(−) 56.6	19.1	8.1	15.3	18.3	8.9	2.8	4.8	7.2	10.5
	45	(−) 31.9	4.2	9.4	4.4	7.1	4.3	2.1	8.4	3.2	8.4
	55	(+) 1.2	19.0	11.0	11.3	3.4	1.7	1.4	6.9	7.9	5.8
	65	(+) 13.3	8.8	13.6	8.4	4.3	3.8	4.5	6.9	4.9	3.2
$\overline{u^*v^*}$	25	(−) 4.4	6.8	5.4	9.7	8.6	8.0	9.0	4.8	4.8	4.6
	35	(−) 1.2	1.5	1.1	0.9	0.2	1.0	2.2	1.8	1.3	0.6
	45	(+) 1.2	1.0	3.3	1.4	3.7	4.7	2.9	1.2	2.4	2.4
	55	(−) 0.8	1.5	1.9	1.7	2.1	1.3	0.4	0.7	0.7	0.5
	65	(−) 0.9	2.2	3.0	2.1	2.6	1.3	1.2	0.6	1.0	1.5

example, consider a simple system of waves defined by

$$u_s = A_s e^{is}$$

$$v_s = B_s e^{is}$$

If A_s and B_s have maxima at $s=2$, say, then the spectra of u and v will show peaks at that scale. However, if one computes the momentum flux we find:

$$u_s v_s = A_s B_s e^{2is}, \qquad (4)$$

so that the spectra of $u_s v_s$ shows a peak at wave number 4.

3. Aspects of the dynamic structure of the southern hemisphere

The dense spatial and temporal nature of the EOLE data provides a unique set of information especially suitable for diagnostic studies of the physics of the atmosphere. Such data allows investigation over the whole gamut of space and time scales, the latter being restricted only by the duration of the experiment and the time interval between successive interrogations of the balloons. In this section, we will restrict ourselves to a planetary space scale and time scales less than the averaging period considered in the last section.

In an experiment involving some 500 balloons varying near randomly in their position in space and in population in time, it is necessary to keep account of how many balloons are where, in a statistical sense, at any specific time. Keeping track of the "center of mass" or mean latitude of the balloon population, for instance, allows some insight into the relative motions of the hemisphere as a whole over the annual cycle.

Because of the various numbers of balloons reporting each day (a number which is a function of satellite and communication malfunctions, as well as the total number of balloons aloft at any one time) it was decided that another quantity was a better measure of balloon population besides the number aloft. This was the per cent of balloons (N) reporting on any one day north of some latitude. Distributions of N for limits of 50°S, 40°S and 30°S for the entire observation period are shown in Fig. 18. The most obvious feature is the general trend of the balloons to move poleward through the spring and summer and generally return with the approach of winter following the seasonal march of the sun.

Superimposed upon this trend are large amplitude cyclic variations which have a period of between 20 and 30 days and which are generally more evident in the middle and higher latitudes. One possible explanation is that the atmosphere is changing its state from a zonal to a perturbed configuration. We will see later that a large value of N refers to a highly perturbed atmosphere, and small N to an atmosphere in a less

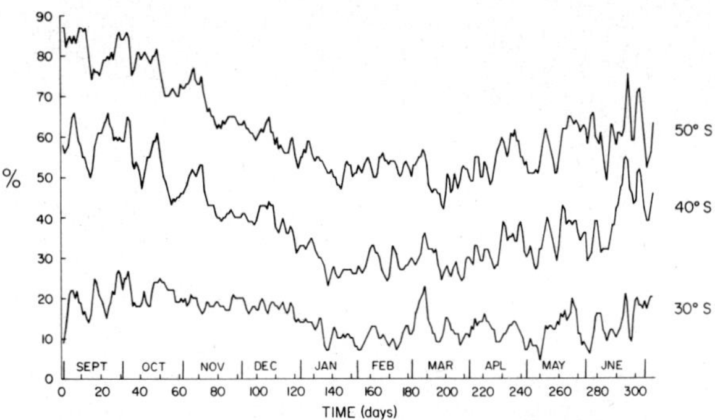

FIG. 18. Plots of N, the percentage of the total number of balloons north of the indicated latitude over the EOLE period.

perturbed state. Further study of Fig. 18 suggests that the variations are fairly strong functions of latitude. Besides being of larger amplitude at higher latitudes, there is also a suggestion of a phase variability.

In the following paragraphs, we shall outline the initial research into the study of the tropospheric rhythm suggested in Fig. 18 and the possibility of its propagation into the stratosphere. This phenomenon has been reported by Webster and Keller (1973a) and in greater detail in Webster (1973a) and Webster and Keller (1973b).

(a) *Tropospheric Rhythms:* The many attempts to find a distinct atmospheric periodicity on a global or hemispheric scale have met with little success. Most notable are the efforts of Willett (1948) and Namias (1950) in the Northern Hemisphere and recently by Taljaard (1973) in the Southern Hemisphere. All studies are similar in that they defined some quantity, a zonal index, which was more or less sensitive to the change of state of the atmosphere. While large variations in the various indicies did occur, no dominant rhythm was identified (Taljaard (1973)).

One other common feature of the previous studies was that the data used came from land-based Eulerian sensors which, due to their grouped geographical distribution, possibly are not suitable for the calculation of an index supposedly representative of a latitude belt or entire hemisphere. To overcome this problem, the dense EOLE data was used to define a zonal index which is extremely sensitive to the transition of the atmosphere from a perturbed to a zonal state. Such an index, R, is defined as the ratio between the perturbation or eddy kinetic energy K_E and the kinetic energy of the mean zonal flow K_Z, i.e.,

$$R = K_E / K_Z$$

where

$$K_E = \frac{1}{\cos\phi} \int_0^{2\pi} \frac{(V - \bar{V})^2}{2} d\phi$$

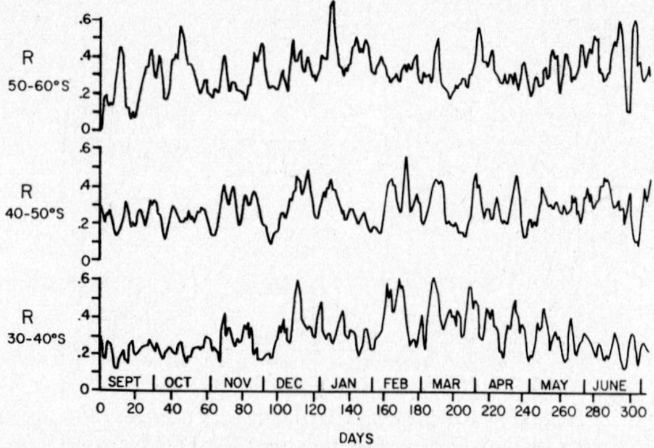

FIG. 19. Plot of $R(t)$ defined in (5) for the latitude bands 50°–60°S, 40°–50°S and 30°–40°S, for the EOLE period.

and

$$K_Z = \frac{1}{\cos\phi} \left[\int_0^{2\pi} \frac{\bar{V}}{2} d\phi \right]^2$$

Here the over-bar represents a time average, ϕ the latitude and V the velocity. It should be noted that a meaningful and representative value of R requires a dense data distribution with little or no longitudinal bias in the population, as is provided by the EOLE experiment.

Time sections of R are shown in Fig. 19 for three 10° latitude bands between 30° and 60°S. Large amplitude variations may be seen with an apparent period of some 20 days, especially in the higher latitudes. These represent regular changes from highly perturbed states (large R) to highly zonal states (small R). Note that R is completely out of phase with the more conventional zonal indicies as defined by Willett and Namias. Superimposed upon this trend are variations of higher frequency and smaller amplitude indicating similar but short lived variations. Towards the equator, this rhythm appears weaker except in the Southern Hemisphere autumn months.

It is interesting to consider representative states of the atmosphere as denoted by the EOLE system for variations in the zonal index R. For example, N_{50} varies by over 10% between 18 October and 4 November, 1971, while N_{40} shows a 15% variation and N_{30} just 4%. The variation of the hemispheric flow may be seen in Fig. 20 which shows three 24-hour distributions of velocity vectors. Although the wave structure is apparent in all three examples shown, the waves appear to be of larger amplitude in the first and third cases. The shaded area denotes the equatorial extent of balloons north of 40°S.

The corresponding values of the zonally averaged perturbation kinetic energy, the zonal mean kinetic energy and the ratio R are shown for the period 10/15/71 to 11/6/71 in Table 3 for the latitude bands indicated. Underlined are the values relating to the

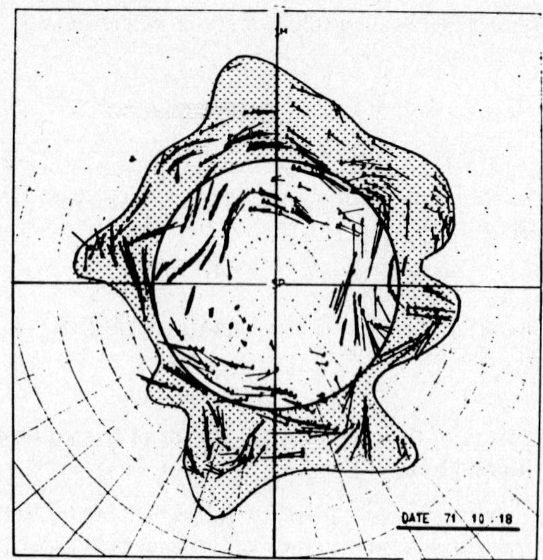

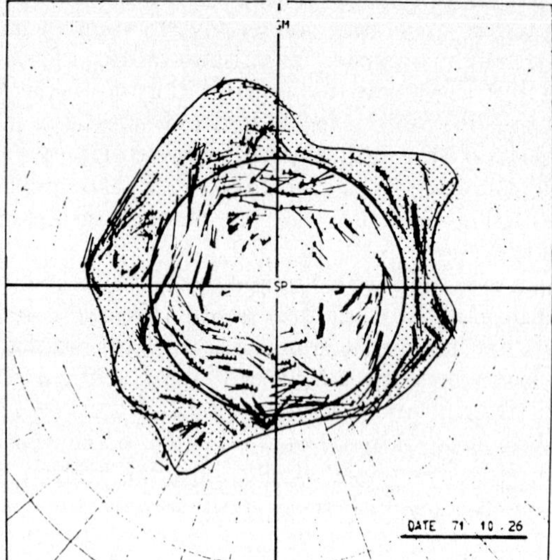

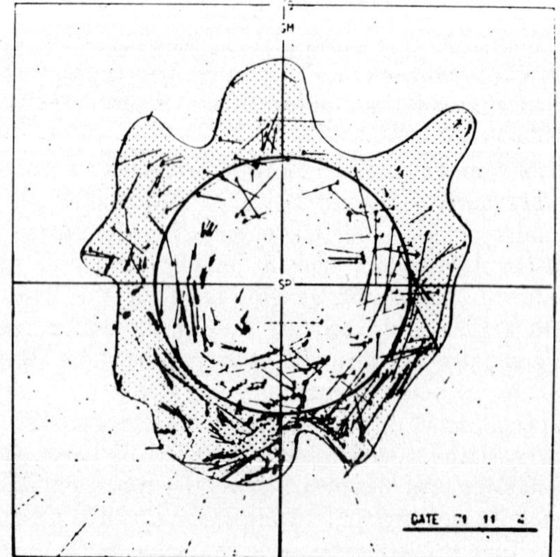

FIG. 20. Distribution of velocity vectors for the three days 10/18/71, 10/26/71 and 11/4/71. Shaded region denotes area occupied by balloons on each day north of 40°S.

TABLE 3. Variation of the Zonal Index R and the component quantities $[KE]$ and $[KE']$ for the period 10/15/71 and 11/6/71. Underlined dates refer to diagrams in Fig. 20.

Lat°S	30–40°			40–50°			50–60°		
	$[KE']$	$[KE]$	R	$[KE']$	$[KE]$	R	$[KE']$	$[KE]$	R
10/15	109	739	0.148	56	546	0.103	114	545	0.253
16	104	697	0.150	66	446	0.150	124	493	0.210
17	118	838	0.141	31	390	0.081	113	543	0.200
18	115	601	0.193	61	432	0.142	102	512	0.178
19	101	651	0.156	77	537	0.144	84	474	0.122
20	73	576	0.127	74	600	0.123	59	483	0.110
21	109	696	0.158	101	649	0.156	41	375	0.125
22	100	760	0.132	106	676	0.158	38	310	0.176
23	96	683	0.140	103	628	0.165	60	346	0.146
24	93	534	0.176	78	546	0.144	60	413	0.114
25	98	491	0.200	65	581	0.112	44	392	0.095
26	117	586	0.201	60	637	0.094	41	440	0.121
27	99	526	0.190	54	556	0.098	44	365	0.102
28	77	414	0.187	41	512	0.081	45	446	0.136
29	70	493	0.144	33	582	0.057	49	362	0.119
30	74	416	0.180	48	521	0.094	43	366	0.081
31	54	468	0.117	53	370	0.145	35	435	0.108
11/ 1	47	527	0.090	58	375	0.156	47	437	0.173
2	34	430	0.080	72	374	0.195	79	458	0.283
3	78	288	0.272	110	355	0.310	116	413	0.311
4	68	453	0.152	173	509	0.341	129	417	0.229
5	63	408	0.154	144	396	0.365	86	378	0.159
6	59	267	0.224	102	432	0.263	80	509	0.179

charts of Fig. 20. In the 40–50°S and 50–60°S bands, R varies as N in Fig. 18, with strong zonal flow, or weak perturbations, between periods of stronger perturbations, or weak zonal flow. In the 30–40°S band, the variation is much less and although variations do occur in both kinetic energies they appear more in phase than in the other two bands.

The times-series spectral analyses of $R(t)$, shown in Fig. 21, tend to support these observations. In all three diagrams, the 18–23 day period band is shaded. It can be seen that in the 50°–60°S latitude spectrum for R, a strong isolated (and significant) peak is apparent suggesting a strong rhythm centered near 20 days in the high latitudes. For brevity we will refer to this as the "20-day peak." As shown by the 40°/50°S spectrum of R, the peak is somewhat weaker and further diminishes into the subtropics. The spectrum of K_E (the center diagram of Fig. 21) shows once again an extremely strong peak near 20 days. Spectrum of the zonally averaged pressure (lower diagram) indicates a weaker periodicity near 20 days, whereas the zonally averaged temperature field does not exhibit as large a variation. This is common to the spectra of the temperature fields at all latitudes. Although not shown here, strong peaks near 30 and 15 days evolve in the temperature spectra further equatorward.

The cross-spectra between the two component energies of R indicate an extreme peak near 20 days. Importantly, in the 50°–60°S band, K_E and K_Z are nearly completely out of phase ($-176°$) and possess a coherence of 0.89. Similar features are seen in the analysis with the 40°–50°S data. This strongly suggests that the 20-day peak in R may be accounted for by the conversion of energy between the eddies and the mean flow, such that a cycle consists of the waves growing at the expense of the mean flow and then the mean flow growing at the expense of the perturbation.

Time-spectral analyses of the variation of the power of the kinetic energy in each longitudinal wave shows the 20-day rhythm to be mainly restricted to the ultra-large scale waves. For example, in the 50–60°S band, the kinetic energy in the first wave in longitude is an order of magnitude greater in the 18–23 day period interval than for any other longitudinal scale.

A study of the momentum flux across the various latitude circles shows a similar 20-day rhythm, which again suggests that this variability is a manifestation of a slow period and very large scale barotropic energy conversion between K_E and K_Z. The barotropic nature is further underlined by the lack of any large 20-day peak in the temperature spectra.

The phenomenon described above seems to be similar in character to the barotropic energy conversion described by Lorenz (1967) and termed the tilted-trough or barotropic energy vacillation in which the trough/ridge orientation changes to facilitate an energy exchange between the mean flow and the perturbation. However, this process is thought to be restricted to a much smaller scale ($\sim$1000 km) and higher frequency motions (period $\sim$4–5 days), and is

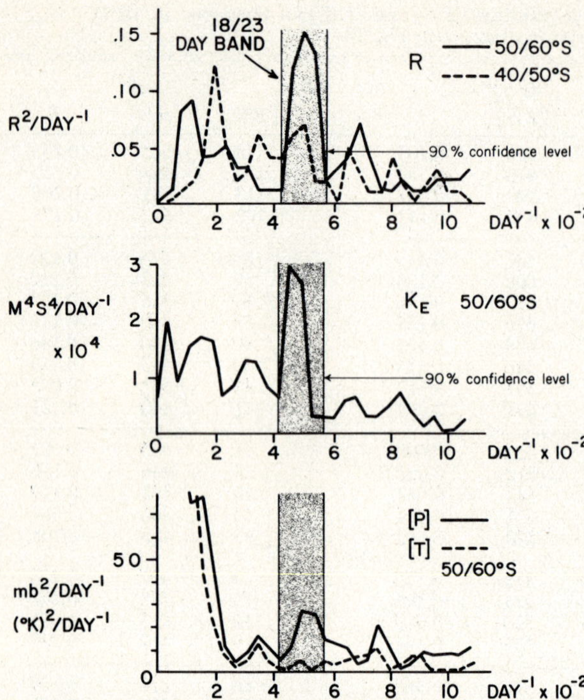

FIG. 21. Time-spectra of the Zonal Index R, the eddy kinetic energy K_E, temperature $[T]$ and pressure $[P]$ calculated from the EOLE data. Units and 90% confidence levels are indicated. Shaded region indicates the 18–23 day period band.

considered to be of secondary importance in the energetics of the general circulation.

In contrast, it is suggested here that the predominant process in the upper troposphere of high latitudes over the time scale of weeks is the barotropic exchange of energy between the ultra-long waves and the zonal flow.

(b) *Stratospheric Rhythms:* Initial attempts have been made to determine to what extent the stratosphere is effected by the large scale, long period oscillations reported above. Due to the scarcity of data and the consequent inability to construct a zonal index for the stratosphere, total ozone data from the few scattered Southern Hemisphere stations was analysed. The choice of ozone as a tracer of stratospheric variability is rather good due to its conservative properties.

Fig. 22 shows the time series spectral analyses of the total ozone for the three stations, Argentine Island (65°S), Macquarie Island (55°S) and Brisbane (28°S). These stations were chosen for the initial study on the basis of data variability and latitudinal spread. Where possible the data were chosen to encompass the EOLE period. The solid curves on the diagrams represent the spectra for the periods indicated whereas the dashed lines are for the EOLE period. The shaded areas denote the 18/23 day period band on each spectrum. Also to remove the effect of a dominating

annual variation, the annual trend was removed *before* the spectral analysis.

The common feature of all three sets of spectra is the evidence of power, to varying degrees, in the 18/23 day period band. This is especially evident in the Argentine Island spectral distribution and at Macquarie Island. Of some surprise is the fact that a station as far equatorward as Brisbane exhibits such a strong peak, especially in the EOLE period.

Whereas the results presented above cannot be considered conclusive, especially with an incomplete ozone study, the evidence of extremely strong spectral peaks in the middle to high latitude troposphere and over a wide latitude spread in the stratosphere is suggestive of a real rhythm near 20-days in both regions of the atmosphere. Evidence is added to this when one remembers that the conclusions were reached from two independent sets of different types of data. Furthermore it would appear that the 20-day rhythm is not a phenomenon of the EOLE period because it is evident in the 1962–4 Argentine Island analysis.

Subject to modifications and clarifications that may arise from future and more thorough investigations of the data and formal theoretical studies, we may summarize the atmospheric process described above, as follows. A large scale, long period oscillation, tied to the barotropic interchange of energy between the perturbations and the mean zonal flow, exists in the upper troposphere of the Southern Hemisphere. The

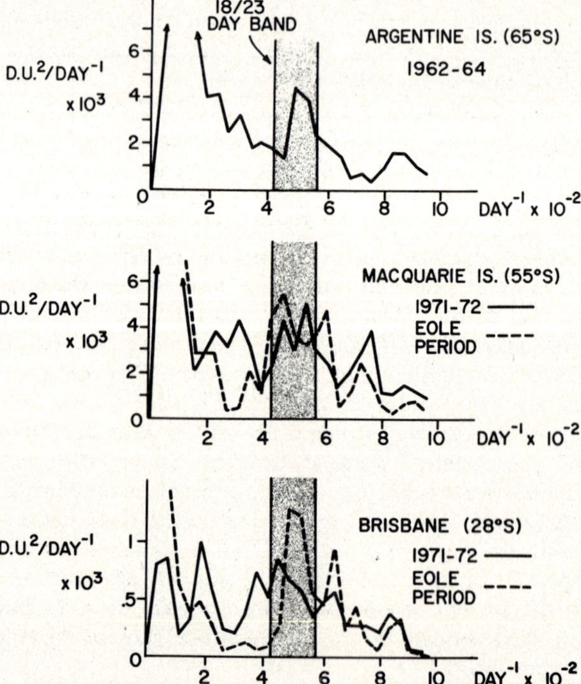

FIG. 22. Time-spectra of the stratospheric total ozone in (Dobson units)² for three stations Argentine Island (65°S), Macquarie Island (55°S) and Brisbane (28°S) for the periods indicated. Shaded region indicates the 18–23 day period band.

period and scale of this phenomenon is such that its vertical influence is not restricted by the structure of the stratosphere as are shorter period and smaller scale synoptic waves in the manner described by Charney and Drazen (1961). On the contrary, the vertical propagation properties must be such that the tropospheric oscillation may be an important energy source for the stratosphere, as is suggested by the 18/23 day period peaks in the ozone spectra. Furthermore, the forced rhythm seems not to be restricted to the middle and high latitudes as it is in the troposphere, but appears to effect the subtropical stratosphere also, as is indicated by the Brisbane ozone spectra.

Acknowledgments. This study represents part of ongoing research into the interpretation of the EOLE balloon data, funded by the National Aeronautics and Space Administration and into the ozone distribution and stratospheric structure, funded by the Department of Transportation through an NSF grant.

REFERENCES

Charney, J. G., and P. J. Drazin, 1961: Propagation of planetary scale disturbances from the lower into the upper atmosphere. *Journal of Geophysical Research*, **66**, 83–109.

Dyer, A., 1973: Do GHOST balloons measure Eulerian mean velocities? *Journal of the Atmospheric Sciences*, **30**, 510–513.

Lorenz, E. N., 1967: *The Nature and Theory of the General Circulation of the Atmosphere*. World Meteorological Organization, No. 218, PT11S, Geneva, 161 pp.

Morel, P., and W. Bandeen, 1973: The EOLE experiment: early results and current objectives. *Bulletin of the American Meteorological Society*, **54**, 298–306.

Namais, J., 1950: The index cycle and its role in the general circulation. *Journal of Meteorology*, **7**, 130–139.

Obasi, G. O. P., 1963: Atmospheric energy and energy calculations for southern hemisphere. *Journal of the Atmospheric Sciences*, **20**, 516–528.

Taljaard, J. J., 1973: Synoptic meteorology of the southern hemisphere. *Meteorological Monographs*, Vol. **13**, No. 35, 139–211.

Webster, P. J., 1973: Dynamic and statistical structure of the southern hemisphere: Preliminary interpretations of the EOLE experiment. Annual Report, NASA Grant NGR-05-007-091, Department of Meteorology, U.C.L.A., Los Angeles, California, 65 pp. September, 1973.

Webster, P. J., and D. G. Curtin, 1974a: Interpretations of the EOLE experiment; (I) temporal variation of Eulerian quantities. *Journal of the Atmospheric Sciences*, **31**, 7, 1860–1875.

Webster, P. J., and D. G. Curtin, 1974b: Interpretation of the EOLE experiment; (II) spatial variation of stationary and transient modes. Submitted to *Journal of the Atmospheric Sciences*.

Webster, P. J., and J. L. Keller, 1974: A strong long period tropospheric and stratospheric rhythm in the southern hemisphere. *Nature*, **248**, 5444, 212–213.

Willett, H. C., 1948: Patterns of world weather changes. *Transactions of the American Geophysical Union*, **29**, 803–809.

Mountain Barrier Effect on the Flow of Stable Air North of the Brooks Range

W. SCHWERDTFEGER

Department of Meteorology, University of Wisconsin

Abstract

When a stable air mass is moving toward a mountain barrier without being heated from below, the iso-thermal surfaces cannot remain horizontal. This implies a modification of the horizontal pressure gradient at surface level, and the appearance of a horizontal temperature gradient (directed toward the barrier) and hence a thermal wind (parallel to it). Such conditions are realized north of the Brooks Range whenever stable, cold air is carried from the north sector across the coast as might be indicated, for instance, by the wind observations at Barrow. The flow then becomes deflected toward the east, and its strength increases markedly along the northern slopes. The frequent occurrence of strong westerly winds in the winter at Barter Island can thus be explained. As there is a pronounced curvature of the streamlines from southward to eastward flow, the ageostrophic component of the wind becomes important for the theory of the phe-nomenon. Dynamically similar conditions, more intense still, have been found on the east coast of the Antarctic Peninsula where very strong, cold surface winds from SSW appear whenever the large scale sea level pressure field suggests a transport of stable, cold air from the east across the ice-covered Weddell Sea. Evidence for and theory of the Brooks Range phenomenon will be discussed.

1. Introduction

The movement of air *over* mountain barriers has been extensively treated in descriptive as well as theoretical meteorology. Favorable for this kind of flow pattern is a near-neutral vertical structure of the lower atmosphere. Situations in which extremely strable air moves toward a mountain range have found much less attention. A short paragraph on the "corner effect" due to the "orographic surplus of pressure on the windward side of a mountain range" by Godske *et al.* (1957) can be mentioned, as well as a study of strong westerly winds at Barter Island (NE Alaska) by Dickey (1961). None of these authors, however, assess quantitatively the effect of the sta-bility of the participating air mass on the strength of the wind-phenomenon. This may be due, in part, to the fact that extremely stable air in the lower layers is characteristic of the winter in rather in-hospitable regions for which regular meteorological observations are understandably scarce.

A classical series of data is known since Bodman (1910) reported on the extremely strong and frequent winds from the SW sector observed at the Snow Hill winter station of Nordenskjöld's Swedish South Polar Expedition 1901/03 (64.4°S, 57.0°W), on the east side of the mountain range of the Antarctic Peninsula. At that time, these icy storms were considered a merely local phenomenon. Later observations, how-ever, in particular those of the Argentine meteoro-logical station Tte. Matienzo (65.0°S, 60.0°W),

strongly support the notion that it is a regional phe-nomenon with important climatological consequences, rather than an effect of local wind-channeling. Indeed, these cold SSW storms appear along the entire east and southeast coast of the mountainous peninsula whenever a broad stream of extremely stable cold air moves from the east over the ice-covered Weddell Sea toward the mountain barrier, south of the circum-polar low pressure trough.

A similar phenomenon occurs in the north polar regions in winter when stable cold air moves from the Beaufort Sea southward and toward the northern slopes of the Brooks Range. In the following, observa-tional evidence and a theoretical explanation for the conditions in northern Alaska will be given. An anal-ysis of the Snow Hill phenomenon will be published elsewhere.

2. Contrasting average flow- and isobar-pattern north of the Brooks Range

Fig. 1 shows the mean sea level pressure field for the month of January, after Orvig and Vowinckel (1970); the "streamlines of the resultant airflow at the surface or 1000 mb, whichever is higher," after Bryson and Hare (1973), based upon data of NAVAIR (1966); and the resultant surface wind vectors com-puted from multi-annual climatological statistics for the three stations Barrow, Umiat, and Barter Island (courtesy of H. W. Searby, regional climatologist for Alaska, NOAA). The maps from which the mean

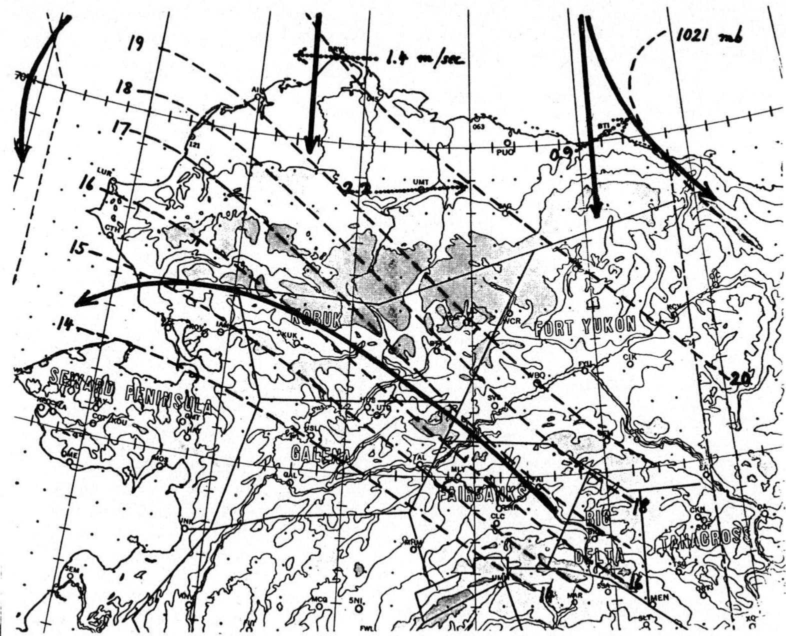

FIG. 1. Streamlines of the resultant air flow near the surface after Bryson and Hare (heavy solid lines), mean sea level isobars after Vowinckel and Orvig (dashed lines), and resultant wind vectors for three stations, northern Alaska, month of January.

isobars and the streamlines have been copied were intended to show the large-scale conditions, and obviously do not reflect smaller, regional patterns of the pressure and wind fields. Nevertheless, serious discrepancies over northern Alaska are revealed in Fig. 1, which suggest that a more detailed study is in order.

The remarkable difference between the resultant wind vectors of Barrow and Barter Island is not restricted to the surface layer; it is found up to about 2000 m, as shown in Table 1. At higher levels, the westerly component of the resultant wind increases upward at both stations, responding to the dominant regime of the cyclonic circumpolar vortex of the middle and upper troposphere.

Another important feature of the wind regime north of the Brooks Range are the differences in the relative frequency of surface winds from the N sector and from the WSW, in winter versus summer, as shown in Table 2.

At the two stations located near the main slope of the mountains (Umiat and Barter Island) winds from the WSW octant occur significantly more frequently in January than in July, and winds from the N-quadrant really are a very rare phenomenon in the winter month. Such contrast is not found at Barrow, about 300 km north of the mountains. It will be shown in the following section that the difference of these wind direction frequencies between Barrow and the other two stations is causally related to the pronounced static stability of the air masses of the lower troposphere which in the winter months pass over

Barrow from the N-sector and for which no heat source is available on their way farther south. For the average of 75 soundings at Barrow with the surface wind from the N quadrant (January 1957–63), the temperature at the surface was −29 C; at 850 mb (1345 m), −21 C. Of course the air coming from the cold sea toward Barrow frequently shows a low level inversion in the summer months also, but in general the stability is much less than in the winter, and must still further decrease as the air then travels over ground with nearly 24 hours of insolation per day.

3. Theoretical considerations

For a simplified theoretical treatment of the flow pattern, let the local time derivative of the vector of horizontal motion be negligible ("steady state"), while finite local space derivatives account for ageostrophic components due to the curvature of the streamlines and to vertical motion. This reduces the equation of motion to the following form (in natural

TABLE 1. Resultant wind vector (azimuth, and speed in m sec⁻¹) for January (1963–72) over Barrow (71.3°N, 156.8°W, 4 m) and Barter Island (70.1°N, 143.6°W, 15 m).

Height	Pressure	Barrow		Barter Island	
Surface	1023 mb	089°	1.4	238°	9.9
550 m	950 mb	094°	3.5	236°	1.1
950 m	900 mb	085°	2.7	268°	0.9
1370 m	850 mb	082°	2.1	299°	1.5
2800 m	700 mb	337°	2.0	328°	3.3

TABLE 2. Relative frequency of winds (>2 m sec^{-1}) from the N quadrant and from the WSW octant and total number of hourly wind observations (n) at three north-Alaskan stations, in January and July.

Station	Month	NW–NE	SW–W	n
Barrow	January	22%	15%	15,149
(1945–68)	July	21%	23%	14,861
Barter Island	January	3%	39%	13,639
(1948–70)	July	19%	15%	14,127
Umiat	January	5%	48%	6,142
(69.4N, 152.1W, 140 m)	July	27%	12%	7,086
(9 years)				

coordinates):

$$\frac{d\mathbf{V}}{dt}=V\frac{\partial \mathbf{V}}{\partial s}+w\frac{\partial \mathbf{V}}{\partial z}=-\alpha\nabla_H p-f\mathbf{k}\times\mathbf{V} \qquad (1)$$

(Haltiner and Martin, 1957, sections 11-10 and 12-16, or Holton, 1972, sect. 3.1.1.) The notation is defined in Table 3. Surface friction effects will only be considered qualitatively, after the wind vector has been determined neglecting friction. The structure of stable air in flow towards higher ground is schematically shown in Fig. 2. The essential, and realistic, assumption is that the upper surface of the cold air mass rises in the same sense, though not necessarily at the same rate, as the terrain itself. The increase of pressure from level 2 to level 1 is inversely proportional to the mean virtual temperature of the layer, and therefore greater at point B than at A. This implies the existence of an additional horizontal pressure gradient at level 1 from B to A, and hence an additional component of the geostrophic wind parallel to the obstacle (toward the viewer).

Another way to appraise such a situation is to use the concept of the thermal wind. Wherever a layer of cold air is sloped, there must exist a horizontal temperature gradient parallel to the slope line, and hence a thermal wind parallel to the obstacle, from the viewer into the plane of Fig. 2. If the temperature

TABLE 3. Definitions of symbols used.

Symbol	Definition
f	Coriolis parameter
g	Acceleration of gravity
$\mathbf{G}$	Slope of the cold air layer
$\mathbf{k}$	Unit vector upward
p	Pressure
s	Distance along the wind trajectory
t	Time
T	Temperature
$\mathbf{V}$	Horizontal wind velocity vector
$\mathbf{V}_T$	Thermal wind velocity vector
$\mathbf{V}_g$	Geostrophic wind. Additional subscripts 1, 2 or 3 refer to the height at which the wind is measured; A or B refer to horizontal position (see Fig. 2).
$\mathbf{V}'$	$\mathbf{V}-\mathbf{V}_g$
$\Delta_s\mathbf{V}_g$	Difference between the geostrophic winds at two points separate by Δs along the trajectory
$\Delta_z\mathbf{V}_g$	Difference between the geostrophic winds at two heights separated by Δz.
w	Vertical velocity, positive upward
z	Vertical coordinate
α	Specific volume ($=$ density^{-1})
Δ	Finite difference
∇	Gradient operator, $\mathbf{i}(\partial/\partial x)+\mathbf{j}(\partial/\partial y)+\mathbf{k}(\partial/\partial z)$
∇_H	Horizontal components of ∇
—(overbar)	Average value over the range given by the associated Δ term

contrast between the cold air near the ground and the warmest air above it is indicated by the difference ΔT and the slope of the cold air layer by $\mathbf{G}$, the thermal wind $\mathbf{V}_T$ must be (Dalrymple *et al.*, 1966)

$$\mathbf{V}_T=-\frac{g}{f}\frac{\Delta T}{\bar{T}}\mathbf{G}\times\mathbf{k} \qquad (2)$$

This thermal wind vector of the layer between the levels 1 and 2 over the slope has to be subtracted from the geostrophic wind at level 2, $\mathbf{V}_{g2}$, to obtain the geostrophic wind vector $\mathbf{V}_{g1}$. In this manner, the geostrophic wind *at surface level* can be determined for any point of the slope line, provided the slope of the terrain and the strength of the inversion are known: Upslope flow must be deflected to the left (northern hemisphere). Consequently, cyclonically curved streamlines result and, as long as the angle between upper wind and thermal wind is not too

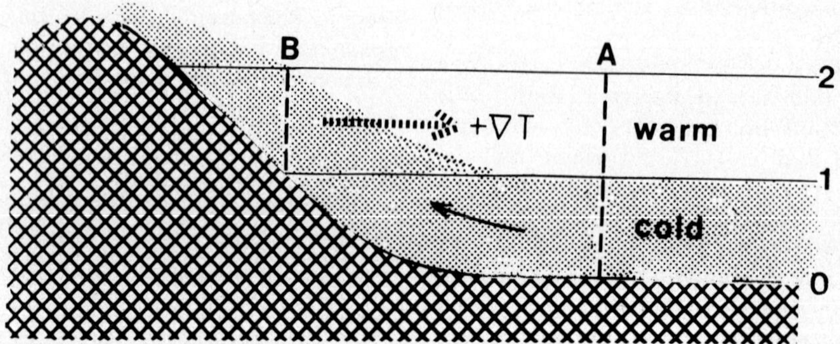

FIG. 2. Schematic vertical cross section of the flow of a stable air mass toward a mountain range.

small, V_g at the lower level must be greater along the slope than over the plain area.

Under such conditions, the possible ageostrophic flow components cannot be neglected. Reference can here be made to Haltiner and Martin's textbook (1957). Since the local time derivative may be disregarded (steady state assumption) the geostrophic departure V' can be approximated in the following form:

$$V' = V - V_g = \frac{\bar{V}}{f}\mathbf{k}\times\frac{\Delta V_{gs}}{\Delta s} + \frac{\bar{w}}{f}\mathbf{k}\times\frac{\Delta V_{gz}}{\Delta z} \qquad (3)$$

It is now important to realize that the difference vector $\Delta_z V_g$ (geostrophic wind at an upper level minus geostrophic wind at a lower level, the height difference of the two levels being denoted by z) is by definition the same as the thermal wind of the layer between the two levels, V_T. Furthermore, $\Delta_z V_g$ is equal in magnitude and opposite in direction to $\Delta_s V_g$ (geostrophic wind at a point downstream minus geostrophic wind upstream along the trajectory, the distance between the two points being s),

$$\Delta_z V_g = -\Delta_s V_g = V_T, \qquad (4)$$

provided the increase of the wind at the lower level is due to the inversion effect only, the wind at the upper level not changing over the area in question. Under such conditions

$$V' = \frac{\mathbf{k}}{f}\times V_T\left(\frac{\bar{w}}{\Delta z} - \frac{\bar{V}}{\Delta s}\right) \qquad (5)$$

where $\bar{V} \gtrless 0$ by definition, and $\bar{w} > 0$ for rising motion. Even if in any real case the above assumption is not exactly valid, one can still expect that the magnitude of V', the vector sum of the two terms on the right hand side of (3), should be smaller than that of the larger one of the two terms. Both are of the same order of magnitude, but only the term due to curvature of the streamlines must increase with stability; this will be discussed in the two following sections. In any case, the wind at surface level, as far as it is determined by horizontal pressure gradient, Coriolis, and inertial accelerations, is

$$V = V_g + V'. \qquad (6)$$

If sufficient information were available regarding the structure and motion of the air before it reaches the slopes of the mountains, V could be computed.

Regarding the effect of surface friction, no detailed analysis is intended. Too much depends on the specific local characteristics of the terrain. It is understood, of course, that the speed of the real wind near the ground must be less than predicted by (6), and its direction deflected to the left.

4. Estimate of the magnitude of the barrier effect

Referring to (2), it may be assumed that

a) very stable cold air is moving from the N toward a W–E mountain range, the upper surface of the cold air remaining parallel to the terrain which slopes at a rate of 700 m/100 km, or $G = 7\times10^{-3}$:

b) the temperature difference between the warm air above and the cold air near the ground is $\Delta T = 10$ C;

c) the mean temperature of the cold air $\bar{T} = 250$ K;

d) the Coriolis parameter at 70°N, $f = 1.37\times10^{-4}$ sec^{-1}.

This combination of values in (2) yields $V_T \cong 20$ m/sec, from the East. Because $\bar{T}$ and f can vary only within rather narrow limits, it is essentially the slope of the terrain, the possible damming-up of the cold air mass, *and* the stability of its vertical structure which determine the magnitude of V_T.

The above example illustrates the main conclusion of the present paper: With a realistic assumption regarding the sloping of the cold air, and with a ΔT value near the average of winter conditions, a remarkably strong thermal wind V_T, parallel to the mountain barrier, appears. It is equivalent to a strong S to N component of the horizontal pressure gradient over the north slopes, and hence indicates the presence of a strong westerly component of the geostrophic wind at the bottom of the cold air over the slope, say, at point B1 in Fig. 2.

To continues the discussion it may be assumed that the isobar pattern at the upper level (level 2 in Fig. 2) is represented by

e) $V_{g2} = 6$ m/sec, from N, not changing from A to B. It follows that $V_{g2} - V_T = V_{g1B} = 21$ m/sec from WNW. And in order to estimate whether the contribution of the geostrophic departure can become important, it may be assumed that

f) $\bar{V} = 14$ m/sec, $\Delta s = 200$ km;

g) $\bar{w} = 4$ cm/sec, $\Delta z = 800$ m.

With these values, (5) gives the magnitude of V' as

$$1.46|5\text{–}7| \cong 3 \text{ m/sec},$$

and its direction 90° to the right of V_T, that is, toward N.

To simplify an illustration of the various wind vectors, it may also be assumed that the horizontal pressure gradient at point A does not change from level 0 to level 2, the notation again referring to Fig. 2. Hence

$$V_{g2B} = V_{g2A} = V_{g1A} = V_{g0A},$$

and

$$V_T = -(V_{g1B} - V_{g0A}),$$

as shown in the vector diagram of Fig. 3.

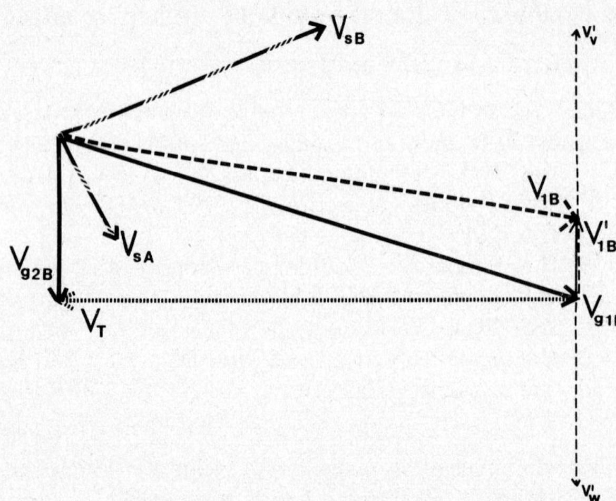

FIG. 3. Wind vector diagram, referring to points and levels of Fig. 2. Interpretation discussed in the text.

In real cases the wind at the upper level may vary somewhat between A and B, and may not be exactly geostrophic either. Then, (4) will not be fulfilled, and the geostrophic departure can be greater than calculated above. Nevertheless, it appears that at least in strong inversion cases the thermal wind effect is overriding. In Fig. 3, the vectors V_{sA} and V_{sB} have been added to suggest the approximate surface winds, about 30° to the left of the vectors V_{g0A} and V_{1B}, respectively, and with reduced speed. Consideration of specific local surface roughness and slope conditions is beyond the scope of this general sketch.

5. Conclusions

The streamlines of a shallow, stable air mass near the ground flowing toward a mountain barrier are deflected to the left (northern hemisphere) over the slopes of the obstacle. The change of direction becomes more pronounced as the temperature inversion (from the cold air near the surface to the warmest air aloft) becomes stronger. A geostrophic departure to the right caused by the positive vertical motion of the cold air [last term in (3)] does not depend upon that temperature contrast. Therefore, the departure to the left due to the curvature of the streamlines becomes the decisive ageostrophic flow component for very stable air. Altogether, then, the strong surface winds approximately parallel to the barrier, the "barrier-effect," which appear when the above conditions are fulfilled, must be directly related to the stability of the cold air mass. Wind statistics for three northern Alaskan stations (Table 2) confirm this concept. The lesson for wind forecasts for low level flight and surface activities is obvious.

REFERENCES

Bodman, G., 1910: Vol. II, Meteorologie, Wissenschaftl. Ergebnisse Der Schwedischen Südpolar-Expedition, 1901–1903. Lief., 1, 22 p, 2, 420 p, 3, 114 p, 4, 160 p.

Bryson, R. A., and K. F. Hare, 1973: The climates of North America. Introduction to Vol. XI. World survey of climatology. Elsevier, Amsterdam.

Dalrymple, P., H. Lettau and S. Wollaston, 1966: South Pole micrometeorology program: data analysis. In: Studies in Antarctic meteorology, M. J. Rubin (editor). Am. Geophys. Union Antarctic Research Series, 9, 13–58.

Dickey, W. W., 1961: A study of a topographic effect on wind in the Arctic. Journ. of Meteorology, 18(6), 790–803.

Godske, C. L., T. Bergeron, J. Bjerknes and R. C. Bundgaard, 1957: Dynamic Meteorology and Weather Forecasting. AMS. Boston, Massachusetts, 800 pp.

Haltiner, G. J., and F. L. Martin, 1957: Dynamical and Physical Meteorology. McGraw-Hill. New York, 470 pp.

Holton, J. R., 1972: An introduction to dynamic meteorology. Acad. Press, New York, 319 pp.

Lettau, H. H., 1967: Small and large scale features of boundary-layer structure over mountain slopes. Proceedings of the Symp. on Mountain Met., Fort Collins, Colorado, 1–74.

NAVAIR, 1966: Components of the 1000 mb winds (or surface winds) of the Northern Hemisphere. Published by direction of the Chief of Naval Operations, NAVAIR 50-1C-51, Washington, D. C., 74 charts.

Vowinckel, E., and S. Orvig, 1970: The climate of the North polar basin. In: Vol. 14 (S. Orvig, editor) of World Survey of Climatology. Elsevier, Amsterdam, 129–251.

Regional Climatonomy of Tundra and Boreal Forests in Canada

H. AND K. LETTAU

University of Wisconsin, Madison, Wisconsin

Abstract

Climatonomy is a basic study of the physical processes by which a planetary surface region gains, stores, and loses its moisture and heat during the course of the seasons. Climatonomical modeling includes the analytical formulation of a forcing function (or input), the parameterization of all the important processes which contribute to the moisture and heat exchange at the earth-air interface, and the rigorous calculation of a response function (or output). The model algorithm consists essentially of one-dimensional differential equations (for soil moisture and for surface temperature) with coefficients expressing the month-to-month variations of respondance and of delay-time of the input-output system.

With the aid of computer programs developed during 1973 a climatonomy study was made of three typical regions: tundra, tundra-forest, and boreal forest, (approximately along the 95th meridian between 65 and 55°N), predicting annual means and month-to-month variations of the two basic response functions: exchangeable soil moisture and surface temperature. The regional extra-atmospheric insolation provides the basic energy input or forcing function. Shortwave radiation attenuation (by scattering and absorption) and albedo effects at the lower as well as upper boundaries of the atmosphere are parameterized. For the moisture regime the basic forcing function of ground-absorbed insolation is combined with and qualified by the mass input of precipitation. The parameterization of the system of evapo-climatonomy permits the solution of the hydrologic balance equation by integral calculus rather than algebraic accounting. Calculated results include monthly rates of evaporation and river runoff. The length of the frost season influences significantly the delay-time parameters.

The forcing function of thermo-climatonomy is ground-absorbed insolation minus latent heat release to the atmosphere as determined by evapo-climatonomy. Parameterization of terrestrial and atmospheric longwave radiation, soil heat conduction, and atmospheric convection of sensible heat produces the differential equation for surface temperature which is solved by numerical forward-integration. It is emphasized that net radiation is not a basic forcing function since it depends on the surface temperature response of the system. Calculated results will be compared with direct climatic observations. It will be shown that with increasing arctic latitude and subsequent reduction of solar forcing, the delay-time parameters tend to increase for soil moisture storage (including snow and ice).

Man's activity may influence a regional climate either by input-control (such as stimulation of precipitation or of cloud formation, heat release by fuel burning, etc.) or, more likely, by parameter modification, such as changing of surface albedo, or vegetation cover, etc. The system of climatonomy permits us to single out selected input or process parameters to simulate their modification and to study the resulting response functions with other conditions either remaining unchanged or affected by physical feedback. Examples of parameter modification will be discussed to explain local anomalies (climatic "oases") of arctic and subarctic regions.

---

1. Definitions

In the "Glossary of Meteorology" (1959) *climate* is defined as the synthesis of weather. More specifically, the climate of a region on earth is said to be represented by the statistical collective of its weather conditions during a specified interval of time (usually at least three decades). It is noted that the term is derived from the Greek word "KLIMA," meaning "inclination" of the sun's rays which reflects the importance attributed by the early students to the sun's influence. Also defined in the "Glossary" are the terms *climatography* (a "thorough quantitative description of climate, particularly with reference to the tables and charts which document the characteristic values of climate elements at a station or over a region"), and *climatology* (the "scientific study of climate, including the analysis of causes of differences of climate, and the application of climatic data to the solution of specific design or operational problems"). An additional term, *climatonomy*, has been defined by us as "the explanation (by physical laws) of causes of climatic differences in space and time, and synthesis of climates (by numerical modeling) for planetary surfaces." Reference can be made to H. and K. Lettau (1969), and endorsement by Landsberg (1957) or Hare (1973).

2. Theoretical models of climate

The "SMIC-Report" (1971) identifies four types of models. We propose to add a fifth type:

(1) *Global-Average Models*—Results are independent of location on earth, and annual variations are nearly completely averaged out.

(2) *Statistical Models*—Results are averaged with respect to longitude, and the effects of atmospheric large-scale motions are treated in a statistical fashion.

(3) *Semi-Empirical Models*—Based in part on empirical relations derived from direct observations using correlation and regression methods.

(4) *Generalized Numerical Models*—Effects of atmospheric large-scale motions are treated explicitly by numerical integration, and the effects of important physical processes are considered in parameterized form.

(5) *Climatonomy Models*—Effects of all important physical processes which determine the budgets of mass (water substance) and energy (heat) at the earth's (or any other planet's) surface are parameterized, with due consideration of storage or delay-time terms. The resulting one-dimensional differential equations (with time as independent variable) for soil moisture and surface temperature are solved by integration methods.

For the study of actual meso- and micro-climates the first two model types can only provide the background features. Numerical models of the type (4) can be considered "general" only with respect to planets that have an atmosphere permitting large-scale motions. There exist, however, planets and satellites without atmospheres. They exhibit surface temperature differentiations of various scales in space (due to equator-to-pole contrast and topography) and time (due to rotation and revolution, also occasional eclipse of the sun) which must be included in modeling of climates.

Climatonomy emphasizes thermal response to solar forcing. As will be shown in Sections 6 and 7, closure is achieved by the modeling of full annual cycles based on transforms of the energy budget equation. For planets without atmospheres, the climatonomy model is a replacement for the types of models listed by SMIC. Even though it can be used as a whole-globe model, it seems more natural to use it for each hemisphere separately but simultaneously in view of the strong annual variations with opposite seasons. For planets with an atmosphere (but optically relatively thin as on our earth), the direct solar forcing dominates in either hemisphere and cross-equator coupling by advection is relatively weak. In the present discussion, the climatonomy model will be applied to regional climates only. Here, advection effects are considered in parameterized form, or could be supplied by the more sophisticated models (3) and (4).

Let us now discuss possible criteria which may be used to decide which type of theoretical model would promise most conclusive results in any operational application. The following listings may serve as a guide:

(1) Comprehensiveness of model formulation for specified resolution in terms of time and area scales.

(2) Physical soundness of algorithm and numerical feedback.

(3) Computer time requirements.

(4) Realistic simulation of terrestrial climates for "natural" regions of micro-, meso-, and macro-scales.

(5) Improvement of theoretical understanding of terrestrial climates through numerical experiments, permitting variations of parameters to clarify feedback processes.

(6) Numerical predictions of climate changes on the basis of documented trends in parameter values, or external forcing.

(7) Application of the model to other planets or satellites.

The third item is one of practical importance. In the "SMIC-Report" on page 142, it is stated that hundreds of hours of IBM 360-91 machine time are required for the one-year integration of some of the "generalized" models. This may be compared with only seconds of machine time per year and station needed for models of regional climatonomy.

The fourth and fifth item are especially important for the modeling of natural regions in polar climates, such as tundra, ice-domes, glacier fields, and other areas under geographic control. Hare and Hay (1973) point out the need for theoretical understanding of the seasonal progression of a snow-melt-line, or the lack of it in other years, and a related "jump to high values of net radiation."

The sixth item concerns the main objective of the SMIC-Report, namely the study of climatic changes due to man's activities. The two last ones refer specifically to climatonomic concepts.

3. Criteria for meso- to micro-scale models of climatonomy

If specific meso- and micro-climates are to be investigated the following criteria should be considered:

(1) Coupling to larger scales by separating *indigenous* from *advective contributions* to the climate's forcing functions.

(2) Explicit treatment of submedium-atmosphere interaction processes with the aid of sets of physical parameters such as: (i) for the submedium: specific heat, heat conductivity, thermal admittance, availability of exchangeable water; (ii), for the interface: energy albedo, emissivity, aerodynamic roughness length, slope inclination, removability of particles; and (iii), for the air: density, composition, shearing velocity based on ground drag.

(3) Response to forcing must include moisture factors of climate in addition to temperatures on both sides of the interface, and, primarily, the annual cycle as the basis for the treatment of diurnal cycles which are different in different seasons.

(4) Explicit formulation of feedback with clear distinction between (i) response-to-process feedback, and (ii) response-to-forcing-function feedback.

(5) Numerical assessment of probable climate changes as consequence of control of process parameters or input parameters.

"Indigenous," in connection with climate factors, corresponds to "eigenbuertig" as used by Flohn (1954). Indigenous forcing is, basically, by radiation. Advective factors refer to "airmass dynamics." Polar latitudes are the source region of "arctic air masses" which implies that indigenous factors are here more important than in temperature regions. For example, a problem which requires a thorough assessment of the relative importance of radiational and advective factors, is the "corelessness" of the annual course of polar surface temperature; reference may be made to a discussion by Schwerdtfeger (1970).

Physical surface conditions in arctic regions are documented in detail by Vowinckel and Orvig (1970). The need for feedback clarification and parameter variation in theoretical model calculations can hardly be overestimated. Control by human manipulation appears feasible in inverse proportion to area-scale of surface parameter modification, but will be justifiable in any case only after a most thorough impact-study is completed which, in turn, requires physical understanding and numerical modeling of meso- and micro-climates.

Climatonomic models are especially suited for application to naturally occurring climatic singularities, or anomalies, over limited areas within a rather uniform climate of the surrounding region. Examples are the "dry valleys" or "oases" of Antarctica. An oasis-effect has also been observed in the arctic tundra region, and it will be shown that a combination of several parameter variants, even though individually not really conspicuous, can when acting together make tundra summers significantly warmer, and winters milder, than in the surroundings.

4. General characteristics of models of regional climatonomy

A region is a "mosaic element" of the planetary or global climate, a physically defined area of the planet's surface and the atmosphere above it. The independently prescribed forcing function is basically the time-series of regionally intercepted solar energy, supplemented by advected heat and moisture. The algorithm of the model is based on the parameterization of all governing processes involved in the mass and energy balance of the regional planetary surface,

TABLE 1. Brief summary of submodel characteristics of regional climatonomy (symbols not specified include a^{**} = top albedo, a^* = surface or ground albedo, G = global radiation).

Submodel	Forcing function	Response-output (partial listings)
I *"Shortwave"*	$F^{(I)} = EI =$ Extra-atmospheric irradiation	Reflection to space $= a^{**}EI$, also ground absorption $= (1-a^*) \cdot G$
II *"Evapo"*	$F^{(II)} = (1-a^*) \cdot G$, also precipitation rate	Exchangeable H_2O, runoff, also evapo-transpiration rate E
III *"Thermo"*	$F^{(III)} = F^{(II)} - E$	Submedium and air temperatures, also fluxes of surface energy budget, including net radiation

and the numerical solution of characteristic one-dimensional differential equations derived from a deterministic use of continuity and balance requirements. The model output, or calculated response functions, are primarily the time-series of surface temperature and exchangeable soil moisture, and, secondarily (making use again of the parameterization), the time-series of net radiation, evaporation and runoff, as well as vertical fluxes of latent and sensible heat. Independent results obtained either from observations or from other models are included in our computer printout as test values for comparisons. Feedback is allowed for by iteration of input and process parameters using output data from tentative applications of the program.

It was found practical to apply the model in three steps by using sequentially the three submodels described in Table 1.

The forcing function EI of the first submodel $F^{(I)}$ is truly externally prescribed. The Shortwave-Submodel is an input-output model in the strict sense of the word, since input is FLUX and output other FLUXES. The ground absorption serves as the energy forcing function for the second submodel while precipitation serves simultaneously, as mass forcing. The output of the second model includes trends of storage of exchangeable soil moisture and fluxes like the evapo-transpiration rate E. This, after conversion to latent heat flux, is subtracted from the energy forcing function of the second model and serves as input for the third and last submodel. The indicated interconnections between submodels can be supplemented further by possible consideration of feedback.

5. Shortwave radiation climatonomy

The forcing function for this submodel ($F^{(I)} = EI$ = extra-atmospheric irradiance) is determined by the sun's emission and distance, and the planet's revolution and rotation. For a specified region, $F^{(I)}$ depends on latitude, the season, and the hour of the day. As a

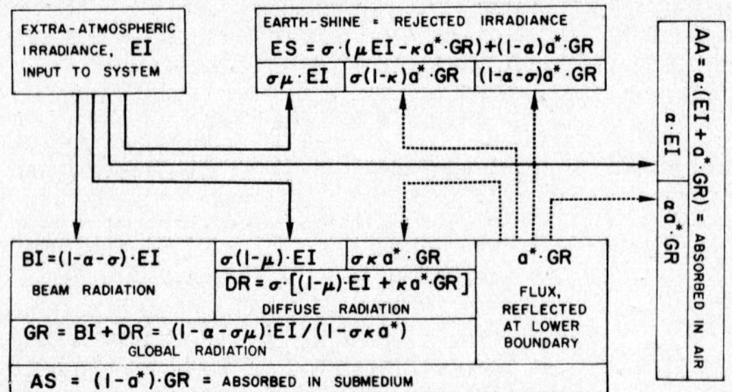

FIG. 1. Quantitative scheme of shortwave radiation transmission, scattering and absorption. Incoming irradiance is represented by the four full arrows, ground-level reflected radiation by the four dashed arrows. Continuity requires that at any instant extra-atmospheric irradiance equals earthshine plus total absorption in air and submedium, $EI = ES + AA + AS$. The scheme shows how multi-component variables like ES, AA, and AS (including ground-level beam radiation, diffuse radiation, and global radiation) are generated by the elementary contributions "boxed-in" at each arrowhead. These flux intensities are expressed in terms of non-dimensional parameters: $a^* =$ ground-level albedo, $\alpha =$ effective absorptance, $\sigma =$ effective scatterance, μ and κ are primary scatterance fractions so that $\mu\sigma$ and $(1-\mu)\sigma$ are the coefficients of earthward and spaceward scattering of incoming irradiance while, correspondingly, $\kappa\sigma$ and $(1-\kappa)\sigma$ are the coefficients of earthward and spaceward scattering of ground-level reflected radiation.

function of time it is quasi-cyclic; diurnal courses are normally described by a truncated cosine-function which is non-zero only from sunrise to sunset. Annual courses of daily totals of insolation are correspondingly non-harmonic for latitudes beyond the arctic circle. The model algorithm requires the parameterization of processes of scattering, absorption, and reflection due to molecules, cloud, and dust particles in the air, also representative values of the ground albedo a^* of the region. Unlike to the subsequent two submodels of climatonomy, delay-time terms are absent since storage of shortwave radiation energy is impossible. Therefore the continuity equation contains only algebraic terms

and the mathematical problem is reduced to the determination of a set of instantaneously valid fractions of EI. Two composite ratios to be calculated are the top albedo and the effective columnar absorptance since these determine the sunlight rejected to space (earth-shine) and the shortwave radiational heating of the air column above the region. Continuity requires that the remainder is absorbed by the ground.

To calculate absorption in the atmospheric column it is necessary to parameterize effects of at least four meteorological variables, namely, atmospheric precipitable water, ozone and other optically active gases, cloud layers, and aerosol. Contributions to scattering by molecules, cloud particles, and aerosol must also be parameterized individually.

A variety of numerical models for the calculation of shortwave energy fluxes are available. An example of one that has been applied to polar climates is "EBBA" by Vowinckel and Orvig (1972). Since our discussion is restricted to the average annual course of shortwave radiation fluxes, we prefer to use our relatively simple climatonomy model; see H. and K. Lettau (1969). The scheme is illustrated in Fig. 1. Actual calculations were carried out by using as independent inputs the monthly values of EI (from Smithsonian Tables), ground albedo a^* according to Hare and Ritchie (1972), and—estimated from a variety of available sources—the climatic means of optical airmass (m), Rayleigh scattering (SR), precipitable water (w), ozone amount (g), and degree of cloudiness (c). These climatic means serve as bases for computing derived variables (as defined on Fig. 1 and in captions of Tables 1 and 2), such as $AW = 0.102 \cdot (m \cdot w)^{0.276}$, $AG = 0.065\ m \cdot g$. We assumed that $SC = 0.41\ c$, and $\mu = (1+c)/2 = \kappa$ as approximately valid for this region with prevailing stratus cloud.

Input variables not directly known are the coefficients of cloud absorption AC/c and, although small,

TABLE 2. Monthly mean shortwave radiation data for the Tundra region near Baker Lake, Canada (65°N, 95°W, 10 m MSL, period 1931–1960). $F^{(I)}$ (ly/day) = extra-atmospheric irradiance = EI; M = optical airmass; a^* = surface albedo; SR, SC, SD = scattering coefficients by molecules (Rayleigh), cloud elements, and dust or haze particles; AW, AG, AC, AD = absorption coefficients by water vapor, other gases (especially ozone), cloud layers, and dust or haze particles; GR, DR, = global and diffuse radiation at the surface (ly/day); a^{**} = resulting top albedo of the region.

	Jan	Feb	Mar	Apr	May	Jun	Jul	Aug	Sep	Oct	Nov	Dec	Ann
$F^{(I)}$	36	137	321	606	851	996	930	706	436	203	59	20	442
M	4.85	3.72	2.45	2.10	1.68	1.70	1.78	1.93	2.26	3.18	5.90	6.46	3.17
a^*	0.79	0.80	0.79	0.74	0.65	0.33	0.20	0.18	0.19	0.38	0.57	0.70	0.53
SR	0.458	0.345	0.226	0.194	0.155	0.158	0.166	0.180	0.210	0.296	0.548	0.608	0.295
SC	0.308	0.279	0.201	0.201	0.234	0.246	0.226	0.250	0.303	0.340	0.377	0.373	0.278
SD	0.08	0.08	0.08	0.06	0.04	0.02	0.04	0.06	0.06	0.08	0.08	0.08	0.063
AW	0.088	0.099	0.099	0.102	0.113	0.125	0.136	0.131	0.126	0.124	0.135	0.122	0.117
AG	0.114	0.092	0.064	0.057	0.044	0.041	0.041	0.041	0.046	0.064	0.123	0.143	0.073
AC	0.008	0.014	0.015	0.025	0.034	0.048	0.055	0.073	0.104	0.116	0.046	0.009	0.046
AD	0.000	0.000	0.000	0.010	0.010	0.010	0.020	0.030	0.030	0.020	0.010	0.000	0.012
GR	21	85	226	415	559	568	491	331	172	72	21	5	248
DR	8	33	77	127	149	111	91	64	32	17	6	3	60
a^{**}	0.572	0.570	0.576	0.530	0.484	0.352	0.300	0.315	0.353	0.411	0.467	0.510	0.453

TABLE 3. Summary of monthly mean shortwave radiation data for three Canadian regions: TU=Tundra region near Baker Lake, OF=Open Forest near Churchill (58°N, 94°W, 35 m MSL), and CF=Closed Forest (about 55°N, 95°W, 250 m MSL). c=fraction of cloud cover; σ=effective scatterance=(SR+SD)$(1-c)+c$ SC; α=effective absorptance=AW+AG+AC+AD; $F^{(II)}=(1-\alpha^*)$GR =solar forcing. Symbols in equations as defined in Table 2.

		Jan	Feb	Mar	Apr	May	Jun	Jul	Aug	Sep	Oct	Nov	Dec	Ann
a^*	TU	0.79	0.80	0.79	0.74	0.65	0.33	0.20	0.18	0.19	0.38	0.57	0.70	0.53
	OF	0.68	0.67	0.62	0.48	0.28	0.19	0.16	0.15	0.19	0.25	0.43	0.60	0.39
	CF	0.34	0.36	0.32	0.25	0.17	0.17	0.18	0.17	0.19	0.18	0.22	0.30	0.24
c	TU	0.75	0.68	0.49	0.49	0.57	0.60	0.55	0.61	0.74	0.83	0.92	0.91	0.68
	OF	0.66	0.52	0.51	0.55	0.62	0.62	0.49	0.53	0.75	0.80	0.82	0.80	0.64
	CF	0.64	0.52	0.49	0.56	0.57	0.55	0.46	0.49	0.68	0.72	0.79	0.73	0.60
σ	TU	0.440	0.415	0.357	0.330	0.318	0.317	0.318	0.344	0.374	0.404	0.427	0.434	0.373
	OF	0.430	0.379	0.339	0.333	0.325	0.316	0.297	0.322	0.368	0.391	0.410	0.434	0.362
	CF	0.411	0.367	0.334	0.329	0.312	0.297	0.287	0.310	0.353	0.377	0.401	0.424	0.350
α	TU	0.209	0.204	0.177	0.191	0.200	0.224	0.252	0.276	0.305	0.324	0.314	0.274	0.246
	OF	0.202	0.173	0.161	0.194	0.195	0.217	0.242	0.270	0.305	0.307	0.243	0.228	0.228
	CF	0.190	0.175	0.165	0.188	0.199	0.216	0.238	0.257	0.292	0.290	0.237	0.217	0.222
a^{**}	TU	0.572	0.570	0.576	0.530	0.484	0.352	0.300	0.315	0.353	0.411	0.467	0.510	0.453
	OF	0.532	0.529	0.506	0.423	0.352	0.311	0.269	0.283	0.350	0.384	0.448	0.504	0.408
	CF	0.423	0.398	0.368	0.339	0.300	0.284	0.266	0.277	0.331	0.353	0.398	0.425	0.347
$F^{(II)}$	TU	4	17	48	108	196	381	393	273	139	45	9	3	135
	OF	18	49	111	249	386	440	435	322	166	83	34	16	192
	CF	51	108	206	214	431	471	442	345	198	116	62	38	232

the aerosol attenuation factors SD and AD. These were adjusted in such a way that the output (ground fluxes of global radiation GR and top albedo a^{**}) agreed with GR-values taken from climatic maps of Canada (1968) and top albedo-values from satellite evaluations as those by Suomi and VonderHaar (1972). Midsummer a^{**}-values of 0.30 to 0.35 were also consistent with interpolations on charts by Raschke and Bandeen (1970), available for July 1966 only. Observational data of average diffuse radiation at ground level would have been helpful to assess effective scattering and absorption processes. Climatic Maps of Canada (1968) give average monthly values of global radiation only, which were used to make the above described adjustments.

We applied the shortwave radiation model of climatonomy to two other regions along the 95th meridian to document parameter variations between three characteristic northern climates: tundra, open forest (tundra-forest transition zone), and closed forest. Observed values of ground albedo and average cloudiness are listed in Table 3 for these three regions; also included are calculated values of effective scatterances and absorptances, top-albedos and, finally, the month-to-month variation of radiation absorbed at the ground which will serve as the energy forcing function for the following application of the evapo-climatonomy submodel.

6. Evapo-climatonomy

Evapo-climatonomy is an operational method to determine moisture storage, runoff, and evapotranspiration resulting from gravitation and the sun's work

on precipitation intercepted by a natural watershed. For a detailed discussion reference is made to Lettau and Baradas (1973). It may suffice here to summarize the main components of the system. They include mass input (of H_2O) described by the time series of precipitation P, in addition to energy input described by the time series of shortwave radiation absorbed by the ground $F^{(II)}=(1-a^*)G$, ly/day, or converted to mm/mo.

The response function is the time series of m=exchangeable soil moisture which is the height of the equivalent water column (mm H_2O) in the representative soil column of the land area (including snowpack and reservoirs) for which the P- and F-series are representative. The process includes runoff (N) concurrently with evaporation (E). The governing equation is the hydrologic balance equation,

$$N+E=P-\Delta m/\Delta t. \tag{1}$$

E and N will involve not only water which is replenished concurrently by P but also water that has been precipitated and subsequently stored during preceeding Δt-periods. We distinguish between "immediate" process rates (E' and N') and "delayed" rates (E'' and N'') so that $E=E'+E''$, and $N=N'+N''$. The physical rationale is to separate out the portion $E'+N'$ of the total process $E+N$ which is, during any time interval Δt, directly coupled with concurrent mass input. We define the "reduced" precipitation rate $P'=P-N'-E'$, so that effective soil moisture changes for finite time steps Δt are exactly determined by reduced input P' and delayed processes $N''+E''$. Writing the storage

TABLE 4. Parameters of evapoclimatonomy for the Tundra region near Baker Lake, Canada. n^* = immediate runoff ratio; P^* (mm/month) = threshold value of precipitation; e^* = immediate evaporivity; t^* (months) = delay time of soil moisture depletion; m^* (mm of liquid water column) = threshold value of soil moisture; e^{**} = delayed evaporivity. (The energy-input parameter a^* = surface albedo is listed in Table 2).

	Jan	Feb	Mar	Apr	May	Jun	Jul	Aug	Sep	Oct	Nov	Dec
n^*	0.0	0.0	0.0	0.0	0.0	0.5	0.8	0.7	0.5	0.0	0.0	0.0
P^*	50	50	50	50	50	50	20	20	40	50	50	50
e^*	0.3	0.3	0.3	0.3	0.3	0.3	0.3	0.3	0.3	0.3	0.3	0.3
t^*	72.5	63.5	37.6	17.0	9.77	3.62	1.08	1.01	1.75	3.95	11.0	22.8
m^*	10	10	10	10	10	10	10	10	10	10	10	10
e^{**}	0.007	0.007	0.007	0.007	0.007	0.007	0.007	0.007	0.007	0.007	0.007	0.007

term as dm/dt, equation (1) can be reformulated as

$$dm/dt = P' - (N'' + E'').\qquad(2)$$

The parameters of the immediate processes, which can be either time-dependent or constant, include a threshold value (P^*) of precipitation and an additional factor, the runoff ratio n^*, so that

$$N' = n^* \cdot (P - P^*).\qquad(3)$$

Immediate evapotranspiration E' does not contribute to dm/dt because it reduces merely the effective mass input $P - N'$. The parameter of "immediate evaporivity" e^* measures the capacity of the land surface to utilize locally absorbed solar energy during a given month for the evapotranspiration of water precipitated during the same month. If the annual, or multi-annual, mean of $F^{(II)}$ is denoted by $\bar{F}$, then

$$E' = e^* \cdot (P - N')F^{(II)}/\bar{F}.\qquad(4)$$

Most important for the delayed processes (N'' and E'') is t^* = delay-time parameter of soil moisture withdrawal expressed in the same units as Δt. We assume that the delayed processes vary in direct proportion to exchangeable soil moisture m. The defining equation is

$$E'' + N'' = m/t^*, \quad \text{or} \quad t^* = m/(E'' + N'').\qquad(5)$$

While E' represents the sun's work on water that is concurrently precipitated, E'' represents the sun's work on stored soil moisture. A relevant physical parameter of a watershed is the delayed evaporivity e^{**}, defined in such a way that

$$E'' = e^{**}F^{(II)}(m - m^*)/m^*,\qquad(6)$$

where m^* = threshold value of m. With the aid of the t^* parameter of the delayed processes Eq. (2) transforms into a one-dimensional or ordinary differential equation for m as the dependent variable,

$$\frac{dm}{dt} + \frac{m}{t^*} = P'.\qquad(7)$$

We define a non-dimensional time variable τ so that

$$d\tau = dt/t^*; \quad \text{or} \quad \tau = \int_{t_0}^{t} (t^*)^{-1}dt.\qquad(8)$$

For either constant or variable t^*, Eq. (7) is solved by

$$m = e^{-\tau} \cdot \left(m_1 + \int_{t_0}^{t} P' e^{\tau}dt\right),\qquad(9)$$

where m_1 = initial value of exchangeable soil moisture. We solve the differential Eq. (7) by integration rather than algebraic accounting of inputs minus withdrawals. This is the salient feature of climatonomy, together with the subsequent utilization of output m from Eq. (9) for the direct calculation of process rates E and N with the aid of Eqs. (3 to 6).

The initial value m_1 can either be independently prescribed (if the problem requires the investigation of climate fluctuations from year to year) or rigorously determined (from the set of 12 normal monthly means of the t^*-parameter and reduced precipitation P') for a stable climate by the mathematical condition that soil moisture of the first month m_1 must be exactly reproduced if the upper integration limit in Eq. (9) is extended to one year plus one month. Namely, in a stable climate, the soil moisture for the thirteenth month must equal that of the first month; or in a more general formulation; $m_{(i+12)} = m_i$ for any i-value from 1 to 12.

Strong annual variations of soil moisture delay-time are typical for arctic climates due to the long season of subfreezing temperatures and snowpack, see Table 4. In our evapo-climatonomy model the spring melt runoff shows up in the abrupt drop of t^*, from winter values of 23 to 72 months to summer lows of close to the possible minimum value of one month (one Δt increment).

Calculations of evapotranspiration for land areas are conventionally based on its "potential" value which has realistic meaning only in regions where soil moisture replenishment is not a limiting factor, whereas evapo-climatonomy takes explicitly into account that every water molecule evaporating from a land surface must have been supplied by preceding or concurrent precipitation (including irrigation or run-in). Consequently, runoff calculations are necessary because this process, too, draws on precipitation. Furthermore, conventional models utilize, normally, net radiation as a forcing function although it is dependent on thermal response, whereas evapo-climatonomy is based on the independent energy supply of solar energy. Results calculated by climatonomical methods are summarized in Table 5 for the Tundra region. To illustrate differences in forcing functions and process rates between Tundra, Open Forest, and Closed Forest, we summarized in Table 6 observed precipitation, global radiation, runoff, and calculated evaporation. Using annual means, $\bar{N}/\bar{P}$, the runoff ratios are between 0.49 and 0.57.

Our model of evapo-climatonomy has been applied to individual years as well as to sequences of several years; reference is made to Lettau and Baradas (1973). Tentative calculations for individual years for the tundra region near Baker Lake have been carried out and will be published in a future report. The problem that needs further elaboration is to establish representative parameter values (especially the highly variable delay-time) as a function of regional soil-water freeze, snowpack, and soil temperature. With reference to discussions in Lettau and Baradas (1973) a pre-requisite for the operational application of the hydrological version of evapo-climatonomy is a thorough "calibration" of the watershed under consideration.

Obviously, Eqs. (4) and (6) give $E=0$ if $F^{(II)}=0$. To obtain evaporation values for periods with no insolation (as during the night phase of diurnal cycles and the polar winter) we have developed a climatonomy model based on the Bowen ratio. This can be applied also to water and ice surfaces as will be discussed in a separate paper.

7. Thermo–climatonomy; theoretical developments

Thermo-climatonomy is an operational method for the calculation of surface temperature (its absolute average, as well as temporal-spatial variability) in conjunction with the determination of all interface

TABLE 5. Results of evapoclimatonomy for the Tundra region near Baker Lake, Canada. Model input and parameter values as summarized in Tables 3 and 4. $F^{(II)}=(1-a^*)G=$ ground absorbed insolation (equivalent mm/month); N', $E'=$ immediate, N'', $E''=$ delayed, N, $E=$ actual runoff and evapotranspiration (mm/month); $m=$ exchangeable soil moisture (mm water equivalent).

	Jan	Feb	Mar	Apr	May	Jun	Jul	Aug	Sep	Oct	Nov	Dec	Ann
$F_{(II)}$	2	8	25	54	102	192	205	143	71	24	5	2	69
N'	0	0	0	0	0	0	28	5	0	0	0	0	3
E'	0	1	1	2	4	22	24	14	9	4	1	0	7
N''	1	1	1	2	3	14	37	21	13	9	5	3	9
E''	0	0	2	4	7	9	8	2	0	1	0	0	3
N	1	1	1	2	3	14	65	26	13	9	5	3	12
E	0	1	3	6	11	31	32	16	9	5	1	0	10
m	77	86	95	97	95	83	48	23	23	38	58	70	66

fluxes of sensible heat, including longwave radiation (LW), submedium conduction (S), and convection (Q) into the lower atmosphere. The forcing input is ground-absorbed insolation minus that fraction of it which is converted to latent heat, that is, the energy equivalent of evaporation (E); see Table 1. The governing equation expresses the energy budget at the atmosphere's lower boundary,

$$(1-a^*)\cdot G-E=F^{(III)}=LWU+LWD+S+Q, \quad (10)$$

where LWU denotes the upward longwave radiation flux emitted by the interface, and LWD the downward flux received from atmospheric radiators as counter-radiation. Because annual courses or climatic month-to-month variations are of primary interest in the present discussion all energy fluxes will be monthly averages in units of cal cm^{-2} (langleys) per day (ly day^{-1}). The novel feature of our deterministic model of thermo-climatonomy is a judicious parameterization of the fluxes of sensible heat which appear on the right-hand side of Eq. (10). The goal is a "budget equation transform" or a mathematical

TABLE 6. Summary of observed monthly averages of precipitation (P), global radiation (G), river runoff (N), and calculated evapotranspiration (E) (all in equivalent mm water per month, period 1966–1971) for three Canadian climates (TU, OF, CF, as defined in Table 3).

		Jan	Feb	Mar	Apr	May	Jun	Jul	Aug	Sep	Oct	Nov	Dec	Ann
	TU	7	14	9	7	10	26	55	27	29	36	25	10	21
P	OF	46	42	38	13	19	43	41	59	45	50	52	44	41
	CF	34	25	18	24	38	66	79	68	63	43	53	54	47
	TU	11	40	118	209	291	286	256	174	87	38	11	5	106
G	OF	29	70	152	242	280	274	270	197	106	57	30	18	144
	CF	40	79	157	211	270	286	282	217	123	73	40	34	151
	TU	1	1	1	2	3	14	65	26	13	9	5	3	12
N	OF	5	4	5	7	24	95	29	17	19	17	12	5	20
	CF	6	6	7	26	114	43	20	16	26	26	20	16	27
	TU	0	1	2	5	11	32	30	15	10	4	1	0	9
E	OF	3	6	14	21	31	53	45	41	20	13	6	2	21
	CF	4	7	13	21	25	44	50	36	20	9	6	5	20

Winter precipitation is reported in "Climate of Canada," as $\frac{1}{10}$ of the depth of newly fallen snow. Independent data (snow course measurements as published by the Atmospheric Environment Service of Canada) suggest that the routine-use of the $\frac{1}{10}$ value for snow density leads to underestimates of snow precipitation. Our values in Table 6 were adjusted according to snow course measurements for the following three stations: Baker Lake (TU), Churchill (OF), and Wabowden (CF).

transformation of equation (10) which associates the climatic forcing $F^{(III)}$ as a prescribed function of time (t) with climatic response of surface temperature as another function of time.

For this purpose we introduce a set of response coefficients which will be called "respondances" (having units of ly day^{-1} per degree Kelvin) and be denoted by r^*S for conduction, and r^*Q for convection. These coefficients control the relative amplitudes of forced fluxes and thermal responses. To account for phase lags between response and forcing cycles we introduce an additional set of parameters which we call "delay-times," t^*S and t^*Q, for conduction and convection, respectively. All t^*-values are expressed in units of the time increment Δt, that is in units of one month for the study of the annual cycle. Defining equations are:

$$S=(r^*S)\cdot[T-\underline{T}+(t^*S)\cdot\Delta T/\Delta t], \qquad (11)$$

$$Q=(r^*Q)\cdot[T-\underline{T}+(r^*Q)\cdot\Delta T/\Delta t], \qquad (12)$$

where T is surface temperature and $\underline{T}$ is its base or annual mean value. Longwave radiation fluxes are parameterized correspondingly, but as departures from their climatic base values $\underline{LWU}$ and $\underline{LWD}$, in the following defining equations:

$$LWU=\underline{LWU}+(r^*LWU)\cdot(T-\underline{T}) \qquad (13)$$

$$LWD=\underline{LWD}+(r^*LWD)\cdot[T-\underline{T} \\ +(t^*LWD)\cdot\Delta T/\Delta t]. \qquad (14)$$

Omitting a delay-time parameter in Eq. (13) is justified by Stefan-Boltzmann's law according to which LWU varies exactly in phase with T if the surface emissivity (ϵ^*) remains unchanged (assumed to be true for the ground areas under consideration).

To complete the process parameterization, the following set of identities are defined:

$$\underline{A}^*=(\underline{LWU}+\underline{LWD})/\underline{LWU}=\text{base value of} \\ \text{the Angstroem ratio,} \qquad (15a)$$

$$r^{**}=r^*LWU+r^*LWD+r^*S+r^*Q=\text{effective} \\ \text{climatic respondance,} \qquad (15b)$$

$$t^{**}=[(t^*LWD)\cdot(r^*LWD)+(t^*S)\cdot(r^*S) \\ +(t^*Q)\cdot(r^*Q)]/r^{**}=\text{effective climatic} \\ \text{delay-time, and} \qquad (15c)$$

$$\Phi=(F^{(III)}-\underline{LWU}-\underline{LWD})/(r^{**}\cdot t^{**})=\text{ef-} \\ \text{fective climatic forcing function.} \qquad (15d)$$

Evidently, the ratio $\underline{A}^*$ is fixed by annual mean values and therefore a constant of the regional climate. r^{**} and t^{**} are composite parameters which may either be climatic constants or, more likely, exhibit month-to-month variations. Annual average and amplitude of Φ determine the thermal climate of the surface for which the system is representative. The governing equation is obtained upon introducing the above parameterization into Eq. (10). After rearranging the

terms and writing dT/dt instead of $\Delta T/\Delta t$, an ordinary one-dimensional differential equation for T as the dependent variable results,

$$dT/dt+(T-\underline{T})/t^{**}=\Phi, \qquad (16)$$

which has the same structure as the governing equation of evapo-climatonomy, Eq. (7). Correspondingly, we define a non-dimensional variable with the aid of the "natural" time increment $d\tau=(dt)/t^{**}$,

$$\tau=\int_{t_0}^{t}(t^{**})^{-1}dt. \qquad (17)$$

For either constant or variable t^{**} Eq. (16) is solved by the "budget equation transform":

$$T-\underline{T}=e^{-\tau}\left[T_1-\underline{T}+\int_{t_0}^{t}\Phi e^{+\tau}dt\right] \qquad (18)$$

where $T_1=$ initial value of surface temperature which may be either independently prescribed (when sequences of individual years are to be investigated), or rigorously determined (from the sets of 12 monthly normals of t^{**} and reduced forcing) by the requirement of climatic stability: the temperature of the first month must be reproduced if the upper limit of integration in Eq. (18) is extended to a thirteenth month, or one year and one month.

After calculating the time series of $T-\underline{T}$ values with the aid of the "budget equation transform," Eqs. (11) to (14) are used to determine individual values for all the fluxes of the surface energy budget. Because the vertical temperature gradient in the lower atmospheric layers depends on the value and sign of Q (inversion for $-Q$, "lapse condition" for $+Q$), we add another parameter, the "height-reduction coefficient" h^*Q, having units of °K ly^{-1} day^{-1}, to calculate monthly means of air temperature at climatic station level, $T(2)$, taking 2 m as the height of the thermometer exposure above the ground,

$$T(2)=T-(h^*Q)\cdot Q. \qquad (19)$$

Net radiation R at the atmosphere's lower boundary is defined as:

$$R=(1-a^*)\cdot G-(LWU+LWD), \qquad (20)$$

and can be calculated with the aid of Eqs. (13, 14 and 18). Its dependence on thermal response explains that net radiation cannot serve as an independent forcing function for evaporation estimates; reference is made to the discussion at the end of Section 6.

It is necessary to relate the coefficients r^{**} and t^{**} to conventional physical parameters; let us begin with Eq. (13). If σ is the universal constant of Stefan-Boltzmann's law,

$$LWU=\epsilon^*\sigma T^4; \text{ and } d(LWU)/dT=4\ LWU/T, \qquad (13a)$$

whereupon, in terms of the finite differences of Eq. (13), and after introducing annual base values of $\underline{LWU}$ and $\underline{T}$,

$$r^*LWU \approx 4\ \underline{LWU}/\underline{T} = 4\ \epsilon^*\sigma\underline{T}^3 = r^*\underline{LWU}. \qquad (13b)$$

In our present program Eq. (13b) is held to be valid within tolerable error limits. Due to this assumption the respondance r^*LWU is a climatic constant for the region under consideration. Correction terms that take into account the non-linearity of Stefan-Boltzmann's law could be incorporated by iterative methods if necessary. With the aid of Eq. (13b) and the base value of the Angstroem ratio, respondance for counter-radiation follows as $(\underline{A}^* - 1)\cdot r^*\underline{LWU}$.

Respondances in conjunction with delay-time parameters are most readily explained by using Eq. (11) for the submedium. Tentatively, we assume that the conductive flux varies in form of a single harmonic with frequency ω. Then, temperature responds with the same frequency but lags by the time-independent phase angle α, so that

$$S = \Delta S \cos(\omega t), \qquad (21a)$$

and

$$T - \underline{T} = \Delta T \cos(\omega t - \alpha);$$
$$\text{or, } \partial T/\partial t = -\omega\Delta T \sin(\omega t - \alpha). \qquad (21b)$$

Elementary expansion of cosine- and sine-terms, elimination of $\sin(\omega t)$ with the aid of the two forms of Eq. (21b), and introducing the resulting $\cos(\omega t)$ term into Eq. (21a) yields

$$S = (\Delta S/\Delta T)\cos\alpha[T - \underline{T} + (\tan\alpha/\omega)(\partial T/\partial t)] \qquad (21c)$$

The comparison with corresponding terms in Eq. (11) shows that

$$r^*S = (\Delta S/\Delta T)\cdot\cos\alpha; \quad \text{and,} \quad t^*S = (1/\omega)\cdot\tan\alpha. \qquad (21d)$$

Conventional parameters are heat conductivity (λ) defined by Fourier's law, and volumetric heat capacity (C) defined by the continuity requirement. Let $\sqrt{\lambda C} = \mu = $ thermal admittance of the conductor. If time (t) and depth (z) below the surface are the only independent variables and no internal heat sink exists, defining identities are

$$\lambda = -S/(\partial T/\partial z) \quad \text{and,} \quad C = -(\partial S/\partial z)/(\partial T/\partial t). \qquad (22)$$

In classical theory it is assumed that we have a homogeneous conductor ($\partial\lambda/\partial z = \partial C/\partial z = 0$) with constant coefficients ($\partial\lambda/\partial t = \partial C/\partial t = 0$), and it is predicted for the conduction of a harmonic heat pulse of frequency ω that

$$\Delta S/\Delta T = (\lambda C\omega)^{\frac{1}{2}} = \mu\sqrt{\omega};$$
$$\text{and, } \tan\alpha = 1; \ (\text{or, } \cos\alpha = 1/\sqrt{2}). \qquad (23)$$

According to Eq. (21d), respondance would be equal, for this highly specialized case, to admittance multiplied by the square-root of $\frac{1}{2}$ of the frequency ($r^*S = \mu\sqrt{\omega/2}$), while delay-time t^*S would be given by the reciprocal of frequency. Specifically, for the annual frequency ($2\pi/12$ months) t^*S would equal 1.91 months, while r^*S would be in the range from 1.5 to 0.8 to 0.3 ly day^{-1} deg^{-1} (depending on the thermal admittance of the submedium) when the μ-value varies from about 0.055 (in ly deg^{-1} sec$^{-\frac{1}{2}}$) as for good conductors like granite, to about 0.03 as for moderate ones like sandy soils, to 0.01 or less for poor admittors like leaf litter, snow, or other porous substances. These μ-values follow from tabulations of typical λ- and C-values in monographs on physical climatology, for example, in Sellers (1965).

Results of classical conduction theory are often unrealistic mainly for the following three reasons: (1) climatic forcing is not strictly harmonic, (2) at any given season, soil strata are hardly ever homogeneous in depth, and (3) soil surface structure varies significantly from month to month due to changes in soil moisture, frost occurrence, snow accumulation, and phenological cycles. While the first two defects can be corrected by considering all harmonics of a Fourier expansion and the use of improved models of thermal diffusion for inhomogeneous media, there is no suitable and satisfactory extension of classical theory to conduction in cases of time-dependent coefficients; Lettau (1951). Therefore, in a significant departure from classical theory, we start from Eq. (11) and let the parameters r^*S and t^*S vary in accordance with actual climatic conditions, from suitably lowered values during months with snowcover, to highest values during early summer when soil moisture is high but vegetation cover not yet developed. A transform of Eq. (11), which parallels exactly the above discussed derivation of Eq. (18) from Eq. (16), will yield an equation of soil surface temperature in response to forcing by any prescribed variation in S-values, solvable by direct methods of numerical forward integration of Eq. (10). However, as in the case of surface albedo a^*, or the parameters of evapo-climatonomy, the truly realistic month-to-month variations of r^*S and t^*S can only be determined by representative measurements of soil heat flux and surface temperature variations, which means by a climatonomic "calibration" of the region.

The remaining five parameters (r^*Q, t^*Q, t^*LWD, $\underline{A}^*$, and h^*Q) are similarly determined by considering the nature of the physical processes involved. For example, assuming a linear increase of eddy diffusivity with height, convection theory predicts that r^*Q should be proportional to the logarithm of frequency (ω) while conduction theory predicts for r^*S a relatively strong effect due to the factor $\sqrt{\omega}$ in Eq. (23). In atmospheric surface layer theory an important scaling parameter is the dimensionless form $N = u^*/z_0\omega$, with $u^* = $ shearing velocity and $z_0 = $ aerodynamic roughness length of the ground surface. Then,

$$r^*Q = c_p\rho u^*(n_1 + n_2 \log N), \qquad (24)$$

where $c_p\rho$ (cal cm^{-3} °K^{-1}) = volumetric heat capacity of the air of density ρ, and n_1, n_2 are numerical factors of semi-empirical nature; reference can be made to Lettau (1951, 1952). In a first order approximation, u^* will vary in direct proportion to anemometric wind speed recordings at a representative climate station, but the factor of proportionality will change with thermal stratification and, thus, with heat flux Q.

Normally, t^*Q will be smaller than t^*S but, again, the effects of thermal stratification and subsequent modifications of the vertical gradient of eddy diffusivity will cause significant month-to-month variations, so that t^*Q may become nearly as large as t^*S in late summer. Delay-time parameters t^*S as well as t^*Q will remain positive which is consistent with flux as "leader" and surface temperature as "follower." However, the delay-time parameter t^*LWD can, and normally will, be negative, because surface temperature passes through maximum and minimum phases ahead of counter-radiation. Namely, LWD-flux depends not only on air temperature aloft, but also on moisture, and the annual course of both will be delayed in comparison with the annual course of surface temperature. The lack of generalized models of submedium conduction as well as atmospheric convection and diffusion forces us to determine the parameters for a given region by climatonomic calibration. This involves comparing model outputs obtained with selected sets of parameters with observations of measureable fluxes, and then adjusting parameters accordingly. Such a

calibration is also needed for the last parameter h^*Q. Atmospheric surface layer theory would predict that in a first order approximation

$$h^*Q = (ku^*c_p\rho)^{-1} \log_e(1 + z/z_0), \qquad (25)$$

where u^*, $c_p\rho$ and z_0 are the same as in Eq. (24), k = Karman's constant = 0.4, and z = height of thermometer exposure above the ground ($z = 180$ to 200 cm for routine observations at standard stations). Here again, corrections may be necessary due to thermal stratification effects. If $c_p\rho = 3 \cdot 10^{-4}$ cal cm^{-3} °K^{-1}, $u^* = 20$ cm sec$^{-1} = 173 \cdot 10^4$ cm day^{-1}, the parameter h^*Q will be between 0.01 and 0.02 deg ly^{-1} day^{-1}, if z_0 is of the order of 1 to 10 cm.

The atmospheric "greenhouse" effect—see Sellers (1965) is expressed by the individual Angstroem ratio, at any time t, $A^* = (LWU + LWD)/LWU$ which varies in accordance with atmospheric water vapor content, temperature and density of cloud layers, haze, and aerosol aloft. The climatonomic method for the iterative determination of the base value $\underline{A}^*$ will be described in the following section.

8. Thermo-climatonomy; operational application

Operational programs for shortwave-, evapo-, and thermo-climatonomy were developed by Peter Guetter of the Department of Meteorology at the University of Wisconsin. Each program requires only seconds of computer time on the university's UNIVAC 1110. Self-explanatory results obtained with the aid of the thermo-climatonomy program for the three Canadian regions are summarized in Tables 7 to 11.

TABLE 7. Monthly values of forcing function $F^{(III)} = F^{(II)} - E$, (ly/day), and parameters of thermo-climatonomy for an Open Forest (OF) and a Closed Forest (CF) (same regions as specified in Table 3): Delay-time (months) for counter radiation (t^*LWD), soil conduction (t^*S), and atmospheric convection (t^*Q); respondances (ly/day per deg K) for soil conduction (r^*S), and atmospheric convection (r^*Q); also: calculated temperature (°C) at climatic station level $T(2)$ and its difference δT from observed 5-year averages. Iterative determination yielded $\underline{A}^*$ base values of 0.2362 for (OF) and 0.2748 for (CF).

		Jan	Feb	Mar	Apr	May	Jun	Jul	Aug	Sep	Oct	Nov	Dec	Ann
$F^{(III)}$	OF	13	23	88	203	294	330	350	242	120	56	22	11	146
	CF	43	92	177	266	383	385	346	274	160	98	49	28	192
t^*LWD	OF	−0.22	−0.10	−0.46	−0.92	−1.16	−0.70	−0.68	−0.68	−0.86	−0.68	−0.48	−0.42	−0.61
	CF	−0.40	−0.20	−1.00	−1.60	−2.20	−1.40	−1.20	−1.60	−1.40	−1.20	−0.80	−0.60	−1.13
t^*S	OF	1.60	1.60	1.60	1.60	1.88	1.91	1.91	1.91	1.91	1.86	1.60	1.60	1.75
	CF	1.80	1.80	1.80	1.84	1.91	1.91	1.91	1.91	1.91	1.91	1.82	1.80	1.86
t^*Q	OF	0.20	0.20	0.20	0.30	0.80	1.20	1.60	1.70	1.80	1.20	0.60	0.30	0.84
	CF	0.20	0.20	0.20	0.00	0.50	0.90	0.60	0.50	0.90	0.70	0.50	0.40	0.48
r^*S	OF	0.48	0.46	0.44	0.42	0.48	0.70	0.64	0.63	0.63	0.63	0.60	0.55	0.56
	CF	0.52	0.50	0.45	0.45	0.62	0.62	0.62	0.62	0.62	0.62	0.58	0.54	0.56
r^*Q	OF	3.2	3.3	3.4	4.0	4.2	4.8	5.5	6.0	6.2	5.8	3.8	3.2	4.5
	CF	2.2	1.8	1.4	3.6	4.9	5.2	4.8	5.1	3.4	2.6	2.3	2.2	3.3
$T(2)$	OF	−26.8	−26.7	−21.5	−11.9	−2.1	5.7	10.5	11.1	6.3	−1.8	−12.5	−22.1	−7.7
	CF	−24.8	−22.5	−15.0	−5.8	3.2	10.3	14.9	14.6	10.0	2.2	−8.2	−18.8	−3.3
δT	OF	−0.7	0.2	1.1	1.1	0.8	0.0	1.5	−0.3	−0.7	−0.0	−1.6	−1.3	0.01
	CF	−0.5	1.7	−0.0	1.6	1.8	1.5	0.8	0.1	−1.7	−0.5	−1.8	−1.2	0.16

TABLE 8. Monthly values of forcing function $F^{III} = F^{II} - E$ (ly/day), and parameters of thermo-climatonomy for the Tundra region near Baker Lake, Canada. Delay-times (months) for counter radiation (t^*LWD), soil conduction (t^*S), and atmospheric convection (t^*Q); also respondances (ly/day per °K) for soil conduction (r^*S) and atmospheric convection (r^*Q). Iterative determination of the base value for the Angstroem Ratio yielded $\underline{A}^* = 0.2309$.

Month	$F^{(III)}$	t^*LWD	t^*S	t^*Q	r^*S	r^*Q
Jan	4	−0.33	1.40	0.30	0.30	3.2
Feb	15	−0.67	1.50	0.30	0.25	3.4
Mar	41	−0.28	1.63	0.15	0.30	4.6
Apr	96	0.04	1.72	0.15	0.38	4.6
May	171	0.26	1.81	0.60	0.45	3.4
Jun	199	−0.66	1.88	1.05	0.55	3.6
Jul	331	−1.94	1.91	1.40	0.58	3.8
Aug	243	−0.06	1.91	1.73	0.58	5.0
Sep	122	−0.20	1.87	1.80	0.55	5.4
Oct	35	−0.63	1.80	1.50	0.54	5.2
Nov	7	−0.45	1.78	1.00	0.53	4.8
Dec	3	−0.05	1.60	0.50	0.35	3.5

The delay-time parameters of thermo-climatonomy (see Tables 7 and 8) are relatively small. This makes the calendar year relatively large on the "natural" time-scale of Eq. (17). Using Δt steps which are smaller than one month would have helped to keep truncation errors within tolerable limits, but the calendar month has advantages as basic time increment. Therefore, we preferred a direct numerical integration of the differential equation (16) rather than using Eq. (18).

In contrast to thermo-climatonomy, the t^* values of evapo-climatonomy (see Table 4) are relatively large on the average. This implies that the "natural" time-scale as defined by Eq. (7) is relatively small for the calendar year and that, therefore, the factor $e^{+\tau}$ in the integrand of Eq. (9) grows relatively slowly. Under such conditions, numerical integration using the simple trapezoidal rule can be performed without significant truncation errors.

Regardless of the technique, our thermo-climatonomy program has two options once the set of monthly values for forcing $F^{(III)}$ and parameters (delay-times t^* for LWD, S and Q, as well as respondances r^* for S and Q; see Table 7 or 8) have been determined. The first option is to prescribe the annual mean base temperature whereupon the computer carries out an iterative search for that value of the base-Angstroem ratio which satisfies (within stated error tolerances) the condition of climatic stability with the given set of parameters. This procedure is most suitable for the climatonomical "calibration" of the region. Namely, for each set of parameters monthly mean calculated temperatures can be compared with observed values, and the parameters may be gradually adjusted to produce by repeated computer runs not only the observed month-to-month changes of temperature but also those of net radiation or other fluxes. The parameter values must, of course, also conform to the physical conditions of the regional climate. In Table 8, for example, the values of soil respondance reflect the duration of snowcover and its insulating effect, while the two maxima of air-respondance in spring and autumn conform to the double maximum of annual variation of wind speed in the region.

The alternate option is to prescribe the base value of the Angstroem ratio whereupon the program carries out an iterative search for the value of the annual mean base temperature (absolute scale because the Stefan-Boltzmann law is used) which satisfies the condition of climatic stability with the given set of parameters in a truly climatonomic procedure.

Results of flux determinations are summarized in Tables 9 and 10. In view of the climatic stability requirements, a sufficient condition for zero values of the annual means ($\bar{S}$ as well as $\bar{Q}$) would be constancy of coefficients. A positive value of $\bar{Q}$, for example, is generated (in Eq. 12) when the r^*Q-values are relatively small for the months of negative $(T - \underline{T})$. This is, indeed, the case even though Q is positive for only five months (see Table 10), and negative for seven months. However, in the Tundra climate $\bar{Q}$ is negative (see Table 9) partly because the summer values of r^*Q (see Table 8) show a relative minimum, and the period of positive Q is reduced to four months. We believe that the slightly positive values of $\bar{S}$ and their increase with geographic latitude were generated because a small but measurable amount of heat is exported downstream following spring-melt. In poleward flowing rivers (McKenzie) snow-melt may occur earlier upstream and heat exported as runoff may help to melt the snowpack in the estuary region.

Delay-time parameters are positive for Q- and S-fluxes consistent with "leading" the annual course

TABLE 9. Thermo-climatonomy of the Canadian Tundra near Baker Lake. Model-generated monthly averages of temperature [$T(0)$ at ground level, $T(2)$ at climatic station level, °C] and heat fluxes in ly/day: S into soil, Q into air, LWU = longwave radiation emitted by the ground, LWD = downward (counter-) longwave radiation; R = net radiation = $F^{(II)} - LWU - LWD$.

Month	$T(0)$	$T(2)$	S	Q	LWU	LWD	R
Jan	−34.0	−33.2	−7	−70	357	−276	−77.1
Feb	−33.5	−32.7	−5	−71	361	−271	−73.4
Mar	−28.2	−27.5	−1	−68	404	−295	−62.1
Apr	−18.1	−17.9	5	−19	488	−378	−1.8
May	−6.5	−6.9	12	43	583	−468	80.6
Jun	3.8	2.8	18	90	668	−477	190.4
Jul	10.0	8.8	17	104	719	−508	182.5
Aug	9.6	8.8	8	72	716	−552	109.4
Sep	2.6	2.7	−2	−16	658	−518	−0.4
Oct	−7.3	−6.7	−7	−52	577	−483	−48.7
Nov	−17.0	−16.3	−12	−69	497	−409	−78.5
Dec	−27.8	−26.9	−12	−75	408	−318	−87.5
Average	−12.2	−12.1	1.3	−10.8	536	413	−11.1

Monthly Angstroem ratios can have an annual average, $[(LWU + LWD)/LWD]$, which may differ from the ratio calculated using annual means, $(\overline{LWU} + \overline{LWD})/(\overline{LWU}) = 0.2295$ in Table 9, which in turn is not the same as the base value $\underline{A}^* = 0.2309$ employed to generate the LW-data for the tundra.

TABLE 10. Thermo-climatonomy of an Open Forest (OF) region and a Closed Forest (CF) region (as specified in Table 3). Model-generated averages of heat fluxes (ly/day): S into soil, Q into air, LWU = longwave radiation emitted by the ground, LWD = downward (counter-) longwave radiation; R = net radiation = $F^{(II)} - LWU - LWD$.

		Jan	Feb	Mar	Apr	May	Jun	Jul	Aug	Sep	Oct	Nov	Dec	Ann
S	OF	−11	−8	−0	6	12	20	17	7	−1	−8	−15	−15	0.4
	CF	−14	−3	1	7	15	17	15	8	−0	−8	−16	−18	0.3
Q	OF	−66	−65	−44	−3	60	112	141	77	1	−38	−49	−57	6
	CF	−50	−33	−15	−10	56	106	98	87	24	−3	−26	−44	16
LWU	OF	399	400	448	538	631	704	749	746	695	620	526	441	575
	CF	408	431	500	583	670	740	780	776	730	656	561	463	608
LWD	OF	−308	−304	−316	−338	−409	−505	−577	−589	−576	−518	−440	−358	−435
	CF	−302	−303	−310	−315	−358	−477	−546	−596	−594	−548	−470	−373	−433
R	OF	−73	−57	−19	46	143	235	246	168	44	−19	−52	−69	49
	CF	−55	−20	16	45	118	209	209	165	62	8	−29	−52	56

of temperature. As outlined at the end of Section 7, the delay-time parameter for longwave counter-radiation is negative. An interesting exception occurs in April and May for the tundra region (see Table 8). The LWD-values listed on Table 9 reveal a very strong rise from March to the end of May followed by a much weaker rise in June and July. The earlier steep rise is probably caused by warm-air advection aloft, while in June the "indigenous" factors prevail. Let us emphasize that the results presented here are tentative and represent a "pilot study" for the testing of climatonomy. To facilitate a judgment of the tentative results, we decided to present the data in tabulated form rather than graphically.

A numerical experiment in climatonomy is exemplified in Table 11. We used the program to perform the iterative search for monthly temperatures for certain parameter modifications. The results are self-explanatory.

A formal "across-the-board" change of Angstroem or evaporivity parameters affects all monthly temperatures in the same sense. A modification of the atmospheric respondance intensifies the annual amplitude without significant change of the annual average. In the last experiment we assumed that the beginning of snow-melt was delayed by one month by using the actual February to June albedo-values for the months March to July, with a corresponding

adjustment for the other snowcover-dependent factors, but leaving counter-radiation unchanged. Such an extension of snowcover would have an extremely strong effect on summer temperatures in the Tundra due to the loss of global radiation during the height of the summer. The results summarized in Table 11 are to be taken as a guide for the explanation of climatic "oases." Let us quote from the experiences of Pryde (1973). ". . . the Baychimo Harbour region, about 80 mi north of Bathurst Inlet (66.8°N, 108.0°W), seemed to be 8 to 10°F warmer than the Perry Island region, (67.7°N, 102.5°W) and accordingly, had a much richer vegetation and wildlife. It was too far north for trees, of course, but some of the willow bushes along the creeks were 6 to 7 feet high and quite dense . . . grass far more lush than anywhere I had seen in the Arctic. Bees, butterflies, some huge moths, and even grasshoppers could be seen . . . ." Unfortunately, Pryde does not specify the suborder of "saltatoria" he encountered at Baychimo Harbor but nowhere else in the Arctic. If this estimate of excess above "normal" temperatures should be confirmed we suggest (with reference to Table 11) that climatonomy could explain this arctic "oasis" as effect of topographical features, possibly the steep cliffs and deep channels, mentioned by Pryde. The cliffsides may favor albedo lowering in spring, the channels, runoff increase at the expense of evaporation.

TABLE 11. Numerical experiments of thermo-climatonomy. Monthly temperatures (T, °C, from Table 9) for the Tundra region calculated as $T + \Delta T$ as effect of parameter variations: $\Delta_1 T$ if atmospheric "greenhouse effect" is enhanced by decrease of Base-Angstroem-Ratio by 2.5%; $\Delta_2 T$ if psychrometric cooling is reduced by decreasing all E-values by 10% (amounting to increased $F^{(III)}$; $\Delta_3 T$ if mixing of the lower atmosphere is reduced by decreasing all respondances by 10%; $\Delta_4 T$ if snowcover disappears one month later (combined effects of albedo, soil insulation, and evaporation changes).

Month	Jan	Feb	Mar	Apr	May	Jun	Jul	Aug	Sep	Oct	Nov	Dec	Ave
T	−33	−33	−28	−18	−7	3	9	9	3	−7	−16	−27	−12.1
$\Delta_1 T$	1.6	1.6	1.6	1.7	1.7	1.7	1.7	1.7	1.7	1.7	1.8	1.7	1.7
$\Delta_2 T$	0.8	1.0	1.0	1.2	1.2	1.4	1.8	1.6	1.4	1.2	1.2	1.0	1.2
$\Delta_3 T$	−1.5	−1.4	−1.2	−0.5	0.6	1.2	1.5	1.4	0.9	0.2	−0.4	−1.1	0.0
$\Delta_4 T$	−0.9	−1.6	−1.3	−0.8	−2.4	−8.6	−8.8	−3.4	−2.0	−1.4	−1.2	−1.3	−2.8

Acknowledgments. This research was supported by Grant GA-10651X, Section on Atmospheric Science, National Science Foundation.

REFERENCES

Climatic Maps of Canada, 1968: Department of Transport, Toronto, Ontario.

The Climate of Canada, 1962. Meteor. Branch Air Services. Department of Transport, Toronto, Ontario.

Flohn, H., 1954: *Klima und Witterung in Mitteleuropa.* Hirzel Verlag, Stuttgart, 214 pages.

Glossary of Meteorology, 1959: (R. E. Huschke, Ed.) Amer. Metero. Soc., Boston, Mass. 638 pages.

Hare, F. K., and J. C. Ritchie, 1972: The Boreal bioclimates. *Geographical Review,* **62**, 333–365.

Hare, F. K., and J. E. Hay, 1973: The climate of Canada and Alaska. *World Survey of Climatology* (H. Landsberg, Ed.) Vol. **11** (Climates of North America).

Landsberg, H. E., 1957: Review of climatology 1951–1955. *Meteor. Monographs* Amer. Met. Soc., **3**, 1–43.

Lettau, H. H., 1951: Theory of surface temperature and heat transfer oscillations near a level ground surface. *Transact. Am. Geoph. Union,* **32**, 189–195.

Lettau, H. H., 1952: Synthetische klimatologie. *Berichte d. Deutschen Wetterdienstes* Nr., **38**, 127–136.

Lettau, H., and K. Lettau, 1969: Shortwave radiation climatonomy. *Tellus,* **21**, 208–222.

Lettau, H. H., and M. W. Baradas, 1973: Evapotranspiration climatonomy II: Refinement of parameterization, exemplified by application to the Mabacan river watershed. *Month. Weather Reveiw,* **101**, 636–649.

Pryde, D., 1973: *Nunaga—Ten Years of Eskimo Life.* Bantam Books Inc., New York, N. Y., 309 pp.

Raschke, E., and W. R. Bandeen, 1970: The radiation balance of the planet earth from radiation measurements of the satellite Nimbus II. *Journal Appl. Meteorol.,* **9**, 215–238.

Schwerdtfeger, W., 1970: The climate of the Antarctic. *World Survey of Climatology* (H. Landsberg, Ed.), Vol. **14**, Chapter 4.

Sellers, W. D., 1965: *Physical Climatology.* University of Chicago Press, 272 pages.

SMIC-Report, 1971: *Report of the Study of Man's Impact on Climate.* (C. L. Wilson, Ed.), MIT Press, Cambridge, 308 pp.

Suomi, V. E., and T. H. VonderHaar, 1972: Reply to comments on measurements of the earth's radiation budget from satellites during a five-year period. *J. Atm. Sciences,* **29**, 602–607.

Vowinckel, E., and S. Orvig, 1970: The climate of the north polar basin. *World Survey of Climatology,* (H. Landsberg, Ed.), Vol. **14**, Chapter 3.

Vowinckel E., and S. Orvig, 1972: *EBBA—An Energy Budget Programme.* Arctic Meteor. Res. Group, Publ. No. 105. McGill Univ., Montreal, Quebec, Canada.

A Model of the Effect of Tundra Vegetation on Soil Temperatures

EDWARD NG AND PHILIP C. MILLER

Department of Biology, San Diego State University, San Diego, Calif. 92115

Abstract

In permafrost areas, the rate and depth of thaw is affected by the vegetation and the soil organic mat. Models of soil temperature, canopy radiation, and turbulent transfer were combined to study vegetation-soil temperature interactions. A preliminary validation was carried out with data from the summer of 1970. Agreement between observed and predicted depths of thaw were good. Sensitivity analysis was also conducted. More recently, better models of canopy radiation and turbulent transfer have been substituted. Data collected during the summer of 1973 will enable a more rigorous validation.

1. Introduction

The purpose of this paper is to describe a simulation model of the vegetation canopy-soil temperature interactions and its preliminary validation. In the literature on the tundra, the effect of the physical environment on biological activity is often cited. Low temperatures, low solar radiation, high wind velocities and low nutrients have been said to restrain plant growth and development, soil fauna activity, and microbial decomposition of organic material. In turn the vegetation affects the local physical environment. The rate and depth of thaw, integrators of various physical

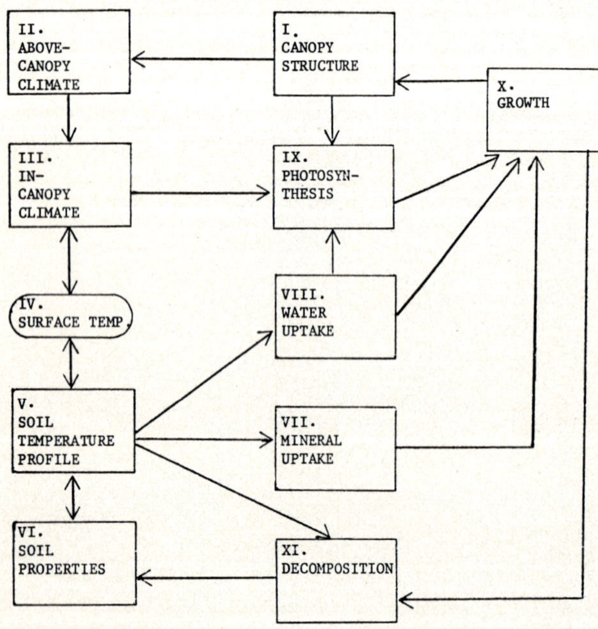

FIG. 1. Block diagram showing the interactions between different sets of processes and submodels involved in the vegetation–soil thermal regime.

factors, have been correlated with vegetative cover (Drury, 1956; Dingman and Koutz, 1974). Removal or modification of the vegetation or soil organic material affects the thaw depths (Corbet, 1972; Brown *et al.*, 1969). These observations suggest interactions between the vegetation, the microclimate, and the soil thermal regime.

The vegetation-soil system modeled is bounded by the top of the vegetation canopy and by the depth of zero annual soil temperature amplitude. Occurring in the system is a complicated set of interactions, illustrated in simplified form in Fig. 1. The vegetation modifies the climatic parameters at the surface (in contrast to those above the canopy) by intercepting and reflecting solar and infrared radiation, by emitting infrared radiation, by changing the air temperature and humidity through convection and transpiration, and by diminishing turbulent transfer. The surface temperature is affected by the canopy microclimate, as defined by the profiles of solar and infrared radiation, air temperature, vapor density, and turbulent transfer, and by the existing soil temperature profiles. The soil temperature profile is determined by the surface temperature and soil properties and influences (1) the soil properties, (2) mineral uptake, and (3) water uptake by plants. Mineral uptake affects growth directly and water uptake affects growth directly and through its influence on photosynthesis. Growth changes the canopy structure, affecting the canopy microclimate, which then affects photosynthesis. The death and subsequent decomposition of leaves, stems, and roots affects the soil properties of thermal conductivity, heat capacity, and soil moisture retention. These interactions are nonlinear and occur simultaneously and continuously, forming the vegetation-soil system.

The vegetation-soil modeling activities have been

centered on I through VI of Fig. 1. In our preliminary effort, models of canopy radiation and turbulent transfer were combined with a soil temperature model. This combined model was tested using input and validation data from the U. S. Tundra Biome IBP sites near Point Barrow, Alaska. Since then, more sophisticated canopy radiation and turbulent transfer models have been substituted to develop a more realistic model. Input and validation data for this second model were collected in the summer of 1973 at Point Barrow, with support from the U. S. Tundra Biome and CRREL. This paper will describe the first model, present output from it, and describe conceptual and data improvements incorporated into the second model.

2. Description of the model

Soil temperature profile

The soil temperature model was adapted from a model by Nakano and Brown (1972). It is an implicit finite differences solution to the one dimensional heat conduction equation with phase change:

$$F\frac{\partial T}{\partial t} = \frac{\partial}{\partial z}\left(K\frac{\partial T}{\partial z}\right), \tag{1}$$

where T is the temperature (°C); z is the vertical distance from the surface (cm); K is the thermal conductivity (cal cm^{-2} min^{-1} °C^{-1}); t is time (min); F is defined by

$$F = C - L\frac{dG'}{dT} \tag{2}$$

where C is the volumetric heat capacity (cal cm^{-3} °C^{-1}); L is the latent heat of fusion (cal g^{-1}); and G' is the ice content of the soil (g cm^{-3}).

The problem is solved in a manner which allows for a non-constant soil regime: i.e., the soil properties are allowed to change with depth and time. Non-equal space increments are incorporated, so that two-thirds of the 313 nodes in the solution mesh are in the upper 40 cm. This allows for better accounting in the surface layers where the greatest temperature changes occur. Solving Eq. 1 requires an initial soil temperature profile, the surface temperature, and function relating thermal conductivity, heat capacity, and unfrozen water content to soil temperature and water content. New soil temperature profiles are produced as output.

Surface temperature

The surface temperature is solved for as the equilibrium temperature in the surface energy budget:

$$S_{abs} + IR_{abs} = IR_s + C + LE + G, \tag{3}$$

where S_{abs} is the solar radiation absorbed by the soil surface; IR_{abs} is the infrared radiation absorbed by the surface; IR_s is the infrared radiation emitted by the surface; C is the energy exchanged by the surface by convection; LE is the surface energy exchange by evaporation; and G is the energy conducted from the surface. All of the preceeding are in cal cm^{-2} min^{-1}. The surface is defined as the level at which conduction is the main mechanism of heat transport downward, and turbulent transfer and radiation are the main mechanisms of transport upward. It may be the top of the moss layer, organic mat or mineral soil.

Canopy microclimate

In the first model the vegetation canopy was treated as a single layer of leaves. The affect of the canopy on the terms in Eq. 3 were evaluated as follows:

The solar radiation reaching the surface under the canopy and absorbed (S_{abs}) was related to the solar radiation above by a negative exponential (Beer's law) relationship. For computational purposes, the solar radiation at the top of the canopy was assumed to be diffuse. Then,

$$S_{abs} = (1-r)S\exp(-K_sF) \tag{4}$$

where r is the albedo of the surface; S is the total solar radiation above the canopy (cal cm^{-2} min^{-1}); K_s is the extinction coefficient for diffuse solar radiation; and F is the total live and dead leaf area index.

The infrared radiation absorbed by the surface (IR_{abs}) is the sum of radiation from three sources: from the sky above the canopy, from the leaves of the canopy, and that emitted by the ground and reflected back downwards by the leaves. Thus,

$$IR_{abs} = \epsilon_g IR_{sky}\exp(-K_sF) + \epsilon_g IR_1$$
$$\times[1-\exp(-K_sF)] + \epsilon_g(1-\epsilon_1)IR_s \tag{5}$$

where ϵ_g is the emittance of the ground surface; ϵ_1 is the emittance of the leaves; IR_{sky} is the infrared radiation from the sky above the canopy (cal cm^{-2} min^{-1}); and IR_1 is the infrared radiation from the leaves (cal cm^{-2} min^{-1}).

Assuming that the air temperature in the canopy is a good approximation to the average leaf temperature on a daily basis, then,

$$IR_1 = \epsilon_1\sigma(T_a+273)^4 \tag{6}$$

where σ is the Stefan-Boltzmann constant and T_a is the air temperature in °C.

The infrared radiation emitted by the ground surface (IR_s) may be evaluated by:

$$IR_s = \epsilon_g\sigma(T_s+273)^4 \tag{7}$$

where T_s is the surface temperature in °C.

To enable solution, the equation for the radiation from the surface is rewritten in terms of the surface temperature and the canopy air temperature by using a first order Taylor series expansion:

$$IR_s = \epsilon_s \sigma (T_a + 273)^4 + 4\epsilon_s \sigma (T_a + 273)^3 (T_s - T_a) \quad (8)$$

where T_a is the air temperature in the canopy at a reference height (°C).

The convectional heat exchange by the surface (C) was assumed to occur by turbulent transfer of heat from the surface. The turbulent transfer coefficient was diminished exponentially with the leaf area index. Then:

$$C = K_h \exp(-K_k F) c_p \rho_a (T_s - T_a) / \Delta h \quad (9)$$

where K_h is the turbulent transfer coefficient for heat above the canopy (cm^2 sec^{-1}); K_k is the extinction coefficient for the turbulent transfer coefficient; c_p is the specific heat of air (cal g^{-1} °C^{-1}); ρ_a is the density of air (g cm^{-3}); Δh is the reference height at which T_a is measured.

The heat exchange by the surface due to evaporation (LE) is assumed to occur by turbulent transfer and is assumed to be affected by the soil moisture availability near the surface:

$$LE = K_c L(\rho_s(T_s) - \rho_w)/\Delta h \quad (10)$$

where K_c is a transfer coefficient which is a function of the canopy air resistance, a soil resistance to water vapor diffusion, and the canopy height. The canopy air resistance was defined by $r_c = (H/K_h) \exp(-K_k F)$, where H is the height of the canopy (cm). The canopy air resistance and the soil resistance were assumed to be in series. $\rho_s(T_s)$ is the saturated vapor density at the temperature of the evaporating surface. ρ_w is the actual vapor density of the air in the canopy measured Δh cm above the soil surface.

Eq. 10 is rewritten in terms of T_s and T_a as

$$LE = \frac{K_c L}{\Delta h} \left[(\rho_s(T_a) - \rho_w) + (T_s - T_a) \frac{d\rho}{dT}\Big|_{T_a} \right] \quad (11)$$

where $d\rho/dT$ is the first derivative of the saturated vapor density vs. temperature curve.

The heat conducted toward the surface (G) is calculated by:

$$G = K(T_s - T_z)/\Delta z, \quad (12)$$

where K is the thermal conductivity (cal cm^{-2} min^{-1}); T_z is the soil temperature at Δz cm below the surface.

Combining and rewriting Eqs. 3, 4, 6–10 and 12, we can solve explicitly for the surface temperature. Then the seasonal course of soil temperatures can be predicted by using the soil temperature model and the canopy models to predict the surface temperature. The necessary input data include the soil properties, an initial soil temperature profile, and the seasonal course of leaf area index, solar radiation, sky infrared radiation, air temperature, turbulent transfer coefficients and vapor density. The flow of computation is as follows:

(1) The soil temperature profile at time t_n and the microclimate input variable at time t_{n+1} is known. The soil surface temperature at t_{n+1} is needed in order to solve for the temperature profile at time t_{n+1}.

(2) Approximate the surface temperature at t_{n+1} with that at t.

(3) Using this approximation, a new surface temperature is calculated with the canopy models.

(4) This new surface temperature is averaged with the preceeding one and a new soil temperature profile is calculated using the soil temperature model.

(5) (3) and (4) are repeated until the surface temperature converges sufficiently.

(6) Following convergence, advance one time step and start at (1) again.

3. Preliminary validation and sensitivity

The preliminary validation was carried out using data from IBP sites near Barrow, Alaska, for the summer of 1970. It was necessary to use several data sources to obtain all the needed input values. Those variables for which no field data were available estimated as reasonably as possible. The seasonal course of thaw for site 2 was chosen for simulation (CRREL, unpublished data). Five observed seasonal courses of soil thaw were available for comparison. Leaf area data was obtained for site 2 from Tieszen and Dennis (1970). The necessary inputs for the soil temperature model were obtained from Nakano and Brown (1972). Radiation, humidity, and air temperature data for 1970 were obtained from Weather Bureau data for Point Barrow Village (ESSA, 1970). Infrared radiation from the sky was assumed to be 0.40 cal cm^{-2} min^{-1} throughout the season. Canopy air temperature at 5 cm height was assumed equal to air temperature above the canopy plus 2 C.

The combined model was run at 10 day intervals from June 25 to August 13. The agreement between the predicted and observed thaw depths was generally good (Table 1).

Sensitivity of the model to a particular input variable was determined by simulating the seasonal course of thaw depth while varying one input variable at a time. In a sensitivity run, the particular variable was changed by adding or subtracting 50% of that variable to the value used in a control run. Sensitivity

TABLE 1. Measured and predicted depths of thaw through July and August 1970. The means ($\bar{x}$) and standard errors (S.E.) for measurements on five control plants (206, 207, 208, 209, 210) are given.

10 day period ending	July			August		
	4	14	24	3	13	23
$\bar{x}$	17.4	21.6	23.4	25.3	26.2	26.3
S.E.	0.5	0.4	0.4	0.2	0.3	0.3
predicted	19	22	25	26	26	27

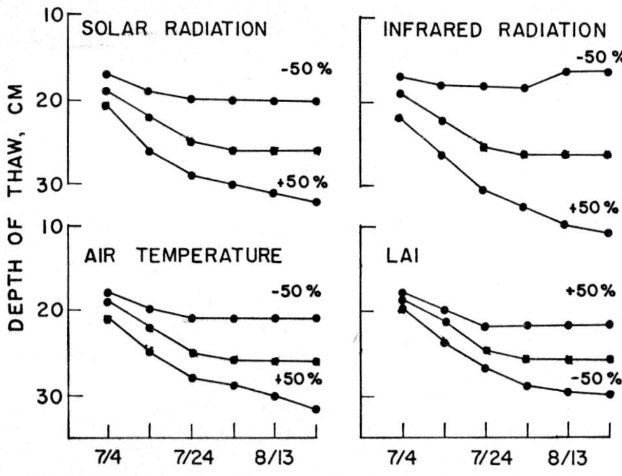

FIG. 2. Results of simulations of the effects of variations in solar radiation, infrared radiation, air temperature, and leaf area index (LAI) on the seasonal course of the depths of thaw for July and August 1970.

runs for solar and infrared radiation at the top of the canopy, air temperature, and leaf area index are shown in Fig. 2. Comparison with the control run, the center curve, shows that by the end of the season, thaw depth differed by 10 cm due to an increase in the infrared radiation by 50%, by 5.5 cm due to an increase in the air temperature, and by 4 cm due to an increase in the leaf area index. Similar but opposite changes occurred when the test variable was decreased by 50%.

Though the agreement between predicted and observed thaw depths was good for Site 2, caution should be exercised since not all the input data were available from measurement for the simulations. A more rigor-

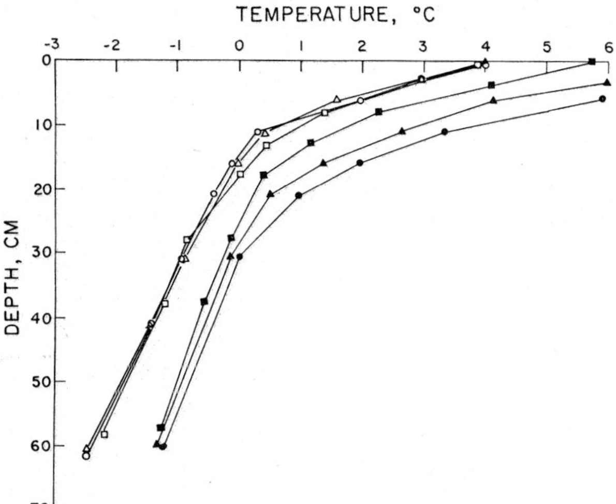

FIG. 3. Temperature profiles at solar time on 1973. ■ is the mulched plot, ▲ for the control plot, and ● for the clipped and cleared plot. Open symbols are for the profiles on July 30, 1973, shortly after treating. Closed symbols are for the profiles on July 30, 1973.

ous test of the model could be conducted if all input and validation data were measured for several plots for at least a season. This was the intent of work conducted at Barrow during the summer of 1973. Five plots, including three controls, one clipped and cleared, and one mulched plot, were instrumented. On each plot soil temperature, air temperature, net radiation, and vapor density were measured. At a central location, total solar radiation, diffuse solar radiation, and sky infrared radiation were measured above the canopy. Point frame measurements of leaf area index were made on nearby plots several times during the season. Preliminary analysis of the data showed that the field trends in comparing a control, the clipped and clear, and mulched plots, agreed qualitatively with the model output, that increased leaf area resulted in colder soil temperatures and shallower thaw depths, and that decreased leaf area resulted in a warmer profile and deeper thaw (Fig. 3).

In addition to collecting more complete input and validation data, improvements have also been made in the models. This was done by replacing the single-layer canopy radiation and turbulent transfer models with models which horizontally stratify the canopy. This allows convective, evaporational, and radiative heat exchanges among canopy layers, and between layers and the ground surface. This new combined model, besides being more realistic, also facilitates interfacing with a photosynthesis model.

In this newer radiation model (Miller, 1974), distinction is made between direct and diffuse solar radiation. Each layer has its own leaf area index, and can absorb direct solar radiation, diffuse solar radiation, reflected solar radiation from other layers or the ground, infrared from the sky, infrared from other layers or the ground, and reflected infrared. The downward reflection of solar radiation by leaves to the ground is a major energy source to the ground surface which was ignored previously.

The new canopy microclimate model, adapted from Waggoner and Reifsnyder (1968) and Waggoner *et al.* (1969), uses a potential and resistance network and a canopy energy budget to solve for the convectional and evaporational heat exchange by each layer. The leaf temperature and vapor density of each layer are also calculated. The temperature and vapor density above the canopy, the absorbed solar radiation by a level, the wind and diffusivity above the canopy, and leaf resistance values are necessary input data.

Reduction and analysis of the 1973 data are not yet complete. The data and a more detailed description of the models will be presented in a subsequent paper after more rigorous validation and sensitivity analyses can be completed.

Acknowledgments. This study was supported by the Cold Regions Research and Engineering Laboratory in cooperation with the U. S. Tundra Biome, I.B.P.

We thank Mrs. Patsy Miller, Mr. Bruce Lawrence, Mr. John Hom and personnel at the Naval Arctic Research Laboratory for their help in the field work in 1973.

REFERENCES

Brown, J., W. Rickard and D. Vietor, 1969: The effects of disturbance on permafrost terrain. U. S. Army Cold Regions and Research Engineering Laboratory (USA CRREL) Spec. Rep. **138**, 13 pp.

Corbet, P. S., 1972: The microclimate of arctic plants and animals in land and in fresh water. Acta Arct., **18**, 1–43.

Dingman, S. L., and F. R. Koutz, 1974: Relations among vegetation, permafrost, and potential insolation in central Alaska. Arctic and Alpine Res., **6**, 37–47.

Drury, W. H., 1956: Bog flats and physiographic processes in the upper Kuskokwim River Region, Alaska. Contr. No. 178, Gray Herb., Harvard University, 130 pp.

Environmental Science Services Administration, 1970: Local climatological data, Barrow, Alaska. U. S. Department of Commerce, Washington, D. C.

Miller, P. C., 1975: A model of radiation for mangrove canopies. (in prep.).

Nakano, N., and J. Brown, 1972: Mathematical modeling and validation of the thermal regimes in tundra soils, Barrow, Alaska. Arctic and Alpine Res., **4**, 19–38.

Tieszen, L., and J. Dennis, 1970: Primary terrestrial production and photosynthesis. In: *Tundra Biome Research in Alaska* (J. Brown and G. C. West, Eds.). The structure and function of cold dominated ecosystems. November, 1970, 29–35.

Waggoner, P. E., and W. E. Reifsnyder, 1968: Simulation of the temperature, humidity, and evaporation profiles in a leaf canopy. *J. Appl. Meteorl.*, **7**, 400–409.

Waggoner, P. E., G. M. Furnival and W. E. Reifsnyder, 1969: Simulation of the microclimate in a forest. Forest Sci., **15**, 37–45.

The Development of a Computer Model of the Annual Snow-Soil Thermal Regime in Arctic Tundra Terrain

CECIL W. GOODWIN AND SAM I. OUTCALT

Department of Geography, University of Michigan, Ann Arbor, Michigan

Abstract

A digital computer model has been developed which simulates the annual evolution of the thermal regime in snowcover and the near surface layers of Arctic soils. The model is a coupled equilibrium-temperature energy budget simulator forced by daily meteorological data. The surface energy budget and the thermal regime of the snow and soil are output. The simulator will eventually be used to approximate the effects of human surface modification and long-term weather trends on hydrologic and thermal-geomorphic evolutionary histories.

1. Introduction

Human modification and natural phenomena contribute to spatial and temporal variation in the annual evolution of temperatures in tundra snow and soil. It is of prime importance to understand the mechanisms which produce the observed variation and to assign that variation to human and background sources if efficient strategies to attenuate man's impact on Northern terrain are to be developed. Disturbances occur at towns, airfields and exploration sites due to the alteration of the thermal-radiative properties of the surface and even as a result of the increased aerodynamic roughness of the structures (Outcalt, 1972b). Heated buildings act as heat sources (Lachenbruch, 1957), and overland traffic, even by surface effect vehicles, may produce subtle alterations to the tundra surface. In addition, buildings, roads and snow fences change the spatial pattern of snow accumulation and, therefore, the pattern of snow and soil temperatures throughout the year.

In concept, temporal step disturbances produced by human activities are interacting with low-frequency background variation produced by climatic change, natural plant succession and geomorphic evolution. Thus, a necessary step in the analysis of human impact is the specification and documentation of the thermal impact produced by the modification of both the near surface thermal-radiative-aerodynamic properties and the pattern of snow accumulation.

Background

During the past two decades analytical solutions to estimate the effect of heated buildings (Lachenbruch, 1957) and road and airfield construction have provided considerable insight into the influence of man on permafrost terrain. These efforts include extremely sophisticated models of active layer evolution which include freeze-thaw effects (Nakano and Brown, 1971). However, all these model structures employ a surface or substrate thermal regime to force their solutions. Other analytical models have been employed to simulate the geomorphic evolution of features ranging in scale from icewedges to pingo hills (Lachenbruch, 1962; Mackay, 1963). These studies indicated the power of mathematical abstraction and as such constitute a major divergence from classical descriptive investigations of Northern terrain.

In nature the thermal regime of the snow or soil surface may be viewed explicitly as a response to the interaction of local weather and the geographically variable surface-substrate radiative, thermal and aerodynamic properties. Viewed in this perspective these models are forced by part of the general solution and cannot be used to study system-sensitivity to the alteration of surface properties. A more generalized model structure must therefore be employed which produces as output both surface-substrate thermal regimes and the surface energy transfer components in physically coupled solutions.

Early in the present decade permafrost researchers stated that the energy conservation approach, which yields coupled solutions for both the soil thermal and surface energy transfer regimes, must constitute a powerful analytical vehicle for the study of permafrost environments (Benninghoff, 1963; Brown, 1963). This, in historical perspective, is part of the wider recognition that the energy conservation (equilibrium temperature) formulation of the surface energy transfer problem is extremely generalized. It is now employed outside the engineering sciences to a wide spectrum of problems ranging from ecosystem analysis to the synthesis of the urban heat island effect (Gates, 1968; Myrup, 1969).

A new era in the study of North America permafrost terrain began with the decision of the Governments of the United States and Canada to exploit their natural gas and petroleum reserves along the Arctic Coast. This event focused attention upon the unique characteristics of the Tundra Ecosystem, where the soil thermal regime is strongly coupled to both geomorphologic and biologic succession. Equilibrium temperature methods have been recently employed to analyze the tundra-atmospheric interface and to simulate spatial variations in primary production processes within the plant canopy (Lord *et al.*, 1971; Miller and Tieszen, 1971).

2. The general scheme of equilibrium temperature simulation

A strategy has been developed which yields both surface energy transfer components and the snow-soil thermal regime in the form of coupled explicit time-dependent functions of local weather and the geographically variable radiative, thermal and aerodynamic properties of the surface (Outcalt, 1972a). The method is based on an equilibrium temperature formulation of the energy conservation rule.

$$R+S+H+L=0. \tag{1}$$

The components of surface energy transfer [net radiation (R), soil (S), sensible (H), and latent (L) heat flow] must have a zero sum across a surface. It follows that if atmospheric and soil properties and variables are all specified at an instant the equation can be written in a transcendental form as a function of surface temperature only. A numerical iterative search using a variation of the interval-halving algorithm is carried out on the energy conservation equation until the component sum is suitably close to zero. The surface temperature which balances the equation is termed the *equilibrium temperature*. Soil temperature phase lag and amplitude attenuation are introduced into the solution by relaxing the finite-difference form of the thermal diffusion equation prior to each equilibrium temperature search.

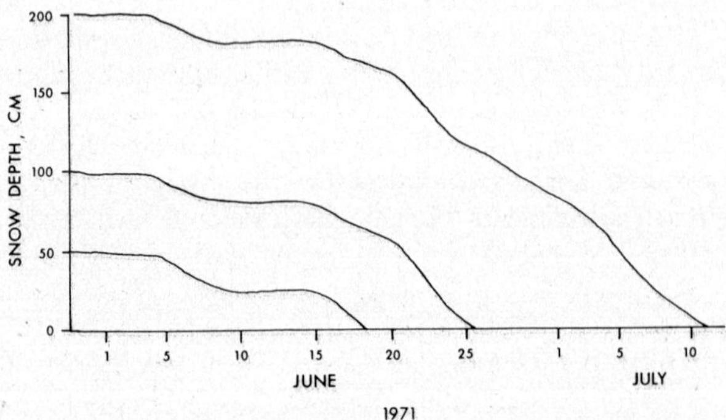

FIG. 1. Course of melt for initial accumulations of 50, 100 and 200 cm of snow.

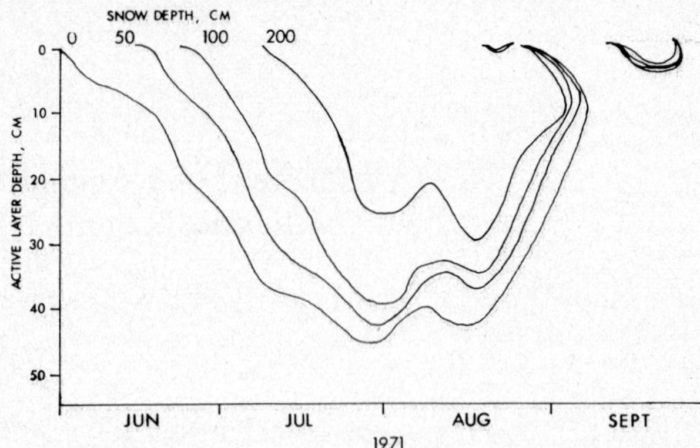

FIG. 2. Active layer evolution as a function of pre-melt snow accumulation.

Surface climate and micro-geomorphic features in frost and permafrost regions are physically coupled by fusion effects and their spatial-temporal variability. As one moves poleward or upward onto mountains, needle ice, seasonal soil heave and active layer effects produce distinctive microgeomorphological features ranging in spatial-temporal scale from pebble depressions resulting from diurnal needle ice growth and ablation to ice-wedge polygons produced by thermal contraction and frost heave during annual cycles in periglacial regions.

The small-scale high-frequency member of this continuum is the diurnal needle ice growth-ablation cycle. The daily phase and amplitude of this geomorphic process was successfully modeled using equilibrium temperature methods (Outcalt, 1971). This encouraged the extension of that methodology to the annual cycle in which the annual march of weather as modified by surface effects is employed to force coupled surface energy budget and snow-soil temperature solutions.

3. The structure of the tundra simulator

The following steps are performed in an annual simulation:

a. A 100 node snow and soil temperature computation vector is established. Spacing is set at 5 cm for the first 80 nodes and is then sequentially increased by a factor of 1.25 throughout the remaining nodes. This operation produces an expanding node spacing which extends the total vector depth well below the annual damping depth to approximately 30 meters. The soil surface is located at node 50 allowing the simulation of up to 245 cm of snowcover.

b. Daily values of incoming solar radiation, cloud cover, air temperature, relative humidity, wind velocity, pressure, and snowfall are read in.

c. The relative snowcover (compared to the maximum value), emergent vegetation height, and length of growing season are employed to scale the daily values of surface albedo and aerodynamic roughness between endpoint values reported by Weller *et al.* (1972).

d. Phase change in the soil was included by making the thermal diffusivity a function not only of depth but also of the temperature at the last iteration. When the temperature was close to 0 C the volumetric heat capacity (C) was calculated as a function of porosity (n), the temperature dependent heat of fusion $[F(T)]$ and the mean value of the layer frozen and thawed values of volumetric heat capacity (c_{ft}) according to Eq. (2) (Martynov, 1959). This description of heat capacity continuous through phase change is compatible with a large experimental program underway at CRREL (Anderson et al., 1973).

$$C = n \cdot [F(T)] + C_{ft}. \qquad (2)$$

The thermal diffusivity in all states (thawed, frozen, phase change) was estimated by dividing the conductivity by the volumetric heat capacity, using values reported in Nakano and Brown (1971). Thus, at each iteration the thermal diffusivity was an explicit function of not only depth but also temperature.

e. If the equilibrium temperature solution converged above 0 C it was reset to 0 C and the energy reaching the snow was calculated as melt.

4. Program flow

The sequence of computation follows a scheme in which the snow-soil thermal diffusion computational loop is nested within the annual iteration loop following the equilibrium temperature search loop. Equilibrium temperature solutions are carried out daily, and following these the soil thermal diffusion equation vector is relaxed at half-hour intervals throughout the daily cycle. An initial snow-soil temperature vector is input. After each daily equilibrium temperature solution, the diurnal energy components, snow-soil thermal structure, snow depth and active layer depth are produced as output.

5. Program application

The sensitivity of active layer evolution to accumulated snow-depth was investigated. In four simulations snow was accumulated linearly on the surface to maximum values of 0, 50, 100 and 200 cm, after which depth was maintained constant until melt began as determined by the equilibrium surface temperature. The course of snow melt for these depths is illustrated in Fig. 1, and consequent active layer evolution in Fig. 2. For these simulations, 1970–71 Weather Bureau data for Barrow, Alaska were input. A bulk snow density of 0.5 was used, and the ground surface was assumed saturated throughout the year. For a maximum snow depth of 38 cm, the course of snowmelt and phase and amplitude of the active layer melting wave are close to that reported by Weller et al. (1972).

6. Conclusion

Initial testing indicates that the equilibrium temperature simulator structure is suitable for annual surface effect analyses in cold regions. Model testing and refinement is facilitated by the highly generalized model structure. Even with gross parameterization, model accuracy is sufficient for some purposes, and ultimate predictive accuracy is largely cost- and data-dependent.

Acknowledgments. This research was conducted under support by the U. S. Army Cold Regions Research and Engineering Laboratory, and by the U. S. Tundra Biome, through the University of Alaska, Tundra Biome Project #3742, "Geomorphic description and modelling of near surface thermal regimes."

REFERENCES

Anderson, D. M., A. R. Tice and H. L. McKim, 1973: The unfrozen water and the apparent specific heat capacity of frozen soils. North American Contributions, 2nd International Conference on Permafrost, National Academy of Sciences, U. S. Government Printing Office, Washington, D. C., 289–295.

Benninghoff, W. S., 1963: Relationships between vegetation and permafrost. Proceedings: Permafrost International Conference, NAS-NRC, Pub. 1287, 9–13.

Brown, R. J. E., 1963: Influence of vegetation on permafrost. Proceedings: Permafrost International Conference, NAS-NRC, Pub. 1287, 20–25.

Gates, D. M., 1968: Toward understanding ecosystems. *Advances in Ecological Research*, **5**, 1–35.

Lachenbruch, A. H., 1957: Three dimensional heat conduction beneath heated buildings. U. S. Geological Survey Bulletin 1052-B, 69 pp.

Lachenbruch, A. H., 1962: Mechanics of thermal contraction cracks and ice-wedge polygons. Special Paper No. 70, Geological Society of America, 69 pp.

Lord, N. W., J. P. Pandolfo and M. A. Atwater, 1971: Simulation of meteorological variation over arctic coastal tundra under perturbed conditions, U. S. Tundra Biome Report 71-4, USIBP-USARP.

Mackay, J. R., 1963: The Mackenzie delta area, N. W. T. Canada Dept. of Mines and Technical Surveys, Geographical Branch, Memoir 8, 202 pp.

Martynov, G. A., 1959: Heat and moisture transfer in freezing and thawing soils. Chapter VI in Principles of Geocryology, Part 1, General Geocryology, Acad. Sci. USSR, U. A. Obruchen Inst. of Permafrost Studies, Moscow, 153–192. Trans.: E. R. Hope, Canada NRC., TT-1065.

Miller, P. G., and L. Tieszen, 1971: A preliminary model of processes affecting primary production in Arctic Tundra. U. S. Tundra Biome Report 71-3., USIBP-USARP.

Myrup, L. O., 1969: A numerical model of the urban heat island. *Jour. App. Met.*, **8**, 908–918.

Nakano, Y., and J. Brown, 1971: Mathematical modeling and validation of thermal regimes in Tundra soils, Barrow, Alaska, U. S. Biome Report 71-5, USIBP-USARP.

Outcalt, S. I., 1971: The climatonomy of a needle ice event. *Arch. Meteor. Geophys. Bioklim.*, **B19**, 325–330.

Outcalt, S. I., 1972a: The development and application of a simple digital surface-climate simulator. *Jour. App. Met.*, **11**, No. 4, 629–656.

Outcalt, S. I., 1972b: The simulation and implications of thermal plumes produced by Arctic construction in smooth terrain. *Arch. Meteor. Geophys. Bioklim.*, **B20**, 261–267.

Weller, G., S. Cubley, S. Parker, D. Trabant and C. Benson, 1972: The tundra microclimate during snow-melt at Barrow, Alaska. *Arctic*, **25**, 291–300.

Description of a Surface Temperature Equilibrium Energy Balance Model with Application to Arctic Pack Ice in Early Spring

WILSON B. GODDARD

Division of Environmental Studies, University of California, Davis, California

Abstract

An equilibrium surface temperature energy balance simulation model (CLISIM) is described. One of the unique features of the model is a simple but thermodynamically sound way of handling the diurnal variations in shelter height boundary condition oscillations of moisture and air temperature. The model is used to simulate conditions on both a cloudy and a clear day in early spring over Arctic pack ice and the simulated results are compared with actual measurements taken during the AIDJEX 1972 Pilot Study at 75°N, 149°W on Arctic pack ice. While the energy balance terms are small during this part of the year in this location the measured and simulated values are in reasonable agreement. The conclusion is drawn that the model can be usefully applied to understanding the Arctic energy balance but that more extensive micrometeorological records are desirable.

1. Introduction

It would be very useful for many purposes if through a modelling technique a single parameter, such as the surface temperature, could dictate the magnitude of the surface energy balance, the degree of atmospheric stability and the strength of the surface shear-stress. An attempt in this direction is the use of surface temperature equilibrium energy balance simulation models which require a thorough understanding of the surface physical characteristics and a detailed knowledge of the atmospheric conditions and of the relationship between each energy balance flux term and the respective physical process which drives the flux. This then requires that each energy balance term be described in terms of the initial boundary conditions, the atmospheric, surface and subsurface physical characteristics and the relationship between these characteristics or boundary conditions and the surface temperature. Surface temperature equilibrium energy balance simulation models have been in use by various groups for many years (Halstead, 1957; Appleby, 1960; Estoque, 1963; Myrup, 1969; Goddard, 1971; Vowinckel, 1972; Outcalt, 1973). The distinctive features of the surface temperature equilibrium energy balance simulation model hereafter referred to as CLISIM (climate simulation model) are first, a simple but thermodynamically sound way of handling the diurnal humidity changes and second, a convectively mixed boundary layer which accurately simulates the diurnal air temperature wave.

The improvement and application of the model CLISIM which is described in this paper has been taking place at U. C. Davis for several years. The model has been used in a variety of applications including land use planning, urban meteorology, agricultural meteorology and snowmelt predictions at high elevations (Goddard, 1971; Myrup *et al.*, 1972; Stowhas, 1973) and has also proved very valuable as a teaching tool in micrometeorology and graduate studies. The simulator was designed to take typically available climatological data as input, coupled with a complete description of the surface characteristics. CLISIM calculates the atmospheric stability which is included in its estimates of shear-stress and in the proportioning of available energy between sensible, latent and conducted heat. This ability to estimate atmospheric stability has made CLISIM useful for air quality modelling in land use analysis (Myrup, 1972). The simulator outputs are surface radiation components, sensible, latent and conducted heat, the friction velocity, atmospheric stability, shelter height and surface temperature, humidity and wind speed, and the estimated height of the convectively mixed boundary layer for each time step. Heat conduction is used to update for each time step the substrate temperature regime. At the completion of each day's simulation, daily totals of energy balance terms are calculated as well as daily average shelter height temperature and humidity.

2. Description of the equilibrium surface temperature energy balance simulation model CLISIM

The basis for equilibrium surface temperature energy balance simulation models is the energy balance at the air-earth interface:

$$Rn + LE + H + G = 0 \qquad (1)$$

where

Rn = net radiation
E = moisture flux
L = latent heat of vaporization/sublimation
H = sensible heat flux
G = substrate heat conduction.

In the following equations fluxes toward the air-earth interface are considered positive; data and results are given in cgs units. A description of each of the energy balance components in Eq. (1) will form the description of CLISIM.

Net radiation

The net radiation calculation requires the solar zenith angle Z:

$$\cos Z = \sin\phi \, \sin\delta + \cos\phi \, \cos\delta \, \cos h \qquad (2)$$

where

Z = solar zenith angle
ϕ = latitude
δ = declination
h = solar hour angle.

The average attenuated intensity of the solar radiation received at the earth's surface can be related to the monochromatic intensity through Beer's Law (Haltiner and Martin, 1957):

$$I_0 T_r^{\sec Z} \cos Z \qquad (3)$$

where

I_0 = solar constant

T_r = atmospheric turbidity coefficient.

Some fraction of the solar incoming will be reflected by clouds and by the surface. The longwave radiation emitted from the surface is given by Stefan-Boltzman gray body emission which is modified by a cloud cover reduction coefficient. The long wave incoming is related to the shelter height temperature after Swinbank (1963). The net radiation is then given by:

$$Rn = I_0(1-n\alpha_c)(1-\alpha_s)T_r^{\sec Z} \cos Z$$
$$- (1-nk_c)\epsilon_0\sigma T_0^4 + \epsilon_2 c\sigma T_2^6 \qquad (4)$$

where

n = percent cloud cover
α_c = cloud albedo
α_s = surface albedo
k_c = longwave cloud reduction coefficient
ϵ_0 = surface emissivity
σ = Stefan-Boltzman constant
ϵ_2 = effective sky emissivity
c = empirical constant = 9.35×10^{-6}
T_0 = absolute surface temperature
T_2 = absolute shelter height temperature.

The net radiation calculated by Eq. (4) under clear sky conditions at Davis, California for 4 May, 1967 using CLISIM simulated values compared to measured values yielded a correlation coefficient of 0.98 where $\alpha_s = 0.22$, $\epsilon_0 = 0.95$ and $T_r = 0.76$ (Goddard, 1971). Net radiation calculations under cloudy conditions using Eq. (4) yield reasonable values but as yet an insufficient number of cloud type cases has been studied to make a thorough analysis.

Momentum, heat and moisture transfer

The simulator makes use of the log plus linear profile description plus a universal function dependent on the Richardson number. The flux-gradient relationships for momentum, heat and moisture are given by:

$$\frac{\partial u}{\partial Z} \frac{kZ}{U_*} = \phi_M(\mathrm{Ri}) \qquad (5)$$

$$\frac{\partial \theta}{\partial Z} \frac{\rho c_p}{H} kZU_* = \phi_H(\mathrm{Ri}) \qquad (6)$$

$$\frac{\partial q}{\partial Z} \frac{\rho}{E} kZU_* = \phi_E(\mathrm{Ri}) \qquad (7)$$

where

u = horizontal wind speed
Z = displacement corrected height
k = von Karman constant taken as 0.41 (Goddard, 1968)
$U_* = \sqrt{\tau/\rho}$ = friction velocity
τ = shear-stress
ρ = air density
θ = potential temperature
c_p = specific heat of air at constant pressure
q = specific humidity
ϕ_M, ϕ_H, ϕ_E = universal stability function for momentum, heat and moisture respectively

$$\mathrm{Ri} = \frac{g}{T} \frac{\partial\theta_*/\partial Z}{(\partial u/\partial Z)^2} = \text{Richardson number}$$

where

T = absolute temperature at height Z
θ_* = virtual potential temperature
g = gravity.

The form of the universal stability function is taken as:

$$\phi(\mathrm{RI}) = (1-\alpha \mathrm{RI})^{-1} \qquad (8)$$

where

RI = bulk Richardson number
α = Monin-Obukhov log plus linear curvature term (Monin and Obukhov, 1954).

The universal stability function form in Eq. (8) has

TABLE 1. Boundary and initial conditions for CLISIM.

Boundary Conditions

ϕ = latitude
δ = declination
α_c = cloud type albedo
k_c = long wave cloud type coefficient
n = percent cloud cover
T_r = atmospheric turbidity coefficient
α_s = surface albedo (may be specified temperature dependent)
ϵ_0 = surface emissivity
ϵ_2 = effective sky emissivity
λ = substrate bulk thermal conductivity
d = depth of substrate layer
c_s = substrate volumetric heat capacity
Z_0 = surface roughness
Z_{ref} = reference height
u_{ref} = wind speed at reference height
RH_{ref}= relative humidity at reference height
LAS = fraction of surface evaporating or transpiring
P = atmospheric pressure
$\gamma(0)$ = strength of inversion lapse rate

Initial Conditions

θ_0 = surface temperature
θ_{ref} = reference height temperature
q_{ref} = reference height specific humidity
T_d = substrate temperature
t = starting time
h = mixing layer height

---

been shown to relate measured fluxes to measured gradients from a Richardson number of -1 past the critical value of 0.25 (Goddard, 1971). The value of α changes from about 0.4 for highly unstable to slightly more than 2 for highly stable conditions (Goddard, 1968). (A value of $\alpha=1$ was used in the pack ice simulation.) The integrated forms of Eqs. (5), (6) and (7) in finite difference form are the following, noting that the diffusivities of heat and moisture are about 1.25 times that of momentum (Goddard, 1971):

$$\text{RI} = (g/T_{\text{ref}})(\theta_{*\text{ref}}-\theta_{*0})(Z_{\text{ref}}-Z_0)/u_{\text{ref}}^2 \qquad (9)$$

$$U_* = ku_{\text{ref}}(1-\alpha\text{Ri})/\ln(Z_{\text{ref}}/Z_0) \qquad (10)$$

$$H = c_p k^2 \rho(\theta_{\text{ref}}-\theta_0)u_{\text{ref}}\,1.25(1-\alpha\text{RI})^2/[\ln(Z_{\text{ref}}/Z_0)]^2 \qquad (11)$$

$$LE = L\rho k^2(q_{\text{ref}}-q_0)u_{\text{ref}}\,1.25(1-\alpha\text{RI})^2/[\ln(Z_{\text{ref}}/Z_0)]^2 \qquad (12)$$

where

Z_0 = surface roughness height
ref = reference height at which climatological or initial condition data is available. Usually this is at shelter height or nominally at 2 meters.

The moisture at the surface is related to that of a free water surface with the percentage cover of evaporating or transpiring surface given. The surface vapor pressure is related to the surface temperature over the range of -50 to 0 C (standard estimate of error 7.96×10^{-3}) by

$$e = 6.084+0.486\,\theta+0.0162\,\theta^2+2.605\times10^{-4}\,\theta^3$$
$$+1.655\times10^{-6}\,\theta^4 \qquad (13)$$

where

$$e = \text{vapor pressure}$$

The surface specific humidity is then calculated from the thermodynamic relationship:

$$q = \frac{0.622\,LAS\,e}{P-0.378\,LAS\,e} \qquad (14)$$

where

LAS = fraction of surface evaporating or transpiring
P = atmospheric pressure.

Substrate heat conduction

The substrate heat conduction has been described in various ways in CLISIM depending on the particular application. Long term snow surface melt applications have required elaborate multi-depth Fourier heat conduction description with variable radiation extinction coefficients and variable thermal properties (Stowhas, 1973). The purpose here is to explore the distribution of energy and not to detail long term ice ablation such as reported by Maykut and Untersteiner (1971). Therefore the simplest description was used, where the surface heat conduction is given by:

$$G = (\lambda/d)(T_d-\theta_0) \qquad (15)$$

where

λ = bulk thermal conductivity
d = depth of layer
T_d = temperature at depth d
θ_0 = surface temperature.

The bulk thermal conductivity is calculated from the individual thermal resistances of each material and their corresponding thickness making up depth d.

3. Climate simulator *CLISIM* operation

Input variables to be specified for CLISIM are listed in Table 1 and a flow diagram of the simulator's computations is shown schematically in Fig. 1. The flow diagram shows the mode of operation where only climatological data is available. In this case the initial conditions are allowed to step through daily cycles until the change in average daily temperature at shelter height corresponds to the available climatological data. For many cases, it can be assumed that the sum of the daily substrate heat conduction is very small, and this can then be an added requirement for an acceptable simulation. These procedures are fully described later.

For each time step of CLISIM Eqs. (4), (9), (10), (11), (12), (13), (14) and (15) are specified in terms of the previous time step conditions and their update and surface temperature. The system is closed and solved by the Newton method of iteration until the equilibrium surface temperature just balances the energy balance, Eq. (1).

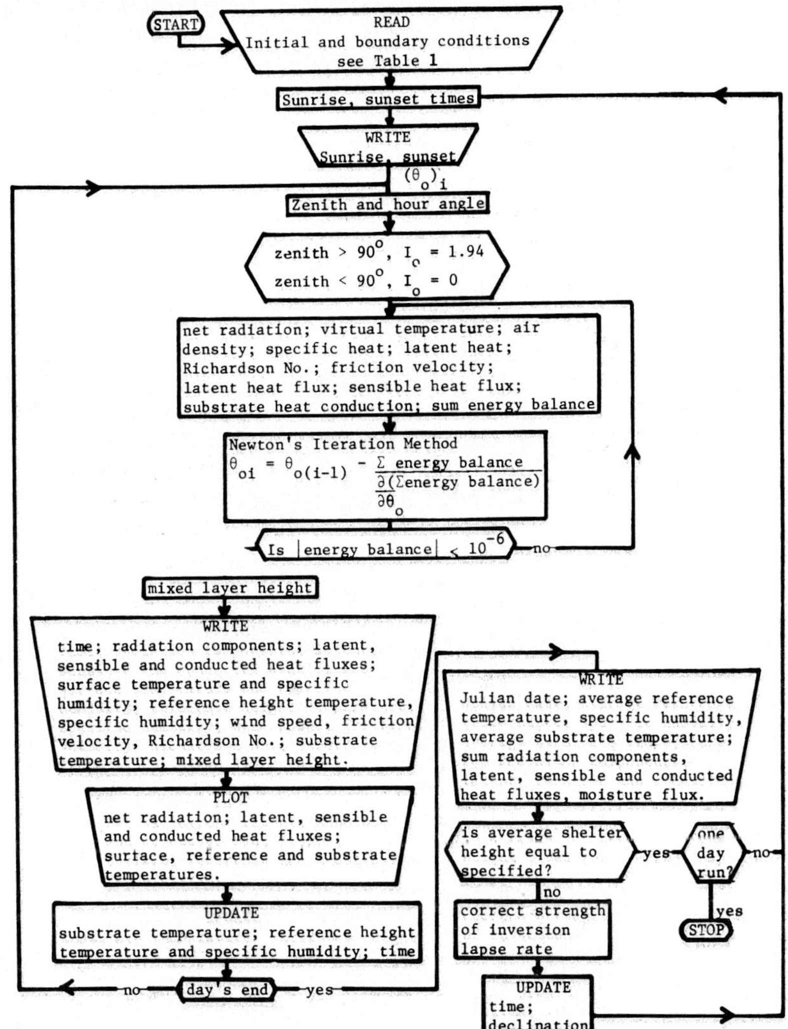

FIG. 1. Flow diagram for the computer model which was used to simulate the relationship between the equilibrium surface temperature and the energy balance at the surface.

Upper and lower boundary conditions

For each time step of CLISIM an update is necessary of the upper reference height temperature and humidity and the lower substrate temperature at depth d. It follows from Eq. (15) that the temperature at depth d will be:

$$T_{di} = T_{d(i-1)} - G\Delta t/c_s d \tag{16}$$

where

T_{di} = substrate temperature update at depth d
$T_{d(i-1)}$ = substrate temperature at depth d
Δt = CLISIM time step, usually 1 hour
c_s = substrate volumetric heat capacity.

The updating of the upper reference height temperature is performed by calculating the atmospheric boundary layer mixing height and the heat capacity and sensible heat flux within this column:

$$\theta_{\text{ref } i} = \theta_{\text{ref}(i-1)} - (H\Delta t/h\rho c_p) \tag{17}$$

where

$$h = \text{mixed layer height.}$$

Under stable atmospheric conditions the mixed layer height is taken as the Monin-Obukhov stability length where for stable conditions, RI positive,

$$h = L = U_* \bigg/ \left(\frac{g}{T}k\frac{H}{\rho c_p}\right) \tag{18}$$

Under unstable atmospheric conditions the mixed layer height is calculated assuming a dry inversion-capped convective unstable layer where for unstable conditions, RI negative,

$$h^2 = 2H\Sigma t/\rho c_p\gamma(0) \tag{19}$$

where

Σt = duration of convective boundary layer growth
$\gamma(0)$ = lapse rate of inversion layer.

The concept of using the Monin-Obukhov stability length as a mixed layer height was proposed by Monin and Obukhov (1954) for stable conditions. The concept of relating the height of the mixed layer under unstable, capped inversion conditions to the strength of the inversion lapse rate and to the surface sensible heat flux was suggested by Ball (1960), improved upon by Deardorff, Willis and Lilly (1969) and thoroughly developed and tested by Carson (1973). In order to avoid indeterminateness at neutral atmospheric stability the height of the atmospheric boundary layer mixed layer height is maintained constant from $-0.001 \leqslant \text{RI} \leqslant 0.001$.

The reference height specific humidity is updated using Eqs. (13) and (14) where a fixed value of relative humidity at reference height is used with the updated reference height temperature. This procedure allows for local advection of dry or moist air or local vertical convection and entrainment of dry air.

An alternative to the use of daily climatological data is to use actual measured initial conditions and to compare the simulated results with collected micrometeorological data. This is the case in the following analysis where CLISIM was used to simulate the equilibrium surface temperature energy balance for Arctic pack ice under early spring conditions.

4. Simulated and measured micrometeorological data comparison for Arctic pack ice

Data measurement

Micrometeorological field data over Arctic pack ice, latitude 75°N, longitude 149°W were obtained during the Arctic Ice Dynamics Joint Experiment (AIDJEX) Pilot Study beginning in mid-March and ending in mid-April. The data consisted of logarithmically spaced temperature, humidity and wind sensors at heights of 25, 50, 100, 200 and 400 cm above the snow surface. The temperature and humidity array consisted of an aspirated, double radiation shielded thermistor and hygristor at each height. The thermistors and hygristors are of the type used in radiosondes and were purchased from VIZ corporation (Stine, 1965). The VIZ hygristors and thermistors are designed for low temperature and low specific humidity applications. The resistance of the hydroxyethylcellulose coating of the hygristor changes as a function of relative humidity. At low temperatures and low vapor pressures, rather than measure directly the specific humidity needed for moisture flux determinations, it is more accurate to measure relative humidity and air temperature and from their thermodynamic relationship to calculate specific humidity. Measurements were made of solar incoming and reflected outgoing radiation using Eppley precision spectral short-wave pyranometers; incoming and outgoing longwave radiation using Eppley precision infrared pyrgeometers; and net radiation using a warm air ventilated flat plate radiometer designed after Gier *et al.* (1949). The radiation instrumentation array was mounted at 2 m and cantilevered over an undisturbed surface. Unfortunately the pyrgeometers measuring longwave radiation were found to be defective so no surface temperature calculations were possible. Substrate temperatures were measured with thermistor probes at 2 cm in the snow and at 30 and 43 cm in the pack ice (measured from the snow surface, which was about 10 to 15 cm thick over the area where the sensors were installed). Substrate heat conduction was measured with two thermopile heat flow plates designed for Arctic pack ice and manufactured by the International Thermal Instrument Company. The design of these plates, which were painted with white epoxy, was such that their conductivity closely approximated that of ice. One heat flow plate was installed at 2 cm in the snow and the other at 22 cm in pack ice, both depths measured from the snow surface.

The data from this instrumentation array, excepting that of the wind sensors, was logged by a data acquisition and computation system. The data logger was allowed to "free run," taking data at its maximum rate, applying each sensor's calibration coefficient to its measured signals and storing the resultant parameter, the square of the parameter and the cube of the parameter in cgs units. Each half hour the system logged on a Teletype 33 the time, mean, variance and third moment of each sensor. In addition, a plot was made automatically each half hour of each temperature and humidity profile and of each of the radiation measurements so that sensor errors could be quickly detected. Paper tape output as well as hard copy was produced from the teletype. The data computation and acquisition system was designed to ensure near on-line data monitoring so as to insure against unknown instrument failure. All sensors were calibrated and checked before and after the field work.

A boundary layer profile system using a tethered kytoon was used to obtain periodic temperature and wind speed profiles up to 500 meters. Robert McBeth, NCAR, operated this system and has reduced the data from it.

Data analysis

During the Arctic pack ice micrometeorological study about 150 half hour wind velocity profiles were obtained. The wind, temperature and humidity profile data were analyzed to obtain estimates of the surface roughness, the friction velocity, and the latent and sensible heat fluxes. The analysis technique used was a least-square fitting of the Monin-Obukhov log-plus-linear profile equation from which estimates of the

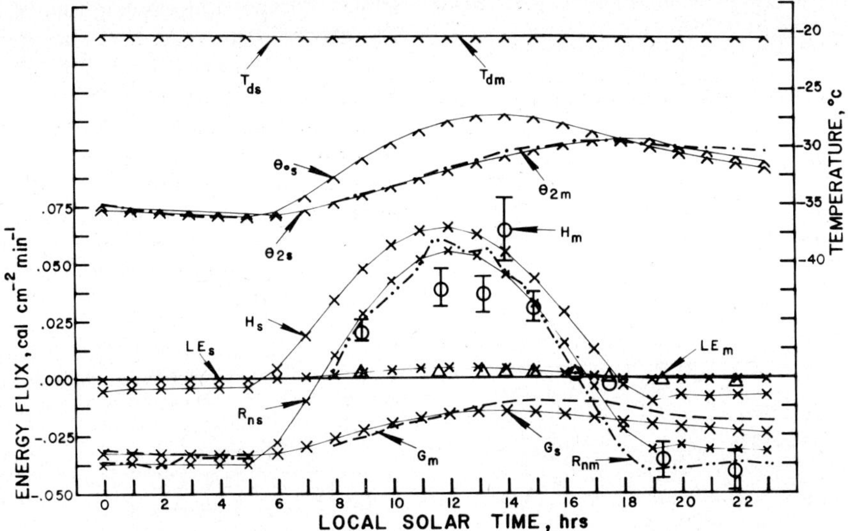

FIG. 2. Simulation-measured comparison for Arctic Pack ice 75°N, 140°25′W Clear Sky,
April 1, 1972; sub s denotes simulated, sub m denotes measured.

fitting parameters yielded the forementioned variables. Completion of this work is still in progress but the technique has been tested previously by Goddard (1971). The radiation array previously described allowed determination of the atmospheric turbidity coefficient and surface albedo. Values for the thermal conductivity of a composite of 15 cm snow and 15 cm of sea ice were obtained from work reported by Maykut and Untersteiner (1971). Analysis of the boundary profile kytoon data showed a progressive increase of the height of the mixed layer beginning near the surface in the early morning to over 100 m by late afternoon. The strength of the lapse rate of the temperature inversion averaged about 0.5 C per 10 m.

5. Equilibrium surface temperature energy balance simulation

A clear sky simulation for April 1, 1972 is shown in Fig. 2 and a cloudy sky simulation for April 13, 1972 is shown in Fig. 3, for 75°N 149°25′W. Table 2 lists the initial and boundary conditions used in the simulations. The measured quantities are shown as heavy solid and dashed lines while the simulated values are shown as inverted V's and crosses (X). The small inverted V mark is the subsurface temperature, the medium size is the 2 m air temperature and the largest inverted V mark is the equilibrium surface temperature. There are four cross marks. The smallest

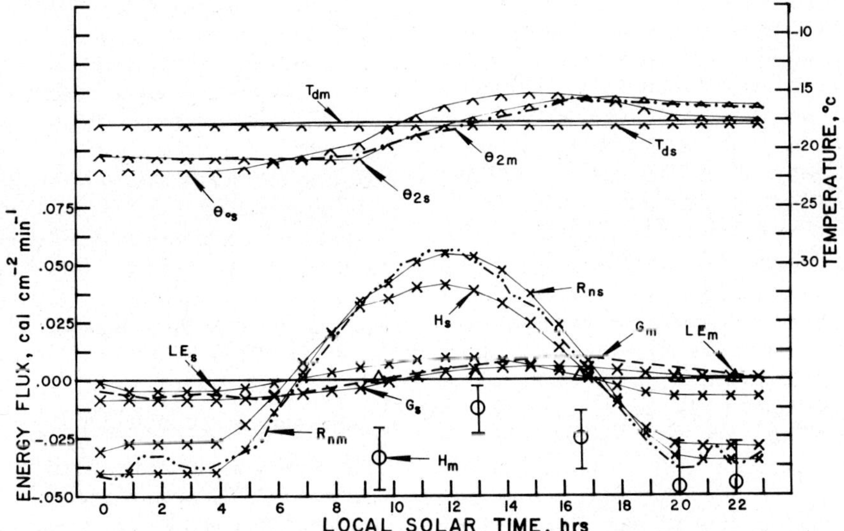

FIG. 3. Simulation-measured comparison for Arctic Pack ice, 75°N, 149°25′W Cloudy Sky,
April 13, 1972: sub s denotes simulated, sub m denotes measured.

TABLE 2. Boundary and initial conditions for CLISIM: Arctic pack ice simulation.

	Parameter	(a) clear sky April 1, 1972	(b) cloudy sky April 13, 1972
Boundary Conditions	ϕ	75	75
	δ	4.41	9.04
	α_c	1.00	0.77
	k_c	0.75	0.73
	n	0.00	1.00
	T_r	0.93	0.93
	α_s	0.79	0.79
	ϵ_0	1.00	1.00
	ϵ_2	1.14	1.00
	λ	1.06×10^{-3}	1.06×10^{-3}
	d	30.0	30.0
	c_s	2.00*	2.00*
	Z_0	0.001	0.001
	Z_{ref}	200	200
	u_{ref}	499	867
	RH_{ref}	1.00	1.00
	LAS	1.00	1.00
	P	1031	1006
	$\gamma(0)$	5×10^{-4}	5×10^{-4}
Initial Conditions	θ_0	-34.99	-20.59
	θ_{ref}	-34.79	-20.39
	q_{ref}	1.4×10^{-4}	5.5×10^{-4}
	T_d	-19.95	-17.75
	t start	0000	0000
	h	10^3	10^4

* Corrected for heat flux from the ocean below.

cross mark is the net radiation, the next largest is the latent heat flux, the next the sensible heat flux and the largest cross mark is the substrate heat conduction. The time step for CLISIM was one hour, hence the hourly marks. To conserve diagram space the plot considers the net radiation as positive toward the surface while the latent and sensible heat fluxes and substrate heat conduction are positive away from the surface. The energy balance flux terms are shown with a greatly expanded scale to aid in their interpretation. The simulation marks are linked with a light line, also as an aid to interpretation. The estimates of sensible and latent heat fluxes determined from profile data are shown as circles and triangles respectively. The error bars shown are based upon an RMS calculated error of $\pm15\%$ and an absolute uncertainty of ±10 cm in instrument height for the sensible and latent heat fluxes. The absolute error in temperatures was calculated from calibration data and field comparisons to be ±0.1 C while the RMS error was ±0.05 C. It was not possible to assign an error to the radiometers since they were operating at the margin of their temperature specifications. Their probable error was about $\pm15\%$ considering the rime ice, low sun angle and low temperature problems. Unfortunately the minimum and maximum absolute errors under these low flux conditions for sensible and latent heat fluxes are much larger than the RMS errors indicate. The largest uncertainty in their determination was instrument height determination under blowing and moving snow conditions. It was admittedly a mistake to make profile measurements at these low elevations (25, 50, 100, 200 and 400 cm), where height determinations lead to large errors. The minimum-maximum absolute errors in sensible and latent heat fluxes averaged $\pm200\%$. Table 3 is a summary of linear regression coefficients comparing measured and simulated temperatures and energy balance fluxes for both the clear sky simulation of April 1, 1972 shown in Fig. 2 and the cloudy sky simulation of April 13, 1972 shown in Fig. 3.

TABLE 3. Linear correlation coefficients measured versus simulated correlation coefficient.

Parameter	Clear 1 April 72	Cloudy 13 April 72
2 m reference temperature	0.96	0.96
30 cm substrate temperature	0.99	0.99
Net radiation	0.99	0.94
Substrate heat conduction	0.93	0.91
Sensible heat flux	0.94	0.79
Latent heat flux	0.97	0.77

Discussion of results

The correlation coefficients in general are high and indicate good agreement between simulated values and measured quantities. The convective mixed layer heights estimated by CLISIM ranged from an early morning low of 16 m to a late afternoon high of 195 m. Balloon soundings indicated for mid March very low inversions in the morning with heights ranging over 90 m in the afternoon. The diurnal character of the 2 m air temperature was well modelled by the convectively mixed boundary layer approach but more data and simulations are needed before conclusions can be drawn.

The net radiation equations (4) used in CLISIM appear to be sufficiently flexible for clear and cloudy sky conditions where sufficient micrometeorological data is available. A much longer micrometeorological data set will be necessary to test the equations thoroughly.

During the cloudy sky April 13, 1972 period blowing snow observations were made. During this day five flux-profile determinations of sensible heat flux showed conditions to be slightly stable while the simulation results estimated unstable conditions. This may have been due to local advection but at this time this is only conjecture.

6. Summary and conclusions

The testing under early April conditions on Arctic pack ice at 75°N of an equilibrium surface temperature simulation model has been presented. While it cannot be concluded from this single case that this type of modelling will be useful under all types of conditions of Arctic pack ice, the results are encouraging. If this type of model can be improved and tested for a complete seasonal cycle it could then form a technique for assessing the consequences of such things as accidental or intentional changes in such parameters as surface albedo. Application of CLISIM along these lines in **an** exploratory way has shown some promise when compared on a monthly basis to work of Fletcher (1965) and Maykut and Untersteiner (1971).

It will be of great assistance for thoroughly testing and improving this type of modelling effort if further micrometeorological data collection as proposed in the AIDJEX experiment is carried out.

Acknowledgments. This work has been sponsored by the National Science Foundation, Office of Polar Programs, Grant No. GVO 29050. Appreciation for able collaboration is extended to Christine B. Goddard, my wife and research assistant.

REFERENCES

Appleby, J. F., and L. Fujikado, 1960: Special cases of simulating the energy budget of the earth/air interface. USAE PG-SIG, 970-30, U. S. Army Elect. Prov. Grd., Fort Huachuca, Arizona, pp. 1–84.

Ball, F. K., 1960: Control of inversion height by surface heating. *Quart. J. Roy. Met. Soc.*, **86**, 483–494.

Brooks, C. E. P. 1949: *Climate through the ages.*, McGraw-Hill, pp. 21–45.

Budyko, M. T., 1966: Polar ice and climate. Proc. of the symposium on the Arctic heat budget and atmospheric circulation, RM-5233-NSF, pp. 1–21.

Carson, D. J., 1973: The development of a dry inversion-capped convectively unstable layer. *Quart. J. Roy. Met. Soc.*, **99**, 450–467.

Deardorff, J. W., G. E. Willis and D. K. Lilly, 1969: Laboratory investigation of non-steady penetrative convection. *J. Fluid Mech.*, **35**, 7–31.

Estoque, M. A., 1963: A numerical model of the atmospheric boundary layer. *J. Geophys. Res.*, **68**, 1103–1113.

Fletcher, J. O., 1965: The heat budget of the Arctic basin and its relation to climate. USAF Project Rand, R-444-PR, pp. 1–17.

Gier, J. T., R. Dunckle and L. Possner., 1949: Measurements of hemispherical radiation and net radiation exchange. Contract N7-0NR-295-Task p, Report #10, Report Code NR-014-062, Dept. of Engineering, Univ. of Calif., Berkeley.

Goddard, W. B., 1968: Momentum transfer near the ground. Master thesis in engineering, Univ. of Calif., Davis, pp. 1–64.

Goddard, W. B., 1971: Heat, mass and momentum transfer processes in the biosphere: theory, analysis and application to agricultural environmental engineering. Ph.D. dissertation in Engineering, Univ. of Calif., Davis, pp. 1–101.

Halstead, M. H., R. L. Richman, W. Covey and J. D. Merryman, 1957: A preliminary report on the design of a computer for micrometeorology. *J. Meteor.*, **14**, 308–325.

Haltiner, G. J., and F. L. Martin, 1957: *Dynamic and physical meteorology.* McGraw-Hill, N. Y., pp. 92–93.

Maykut, G. A., and N. Untersteiner, 1971: Some results from a time-dependent thermodynamic model of sea ice. *J. of Geophys. Res.*, **76**, 1550–1575.

Monin, A. S., and A. M. Obukhov, 1954: Basic regularity in turbulent mixing in the surface layer of the atmosphere. U. S. S. R. Acad. of Sci., Works in Geophysical Institute, #24(131), 30.

Myrup, L. O., 1969: A numerical model of the urban heat island. *J. Applied Met.*, **8**, 908–918.

Myrup, L. O., and D. L. Morgan, 1972: Numerical model of the urban atmosphere. Volume I, The city-surface interface, contributions to Atm. Sci. #4, Univ. of Calif., Davis, 64–107.

Outcalt, S. I., 1973: The development and application of a simple digital surface-climate simulator. *J. Applied Met.*, **11**, 629–636.

Stine, S. L., 1965: Carbon humidity elements—manufacture, performance and theory. *Humidity and moisture* Vol. 1, New York Reinholdt, pp. 316–330.

Stowhas, L. A., 1973: Simulation of snow melting process. Master's theisis in engineering, Univ. of Calif., Davis.

Swinbank, W. C., 1963: Long wave radiation from clear skies. *Quart. J. Roy. Met. Soc.*, **89**, 339–348.

Vowinckel, E., and S. Orvig, 1972: An energy budget programme. Arctic Met. Res. Group, Dept. of Met., McGill, Univ. Montreal, Publ. in Met., #105, pp. 1–150.

The Radiation Matrix in the Arctic

G. WELLER, S. BOWLING, B. HOLMGREN, K. O. L. F. JAYAWEERA, T. OHTAKE AND G. SHAW

Geophysical Institute, University of Alaska

Abstract

Radiative processes in the earth/atmosphere system can be represented schematically in matrix form. Some of the matrix elements in the arctic regions, in particular the radiation-aerosol interaction are described, presenting experimental data from the Arctic Basin. Vertical profiles of the optical extinction coefficient measured by airborne photometer near Barrow, Alaska, show a peak in the extinction coefficient in the lower troposphere (300 m) in spring; this is attributed to ice crystal aerosols. A secondary peak at about 2 km height is considered to be a semi-permanent haze layer, possibly of man-made origin, which is advected into the Arctic Basin. Seasonal variations of both the Ångström and optical extinction coefficients, which were measured, indicate turbidities which are lower in summer than in spring. Several case studies are presented. Data on the composition of arctic stratus clouds and ice nuclei concentrations, which are required for models of radiative transfer through these persistent summer cloud decks are also given.

1. Introduction

Weather and climate in the arctic and sub-arctic regions are strongly affected by the state of the Arctic Ocean and the atmosphere, and by the effective coupling between them. The polar regions occupy the role of the heat sink, as part of the global heat engine which drives the general circulation—studies of these heat sinks are important in understanding weather and climate not only on a regional scale, but on a global scale as well.

Radiative processes in the earth/atmosphere system, which are responsible for the existence of the heat sinks in the polar regions, can be described by a fairly simple radiation-balance matrix (Fletcher, 1966, p. 339).

In the Arctic Basin, two important components of the environment strongly influence the radiation-balance matrix—these are the presence of pack ice throughout the year and of low stratus cloud decks during summer. In addition to these, we have accumulated evidence that suggests that aerosols or particulates in the clear Arctic atmosphere may also play an important role in the radiative heat exchange processes. Thus, our studies to date have concentrated on determining the physical characteristics of both pack ice, clouds and free air particulates as they affect the Arctic radiation regime. At Barrow, flights through stratus clouds with an aircraft-mounted continuous cloud particle sampler have determined number and mass densities, particle size distributions, and ice crystal contents of these clouds over a wide temperature range (Jayaweera and Ohtake, 1973). Simultaneously, light intensity and reflectivity measurements were carried out to determine the optical properties of these clouds. Studies were also made of the concentration of freezing nuclei in the Arctic atmosphere.

Although the air is fairly "clean" over the Arctic Ocean, aerosol concentrations are apparently high

THE RADIATION MATRIX

Input (energy)	Output (energy)
ATMOSPHERE	
1. Solar radiation (direct) $\sim >1\,\mu$ absorbed by water vapor, CO_2, particulates.	1. Solar radiation reflected by clouds, and scattered by particulates.
2. Terrestrial radiation (emitted) $\sim >6\,\mu$ absorbed by water vapor and CO_2.	2. Longwave radiation emitted by the atmosphere.
3. Solar radiation reflected by ground and/or scattered by atmosphere (absorbed by water vapor, CO_2, and particulates).	
4. Longwave radiation emitted by the atmosphere and reabsorbed by atmosphere.	
SURFACE	
1. Solar radiation absorbed by surface or subsurface layer (water, or particulate matter absorbing in certain wavelengths).	1. Longwave radiation from surface.
2. Longwave radiation from atmosphere.	2. Shortwave radiation (solar) reflected by surface.
3. Longwave radiation from earth scattered back to surface.	3. Longwave radiation from atmosphere reflected by surface.

enough to be important in scattering and absorbing solar and thermal radiation. To study the aerosols in the atmosphere we carried out a series of ground-based actinometer measurements (Holmgren, Shaw and Weller, 1974). Also, an aircraft-mounted photometer has provided data that allowed deduction of clean air particulate profiles up to 4000 meters (Shaw, in press).

Routine monitoring of components of the radiation balance has been carried out at Barrow, Prudhoe Bay, Ice Island T-3 and during the various field experiments of the Arctic Ice Dynamics Joint Experiment (AIDJEX) on the pack ice north of Pt. Barrow. Coupled with this were studies of surface inhomogeneities, such as hummocks, snow dunes, leads and pressure ridges, and the effects of these features on the surface albedo and temperature. Of particular interest were the measurements over refreezing leads, both artificially-made and natural ones, showing extraordinary modification of the radiation balance during the freezing process (Holmgren and Weller, 1974). Finally, light extinction measurements in snow, ice and sea water, using photocells, allowed the construction of a typical extinction nomogram for these substances (Weller *et al.*, 1972).

One important part of our work has been theoretical modeling in order to synthesize our observations of radiation fluxes and of surface and atmospheric radiation characteristics. For infrared fluxes we have developed a model which allows computation of radiative transfer in an atmosphere with several cloud layers. For short wave fluxes we have so far developed a rough model which shows the effect of a thin cloud layer on the radiation balance of the earth-atmospheric system at various latitudes and seasons. Our data have also been used by Wiscombe (1975) to model radiative transfer through Arctic summer stratus clouds.

In this paper we will discuss primarily the experimental results concerning the radiative and physical properties of Arctic aerosols and Arctic stratus clouds.

2. Composition of Arctic clouds

Studies of the composition of arctic stratus clouds were made at Barrow, Alaska: the first series of measurements was performed in September 1971 and the second in April 1972, others have followed these. The cloud particles were collected continuously in flight using an MRI cloud particle sampler extending through the door of a Cessna 180 aircraft so that the sampling point was well outside the disturbed propeller wake. The air was sampled at the rate of about 1.5 l/sec at 100-knot flight speeds. 16 mm clear leader film was continuously coated with a 4% solution of formvar in chloroform just before exposure to the cloudy air through a small rectangular orifice. Permanent replicas of the cloud particles, formed in the hardening formvar, were later analyzed in the laboratory. We found film

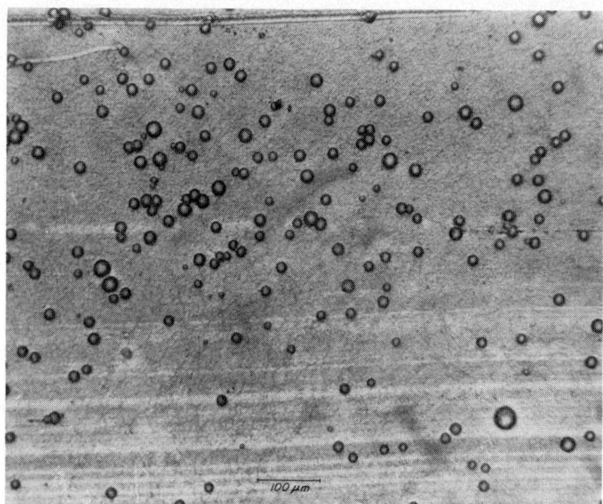

FIG. 1. An example of water droplets collected from the arctic stratus clouds by the MRI cloud particle sampler.

speeds of 11 cm per second during sampling to be the most satisfactory rate.

The clouds that we sampled during the measuring series in September were probably rather typical for stratiform clouds in the Arctic during fall. In most cases they consisted of two and sometimes three separate layers. Each of the cloud layers was about 1000 m thick and they were separated from one another by a few hundred meters. Weak or no updrafts were indicated within the clouds. We found clouds extending from nearly 200 m to over 4000 m above the ground, hence we were able to sample clouds at temperature levels from $+2$ C to -11 C. Sampling was done by flying at a fixed height or constant temperature for about 5 minutes, so that about 500 liters of air were sampled.

The ice crystal concentrations were determined by analyzing sections of at least 6 meters of film at a time, frame by frame, using a stop motion projector and counting the number of ice crystals within each section. The ice crystals were all columnar and unrimed.

The water droplet concentration and size distribution were determined by photographing, at about 30 cm intervals, the formvar replicas under a microscope. One such photograph is shown in Fig. 1. The concentration of droplets averaged about 90 per cm^3 at all levels. It must be mentioned, however, that the concentrations generally varied, owing to the patchy nature of the clouds, from almost zero to about 150 per cm^3. The liquid water content was about 0.2 gm m^{-3}. The size distribution did not show significant variations at different levels, hence the overall size distribution for all the levels is shown in Fig. 2. This, of course, was corrected for the droplet spread and collection efficiency of the sampler. The 3 μm cutoff is a result of the zero collection efficiency of the sampler for droplets below this size.

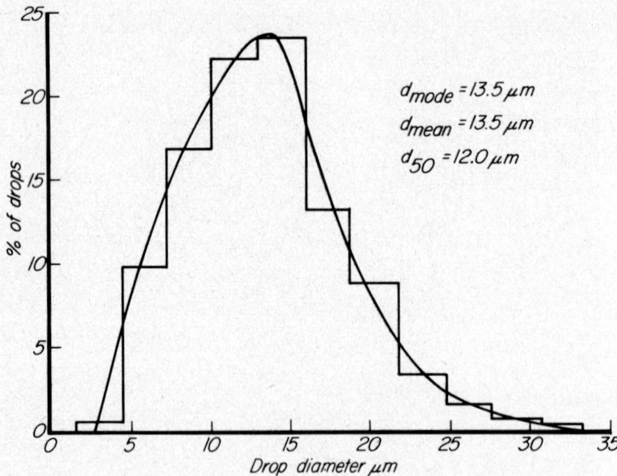

FIG. 2. Average drop size spectrum for the arctic stratus clouds.

In the April 1972 experiments, the clouds were again stratiform, except on one occasion when strato-cumulus was observed. On two occasions the sampling was done in a cloud which was producing snow on the ground. The cloud temperatures were on the average lower than in the September experiments, with the lowest sampling temperature being −15 C. Our analysis indicates that the concentration of ice crystals corresponds to that expected from observed concentrations of ice nuclei active at −15 C (Fig. 3). In these temperature regions the ice crystals are plate-like and dendritic. Although we used a decelerator to reduce the air speed to one-fifth of the aircraft speed, the dendritic crystals were all found to have shattered on impact. The pieces of the shattered ice crystals were found in clusters on the film. However, solid hexagonal plates were found intact.

Summarizing the results, we could say that the non-precipitating stratus clouds over the arctic, within the temperature range of our measurements, have a narrow droplet spectrum typical of stratus clouds of lower latitudes. Ice crystal concentrations are low and can be predicted from the ice nuclei concentration.

3. Ice nucleus concentrations in the Arctic regions

Ice nuclei are particles necessary to form ice crystals in the atmosphere. In the natural atmosphere they are not present in abundant quantities compared to condensation nuclei. To initiate precipitation in cold regions, ice crystals must be present, at least in small quantities, in supercooled water clouds; hence it is important to know the concentration of ice nuclei in the atmosphere.

During April 1972, concentrations of ice nuclei were observed at Barrow, Alaska, by the following two methods:

1) Cloud-settling chamber for counting ice nuclei (Ohtake, 1971). Outside air is introduced into a 10 l

chamber using a vacuum pump. After the air is cooled to the desired temperature (−15 C or −20 C), cloud droplets are introduced into the chamber to give water saturation values exactly equal to those found in natural clouds. If any ice nuclei exists in the chamber, these will nucleate ice crystals, which will then fall into a supercooled sugar solution and grow to visible size. The number counted will be the number of ice nuclei in the 10 liters of air. Fig. 3 shows all the data points we obtained at −15 C and −20 C; they are compared with concentrations of ice crystals in the atmosphere and agree well with the latter.

2) Millipore filter method. In this method air containing ice nuclei was drawn in through two Millipore filters; volumes of air sampled daily were 250 liters

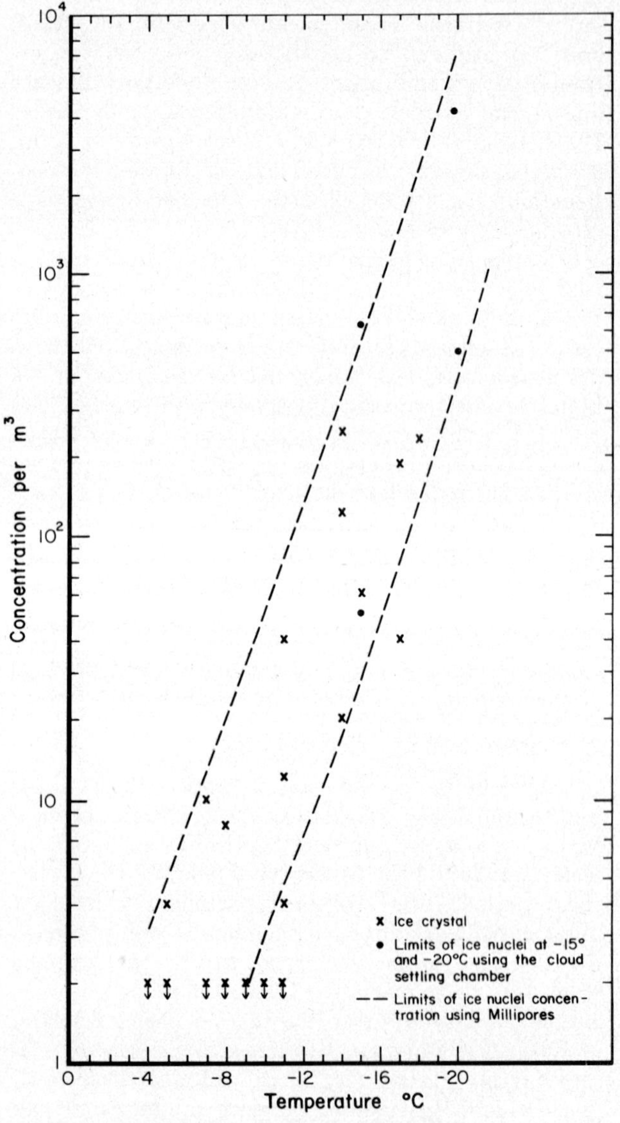

FIG. 3. Comparison of the concentration of ice crystals in the stratus clouds and the concentration of ice nuclei present in clear air at Barrow, Alaska.

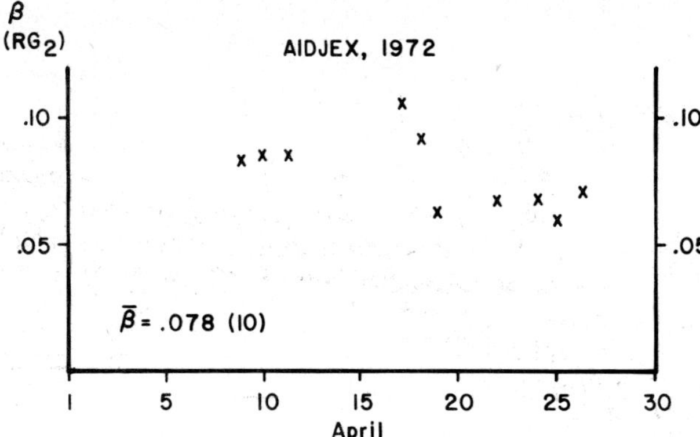

FIG. 4. Daily values of the turbidity coefficient β determined from actinometer measurements during 1972 AIDJEX.

and 360 liters. The filters were developed in a manner similar to that used by Stevenson (1968); processing was done in the laboratory at the Geophysical Institute by cooling the filters to -20 C and subjecting them to water saturation in the processor for 20 minutes. The number of ice crystals formed on a filter indicated the number of nuclei of the sample volume.

We also observed condensation nuclei concentrations with a commercial counter. Condensation nuclei counts consistently increased when winds shifted to directions from inhabited areas, even though absolute numbers in a unit volume of air were quite small compared with other areas in Alaska. On the other hand, ice nuclei concentrations were unaffected by winds from inhabited areas. It is therefore suggested that these two types of nuclei have different origins.

4. Clear air particulates in the Arctic atmosphere

During the AIDJEX pilot study in April 1972, we made approximately 100 measurements of the direct solar intensity using a Linke-Feussner actinometer furnished with Schott color bandpass filters OG1 and RG2. These measurements, representing in all ten days with clear sky conditions (although in some cases there were visible ice crystal aerosols from open leads) have been analyzed to determine the Ångström turbidity coefficient β (Fig. 4) and the total water vapor absorption F (Fig. 5) according to the method of Hoelper (1935). The average β value for the ten days was found to be 0.078, which is higher than expected for clear polar air. On the other hand, the corresponding F values seem to be somewhat low compared to earlier measurements in polar regions (Liljequist, 1965). There are indications, judging from the low F value and also from the relationships between F and air mass m, that our β values for some reason or other may be too high by 0.001–0.010 units. An accurate determination of the atmospheric turbidity parameters requires well-calibrated instruments. Preferably, we should have used a standard pyrheliometer to

support the factory calibrations to ensure maximum reliability of the data.

With these qualifications in mind, it is obvious that the scattering and absorption by particles in the Arctic atmosphere cannot be neglected in considerations of the energy budget of the surface-atmosphere system. For instance, with a solar elevation of 30°, our β values correspond to a decrease of the direct solar radiation by about 20%, compared with conditions in an atmosphere without dust scattering. On the other hand, the influence of the particulates depends on the ratio of absorption to scattering and on the size distribution of the particles, so the effect of the aerosols on the heat budget may be positive or negative. Clearly more work needs to be done in this regard.

The conventional measurements of the direct solar radiation were supplemented with experiments using a sun photometer carried aloft by an aircraft to determine the vertical profile of the optical extinction coefficient. This profile was derived by measuring, at different altitudes, the depletion of monochromatic direct solar radiation due to scattering and absorption by the atmospheric aerosols. Details of the instrumentation and the methods applied are given by Shaw (in press).

We found by using this method that the particulate concentrations in the spring months were generally larger than those found for clear periods in summer (Fig. 6). Earlier measurements of β in the Arctic indicated a seasonal variation with relatively high values in the early spring perhaps due to ice crystals, and markedly lower values in summer (Shaw and Wendler, 1972). Fletcher (1965) points out the prevalence of ice crystals, especially during the dark months and discusses their effect on the long wave radiation budget of the surface-atmosphere systems.

It has been speculated that high turbidities sometimes observed in the Arctic/Subarctic may arise

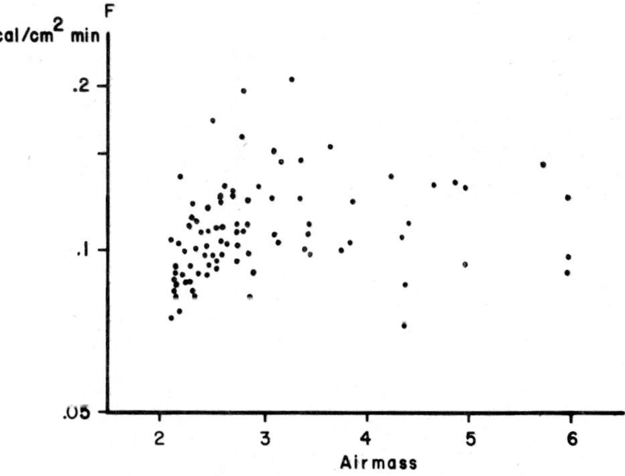

FIG. 5. Water vapour absorption F of solar radiation determined by applying the Ångström-Hoelper method to actinometric measurements during 1972 AIDJEX.

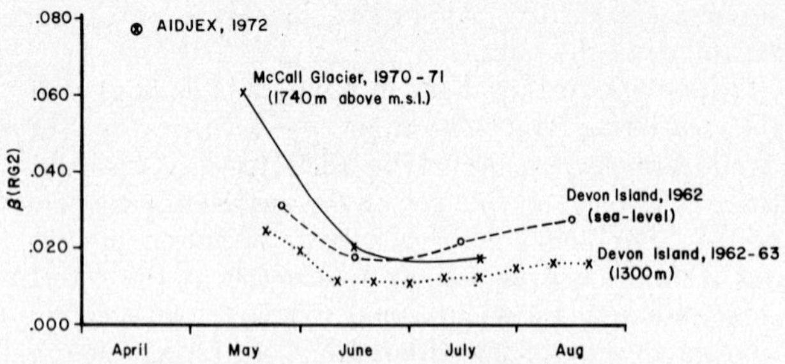

FIG. 6. Variation of the turbidity coefficient β as measured at selected stations in the Arctic.

from the presence of thin sub-visible layers of cirrus ice clouds. Our measurements indicate that this is not the case; instead, the extinction results from particulates that are distributed throughout the troposphere. The highest extinction coefficients are usually found at or near the ground level. At times the extinction coefficient falls off with height in roughly an exponential fashion with a "scale height" ranging from about 1.0 to 1.5 km (Fig. 7). The exponential relationship between extinction coefficient and height is approximate, and on occasion we have observed structure in the height profile. Fig. 8 shows an example of structure observed during the spring 1974 field season. The predominant features shown in Fig. 8 are the two elevated haze layers at altitudes of 300 and 1600 meters. When viewed horizontally from aloft the upper haze layer appeared browning/yellowish, indicating the presence of absorbing material which may have been advected in from large distances. A rough trajectory analysis at the 850 mb level indicates that the airmass had originated from the northeast coast of the United States some four to five days prior to the measurements.

The lower haze layer at 300 meters is associated with ice crystals which form in a supersaturated

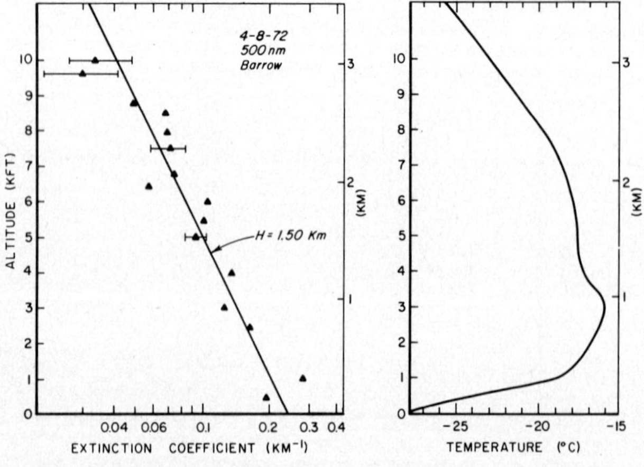

FIG. 7. a) Vertical profile of aerosol volume extinction coefficient (km⁻¹) evaluated at a mean wavelength of 500 nm, near Barrow, Alaska, on April 8, 1972. b) Air temperature profile measured with an airborne thermistor.

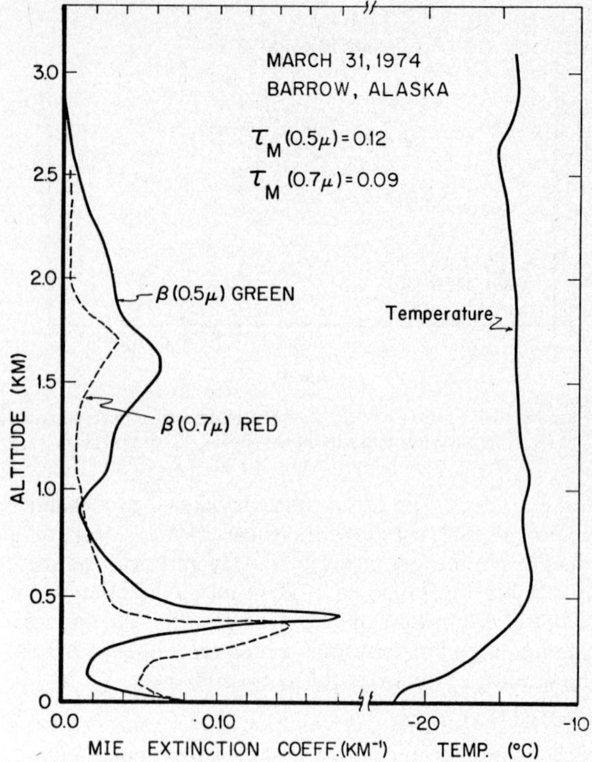

FIG. 8 a) Vertical profile of aerosol volume extinction coefficient (km⁻¹) evaluated at $\lambda = 500$ nm, and 700 nm, near Barrow, Alaska, on March 31, 1974. b) Air temperature.

region near the top of the planetary boundary layer (Holmgren, Shaw and Weller, 1974; Holmgren and Spears, 1974). Both lower ice crystal and upper haze layers play an important role in the radiative transfer in the Arctic atmosphere.

One can interpret the curves of optical extinction coefficient as being at least approximately proportional to aerosol concentration as a function of altitude. A particulate concentration which falls off with height exponentially as in Fig. 7 suggests that the particles may be generated at the surface and mixed upwards through the boundary layer by eddy diffusion processes. As already mentioned, there may also be times when aerosols are advected in from afar to produce elevated haze layers such as those shown in Fig. 8.

Unfortunately no direct samples of the particulates in the haze layers could be collected during these experiments, so we can only speculate about their chemical composition. Fenn *et al.* (1963) found a polar background aerosol over the Greenland icecap with a mass loading of 1 μg m^{-3}. The majority of the aerosol mass was in the size range $0.4 < d < 1.5$ μm; chemical analysis showed that approximately 40% of the particulates were sulphates. Since the vapor pressure over sulphate compounds is low, they can have a long life time in an environment with zero constituent vapor pressure (Junge, 1963). For example, the sublimation time for ammonium sulphate is of the order of four days. This residence time is consistent with the hypothesis that sulphate compounds may be advected into the Arctic from great distances and may perhaps be responsible for the elevated haze layers over the Arctic Basin.

The vertical particulate profile during summer was derived from three flights during July 1972. The total optical extinction was markedly lower than in spring, but variable. It is difficult, of course, to make general statements about seasonal variability with these few measurements only. As an example of the summer data, Fig. 9 shows a typical vertical profile of the extinction coefficient. As can be seen, the lower troposphere was essentially devoid of aerosols on July 11, reinforcing the view that the peaks in the extinction coefficient seen in spring at lower observations are due to ice crystals. On July 12 the troposphere was invaded by aerosols in the height interval from three to twelve kilometers. The aerosols were distributed approximately in an exponential fashion with height with a scale height of 1.3 km, and the aerosol height profile changed little during the following 24 hours. Analysis of the synoptic charts showed that a cold frontal system had passed through Barrow approximately 20 hours prior to the first flight of July 11, 1972. During the passage of this system a polar airmass, which had a relatively low aerosol content, intruded into the region. In the following twenty four hour period, a cyclonic pressure system located to the southwest apparently advected aerosols into the area, causing the observed increase.

To summarize, we see that the vertical aerosol profile over the Arctic Basin is complex and variable. A meaningful aerosol climatology must, of course, be based on a large sample of data. However, from our relatively limited measurements we tentatively identify high springtime turbidities with ice crystals in the boundary layer. One would assume that the ice crystal concentrations during the winter months in the Arctic must also be quite large. Since ice has strong absorption features in the 8–12 μ window (Irvine and Pollock, 1968) it is likely that ice crystals would affect the heat budget of the polar regions. In winter, when solar radiation is negligible, their presence would lead to a net heating of the surface; however, the net heat loss from the earth-atmosphere system could either increase or decrease depending upon the vertical distribution of ice crystals and the temperature structure.

The elevated haze layers show indications of being composed of absorbing material, and their presence in conjunction with the high albedo surface would almost certainly lead to a surface heating (Chylek and Coakley, 1974).

5. Concluding remarks

We consider our measurements of the physical and radiative properties of the atmospheric clouds and

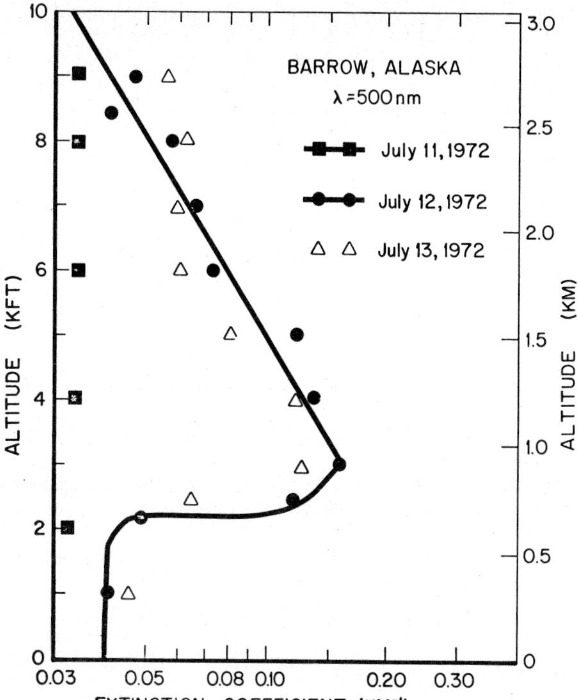

FIG. 9. Vertical profile of aerosol volume extinction coefficient ($\lambda = 500$ nm) near Barrow, Alaska, for three consecutive days in July 1972.

aerosols as a start for more extensive investigations. Obviously, we need to know much more about the day-to-day and also seasonal variations of the radiative properties of the Arctic atmosphere. One of our next experiments will be to investigate the water vapor transport, ice crystal production and the radiative exchanges that are associated with open leads in winter and in early spring. We may then be able to state more definitely the connection between the crystal aerosols found over open leads and the high turbidity values found in spring. The ultimate objective of our measurements is to provide input data for models of the radiative transfer in the Arctic. Data on size, shape, refractive index and the vertical height distribution of the aerosols, concentrations of droplets and ice crystals in the clouds, surface reflectivities and optical properties of snow, pack ice, etc., are required in much greater detail.

Acknowledgments. It is a pleasure to acknowledge the financial support of the Office of Naval Research and the logistical assistance of the Naval Arctic Research Laboratory at Barrow, Alaska.

REFERENCES

Chylek, P., and J. A. Coakley, Jr., 1974: Aerosols and climate. *Science*, **183**, 4120, 75–77.

Fenn, R. W., W. E. Gerber and E. Wasshausen, 1963: Measurements of the sulphate and ammonium composition of the arctic aerosol of the Greenland icecap. *J. Atmos. Sci.*, **20**, 466.

Fletcher, J. O., 1965: The heat budget of the Arctic Basin and its relation to climate, RAND Rept. No. 12-444-PR.

Fletcher, J. O., 1966: *Proceedings of the Symposium on the Arctic Heat Budget and Atmospheric Circulation.* Jan. 31 through Feb. 4, 1966, Lake Arrowhead, California, RAND Corp., Rm 5233 NSF.

Hoelper, O., 1935: "Deutsches Meteorologisches Jahrbuch fur das Jahr 1933", Herausgegeben im Auftrage des Reichsamtes fur Wetterdienst, Aachen.

Holmgren, B., G. Shaw and G. Weller, 1974: On the turbidity of the Arctic atmosphere. *AIDJEX Bulletin,* 27.

Holmgren, B., and L. Spears, 1974: Sodar investigations of the effect of open leads on the boundary layer structure over the Arctic Basin. *AIDJEX Bulletin,* 27.

Holmgren, B., and G. Weller, 1974: Local radiation fluxes over open and refreezing leads in the polar pack ice. *AIDJEX Bulletin,* 27.

Irvine, W. M., and J. B. Pollack, 1968: Infrared optical properties of water and ice spheres. *Icarus,* 8, 324.

Jayaweera, K. O. L. F., and T. Ohtake, 1973: Concentrations of ice crystals in Arctic stratus clouds. *Journ. de Recherches Atmospheriques,* 200–207.

Junge, C. E., 1963: *Air Chemistry and Radioactivity.* International Geophysics Series, Vol. 4, New York, Academic Press, 1–100.

Liljequist, G. H., 1956: "Energy exchange of an Antarctic snowfield. Part 1A: Short-wave radiation," Norwegian-British-Swedish Antarctic Expedition, 1949–52, *Scientific Results,* Vol. II, Oslo.

Ohtake, T., 1971: Cloud settling chamber for ice nuclei count, Proceedings of Inst. Conf. on Weather Modification, Sept. 1971, Canberra, Australia, 38–41.

Shaw, G. (in press): The vertical distribution profile of tropospheric aerosols at Barrow, Alaska, *Tellus.*

Shaw, G., and G. Wendler, 1972: Atmospheric turbidity measurements at McCall Glacier in Northeast Alaska. Conference on Atmospheric Radiation, August 1972, Ft. Collins, Colorado. Preprint Vol. 181–187, AMS, Boston.

Stevenson, C. M., 1968: An improved Millipore technique for measuring the concentration of freezing nuclei in the atmosphere. *Q. J. Roy. Met. Soc.,* 94, 35–43.

Weller, G., S. A. Bowling, K. O. L. F. Jayaweera, T. Ohtake, S. Parker, G. Shaw and G. Wendler, 1972: The solar and terrestrial radiation fluxes over arctic pack ice. Technical Report No. 2, ONR Contract N00014-71-A-0364-0001, Geophysical Institute, University of Alaska.

Wiscombe, W. J., 1975: Solar radiation calculations for arctic summer stratus. AAAS-AMS Conference: Climate of the Arctic, Eds. G. Weller, and S. A. Bowling, Geophysical Institute, University of Alaska.

Solar Radiation Calculations for Arctic Summer Stratus Conditions

WARREN J. WISCOMBE*

Systems, Science and Software, La Jolla, California

Abstract

A new and highly detailed model for one-dimensional radiative transfer in the atmosphere, accounting for the combined effects of line absorption and multiple scattering is applied to the problem of solar radiative fluxes in the presence of typical Arctic summer stratus. The model is verified against measurements by Weller *et al.* (1972) and then used as a predictive tool. Simple two-stream multiple cloud-ground reflection approximations are shown to be useful in reproducing the results of the detailed model, but only when it is recognized that the cloud has a different albedo and absorptivity for the unidirectional, undepleted radiation incident from above than for the diffuse, depleted radiation incident from below. The solar fluxes are parameterized in a simple way as functions of cloud droplet density, surface albedo, and solar elevation, and the dependence of the multiple-reflection model parameters on these same variables is investigated. Finally, some new and interesting conclusions *re* solar absorption in the atmosphere are offered, notably that this absorption is sensitive neither to the amount of cloud present nor to the surface albedo.

1. Introduction

Radiation tends to dominate the Arctic heat budget at all seasons (cf. Fletcher, 1965). The fluxes of incoming solar and outgoing long-wave radiation greatly exceed the other terms in the Arctic energy balance relation. These fluxes are substantially influenced by the extensive low stratus prevalent in the Arctic during late spring, summer, and early fall. The flux of solar radiation into the surface under this stratus layer is the most important determinant of pack ice and snow melt, and this summer melt in turn drastically lowers the albedo, which in a complicated fashion (because of multiple reflections between cloud and surface) reacts back on the radiation income at the surface. To follow this process in the necessary detail demands theoretical models and experiments of the greatest possible sophistication. In particular, the theoretical models must predict the radiation flux as a function of atmospheric temperature and humidity, cloud and aerosol content, solar elevation, surface albedo, and ozone amount if realistic heat budget calculations are to be made.

The most ambitious program of theoretical radiation calculations directed specifically to the Arctic stratus problem was that of Feigelson (1964). However, there are a number of approximations in her work, most particularly with respect to the treatment of line absorption and cloud droplet scattering, which leave lingering doubts about the generality of the results. Furthermore, no consideration was given to

the effects of surface reflection. Therefore, in order to remove the limitations inherent in Feigelson's work, and in order to develop simple parameterizations of solar flux for use in heat budget calculations, an extensive series of highly detailed solar radiation calculations in the presence of typical Arctic stratus has been made. The theoretical model used to perform these calculations is described in Section 2. Section 3 presents the model atmosphere chosen for this study. In order to demonstrate that the model is physically realistic, comparisons are presented in Section 4 between the model and some experimental results of Weller *et al.* (1972). Selected predictions of the series of calculations are presented in Section 5 and interpreted in terms of a lumped-parameter, two-stream, one-spectral-interval approximation. The importance of distinguishing between cloud albedo and absorptivity viewed from above and viewed from below is demonstrated. In Section 6, new and simple analytic formulas are given for the surface and cloud-top fluxes (as functions of surface albedo, solar elevation, and cloud thickness) which agree well with the detailed predictions. Finally, the question of solar absorption in the Arctic atmosphere [the most uncertain component of the Arctic heat budget according to Fletcher (1965)] is taken up in Section 7, with a particular view to whether or not it is "anomalously high" as often speculated.

2. The theoretical model

The theoretical model used to perform the computations is the most detailed model of broad-band atmospheric radiative transfer currently in existence,

---

* Present address: National Center for Atmospheric Research, Boulder, Colorado.

short of a prohibitively expensive line-by-line calculation. The goal in the formulation of this model was to make as few approximations and to keep as closely to first principles as possible in order to provide benchmark predictions of radiative fluxes against which to test simpler models. The most important approximations made in the model are that:

(1) the atmosphere is plane-parallel and horizontally homogeneous;

(2) aerosols (including clouds) are composed of spherical particles of uniform composition;

(3) polarization may be neglected;

(4) the pressure scaling approximation of McClatchey *et al.* (1970) satisfactorily accounts for the pressure variation of absorption line width;

(5) Eq. (7) below is valid.

The first assumption is well-satisfied throughout most of the Arctic, with the significant exceptions that leads in the pack ice violate horizontal homogeneity and that the sphericity of the atmosphere becomes non-negligible for solar elevations less than about 5°. The second assumption permits the use of Mie scattering theory to compute aerosol optical properties; this theory hax been shown to be useful for irregular non-spherical particles as well, although its application to ice-crystal aerosol is an open question. The neglect of polarization is an excellent assumption when only fluxes are to be computed. The largest uncertainties are really associated with the last two assumptions. The limitations of pressure scaling approximations have been discussed in the literature in a general way but no precise error estimates exist for the McClatchey scheme, which, nevertheless is the most sophisticated. The assumption embodied in Eq. (7), while it can be made plausible on various grounds, and which enables the model to treat combined line absorption and scattering without resorting to line-by-line calculation, has yet to be rigorously tested against a line-by-line calculation. However, the current results of the model are insensitive to the validity of Eq. (7) because the continuum absorption due to liquid water is generally much larger than the line absorption in the cloud.

The equation for the transfer of monochromatic radiation in plane-parallel horizontally-homogeneous geometry, together with appropriate boundary conditions, is*

$$\mu\frac{\partial\bar{I}}{\partial z}=-\kappa\bar{I}+\alpha B(T)+\frac{\beta}{2}\int_{-1}^{1}\bar{P}(z,\mu,\mu')\bar{I}(z,\mu')d\mu' \quad (1)$$

Top: $\qquad \bar{I}(0,\mu)=\frac{S}{2\pi}\delta(\mu-\mu_{\text{sun}}) \quad (0<\mu\leqslant1) \quad (2)$

---

* For further details, see Freeman, Wiscombe and England (1972a, b).

Bottom: $\bar{I}(z_0,\mu)=\epsilon(|\mu|)B(T_g)+\rho_s(|\mu|)\bar{I}(z_0,-\mu)$

$$+2\int_{0}^{+1}\mu'\bar{\rho}_d(|\mu|,\mu')\bar{I}(z_0,\mu')d\mu' \quad (-1\leqslant\mu<0) \quad (3)$$

The independent variables are z, the vertical coordinate measured from the top of the atmosphere ($z=0$) to the surface ($z=z_0$); μ, the cosine of the nadir angle measured away from the vertical; and ν, the frequency, on which all non-independent variables depend implicitly. A fourth independent variable, the azimuthal angle ϕ, measured around the vertical, does not appear because Eq. (1) has been averaged over azimuth. $\bar{I}$ is the azimuthally-averaged radiation intensity; α, β and κ are the absorption, scattering and extinction coefficients, respectively ($\kappa=\alpha+\beta$), which depend implicitly on pressure $p(z)$ and temperature $T(z)$; $B(T)$ is the Planck function; $\bar{P}$ is the azimuthally-averaged scattering phase function; S is the solar flux at $z=0$; μ_{sun} is the cosine of the solar zenith angle; ϵ, ρ_s, and $\bar{\rho}_d$ are directional emissivity, specular reflectivity, and azimuthally-averaged bi-directional reflectivity of the surface, respectively and T_g is the surface temperature. Often optical depth

$$\tau=\int_{0}^{z}\kappa dz$$

is used in place of z, although the concept of optical depth loses utility across broad spectral regions. Once $\bar{I}$ is known, the vertical flux F is obtained from

$$F(z)=2\pi\int_{-1}^{1}\mu\bar{I}(z,\mu)d\mu \quad (4)$$

(the down-flux and up-flux are given by the same expression with integration limits of 0 to 1 and 0 to -1, respectively). In practice one does not solve directly for $\bar{I}$ but for the diffuse intensity i resulting from subtracting the solar beam and its specular reflection from $\bar{I}$:

$$i=\begin{cases}\bar{I}-\bar{I}^{\text{spec}} & 1\leqslant\mu<0 \\ \bar{I}-\bar{I}^{\text{sol}} & 0<\mu\leqslant1\end{cases}$$

where

$$\bar{I}^{\text{sol}}=\frac{S}{2\pi}e^{-\tau/\mu_{\text{sun}}}\delta(\mu-\mu_{\text{sun}})$$

$$\bar{I}^{\text{spec}}=\frac{S}{2\pi}\rho_s(\mu_{\text{sun}})e^{-(2\tau_0-\tau)/\mu_{\text{sun}}}\delta(\mu+\mu_{\text{sun}})$$

Appropriate modifications are made in Eqs. (1–4) to phrase them in terms of i. This transformation eliminates the problematical (from a numerical point of view) δ-function in the top boundary condition, Eq. (2).

Equation (1) is essentially a conservation law for photons along the ϕ-averaged beam making an angle $\theta = \cos^{-1}$ with the vertical. Absorption and scattering deplete the beam according to Lambert's Law ($-\kappa \bar{I}$ term) while thermal emission (αB term) and scattering into the beam from other beams (term involving $\bar{P}$) augment it. No general analytic solution to Eq. (1) is known, as one might surmise from its integro-differential character, although a good deal of mileage has been gotten out of the special solutions for no scattering and Rayleigh scattering. Therefore, one must resort to numerical methods. A number of iterative schemes have been used to solve Eq. (1) in the past, but these break down for optical depths larger than about 5 and have now been made obsolete by the discovery of the Grant-Hunt (1969) method, which is a non-iterative, flux-conserving solution to Eq. (1) valid for arbitrary optical depths. The Grant-Hunt method, augmented by the source doubling techniques of Wiscombe and Freeman (1972), forms the nucleus of our detailed model.

If a line-by-line calculation were feasible, it would then be a simple matter of stepping through the spectrum with the Grant-Hunt method, using frequency steps small enough to resolve individual absorption lines, and summing the resultant intensities to obtain broad-band intensities. To do the full solar and IR spectrum in this manner, however, would require millions of frequency steps, and it can be shown that the computation time required would be prohibitive. Therefore, some method must be devised for taking steps $\Delta \nu$ large compared to individual line widths but still small enough to resolve the comparatively slowly-varying $B(T)$, $\bar{P}$, β, S, ϵ, ρ_s and $\bar{\rho}_d$. Any attempt to average Eq. (1) over such a frequency interval $\Delta \nu$ founders upon the term $-\alpha \bar{I}$, for both factors in this term vary rapidly with ν inside $\Delta \nu$ and thus neither may reasonably be computed with the frequency average. In an attempt to get around this difficulty, it is natural to go to the integral formulation, which is obtained by integrating Eq. (1) like a differential equation to get

$$\bar{I}(z,\mu) = \bar{I}_b(\mu) e^{-(\tau - \tau_b)/\mu} + \frac{1}{\mu} \int_{z_b}^{z} J(z',\mu) e^{-(\tau - \tau')/\mu} dz' \quad (5)$$

where subscript b refers to a boundary $z = z_b$, $\tau' = \tau(z')$, and J is the sum of the thermal and scattering source terms. Eq. (5) cannot be readily averaged over $\Delta \nu$ either, since τ, τ', τ_b, $\bar{I}_b$ and the $\bar{I}$-term in J all vary rapidly across $\Delta \nu$ in general. Nevertheless, an idea suggested by Yamamoto (1971) enables us to derive a plausible frequency-averaged form of Eq. (5). First, we direct attention specifically to the line absorption part

$$\tau_{\text{line}} = \int_{0}^{z} \alpha_{\text{line}} dz$$

of the optical depth since the other parts vary relatively slowly with ν. The scaling approximation assumes that α_{line} is the product of a function of frequency and a function of pressure and temperature, so that

$$\tau_{\text{line}} = k_\nu u(z)$$

where u is called the "scaled" absorber amount. Let the (line) transmission function $T_{\Delta\nu}$ for an absorber amount u be

$$T_{\Delta\nu}(u) = \frac{1}{\Delta\nu} \int_{\Delta\nu} e^{-k_\nu u/\mu} d\nu$$

As $\Delta\nu \to 0$, this reduces to the monochromatic transmission $e^{-k_\nu u/\mu}$; however, for $\Delta\nu$ large enough to include many lines $T_{\Delta\nu}$ has a decidedly non-exponential character. But Yamamoto's idea was that $T_{\Delta\nu}$ could still be represented as a *sum* of exponentials,

$$T_{\Delta\nu} = \frac{1}{\Delta\nu} \int_{\Delta\nu} e^{-k_\nu u/\mu} d\nu \cong \sum_{i=1}^{M} a_i e^{-k_i u/\mu} \quad (6)$$

(although he assumed $a_i = 1/M$) and, furthermore, that in this manner one could reduce the problem to a series of monochromatic problems, each with absorption coefficient $k_i(du/dz)$. There remained two gaps in this procedure, however, first that the key underlying assumption was not made explicit nor justified, and second that a computational procedure to obtain exponential-sum fits to transmission data was not available. Freeman *et al.* (1972a) have shown that the underlying assumption is

$$\frac{1}{\Delta\nu} \int_{\Delta\nu} \bar{I}_\nu e^{-k_\nu u/\mu} d\nu = \sum_{i=1}^{M} a_i \bar{I}_i e^{-k_i u/\mu} \quad (7)$$

where the $\bar{I}_i$ are defined to be solutions of the corresponding monochromatic problem with line absorption coefficient $k_i(du/dz)$, and where the averaged intensity for $\Delta\nu$ is

$$\bar{I}_{\Delta\nu} = \frac{1}{\Delta\nu} \int_{\Delta\nu} \bar{I}_\nu d\nu = \sum_{i=1}^{M} a_i \bar{I}_i \quad (8)$$

Freeman *et al.*, argue for the plausibility of Eq. (7) based on the observation that Eq. (6) furnishes a Lebesgue quadrature rule for the integral on the left and that this quadrature rule should also be applicable to the integral in Eq. (7). As for the determination of the a_i and k_i, Evans and Wiscombe (in preparation) have devised a stable numerical algorithm with guaranteed convergence which fits exponential sums to transmission functions in the least squares sense. The transmission data actually fitted are those of McClatchey *et al.* (1970) which account for all known atmospheric absorbers across the full solar and IR

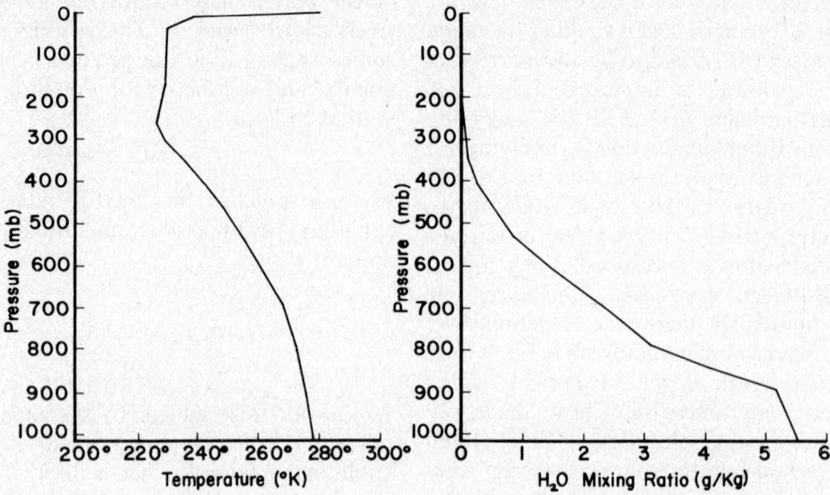

FIG. 1. Atmospheric temperature and mixing ratio profiles—Arctic stratus problem.

spectrums, and which have a basic averaging interval $\Delta\nu$ of 20 cm^{-1}.

When the approximation (6), the assumption (7), and the definition (8) are all placed into the frequency-averaged form of Eq. (5), and the right- and left-hand sides are equated term-by-term, we are left with M monochromatic problems which can be solved by the Grant-Hunt method and whose results can be assembled according to Eq. (8) to give $\bar{I}_{\Delta\nu}$. This, in abbreviated form, is the theoretical basis of the model whose results we shall now examine. A more definitive treatment is available in Freeman, Wiscombe and England (1972a, b).

3. The model atmosphere

We present here the atmospheric input data required by the detailed model and used in the present computations. The temperature and humidity profiles, shown in Fig. 1, are taken from the Air Force Hand-

book of Geophysics (Valley, 1965) supplemental standard atmosphere for July and for 75°N; however, the relative humidity within and below the cloud has been increased to 100%. The total water vapor amount is 1.65 g cm^{-2}, of which 0.33 g cm^{-2} is between the surface and the cloud base ($\frac{1}{2}$ km) and 0.30 g cm^{-2} is within the cloud ($\frac{1}{2}$–1 km). The sub-Arctic summer ozone profile of McClatchey *et al.* (1970), with a total ozone amount of 0.33 atm-cm, is also used. The cloud location ($\frac{1}{2}$–1 km) is typical for Arctic summer stratus according to Huschke (1969). The cloud is assumed to be vertically homogeneous and to have the droplet size distribution shown in Fig. 2, which was measured by Weller *et al.* (1972). Optical properties of the cloud were computed using the liquid water index of refraction data of Hale and Querry (1973). Finally, surface albedos, solar elevations, and dates on which these measurements were taken (Weller *et al.*, 1972) are given in Table I.

It should be noted that the computed solar fluxes are almost totally insensitive to physically realistic variations of the temperature profile, ozone profile, and cloud base altitude, for reasons which space

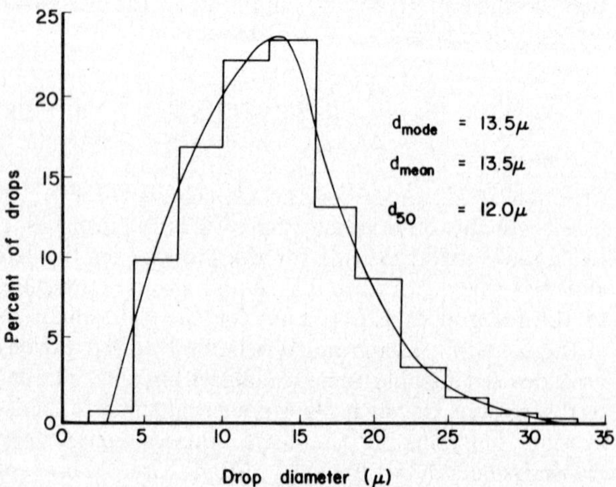

FIG. 2. Droplet size distribution of Arctic stratus cloud at Barrow, measured by Weller *et al.* (1972).

TABLE I. Comparison of solar flux measurements (in cal cm^{-2} min^{-1}) of Weller *et al.* (1972) with detailed calculations. (Calculated fluxes have been rounded to two significant figures since measurements are only quoted to this accuracy).

Date (1971)	Pt. Barrow, Alaska		
	June 2	June 10	June 29
Albedo	79%	58%	20%
Mean solar elevation	31°	24°	21°
Measured surface down-flux	0.56	0.38	0.26
Predicted surface down-flux	0.60	0.38	0.26

limitations do not allow us to pursue. We also speculate that there is a similar insensitivity to the precise form of the droplet size distribution. Therefore, the important parameters are the surface albedo, solar elevation, humidity profile, and cloud liquid water amount (which is proportional to droplet number density since cloud thickness is fixed in this problem). In the following we shall examine how solar radiation fluxes vary with all of these except humidity profile, which is fixed.

4. Comparison with measurements

The incoming solar flux at the surface was measured by Weller *et al.* (1972) at a site near Point Barrow, Alaska, during the June thaw when the albedo was decreasing rapidly. The results for three days are shown in Table I. Cloud conditions were judged to be similar on the three days, and therefore the decrease in downward flux as the thaw progressed was ascribed primarily to the decreasing importance of multiple cloud-ground reflections. The detailed calculations bear out this conjecture.

Unfortunately, no measurements of cloud droplet number density were made on these days. Therefore, the model was iterated to determine the value of droplet number density (which turned out to be 28.35 cm^{-3}) that would force agreement with the downward flux measurement on June 29. The same value of droplet number density was used to calculate fluxes for the other two days. Agreement with measurement was exact for June 10, while the calculated downward flux was too high by about 7% for June 2. Thus, the model seems capable of prdoucing physically realistic flux predictions.

The discretization of altitude, angle, and frequency used in the computations should be stated. Using the notation that $Z_1(\Delta Z) Z_2$ means $Z_1, Z_1 + \Delta Z, Z_1 + 2\,\Delta Z, \cdots, Z_2$, the zone structure, in km, was $0(\frac{1}{2})4(1)10(2)24(6)30(20)50$, for a total of 21 zones. The 75 spectral intervals used to span Weller's instrumental response range (roughly 0.2–2.8 μ) were, in cm^{-1}, $3600(240)4800(320)8000(500)32000(1000)35000(1500)48500$. A large number of spectral intervals are needed in the visible in order to resolve the rapidly-varying Rayleigh scattering coefficient. Twelve (Gaussian quadrature) angles were used to resolve the intensity in each spectral interval.

Putting aside questions of flux measurement error and flux prediction error, it is interesting to use the detailed model to determine what changes in input parameters would bring measurement and calculation into agreement on June 2. We find that agreement could be obtained by any one of the following:

(a) decreasing solar elevation to 29°,
(b) decreasing albedo to 65%,
(c) increasing droplet density to 43.5 cm^{-3}.

The drastic changes in albedo (18%) and droplet density (53%) necessary are surprising in view of the relatively minor (7%) flux disagreement. It indicates that the solar down-flux at the surface is relatively insensitive to albedo and droplet density and that, therefore, the most likely source of the disagreement (among the three being considered) is Weller's value of solar elevation. There is a pronounced sensitivity to solar elevation, for a 2° (6%) change in it fully accounts for the 7% flux disagreement. Since the sun's position was not directly observable during the measurements, it must have been calculated and averaged over the measurement period. Even if that calculation was correct, there still remains an uncertainty in the proper "mean solar elevation" with which to associate the flux measurement. Small errors at any step of this process, coupled with the effects of rounding to the nearest whole degree, could more than explain the disagreement. In light of this discussion, it is recommended that experimenters state the times during which their flux measurements were taken rather than "mean solar elevations," which are processed data and, therefore, more subject to error.

5. Multiple reflection models

Multiple reflection models are special cases of the "two-stream" approximation in radiative transfer in which the reflection and transmission properties of each atmospheric layer are lumped into two parameters (per layer): an albedo α and an absorptivity a. The simplest such model, for a cloud with albedo α_c, absorptivity a_c, and transmissivity $T_c = 1 - \alpha_c - a_c$ overlying a transparent cloud-to-ground (cg) layer, above a ground surface with albedo ρ, is shown schematically in Fig. 3. (The notations ct for cloud top, cb for cloud base, g for surface, $F^{\downarrow}$ for downward flux, $F^{\uparrow}$ for upward flux, and $F = F^{\downarrow} - F^{\uparrow}$ for net flux are used in the remainder of this paper.) The various

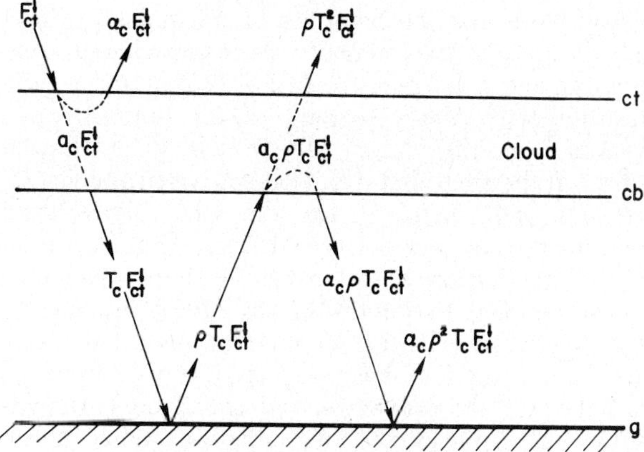

FIG. 3. The simplest multiple cloud-ground reflection model. $F_{ct}{\downarrow}$, α_c, a_c, T_c and ρ are the solar down-flux at the cloud top, the cloud albedo, the cloud fractional absorptivity, the cloud transmission, and the surface albedo, respectively.

TABLE II. Multiple-reflection model parameters determined from the detailed model (from $\rho=0$, 10% cases) for droplet density 28.35 cm^{-3} and various solar elevations.

Solar elev. (θ_s)	α_c	α_d	α_{cg}	a_c	a_d	a_{cg}
10°	0.597	0.376	0.005	0.018	0.011	0.004
20°	0.516	0.373	0.006	0.022	0.011	0.006
30°	0.440	0.370	0.006	0.024	0.012	0.007
40°	0.370	0.367	0.006	0.025	0.013	0.008

fluxes in Fig. 3 may be obtained simply by summing geometric series, e.g.,

$$F_g{}^\downarrow = \{1+\alpha_c\rho+(\alpha_c\rho)^2+\cdots\}T_cF_{ct}{}^\downarrow = \frac{T_c}{1-\alpha_c\rho}F_{ct}{}^\downarrow$$

It becomes very difficult to draw correct pictures of the type of Fig. 3 when more than one layer has an albedo, however, and since in general the cg layer has an albedo α_{cg} (due to Rayleigh and aerosol scattering), an absorptivity a_{cg} (due to molecular and aerosol absorption), and, therefore, a non-unit transmissivity $T_{cg}=1-\alpha_{cg}-a_{cg}$, we shall want a more general procedure. Such a procedure is furnished by the "interaction principle" of Grant and Hunt (1969), specialized to the case of only two streams of radiation and no internal sources. The interaction principles for the cloud and cloud-ground layer (plus the surface boundary condition) are

$$F_{ct}{}^\uparrow = \alpha_cF_{ct}{}^\downarrow + T_dF_{cb}{}^\uparrow \tag{9}$$

$$F_{cb}{}^\downarrow = \alpha_dF_{cb}{}^\uparrow + T_cF_{ct}{}^\downarrow \tag{10}$$

$$F_{cb}{}^\uparrow = \alpha_{cg}F_{cb}{}^\downarrow + T_{cg}F_g{}^\uparrow \tag{11}$$

$$F_g{}^\downarrow = \alpha_{cg}F_g{}^\uparrow + T_{cg}F_{cb}{}^\downarrow \tag{12}$$

$$F_g{}^\uparrow = \rho F_g{}^\downarrow \tag{13}$$

It should be obvious how such equations are written down. Note that the cloud has been assumed to have albedo α_c and transmissivity T_c when viewed from the top, and a different albedo α_d, absorptivity a_d, and transmissivity $T_d=1-\alpha_d-a_d$ (d for diffuse) when viewed from the bottom. The necessity for this, in spite of the fact that the cloud is vertically homogeneous and, therefore, has the same bidirectional reflectivity top and bottom, derives rigorously from the interaction principle but can be simply explained by noting that the albedo of any object depends on the angular distribution of incident radiation. Since the cloud top is subjected primarily to collimated radiation at the sun angle, and the cloud bottom is subjected to almost isotropic radiation, which, in addition, has been preferentially depleted in the wavelengths most strongly absorbed by the clouds, it is natural they should have different effective albedos and absorptivities. By this reasoning, it is also logical

that α_d and a_d are independent of solar elevation, which we shall see later is true. We shall also see the consequences of assuming $\alpha_d=\alpha_c$ and $a_d=a_c$, which has in the past been customary.

Eqs. 9–13 may be solved for all fluxes in terms of $F_{ct}{}^\downarrow$. Selected results are

$$F_g{}^\downarrow = \gamma_1 T_{cg}F_{ct}{}^\downarrow \tag{14}$$

$$F_{ct}{}^\uparrow = (\alpha_c+\gamma_2 T_d)F_{ct}{}^\downarrow \tag{15}$$

$$(\Delta F)_c = F_{ct}-F_{cb} = (a_c+\gamma_2 a_d)F_{ct}{}^\downarrow \tag{16}$$

$$(\Delta F)_{cg} = F_{cb}-F_g = \gamma_1 a_{cg}[1+\rho(T_{cg}-\alpha_{cg})]F_{ct}{}^\downarrow \tag{17}$$

where

$$\gamma_1 = \frac{T_c}{(1-\alpha_d\alpha_{cg})(1-\rho\alpha_{cg})-\rho\alpha_dT_{cg}{}^2} \tag{18}$$

$$\gamma_2 = [\rho T_{cg}{}^2+\alpha_{cg}(1-\rho\alpha_{cg})]\gamma_1 \tag{19}$$

In the following, only the ratios of $F_g{}^\downarrow$, $F_{ct}{}^\uparrow$, $(\Delta F)_c$, and $(\Delta F)_{cg}$ to $F_{ct}{}^\downarrow$ will be considered, since the value of $F_{ct}{}^\downarrow$ is an input datum for the multiple-reflection model.

Let us compare the predictions of the multiple reflection model (Eqs. 14–19) and the detailed model for the albedos $\rho=20\%$, 58%, 79% and the solar elevations $\theta_s=10°$, $20°$, $30°$, $40°$. The multiple reflection model has six unknown parameters; therefore, we use the detailed model to determine them. In any one run of the detailed model, only four data are usable for this purpose ($F_{cb}{}^\downarrow$, $F_{cb}{}^\uparrow$, $F_g{}^\downarrow$, $F_{ct}{}^\uparrow$). Thus, two "parameterization" runs of the detailed model were made for each solar elevation, one for $\rho=0$ and the other for $\rho=10\%$; these extra pairs of runs enabled us to solve for the six parameters as functions of θ_s. The results are shown in Table II. Several important observations may be made regarding Table II. First and foremost, the "diffuse" albedo α_d and absorptivity a_d are indeed practically independent of θ_s, indicating that the under-cloud radiation field approaches isotropy as conjectured. The cloud top albedo α_c is a strong (and almost linear) function of θ_s and exceeds the cloud bottom albedo α_d for all θ_s (although the two become practically equal for $\theta_s=40°$). The cloud absorptivity for direct downward solar radiation a_c ($\sim2\%$) is $1\frac{1}{2}$ to 2 times larger than the cloud absorptivity for diffusely reflected radiation a_d ($\sim1\%$), which is partly due to the fact that on the downward pass through the cloud the strongly absorbed frequencies are depleted and the cloud is more transparent to the remaining radiation on subsequent upward passes. The albedo α_{cg} and absorptivity a_{cg} of the cloud-to-ground layer are small, of the order of $\frac{1}{2}\%$, and have a correspondingly small effect on the flux predictions of Eqs. (14–17).

The predictions of the 6-parameter multiple reflection model (Eqs. 14–17), with parameters from Table II, are compared with the predictions of the detailed

TABLE III. Comparison of 6-parameter multiple-reflection model (unparenthesized) and detailed model (parenthesized) predictions for surface down-flux $F_g\!\downarrow$, cloud-top up-flux $F_{ct}\!\uparrow$, net flux change across the cloud $(\Delta F)_c$, and net flux change between cloud and ground $(\Delta F)_{cg}$, all normalized to the cloud-top downflux $F_{ct}\!\downarrow$.

Solar elevn.	Surface albedo	$F_g\!\downarrow/F_{ct}\!\downarrow$	$F_{ct}\!\uparrow/F_{ct}\!\downarrow$	$(\Delta F)_c/F_{ct}\!\downarrow$	$(\Delta F)_{cg}/F_{ct}\!\downarrow$
10°	20%	0.414 (0.414)	0.648 (0.648)	0.018 (0.018)	0.002 (0.002)
	58%	0.490 (0.490)	0.771 (0.771)	0.021 (0.020)	0.003 (0.003)
	79%	0.545 (0.545)	0.859 (0.860)	0.022 (0.022)	0.004 (0.004)
20°	20%	0.494 (0.494)	0.578 (0.578)	0.023 (0.023)	0.003 (0.003)
	58%	0.583 (0.583)	0.724 (0.725)	0.026 (0.025)	0.005 (0.005)
	79%	0.648 (0.648)	0.830 (0.831)	0.028 (0.027)	0.006 (0.006)
30°	20%	0.573 (0.573)	0.512 (0.512)	0.025 (0.025)	0.005 (0.005)
	58%	0.675 (0.675)	0.681 (0.681)	0.029 (0.029)	0.007 (0.007)
	79%	0.748 (0.748)	0.803 (0.804)	0.031 (0.031)	0.009 (0.008)
40°	20%	0.645 (0.645)	0.451 (0.451)	0.026 (0.026)	0.006 (0.006)
	58%	0.758 (0.758)	0.642 (0.643)	0.030 (0.030)	0.009 (0.009)
	79%	0.839 (0.840)	0.779 (0.781)	0.033 (0.033)	0.012 (0.010)

model in Table III. To three decimal places, which is the estimated accuracy of the detailed model, they agree almost exactly for all solar elevations and all surface albedos. Thus, we are able to recover the results of our 75 spectral interval, 12 stream model from a much simpler model having only one spectral interval (the full solar spectrum) and two streams. The catch is, of course, that the detailed model was used to parameterize the simple one; however, a suitable experimental program can also furnish the requisite parameters. And, the detailed model can furnish guidance in extrapolating the measured parameters to other solar elevations, other cloud droplet densities, etc.

Fletcher (1965) has emphasized that "the largest quantitative uncertainty in the heat budget is the amount of solar radiation absorbed directly by the atmosphere," in particular by clouds. Therefore, the two ΔF calculations in Table III deserve close scrutiny. The fractional absorption by the cloud, $(\Delta F)_c/F_{ct}\!\downarrow$, is about 2–3% for all ρ's and θ_s's (it varies only weakly with ρ and θ_s) and varies more rapidly for low solar elevations ($\leqslant 20°$) while seemingly approaching an asymptote for larger solar elevations ($>20°$). The increase of $(\Delta F)_c/F_{ct}\!\downarrow$ with θ_s is related to the decrease of cloud-top albedo α_c with θ_s (see Table II), which allows a larger fraction of $F_{ct}\!\downarrow$ to penetrate the cloud and be subjected to absorption. The slow increase of $(\Delta F)_c$ with ρ is, of course, due to the increasing amount of ground-reflected radiation passing upward through the cloud and being absorbed there, but the majority of the cloud absorption occurs on the first (downward) pass through the cloud, and increasing ρ from 20% to 79% only augments this initial absorption by about 25%. This is undoubtedly related to the fact, mentioned earlier, that, after the initial pass through the cloud, the spectral composition of the flux is distorted in favor of frequencies to which the cloud is transparent.

The fractional cloud-to-ground absorption, $(\Delta F)_{cg}/F_{ct}\!\downarrow$, varies from 0.2% to 1.2% and increases nearly linearly with both ρ and θ_s. At its smallest ($\theta_s=10°$, $\rho=20\%$) it is a factor of 10 smaller than the cloud fractional absorption $(\Delta F)_c/F_{ct}\!\downarrow$, but at its largest ($\theta_s=40°$, $\rho=79\%$) it is only a factor of 3 smaller due to the high level of multiple reflection. Thus, the cloud-to-ground layer may play a significant although not dominant role in the atmospheric absorption.

The ratio $F_{ct}\!\uparrow/F_{ct}\!\downarrow$ (which is also called the "cloud albedo" by some since this quantity, not α_c, is in fact what one measures) is an important determinant of the radiation uptake of the polar regions. The upward flux at the cloud top is essentially lost to space; according to the detailed model, in no case does $F\!\uparrow$ change by more than a few percent between the cloud top and the top of the atmosphere. The ratio $F_{ct}\!\uparrow/F_{ct}\!\downarrow$ functions as a "valve" determining how much radiation will be available for heating the Earth-atmosphere system below the cloud top. Aside from the obvious facts (see Table III) that this ratio is a strongly increasing function of ground albedo ρ and a decreasing function of solar elevation θ_s, we remark that it exhibits only a small variation with θ_s under high-albedo conditions (78%–86% for $\rho=79\%$) and that, in general, it exceeds the surface albedo except for the anomalous case $\theta_s=40°$, $\rho=79\%$. These observations imply that, in general, more of the solar income is reflected back to space when Arctic cloud is present (a crucial assumption in one proposed climatic feedback mechanism), but over a high-albedo surface this reflection augmentation is very weak.

If one were to ignore the difference between upward and downward cloud parameters and assume $\alpha_d=\alpha_c$ and $a_d=a_c$, then one would have a 4-parameter model which could be parameterized from a single run of the detailed model. As an example, we show in Table IV the comparison between the 4-parameter model, parameterized from the detailed model for $\rho=0$, and the detailed model, for solar elevation 30°. (The sense and size of the errors is almost identical when we parameterize from the detailed model for $\rho=10\%$.) The 4-parameter model predictions of surface down-flux and especially of cloud-absorbed flux are significantly in error, the more so the larger the surface albedo (ρ). However, its predictions of up-flux to space, $F_{ct}\!\uparrow$, are only in error by about 3%. Nevertheless, it must be concluded that a 4-parameter

TABLE IV. Comparison of 4-parameter multiple reflection model (unparenthesized) with detailed model (parenthesized) flux ratio predictions for $\theta_s=30°$ (see Table III for notation).

Surface albedo	$F_g\!\downarrow/F_{ct}\!\downarrow$	$F_{ct}\!\uparrow/F_{ct}\!\downarrow$	$(\Delta F)_c/F_{ct}\!\downarrow$	$(\Delta F)_{cg}/F_{ct}\!\downarrow$
20%	0.582 (0.573)	0.503 (0.512)	0.027 (0.025)	0.005 (0.005)
58%	0.710 (0.675)	0.660 (0.681)	0.034 (0.029)	0.008 (0.007)
79%	0.810 (0.748)	0.781 (0.804)	0.039 (0.031)	0.010 (0.008)

multiple-reflection model will only be useful in situations where flux errors of up to 10% and cloud heating rate errors of up to 25% may be tolerated.

6. Empirical formulas for flux

In the preceding section the dependence of various quantities on ρ and θ_s was analyzed in a qualitative way, for fixed cloud droplet density ($n_c = 28.35$ cm^{-3}). Let us now analyze the dependence on n_c and show how it may be simply parameterized. This in turn will lead to simple empirical formulas for the fluxes $F_g\uparrow$ and $F_{ct}\uparrow$ as functions of all three variables ρ, θ_s and n_c.

We begin by presenting in Table V calculations of the multiple-reflection model parameters (see Section V) for $\theta_s = 30°$ and for a range of typical Arctic stratus droplet densities. Note that the cloud-to-ground properties (α_{cg} and a_{cg}) are independent of n_c. The up-flux absorptivity a_d ceases to increase significantly for $n_c \geqslant 50$ cm^{-3}, indicating that, for upward radiation, the liquid water absorption bands are already "saturated" (absorbing only in the wings) at 50 cm^{-3}. Since the down-flux absorptivity a_c is still increasing at 90 cm^{-3}, however, a similar saturation point has not been reached for downward radiation. The albedos α_c and α_d also increase as n_c increases, but ever more slowly the larger n_c is. Again (as we have observed previously) $\alpha_c > \alpha_d$, but the two albedos become ever more nearly equal as n_c increases.

In searching for a simple analytic fit to the results of Table V, we were naturally led by the success of the two-stream multiple-reflection model (see Section V) to employ other results from two-stream theory. In particular, Schuster (1905), who first proposed the two-stream approximation, showed that the monochromatic (flux) transmissivity of a purely scattering layer of optical depth τ should follow the law $1/1+\tau$. Since the cloud optical depth is proportional to n_c, it would be reasonable to try the form $1/a+bn_c$ for the monochromatic cloud transmissivity; a and b would depend on frequency, however, so it is not obvious that the same form would be useful for the spectrally-averaged cloud transmissivities T_c or T_d. Nevertheless, such was found to be the case, and the

data of Table V are excellently approximated by

$$T_c = 1 - \alpha_c - a_c = \frac{0.8255}{1 + 0.01943 n_c} \qquad (20)$$

$$T_d = 1 - \alpha_d - a_d = \frac{0.9273}{1 + 0.01768 n_c} \qquad (21)$$

(these fits are in fact good all the way out to $n_c = 300$ cm^{-3}). The fact that these fits do not have reasonable limiting values as $n_c \rightarrow 0$ is not disturbing, for the cloud approaches less and less to a purely scattering layer as $n_c \rightarrow 0$ and, thus, the $1/1+\tau$ law may be expected to break down. It may further be discovered (cf. Table II) that T_c is almost linear in θ_s, and that

$$T_c = \frac{0.4854 + 0.01135 \theta_s}{1 + 0.01948 n_c} \qquad (22)$$

fits T_c for all θ_s (10°–40°) and all n_c (28.35–90) to an average r.m.s. error of better than 0.002. (T_d is, as noted previously, practically independent of θ_s.) Similar fits may be obtained for α_c, a_c, α_d and a_d; in particular, α_c is excellently fit by

$$\alpha_c = \frac{0.5178 - 0.01198 \theta_s + 0.01875 n_c}{1 + 0.01968 n_c} \qquad (23)$$

which has an average r.m.s. error (over 16 fitted values of α_c) of only 0.0025. The slight differences in the denominators of Eqs. (20), (22) and (23) are insignificant when one considers that the various fractions (α_c, etc.) being fitted are only estimated to be accurate to ± 0.001. The denominators in the T_c- and T_d-fits (Eqs. 21 and 22) are, however, significantly though not substantially different, which may be ascribed to the effects of cloud absorption on the spectral composition of the radiation.

Now that we have simple formulas for the various multiple-reflection model parameters in terms of θ_s and n_c, we may use them in the multiple-reflection model itself (Eqs. 14–19) to obtain the solar fluxes as simple functions of θ_s, n_c and ρ. Beginning with the surface down-flux $F_g\downarrow$, we note that $F_g\downarrow/F_{ct}\downarrow$ equals γ_1 apart from a constant factor (cf. Eq. 14). γ_1 (Eq. 18) depends on θ_s only through the factor T_c. Since T_c is linear in θ_s (Eq. 22), γ_1 is linear in θ_s. The denominator of γ_1 is obviously linear in ρ and depends on n_c only through being linear in α_d. Putting all these facts together, we may postulate a form for $F_g\downarrow/F_{ct}\downarrow$ with unknown constants and then adjust those constants to obtain the least-squares fit. The result is

$$\frac{F_g\downarrow}{F_{ct}\downarrow} = \frac{0.4920 + 0.01094 \theta_s}{1 - 0.0477 \rho + (0.01964 - 0.01858 \rho) n_c} \qquad (24)$$

TABLE V. Multiple reflection model parameters determined from the detailed model (from $\rho = 0$, 10% cases) for solar elevation 30° and various droplet densities.

Droplet density (n_c)	α_c	α_d	α_{cg}	a_c	a_d	a_{gc}
28.35 cm^{-3}	0.440	0.370	0.006	0.024	0.012	0.007
50 cm^{-3}	0.552	0.493	0.006	0.029	0.015	0.006
70 cm^{-3}	0.617	0.569	0.006	0.033	0.016	0.006
90 cm^{-3}	0.663	0.625	0.006	0.036	0.016	0.006

This formula approximates the detailed model predictions to an average r.m.s. error of 0.002. As for the up-flux at the cloud-top, $F_{ct}\uparrow$ (Eq. 15), it involves α_c and T_d, which we have already parameterized in Eqs. (21) and (23) and γ_2, which is defined in Eq. (19). Since α_{cg} is small,

$$\gamma_2 \cong \rho T_{cg}^2 \gamma_1 = \rho T_{cg} \frac{F_g\downarrow}{F_{ct}\downarrow}$$

whereupon

$$\frac{F_{ct}\uparrow}{F_{ct}\downarrow} = \frac{0.5178 - 0.01198\theta_s + 0.01875 n_c}{1 + 0.01968 n_c} + \frac{0.9180\rho}{1 + 0.01768 n_c}\left(\frac{F_g\downarrow}{F_{ct}\downarrow}\right) \quad (25)$$

with $F_g\downarrow/F_{ct}\downarrow$ given by Eq. (24). The accuracy of Eq. (25) is comparable to that of Eq. (24). Finally, the fractional absorption between cloud top and ground is

$$\frac{(\Delta F)_{ct-g}}{F_{ct}\downarrow} = \frac{F_{ct} - F_g}{F_{ct}\downarrow} = 1 - \frac{F_{ct}\uparrow}{F_{ct}\downarrow} - (1-\rho)\frac{F_g\downarrow}{F_{ct}\downarrow}$$

where the two flux ratios may be taken from Eqs. (24) and (25). However, this formula involves cancellation of significant digits and is not as accurate as the preceding ones. Also, it implies that the fractional absorption is linear in θ_s which is not borne out by Table III.

Simple formulas such as Eqs. (24) and (25) should prove extremely useful in a variety of applications, among which we might mention temporally and spatially extended heat budget calculations, predictions of ice thaw and refreezing, and predictions of the general circulation of the Arctic atmosphere.

7. Absorbed solar flux

Because of the previously noted concern about the amount of solar radiation which is absorbed in the Arctic atmosphere, some of our detailed model's predictions for flux changes across various layers in the atmosphere are presented in Table VI. In particular, the flux differences $(\Delta F)_{ct-g}$ from cloud top (1 km) to ground, $(\Delta F)_{5\ km-g}$ from 5 km to the ground, and $(\Delta F)_{top-g}$ from the top of the atmosphere (1 mb) to the ground are shown normalized by the down-flux $F_{top}\downarrow$ at the top of the atmosphere, as functions of the cloud droplet concentration n_c and surface albedo ρ for fixed $\theta_s = 30°$. The case $n_c = 0$, corresponding to clear sky, is included for comparison with the Feigelson (1964) calculation cited by Fletcher (1965) showing that "absorption of solar radiation in the atmosphere is over 50% greater when the cloud is present than when the sky is clear."

TABLE VI. Solar flux differences from cloud top to ground $(ct-g)$, from 5 km to ground, and from top of the atmosphere to ground, as predicted by the detailed model for $\theta_s = 30°$ and normalized to the down-flux at the top of the atmosphere.

Droplet density (n_c)	Surface albedo (ρ)	$\dfrac{(\Delta F)_{ct-g}}{F_{top}\downarrow}$	$\dfrac{(\Delta F)_{5\ km-g}}{F_{top}\downarrow}$	$\dfrac{(\Delta F)_{top-g}}{F_{top}\downarrow}$
0	20%	0.016	0.076	0.168
	58%	0.020	0.083	0.180
	79%	0.022	0.087	0.187
28.35	20%	0.025	0.091	0.187
	58%	0.029	0.097	0.195
	79%	0.033	0.101	0.201
90	20%	0.033	0.101	0.200
	58%	0.037	0.106	0.206
	79%	0.040	0.110	0.210

Some important features of solar absorption in the Arctic atmosphere may be deduced from Table VI. Perhaps the most striking feature is that, whatever the surface albedo, changing from a clear to a very cloudy ($n_c = 90$ cm^{-3}) sky has only a small impact on the total absorption. For a clear sky, 17–19% of the incident solar flux is absorbed, and this only increases to 20–21% for a very cloudy sky. Thus, for the atmosphere as a whole, water vapor absorption (coupled with the much smaller O_3 absorption) far outdistances liquid water absorption in Arctic stratus. However, considering only the ct-g layer, the presence of the 90 cm^{-3} cloud doubles the absorption (from $1\frac{1}{2}$–2% up to 3–4%). The change in the 5 km-g layer absorption, from $7\frac{1}{2}$–9% to 10–11%, is closest to Feigelson's 50% estimate.

The predominance of water vapor absorption can be rationalized on two counts. First and probably most important, liquid water and water vapor absorb in similar spectral regions (0.8–2.8 μ), and the water vapor has the opportunity to absorb the solar radiation before it reaches the cloud. To the argument that, conversely, the cloud has the opportunity to absorb the up-flux before it passes through most of the water vapor, we point out that (as is borne out by Table VI) most of the absorption occurs on the downward pass. Changing the surface albedo from 20% to 79%, which dramatically increases the up-flux, results in only a modest increase in total absorption. Second, on its passage through the above-cloud air, the solar beam traverses a relatively long optical mass of absorber due to the low sun angle, while in the cloud, due to multiple scattering, many of the photons are able to travel a more nearly vertical path. This effect can only be accentuated for sun angles lower than the 30° of Table VI.

8. Conclusions

A new and highly detailed model for one-dimensional radiative transfer in the atmosphere, accounting for the combined effects of line absorption and multiple scattering, has been applied to the problem of solar radiative fluxes in the presence of typical Arctic summer stratus. The model has been verified against measurements of Weller *et al.* (1972) and then used as a predictive tool. Simple two-stream multiple cloud-ground reflection approximations have been shown to be useful in reproducing the results of the detailed model, but only when it is recognized that the cloud has a different albedo and absorptivity for the unidirectional, undepleted radiation incident from above than for the diffuse, depleted radiation incident from below. The solar fluxes have been parameterized in a simple way as functions of cloud droplet density, surface albedo, and solar elevation, and the dependence of the multiple-reflection model parameters on these same variables has been studied. Finally, some new and interesting conclusions *re* solar absorption in the atmosphere have been offered, notably that this absorption is sensitive neither to the amount of cloud present nor to the surface albedo.

REFERENCES

Feigelson, E. M., 1964: Radiation processes in stratified clouds Academy of Sciences, Moscow, U.S.S.R.

Fletcher, J. O., 1965: The heat budget of the Arctic Basin and its relation to climate. RAND Report R-444-PR, RAND Corp., Santa Monica, California.

Freeman, B. E., W. J. Wiscombe and W. G. England, 1972a: The effects of meso-scale and small-scale interactions on global climate II. Report 3SR-1034, Systems, Science and Software, La Jolla, California.

Freeman, B. E., W. J. Wiscombe and W. G. England, 1972b: The effects of meso-scale and small-scale interactions on global climate III. Report SSS-R-73-1255, Systems, Science and Software, La Jolla, California.

Grant, I., and G. Hunt, 1969: Discrete space theory of radiative transfer I. Fundamentals. *Proc. Roy. Soc. London,* **A313**, 183–205.

Hale, G., and M. Querry, 1973: Optical constants of water in the 200-nm to 200-μ wavelength region. *Appl. Opt.,* **12**, 555–563.

Huschke, R., 1969: Arctic cloud statistics from "air-calibrated" surface weather observations. RAND memorandum RM-6173- PR, RAND Corp., Santa Monica, California.

McClatchey, R., *et al.*, 1970: Optical properties of the atmosphere. AFCRL-70-0527, Air Force Cambridge Research Labs, Bedford, Massachusetts.

Schuster, A., 1905: Radiation through a foggy atmosphere. *Astrophys. J.,* **21**, 1–22.

Valley, S. L., Ed., 1965: Handbook of geophysics and space environments. McGraw-Hill, New York, New York.

Weller, G., *et al.*, 1972: Studies of the solar and terrestrial radiation fluxes over Arctic pack ice. ONR Technical Report #2. Geophysical Institute, Univ. of Alaska, Fairbanks, Alaska.

Wiscombe, W., and B. Freeman, 1972: A detailed radiation model for climate studies. Conference on Atmospheric Radiation (August 1972) pre-print volume, Amer. Meteor. Soc., Boston, Massachusetts.

Yamamoto, G., M. Tanaka and S. Asano, 1971: Radiative heat transfer in water clouds by infrared radiation. *JQSRT,* **11**, 697–710.

The Climate of Plateau Station

M. H. Kuhn, A. J. Riordan and I. A. Wagner

Institut für Meteorologie und Geophysik der Universität Innsbruck, Austria

Abstract

The climate of Plateau Station (79°15′S, 40°30′E, 3625 m a.s.l.) is typical of several million square kilometers of the East Antarctic Plateau. Nonetheless it must be classified as a microclimate since all over this area temperature, wind speed and direction, humidity, visibility, and precipitation are controlled by a shallow, extreme surface inversion and experience drastic vertical variation in the lowest 100 meters. Pressure, cloudiness, and solar radiation are the climatic factors that are independent of the thermodynamic processes in the surface layer but are largely dominated by high station latitude and altitude.

Standard synoptic observations of the USWB carried out in the three years 1966–1968 and data from a micrometeorological tower of 1967 furnished a limited basis for statistical analysis. In terms of atmospheric pressure, absolute temperature, and temperature variability the sunlit and transitional seasons are clearly distinguishable from the dark season. The climatonomical forcing function for the summer season is solar short wave radiation. Daily sums of radiation absorbed by the snow surface do not differ by more than ten percent in December, regardless of cloud cover, due to the near absence of opaque clouds over the plateau. Since the surface acts as heat source by absorption the inversion is reduced in summer and its strength follows the daily march of solar elevation. The additional possiblity of warm air advection in December causes yearly maximum temperatures of between −19.3 and −26.6 C in four summers, while minimum temperatures of three winters vary only between −84.2 and −86.2 C as measured 1.5 m above the surface.

The dark season represents a well-developed coreless winter. Cooling trends between May minimum and absolute annual minimum vary between 5.5 and 6.7 C. This probably reflects the simultaneous cooling rates of stratospheric air. From radiation measurements it was found that the effective black body temperature of the sky is approximately 10 C lower than the surface temperature. The very effective radiative cooling is interrupted by warm spells frequently reaching −45 C, which is likely to be the winter temperature of the lower troposphere above the inversion layer. Three mechanisms can be distinguished by which surface temperature is increased: vertical advection by large scale subsidence or local divergence; mixing of the inversion layer by strong gradient winds; or radiative heating from clouds without increase in windspeed. The latter two mechanisms usually operate together during the passage of frontlike disturbances. After such incidents radiative equilibrium appears to be reestablished within 48 hours. In this sense the cause and course of the coreless winter depends on both internal (local) and external (advective) influences. Due to the limited memory of the surface layer for advective processes the minimum temperature is determined by the local snow heat flux and by stratospheric temperatures.

Correlations of daily pressure, temperature, and wind values as well as their interdiurnal variability yield coefficients of less than ±0.4 providing strong evidence that the climate of the surface layer, expressed by wind and temperature, is independent of free air climate represented by atmospheric pressure.

---

1. Introduction

In December 1965 Plateau Station was established in the heart of the East Antarctic Plateau, at 79°15′S, 40°30′E at an elevation of 3625 m a.s.l. It is situated on the very gentle slope near the crest of the inland ice dome. The uniform terrain experiences little erosion by the steady winds of the inversion layer; sastrugi and dunes seldom reach heights of 30 cm. They are formed and modified by occasional strong winds associated with the passage of cyclonic disturbances and frequently contain snow of several years. This is not surprising in view of the small mean annual accumulation of 3 g cm⁻². The dryness, which puts the plateau among the great deserts of the world, is a result of large distance from the coast (approximately 1150 km from either Syowa or Roi Baudouin Stations) and of both high altitude and low air temperature which remove much of the atmospheric moisture from air masses reaching the interior of the continent. Likewise, sky cover is minimal and usually consists of high cirrus clouds. Opaque clouds are an exception observed on less than 10 days per year. As a consequence, snowfall, in the strict sense of conglomerates of several crystals precipitating from low and middle clouds, is negligible. On the other hand, there is nearly daily precipitation of ice crystals either from high cirrus or very frequently from a cloudless sky. The year-round existence of a temperature inversion over the East Antarctic Plateau creates a condensation sinking level where moist air is mixed into the cold surface layer. The inversion extends over a layer of several hundred meters on the average. It reaches intensities of up to

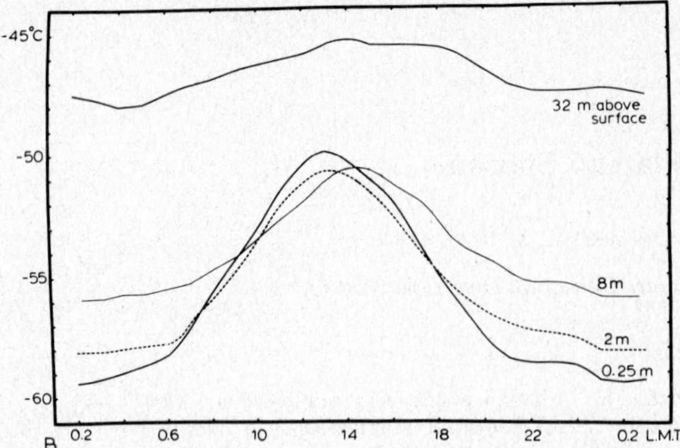

Fig. 1. Mean diurnal variation of temperatures, March 1967.

30 C in the lowest 30 m in winter and has a marked diurnal variation from 1 to 10 C in the sunlit season. An example of the diurnal variation of the inversion is illustrated in Fig. 1 for the month of March. During the months when the sun was continuously above the horizon the inversion generally maintained itself at about 0.1 to 0.2 C m^{-1} during the warmest hours of the day and reached values of 0.5 C m^{-1} near local midnight.

The strong vertical temperature gradients cause a noticeable baroclinity of the boundary layer over the terrain slope of about 1/1000. The ensuing thermal wind shears act together with surface friction to create a wind field in the inversion layer that exhibits extreme vertical variations and can by no means be used to estimate the synoptic pressure distribution. In this sense, surface records of temperature and wind describe a microclimate. Although conditions are typical for a thousand kilometers of horizontal distance, their vertical validity is limited to 10–100 m

above the surface. The scales of vertical layering have the following orders of magnitude:

Inversion layer: 50–500 m

Friction (or Ekman) layer: 30–300 m

Surface boundary layer: 1–10 m defined either by constancy of stress direction or as the height of maximum eddy flux divergence.

Under these circumstances the position of instruments is crucial to the data interpretation. In the three years 1966–1968 standard USWB equipment was used at Plateau Station. Temperature was recorded 1.5 m above the surface with a ventilated thermohm (resistance thermometer). Wind speed and direction were obtained from a Bendix Aerovane installed 8 m above the surface. Pressure was recorded on a Belfort barograph and checked with a Fortin station barometer. Synoptic observations were made at least every six hours and on most days every three hours. Visual observations such as sky cover, visibility, and precipitation (ice crystal versus snow fall) reflect to a certain degree the individuality of the six observers. They are, however, consistent within each year after mutual agreement and concessions among the residing meteorologists.

In 1967 and 1968 micrometeorological data were recorded on a 32 m tower equipped with 10 sensors each of wind speed, wind direction, and temperature. Unless otherwise noted, data of T and v referred to in this report are those of the USWB records. Data of radiation fluxes are the result of an extensive program of redundant instrumentation. They are expressed in the international Pyrheliometric Scale 1956 and should have an accuracy of ± 3 per cent for shortwave fluxes and ± 10 per cent for longwave fluxes.

TABLE 1. Climatic table for Plateau Station. (From Schwerdtfeger, 1970.)
Latitude 79°15′S, longitude 40°30′E. elevation 3,625 m.

Month	Mean Sta. press.[a] (mbar)	Temperature[a] (C) Daily mean	Daily range	Extremes max.	min.	Number of days with[c] Drifting snow	Snow fall	Ice crystals	Mean cloudiness[a] (%) 0-3/ 10	4-7/ 10	8-10/ 10	Mean wind speed[a] (m sec⁻¹)	Most frequ. wind dir.[c]	Peak gust[d] (m sec⁻¹)	Net radiation ly mo⁻¹ (IPS 1956))	Wind chill kcal m⁻² hr⁻¹
Jan.	619.0	−33.9	10.4	−18.5	−48.9	4	8	20	52.5	32.4	15.1	3.0	N	9	—	1490
Feb.	615.7	−44.4	11.8	−24.9	−60.8	8	10	28	35.8	43.4	20.8	4.2	NW	12	−340	2070
Mar.	612.7	−57.2	9.9	−35.9	−75.3	8	8	28	47.3	43.0	9.7	5.0	N	16	−920	2510
Apr.	606.7	−65.8	8.1	−42.7	−78.0	6	3	22	64.2	28.9	6.9	5.2	NNE	18	−970	2770
May	609.3	−66.4	9.4	−38.9	−80.6	6	1	25	74.5	20.2	5.4	5.4	N	16	−970	2810
June	606.3	−69.0	9.0	−32.8	−82.2	5	—	26	71.9	15.6	12.5	5.0	N	22	—	2840
July	605.3	−68.0	9.1	−43.9	−86.2	9	2	30	70.9	21.8	7.3	5.8	N	13	−950	2900
Aug.	597.3	−71.4	9.1	−41.2	−85.0	11	—	28	60.2	28.7	11.1	5.9	NNW	16	−950	3010
Sept.	602.0	−65.0	12.0	−37.8	−84.4	11	2	27	33.4	43.7	22.9	5.7	NNW	20	−960	2800
Oct.	604.0	−59.5	15.4	−37.1	−80.0	5	5	25	61.5	27.2	11.4	5.1	NNW	13	−930	2580
Nov.	613.3	−44.4	12.9	−26.7	−66.1	10	6	29	59.6	23.5	16.9	4.6	N	25	—	2110
Dec.	619.3	−32.3	13.6	−20.6	−47.8	7	6	28	47.6	32.9	19.5	3.8	NNW	12	—	1700
Annual	609.2[b]	−56.4	10.9	−18.5	−86.2	90	51	316	56.6	30.1	13.3	4.9	N	25	—	2470

[a] XII/65–XII/68.
[b] Boiling point of water at average station pressure is 86.3°C.
[c] I/67–XII/68.
[d] III/66–XII/68, except XII/66.

TABLE 2. Climatic classification criteria after Dalrymple.

	Cold interior	Cold central core	Plateau
$\bar{T}$	−40 C to −50 C	<−50 C	−56.4
T_{min}	−70 C to −80 C	<−80 C	−86.2
T_{max}	−10 C to −20 C	<−20 C	−18.5
$\bar{v}$	5 to 7 m sec^{-1}	3 to 5 m sec^{-1}	4.9
Drifting snow (DS) frequency ($v>7$ m sec^{-1})	30 to 55%	5 to 20%	25% of all days (48% of all days)
Blowing snow (BS) frequency ($v>12$ m sec^{-1})	0 to 10%	<2%	1.9% of all days in 1967 (3.3% of all days)
Mean annual precipitation g cm^{-2}	0 to 30	0 to 15	2.9
Mean annual windchill kcalcm^{-2} hr^{-1}	2300 to 2500	2200 to 2600	2470
Max monthly windchill kcalcm^{-2} hr^{-1}	2500 to 3000	2500 to 3200	3030

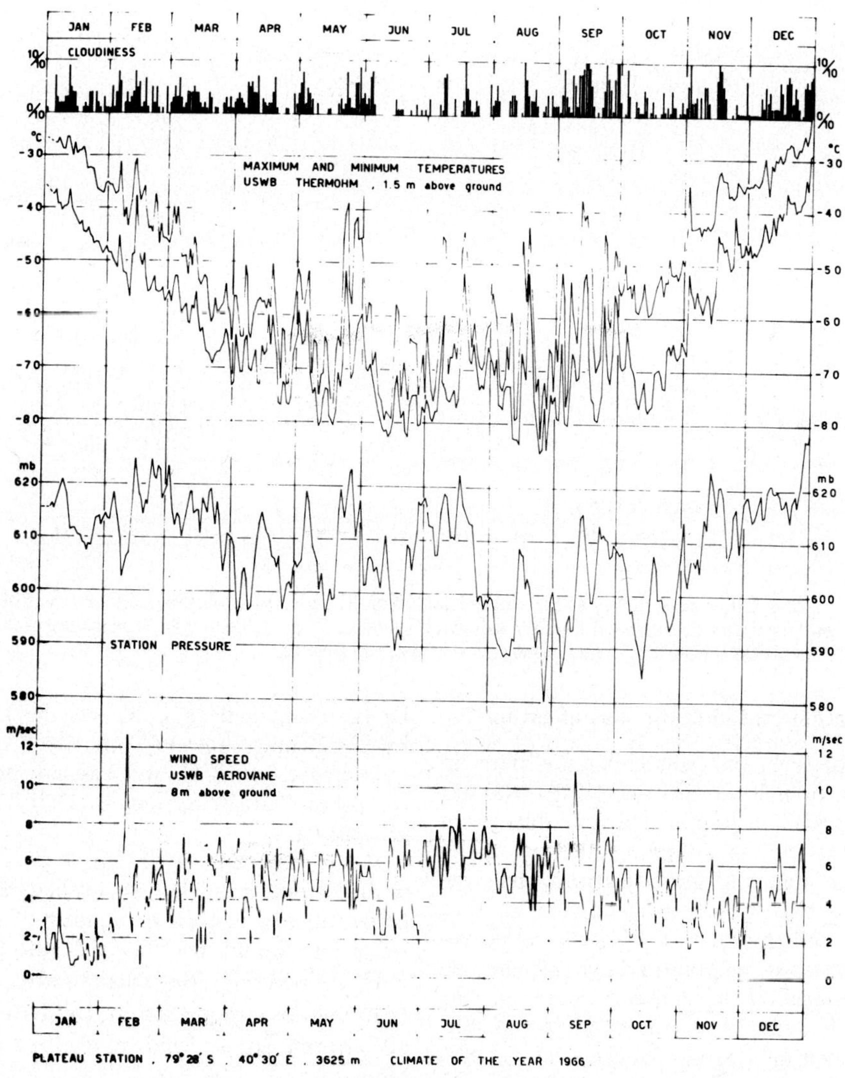

FIG. 2. Climatic elements at Plateau Station, 1966. Cloudiness in tenths, daily extremes of temperature in C, station pressure in mb, wind speed in m sec^{-1}. Temperature was measured 1.5 m above the surface, wind speed at 8 m above the surface.

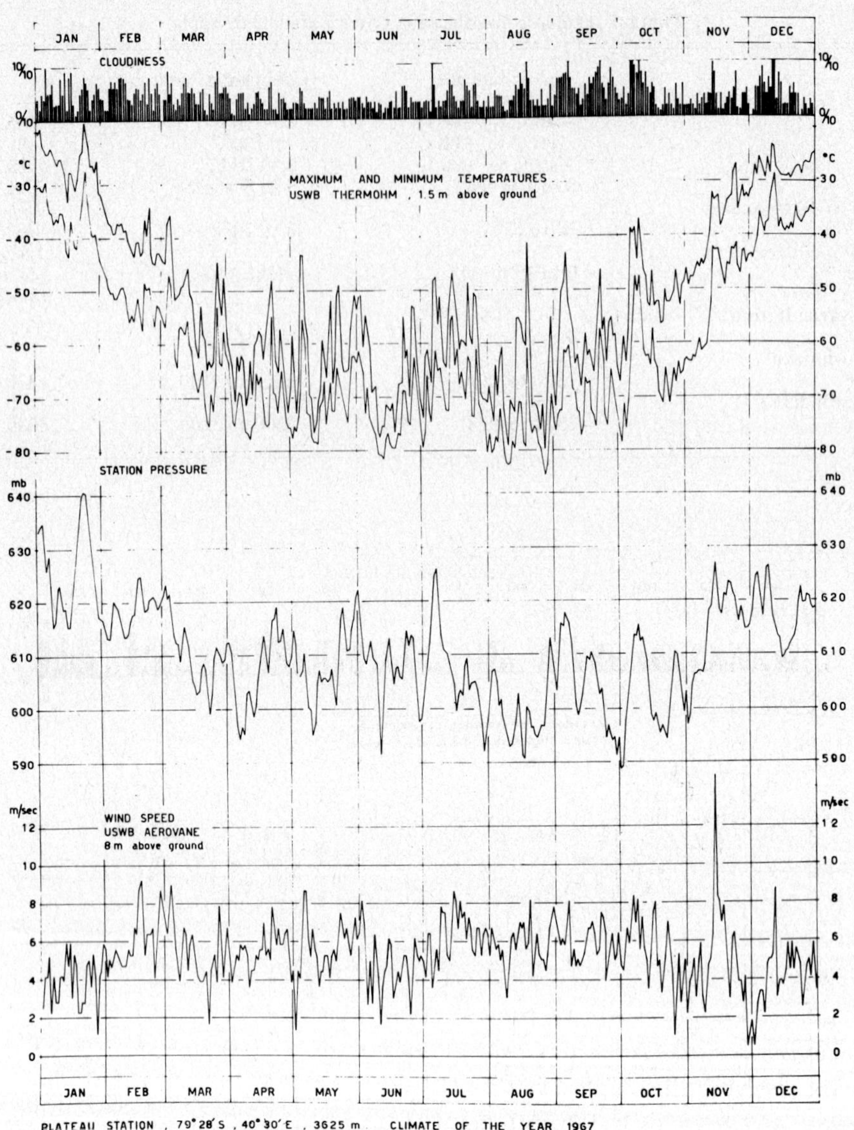

Fig. 3. Climatic elements at Plateau Station, 1967. Cloudiness in tenths, daily extremes of temperature in C, station pressure in mb, wind speed in m sec^{-1}. Temperature was measured 1.5 m above the surface, wind speed at 8 m above the surface.

2. Data presentation and climatic classification

Except for radiation and windchill, the data in Table 1 are taken from Schwerdtfeger (1970) who has accumulated in a similar fashion climatic data from 34 other antarctic and subantarctic stations up to 1968. In order to find the gross features that the climate of Plateau Station has in common with that of other stations and in order to discover some distinguishing factors it is helpful to have recourse to Dalrymple's classification of climatic zones on the East Antarctic Plateau. Dalrymple (1966) distinguishes four zones on the degree of severity of climate: Cold Transitional—Cold Katabatic—Cold Interior (CI)—Cold Central Core (CCC). From its high elevation and central situation Plateau Station seems to

be best qualified as CCC. Of the nine criteria used by Dalrymple, however, one does not fulfill the requirements for CCC, and two are uncertain. Table 2 compares Plateau Station to Dalrymple's criteria for CI and CCC.

If the frequencies of DS and BS (or their substitute wind speeds) were evaluated on the basis of hourly means instead of number of days with occurrence they would most likely fit into the CCC bracket.

If, in addition, the mean yearly maximum rather than the absolute maximum had been used in Table 2, all criteria for a cold central core climate would be met.

As can be seen from the diagrams of daily observations (Figs. 2, 3 and 4) both T and v have a tendency

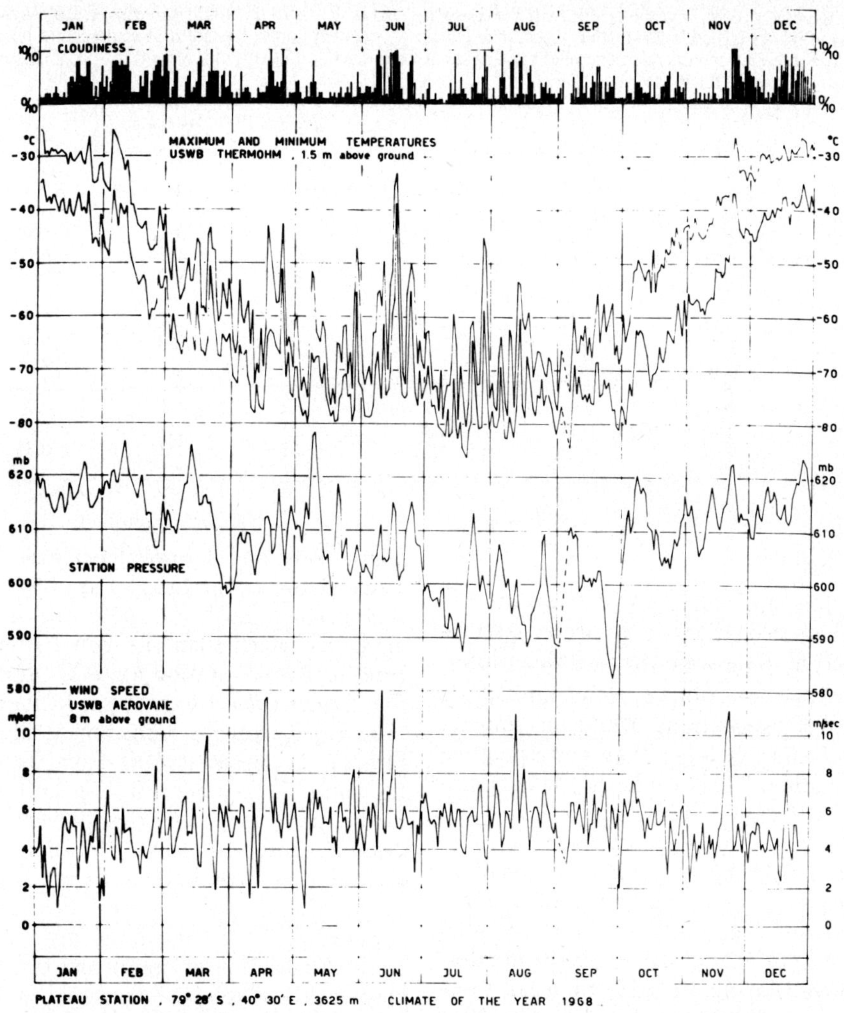

FIG. 4. Climatic elements at Plateau Station, 1968: Cloudiness in tenths, daily extremes of temperature in C, station pressure in mb, wind speed in m sec⁻¹. Temperature was measured 1.5 m above the surface, wind speed at 8 m above the surface.

for strong positive deviation. The deviation of the absolute maximum, -18.5 C, from the pentade mean maximum of three years, -31 C, is six times the standard deviation (σ) of 1.9 C in the sunlit season. The maximum negative deviation was only half as large, $-3\ \sigma$, in summer. In winter, $\sigma = 4.7$ C, and deviations from the three year pentade averages range again within the extremes of $-3\ \sigma$ and $+6\ \sigma$, as in summer.

Wind velocities in Figs. 2, 3 and 4 are means of four daily observations. As was mentioned, the wind speed at 8 m height is strongly influenced by the inversion and by the height of the friction layer. A detailed statistical analysis is therefore of restricted use unless all profile characteristics measured on the tower are discussed simultaneously. It suffices to point out that monthly means at 8 m are highest in the dark season when the inversion is best developed.

The storms of 12–14 February 1966 (maximum gust 19 m sec⁻¹), of 13–15 November 1967 (maximum gust 25 m sec⁻¹), and of 20–23 November 1968 (maximum gust 18 m sec⁻¹) reached daily mean wind speeds that were more than twice as high as any other daily mean during the months mentioned.

The correlation between wind speed and the onset of drifting snow (DS) is impaired by two facts: i) the surface stress is not unambiguously determined by 8 m wind speeds, and ii) with the extremely low accumulation of snow the surface was often hardened or protected by crusts so that in all cases the onset of snow drift had a higher threshold than its end. DS was observed on one day with a peak gust of only 5.2 m sec⁻¹, while it was *not* observed on four days having peak gusts in excess of 9 m sec⁻¹. These figures compare well with frequencies given by Schwerdtfeger (1970) for South Pole and Byrd Station.

TABLE 3. Pressure data of 7 antarctic stations. Plateau Station PL, Vostok V, Byrd B, Little America V LA, McMurdo McM, Syowa SY, South Pole SP. Amplitudes $C_{1,2}$, Phase shifts $t_{1,2}$, and Variances $V_{1,2,1+2}$ explained by the first and second harmonic. $\sigma(\bar{p}-\bar{p}_{1+2})$ is the standard deviation of monthly means from the resultant of the first and second harmonic. $R=(\bar{p}_{max}-\bar{p}_{min})/\bar{p}$. All data are based on monthly means given by Schwerdtfeger (1970).

		PL	V	B	LA	McM	SY	SP
Latitude	°S	79	78	80	78	78	69	90
Elevation	m	3625	3488	1533	40	24	15	2800
$\bar{p}$	mb	609	624	806	982	988	986	681
C_1	mb	8.06	5.10	5.39	6.51	3.62	1.83	4.35
t_1	months	1.5	1.7	1.9	2.4	2.3	2.7	2.0
V_1	%	64	51	52	57	35	13	62
C_2	mb	3.56	4.50	4.77	4.30	2.76	2.23	2.86
t_2	months	0.1	0.7	0.5	0.6	0.8	0.3	0.6
V_2	%	12	40	41	25	21	19	27
V_{1+2}	%	78	91	93	82	56	32	89
R	%	3.6	2.4	2.1	1.8	1.1	0.7	1.9
$\sigma(\bar{p}-\bar{p}_{1+2})$	mb	1.4	0.7	1.3	1.2	2.1	1.4	1.3
C_1/C_2		2.26	1.13	1.13	1.51	1.31	0.83	1.52

3. The pressure regime

Comparison of pressure variations at Plateau Station with those measured at other antarctic stations depends greatly on the time scale chosen. Mean interdiurnal pressure variations, $|\overline{dp}|/\bar{p}$, as computed by Schwerdtfeger (1970) range from 0.0031 in summer to 0.0048 in winter and are lower than corresponding values for other stations. This confirms the expectation that the central region of East Antarctica should be subject to the least degree of cyclonic activity. Additional evidence favoring this view is given by the respective magnitudes of uninterrupted changes of daily mean pressure. The maximum uninterrupted increase was 31.7 mb, or 5.2%, the maximum uninterrupted decrease was 27.5 mb, or 4.5% of mean pressure. From data of Little America V (February 1957 through February 1958) which were kindly supplied by H. Hoinkes, the corresponding amounts are: decrease, 60 mb, or 6.1%; increase, 49 mb, or 5.0% of mean pressure. Plateau Station experienced an uninterrupted change of more than 3.5% on 23 occasions in a three year period, which compares well with only 7 cases found in the one year IGY record of Little America V. While mean daily changes are considerably higher in coastal areas, there seems to exist no significant difference in either magnitude or frequency of extreme variations in the time scale of several days.

From work done by Schwerdtfeger (1962) and van Loon (1967) it is well established that the annual and semiannual pressure oscillations in high southern latitudes are directly linked to seasonal differences in the meridional temperature gradient and display a significant latitudinal effect. Table 3 gives the first two harmonics computed from 12 monthly means of several stations. For a discussion of seasonal or monthly pressure variations at Plateau Station, four stations of approximately the same latitude can be compared, i.e., Byrd, Little America, McMurdo and Vostok.

South Pole and Syowa have also been included in Table 3 for comparison. Van Loon (1967) observed that between 50°S and 65°S the second harmonic is more important than the first harmonic. This is still true for Syowa Station at 69°S. Further to the south the annual cycle becomes predominant again and the ratio C_1/C_2 reaches a maximum of 2.3 over Plateau Station. It seems evident from Table 3 that within the antarctic continent, further latitude increase ceases to be important for the pressure harmonics, and distance from the coast, elevation, and the position of a station with respect to the irregular, asymetric shape of the polar vortex become the controlling parameters. In other words, inside the continent the seasonal variation of meridional temperature gradients play a lesser role, cyclogenesis is restricted to the coastal belt from where inland penetration of traveling disturbances depends on orography rather than latitude. The phase lag t_1 of the annual maximum is larger for coastal than for continental stations and can be taken as one of the measures of continentality. The distance from the coast is so closely linked to station elevation that these two parameters cannot be analyzed separately. Since the variance explained by the first and second harmonics is rather low for coastal stations (Syowa, 32%; McMurdo, 56%) it must be assumed that cyclogenesis produces not only the latitude-dependent second harmonic but oscillations of higher frequencies as well. As these are apparently more important than seasonal variations, the yearly range is kept small. Provided furthermore that cyclonic activity is most pronounced in the lower troposphere, the yearly range of pressure must increase both with distance from the coast and with station elevation. This is illustrated in Table 3 by the normalized range of monthly mean pressure which has a maximum over the high, central Plateau Station. Also, those stations that lie within the circle of the polar-night jet stream in winter should be expected to experience large negative deviations of monthly pressure from the yearly average, also contributing to the increase of the range of monthly means.

Finally, the standard deviation of monthly means from the curve prescribed by the first and second harmonic was computed. It is not proportional to the variance due to all harmonics higher than order two but rather reflects the significance of monthly oscillations. This quantity is twice as high for Plateau Station than for Vostok and may be interpreted as a consequence of the varying position of the polar vortex and of the circumpolar jet. In this view either Vostok is mostly inside the jet while Plateau Station is affected by its meandering, or the pressure cell over East Antarctica is occasionally divided into two cells, temporarily placing Plateau Station into a trough between them.

At Plateau Station the seasonal variation of pressure is well correlated with variations in both temperature and wind speed. From mean monthly values of p and T a linear correlation of 0.91 was computed, and of -0.90 for p and v. However, a consideration of the physical reasons for the seasonal trends of p, T and v reveals that the high degree of correlation is mostly of a statistical nature. Pressure is, for all practical purposes, independent of the strength of the inversion. The 8 m wind speed on the other hand, as was already mentioned, is greatly influenced by the shear and friction in the stable surface layer. Although pressure and temperature are linked in the mechanisms that drive the atmospheric circulation, it is the temperature of the free atmosphere and its gradients that play a role, and not the temperature of the shallow inversion. The influence of the inversion on the variations of windspeed and temperature is best documented by the total lack of correlation between p, T and v on a daily basis. Results of analysis of mean daily values as well as interdiurnal variability are given in Table 4.

The forcing function for the temperature and for the strength of the inversion is the radiation budget of the surface, or predominantly the shortwave radiation in summer and the longwave fluxes in winter. The different response of atmosphere and snow surface to these radiation fluxes and the different structure of the inversion in winter and summer make it neces-

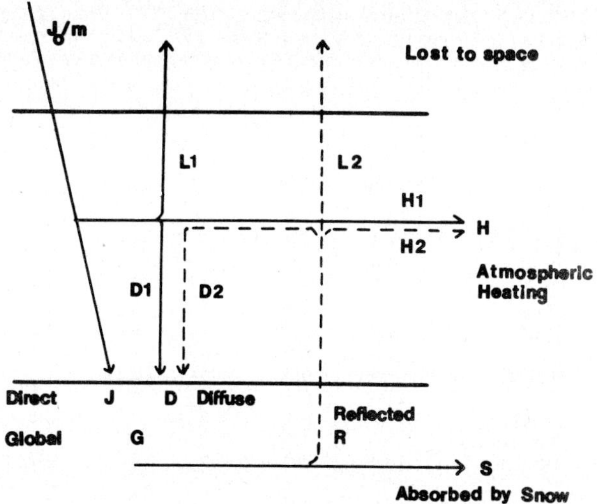

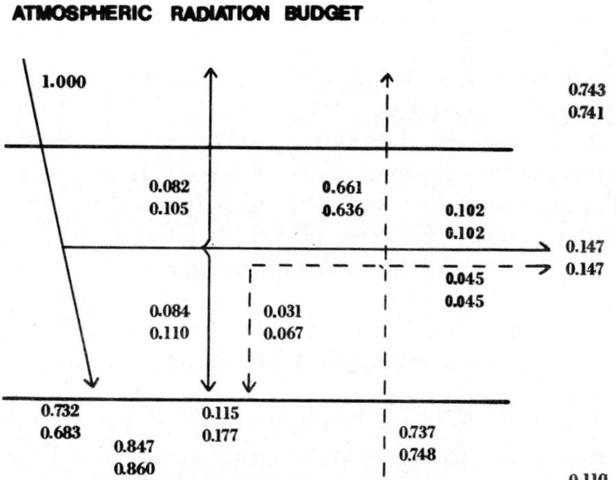

FIG. 5. Effect of broken ci and cs on the short-wave radiation budget.

sary to discuss the temperature regime of the two seasons separately.

4. The sunlit season

From the first sunrise on about 21 August until the last sunset on 24 April, the temperature at 1.5 m closely follows the march of solar radiation. The pentade averages of mean daily temperature for 1966–1968 are almost exactly symmetrical about the annual maximum occurring near 31 Dec, except that from Nov 14 to Dec 9 temperatures were 3 to 5 C warmer than from Jan 28 to Feb. 22. Solar radiation values show little effect of cloud cover, as was found in an investigation of direct and diffuse shortwave fluxes for periods of broken cloudcover. Fig. 5 compares the means of a period with an average of 8/10 Ci to clear sky conditions. The amount of energy depleted from

TABLE 4. Correlations of daily means.

	Temp—wind	Temp—pressure	Wind—pressure
Annual	−0.19	+0.22	−0.15
Correlations of interdiurnal changes			
Annual	0.39	0.19	−0.04
Dec and Jan	0.27	0.61	0.15
Nov and Feb	0.22	0.48	0.16
March through October	0.32	0.48	0.05

TABLE 5. Mean diurnal temperature range (C°). Comparison of Inland Stations (after Schwerdtfeger, 1970). The three-year mean of absolute values of mean interdiurnal temperature variation, $A = |\overline{T_2} - \overline{T_1}|$, is given in the last column for Plateau Station.

	Plateau Station	South Pole	Byrd	Eights	$\bar{A}$
January	10.7	2.9	5.5	5.6	1.3
February	11.9	3.8	6.7	5.4	2.1
March	9.9	5.0	7.5	6.4	3.0
April	8.7	5.7	9.0	7.0	4.1
May	9.4	6.3	8.7	8.1	4.3
June	8.8	6.7	8.8	9.5	4.2
July	9.0	6.5	8.8	7.8	4.7
August	9.5	6.2	8.5	8.2	4.7
September	11.3	6.2	8.1	8.3	4.4
October	15.2	4.1	8.5	6.8	2.5
November	13.1	2.6	6.2	6.4	1.7
December	10.3	2.0	5.2	6.8	1.2
Annual	10.9	4.8	7.6	7.2	3.2

the direct beam is approximately compensated for by multiple scattering.

The persistant dominate of solar radiation in determining air temperature is reflected in the interdiurnal variability which is greatly reduced from winter values. For the period 1 January through 25 February and 18 October through 31 December 1967 when the sun was totally above the horizon, the standard deviation of daily mean temperature was 1.9 C compared with 4.7 C during the 123 day sunless period.

Table 5 illustrates monthly values of interdiurnal temperature variation and diurnal ranges for 1966–1968 and for three other inland stations taken from Schwerdtfeger (1970). The interdiurnal variation reaches a minimum in the sunlit months and its seasonal variability is also lowest in December and January. That is, the standard deviation of daily values is about 1.0 C in December as compared to 3.8 C in August. Both the lower interdiurnal change and its reduced variability in summer are most likely linked to the dominant role of the persistent march of solar radiation.

The mean diurnal range is the difference of the monthly average of the daily maximum and the daily minimum temperature for 1966–1968. Values reach annual maxima in February and October and reflect larger diurnal ranges in summer than in winter. The higher summer values and pronounced spring and fall maxima are not found at other inland stations such as South Pole, Byrd, or Eights.

South Pole, of course, has no diurnal variation of radiation fluxes, the mean diurnal temperature range merely represents average interdiurnal trends. Byrd shows some tendency for maxima near the equinoxes. Eights, finally, does not show any significant effect of daily solar heating as compared to the dark months. The diurnal range of net radiation at Plateau Station

that is responsible for the maximum diurnal temperature range of 15 C in October is from +0.035 to −0.070 ly min⁻¹. Maximum values of global shortwave radiation are 990–1000 ly day⁻¹.

Several instances of pronounced warm temperature during summer which seem to bear no connection with the solar radiational maximum at the end of December can be seen in Figs. 2, 3 and 4. The occurrence of 15 well-defined maximum temperature anomalies during the period from 18 October through 25 February 1966–68 were associated with either mean wind speeds of over 6 m sec⁻¹ or with mean daily cloudiness of at least 6/10 or more, or both. The importance of the disturbance phenomenon in summer is underlined by the fact that the highest temperature recorded at the station (−18.5 C) occurred on 23 January 1967, well after the usual date of the seasonal maximum, during such a disturbance. A similar situation was reported by Dalrymple (1966)

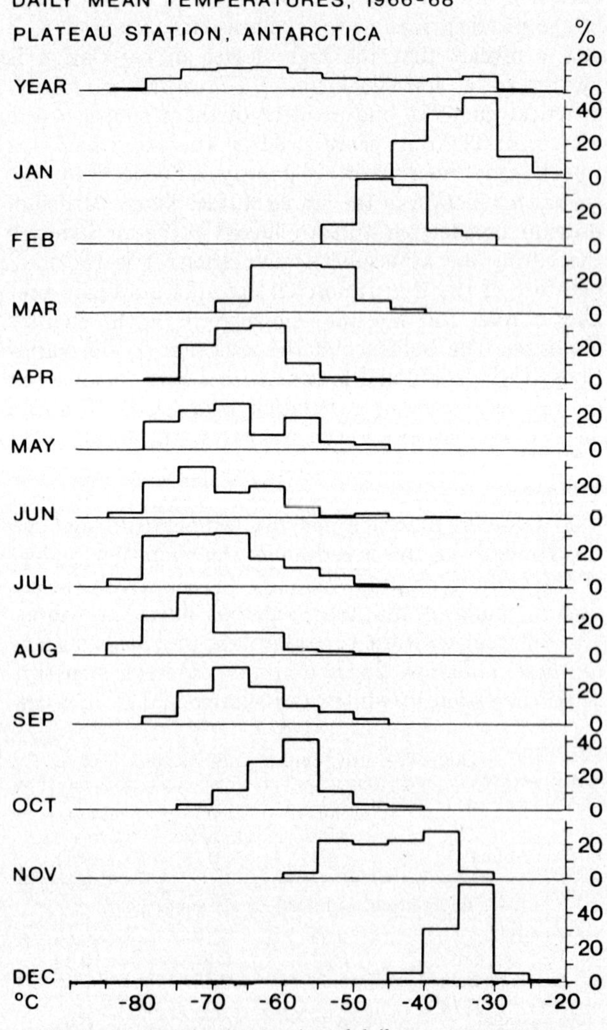

FIG. 6. Frequency distribution of daily mean temperatures, 1966–68, Plateau Station, Antarctica.

for South Pole. The large year-to-year difference in maximum temperature further reflects the same atmospheric process causing extreme warming in summer and in winter. Since Plateau Station is situated in the cold central core, there is little probability of cold air advection, and frequency distribution of temperature for any period of the year must be strongly positively skewed. Fig. 6 illustrates the temperature distributions for each month. The skewness of the summer months is masked by the seasonal trends so that shorter periods would have to be examined.

In terms of monthly means the four summer seasons on record do not show conspicious differences. The subjective impressions of persons working outside, however, do distinguish the summer of 1968/69 from the previous ones. The term "Plateau weather" was coined by station personnel for days with comfortable outside conditions, calm spells or little wind, dark blue sky and unlimited visibility. In the summers of 1966/67 and 1967/68 cumulus clouds, *cu humilis* and a few *cu mediocris*, were observed on such occasions, while nightly fog development was missing. In the summer of 1968/69 such typical Plateau weather was not felt. In objective terms it was certainly not typical even for the previous years since human recollection has a tendency not to integrate sensations but rather to overemphasize extremes. A physical description of Plateau weather should therefore concentrate on extremes of windspeed and temperature, and, as personal comfort is involved, on cooling power or windchill. From the observed state of the sky the synoptic situation seems to be that of anticyclonic subsidence. The development of cumulus clouds requires a strongly positive energy budget of the snow surface in order to destroy the temperature inversion and to supply moisture by the evaporation of snow. With little or no gradient wind the convection over the homogeneous surface is likely to result from shallow, local convergences (Kuhn, 1969), often from lines of convergence as the clouds favored alignment in bands. Since wind data above 32 m are missing it cannot be determined whether the cloud bands were not due also to instabilities in the Ekman layer. Order of magnitude estimates of the distance between bands, 1–2 km, would agree with computations by Faller (1965) of the wavelength of helical circulation in an unstable friction layer.

Daily means of wind speed of less than 1.2 m sec^{-1} appear frequently in the summer records (Figs. 1, 2 and 3), except for November and December 1968. During these two months, moreover, periods of low wind were accompanied by relatively high cloudiness, which spoils the impression of Plateau weather. For an average temperature of -27 C the windchill formula of Siple–Passel [$K = (\sqrt{100v} + 10.45 - v)\,(33 - t^\circ C)$ as quoted by Dalrymple, 1966] yields the following losses, K:

v	5	4	3	2	1	0	m sec^{-1}
K	1668	1587	1486	1355	1167	627	kcal m^{-2} hr^{-1}

Since the windchill factor describes only the losses due to ventilation and longwave radiation, the overall human heat budget can be crudely estimated by adding the gain from solar shortwave radiation, global and reflected from the snow. Assuming the surface of a person to be 1.5 m^2 and to be irradiated by 1 ly min^{-1}, on the average, this gain becomes 900 kcal m^2 hr^{-1}. The zero level of discomfort is then maintained in wind speeds of 0.25 m sec^{-1}, neglecting metabolic heat production. This threshold of windspeed may well have played a role in the subjective classification of different types of summer weather.

5. The coreless winter

In the sunless period from late April to late August the atmospheric boundary layer responds to the heat balance of a snow surface no longer influenced by shortwave radiation. In 1967 daily sums of net radiation dropped below zero on 15 February and stayed negative, with a few exceptions, till 20 October. By the beginning of March daily maxima of shortwave balance of about 0.1 ly min^{-1} are compensated for by equal amounts of longwave balance. Diurnal variations dissappear with sunset which was four days later than predicted due to the influence of strong atmospheric refraction. The energy gain of the surface of about 100 ly day^{-1} in December is little disturbed by occasional warm air advection so that solar radiation is the climatonomical forcing function in summer. Daily losses due to net radiation of up to -60 ly day^{-1} in the dark season rapidly build up a strong temperature inversion. Since the most frequent value of net radiation in the dark period is about -30 ly day^{-1}, the temperature regime in winter is more easily upset by turbulent gains of sensible heat than in summer. In other words, radiative cooling works more slowly than advective heating, and both processes have absolute magnitudes several times smaller than absorption of global shortwave radiation in summer. These conditions are significantly different from coastal stations like Little America V where Hoinkes (1970) found absolute values of shortwave balance approximately equal to longwave balance in the four summer months October 1957 to January 1958, and daily net radiation losses exceeding -95 ly day^{-1} at least once a month in the dark season. Apparently, the surface temperature of the plateau region stays closer to radiative equilibrium at all times of the year.

For an average longwave loss of -30 ly day^{-1} in winter and a surface temperature of -80 C the equivalent black body temperature of the sky is computed at -90 C. While the snow surface is indeed a black body, the atmosphere is highly transparent to long-

TABLE 6. Minimum temperatures of May and winter minimum
at Plateau Station.

1966	−80.3 C on 11. May	−85.2 C on 24. August
1967	−78.5 C 13. May	−84.2 C 27. August
1968	−79.9 C 6. May	−86.2 C 20. July

Mean difference −6.2 C per 100 days

wave radiation and will radiate from all levels at temperatures from −40 C in the lower troposphere to below −80 C at the tropopause. The physical significance of the equivalent sky temperature can only be speculated on since vertical profiles of the most effective emitters in the atmosphere, i.e., H_2O, CO_2, O_3, and aerosols are largely unknown. H_2O amounts of less than 0.1 g cm^{-2} (or 1 mm precipitable water) were inferred from radiation measurements at Plateau Station (Kuhn, 1972a). CO_2 concentrations differ only slightly from other places in the world (Keeling, 1960). Ozone concentrations near the surface indicate significant downward transport through the troposphere (Wexler, Moreland, and Weyant, 1960). Since ozone is being destroyed chemically and photochemically while aerosols do not dissolve during the subsidence from the layer of high concentration near the tropopause (Hofmann et al., 1972; Kuhn, 1972b) they will experience less vertical variation over the antarctic interior. The contribution of the troposphere to radiative equilibrium temperature thus cannot be neglected inspite of the low value of −90 C. In view of the different cooling rates observed in the antarctic troposphere and stratosphere, the changes in radiative equilibrium temperature during winter can tentatively be understood as originating from two layers having mean temperatures of −45 C and −75 C and emissivities of 0.3 and 0.2, respectively, the remaining 50% of the flux from the surface being lost to space. Note that in this crude approximation the three layers (troposphere, stratosphere, space) do not radiatively interact, so that their emissivities have only mathematical and no physical meaning. The mean loss of −30 ly day^{-1}, or 0.021 ly min^{-1}, consists then of three components, the indices 0, T, S denoting surface, troposphere and lower stratosphere, resp.

$$-0.021 = -8.1 \times 10^{-11}(T_0{}^4 - 0.3T_T{}^4 - 0.2T_S{}^4) \text{ (ly min}^{-1})$$

which is fulfilled for the temperatures mentioned above. Taking time derivatives of temperatures while keeping the net radiation constant,

$$T_0{}^3 \cdot dT_0/dt = 0.3T_T{}^3 \cdot dT_T/dt + 0.2T_S{}^3 \cdot dT_S/dt.$$

The decrease from the minimum temperature of May to the absolute minimum in August or July is taken as a representative value for dT_0/dt. These minima are given for the three years on record in Table 6.

Upper air temperature data of South Pole given by Wexler (1959) show a decrease of 15 C from mid May to mid August for layers between 200 mb and 20 mb. Similar averages are reported for the 50 mb level by Rubin (1964). From numerous investigations of the stratospheric spring warming these cooling rates seem to be applicable also for the period of measurements at Plateau Station. Midtropospheric cooling rates in winter show regional differences and are not as constant with time as those of the stratosphere. The reports quoted (Wexler, 1959; and Rubin, 1964) indicate a cooling rate of −5 C from May to August as well within the possible range of values. Inserted in the above equation in degrees Kelvin,

$$7.2 \times 10^6 \times 6 = 0.3 \times 11.9 \times 10^6 \times 5$$
$$+0.2 \times 7.8 \times 10^6 \times 15 + 2 \times 10^6,$$

the last term on the right hand side indicates a remainder due to inaccuracy of 5%. These values substantiate the very simple model used for the explanation of radiative equilibrium temperatures observed at Plateau Station.

Thus, if the surface temperature were controlled by radiative energy exchange with troposphere and stratosphere alone there would be a slow, continuous temperature decrease of the order of 10 C in the dark season, little compared to the heating of about 50 C in spring caused mainly by the absorption of solar shortwave radiation.

Superimposed on the slow monthly cooling rate during the sunless period are sharp upward temperature displacements typically attaining values of half the annual amplitude. These temperature disturbances are the direct result of a rapid destruction of the surface inversion and probably reflect simultaneous temperatures in the mid to lower troposphere. From May through August 1966–1968 there were 66 cases of mean daily temperature increase of at least 5 C. All but two were associated with either a mean wind increase, or cloudiness of 5/10 or more, or both. The stronger temperature increases of 8 to 19 C per day were more often associated with both high wind and cloudiness. Thus, the destruction of the strong surface inversion is accomplished rapidly by mechanical mixing due to the onset of winds of over 7 m sec^{-1} at the 8 m level and by radiative heating from the troposphere

TABLE 7. Destruction of inversion on August 18–19, 1967.

Hour ending GMT	Windspeed m sec^{-1}			Inversion °C	Net radiation
	8 m	32 m	diff.	32−1 m	ly min^{-1}
0600	4.2	8.3	4.1	14.3	−0.027
0900	4.6	10.4	5.8	13.2	−0.021
1200	4.5	10.4	5.9	11.2	−0.010
1500	5.2	11.7	6.5	7.8	−0.021
1800	5.5	10.4	4.9	7.8	−0.021
2100	5.4	9.8	4.4	5.8	−0.024
0000	6.4	9.6	3.2	1.0	+0.023
0300	9.4	12.7	3.3	0.4	+0.033

above the inversion. Often both phenomena were linked and occurred simultaneously; a typical case of this kind is illustrated in Table 7.

Other, less drastic temperature changes were caused by local sinking or by wave motion in the inversion layer. Vertical motion of 1 mm sec^{-1} and a temperature gradient of 1 C m^{-1} give rise to a temperature change of 3.6 C h^{-1}. Temperature oscillations of this magnitude were observed on several occasions under extremely stable conditions. Such oscillations hardly affect daily mean temperatures so that interdiurnal warming in winter should entirely be explained by warm air advection that acts both by raising net radiation and mechanical destruction of the inversion. Warming is accomplished at a faster rate than cooling as illustrated in Fig. 7 but it is surprising to note how rapidly a return to conditions of radiative equilibrium is attained once the influence of clouds or high winds is removed. For cases where clearing took place within 24 hours and winds were not appreciably higher than monthly means, the return to equilibrium was accomplished within 24–48 hours. Table 8 illustrates this for 17 cooling periods.

The number of cases applicable is low compared to the 360 dark days used for the statistic. It reflects the high frequency of disturbances that is also evident in Figs. 2, 3 and 4. The rapid return to equilibrium conditions is no doubt due to the poor thermal admittance versus high radiative emittance of the snow.

TABLE 8. Average decrease of daily mean temperatures after the passage of a disturbance, 1966–1968, winter months.

	Days after disturbance				
	0	1	2	3	4
Cloudiness	6/10	3/10	3/10	3/10	3/10
$\bar{T}$, °C	−62.2	−71.5	−73.0	−74.5	−75.5
Number of cases	17	17	13	6	3

Heat fluxes in the snow are generally one order of magnitude smaller than net radiation or eddy heat flux, which is true at most interior stations of Antarctica (Hoinkes, 1964; Dalrymple, Lettau and Wollaston, 1966; Lettau, Wollaston and Dalrymple, 1967; Liljequist, 1956).

The heat capacity of the snow is its memory for temporary disturbances of the surface heat budget. Obviously this memory is short, as, regardless of frequency and magnitude of advection, the minimum temperatures found each year do not differ by more than 2 degrees, and the prediction of the winter minimum on the basis of the May minimum by a 6-degree cooling is even more accurate.

It is interesting to note that most minima of T in winter are accompanied, or shortly preceeded, by minima of p. This should not be interpreted as the effect of higher atmospheric transparency due to less mass over the emitting surface, but rather a disturbance of the heat budget of the layers with which the surface is in radiative exchange. Schwerdtfeger (1970) reports radiative cooling rates at 50 mb of 40 C month^{-1}. The difference from the observed cooling rate of 5 C month^{-1} is then compensated for by advection. If this advection is temporarily interrupted, both temperature and surface pressure will be directly affected, with cooling rates increasing while the surface pressure drops. The surface temperature then reacts to the rapidly cooling upper air by radiative exchange. This twofold effect of short term interruption of stratospheric circulation might explain the early occurrence of minimum temperature in winter 1968.

It is tempting to divide the different modes of temperature changes into internal and external ones. Internal processes are those taking place locally, i.e., within the snow and in the inversion layer. External processes are those caused by advection, steady or disturbed, in the troposphere and above the tropopause where circulation behaves quite differently.

Local parameters are:

a) the thermodynamic stability of the inversion layer, or its resistance to turbulent downward transport of advected heat.

b) the relative magnitude of heat flux from or into the snow compared to other components of the surface energy balance, in other words, the memory of the snow surface for previous temperature changes.

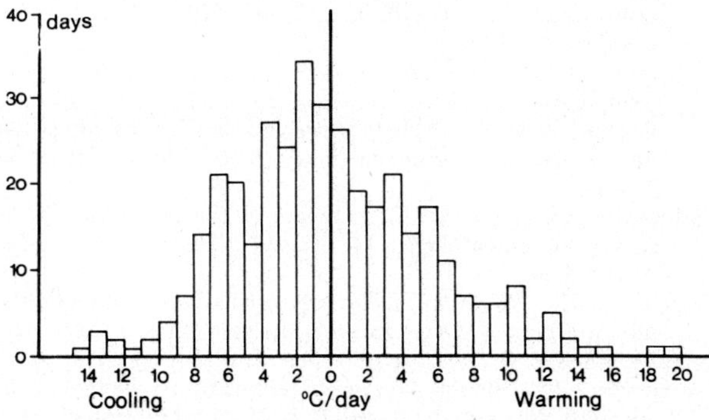

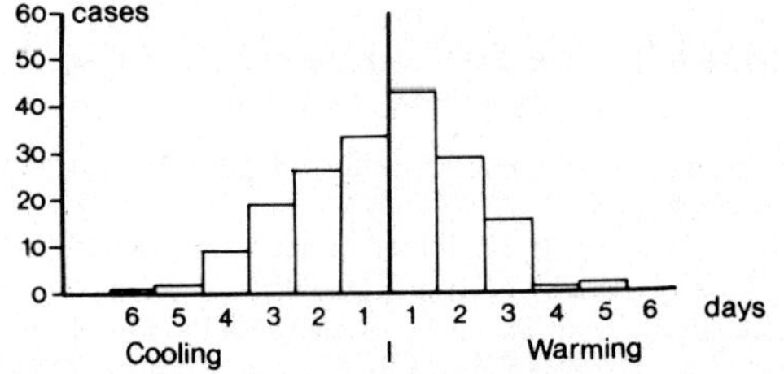

FIG. 7. Frequency of warming and cooling rates, Plateau Station, May–August 1966–1968.

TABLE 9. Temperature harmonics of 5 antarctic stations. For explanation of symbols, see Table 3. $t=0$ on December 20.

		Plateau	Vostok	South Pole	Bryd	Vanda
$\bar{T}$	C	-56.4	-55.6	-49.3	-27.9	-20.0
C_1	C	17.25	16.95	14.39	10.33	18.91
t_1	months	1.0	0.5	0.5	0.9	0.6
V_1	%	85	86	79	87	92
C_2	C	6.25	6.85	7.38	3.77	4.64
t_2	months	0.0	0.4	0.4	0.2	0.1
V_2	%	11	14	21	12	6
V_{1+2}	%	96	100	100	99	98
C_1/C_2		2.8	2.5	1.9	2.7	4.1

External, or advective parameters are:

c) mean meridional advection of heat in troposphere and stratosphere working against the radiative cooling of these layers. This advection takes place in low wavenumbers of the circumpolar circulation.

d) mesoscale eddy advection at medium wave numbers of circumpolar circulation, which temporarily raise the temperature of the troposphere and destroy the inversion by small scale eddy mixing and radiative heating.

Factors (a) and (c) are responsible for the build-up of the inversion and explain the slow decrease of minimum temperatures during winter. Moreover, they explain the different degrees of corelessness found on the basis of 500 mb and surface temperatures. Both yearly ranges and interdiurnal variability of temperatures are higher at the surface than at 500 mb due to the existence of the inversion.

Factor (d) determines the corelessness of winter temperatures, which would be more prominent if it were not for the restoring action of (b). Corelessness can be described, among other possibilities, by low values of the ratio of the first to the second harmonic of the yearly temperature variation, C_1/C_2. Table 9 gives those values for several antarctic stations.

In this regard, South Pole Station experiences the best developed coreless winter while Plateau Station does not differ much from other antarctic stations. The climate of the dry valley station Vanda (Riordan, 1973) displays a remarkably different character.

Note: Many papers not directly referenced in this report present significant contributions to the understanding of processes governing the climate of Plateau Station. These are listed at the end of the referenced bibliography.

Acknowledgments. The authors wish to thank the many who contributed to this report by help in data reduction and in discussions and suggestions. The work was sponsored by the Office of Polar Programs of the National Science Foundation through grants to the Ohio State University.

REFERENCES

Faller, A. J., 1965: Large eddies in the atmospheric boundary layer and their possible role in the formation of cloud rows. *J. Atm. Sci.*, **22**, 176–184.

Dalrymple, P. C., 1966: A physical climatology of the Antarctic plateau. Studies in Antarctic meteorology, Ed., M. J. Rubin, Am. Geoph. Union, Antarctic Research Series, **9**, 195–231.

Dalrymple, P. C., H. H. Lettau and S. H. Wollaston, 1966: South Pole micrometeorology program: Data analysis. Studies in Antarctic meteorology, Ed., M. J. Rubin, Am. Geoph. Union, Antarctic Research Series, **9**, 13–58.

Hofmann, D. J., J. M. Rosen and N. T. Kjome, 1972: Measuring submicron particulate matter in the antarctic stratosphere. *Antarctic J. U. S.*, **7**, 122–123.

Hoinkes, H. C., 1964: Glacial meteorology. Research in geophysics, Ed., H. Odishaw, **2**, 391–424. M. I. T. press, Cambridge, Mass.

Hoinkes, H. C., 1970: Radiation budget at Little America V, 1957. Proc. ISAGE Symposium, Hanover, N. H., 1968. IASH publ. No. 86, 263–284.

Keeling, C. D., 1960: The concentration and isotopic abundances of carbon dioxide in the atmosphere. *Tellus*, **12**, 200–203.

Kuhn, M. H., 1969: Preliminary report on meteorological studies at Plateau Station, Antarctica, 1967. Univ. of Melbourne, Met. Dept. publ., 20 pp.

Kuhn, M. H., 1972a: Die spektrale Transparenz der antarktischen Atmosphäre. *Arch. Met. Geoph. Biokl.*, Ser. B, **20**, 299–344.

Kuhn, M. H., 1972b: Global pollution in antarctic air documented by solar radiation depletion. *Antarctic J. U. S.*, **7**, 35–37.

Lettau, H. H., S. H. Wollaston and P. C. Dalrymple, 1967: Little America V micrometeorology program, Data analysis. U. S. Army Materiel Command, Natick, Mass., ES-29, 253 pp.

Liljequist, G. H., 1956: Energy exchange of an Antarctic snowfield, long-wave radiation and radiation balance. Norwegian-British-Swedish Antarctic expedition, 1949–52, Scientific Results, Vol. II, Part 1B. Norsk Polarinstitutt, Oslo.

Riordan, A. J., 1973: The climate of Vanda station. Proc. 24th Alaskan Science Conference, August 1973, Fairbanks, Alaska.

Rubin, M. J., 1964: Antarctic weather and climate. Research in geophysics, Ed., H. Odishaw, **2**, 461–478, M. I. T. press, Cambridge, Mass.

Schwerdtfeger, W., 1962: Die halbjährige Periode des meridionalen Temperaturgradienten in der Troposphäre und des Luftdrucks am Boden im Südpolargebiet, ihre Erscheinungsform und kausalen Zusammenhänge. *Beitr. Phys. Atm.*, **35**, 234–244.

Schwerdtfeger, W., 1970: The climate of the Antarctic. World survey of climatology, **14**, 253–355. Elsevier Publ. Co., Amsterdam.

Van Loon, H., 1967: The half-yearly oscillations in middle and high southern latitudes and the coreless winter. *J. Atm. Sci.*, **24**, 472–486.

Wexler, H., 1959: Seasonal and other temperature changes in the antarctic atmosphere. *Quart. J. R. M. S.*, **85**, 196–208.

Wexler, H., W. B. Moreland and W. S. Weyant, 1960: A preliminary report on ozone observations at Little America, Antarctica. *Mo. Wea. Rev.*, **88**, 43–54.

BIBLIOGRAPHY OF METEOROLOGICAL RESEARCH AT PLATEAU STATION

Dabbert, W. F., 1970: A selective climatology of Plateau Station, Antarctica. *J. A. M.*, **9**, 311–315.

Dalrymple, P. C., 1969: Micromet programs in East Antarctica and Thailand. *Bull. A. M. S.*, **50**, 80–81.

Dalrymple, P. C., and Th. O. Frostman, 1971: Some aspects of the climate of interior Antarctica. Research in the Antarctic, Ed. by L. Quam. AAAS publ. No. 93, 429–442. Washington, D. C.

Dalrymple, P. C., and L. A. Stroschein, 1966: Antarctic plateau radiation climatology. *A. J. U. S.*, **1**, 199.

Dalrymple, P. C., and L. A. Stroschein, 1967: Radiation climatology at Plateau Station. *A. J. U. S.*, **2**, 159.

Dingle, R. W., U. Radok, P. Schwerdtfeger and G. Weller, 1967: Surface and subsurface micrometeorology at Plateau Station. *A. J. U. S.*, **2**, 162.

Frostman, Th. O., 1969: Plateau Station micrometeorology. *A. J. U. S.*, **4**, 224.

Kuhn, M. H., 1969: Preliminary report on meteorological studies at Plateau Station, Antarctica, 1967. 20 pp. Univ. of Melbourne, Met. Dept.

Kuhn, M. H., 1970a: Analysis of direct solar radiation at Plateau Station 1966–1968. *A. J. U. S.*, **5**, 175.

Kuhn, M. H., 1970b: Ice crystals and solar halo displays, Plateau Station. 1967. Proc. ISAGE Symp., Hanover, N. H., 1968. IASH publ. No. 86, 298–303.

Kuhn, M. H., 1971: Elevated temperature minima at Plateau Station. *A. J. U. S.*, **6**, 217–218.

Kuhn, M. H., 1972a: Die spektrale Transparenz der antarktischen Atmosphäre. *Arch. Met. Geoph. Biokl., Ser. B*, **20**. Part I: pp. 207–248, part II: pp. 299–344.

Kuhn, M. H., 1972b: Global pollution in antarctic air documented by solar radiation depletion. *A. J. U. S.*, **7**, 35–37.

Kuhn, M. H., 1973: Natural illumination of the Antarctic Plateau. *Arch. Met. Geoph. Biokl., Ser. B*, **21**, 55–66.

Kuhn, M. H., 1975: Spectral radiation fluxes over the Antarctic Plateau. Proc. Symp. Energy Fluxes over Polar Surfaces, XV Gen. Assembly IUGG, Moscow, 1971. IAHS Publ. 104.

Kuhn, M. H., and A. J. Riordan, 1973: Some characteristics of the friction layer over the antarctic plateau. *A. J. U. S.*, **8**, 236–238.

Lettau, H. H., 1971: Antarctic atmosphere as a test tube for meteorological theories. Research in the Antarctic, Ed. by L. Quam, AAAS publ. no. 93: 443–475. Washington, D. C.

Lettau, H. H., and W. F. Dabberdt, 1970: Variangular wind spirals. *Boundary Layer Met.*, **1**, 64–79.

Miller, S., and W. Schwerdtfeger, 1972: Ice crystal formation and growth in the warm layer above the antarctic temperature inversion. *A. J. U. S.*, **7**, 170–171.

Radok, U., P. Schwerdtfeger and G. Weller, 1968: Surface and subsurface meteorological conditions at Plateau Station. *A. J. U. S.*, **3**, 257–258.

Riordan, A. J., 1972: Atmospheric stability at Plateau Station. *A. J. U. S.* **7**, 69–170.

Schwerdtfeger, W., 1969: Ice crystal precipitation on the antarctic plateau. *A. J. U. S.*, **4**, 221–222.

Schwerdtfeger, W., 1971: Remarkable windshifts and speeds a few meters above the surface of the antarctic plateau. *A. J. U. S.*, **6**, 218–219.

Schwerdtfeger, W., 1970: Theory and observations of the wind in the friction layer over the antarctic plateau. *A. J. U. S.* **5**, 175–176.

Sponholz, M. P., 1968: Meteorological studies on the antarctic plateau. *A. J. U. S.*, **3**, 189–190.

Weller, G., and P. Schwerdtfeger, 1970: Thermal properties and heat transfer processes of the snow of the central antarctic plateau. Proc. ISAGE Symp., Hanover, N. H., 1968. IASH publ. No. 86, 284–297.

Weyant, W. S., 1967: Meteorological studies on the antarctic plateau. *A. J. U. S.*, **2**, 164–165.

Wong, E., and A. J. Riordan, 1971: Micrometeorology at Plateau Station. *A. J. U. S.*, **6**, 215–217.

The Climate of Vanda Station, Antarctica

A. J. RIORDAN

Institut für Meteorologie und Geophysik der Universität Innsbruck, Austria

Abstract

Vanda Station, located in the Wright Valley which forms part of the McMurdo Oasis, has a climate which contrasts markedly from that of the antarctic ice sheet. Due to topographic obstruction and a reduced ice level on the plateau to the west, the region is free of glacial ice. The resulting climate does not permit appreciable snow accumulation during any season but perpetuates the anomalous ice-free character of the oasis. Nearly two years of weather and radiation measurements at Vanda Station in 1969 and 1970 as well as detailed wind studies and observations in 1969 show that several interrelated factors are responsible for the snowlessness.

The area is indeed a desert, with 8.4 cm of total snowfall in 1969 and only 0.7 cm in 1970. Significantly, snowfall almost always occurred with winds of less than 5 m sec^{-1} and formed a uniform cover over the valley surface which lay undisturbed for an average of one week. Winds of 15 to 20 m sec^{-1} associated with low pressure disturbances were noted several times per month in 1969. Their occurrence immediately disrupted the snowcover leaving generally less than half the valley surface covered by drifts. Westerly wind originating on the ice sheet some 2000 m above the level of the valley was particularly effective in removing snowcover during the winter and was associated with sudden warmings of up to 35C day^{-1}. During the summer, a shallow diurnal east–west wind regime became established and uniform snow cover was rare. Occasional large cumulus clouds produced snowfall which often did not reach the valley floor.

The measured annual global radiation at the station was slightly less than that at Oasis Station (66.3°S, 100.7°E) and much less than that measured at continental stations on the ice sheet. However, the albedo of the snowless surface averaged from 0.20 to 0.24 and thus the total effective shortwave radiation was many times greater than that of a snow surface. Using albedo, Angstroem ratio, and emissivity estimates, the sensible heat flux density can be estimated from the heat balance equation. Despite uncertainties regarding the longwave balance, it is certain that a significant upward heat flux component is available to the atmosphere. It is possible that a warm-core circulation system results which isolates the oasis from cyclonic disturbances during the summer and acts as a feedback mechanism which maintains a snowless surface during the insolation period.

---

1. Introduction

Vanda Station (77°31′S, 161°40′E) is located in the Wright Valley, which forms an east–west trough 46 km long and 2 km deep. Its width is only 8 km from the summits of the Asgard Range to the south to those of the Olympus Range to the north. It is part of the 1600 km² ice-free area in the mountains of South Victoria Land approximately 100 km west of Ross Island. The station is situated at the eastern end of Lake Vanda at the lowest point in the valley—about 75 m above sea level, and about 2000 m below the level of the Antarctic ice sheet 35 km to the west. The close proximity of the Olympus Range causes a marked reduction in sunlight reaching the station, so that direct insolation begins and ends at the spring and autumn equinoxes.

The valley surface remains snow free throughout most of the year. It is composed of brown granitic sand, pebbles 1–2 cm in diameter, and stones 10–15 cm in diameter, with large dolerite boulders 1–3 m in diameter found principally along the north and south

slopes. The terrain in the western third of the valley near Lake Vanda is intersected by dark grey dolerite dykes 3–6 m high, aligned northeast-southwest across the valley floor. About 4 km east of the lake the valley surface is flat and sandy for a distance of about 7 km.

Lake Vanda, which measures 5 km by 1¼ km, remains almost entirely covered throughout the year by extremely rough ice except for shallow portions within about 20 m of the shoreline. Water temperatures at a bottom depth of 70 m are maintained at 25 C by geothermal heating and stratified saline layering (see Ragotzkie and Likens, 1964). The lake has no outlet but receives annual inflow from the Onyx River, which flows westward from the eastern end of the valley for 4–6 weeks in summer.

The anomalies of both the lake temperature and the climate of the entire oasis region have been the subject of intensive interest and investigation since 1957. The most widely accepted theory explaining the lack of glacial cover in the region was proposed by McKelvey and Webb (1962). A decrease in the eleva-

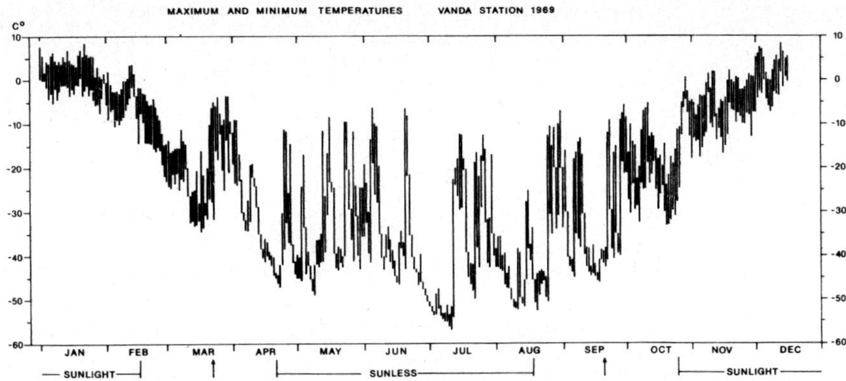

FIG. 1. Daily maximum and minimum temperatures for 1969.

tion of the inland ice sheet coupled with the presence of rock thresholds along the western boundary of the oasis apparently nearly halted the flow of ice into the region. Accumulated evidence shows that an important and massive series of glaciations from the west occurred about 4 million years before present. These were followed by a more recent series of advances from the east from Alpine glaciers which is probably concurrent with the Wisconsin glaciation (Nichols, 1971, Denton, Armstrong, and Stuiver, 1971). Interestingly, the ice sheet to the west of the Wright Valley now seems to be at its maximum level since before the Wisconsin glaciation (Denton *et al.*, 1971). The establishment of New Zealand's Vanda Station in December 1968 has provided two years of continuous weather records through which the climate can be quantitatively described, and some insight into the mechanism which maintains the snowless anomaly can be gained. Nearly all data presented here were kindly supplied by D. C. Thompson (Thompson, Craig and Bromley, 1971).

2. Temperatures

Air temperatures at Vanda Station, measured in a standard instrument shelter 1.5 m above the surface, averaged near -20 C for the two-year period beginning in January 1969. Summer temperature averaged about 5 C warmer than at McMurdo Station, while winter temperatures averaged 10–12 C colder due to long periods of calm winds and clear skies. The daily temperature extremes for 1969 are illustrated in Fig. 1. The shape of the annual temperature cycle is generally similar to that measured at other antarctic stations, but important differences which are characteristic of Vanda Station include high summer air temperatures and unusually large upward temperature displacements in winter. Summer monthly mean temperatures in December and January of both 1969 and 1970 averaged greater than or equal to $+1.0$ C with mean maxima greater than 4.0 C. An extreme maximum of $+10.4$ C was measured in January 1970. Such high air temperatures invariably occurred as a result of

high radiation absorption at the surface during clear skies and calm conditions. On several such occasions temperatures on the rock surface were measured at near 20 C. Previous short term air temperature measurements by Colin Bull throughout the oasis area from 1958–1962 have shown similar temperature maxima (Bull, 1966).

During the period from 25 April through 18 August when the sun was below the horizon, temperatures steadily decreased if skies were clear and winds were light. The 1969 minimum temperature of -56.9 C, for example, occurred at the end of a gradual temperature decrease during a 19 day calm period. Temperature increases of 25–35 C within 24 hours occurred on an average of twice per month during winter when a foehn wind from the west penetrated the surface inversion. Several typical examples of sudden warming are shown in Fig. 2. Often during calm conditions the sound of wind could be heard from the peaks of the Olympus Range and blowing snow could be seen on the Upper Wright Glacier near the ice sheet beyond the west end of the valley. On many instances gusty variable winds would commence at the station within a few hours and, after a 30–60 minute period of highly erratic temperatures and winds, warm temperatures and sustained winds of 10–20 m sec^{-1} would continue for several days.

3. Winds

Winds at Vanda Station, summarized in Table I, were measured from a height of approximately 8 m as part of the instrument program of the New Zealand Meteorological Service. In addition, during 1969 five remote wind recording stations were established within 6 km of Vanda Station as shown in Fig. 3. Wind speed and direction were measured at 1.5 m above the ground and were continuously recorded using a Rustrak recorder powered by an insulated heavy duty lead-acid battery. Simultaneous operation of all five recorders was achieved only during summer periods. However, at two locations nearly continuous wind records were obtained throughout the winter.

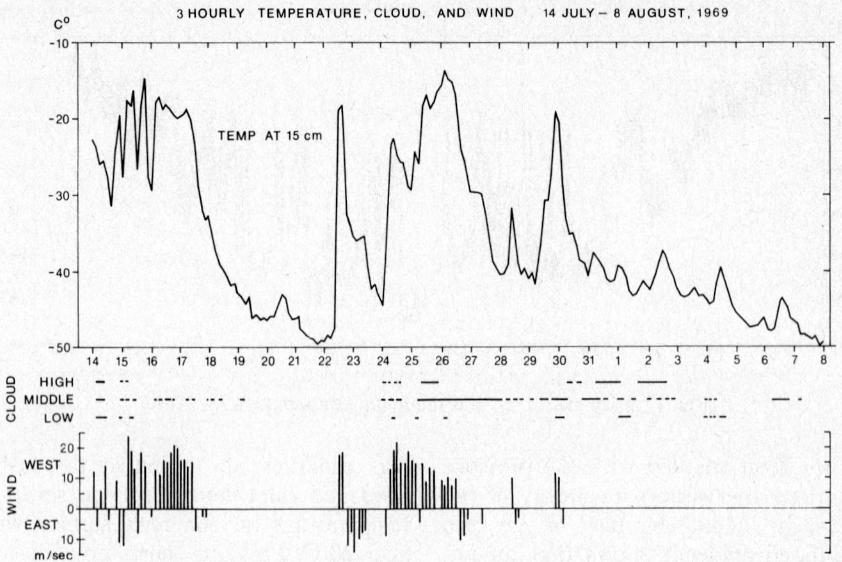

FIG. 2. 3-hourly temperature, cloud cover, and wind 14 July–8 August, 1969.

Two general types of wind regimes predominate throughout the valley. The first, which occurred only during sunlit months, is a diurnal-based periodic wind characterized at the station by east winds during the afternoon and evening, and calm periods or west winds in the morning. Interesting differences at various locations show this to be a complex phenomenon. The second wind type is of external origin and occurred throughout the year when winds from synoptic disturbances reached the valley surface from aloft. These winds were often strongly deflected by the valley alignment and blew from either east or southwest to west.

The diurnal wind cycle

From November through mid February a diurnal wind cycle predominated at Vanda Station with east winds averaging 6–10 m sec⁻¹ between 1200 and 0000 hours local time. In some instances this was preceeded by west wind between 0000 and 1200 hours. The pattern is illustrated in the frequency diagram in Fig. 4.

The summer period is characterized by steady winds. There is a marked reduction in gustiness from that of winter months, and periods of wind less than 5 m sec⁻¹ are only of several hours duration. Thus, mean wind speeds for November through February in Table I are representative of the usual conditions at the station.

A similar diurnal pattern of east and west winds prevails at the outlying sites. Along the north and south slopes a katabatic-anabatic regime is superimposed upon the flow along the valley with uphill flow when the slope was in sunlight and downhill drainage when the slope was in shade. This can be

TABLE I. Wind data (m sec⁻¹) for Vanda Station, 1969.

Month	Mean wind speed	Maximum gust and direction		Number of days with Maximum gust greater than 20 m sec⁻¹	Number of days with Maximum gust less than 6 m sec⁻¹
January	6.4	—	—	—	—
February	6.2	25	206°	3	0
March	3.9	28	270°	8	11
April	1.5	37	270°	4	19
May	1.9	27	270°	3	18
June	2.1	26	260°	6	16
July	4.6	37	280°	12	11
August	2.3	40	280°	5	20
September	3.2	34	210°	10	14
October	4.9	32	270°	9	5
November	7.2	30	270°	9	0
December	6.6	—	—	—	—

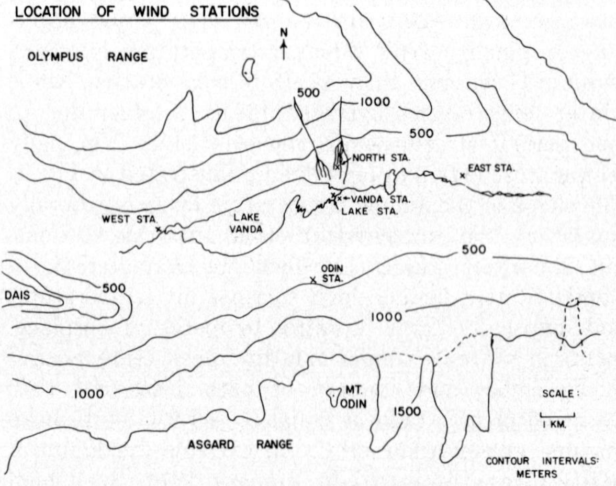

FIG. 3. Location of wind stations.

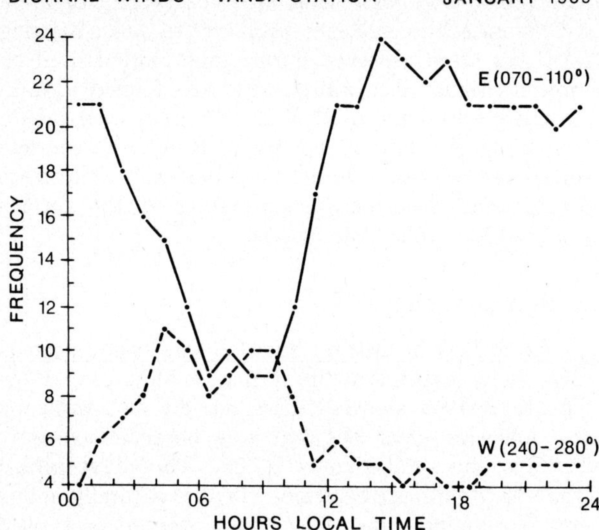

FIG. 4. Diurnal wind frequency for winds measured at
Vanda Station during January, 1969.

seen in Fig. 5 which illustrates winds measured at
Odin station from 24 September through 12 November,
1969, during wind speeds of less than 5 m sec⁻¹.
During periods with wind greater than 5 m sec⁻¹, the
mountain slope flow is less noticeable.

A comparison of records from the Odin site with
those from the lake and east stations for the same
period is illustrated in Fig. 6. East winds at the Odin
site account for less transport than at either the lake
or the east sites. Intermittent records at the west
station suggest that the occurrence of east wind in
the area north of the dais and west of the lake is less
frequent and that westerly winds are more common
than at sites to the east. On several occasions when
a well established east wind was observed at Vanda
Station, calm conditions or west winds were observed
along the slopes at about 800 m above the valley
floor north of the station. Both observations suggesting the limited extent of the summer diurnal wind
pattern are confirmed by Bull (1966), who observed
that on 15 days with a strong east wind at the valley
floor, the winds were calm or light and variable
above 1200 m on the valley walls. Furthermore, he
observed that winds at the eastern end of the valley
were practically never from the west.

It is possible that the shallow nature of the summer
flow pattern may be the result of the temperature
anomaly of the entire oasis region. Thermally induced
circulation in the summer may be a large determining
factor in maintenance of a snowfree surface. A warm-
core circulation could be accompanied by a wind
reversal with height characterized by anticyclonic
(counter-clockwise) circulation above the valley system. This remains speculative, however, since upper
air data above the oasis region is not available.

WINDS AT ODIN STATION: 24 September-12 November 1969

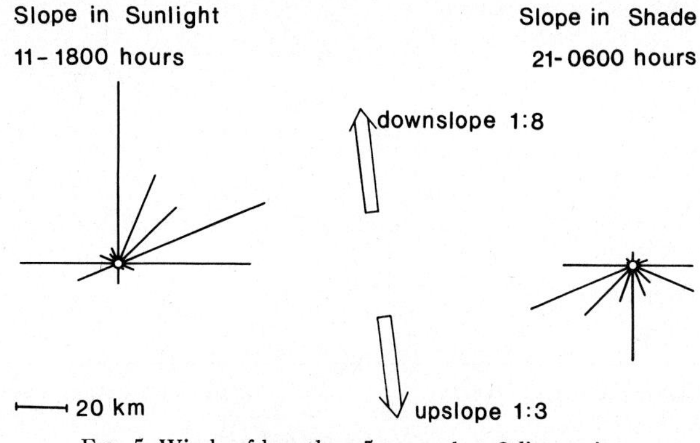

FIG. 5. Winds of less than 5 m sec⁻¹ at Odin station
24 September–12 November, 1969.

Winds of synoptic scale origin

Winds at Vanda Station from March through
September, 1969, were less frequent but more intense
than during the summer. Table I illustrates the increase both in the number of days with winds of less
than or equal to 5 m sec⁻¹ and in maximum wind

WIND COMPARISON AT THREE SITES

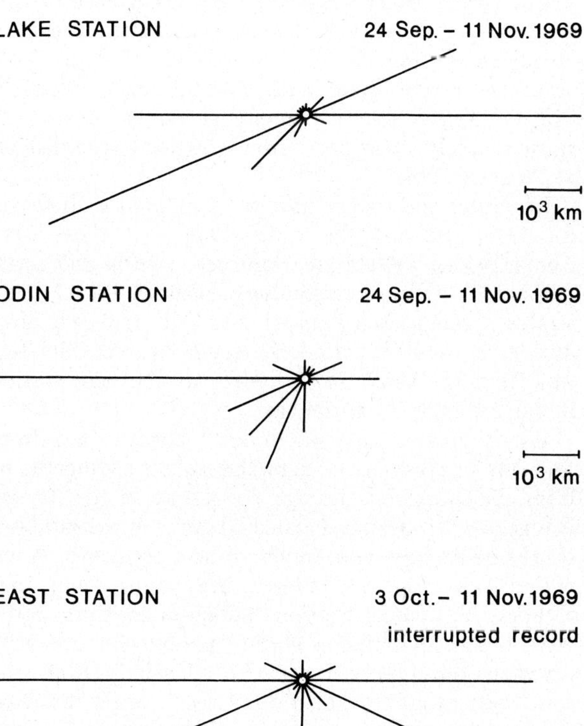

FIG. 6. Winds at three valley locations during the
transitional and early sunlit period, 1969.

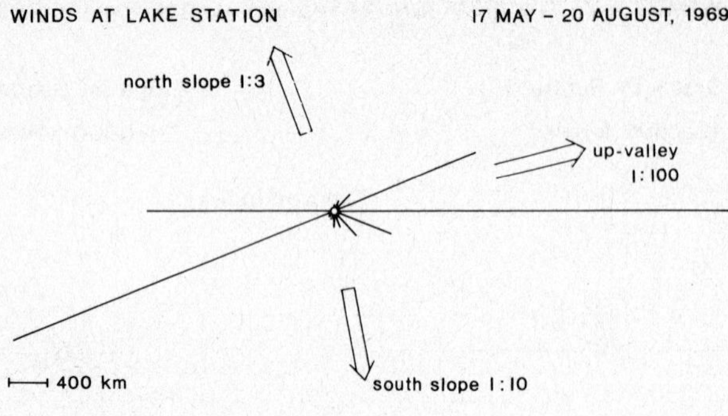

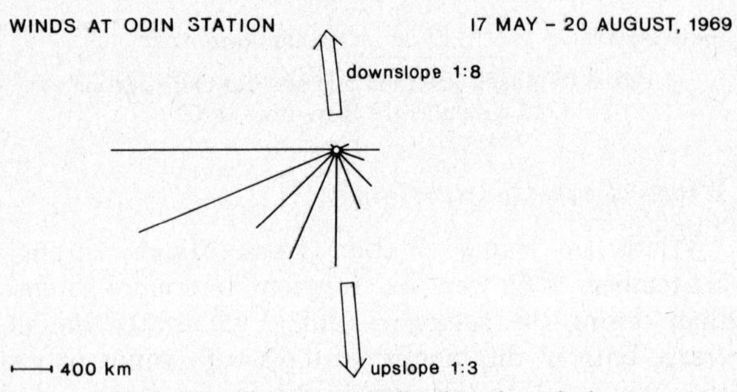

FIG. 7. Winds at two valley locations during the sunless period, 1969.

speed. Nearly every sustained wind occurrence of this type was associated with low barometric pressure. Sustained 10 minute wind speeds of 15–20 m sec⁻¹ occurred several times each month during westerly winds. The highest 10 minute sustained speed was approximately 28 m sec⁻¹ from the west recorded on 31 August, 1969.

In winter there were also wind differences between the Odin site and the valley floor, but these were primarily due to cold air drainage patterns and topographical deflection of southerly airflow. Fig. 7 illustrates a comparison between the Odin and lake sites during the sunless period. Drainage at the Odin site was from the south sector, while at the lake station it was generally from the east.

Winds greater than 4.5 m sec⁻¹ always blew from the east or west, parallel to the valley alignment, or from the southwest through the passes in the Asgard Range. One pass was located about 4 km southwest of the Odin site and much of the southwest wind recorded at the site entered the valley from that location. At Vanda Station sudden wind shifts often were observed during a stormy period. On one such occasion the observer experienced winds from the southwest estimated at 15–20 m sec⁻¹, while the wind vane and anemometer at the main station site approximately 100 m to the east measured a 26 m sec⁻¹ gust from the northeast. Similar conditions were common in both summer and winter when winds blew from the southwest and were subject to large deflections. Mean wind speed was lower than with west or east winds, but gusts sometimes reached 25 or 30 m sec⁻¹ from calm conditions within 30 seconds. Blowing sand was often observed during these periods and on three occasions dust whirls, with well-defined tubular structure estimated at 20–30 m in height, were briefly seen along the base of the Asgard Range. These were considered to be of purely mechanical origin since during their occurrence temperatures at the surface were 4–10 C cooler than at 2 m.

4. Precipitation

Due to lack of drifting, snowfall was easily measurable. Snow occurred at the station on 59 days in 1969. The total 1969 snowfall measured 8.4 cm, while on the following year snowfall was observed on only 11 days and totalled only 0.7 cm. The entire period from May through November 1970 was totally snowless. It is uncertain which years represents typical conditions, but high precipitation variability is itself characteristic of most extremely dry regions. These values suggest a total annual water equivalent of only 1 g cm⁻² or less, contrasting markedly to a net annual accumulation value of about 15 g cm⁻² on the plateau within 100 km to the west (Bull, 1971). One must bear in mind that the latter is a net balance figure, and total annual accumulation on the plateau might be somewhat higher. Precipitation statistics for February through November 1969 are given in Table II. In 1969 nearly all cases of snowfall from March through September were accompanied by a stratus layer at about 800–1000 m drifting from the east, although in a few instances measurable snow fell from cloudless skies or from altostratus layers above 2000 m. There was never noticeable drifting during snowfall. Significantly, snowfall at the station was observed on only about half the number of occasions when snowfall was observed in the valley. The eastern half of the valley received snow more frequently than the western half. Fall of ice prisms, observed on 23 days with clear skies and surface temperatures below −40 C during July through September 1969, contributed negligible amounts to the annual total. During the months of October through February snowfall also occurred as showers originating from cumulus clouds. Often such snowfall either was confined to higher elevations and did not reach the valley floor, or occurred only over small local areas of the order of 5×5 km, as shown in Fig. 8

Uniform snow cover on the valley floor presents an important albedo modification, especially in summer. Initially, uniform cover occurred immediately after a widespread snowfall of the type first described, and thus was more characteristic of the winter season than the summer. Drifting occurred with the onset of winds of over 5 m/sec after an average of six days with uniform cover, and the snow cover was immediately reduced to about 50% total coverage. Table II

TABLE II. Precipitation and snowcover data for February–November, 1969.

Month	Total snowfall at station (cm)	Snow at station	Snow in valley	Ice prisms	Measurable uniform snow cover	Frost	Average % of ground covered
February	Trace	3	10	0	0	1	0
March	1.2	7	12	0	12	2	39
April	0.6	4	10	0	13	19	47
May	2.9	9	12	0	13	16	57
June	2.2	8	12	0	5	14	52
July	Trace	2	3	9	0	17	33
August	1.2	4	4	12	9	25	39
September	0.0	0	5	1	0	22	13
October	0.3	3	9	0	2	10	11
November	Trace	2	11	0	0	0	3

gives the mean monthly percentage of the valley surface covered by snow. By the time direct sunlight began reaching the valley floor in September, much of the surface was already free of snow cover. Total snow coverage in the western half of the valley in mid-September was estimated at 12%. Cover was generally less in flat sandy areas, but was 20–30% in the dyke areas south of the lake from the dais to the lake penninsula. At the base of Mt. Odin 25% of the valley was covered by drifts, but farther west along the foot of the Asgard Range south of the dais there was no snow at the time of sunrise in 1969.

5. Albedo

Albedo was measured over various surfaces with a pair of silicon photocells mounted within upward- and downward-directed integrating spheres. Readings ranged from 0.12 to 0.14, obtained along dolerite dykes, to 0.31, obtained over the whitest snow- and ice-free surface, but most measurements averaged from 0.20 to 0.24. Considering the relative amounts of lighter and darker material, the latter seems a reasonable estimate of albedo for the snowless surface.

6. Annual heat budget

The annual heat budget can be estimated using the balance relation

$$(1-a)\overline{SW{\downarrow}} = \overline{LW{\downarrow}} + \overline{LW{\uparrow}} + \bar{E}_0 + \bar{Q}_0 + \bar{S}_0. \qquad (1)$$

Surface heat gain on the left side of Eq. (1) is balanced by surface heat loss on the right. Downward arrows denote mean heat flux density directed toward the surface. The first term represents the mean annual solar radiative heat flux density absorbed by the surface, where a is the mean surface albedo and $\overline{SW{\downarrow}}$

FIG. 8. An example of precipitation in summer.

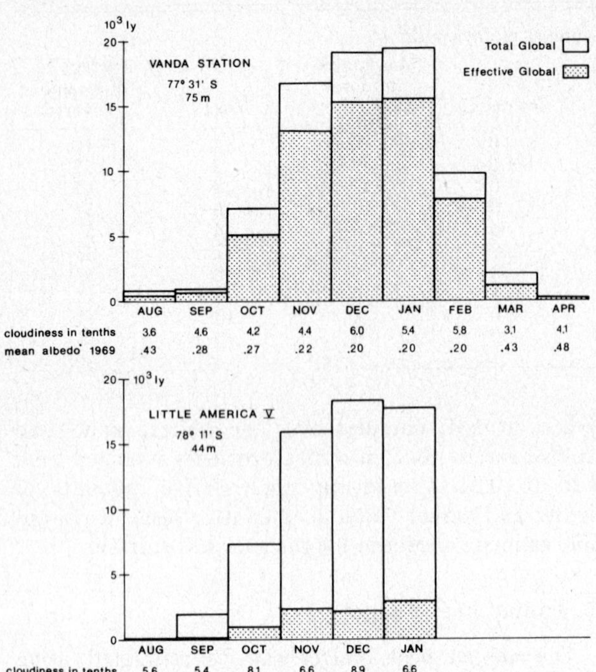

FIG. 9. Comparison of shortwave radiation values at Vanda and little America V.

is the total global radiation. The second term is the net longwave heat flux density, where $LW\downarrow$ is the heat flux density directed from the atmosphere toward the surface and $LW\uparrow$ is the longwave heat flux density emitted by the surface. The last three terms on the right in Eq. (1) are mean annual heat flux densities denoting surface loss due to latent (evaporative), sensible, and subsurface heat flux processes. Note that all terms on the right are positive when directed away from the surface. Thus, $LW\downarrow$ is negative and a positive $\bar{S}_0$ denotes a downward heat flux density.

Fig. 9 gives mean monthly solar radiation values (Thompson, Craig and Bromley, 1971) as measured at Vanda Station by a CSIRO radiometer. Values for April through November represent means of two years of measurement. The total global radiation measured during the year averaged 75,400 ly which is clearly less than the average annual measurements of between 100,000 and 110,000 ly measured at Vostok, Pioneerskaya, and South Pole, and slightly less than the 89,100 ly measured at Oasis Station (data summarized in Schwerdtfeger, 1970). The limited record at Vanda suggests that large year to year variations in radiation may be expected due to large variations in summer cloudiness. For example, 18.3×10^3 ly was measured in December 1969, with a mean cloudiness of 7/10, whereas in December 1970, 19.7×10^3 ly was measured with a mean cloud cover of 5/10. The effective solar radiation absorbed by the surface is estimated based on albedo and snow cover statistics for 1969. The estimated albedo of the bare valley surface of 0.2 was weighted by the mean monthly percentage of snow cover. Snow lying on the valley floor was assumed to have an albedo of 0.8, a value somewhat reduced from 0.85 to 0.95 due to the limited depth of uniform snow cover.

For comparison, values of shortwave measurements and effective shortwave values based on measured albedo at Little America V for August 1957 through January 1958 (Hoinkes, 1968) are also illustrated in Fig. 9. It is apparent that, in spite of topographic obstructions, the monthly solar radiation values are 5–10% higher at Vanda for November through January, due to reduced mean cloudiness. However, the surface absorption of available radiation at the two locations is markedly different with 5.8 times more shortwave radiation absorbed by the rock surface than by the snow during the 6 month period.

The mean annual absorbed solar radiation flux at Vanda, based on the limited $1\frac{1}{2}$ year sample, is tentatively estimated at 114 mly min^{-1}. Assuming a Stefan-Boltzmann constant of $\sigma = 8.13 \times 10^{-8}$ mly min^{-1} K^{-1}, a mean annual Ångstroem Ratio, Å, of 0.21 (where Å $= (LW\uparrow + LW\downarrow)/LW\uparrow$), a surface emissivity, ϵ, of 0.96, and using a mean annual surface temperature Of -20 C and the relation $LW\downarrow + LW\uparrow = \epsilon \sigma \text{Å} \bar{T}^4_0$, a net outgoing longwave flux density of 67 mly min^{-1} was computed. If mean annual latent and soil heat flux densities are assumed to be upward at 0–1 mly min^{-1} each due to negligible surface moisture and above normal geothermal heating, then a mean upward sensible heat flux density value of 47 mly min^{-1} is obtained as a remainder term in the heat balance equation. This is an extremely rough computation intended only to illustrate the relative magnitudes of the heat flux terms. Tentative values for Oasis and Vostok (Schwerdtfeger, 1970), as well as Maudheim (Lilje-

TABLE III. Comparison of annual radiation balance (mly min^{-1}) for four antarctic stations. The terms are as defined in the text with the addition of $\bar{R}_{net} = (1-a)\overline{SW}\downarrow - \overline{LW\downarrow + LW}\uparrow$.

	$\overline{SW}\downarrow$	$(1-a)\overline{SW}\downarrow$	$\bar{R}_{net}$	$\bar{E}_0$	$\bar{S}_0$	$\bar{Q}_0$	$\overline{LW\downarrow + LW}\uparrow$	$\bar{T}$
Vanda	143↓	114↓	47↓	1	−1	47	67↑	−20C
Oasis	170↓	130↓	71↓				59↑	
Vostok	206↓	37↓	12↑				49↑	−56C
Maudheim			17↑	−3	0	−14	46↑	−18C

quist, 1956, and Schytt, 1960) are illustrated for comparison in Table III.

The value of the net longwave radiation flux at Vanda appears to be the most uncertain factor in the balance relation. Measured values of net radiation for a $1\frac{1}{2}$ year period indicate a net annual outward longwave flux density of 97 mly min^{-1}. Assuming the same mean annual surface temperature and emissivity as above, the mean Angstroem ratio becomes 0.30, a value somewhat larger than expected in view of measurements of 0.13–0.21 at Oasis Station (Schwerdtfeger, 1970). It seems certain, however, that due to low albedo, the effective solar radiation in the Wright Valley is substantially increased and both anomalously high surface temperature and upward sensible heat flux are the result.

7. Conclusion

The low summer albedo is only partially maintained by solar radiation. The principal factors which maintain a mostly snowless surface are the intermittent occurrence of foehn winds throughout the year, which greatly reduces the thin snow cover, coupled with the extremely small amount of annual snowfall.

It is likely that surface elevations nearly 2000 m lower than that of the ice sheet and consequent adiabatic warming produce the additional dryness which reduces the precipitation reaching the surface in summer and produces dry foehn conditions during synoptic disturbances throughout the year. The occurrence of major snowfall is thereby reduced to those cases where there is moist advection aloft with nearly calm conditions at the ground. The possible presence of a warm-core circulation over the oasis region in summer may further reduce cloudiness and precipitation, thus providing a feed-back mechanism by which the snowless anomaly maintains itself. Thermal winds over ice domes and desert regions as coupled with terrain effects are discussed by Lettau (1967). Such systems probably play a key role in maintenance of large dry regions as well as continental ice sheets. Whether such a system is present over the limited area of the oasis region is not certain.

However, the existence of the oasis illustrates a paradox whereby once glacial ice is removed from a region, that region can easily maintain itself alongside a permanent ice sheet. One may speculate that the only necessary conditions are that the surrounding ice surface be significantly higher than the oasis and that no glacial ice be permitted to flow into the region.

REFERENCES

Bull, Colin, 1966: Climatological observations in ice-free areas of southern Victoria Land, Antarctica. *Antarctic Research Series*, 9, 195–231. Amer. Geophys. U.

Bull, Colin, 1971: Snow accumulation in Antarctica. *Research in the Antarctic*, 367–421. Edited by Louis Quam, American Assoc. Adv. Sci., Publ. 93, Washington, D. C.

Denton, George, Richard Armstrong, and Minze Stuiver, 1971: The late Cenozoic glacial history of Antarctica. *The Late Cenozoic Glacial Ages*, 267–306. Edited by Karl Turekian, Yale U. Press, New Haven and London.

Hoinkes, H. C., 1957: Radiation budget at Little America V, 1957. *International Symposium on Antarctic Glaciological Exploration*, Publ. No. 86, 263–284.

Lettau, H. H., 1967: Small to large-scale features of boundary layer structure over mountain slopes. *Proceedings of the Symposium on Mountain Meteorology*, 26 June 1967, Colorado State U, Ft. Collins, Col.

Liljequist, G. H., 1956: Energy exchange of an antarctic snowfield. *Norwegian-British-Swedish Antarctic Expedition 1949–1952, Scientific Results*, Part 1, Vol. 2, Oslo.

McKelvey, B. C., and P. N. Webb, 1962: Geological investigations in southern Victoria Land, Antarctica, 3, Geology of the Wright Valley. *New Zealand Journal of Geology and Geophys.*, 5, 143–162.

Nichols, Robert L., 1971: Glacial geology of the Wright Valley McMurdo Sound. *Research in the Antarctic*, 293–340. Edited by Louis Quam, Amer. Assoc. Adv. Sci. Publ. 93, Washington, D. C.

Ragotzkie, R. A., and Gene Likens, 1964: The heat balance of two antarctic lakes. *Limnology and Oceanography*, 9, 412–425.

Schwerdtfeger, W., 1970: The climate of the Antarctic. *World Survey of Climatology*, 14, 256–261. Edited by H. E. Landsberg, Amsterdam.

Schytt, Valter, 1960: Snow and ice temperatures in Dronning Maud Land. *Norwegian-British-Swedish Antarctic Expedition 1949–1952, Scientific Results*, Glaciology II. Oslo.

Thompson, D. C., R. Craig and A. Bromley, 1971: *Climate and Surface Heat Balance in an Antarctic Dry Valley*. Technical Note 193, New Zealand Met. Service, Wellington, N. Z.

Upland Climatic Parameters on Subarctic Slopes, Central Alaska

C. W. Slaughter

Alaskan Division, USACRREL

AND

K. P. Long

ASL Met Support Activity, Ft. Wainwright, Alaska

Abstract

A cooperative program of climatic data acquisition has been undertaken in the Yukon-Tanana Uplands of central Alaska. Data acquisition efforts are briefly described; examples of results available to data include comparison of air and ground temperatures at the same elevation on opposing (north and south) forested slopes, and upland precipitation measurements.

1. Introduction

Climatic and hydrologic information from the uplands of central Alaska has been and remains extremely scarce. Most stations reporting data to the National Weather Service are in valley locations (Environmental Data Service, 1972), and upland stations with appreciable record length are rare. Even in the vicinity of Fairbanks, population center for the entire Alaskan "Interior," reporting stations have been limited to lowland sites. Haugen *et al.* (1971) analyzed available climatic data for all of interior Alaska; without exception, the record at upland stations is spotty and *no* stations removed from valley locations were reporting data at the time of their compilation. Similarly, streamflow information until recently has been available only for major streams; partial records (crest-stage gage record, spot measurements) are available for some upland locations (USGS, 1971).

In the late 1960's a clear need was seen for developing increased understanding of the hydrologic behavior of streams draining the Yukon-Tanana uplands, and concomitantly, to develop a climatic parameter data base appropriate for analysis of hydrologic regimen. At the same time, the desirability of establishing a study area encompassing complete drainage units for inter-disciplinary research and experimentation in the upland subarctic environment was recognized. These concerns and needs led to establishment of the Caribou-Poker Creeks Research Watershed, about 50 km north of Fairbanks. Development efforts, physical layout and basin description, and research results have been reported elsewhere (for example, Slaughter, 1970; Quirk and Sykes, 1971; Rieger *et al.*,

1971; Kane and Slaughter, 1973; Carlson, 1972; Ford, 1973; Troth *et al.*, 1973).

This paper provides examples of upland climatic data acquired in this endeavor, along with a consideration of the means employed to obtain what would perhaps be "routine" information in more temperate locales. The work reported is carried out under the aegis of the Inter-Agency Technical Committee for Alaska, a group chartered by the Water Resources Council, Washington, D. C. (IATCA, 1970).

2. The research area

An initial decision was made to concentrate baseline data acquisition in the Caribou Creek drainage of the research watershed (Fig. 1). This decision stemmed in part from logistics considerations—Caribou Creek was relatively more accessible than Poker Creek—and in part from the opportunity presented in Caribou Creek for study of two contrasting, undisturbed, similar-sized watersheds: C-2, south-draining, largely free from permafrost, with extensive deciduous vegetation; and C-3, north-east draining, largely underlain by permafrost at shallow depth, with a dominantly coniferous overstory. It was reasoned that these two watersheds, if adequately analyzed, could yield valuable information on such questions as hydrologic response and local climatic regimen in upland subarctic settings. The need for such information has been clearly expressed by a variety of agencies, such as the National Weather Service (Audsley, personal communication, 1972).

Consequently, available instrumentation was concentrated in Caribou Creek, with emphasis on subdrainages C-2 and C-3. Parallel installations at 340 m,

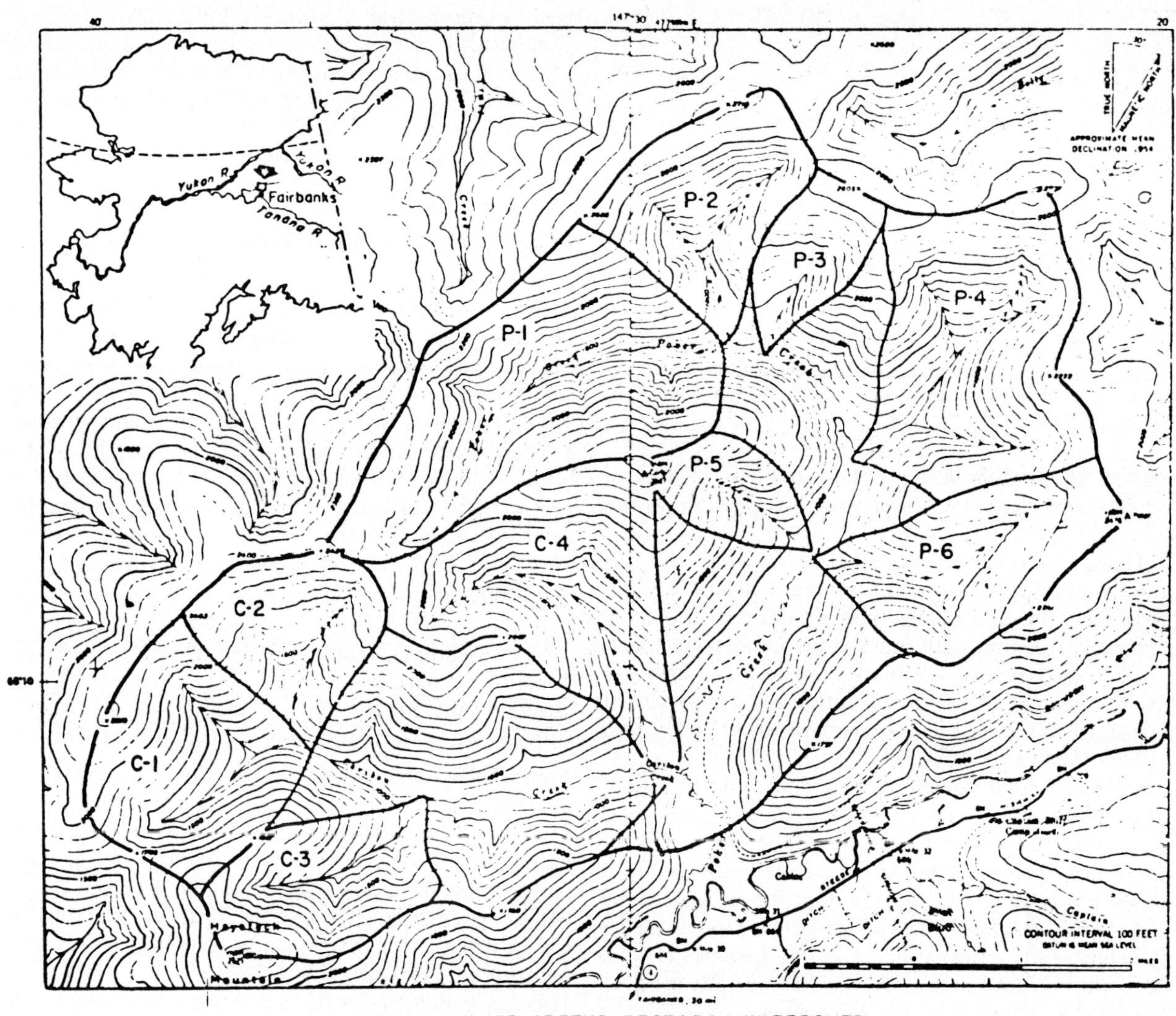

FIG. 1. Caribou-Poker Creeks research watershed, Tanana River Basin, Alaska.

490 m, and 640 m MSL were intended to monitor air temperature, ground temperature (at the 490 m stations), and precipitation. A "main site" was established in the Caribou Creek valley, where a permanent stream-gaging station was installed by the US Geological Survey, and a recording "snow pillow" was installed by the Soil Conservation Service.

3. Data acquisition

A number of climatic instruments have been employed in the research watershed, with results being a decidedly "mixed bag."

The Wainwright Detachment, ASL Alaska Met Team (Ft. Wainwright) is currently responsible for servicing the majority of the meteorological equipment located in the Caribou Watershed area. Currently, there are eleven sites instrumented with hygro-thermographs, distant probe thermographs, mechanical weather stations, weighing and dip stick type rain gages, and an occasional new type of mechanical instrument. It should be noted that equipment varies from site to site; no site contains all types.

Since neither commercial nor generator power is available at these sites, it was necessary to limit instrumentation to either mechanical or battery-driven equipment. Heretofore, the thermographs, hygrothermographs, and rain gages were driven by eight-day spring-wound chart drives. Due to the uncertainty of entry into the watershed and lack of personnel to service the sites on a weekly basis, the eight-day clocks have been replaced with 31-day electric and/or spring-driven chart drives. The 31-day electrical drives have proven fairly reliable through one winter's operations. They have yet to be tested by the forthcoming

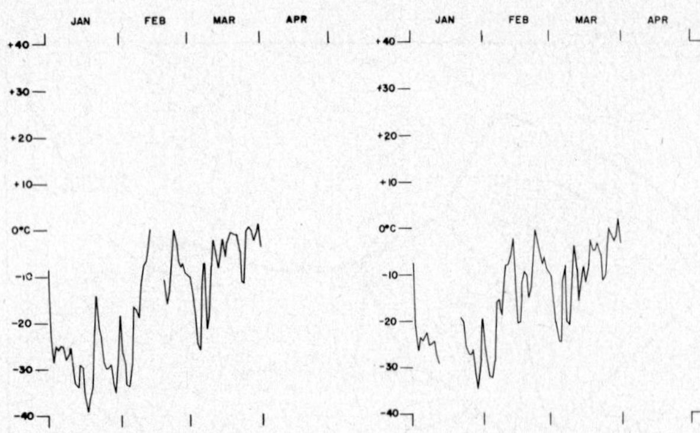

FIG. 2. A. Mean daily air temperature, Watershed C-2, 490 m elevation, 1970. B. Mean daily air temperature, Watershed C-3, 490 m elevation, 1970.

winter. Installation of these units has provided more reliable and continuous data than was possible in the past.

These instruments (hygrothermographs, thermographs, rain gages) are all of the mechanical recording type and, therefore, have their limitations insofar as accuracy, real time, and quick response are concerned. They are considered adequate, however, for field use and are simple enough in operation for inexperienced personnel to service under extreme weather conditions.

The Mechanical Weather Station (MRI)* is a self-contained system capable of recording wind direction, wind speed, air temperature, and rainfall at remote, unattended sites. It is available in either 30- or 60-day operation, spring wound, or electrically driven. Both types have been used in the Watershed since 1969 and experience has shown them to be reliable down to about −20 C, thereafter, operation becomes erratic. This, plus a $2000-plus cost, does not warrant installation of these units at all recording sites.

A Leupold-Stevens Type A-71* recorder with distance/temperature probe has come into recent use by the Met Team. The only experience we have is a one-year operational period of two instruments in the Eagle Summit area (Mile 106 Steese Highway). Both ran through the entire 72–73 winter season and functioned perfectly insofar as inking, timing, and accuracy are concerned. This appear to be a trustworthy instrument and quite versatile because it can be had in many configurations for recording water level, precipitation, temperature, and (with minor modification) wind passage through the use of a contact anemometer. It is driven by the dependable Chelsea clock system and will run for up to six months on one winding. Its only drawbacks are size and weight.

Based on this operational experience, and other favorable reports on the reliability of this recorder system, four custom-built precipitation recording storage gages have been installed in the Research Water-

---

* Use of trade names is for illustration only, and does not imply Government endorsement or criticism of any commercial product.

shed, using a design supplied by L. Mayo, U. S. Geological Survey (Mayo, personal communication, 1972). These gages store 1500 mm of precipitation. The A-71 recorder utilized will run $4\frac{1}{2}$ months unattended, and is equipped with a 15 m temperature probe for monitoring air temperatures in a standard shelter.

4. Examples of initial results

In the course of a study of precipitation and consequent streamflow in Caribou Creek, Ford (1973) has provided a brief summary of Caribou Creek climatic data collected by other investigators. He noted that summer temperatures in the upper Caribou Creek valley (at 340 m MSL) were lower than temperatures at Fairbanks (140 m MSL), in the margin of the broad Tanana Valley flood plain. As would be expected, the Caribou Creek valley temperatures observed were consistently higher than those at Caribou Peak (773 m MSL). Mean air temperatures for Summer 1969 are:

		Upper	
	Caribou Peak	Caribou Creek	Fairbanks
June	11 C	—	18.5 C
July	5.5 C	13.5 C	15.5 C
August	3 C	7 C	10 C

Ford (1973) also commented on the strong inversion observed during winter in this locality. Winter inversions in central Alaska have long been of interest, as noted by Benson (1970). In January 1970, mean daily temperature was −20.5 C at Caribou Peak (773 m MSL), *vs* −24.5 C at 340 m MSL in the Caribou Creek valley. (The corresponding monthly mean temperature at Farbanks was −26.5 C.)

Possible differences in local climate between south-facing and north-facing slopes are relevant to hydrologic study, plant community analysis, and wildlife habitat study, to name a few concerned disciplines. The stations at 490 m MSL, at about mid-slope in both C-2 and C-3, provide some information on local climatic parameters. Air temperature and ground temperature data for these two stations for one winter period (Jan–Mar 1970) and two summer periods (July–August 1970 and June 1971) are shown in Figs. 2–6. Measurement was by a Thies Model L-597-7 recording distance thermograph. Of immediate interest is the very close correspondence of both air and ground temperatures during the winter months (Figs. 2 and 3). The correlation coefficients (Snedecor, 1956), based on mean daily temperatures (derived by averaging hourly values for the winter period shown) for air temperature and ground temperature are $r=0.998$ and $r=0.999$, respectively. The lack of temperature differences in winter between these slopes at the same elevation is to be expected; this is the period of least solar radiation input (the dominant energy source in this environment) and low air temperatures.

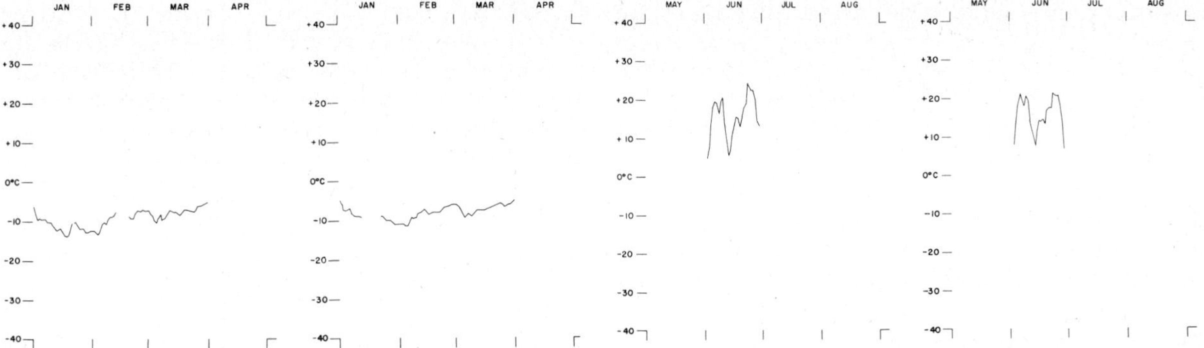

FIG. 3. A. Mean daily ground temperature, Watershed C-2, 490 m elevation, 1970. B. Mean daily ground temperature, Watershed C-3, 490 m elevation, 1970.

FIG. 5. A. Mean daily air temperature, Watershed C-2, 490 m elevation, 1971. B. Mean daily air temperature, Watershed C-3, 490 m elevation, 1971.

During summer months a marked difference in observed mean daily air temperatures between the south-facing and north-facing slopes might be expected. However, data acquired in this study do not immediately reflect such an anticipated difference; the comparative record for June–July 1970 (Fig. 4) shows little difference for the two sites. June 1971 data (Fig. 5) yield a similarly small difference in daily mean temperatures. Statistical comparison of daily mean temperatures showed that these means did not differ significantly for the periods shown.

We would still anticipate measurable differences in thermal regimen of these two slopes at this latitude. Soils of the north facing site are Ester silt loams, underlain by permafrost at shallow depth; soils of the south-facing site are permafrost-free Gilmore silt loams (Rieger *et al.*, 1971). Calculated "equivalent latitude," an index of potential solar radiation input (Dingman, 1970), for both sites yields an "equivalent latitude" value of 80°N for the north-facing C-3 site, *vs* an "equivalent latitude" of 50°N for the south-facing C-2 site (Koutz and Slaughter, 1973). These factors indicate that, even though available air temperature data fail to indicate major thermal environment differences, such must exist.

The summer ground temperature data (measured at the litter-mineral soil interface) do show such a difference (Fig. 6). July–August 1970 ground temperatures measured differ by 4 C to 7.5 C, the south-facing slope showing consistently warmer soils. The difference increases as summer progresses.

Further, the daily temperature *range* for the south-facing site was markedly greater than that for the north-facing station. In June 1971 the average range at C-2 was 20.6 C, *vs* 12.1 C at C-3; this difference was significant at the 0.01 probability level, as measured by "*t*"-test of means. Daily maximum temperatures were also consistently higher at C-2 (26 out of 27 days in June 1971), the difference again being significant at the 0.01 probability level.

Without further analysis, these data indicate that air temperatures at shelter height may not be an adequate indication of the near-ground environment (this is not a novel observation!). They also indicate that the local "slope climates" of these sites are measurably different, if appropriate parameters are monitored. As further data become available from these sites, and those at both higher and lower elevations in these same subdrainages, it should be possible to more closely characterize local climatic parameters.

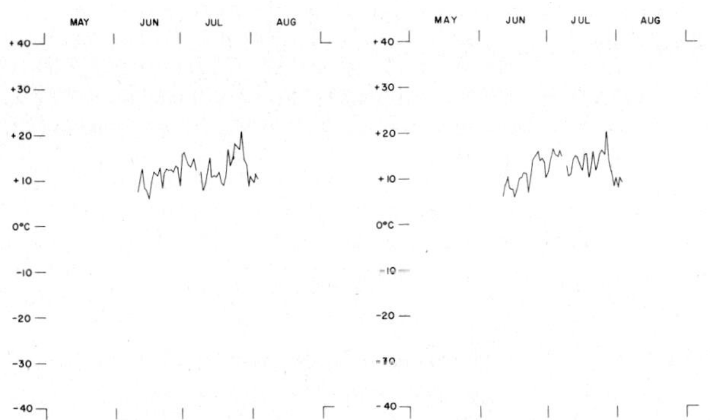

FIG. 4. A. Mean daily air temperature, Watershed C-2, 490 m elevation, 1970. B. Mean daily air temperature, Watershed C-3, 490 m elevation, 1970.

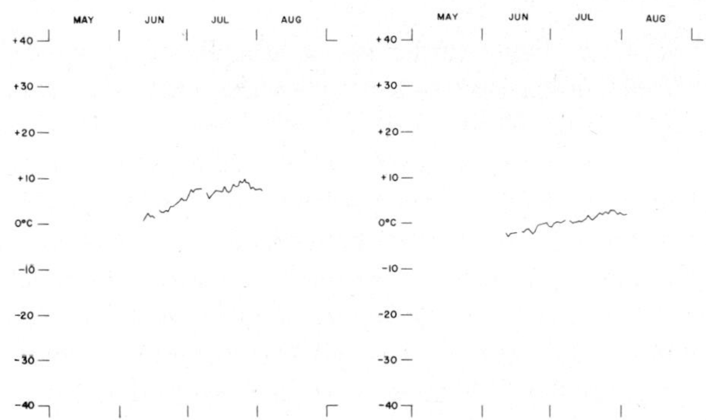

FIG. 6. A. Mean daily ground temperature, Watershed C-2, 490 m elevation, 1970. B. Mean daily ground temperature, Watershed C-3, 490 m elevation, 1970.

Summer precipitation is similarly of interest in these upland sites. As indicated previously, continuity of record for recording precipitation gages has been less than satisfactory. From the available data we have extracted data to exemplify upland precipitation input for two sets of precipitation gages.

Storage gage data are available for 490 m C-2 and for the Caribou Creek valley "main site," for 20 May to 23 September 1970. Storage gage catch for this period was 259 mm water at the main site (elevation approximately 270 m MSL), and 343 mm water at the 490 m C-2 site. Data for the 490 m C-3 site are missing for the periods 22–29 July and 2–23 September; even with this period missing, a total of 267 mm was measured (14 mm precipitation was measured at the main site during those periods when the C-3 site was not operating; 55 mm was measured at 490 m C-2 during the same time).

Recording (weighing) rain gage data are available for a more limited period for the 640 m MSL elevation of C-2 and C-3, and for the Caribou Creek "main site." Direct comparison of precipitation input at these locations is possible only for the period 5 August to 9 September; precipitation recorded for these periods was:

C-2,	640 m	62 mm
C-3,	640 m	66 mm
Main site,	270 m	61 mm

More complete data are obviously needed prior to any attempt at defining precipitation input to the upland basin. It is worth noting, however, that available climatic summaries, such as that of Feulner *et al.* (1971), show this areas as receiving around 508 mm precipitation (annually); as with most "standard" observations, that extrapolation is based largely on low-elevation climatic stations and reasoned inferences regarding elevation and physiographic effects on precipitation input.

5. Conclusions

We have briefly outlined some aspects of an upland, subarctic taiga environmental research endeavor, and have attempted to illustrate the types of data obtained. The potential for more intensive study of data already available for the Caribou-Poker Creeks catchment, as well as for developing more reliable means of obtaining relevant valid data, is clear. This area is one of a very few designated sites in Alaska's subarctic where both process and experimental research can be undertaken on a watershed scale; improved understanding of the physical setting, including slope climates, is a basic prerequisite to truly comprehensive environmental research.

Acknowledgments. This paper reports one phase of a larger research endeavor to which a number of persons have contributed in field activities and data tabulation. Special acknowledgment is due the efforts of W. Hobgood, D. Kane, J. Gilchrist, P. Quinn, D. Ludwig and P. Delp. This work has been supported in part by the US Army Corps of Engineers Work Unit, CWIS No. 31003, "Watershed Studies in Cold Regions."

REFERENCES

Carlson, R. F., 1972: Development of a conceptual hydrologic mocel for a subarctic watershed. Institute of Water Resources, University of Alaska, Fairbanks, Alaska, 58 p.

Dingman, S. L., 1970: Hydrology of the Glenn Creek watershed, Tanana river drainage, central Alaska. Ph.D. thesis, Harvard University, Cambridge, Massachusetts, 122 p. (Also published as Research Report 297, USACRREL, 1972).

Environmental Data Service, 1972: Climatological data, Alaska. EDS, NOAA, U. S. Department of Commerce.

Feulner, A. J., J. M. Childers and V. W. Norman, 1971: Water resources of Alaska. Open-file report, U. S. Geological Survey, Water Resources Division, Alaska District, Anchorage, Alaska, 60 p.

Ford, T. R., 1973: Precipitation-runoff characteristics of the Caribou Creek research watershed near Fairbanks, Alaska. MS thesis, University of Alaska, Fairbanks, Alaska, 151 p. (Unpublished).

Haugen, R. K., M. J. Lynch and T. C. Roberts, 1971: Summer temperatures in interior Alaska. Research Report 244, USACRREL, Hanover, N. H., 37 p.

Inter-Agency Technical Committee for Alaska, 1970: Alaska ten-year comprehensive plan for climatologic and hydrologic data, third edition. IATCA, Hydrology Committee, Water Resources Council.

Kane, D. L., and C. W. Slaughter, 1973: Seasonal regime and hydrological significance of stream icings in central Alaska. Paper presented at International symposium on the role of snow and ice in hydrology, September 1972, Banff, Alberta. UNESCO/WMO/IAHS Publication, 528–540.

Koutz, F. R., and C. W. Slaughter, 1973: Equivalent latitude (potential insolation) and a permafrost environment: Caribou-Poker Creeks research watershed, interior Alaska. Technical Note, USACRREL, Hanover, N. H., 33 p.

Quirk, W. A., and D. J. Sykes, 1971: White Spruce stringers in a fire-patterned landscape in interior Alaska, p. 179–197 in Proceedings, Fire in the Northern Environment: A symposium. Slaughter, C. W., R. J. Barney, and G. M. Hansen, Editors. Pacific Northwest Forest and Range Experiment Station, U. S. Forest Service, Portland, Oregon.

Rieger, S., C. E. Furbush, D. B. Schoephorster, H. Summerfield, Jr. and L. C. Geiger, 1971: Soils of the Caribou-Poker Creeks research watershed, interior Alaska. Technical Report 236, USACRREL, Hanover, N. H., with Soil Conservation Service, USDA, 10 p.

Slaughter, C. W., 1971: Caribou-Poker Creeks research watershed: Background and current status. Special Report 157, USACRREL, Hanover, N. H., 11 p.

Snedecor, G. W., 1956: Statistical methods applied to experiments in agriculture and biology. The Iowa State University Press, Ames, Iowa, 534 p.

Troth, J. L., F. J. Deneke and L. M. Brown, 1973: Subarctic plant communities and associated litter and soil profiles in the Caribou Creek research watershed, interior Alaska. Research Report, USACRREL, Hanover, N. H. (In press).

U. S. Geological Survey, 1971: Water resources data for Alaska, 318 p.

Climatic Conditions in Agricultural Areas in Alaska

Harold W. Searby

University of Alaska, Sea Grant Office, Anchorage, Alaska

AND

C. Ivan Branton

Institute of Agricultural Science, Palmer, Alaska

Abstract

Settlement of the native land claims in Alaska created some new problems for the state. Over 90% of Alaska is federal land. In the near future large areas will be selected by the natives and by the state itself. Other areas will remain federally owned but designated as parks, wilderness, etc. Many people believe that multiple use of land should be a basic principle. One of the multiple uses should be agriculture. It is entirely feasible that Alaska will eventually be called upon to meet some of the future needs of the food market outside of Alaska. Planning for this dictates that we know now what the potential is for agriculture within the state. The Soil Conservation Service, a branch of the Department of Agriculture, has surveyed most of the soils of Alaska, with those soils suitable for agriculture indicated on a map of the state. The climate of each of these areas was determined. The primary factors for this were water and temperature. The distribution of precipitation in Alaska, which is light rainfall in the spring and early summer, building up to a maximum in August and September, is less than ideal for agriculture. For this reason, irrigation must be considered as desirable and in many cases necessary for crop growth in any of the areas where suitable soils exist. If we make this assumption, then temperature becomes the basic determining factor. Temperature is used in three ways. They are length of growing season, growing degree days, and frequency of frost during a growing season. Each of these three factors, which are defined in the body of the paper, has been computed for all of the areas under consideration, and a rating factor determined, using minimum acceptable requirements. The conclusion is that through proper choice of crops, irrigation, and use of existing methods for combating frost, large areas of the state can be profitably used for commercial agriculture.

---

1. Introduction

The purpose of this paper is to evaluate climatic conditions of those areas of the state where soil conditions have been judged suitable for tillage for agriculture. The total area of tillable land has been divided into about a dozen separate areas to facilitate discussion. The individual areas were delineated on the basis of geographic and climatic coherence. Each of these areas is discussed; some in greater detail than others where numerous considerations required recognition to adequately describe the climate of the area. In relating Alaska's climate to the state's potential agricultural development, our discussion will, at times, be both subjective and general. This is because of the absence in some instances of climatological data to support the conclusions made. Climatic parameters are discussed generally to provide a better understanding overall, and are then offered in more detail in relation to specific areas possessing agricultural potential.

Alaska is normally divided into four climatic zones: arctic, continental, maritime, and transitional (a zone between continental and maritime). The *arctic zone* has no value for traditional agriculture; temperatures are much too cold and precipitation too light. Only the herding and management of reindeer or muskox could succeed in this extreme environment. The *maritime zone* is marginal, and for the most part, suited to rangelands supporting livestock. The climate of the *transition zone* is more favorable for agriculture, but is limited by a shortage of suitable soils. The two possible exceptions to this are the Matanuska and Susitna Valleys, and it is questionable whether these valleys should be considered as being in the transition zone. The remaining area is the *continental zone*, which is best from the consideration of both climate and soils.

2. Temperature

The temperature pattern for a particular area is determined by many factors. Latitude is the controlling factor on the amount of incoming solar radiation that reaches the surface of the earth's atmosphere. Many things affect solar radiation as it passes through the atmosphere, but the major influence is water vapor, particularly in the form of clouds. Average cloudiness in Alaska is high. Another factor is elevation. The air over us cools with increasing altitude.

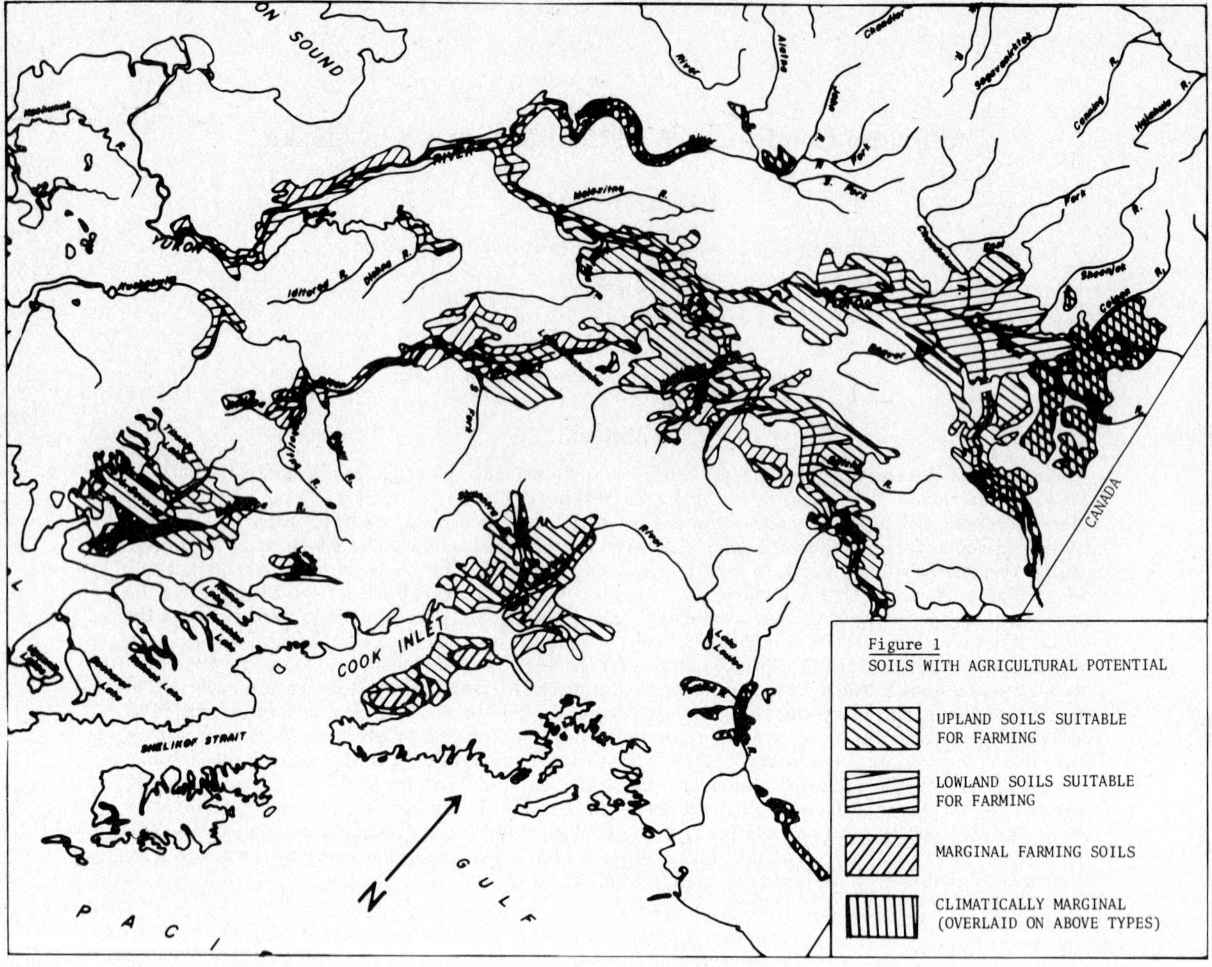

Fig. 1. Soils with agricultural potential.

Cooling also is modified with the slope of the land. South- and west-facing slopes receive more heating from the sun than a flat surface. North- and east-facing slopes are cooler than flat surfaces. North slopes in Alaska usually are not suitable for an agricultural crop, while a south slope may be better than a horizontal area. Permafrost is much more persistent on north slopes, and the probability of frost during the growing season is greater.

Proximity of large bodies of water tends to ameliorate temperature changes, with an end result of lower maximum and higher minimum temperatures than areas not similarly influenced. The effect of wind on temperature is common knowledge; frosts that occur during the period June through August are always under calm wind conditions.

"Tree line" represents the highest elevation suitable for tree growth and the elevation of the line differs in different climatological environments. In this study, tree line minus 500 ft is considered to be the upper topographic limit of areas useful for agriculture.

3. Precipitation

Seasonal distribution of rainfall in Alaska is not ideal for agriculture. The usual pattern is very light precipitation in late spring and early summer, building up during late June and July to a maximum in August, then decreasing slowly through October (Table 2). The amount of seasonal rainfall is marginal in a few areas, as well as poorly distributed, making irrigation desirable, if not necessary. The ground usually freezes with an adequate moisture content for the start of plant growth the following growing season. Precipitation in the form of snow usually is of little value to agriculture, because it occurs after the ground freezes and it runs off in the spring before the ground is thawed. A good snow cover is beneficial to overwintering crops, due to its insulating effect, protecting plants from extremely low air temperature and decreasing the depth of frost penetration into the ground.

4. Surface winds

Surface winds were not specifically mentioned above as an item of particular importance to agriculture, but in local areas they can be a serious deterrent. The strongest winds usually do not occur during the growing season. Except for coastal areas, where relatively strong winds are continuous, winds with velocities that cause damage occur in narrow bands. They are found where the valleys exist perpendicular to the mountain ranges.

The Matanuska River Valley winds are a good example. They are relatively frequent and reach their greatest speeds during the winter and early spring, exerting considerable influence in removing snow cover from open fields. The loss of this insulating cover contributes to extensive winter-kill of perennial crops when followed by extremely cold temperatures. Occasionally after the snow cover has been removed, extensive soil erosion in unvegetated areas occurs. Snow removal by winter winds does, however, have a beneficial effect also. Without the delay occasioned by snow melting, soils warm and dry sooner, permitting earlier tillage and earlier spring growth of perennial crops.

5. Soil types

To be utilized for agriculture, an area must have suitable soils as well as a favorable climate. The Soil Conservation Service has developed a soil map which delineates areas where soils are suitable for crop growth. Following are descriptions of climates for those particular areas of Alaska.

6. Figures, tables and data

Fig. 1 is a map of soil areas suitable for agriculture. Figs. 2 and 3 depict annual rainfall and snowfall for the state as a whole. Figs. 4 through 12 present graphic comparisons among reporting stations on the basis of three computations from climatic data: (a) freedom from summer frost, (b) growing degree days, and (c) length of growing season. Table 1 gives frost records for each of the observing sites, and Table 2 presents precipitation by months and also shows seasonal and annual totals. All data were taken from the Department of Commerce publication "Climatological Data—Alaska," published monthly and annually.

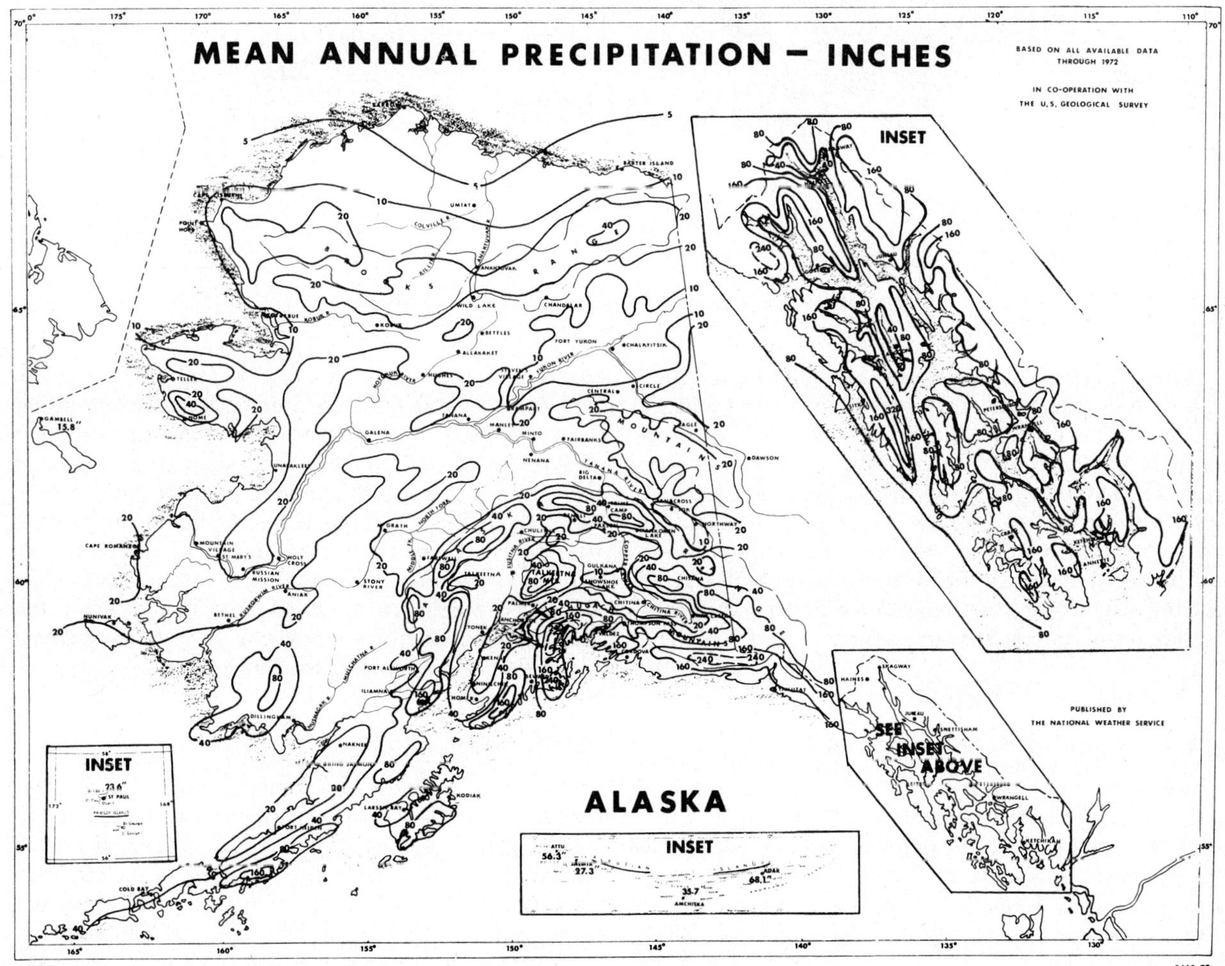

FIG. 2. Mean annual precipitation in inches for the state of Alaska.

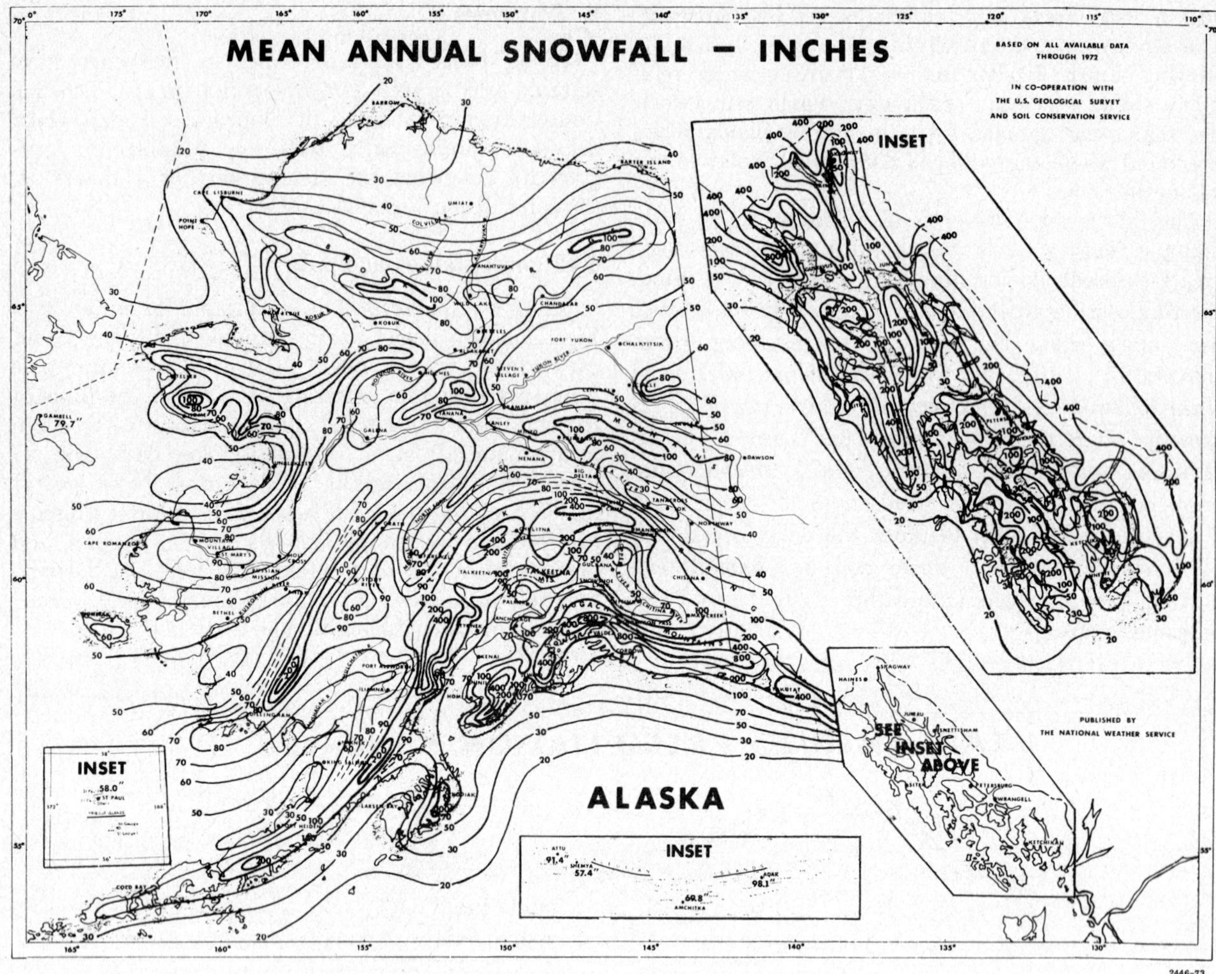

FIG. 3. Mean annual snowfall in inches for the state of Alaska.

Environmental characteristics of particular importance to agriculture are water and temperature. Water is usually available—if not as rainfall, in the form of groundwater. Temperature as it affects agriculture can be categorized in various ways such as growing degree days, length of growing season, and frequency of frost during the growing season. In the following discussions, these three temperature items are the primary factors used in determining the climatic suitability of an area for agriculture.

7. Explanation of charts

Rating—freedom from summer frosts

The "freedom-from-frost" rating is empirical, and is derived by the following series of operations. First, a survey of at least 10 years of climatic data was made, where available, to record the number of occurrences of 32 F (or lower) temperatures in the 24 five-day periods between May 1 and August 31. These data are recorded in Table 1. Next, a count was made of the number of five-day periods recorded on Table 1 that experienced no frost, frost on two or less percent of the days, and frost on four or less percent of the days. A rating was derived by adding the products of three times the number of periods with zero percent frost, two times the number of periods with two or less percent frost, and one times the number of periods with between one and four percent of days showing frost. The product is an empirical rating which gives a greater weight to a record showing no frost, but gives some credit for periods with four or less percent of the days showing freezing temperatures.

Growing degree days

The growing-degree-day determination is an accumulation of values for each day after the minimum temperature ceases to go below 32 F and until a 32 F reading is reached later in the year. It is obtained for each day by adding the maximum and minimum temperatures, then dividing by two. If the result is greater than 40, the growing degree days for that day is the difference between that value and 40. For example: 70 (max)+42 (min)=112, 112/2=56; 56—40 =16 growing degree days for that particular day. In this discussion only growing degree days computed using a base of 40 F will be used. More southerly states use a base of 50 F, so direct comparisons between those computations and ours for Alaska are not valid. A requirement for growing days is that the minimum temperature must remain above 32 F. It usually does with a mean temperature of 40 F, but there are exceptions. There are crops that will tolerate temperatures down to about 28 F, but the 32 F temperature was chosen because it is measured at five feet above ground, and under calm wind conditions the ground temperature can be considerably colder than a measurement of 32 F at the five foot level.

Length of growing season

This parameter is closely related to growing degree days, in that the criterion of a minimum temperature of more than 32 F is also a factor in determining its beginning and ending. For the purpose of this discussion, a growing season is defined as beginning when the mean temperature (average of the maximum and minimum) reaches 40 F *and* the minimum no longer dips to 32 F or lower. The growing season ends later in the same year when the minimum again dips to 32 F. When these restrictions on crop growth occur, the season is considered terminated, even though the mean temperature is still 40 F or higher. The assumption is made that the ground temperature was less than 32 F and growth of all crops has terminated. This concept may not be totally valid, but it does keep from over-estimating the length of the growing season.

8. Upper Yukon

One of the very large areas with suitable soils for agriculture is included in a roughly triangular-shaped block of land with Stevens Village at its western extent, Old Rampart at the northeast, and Eagle at the southeast. Of this, the southeastern portion consists of rolling hills where grazing is probably its highest use. From Eagle to Circle along the Yukon River the valley averages about five miles in width by 120 miles in length. Elevations from Eagle to Woodchopper are just under the 1000 foot level with the hills on either side of the valley rising sharply. From Woodchopper to Circle, the valley begins to widen and the drop in elevation is much more rapid with the elevation at Circle 650 feet.

The Porcupine River Valley is a second major valley in the eastern portion of this area. It is a wider valley with elevations generally between 600 and 800 feet in the upper portion, dropping to about 400 feet where the Porcupine joins the Yukon in the Fort Yukon area. Climatological data for the upper Yukon is limited to three locations, Fort Yukon, Eagle, and

Chalkyitsik. Records for the latter station are rather short term and should not be considered as completely representative of the area. Large variations in climatic conditions occur over short distances in Alaska; examination of the data for these three sites (Table 1 and Fig. 4) shows that this area is no exception. Length of growing season, growing degree days, total precipitation and its distribution are all variable factors.

The greatest potential for agriculture within this large area is centered around Fort Yukon, where climate and soils are the most favorable. If we compare this location to an already proven agricultural area such as the Matanuska Valley, and specifically to the Matanuska AES, Fort Yukon has nearly as many growing degree days but a much shorter growing season. This apparent contradiction is explained by warmer temperatures during the summer months, thus providing about the same number of growing degree days in a shorter period of time.

On the adverse side, precipitation amounts are considerably less and the frequency of frost during the growing season is greater at Fort Yukon. Annual ice-jam flooding is expected somewhere along the Yukon every year, but has little or no effect on agriculture since the flooding is usually during spring months before crops are planted. Comparison of data from Fort Yukon, Eagle, and Chalkyitsik shows somewhat less favorable conditions at the latter two locations. From the standpoint of climate, however, this entire area appears to have reasonably good potential for agriculture.

9. Central Yukon

This area includes the Yukon River Valley from Galena to Tanana and the Tanana River Valley from Tanana to Nenana; it includes considerable variation in terrain. Most of the land on the south side of the two valleys is flat or gently sloping. On the north side of the two valleys, from Tolovana westward, most of the area has relatively rough terrain extending from the river's edge northward. This portion is subjected to more frequent occurrences of frost during the growing season than areas with flat terrain. Cold air drainage down valleys perpendicular to the main range of the hills will be fairly common. Climatological data is available from Galena, Tanana, Manley Hot Springs, and Nenana; although it is out of the valley, data for Hughes is presented here also (Fig. 5).

The greatest consistency among these sites is in growing degreee days. The range is from 1667 at Tanana to 1852 at Nenana. Less homogeneity is found in length of growing season (base of 40 F). Galena with 96 days is the longest, and Manley Hot Springs with only 50 days is the shortest. These are considerably shorter growing seasons than in the Matanuska Valley. Growing degree days are also less than

TABLE 1. Percentage frequency of frost occurrences during growing season. The percentage frequency of occurrence figures in the five day period. If the figure is a 10, then on the average 10% of the days within that five day period will experience frost. The bottom within that five day period.

Station	May						June					
	1–5	6–10	11–15	16–20	21–25	26–31	1–5	6–10	11–15	16–20	21–25	26–30
Upper Yukon	88	76	68	48	26	24	16	6		2	4	
Eagle	100	100	100	90	80	70	40	20		10	20	
	92	86	70	34	20	6	6	4				2
Fort Yukon	100	100	100	80	50	20	10	10				10
	96	72	80	80	64	32	8					
Chalkyitsik	100	100	100	100	100	80	20					
Central Yukon	88	62	58	58	26	24	8	4				
Tanana	100	90	80	100	60	40	20					
	84	84	56	26	14	12	4					
Nenana	100	100	100	50	50	30	20					
	84	68	62	56	22	26	22	4	12	10	12	4
Manley Hot Springs	100	100	100	100	70	70	40	40	50	30	30	21
	72	40	36	4	10		2					
Galena	100	70	70	10	20		10					
	84	82	64	56	14	16	8	2	4	8	2	
Hughes	100	100	100	80	60	60	20		10	10	20	10
Tanana Basin	65	47	45	17	5	2		1				
Big Delta	90	75	80	40	15	10		5				
	90	78	88	78	45	35	23	23	3	6	3	
Clearwater	100	100	100	100	88	75	63	50	25	29	14	
	78	64	58	54	28	26	14	10		2		
Richardson Roadhouse	90	100	100	100	80	70	50	30		10		
	76	68	48	30	16	4	6	2	2			
University Exp. Sta.	90	90	90	60	40	20	30	10	10			
	94	94	71	71	66	33	37	29	6		3	2
Dot Lake	100	100	100	100	100	100	71	71	29		14	14
Kuskokwim River Valley	76	52	48	28	8	2	2					
Minchumina	90	90	90	70	20	10	10					
	70	54	40	12	12	2	10					
McGarth	100	80	90	50	40	10	30					
	87	67	60	53	20	10	20	17	13	3		
Sleetmute	100	100	100	33	50	50	67	50	33	17		
Lower Yukon	72	40	36	4	10		2					
Galena	100	70	70	10	20		10					
	92	60	42	40	24	4	8				2	
Holy Cross	100	100	70	80	80	10	70				10	
	83	90	50	37	47	31	13	77		4		
Russian Mission	100	100	100	67	83	67	33	17		17		
	72	74	62	34	27	20	2			2		
Mountain Village	100	100	100	90	80	70	30	10		10		
	86	70	52	28	6	4	8		2	2		
Aniak	100	100	100	50	10	20	30		10	10		
Dillingham Area	68	72	54	48	26	18	10	2	2	6	4	4
Dillingham	60	50	37	23	23	33	11	14	9	6		
Aleknagik	83	100	100	83	67	100	57	71	43	29		
Kenai Peninsula	70	58	44	36	16	14	2	4				
Homer FAA	80	100	80	90	70	40	10	20				
	86	46	43	31	20	11	8		3			
Venta (59°50′N 105°58′W)	100	100	86	86	43	29	25		14			
	62	58	52	38	38	25	22	16	8	14	2	
Sterling	90	100	100	90	80	80	60	40	30	50	10	
Susitna Valley	84	72	42	38	28	8	10	6	2			2
Talkeetna	100	100	80	100	60	40	30	20	10			10
	83	53	49	40	40	9	4	4				2
Caswell	100	88	100	100	78	33	22	1				11
	78	54	28	28	12	2	14	2				
Skwentna	100	100	50	60	50	10	30	10				
	84	78	53	60	33	26	10	10				
Willow	100	100	78	100	67	78	30	40				
Matanuska AES	47	36	24	17	11	4		1				
Matanuska	87	10	80	53	40	26		7				
	58	30	14	2	2							
Anchorage	100	70	40	10	10							
Kodiak	28	16	16	8	4	3	2					
Kodiak	60	40	30	40	10	10	10					
Copper River Valley	94	78	64	64	28	28	4	4	2	6		
Gulkana	100	100	100	90	70	70	20	20	10	20		
	93	73	40	65	25	58	35	30	15	5	10	
Copper Valley School	100	100	100	100	50	100	75	75	75	25	50	
	97	97	77	97	63	63	23	33	40	50	27	30
Kenney Lake	100	100	100	100	100	100	50	83	83	83	83	50
	68	68	34	20	30	8	4			2		2
Chitina	100	100	60	50	80	30	10			10		10

following table provide two sets of information. The top line for each station gives the average frequency of frost by days within each row treats the five day period as a unit. For example, the number 50 means that five out of every 10 years frost will occur some time

| July | | | | | | Aug | | | | | | Elevation |
1–5	6–10	11–15	16–20	21–25	26–31	1–5	6–10	11–15	16–20	21–25	26–31	(in feet)
					2	4	4	10	4	16	36	
					10	10	10	10	20	40	70	825
2						2	2	6	6	20	16	
10						10	10	30	20	30	70	419
		4		8	4		4	16	16	4	28	
		20		40	20		20	20	40	20	80	560
			2				4	10	6	10	26	
			10				20	30	30	30	60	232
						2		2		2	14	
						10		10		10	40	356
2	2	2	2			8	10	10	30	22	28	
10	10	10	10			30	30	40	80	20	60	275
										4	2	
										10	10	120
						6	8	6	10	16	12	
						30	30	30	30	60	40	545
1											4	
5											15	1268
			9	6	6	7	10	27	20	20	73	
			29	29	29	33	17	50	67	50	100	1100
2		2			3	2	4	18	8	20	13	
10		10			20	10	10	20	20	50	60	890
						4	2	2	2		2	
						10	10	10	10		10	475
3			3	9	2	5	7	38	23	15	65	
14			14	14	14	13	25	63	63	50	100	1100
												701
										2	10	
										10	20	344
										3	3	
										17	33	285
										4	2	
										10	10	120
										2		
										10		150
									4	8	4	
									20	20	20	50
		6	2									
		20	10									39
						2			2	2	4	
2						10			10	10	40	81
2									2	2	2	
						10			10	10	10	50
					2	9	4	4		7	9	
					11	33	11	11		33	22	70
											2	
											10	67
									3			
									13			150
8	2							2	8	6	18	
40	10							10	40	30	70	250
								2	6		2	
								10	20		10	345
					2			7	2	2	7	
					11			22	11	11	22	290
								2	8	6		
								10	20	20		153
2						3	5	9	5	5	17	
8						17	9	9	9	9	33	251
											1	
											7	150
												114
												21
		2	2	2		6	14	4	12		36	
		10	10	10		10	30	20	40		70	1572
8	4		4			4	4	8	12	16	30	
40	20		20			20	20	40	40	40	60	1030
23	20	27	7		7	10	25	38	23	15	70	
33	33	50	33		17	38	63	75	75	50	100	1200
						2			2	4	14	
						10			10	10	50	600

TABLE 2. Precipitation, seasonal and annual (inches)

Area and station	Apr	May	Jun	Jul	Aug	Sep	Snl	Year
Upper Yukon								
Fort Yukon	0.18	0.32	0.64	0.89	1.14	0.78	3.95	6.52
Chalkyitsik	0.31	0.23	1.04	1.14	0.78	0.35	3.85	5.85
Eagle	0.40	0.79	1.58	1.88	2.06	1.25	7.96	11.11
Central Yukon								
Tanana	0.32	0.75	1.29	2.33	2.99	1.92	9.60	13.75
Nenana	0.33	0.66	1.44	2.06	2.50	1.26	8.25	11.56
Manley Hot Springs	0.46	0.73	1.63	2.50	3.58	1.20	10.10	14.99
Galena	0.52	0.79	1.25	2.32	2.81	1.59	9.28	14.02
Hughes	0.20	0.45	1.02	1.97	2.50	1.43	7.57	12.74
Tanana Basin								
Big Delta	0.29	0.90	2.17	2.50	1.93	1.22	9.01	11.37
Clearwater	0.57	1.04	2.11	2.52	1.59	1.38	9.21	14.69
Richardson Roadhouse	0.25	0.81	1.87	2.79	2.05	1.03	8.79	12.17
University Exp. Sta.	0.24	0.80	1.48	2.10	2.44	1.36	7.87	12.31
Dot Lake	0.58	1.63	1.64	1.56	1.41	1.75	8.57	12.35
Kuskokwim River Valley								
Minchumina	0.43	0.77	1.74	2.40	3.07	1.35	9.76	13.35
McGarth	0.65	0.81	1.64	2.19	3.18	2.18	10.65	16.67
Nikolai	Not enough data for representative averages							
Sleetmute	0.92	1.45	1.85	3.13	3.22	3.32	13.89	20.74
Lower Yukon								
Galena	0.52	0.79	1.25	2.32	2.81	1.59	9.28	14.02
Holy Cross	0.48	0.82	1.16	2.06	3.90	2.78	11.20	18.00
Russian Mission	1.28	0.66	1.43	2.86	2.99	1.18	10.40	18.76
Mountain Village	0.28	0.61	1.09	1.66	4.35	2.76	10.75	15.55
Aniak	0.66	1.00	1.47	2.37	4.91	2.97	13.38	19.79
Dillingham Area								
Dillingham	1.16	1.78	1.69	2.57	3.99	3.46	14.65	25.76
Aleknagik	2.63	2.70	2.87	2.66	5.14	4.83	20.83	34.31
Kenai Peninsula								
Homer FAA	1.08	0.98	0.98	1.69	2.56	2.76	10.05	23.08
Venta	1.35	1.15	1.29	1.79	1.92	3.04	10.54	23.93
Sterling	0.70	0.70	1.03	2.57	2.56	2.47	10.03	16.88
Susitna Valley								
Talkeetna	0.75	1.34	1.77	3.19	5.33	4.46	16.84	28.02
Caswell	0.89	0.63	2.42	2.85	3.77	3.55	14.11	26.01
Skwentna	0.98	1.21	1.70	3.02	3.99	4.64	15.54	28.67
Willow	1.20	1.61	1.99	2.46	2.81	3.36	13.43	24.93
Matanuska Valley								
Matanuska AES	0.47	0.73	1.41	2.22	2.76	2.47	10.06	15.65
Anchorage	0.42	0.52	0.98	1.86	2.57	2.50	8.85	14.71
Kodiak								
Kodiak	3.59	4.47	4.24	3.62	4.38	6.25	26.55	57.39
Copper River Valley								
Gulkana	0.19	0.61	1.35	1.88	1.67	1.72	7.42	11.25
Copper Valley School	0.09	0.82	1.56	1.52	0.96	0.89	5.84	9.06
Kenney Lake	0.97	0.31	1.45	1.51	1.29	1.39	6.92	15.76
Chitina	0.25	0.38	0.70	1.30	1.38	1.66	5.67	12.19

in the Matanuska Valley, but not by a large amount. Adequate water should be available, either from rainfall or ground water. This area has potential for agriculture, but somewhat less than the Upper Yukon.

10. Tanana Basin

This is the second most important existing agricultural area in Alaska. Climatological conditions are

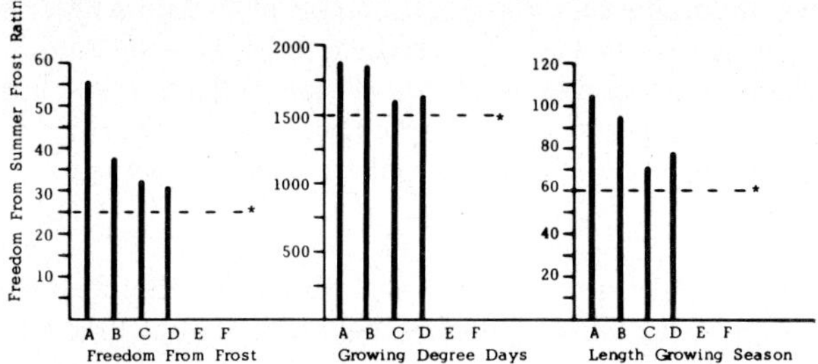

FIG. 4. Climatic data affecting crops at selected locations in upper Yukon area: A. Matanuska—Elevation 150 feet; B. Ft. Yukon—Elevation 419 feet; C. Chalkyitsik—Elevation 560 feet; D. Eagle—Elevation 825 feet.

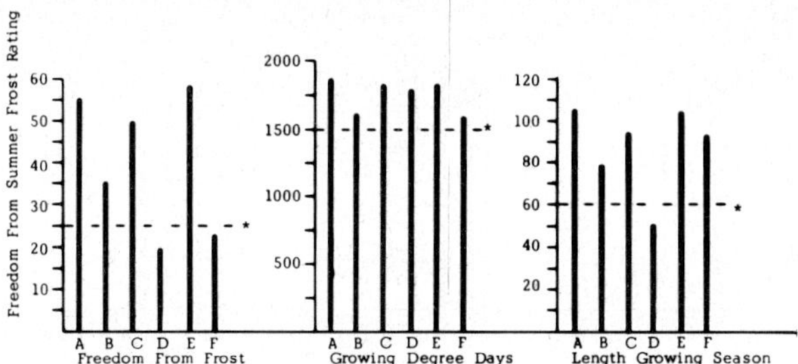

FIG. 5. Climatic data affecting crops at selected locations in central Yukon area: A. Matanuska—Elevation 150 feet; B. Tanana—Elevation 232 feet; C. Nenana—Elevation 356 feet; D. Manley Hot Springs—Elevation 275 feet; E. Galena—Elevation 120 feet; F. Hughes—Elevation 545 feet.

not quite as favorable as for the Matanuska Valley (Fig. 6). Along with the Upper Yukon area, this part of the state experiences the greatest extremes of temperatures, having both the coldest winters and the warmest summers. Warming and cooling trends in spring and autumn are quite rapid. The frequency of frosts during the growing season is greatest at the highest elevations except for Big Delta, where the data shows just the opposite to be true. The figures indicate that Big Delta has fewer frosts in summer than Fairbanks. The contrast is even greater when comparing it to Clearwater. Both Big Delta and Clearwater are on a flat plain with only about 150 feet difference in elevation. Similar conditions should be expected for both, but the data show considerable differences with the Clearwater area least suitable for crop growth. Limited data from a third site nearby, Delta Junction, supports the representativeness of the Clearwater data over that from Big Delta. These inconsistencies concerning Big Delta probably are due to the fact that the thermometers there are located between buildings and near a large asphalt parking ramp, influencing the temperature readings on the high side and eliminating the occurrences of frost during the growing season that are so frequent at Clearwater and Delta Junction.

Table 1 contains data for Dot Lake, Big Delta, Clearwater, Richardson, and the University Experiment Station. No wind data is included; although narrow bands of relatively strong winds occur in winter, this problem is minor in summer. Crop growth in the Upper Tanana Basin, where elevations are above 1000 feet, will be difficult except for extremely hardy types that can resist frequent temperatures as low as 25 to 30 degrees. Growing degrees are considerably less and the season much shorter there than at lower elevations.

11. Kuskokwim River Valley

The most suitable soils for agriculture in this area are found in the upper part of the valley from approximately Minchumina south to Nikolai, and from the Alaska Range westward to the Kuskokwim

Mountains. Unfortunately, there are no data from within this area. A climatological station exists at Nikolai but the record at present is only between one and two years in length and, therefore, is of little help. Data for Minchumina and McGrath are presented in the tables. To make use of the Nikolai data that is available, it was compared with concurrent data from McGrath. There is no Minchumina data for the same time period.

To evaluate this portion of the Kuskokwim River Valley, elevation and terrain features were studied. It is probable that all three locations have local influences that affect their temperatures, particularly McGrath and Minchumina. McGrath is surrounded on three sides by the river, and the observing site is close to a paved runway. At Minchumina, the observing site is close to a large body of water on two sides. Considering the terrain and elevation of these two stations, their frequency of frost record could be expected to show at least isolated occurrences during both June and July. Minchumina had one occurrence in ten years of data during the first five days in June, and none in July or August. McGrath had three years in ten with frost during the first five days in June, then none until the 26th of August in one year in ten. It is highly probable that both sites experience warmer

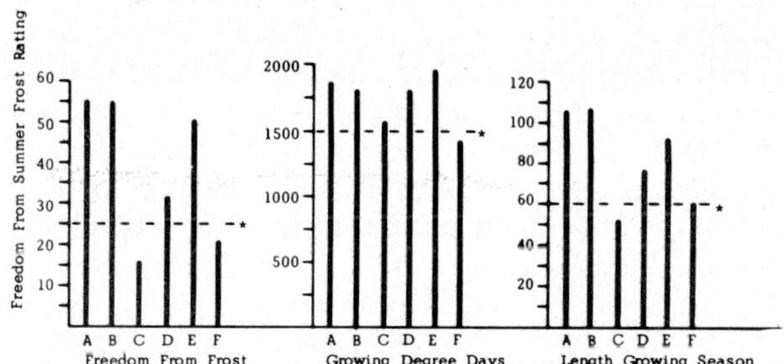

FIG. 6. Climatic data affecting crops at selected locations in Tanana Basin: A. Matanuska—Elevation 150 feet; B. Big Delta—Elevation 1268 feet; C. Clearwater—Elevation 1100 feet; D. Richardson Road House—Elevation 890 feet; E. Fairbanks Experimental Farm—Elevation 475 feet; F. Dot Lake—Elevation 1100 feet.

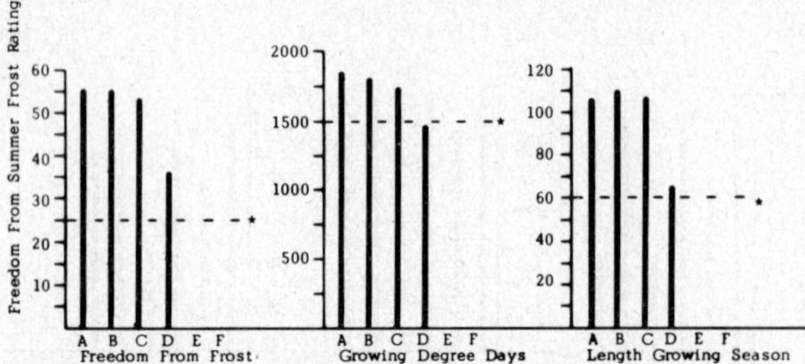

FIG. 7. Climatic data affecting crops at selected locations in Kuskokwim River Valley: A. Matanuska—Elevation 150 feet; B. Minchumina—Elevation 701 feet; C. McGrath—Elevation 344 feet; D. Sleetmute—Elevation 285 feet.

night-time temperatures than is typical for the general area because of their proximity to heat-retaining water.

Nikolai Village is located on the north side of the south fork of the Kuskokwim River. The area in general is dotted with small lakes and much of the vicinity is marshy. Although temperatures at Nikolai probably are modified by the bodies of water in the area, it would not be to the extent that McGrath and Minchumina are. Data for Nikolai covers only the 1971 and 1972 growing seasons. During the first season, frost occurred on four different days during July, shortening the season to about 35 days. During 1972 there were two frost days early in June and none during July. Although the August data were missing, we know that the growing season was at least 55 days and probably longer.

Precipitation figures for this area appear to be similar to those for a large part of the interior of Alaska. Amounts are adequate to support growth, but the distribution is not good. It is probable that climatic conditions for this area are adequate for agriculture but not quite as good as is indicated by the unusually frost-free growing seasons shown for McGrath and Minchimina.

Less desirable soils exist along the Kuskokwim River from McGrath southward to Sleetmute and along the Holitna to the south of Sleetmute. This is hilly country which should experience a higher frequency of summer frosts because of cold air drainage down valleys perpendicular to the main river valley. The growing degree days for Sleetmute, based on six years of data, are low and the growing season is short. On the basis of climate, the potential for agriculture in this southern portion of the Kuskokwim River Valley appears marginal. Fig. 7 graphically shows the agricultural potential for this area.

12. Lower Yukon

This area includes that portion of the Yukon River Valley from Galena downstream through Holy Cross and Russian Mission to Mountain Village. As stated earlier, climatic conditions in the vicinity of Galena

are favorable for crop growth. The next reporting site downstream is Holy Cross. Length of growing season there is about the same as in the Galena area, but growing degree days are 9% fewer. The frequency of frost during the growing season is not a serious deterrent to agriculture. Southward in the area of Russian Mission, climatic conditions are progressively poorer for agriculture. The growing season is significantly shorter and growing degree days are fewer. Freedom from frost during the growing season is good. Farther west at Mountain Village, growing degree days are markedly fewer at 1174. The length of growing season and the record of frost frequency is similar to that of Russian Mission. Obviously, the progressively poorer growing conditions from north to south is due to cooler maximum daytime temperatures, resulting in fewer growing degree days. Agricultural crops in the southern portion of this area must tolerate low growing season temperatures to be successful. (See Fig. 8.)

13. Dillingham Area

This area is fairly large. It extends over a hundred miles northeast from Dillingham and is 40 to 60 miles wide. It contains several streams, the largest of which are the Nushagak and the Mulchatna Rivers. Elevations are not high (generally below 500 feet) except in the area of the headwaters of the Mulchatna River. Even there the river valley is well below 1000 feet, with isolated areas on both sides of the valley extending somewhat above 1000 feet.

During summer months, the prevailing air flow is from the south, off of Bristol Bay. This air is moist and produces considerable cloudiness which in turn affects temperatures. Cloud cover lowers the daytime maximums through shading, and raises the minimum temperatures by limiting nighttime heat loss through back-radiation from the earth's surface. Conditions favorable for a land to water breeze probably do not develop very often because of the long hours of daylight warming the land and nights too short for much radiational cooling.

Away from the water's influence (further inland)

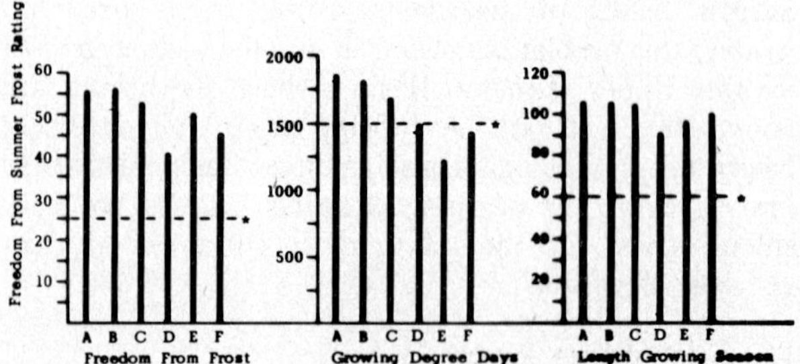

FIG. 8. Climatic data affecting crops at selected locations in lower Yukon: A. Matanuska—Elevation 150 feet; B. Galena—Elevation 120 feet; C. Holy Cross—Elevation 150 feet; D. Russian Mission—Elevation 50 feet; E. Mountain Village—Elevation 39 feet; F. Aniak—Elevation 81 feet.

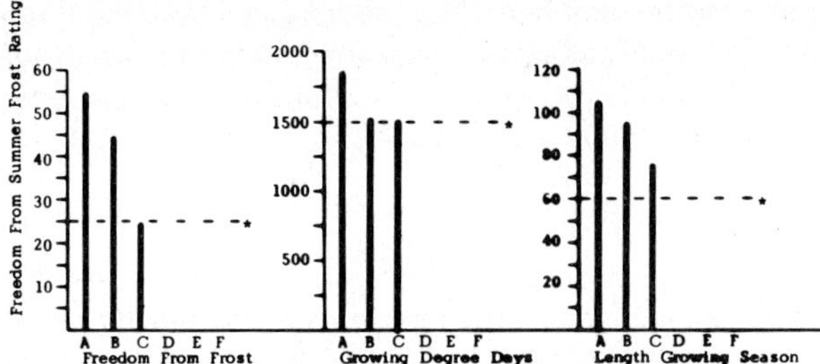

Fig. 9. Climatic data affecting crops at selected location in Dillingham area: A. Matanuska—Elevation 150 feet; B. Dillingham—Elevation 50 feet; C. Aleknagik—Elevation 70 feet.

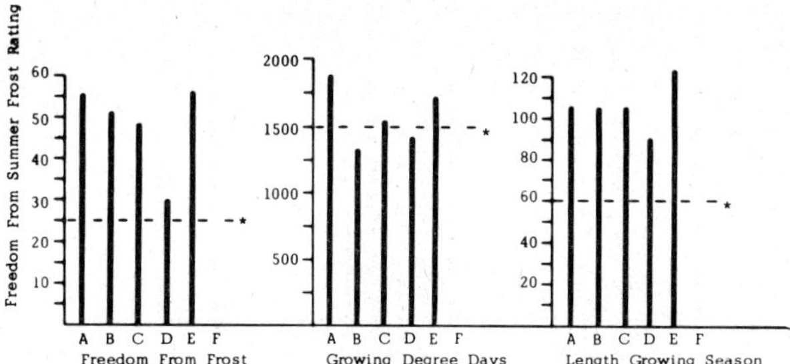

Fig. 10. Climatic data affecting crops at selected locations in Kenai Peninsula and Kodiak: A. Matanuska—Elevation 150 feet; B. Homer—Elevation 67 feet; C. Venta—Elevation 150 feet; D. Sterling—Elevation 250 feet; E. Kodiak—Elevation 21 feet.

the southerly winds are lighter because of surface friction, the air stabilizes at night and the clouds disappear leaving favorable conditions for nighttime negative radiation. The total growing degree days do not differ much from location to location within the area; however, the length of growing season does differ and the frequency of frost during the growing season is slightly greater inland than along the coast. Since the number of growing degree days is rather low, agricultural crops would have to be selected carefully in order to make commercial ventures successful (see Fig. 9).

14. Kenai Peninsula

This area is made up of portions of the peninsula to the west of the Kenai Mountains. It is characterized generally by considerable cloudiness which keeps maximum temperatures relatively cool. Frosts are fairly frequent until mid-June in all areas, and occur as late as early July in some. In a narrow band along the coast, the growing season is long enough for good crop growth, but the number of growing degree days is marginal because of cool temperatures.

Inland areas are warmer in summer but frosts end later in the spring and begin earlier in the fall. Areas closest to the mountains are subject to cold air drainage from glaciers of the massive Harding Ice Field, resulting in frost problems, fewer growing degree days and shorter growing seasons. Crops raised in most areas of the Kenai Peninsula will have to be carefully selected for their tolerance of frosts (see Fig. 10).

15. Kodiak Island

Favorable considerations for the Kodiak Island area include adequate rainfall (possibly too much) and a long growing season. On the negative side are relatively cool temperatures resulting in only 1646 growing degree days despite the fact that the growing season averages 148 days in length.

16. Susitna Valley

This area encompasses soils and topography suitable for agriculture on both sides of the Susitna River from

a point about 25 miles north of Talkeetna southward approximately to Willow. Data-reporting stations are Talkeetna, Caswell, Skwentna, and Willow. The growing season extends from the first half of June to about the middle of August. Growing degree days are 1700 or greater in all areas. The length of growing season is shorter than in the Matanuska Valley but long enough to mature crops, and the record shows a favorable absence of frosts during the growing season. There undoubtedly are localized areas where cold air drainage will make the frequency of frost higher than for the general area (see Fig. 11).

17. Matanuska Valley

This is the major agricultural area within the state at the present time, and probably will remain so. The reason for this is that it not only has good soils, but also has a suitable climate for agriculture, is readily accessible by road, and near the state's major center of population. There are many locations within Alaska where maximum temperatures are higher, resulting in a faster accumulation of growing degree days, but other factors become restrictive to agriculture. The Anchorage area, for our purposes, is considered to be a part of the Matanuska Valley (see Fig. 11).

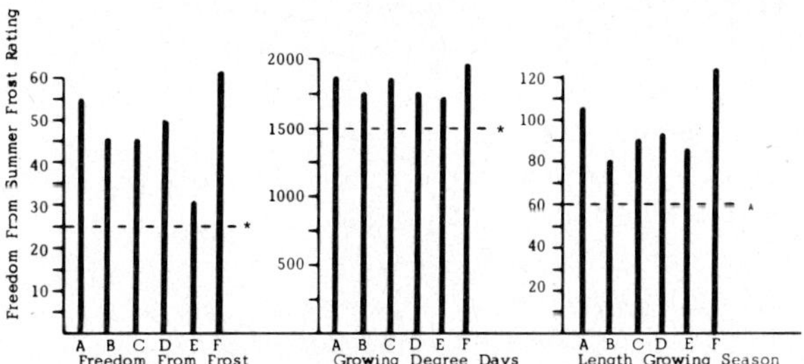

Fig. 11. Climatic data affecting crops at selected locations in Susitna Valley: A. Matanuska—Elevation 150 feet; B. Talkeetna—Elevation 315 feet; C. Caswell—Elevation 290 feet; D. Skwentna—Elevation 153 feet; E. Willow—Elevation 251 feet; F. Anchorage—Elevation 114 feet.

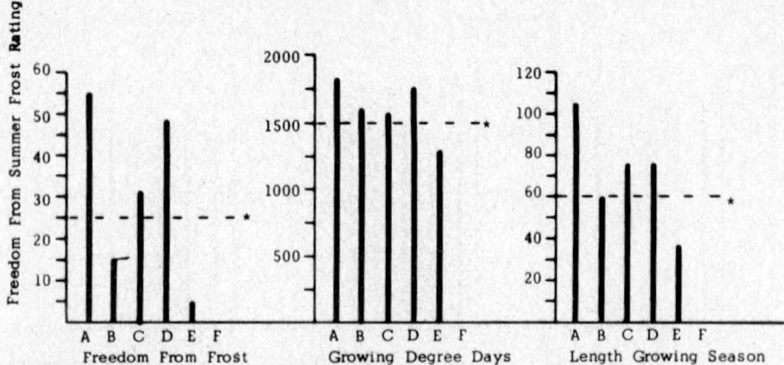

FIG. 12. Climatic data affecting crops at selected locations in Copper River Valley: A. Matanuska—Elevation 150 feet; B. Copper Valley School—Elevation 1030 feet; C. Gulkana—Elevation 1572 feet; D. Chitina—Elevation 600 feet; E. Kenny Lake—Elevation 1200 feet.

18. Copper River Valley

Climatic data for this area is available from Gulkana, Copper Valley School, Kenny Lake, and Chitina. The direct relationship between elevation and frequency of frost is demonstrated here. Chitina, with lowest elevation (600 ft), has the lowest frost frequency and Kenny Lake (1200 ft) has the highest. Gulkana, with the highest elevation (1572 ft), actually ranks next to Chitina, but this is another instance of an observing site in close proximity to a large paved area that retains heat and modifies minimum temperatures upward. Considered as a whole, this area is marginally suited to agriculture, not only because of

temperature problems, but because it experiences low precipitation amounts and ground water for irrigation has been difficult to find; in some areas it has been impossible to find (see Fig. 12).

19. Chitina River Valley

Except for Chitina, there are no other sites that have accumulated data for this area. Although elevations on the average are lower, the comments on the Copper River Valley are considered applicable here. In addition, most of the soils are marginal. This area is not recommended for agriculture (see Fig. 12).

20. Other areas

There are many other areas in Alaska, limited in extent, with soils suitable for tillage that are not identified on the soils map nor discussed here from the standpoint of climate. To do so would require extension of this discussion beyond desired limits.

Examples of these areas include certain coastal areas as near Yakataga and in the southern Panhandle, and many small areas in interior Alaska. Omission from discussion here does not infer unsuitability for gardening or agriculture of limited scope. In some instances, climatic conditions of these small areas can be extrapolated roughly from discussions of climate prevailing in larger areas which are located in the same climatic zone.

Acoustic Soundings of the Fairbanks Temperature Inversions

B. Holmgren,* L. Spears, C. Wilson and C. Benson

Geophysical Institute, University of Alaska, Fairbanks, Alaska

Abstract

In cooperation with the Wave Propagation Laboratory of NOAA in Boulder, Colorado, the Geophysical Institute of the University of Alaska is operating an acoustic sounder to study the dynamics of the formation and dissipation of the Fairbanks inversions. The acoustic sounder is generally operated in a monostatic mode, with receiving and transmitting antennas collocated. In the monostatic mode the recorded backscatter is supposedly due only to small-scale temperature fluctuations. The interpretation of the acoustic records is augmented by vertical profile measurements of wind and temperature using a captive-balloon-borne instrument package with telemetric link to the ground.

The Fairbanks inversions are quite complex, as indicated by the multi-layered structures of the acoustic records. There may be as many as 10–20 separate, quasi-horizontal backscatter bands within the height interval from the surface up to 500 m in situations with well-developed inversions. During these mutli-layered conditions the profile measurements using conventional wind and temperature sensors on a tethered balloon show a conspicuously strong temperature gradient in the lowest few tens of meters, and a wind speed at the 2 m level that is less than the starting speed of our anemometer ($\simeq$0.5 m s^{-1}). Above this extremely stable surface layer there is often a step-like build-up of the inversion; between layers of small temperature gradients, positive or negative, there are thin layers of sharp inversions. As for the winds aloft, one may typically recognize, in the lowest 500 m, two or more low-speed jets, often in diametrically opposed directions.

So far we have not been consistently able to relate the acoustic echo patterns to the simultaneously observed wind and temperature profiles. We are especially intrigued by the many thin backscattering bands which appear in layers of great stability, and which cannot be related either to marked wind shear or sharp temperature inversions. Although our present knowledge thus does not allow us to state unambiguously what is causing all the echo patterns, the acoustic soundings may still be used to deduce information on mesoscale processes in the boundary layer. Some examples of mesoscale processes that may be studied using acoustic records are: 1) the structure of surface inversions in connection with light or strong winds, 2) the formation of a convective or mixing layer below a capping inversion resulting from radiational heating of the surface, 3) the breakup of inversions due to increasing winds aloft and 4) the behavior of breaking waves associated with positive and negative wind shear. When used on a real time basis, the acoustic sounder should be a valuable tool for the local weather forecasts in Fairbanks, particularly for prediction of ice fog conditions.

---

1. Introduction

The acoustic sounder has in the past few years become recognized as a valuable remote sensing tool for studying the structures of the lower troposphere. The introduction of facsimile recording (McAllister, 1968; McAllister *et al.*, 1969), which gives a visual display of the height versus time variations of the atmospheric structures, was perhaps one main reason for the initial success. Acoustic sounding techniques have since been developed for quantitative measurements of vertical and horizontal wind velocities (Beran *et al.*, 1971). A review of the recent experimental progress is given by Ottersten *et al.* (1973).

In cooperation with the NOAA Wave Propagation Laboratory in Boulder, Colorado, the Geophysical Institute of University of Alaska is operating an acoustic sounder, mainly to study the dynamics of

the formation and the breakup of the Fairbanks inversions.

The city of Fairbanks, 148°W, 65°N, is situated on the flat, almost horizontal valley floor of the Chena-Tanana River Basins in central Alaska (Fig. 1). Fairbanks is sheltered; on three sides nearby hills rise to maximum elevations of 300–500 meters. Fifty km to the south the foothills of the Alaska Range form another barrier. Considering the local topography, the distance from the sea, and the high latitude, it is perhaps not surprising that the wintertime surface inversions in Fairbanks are considered to be among the strongest in the world, even when measured by Arctic and Antarctic standards (Bilello, 1966; Benson and Weller, 1969). These strong and persistent inversions create serious air pollution problems, with high concentrations of combustion products, notably carbon monoxide (Winchester *et al.*, 1967) at any temperature, as well as ice fog when the temperature decreases below about -30 C (Benson, 1970). The

* Present address; Meteorologiska Institutionen, Uppsala, Sweden.

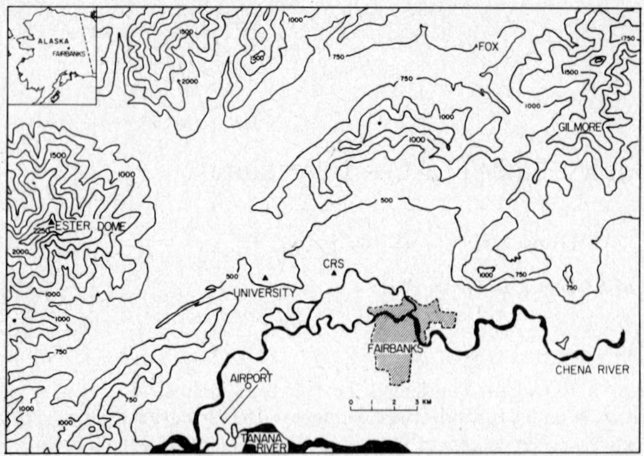

FIG. 1. Map showing location of the acoustic sounder at CRS (College Road Site). The site is situated outside the main city limits and is generally not so much affected by ice fog. Elevations are in feet.

object of this paper is to discuss some features of the Fairbanks inversions as observed using the acoustic sounder, in some cases complemented by tethered balloon soundings using more conventional wind and temperature sensors.

2. Instrumentation

All measurements are made at College Road Site (C.R.S.) northwest of the main city (Fig. 1). The surrounding area is sparsely forested with spruce, birch and willow. A simplified diagram of the acoustic sounder design is given in Fig. 2. A detailed description of a similar design is given by Simmons *et al.* (1971).

Briefly, a tone burst of the carrier frequency is passed via a time code generator into a power amplifier. The amplified tone burst is emitted as a sound pulse into the atmosphere via a 100 Watt audio transducer, which is mounted at the focus of a 1.2 m parabolic dish (reflector). The overall efficiency of the transducer-antenna system allows for a beam of radiated acoustic power of about 10 Watts during the period of transmission. Ordinarily we apply a tone burst of a duration of about 60 milliseconds, which gives a reasonable balance between the vertical resolu-

tion and the strength of the backscattered echoes. A collocated, identical transducer-antenna is used as a receiver of the backscattered acoustic power during the intervals between the tone bursts. The pulse repetition period is about 4 sec, corresponding to a tracking range of elevation of 600–700 meters. The received echo signals are amplified linearly with time to compensate for the loss of acoustic pressure at increasing range. During cold weather conditions a frequency of between 2000 and 3000 Hertz and a bandwidth of 100 Hertz are found to give the best results.

In order to increase the spatial resolution of the echoes and to reduce unwanted back-ground noise, the beamwidths of the transmitted and received signals are narrowed by sound absorbing cuffs surrounding both antennas. The sidelobes of the antenna gain patterns are thereby suppressed to correspond to an effective beamwidth of about 10°. The backscattering acoustic power P_r is related to the transmitted acoustic power P_t by the so-called radar equation:

$$P_r = P_t \sigma(\theta) \frac{ctA}{2l^2} \Upsilon^2 G$$

where $\sigma(\theta)$ is scattering cross section ($=$ the scattered power per unit volume per unit incident flux per unit solid angle at the angle θ between the direction of incident flux and the scattering flux), c is the speed of sound, t is the duration of the transmitted acoustic signal, A is the antenna area, l is the range, Υ is the transmittance of the atmosphere for the acoustic power from the antenna to be scattering volume, and G is the gain factor of the antenna. The facsimile records shown here depict echoes above a certain power level. Further semi-quantitative information on the strength of the echoes is obtained by a grey scale of six shades with the darkest shade corresponding to the strongest echoes.

The balloon-borne instrument package with telemetric link to the ground (Fig. 3) is a modified version of a Boundary Layer Profiler (BLP) developed at NCAR in Boulder, Colorado. The sensors include a linearized set of thermistors with a response time of about 1 sec for a $1/e$ adjustment to a sudden tem-

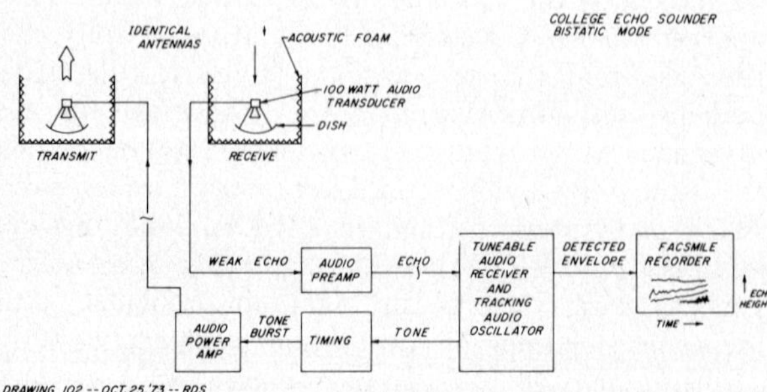

FIG. 2. Schematic of the acoustic sounder showing its main components and mode of operation.

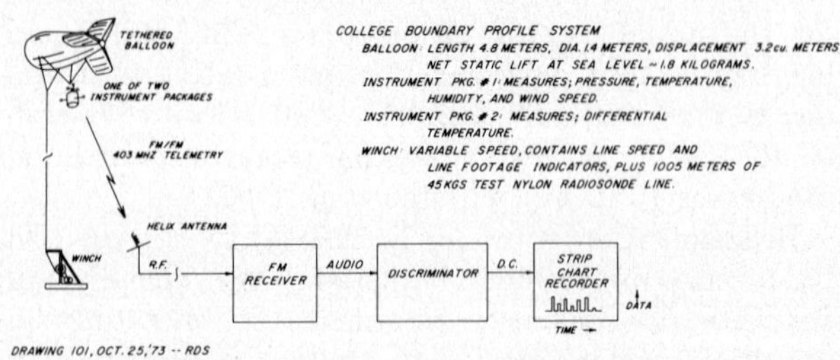

FIG. 3. Schematic of the Boundary Profile System. Two instrument packages may be applied. Only package #1 is described in the text.

perature change, a cup anemometer with a starting speed of about 0.5 m sec^{-1} and a pressure sensor allowing height determinations within an accuracy of a few meters. The tethered balloon is generally given a rate of ascent of 0.2–0.3 m sec^{-1}. One may show that the lag coefficient of the temperature sensor has no noticeable effect on the shape of the temperature profiles with the height scale that is used on the records. On the other hand, one may also show that time variations of the temperature and the wind in the layers traversed by the sensors, and also the vertical wind speeds associated for instance with gravity waves, may induce marked distortions of the measured wind and temperature profiles. These facts must be considered when interpreting the details of the measured profiles.

3. Theoretical interpretation of the backscatter

In a homogeneous atmosphere with continuously varying wind and temperature fields no scattering of sound would be obtained. The scattering is associated with wind, temperature and humidity, inhomogeneities in the atmosphere, which give rise to variations of the refractive index for sound propagation. The speed of sound c in relation to a fixed observer may be given by:

$$c = 20.05 T^{\frac{1}{2}}\left(1 + 0.14\frac{e}{p}\right) + V\cos\phi$$

where T is the absolute temperature, e is the water vapor pressure, p is the atmospheric pressure, $V\cos\phi$ is the wind speed component in the direction of the wave propagation vector. An acoustic refractive index n_a may be defined (Ottersten *et al.*, 1973) by:

$$n_a = \frac{c}{c_0} = \frac{T_0 - T}{2T_0} - 0.14\frac{e}{p} - \frac{V\cos\phi}{c_0}$$

where c_0 is the speed of sound of a dry reference atmosphere at temperature T_0. Fluctuations of temperature of 1 C, vapor pressure of 1 mb, and wind-speed of 1 m sec^{-1} correspond, according to this formula, to a change of the acoustic refractive index of 1700, 140 and 3000 respectively. These values may be compared with the corresponding changes of the microwave refractive index of 1, 4 and 0 respectively. Obviously the large variations of the acoustic refractive index make acoustic soundings attractive as remote sensing tools. On the other hand, the absorption of the sound waves is typically several orders of magnitude higher than for microwaves. Except for the most powerful acoustic systems presently in use, the range of acoustic sounding is therefore generally limited to the lowest 1–2 km of the atmosphere.

The fluctuations of the refractive index may be expressed as fluctuations of wind and temperature, neglecting humidity fluctuations. The scattering theory, reviewed for instance by Little (1969), predicts that the backscattering cross-section is given by:

$$\sigma(\theta) = 0.03 k^{\frac{1}{3}}\cos^2\theta\left(\frac{C_v^2}{c^2}\cos^2\frac{\theta}{2} + 0.13\frac{C_T}{T^2}\right)\left(\sin\frac{\theta}{2}\right)^{-11/3}$$

where k is the angular wave number, θ is the angle between the initial propagation direction and the scattering direction, and C_v and C_t are the so-called structure parameters for wind and temperature, respectively, given by

$$C_v^2 = \frac{\overline{[\bar{V}(\bar{r}_1) - \bar{V}(\bar{r}_2)]^2}}{|\bar{r}_1 - \bar{r}_2|^{\frac{2}{3}}} \qquad C_T^2 = \frac{\overline{[T(\bar{r}_1) - T(\bar{r}_2)]^2}}{|\bar{r}_1 - \bar{r}_2|^{\frac{2}{3}}}$$

where $\bar{r}_1$ and $\bar{r}_2$ are two arbitrary position vectors. The derivation of the backscattering cross-section is based on a so-called Kolmogorov spectrum, assuming among other things a homogeneous isotropic turbulence, within the spatial scale given by approximately one half the acoustic wave length. With the two antennas side by side and pointing in the same direction (Fig. 2), we get $\theta \cong 180°$. The backscattering is then given by:

$$\sigma(\theta) = \frac{0.0039 k^{\frac{1}{3}} C_T^2}{T^2}$$

i.e., the backscattering is due to random temperature fluctuations only. One may note that $\sigma(\theta)$ is a rather slowly varying function of the acoustic wave number. In the derivation of $\sigma(\theta)$ it also appears (Kallistrova, 1961) that the backscattering mainly arises from fluctuations on the spatial scale of one half of the acoustic wave length $\lambda (= 2\pi/k)$.

The validity of the above formulas for all stability conditions seems to be in doubt (Beran *et al.*, 1973). It has been suggested that part of the energy returns may be due to coherent specular reflections at thin layers of sharp inversions. This matter is discussed briefly in connection with some observations of echoes obtained for varying angles of incidence of the transmitted acoustic beam at thin quasi-horizontal inversion layers (Section 6).

4. General characteristics of backscattering in stable and unstable stratifications

The facsimile records of the acoustic soundings in Figs. 4 and 5 illustrate the fundamentally different turbulent structures of the boundary layer during stable and unstable conditions respectively. During stable conditions the backscatter is confined mainly to multi-layered, quasi-horizontal bands. Individual bands may be traced continuously for many hours. The thickness of some bands corresponds to the dura-

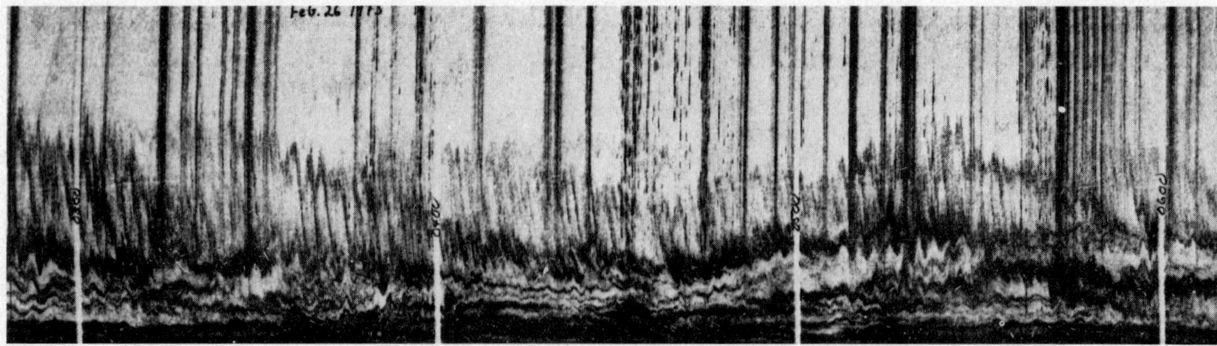

FIG. 4. Facsimile record of acoustic soundings between 2^h48^{min} a.m. and 6^h08^{min} on February 26, 1973. The distance from the bottom to the top of the record corresponds to about 650 meters. The quasi-horizontal bands are the backscattering echoes. The vertical lines are due to traffic noise.

tion of the transmitted pulse, i.e., the backscattering layer can then be expected to be very thin. Fig. 4 depicts a typical event. We have counted up to 20 layers during situations with strong inversions.

During unstable conditions the echo patterns are vertically oriented. The spacing of the echoes indicate that the convection is organized in thermal plumes (McAllister, 1968). The upper limit of the echoes does not, however, correspond to the maximum range of the convective plumes. The echoes merely indicate that the small-scale temperature fluctuations are more marked in the lower part of the plumes and in the (superadiabatic) surface layer on which the plumes feed. Within the plumes, the kinetic turbulent intensity as well as the temperature gradients probably diminish with elevation, i.e., also the small-scale temperature fluctuations may be expected to decrease. Outside the plumes the air is sinking, stable and of small turbulent intensity (Priestly, 1955).

The dark vertical bands seen in the upper part of the records of Figs. 4 and 5 are due to noise from road traffic and airplanes. The intense short dashes above the horizontal layers in Fig. 4 are due to howlings of dogs at an adjacent kennel.

In most of the multiple echo layers of Fig. 4, one may trace waves, many of quite regular sinusoidal shape, others of more diffuse nature. The uppermost backscattering band is broadened with streaks of echoes tilting to the left in a 200–300 meter deep layer. Structures of this kind are generally associated with marked wind shears (see Section 5), and are believed to be due to Kelvin-Helmholtz instability waves or breaking waves (e.g., Bean, 1972). One striking feature of the wave patterns is the close relationships between the breaking waves at the top of the boundary layer and the waves of periods of 2–4 minutes at lower elevations. From time to time the upper breaking waves become cusp-shaped and increase in

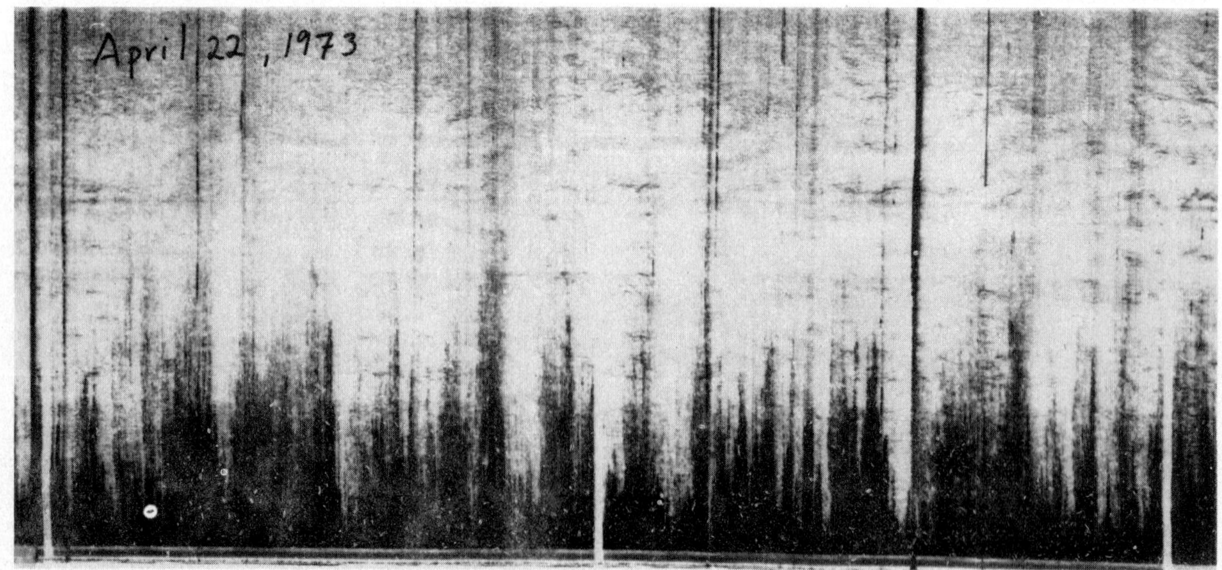

FIG. 5. Facsimile record of convective plumes during about two hours around noon on April 22, 1973. The distance from the bottom to the top of the diagram corresponds to about 650 meters.

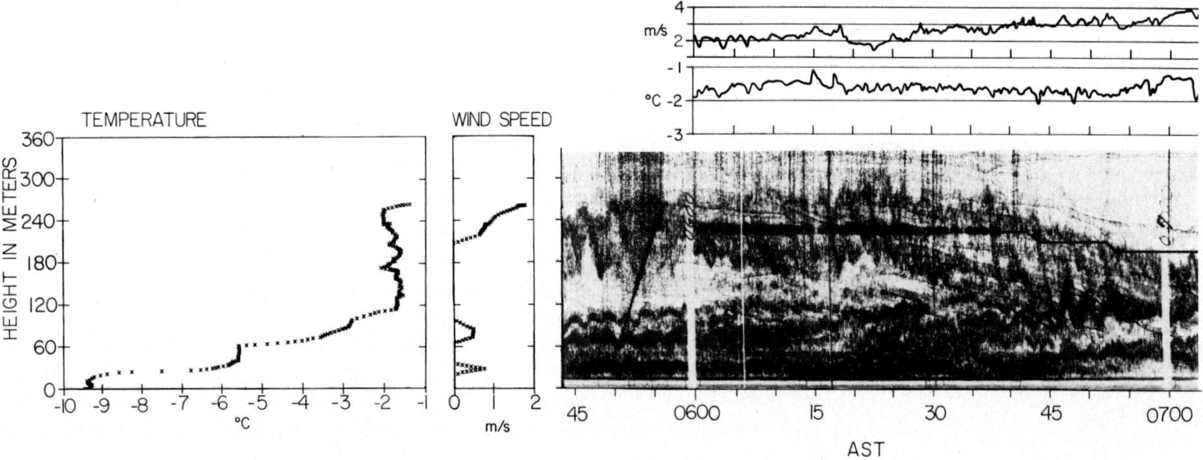

FIG. 6. Temperature and wind speed variations as obtained from the Boundary Layer Profiler, together with the simultaneous acoustic record. The height scales of the wind and temperature profiles are the same as for the acoustic record.

amplitude. During this process they appear to induce marked wave trains that are in phase vertically throughout the boundary layer. Most of the time, the amplitudes decrease downwards from the breaking waves. This pattern suggests that the wave energy is primarily derived from the wind shearing layer. The wave amplitudes in the low layer are very small and the corresponding particle motions are probably of little consequence for the turbulent conditions there.

It should be observed that the geometry of the real waves in the atmosphere may differ markedly from the wave shapes as they appear on the facsimile records. The horizontal scale is in fact a time scale. For instance, a wave of a three minute period propagating at a speed of 5 m s^{-1}, which incidentally seem to be typical values for gravity waves in the Fairbanks area as determined by Fahl (1969) using an infrasonic sensor array, would have a horizontal wave length 25 times larger than the apparent wave length on the facsimile record. In other words, even the sinusoidal waves with the largest amplitudes in Figure 4 correspond to interfaces that are in reality probably not very far from horizontal.

The acoustic records generally show a wide range of wave frequencies, both higher and lower than the more obvious waves of 2–4 minute periods discussed so far. For instance, in Fig. 4 there is an indication that the whole boundary layer fluctuates with a period of an hour or so. The fluctuations may or may not be related to internal seiches in the pool of cold air confined by the local topography as suggested by Benson (1965) and Haurwitz (1967). It seems obvious, though, that acoustic soundings may conveniently be used to study such long-period oscillations, for instance how they are related to the shearing of the upper winds.

On the high-frequency side, the resolution of the acoustic sounder system using a 60 millisecond sound pulse does not allow identification of wave periods less than about one minute. A few times we have used a 10 millisecond pulse to increase the vertical resolution of the backscattering layers. Using the higher resolution it appears that many oscillating thin bands similar to those seen in the low layer on the record of Fig. 4 actually have a substructure suggesting high-frequency waves of a period less than one minute. Similar observations concerning the nature of thin backscattering layers have been made using FM-CW (Frequency-Modulated Continuous Wave) radar (Gossard et al., 1971).

5. Acoustic backscatter in relation to wind and temperature variations

Ground-based inversions

In Fig. 6 an acoustic record is shown with associated wind and temperature profiles obtained shortly after sunrise on a day with a clear sky in early spring. The dark line rising at 05:48 AST and reaching a maximum elevation of 260 m at 05:52 AST is the echo from the balloon that, in sufficiently light winds, rises nearly vertically above the acoustic antenna. From 06:00 to 06:42 AST the balloon is parked at an elevation of 230 m. After 06:42 the balloon is lowered a short distance twice. Except in the lowest few meters, where the influence of the solar heating in the early morning may be traced, there is a strong, steplike inversion up to about 120 m. At higher elevations, the temperature profile is rather irregular with approximately isothermal conditions on the average. The wind profile shows two low-speed jets within the

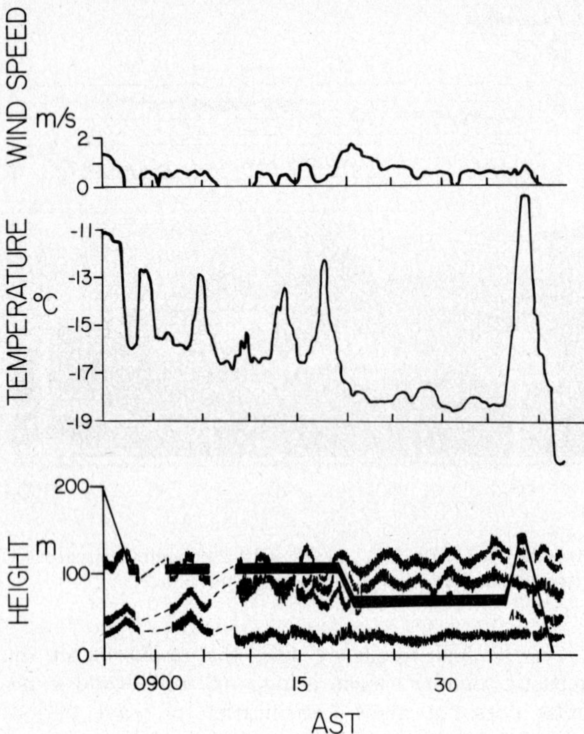

FIG. 7. Wind and temperature variations with the simultaneous acoustic record on 5 November 1972. The acoustic record was of poor technical quality, and was redrawn for this figure.

inversion layer, and a marked shearing layer from about 210 m to the top of the sounding at 260 m.

As nearly as the height resolution permits, the three dark layer echoes of the acoustic sounding can be associated with the three layers of sharp inversions in the lowest 120 meters. The breaking waves are found in a layer with relatively strong shearing, but with a small average temperature gradient. The temporal variations of wind and temperature within the shearing layer, presented in the upper right of Fig. 6, give much the same impression as irregular turbulent fluctuations. No obvious connections are found among the wind, temperature, or wave fluctuations. At the start of the acoustic record, the breaking waves are apparently not in phase vertically with the sinusoidal waves at lower levels. Not until the breaking waves descend and merge with the upper part of the strong inversion do the phases seem to agree in all the layers (compare Fig. 4). As a general feature of the wave patterns in situations with a strong groundbased inversion, we may point out that the wave amplitudes are small in the lowest layer. Inspection of acoustic records during various stability conditions shows that the waves tend to be of larger amplitude when the stratifications are only moderately stable. The strong ground-based inversions appear to have a strong damping effect on the wave activity in the lower layers.

The relationships between the backscattering layers and the wind and temperature profiles are generally analysed in terms of the gradient Richardson number Ri, defined by:

$$\mathrm{Ri} = \frac{g}{T} \frac{(\partial\theta/\partial z)}{(\partial u/\partial z)^2}$$

where g is the gravitational acceleration, T is the absolute temperature, θ is the potential temperature, u is the horizontal wind component (assumed to vary in one direction only), and z is the vertical coordinate. In practice, the Ri-numbers are calculated for selected height intervals rather than for specific elevations.

From the remarks made in Section 2 concerning the influence of temporal variations and of vertical wind speeds on the profile shapes, it is apparent that we cannot determine the Ri-numbers with very great accuracy, especially for a small height interval. On the assumption of an average wind speed difference of 3 m s^{-1} and isothermal conditions, the overall stability of the upper shearing layer would correspond to a Ri-number of roughly 0.5. The stability of the lowest 120 meters corresponds to a Ri-number of several units even if the absolute sum of all wind shears involved is used in the calculations, i.e., non-turbulent conditions might be expected. In both regions there may, however, be laminae where the Ri-number may be much smaller, perhaps below the critical limit of 0.25 that according to both theoretical and experimental investigations seem to be necessary to initiate small-scale wave instabilities (Taylor, 1931; Miles, 1961; Chimonas, 1970). If the wind shear layer is deep, these instabilities may grow in amplitude over a layer which may be several times as thick as the generating region, until they ultimately roll and break. It has been suggested (Bean, 1972) that the Ri-number increases during the growth stage (since the wave energy is derived from the wind shearing) to reach a maximum value of 0.5 at the breaking stage. Although our observations do not allow any detailed investigation, well-developed breaking wave patterns do seem to be associated with Ri-numbers of this order of magnitude.

Since the stability may vary drastically over a short vertical distance, we cannot with certainty determine the stability of the thin layers of enhanced backscatter. This difficulty is further demonstrated by another example of thin layer echoes in connection with a strong inversion and light winds (Fig. 7). As seen in the left half of this figure the marked temperature variations are in antiphase with the undulations of the backscatter layers. The temperatures were measured with the balloon system at 100 m. The upper undulating dark bands are obviously associated with a sharp inversion. The total temperature difference across the bands is of the order 6–8 C. The wind speed variations are not related in a systematic

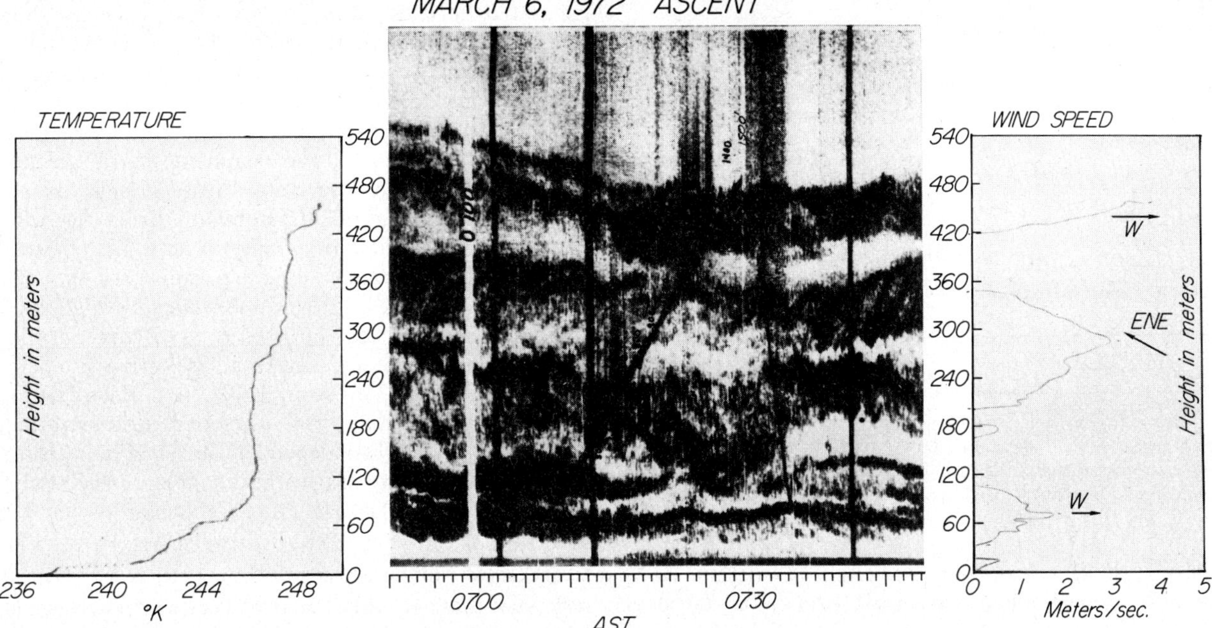

FIG. 8. Low speed windjets, steplike temperature profile and layered backscattering structures.

way to the wave pattern. The wind shear across the echo layers appears to be small on the average, and there is hardly any indication that the windshear is accentuated across the steep inversion. The overall stability is very high.

In the cases seen so far the thin undulating echo layers are obtained in connection with strong inversions and light winds, whereas the "braided" backscatter structure of the upper part of Fig. 6 is obtained in an approximately isothermal, high wind shear region. The wind profile of Fig. 8 includes two jets, one westerly with a maximum speed of 2 m s^{-1} and one east-northeasterly with a maximum speed of 3 m s^{-1}, and one shear layer due to a westerly wind with a maximum speed of 3.5 m s^{-1} at the top of the boundary layer. The temperature profile has a steep inversion in the lowest few tens of meters. At higher elevations there are two sharp inversions between nearly isothermal layers. The strong temperature gradients are not consistently related to the echoes. For instance, the inversion layer between 270 and 300 meters is not associated with a definite backscatter band. Instead, the backscatter bands appear to be rather well correlated with the wind shear layers. The three uppermost bands are "braided" and of somewhat diffuse appearance suggesting that, at least intermittently, there may be well mixed conditions in the shear zones. The layer stabilities, as given by Ri-numbers calculated for the wind shear regions, are roughly 1.4, 0.7, 0.7, 0.3 and 0.2 as counted from the lowest layer and upwards. It should be noted that the width of the backscatter bands and the width of the shear regions

are not exactly the same. The Ri-numbers therefore do not quite represent the backscatter bands.

The substructure of the individual bands appears to be rather intriguing. Occasionally, however, the darkest lines indicate organized air movements. For instance, between 07:35–07:50 AST, the layer of positive wind shear in the lower part of the east-north-easterly jet in Fig. 8 is associated with dark lines tilting to the left, whereas the negative shear at the upper part of the jet is associated with dark lines tilting to the right. This strongly suggests that breaking gravity waves are induced by the wind shear according to the scheme in the upper part of Fig. 9. At elevations corresponding to the maximum wind speed and also in the calm regions between the jets, there is generally less backscatter. This allows for a rather safe interpretation of the jets directly from the acoustic records, when wave breaking takes place.

The jets within the boundary layer may occasionally interact strongly as is demonstrated on an acoustic record with associated balloon sounding (Fig. 10) obtained about two hours before the sounding of Fig. 8. No wind directions were observed at this time because the darkness of the night prevented determinations of the orientation of the balloon (Fig. 3). In the shear layer from 90 to 250 meters, between the two jets, a sudden amplification of the gravity waves starts at 05:03. The substructure of the backscatter shows cusp-shaped waves with an amplitude of about 50 m and with a tendency to break in the upper part of the layer. These waves are in phase vertically with a train of very regular sinusoidal waves with an am-

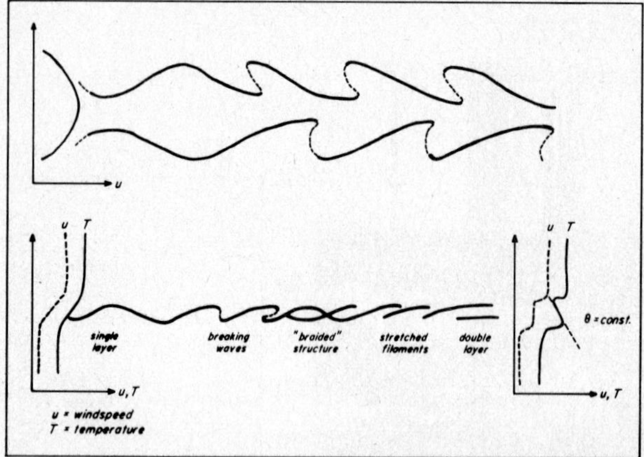

FIG. 9. Upper part: Breaking waves in connection with positive and negative wind shearings. Lower part: Formation of thermoclines in connection with turbulence induced by a wind shearing and breaking waves (Redrawn from Browning and Watkins, 1970, and Hardy, 1972).

plitude of 10 m at a height of about 60 meters. However, a corresponding wave train cannot be traced at elevations above 300 meters, as is indicated by the backscatter band at about this level in Fig. 10. In this case, then, the gravity waves are caused by the wind shear between the jets within the boundary layer, rather than by the wind shear at the upper part of the boundary layer as is shown in Fig. 4.

Wind jets appear to be rather common in the Fairbanks area in situations with deep inversions. The acoustic soundings indicate that the the jets can induce a great deal of turbulence via breaking waves. Occasionally, long-period variations of the vertical-

distance between the backscatter bands of the jets suggest a pulsating flow pattern. The jets may show rapid ascents or descents within the boundary layer. Dynamical features of this kind may conveniently be studied using acoustic soundings.

Although this paper aims mainly at a description of acoustic records, a brief comment on the general shape of the wind and temperature profiles is appropriate at this point. It is obvious, from the wind and temperature profiles of Figs. 8 and 10, obtained in situations with a net outgoing radiation, that the stability next to the ground is extremely high with stagnant air near the surface. It is because of this stagnant layer that the severe air pollution problems of Fairbanks arise (Benson, 1970). A surface friction layer, characterized by well-developed turbulence and approximately height-independent fluxes of momentum and heat, does not exist during these very stable conditions. At higher elevations, the build-up of the inversion is often stepwise: between layers of relatively small temperature gradients, either positive or negative, there are thin layers of very sharp inversions. Similar sharp inversions have been observed earlier, in the polar regions notably by Sverdrup (1933), using captive balloons over the arctic pack ice, and by Liljequist (1957), who made observations of "thermoclines" in the surface layer over an Antarctic shelf ice. Bowling (1972) has described observations of inversions "so sharp as to approach discontinuities" at or near the top of dense and thick ice fog in the Fairbanks area. The thermoclines presented here, all represent clear weather situations without ice fog at

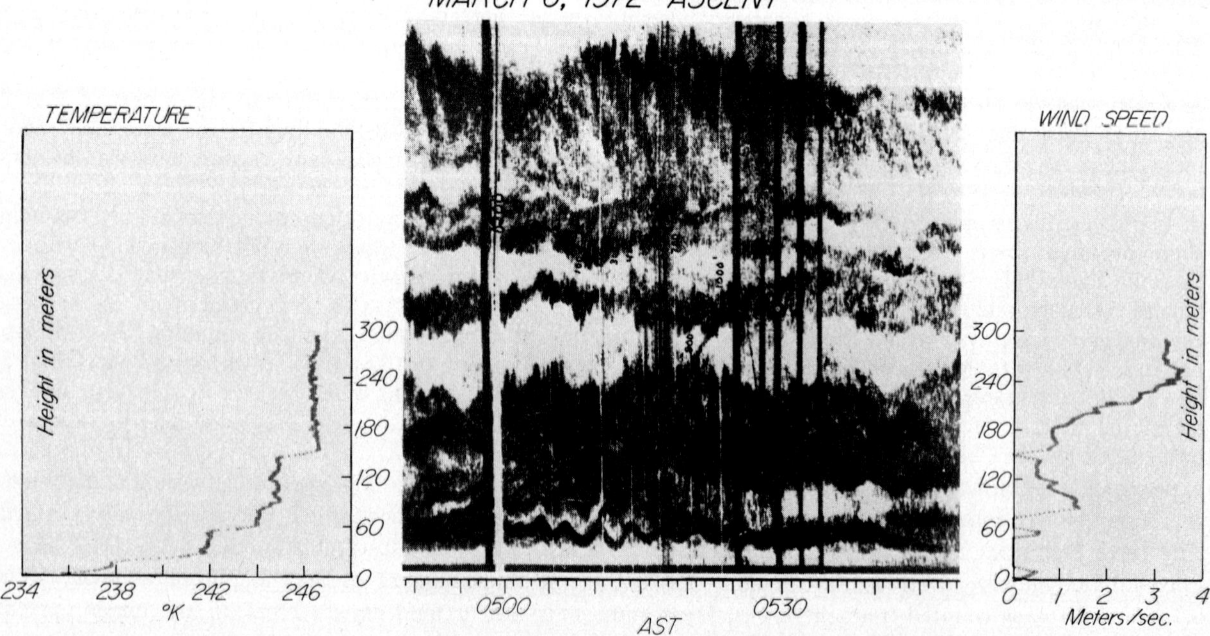

FIG. 10. A sinusoidal wave train in the low layer appears to be induced by breaking waves in a wind shearing layer between two local windjets. Note marked step structure of the temperature profile.

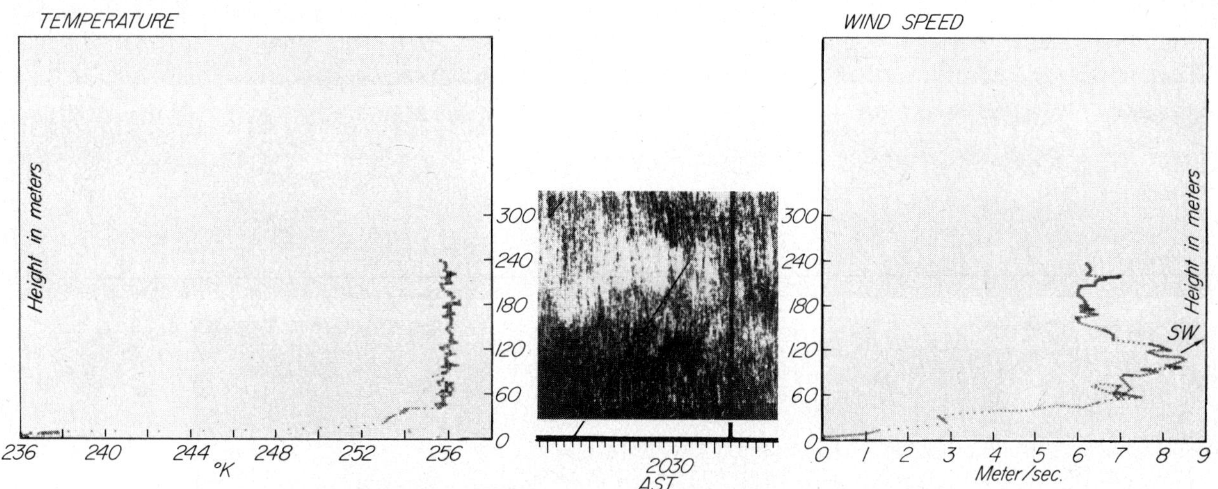

FIG. 11. Acoustic record together with wind and temperature profiles in a situation with a strong surface inversion and strong winds above the surface layer.

the measuring site or, at the most, with low ice fog over the city of Fairbanks.

One appealing scheme for the formation of thermoclines has been suggested by Browning and Watkins, 1970 (lower part of Fig. 9). Our observations indicate, however, that the thermoclines may appear, rather unsystematically, within as well as outside of wind shear regions. The scheme of Fig. 9 may be too simplified to correspond to the actual conditions.

During strong inversion conditions the main flow direction within the boundary layer in the Tanana Valley appears to be easterly or down the valley (Benson and Weller, 1969). In the Fairbanks area the flow pattern becomes extremely complex because of the influence of low-level katabatic winds (Benson and Weller, 1969), seiches (Benson, 1965), the "heat island" effect, and the "cold dome" effect by the ice fog (Bowling, 1972). As for the wind profile of Fig. 8, it might be suggested that the upper westerly wind corresponds to the gradient wind above the main inversion layer. The east-northeasterly jet may be part of the main katabatic flow down the Tanana Valley, at lower levels it is reduced by a westerly wind caused by the local topography. The drifting of the smoke from stack plumes within the topographical bowl of Fairbanks sometimes suggest eddy circulations driven by the main easterly flow. The low westerly jet may be related to such an eddy, perhaps reinforced by a katabatic wind from the nearby hills.

Strong winds

The backscattering echoes discussed so far are all related to light or fairly moderate winds. The acoustic record of Fig. 11 is obtained in connection with winds increasing from calm at the surface to 7–8 m s⁻¹ at an elevation of 60–120 meters. Remarkably enough, there is an inversion of about 20 C in the lowest 50 meters in spite of the strong upper winds. At higher elevations near-isothermal conditions prevail. The thin, multi-layered structures typical for the conditions with light winds are now gone. The backscatter is diffuse, showing a tendency for division of the darkest echo into two parts. The lowest echoes may correspond to intensive mixing and enhanced small-scale temperature turbulence in the shear zone between the upper part of the inversion layer and the lower part of the isothermal layer. The upper echoes may correspond to a layer of increased static and decreased dynamic stability at an elevated inversion that forms in connection with the downward turbulent transfer of heat within the mixing layer. The wind and temperature profiles indirectly demonstrate the sheltered environment at the site of the acoustic sounder. At the surface the winds are effectively suppressed by the combined effect of the strong temperature gradient, the surrounding hills and the surface roughness elements like trees and houses.

The acoustic records of Fig. 12 show the development of the backscatter structure in connection with strong gradient winds during a night with clear skies. At the start of the record in the upper left of the diagram, the wind speed is 7–8 m s⁻¹ as measured at an elevation of about 10 m at the Fairbanks Airport, 6 km from C.R.S. The winds gradually decrease to 2–3 m s⁻¹ at the end of the recording period. At the same time the temperature difference between the surface and the 500 m level changes from a lapse of 5 C to an inversion of 11 C.

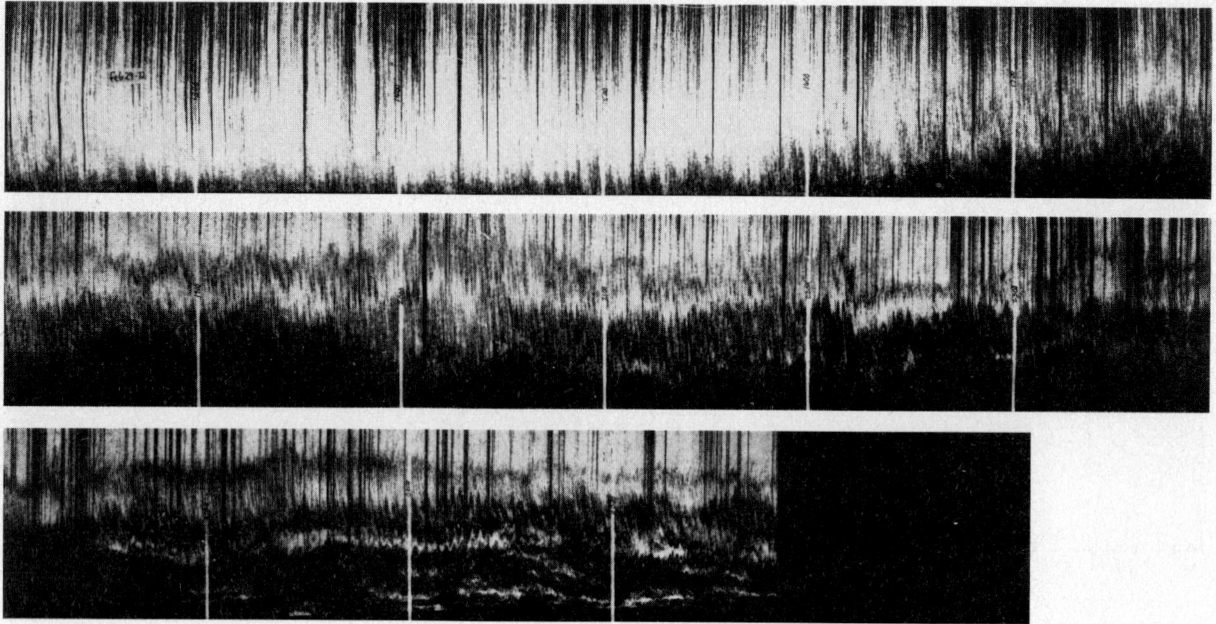

FIG. 12. The development of a surface inversion as indicated by the acoustic sounding record between 12^h a.m. on February 29 and 5^{h}50^{min} a.m. on March 1, 1972. The surface winds were initially moderate to strong, but died down to 2–3 m s^{-1} towards the end of the recording period.

At noon and in the early afternoon the acoustic record shows diffuse echoes in the lowest 100 m or so, indicating turbulent small-scale mixing in the adiabatic surface layer. As the inversion develops later in the afternoon the vertical extent of the echoes increases. Simultaneously the echoes gradually split into several layers. Some of the layers may be traced for hours as they develop from diffuse echoes into marked breaking-wave or "cat-eye" structures. In the early morning hours the echoes at lower elevations are mostly relatively thin backscatter banks, at higher elevations the echoes are diffuse or of breaking-wave type.

During the build-up of the inversion in connection with a strong gradient winds there is obviously a complete reorganization of the turbulent structure of the boundary layer. The backscatter echoes indicate that the turbulent mixing in the initial stages occurs over deep layers. As the stability increases, the enhanced small-scale temperature fluctuations appear in quasi-horizontal bands, perturbed by the wave activity. There is probably little mixing vertically at this stage. Of special interest is the gradual transition of the diffuse bands into breaking wave patterns and then further into relatively thin, undulating bands.

Mixing layers with capping inversions

During midwinter, there is practically no diurnal temperature variation in Fairbanks (Wendler, 1969). However, by mid-February the solar elevations are high enough to cause marked diurnal variation of the surface temperature and the stratification in the low layer. In spite of snow covered ground, the regional albedo in the Fairbanks area is surprisingly low, because of trees, houses, etc. The solar heating can, even at low solar elevations, in a matter of an hour or so remove the sharp shallow surface inversion that forms at night. When the surface inversion disappears, a mixing or convective layer generally develops under an upper capping inversion (Fig. 13). The acoustic record shows diffuse, but mainly vertically oriented, echoes below a dark continuous quasi-horizontal band. At higher elevations there are several layer echoes.

The temperature profiles in Fig. 13 show approximately dry adiabatic lapse rate within the convection layer. Close to the surface, the temperature conditions appear to be somewhat variable as seen when comparing the ascent and descent of the balloon. Normally, a superadiabatic lapse rate might be expected close to the surface. However, many of our profiles collected at other times over snow at daytime do show near-neutral or stable conditions in the low layer, and adiabatic lapse rates above. The main reason for this discrepancy is probably that the warming of the air mainly takes place via the vegetation rather than the snow-covered ground. This is especially apparent when the snow starts to melt.

The mixing layer is capped by a sharp inversion which seem to correspond to the lowest backscattering band during the ascent as well as the descent. Very light, somewhat variable winds prevail in the mixing layer and also in the inversion layer above.

The temperature profiles and the acoustic record of Fig. 13 seem to agree, on the whole, with a model of convective layers suggested by Ball (1960), and later modified and elaborated by Lilly (1968), Deardorff *et al.* (1969). Briefly, thermals rise from a superadiabatic surface layer into the convective layer of nearly dry-adiabatic temperature gradient. When the thermals meet the inversion layer, the kinetic energy associated with their organized vertical motion may be transformed either into potential energy by penetrative convection or into turbulent energy by mixing. The latter transformation may take place in a shearing zone as the plumes stretch and spread laterally, perhaps via Kelvin-Helmholtz instabilities. The inversion will normally be displaced upwards either by entrapping warm air into the convective layer by the over-shooting of cold air, or by entrainment, across the inversion, of the warm stable air into the cold air of higher turbulent intensity. Either process may be expected to induce small-scale turbulence. In fact, a dark backscatter band capping a mixing layer is one of the more persistent features on the acoustic records in daytime during fine-weather periods in late fall, winter and early spring. During these periods the capping inversion is confined to relatively low levels and can generally be traced on the acoustic records throughout the day. It should be remarked that the capping backscatter bands are often much more perturbed than indicated on Fig. 13, which probably represents not too vigorous convection. During the summer season, the convection layers extend too high to be recorded by the acoustic sounder other than occasionally in the mornings during the breakup of the night inversions.

The maximum height of the mixing layer appears in the afternoon on the average. Large deviations occur, however. The structure and the behavior of the capping inversions in varying weather situations offer insight into interesting meso-scale processes. The reverse development of the convection layer, which takes place when the heat transfer from the surface becomes zero and changes sign, has been recognized (Plate, 1971) as one of the most important areas of boundary layer research. Some modes of reversals of convective layers are demonstrated in Fig. 14 showing excerpts of acoustic records on four days from around noon to the afternoon or evening in March 1972.

The upper record shows a convective layer with an upper boundary that suggest perturbations of the inversion layer above by convective plumes. The record is unfortunately too dark to permit identification of any substructures within the convective layer. In the early afternoon the capping backscatter band splits into one ascending and one descending branch. The ascending branch has dark streaks tilting to the right, indicating that a jet has formed with the maximum speed probably somewhere in between the echoes. Record No. 2 in Fig. 14 shows a backscatter band at approximately constant elevation after the end of the convection. As the new surface inversion builds up, the space below the capping inversion is gradually filled by bands rising from the surface. The third record, which is a 2-channel record, and the fourth record show descending capping inversions in the early afternoon and in the middle of the day. Above the mixing layers breaking waves indicate strong positive wind shear.

The structure and the behavior of the capping inversion may be expected to be determined by the character of the turbulence on both sides of the inversion. Changes of the elevation of the capping inversion should be related to the rate of the entrainment of air across the inversion. Laboratory experiments by Turner (1968) suggest that the entrainment rate

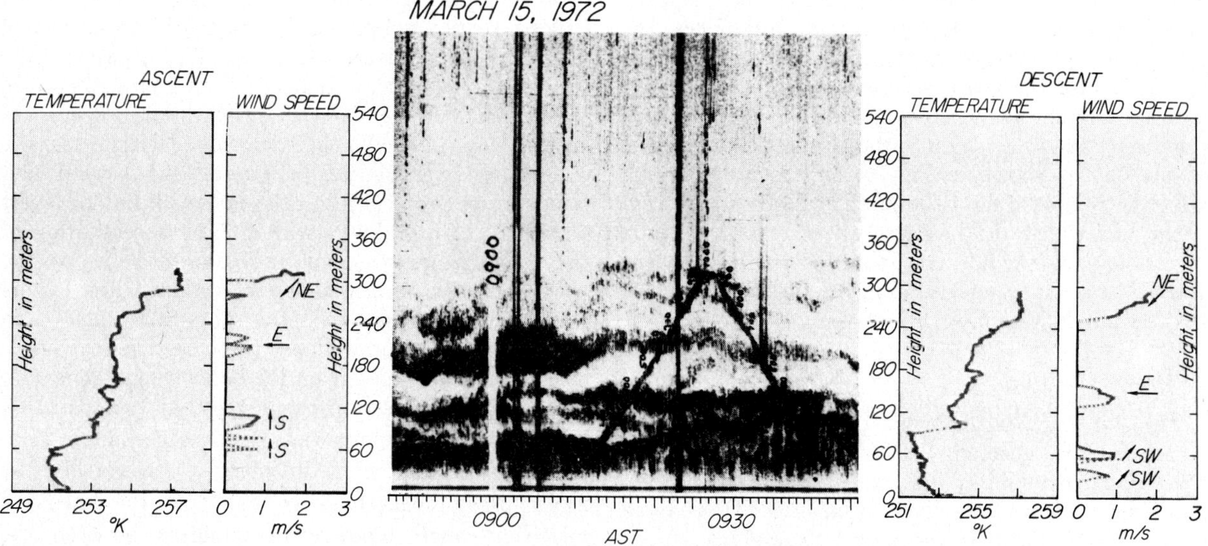

FIG. 13. A mixing layer with a capping inversion as observed by the Boundary Layer Profiler and the acoustic sounder.

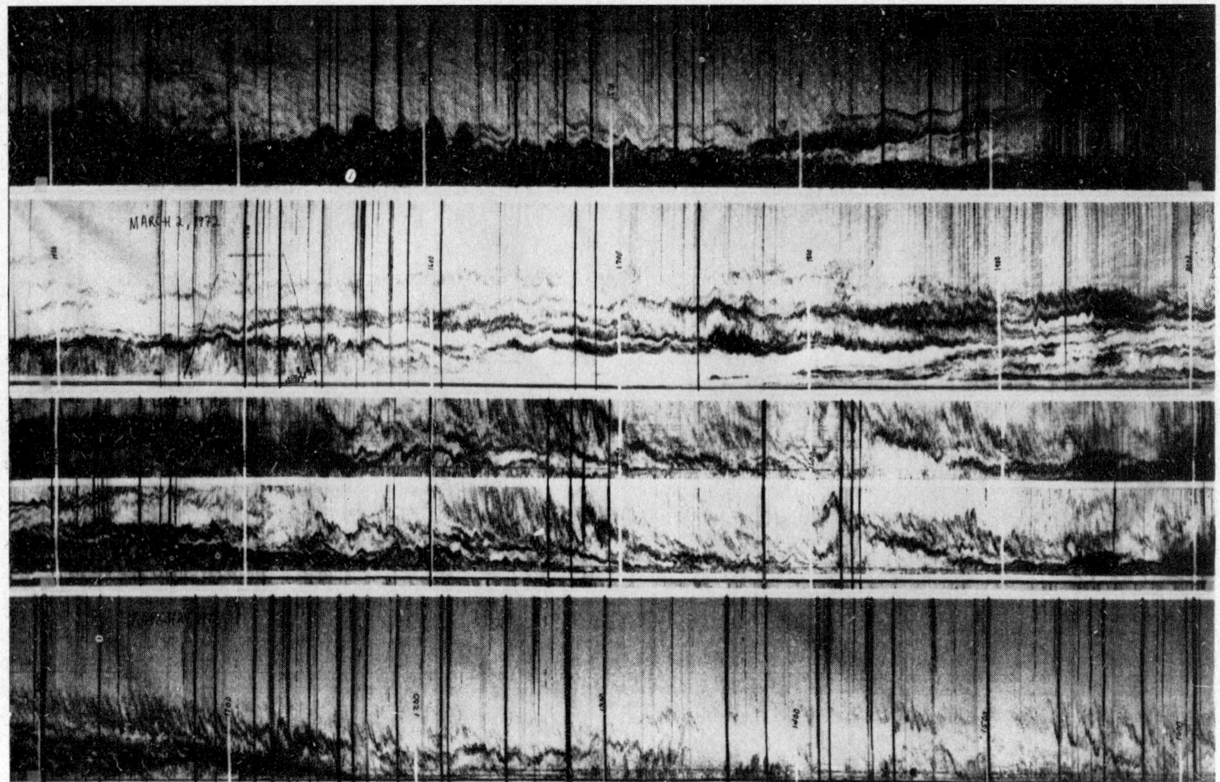

F IG. 14. Various modes of reversal of mixing or convective layers. From above the acoustic records represent these periods : 1) 11^{h}45^{min} a.m.–06^{h}10^{min} p.m. on March 1, 1972; 2) 13^{h}40^{min} a.m.–08^{h}05^{min} p.m. on March 2, 1972; 3) 11^{h}40^{min} a.m.–06^{h}05^{min} p.m. on March 7, 1973. (This is a dual-channel record obtained by operating two antennaes simultaneously. The upper half of this record corresponds to an antenna tilting 45°, and the lower part corresponds to an antenna pointing vertically). 4) 09^{h}50^{min} a.m.–04^{h}15^{min} p.m. on March 24, 1972.

across a density interface is fastest into the layer of highest turbulent intensity. In analogy, with light winds above an active convective layer, the warm stable air above the capping inversion will generally be entrained into the convective layer. With strong winds and marked wind shear above the capping inversion, inducing relatively intensive turbulence, the air of the convective layer might instead be entrained primarily into the warm air above. This may explain how the capping inversion may descend right through the convective layer down to the surface in the middle of the day as shown in Fig. 14 on the 3rd and 4th records. On the same assumption, record No. 2 from above, on which the height changes of the capping inversions are small, may indicate small turbulent activity, and rates of entrainment, on both sides of the capping inversion.

6. Discussion

The thin backscatter bands caused by atmospheric structures are generally believed to be caused by small-scale instabilities in regions of enhanced temperature gradient and some wind shear (Ottersten et al., 1973). There is theoretical as well as experimental evidence that the wind shear may be accentuated by gravity waves in the boundary layer that are either untrapped (Gossard et al., 1971) or trapped (Gossard et al., 1973). Whether all the thin backscatter bands seen in layers of very stable stratification can be ascribed to wave-induced instabilities cannot be resolved from our measurements. With our balloon sounding system, the temporal variations of wind and temperature are so hard to separate from the vertical variations, that the wind and temperature profiles cannot be determined with any degree of accuracy over a small height interval. On some acoustic records with associated balloon-measured wind and temperature profiles, thin echo layers appear in layers of overall high stability without any accentuation of the temperature gradient (not shown here) or the wind shear at corresponding elevations. The factors causing these echoes in terms of vertical wind and temperature structure appear to be so small that they cannot be determined from the balloon soundings.

Some of our observations suggest that not all thin backscatter layers are caused by shear-induced instabilities of the sharp inversions. Occasionally the lowest Ri-numbers may be found in the layers of relatively small temperature gradient between the sharp inversions. In that case one might expect that small-scale turbulent velocity fluctuations, if existing, would coincide with the layer of low Ri-numbers and that the fluctuations would be strongly damped at the sharp inversions. In a zone close to the sharp inversion, the small-scale temperature fluctuations, as expressed for instance by the C_T values, may increase both because of increased temperature gradient and because of a shift of the spectrum of fluctuations towards the high-frequency side. That sharp density interfaces do develop in turbulent flows with density gradients under special circumstances is observed in the laboratory as well as the atmosphere and the ocean (for a summary of laboratory investigations see Turner, 1972). One of the present authors has observed the formation of sharp inversions in regions of small shear above a turbulent surface layer on an ice cap in the Arctic Canada. (Holmgren, 1971) Such sharp inversions next to turbulent layers seem, incidentally, to develop especially in connection with katabatic winds.

Although we cannot at the present time state unambiguously what is causing all the echoes, many backscatter features like breaking waves and convective plumes may be positively identified. The continuity of backscatter features often allows visual interpretation of boundary layer processes. The gradual break-up of a deep inversion by breaking waves associated with increasing wind speeds aloft, the variations of the depth of the mixing layer and the character of the capping inversion above, and low-speed wind jets within the boundary layer are all examples of processes that can be monitored by the acoustic sounder. These are all processes that relate to the air pollution situation in Fairbanks. Used on a real time basis as a tool in addition to synoptic, climatic, radiosond etc., data, the acoustic sounder should be a valuable aid in local weather forecasts.

Acknowledgments. This research is supported by N.S.F. Grant GV 27697. Members of the NOAA Wave Propagation Laboratory in Boulder developed our acoustic sounding equipment and gave us excellent introduction into sounding techniques. R. G. Siegrist assisted significantly in the data acquisition and prepared the instrument diagrams.

REFERENCES

Ball, F. K., 1960: Control of inversion height by surface heating. *Quart. J. Roy. Meteorol. Soc.*, **86**, 483–494.

Bean, B. R., 1972: Application of FM-CW radar and acoustic echo-sounder techniques to boundary layer and CAT studies. Remote sensing of the troposphere, Natl. Oceanic Atmos. Admin. W. P. L., Boulder, Colorado.

Benson, C. S., 1965: Ice fog: low temperature air pollution defined with Fairbanks, Alaska as type locality. Geophysical Institute Report, UAG R-173, University of Alaska.

Benson, C. S., 1970: Ice fog: Low temperature air pollution. CRREL Research Report 121.

Benson, C. S., and G. E. Weller, 1969: A study of low-level winds in the vicinity of Fairbanks, Alaska. Report to Earth Resources Company, Geophysical Institute, University of Alaska, Fairbanks.

Beran, D. W., C. G. Little and B. C. Willmarth, 1971: Acoustic Doppler measurements of vertical velocities in the atmosphere. *Nature*, **230**, 160–162.

Beran, D. W., W. H. Hooke and S. F. Clifford, 1973: Acoustic echo-sounding techniques and their application to gravity-wave, turbulence, and stability studies. *Boundary Layer Meteorology*, 4, 133–153.

Bilello, M. A., 1966: Survey of arctic and subarctic temperature inversions. CRREL Technical Report 161.

Bowling, S. A., 1970: Radiative cooling rates in the presence of ice crystal aerosols. Ph.D. dissertation Geophysical Institute University of Alaska (unpublished).

Bowling, S. A. (1973). Calculation of radiative cooling rates in fogs. III. The effect of ice fog on thermal stability (unpublished).

Browning, K. A., and C. D. Watkins, 1970: Observations of clear air turbulence by high power radar, *Nature*, **227**, 260–263.

Chimonas, G., 1970: The extension of the Miles-Howard theorem to compressible fluids. *J. Fluid Mech.*, **43**, 883–836.

Deardorff, J. W., G. E. Willis and D. K. Lilly, 1969: Laboratory investigation of non-steady penetrative convection. *J. Fluid Mech.*, **35**, 7–31.

Fahl, C. B., 1969: Internal atmospheric gravity waves at Fairbanks, Alaska. M.S. thesis, University of Alaska, Fairbanks.

Gossard, E. E., D. R. Jensen and J. H. Richter, 1971: An analytical study of tropospheric structure as seen by high-resolution radar. *J. Atmos. Sci.* **28**, 794–807.

Gossard, E. E., J. J. Richter and D. R. Jensen, 1973: Effect of wind shear on atmospheric wave instabilities revealed by FM/CW Radar observations. *Boundary-Layer Meteorology*, 4, 113–131.

Hardy, K. R., 1972: Studies of the clear atmosphere using high power radar. Remote sensing of the troposphere, Natl. Oceanic Atmos. Admin. W. P. L., Boulder, Colorado.

Haurwitz, B., 1967: Oscillations in a basin of cold air. Geophysical Institute note, University of Alaska (unpublished).

Holmgren, B. E., 1971: On the katabatic winds over the northwest slope of the Devon Island ice cap. Variations of the surface roughness. Meddelande Nr 109, Meteorologiska Institutinen, Uppsala Universitet, Uppsala.

Kallistrova, M. A., 1961: Experimental investigation of sound wave scattering in the atmosphere. Trudy Inst. Tiz. Atmos., Atmos. Turbulentnost No. 4, 205–256, USAF FTD translation TT-63-441.

Liljequist, G. H., 1957: Energy exchange of an Antarctic snowfield. Part 1C: Wind structure in the low layer. Norwegian-British-Swedish Antarctic Expedition, 1949–52. Scientific Results, Vol II, Norsk Polarinstitutt, Oslo.

Lilly, D. K., 1968: Models of cloud-topped mixed layers undre strong inversions. *Quart. J. Roy. Meteorol. Soc.*, **94**, 292–309.

Little, C. G., 1969: Acoustic methods for the remote probing of the lower atmosphere, Proc. IEEE **57**, 571–578.

McAllister, L. G., 1968: Acoustic sounding of the lower troposphere, *J. Atmos. Terr. Phys.*, **30**, 1439–1440.

McAllister, L. G., J. R. Pollard, A. R. Mahoney, and P. J. Shaw. 1969: Acoustic sounding—A new approach to the study of atmospheric structure, Proc. IEEE, **57**, 579–587.

Miles, J. W., 1961: On the stability of heterogeneous shear flows. *J. Fluid Mech.*, **10**, 496–508.

Ottersten, H., K. R. Hardy, and C. G. Little, 1973: Radar and solar probing of waves and turbulence in statically stable clear-air layer. *Boundary Layer Meteorology*, 4, pp. 47–89.

Plate, E. P., 1971: Aerodynamic characteristics of atmospheric boundary layers, AEC critical review series. U. S. Department of Commerce, Springfield, Virginia.

Priestly, C. H. B., 1955: Free and forced convection in the atmosphere near the ground. *Quart. J. Roy. Meteorol. Soc.*, **81**, 139–143.

Simmons, W. R., J. W. Wescott and F. F. Hall, Jr., 1971: Acoustic echo sounding as related to air pollution in urban environments, Natl. Oceanic Atmos. Admin. Tech. Report. ERL 216 WPL 17, Boulder, Colorado.

Sverdrup, H. U., 1933: Meteorology, Part 1, Discussion. The Norwegian North Polar Expedition with the "Maud" 1918–1925, Scientific Results, Vol. II, Bergen.

Taylor, G. J., 1931: Effect of variation in density on the stability of superposed streams of fluid. Proc. Roy. Soc. A **132**, 499–523.

Turner, J. S., 1968: The influence of molecular diffusivity on turbulent entrainment across a density surface. *J. Fluid Mech.*, **33**, 639–656.

Winchester, J. W., W. H. Zoller, R. A. Duce, and C. S. Benson, 1967: Lead and halogens in pollution aerosols and snow from Fairbanks, Alaska. Atmospheric Environment, **1**, 105–119.

Wendler, G. D., 1969: Heat balance studies during an ice-fog period in Fairbanks, Alaska. *Monthly Weather Review*, **97**, 512–520.

Climate and Air Pollution at High Latitudes

P. E. Nicpon

Geophysical Institute, University of Alaska, Fairbanks, Alaska 99701

Abstract

An interest exists concerning the relationship between air quality and climatology at high latitudes, especially in regard to the air pollution climatology of urban centers in these regions. The effect of geographical and meteorological factors on the transport and diffusion of air pollutants in such an environment is of major concern. But the effects of weather elements such as temperature, solar radiation, and precipitation on the atmospheric processes which naturally remove pollutants must also be examined at high latitudes if one is to assess the magnitude and nature of potential air pollution problems in northern climates.

Relatively few studies have been made concerning the effect of air pollutants on the ecological and climatic parameters which characterize high latitudes. Kay (1968) has suggested that development of the Arctic in the same pattern followed in more temperature zones could possibly result in even more serious environmental contamination problems due to a combination of meteorology, geology, and geography.

At high latitudes where no spring runoff occurs, year-by-year accumulation of air-discharged pollutants could result in high concentrations of the contaminants on the surface. Arsenic trioxide discharged to the air by ore-roasters in the recovery of gold in the Northwest Territories of Canada contaminated a surrounding townsite to the extent that poisoning cases involving humans and domestic animals occurred (Kay, 1968). In this sub-Arctic case, the arsenic from the smelting process accumulating on snow led to high drinking-water concentrations of this toxic material during the short melting period. Surface accumulations from the air discharge of arsenic during the frozen period were up to fifty times greater than found in July after the break-up period.

Schofield and Hamilton (1969) have reviewed the possible damage to Arctic ecosystems through air-pollution effects on lichens. They note that the destructive effects of air pollution on lichens are due, in large part, to sulfur dioxide. They further point out the potential hazards of sulfur dioxide pollution on Alaska's North Slope.

Strong temperature inversions frequently occur in the surface layers of the Arctic and sub-Arctic atmosphere due to radiative cooling. While these are fairly common in the summer period, they are more frequent in the winter (Bilello, 1966). Furthermore, inversions in combination with low topographic relief and low wind velocities in many places at high latitudes can result in exceptionally stable air masses which are easily polluted. In addition, water and ice fogs are common under these conditions and fogs have been a factor in many of the world's fatal air-pollution episodes.

But, in general, we know very little concerning how atmospheric reactions, dispersion, and removal of pollutant species are modified by climatic elements at high latitudes. Nor do we know the full consequences of such modifications for man in northern climates.

For example, what is the effect of low temperatures and absence of solar radiation on the reactions of atmospheric pollutants? Water vapor plays a prominent role in atmospheric reactions. What is the effect of low water-vapor contents of air at low temperature on the removal of atmospheric contaminants? Atmospheric residence times of some pollutant gases and aerosols have been determined in more moderate climates to be fairly short. Would climatic factors result in long resistence times when such pollutants are injected at high latitudes? Low amounts of precipitation in the Arctic, for example, might result in longer residence of pollutants in the atmosphere because rain and snow play a role in scavenging pollutant species. Similarly, what is the nature of atmospheric aerosols—their chemistry and size distribution—in remote areas of the Arctic and sub-Arctic and what effect would they have on neutralization of acidic pollutant gases?

Atmospheric particles and aerosols due to man's activities occur at urban centers in the Arctic and sub-Arctic. Adsorption of pollutant gases on these followed by deposition may be an important removal mechanism at extremely low temperatures. Under atmospheric stagnation conditions at high latitudes the ground snow cover may also serve as a sink for air pollution gases by adsorption. If the low-temperature adsorption processes were reversible, then it might be possible for these sinks to act as sources at subsequent higher temperatures. Any model describing the dispersion or concentration of atmospheric pollutants in an urban Arctic or sub-Arctic environment would have to take such sinks into account—that is if they do, indeed, exist.

Another aspect is the effect of temperature on the physical and chemical nature of air pollutants at low temperatures. The conversion of normally gaseous organic species to solid or liquid aerosols might occur when automobile exhaust effluents are released at low temperatures. Another example is the nature of nitrogen oxides occurring in a polluted atmosphere at low temperature. Combustion processes at high temperatures involving air result in the formation of nitric oxide (NO). Nitric oxide is then oxidized to nitrogen dioxide (NO_2) in the atmosphere. Reaction rates usually decrease at lower temperatures but the rate constant for this reaction is unusual in that it has a negative temperature coefficient, at least over the temperature range of 400–0 C (Bodenstein, 1922). The rate of formation of nitrogen dioxide increases with decreasing temperature but one does not know if this would occur at temperatures on the order of −20 or −40 C. At low temperature and in the absence of solar radiation, the interest in nitrogen oxides is not because of the role these play in photochemical reactions. Rather, knowledge of which of the nitrogen oxides are prevalent at low temperatures might enable one to better understand how it is dispersed and removed. But there is also a health aspect. Nitric oxide is reported to have a relatively low toxicity compared with nitrogen dioxide (Stokinger and Coffin, 1968). Finally, nitrogen dioxide and dinitrogen tetroxide (N_2O_4) exist in a strongly temperature-dependent equilibrium; one would expect dinitrogen tetroxide to predominate at low temperature. What are the health consequences of atmospheric dinitrogen tetroxide?

The effect of air pollutants in general on man under cold-environment stresses should be examined in greater detail. No knowledge is available, for example, concerning the toxicity of pollutants in conjunction with ice fog such as occurs in the Fairbanks area. Indeed, up until recently there has been little study concerning the general nature of atmospheric pollutants during ice-fog conditions. The low-temperature and lack-of-solar-radiation aspects of air pollution at high latitudes here are modified by the presence of a large input of water vapor—more than the cold air can hold—which condenses, supercools, and then freezes. Removal of pollutants under such conditions might resemble in-cloud scavenging processes.

Furthermore, the solubility of gases in water increases at lower temperatures. Cloud physicists (Pena, Pena, and Hosler, 1969) studying the freezing of supercooled water droplets in equilibrium with different gases have shown that some gases (carbon dioxide, for example) were expelled when the droplets froze. When low partial pressures of other gases (sulfur dioxide, for example) were examined, however, no gas was found to be expelled during freezing; all the gas separated from the ice is immediately dissolved in the remaining solution thereby lowering its freezing point.

In a review concerning reactions in frozen systems, Pincock (1969) has noted that increased reaction rates in ice for certain chemical species are due to the crystallization of water as ice resulting in high concentrations of reactants in liquid regions of the frozen system. Pincock also points out that the frequent existence of liquid in equilibrium with a solid at temperatures below the freezing point is often neglected. An apparently solid material may contain liquid phase at any temperature if the system is above its eutectic temperature. While chemical reaction rates in general slow down as the temperature decreases, freezing droplets under ice fog conditions might tend to concentrate atmospheric species in liquid regions and increase reaction rates.

Finally, the likelihood of photochemical atmospheric reactions becoming a problem at high latitudes with increasing development should be examined, since temperature inversions are also fairly common in the Arctic and sub-Arctic during the summer when daylight may be continuous or nearly continuous. However, the difference in spectral energy distribution and intensity of sunlight between the temperature zone and high latitudes has yet to be examined for its effect on photochemical reactions in the lower atmosphere (Kay, 1968).

REFERENCES

Bilello, M. A., 1966: Survey of Arctic and sub-Arctic temperature inversions. CRREL, Technical Report 161.

Bodenstein, M., 1922: Bildung und Zersetzung der Höheren Stickoxyde. *Z. Physik. Chem.* **100**, 62–123.

Kay, K., 1968: A look at the future of hazardous contamination of the circumpolar environment. Archives of Environmental Health, Vol. 17, No. 4, 653–661.

Pena, J. A., R. C. de Pena and C. L. Hosler, 1969: Freezing of water droplets in equilibrium with different gases. *J. Atmos. Sci.*, **26**, 309–314.

Pincock, R. E., 1969: Reactions in frozen systems. *Acc. Chem. Res.*, **2**, 97–103.

Schofield, E., and W. L. Hamilton, 1969: Probable damage to Arctic ecosystems through air-pollution effects on lichens. Proceedings of the 20th Alaskan Science Conference, College, Alask, August 24–27, 271–291.

Stokinger, H. E., and D. L. Coffin, 1968: Biologic effects of air pollution. *Air Pollution*, Ed. A. C. Stern, Vol. I, 2nd Edition, Academic Press, New York, 1968, 445–546.

The Sub-Arctic Urban Heat Island as Studied at Fairbanks, Alaska

C. S. BENSON AND S. A. BOWLING

Geophysical Institute, University of Alaska, Fairbanks, Alaska

Abstract

Changes in surface properties and addition of man-made heat combine to make cities generally warmer than their surroundings. This effect is known as the 'urban heat island.' The surface properties involved in the changes are: Albedo and thermal properties (building materials vs. soil), which affect response to solar radiation; moisture (vegetation or wet soil vs. pavement or, in desert climates, the reverse situation of dry land vs. irrigated areas), which affects latent heat exchange; surface roughness, which affects turbulent heat exchange due to wind action; and atmospheric clarity (smog vs. clear air), which affects the infrared energy exchange with the atmosphere. The arctic/sub-arctic heat island in winter is of considerable theoretical interest in that solar radiation is negligible and moisture contrast is cancelled by a uniform snow cover and dormant vegetation. Additionally, in the Fairbanks area wind speeds are generally very low, minimizing roughness effects. Thus the Fairbanks heat island provides a natural laboratory for the study of the interaction of added man-made heat and infrared (thermal) radiation in producing a heat island.

The Fairbanks winter heat island was studied prior to 1965 as part of the ice fog studies carried out at that time by one of us. Considerable changes in land use have taken place since that time. Furthermore, the effect of a heat island on pollutant dispersal has become a pressing theoretical and practical problem. Preliminary reconnaissance early in 1973 indicates that the heat island covers a larger area and is less sharply defined near its core than was previously the case. These changes parallel, and are probably related to, an increase in the area covered by ice fog. Even as early as 1962, however, the Weather Bureau (airport) temperature at 135 m was found to be consistently higher than the mean of the other flatland stations (one at 130 m and one at 140 m), and frequently higher than either. This suggests the possibility that the airport was actually within the Fairbanks heat island, or producing its own small heat island. On this basis, it will be necessary to extend the traverses beyond the areas studied so far to obtain good background temperatures.

Cities affect their own temperatures in several ways. Building materials have albedos different from natural surfaces, which leads to differences in the absorption of solar radiation. Thermal diffusivities also differ, which results in a reduced amplitude of the daily temperature wave in cities. The increase in surface roughness length observed in cities has the same effect (Nappo, 1972). Differences in vegetative cover between a city and its surroundings, however, will lead to a general increase in the temperature of the less vegetated areas (usually the city). Energy consumed within the city, whether for heating, cooling, or mechanical work, will ultimately degrade to heat which raises the city temperature (SMIC report, 1972; Myrup, 1969). Finally, city air pollution may affect both the visible and infrared radiative balances (Atwater, 1971; Bowling, 1970).

The change in temperature is not confined to the surface layer of the atmosphere, but may extend upward for several hundred meters. Air near the top of the affected layer may even be colder than that in surrounding areas—a phenomenon known as "crossover." (Duckworth *et al.*, 1954). The resulting baroclinicity may affect local wind systems. This, together with the direct influence of changes in the stability of the thermal lapse rate, make the city heat island an important influence on patterns of pollutant dispersal. Thus prediction of heat island effects may become an important factor in the prediction of air pollution potential.

Because the generalized heat island is dependent on so many, often conflicting, parameters, cases in which only a few variables need be considered are of considerable theoretical interest. One such case is the sub-arctic winter heat island, as exemplified in Fairbanks, Alaska. Not only is solar radiation minimal (on the order of 5 cal cm^{-2} day^{-1} at winter solstice) but a blanket of snow and dormant vegetation virtually eliminate differences in substrate thermal properties, albedo, and evapotranspiration. Roughness length differences between the forested portion of the surroundings and the one-story portion of the city are probably minor, and even the contrast between agricultural land and the core business district is minimized by the very low wind speeds observed (typically less than 3 mps). These same low wind speeds, plus extreme ground inversions, allow considerable pollutant buildup in the city area. Furthermore, at the extremely low temperatures observed (often < -40 C) water vapor input greatly exceeds the holding capacity

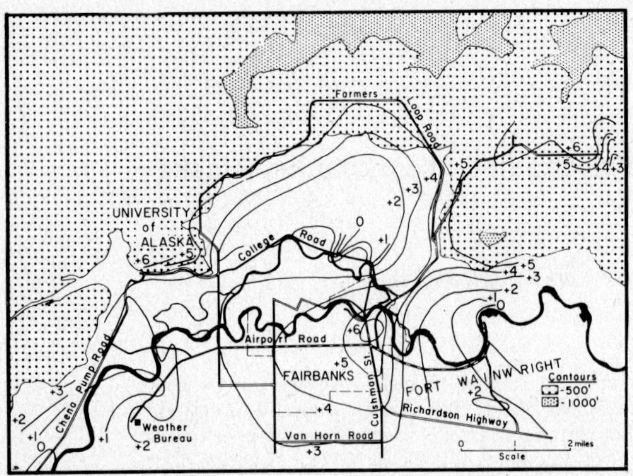

Fig. 1. The Fairbanks heat island, generalized from three traverses. Contours are labeled in °C above the lowest temperature encountered (−33, −45 and −46 C in the actual surveys). All roads shown were utilized in at least one traverse; dash-filled roads were used in the pre-1965 surveys. Fairbanks city limits are shown as of 1965. Road elevations from College Road south are 430 to 445 feet m.s.l.

of the ambient air (Benson, 1965, 1970). Surplus water vapor crystallizes out in the form of ice fog, which is highly active in the thermal infrared. Low temperatures also encourage one of the highest per capita energy consumption rates in the world—slightly higher than for Manhattan Island (SMIC, 1971). Thus the Fairbanks heat island is dominated almost entirely by anthropogenic heating and a disturbed infrared flux—terms which in most other heat island situations are swamped by other effects.

Sporadic observations of the Fairbanks heat island have been made since before 1965 (Benson, 1965, 1970). The isolation of the area makes calculation of the anthropogenic heat production relatively simple, and fuel inventories were made prior to 1965. This survey badly needs updating, and we hope to be able to do this updating in the near future. The purpose of this paper is to outline the results of recent surface observations of the heat island in combination with reexamination of some of the pre-1965 data, and, on the basis of these observations, to suggest additional measurements which should be made in an extended study.

The geometry of the surface temperature distribution around Fairbanks is critically dependent on the local topography. Fairbanks itself is located on the virtually flat flood plain of the Chena River, just upstream from the Chena-Tanana confluence. The divide between the two flood plains at this point is low and largely artificial, so, as far as low-level airflow is concerned, flat ground extends south to and across the Tanana River almost to the Alaska Range. The large-scale low-level air drainage under inversion conditions follows the Tanana drainage westward. From northeast to southwest, however, the city is sur-

rounded by a rough semicircle of hills rising 300 to 600 m above the flood plain. Low level flow within this semicircle tends to include one or more eddies and is very probably influenced by the existence of the city. The majority of the visible ice fog export, however, is to the southwest and down the Tanana. Near-surface temperatures are strongly influenced by topography, with temperatures on the flood plain under clear skies naturally being 6–10 C or more colder than temperatures 100 m higher, on the hillsides. As one result, considerable residential development is taking place on the hill slopes. Most of the low land around Fairbanks is also being covered by residential area except for the Creamers field area just north of the city between Farmers Loop and College Roads (see map).

Temperature traverses were made prior to 1965 along two routes—a north–south run with a loop in the core area and an east–west run. The south end of the cross thus formed was in relatively undisturbed country. Lowest temperatures were normally observed about a mile east of the airport, or occasionally on Ft. Wainwright.

During the winter of 1972–73, three additional traverses were made, using various expanded road nets. Since no two of the traverses covered quite the same area, all three are combined with an arbitrary temperature scale in Fig. 1, which also shows the routes used. All temperature measurements in both series were made with a thermistor mounted 2 m above the front bumper of the traverse car, and measurements were made while the car was moving faster than 10 mph. The severity of ice fog increased markedly during the 1967–68 winter and has remained higher than pre-1967 values to the present. In making our 1972–73 traverses, it was observed that virtually the entire area covered by the pre-1965 surveys is now under at least light ice fog, the only exception being the extreme east end of Fort Wainwright. To some extent this increase in fog is due to increased development along the traverse—much of Airport Road, for instance, has been changed from ordinary 2-lane to 4-lane limited access. Also, fog generated over Fairbanks speads over the surrounding area. Some of this spreading goes to the Creamer's field area north of Fairbanks where air stagnation seems most pronounced. However, most of the Fairbanks ice fog drifts off to the southwest. This drift is clearly visible at times from the University, and is reflected in the isotherm pattern as well.

Even with the extended traverse there is a real problem in finding an undisturbed background temperature. The area south of town is clearly contaminated, and the situation near the airport is highly variable—local temperature maxima have been recorded at the site of the minimum shown. Temperatures comparable to those in the city on the higher ground north of town are controlled by elevation. Along

College Road there seems little doubt that the sharp horizontal temperature variations (the exact position and intensity of which varied between traverses) were due to cold air spilling across the road from the Creamer's field area. This farm land is poorly drained and somewhat swampy, but it is a northward extension of the flood plain rather than a depression. Thus there is no a priori reason for its temperature to differ from that of the downtown area in the absence of anthropogenic effects. Future traverse work will include penetration of this area, much of which is now a game refuge, and temperatures from this area will probably be used for baseline temperatures. The only alternative site is the east part of Fort Wainwright.

Data collected prior to 1965 included thermograph records with frequent calibration from an extensive station network as well as the traverses mentioned above. Two of the thermograph stations were located in undeveloped areas at 130 m and 140 m m.s.l. elevation, while the Weather Bureau station at the airport is 135 m m.s.l. In comparing temperatures from these three flood-plain stations, the Weather Bureau temperatures were found to be consistently higher than those of either of the other two stations. Thus the possibility of heat island effects at the airport during the early study must be considered.

Thermograph records from hill-slope and hill-top stations during the same period (January 1963) were compared with soundings obtained by the Weather Bureau. Records from 2 m above the surface on hill-top stations were found to be generally unreliable as indicators of free-air temperature even with strong winds. Differences of 5 C or more were common, with hill-top station temperatures generally being lower than the free air temperature. Hill-slope temperatures, however, were normally within 2 C of the sounding temperature for the same height and time. This suggests that hill-slope traverses may help define vertical temperature structure in the free air, at least near the edges of the basin, whereas hill-top temperatures are not as reliable.

REFERENCES

Atwater, Marshall A., 1971: The radiation budget for polluted layers of the urban environment. *J. A. M.*, **10**, 205–214.

Benson, Carl S., 1965, 1970: Ice fog—Low temperature air pollution defined with Fairbanks, Alaska as type locality. Geophysical Institute Report UAG R-173, 1965, Revised edition published as CRREL Research Report 121, June 1970.

Bowling, Sue Ann, 1970: Radiative cooling rates in the presence of ice crystal aerosols. Ph.D. Dissertation, University of Alaska, May 1970.

Duckworth, Fowler S., and James S. Sandberg, 1954: The effect of cities upon horizontal and vertical temperature gradients. *Bull. A. M. S.*, **35**, 198–207.

Myrup, Leonard O., 1969: A numerical study of the urban heat island. *J. A. M.*, **8**, 908–918.

Nappo, Carmen J., Jr., 1972: A numerical study of the urban heat island. Conference on the Urban Environment and Second Conference on Biometeorology, A. M. S., Philadelphia, Oct. 31–Nov. 2, pp. 1–4.

SMIC Report 1971: Inadvertent climate modification. Report on the study of man's impact on climate, MIT Press, Cambridge, 307 p.

Tundra Environmental Changes Induced by Urbanization

M. A. ATWATER AND J. P. PANDOLFO

The Center for the Environment and Man, Inc., Hartford, Connecticut 06120

Abstract

A three-dimensional numerical model based on the Eulerian conservation equation for momentum, heat, and water vapor is examined for environmental changes that may be induced by urbanization in the tundra. Advective, vertically diffusive, and radiative processes are explicitly induced in the differential equations. The numerical model simulates the relative magnitude of thermal, momentum, and moisture changes induced by a city in the tundra. Results are compared with observations of the mid-latitudes.

1. Introduction

During the past couple of centuries, urbanization and industrialization have caused inadvertent microscale and mesoscale changes in weather and climate. With most of the cities being in the mid-latitudes, the weather and climate changes in these latitudes have been examined in relatively great detail, both by observation and with numerical studies. Most studies have examined the thermal structure. Atwater (1972) concluded that changes in the physical properties were responsible for many of the urban thermal characteristics.

The discovery of oil on the Alaskan north shore gives the potential for the development of a city in this area. At present an ecological study is being undertaken as part of the IBP Tundra Biome program at Point Barrow. In conjunction with this program, a numerical model has been used to simulate meteorological variables in the tundra (Lord *et al.*, 1972). Experience obtained with the model at other latitudes has suggested the validity and utility of the computer solutions (Pandolfo, 1969; Pandolfo and Jacobs, 1973). The model will be applied here to estimate changes in

microclimate that might be induced by urbanization in the tundra.

2. The numerical model

The numerical model is based on four Eulerian conservation equations given in Table 1 where $x_i \equiv x_i(x,y,z,t)$

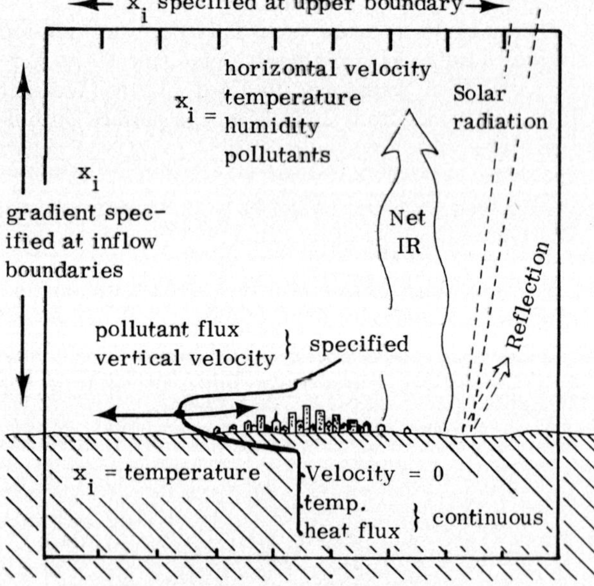

FIG. 1. Schematic diagram of the influences which were analyzed by the urban boundary layer model.

TABLE 1.

$$\frac{\partial}{\partial t}x_i + \mathbf{V}\cdot\nabla x_i + w\frac{\partial x_i}{\partial z} = S_i(x,y,z,t) + \frac{\partial}{\partial z}\left(K_z\frac{\partial x_i}{\partial z}\right) \quad (1)$$

i	x_i	S_i
1	u—eastward velocity	$f(v-v_g)$—geostrophic deviation
2	v—northward velocity	$f(u_g-u)$—geostrophic deviation
3	T—temperature	R,E—radiative and evaporative heat fluxes
4	q—specific humidity	E—evaporation
5	p_1—pollutant (aerosol)	Q—specified emissions

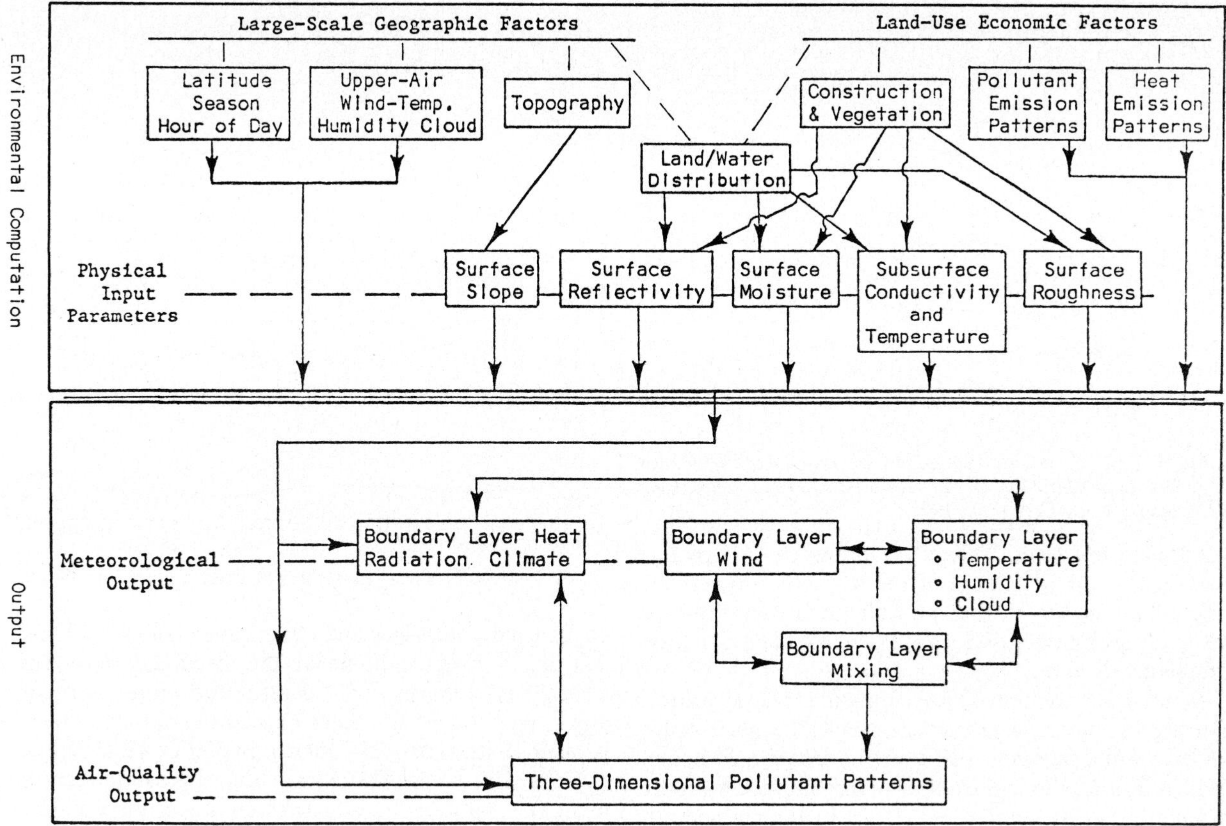

FIG. 2. Schematic diagram showing interaction of various input and computed parameters.

is the dependent variable, $\mathbf{V}$ is the horizontal wind vector, w is the vertical velocity, which is derived from the mass continuity equation, S_i is an appropriate source term, K_z is the vertical eddy diffusion coefficient, t is time, f is the Coriolis parameter, and z is height. The i variables and their corresponding source terms are listed in Table 1.

Pollutants, which can be included in the model, were omitted from these simulation experiments. Clouds, specified as a function of time, are included in the model. A schematic diagram is shown in Fig. 1.

The dependent variables are held constant at the upper boundary, about 2 km. The horizontal gradients are specified at the inflow boundaries, and the temperatures at the lower boundary of 1 to 3 m are held constant. The auxiliary variables are computed using a time step of 4.8 minutes. The finite-difference technique uses upwind differencing to approximate horizontal spatial differences. Center differences are used in vertical terms and are implicit in time. An alternative schematic diagram is shown in Fig. 2. This shows the interaction among various input and computed variables.

The major change from previous versions was in the thermal energy balance equation at the interface. Previously (Atwater, 1972), the heat source due to man was held constant. This was modified to make the heat source a function of temperature of the previous time step. The artificial heat term is now given by

$$R_x = R_c + R_v (65 - T) \quad T \leqslant 65 \text{ F}$$
$$R_x = R_c \qquad\qquad\qquad T > 65 \text{ F}$$

where R_x is the artificial heat, R_c is the artificial heat constant and R_v is the artificial heat variable.

In a paper being prepared for publication, the reliability of the model-generated daily fluxes have been compared with observations of Weller and Cubley (1972). Weller and Cubley made observations for five periods from May through September 1. Our simulated values were made for September 21. The daily fluxes as a function of date are shown on Fig. 3.

3. Experimental data

The experiments are designed to simulate the microclimate response to a hypothetical urban area in a

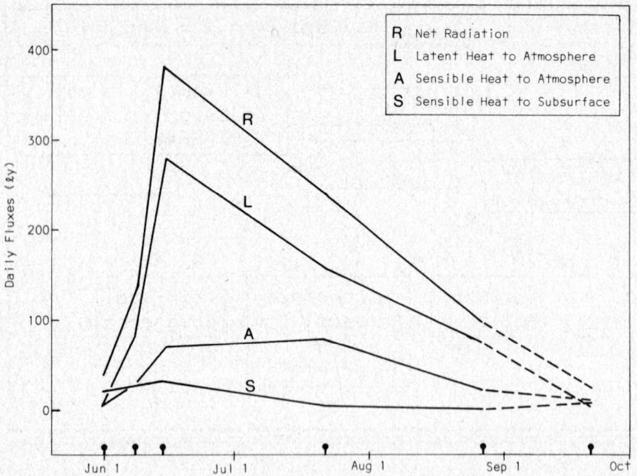

FIG. 3. Daily fluxes as a function of time using measured values of Weller and Cubley (1972) and simulated values for September 21 (from paper by Lord *et al.*, 1973).

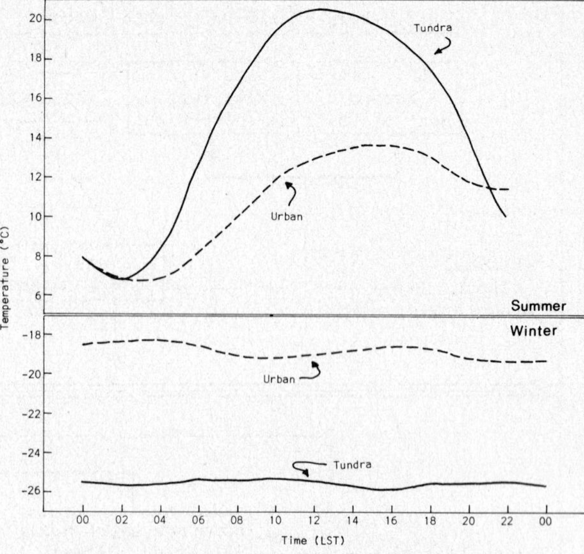

FIG. 4. Temperature at the interface as a function of time of day.

tundra environment. This is accomplished by a variation in the characteristics of the surface. A five-point grid is assumed in an east-west direction with distance between grid points of 8 km. The large-scale synoptic gradients are zero.

Simulations were made for both summer and winter. During the summer, the sun is above the horizon for 24 hours, and in winter below the horizon for 24 hours. The initial profiles and clouds for the summer were the same as used by Lord *et al.* (1974) in their report on tundra simulations. In the winter, a standard arctic sounding and climatological clouds were used. Values of the surface parameters in summer and winter are shown in Table 2.

Both summer and winter simulations start at midnight and run for 24 hours.

4. Results

The temperature in the summer lags the rise and fall of the sun. The temperature lag is less than two hours at the tundra interface and about seven hours at 100 m. The lag is about 4 hours at the urban interface. An example is shown in Fig. 4. During the winter, without any forcing by the sun, there are small variations of temperature with nearly the inertia period of 12.75 hours.

It is seen in the figure that the city is warmer at night (i.e., winter) than the surrounding countryside by

TABLE 2. Numerical value of interface parameters.

Parameter	Summer		Winter	
	Tundra	Urban	Tundra	Urban
Roughness height (cm)	1	100	1	100
Albedo	0.2	0.2	n.a.	n.a.
Soil-snow density (g cm^{-3})	2	2	0.5	0.7
Specific heat (cal °C^{-1} cm^{-3})	0.52	0.55	0.22	0.25
Moisture parameter*	0.1	0.05	0.05	0.05
Artificial heat constant (ly sec^{-1})	0	0.001	0	0.001
Artificial heat variable (ly sec^{-1} °C^{-1})	0	0.00016	0	0.00016
Soil thermal diffusivity (cm^2 sec^{-1})	0.02	0.02	0.014	0.009

* See Lord *et al.*, 1972.

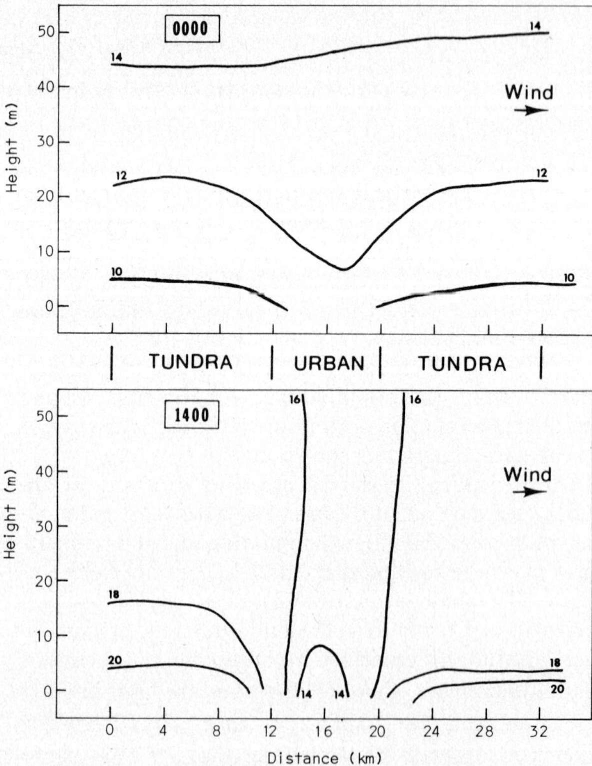

FIG. 5. Vertical temperature structure over a simulated urban area in the arctic in summer.

about 7 C. This is comparable to what has been observed in mid-latitude cities. The rural temperature excess during the day has been simulated by Nappo (1972) in the mid-latitudes and observed by Mitchell (1961) and by Hage (1972). Nappo stated for the mid-latitude that this occurs when there is little difference between rural and urban surface moisture sources.

The resultant vertical thermal structure is shown in Figs. 5 and 6. Fig. 5 is for summer, where at night the atmosphere is warmer over the urban area below heights of 20 m, and during the day the city and the air above the city up to 400 m is cooler than the surroundings. Fig. 6 shows the vertical thermal structure in the winter. The urban heat excess at the surface is 7 C, comparable with observation of the mid-latitude. There is little difference in rural and urban temperature above 100 m.

The specific humidity was up to 25 percent higher in the city during the summer day, with a reduced moisture availability. During the night and during the winter, there were no significant differences in specific humidity.

The simulation also shows some effects of the hypothetical urban area on the wind field. In the summer the wind speed was reduced up to 50 percent in the lowest 100 m over the simulated city. There were small changes at higher levels. In the winter, urbanization increased the wind speed below 50 m above the urban area and reduced wind speeds from 50 to 100 m. Landsberg (1970) has shown average reduction in wind speeds caused by urbanization to be about 20 to 30 percent in mid-latitudes.

Atmospheric vertical velocities are upward upwind of the city and downward downwind of the city during both summer and winter simulations. The simulated values are on the order of 1 cm sec,$^{-1}$ which is not insignificant when compared to natural vertical velocities.

The depth of the mixing layer in winter is increased by about 50 m over the city. In the summer, the depth of the mixing layer is reduced from greater than 1000 m to less than 100 m, as a result of the lower surface temperatures. This reduction should significantly increase the problem of air pollution in a future arctic city. In general, a reduction of this magnitude in the mixing layer would lead to an increase by a factor of 10 in the pollution concentrations.

5. Summary

Many of the environmental changes induced by urbanization in the mid-latitudes are found in the simulations of a city in the arctic tundra. This would include reduced wind speeds and an urban heat island when the sun is below or near the horizon. The vertical velocities are similar to those calculated in mid-latitude. The major differences in these simulations, when compared with simulations and observations of the mid-latitudes, is the much larger summer urban deficit of

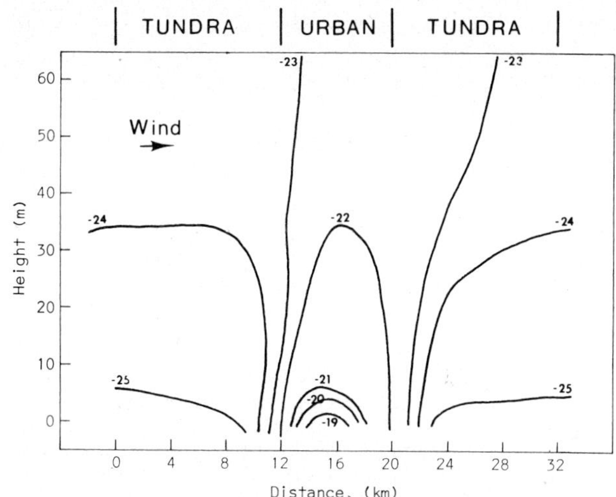

FIG. 6. Vertical temperature structure over a simulated urban area in the arctic in winter.

temperature compared with the surrounding area. Further, this results in a more shallow mixing layer. The results of this would be to increase the problem of pollutants in a city in the arctic tundra.

Future work will be to repeat these simulations with the inclusion of pollutants.

Acknowledgements. This work was part of, and funded by, the International Biological Program (Tundra Biome) of the National Science Foundation (Grant GB-25064). The numerical computations were performed at the University of Connecticut Computer Center.

REFERENCES

Atwater, M. A., 1972: Thermal effects of urbanization and industrialization in the boundary layer. A numerical study. *Boundary-Layer Meteor.*, **3**, 229–245.

Hage, K. D., 1972: Nocturnal temperature in Edmonton, Alberta, *J. Appl. Meteor.*, **11**, 123–129.

Landsberg, H. E., 1970: Climate and urban planning, *Urban Climates* (Geneva, Secretariat of WMO), p. 372.

Lord, N. W., J. P. Pandolfo and M. A. Atwater, 1972: Simulation of meteorological variation over Arctic coastal tundra under perturbed physical interface conditions. *Arctic and Alpine Res.*, **4**, 189–209.

Lord, N. W., M. A. Atwater and J. P. Pandolfo, 1974: Influence of the interaction between tundra thaw lakes and surrounding land. *Arctic and Alpine Res.*, **6**, 143–150.

Mitchell, J. M., Jr., 1961: The temperatures of cities. *Weatherwise*, **14**, 224–229.

Nappo, C. J., 1972: A numerical study of the urban heat island. *Proc., Conf. on Urban Environment*, Amer. Meteor. Soc., 1–4.

Pandolfo, J. P., 1969: Motions with inertial and diurnal period in a numerical model of the navifacial boundary layer. *J. Mar. Res.*, **27**, 301–317.

Pandolfo, J. P., and C. A. Jacobs, 1973: *Tests of an Urban Meteorological-Pollutant Model Using CO Validation Data in the Los Angeles Metropolitan Area*, Vol. 1, CEM Rpt. #490a, Final Report for EPA, Contract 68-02-0223, 176 pp.

Weller, G., and S. Cubley, 1972: Microclimates of the Arctic tundra. *Proc., 1972 Tundra Biome Symposium*, Lake Wilderness Center, University of Wash., 5–12.

Low Cloud Cover and the Winter Temperature of Fairbanks

K. O. L. F. JAYAWEERA, G. WENDLER AND T. OHTAKE

Geophysical Institute, University of Alaska, Fairbanks, Alaska 99701

Abstract

The paper will discuss the effects of low level cloud cover on the changes of the temperature of Fairbanks. Because Fairbanks is located in a valley in the interior of Alaska, the results presented in this paper may be applicable to similar locations in the Arctic land masses. The paper will be divided into three parts.

The first part will discuss the decrease of air temperature with time at various heights above Fairbanks, after clearing of the sky. Graphs showing the temperature at 2.5 cm, 1, 4, 8, 16 and 200 m at various times will be shown in order to illustrate the cooling at various levels and the formation of surface inversions. Energy balance computations will be presented which show that the radiation loss under clear skies is compensated mainly by sensible heat (62%) and soil heat flux (32%) while condensation contributes only a small 6%.

The second part of the paper will discuss the increase of the 1 m air temperature of Fairbanks when the sky is completely cloud covered after a clear period. Here only cases of low clouds (below 7000 ft, cloud base) and 100% cloud cover will be considered. The increase in surface temperature is plotted as a function of time with cloud base temperatures grouped in 5 C ranges varying from 0 to −25 C. The rate of increase of temperature will be compared with the expression of Brunt and the discrepancies discussed.

The final part of the paper will discuss the theory and experiments behind the generation of artificial clouds over an area under clear sky so as to inhibit radiative cooling. The results of the 1972/73 experiments showing the number of occasions suitable conditions existed for forming artificial clouds and the radiation effects of these clouds will be discussed. The small amounts of cloud cover that were produced during the experiments were not sufficient to obtain any significant change in the hemispherical radiation or the ground temperature but an indication of the radiative properties of these clouds were obtained using the Linke-Feussner actinometer with a 5° angle of view.

---

1. Introduction

The polar regions are the sinks in the earth's heat balance, especially in winter, due to lack of solar radiation. When clouds are present, a radiation balance near equilibrium between the lower boundary of the clouds and the earth's surface will be reached. However, when the sky is clear there is a steady loss from the surface owing to the negative long-wave radiation balance. A strong surface inversion is thereby developed, and temperatures below the mean for the season are observed to affect the climate near the surface, where it matters most as far as human activity is concerned.

Bilello (1966) has found by analysing the radiosonde data for 9 years that for Fairbanks (64°50′N and 147°40′W), a typical town situated in the continental climate of Central Alaska near the arctic circle and surrounded on three sides by hills, that the frequency of surface inversions for both day and night is highest at 82% for the coldest months (Dec.–Jan.), and averages 68% for the winter months (Nov.–April), and 37% for the summer (May–Oct.). A strong connection between the occurrence of lowest temperatures in Fairbanks with high pressure systems and clear skies has been found by Bowling *et al.* (1968). When the cloudiness decreases, a sharp temperature drop at the surface is observed and the surface inversion is built up. On the other hand with the onset of cloudiness the temperature increases and reaches a maximum determined by the temperature of the cloud.

This paper is an attempt to explain such drastic changes in the surface temperature with the change in cloudiness in terms of the various energy fluxes and discuss the theory and experiments on the formation of artificial clouds to reduce the radiative losses of the ground.

The paper will be divided into three parts:

The effect of a decrease in cloudiness on the air temperature and the development of inversions.

The effect of the onset of cloudiness on the increase in surface temperature.

Studies on the formation of artificial clouds.

2. The effect of decrease in cloudiness on the air temperature and the development of inversions

Descriptions of the observations

We have in this study used the meteorological data for Fairbanks, which is a typical city of the polar regions. Meteorological data is readily available for

Fairbanks and discussions on its climate as a case study for polar regions are available in the literature, thereby aiding the present sudy.

The effects of decreasing cloudiness can be studied best when the diurnal temperature variation is small. Therefore midwinter, when solar effects on the diurnal temperature variation tend to be small (U. S. Army 1966/67), is the ideal time for this study. We have investigated only five cases, which occurred during the periods 15 Nov. 1966 to 28 Feb. 1967 and 15 Nov. to 31 Dec. 1967. This limitation was imposed by the following reasons: (1) Only during these periods were detailed micrometeorological measurements pertinent to our study available. (2) The cloudiness had to be >8/10 for at least 12 hours and thereafter should drop to <2/10 within 9 hours. Owing to these relatively strict requirements, which were necessary to study the cooling rates, only five cases were available during the time of detailed observations.

Our analysis was based on the following measurements which were carried out by the U. S. Army (U. S. Army, 1966/67) and the Weather Bureau (Haggard 1966/67). The air temperatures were measured at 5 different levels (1, 2, 4, 8 and 16 m) with ventilated thermocouples, the outputs of which were continuously recorded. Furthermore, the surface temperatures, the snow/soil interface temperatures, and the soil temperature at 2.5, 15 and 50 cm in depth were measured. The wind speeds were obtained at four altitudes (1, 4, 8 and 16 m) with cup anemometers, the relative humidity was recorded at one height (2 m) and

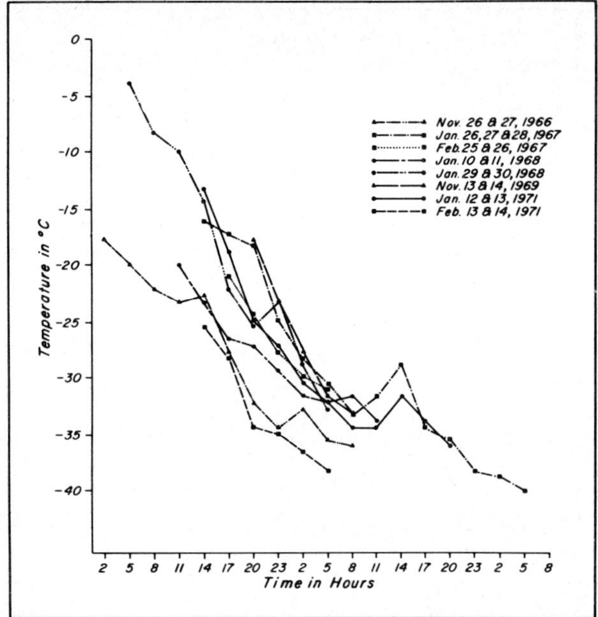

FIG. 1. The decrease in air temperature in winter, after the sky had become clear, for individual events in Fairbanks, Central Alaska. The data presented are for selected winter values during the years 1966–1971. Note that the cooling rate is fairly similar for most of the cases, though sometimes disturbed by the diurnal temperature variation.

the cloudiness was observed every 3 hours. The net radiation was measured with ventilated Beckman and Whitley radiometers, the outputs of which were con-

TABLE 1. Some climatological data for the five periods when rapid surface cooling was observed in Central Alaska. Notice the strong surface cooling in the valley, while on Birch Hill, which is situated 200 m above the valley floor, cooling rates were small and in one case (No. 4) even a slight warming was observed.

Period no.	1	2	3	4	5	Units
Date	26–27 Nov 66	25–26 Feb 67	26–27 Jan 67	10 Feb 67	25 Nov 67	
Length of period	16	16	14	8	6	hours
Air temp in valley at beginning of period	−23.8	−19.0	−20.3	−17.6	−20.6	°C
Air temp in valley at end of period	−39.9	−33.5	−36.1	−30.2	−29.4	°C
ΔT (valley)	−16.1	−14.5	−15.8	−12.6	−8.8	°C
ΔT/hour (valley)	−1.01	−0.91	−1.13	−1.58	−1.47	°C hr^{-1}
Air temp Birch Hill at beginning of period	−17.1	−17.2	−16.8	−17.3	−17.4	°C
Air temp Birch Hill at end of period	−19.1	−20.1	−21.6	−16.2	−18.2	°C
ΔT (Birch Hill)	−2.0	−2.9	−4.8	+1.1	−0.8	°C
ΔT/hour (Birch Hill)	−0.13	−0.18	−0.34	+0.14	−0.13	°C hr^{-1}
Mean wind speed 16 m (valley)	50	42	52	56	67	cm sec^{-1}
Net radiation, valley	−53.0	−42.0	−49.0	−22.5	−27.5	cal cm^{-2} period^{-1}
Mean net radiation, valley	−3.3	−2.6	−3.5	−2.8	−4.6	cal cm^{-2} hour^{-1}
Snow depth, valley	80	57	55	57	17	cm

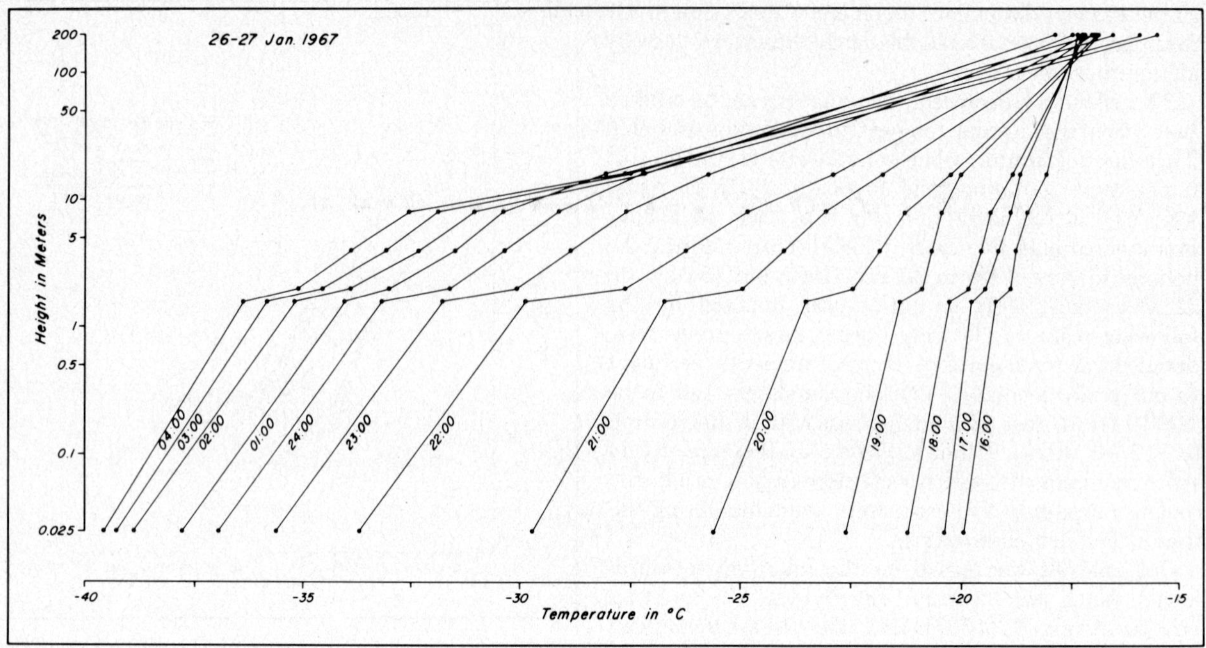

FIG. 2. The temperature in the lowest 200 m in Fairbanks, Central Alaska, on 26/27 Jnauary 1967. The temperature profile is given in hourly intervals, after the sky had become clear. Notice how the inversion becomes stronger with time.

tinuously recorded. The instrument measures the sum total of long and short wave radiation, which in our case is almost equal to long wave balance, as the short wave radiation is negligible. Furthermore, the air temperature was measured on Birch Hill, a hill situated 7 km NNE of the valley station and 200 m above the valley floor.

Results

The rate of decrease of temperature with time, after the sky has become clear ($<2/10$), was in excess of 1 C per hour for the first 10 hours after which the cooling rate slowed down somewhat. This rate of cooling is rather typical for Fairbanks valley, as can be seen from the individual cases shown in Fig. 1. The very similar cooling rates, in most cases, show that the five cases we selected for detailed analysis are not exceptional.

In Table 1 the climatological data are given for the 5 periods. The length of the cooling time was in some cases limited by the mid-day heating, which disturbs the smooth decrease in temperature (see Fig. 1). Thus, all calculations were terminated by mid-morning, and the periods discussed here varied in length from 6 to 16 hours. At the beginning of the cooling period when the cloud cover was $>8/10$, temperatures around -20 C, which is near the long-term mean for this season (Searby, 1968), were observed. During the next 6–16 hours, with the cloudiness dropping to $<2/10$, the temperature decreased to between -30 C and -40 C, which is even below the long-term mean low.

During these times the wind speeds were low (Table I), which is in agreement with values found for

cold spells by Benson and Weller (1970) and Wendler (1969). The net radiation was negative and values around -3 cal cm^{-2} hour^{-1} were found, while the depth of the snow cover depended, naturally, on the time of the year.

In order to illustrate the change of the vertical temperature profile between the valley and Birch Hill (200 m) after the initiation of a cooling period, and the higher rate of cooling of the valley during the initial stages of cooling, we have plotted in Fig. 2 the hourly temperature at various heights above the valley for one of the five periods we selected, 26/27 Jan. 1967. On this day the cooling period began at 14:00 AST on the 26th and continued until 04:00 AST next day. The temperature at Birch Hill remained very much the same between -15 C and -18 C all through the period while the valley temperature dropped from -20 C to -40 C. The largest value for cooling in the valley was observed in the first 7 hours, in which time the temperature dropped to -36 C, giving a cooling of 16 C, while in the next five hours the cooling was only by 4 C.

Calculation of the energy balance

For any given period, the simplified heat balance fluxes across a surface are expressed by the following equation:

$$R+S+L+B=0,$$

where

$R=$ Radiation flux
$S=$ Sensible heat flux
$L=$ Latent heat flux
$B=$ Soil heat flux.

TABLE 2. The heat balance for the 5 cooling periods.

Period no.	1	2	3	4	5	
Radiation-balance (R)	−53.0	−42.0	−49.0	−22.5	−27.5	cal cm^{-2} period^{-1}
Sensible heat flux (S)	35.6	21.6	31.3	16.0	10.6	cal cm^{-2} period^{-1}
Latent heat flux (L)	3.5	2.1	2.8	1.6	1.2	cal cm^{-2} period^{-1}
Soil heat flux (B)	13.9*	18.3*	14.9*	4.9*	14.2	cal cm^{-2} period^{-1}
Radiation balance (R)	−3.3	−2.6	−3.5	−2.8	−4.6	cal cm^{-2} hour^{-1}
Sensible heat flux (S)	2.2	1.4	2.2	2.0	1.8	cal cm^{-2} hour^{-1}
Latent heat flux (L)	0.2	0.1	0.2	0.2	0.2	cal cm^{-2} hour^{-1}
Soil heat flux (B)	0.9*	1.1*	1.1*	0.6*	2.3	cal cm^{-2} hour^{-1}

* means that this value was obtained as the remainder of the heat balance equation.

All fluxes towards the surface are considered to be positive and those away from the surface, negative. We will now proceed to estimate the four components of the fluxes from the available measurements.

(a) RADIATION FLUX

The flux of radiation was measured with the previously described instrument and hourly values of the radiation budget are given in lines 2 and 6 of Table 2.

(b) SENSIBLE HEAT FLUX

Sensible heat flux can be calculated from the wind and temperature profiles according to the theories presented by Prandtl (1956) and Lettau (1939, 1949). The calculated values using the measured wind and temperature profiles are given in lines 2 and 4 of Table 3. The theories used in this calculation, however, are based on the assumption that the atmosphere is adiabatic and no advection occurs. But in our case very stable conditions are present, which suppresses mixing, resulting in estimates for the calculated values of S which are too high. To correct for this by use of the Richardson number (e.g., Ambach, 1963) was not possible, as the correction formula is not applicable for the very high Richardson numbers characteristic of our case. The sensible heat could also be estimated from the amount of energy released during the cooling of the atmosphere provided that there is no advection of cold air. This amount of energy K is given by the equation:

$$K = c_p \rho \int_{Z_2}^{Z_1} (\Delta T) dZ$$

TABLE 3. The observed cooling of the air (K) and the sensible heat flux (S) calculated after Lettau (1939, 1949) for 5 periods in Fairbanks, Central Alaska.

Period no.	1	2	3	4	5	
K	50.0	29.0	52.0	10.4	9.8	cal cm^{-2} period^{-1}
S	35.6	21.6	31.3	16.0	10.6	cal cm^{-2} period^{-1}
K	3.1	1.9	3.7	1.3	1.6	cal cm^{-2} hr^{-1}
S	2.2	1.4	2.2	2.0	1.8	cal cm^{-2} hr^{-1}

where

c_p = specific heat of air
ρ = density of air
Z_1 = surface height
Z_2 = height where the temperature change is zero
ΔT = temperature change at an arbitrary height Z.

K was calculated for the five cases and the results are given in lines 1 and 3 of Table 3.

In these calculations we have assumed that the temperature, either 2 m or 16 m above the ground at Birch Hill, corresponds to the free air temperature at the same elevation directly above the valley station. By doing so, a certain amount of error may be involved. But this error will be similar throughout the cooling period. Since we have used the difference in temperature at the end and beginning of the cooling period in calculating D, the error of temperature difference involved in the calculation is small. Further, much higher winds at Birch Hill than in the valley (Wendler, 1971, U. S. Army 1966/67) tends to minimize the temperature differences at the same elevation.

The calculated value of K represents the total amount of heat released during the cooling of the air above the valley. If no advection or drainage of cold air took place, then this value of K can be assumed to represent the net balance of sensible heat flux. But comparison of K with S suggests that for the two short periods S is larger than K (No. 4) or the agreement is good (No. 5). However, for longer periods (Nos. 1 to 3), K is bigger than S, even though values for S represent rather an upper limit. The most plausible explanation for this could be that advection of cold air has taken place from the surrounding hills into Fairbanks valley adding to the accumulation of cold air. Understandably, therefore, the longer the cooling period the larger is the effect due to drainage of cold air. Confirmation of this occurrence of cold air advection is seen from the observations of Benson and Weller (1970). Comparison for the values for K and S for longer periods suggests that drainage of cold air contributes to about a third of the observed heat loss of the air layer above the valley.

(c) Latent heat flux

To calculate the latent heat flux, water-saturated air was assumed for the lowest meters of the atmosphere. This is normally the case, since after a sharp temperature decrease, saturation is realized very quickly. With this assumption the latent heat flux can be calculated by knowing the temperature profile for the cases considered. In the five cases we studied, this flux is positive and small (0.2 cal. cm^{-2} hr^{-1}, see Table 2, line 8) in comparison to the other heat fluxes. Because of this small contribution of the latent heat flux to the heat balance as a whole, the possible error which would occur, even if saturation were not present in the air at all times, is negligible.

(d) Soil heat flux

The soil heat flux could not be calculated, as the temperature profile in the snow cover was not measured. However, in case No. 5, the snow cover was thin enough (17 cm) so that the temperature change could be estimated by knowing the surface temperature as well as the temperature profile of the soil. The value of B calculated for this case together with the other heat fluxes satisfy the heat balance equation very well. Because of this agreement, the values for B for the other cases were assumed to be the remainder of the heat balance equation when R, S and L are substituted.

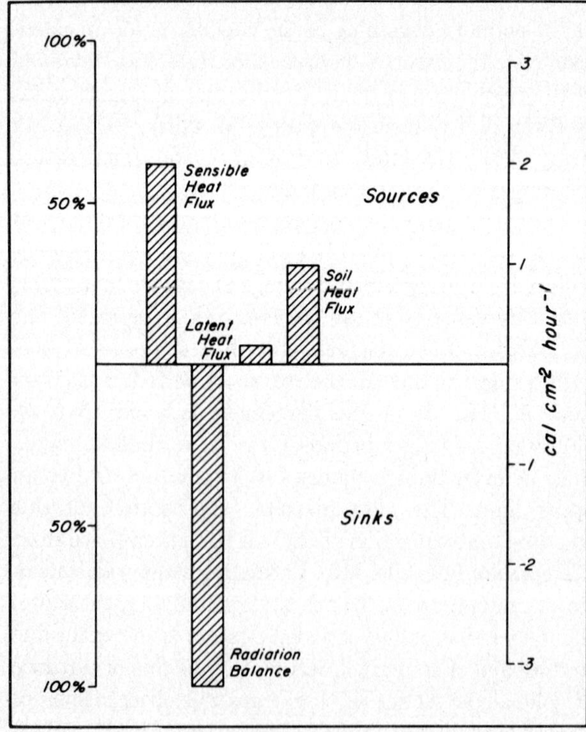

Fig. 3. An estimate of the heat balance for the mean of the 5 periods as the sky becomes clear. The only energy sink is the radiation balance. This loss is compensated by sensible 62%, latent 6% and soil heat flux 32%.

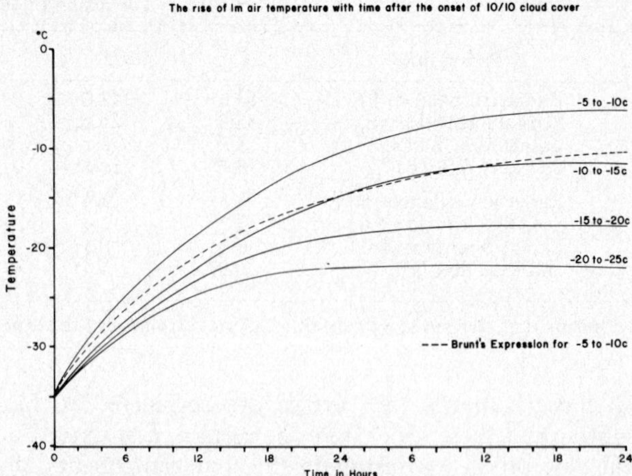

Fig. 4. The rise of 1 m air temperature with time after the onset of 10/10 cloud cover. The initial time is selected when the air temperature is −35 C.

Mean energy fluxes

The five cases we discussed represent typical cooling conditions for the coldest months in Fairbanks under clear skies. The energy fluxes of the five periods were used to determine their relative importance in the heat balance of Fairbanks in which the three non-radiative fluxes should together balance the radiative loss. In Figure 3 we have plotted the mean fluxes for the five periods in absolute units as well as a percentage of the total negative radiation balance. From this figure we see that the sensible heat flux compensates 62% of the radiation loss; soil heat flux, 32% and latent heat a small 6%. The low contribution by latent heat indicates that the amount of condensation is small during these cooling periods. The values found here agree in general with those for other areas under similar conditions (Niederdorfer, 1933; Miller, 1956; Wendler, 1971).

3. The effect of cloudiness on the surface temperature

Analysis of data.

In contrast to the case of clear skies, the increase in surface temperature with the onset of cloudiness depends on the cloud cover, cloud base temperature and the cloud height. Therefore we have to impose further limitations for this study in addtion to those discussed in Section 1.1. Our analyses were confined only to cases where the sky was completely covered ($>8/10$) with low stratus (<7000 ft base height) after a period of at least twelve hours of $<2/10$ cloudiness. The change in cloudiness from 2/10 to 8/10 should occur within 9 hours and the clouds had to remain for at least 24 hours. These conditions were arbitrarily chosen so that the change in cloudiness would show a real effect on the 1 m air temperatures and not a transient effect. The clouds were divided into different categories according to the base temperature. We grouped the clouds in 5 C temperature intervals covering a range from −5 to −25 C. The 1.5 m air temperature recorded by the National Weather Service, Fairbanks, were then plotted for various groups of clouds as a function of time.

The individual temperatures plotted against time showed a considerable scatter. However if the time axis were shifted so that zero time corresponded to a fixed temperature of −35 C, they showed remarkable similarity in the shape, so that it became possible to draw a mean curve. In Figure 4 these curves for the 4 different cloud base groups are shown.

Results

All the temperature-time curves with onset of cloudiness showed that initially the temperature rose sharply and later settled to a constant temperature within the temperature range of the clouds. These indicate that on the average, the air temperature can be expected to reach the cloud temperature thereby establishing radiative equilibrium with the cloud. Another important observation is the time lag that is required to reach equilibrium. This time increases as the temperature differential between cloud and ground increases from about 18 hours for a cloud temperature between −20 and −25 C to a mean of about 36 hours for cloud temperature between −5 to −10 C.

Due to the lack of any other numerical expression with which to compare this observed mean rate of heating, we have used the expression given by Brunt (1939) in which temperature change (ΔT) for a given interval of time in the absence of solar radiation is given by:

$$\Delta T = \frac{-2}{\pi} \frac{(\sigma T_0{}^4 - R_A)}{\rho c \lambda} t$$

where

$\sigma T_0{}^4$ = outgoing long wave radiation
R_A = incoming long wave radiation = $\sigma T_c{}^4$
ρ = density of the surface material
c = specific heat of the surface material
λ = thermal conductivity of the surface material
t = time
T_0 = surface temperature
T_c = mean temperature of cloud base

This equation is applicable for periods of our study because there is no incoming solar radiation and $\sigma(T_c{}^4 - T_0{}^4)$ represents the net incoming radiation. Since the surface is snow, the density, specific heat and thermal conductivity are known to reasonable accuracy. Therefore this equation can be used to calculate the warming within a given interval of time. The increase of temperature with time using this expression is shown in Fig. 4 for the mean cloud temperature of −7.5 C. The theoretical curve consistently gives a slower rise of temperature than observed. The lower heating predicted by Brunt may be the consequence of neglect of convection or advection that may take place with the warming of the surface.

4. Studies on the formation of artificial clouds

Introduction

The formation of a cloud in the atmosphere at a temperature below 0 C can be accomplished by the introduction of ice crystals into air containing more water vapor than would be present at the saturation point with respect to ice. Seeding with dry ice powder or liquid propane, which produces temperatures of approximately −80 C, results in the condensation of water vapor from the air followed by the spontaneous freezing of the water droplets thus formed. In ice-supersaturated air, such ice crystals grow to larger sizes and a cloud is formed. In order to find out whether the air is ice-saturated or not, it is useful to employ in addition to a radiosonde another small balloon onto which is attached a small piece of dry ice in a thin cloth bag. When the dry ice penetrates the ice-saturated air, it forms a condensation trail which produces a small-scale seeding of the atmosphere. If the trail persists or grows, this indicates that the air is ice-supersaturated. This is a usable technique to compensate for the relatively unreliable measurement of humidity by radiosonde hygristor sensors (humidity sensors) at low temperatures.

The preliminary experiment was carried out on 18 January 1972 in the Fairbanks area. At 13:00 A.S.T. a rawinsonde balloon onto which was attached about 200 g of dry ice detected ice-saturated air in a layer between 1000 and 2000 feet (300 and 600 m) from the ground. The radiosonde reported an isothermal temperature of −26 C in this layer.

Using a light aircraft, we seeded clear air at a height of 2000 feet (temperature, −20 C) above the ground level (ground temperature, −32 C) at 13:40 A.S.T. with about 5 kg of dry ice powder. Just after seeding, we observed the formation of cloud cells which grew and merged into a larger, uniform thin cloud. The size of the cloud 20 minutes after seeding was approximately 1 km in diameter with a thickness of a few hundred feet. There were no other clouds in the sky, and there was a slight wind from the east-southeast. The cloud grew to a greater depth (approximately 500 feet or more) and drifted out of sight $1\frac{1}{2}$ hours later.

In the winter of 1972–73 similar experiments were performed to determine the following: (1) the number of occasions on which suitable conditions occur for cloud making and (2) the radiative properties of these clouds.

In order to determine the first objective pilot balloons with dry ice were released on all clear days when the surface temperature was below −20 C. If suitable conditions occurred all attempts were made to produce artificial clouds.

The radiative properties of these clouds were measured using a PD-4 Davos radiometer and a Linke-Feussner actinometer. The PD-4 was used to measure the total hemispherical radiation if a large cloud was made. The Linke-Feussner was used to infer the radia-

TABLE 4. Statistics on the relevent meteorological conditions pertaining to cloud formation during the winter 1972–73 for Fairbanks.

Month	Number of clear days <3/10 cloud cover	Number of clear days with ice saturated layers between 0 to 2000 m	Number of clear days with surface inversions and temperature −25 C	Ice fog days	Suitable days cloud formation
November	7	0	0	0	0
December	11	4	9	6	4
January	20	11	4	17	4
February	15	0	2	0	0

tive temperature of these clouds. This instrument has the advantage of finding the radiative temperature even of a small cloud.

Results

The winter of 1972–73 was a relatively warm one for Fairbanks, Alaska. The temperatures for all the winter months except January were above normal. Table 4 summarizes the number of clear days and suitable occasions for seeding. These results were based only on daylight conditions because the balloon observations cannot be made otherwise. Although the month of December was relatively warm last year, the proportion of the number of clear days to ice fog events and days with inversions was typical for this time of the year. Of the 11 clear days, 9 had temperatures below −25 C with surface inversions, and ice fog events were recorded by the National Weather Service on 6 days. In January, on the other hand, conditions were far from typical. Of the 20 clear days with 17 days of recorded ice fog only 4 days had a surface inversion. The rest of the 16 days there was no surface inversion and nearly isothermal conditions existed up to 2000 m. As a result, the fog extended high above the ground and the National Weather Service reported 100% cloud cover and no ceiling. These days were not suitable for seeding. Hence during the whole winter period only 8 days were suitable for cloud formation, although for 15 out of the 31 clear days ice-saturated conditions suitable for cloud making existed between the ground and 2000 m. The small number of occasions suitable for cloud formation was a reflection of the unusually warm winter conditions this year. It is very unlikely that such conditions will occur again, hence we hope there will be more occasions for cloud formation in the coming winters.

The amount of dry ice used for any experiment was about 150 lbs. This was curshed to about 1 cm size particles and manually dispersed from an open door in the aircraft. This method was very inefficient due to the following:

1) The dry ice pellets coagulate and tend to fall as a lump.

2) The dispersion was intermittent and no control on the amount or rate of dispersion could be made.

3) The dry ice pellets fall through the layer to the ground at a high speed so that only a small fraction of the actual mass is utilized for cloud formation.

The clouds that were made during these experiments were thin and patchy. The maximum cloud cover never exceeded more than 2/10. Hence the PD-4 Davos radiometer showed no response. However the Linke-Feussner actinometer showed a considerable effect from the cloud. It indicated that the radiation emitted from these clouds was about 60% of that of a black body having the cloud temperature.

The inability to form a cloud over an area the size of Fairbanks (10 km²) and hence the inability to find an appreciable effect on the temperature, we feel is due to the inefficient dispersion system used for dry ice and the inability to utilize the full extent of the supersaturated layer. Therefore we propose to continue the experiment during the next winter with the dry ice dispersed in a near-powder form from an on-board crusher, either manually operated or battery powered. The dry ice will be dispersed by means of a tube passing through a hole in the aircraft rear door.

Acknowledgment. This work was supported by National Science Foundation Grant GI-35664 and State of Alaska funds.

REFERENCES

Ambach, W., 1963: Untersuchungen zum Energieumsatz in der Ablationszone des Grönländischen Inlandeises. *Meddelser om Gronland*, **174**, 4, 311 p.

Benson, C., and G. Weller, 1970: A study of low-level winds in the vicinity of Fairbanks, Alaska. Report to Earth Resources Co., Geophysical Institute, University of Alaska, College, Alaska.

Bilello, M. A., 1966: Survey of Arctic and sub-Arctic temperature inversions. CRREL, Technical Report 161, 36 p.

Bowling, S., T. Ohtake and C. Benson, 1968: Winter pressure systems and ice fog in Fairbanks, Alaska. *Journal of Applied Meteorology*, **7**, 6, 961–968.

Brunt, David, 1939: Physical and dynamical meteorology, 2nd ed. Cambridge, Eng., Cambridge University Press, 428 pp.

Haggard, H., 1966–67: Local climatological data, Fairbanks, Alaska, International Airport. U. S. Department of Commerce, ESSA.

Lettau, H., 1939: Atmosphärische Turbulenz. Akademische Verlagsgesellschaft, Leipzig.

Lettau, H., 1949: Isotropic and non-isotropic turbulence in the atmospheric surface layer. Geophysical Res. Pap., No. 1, Cambridge, Mass.

Miller, D. H., 1956: The influence of snow cover on local climate in Greenland. *Journal of Meteorology*, **13**, 112–120.

Niederdorfer, E., 1933: Messungen des Wärmeumsatzes über schneebedecktem Boden. *Meteorologische Zeitschrift* **50**, 201–208.

Prandtl, L., 1956: Führer durch die Strömungslehre. 4. Auflage Braunschweig, F. Vieweg und Sohn, 407 p.

U. S. Army Meteorological Team Data, Ft. Wainwright, Alaska. U. S. Army Electronics Command Fort Huachuca, Arizona, 1966/67.

Wendler, G., 1969: Heat balance studies during an ice-fog period in Fairbanks, Alaska. *Monthly Weather Review*, **97**, 512–520.

Wendler, G., 1971: The estimate of a heat balance for a valley and a hill station in central Alaska. *Journal of Applied Meteorology*, **10**, 4, 684–693.

Operational Cold Fog Dissipation in Alaska

JAMES L. WISE

11th Weather Squadron, Elmendorf AFB, Alaska

Abstract

This paper describes the theoretical basis for cold fog dissipation, the history of cold fog dissipation at Elmendorf AFB, and concludes with the present propane dispensing cold fog dissipation system. The theoretical basis for the dissipation of cold fog; (i.e., fog in which the visibility restriction is composed of suspended liquid water droplets at temperatures below 0 C) is the Bergeron-Findeisen ice crystal process. Because of structural differences, an ice crystal has a lower vapor pressure than a water droplet at the same temperature. Therefore, the introduction of ice crystals into a supercooled cloud mass or fog results in the growth of the ice crystals at the expense of the cloud droplets. The ice crystals grow to a size too large to be supported in the cloud and then precipitate as snow. The process requires 45 minutes to one-and-one-half hours for clearing to be effected.

The history of cold fog dissipation began at Elmendorf in the 1965–66 winter season. In early experiments, generation of ice crystals in the cold fog was accomplished by attaching small cakes of dry ice to free or tethered balloons. Due to the late start in that season, testing of the same procedure was again conducted in the 1966–67 winter season. At the end of the 1966–67 season it was concluded that fog dissipation by the use of dry ice attached to free or tethered balloons was neither effective nor practical due to the manpower involved to comply with flying safety requirements, the inaccessibility of the area to be seeded upwind from the runway, and the amount of time required to position men and material.

During the winter season of 1967–68, Air Weather Serivce tested the airborne seeding of cold fog with crushed dry ice dispensed from a WC-130 aircraft. Seeding patterns and rates were theoretically determined and empirically refined. Cold fog dissipation by airborne seeding with crushed dry ice became a routine operation for the following five winters. Airborne seeding required the flying of a specific pattern in which an area no smaller than 2 by 5 miles was seeded in lanes 3000 to 6000 feet apart, 45 minutes to one-and-one-half hours upwind from the Elmendorf AFB runway complex. During this period operational clearing of cold fog was a success; however, several drawbacks remained. The operation of the system, including maintenance of the aircraft, costs for aircrews, maintenance personnel, dry ice and other expendable supplies, amounted to 300 to 500 thousand dollars per season. Total costs varied with the amount of cold fog and the number of seeding aircraft involved.

In the meantime another system for clearing cold fog became operational at Orly Airport, France. This method consists of spraying liquid propane into the cold fog in order to generate ice crystals. This system was initially tested and put into operation at Fairchild AFB, Washington, in the winter of 1967–68. Programming for a propane dispensing system at Elmendorf AFB began in the fall of 1970. The installation was ready for operation by the end of 1971. However, little or no cold fog occurred in early 1972. Operational testing and evaluation of the propane system was completed during the 1972–73 winter. The airborne system acted as back-up and was also an observational platform for recording the success or failure of the propane dispensing system. There were some phenomenally successful cold fog dissipation cases early in the season. However, there were also failures during periods of calm winds and patchy ground fog when the air mass containing the fog did not flow from the locations of the dispensers to the runway area. The propane system has several advantages over the airborne system, the most obvious of which is reduced cost. Since the propane dispensing sites are remotely controlled by radio, the reaction time for initiating clearing actions is reduced.

The paper further discusses measures of success in cold fog dissipation, local terrain features in the vicinity of Elmendorf AFB, the physical layout of the propane dispensing system, environmental aspects on the use of odorless liquid propane, and anticipated actions to improve the performance of the system during periods of calm or very light winds.

For the purpose of this presentation, we will define three forms of fog: ice fog, cold fog and warm fog. ICE FOG is that fog in which the visibility restriction is due to ice crystals suspended in the atmosphere. It is usually caused by human activity but in the polar regions it can form naturally with temperatures colder than −20 F. More often it is found in the vicinity of man and his activities which introduce moisture into the atmosphere by the combustion of fossil fuels.

COLD FOG, sometimes called super-cooled fog, is that fog in which the visibility restriction consists of liquid water droplets at temperatures below freezing. It is quite common at several locations in Alaska. This type of fog is unstable and can be dissipated by the introduction of sublimation or freezing nuclei, in the form of ice crystals or a glacogenic material such as silver iodide. This type of fog has been successfully dissipated at several locations for the past 5 to 10 years.

WARM FOG is that fog where the visibility restriction consists of water droplets at temperatures above freezing. Cold fog dissipation techniques are not effective with this type of fog.

The theory for the physical process used in the dissipation of cold fog has been around for quite some time. Experiments in dissipating stratus type clouds date back to the 1940's. The process is the application of the Bergeron-Findeisen theory of the growth of precipitation. The basis of this theory is the fact that the equilibrium vapor pressure of water vapor with respect to ice is less than that with respect to water at the same subfreezing temperature. Thus, within an admixture of these particles, and provided that the total water content were sufficiently high, the ice crystals would gain mass by sublimation at the expense of the liquid drops which would lose mass by evaporation. Upon attaining sufficient weight, the ice crystals fall as snow and very likely become further modified by accretion, melting, and/or evaporation before reaching the ground. The theory was first proposed by T. Bergeron in 1933 and further developed by W. Findeisen. Certain of its features had been suggested by A. Wegener as early as 1911. The process is not instantaneous but requires a minimum of 45 minutes for snow to precipitate out and visibility to improve. Fog does not completely dissipate but a sufficient reduction in the amount of fog can take place to allow for safe aircraft operations.

Elmendorf AFB is located on the Knik Arm of the Cook Inlet. The approach end of the primary runway is about one mile from the water's edge. The Cook Inlet is subject to large tides often on the order of 30 ft difference between high and low tides on a particular day. Therefore, the inlet seldom freezes completely, even in the coldest winters. With high and low tides, fresh, relatively warm water is exposed to the colder air present during the Alaska winters. As a result, Elmendorf AFB receives, on the average, 107 hours of cold fog with conditions less than 200 ft ceiling and/or $\frac{1}{2}$ mile visibility per year. This is considerably more than any other location in the state where extensive flying operations are conducted. Therefore, cold fog dissipation is generally cost effective.

Cold fog dissipation began at Elmendorf AFB in the 1965–66 winter season. At that time the creation of ice crystals in the cold fog was accomplished by attaching small cakes of dry ice to balloons. Dry ice cakes were made locally with a mold and a cylinder of liquid carbon dioxide. The balloons were either released into the air as free balloons, tethered at fixed locations, or attached to a vehicle and moved around the runway area. It was early 1966 before the testing routine was underway and, for the remainder of the season, testing was too infrequent to be conclusive. This procedure was continued in the 1966–67 winter season. The conclusion was that the dissipation of cold fog by the use of dry ice cakes attached to balloons was neither effective nor practical. Considerable manpower was involved to comply with flying safety requirements to reduce the hazard caused by the balloons. In addition, to be effective, the area seeded must be 45 minutes to one and one-half hours upwind from the runway complex. These areas were often inaccessible due to snow clogged roads or lack of roads. Also, the time required to get men and materiel in place to initiate the clearing process was excessive. It was too costly to maintain crews in place for long periods of time when fog threatened. Danger of frostbite in the bitter cold was ever-present unless adequate relief crews were available.

In the 1967–68 winter seaon, airborne seeding of cold fog with crushed dry ice and silver iodide pyrotechnics was begun. Seeding was done with Air Weather Service WC-130 type aircraft (Hurricane Hunters). The seeding with dry ice was declared operational during the first season. Dry ice seeding was found to be effective at temperatures of −1 C or colder. Seeding was done at no more than 500 ft above the fog. Particle size was no larger than $\frac{3}{8}$ in. in diameter. The larger particles lasted long enough to fall into the fog and initiate the clearing process. Silver iodide was seeded from a pod attached to the wing of the WC-130 aircraft. Silver iodide was effective with temperatures colder than −4 C provided the material was introduced directly into the tops of the fog. Flying in the fog was considered unsafe in the vicinity of Elmendorf due to the local terrain. There is a moraine which rises to over 300 ft elevation just north of the runway which was very near the fog tops. This made seeding in the tops unsafe. Therefore, the use of silver iodide pyrotechnics never became routine. Testing of the pyrotechnics was done in open areas away from cities and aircraft traffic.

Cold fog dissipation by airborne seeding with crushed dry ice under Operation COLD COWL was conducted for five winter seasons. Initially, the dry ice was crushed on the ground and loaded into the aircraft. However, this delayed departures and also resulted in the dry ice becoming caked and not dispensing evenly. During the last few seasons the dry ice was crushed and dispensed from equipment on board the seeding aircraft. In actual operation an area no smaller than 2×5 miles was seeded 45 minutes upwind from the base. Parallel lanes 3000 or 6000 ft apart were seeded with 15 lbs/nm. Lane spacing and the size of the area to be seeded depended on the strength of the winds. Wider spacing and larger areas were seeded with stronger winds. The measure of success used during the operation COLD COWL was the number of aircraft movements assisted and the lack of aircraft diversions due to cold fog. During operation COLD COWL, clearing was initiated based on known aircraft traffic. On occasions when there were two seeding aircraft available, preventive seeding was successful as long as the fog was of sufficient depth and moved with a steady flow. The limiting factors were the availability of dry ice and fuel, and the endurance of the crews and aircraft.

Some drawbacks of the airborne seeding were due to the state of the art of fog forecasting. A system of alerts was established whereby aircrews were required to be airborne anywhere from 45 minutes to 15 hours after notification of the danger of cold fog. When the danger of cold fog was low, the WC-130's flew weather reconnaissance missions and were not immediately available for fog seeding. Unexpected cold fog would develop and dissipate on occasion before aircrews could react to it. With one aircraft available, maintenance difficulties occasionally denied success. Though judged to be cost effective, based on the savings resulting from being able to operate aircraft on schedule, it was still an expensive operation except under emergency or wartime conditions. The cost was 300 to 500 thousand dollars per year depending on the amount of cold fog, the number of seeding aircraft used, and the length of the operational season.

In the meantime, another system for clearing cold fog from an aerodrome had been developed and was in operation at Orly Airport, France. This method consists of spraying liquid propane into the cold fog from ground based dispensers. This system was initially tested by the Air Weather Service at Fairchild AFB, Washington, under Operation COLD WAND in the winter of 1967 to 68. It was declared operational the following season. The system at Fairchild has 18–20 dispensers in an arc from south to east to north. Distance of the dispensers from the target area, the approach end of the runway, is $\frac{1}{4}$ to two miles. Testing and programming for the installation of a propane system for dissipating cold fog at Elmendorf AFB was begun in the fall of 1970. The system was ready for operational testing by the end of 1971. There was insufficient fog to test the system in early 1972, so operational testing and evaluation was done this past season. The system was declared operational late in the season.

The ground based cold fog dissipation system at Elmendorf AFB consists of a series of nineteen propane dispensing sites. Each site is equipped with a 1000 gallon tank of propane, a 20 ft mast with dual nozzles, and a module for remote control of each dispenser. In actual operation for any wind direction only 4 to 6 of the dispensers are used simultaneously. In operation the propane solenoid control valve opens. Liquid propane is carried from the tank through hoses, up the mast to the nozzles. The liquid propane vaporizing through the nozzles cools adjacent fog droplets to near −40 F, at which temperature spontaneous freezing occurs. Thence the droplets freeze into ice crystals and begin the fog dissipation process. The Bergeron-Findeisen theory operates the same as in the airborne system except the source of the ice crystals is different. Natural diffusion spreads the ice crystals to the top of the fog, effecting dissipation through its entire depth. Command and control is achieved through a radio control system operated from the base weather station. Each dispenser can be turned on and off independently. The system is designed so that in the event the storage battery, which operates the control module at each site, becomes weak, the solenoid control valve will close and prevent waste of the propane. While in operation, a roving observer sees that the dispensers in use are actually in the fog. He also makes observations of winds at the sites and subjective remarks on the apparent success or failure of a seeding. When the system is shut down he also sees that the flow of propane has stopped at all dispensers. Each observer is in continuous contact with the control center at the base weather station either by radio in a 4 wheel drive vehicle or a hand held radio. Each site is fenced in to protect the equipment from moose and man and man himself from the equipment.

Not only personnel safety but also environmental ecology are important considerations in operating the ground based cold fog dissipating system. Two factors have been repeatedly examined for their potential for harm: explosive possibility and toxicity. The explosive danger turns out to be minor. Propane is flammable when mixed with air in the proportion of 2 to 10%. These proportions exist in the plume of vaporizing propane to a distance of approximately 4 feet from the dispenser. Deliberate ignition of the plume within this distance of the nozzle, at 20 feet above the ground causes a noise but no damage. In tests carried out when the wind was greater than 4 knots, the dispensers would not remain ignited. Also, it was found that the propane did not collect in depressions to a detectable level downwind from the dispensers. The propane itself is not poisonous. It kills the same way as water does, by excluding oxygen. The molecules of gaseous propane are photochemically inert and are harmless to plant and animal life. Quantities of propane used in seeding are so small, approximately 10 gallons per hour per dispenser, that there is no accumulation leading to a pollution problem. Though propane itself has no smell, it is commercially stenched as a safety measure when used for cooking or heating. The smell immediately calls attention to undesired leaks. Since the presence of the stenching agent (Methyl Mercaptan) is immediately detectable downwind and, in fact, is noxious at small concentration, unstenched propane is used. The propane we use is produced in Kenai, Alaska, and is remarkably free of impurities. According to the Petrolane Company and the Alaska Testlab of Anchorage, the propane is 98% pure. An examination of this safety problem by the Air Force Environmental Health Laboratory resulted in this conclusion: "No appreciable danger to persons in the vicinity of a propane dispenser is believed possible."

Beyond safety, the laboratory examined the ecological implications and concluded, "Propane is biologically inert. It is also relatively non-reactive photochemically. No significant increase in the air pollutant burden of any area is expected from usage of unstenched propane in cold fog dissipation." (USAF Environmental Health Laboratory, 1970.)

In designing the system, an attempt was made to position the dispensers 30 minutes to one hour upwind from the desired clearing area (the approach end of the primary instrument runway). Thus, 5 dispensers were positioned close to the end of the runway to be used in absolutely calm conditions, and fourteen dispensers were positioned in a semi-circular pattern from north to southeast, approximately two miles from the desired clearing area. The placement of the dispensers was also dependent on the availability of roads to reach them for servicing and maintenance. The south-southeast through northwest arc was not protected for two reasons. Records show that less than 4% of the cold fog occurs with wind directions south-southeast through northwest. Also, the location of the Knik Arm of the Cook Inlet to the west and north of the base precluded the placement of dispensers two miles out in the southwest through west-northwest directions. In addition, much of the land southeast through southwest is populated, privately owned land of the City of Anchorage; whereas, the present array of dispensers is located entirely on U. S. government property. The primary cold fog source is the Eagle River Mud Flats to the north-northeast of Elmendorf AFB. Under conditions of a steady 3 knot wind from the northeast through east directions, the system works beautifully. The fog is seeded by the outer row of dispensers. The bulk of snow generated as part of the clearing process falls between the dispensers and the runway area. So the air is relatively fog free when it reaches the base. If the wind flow is too strong, the snow falls on the base and actually worsens conditions.

There are several factors unfavorable to adequate fog dissipation. Patchy or thin fog elements are difficult to clear or dissipate with ground based seeding. Under light and variable wind conditions, the local effect of the Elmendorf moraine has been to channel the clearing produced out over the Knik Arm of the inlet or toward Fort Richardson. This coming season, four of the lesser used dispensers will be moved to the crest of the Elmendorf moraine to take advantage of the cold air drainage effects. Study of the low level wind flow will continue in an effort to determine if a different placement of the dispensers will be more effective.

How well does the system work? Aside from the problems of clearing the field under adverse wind conditions, there have been several other problems. One is that nozzles ice up due to premature vaporization of the propane. One cure for this is a different design of the nozzles. The nozzles installed are of the "Whirljet" variety which have a chamber for expansion of the propane before it reaches the outside air. A different nozzle consisting of a calibrated opening in a pipe cap will be tried in the future. On some occasions, where there are tall trees in the vicinity of the dispensers, the ice crystals generated were captured by the trees and were ineffective. This year we will extend the masts up to 75 ft. With extensions of over 40 ft, additional pressure will have to be added to the propane tanks with compressed nitrogen or some other inert gas. This will increase the cost of the installation and complicate maintenance and filling of the tanks. The batteries used with the control modules are automotive type lead storage batteries. They weaken after prolonged operation in the extremely cold weather. However, with frequent changes and charges, the batteries have not been a major problem.

What is a reliable measure of success for the ground based propane system? In the airborne seeding operation, the assumption was made that aircraft movements that occurred within two hours of a successful seeding were saves for the system. In the philosophy of preventive seeding (that is, keeping the base above instrument minima at all times when the area is threatened by fog), it is not conclusive whether improved visibility is the result of seeding or the natural variability of the cold fog occurrences. This past season a subjective evaluation of each occurrence was made to determine success or failure of the system. In the future, a possible measure of effectiveness may be a long term change in the average number of hours per year that visibilities in cold fog of various threshold values occur.

Some advantages of the propane system over the airborne system are:

1. Cost of operation is a fraction of the airborne system. Propane costs are about $8000 per season; manpower costs are one additional maintenance man and one additional weather observer, plus a radio maintenance contract and battery charging expenses.

2. The reaction time is much faster since all that is required to initiate the system is to turn on the dispensers by remote control radio.

3. A longer season of operation is possible as the system is very inexpensive to maintain in a standby status. All that is required is to keep the batteries charged, the radio control sets operating and the tanks filled with a sufficient supply of propane.

4. Propane is less of a pollutant than are the exhaust gases of operating an aircraft the size of a WC-130.

The major disadvantage of the system is that there are some occurrences in which the airborne system can be effective and the propane system cannot; for instance, the rare occurrences of fog with winds from south-southeast through west-northwest. In this past season 324 aircraft movements occurred which were credited to the propane dispensing system. If the operator can accept the occasional failure of the ground based propane system, it is far more cost effective than the airborne system in most fog cases.

REFERENCE

USAF Environmental Health Laboratory, 1970: Use of propane in cold fog dissipation. Letter from USAF Environmental Health Laboratory at McClellan AFB, California to Air Weather Service Headquarters, Scott AFB, Illinois, dated August 12, 1970.

Cloud seeding in Alaska: A program to aid in the control and prevention of wildfires

JAMES W. FRANKS

Alaska Weather Modification Project, Bureau of Land Management, Anchorage, Alaska 99501

Abstract

The Bureau of Land Management conducted a two month summer cloud seeding program during 1973 in interior Alaska to aid in the prevention and control of wildfires by reducing the number and intensity of cloud-to-ground lightning strokes. Three seeding aircraft dispensed silver iodide into the tops of potential thunderstorm clouds over 10 primary target areas. Evaluation of seeding effects on the electrical character of the cloud was conducted by a specially equipped aircraft instrumented, directed and sponsored by the United States Forest Service.

Upper air soundings were taken at 6 locations, four of which were operated in conjunction with the project during the summer months to obtain meteorology for determining seedable areas.

Effective glaciation resulting from seeding was construed as having met the project objective of converting the majority of supercooled water to ice, therefore reducing the electrical charging and separation mechanism, and thus preventing lightning.

1. Introduction

Wildfires destroy millions of acres of resources annually. Lightning causes 10,000 fires per year in the United States. About 30 percent (Barney, 1969; 1971) of the wildfires in Alaska are lightning caused and these fires are responsible for about 80 percent of the annual acreage burned (one million acres).

Lightning was discussed by Aristotle, and its electrical nature was proven by Benjamin Franklin with his famous kite experiment in 1752.

Lightning has been responsible for many conflagrations and disastrous forest fire situations. In response, the United States Forest Service has conducted lightning fire research for more than 25 years (Fuquay and Baughman, 1969) seeking ways to prevent or reduce lightning-caused fires. One of the conclusions of the research was that lightning can be characterized as hot or cold depending upon its temperature range. It was been found to range from 15,000 to 60,000 F, hotter than the 11,000 F temperature of the sun's surface. The greater temperature is derived from longer sustained lightning discharges.

Research have brought forward several theories which may explain electrical charging and separation in the clouds. Among these the Reynolds-Brook Charging Mechanism (Reynolds, Brooks and Gourley, 1957) appears to provide a reasonable explanation and agrees with observations. It will be discussed later in the text. The Alaska Weather Modification Project was modeled after the Reynolds-Brook Charging Mechanism as reported by Stow (1969).

2. Weather modification: an aid to fire control

Since the late 1940's man has looked for more technical ways to prevent and suppress forest fires.

The use of the wet burlap sack and spruce bough needed supplementing because sufficient manpower was not always readily available where the fire occurred. Time delays give nature great odds against the little persuasive effort man could muster in suppression of the fire. More mechanization and technological schemes with faster action were needed. Why not cloud seeding as a prevention and suppression tool?

Cloud seeding has been used for precipitation enhancement, primarily for drought relief and to augment water reserves. Sustained water management programs became prominent in the early 1960's through special appropriations and supplemental funds provided by federal and state governments and local private organizations. As the knowledge grew in cloud seeding techniques the application of cloud seeding spread to many uses, such as hail suppression and precipitation suppression for special use areas.

In 1969 the BLM initiated a pilot program in Alaska to seed clouds in the vicinity of wildfires as an aid to their control. The results of the pilot project, reported by Davis (1969), encouraged a further expansion of the effort for rain augmentation in the summers of 1970 through 1972.

In 1972 and 1973, as a part of the cloud seeding project, the Bureau seeded clouds in an effort to prevent lightning-caused fires. Cold cloud seeding techniques were used.

Understanding the Reynolds-Brook theory for charging will provide both the background for the seeding techniques and the purpose of seeding for lightning fire prevention.

3. Reynolds-brook charging mechanism

Water ionizes into H+ and OH− ions. Consider a piece of ice in equilibrium with the environmental

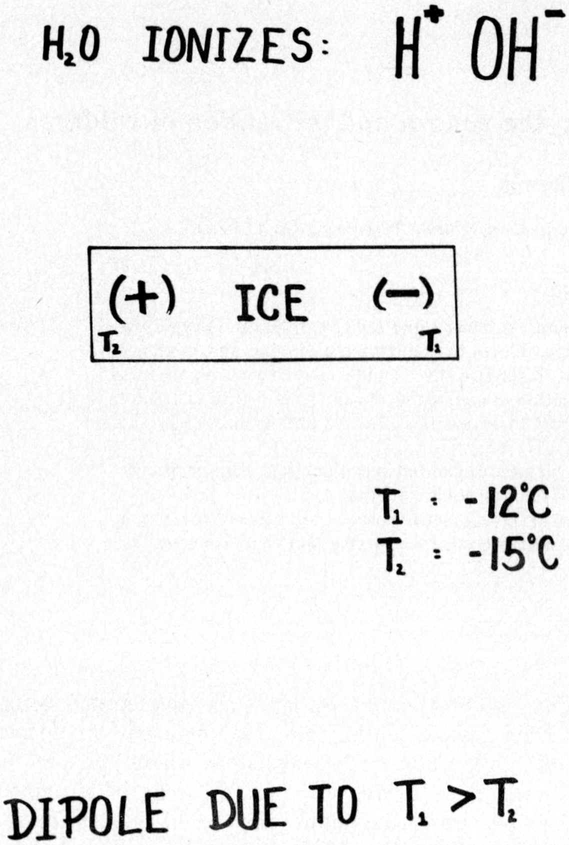

FIG. 1. Ionization in an ice particle due to temperature differential.

temperature. The ions are evenly distributed throughout, therefore, no net positive or negative charge exists within the ice particle. However, if a part of the ice particle becomes warmer than the other the positive ions concentrate in the colder region and the negative in the warmer region. Thus a dipole is formed (Fig. 1).

The Reynolds-Brook theory, as reported by Reynolds, Brook and Gourley (1957), and Stow (1969), states that charge formation and separation occurs within a cloud zone which contains three types of water: supercooled water droplets (temperature below freezing), small ice particles or crystals, and ice pellets or small soft hail whose diameter or mass is larger than either the ice crystals or water droplets. With this mix of water types there obviously is a lack of equilibrium with the ambient air and the heat of fusion causes ion movement thus an adjustment and mixing of charges. By removing one of the types of water, the charging mechanism can be controlled. This has been confirmed by researchers and is explained in the following way.

The large ice pellets collide with water droplets with the result that the water coalesces with the ice. The heat of fusion due to this freezing causes the ice pellet to be warmer than the cloud environment.

The ice pellet remains warmer than the surrounding environment as long as water is available to collide and freeze. When the small ice crystals collide with the larger ice pellet the charged ions separate in the dipole fashion. Thus the ice crystals become positively charged and the ice pellet becomes negatively charged on contact.

Since both ice particles are in the ice phase, the small ice crystals bounce off the ice pellet carrying the net positive charge with it, and at the same time leaving the large ice pellet with a net negative charge (Fig. 2).

Consider a natural cloud where the temperatures are between −5 C and −25 C or about 10 to 18 thousand feet in height. A natural convective cloud contains a mixture of the three types of water described above, i.e., small supercooled liquid water droplets, small ice crystals, and large ice pellets or hail. The Reynolds-Brook charging mechanism generates and separates charge so that the mature cloud has a top which is positive and a base which is negative. This dipole effect is the result of convective air currents carrying the lighter ice particles (+) upward and the heavier ice pellets (−) falling due to size and mass overcoming convection (Fig. 3).

The negatively charged cloud base induces a positive charge within the ground beneath the cloud, which follows the cloud in a shadow effect as it migrates. When the charge difference between positive and negative areas becomes great enough step leaders of

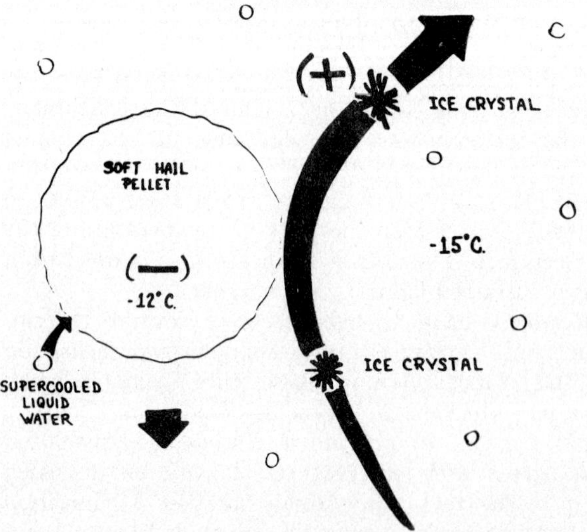

FIG. 2. The Reynolds-Brook charging mechanism.

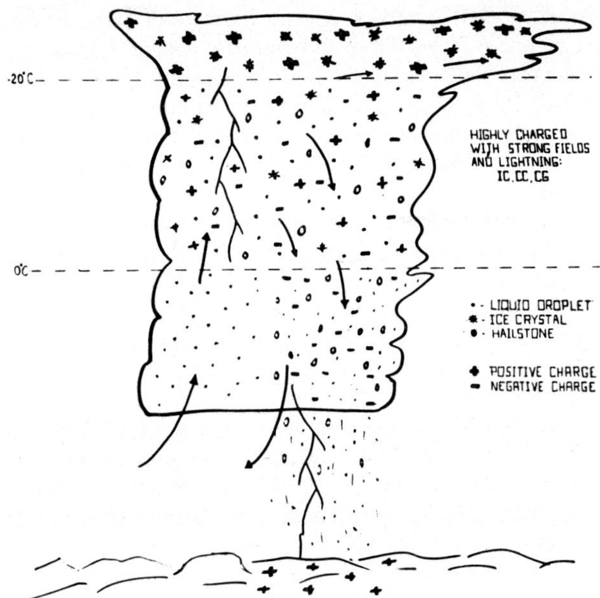

FIG. 3. Mature natural cloud.

opposite charge develop, which then attract each other. As the electrical field gets strong enough the leaders connect, thus releasing a charge. This discharge is seen as lightning. The resulting current dissipates the two charged areas and the process starts over again as long as there are the three water types available to mix and cause charge separation.

Using silver iodide (artificial ice nuclei) to seed clouds at the −5 C to −25 C region causes the supercooled water droplets to freeze into ice crystals. The conversion of water droplets to ice creates heat of freezing. The buoyancy released causes nearly immediate growth in cloud height. This occurs until the supercooled water droplets all freeze, thus causing the cloud environment to come into equilibrium with the surrounding atmosphere and cease growing. Ice nuclei are introduced into the cloud, on the order of 100 per liter of cloud mass. The nuclei available provide numerous opportunities for the water to come in contact, therefore, water droplets are frozen by attaching to the massive number of nuclei and will not grow into large ice pellets and thus the cloud becomes a mass of ice crystals. Some growth does occur from diffusion. Therefore when the ice crystals collide or strike the large ice pellets no ion separation occurs and no charge formation of separation occurs.

This process is the ideal situation and seeding can slow down the charging process or prevent it from developing. With timely seeding in the life cycle of the cloud the electrification process can be modified resulting in lightning discharges of lower amperage and less duration and fewer cloud-to-ground discharges (Fig. 4).

The Forest Service research reported by Fuquay and Baughman (1969) showed that lightning preven-

tion may be possible. It found that massive seeding with silver iodide did reduce the occurrence of lightning. Seeded storms produced 66% fewer cloud-to-ground discharges and 54% less total lightning than clouds that were not seeded. Cloud-to-ground discharges averaged a maximum of five flashes in five minutes as compared to 8.8 discharges for non-seeded storms during the same time period.

Seeded storms had a significantly lower level of electrical current. The average duration of discharges decreased from 235 milliseconds for unseeded storms to 182 milliseconds for seeded storms. The decrease in discharge duration would have an effect upon ignition in forest fuels. The longer duration discharges were responsible for ignition in Montana forest fuels according to Fuquay, Boughman, Taylor and Hawe (1967).

Encouraged by results of the Forest Service research, the BLM initiated cloud seeding on a selective basis to prevent lightning-caused fires in seven primary resource areas, each given descending priority order for seeding.

4. Seeding techniques and instrumentation

Three twin-engine Cessna 421 aircraft were equipped and based at Fairbanks to conduct cloud seeding missions. Each aircraft had ejector racks capable of holding 104 flares and wing booms carrying 24 flares. All were fired electrically from a control panel in the aircraft operated by a flight meteorologist.

The ejector flares were made available in 24, 60 and 150 gram units of silver iodide. Wing flares were available in 75 and 225 gram units of silver iodide. The larger ejector type flare had a 10 second delay

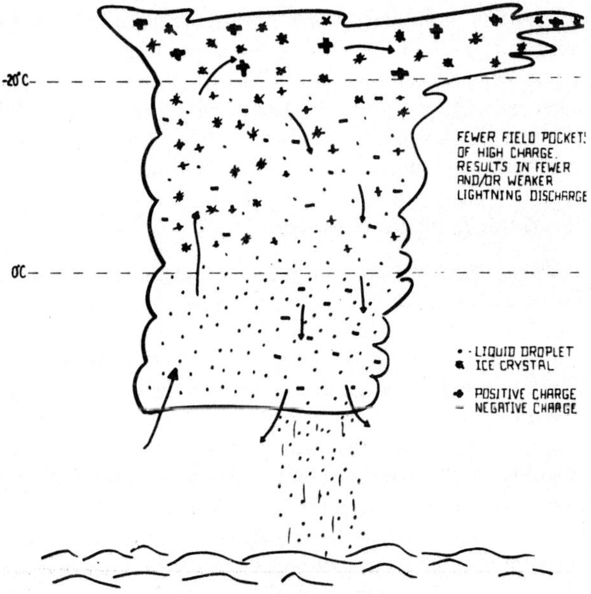

FIG. 4. Mature seeded cloud.

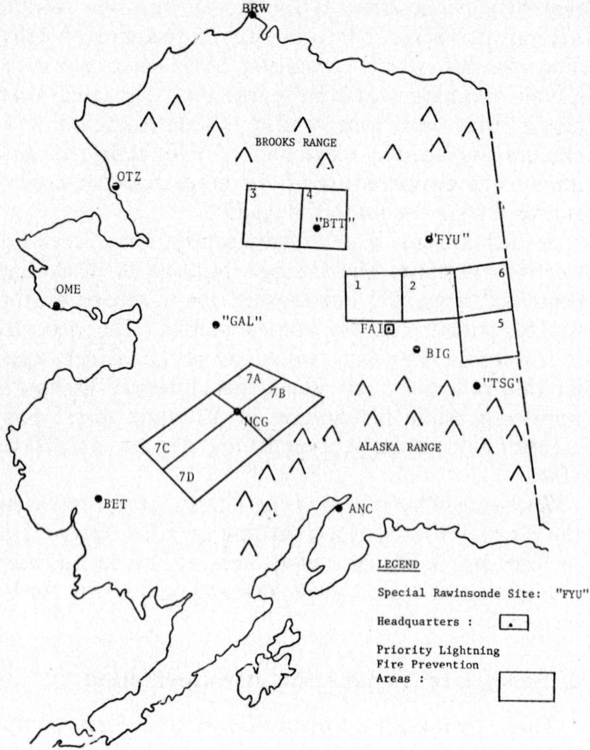

Fig. 5. Map of priority lightning fire prevention seeding areas.

burn built in so that it could be ejected into the primary zone of clouds with a minimum of cloud penetration by the flight crew.

Generally cloud top seeding was conducted, releasing one 150 gram unit each two seconds over or within the convective cloud of interest. Generally the seeding rate was 1000 grams per hour per cloud or an average of 830 grams AgI per seeded cell. Each cell which exhibited hard features or rapid growth within the $-15\,C$ or $-18\,C$ range was seeded on days when potential thunderstorm development was forecast. The majority of the seeding was conducted within the seven priority areas, with areas one and two receiving the majority of flights (Fig. 5).

5. Meteorological considerations

Three primary conditions are necessary for the formation of thunderstorms. Sufficient low level moisture, atmospheric instability, and a triggering mechanism of the right amount create thunderstorms. Alaska generally is endowed with sufficient low level moisture, so moisture is rarely a limiting factor in forecasting Alaska thunderstorms. Atmospheric instability is a combination of warm temperatures at low levels and relatively cool temperatures at high levels. These latter two elements, since they are relative to each other, fluctuate constantly as a result of both low and high level air patterns as well as the degree of surface heating be the sun. It is surface

heating that plays such an important part in the occurrence of Alaska thunderstorms. Triggering mechanisms at lower latitudes are usually fronts, dry lines, squall lines, orographic lifting or differential temperature advection. However, differential temperature advection accounts for only a few thunderstorms in Alaska.

The most important triggering mechanism in Alaska is solar heating of the surface, particularly on mountain slopes which face the afternoon and evening sun. These storms are air-mass thunderstorms triggered by local heating of near-surface air by the sun to cause localized convection during periods of clear sky conditions.

The low sun angle produces more solar heating per unit area on the slopes of hills and mountains than on the flat valley floor. This differential heating produces early convection over the higher terrain and in general convection is very terrain oriented.

The long duration of sunlight means there is much less diurnal effect than at lower latitudes. In other words, convection can take place for a longer period during the day with solar heating available for a longer time. Because of this, the thunderstorm potential time can be as long as 12 hours in a day.

Thunderstorms generally occur from the last week in May through August with the peak activity ending the first week in July. The tropopause in the summer reaches heights near 40,000 feet (12,000 m) and the thunderstorms do penetrate the tropopause.

Well-organized convection in turn causes charge generation and separation responsible for cloud-to-ground lightning of sufficient duration to start wildfires.

Synoptic weather patterns conducive to the formation of thunderstorms in Alaska and conditions previously discussed include:

Low level convergence indicated by surface low pressure areas or low level troughs.

Lack of cloud cover to allow good surface heating (Interior temperatures in the range of 80 to 100 F)— usually associated with 18,000 foot (500 mb) ridge over interior Alaska (best orientation is northwest to southeast into Canada).

An 18,000 foot (500 mb) low pressure center in the northern Gulf of Alaska with cold air being pumped northward on its east side.

A temperature difference of 28 C or greater between the 850 and 500 mb levels.

Wind shear of less than 20 knots between cloud base and top so that the cloud tops are not sheared off.

6. Operations

Area and objectives

The general operating area included the greater interior of Alaska from the Canadian border to the

TABLE 1. Alaska—Seeding Summary For Summer, 1973.

Date	Lightning suppression	Rain augmentation	Seeding areas	No. runs	No. and type* flares	Total AgI	No. flts w/seeding	Total flt. time (hrs)	Fire starts in/out**	
6/5/73	x		SE 5–10 TSG	2	8A, 1D	1,425g	2	9.0	0/0	
6/6/73	x		1, 2	57	243A	36,450g	4	11.0	0/0	
6/7/73	x		1, 3, 4 30W FYU	17	135A	20,250g	3	9.4	0/0	
6/8/73	x		100E FYU	3	9A	1,350g	1	7.2	0/0	
6/10/73	x		Vicin FYU, 20N 6, 30W Area 5	8	41A	6,150g	3	1.0	0/0	
6/11/73	x		1, 2, 6	29	252A	37,800g	3	12.3	3/2	
6/12/73	x		1, 2, 3, 4	32	263A	39,450g	6	12.8	0/0	Lightning fire
6/14/73	x		1, 2, 6	56	319A	47,850g	5	10.9	3/4	starts on days
6/15/73	x		2, 6 NE 7B	9	45A	6,750g	3	12.6	6/3	of no seeding
6/16/73	x		7A, B, C, D	38	219A	32,850g	4	10.3	3/6	in/out of
6/18/73	x		100 E GAL, 7B	23	154A, 23B	24,480g	4	13.7	0/0	seeding areas.
6/19/73	x		1, 2	41	284A	42,600g	4	10.4	0/0	
6/27/73	x		2, 6	15	65A	9,750g	2	8.4	0/1	13 June 0/1
6/28/73	x		1, 2, 3, 4, 5, 6	46	179A, 25D	32,475g	6	19.5	0/3	17 June 1/3
6/29/73	x		1, 2	36	168A, 21D	29,925g	4	13.3	0/0	20 June 0/1
6/30/73	x		1, 2	49	79A, 121D	39,075g	4	22.1	1/3	23 June 1/0
7/1/73	x		1, 2, N of 1	37	92D	20,700g	8	19.8	2/19	6 July 1/4
7/2/73	x	x	1, 90N GAL	27	70B, 32D	11,400g	4	20.8	8/9	7 July 0/3
7/3/73	x	x	1, 2, 3, 4	18	37D, 59A, 10E	17,925g	6	18.2	7/3	9 July 1/1
7/4/73	x		1, 2, 6 ,FYU	15	30D, 80E	12,750g	6	23.8	8/5	12 July 0/2
7/5/73	x		6	2	15A, 3E	2,475g	2	11.0	0/4	13 July 1/0
7/10/73	x		30SE+60–100 NE FYU	4	27A	4,050g	2	11.6	0/1	23 July 0/1 24 July 1/3
7/29/73	x		60 N FYU	10	90A	13,500g	2	7.3	0/0	26 July 1/1
23 38% of 61 days				591	3201 drops 832 gm/cld	491,430	88	302.4 3.44 hrs/flt	41/63 104	7/20 27

* A: 150 gm cartridge, 20 sec delay; B: 60 gm cartridge no delay; C: 24 gm cartridge, no delay; D: 225 gm end burning; E: 75 gm end burning.

** Fire starts in and out of primary areas—Lightning started only.

west coast, bounded on the north and south by the Brooks and Alaska Mountain Ranges, but excluding Fairbanks, its watershed and the Tanana Valley. Specific seeding areas were designated for priority seeding for lightning fire prevention. These consisted of areas of about 6000 square miles or more each. These areas were chosen based upon resource values and lightning fire history. Ten areas in all were designated, however, seeding was concentrated in the first two priority blocks, with intermittent seeding occurring in other designated areas (Fig. 5).

A version of the Weinstein-Davis Numerical Cloud Model was used to analyze the upper air data to determine cloud growth, amounts of precipitation expected following seeding and the time convection may occur for each upper air station location. These data were used to forecast areas of probable thunderstorms. The use of the cloud model may provide an easy analysis and technique to determine possible thunderstorm propagation areas. By routine daily surveillance of the priority areas, comparisons of actual observations were made with the model prediction to determine the reliability of the model to forecast thunderstorms and seedable conditions.

Project headquarters was located at the Fairbanks District Fire Control Station with aircraft based at Ft. Wainwright army airfield about 5 miles away.

Project objectives were:

A. To prevent lightning-caused fires through modification of convective clouds.

B. To induce precipitation to aid in the control of wildfires.

C. To evaluate the use of the Weinstein-Davis numerical cloud model as a tool to determine seedable conditions and predict thunderstorm areas.

Procedure

Upper air soundings were taken from 6 locations in interior Alaska. Four of these stations were operated in conjunction with the cloud seeding program; the others were National Weather Service stations. The four project stations were operated from late May through mid-August.

An analysis of the synoptic weather and upper air data was made and a forecast issued daily by 9 a.m. Alaska Daylight Time. The upper air data was analyzed using a modified version of the Weinstein-Davis numerical cloud model (Weinstein and Davis, 1967), to calculate cloud heights, bases, amounts of precipitation expected from the seeded cloud and the predicted convective temperature and time of convection for each station location. This data assisted the forecaster in making a prediction of thunderstorm development by priority work areas.

Following the daily weather briefings a decision was made on locations for seeding missions and aircraft with flight crews were dispatched to the forecast areas. Each aircraft flight crew consisted of a pilot and flight meteorologist. Four flight crews were available for the summer operation.

Results

During the two month (June and July) project, 88 flights were flown for a total of 302 hours or about 3.5 hours per flight. Seeding was conducted on twenty-three days, sixteen of which were in June. About 491 kilograms of silver iodide were dispensed in 591 seeded cases. The majority of the seeded cells glaciated well. Some, however, either did not respond or were not observed from the seeding or observation aircraft during the time limited to subjective evaluation (Table 1).

Where seeding resulted in effective glaciation it was construed that the objective of lightning suppression had been accomplished. There were no means for determining whether the clouds in fact had an electrical field prior to or following seeding except for the cases observed by the Forest Service evaluation aircraft. Some cases may have been seeded which would not have produced lightning in their natural

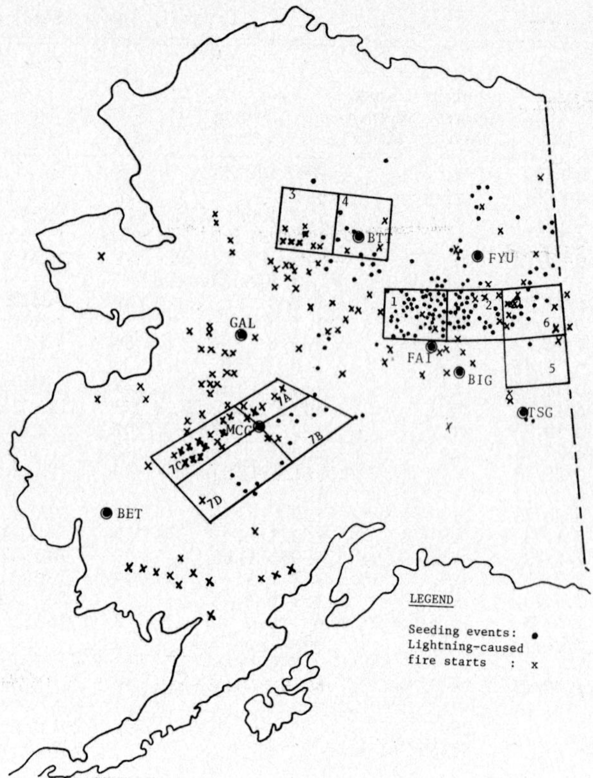

FIG. 7. Composite of seeding events and lightning-caused fire starts, June and July 1973.

development. These cases cannot be distinguished on the basis of the subjective evaluation.

Fewer lightning-caused fires were reported in areas of concentrated cloud seeding (Figs. 6 and 7).

Evaluation

The effectiveness of a seeding event was evaluated by observing and recording the amount of glaciation exhibited by the seeded cloud. This was recorded both on flight records and in photographs.

A Forest Service instrumented evaluation aircraft was capable of measuring changes in electrical field, the number of lightning strokes, and the types of strokes occurring: whether cloud-to-cloud or cloud-to-ground, and whether cloud-to-ground strokes were hybrid or discrete types.

The Forest Service observed both seeded and non-seeded cases, and the results of the observations will be reported later after evaluation of the data.

The subjective evaluation of seeding events recorded by the flight meteorologist indicate that the majority of the seeding events glaciated well. The remainder were not observed or showed only slight glaciation during the observation period.

Glaciation reflects the conversion of supercooled water droplets to ice particles. The rate of glaciation is accelerated by increasing the ice nuclei from about

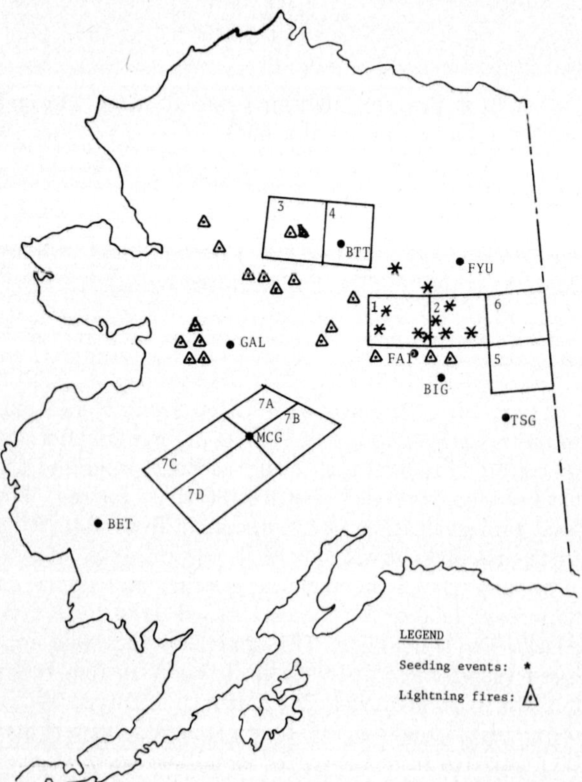

FIG. 6. Seeding areas July 1, 1973, with reported lightning fires.

one liter^{-1} naturally to 100 liter^{-1} by introducing silver iodide crystals into the supercooled (at about -20 C) water region of the cloud.

Effective glaciation resulting from seeding was construed as having met the project objective of converting the majority of supercooled water to ice, thereby reducing the electrical charging and separation mechanism, and thus preventing lightning.

REFERENCES

Barney, Richard J., 1969: Interior Alaska wildfires 1956–1965. USDA Forest Service, Pacific Northwest Forest and Range Experiment Sta. 47P.

Barney, Richard J., 1971: "Wildfires in Alaska, some historical and projected effects and aspects." A Symposium—Fire in the Northern Environment, College, Alaska April 13–14, 1971.

Davis, L. G., 1969; Cloud seeding tests on fires in Alaska. Final report on Contract 08-550-CT-0-1, EG&C, Inc., Boulder, Colorado.

Fuquay, D. M., and R. G. Baughman, 1969: Project skyfire lightning research. Final report to NSF under Grant No. GP-2617, December, 1969.

Fuquay, D. M., R. G. Baughman, A. R. Taylor and R. G. Hawe, 1967: Characteristics of seven lightning discharges that caused forest fires. *Journal of Geophysical Research*, **72**, 6371–6373.

Reynolds, S. E., M. Brook and M. F. Gourley, 1957: Thunderstorm charge separation. *Journal of Meteorology*, **14**, 426–436.

Stow, C. D., 1969: On the prevention of lightning. *Bulletin American Meteorological Society*, **50**, 514–520.

Weinstein, A. I., and L. G. Davis, 1967: A parameterized numerical model of cumulus convection. Report Number 11 to National Science Foundation (NSF GA-777), Department of Meteorology, The Pennsylvania State University.

Glacio-Meteorological Studies of McCall Glacier

G. WENDLER, C. BENSON, C. FAHL, N. ISHIKAWA, D. TRABANT AND G. WELLER

Geophysical Institute, University of Alaska, Fairbanks, Alaska 99701

Abstract

In the spring of 1969 the Geophysical Institute began a glaciometeorological study on McCall Glacier in the Brooks Range of Northern Alaska. This paper summarizes the results obtained so far. The mass balance of the glacier has been negative for all four years of the study; comparisons of ice, water and heat balances lead to similar results. A northerly exposure and steep mountains surrounding the glacier are shown to affect the heat balance significantly. Aufeis (overflow ice) features have been mapped repeatedly and are described. Glacier movement studies show a surface velocity maximum of 18 m year^{-1} and meltwater percolating into the firn produces a matrix of ice lenses and anomalously high temperatures in the firn.

1. Introduction

McCall Glacier lies in the eastern part of the Brooks Range in Alaska, in the Romanzof Mountains, at latitude 69°18′N, longitude 143°48′W. The glacier has an area of 6.22 km² and an altitude span from 1340 to 2720 m. It is one of the few small glaciers which exist in the Brooks Range. These glaciers generally have northern exposures and lie at altitudes above 1000 m.

In 1969, a study of the combined heat-, ice-, and water-balance was started by members of the Geophysical Institute, University of Alaska, as part of the International Hydrological Decade (IHD). McCall Glacier is the only arctic glacier currently being studied in the United States of America, and is of special importance as it lies at the intersection of two glacier "chains" recommended for intensive study in the IHD: the Arctic Circle and the American chains. It had been studied previously during the IGY (e.g., Keeler 1959; Orvig 1961; Orvig and Mason 1963).

This paper summarizes the results obtained so far, with the exception of the results relating to: (1) the thermal regime of the glacier, and (2) synoptic scale mean sea level pressure pattern anomalies. These two topics are being reported on separately later in this volume by Harrison *et al.* (1975) and Fahl (1975).

2. Mass balance studies

Seventy ablation/accumulation stakes were installed on McCall Glacier in 1969, and the data obtained from these were used to calculate the mass balance. It was found to be negative for all four years.

A mean annual balance between −15 and −35 cm of water equivalent has been found (Wendler *et al.*, 1972a; Trabant *et al.*, in press). These values would be near equilibrium for a glacier in southern Alaska but for the Brooks Range, where accumulation (about 50 cm annual precipitation) and ablation (maximum value at the glacier terminus of about −200 cm) are small, these values are considered quite "unhealthy" for the glacier.

3. Hydrology of McCall Glacier Basin

In June 1969, a stilling well with a water level recorder was installed about 2 km downstream from the glacier terminus. The water level recorder was calibrated with an OTT current meter. Data for the 1969, 1970 and 1971 summers have been obtained (Wendler *et al.*, 1972b). Maximum discharge values of up to 5000 l sec^{-1} were measured during periods of heavy precipitation and high temperatures. During normal ablation periods, discharge values between 750 and 1250 l sec^{-1} were found. These discharge rates are equivalent to daily melt of approximately 10 mm water equivalent over the whole glacier surface. Greater values are nearly always connected with liquid precipitation while lower values are due to cold spells. A strong diurnal variation in the amount of discharge was related to the diurnal ablation cycle. The time of day during which peak flow occurred gradually changed during the season from late afternoon to early afternoon as the efficiency of runoff channels on the glacier gradually increased.

The amount of ablation measured by the water balance was compared with the stake measurements of snow and ice ablation. Snow and ice ablation values calculated from direct measurements were about 16% lower than those calulated by the hydrologic method. Possible reasons for this discrepancy are: 1) insufficient knowledge of the distribution of liquid precipitation; 2) insufficient number of ablation stakes; 3) changes in the stream cross section; and 4) changes in the liquid water storage within the basin.

In summary, the agreement between ablation values calculated by these two methods is not good, but is satisfactory. Perhaps, in view of the sources of errors pointed out above, a better agreement would have been surprising.

4. Heat balance

A micrometeorological station was established near the middle of the ablation zone at an altitude of 1730 m in August, 1969. This station consisted of four sets of continuously recording temperature, humidity, and wind speed sensors at 0.5, 1, 2 and 4 m above the glacier surface. Ice temperatures to a depth of 8 m and the in- and outgoing short and long wave radiation were also measured.

For a short period in the 1971 summer the heat balance of this station was compared with the heat balance over rock and snow (Wendler and Ishikawa, 1972b). Rock, ice and snow are the three dominant surface types found in the McCall Creek Basin. It was found that energy from the radiation balance accounted for 56% of the ice and 63% of the snow ablation measured. Evaporation was somewhat higher than condensation, the effect being more pronounced for snow than for ice surfaces. Analysis of the data for a longer period in the summer of 1970 confirmed that radiation is the most important heat source for snow and ice melt (Wendler and Weller, 1973). The melting period itself is only 11 weeks long, which is quite short. Evaporation overcompensates for what little condensation occurs, and amounts to about 2% of the total ablation. Evaporation is most important in the spring, becoming decreasingly important during the summer. The melt water which percolates into the snow pack and refreezes at a lower level is a more effective way of transporting energy into the snow and ice than conduction, and is of importance during the beginning of the melt period.

The summer balance at the glacier is considerably less energetic than it is over the tundra north of the Brooks Range. The main differences are a higher surface albedo and the protected situation of the glacier in a deep valley on a north–south axis. Most of the glacier's slopes have a northerly exposure, with an inclination between 5 and 15°. The reduction in direct solar radiation owing to this northerly exposure is small (1.7%) during the summer ablation period when the solar declination is approximately 20°. The reduction in radiation received on these north slopes during the noon hours is almost compensated for by the increase of radiation received during the "night" hours, as the sun does not set at this latitude in summer. Later in the year, the decrease in direct solar radiation received on the glacier surfaces as compared with a horizontal becomes more important. At the equinox the loss is 24.8%, and at a solar declination of −10° (20 October or 24 February) even higher with 32.6%.

A further reduction in solar radiation is caused by the steep mountains which surround the McCall Glacier. These reduce the duration of sunshine during the abla-

tion period by nearly 40%. However, this reduction represents an energy loss of only 13.4% as the screening effect of the mountains is most important during low solar angles; at these times the total energy received at the surface is small. The screening effect of the mountains becomes more severe with lower sun angles and shorter paths of the sun. During the equinox a loss in duration of 67.6%, and in energy of 55.7% is observed. For a solar declination of −10°, there is hardly any direct sunshine on the glacier at all. There is then a loss in duration of 93.6%, resulting in a loss of energy of 87.7%.

Together, northerly exposure of the glacier and the screening effect of the surrounding mountains reduce the direct solar radiation by about 15% in the ablation period, 67% at the equinox and more than 90% at a solar declination of −10° (Wendler and Ishikawa 1973c).

5. Combined ice-, water-, and heat-balance

It is a very difficult task to carry out a combined ice-, water-, and heat-balance study for a glacier basin. Hence, a comparison was made first for one point on a short term basis (Wendler and Ishikawa, 1973a) with good agreement. After accomplishing this the combined heat, ice and water balance was calulated for the entire McCall Glacier Basin (30.6 km²) for a 36 day period in the summer of 1971 (Wendler and Ishikawa 1973d). This period represents about half the ablation period in this region. The heat balance was measured by detailed observations over ice, and secondary stations were established over snow and moraine surfaces. The heat balances calculated for stations located on ice and snow surfaces, respectively, were assumed to be representative of all such surfaces. The moraine station was only used to obtain evaporation data for non glacier-covered areas of the basin (totalling about 70%). Corrections were made to the radiative fluxes owing to screening of the surrounding mountains and the exposure of the glacier.

The ice-balance was calculated using 70 ablation/accumulation stakes and the discharge was measured with a water level recorder, which was calibrated with a current meter. The precipitation was measured with a network of seven rain gauges.

Compared with the direct run-off measurements, the calculated values from the heat balance gave a 5.5% higher value, and the stake measurements an 8.9% lower value. This agreement is considered satisfactory and increases confidence in the methods employed in each of the three individual calculations.

6. Climatology

Four years of data from an automatic weather station at an altitude of 2275 m on the glacier were compared with simultaneous, long-term observations at the nearer permanent meteorological stations. The high level location was found to differ greatly in temperature and wind regime from both the interior valleys and the arctic coast. In particular, the calculated annual precipitation of approximately 500 mm is much higher than that at any other station in the region and considerably higher than other estimates for the higher part of the Brooks Range (Wendler *et al.*, 1973).

7. Aufeis

An extensive perennial aufeis deposit exists in the McCall Creek immediately below the terminus of the Glacier. The water which runs from within the glacier and forms the aufeis continues to flow all winter. It freezes whenever it is forced to the surface and continues to add ice to the surface until the beginning of summer. Then the water, instead of freezing and adding to the aufeis, begins to erode channels in it. This transition, from accretion to erosion in the aufeis deposit of McCall Creek, has been observed during 1970, 1971 and 1972 before surface melt occurred on the glacier. The melt channels are complex and the aufeis at the end of summer consists of continuous areas cut by channels, some of which extend to the stream bottom, and other areas of jumbled ice blocks which are too complex to map in detail. The basic network of channels in the ice was very similar from year to year for the first three years but considerably different during the fourth year.

In the fall of 1969, six reference markers were placed in rocks, and ice cross sections were surveyed between these fixed points. This was followed by detailed topographic surveys of the aufeis in the spring and fall of 1970, 1971 and 1972. The surveys were made using a Wild RK1 Alidade and Plane Table in combination with photography from the air and from selected points on the ground. A total of seven maps of the aufeis are being prepared at a scale of 1:2000 with a contour interval of 1 meter. Some of these will require considerably more work than others. The network of fixed points was expanded to 26 points during spring 1971; all seven maps will be drafted over a single base map of these fixed points. The fall and spring maps, which bracket each winter season, will be compared to determine the amount of ice stored during the winter. This will give a minimum estimate of the amount of winter runoff from the glacier.

The aufeis may contain 80 to 90% of the runoff which takes place between October and May. During September and October, where there is no surface runoff from the glacier, we have observed running water under the snow and thin ice cover of McCall Creek. At some time in October the limited running water probably freezes before it traverses the 12.5 km channel of McCall Creek. The aufeis deposit then starts to grow. In early May, the aufeis extends 2 km downstream from the glacier and is still growing by the freezing of overflow water. The maximum dimensions of the aufeis in late spring are approximately: length 2 km, width 90 m,

thickness 13 m. The minimum dimensions in early fall are approximately: length 1 km, width 70 m, thickness 8–10 m.

8. Glacier movement

At the inception of the McCall Glacier project a survey of the complete set of accumulation/ablation stakes was made in order to establish the positions of the stakes for the purposes of the mass balance analysis. Once this was done, relatively little additional effort was necessary to repeat the survey in order to gain the data necessary for a complete vector analysis of the surface motion of the glacier.

A computer program was developed in September of 1970 and the data from the surveys of 1969–70 were analyzed. At present, all data from the surveys of 1969–72 have been analyzed. The computer program computes: 1) the position of the stake according to the Universal Transverse Mercator grid, and 2) the magnitude of the total motion; it also resolves the total motion into its horizontal and vertical components. The vertical component must then be corrected for the effect of surface slope and for the net accumulation or ablation.

Surface velocities range from about 1 m year^{-1} in the upper firn areas and gradually increase to a maximum of 16–18 m year,$^{-1}$ 2 to 3 km below the firn line (where the surface slope is not above average at 6–10°) then decrease to 3–5 m year^{-1} near the terminus. Two aspects of this velocity field are of interest:

1) The very slow velocity maximum (20 m year^{-1} is usually considered to be very slow) may indicate an extended period of negative balance or may be, in part, due to the rheology of "cold" ice and the absence of basal slip.

2) The fact that the maximum velocities are below the firn line is an indication that the glacier is not in equilibrium, but has a negative mass balance.

9. Snow and ice stratigraphy

Pits were excavated at many places in the seasonal and perennial snow of the McCall Glacier during each of the four field seasons: 1969, 1970, 1971 and 1972. The pits were selectively placed at representative points in each cirque as well as in the main north–south trending lower part of the glacier. Detailed profiles of temperature, density, ram hardness, and grain size together with a description of the strata were made for the snow and ice at each pit site. The data from these pits have been used for two main purposes: First, they enable us to determine the water equivalent of the annual accumulation increments (thus they are critical to our determination of mass balance); second, they provide information on the physical properties of the snow and on the physical processes which occur within it. The latter includes a study of the mechanisms involved in transforming the snow into glacier ice. The information from pit studies has also enabled us to determine that the McCall Glacier fits into a part of the glacier facies spectrum which has not been studied in detail before.

The basic structure of the seasonal snow cover on the McCall Glacier is essentially the same as that all over the Arctic Slope. Briefly, it consists of two layers: 1) a medium to fine grained, often very hard, wind packed layer at the top, with density in the range of 0.35 to 0.50 g cm^{-3}; 2) a depth hoar layer on the bottom, consisting of large, loosely bonded crystals with density less than 0.30 g cm^{-3}. This snow is subject to drastic change during the summer at all levels on the glacier. It melts completely on the tundra and on the lower half of the glacier. Part of it transforms to superimposed ice directly onto the glacier ice in the lower cirque and up to an altitude of about 2300 m in the middle and upper cirques. At higher altitudes there are areas of perennial firn where the melting and densification processes become more complex.

The physical properties of the firn have been studied in the upper cirque at stake 26 (2375 m) and stake 24.5 (2335 m). Six deep pit studies were made at stake 26, in addition to the studies made every spring to determine the seasonal snow accumulation. The deep pits varied from 4 to 7 m in depth with core drilling, from the pit floor, to total depths as deep as 18 m. One deep pit was made at stake 24.5 in 1972 with Dr. Wakahama's group from the Institute of Low Temperature Science, Hokkaido University, Sapporo, Japan.

The entire annual increment of snow reaches the temperature of 0 C and becomes wet at all altitudes on the McCall Glacier. Part of the melt water percolates downward into the accumulation of the previous two and in some cases three years. The melt water partly refreezes in the firn to form a complex network of ice glands, lenses and layers. The process of meltwater refreezing on pre-existing ice lenses and layers is essentially the same as the process of forming superimposed ice directly on glacier ice as happens at lower altitudes. The complexities of the processes in the firn region are: 1) part of the mass from one annual unit is transported to underlying annual units in variable quantity each year; 2) the refreezing of melt water in the firn adds enthalpy to the system and results in significantly higher temperature (-1 or -2 C at a depth of 10 m below the snow surface) in the firn region than in the lower-lying ice region (-8 to -10 C at the 10 m depth) where melt water percolation is markedly reduced in the solid ice; and 3) the mass transfer by fluid motion (both vapor and liquid) in the firn gives rise to anomalously low density values (of 0.35 g cm^{-3}, for example) at depths of 3 to 4 m below the surface. The low density values are especially striking since the seasonal snow each year attains density values in excess of 0.40 g cm^{-3} during the summer. Therefore, there is not only a low rate of densification of the snow but some snow strata appear to decrease in density as they are buried.

An analysis of the stratigraphic data from the deep pits is currently under way. At present we are comparing the densification rates with similar data from Greenland, Antarctica and high mountain areas of Alaska and Canada. It has proved to be a complicated and interesting study.

10. Atmospheric turbidity measurements on McCall Glacier

The direct component of solar radiation was measured at McCall Glacier with a Linke-Feussner actinometer equipped with standard Schott glass OG1 and RG2 filters to isolate different wavelength intervals. Measurements were made during the spring and summer months of 1970 and 1971.

Analysis of the data for clear days shows that the turbidity is higher in the spring months than it is during the summer months; this agrees well with values found almost a decade earlier from Devon Island in the Canadian Artic. It may suggest that there has not been any significant change in the global background turbidity over the past several years (Shaw and Wendler, 1972).

Acknowledgment. This investigation was supported by the Atmospheric Sciences Section, National Science Foundation, under Grants GA-10090, GA-28278x, and GA-37306.

REFERENCES

Fahl, C. B., 1975: Mean sea level pressure patterns relating to glacier activity in Alaska. Proceedings of Climate of the Arctic Conference, University of Alaska, Aug. 15–17, 1973.

Harrison, W. D., D. Trabant and C. Benson, 1975: Thermal regime of McCall Glacier, Brooks Range, Northern Alaska. Proceedings of Climate of the Arctic Conference, University of Alaska, Aug. 15–17, 1973.

Keeler, C. M., 1959: Notes on the geology of the McCall Valley area, *Arctic*, 12, 2, 87–97.

Orvig, S., 1961: McCall Glacier, Alaska: Meteorological Observations 1957–1958, Arctic Inst. N. Amer. Res. Paper No. 8 (Montreal).

Orvig, S., and W. Mason, 1963: Ice temperatures and heat flux, McCall Glacier, Alaska. Intn'l Assoc. Sci. Hydrol. Publ. 61, 181–188.

Shaw, G., and G. Wendler, 1972: Atmospheric turbidity measurements at McCall Glacier in Northeast Alaska. Preprint Volume of the Conference on Atmospheric Radiation, Aug. 7–9, Fort Collins, Colorado, published by AMS, Boston, Mass., 181–187.

Trabant, D., C. B. Fahl and C. S. Benson, 1973: Mass balance of McCall Glacier, Brooks Range, Alaska, 1971 and 1972 Hydrologic Years. *Journal of Glaciology* (in press).

Wendler, G., C. Fahl and S. Corbin, 1972a: Mass balance studies on McCall Glacier, Brooks Range, Alaska, *Arctic and Alpine Research*, 4, 3, 211–222.

Wendler, G., *et al.*, 1972b: On the hydrology of a partly glacier-covered Arctic watershed, by G. Wendler, D. Trabant and C. Benson, Preprint of the Conference of the Role of Snow and Ice in Hydrology, Banff, Sept. 1972.

Wendler, G., and N. Ishikawa, 1973a: Experimental study of the amount of ice melt using three different methods, *Journal of Glaciology*, **12**, 66, 399–410.

Wendler, G., and N. Ishikawa, 1973b: Heat balance investigation in an Arctic mountainous area in Northern Alaska, *Journal of Applied Meteorology*, **12**, 955–962.

Wendler, G., and N. Ishikawa, 1973c: The effect of slope and exposure and the screening effect of the surrounding mountains on the solar radiation of McCall Glacier, Alaska, *Journal of Glaciology*, **13**, 68, 213–226.

Wendler, G., and N. Ishikawa, 1973d: The combined heat-, ice-, and water-balance of McCall Glacier, Brooks Range, *Journal of Glaciology*, **13**, 68, 227–241.

Wendler, G., *et al.*, 1973: A note on the climate of the McCall Glacier, Alaska in relation to its geographical setting, by G. Wendler, N. Ishikawa, and N. Streten. *Arctic and Alpine Research*, **6**, 3, 307–318, 1974.

Wendler, G., and G. Weller, 1973: A heat balance study on McCall Glacier, Brooks Range, Alaska, *Journal of Glaciology*, **13**, 67, 13–26, 1974.

Mean Sea Level Pressure Patterns Relating to Glacier Activity in Alaska

CHARLES B. FAHL[1]

Geophysical Institute, University of Alaska, Fairbanks, Alaska

Abstract

Relationships between climate and glaciers were investigated for three glaciers in mainland Alaska: McCall Glacier in the Brooks Range, Gulkana Glacier in the Alaska Range, and Wolverine Glacier in the Kenai Range. Mean pressure maps (MPM's) were constructed for each glacier for particular seasons and particular climatic conditions that contributed either to the growth of the glacier or to the decay of the glacier. The synoptic patterns revealed by the MPM's for summer snowfall on McCall Glacier resembled other investigators' theoretical July maps for ice age conditions. A low was found near 70°N, 130°W. A northward shift of 2–3 degrees of latitude was noted in the summertime cyclogenetic zone of extreme northwestern Canada. Precipitation at McCall Glacier was enhanced when the Pacific High was stronger than normal, steering cyclones around Alaska into the Beaufort Sea. Ablation on McCall Glacier increased when the Aleutian Low was stronger than normal resulting in generally southerly drier air at the glacier. Snowfall on Gulkana Glacier was enhanced throughout the year when the mean Aleutian Low was shifted eastward 10–20° and the axis of the low was rotated counterclockwise about 10° from its normal east-west orientation. Ablation increased when the Beaufort Sea High was stronger than normal. Snowfall on Wolverine Glacier was enhanced when the mean Aleutian Low was intensified and shifted westward to a slightly more southerly position than that noted for Gulkana Glacier. A stronger than normal Pacific High contributed to increased ablation on Wolverine Glacier during the summer and reduced accumulation during the winter. Thus, a strong Aleutian Low was found to favor glacial growth in the Alaska and Coastal (Kenai and Chugach) mountain ranges while it favored glacial decay in the Brooks Range. Conversely, a weak Aleutian Low (implying a strong Pacific High) favored glacial growth in the Brooks Range and glacial decay in the Alaska and Coastal Ranges. Altogether, though, conditions in the recent historical period (1900–1970) have been unfavorable for glaciation in these three Alaskan mountain ranges.

---

1. Introduction

The main results presented in this paper are a series of weather maps, each of which shows the mean sea level pressure for a particular climatic condition which is conducive for either growth or decay of one of three glaciers in mainland Alaska. These three glaciers are located one each in the principal mountain ranges of mainland Alaska: McCall Glacier in the Brooks Range, Gulkana Glacier in the Alaska Range, and Wolverine Glacier in the Coastal Range (composed of the Kenai and Chugach Mountain Ranges). These three mountain ranges separate Alaska into four climatic zones: (1) an arctic zone north of the Brooks Range, (2) a continental zone between the Brooks and Alaska Ranges, (3) a transitional zone between the Alaska and Coastal Ranges, and (4) a maritime zone south of the Coastal Ranges. The three glaciers thus represent a cross section of glaciers from strongly maritime to strongly continental; Wolverine Glacier is the most strongly maritime in character while McCall Glacier is the most strongly continental in character. The circulation patterns and climate that are either conducive or not for glacier growth can be established

by averaging weather maps for only those days when certain climatic conditions occur. For example, if it is desired to learn what the summer circulation patterns would be during periods when glaciers are growing, those summer days when snow of a prescribed quantity fell on the glacier can be selected and the sea level pressure for those days averaged. The result is a mean pressure map (MPM) that approximates a circulation pattern that enhances glacier growth, and perhaps a pattern that existed during the last ice age. The opposite can also be done such that a circulation pattern that enhances glacial decay is produced. Such a circulation pattern might approximate one that perhaps existed during the period when the last great ice age was ameliorating.

For each MPM produced two associated or derived maps are also produced which amplify the significant features of the MPM. One map shows the normal pressure pattern for the particular time that the events constituting the MPM occurred in. These normal patterns are monthly normals based on the 25-year period from 1947 to 1971. The other derived map is the pressure anomaly map which shows the difference in pressure between the MPM and the normal map; it shows those areas where the MPM differs the most from the normal map.

---

[1] Presently affiliated with Dames and Moore, Anchorage, Alaska.

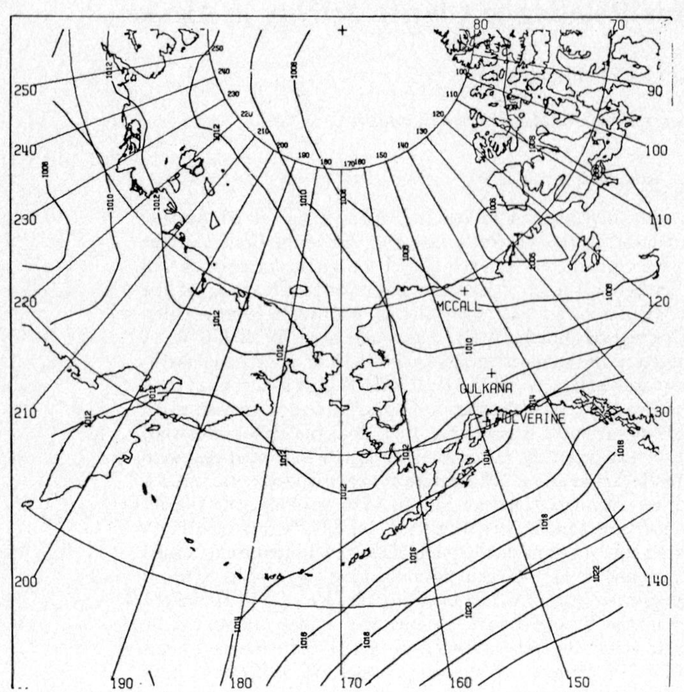

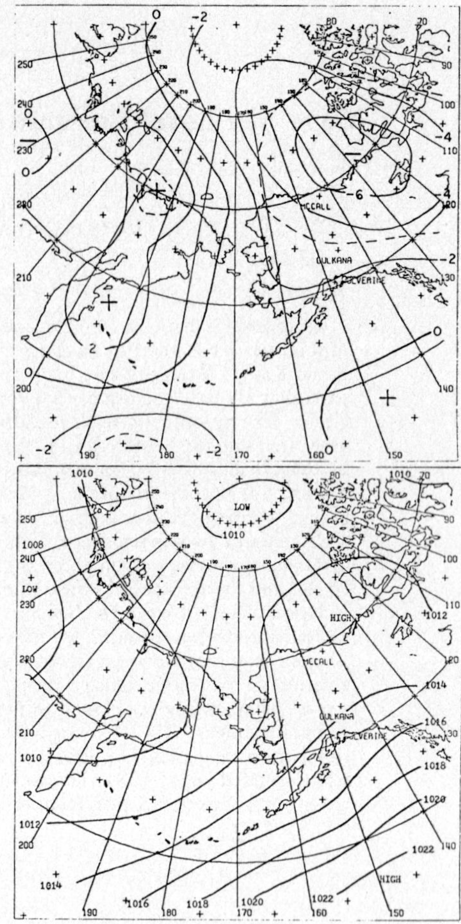

Fig. 1. (a) Mean pressure map for 23 summer snowfalls, McCall Glacier; (b) mean pressure anomaly pattern; (c) normal summer (July) sea level pressure (mb).

Note: Pressure anomalies (2-mb intervals) from 1947–1971 normals. Broken lines enclose areas where anomalies are significantly different from zero at the 95% level according to *t*-test.

2. Results

Summer snowfall

The MPM for the climatic condition of summer snowfall on McCall Glacier was derived from 23 separate maps. A snowfall of at least 2.5 mm water equivalent (w/e) in the 12 hour period centered around the synoptic observation times of 0000 GMT or 1200 GMT constituted a snowfall event. The summers of 1969 through 1972 were investigated; thus there were 23 days during this period when summer snowfalls of the prescribed quantity occurred on McCall Glacier. These 23 maps were then averaged producing a MPM (Fig. 1). The principal features of this MPM are the low pressure system near 70°N, 130°W, the low pressure pattern throughout all of the Arctic Ocean, and the mean northerly flow near McCall Glacier, a flow which allowed orographic uplift to augment precipitation in this area. The pressure anomaly map and the normal pressure pattern are also shown in Fig. 1. It is seen that the normal pressure pattern, for the month

of July, differs considerably from the pattern shown in the MPM. This difference is accentuated on the anomaly map where a strongly negative anomaly area to the northeast of McCall Glacier is shown.

Fig. 2 shows the MPM for the climatic condition of summer snowfall on Gulkana Glacier. Once again the four summers of 1969 through 1972 were used; however, the threshold level of snowfall used here was 7 mm (w/e) in 12 hours. A special feature of this map is the southwest–northeast trough across Alaska with the long axis lying to the northwest of Gulkana Glacier. The indicated geostrophic flow is southwesterly at low levels. The mean storm track is also southwesterly along the axis of the trough, a track favoring the influx of moisture from the Bering Sea and North Pacific Ocean. The normal map and the anomaly map illustrate the anomalies of this MPM showing the negative anomaly area centered to the east of Gulkana Glacier and extending over all of Alaska and much of northwest Canada. There is a small positive anomaly area in the central Aleutians. The orientation of these anomaly areas implies more cyclonic activity than normal in central Alaska during these snowfall events, an increase in cyclonic activity that can be attributed to an eastward shift of the Aleutian Low.

Winter snowfall

In Fig. 3, the MPM for the condition of winter snowfall at McCall Glacier is depicted. The most interesting feature of this map is the Aleutian Low near 57°N, 175°E. There is also a weak low located near McCall Glacier; convergent circulation is indicated in the McCall Glacier region. Consideration of the anomaly and normal maps helps to illustrate the pressure patterns and the dynamic conditions contributing to winter snowfall on McCall Glacier. The strongly positive pressure anomaly area in the Gulf of Alaska implies that cyclones were steered around Alaska into the Arctic Ocean. The existence of the negative anomaly area near McCall Glacier itself is a further example of this steering affect.

The MPM for winter snow at Gulkana Glacier (Fig. 4) is characterized by a southwest–northeast orientation of an extension of the Aleutian Low into central Alaska. The orientation of this trough indicates a mean storm track into central Alaska. Consideration of the anomaly pattern shows again a strong negative anomaly over Alaska centered to the north of Gulkana Glacier, and a strong positive anomaly in the eastern Gulf of Alaska indicating that storms are being steered away from this area into central Alaska.

The MPM for winter snowfall at Wolverine Glacier (Fig. 5) is marked by a strong pressure gradient indicating intensification of the Aleutian Low. The resultant geostrophic flow at Wolverine Glacier is very strong, about 10 m s^{-1} from the southeast. The intensification of this low and its shift to the east is vividly displayed on the anomaly map which shows negative pressure anomalies greater than 16 mb in the vicinity of the Alaska Peninsula.

Summer hot spells

Figs. 6, 7 and 8 show the MPM's and their derived maps for the climatic conditions of hot spells at each

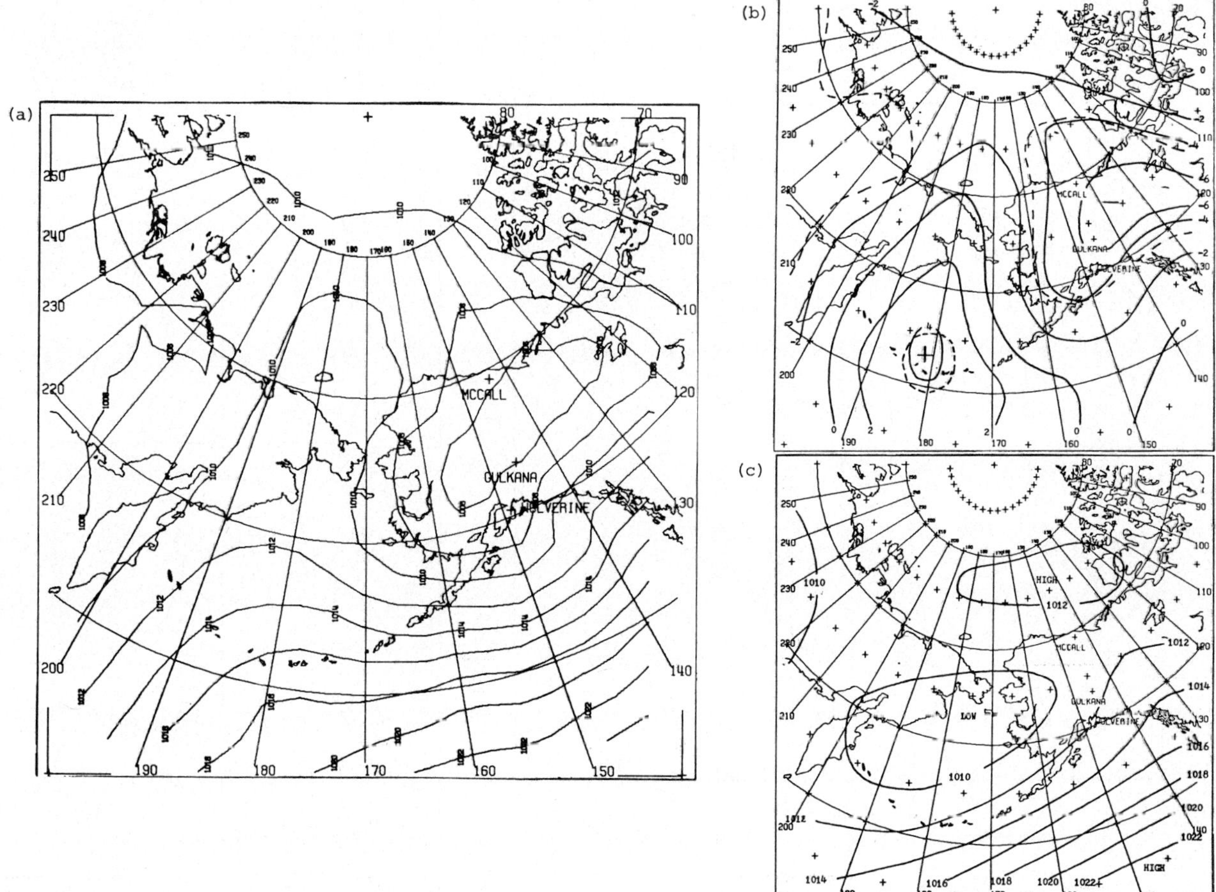

FIG. 2. (a) Mean pressure map for 27 summer snowfalls, Gulkana Glacier; (b) mean pressure anomaly pattern; (c) normal summer (August) sea level pressure (mb). See note at foot of Fig. 1.

of the three glaciers. These hot spells were selected to represent those patterns that would be conducive for ablation; that is conducive for decay of the glaciers.

The MPM for McCall Glacier (Fig. 6) shows that the Aleutian Low, located near 53°N, 176°W, is well defined. Weak pressure gradients are evident near McCall Glacier itself and the geostrophic flow there is southeasterly. The normal and anomaly maps show that an intensification of the Aleutian Low is significant for hot spells at McCall Glacier.

The MPM for hot spells at Gulkana Glacier (Fig. 7) is characterized by a strong high pressure system in the Arctic Ocean and a weakened and westward shifted Aleutian Low. Only a very weak northerly flow at Gulkana Glacier is indicated. Inspection of the anomaly map along with the normal map shows that the Beaufort Sea High is above normal by several mb.

The MPM for hot spells at Wolverine Glacier (Fig. 8) is markedly different than those for McCall and Gulkana Glaciers. Essentially, the normal North Pacific High has been stretched northwards and covers all of Alaska. This northward stretching or shifting is strongest in southwest Alaska, a positive anomaly

of 8 mb being indicated on the anomaly map. The indicated geostrophic flow at Wolverine Glacier is weak and from the northwest, a direction of flow which is perhaps critical for ablation there due to the fact that the air reaching the glacier can be heated while passing overland; other directions of flow would not allow as much heating as the overland passages have less extent or are virtually nil.

3. Discussion

McCall Glacier

The circulation patterns and weather systems that contributed to the growth or decay of McCall Glacier were more complex than those affecting the other two glaciers. Conditions in the Beaufort Sea, Northwest Canada, the Bering Sea, and the North Pacific Ocean were all critical. Growth occurred when the patterns interacted to produce northerly flow at the glacier. A low in the Beaufort Sea to the north and/or to the east as well as one in extreme northwestern Canada was frequently the agent of such flow. A blocking high in the North Pacific Ocean steered storms around

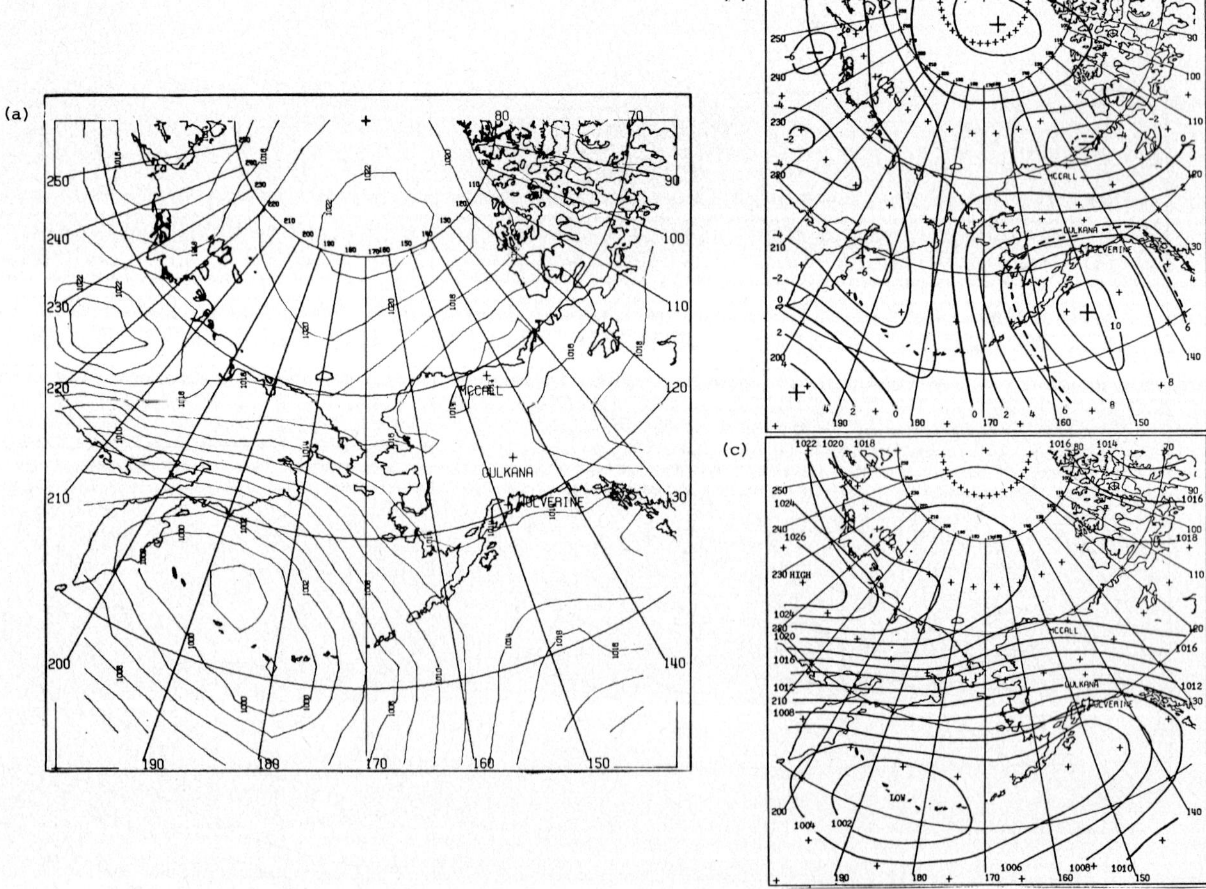

Fig. 3. (a) Mean pressure map for 29 winter snowfalls, McCall Glacier; (b) mean pressure anomaly pattern; (c) normal winter (December–February) sea level pressure (mb). See note at foot of Fig. 1.

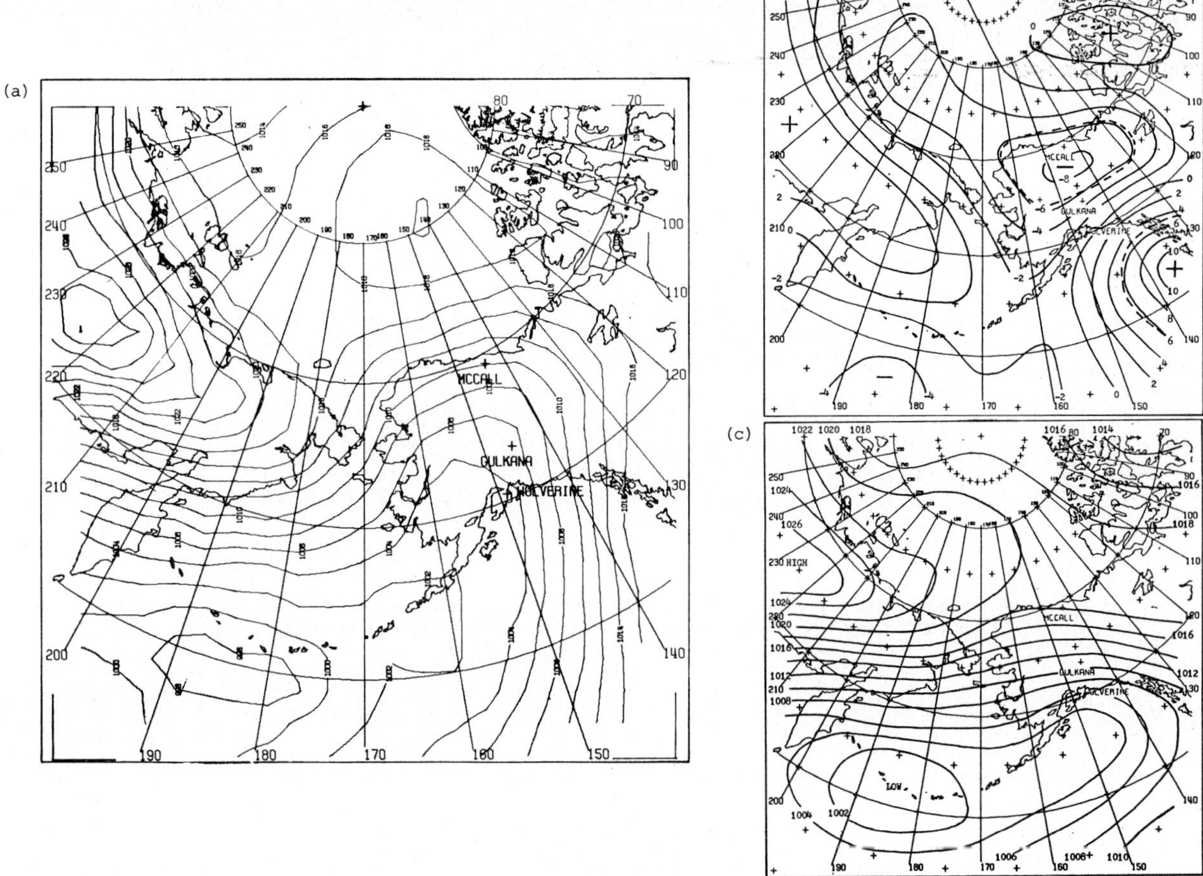

Fig. 4. (a) Mean pressure map for 29 winter snowfalls, Gulkana Glacier; (b) mean pressure anomaly pattern; (c) normal winter (December–February) sea level pressure (mb). See note at foot of Fig. 1.

Alaska into the Arctic Ocean and was, therefore, a favorable pattern for growth. Decay occurred when the patterns produced southerly flow at the glacier. Such flow was drier as the air had passed over at least the Brooks Range and possibly the Alaska Range and Coastal Ranges as well. In addition, orographic uplift could not increase precipitation when the wind was from the south. A very strong Aleutian Low produced southerly flow. Such a strong flow can be considered a manifestation of broader scale flow restricting cyclonic activity north of the Alaska range. Also, a strong Aleutian Low implies the compensatory formation of the Beaufort Sea High. In summer a strong Beaufort Sea High favored ablation on McCall Glacier while in winter it hindered accumulation.

Gulkana Glacier

The Aleutian Low was the most critical circulation pattern affecting the growth of Gulkana Glacier. Growth occurred there with southerly flow; moisture was brought by storms from the southwest. An easterly shift of the Aleutian Low was always observed during snowfall on Gulkana Glacier. Decay occurred when these factors did not operate; thus a westward shifted Aleutian Low was unfavorable. The build up of the Beaufort Sea High in the summer increased ablation on Gulkana Glacier.

Wolverine Glacier

Only circulation patterns in the Pacific Ocean affected growth and decay at Wolverine Glacier. Growth occurred when the Aleutian Low was very intense and shifted to the east. A slightly more southerly position of this low than found for Gulkana Glacier occurred. Southerly to southeasterly flow at Wolverine Glacier favored growth. When these conditions did not evolve decay was favored. A strong blocking high in the north Pacific Ocean was the single most important feature whose appearance caused decay. In winter it acted to steer storms away from the glacier preventing accumulation, while in summer its appearance enhanced ablation.

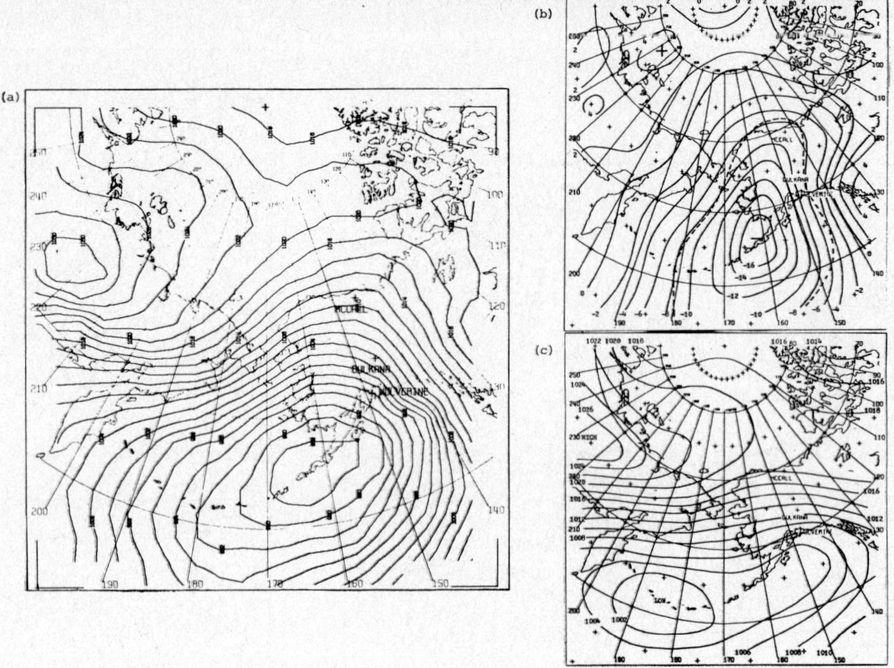

FIG. 5. (a) Mean pressure map for 22 winter snowfalls, Wolverine Glacier; (b) mean pressure anomaly pattern; (c) normal winter (December–February) sea level pressure (mb). See note at foot of Fig. 1.

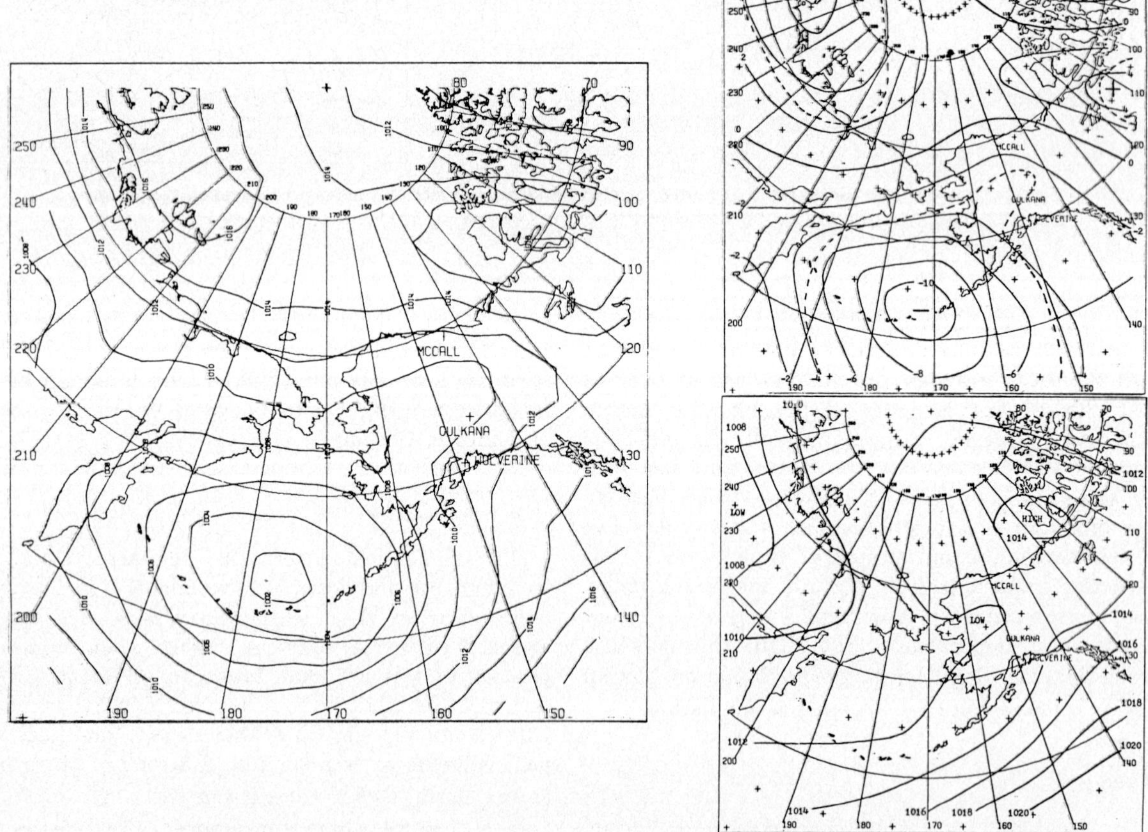

FIG. 6. (a) Mean pressure map for 12 hot spells, McCall Glacier; (b) mean pressure anomaly pattern; (c) normal summer (June–July) sea level pressure (mb). See note at foot of Fig. 1.

344

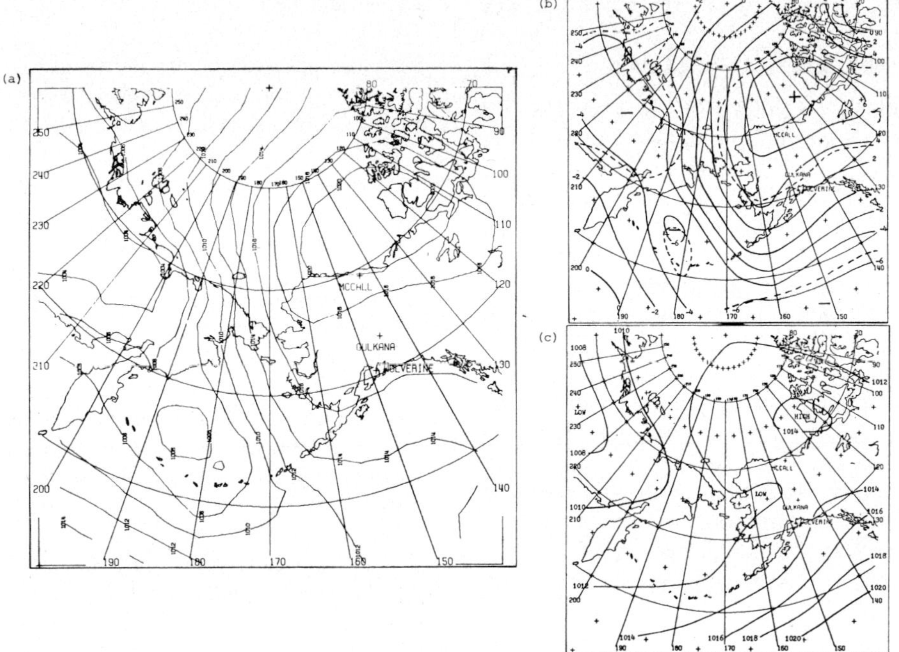

FIG. 7. (a) Mean pressure map for 10 hot spells, Gulkana Glacier; (b) mean pressure anomaly pattern; (d) normal summer (June–July) sea level pressure (mb). See note at foot of Fig. 1.

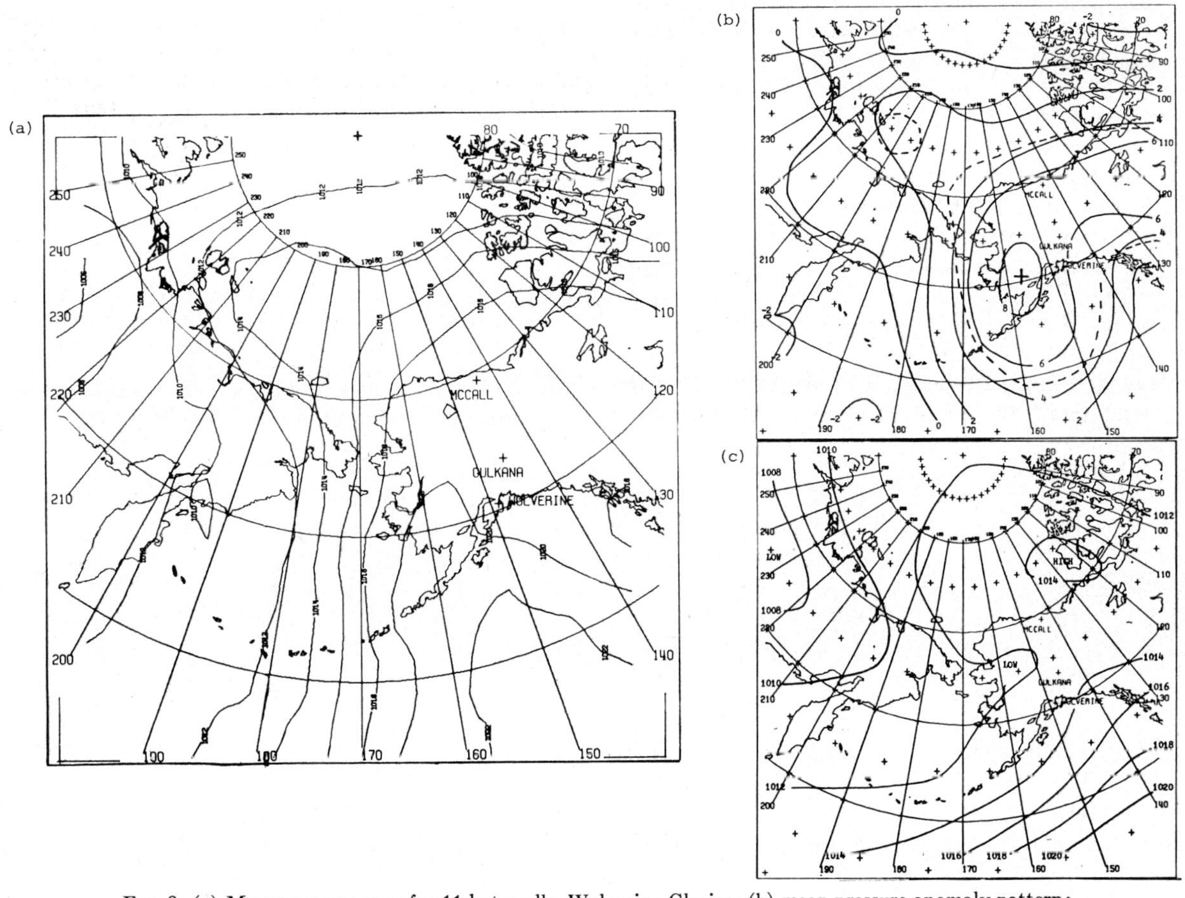

FIG. 8. (a) Mean pressure map for 11 hot spells, Wolverine Glacier; (b) mean pressure anomaly pattern; (c) normal summer (June–July) sea level pressure (mb). See note at foot of Fig. 1.

4. Comparison with other investigations

The features shown on the MPM's in Figs. 1 and 2 (MPM's for summer snowfall on McCall and Gulkana Glaciers, respectively) are similar in form to those features found on theoretical ice age period mean pressure maps. Both Lamb and Woodroffe (1970, Fig. 9a, p. 50) and Williams and Barry (1975) have shown troughs or closed lows in the vicinity of 70°N, 130°W. The MPM for summer snowfall on McCall Glacier (Fig. 1) shows a low pressure cell in this area. The presence of a low pressure system here during the summer is reasonable as a pattern conducive to the nourishment of a continental ice sheet lying to the south. When a low such as this existed during the middle of an ice age we can speculate that frequent snowfalls would occur along the margin of the ice sheet, nourishing it as well as glaciers in the nearby Brooks Range.

5. Conclusion

For all three glaciers it was found that growth occurred when the low level flow was from the nearest large body of water; there was an adequate supply of moisture. Decay occurred when these conditions were not met, there was not an adequate supply of moisture. Since the influx of moisture is expected for glacier growth the fact that the MPM's for "good" circulations showed patterns favorable for moisture influx is a further proof that they are reasonable and realistic patterns. Flow from the direction of the nearest body of water was partially happenstance for McCall Glacier. Other bodies of water were moisture sources for McCall Glacier, especially in the winter and spring. However, whatever the moisture source, most significant accumulations there occurred if the low level flow was northerly. This direction allowed orographic uplift to operate and increase precipitation amounts.

Synoptic patterns favorable for glacier growth were not the same for each glacier. Features that favored growth of McCall Glacier were a blocking high over the Gulf of Alaska and/or mainland Alaska and a westward shifted Aleutian Low. Such systems resulted in decay of Gulkana and Wolverine Glaciers. However, glacial growth or decay at all three glaciers is not necessarily mutually exclusive. A proper alternation of individually favorable or unfavorable conditions for the three glaciers might occur in a particular year such that all three would experience either a positive or a negative annual balance. Identification of the patterns that might be responsible for such occurrences was not made here, as investigation of the hemispheric flow at higher levels would probably be required.

Acknowledgments. This work was used to satisfy, in part, the requirements for the Ph.D. degree at the Geophysical Institute at the University of Alaska, Fairbanks. Financial support was provided by the Atmospheric Sciences Section of the National Science Foundation under Grants NSF GA-10090 and GA-28278X. The author wishes to thank his co-workers on the McCall Glacier project, notably Drs. G. Wendler, C. Benson, and G. Weller, and Mr. D. Trabant who in part gathered the McCall Glacier climatological data used in this study. Mr. Larry Mayo of the U. S. Geological Survey, Fairbanks, Alaska, kindly furnished climatological data from Gulkana and Wolverine Glaciers.

REFERENCES

Lamb, H. H., and A. Woodroffe, 1970: Atmospheric circulation during the last ice age. *Quaternary Research*, **1**, 29–58.

Williams, J., and R. Barry, 1975: Ice age experiments with the NCAR general circulation model: conditions in the vicinity of the northern continental ice sheets. 24th Alaska Science Conference, University of Alaska, Fairbanks, August 15–17, 1973.

Thermal Regime of McCall Glacier, Brooks Range, Northern Alaska

Dennis Trabant

U. S. Geological Survey, Water Resources Division, Fairbanks, Alaska, 99701

W. D. Harrison and Carl Benson

Geophysical Institute, University of Alaska, Fairbanks, Alaska 99701

Abstract

The thermal regime of McCall Glacier, a small valley glacier located in the Romanzof Mountains of the northeastern Brooks Range, Alaska, is discussed. Near-surface temperatures are warmer in the accumulation zone than in the ablation zone, and show uneven spatial variability, apparently in response to non-uniform water permeability of the firn. Although the accumulation of the current year, and perhaps the two previous years, is warmed to 0 C in the summer, the glacier is cold throughout most of its thickness in both the accumulation and ablation zones. At least in some areas bottom temperatures appear to reach 0 C, and there is probably a finite thickness of 0 C ice. Some implications of this thermal regime are considered.

The temperature of a glacier has a profound effect on most aspects of its behavior; ice flow, surface geometry, hydrology, basal sliding and erosional processes are all in this category. Although glacier temperature is ultimately controlled by climate, there is not necessarily any simple relationship between micrometeorology and glacier temperature, except perhaps in temperate glaciers, which are at 0 C throughout, or in some glaciers that are so cold that there is never any surface melting. Often conductive, advective, and latent heat transport in the ice or snow are all important, along with frictional and geothermal heating. In this situation the determination of glacier thermal regime may require considerable experimental effort. We are reporting here on part of an ongoing project to determine the thermal regime of McCall Glacier, and to study the factors controlling it. It is thought that this glacier, located in the Romanzof Mountains of the northeastern Brooks Range, may be typical of many other Arctic glaciers.

Fig. 1 is a map of the glacier showing the usual position of the firn line and the temperature measurement sites. The near surface temperature measurements were made with thermocouples in holes ranging from 8 to 20 meters deep, which were made with a coring auger or a steam drill. Temperatures at a depth of 10 m below the snow or ice surface are shown in Fig. 2. Although seasonal 10 m temperature variations are usually thought to be small, this is not true in the accumulation area of McCall Glacier, where 1 C variations are typical. The 10 m temperature seems to be everywhere warmer than the mean annual air temperature, which at 1700 m is approximately −12 C.

It is seen in Fig. 2 that the data points obtained below the firn line can be connected with a smooth curve showing a slight decrease in temperature with altitude, while no smooth curve can be drawn through the data obtained in the firn areas. Obviously the situation is more complicated in the firn area, although it can be said that temperatures are considerably higher there than below the firn line, and show a rough trend to warming with altitude.

Evidently the temperature in the firn area is influenced by the permeability of the snow and firn. The highest temperatures are found where the percolation of liquid water is thought to be greatest, and temperatures decrease in response to the decreasing permeability in the direction of the firn line. The decrease in permeability is due to the accumulation of ice lenses and layers within the snow and firn. In the summer, the freezing of percolating water raises the snow temperature to 0 C. Pit studies at one site in the accumulation zone (Fig. 1) indicate that there this process extends to a depth which usually includes three annual increments of accumulation, although the lower 0 C boundary is irregular. In spite of this, the glacier is definitely not temperate. The freezing of percolating water has a significant effect on the mass balance of such glaciers (Trabant *et al.*, in press).

These near-surface temperatures can be thought of as the upper boundary condition which, together with effects of ice motion and geothermal heat, determine deep ice temperature. So far, deep temperature measurements have been made at only two sites. A 90 m deep thermocouple chain placed in the accumulation zone (Fig. 1) by an I.G.Y. team (Orvig and Mason, 1963) showed a fairly constant temperature of about −1 C or −1.5 C below the depth of seasonal varia-

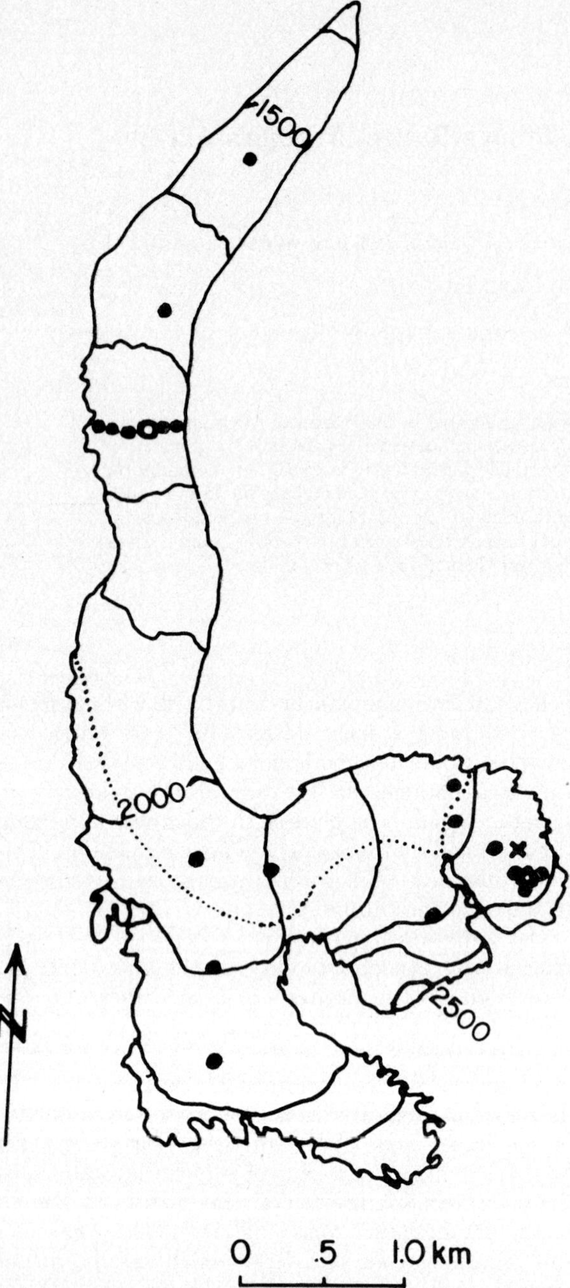

FIG. 1. Map of McCall Glacier showing the location of temperature measurement stations, average firn line and deep snow pit. ··· Average firn line. ● Temperature probe site. ○ 75 m deep temperature site. × 90 m deep IGY temperature site. △ Snow pit location.

tions. We have not yet attempted an analysis of these data. In 1972 we placed a 75 m deep thermistor chain near the center of the ablation zone (Fig. 1). Both chains were placed with electro-thermal drills.

Our deep temperature data are shown in Fig. 3. These data were fitted with a simple time-independent temperature model which includes the effect of vertical

advection:

$$\kappa\frac{d^2T}{dy^2} - v\frac{dT}{dy} = 0,$$

where T is the temperature, κ is the thermal diffusivity of ice, y is the surface-normal coordinate, and v is the surface-normal velocity. The magnitude of the omitted longitudinal advection term was estimated from the 10 m longitudinal temperature gradient (Fig. 2) and the observed surface velocity (16 m/year), and found to be small. The fit given by the solid curve of Fig. 3 was obtained using a constant surface-normal velocity (v) of 0.8 m/year, a value consistent with surface velocity measurements in the vicinity.

An effort was made to find the temperature at the bed of the glacier by extrapolation. The $v=$constant fit implies that the 0 C isotherm should lie at a depth of 127 m. A slightly different extrapolation, made by allowing v to decrease linearly to zero between 75 m

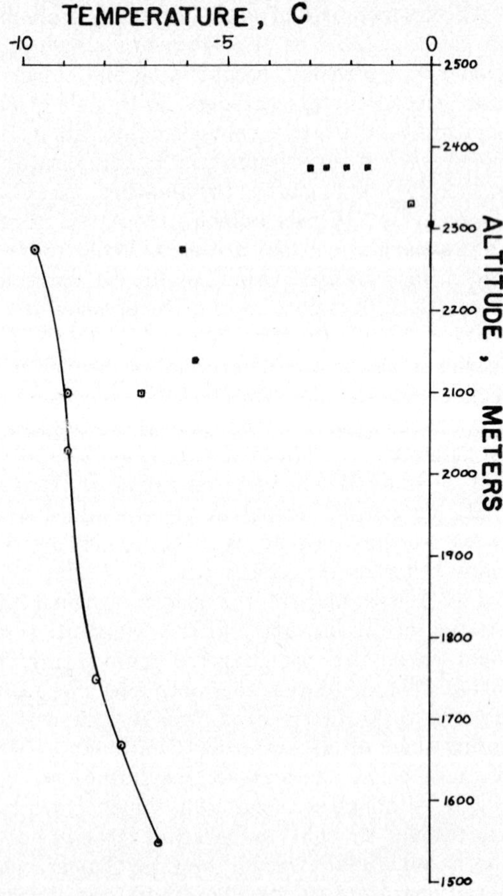

FIG. 2. Ten meter deep temperatures from measurements made October 4 and 5, 1972, on McCall Glacier. The circles are temperatures from sites below the firn line and the squares are temperatures from sites above the firn line.

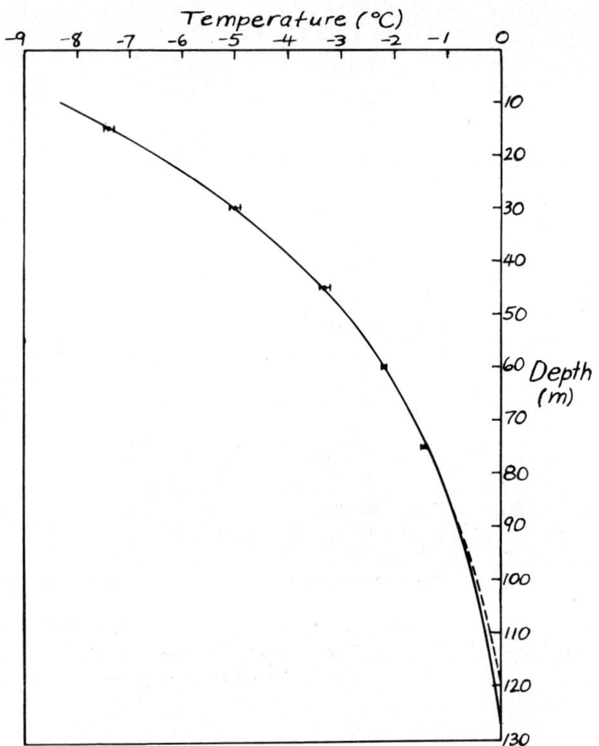

Fig. 3. Temperature of McCall Glacier at 1730 m altitude in the middle of the ablation area. The solid curve is for a constant surface-normal velocity (v). The broken curve is for a surface-normal velocity which decreases with depth below 75 m.

and the bed, implies that the 0 C isotherm is at 119 m depth (broken curve in Fig. 3). These depths are to be compared with the estimate of 150 m for total depth, which was made from a consideration of surface slope and velocity, using the mechanics of Budd and Allison (1975). According to these extrapolations, the temperature gradient at the 0 C isotherm is about 1.8 deg/100 m. A more elaborate extrapolation, which would include the effect of heat dissipation by glacier flow, would lower the 0 C isotherm but also rapidly decrease the temperature gradient there. For example, if the 0 C isotherm were below the estimated position of the glacier bed, the temperature gradient at the bed would be much less than 1.8 deg/100 m, while a gradient of 2.2 deg/100 m would be needed to transport normal geothermal heat. Therefore the glacier bed appears to be at 0 C at this site. Probably there is a finite thickness of 0 C ice, in which case no geothermal heat would enter the glacier here.

It seems likely that basal sliding and erosional processes associated with temperate glaciers occur under McCall Glacier. But because the greater portion of the glacier thickness is below 0 C, one would be surprised to find any process requiring penetration of surface water to the bed. For the same reason, storage of large amounts of liquid water would not be expected either.

Acknowledgments. This research was supported in part by the Atmospheric Sciences Section, National Science Foundation, under Grants GA-10090 and GA-28278x, and in part by State of Alaska funds.

REFERENCES

Budd, W. F., and I. Allison, 1975: An empirical scheme for measuring the dynamics of unmeasured glaciers: International Union of Geodesy and Geophysics, International Association of Scientific Hydrology, General Assembly, Moscow, IAHS Publ. 104.

Orvig, Svenn, and R. W. Mason, 1963: Ice temperatures and heat flux; McCall Glacier, Alaska: International Union of Geodesy and Geophysics, International Association of Scientific Hydrology, General Assembly, Berkeley, 181–188.

Trabant, D., C. Fahl and C. Benson, 1975: Mass balance of McCall Glacier, Brooks Range, Alaska, 1971 and 1972 Hydrologic years. *Journal of Glaciology* (in press).

Temperature Measurements on Black Rapids Glacier, Alaska, 1973*

W. D. Harrison

Geophysical Institute, University of Alaska, Fairbanks, Alaska

L. R. Mayo and D. C. Trabant

U. S. Geological Survey, Fairbanks, Alaska

Abstract

As part of reconnaissance work on Black Rapids Glacier, we measured near-surface temperatures in early April and July, 1973, at three sites. The highest site is at 1860 m altitude in the accumulation area. In April the 0 C isotherm was found at a depth of 9 m below the 1972 summer surface; by July the snow and firn were isothermal at 0 C at all depths of temperature measurement. It is fairly likely that this condition is typical of the entire accumulation area. The second site is at an altitude of 1550 m, about 7 km below the equilibrium line. There the April and July temperatures were, respectively, −1.0 and −1.7 C at 10 m below the 1972 summer surface. The third site is at 1140 m in the ablation area and the temperatures were −0.6 and −1.2 C.

Our measurements favor the classification of Black Rapids Glacier as temperate, except for the colder surface layer. In this case its surge behavior would not be due to thermal instability associated with alternation between freezing and melting conditions at the bed.

Several hundred glaciers in Alaska periodically flow at speeds 10 to 100 times greater than their "normal" flow rate; these are called surging glaciers. To date no satisfactory explanation of this surging behavior exists. A leading hypothesis (Robin, 1955; Hoffman and Clarke, 1972) states that a surging glacier is normally frozen to its bed and that surging recurs periodically when the bed is warmed to 0 C as the ice in the "ice reservoir" area gradually thickens while the glacier recovers from its previous surge. The inference is that no temperate glacier, one that is at 0 C throughout except for a thin surface layer subject to seasonal temperature fluctuations, may surge, at least by this mechanism.

Black Rapids is a famous surging glacier in the central Alaska Range. The glacier has surged periodically in the past; the last surge was in 1936–37. The Richardson Highway is built over moraines associated with earlier, somewhat larger surges which blocked the Delta River. A joint project on the Black Rapids Glacier by the U. S. Geological Survey, Water Resources Division, the University of Alaska and the University of Washington is designed to study the mechanism of surging. As part of our work we are attempting to determine the thermal regime.

Three holes were steam drilled in firn and ice on October 18–19, 1972 (Fig. 1). An array of three thermocouples spaced at 4 m intervals was placed in each hole. The temperature at each thermocouple was measured in April and July, 1973; the uncertainty is about ±0.15 C. Overlying snow temperatures were obtained at the same time using a bimetallic dial thermometer in the walls of snow pits; the uncertainty is about ±0.4 C for temperatures in the snow and somewhat greater for the snow surface temperatures.

Temperature data from the highest altitude station, at 1860 m, near the center of the accumulation area are presented in Fig. 2. The April 3 measurements revealed that the winter cold wave had penetrated about 9 m below the summer surface. By July 19,

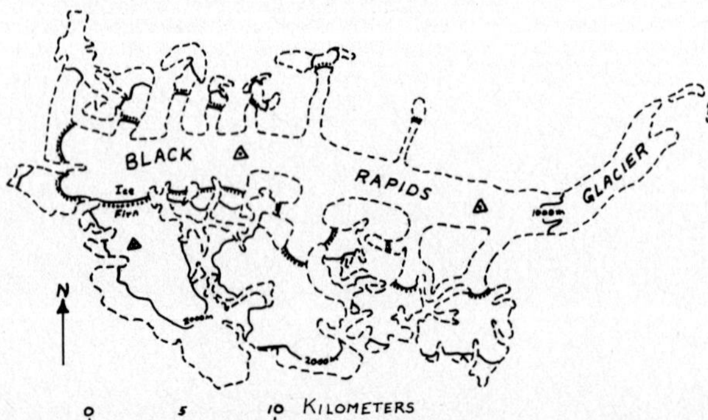

Fig. 1. Map of Black Rapids Glacier showing the location of temperature measurement stations and the average firn edge.

* Publication authorized by the Director, U. S. Geological Survey.

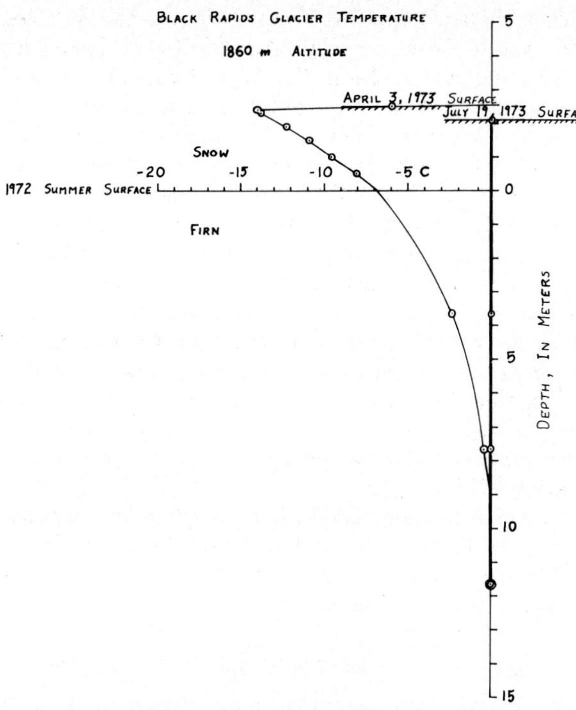

FIG. 2. Temperature of Black Rapids Glacier at 1860 m altitude in the accumulation area. The snow depths at the times of measurement are also shown.

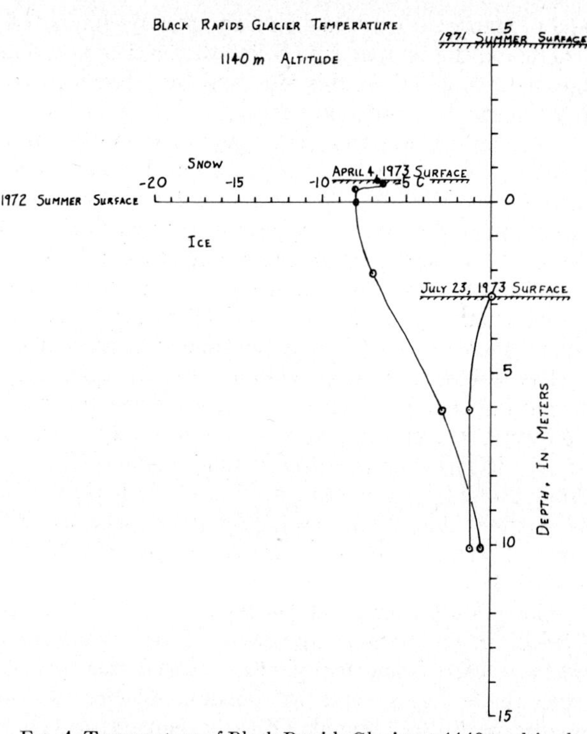

FIG. 4. Temperature of Black Rapids Glacier at 1140 m altitude, low in the ablation area. The April snow depth and ice ablation by July are also shown.

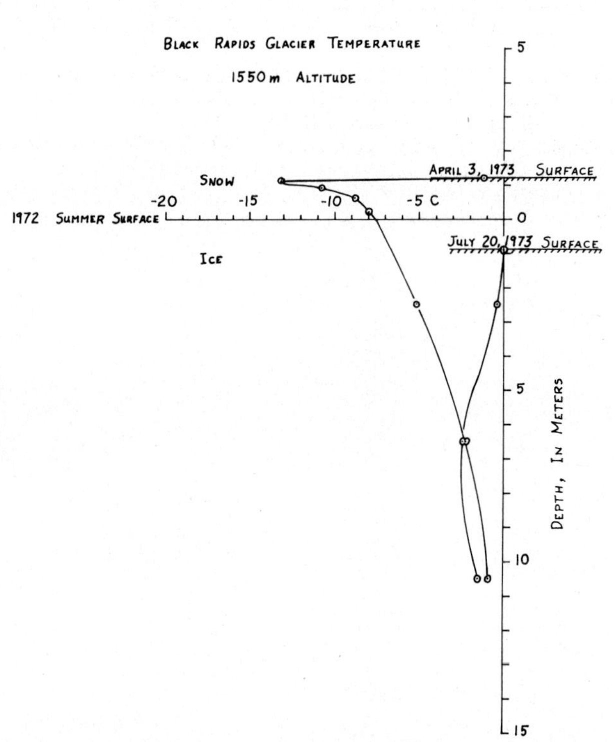

FIG. 3. Temperature of Black Rapids Glacier at 1550 m altitude, high in the ablation area. The April snow depth and ice ablation by July are also shown.

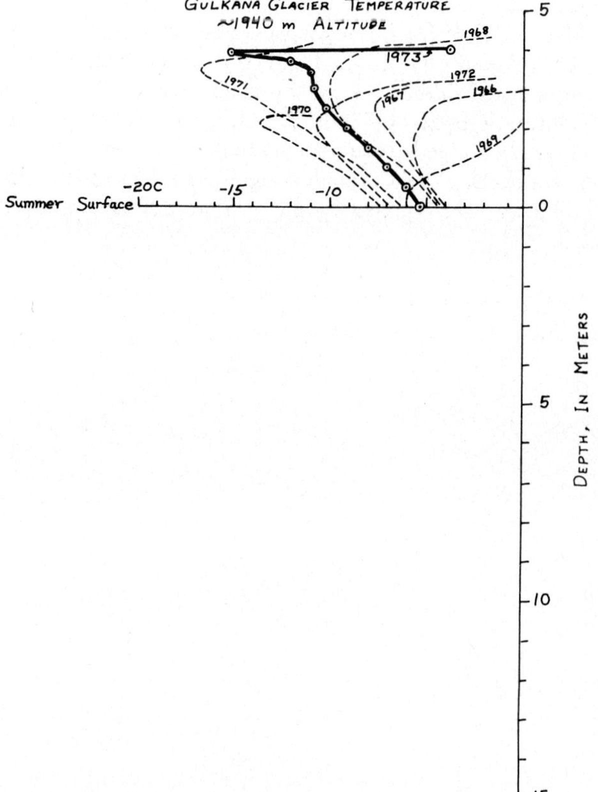

FIG. 5. Eight years of Gulkana Glacier spring snow cover temperatures. The 1973 spring temperatures were not extreme.

and probably earlier, it had been completely eliminated. Therefore, the temperature below the level of seasonal fluctuations is 0 C at this site, and by inference over most of the accumulation basin.

Ice temperatures from the upper part of the ablation area, 7 km below the equilibrium line and at an altitude of 1550 m, are shown in Fig. 3. Seasonal temperature fluctuations appear to be nearly damped out at 10 m depth, where the temperature is between −1.0 and −1.7 C. Note that depths have been referenced to the 1972 summer surface rather than the actual snow or ice surface at the time of measurement.

The lowest site is at 1140 m altitude, somewhat below the center of the ablation area. Here the April and July temperatures are −0.6 and −1.2 C, respectively, 10 m below the 1972 summer surface (Fig. 4). Annual ablation removes 3 to 5 m of ice here, and it is possible that 10 m below the ice surface at any time of year the temperature is continuously higher than −1 C.

The question arises as to whether these data are typical or, for example, the result of an exceptionally warm winter. Snow temperature measurements have been made for 8 years at Gulkana Glacier, 30 km southeast of Black Rapids Glacier. Temperatures from March through May, at approximately 1940 m altitude (Fig. 5) were compared with the April 1973 Black Rapids temperatures. The snowpack base, or summer surface, has varied from −4 to −7.4 C. On March 31, 1973, the snowpack base was −5.4 C and the temperature gradient in the lower part of the snow was similar to all previous years. From this information, the 1973 Black Rapids Glacier temperatures are judged to be near normal.

Black Rapids is typical of many glaciers in that its ablation area is cooler than its accumulation area. This is because the impermeable ice in the ablation area cannot be warmed by the freezing of downward percolating water. Both the 10 m temperatures and the annual ice loss in the ablation area are similar to those of Athabasca Glacier in Canada's Jasper National Park, which is temperate in the ablation area below a depth of roughly 15 m (Paterson 1971, 1972). It is likely that Black Rapids Glacier is similar. In this situation, probably typical of many glaciers, latent heat is released at the lower boundary of the cool surface layer by the freezing of small amounts of liquid water contained in the upward moving ice. We have not yet measured deep temperatures, and it is possible that the temperature structure here is complicated by the slow freezing of water trapped in deep crevasses during the 1936–37 surge (Jarvis and Clarke, 1974).

In summary, the near-surface temperature measurements we have made to date favor the classification of Black Rapids as a temperate glacier, in which case its surge behavior could not be thermally controlled.

REFERENCES

Hoffman, J. W., and G. K. C. Clarke, 1972: Periodic temperature instabilities in sub-polar glaciers. International Symposia on the Role of Snow and Ice in Hydrology, Banff Symposium, UNESCO-WMO Conference. Proceedings, 1, 445–450.

Jarvis, G. T., and G. K. C. Clarke, 1974: Thermal effects of crevassing on Steele Glacier, Yukon Territory, Canada. *Jour. Glaciology*, 13, 68, 243–254.

Paterson, W. S. B., 1971: Temperature measurements in Athabasca Glacier, Alberta, Canada. *Jour. Glaciology*, 10, 60, 339–349.

Paterson, W. S. B., 1972: Temperature distribution in the upper layers of the ablation area of Athabasca Glacier, Alberta, Canada. *Jour. Glaciology*, 11, 61, 31–41.

Robin, G. de Q., 1955: Ice movement and temperature distribution in glaciers and ice sheets. *Jour. Glaciology*, 2, 18, 523–532.

Observations of Stage, Discharge, pH and Electrical Conductivity During Periods of Ice Formation in a Small Sub-Arctic Stream

T. E. OSTERKAMP, R. E. GILFILIAN AND C. S. BENSON

Geophysical Institute, University of Alaska, College, Alaska 99701

Abstract

Ice formation in a small, sub-Arctic stream modifies the stage, velocity profiles, discharge and electrical conductivity while the pH remains nearly constant. Frazil ice crystals suspended in the flow reduce the velocity profiles and increase the stream level for a constant discharge. Anchor ice and border ice growth may decrease the discharge by as much as 55%. As some of the discharge goes into storage, the stage decreases. Continued ice growth overnight restricts the stream channel cross section and consequently the stage increases until the following day when the anchor ice is removed from the stream. The electrical conductivity of the stream water increased during periods of ice production and this increase was related to the concentration of ice in the stream. Ice concentrations calculated from this increase in conductivity ranged from 0.9% to 4.7% (by volume) for 150 minutes of ice production.

---

1. Introduction

Ice formation in a stream may be divided into three regimes based on the flow velocity (Carstens, 1970; Michel, 1971). When the flow velocity is "high" ($v > 1.2$ m s^{-1}), frazil ice crystals both are suspended in the flow and accumulate on the bottom as anchor ice. For "medium" flow velocities (0.6 m s$^{-1} < v < 1.2$ m s^{-1}), frazil ice crystals are carried on the surface as frazil slush, and there is little accumulation of anchor ice. When the flow velocity is "low" ($v < 0.6$ m s^{-1}), there is very little underwater ice (frazil ice and anchor ice), and a solid ice cover tends to form on the surface of the stream. While this classification of ice formation in streams is not rigorous, it serves as a rough measure for predicting the occurrence of underwater ice in a stream.

Physical considerations of a suspension of frazil ice crystals in the flow predict that the rate of energy dissipation and the effective viscosity will be greater than for the pure fluid phase (McCormack and Crane, 1973). These changes may be expected to modify the velocity profiles and thus the discharge and stage of the stream. In addition, the impurity content of the stream water will increase due to rejection of impurities by the ice phase during growth. This increased impurity concentration increases the electrical conductivity of the stream water and may possibly change its pH.

The above changes in velocity profiles, discharge, stage, electrical conductivity and pH of the stream may be expected to be more pronounced when ice formation consists of underwater ice rather than the layer of skim ice that usually forms at lower stream velocities.

Recent investigations elaborating on the sequence of events and the physical mechanisms involved in underwater ice production were carried out by Michel (1971) and Carstens (1966). Carstens (1968) also investigated the hydraulics of a suspension of frazil ice crystals in flowing water and used his results to model power plant design. Recent measurements have been made of velocity profiles prior to ice formation and after an ice cover formed on the stream (Tsang, 1970; Ohashi and Hamada, 1970; Ashton and Kennedy, 1970); however, there does not appear to be much information on velocity profiles taken during periods of underwater ice formation in streams. Reductions in stream discharge (up to 30%) have been reported by Arden and Wigle (1973) for the Niagara River. Kreitner (1969), Gilfilian *et al.* (1972) and Ferguson and Cork (1973) have reported stage increases attributed to underwater ice formation; Benson (1973) observed similar stage increases for several years at Goldstream Creek.

A typical period of underwater ice production usually begins in the evening hours or at night with a large rate of heat extraction through the stream surface until the stream is supercooled (i.e., the water temperature is less than the equilibrium freezing point of the water) (Altberg, 1936; Barnes, 1928; Devik, 1944). Subsequent nucleation and growth of frazil ice and anchor ice leaves the stream with anchor ice growing on the stream bottom and frazil ice crystals suspended in the flow. Frazil ice crystals evolve into frazil flocs and finally into frazil pans because of an unexplained tendency to stick together when they collide. These flocs and pans are concentrated at the stream surface since they are sufficiently buoyant to overcome turbulent forces and are not entrained in the flow (Carstens, 1970; Michel, 1971). On the morning following a night of underwater ice produc-tion, the stream usually contains frazil ice pans on its surface and anchor ice on the stream bottom (anchor ice up to 10 cm in thickness covering most of the stream bottom has been observed at our test site). Near midday, when the water temperature in-creases slightly above 0 C by absorption of solar radiation, this anchor ice usually floats to the surface and is flushed downstream leaving the stream free of ice (Devik, 1949; Benson, 1973).

Under favorable meteorological conditions, the stream may undergo several periods of underwater ice production before a complete ice cover forms at its surface. Thus, streams with high velocities produce much more ice during freeze-up than do streams with very low velocities.

2. Electrical conductivity and ice discharge

Increases in the electrical conductivity of a stream during periods of underwater ice formation have been observed by Benson (1973) and Kristinson (1970). Kristinson (1970) measured the electrical conductivity of frazil slush floating on the surface of a stream as it passed through a specially designed conductance cell. The frazil ice was sensed as a change in the electrical conductivity between the electrodes of the cell. The amount of frazil ice in the water was determined empirically to be

$$n = \frac{\Delta\sigma}{\sigma} = \frac{\Delta V}{V}, \tag{1}$$

where σ is the electrical conductivity of the water, $\Delta\sigma$ is the change in conductivity due to the presence of ice in the water, V is the total volume of ice and water mixture sensed by the cell and ΔV is the ice volume. The total frazil ice discharge was obtained by multiplying the ice density by the surface velocity and integrating over the width of the river. Rubanenko (1939) used a similar technique but with a different cell geometry to determine frazil ice concentrations.

An alternative method for determining the amount of ice in the stream involves a measurement of the increase in electrical conductivity of the stream water caused by the rejection of impurities by the ice during its growth (Benson, 1973; Gilfilian *et al.*, 1972; and Gilfilian, 1973).

Suppose the initial concentration of impurities in the water is

$$C_0 = \frac{M}{V_0} \tag{2}$$

where M is the mass of ionic impurities and V_0 is an initial volume of water. Assume that the ice crystals

reject all ionic impurities during their growth. Then the mass of impurities in the water remains un-changed and the impurity concentration after freezing a volume of ice, V_i, is

$$C_f = \frac{M}{V_0 - V_i}. \tag{3}$$

Using Eqs. 2 and 3, the ratio of the concentration of impurities before and after a period of underwater ice formation is

$$\frac{C_0}{C_f} = 1 - \frac{V_i}{V_0}. \tag{4}$$

This ratio may also be written in terms of the defini-tion of the electrical conductivity of the water as

$$\frac{C_0}{C_f} = \frac{\sigma_0}{\sigma_f} \tag{5}$$

where σ_0 and σ_f are the initial and final electrical conductivities of the water. Equating the right hand sides of Eqs. 4 and 5 and rearranging terms

$$\frac{V_i}{V_0} = \frac{\sigma_f - \sigma_0}{\sigma_f}. \tag{6}$$

Eq. 6 is similar in form to Eq. 1; however, its ap-plication and interpretation is different. When Eq. 6 is used to determine the amount of frazil ice in the stream, it is the change in electrical conductivity of the water caused by impurity rejection of the ice during growth that is sensed rather than the change in electrical conductivity caused by the presence of ice in the region between the electrodes of the mea-suring cell.

3. Experimental

Goldstream Creek is a small, sub-Arctic stream near Fairbanks, Alaska, flowing in a southwesterly direction in a valley underlain with permafrost. The stream width at the test site was about 8 m and the stream depth was 0.6 m or less. Its bed consists of gravelly sand material ranging in size from very fine-grained silt to pebbles. The channel is well-defined with moderate banks and an average bed gradient of about 2 m km^{-1}. The slope of the water surface at the test site was 0.0012.

Both a staff and a Stevens Type F, Model 61 water level recorder were used to measure the stream level. Water samples were collected from the stream at frequent intervals and returned to the laboratory to measure their electrical conductivity and pH. The electrical conductivity was measured with a Leeds and Northrup Model 4959 electrolytic conductivity bridge and pH was measured with a Beckman Elec-

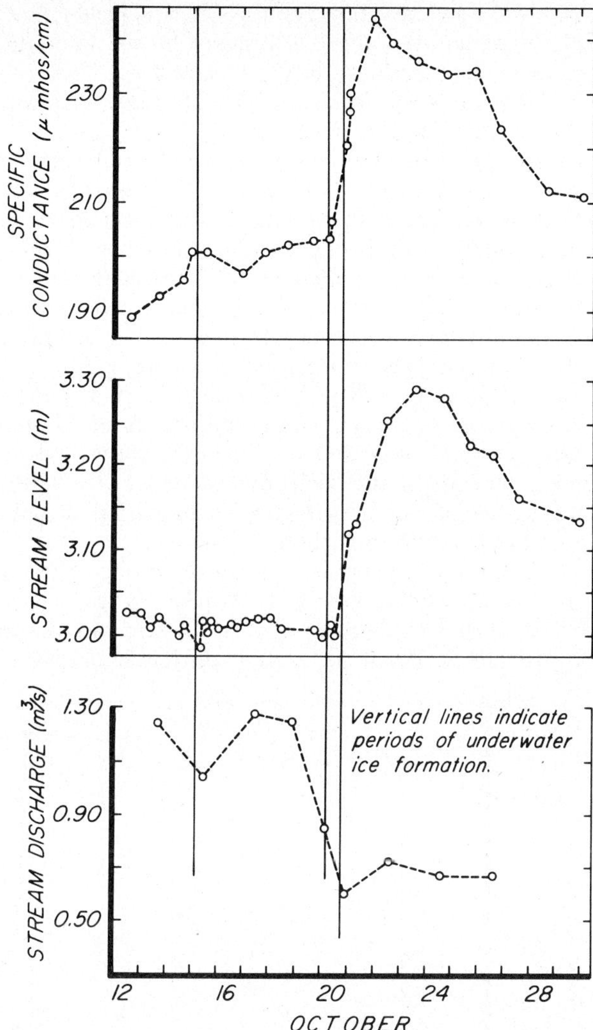

Fig. 1. Specific conductance, stream level and stream discharge during the 1971 freeze-up priod.

tromate pH meter, Model 1009. Measurements of the stream velocity were made with a Gurley pygmy current meter. The stream discharge was obtained by velocity integration over the cross-sectional area.

4. Results and discussion

The electrical conductivity of the stream water and the stage and discharge of the stream are shown as functions of time in Figs. 1 and 2 for the 1971 and 1972 freeze-up periods, respectively. While these graphs illustrate the gross behavior of the stream during freeze-up, they are too coarse to discern the detailed behavior of the stream during periods of underwater ice production. The reason is that underwater ice production usually occurs at night over a time span of a few hours. Figs. 3 and 4 show the variation of stream level compared to the stream temperature during periods of underwater ice production. These

graphs are typical of observations taken during several periods of underwater ice production.

The initial increase in stream level shown in Figs. 3 and 4 occurred immediately after frazil ice crystals formed in the stream and may be attributed to changes in the characteristics of the flow. Frazil ice crystals suspended in the flow increase the rate of energy dissipation and the effective viscosity of the suspension is greater than the viscosity of pure water. These changes in the rate of energy dissipation and the effective viscosity reduce the velocity profiles and produce a corresponding increase in stage (assuming that the discharge remains constant). The decrease in level after a few hours may be due to several factors. Frazil ice crystal growth and agglomeration into frazil flocs and pans tends to cause an accumulation of ice on the surface of the stream and thus removes the frazil ice crystals from the main part of flow. In addition, some of the discharge goes into storage because of anchor ice and border ice growth. Continued anchor ice and border ice growth eventually results in channel restriction which again causes the level to increase as shown in Figs. 3 and 4. The sharp decrease in stage when the anchor ice flushes downstream near midday is illustrated in both Figs. 3 and 4.

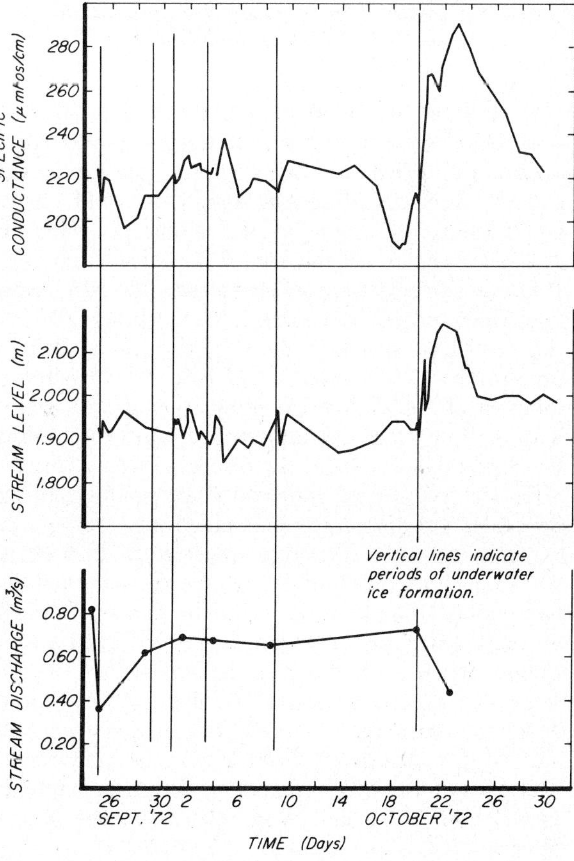

Fig. 2. Specific conductance, stream level and stream discharge during the 1972 freeze-up period.

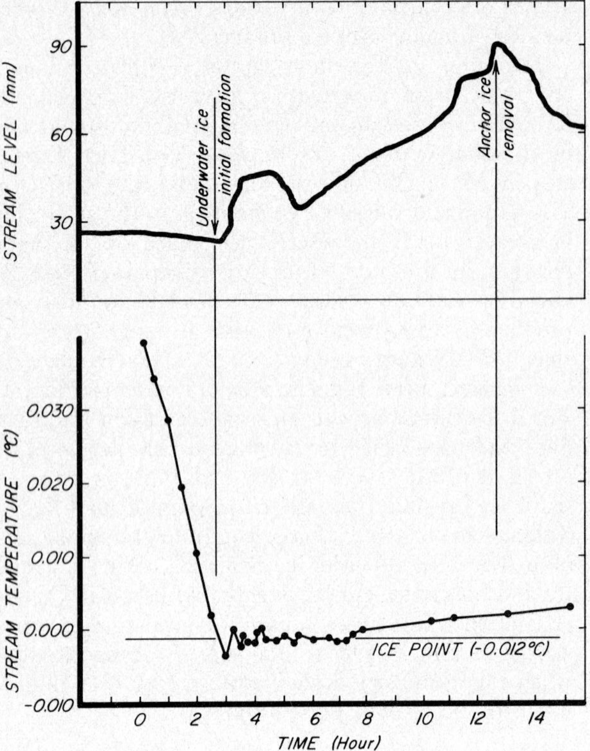

Fig. 3. Stream temperature and level during a period of underwater ice formation in 1971.

During the freeze-up period, the stream discharge was relatively constant except during periods of ice production. When the stream produced underwater ice, the discharge decreased significantly which may be attributed to some of the discharge going into storage as anchor ice and border ice (Arden and Wigle, 1972) and to upstream water storage due to increased flow resistance in the stream. On October 20, 1971, the discharge was 1.23 m^3 s^{-1} prior to a period of underwater ice production and 0.85 m^3 s^{-1} after 125 minutes of undewater ice production in the stream, with 0.38 m^3 s^{-1} of discharge transformed into storage. On September 25, 1972, the discharge was 0.76 m^3 s^{-1} after 140 minutes of underwater ice production, with 0.42 m^3 s^{-1} of discharge transformed into storage. It is expected that the discharge transformed into storage (0.38 m^3 s^{-1} and 0.42 m^3 s^{-1}) will be the same for these two periods of underwater ice production since transfer of the latent heat of fusion of the ice to the atmosphere depends on the heat balance which was the same for these two periods (Gilfilian, 1973). The decrease in discharge for these two periods was 31% and 55%, respectively, which may be compared to decreases of 20–30% observed by Ferguson and Cork (1972) and Arden and Wigle (1972) on the Niagara River.

The pH of the stream water was measured during the 1971 freeze-up. It remained nearly constant between 7.5 and 7.8 and was not affected by ice produc-

tion in the stream. However, the electrical conductivity of the water was affected strongly by ice formation in the stream as shown in Figs. 1 and 2.

The relative concentrations of ice in the stream were calculated with Eq. 6 to be 1.8%, 0.9% and 4.7% for three periods (150 minutes each) of underwater ice production during the 1971 and 1972 seasons. Unfortunately, there is no satisfactory technique for measuring these ice concentrations; however, Gilfilian et al. (1972) and Gilfilian (1973) have estimated the ice concentrations from heat balance measurements. These estimated ice concentrations corresponding to the above periods of ice production are 1.1%, 1.6% and 2.3%, respectively. While there is general agreement between the ice concentrations obtained from the electrical conductivity and the heat balance measurements, it is obvious that more data are needed during periods of underwater ice formation in order to make a valid comparison.

Stream velocity profiles measured during freeze-up in 1971 are shown in Fig. 5. A velocity profile measured when no ice was present in the stream is shown by profile A. When the stream produced underwater

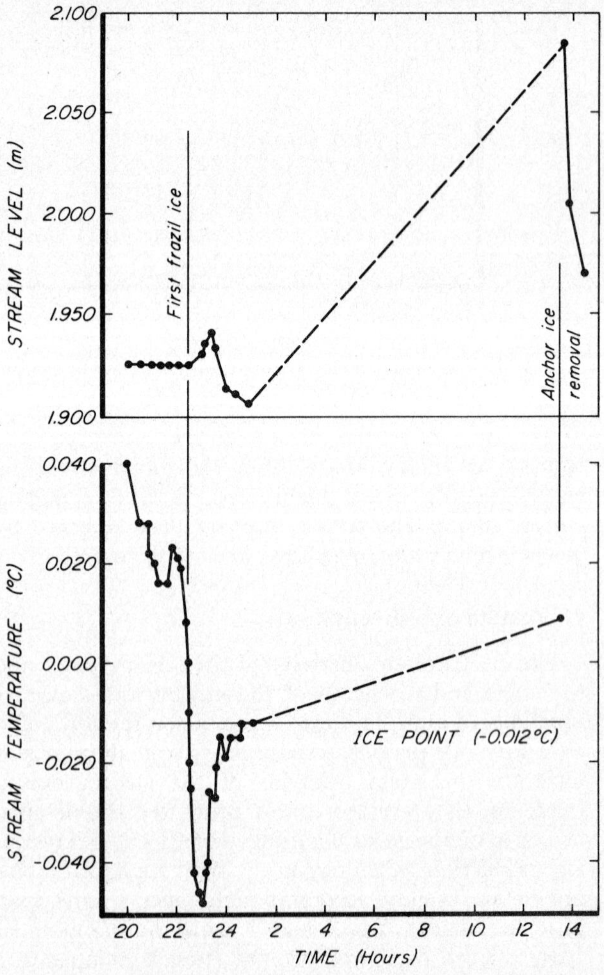

Fig. 4. Stream temperature and level during a period of underwater ice formation in 1972.

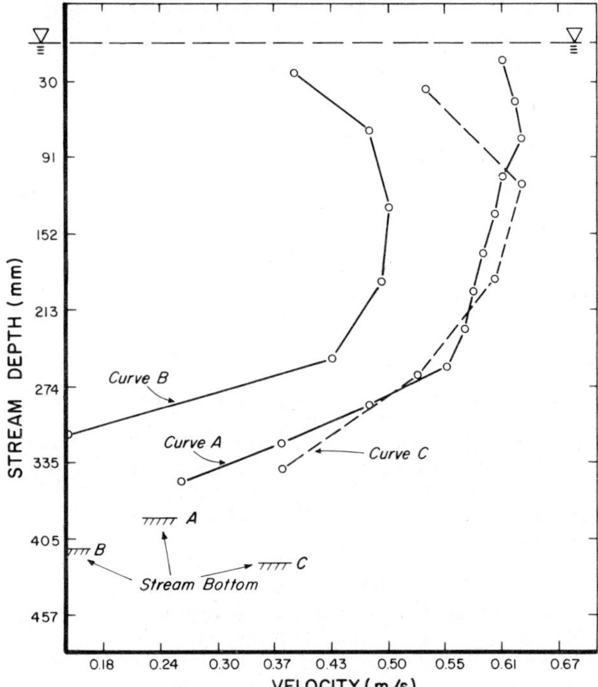

Fig. 5. A comparison of velocity profiles measured during the 1971 freeze-up period.

ice, the velocity profile shifted to the left, as shown by profile B, due to frazil ice entrained in the flow and anchor ice on the stream bottom. Profile C was measured after a continuous ice cover formed on the stream. The decrease in velocity in profile C at the surface is a result of the surface ice cover.

5. Conclusions

Observations made during periods of underwater ice production in a small stream show that the stage, velocity profiles, discharge and electrical conductivity change and that the pH of the stream water remains nearly constant. The stage increases, due to a reduction in the velocity profiles, when underwater ice initially forms in the stream. Following this increase, there is a short-term decrease in stage which may be attributed to evolution of frazil ice crystals into frazil ice pans and the reduction of the discharge by its transformation into storage as anchor ice and border ice. Continued ice production in the stream restricts the stream channel, and the stage increases until mid-day when the anchor ice is flushed from the stream. The electrical conductivity of the stream water increases during periods of underwater ice production, and the change in conductivity is related to the concentration of ice in the stream. An equations was derived to calculate the ice concentrations in the stream, which ranged from 0.9% to 4.7% for a 150 minute period of ice production. This agrees favorably with the ice concentrations in the stream calculated from measurements of heat loss from the stream.

Acknowledgments. This paper is based on material prepared for and included in a M.S. thesis written by Gilfilian (1973) under supervision of Dr. T. E. Osterkamp. Mr. D. Kane measured the velocity profiles and furnished the discharge data. This research is supported by the Earth Science Section, National Science Foundation, NSF Grant # GA-30748.

REFERENCES

Altberg, W. J., 1936: Twenty years of work in the domain of underwater ice formation (1915–1935), IUGG-IASH, p. 373–407.

Arden, R. S., and T. E. Wigle, 1973: Dynamics of ice formation in the upper Niagara River. Proceedings Int. Symp. on the Role of Snow and Ice in Hydrology, Banff, Canada, September, 1972, UNESCO/WMO/IAHS, 1296–1313.

Ashton, G. D., and J. F. Kennedy, 1970: Temperature and flow conditions during the formation of river ice, in Proc. IAHR Symp., Ice and its action on hydraulic structures, p. 2.4, Reykjavik, Iceland, September, 1970.

Barnes, H. T., 1928: Ice Engineering, Renowf Publishing Co., Montreal, Canada.

Benson, C. S., 1973: A study of the freezing cycle in an Alaskan stream, Report No. IWR-36, Inst. of Water Resources, Univ. of Alaska, Fairbanks, Alaska.

Carstens, T., 1966: Experiments with supercooling and ice formation in flowing water, *Geofys. Publ.* **XXVI**, 9, 1–18.

Carstens, T., 1968: Hydraulics of river ice, La Horrible Blanche, No. 4, 271–284.

Carstens, T., 1970: Heat exchanges and frazil formation, in Proc. I.A.H.R. Symp., Ice and its action on hydraulic structures, p. 2.11, Reykjavik, Iceland.

Devik, O., 1944: Ice formation in lakes and rivers, *The Geophysical Journal*, **CIII**(5), 193–302.

Devik, O., 1949: Freezing water and supercooling, *Journal of Glaciology*, **1**, 307–309.

Ferguson, H. L., and H. F. Cork, 1973: Regression equations relating ice conditions in the upper Niagara River to meteorological variables. Proceedings, Int. Symp. on the Role of Snow and Ice in Hydrology, Banff, Canada, September, 1972, UNESCO/WMO/IAHS, 1314–1327.

Gilfilian, R. E., W. L. Kline, T. E. Osterkamp and C. S. Benson, 1972: Ice formation in a small Alaskan stream, paper presented at the Int. Symp. on the Role of Snow and Ice in Hydrology, Banff, Canada, September, 1972.

Gilfilian, R. E., W. L. Kline, T. E. Osterkamp and C. S. Benson, 1973: Winter history of a small sub-arctic Alaskan stream, M.S. thesis, University of Alaska, Fairbanks, Alaska.

Kristinson, B., 1970: Ice monitoring equipment, in Proc. I.A.H.R. Symp., Ice and its action on hydraulic structures, p. 1.1, Reykjavik, Iceland, September, 1970.

Michel, B., 1967: Morphology of frazil ice, in Physics of Snow and Ice, Edited by H. Oura, Institute of Low Temperature Science, Hokkaido University, Sapporo, Japan, 119–128.

Michel, B., 1971: Winter regime of rivers and lakes, CRREL Monograph III-Bla, CRREL, Hanover, New Hampshire.

McCormack, P. D., and L. Crane, 1973: Physical Fluid Dynamics, Academic Press, New York, New York.

Ohashi, K., and T. Hamada, 1970: Flow measurements of ice-covered rivers on Hokkaido, in Proc. I.A.H.R. Symp., Ice and its action on hydraulic structures, p. 1.4, Reykjavik, Iceland, September, 1970.

Rubanenko, B. K., 1939: Instrument to determine the concentration of frazil ice, *Meteorologiia i Gidrologiia*, **5**(4), 132–134.

Tsang, G., 1970: Change of velocity distribution in a cross-section of a freezing river and the effect of frazil ice loading on velocity distribution, in Proc. I.A.H.R. Symp., Ice and its action on hydraulic structures, p. 3.2, Reykjavik, Iceland, September, 1970.

A Study of the Breakup on the Arctic Slope of Alaska by Ground, Air and Satellite Observations

B. HOLMGREN,* C. BENSON AND G. WELLER

Geophysical Institute, University of Alaska, Fairbanks, Alaska 99701

Abstract

Satellite imagery, with support of air and surface photography, radiation and climatological data, is used to describe characteristics of the 1973 breakup including the stream flow in a 300 km long north-south transect across the Arctic slope from the Arctic Ocean to the divide of the Brooks Range. Data from three ERTS satellite passes, one from the pre-breakup, the second from the middle and the third from the end of the breakup periods, demonstrate a number of snow accumulation as well as ablation features of interest in the study of the hydrology of the Arctic slope. The snow distribution is largely determined by wind deposition and erosion through drifting. On steep mountainsides and in north-facing valleys in the Brooks Range, as well as in the upper foothills, there are extensive areas of thin or discontinuous snow in early spring. On the regional scale, these areas are also clearly brought out by the images from the NOAA 2 satellite. The areas of thin snow cover appear to serve as nuclei for intensified ablation, by melting and/or evaporation with early runoff into the low-lying areas, where the ablation generally does not start until a few weeks later. In the middle of the breakup, the valleys of the major rivers appear on the ERTS photos as dark bands on the snow-covered tundra, indicating a relatively advanced state of breakup along the rivers. In the foothills, the ridges melt out first leaving extensive snow drifts in the gullies, the distribution and areal extent of which may be determined from the ERTS images. On the flat tundra, the snow pack disintegrates into patches after a few days of melting, the longest-lasting snow features being sastrugi of length and width of the order of several meters, and elongated snow drifts several kilometers long along river and lake banks.

Climatological and micrometeorological data from the coastal plains, where the average snow depth before breakup is 30–40 cm, indicate that evaporation plays a rather insignificant role in the ablation process. Immediately after snow melt, however, the rates of evaporation are high, amounting to maximum values of about 5 mm per day. In those areas where the snow cover in early spring is thin or discontinuous, the potential energy available for evaporation of snow will be much higher. The satellite data may be used to monitor snow areas of relatively low reflectance in early spring, and perhaps to discuss the importance of melting compared with evaporation in the early retreat of the snow cover.

As a point of special interest, it may be noted that, in the Prudhoe Bay oil exploration area, the influence of roads, oil camps, etc. on the breakup may be readily traced on the ERTS photos. At the present level of activities the artificial disturbances are small when compared with the natural variations of the breakup. With the expected increase of the activities in this area, the ERTS data will certainly be of value for monitoring the effect of the man-made disturbances on the sensitive tundra ecology.

---

1. Introduction

The Arctic slope is the area north of the divide of the Brooks Range in Alaska, covering about 196,000 km² which corresponds to about 13% of the land area of Alaska. The surface is underlain by permafrost and covered by tundra-type vegetation without forest. Some main characteristics of the annual temperature regime are summarized in Fig. 1. From a hydrological point of view, the Arctic slope may be divided into three main physiographic types: the oriented lakes district with a flat, almost horizontal surface, the foothills of the Brooks Range with elevations ranging between a few hundred and about 800 meters, and the mountains of the Brooks Range

with maximum elevations of 2000 to 3000 meters. The National Weather Service mean annual precipitation map, prepared in cooperation with the U. S. Geological Survey and based on all "available information" through 1972, shows values ranging from about 100 mm in the coastal zone to about 500 mm in the upper foothills, and with maximum values of about 1000 mm in the high-mountain regions. The mean annual snowfall shows similar distribution patterns (Fig. 2).

There is no permanent inland climate station in operation at present, and within this whole extensive region only a few climate stations exist on the coast. For the past few years, U. S. Geological Survey has collected streamflow data in the Putuligayuk, Kuparuk and the Sagavanirktok basins (Fig. 3). No permanent snow surveys are established on the Arctic slope. The

---

* Present affiliation; Meteorologiska Institutionen, Uppsala, Sweden.

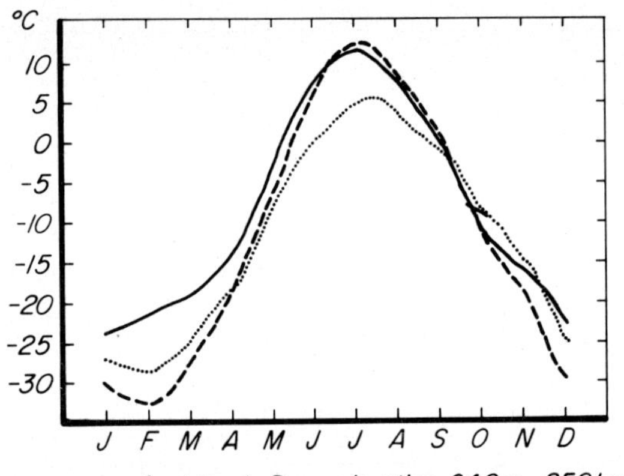

FIG. 1. Average monthly temperatures at Anaktuvuk Pass (1953–56), Umiat (1947–53) and Barrow (1947–53). Note that the temperature data are not from the same time period (from Conover, 1960).

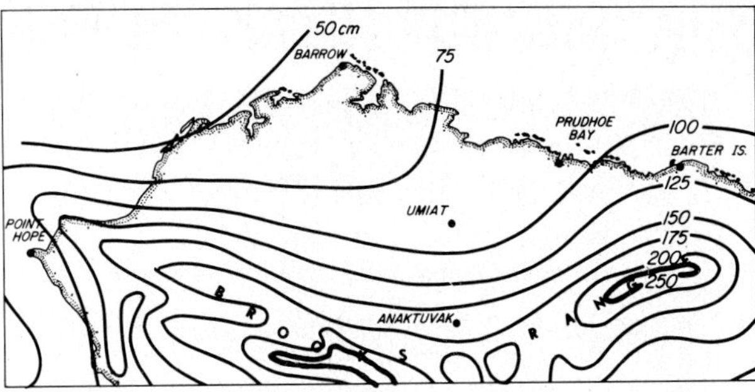

FIG. 2. Total annual snowfall on the Arctic slope. Redrawn from a U.S.W.B. map prepared in cooperation with U. S. Geological Survey (1973).

sparsity of the meteorological and hydrological stations may be illustrated by the fact that many ERTS scenes each corresponding to an area 180×180 km, do not include one single observational station. It would therefore appear logical to use satellite imagery for determining characteristics of the seasonal snow cover on the Arctic slope. Knowledge of the hydrology of the Arctic slope becomes increasingly important as man's activities increase in that area. The objective of this paper is to discuss some aspects of the breakup as observed, using primarily ERTS images of a north-south transect located in the central part of the Arctic slope.

2. General observations of the snow cover characteristics

Figs. 4, 7 and 8 each show a sequence of three ERTS scenes approximately centered on the Colville River and covering a distance over land of about 300 km from the coast in the North to the Brooks Range in the South. The transects represent respectively pre-melting conditions on 16 March, the main melting period on 27 May and the post-melting period on 14 June. The last transect is partly obscured by clouds. Some features of the snow cover (Fig. 4) are summarized as follows:

1. In winter the snow cover is, on the whole, continuous. There are, however, exceptions from that general rule that will be discussed later.

2. The main rivers stand out clearly either because of the micro- or meso-topography of the river channels, or dense vegetation on islands in the rivers or because of overflows.

3. The meso- and large-scale topography may be recognized through the snow cover because of varia-

tions of intensity of the reflected radiation, mostly related to surface aspect and exposure.

4. In many areas, notably west of the Colville River, lakes appear darker than the surroundings because of a thin snow cover on the ice surface.

5. The coast of the Arctic Ocean is barely recognizable because of the nearly equal reflectance levels of

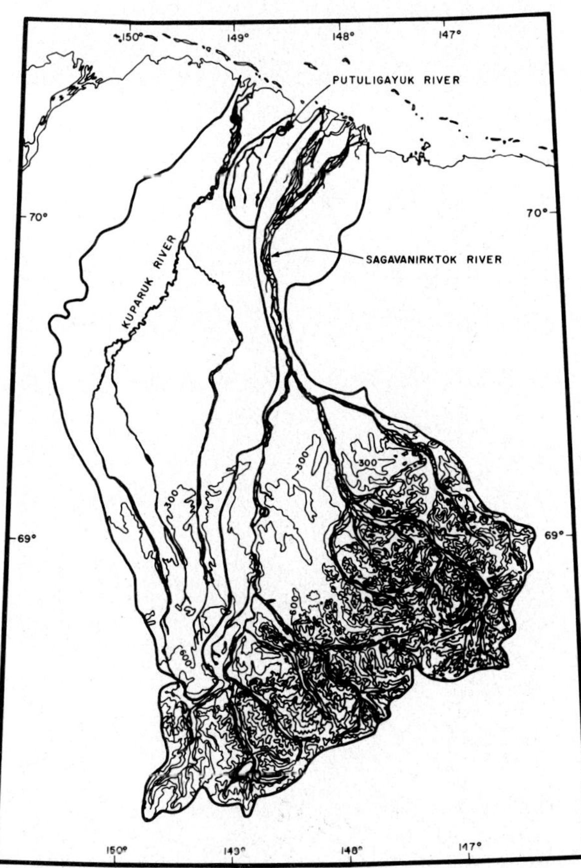

FIG. 3. Map of the Putuligayuk, Kuparuk, and Sagavanirktok Basins. Gauging stations are indicated by open circles. Elevations are in meters. The highest mountains are between 2000 and 3000 meters. Drainage area of the gauging stations: Putuligayuk: 456 km²; Kuparuk: 8107 km²; Sagavanirktok: 5719 km².

16 MARCH 1973 BD6

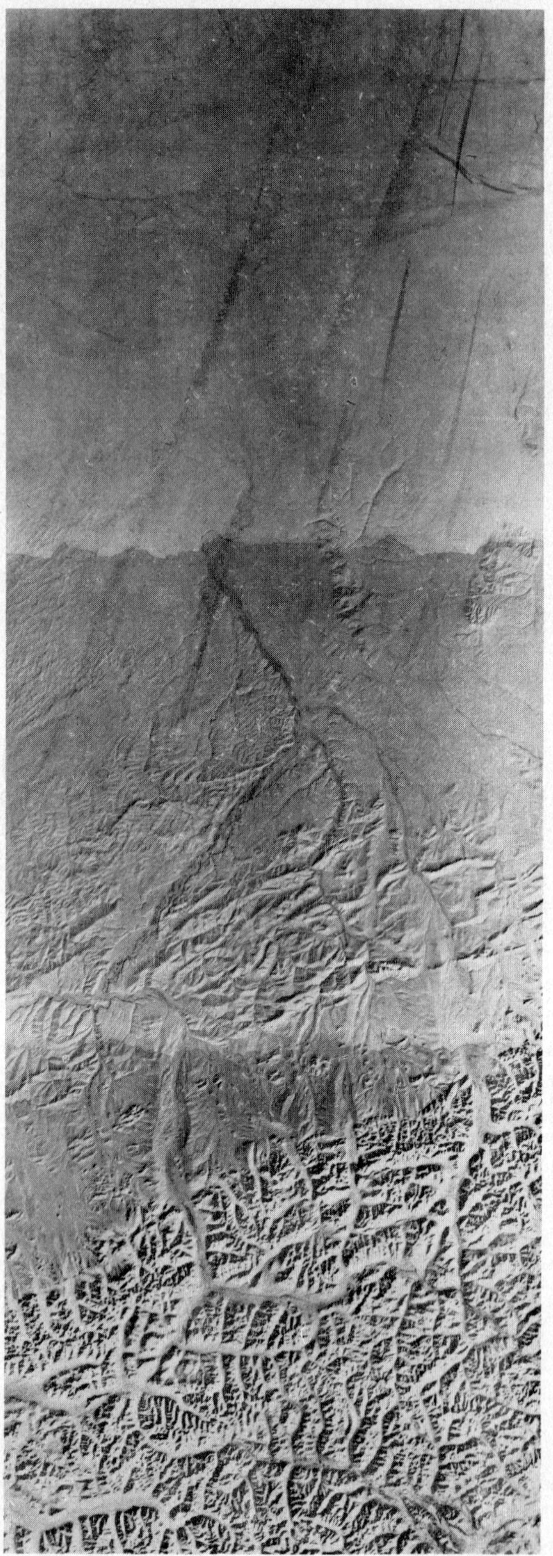

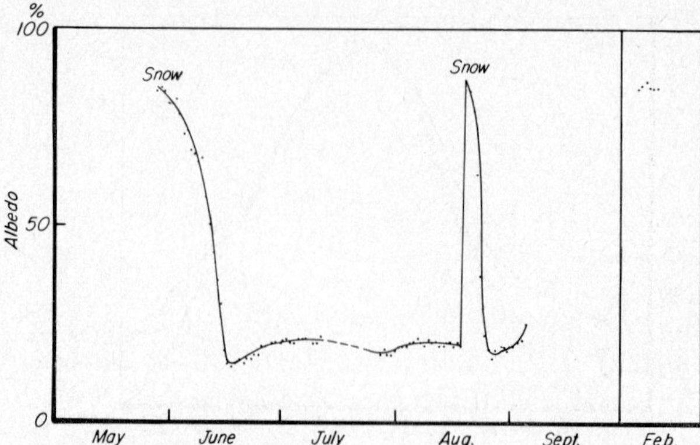

FIG. 5. Variations of albedo as measured at Barrow during the summer of 1971 (after Weller and Holmgren, 1974).

the snow-covered shorefast ice and the tundra. The pack ice, on the other hand, has a lower reflectance, probably because of surface roughness elements like pressure ridges and hummocks. Several relatively new, but ice-covered leads are visible.

On the whole, the winter and early spring snow on the North Slope may be described as an almost con-

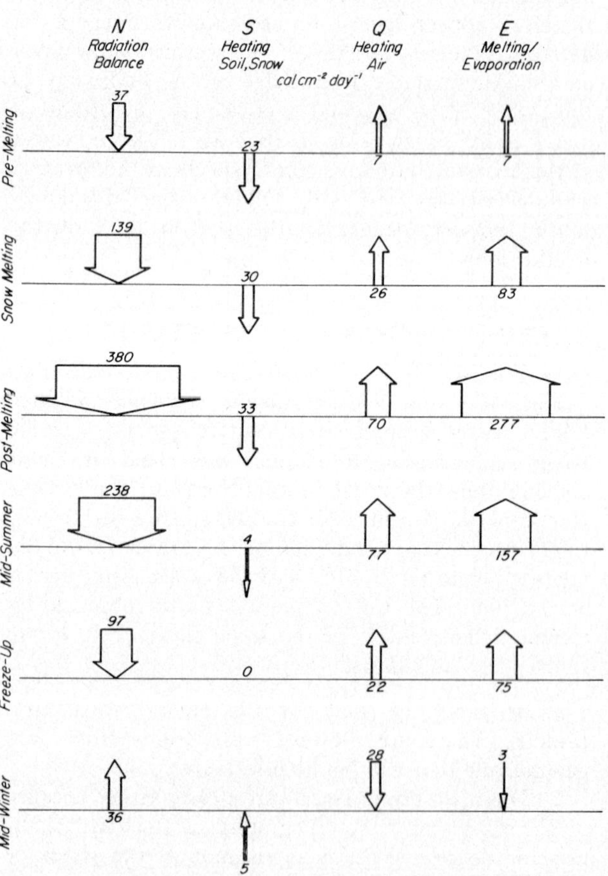

FIG. 6. Heat balances at Barrow for six different characteristic periods during the summer of 1971 and the winter of 1971–72 (after Weller and Cubley, 1972).

FIG. 4. Mosaic of ERTS scenes 1236–21292, 1236–21294 and 1236–21301, all in Band 6 (near infrared).

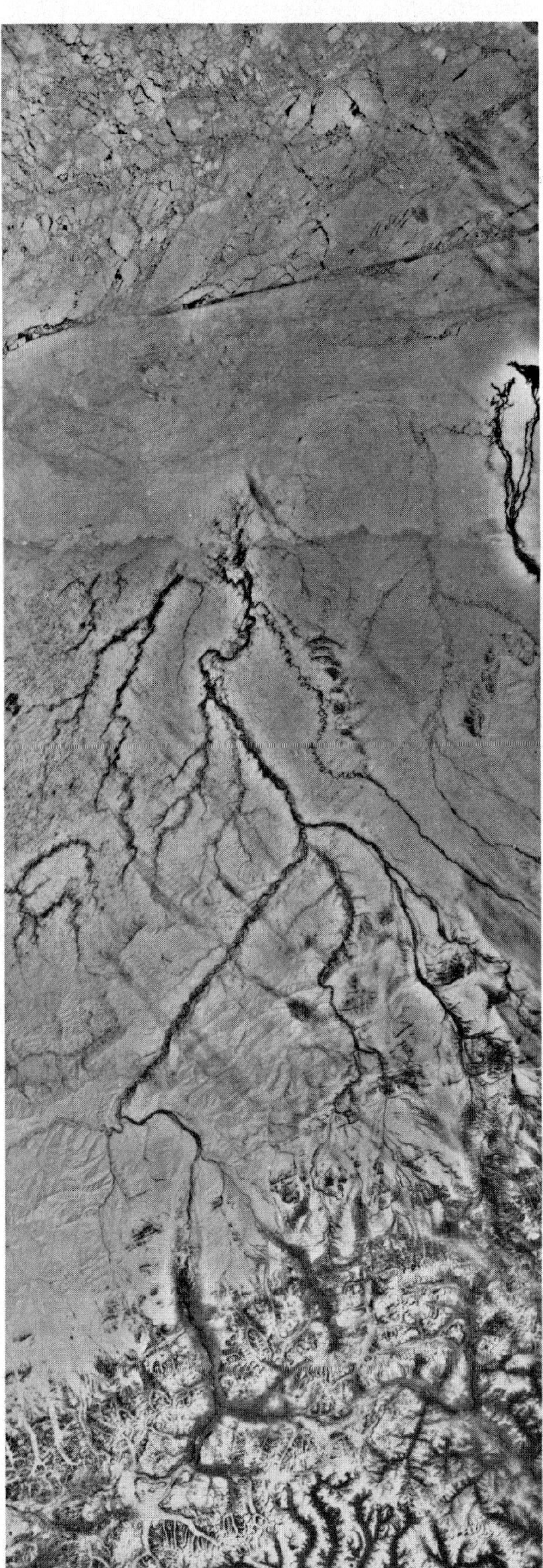

tinuous and highly reflective cover, in many respects resembling the surface of the Greenland and Antarctic ice sheets. Measurement of the surface albedo, corresponding to the whole solar spectral interval, gives values of 80–90% over flat snow-covered tundra, i.e., most of the incoming radiation is reflected at the surface. When the air temperature increases towards 0 C, the snow starts to melt with a sharp drop of the albedo as a consequence (Fig. 5). As the bare ground becomes visible, the snow melt often accelerates due to a rapid decrease of the albedo.

In connection with the snow melt, there is a drastic increase of the energy available for ablation of the snow cover (Fig. 6). At the snow surface most of the energy goes into melting; evaporation is relatively insignificant for the ablation. The values in Fig. 6 are representative for the tundra on the coastal plains with an average snow depth of 30–40 cm at the start of the ablation period. From these heat budget studies it may be concluded that solar radiation has little affect on the snow cover during the pre-melting period or as long as the albedo of the snow pack is high. After the snow melt, however, in connection with a rapid warming of the surface the rates of evaporation become high, up to about 5 mm per day (Weller and Cubley, 1972).

Vegetation that is visible through the snow cover may lower the overall albedo and increase the rates of evaporation as discussed by Benson (1969). On many ERTS images from the pre-breakup season there are two easily detectable features: aufeis and areas which either have thin snow cover or are blown bare of snow. Both surface types have a heat budget that is markedly different from that of a continuous snow cover.

Fig. 7 shows that the breakup at the end of May is obviously further advanced in the upper parts of the water sheds than in the lower parts. The major valleys of the Brooks Range are more-or-less snow free. However, a close inspection reveals that the gullies on the mountainsides are often filled with snow drifts extending to the valley bottom. The highest mountain tops are generally snow-covered but varying shades of the gray scale indicate a snow cover consisting of isolated patches. In the foothills, the ridges melt out first leaving snow in the gullies. The dark ridge patterns often resemble herring-bones. On the coastal plains many lakes appear darker than the surroundings, probably because of standing water and slush on the ice. The major rivers have developed, or are in the process of developing, continuous open water streams. The riverbeds generally appear as dark bands probably because of flooded areas and because of further advanced melting along the rivers than on

Fig. 7. Mosaic of ERTS scenes 1308–21290, 1308–21292 and 1308–21297, all in Band 7 (near infrared). Major rivers at coast counted from left to right: Fish Creek, Colville, Kuparuk, Sagavanirktok. The Prudhoe Bay road system is faintly visible, extending between Kuparuk and the westernmost channel of the Sagavanirktok delta.

FIG. 8. Mosaic of ERTS scenes 1326–21284, 1326–21291, 1326–21293. All in Band 5 (red). A band of clouds obscures the middle part of the mosaic. Much of the Brooks Range is also obscured. Water may be observed flooding the sea ice outside the delta of major rivers.

the surrounding tundra. At the outlet, the Sagavanirktok (to the far right in Fig. 7) spreads out in an enormous plume flooding the delta area and the sea ice, but the runoff from the Colville into the sea seems to take place almost entirely below the ice at the time this image was made. It should be expected (Arnborg *et al.*, 1966) that the Colville will show a similar plume on the sea ice at a later stage. It is also of interest to see that the development of the drainage in the Kuparuk and the Putuligayuk Rivers, with source regions restricted to the foothills and the coastal plains (Fig. 3), lags in breakup when compared to most rivers originating in the Brooks Range. Examples elsewhere, as for instance in the Mackenzie River Delta (Gill, 1973), show that local melting of the snow pack along the river occurs much earlier because of flooding by melt water originating further upstream. This also has a considerable effect on the local climate by modification of the surface albedo.

In the Prudhoe Bay area, it is of particular interest to note that the road systems between the oil camps, airfields, etc. are readily visible. On the leeside of the major oil camps, dark areas extend for 2–3 km in the direction of the prevailing winds from E-NE. This indicates the effects of disturbances from the camps through wind-carried dust and complex snow distribution changes, causing earlier melting. The roads are partly visible because of road dust plumes extending mainly towards the west, as also shown by photos taken from the ground on May 23, or 4 days before the ERTS pass. These man-made disturbances were observed to cause an advance of the melt season in the Prudhoe Bay area during the spring of 1972 and 1973. However, at the present level of operations, the overall effect of the man-made disturbances on the regional breakup on the Arctic slope are small compared with natural causes as shown in the ERTS images. Chief among these natural variations are, for instance, wide areas of sand dust transported by winds from river beds, onto the snow, as well as the more direct effects of the rivers mentioned above. With the expected increase of industrial activities on the Arctic slope, the ERTS data might be useful for studying various ecological effects of man-made disturbances on the sensitive tundra environment.

Compared to the conditions of 16 March (Fig. 4) the pack ice is much more broken up on 27 May (Fig. 7) with many open leads, indicating that a positive radiation balance in combination with higher air temperatures prevents the leads from freezing over in May. Direct radiation measurements over open leads during the 1972 AIDJEX experiment in the Beaufort Sea (Weller *et al.*, 1972) indicate that the radiation balance becomes positive during the second half of April.

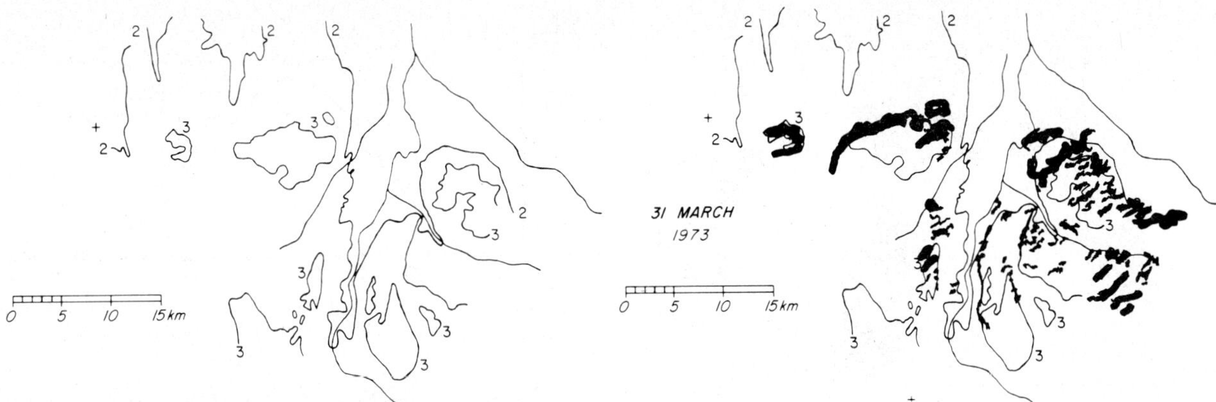

FIG. 9. Simplified topography of an area with center at 149°31″W, 68°45′N. Elevations are in thousands of feet.

FIG. 10. Same area as in Fig. 9. Dark areas are snowfree.

During the ERTS pass on June 14 (Fig. 8), the snow cover on the Arctic slope was mainly gone. Elongated snow drifts remain in the gullies of hilly areas. In the lowlands one may recognize snow drifts along riverbanks, some of them extending for many tens of kilometers. Most lakes are ice covered. Aufeis fields along the river channels are clearly visible. Snow also remains in the mountain areas in the northern part of the Brooks Range. The presence of clouds makes the identification difficult there, however.

The snow melt patterns found on the mosaics of May 27 and June 14 thus clearly show the profound influence of snow drifting on the Arctic slope, including the Brooks Range. This was also clearly apparent during a helicopter flight over the Arctic slope on June 5, i.e., approximately midway between the two ERTS passes and with roughly half of the snow cover melted in the coastal region. The accumulation patterns on the tundra are, in fact, best recognizable after the main snow cover has disappeared leaving the snow drifts readily visible. On the flat tundra the most abundant snow drifts are sastrugi features of a length and width of the order of several meters. Along river banks elongated snow drifts occur which have widths varying from a few meters to several tens of meters and which extend laterally for many kilometers. The processes involved in the formation of these drifts together with their physical properties, have been described in detail by Benson (1969).

The drainage of the flat tundra is typically very slow. At the middle and towards the end of the breakup, this area may be regarded as an extensive lake as far as the surface conditions go. In the hilly areas the snow accumulation on the ridges is much less than in the gullies. Wind speeds on the crests are higher than in the valleys, and the snow tends to accumulate where the wind speeds are low. The hill crests melt out first, leaving the gullies snow filled. The drainage develops rapidly. In the high mountains, the snow accumulation patterns are very complex.

In many cases there is little or no relationship between the snow distribution and either altitude or aspect, especially in the early stages of the ablation period. The major snow drifts observed in the foothill regions, as well as the lake ice and the aufeis, persist during a major part of the summer, as may be seen on the ERTS photos of the very same region during the pass on 2 July. In fact, many snow and aufeis features on the Arctic slope are perennial.

3. Areas of thin snow cover and the breakup

As indicated by a low reflectance on ERTS images from winter and early spring, many north-facing valleys and also many mountainsides in the Brooks Range have a relatively thin or discontinuous snow cover. These areas naturally become bare earlier than areas of deeper and more continuous snow.

In order to illustrate this early ablation of the snow cover, we have selected an area, about 40×60 km, in the northern foothills. A simplified topography of this area is shown in Fig. 9. Figs. 10, 11 and 12 show the successive retreat of the snow cover as depicted from ERTS images on three different dates. These figures were drawn by using a zoom transfer scope to overlay ERTS negatives on a U. S. Geological Survey

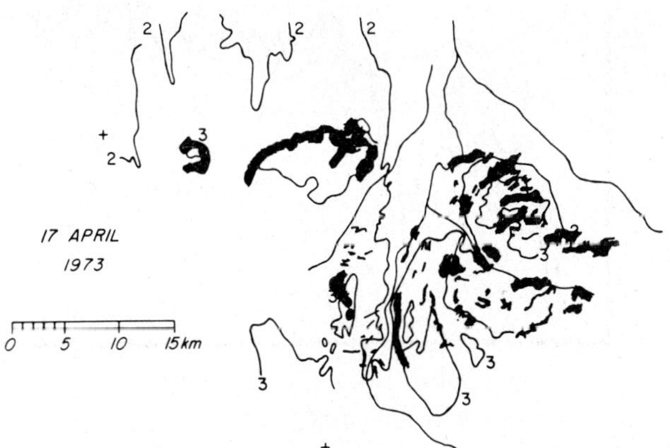

FIG. 11. Same areas as in Fig. 9.

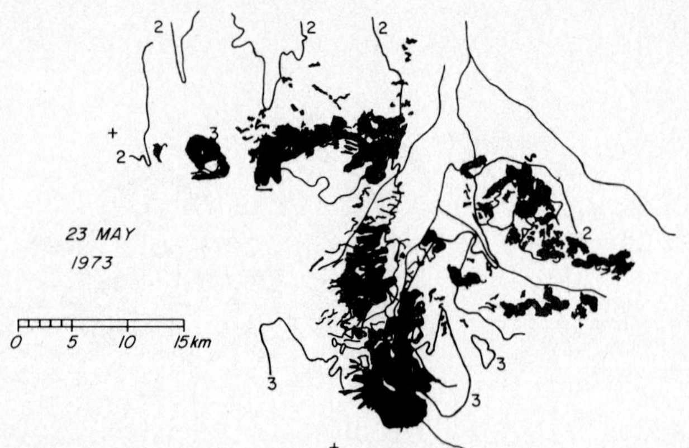

FIG. 12. Same area as in Fig. 9.

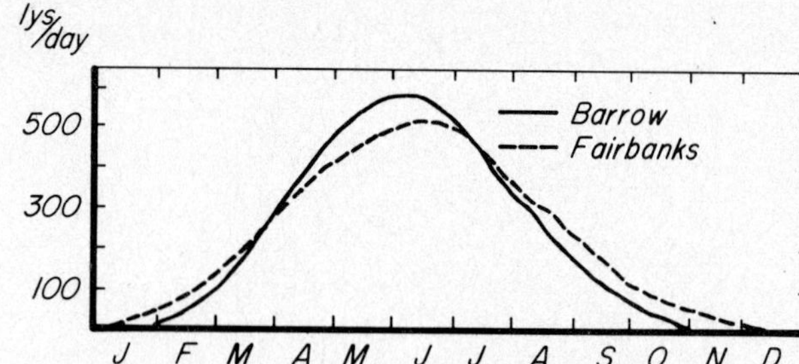

FIG. 14. Insolation in Langley per day at Barrow (1951–54) and Fairbanks (1933–49). Redrawn after Conover (1960).

topographic map (scale 1:250,000). The snow-free areas in winter and early spring are clearly related to the topography. Steep slopes and hill crests tend to be blown bare of snow. Later during the breakup, these snow-free areas expand, appearing to serve as nuclei for intensified ablation. Because of lack of supporting climatological and micrometeorological data from this area, we cannot at the present time definitely state the possible role of evaporation in the ablation process. Although this is true, it may still be of interest to discuss the ablation in reference to the general climatological conditions on the Arctic slope. Fig. 1 indicates that during spring, a positive horizontal temperature gradient exists from the Arctic coast to the Brooks Range; this may be expected, considering the decreasing latitude, but occurs in spite of a 650 m rise of elevation over this distance. The main melting will thus normally start around mid-May in the upper foothills. During spring 1973, air temperatures increased towards the melting point and significant melting started at the end of May on the coast of

the Arctic ocean (Fig. 13). Fig. 14 demonstrates the relatively small latitudinal variation of the incoming shortwave radiation in spring. Also, the incoming solar radiation during April-May is of the same order of magnitude as during June-July, i.e., the solar energy potentially available for snow ablation is high in early spring. Possible duration of sunshine at 60N latitude is about 16 hours in mid-April, 22 hours in mid-May, and 24 hours in mid-June and mid-July.

The importance of the areas of thin snow cover and early melt from a hydrological point of view is quite evident from Fig. 8, and other ERTS images, showing melt streams from the Brooks Range flowing out over the lower tundra regions that are much less affected by the melting. How widespread these areas were during the 1973 spring, may best be studied by reference to satellite images with a greater field of view than the ERTS satellites. The NOAA 2 image of Fig. 15 from May 10 depicts a dark band stretching over the major part of the northern foothills. In the

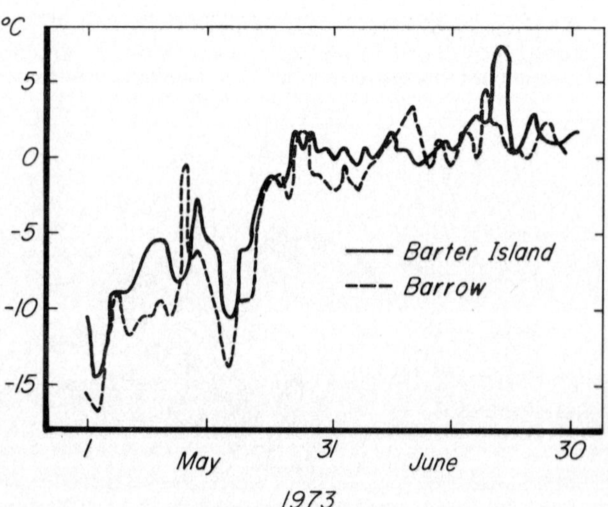

FIG. 13. Climatological temperature data from Barter Island and Barrow, Spring 1973.

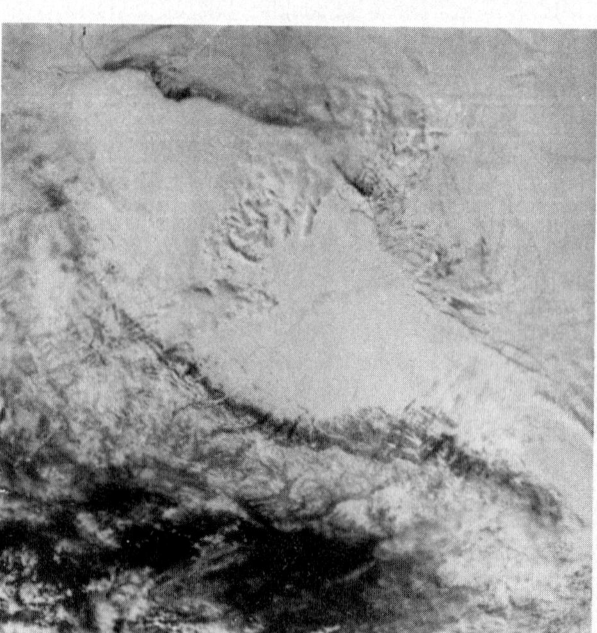

FIG. 15. NOAA 2 satellite photo in the visible part of the spectrum from May 10, 1973.

western part of the Brooks Range this band is less distinct, although obscuring clouds may contribute to this impression. South of the Brooks Range, the Yukon Valley forms an extensive dark area because of forests and advanced melting. In the southern foothills of the Brooks Range, the snow ablation has not progressed so far as at corresponding altitudes in the northern foothills, as indicated by the brightness levels.

The reason for the low snow accumulation in the northern Brooks Range is somewhat obscure. One may suspect that in part a redistribution of the snow by strong winds may be involved. However, to our knowledge there are no wind records available from the upper foothills or the valleys of the Brooks Range. The pattern of snow-free areas in the valleys in winter and early spring may suggest that the snow erosion is caused by lee-winds on the northern side of the Brooks Range channeled into the north-facing valleys. Strong winds might be generated by standing waves in situations with a general south to north flow across the Brooks Range. Katabatic winds in the valleys caused by temperature inversions may also play a part in the snow erosion. It should be pointed out, however, that wind measurements from the Arctic slope elsewhere generally indicate that the strongest winds are predominantly westerly.

The areas of low albedo should significantly influence their own microclimate to increase both the evaporation and the melting rates of snow. When snow starts to melt, the reflectance levels decrease, especially in the spectral region corresponding to Bands 6 and 7 (infrared) because of increased absorption by the free water in the uppermost part of the snow pack. An attempt was made to determine the state of the snow surface in the area of Fig. 9 by analyzing the reflectance levels in Bands 5 and 7 using data obtained from ERTS digital tapes. The result of this analysis, which will be reported elsewhere, appears somewhat inconclusive for reasons, partly of a technical nature, that will not be discussed here.

4. Stream discharge on the Arctic slope

Figure 16 shows preliminary discharge records from gauging stations in the Putuligayuk, Kuparuk and Sagavanirktok Basins (Fig. 3). For simplicity, these rivers will be referred to as Put, Kup and Sag. A few features of the hydrographs as they relate to the satellite data will be pointed out. Most obvious, of course, is the similarity between the hydrographs of Put and Kup, which are completely dominated by the spring flood. The Sag streamflow is much more evenly distributed during the summer. After a sharp rise starting on June 5 or 6 the flow of Put peaks on June 9 with a maximum of about 250 liters per square kilometer per second ($1\ \mathrm{km^{-2}\ sec^{-1}}$). On June 14, the day of the ERTS pass (Fig. 8) the flow has de-

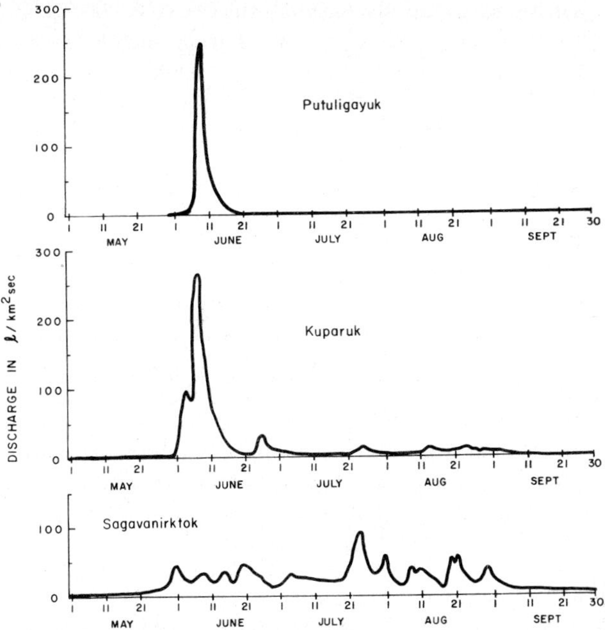

Fig. 16. Preliminary streamflow data for May–September, 1973. Courtesy of the Water Resources Laboratory, U. S. Geological Survey, Fairbanks.

creased to 18 $1\ \mathrm{km^{-2}\ sec^{-1}}$, and after a few more days the flow is of the order of 1 $1\ \mathrm{km^{-2}\ sec^{-1}}$ or less. This low flow regime then prevails throughout the summer.

A discussion of the regime of a small river in the Barrow region in relation to physiography, temperature and precipitation was given by Brown *et al.* (1968). Among the findings was that only about 5% of the thaw season precipitation runs off. After rainstorms only part of the watershed normally contributes to the runoff because of the storage capacity of the depressed topography. Carlson (1972) and Dingman (1973) have modeled the spring peak flows on the Arctic coastal plain. Their work shows among other things the importance of allowing (1) for a large storage capacity of the subdued tundra terrain, and (2) for the aerial variability of the snow pack in the generation of meltwater. Our observations, which include air photos in the Put area on June 4 and 5 indicate that damming of meltwater by snow drifts, bridging over many natural small-scale drainage channels and the increased accumulation in depressions may be an important factor for determining the shape of the hydrograph curve. Similar observations have been made during earlier breakups in this area (L. Mayo, personal communication). As the snow drifts disappear, in connection with increased melting rates at the end of the melting period, the physical setting of the basin is suddenly changed, allowing a rapid discharge of the dammed water.

The spring flood of Kup, although extending over a period which is roughly a week longer than that of Put, is also remarkably sharp, considering the extensive area and the height interval of 0–900 meters involved (Fig. 3). One contributing factor for the narrow peak of the spring regime, could be the early ablation in the foothill areas. On the ERTS transect of May 27 (Fig. 7), one can see areas of meltwater flooding the river channels in the upper part of the basin. From the hydrograph it appears that a water front reaches the outlet about 4 days later, or on May 31. From this day and onwards the discharge increases rapidly to reach its main maximum on June 8. At this time the contribution from the lower foothills and the coastal plains is at its maximum as indicated by the Put hydrograph. The observed snow breakup patterns thus qualitatively allow for the sharp peaks of Put and Kup. The Kup summer regime is characterized by a remarkably low runoff with little variation. Estimates of the meltwater contribution from snow drifts in the gullies of the foothill areas (Fig. 8), indicate that the Kup streamflow should, on a percentage basis, be noticeably influenced by the remaining snow drift until late in summer.

The upper part of the Sag Basin is a high-mountain area with peaks between 2000–3000 meters. The period of significant flow is distributed over the entire thaw season. The spring peak occurs already on May 31, which may qualitatively be explained by the early retreat of the snow as observed on the satellite data. There is no marked transition between the spring and summer regimes. The highest peaks were observed on July 24 with a discharge per unit area amounting roughly to two-fifths of the spring peaks of Put and Kup. The summer peaks of the Sag hydrograph may be due to increased rate of melting or liquid precipitation or both.

5. Conclusions

Due to lack of ground observations, meteorological as well as hydrological, quantitative assessments of the snow hydrology on the Arctic slope are not possible at the present time. The satellite data offers insight into interesting relationships between physio-graphic and climatic parameters. The ERTS data can be used to determine snow characteristics in detail, like the areal extent of snow drifts and reflectance levels of frozen, melting or dust-contaminated snow. For the Arctic slope environment, the high-resolution capability may be valuable for monitoring man-made effects on the snow breakup as the level of activity increases.

Acknowledgments. This work was supported by NASA Contract NAS 5-21833 and NSF Grant GV-29342. The Water Resources Laboratory of the U. S. Geological Survey in Fairbanks, Alaska provided the stream flow data. Mr. Larry Mayo of the U. S. Geological Survey of Fairbanks gave us valuable advice on the topics of this paper.

REFERENCES

Arnborg, L., H. J. Walker and J. Peippo, 1972: Water discharge in the Colville River, *Geografiska Annalen*, **48A** (1966), 4.

Benson, C. S., 1969: The seasonal snow cover of Arctic Alaska, Arctic Institute of North America Research Paper No. 51.

Brown, J., S. L. Dingman and R. J. Lewellen, 1968: Hydrology of a drainage basin on the Alaskan costal plain, CRREL Research Rept. 240.

Carlson, R., W. Norton and R. Britch, 1972: Modeling snowmelt runoff in an Arctic coastal basin, International Symposia on the Role of Snow and Ice in Hydrology, Symposium on Measurement and Forecasting, Banff.

Conover, J. H., 1960: Macro- and micro-climatology of the Arctic slope of Alaska, Quartermaster Research E. Engineering Center Environmental Protection Research Division, Technical Rept. EP-139.

Dingman, S. L., 1973: Development of a snow melt-runoff model for the U. S. Tundra Biome, U. S. Biome Rept. 73–3.

Gill, D., 1973: The summer climate of McKenzie River Delta, 24th Alaska Science Conference, 1973 (abstract).

Weller, G., S. A. Bowling, K. O. L. F. Jayaweera, T. Ohtake, G. Shaw and G. Wendler, 1972: Radiation fluxes in the Arctic, Annual Report, ONR Contract No. N00014-71-A-0364-0001.

Weller, G. and S. Cubley, 1972: The microclimates of the Arctic tundra, Proceedings, 1972 Tundra Biome Symposium, Lake Wilderness Center, University of Washington, Seattle, July 1972.

Weller, G. and B. Holmgren, 1974: The microclimates of the arctic tundra. *Journal of Applied Meteorology*, **13, 8**.

Hydrology of Alaska's Arctic

ROBERT F. CARLSON AND DOUGLAS L. KANE

Institute of Water Resources, University of Alaska, Fairbanks, Alaska 99701

Abstract

The Institute of Water Resources, in 1969, began a long term study of the water resources of Alaska's Arctic in response to the area's large scale petroleum exploration and extraction activities. A summary of the work is presented through a discussion of the basic features of the hydrologic system—the physical system, climatic input, and hydrologic output, with particular emphasis given to the Kuparuk, the Sagavanirktok, and the Putuligayuk Rivers. Precipitation acts as the controlling input function for the overall system. It occurs as snowfall in the eight winter months and as rainfall in June, July, August, and most of September. Comparison of precipitation records are made for Barrow, Barter Island and Prudhoe Bay. Other input variables which were examined are solar radiation, wind speed, and temperature. The output variables of the hydrologic system are evaporation and streamflow. Streamflow values collected by the U. S. Geological Survey for a two to three year period for the Putuligayuk, the Kuparuk, the Sagavanirktok Rivers indicate peak values and approximate summer mean values of 25, 20 and 20 cfs mi^{-2} and .01, 0.1, 1.0 cfs mi^{-2}, respectively. The streamflow begins with a precipitous rise at the beginning of June and recedes to a sustained amount for the remainder of the summer until September, after which the winter flow becomes nearly negligible. The most severe restriction on hydrologic studies in this and other arctic areas is the lack of long term data. Yet, in spite of the accelerating resource development, few additional water resource data activities are being funded.

---

1. Background

Extensive resource exploration and extraction activities in Alaska's Arctic began in 1969. Of the many problems faced by this resource development, an important facet will be water resources. In 1969, the Institute of Water Resources at the University of Alaska began a long term study of collection of data, field measurement, and analytic studies pertaining to the area's hydrology and water resource system. The project is now complete and has resulted in a compilation of literature on arctic water resources (Hartman and Carlson, 1970), and in an exploratory analytic study of the area's spring runoff by mathematical modeling (Carlson, Britch and Norton, 1972; and Carlson and Norton, 1973). An attempt to explore the interrelationship between arctic lakes and the subpermafrost aquifer was completed (Hartman and Carlson, 1973). Finally, a comprehensive report of the general nature of the hydrology in Alaska's Arctic has been published by Kane and Carlson (1973). This paper is a summary of the last report with an emphasis on the need for more intensive data gathering activity in Alaska's Arctic.

The physical system, climatic input, and hydrologic output of the hydrologic system are discussed in turn. Except for one instance, the discussion will be limited to three adjacent river basins in the vicinity of the Prudhoe Bay oil development area: Kuparuk, Sagavanirktok and the Putuligayuk (Fig. 1).

2. Geography

Alaska has been divided by Wahrhaftig (1965) into three physiographical divisions. The Sagavanirktok and the Kuparuk Rivers transect all three regions, beginning in the Brooks Range, flowing through the Arctic Foothills and emptying into the Beaufort Sea after flowing across the Arctic Coastal Plain. The Putuligayuk River is confined entirely to the Arctic Coastal Plain. The southernmost extent of the study area extends into the Brooks Range with peak elevations ranging from 6000 to 8200 feet. No glaciers and few lakes are found in this part of the Kuparuk and Sagavanirktok River basins. The area is considered to be underlain with continuous permafrost. The middle section of the Sagavanirktok and Kuparuk Rivers, the Arctic Foothills, consist of broad east-trending ridges ranging in elevation from 600 to 3500 feet. Few lakes are found in the valley bottoms. The Arctic Coastal Plain, the northernmost portion of the Sagavanirktok and Kuparuk River basins and the entire Putuligayuk River basin, extends from the Arctic Foothills to the Beaufort Sea. The plain is approximately one hundred miles in width beginning just a few feet above sea level and reaching a maximum elevation of 600 feet. The general area has very poor drainage, numerous lakes, and extensive permafrost. The topographic distribution of the Kuparuk and Sagavanirktok Rivers are indicated both by the isometric curves of Fig. 2

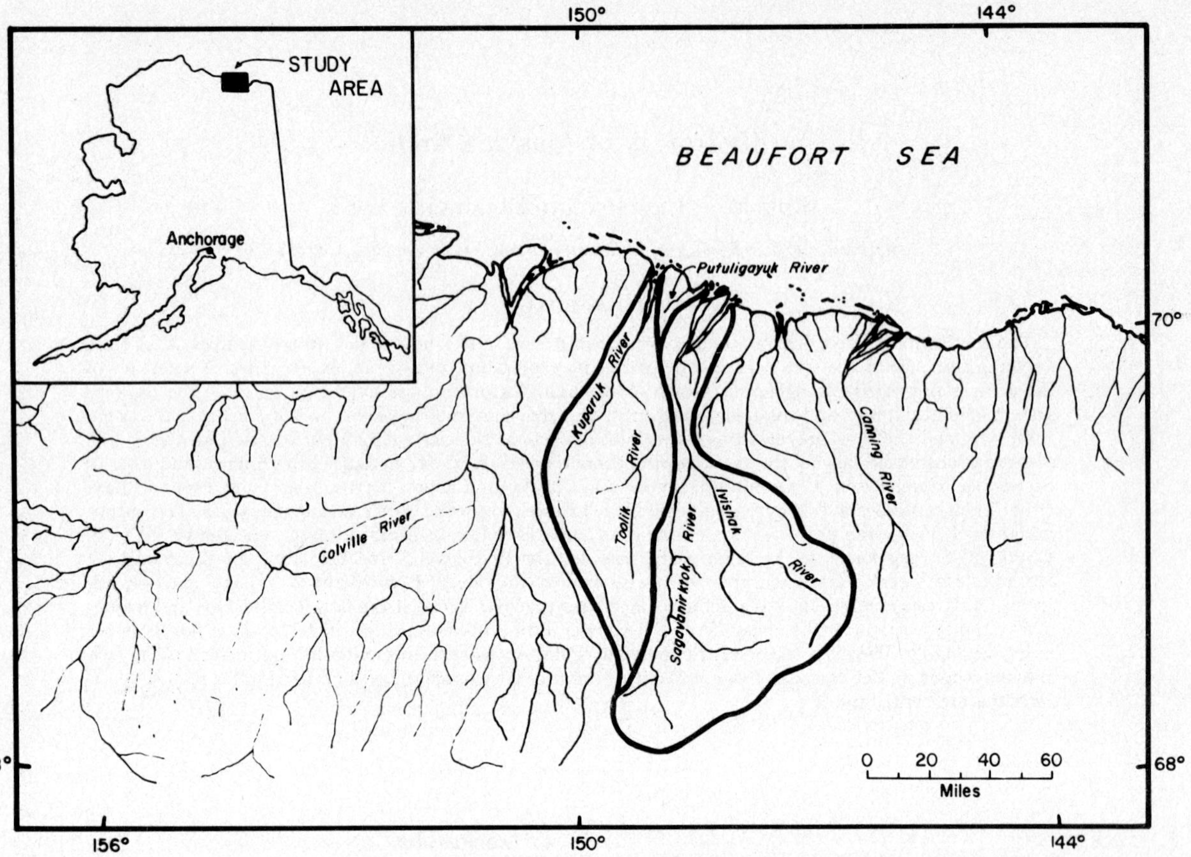

FIG. 1. Location map showing the major drainages in Prudhoe Bay area.

and the area elevation curves in Fig. 3. Because of the low relief, the Putuligayuk River is not shown as part of these figures.

Approximately 30% of the Putuligayuk River basin is covered with lakes and ponds while less than 2% of the Sagavanirktok and Kuparuk River basins are covered with lakes.

3. Climatic input

The most important climatic input is precipitation. The obvious dominant feature of precipitation in these arctic basins is the division between winter and summer. Most of the winter precipitation occurs from mid-September through May in the form of snowfall. The summer precipitation occurs in June, July, August, and most of September in the form of rainfall. Most of the water equivalent occurs in the months of July, August, September and October as shown in Fig. 4. Practically all of the water is made available to the active hydrologic system only in the four summer months.

The main difficulty with analyzing the hydrology of Alaska's Arctic, as with most arctic regions, is the extreme paucity of data. The only long term precipitation information for this region is available at Barrow and Barter Island to the west and east of the study site, respectively. The monthly distribution at each of the precipitation stations is shown in Fig. 4. The cumulative precipitation for the period from 1949 to

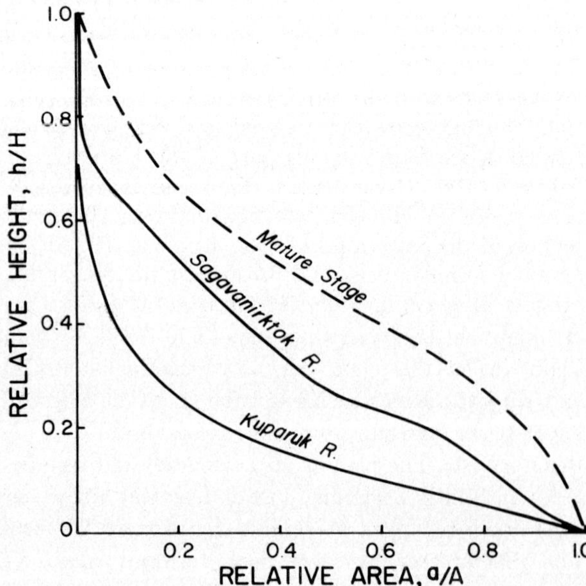

FIG. 2. Hypsometric curve, H = maximum elevation, A = total drainage area, and a = drainage area above a given elevation h.

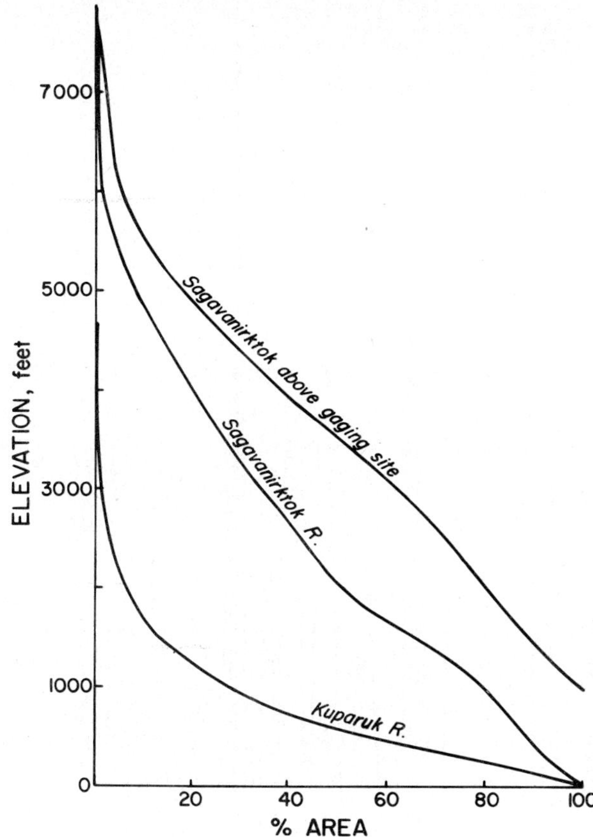

FIG. 3. Area-elevation curve illustrating the percentage of the total drainage area above a given elevation.

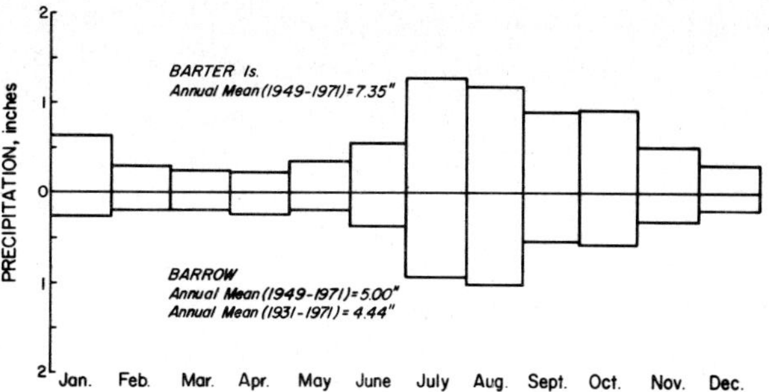

FIG. 4. Mean monthly precipitation at Barrow and Barter Island, 1949–1971. (Data source: U. S. Weather Bureau.)

day to day and a pronounced seasonal trend, peaking, as one might expect, in the month of June and slowly decreasing throughout the summer months. One important item to notice is that, because of the low air temperature in arctic regions, snowmelt runoff seldom begins in this area before the first of June. By this time, solar radiation is near its maximum with the result that snowmelt phenomena proceeds at a very dramatic, rapidly increasing rate.

1971 at two stations is shown on Fig. 5. The precipitation record of these stations seems to be quite consistent with time and there is a definite bias of higher precipitation toward Barter Island. One would expect that the precipitation available at the three basins under discussion would be approximately midway between the two at comparable elevations.

This hypothesis was checked during the field measurement season in 1971. The results are shown in Fig. 6. Again, the indicated precipitation at Prudhoe Bay is approximately midway between the records at Barrow and Barter Island. Weller and Brown (1972) at Prudhoe Bay indicate some deviation from the others. The IWR station at Prudhoe Bay was located approximately 15 miles to the west of the Deadhorse airstrip, center of most of the development activity.

Another important but often neglected input to the hydrologic system is solar radiation. It is particularly important in arctic regions because of the importance of snowmelt to the total hydrologic system. Solar radiation is estimated from available climatic data such as cloud cover taken at the U. S. Weather Service stations. Standard mechanical pyranometer measurements taken in 1971 at Prudhoe Bay are shown in Fig. 7. There is great variation of solar radiation from

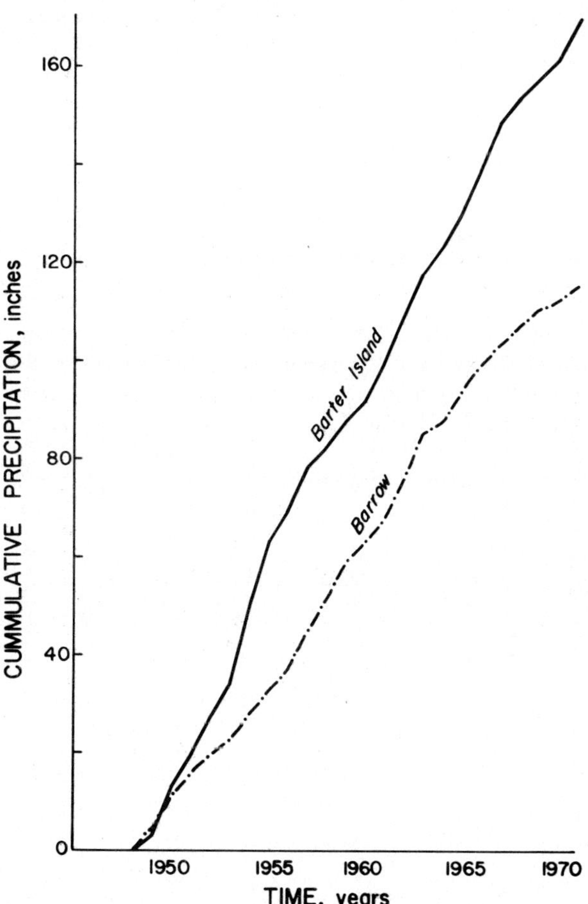

FIG. 5. Cumulative precipitation at Barter Island and Barrow, 1949–1971. (Data source: U. S. Weather Bureau.)

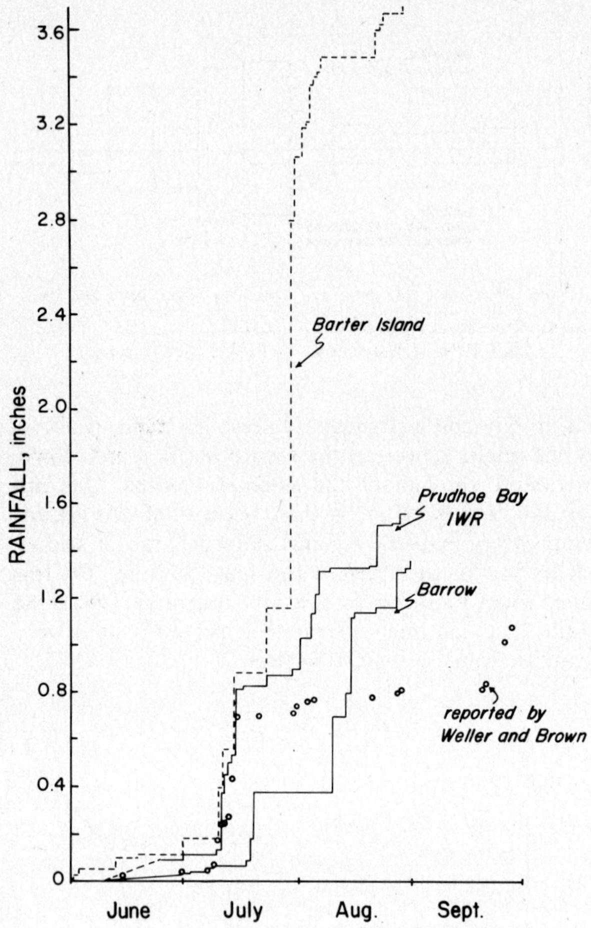

FIG. 6. Cumulative plot of daily precipitation at selected sites, summer, 1971.

The next input variable of the hydrologic system is wind speed, usually expressed in terms of average daily wind speed in miles per hour. It was measured during the IWR study in 1971 (Fig. 8). Wind speed also varies greatly from day to day but tends to be fairly consistent during summer when averaged over

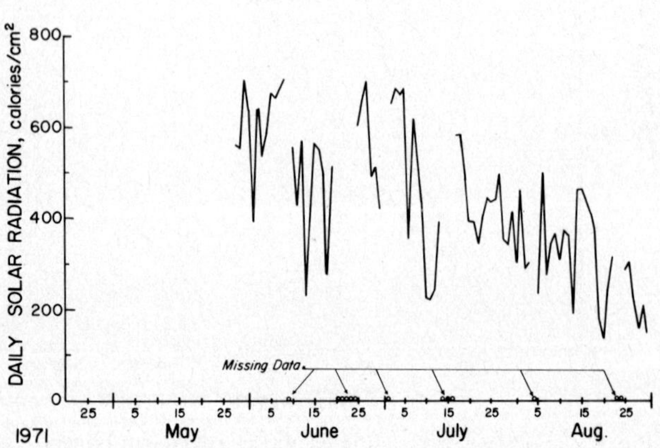

FIG. 7. Daily solar radiation near Prudhoe Bay.

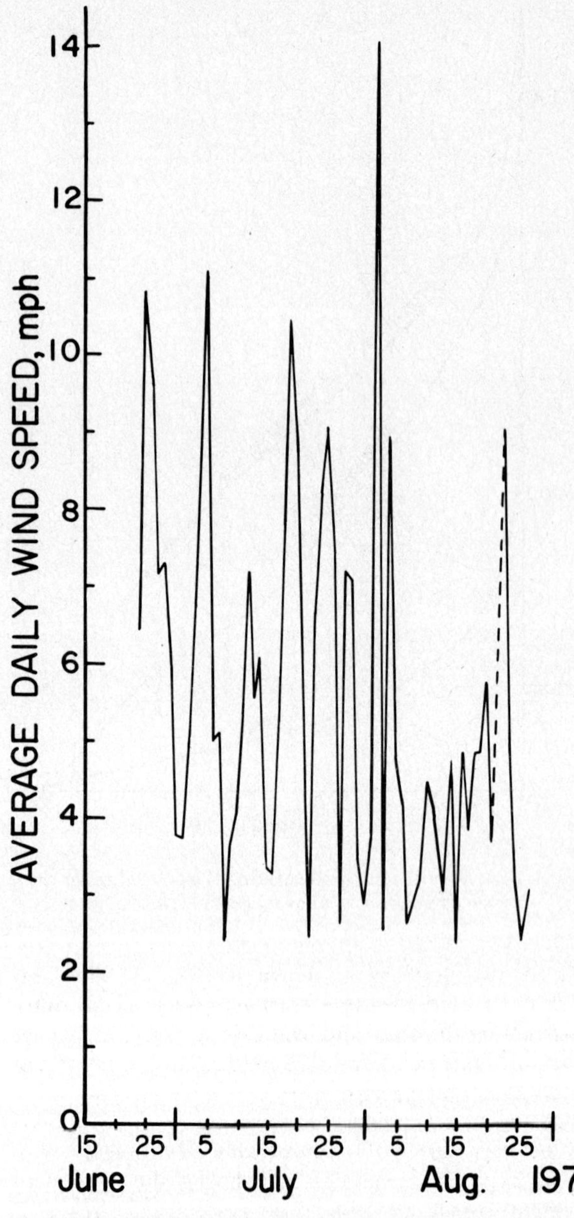

FIG. 8. Average daily wind speed (miles/hour) near Prudhoe Bay.

a month's time. This variable exerts its main influence through calculations of snowmelt and evaporation.

As one might expect, the temperature variable provides an important input in determining the characteristics of the hydrologic system in arctic regions. The main quantitative effect is made through calculation of snowmelt and evaporation rates. Its other important effect is determining whether a snowfall or rainfall event has occurred. A more qualitative aspect is an indicator of the beginning of the spring breakup of snowpack and water courses and as an indication of the freeze up in the fall. The mean daily air temperatures at Prudhoe Bay are shown in Fig. 9 for the summer season. The data portray a typical year

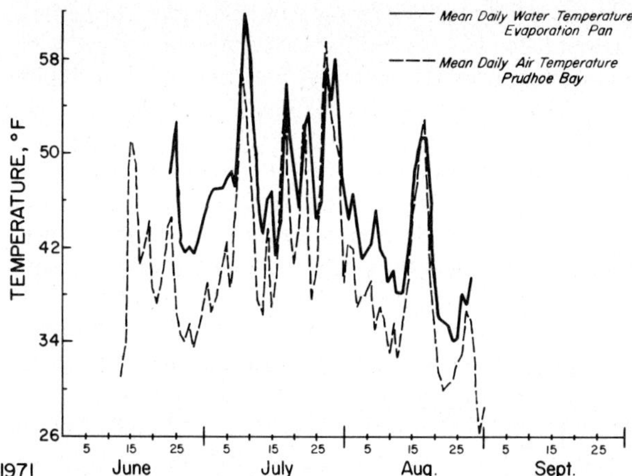

FIG. 9. Comparison of mean daily water temperature in evaporation pan to mean daily air temperature near Prudhoe Bay.

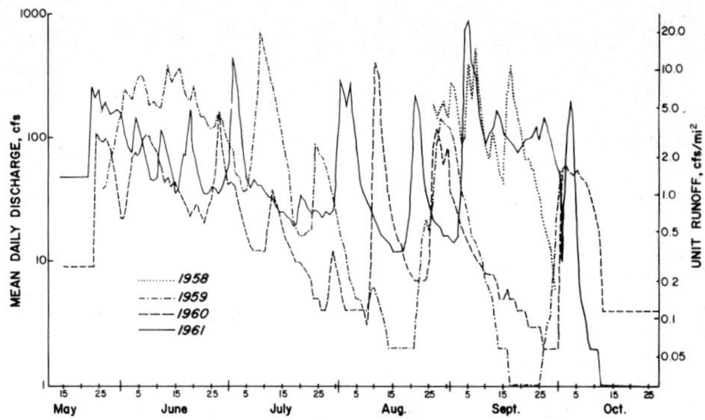

FIG. 11. Hydrograph of mean daily discharge, Ogotoruk Creek near Pt. Hope. (Data source: U. S. Geological Survey.)

in which only the months of June, July, and August have air temperature consistently above 0 C.

4. Hydrologic system output

The most persistent but often neglected output variable is that of evaporation and its partner, evapotranspiration. Measurements are regularly taken at only two places in Alaska, Fairbanks and Palmer. This parameter is becoming increasingly important, especially in the design of wastewater treatment lagoons and reservoirs. It has been measured or even estimated only a few times in arctic regions. Mather and Thornthwaite (1958) measured and computed the evapotranspiration for several sites near Barrow. Their calculation was based on a modified Penman method. Other calculations were made by Patric and Black (1968) who determined yearly potential evapotranspiration estimates by the standard Thornthwaite method. They reported a value of 8 inches of 20 cm. Kane and Carlson (1973) reported measurements of pan evaporation and calculations of lake evaporation for the Prudhoe Bay area for the summer months

of 1971. These measurements are plotted in Fig. 10. In addition, a water level recorder was maintained on a closed lake near the Putuligayuk River and is also plotted on Fig. 10. A close agreement is indicated between the measured pan evaporation, calculated lake evaporation, and calculated lake levels. As the measurements were begun only after the first of June, it appears that the pan evaporation rate is nearly 8 inches over the summer season. It compares very favorably to the calculated lake evaporation and the declining lake level, as these measurements do not begin until the latter part of June. As indicated by the comparison of the two slopes, the rates are very nearly equivalent.

The last component of the hydrologic system to be discussed is the surface runoff. This, both peak flow from snowmelt and rainfall, and low flow, is clearly the most important element from an engineering point of view. The former is needed for design of natural drainage crossings and occupation of the flood plain, and the latter is needed for low flow estimates for water supply and waste discharge. The collection of surface runoff data has been extremely sparse in Alaska's Arctic. Until recently, only miscellaneous measurements have been made. The first stream to be measured for an extended period of time was Ogotoruk Creek near Point Hope. Its record in terms of mean

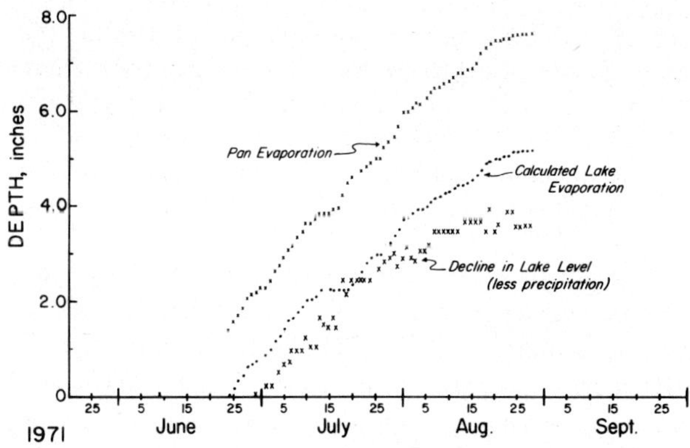

FIG. 10. Calculated and measured rates of evaporation from a small lake near Prudhoe Bay.

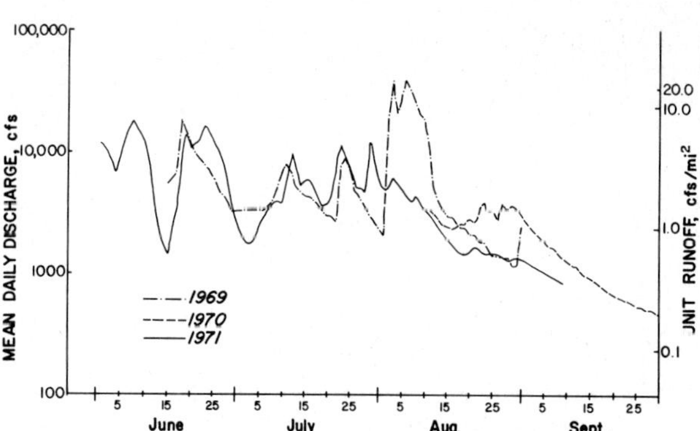

FIG. 12. Hydrograph of mean daily discharge, Sagavanirktok River. (Data source: U. S. Geological Survey.)

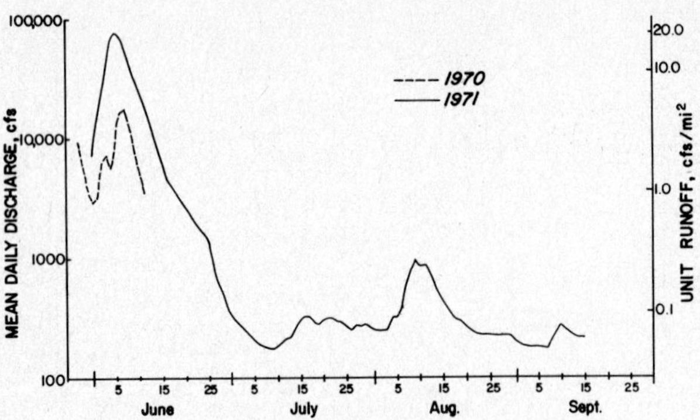

FIG. 13. Hydrograph of mean daily discharge, Kuparuk River. (Data Source: U. S. Geological Survey.)

daily discharge and discharge per square mile is shown in Fig. 11 for four years, 1958 to 1961. The maximum instantaneous discharge, not shown on that figure, is 41 cfs mi^{-2}, nearly twice the maximum unit runoff of 25 cfs mi^{-2}. Measurements on the Colville River by Arnborg *et al.* (1966) indicate a peak runoff of 11 cfs mi^{-2} and an average discharge during the summer months of 2.3 cfs mi^{-2}. Brown *et al.* (1968) measured discharge on a small stream near Barrow from 1963 to 1966. Because the area of the stream is only 0.6 mi^2, the data is too erratic to extend to larger areas. Beginning in 1969, the U. S. Geological Survey began a series of regular measurements on three arctic river basins: the Sagavanirktok, Kuparuk, and Putuligayuk. These streamflow hydrographs are presented in Figs. 12, 13 and 14.

These hydrographs show, at least for these few years, that most of the runoff for the Kuparuk and Putuligayuk Rivers occurs during the spring snowmelt, whereas the Sagavanirktok River has large

volumes of water discharge continuously throughout the summer. The reason for this difference is probably due to the greater percentage of the area at higher elevations drained by the Sagavanirktok River which would lead to a greater dominance of snowmelt throughout the summer. The Putuligayuk River, on the other hand, is located entirely on the Arctic Coastal Plain which would lead one to expect a very sharp spring break-up and a continuous recession throughout the summer months. The reader should be warned that all four figures of the streamflow were plotted on a semi-log scale so that the peaks are greatly suppressed. Several summer storm events are evident on both the Kuparuk and Putuligayuk Rivers. The U. S. Geological Survey rates these records as only fair because of the extremely hazardous conditions under which they must be obtained, especially during the spring breakup period. These three basins have peak flows of approximately 25, 20, and 20 cfs mi^{-2}, respectively, for the Putuligayuk, Kuparuk and Sagavanirktok Rivers. Mean flows on the other hand are approximately 0.01, 0.1 and 1.0 cfs mi^{-2} for the summer discharge period.

In summary then, the main characteristic of the runoff hydrograph is a very precipitous rise beginning about the first of June followed by a sustained flow throughout the rest of the summer months. The nature of the winter flow can only be guessed at but the consensus is that the flow becomes nearly negligible throughout the winter months.

5. Conclusions

The previous discussion has presented a summary of the available data and of the various components of the hydrologic system of Alaska's Arctic. A more complete account is available in the report by Kane and Carlson (1973).

In attempting to form a hypothesis of the characteristics of the arctic hydrologic system, a most severely limiting factor is availability of basic data, particularly climatic data and streamflow. Most work has tended to be short term data collected for research purposes such as the IWR data reported here. Generally, the value of such short term data is very limited. There is a great need for long term data stations particularly with attention to distribution with elevation. As is true in much of Alaska, most data recorded in the Arctic is at sea level while most of the area is much higher.

Although basic hydrologic data is essential to most resource development activities, data collection efforts have been quite minimal. The present data plan is particularly incongruous in view of the rapidly accelerating resource extraction development in the Arctic which is of great importance to the nation and the world as a whole.

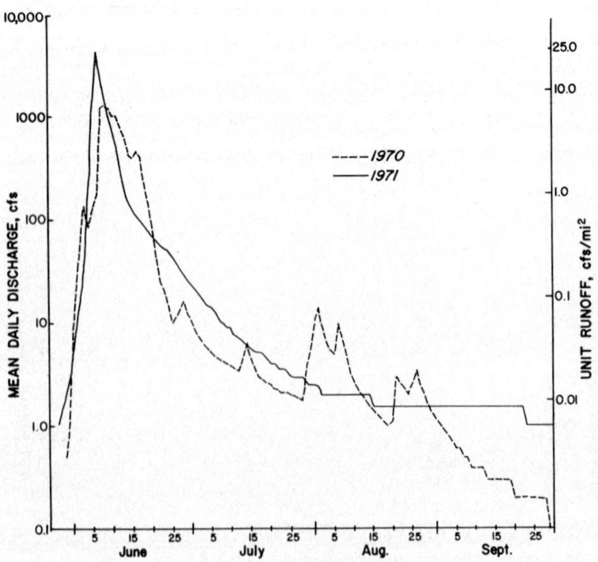

FIG. 14. Hydrograph of mean daily discharge, Putuligayuk River. (Data source: U. S. Geological Survey.)

REFERENCES

Carlson, R. F., W. Norton and R. Britch, 1972: Modeling snowmelt runoff in an Arctic Coastal Basin. Proc. of Symposia on the Role of Snow and Ice in Hydrology, Banff, Canada, Sept. 1972, UNESCO-WMO-IAHS 1004-1016.

Carlson, R. F., and William Norton, 1973: Modeling snowmelt runoff in an Arctic Coastal Plain. Institute of Water Resources, University of Alaska, Report No. IWR-43.

Hartman, C. W., and R. F. Carlson, 1970: Bibliography of arctic water resources. Institute of Water Resources, University of Alaska, Report No. IWR-11.

Hartman, C. W., and R. F. Carlson, 1973: Water balance of a small lake in a permafrost region. Institute of Water Resources, University of Alaska, Report No. IWR-42.

Kane, D. L., and R. F. Carlson, 1973: Hydrology of the central arctic river basins of Alaska. Institute of Water Resources, University of Alaska, Report No. IWR-41.

Mather, J. R., and C. W. Thornthwaite, 1958: Microclimatic investigations at Point Barrow, Alaska, 1957-1958. Drexel Inst. of Technology, Laboratory of Climatology Volume 11, No. 2.

Patric, J. H., and P. E. Black, 1968: Potential evapotranspiration and climate in Alaska by Thornthwaite's classification. U.S.D.A., Forest Service Research Paper PNW-71.

Weller, G., and J. Brown, 1971: Abiotic overview. The structure and function of tundra ecosystem. International Biological Program, Volume 1, Progress Report and Proposal Abstracts, 173-179.

Runoff in the Canadian Arctic Archipelago

E. R. WALKER AND R. A. LAKE

Frozen Sea Research Group, Marine Sciences Directorate (Pacific Region), Federal Building, Victoria, B. C., Canada

Abstract

The Canadian Arctic Archipelago has been described as an "Arctic Desert." However, the volume of precipitation falling over the Archipelago north of the mainland and north of Baffin Island has, using climatic normal values of precipitation, been estimated as 2×10^{11} m³ of water per year. This may be compared with estimates of annual precipitation volume of 6×10^{11} m³ of water per year falling on the drainage area of the Mackenzie River, and 1×10^{11} m³ of water per year falling on the remainder of the area draining to the Arctic coast of mainland Canada west of Hudson Bay.

Within the Archipelago slightly over half the total area is land. There is increasing interest in the runoff of this precipitation. As oceanographers we are concerned with amounts, distribution and timing of runoff both on a large and small scale. Useful estimates by oceanographic methods seem unlikely in the near future, so meteorological methods must be used. Even here there are difficulties.

One almost overwhelming difficulty lies in the sheer extent of poorly known country, with an extreme paucity of weather stations. Another is the well known difficulty of measuring snowfall. Air temperatures are above freezing only from June to September. The latest precipitation normals suggest that about 60% of total precipitation is in the form of snow. If the amount of snowfall is underestimated then correction to the snowfall measurements may be possible. That this correction is needed is suggested by comparing cumulative snowfall water content, with snow depth and water content measured on snow courses at the meteorological stations. However, these comparisons suggest that the snow depth measurements may not always adequately represent conditions at the meteorological site. This is supported by comparing the very few runoff records in the Archipelago with volumes of water available in the basin estimated from meteorology.

In most parts of the Archipelago evaporation and percolation may be quantitatively rather unimportant insofar as the usually explosive runoff peak is concerned. The question of the runoff from glaciers which occupy 1×10^5 km² in the eastern Archipelago cannot be as easily dealt with as runoff from non-glaciated Arctic areas. Runoff from both types of areas needs research efforts rather more intensive and extensive than those of the present, if urgent runoff questions are to be answered on a useful time scale.

The Canadian Arctic Archipelago has been described as an "Arctic Desert." Certainly if snow be substituted for sand and gloom for glaring sun, this may seem appropriate in winter. However, the "desert" classification may be questioned by those who have tried to slog through the gumbo of summer, or experienced the torrents of spring.

This paper reviews in a broad way some of the latest official statistics, especially those of precipitation, over the archipelago west and north of Baffin Island. To review the latter island would be a project in itself. The area is shown in Fig. 1. Physically a glaciated backbone runs along the mountainous eastern rim. The western parts of the archipelago tend to be lower and rolling. Some areas, of course, are very flat indeed, with confused drainage. Apart from the DEW-line Stations along 70°N and stations on Baffin Island, the weather statistics over this vast area (2×10^6 km²) come from the seven weather stations marked on Fig. 1.

The latest thirty year (1941–70) precipitation normals (Anon., undated) are shown in Fig. 2. The isohyets we drew ourselves. They are generally similar to those appearing on charts based on the 1931–60 normals. Over the Arctic Islands the normals are based on weather stations established in the late 1940's. For most stations the current normal values of precipitation are very slightly higher than past normals but we have not investigated the details or significance of this increase.

Although the isolines in Fig. 2 are engagingly smooth and simple, undoubtedly, particularly in the more mountainous east, fine scale detail of the sort published for rough terrain with more adequate gauging must exist. A suggestion of this has been allowed to creep into the area around Eureka. Surrounded by mountains, the Eureka station records the lowest amount of precipitation in the Arctic. On nearby glaciers estimates of accumulation and average annual precipitation (Hattersley-Smith, 1960; Muller, 1963) have ranged far above 12 cm year⁻¹ compared to Eureka's 1941–70 normal of 2.3 inches or 5.8 cm. However the statistics say that over most of the Archipelago the precipitation averages between 4 and 6 inches water equivalent.

The areas involved are so vast that the volume of

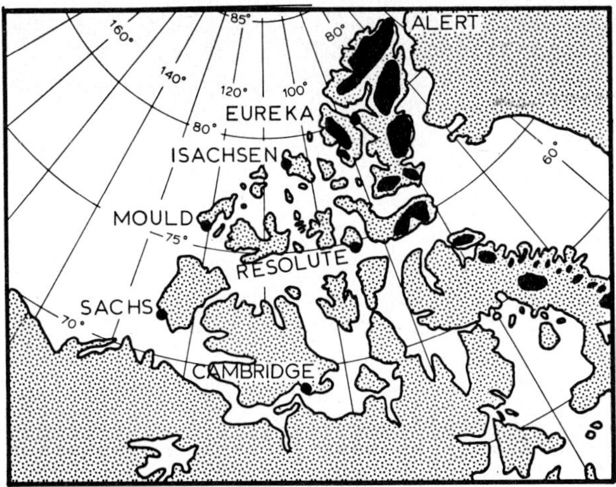

CANADIAN ARCTIC ARCHIPELAGO

FIG. 1. The Canadian Arctic Archipelago, showing High Arctic weather stations and glaciated areas.

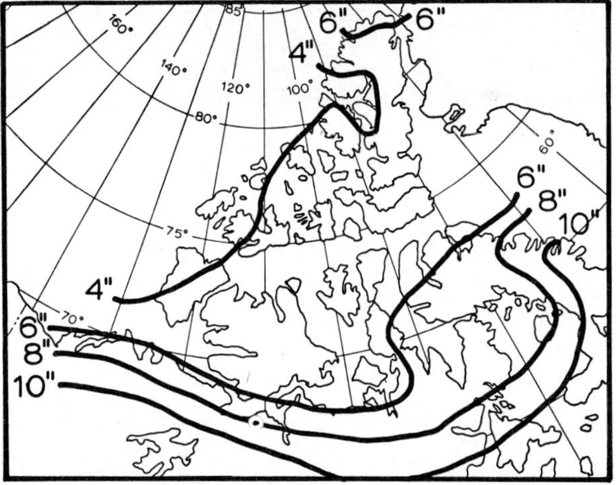

NORMAL PRECIPITATION 1941–1970 (AFTER AES)

FIG. 2. Total annual precipitation normals (1941–70) over the Canadian Arctic Archipelago in inches of water (after AES).

precipitation falling annually over the area with which we are dealing is about 2×10^{11} m³ of water. This may be compared with our estimates of 6×10^{11} m³ of water falling onto the drainage area of the Mackenzie River, and 1×10^{11} m³ of water falling on the area draining into the Arctic coast of Canada between Hudson Bay and the Mackenzie drainage.

Within the Archipelago slightly over half the total area is land. There is increasing interest in the runoff on land in order to choose safe and economical sites for the increasing exploitation of natural resources. As oceanographers we are concerned with amounts, distribution and timing of runoff from the land, both on a large and small scale. On the large scale the total precipitation, disregarding evaporation, would put about 0.25 m of fresh water in the channels of the Archipelago. Within the channels somewhere between 1 and 2 m fresh water is added every summer from melting sea ice. The volume flow through the Archipelago is estimated at 3×10^{13} m³ per year so the precipitation volumes are not in general practicably measurable. Presumably runoff fresh water depth will be greater in restricted water areas with a larger ratio of drainage area to water surface. Even so, useful estimates of runoff by oceanographic measurements seem unlikely in the near future, so meteorological methods must be used. Even here there are difficulties.

One almost overwhelming difficulty lies in the sheer extent of poorly known country with the extreme paucity of weather stations shown earlier in Fig. 1. Another problem is obtaining a correct measurement of precipitation, particularly snow. In the area of the Archipelago with which we deal air temperatures are above freezing only from June to September. The annual course of normal air temperatures is shown

in Fig. 3. At Eureka in northern Ellesmere the winters are long and cold. In fact February 1973 had a mean air temperature of -46 F at Eureka. We noted that the air temperature normals for 1941–70 are slightly colder than earlier normals. To return to Eureka, note the very rapid warmup in April–May with cool summer temperatures because of ice choked channels. Resolute is not quite as cold in winter as Eureka but is cool in summer. Cambridge Bay in the south has occasional summer airflow from the warmer continent.

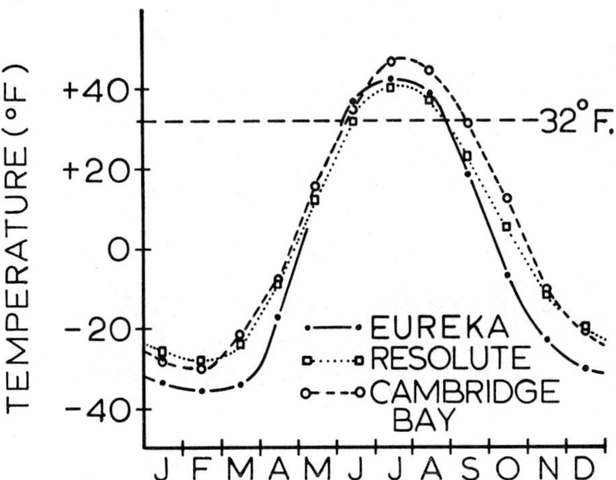

AIR TEMPERATURE NORMAL 1941–70 (AFTER AES)

FIG. 3. Normal (1941–70) air temperatures at Eureka, Resolute and Cambridge Bay weather stations (°F.) (after AES).

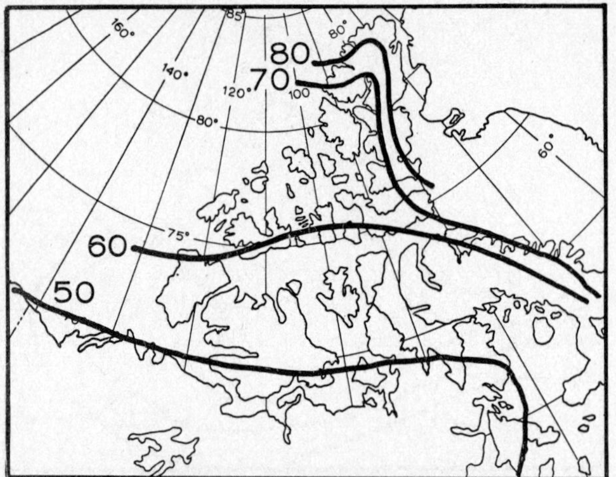

FIG. 4. Percentage of normal (1941–70) annual precipitation falling as snow over the Canadian Arctic Archipelago (after AES).

With such air temperatures one may expect more snow than rain. The 1941–70 normals, for the low altitude weather stations of course, give the percentage contributions of snow to total precipitation shown in Fig. 4. Over most of the Archipelago it is between 50 and 70%. Fig. 5 shows the normal course of rainfall and snowfall at three stations from Eureka in the north to Cambridge Bay in the south.

Are the precipitation quantities as they appear in official statistics correct? We know that techniques of measurements of rainfall and even more so of snowfall contain sources of possible errors. Experts on the subject suspect that on the average rain gauges underestimate rainfall by 9% while snowfall is underestimated by 40%. If this is so then at Resolute, for example, the corrected and real values might be 2.52 inches of rain and 4.28 inches water equivalent of snow, instead of normals of 2.31 and 3.06 inches, respectively.

Until the early 1960's snowfall water content was estimated by measuring the depth of newly fallen snow and assuming a density of 0.1 gm cm^{-3}. The 1941–70 normals indicate a snow density of either 0.09 or 0.10 for the Arctic stations. Since the mid-sixties snow has been caught and melted. The fresh snowfall is still measured nearby. For the years 1968 to date we examined the density of newly fallen snow by dividing reported monthly snowfall depths into the water content of total precipitation for the months of October through April. The values varied somewhat as might be expected. There seemed to be no seasonal variability. A summary of statistics is given in Table 1.

As can be seen, the density of newly fallen snow tends to be less than 0.10 gm cm^{-3}.

In addition, total snow depth and snow water content are measured twice monthly during the winter. We compared the total precipitation amounts accumulated monthly from September to the time the snowpack began to decrease, ranging from the end of April to the end of May in the far north. The accumulated water content of precipitation divided by the water content of the snowpack at the end of winter is shown for 1968–72 in Table 2. The figures are extremely variable, particularly in the western Archipelago. On the whole, the water content of the snowpack was larger than the water equivalent of precipitation. It was markedly and consistently so at

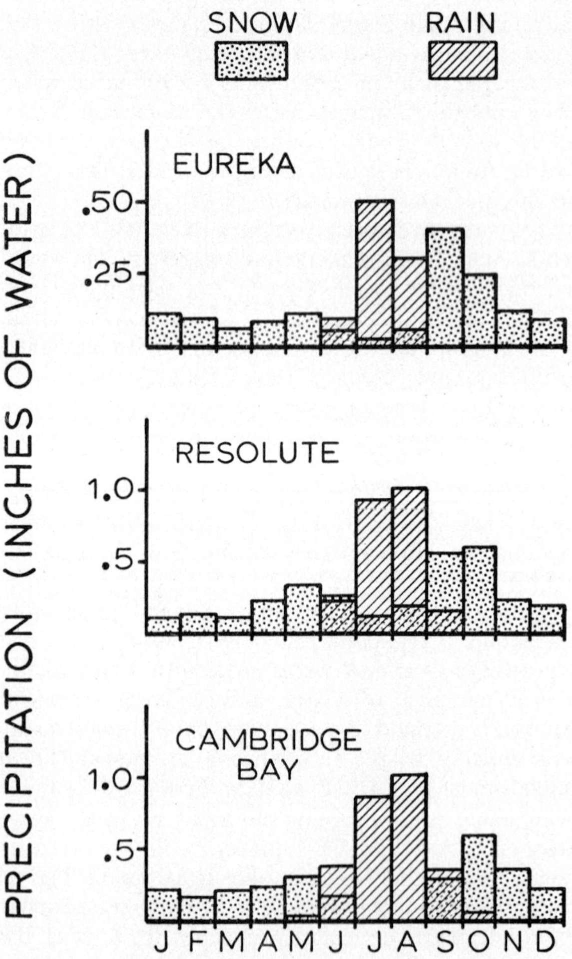

FIG. 5. Monthly normals (1941–70) of rainfall and snowfall water equivalent over the Canadian Arctic Archipelago (inches of water) (after AES).

TABLE 1. Density (gm cm⁻³), means and variability of newly fallen snow over the Canadian Arctic Archipelago from 1968–1973. Obtained by dividing water content of monthly precipitation by monthly values of snowfall. Months October through April (after AES).

Station	No. of months	Mean density	Standard deviation	Lowest value	Highest value
Alert	39	0.094	0.023	0.04	0.15
Cambridge Bay	38	0.078	0.026	0.03	0.20
Eureka	38	0.097	0.007	0.08	0.11
Isachsen	37	0.097	0.009	0.06	0.11
Mould Bay	37	0.084	0.022	0.05	0.14
Resolute	38	0.092	0.012	0.06	0.11
Sachs Harbor	37	0.087	0.013	0.05	0.10

TABLE 3. Density (gm cm⁻³), means and variability of snowpack over months October through April, 1968–1972, over the Canadian Arctic Archipelago (after AES).

Station	No. of months	Mean density	Standard deviation	Lowest value	Highest value
Alert	32	0.316	0.057	0.17	0.40
Cambridge Bay	26	0.329	0.059	0.14	0.43
Eureka	27	0.285	0.063	0.15	0.37
Isachsen	31	0.305	0.055	0.15	0.42
Mould Bay	30	0.283	0.084	0.14	0.38
Resolute	32	0.299	0.052	0.16	0.38
Sachs Harbor	30	0.303	0.051	0.22	0.38

Eureka. Other stations tended to be more disturbed, the value of 2.58 in 1969 at Resolute for example being caused by an inexplicable drop in snowpack water content as measured in April and May 1969. Examination of meteorological conditions suggests no reasonable explanation. Attention is drawn to this as an example of inconsistencies which are not infrequent in the records.

Density of the snowpack, examined monthly from October through April, gives values shown in Table 3 and Fig. 6. The anomalous point at the end of October came from Cambridge Bay and might possibly be due to rainfall on the snowpack. The anomalously high point at the end of November came from one measurement at Eureka which was clearly in error. If this one measurement is removed, the point would fall with the others.

In contrast to snowpack densities in more southerly latitudes (McKay and Findlay, 1971), there was little seasonal variation. These densities are more stable than other statistics. Combined with more adequate snow depth measurements over wide areas they would suffice to determine snowpack water content sufficiently well for many purposes.

Further support is given to the suspicion of under-measurement of snowfall by comparing the very few river runoff measurements with snowpack water content in the river basin. In three examples for years 1970, 71 and 72 for basins of size 80 or 400 km² the ratios of measured runoff to basin water estimated from snowfall (without any evaporation) at nearby

TABLE 2. Accumulated water equivalent of winter precipitation divided by water content of snowpack at the end of winter for stations in the Canadian Arctic Archipelago (after AES).

Station	1968	1969	1970	1971	1972
Alert	0.87	0.66	0.76	1.06	0.66
Cambridge Bay	1.06	1.72		0.96	1.00
Eureka	0.64	0.38	0.43	0.35	0.43
Isachsen	0.91	1.27	5.53	2.20	0.84
Mould Bay	0.77	0.57	0.71	1.05	2.05
Resolute	0.83	2.58	0.55	0.43	0.51
Sachs Harbor	0.73	—	1.37	1.59	1.80

Resolute were 2.3, 1.6 and 1.7 in the respective years while the ratios of runoff to basin water estimated from snowpack water content were 1.5, 1.2 and 1.2 in the respective years. The runoff figures are much more uncertain for 1970 than the other two years. The latter suggests that (a) snowfall is underestimated, (b) acceptable runoff estimates can be made from snowpack water content.

The Archipelago is underlain by permafrost (Brown, 1972). The ground near our base in northern Ellesmere Island thaws to a depth of less than one half meter. At Resolute the active layer is about one half meter so presumably over most of the Archipelago the thaw depth is less than a meter. This certainly reduces percolation problems compared to southern latitudes, as is borne out by the river flow studies mentioned above.

The snow stays late over the Archipelago. The albedo remains high. Examples of net radiation averaged over the last few years are shown in Fig. 7. Even in these curves, which represent measurements near weather stations where the surface might be

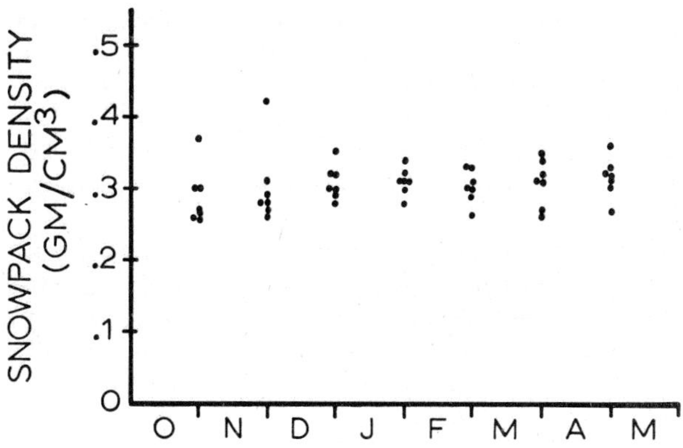

SNOWPACK DENSITY (GM/CM³)
ARCTIC ARCHIPELAGO
1968–1973

FIG. 6. Density of snowpack (gm cm⁻³) at month's end, October, to April, averaged over 1968–73 for weather stations in the Canadian Arctic Archipelago (after AES).

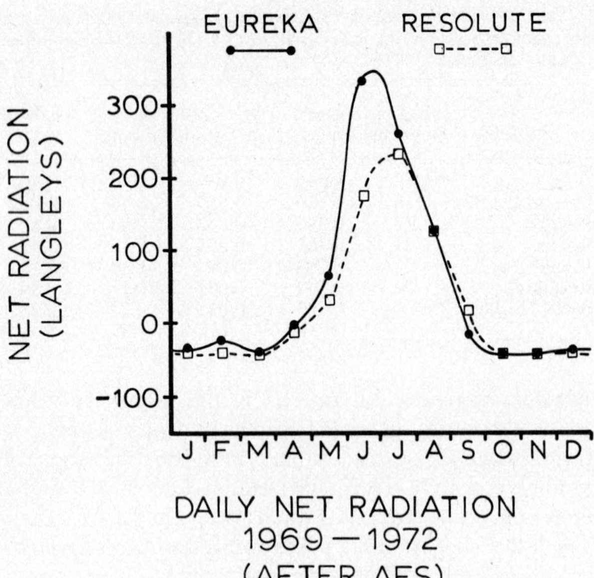

Fig. 7. Daily net radiation (langleys) averaged over 1969–72 at Eureka and Resolute (after AES).

dirtier than in the hinterland, the curves are by no means symmetrical about midsummer. Another peculiarity in Fig. 7 is the higher and earlier values of net radiation at Eureka within its encircling mountains compared to Resolute over 5 degrees farther south. This can be accounted for in large part by the approximately 50% greater cloud cover at Resolute. This radiation regime is borne out by dates of runoff from small low level streams. In our area near Eureka, peak runoff in a stream with a basin of about 40 km² occurred on June 24th–26th, 1973 while McCann *et al.* (1972) reported spring peaks in early July in 1970 for streams near Resolute. We think this time difference is typical of most years. All streams were on sloping ground and spring runoff was very rapid. We estimate more than half the spring runoff from our stream went out in five days. While in other, larger basins in flatter terrain spring flow may not be quite as explosive, the general rule that the farther north one goes the faster things happen must remain true.

Later in the summer, ponding and evaporation assume importance. Vegetation, evapotranspiration and storage in bogs undoubtedly must be considered. At the moment accumulation of knowledge of the distributions of terrain types important in these respects is still in early stages.

Another problem which we have not touched upon is runoff from the glaciated areas (1×10⁵ km²) in the eastern Archipelago. We will content ourselves in this regard with outlining our own problem concerning glacier runoff.

We are interested in amount and timing of runoff into the small d'Iberville Fiord in northern Ellesmere Island. The fiord water surface is 213 km². Nine rivers flow into the fiord from unglaciated basins with a total area of 910 km². With these we are more or less prepared to cope. But 2800 km² of drainage is occupied by a very active glacier. It must put out a great deal of meltwater (as yet unmeasured). In addition it puts out icebergs as a fair rate. About fifty per cent of the years that we have operated in the area the sea ice does not clear from the fiord but keeps the icebergs penned against the glacier snout. In other years (e.g., 1969) the sea ice clears and icebergs fill the fiord. We estimated that 95 per cent of the icebergs melted in the fiord. An estimate made on the spot was that over 1×10⁸ m³ of fresh water was added by this melting. This is about 80 percent of the average annual precipitation of the nearby Eureka weather station over the glacier drainage area. That is our problem and I trust for other people's sakes their glaciers are less active.

REFERENCES

Anonymous, undated: Temperature and precipitation, 1941–1970, the North—Y.T. and N.W.T. Environment Canada, Atmospheric Environment Service, 4905 Dufferin Street, Downsview, Ontario, pp. 24.

Brown, R. J. E., 1972: Permafrost in the Canadian Arctic Archipelago. *Zeit. fur Geomorphologie, Neue Folge, Supp.* **13**, 102–130.

Hattersley-Smith, G., 1960: Studies of englacial profiles in the Lake Hazen area of northern Ellesmere Island. *Jour. Glaciology*, **3**, 27, 610–625.

McKay, G. A., and B. F. Findlay, 1971: Variation of snow resources with climate and vegetation in Canada. Presented at the Western Snow Conference, 39th Annual Meeting, April 20–22, 1971, Billings, Montana.

Muller, F., 1963: Investigations in an ice shaft in the accumulation area of the McGill Ice Cap. In Preliminary Report 1961–1962, Axel Heiberg Island Research Reports, McGill University, Montreal, P.Q., 27–36.

McCann, S. B., P. J. Howarth and J. G. Cogley, 1972: Fluvial processes in a periglacial environment, Queen Elizabeth Islands, N.W.T., Canada. Transactions of the Institute of British Geographers, Publication No. 55, March 1972, 69–82.

Satellite Observations of Sea Ice Movement in the Bering Strait Region

LEWIS H. SHAPIRO

Geophysical Institute, University of Alaska, Fairbanks, Alaska

AND

JOHN J. BURNS

Alaska Department of Fish and Game, 1300 College Road, Fairbanks, Alaska

Abstract

This paper describes a short-term episode of rapid southward displacement of sea ice through the Bering Strait which occurred during early March, 1973. The area was imaged by the ERTS-1 satellite on March 6, 7 and 8. The movement of individual ice floes was mapped directly from the 9×9 photographic products of the MSS data acquired at that time. Additional coverage for the first 10 days of March was available from the Air Force DAPP system, which provided imagery of the area from the southern limits of the pack ice in the Bering Sea to north of Point Barrow. Thus, the process of break-up and movement of the pack ice was observed on a regional scale. Weather data from Wales, Alaska indicated that the wind blew steadily from the north or northeast at 15 to 25 knots during the first 10 days of March, 1973. Break-up of the ice north of the Bering Strait began on March 6 and involved the extensive development of tension and shear fractures. Displacement vectors of individual floes for the period March 6 through 8 range from about 20 kilometers near Point Hope to greater than 50 kilometers near Bering Strait. Data from the DAPP system indicates that the movements continued at least through March 10, accompanied by a significant southerly shift of the edge of the pack ice in the Bering Sea.

1. Introduction

The period during which sea ice is present in the Bering Strait region extends, in general, from mid-November to late June. Major and essentially predictable aspects of this annual ice cycle include the early winter formation, progressive increase in thickness which occurs throughout the freezing period and the spring break-up involving both the thawing of sea ice and its rapid northward movement. Within the framework of these major occurrences there are numerous episodes of short-term ice movement and deformation, triggered by a variety of atmospheric and oceanographic factors which operate as semi-independent processes.

In this paper we will describe a late winter, short-term episode of rapid deformation of the pack ice in southeastern Chukchi Sea and its transport southward through Bering Strait and into Bering Sea. This episode occurred during several days in early March 1973, while there was almost no cloud cover and temperatures well below the freezing point of sea water prevailed. From photographic products of data acquired by two observational satellites, NASA's ERTS-1 and the U. S. Air Force DAPP system, it was possible to map the displacement of individual ice floes and changes in the geometry of the pattern of leads associated with these movements. This provided sufficient information for a description of the sequence of break-up and transport of

the ice, and for advancing an explanation of the mechanics of the process.

2. Method of study

The data used in this study were primarily the photographic products of the data acquired by the MSS (Multispectral Scanner) system of the ERTS-1 satellite and the Air Force DAPP system. The characteristics of the ERTS-1 system have been described elsewhere (see, for example, Lathram, 1973). For the purpose of this paper, it is sufficient to note only that the resolution of the MSS system permits elements of moderate contrast and linear dimensions of less than 100 meters to be discriminated. Distortions in the imagery tend to be systematic (Southard and MacDonald, 1973) and in general, the root mean square error of position for points on any MSS image ranges from 200 to 450 meters, with no detectable additional error associated with image duplication or enlargement (Colvocoresses and McEwen, 1973).

In order to map the position of a particular ice floe on successive days, some means of registering sequential images is required. In general, this cannot be done by reference to the coordinates of the scenes as determined from the orbital information (Colvocoresses and McEwen, 1973), which tends to limit the usefulness of the ERTS-1 data for mapping sea ice movements. In

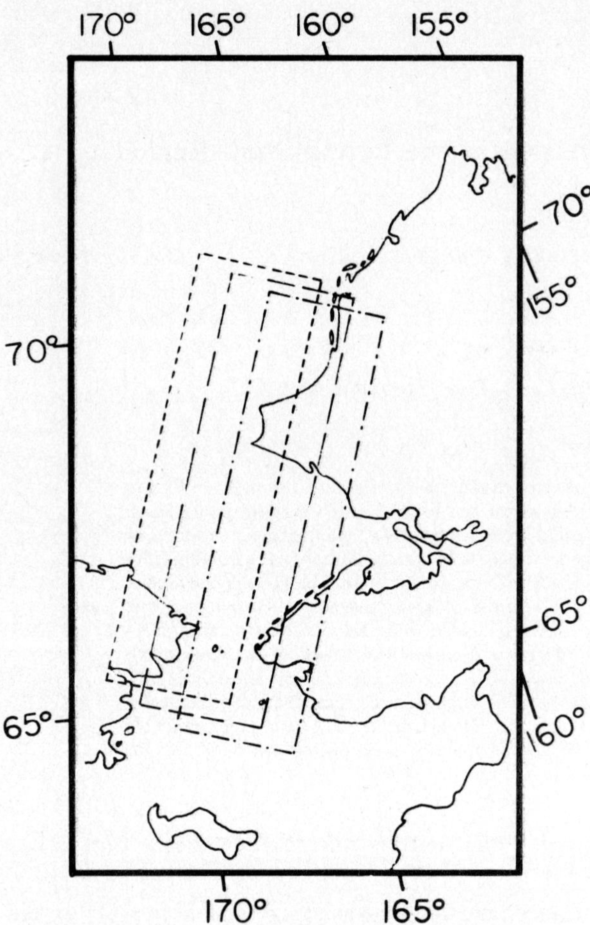

Fig. 1. Location map of the study area showing the ERTS-1 coverage available. Area imaged on March 6 is outlined by dot-dash line, March 7 by long dashes, and March 8 by short dashes. Note the degree of repetitive coverage.

the present study, however, the area of interest is close to shore and, in fact, land areas are shown in all of the images examined. Thus, it was possible to register sequential images by registering land areas. This was done on a light table by overlying 9×9 inch positive transparencies (scale 1:1,000,000) of images acquired on successive days. Registration on base maps of the same scale appeared perfect to the naked eye, and it is estimated that, at the scale of the transparencies, errors of registration of less than 500 meters would have been easily detectable. Assuming this relationship to be valid, the errors discussed above have no effect on the results of this study.

The orbit of the ERTS-1 satellite was selected to provide a 10% overlap of images acquired on successive days at the equator. This overlap increases at higher latitudes, and reaches about 65% at the latitude of the Bering Strait, providing overlapping coverage of a strip about 135 kilometers wide along the orbital path for two successive days. An overlapping strip about 65 kilometers wide is covered in three successive passes. Data from three consecutive ERTS-1 passes (March 6,

7 and 8) were used for this study. The area covered is shown in Fig. 1. Samples of the data are shown in Fig. 2.

The accompanying maps of ice floe displacement vectors (Figs. 3, 4 and 5) were prepared by connecting the positions of recognizable floes on successive images using the registration procedure outlined above. Thus the maximum error in the position of any floe on the second or third day of observation, relative to its initial position, is less than 500 meters. It should be emphasized that the vectors illustrated are only a small sample of the total which we measured and were selected as representative of each area.

Maps of open leads and polynya for March 7 and 8 are shown in Figs. 6 and 7. These were traced directly from the ERTS-1 images. The techniques involved in identifying these are noted below.

Photographic images available from the DAPP system were in both visible and infrared bands, with a resolution of about 0.5 km and on a scale of approximately 1:15,000,000. One scene for each of the first ten days of March 1973 was examined. No attempt was made to accurately map specific leads or to track the movement of ice floes visible on these images. Instead, the data were used only to provide qualitative information on the overall regional aspects of the problem under study.

3. Weather and currents

Weather conditions in the area of interest during the first ten days in March 1973 were dominated by a large high pressure system which remained relatively stationary over northeastern Siberia. As a result, winds in the Bering Strait region had strong northerly components during this time. Observations of surface winds at Wales on the western tip of the Seward Peninsula indicated that the volocities at that station ranged from about 10 to 16 knots from the north and northeast from March 1 to 5, and then increased to 20 to 25 knots from March 6 to 10 when the main movements occurred (Bloom, pers. comm., 1973). Ambient air temperatures ranged from about −15 C to −35 C.

It has long been recognized that water transport through Bering Strait is mainly northward (Bloom, 1964; Fleming and Haggarty, 1966) with velocities averaging about 1 knot. These currents prevail throughout the water column. South setting currents with velocities approaching 1 knot have been periodically recorded (Bloom 1964, pers. comm., 1973), and these may be associated with intense high pressure cells north of the Bering Strait, with their attendent strong northerly winds. However, the cause-effect relationship has not been reliably established (Bloom, pers. comm., 1973). Unfortunately, data concerning the direction and velocity of currents at various depths were not available for the time period under discussion. Therefore, we do not know whether winds and ocean currents were operating in concert to produce the ice movements observed,

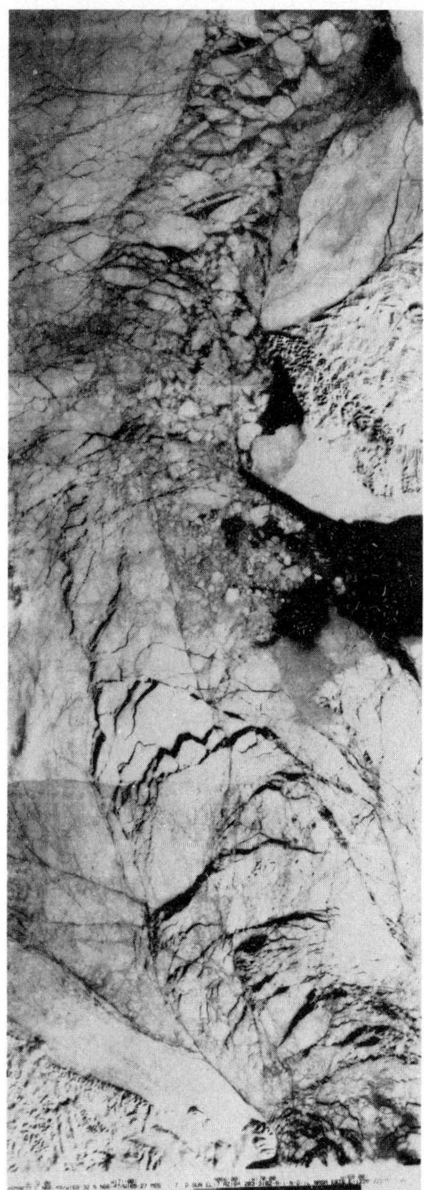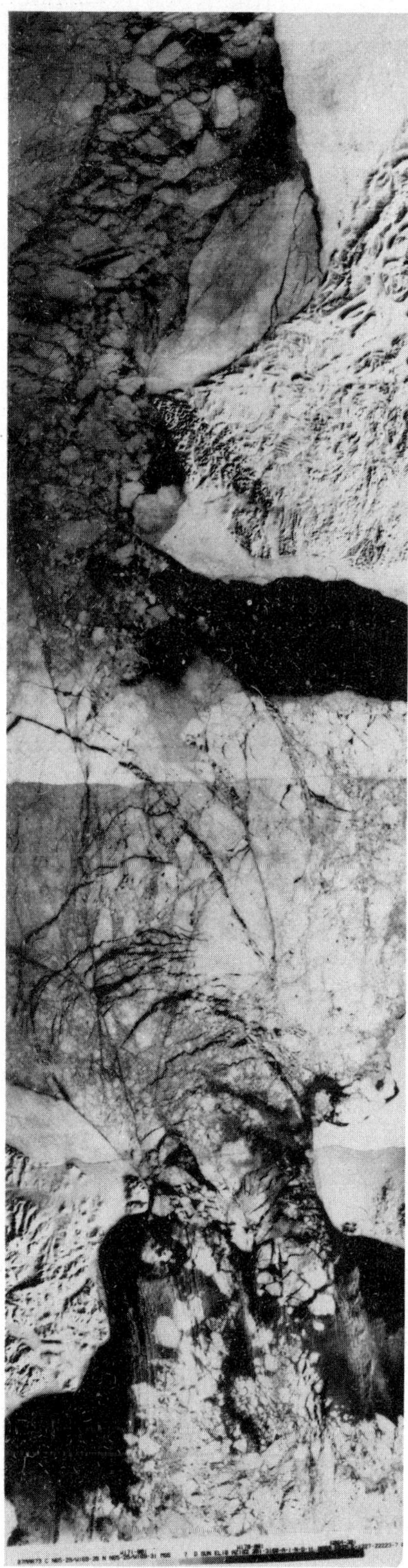

Fig. 2. Mosaics prepared from ERTS-1 MSS band 7 images acquired on March 7 (right) and March 8 (left), 1973. Similar data for March 6 were also utilized. Note the ease with which open leads can be distinguished and the same ice floe identified on successive days.

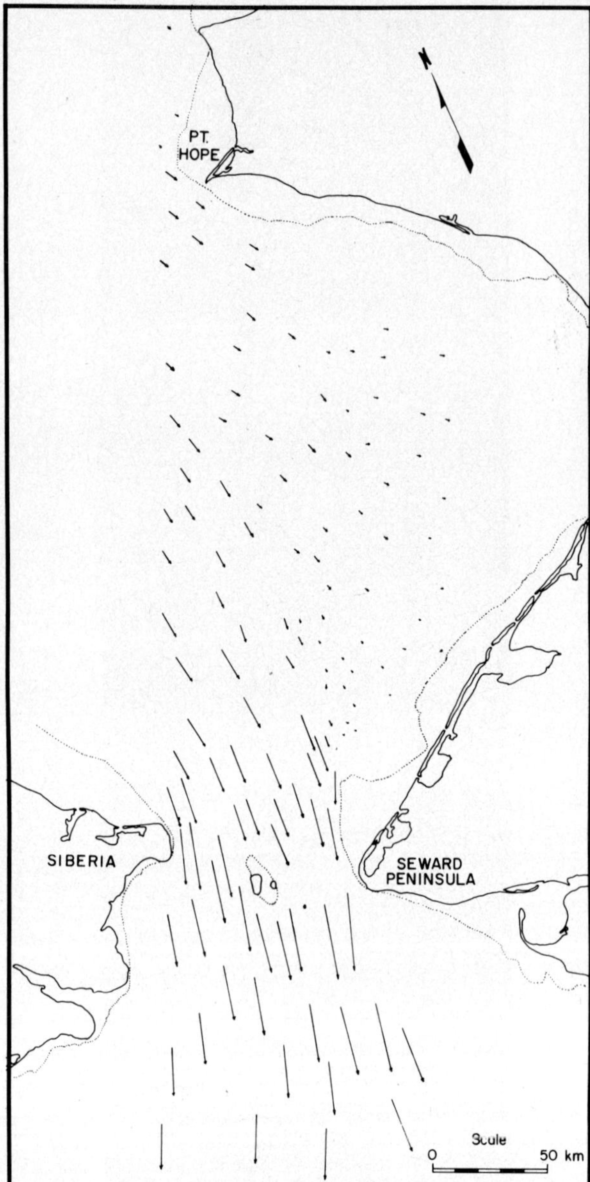

FIG. 3. Displacement vectors for the interval March 6 to 7. Each vector represents the change in position of an individual ice flow or recognizable point on a larger ice mass. Scale of the vectors is the same as the map scale. Dotted line is the edge of land fast ice.

or if the wind was causing the ice to move against the current.

4. Interpretation of ERTS-1 images

The problem under discussion is such that detailed information about the distribution of specific types of ice within the area of interst is not required. A simplified classification recognizing the following general types of ice was adopted:

new and nilas ice—ice formed in leads and polynya as they are developing

pack ice—any other drifting ice with no connotation as to age, thickness, etc.

landfast ice—ice which remains fixed to shore during the time covered by this report, and in which no movement was detected.

The distinction between new and nilas ice and pack ice was obvious in comparisons of the photographic

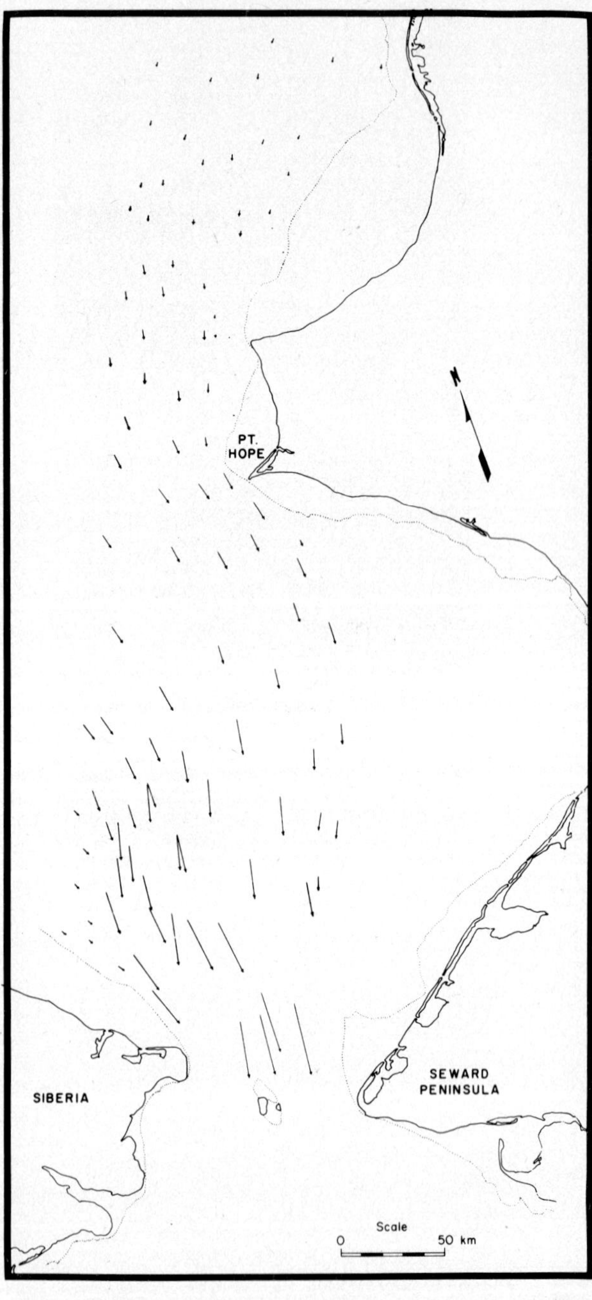

FIG. 4. Displacement vectors for the interval March 7 to 8. Other features the same as Fig. 3.

images of MSS gand 4 (0.5–0.6 micrometers) with MSS band 7 (0.8–1.1 micrometers). New and nilas ice is represented by the darker gray tones in both bands. However, pack ice tends to be uniformly light gray on

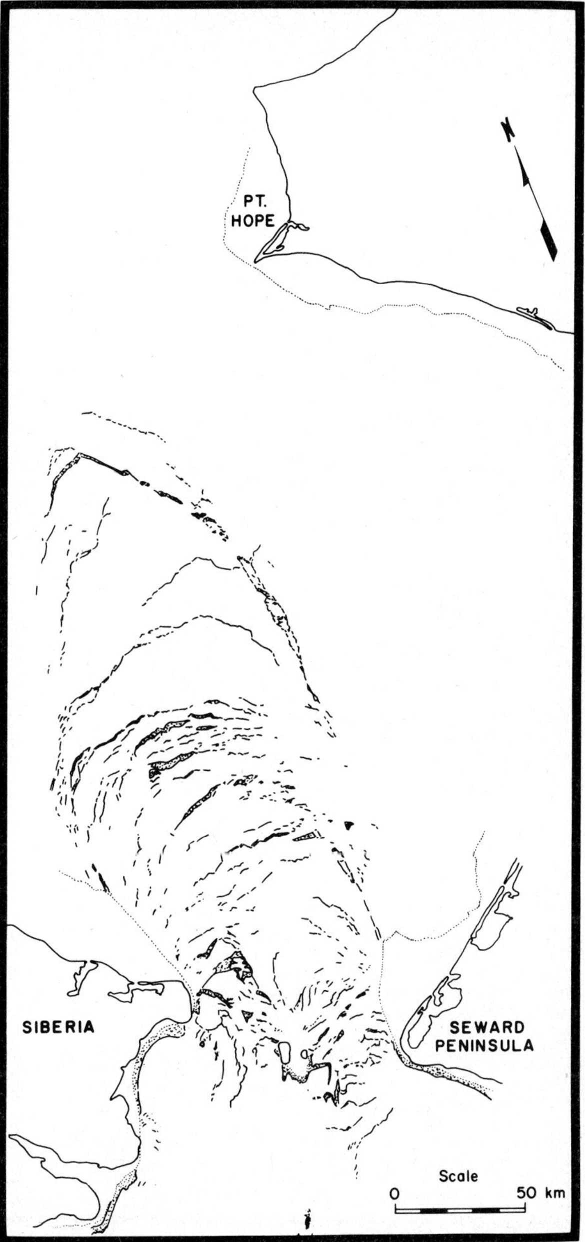

FIG. 6. Map of newly formed leads traced directly from images of March 7. Stipled areas are open water or new ice. Dotted line is the edge of land fast ice.

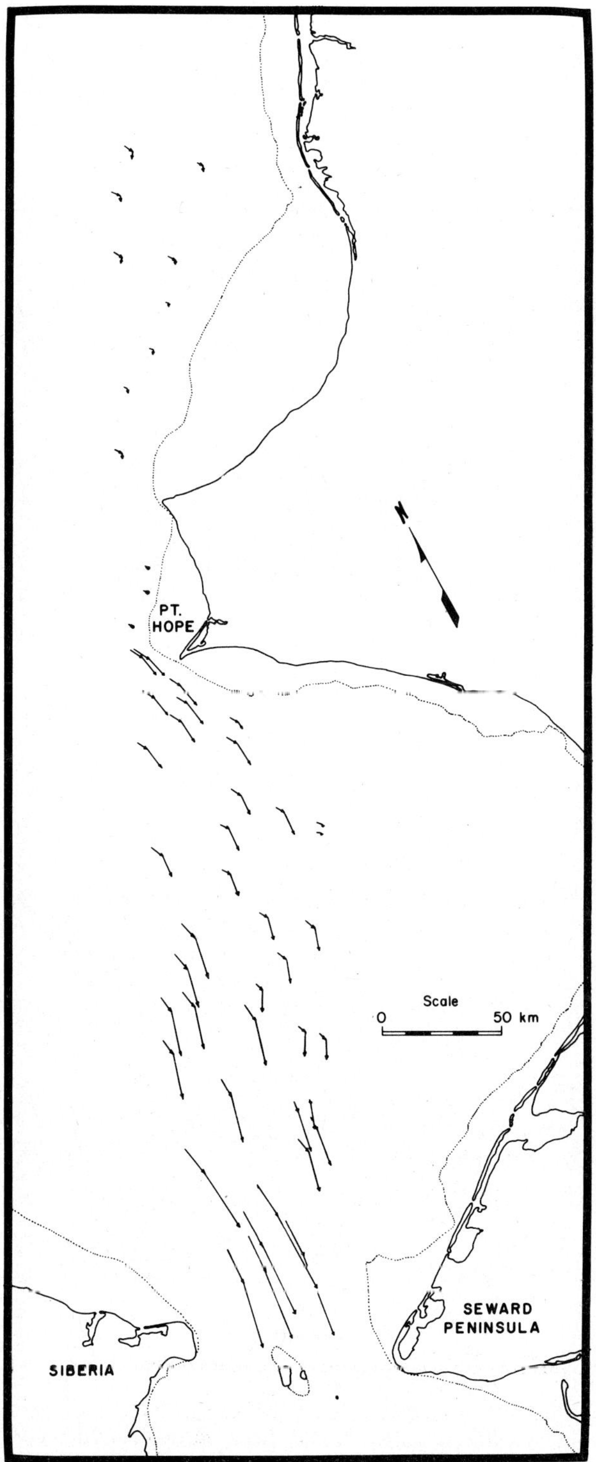

FIG. 5. Displacement vectors for the area imaged on all three days. Other features the same as Fig. 3.

band 4, while numerous dark patches, which may be interpreted as new and nilas ice, appear in the fields of pack ice in band 7. Accurate recognition of new and nilas ice was facilitated by observing its formation in images of developing leads and polynya on two successive passes (Fig. 2).

The problem of distinguishing cloud cover from ice is generally not difficult, particularly when sequential images are used (Barnes and Bowley, 1973). Open water appears black on all bands.

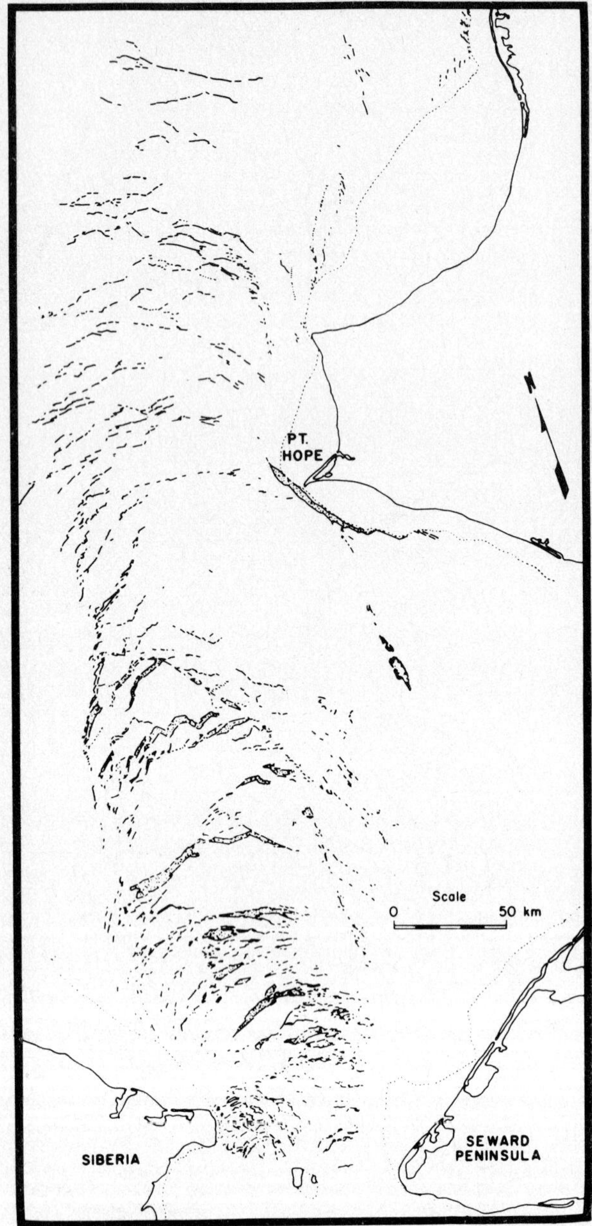

FIG. 7. Map of leads and new ice traced from images of March 8. Other features the same as Fig. 6.

5. Observations

The pattern of displacement vectors and of lead development appears to result directly from a relationship between the regional drift of the pack ice during the period under discussion and the configuration of the boundaries with which it interacts. Fig. 8 is a map of the Bering Strait region showing the shore line and the distribution of land fast ice, superimposed on contours of water depth. These define most of the boundary. The exception is in the mouth of Kotzebue Sound where the boundary is variable, and probably depends upon the rate at which the pack ice can drift into this ice covered

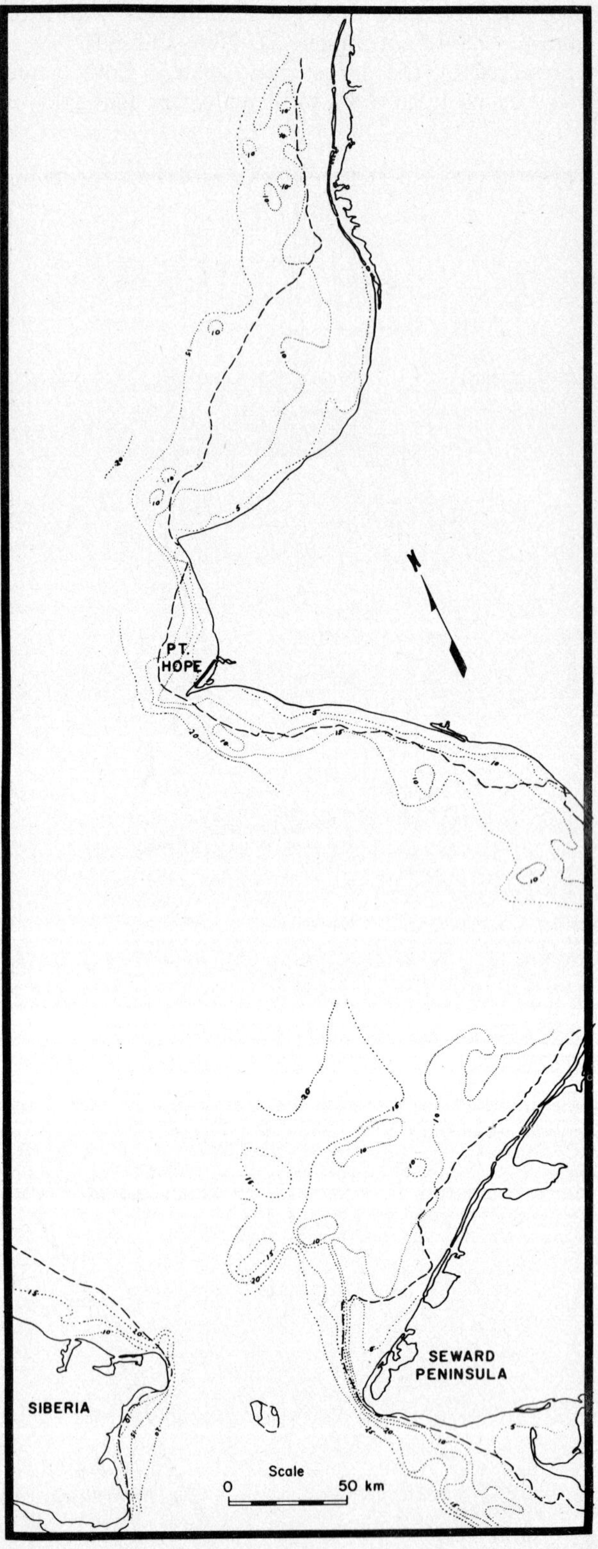

FIG. 8. Distribution of land fast ice as traced from ERTS images of March 6, 7 and 8, 1973. Heavy dashed line is the edge of land fast ice. Dotted lines are depth contours. Depths in fathoms were traced from nautical chart number 9400, U. S. Department of Commerce.

cul-de-sac. The influence of the boundaries on the flow pattern are apparent in Figs. 3 and 4. Examples of decreased magnitude of the displacement vectors near a boundary, and of deflection of flow by the boundaries are readily observed. In addition, it is apparent that the area of moving ice can be divided into several fields, each characterized by displacement vectors of similar or smoothly varying magnitudes and directions. These fields are, in turn, separated by shear zones, across which abrupt changes in the magnitude and/or direction of the displacement vectors are apparent from the figures.

The zone of intense lead development in Fig. 6 (March 7) is confined to an area extending north from the Bering Strait for approximately 250 kilometers. These leads were absent in the imagery acquired on March 6, with the exception of a few curving leads extending across the Bering Strait proper, so that the deformation occurred in, at most, one day. The pattern observed on March 7 consists of a series of east–west trending tension leads bounded by shear zones which intersect at the north end of the fractured zone. These clearly originate on opposite sides of the Bering Strait, and are easily identified over their entire length by the presence of local shear leads.

Fig. 7 shows the lead pattern traced from the ERTS imagery of March 8. The extension of the fractured zone to the north is apparent and is directly related to significant displacement of ice southward through Bering Strait. Examination of imagery acquired by the DAPP system for the same day shows that the zone probably does not extend farther north than indicated in Fig. 7. However, the DAPP images for March 9 and 10 show that fracturing had, by that time, extended north along the entire coast of Alaska as for as Point Barrow. Note that the major shear zones described above are still present on March 8 in essentially the same position they occupied on March 7.

Comparisons of Figs. 6 and 7 with the maps of displacement vectors indicate that the major shear zones enclose the area in which the largest displacement vectors north of the Bering Strait are found. The pattern of these vectors indicates a funneling effect of the Strait, and their length reflects the rapid rate of lead opening within the zone.

6. Discussion

The descriptions above clearly indicate the relationship between the patterns of displacement vectors and leads, and the geometry of the boundaries of the moving pack ice. It is reasonable to seek a hypothesis which combines these factors into a coherent working model. The approach adopted for our purposes was to identify some simple mechanical model which includes the most important elements of the observed process while idealizing these elements to avoid complications which obscure the simplicity of the model.

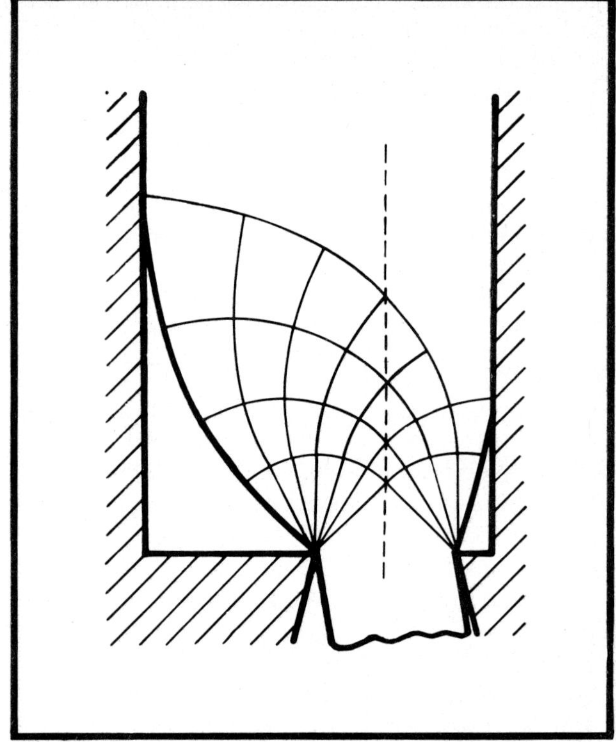

FIG. 9. Slip-line field for a perfectly plastic material extruded through a rough, unsymmetric die (*from* Johnson and Kudo, 1962). Note the zone of "dead" material in the lower left corner of the figure.

For the purpose of formulating a model the process described above can be characterized as a two-dimensional problem involving the flow of the pack ice through a constricted channel under the influence of a driving force which originates upstream from the constriction. That is, the ice is extruded through the constriction rather than being drawn through. The positions of the shear zones trending north from the boundaries of the Bering Strait are clearly related to the geometry of the boundary and must result from failure of the moving ice sheet under an internal stress field reflecting the interaction of the ice with the boundary. The similarity in the position of these zones during the period of observation suggests that the process has achieved a short-term steady-state condition.

A simple mechanical analogy to the process described above can be found in the theory of plasticity, notably in the application of the theory of plane-strain slip-line fields to extrusion problems. Fig. 9 (from Johnson and Kudo, 1962) shows the solution to the problem of extrusion of a perfectly plastic material through a rough, unsymmetric die. The envelopes of the family of curves radiating from the corners of the die opening mark the boundaries of the zone in which the material is being deformed in a state of unrestricted plastic flow. These curves define the locus of points within the stress field at which the yield stress of the material is reached. The geometric similarity between the shape of these theoretical curves and their relationship to the die opening, and the actual major shear zones observed north of Bering Strait are apparent. Note also the correspondence between the zone of "dead" material in Fig. 9 and the expanse of landfast ice on the north side of the Chukchi Peninsula. Reference to Fig. 8 shows that this ice persists, although it occurs over deep water along an exposed coast line. The position of this land-fast ice is analogous to that of the "dead" material in the extrusion flow field, which may account for its stability during the episode under discussion.

The above comments are not meant to imply that the pack ice can be modeled as a perfectly plastic material, nor that plain-strain slip-line field theory can be applied to problems of drifting ice in general. However, in this specific instance slip-line field theory does seem to identify a two-dimensional stress field with geometric properties similar to those deduced from analyses of the data discussed in this paper. A more thorough examination of the applicability of this approach to the present problem is in progress.

Acknowledgments. This research was supported by State of Alaska funds, and by NASA Contract NAS-5-21833 (tasks 1 and 7) to the University of Alaska ERTS program. We wish to thank Dr. E. P. McClain of NOAA for supplying us with the DAPP imagery.

REFERENCES

Barnes, J. C., and C. J. Bowley, 1973: Mapping sea ice from the Earth Resources Technology Satellite. *Arctic Bull.* **1**(1), 6–13.

Bloom, G. L., 1964: Water transport and temperature measurements in the eastern Bering Strait, 1953–1958. *J. Geophys. Res.* **69**(16), 3335–3354.

Colvocoresses, A. P., and R. B. McEwen, 1973: Progress in cartography, EROS program. Symposium on Significant Results Obtained from ERTS-1 NASA/GSFC, March 5–9, 1973.

Fleming, R. H., and D. Haggarty, 1966: Oceanography of the southeastern Chukchi Sea. *In* Environment of the Cape Thompson Region, Alaska, N. J. Wilimovsky and J. N. Wolfe, Eds. U. S. Atomic Energy Commission, Division of Technical Information, p. 877–924.

Johnson, W., and H. Kudo, 1962: "The Mechanics of Metal Extrusion," Manchester University Press, Manchester, England.

Lathram, E. H., 1973: EROS program, ERTS satellites and Arctic applications. Proc. Int. Congr. "Arctic Oil and Gas, Problems and Possibilities," 5th, Foundation Francaise d'Etudes Nordique, Le Harve, France, May 1973.

Southard, R. B., and W. R. MacDonald, 1973: The cartographic and scientific applications of ERTS-1 imagery in polar regions. Symposium on Approaches to Earth Survey Problems through the Use of Soace Techniques, Konstanz, FRG, May 23–25, 1973.

The Steady Drift of an Incompressible Ice Cover in the Arctic Ocean

D. A. ROTHROCK

Department of Atmospheric Sciences, University of Washington, Seattle, Washington 98195

Abstract

The steady drift of sea ice in an idealized Arctic Basin has been calculated assuming that the ice is incompressible and inviscid. The momentum and continuity equations for the ice are solved for the velocity and the ice pressure. The divergence of velocity is assumed to be 0.33×10^{-8} sec^{-1}. The drift can be characterized as nearly non-divergent and predominantly wind-driven. The boundary conditions require that no ice flows across coastal boundaries, but that ice flows out of the basin into the Greenland Sea, and into the basin from the Kara Sea.

The patterns of calculated velocities and vorticities are realistic, but their magnitudes are higher than observed values. Realistic speeds and vorticities can be obtained by varying the specified wind stress and water drag coefficient within the limits of the uncertainties in their measured values. The maximum calculated ice pressure of about 10^8 dyne cm^{-1} (pressure integrated through the ice thickness) is marginally able to ridge thick ice, according to the ridging model of Parmerter and Coon (1973). These maximum values occur near Greenland where Wittmann and Schule (1966) report intense ridging. Coastal shear zones on the order of 100 km wide might be represented by the added effect of a shear viscosity of about 6×10^{12} gm sec^{-1}.

The current areas of interest to the AIDJEX Modeling Group are briefly described; they include the characterization of ice properties by an ice thickness distribution and the assumption of a rigid-plastic constitutive law for ice deformation.

The work described in this paper is related to the general question of why sea ice moves as it does over the surface of a polar ocean. If we observe the location of a piece of ice, follow it through time, we find a rather jagged, contorted drift track. The drift tracks of several pieces of ice, which may have started within several hundred kilometers of each other, will remain close together and show a close temporal correlation. If we apply a suitable low-pass filter to these trajectories, a fairly well-defined mean drift track emerges. Since there have been over two dozen drift tracks in the Arctic, most of them within the last twenty years, there are sufficient data to acquire a rather accurate picture of the long-term mean drift, which is shown in Fig. 1. The major features of the ice, which covers this whole basin, are a gyre in the Beaufort Sea and a transport drift stream. Typical speeds are 2 or 3 cm sec^{-1}. Thus, ice island T-3 circled the gyre in about four years, and Arlis II drifted from near Barrow to the Greenland Sea in about the same length of time. This is the motion which the model presented here and in more detail by Rothrock (1973) seeks to describe.

There are two aspects of modeling the movement of sea ice which are not well understood, and which have been treated in different ways by different scientists. First, we would like to know in what way an elementary area of sea ice will deform if stress is applied to its boundaries. In the past, the assumption that the material sea ice has a shear viscosity has been used by Ruzin (1959), Cambell (1965) and others. A different assumption has been that the ice behaves like a cavitating material. That is, it cannot support tension and will simply open up if one tries to put tension on it. But under compression it is incompressible. The assumption used in the present model is simply that the ice is incompressible, this being a simplification of the cavitating assumption. The ice is assumed to support no shear stress.

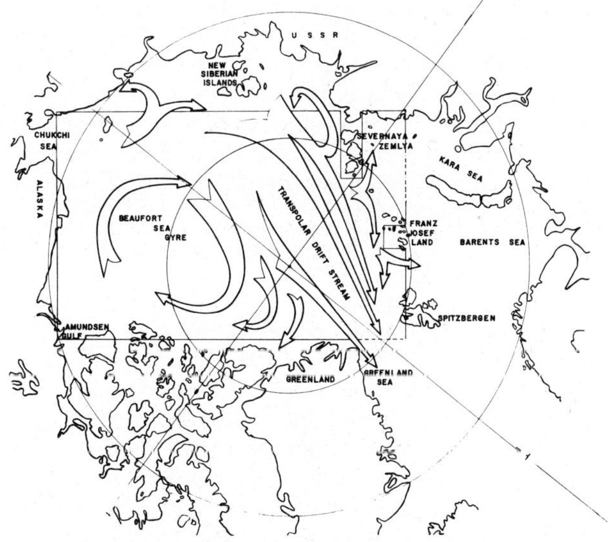

Fig. 1. The pattern of the mean drift of sea ice in the Arctic Ocean, adapted from Gordienko (1958).

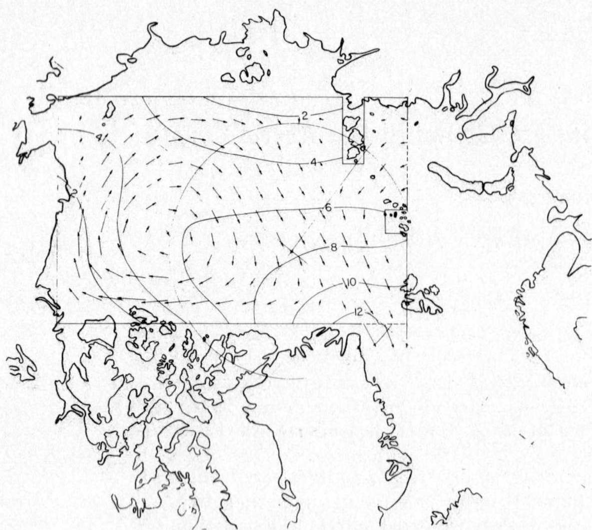

Fig. 2. The calculated velocities and isobars for the standard case in which the ice is incompressible. A velocity vector one grid space long represents 10 cm sec^{-1}. The isobars are labeled in units of 10^7 dyne cm^{-1}. Grid points are 200 km apart.

The second major element in any model of ice dynamics is the state variables which are used to describe the ice cover. In the past, some scientists have assumed that it is characterized simply by its mass per unit area. Soviet scientists have done considerable work assuming that the only relevant state variables are a mean thickness and a mean compactness, which is the local fraction of the ocean surface covered by ice. In the present model the assumption is again of a uniform mass per unit area. At the end, a brief description will be given of ways in which the AIDJEX modeling group is trying to use more realistic assumptions in the categories both of the stress-deformation law and the choice of state variables.

The purpose of doing this calculation was first to see if realistic flow fields could be calculated, and, more importantly, to see whether the pressure field within the ice cover can be interpreted sensibly in the light of known ice conditions in different areas of the basin. The momentum equation reduces to a statement that the sum of forces acting on the ice cover is zero because the advective acceleration is negligible, and the problem is steady. Thus, we have

$$-mf_c\mathbf{k}\times\mathbf{u}+\boldsymbol{\tau}_w+\boldsymbol{\tau}_a-\boldsymbol{\nabla}p-m\hat{g}\boldsymbol{\nabla}H=0$$

where $\mathbf{u}$ is the unknown ice velocity in two horizontal dimensions, $\mathbf{k}$ is the unit vector in the vertical, f_c is the Coriolis parameter, and m is the mass per unit area. The other terms are the water stress $\boldsymbol{\tau}_w$, the air stress $\boldsymbol{\tau}_a$, the gradient of the internal ice pressure (true stress integrated through the thickness of the ice), and the gravitational acceleration down the sloping sea surface, where $\hat{g}$ is the acceleration of gravity and H is the local height of the sea surface. Mathematically, the sea surface tilt term, the air stress term, and part of the water stress term are inhomogeneous terms, specified by sur-

face pressure given by Fel'zenbaum (1958) and by sea-surface topography given by Coachman (1962). A modified Ekman layer has been assumed in which the wind stress is proportional to the geostrophic wind with an eddy coefficient of 3×10^4 cm^2 sec^{-1} and an angle of turning in the boundary layer of 20°. The same is assumed in the water boundary layer, but there the stress is proportional to the relative velocity between the ice and the water, producing a term in the unknown ice velocity as well as a term in the geostrophic water velocity. The eddy viscosity used in the water is 24 cm^2 sec^{-1}, after Hunkins' (1966) observation. The momentum equation can be written as

$$-A\mathbf{u}-B\mathbf{k}\times\mathbf{u}-\boldsymbol{\nabla}p+\boldsymbol{\tau}=0$$

where $\boldsymbol{\tau}$ contains all inhomogeneous terms.

The second equation is the continuity equation, which reduces simply to the statement that the divergence is specified.

$$\text{div}\ \mathbf{u}=\Phi$$

Furthermore, it is specified to be uniform and taken to be the mean divergence $(0.33\times10^{-8}$ sec$^{-1})$ obtained by estimating the fluxes all the way around the basin and applying Gauss' theorem.

The unknown velolity $\mathbf{u}$ and pressure p are found from the momentum and continuity equations. The boundary condition that has been used is that the component of velocity normal to the boundary be specified everywhere around the basin. It is taken to be zero on coastal boundaries. The standard solution, shown in Fig. 2, was obtained with a wind stress typically 0.5 dyne cm^{-2}. The pattern of flow is realistic. The speeds are typically twice the observed speeds. The vorticities likewise are a factor of 2 or 3 higher than observed values. If the wind stress is reduced by about a factor of 3, then both the speeds and the vorticities become quite realistic. Thus, it appears that by assuming that ice has resistance to compression and by restricting its divergence to be a reasonable value, realistic flow patterns can be calculated. If the wind is adjusted within the limits of its uncertainty, realistic speeds are found. It seems that resistance to compression is an important mechanical property.

The flow pattern here is very much wind driven. The small divergence and the difference in the import and export have little effect on the gyre and the transpolar drift stream in the interior of the basin. This is due to the smallness of the divergence, and the fact that the only significant import and export are assumed to occur on the Atlantic side of the basin. Thus, it turns out that the assumption of uniform divergence is not as restrictive as it might seem at first.

The pressure field has features which correlate fairly well with observed ice conditions. One point of interpretation needs to be handled with a little caution. The zero of pressure is not determined by differential equations or by the boundary conditions, so it has been chosen arbitrarily to be the minimum calculated value. The interpretation is made that low pressure is associated with open water and high pressure is associated with ridging. In Fig. 2, low pressures occur in the Amundsen Gulf area and in the area of the New Siberian Islands. These areas correspond to areas which show open water earlier in the spring and later into the fall than other peripheral areas of the basin, as illustrated in Fig. 3. The high pressure region near Greenland is presumably associated with intense ridging seen in Fig. 4.

It appears reasonable that the long-term pressure field is the cause of the observed ridging distribution. However, ridging must also be driven to some extent by transient stresses associated with higher frequency phenomena, such as storms. But internal stresses in the ice are proportional to the product of surface stresses (such as wind stress) and their fetch, and it has not yet been established whether this product is greater for transient phenomena or for the steady case being considered here.

The values of pressure have been compared with the kinematic ridging model developed by Parmerter and Coon (1973), which suggests that the maximum pressure found here can marginally ridge 3-meter thick ice. Ice one meter thick, however, can be ridged almost anywhere in the basin.

The shape and magnitude of the pressure field correlate well with observed ice conditions. However, there is one detail that is troublesome. The positive pressure in the corner near Greenland is not consistent with the presence of a free boundary of zero pressure in that vicinity. Within the framework of this theory, this corner pressure is sensitive to the intensity of the wind

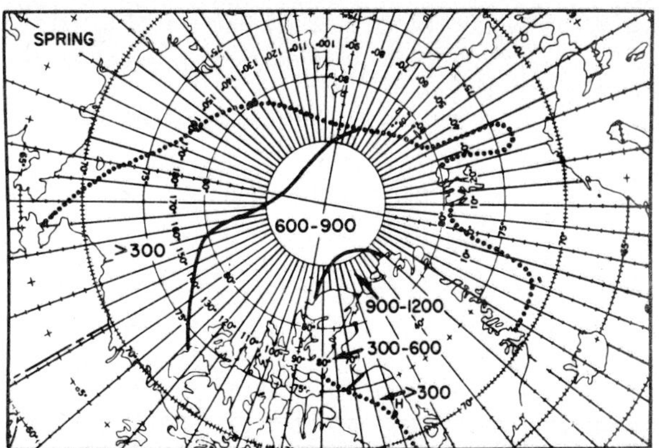

FIG. 4. The observed ridging index, defined as the number of ridges per 30 nm, after Wittmann and Schule (1966).

stress, which is not known very well, to the local details of the flow, which have been somewhat crudely represented here, and to the magnitude of the flux through the outlet, which again is known only approximately. With some modification of those factors, the pressure in that region can be changed considerably and can become much lower.

Uncertainty in the magnitudes of the wind stress and the water stress have made some conclusions tenuous. In particular, one cannot really say whether high velocities and vorticities calculated in the standard case are due to overestimates of wind stress or underestimates of the water drag coefficient or to an unrealistic constitutive equation for the pack ice.

Whether or not the inviscid incompressible approximation is sufficiently realistic, it does not appear that shear viscosity can be invoked to improve the prediction of flow velocities in the interior of the basin. The reason for this statement is the observation that when T-3 drifted about 100 km off the Canadian archipelago, it was rotating in the same sense as the interior of the gyre, that is, clockwise. If there were a viscous boundary layer on the coast, there would be some coastal region of thickness

$$\left(\frac{\text{shear viscosity}}{A}\right)^{\frac{1}{2}}$$

with counterclockwise vorticity. Thus, we can put an upper bound on a shear viscosity of about 6×10^{12} gm/sec. It might be proper to describe the so-called "shear zones" by viscous boundary layers, although they might also be described by other material properties, such as plasticity. But it appears that shear viscosity can do no more than provide these shear zones. It cannot control the whole interior flow.

Because this session is focused on future research, it is fitting to describe our current thinking in the AIDJEX Modeling Group. The formulation we are now pursuing involves describing the state at each point and at each time by an ice thickness distribution $g(h)$, where

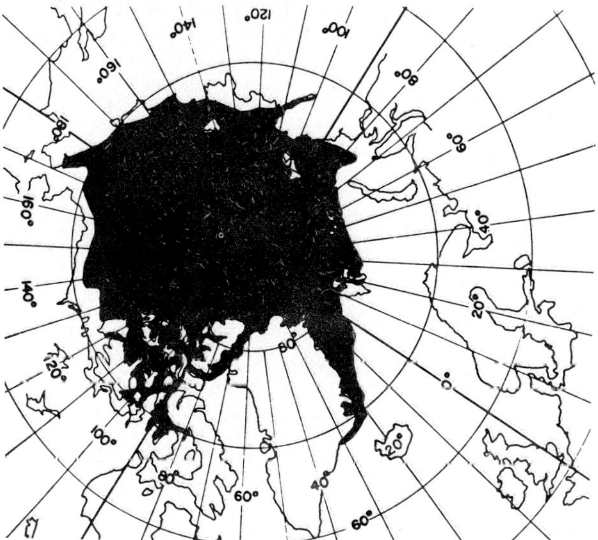

FIG. 3. September extent of sea ice with compactness greater than 4/10 (shown as dark area). These data, from the Meteorological Office Monthly Ice Charts, represent a six-year mean.

ice of thickness between h and $h+dh$ covers a fraction $g(h)dh$ of the local area. The balance equation for this material property is

$$\frac{\partial g}{\partial t} = -\mathrm{div}(\mathbf{u}g) - \frac{\partial}{\partial h}(fg) + \psi[g(h),E_1,E_2]$$

where f is defined as dh/dt (in analogy with the definition of $\mathbf{u}$ as $d\mathbf{x}/dt$), and ψ is a mechanical redistribution function and is a function of the state and the strain-rate invariants representing divergence and the rate of shear. The first term on the right-hand side is the advective change in the thickness distribution, the second is the thermodynamic change, and the last represents the volume conserving mechanical processes which actually break up or pile up thin ice and produce ridges. A discussion of the integral of this equation, its properties, and the general effects of f and ψ has been given by Thorndike and Maykut (1973).

The second element of the theories now being examined involves an assumption that ice is rigid under low stress and behaves plastically only when the stress reaches a yield surface in stress space. If the stress state is inside the yield surface, the ice may be part of a rigid body rotation, but is not deforming. If the stress is then increased until it lies on the yield surface, plastic flow will occur. At this point, ψ becomes operative, changes the g distribution, and probably changes the yield surface somewhat. The stress state may stay on the yield surface or may not. It can never be outside the yield surface. This plasticity formulation was suggested by Coon (1972) in analogy with some work in soil mechanics. These are the kinds of systems of equations that are being considered. We are now trying to synthesize these elements—the yield surface, the thickness distribution, and the redistribution function ψ—and examine them in the light of the knowledge that we are

gaining of small-scale processes of rafting and ridging. Recent progress is described by Rothrock (1974).

REFERENCES

Campbell, W. J., 1965: The wind-driven circulation of ice and water in a polar ocean. *Journal of Geophysical Research*, **70**, 3279–3301.

Coachman, L. K., 1962: Water masses of the arctic. In *Proceedings of the Arctic Basin Symposium, October 1962*. Arctic Institute of North America, Washington, D. C., 143–167.

Coon, M. D., 1972: Mechanical behavior of compacted arctic ice floes. In *Preprints of the Offshore Technology Conference, May 1972*. Houston, Texas. Paper No. OTC 1684.

Fel'zenbaum, A. I., 1958: Teoriya ustanovivshegosya dreifa l'dov i raschet srednego mnogoletnego dreifa v tsentral'noi chasti Arkitcheskogo Baseina (The theory of steady drift of ice and the calculation of the long period mean drift in the central part of the Arctic Basin. English transl. *Problems of the North*, No. 2, 13–44, 1961). *Problemy Severa*, No. 2, 16–46.

Hunkins, K., 1966: Ekman drift currents in the Arctic Ocean. *Deep-Sea Research*, **13**, 607–620.

Meteorological Office, Climatological Services (Met. 0.3), Eastern Road, Bracknell, England RG 12 2UR.

Parmerter, R. R., and M. D. Coon, 1973: On the mechanics of pressure ridge formation in sea ice. In *Proceedings of the Offshore Technology Conference, May 1973*. Houston, Texas. Vol. I, 733–742.

Rothrock, D. A., 1973: The steady drift of an incompressible arctic ice cover. *AIDJEX Bulletin No. 21*, 49–77. NTIS Accession No. PB 223 387.

Rothrock, D. A., 1974: Redistribution functions and their yield surfaces in a plastic theory of pack ice deformation. *AIDJEX Bulletin No. 23*, Univ. of Washington, Seattle, Wash. 98105.

Ruzin, M. I., 1959: O vetrovom dreife l'dov v neodnorodnom pole davleniia (The wind drift of ice in a heterogeneous pressure field.) *Trudy Arktiki i Antarktiki Nauchno-Issle. In-ta.*, Vol. 226, Leningrad, 123–135.

Thorndike, A. S., and G. A. Maykut, 1973: On the thickness distribution of sea ice. *AIDJEX Bulletin No. 21*, 31–47. NITS Accession No. PB 223 387.

Wittmann, W. I., and J. J. Schule, 1966: Comments on the mass budget of arctic pack ice. *Proceedings of the Symposium on the Arctic Heat Budget and Atmospheric Circulation*. RAND Memorandum RM-5233-NSF. The RAND Corporation, Santa Monica, Calif.

Some Observations of Variations in North Water Surface Area and in Certain Atmospheric Parameters

ROBIN D. MUENCH

Institute of Marine Science, University of Alaska, Fairbanks, Alaska 99701

Abstract

Satellite photographs obtained during March–July 1969 and 1970 were sufficient for estimation of variations in surface area of the northern Baffin Bay polynya known as the North Water. These surface area variations are compared with selected meteorological parameters obtained from the Canadian Arctic Archipelago and Thule AB, Greenland.

The overall spring expansion and break-up pattern of the North Water showed no significant anomalies, relative to previous seasons, during the springs of 1969 and 1970. The increase in open water area during break-up appeared to be due primarily to seasonal warming, while the pattern of break-up could be explained satisfactorily on the basis of underlying water circulation.

Fluctuations, short-term relative to the time scale of spring break-up in the surface area of the North Water are compared with computed geostrophic wind speed and direction and with wind speed and direction, surface air temperature, dew point and cloud cover observed at Thule AB, Greenland. Small correlations were found between surface area fluctuations, geostrophic and observed wind directions; correlations between surface area fluctuations and the remaining meteorological parameters were negligible.

The lack of significant correlation between surface area fluctuations and fluctuations in meteorological parameters suggests that oceanographic processes, particularly currents, may exert a significant control on short-term fluctuations in the open water surface area. Oceanographic knowledge of the region suggests, moreover, that currents sufficient to cause the observed variations may exist.

1. Introduction

The North Water is a polynya located in northern Baffin Bay (Fig. 1). It is of particular scientific interest because it represents, throughout the winter months, an open water area in a region where climatic conditions would seem to dictate the formation of 1–2 m. of ice as observed in surrounding oceanic regions. Presence of such a polynya, or open water area, during winter in a region where ice would be expected to form must be due to: (1) upwelling of subsurface water containing heat sufficient to prevent ice formation; (2) mechanical removal of the ice, as it forms, by winds, currents or a combination of these; or (3) some combination of the above.

It now appears that the North Water is maintained primarily by mechanical removal of the ice as it is formed. It has been shown unlikely that sufficient heat is present in the water column to prevent ice formation (Muench, 1971; Muench & Sadler, 1973). Studies devoted primarily to the observation, via satellite or aircraft, of surface area variations in the North Water have contributed further to this hypothesis, as Dunbar (1970, 1971 and 1972) has noted that light ice cover does indeed appear to form on the North Water but that it is continually swept southward, never attaining an appreciable thickness or degree of cover. This same pattern of freezing and removal has also been suggested by the observations of Aber and Vowinckel (1972), who used satellite data to observe ice distribution during spring 1969 and 1970.

Observations of the North Water have revealed that its most consistent feature is the arch-shaped fast ice edge which forms its northern boundary in Smith Sound and appears to effectively block all southward flow of ice through Smith Sound. Ice concentrations increase southward, from virtually open water just south of this arch to 10/10 ice cover in Baffin Bay, in a gradual fashion which has made it difficult to define the actual southern boundary of the North Water at any given time. This pattern of ice distribution is suggestive of a mechanism whereby ice forms in the northern portions of the North Water, then is swept southward to create the observed southward increase in ice concentration.

This hypothesis for formation of the North Water agrees qualitatively with existing knowledge of the wind and current regimes in northern Baffin Bay. The summer baroclinic transport of water is southward through the North Water region, and limited oceanographic data suggest that the winter circulation is similar (Muench, 1971; Muench and Sadler, 1973). Meteorological records reveal that the North Water region is characterized during the summer months by relatively weak and

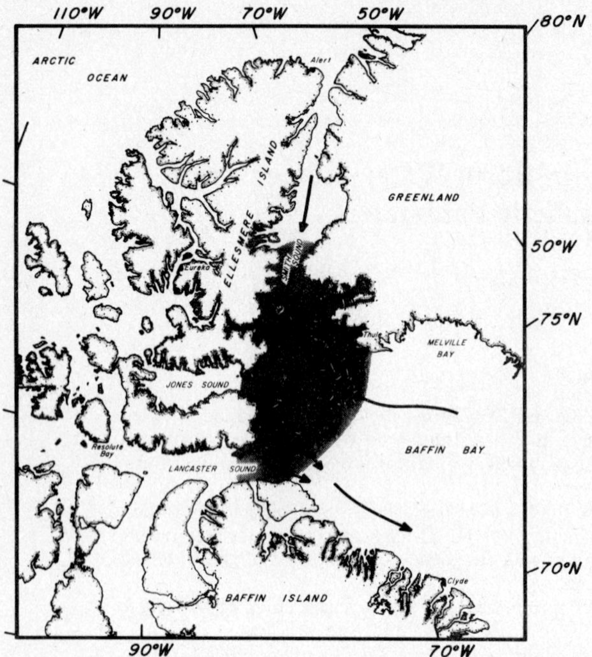

FIG. 1. Geographical locations in the North Water region, indicating the locations of the meteorological stations from which data were obtained for the analysis. The study area is shown as shaded, and arrows indicate the general known summer circulation and suspected winter surface circulation pattern.

variable winds which become stronger and north-northeasterly during the winter, with the intensification of the Baffin Bay low pressure trough. These winds and currents would be expected to remove ice southward from the Smith Sound region and so tend to uphold the mechanical removal hypothesis for formation of the North Water.

2. The North Water during spring 1969 and 1970

During mid-March through mid-July 1969 and 1970 satellite photos were obtained, in the visible wavelengths, of the North Water region. These photos have been compiled and analyzed by Aber and Vowinckel (1972) to obtain a picture of fluctuations in the open water area during those periods. (The term "open water" used hereinafter refers to areas having less than 25% ice cover, this being the maximum attainable resolution using the satellite photos.) Photographic coverage was limited prior to mid-March due to winter darkness, after mid-July by developing cloud cover. Since the open water area is at its minimum extent in March (Dunbar, 1970, 1971 and 1972), and by mid-July the breakup has progressed to the point where the North Water has begun to lose its identity and is part of the drift path for the south-flowing ice from Smith Sound, the records covered a period inclusive of mid-

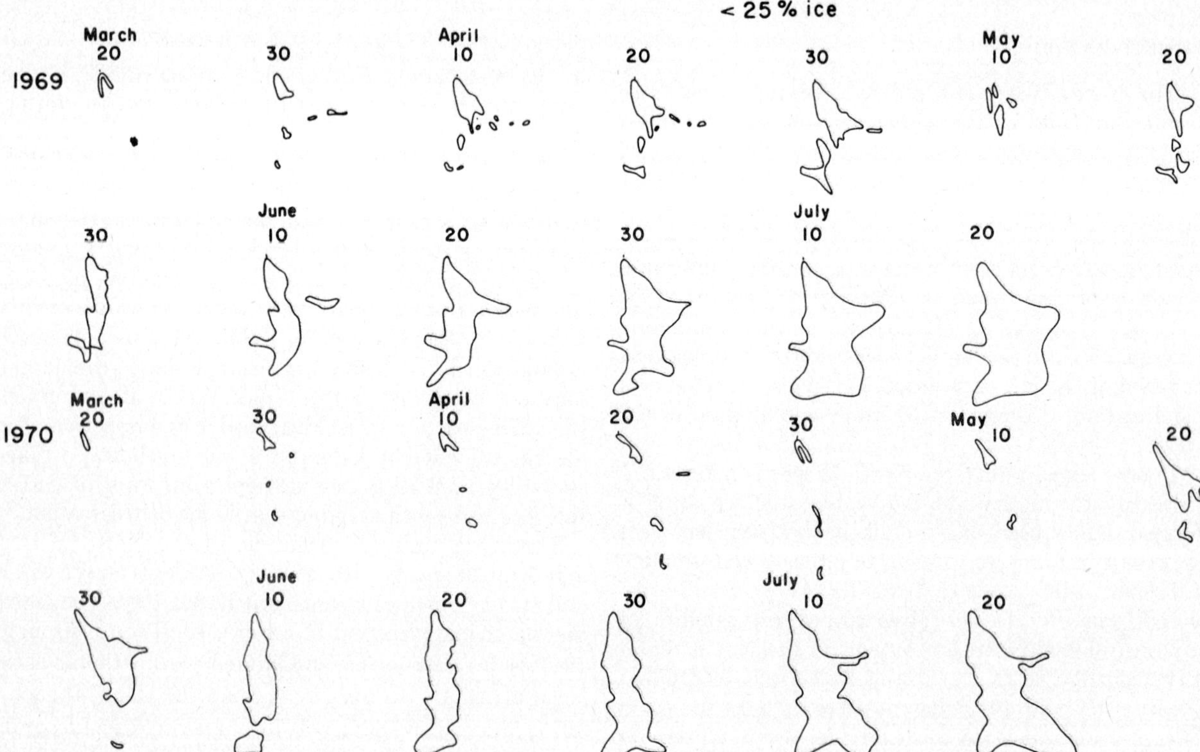

FIG. 2. Plan view showing surface area fluctuations during spring 1969 and 1970 (from Aber and Vowinckel, 1972).

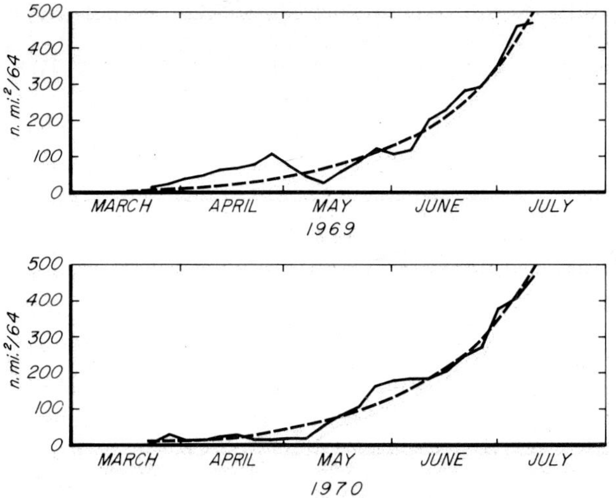

FIG. 3. Variations with time of 5-day mean areas having less than 25% ice cover. The broken curve represents a visual average of these areas.

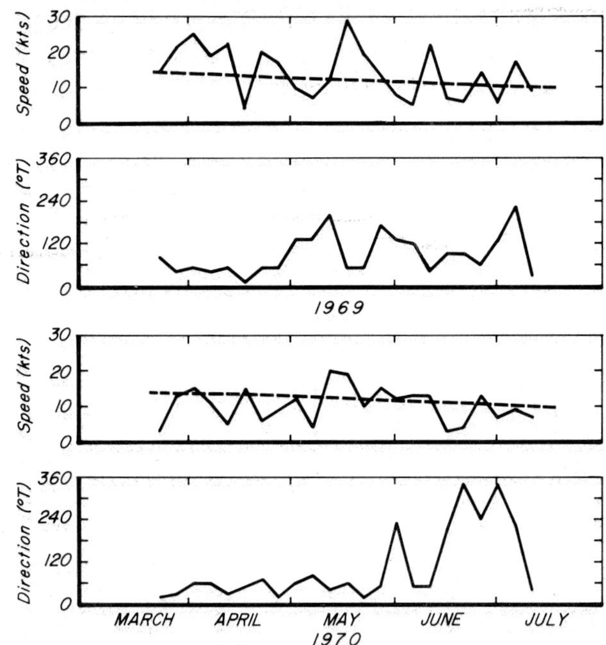

FIG. 4. Variations with time of computed geostrophic wind over the North Water region. The broken curve respresents a visual average of wind speed.

winter conditions through spring breakup. The data were adequate, in addition, for detection of open water area fluctuations having time scales short relative to the overall time scale of the break-up.

While no oceanographic information was obtained concurrently with the periods of satellite data acquisition, oceanographic cruises were made to northern Baffin Bay during the summers of 1968, 1969 and 1970 (Muench, 1972). Comparison of data from these cruises with each other and with data obtained previously suggested that no significant anomalies in physical oceanographic conditions existed during the period from summer 1968 through summer 1970.

The observed surface area variations were presented by Aber and Vowinckel (1972) both as plan views (Fig. 2) and as plots vs time of the open water area. Variations of less than 5 days duration were barely detectable from the original plots and were felt to be insignificant relative to longer term changes. Aber & Vowinckel's plots were therefore used to compute 5-day mean values of the open water area which were then plotted vs time (Fig. 3).

Prominent features of the open water area during spring 1969 and 1970 were the remarkable stability of the northern boundary and the southward expansion during breakup beginning in mid-May. There was a tendency for the open water to extend westward into Jones and Lancaster sounds and, later, eastward into Melville Bay. The open water areas were at times discontinuous, particularly in the southern portions and during April and May of both 1969 and 1970. These features, which agree with those noted by Dunbar (1970) from historical information, qualitatively support the hypothesis that winds and currents sweep ice southward as it is formed while the fast ice arch in Smith Sound prevents additional ice from flowing southward to fill the void. The observed westward expansion

of the open water into Jones and Lancaster sounds may be due to transport of ice by water currents; cyclonic circulation of Baffin Bay surface water into these channels has been observed during the summer (Muench, 1971). The eastward extension into Melville Bay may have been due in part to westerly winds which developed at that time during 1969 and 1970 (Figs. 4 and 5).

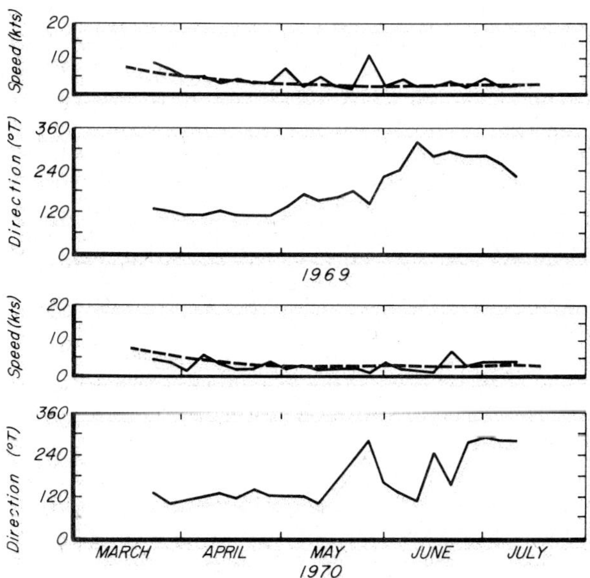

FIG. 5. Variations with time of surface winds at Thule, Greenland. The broken curve represents a visual average of wind speed.

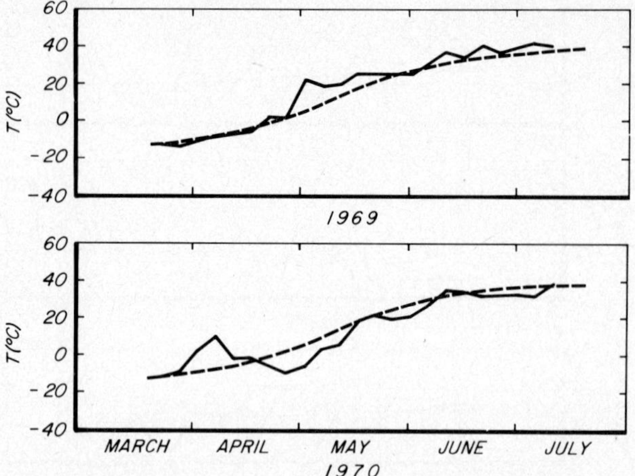

FIG. 6. Variations with time of surface air temperature at Thule, Greenland. The broken curve represents a visual average temperature.

The 5-day mean surface area values illustrate more clearly than the plan views the overall areal increase during spring 1969 and 1970 (Fig. 3). For purposes of illustrating this increase, as well as for analyzing short-term areal variations, a visual average of both curves has been compiled and is superposed upon them. From a minimum during March the area increases, gradually through April, with the increase becoming more rapid through May and June to become undefined by mid-July due both to lack of observations and the fact that the North Water loses its identity as it merges with other open water areas in northern Baffin Bay. This pattern of expansion is similar to that deduced by Dunbar (1970).

Using the bulk aerodynamic method in conjunction with meteorological observations obtained from Thule, Greenland, it is possible to compute a regional heat budget which can explain the overall open water area increase in terms of heat input to the ice-water system from the atmosphere and solar radiation. These computations, carried out by Muench (1971) using mean annual meteorological data revealed that the air-sea heat exchange reverses from a net upward to a net downward flux in early May, when the increase in open water area begins to accelerate markedly. The influx of heat following early May is sufficient to melt the ice remaining at that time.

The heat flux computations are subject to errors since: (1) the actual parameters used in the computation equations are uncertain (see, e.g., Doronin, 1970); (2) the effect of the observed cloud cover on the radiative flux is not well known. Cloud cover is normally recorded in tenths, which yields no information concerning cloud or height number and thickness of decks; and (3) the assumption that conditions at Thule are representative of upstream atmospheric conditions for the North Water may not be realistic at all times, particularly during the later portions of the 1969 and

1970 break-up periods when the winds become westerly. No attempt was therefore made to carry out heat flux computations specifically for 1969 and 1970, particularly since the overall patterns of breakup appeared to be normal during both those years.

3. Shorter term fluctuations in open water area

The plot of 5-day mean surface areas vs time (Fig. 3) reveals surface area fluctuations of a shorter time scale than the overall break-up period. The most prevalent of these fluctuations was the sudden decrease in open water area from late April–early May 1969, leading to low values during mid-May 1969. Aber and Vowinckel (1972) noted the existence of these fluctuations but did not attempt to explain them.

If it is assumed that the North Water is maintained by a combination of winds and currents as hypothesized, it would be expected that short-term variations in area would show some correlation with wind and current fluctuations. Unfortunately, no current measurements were made in the North Water region during the study period. Atmospheric measurements were sufficient, however, to allow a comparison between areal fluctuations, geostrophic winds over the region and observed winds at Thule, Greenland. In the interest of completeness, and also to rule out other factors as much as possible, it was decided to include fluctuations in the air temperature, dew point and cloud cover at Thule in the comparison. For compatability with the areal data, atmospheric data were compiled into 5-day means and plotted vs time (Figs. 4–8). Visual averages of the wind speeds, air temperatures, dew points and cloud covers were constructed and are shown superposed on these plots.

Geostrophic winds were computed using atmospheric surface pressure data from 5 eastern Arctic weather stations (Fig. 1). Daily mean pressures were calculated

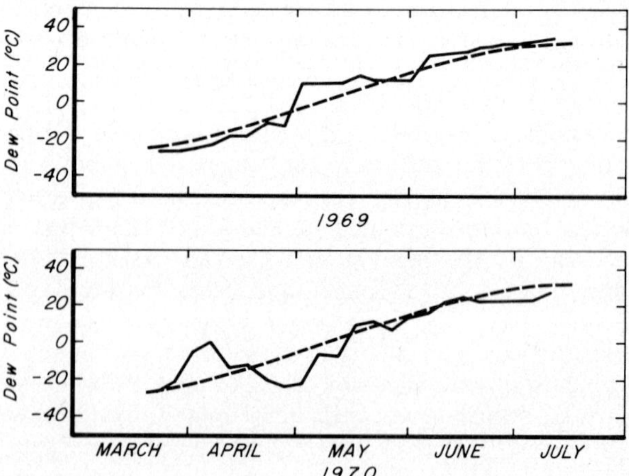

FIG. 7. Variations with time of surface dew point at Thule, Greenland. The broken curve represents a visual average dew point.

for each station, isobars constructed for that day, geostrophic wind speed and direction over the North Water obtained from the isobars and vector averaged 5-day means obtained from the daily values (Fig. 4). In drawing the isobars, minimum curvature was allowed and linear interpolation was used between known surface pressure points. Experimentation with some extreme cases suggested that directions are good to better than $\pm 20°$ while speed is accurate to $\pm 10\%$.

A linear regression analysis was carried out on the geostrophic wind speeds and directions, as u–v components, and those observed at Thule, Greenland. Aagaard (1969) has observed that under unstable atmospheric conditions the computed geostrophic winds may agree closely with observed surface winds. Due however to the topographic effects, coupled with the effects of local adiabatic winds expected at Thule, it was not *a priori* expected that a large correlation would be found between the two; the correlation coefficient for 1969 was in fact about 0.4 while that for 1970 was negligible. This suggested that the winds at Thule were controlled to some extent during 1969 by the geostrophic wind field, but that during 1970 local effects predominated.

The plots showing variations in atmospheric parameters with time (Figs. 4–8) can be compared directly with the surface area variations (Fig. 3). The prominent surface area variation during 1969 was the abnormally high value during April followed by a sudden decrease to a low during May. During April the winds observed at Thule were light (3–5 kts) and east-southeasterly. The geostrophic winds during this period were higher (12–15 kts), with a minimum of less than 5 kts in mid-April, and northeasterly. During early May the observed winds increased slightly in speed (up to about 5 kts) and by mid-May the direction had changed from east-southeasterly to southerly. The geostrophic wind speeds had dropped off to less than 10 kts by mid-May but then increased to as high as 30 kts by late May. Geostrophic winds became southerly in early May and remained so throughout the month. The sudden surface area decrease in early May therefore coincided with southerly observed and geostrophic winds, while the abnormally large area during April coincided with northerly winds. The fluctuations in surface area during April–May 1969 appeared, therefore, to be qualitatively correlated with the wind direction as would be expected if wind exerts an influence over the open water area.

Surface area variations were less pronounced later in 1969 than during April and May. A low value of area in late May–early June coincided with south-southeasterly geostrophic winds, but later anomalies in area did not coincide with any particular wind pattern.

A visual comparison between surface area variation and temperature, dew point and cloud cover observed at Thule, Greenland suggests that no correlation was present between these parameters.

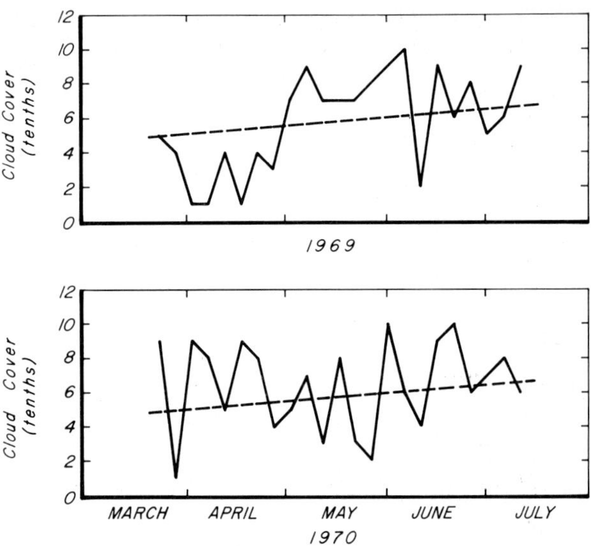

FIG. 8. Variations with time of cloud cover at Thule, Greenland. The broken curve represents a visual average cloud cover.

Short-term surface area fluctuations during 1970 were less pronounced than during 1969, and consisted primarily in low values during late April–early May followed by high values during late May–early June. There was no obvious visual correlation between wind speed, direction and surface area fluctuations during 1970. Surface area showed, moreover, no correlation with the other atmospheric parameters during 1970.

Linear regression analyses were run on the observed variations in an attempt to verify the results of the visual comparisons. Differences between the actual measured values of each parameter (except wind direction) and the visually averaged curves were taken as the quantities to be correlated, e.g., the high surface areas observed during April 1969 would be positive anomalies while the following low values would give negative anomalies, these anomalies being the quantities compared in the analyses.

Comparisons between the areas and wind directions were made using the hypothesis that a southerly wind would tend to decrease the surface area while northerly winds would increase the area. A wind from $180°T$ would have a value of $-90°$ (maximum tendency to decrease the area), a wind from $0°T$ would have a value of $+90°$ (maximum tendency to increase the area), and winds from either $90°T$ or $270°T$ would have values of $0°$ (no effect on surface area). These directions allow for the deviation of the channel from true north in conjunction with the tendency for ice to move to the right of the surface wind direction.

Results of the regression analyses revealed that correlations between the surface area fluctuations and all atmospheric parameters except wind directions during 1969 were negligible. During 1969 there was a weak correlation ($r=0.4$) between both geostrophic and observed wind directions and surface area fluctuations.

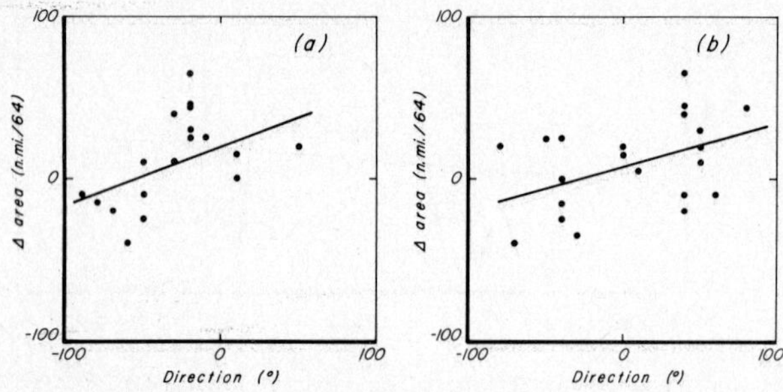

FIG. 9. Data points and regression curves showing the relation between surface area fluctuations and observed wind direction (left) and geostrophic wind direction (right) during March–July 1969.

The points representing this correlation, along with the linear regression curve, are shown in Fig. 9.

4. Discussion

The results of the comparison between short-term surface areal fluctuations and fluctuations in meteorological parameters suggests that, during some periods, winds may play a role in influencing area. Specifically, a southerly wind may decrease the area while a northerly wind may increase the area. The lack of any apparent correlation during 1970 suggests, however, that such areal fluctuations must at times be due to factors other than wind.

Comparisons between surface area and air temperature, dew point and cloud cover observed at Thule, Greenland suggested that no correlation was present between the former and either of the three latter quantities. It might have been expected *a priori* that a period of high temperatures and low cloud cover would have led to increased melting of sea ice and a concurrent increase in surface area for the North Water. That this does not appear to be the case suggests that either:

(1) the conditions observed at Thule are not particularly representative of conditions over the North Water. The degree to which conditions at Thule represent those over the North Water must depend in part upon the prevailing wind directions. Easterly winds would transport air from Thule out over the North Water, so that air temperatures there would then be representative of upstream conditions from the North Water. Westerly winds would dictate that the air at Thule be conditioned by, rather than acting upon, the North Water. The role of local effects on the measurements at Thule is difficult to assess here; it was noted that, during 1970, the geostrophic winds were only poorly correlated with the surface winds at Thule. Apparently local wind conditions were dominant in the Thule region during that period, and it might be expected that this would have applied to other atmospheric parameters and hence that such parameters as air temperature would not apply far outside the actual region of measurement. Measurements within the actual boundaries of the North Water would have been required to resolve this; or

(2) the effects of high air temperatures, etc. are present but are negligible in relation to fluctuations caused by variations in other parameters. The ice cover would be expected to react instantaneously to a change in wind direction, while reaction to a change in air-sea heat exchange would be slower. It thus seems probable that any changes due to, e.g., insolation might be masked by larger changes due to winds.

Based on what is known about water circulation in the North Water region, some speculation concerning the effects of currents on the open water area is possible. Observations have been sufficient to establish that the current through Smith Sound fluctuates, being predominantly southerly but flowing in a northerly direction at times. These observations are based on both direct measurements, although these are somewhat limited in number, and indirect measurements utilizing ice drift (Nutt, 1966; Day, 1968; Muench, 1971; Avis and Coachman, 1971). Current measurements have been obtained for short periods in Kane Basin north of Smith Sound, in Smith Sound and in northern Baffin Bay southwest of Thule. The first two sets of measurements revealed a net southerly flow with northerly flow during the flood tide. Tidal currents were on the order of 15–20 cm sec^{-1} in Smith Sound but considerably less in Kane Basin. The measurements off Thule substantiated that a cyclonic circulation was present in northern Baffin Bay during late summer and revealed semidiurnal tidal currents on the order of 10–15 cm sec^{-1}.

That tidal noise is the cause of apparent surface areal fluctuations is unlikely. Assuming a peak tidal current speed of 15 cm sec^{-1} in the southern portion of the North Water region, and assuming that the ice drifted freely with the water, displacement of the ice over one-half of a diurnal tidal cycle would only be about 1 nautical mile. If the mean channel width is taken to be 60 n.mi., then the areal change is only 60 n.mi.², or far less than the observed fluctuations which were on the order of several thousand n.mi.².

Reference to the plan views (Fig. 2) reveals that a major proportion of the areal variations not correlated with winds occurred well to the south of the constriction in Smith Sound; far enough south, in fact, so that it would be within the bounds of the cyclonic circulation extending from northern Baffin Bay toward Smith Sound. It therefore would be possible for ice to be advected from Melville Bay into the southern parts of the North Water, and a varying advection rate could help explain the observed variations in ice cover. Both available summer circulation information (Muench, 1971) and information based on drifting ice during the winter (Aber and Vowinckel, 1972) suggest that the circulation could have this effect. Ice would then be removed, at variable rates, from the southwestern portion of the North Water by the southerly branch of the cyclonic circulation cell these. Unfortunately, too little is known quantitatively of the circulation to make more specific estimates of the effects, particularly in the Melville Bay region.

5. Summary and conclusions

Time series data showing surface area variations in the North Water and variations in selected atmospheric parameters over the North Water have been compared for the winter-spring periods of 1969 and 1970. These comparisons suggested a weak and intermittent correlation between the open water area and wind direction, with no correlation between short-term surface area variations and other atmospheric parameters.

It is possible to qualitatively explain the variations not correlated with wind direction variations in terms of the water circulation in northern Baffin Bay. Melville Bay might act as a source of ice via the cyclonic circulation in northern Baffin Bay, while the southerly branch of this cyclonic circulation, off Jones and Lancaster sounds, might act to remove ice. The ice concentration in all but the northernmost portions of the North Water would be affected by this mechanism and would vary as the water circulation. The fact that little areal variation was observed in the extreme northern portion, which would be outside the range of the cyclonic circulation, substantiates this hypothesis; this northernmost portion would be kept open by the relatively constant southerly flow through Smith Sound.

Acknowledgments. Acknowledgment is given to the Arctic Institute of North America and the Institute of Marine Science, University of Alaska, both of which have provided support for this work.

REFERENCES

Aagaard, K., 1969: Relationship between geostrophic and surface winds at Weather Ship M. *Jour. Geophys. Res.*, 74, 13, 3440–3442.

Aber, P. G., and E. Vowinckel, 1972: Evaluation of North Water spring ice cover from satellite photographs. *Arctic*, 25, 4, 263–271.

Avis, R. A., and L. K. Coachman, 1971: Current measurements in Smith Sound-northern Baffin Bay, September 1968. The Baffin Bay-North Water Project Scientific Report No. 2, AINA, 27 pp.

Day, G. G., 1968: Current measurements in Smith Sound, summer 1963. U. S. Coast Guard Oceanographic Report No. 16, 75–84.

Doronin, Y. P., 1970: Thermal interaction of the atmosphere and the hydrosphere in the Arctic. U. S. Dept. of Commerce, 244 pp.

Dunbar, M., 1970: The geographical position of the North Water. *Arctic*, 22, 4, 438–441.

Dunbar, M., 1971: Winter ice reconnaissance in Nares Strait, 1970–71. DREO Technical Note No. 71–34, 29 pp.

Dunbar, M., 1972: Winter ice reconnaissance in Nares Strait, 1971–72. DREO Technical Note No. 72-30, 8 pp.

Muench, R. D., 1971: The physical oceanography of the northern Baffin Bay region. The Baffin Bay-North Water Project Scientific Report No. 1, AINA, 150 pp.

Muench, R. D., 1972: Oceanographic conditions in the northern Baffin Bay region—1970. U. S. Coast Guard Oceanographic Report No. 54, 113 pp.

Muench, R. D. and H. E. Sadler, 1973: Physical oceanographic observations in Baffin Bay and Davis Strait. *Arctic*, 26, 1, 73–76.

Nutt, D. C., 1966: The drift of ice island WH-5. *Arctic*, 19, 3, 244–262.

Subsurface Eddies in the Arctic Ocean and Baroclinic Instability*

KENNETH L. HUNKINS

Lamont-Doherty Geological Observatory of Columbia University, Palisades, N. Y. 10983

Abstract

On four occasions during the AIDJEX field program in March and April of 1972 transient undercurrents associated with eddies were observed at depths between 50 and 300 m. The velocity profile was parabolic with a maximum of 40 cm sec^{-1} at 150 m. A distortion of the salinity and temperature field accompanied these currents, and gradient equilibrium was closely approached in each case. Two of the eddies were anticyclonic and two, cyclonic. The lifetime of the eddies is not known but they persisted for at least several days and probably endured much longer. The eddies were 10 to 20 km in diameter and separated by 20 to 50 km from each other although the time and space scales were not always clearly resolved in these measurements. The subsurface currents in the eddies were swifter than the wind-driven currents in the upper mixed layer which usually had speeds of less than 10 cm sec^{-1}, and there seemed to be little correlation between the two levels. Evidence of similar eddies has been noted by other investigators, both Soviet and American, in different parts of the Arctic Ocean and in different seasons, but the present data are the most revealing, especially of horizontal scale.

The eddies are believed to have their origin in the instability of the basic baroclinic current. The large-scale geostrophic current was about 1 cm sec^{-1} in the upper few hundred meters of the observation area in the permanent arctic anticyclonic gyre. The gyre has a lens-shaped surface water mass of low salinity produced in the Arctic, overlying high-salinity water originating in lower latitudes. There is thus a large-scale horizontal salinity gradient produced by global conditions of oceanic precipitation-evaporation and modified by wind conditions. It can be shown that the currents accompanying such a density gradient are not stable but rather lead to growing disturbances. As the disturbances amplify, the potential energy of the horizontal density gradient is converted into the kinetic energy of eddies. Theory predicts that the fastest growing disturbance will have a horizontal wavelength on the order of the Rossby radius of deformation, which is 10 to 20 km in the Arctic Ocean. The observed horizontal scale agrees fairly well with this.

---

1. Introduction

The interactions between the atmosphere, the ocean and sea ice are of importance for a number of problems ranging from ice forecasting and climate prediction to oil production and polar transportation. The Arctic Ice Dynamics Joint Experiment (AIDJEX) is a coordinated program of field experiments and analysis which is designed to further understanding of these interactions. AIDJEX involves measurements from arrays of manned and unmanned drifting ice stations. The main AIDJEX experiment, which will run for 14 months, is scheduled to begin in February, 1975. In 1971 and 1972 arrays were deployed in pilot programs, and the present paper describes oceanographic results from the 1972 experiment. The 1972 manned array was located 400 km north of Barrow, Alaska and contained three stations separated by about 100 km (Figs. 1 and 2). During their six-week occupation the stations drifted generally westward covering about 100 km. This westward drift followed the mean ice circulation on the southern side of the clockwise gyre in this part of the Arctic Ocean.

The AIDJEX array was located over the featureless Canada Abyssal Plain with uniform depths of 3800 m.

A program of current, salinity and temperature measurements was conducted at the main station by investigators from Lamont-Doherty Geological Observatory. Profiles of currents at ten-meter intervals were taken twice each day with a Savonius rotor current meter lowered by hand to 170 m. These hand-lowered observations were referenced to magnetic north and extended from March 15 to April 19, 1972. Continuous current readings were obtained with Savonius rotor meters attached rigidly to inverted masts. Currents were sampled at one minute intervals at ten fixed levels down to 100 m with direction referenced to true north determined astronomically. The continuous current data were recorded digitally on magnetic tape. Since these current measurements are relative to the drifting ice platform, the ice drift was removed to obtain currents relative to the earth. The drift of the ice was closely monitored with satellite navigation systems and ice velocity data derived from the positions was vectorially added to the observed currents to produce the true currents used in this paper. A salinity-temperature-

* Lamont-Doherty Geological Observatory Contribution #2170

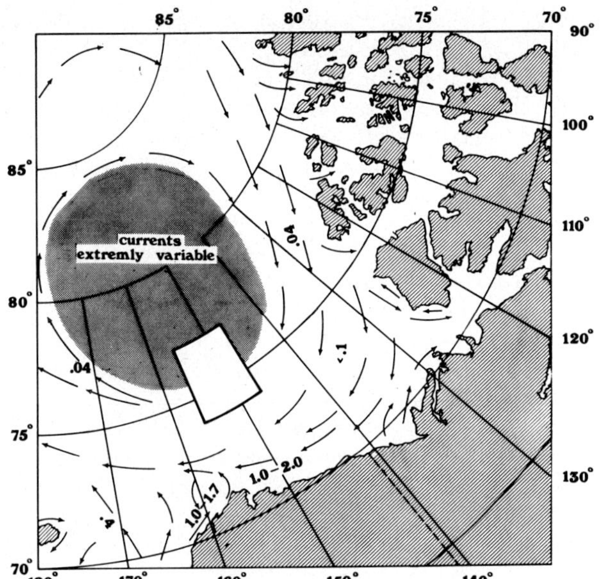

FIG. 1. Ice circulation in the Arctic Ocean (adapted from U. S. Naval Oceanographic Office Atlas). Area of Fig. 2 is outlined. Drift speeds in knots.

depth-recorder (STD) was operated between 13 March and 25 April, obtaining a total of 112 stations. Other oceanographic observations were made by the University of Washington. These included hydroagrphic stations with Nansen bottles and reversing thermometers twice each day between March 12 and April 11 at all three stations. Preliminary reports on the 1972 pilot project appeared in AIDJEX Bulletin No. 14 (1972) and in subsequent bulletins. Much of the data is stored in the AIDJEX data bank, where it is accessible to other researchers.

2. Oceanographic background

A surface mixed layer from 25 to 50 m thick is generally found throughout the Arctic Ocean. Beneath the mixed layer there is a steep gradient of salinity and density to about 300 m. Properties in the deep water, below 300 m, change little with depth. A vertical profile made at the AIDJEX array illustrates these features (Fig. 3). Density, the dynamically important parameter, is almost entirely a function of salinity in this ocean. Since salinity, and therefore density, increase continuously with depth the ocean is statically stable. Temperature oscillates with depth and serves as a tracer of water masses. The salinity contrast between the surface and deep water masses is due to differing origins. The high-salinity deep water is formed at low latitudes in the Atlantic where evaporation exceeds precipitation.

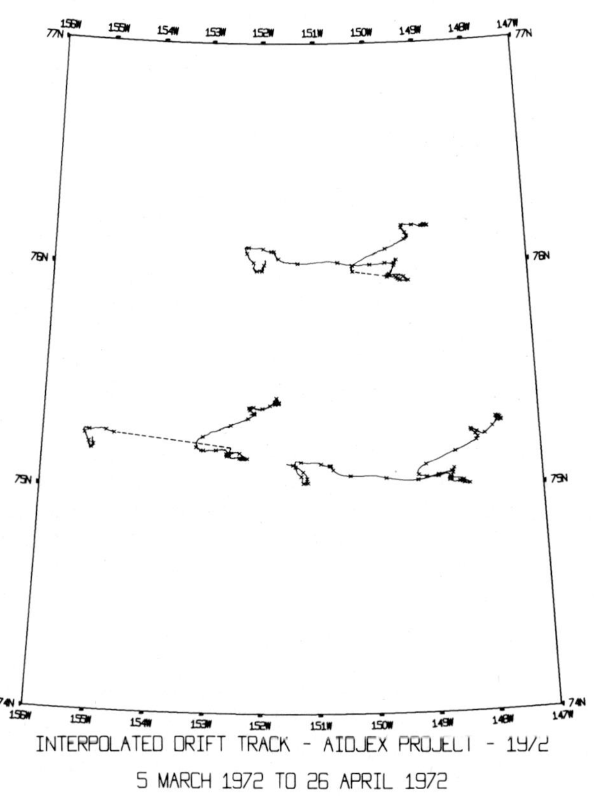

FIG. 2. Drift track of ice stations from March 5 to April 26, 1972. Main camp is on the southeast. Dashed lines indicate lack of navigation data.

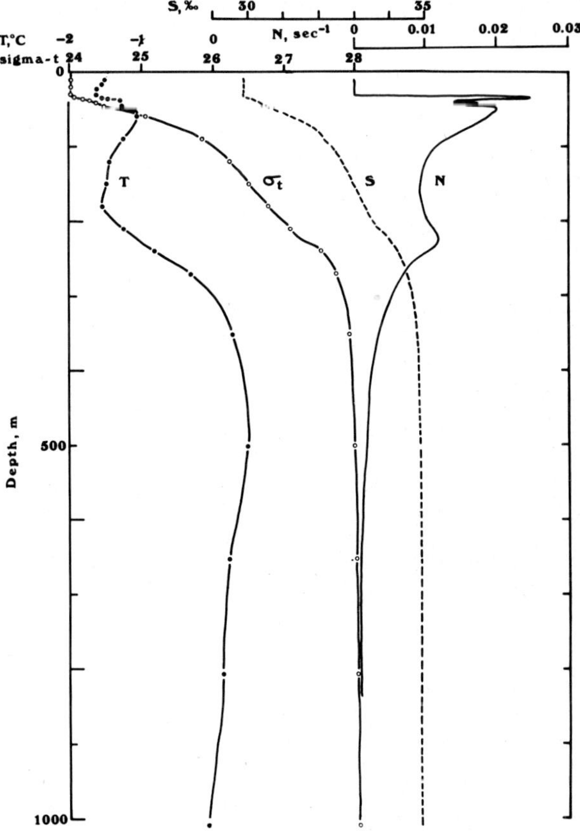

FIG. 3. Vertical profile of temperature (T), salinity (S), density (σ_t) and Väisälä frequency (N) on March 25, 1972 at 75°07′N 149°00′W.

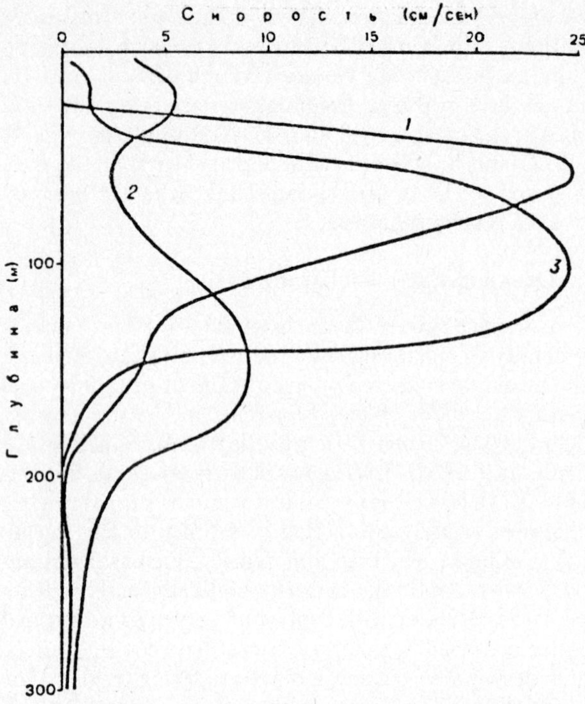

FIG. 4. Vertical profiles of subsurface current maxima from Soviet ice stations (Belyakov, 1972). 1. North Pole–1; 2. North Pole–8, 9/10/59; 3. North Pole–8, 1/11/60. Abscissa represents velocity in cm/sec. and ordinate, depth in meters.

It is then advected into the Arctic Basin where it is modified at the surface by the excess of precipitation over evaporation, producing an upper layer of low salinity. The surface waters and pack ice circulate in a clockwise gyre. The dynamic topography of the sea surface, based on hydrographic observations, reflects this gyre showing high pressure at the center. The density surfaces below the center of the gyre are depressed, limiting the clockwise circulation to the upper few hundred meters. These are currents with a time scale of years and a space scale of thousands of kilometers. The mean geostrophic currents for one month over the AIDJEX array indicate a southwestward current of about 2 cm sec^{-1} which decreases with depth.

This circulation with a time scale of months and a distance scale of hundreds of kilometers agrees in magnitude and vertical shear with the larger scale conception.

There was close agreement between the average ice drift, 2.4 cm sec^{-1} to the southwest, and the mean geostrophic currents at 30 m, 1.8 cm sec^{-1} in the same direction.

Direct current observations at a single station contrast with the mean circulation. Much swifter currents are superimposed on the slow mean circulation at times. Currents driven by the drifting ice may reach 10 to 15 cm sec^{-1} in the upper 10 meters but the swiftest and most striking currents are found considerably deeper. Current speeds of up to 40 cm sec^{-1} were observed at a depth of 150 m on occasion at the main camp during the 1972 AIDJEX program.

Transient undercurrents similar to those observed at the AIDJEX site were originally noted by Shirshov in 1937 during the drift of the first Soviet ice research station, NP-1. Belyakov (1972) has discussed these and later measurements from other Soviet ice stations (Fig. 4). Somewhat similar currents have also been measured at Fletcher's Ice Island (T-3), (Bernstein, 1972; Galt, 1967). These observations from different regions of the Arctic Ocean, as well as from different seasons and years, suggest that the phenomenon of transient undercurrents is fairly widespread through the Arctic Ocean.

The AIDJEX pilot program provided the best opportunity yet to investigate the nature of these currents. The accurate positioning and the multiple stations allowed the first accurate determination of the true current speeds in these undercurrents, and an estimate of their horizontal scale.

3. Structure of Arctic subsurface eddies

A prominent velocity maximum is the most characteristic feature of vertical current profiles taken within subsurface eddies (Fig. 5). The vertical profile has a generally smooth shape between depths of 50 and 300 m with the swiftest current at about 150 m. The current coincides with the steep density gradient shown in Fig. 3. There is little motion in the mixed layer or in the deep layers below 300 m. Strong subsurface currents were noted on four occasions during the six weeks of observations, persisting for one to four days on each occasion. This is not necessarily the lifetime of the features. It is likely that they last for a time much longer than several days but that the ice station drifts over them. During the course of a day, current directions within the features may change as much as 180°.

The interpretation of time- and space-dependent current patterns observed from a drifting platform presents difficulties. The clearest resolution occurs when the ice is drifting rapidly relative to these current systems, which then appear to be relatively stationary. But presenting the data in different types of plots which emphasize different aspects of the observations gives insight into the structure and behavior of less ideal cases. Since the observations suggest that the features are closed circulation systems, the general term eddy will be used.

Several strong eddies appear in a plot of current speed and depth of density surfaces versus time (Fig. 6). This presentation obscures the horizontal dimensions of the eddies but clearly shows the presence of current maxima and the relation between the velocity and density fields. The two most pronounced eddies appeared on March 15–17 and on March 29–April 2. There were weaker events on March 26–28 and on April 3–5. The latter, on basis of the drift track, is apparently a

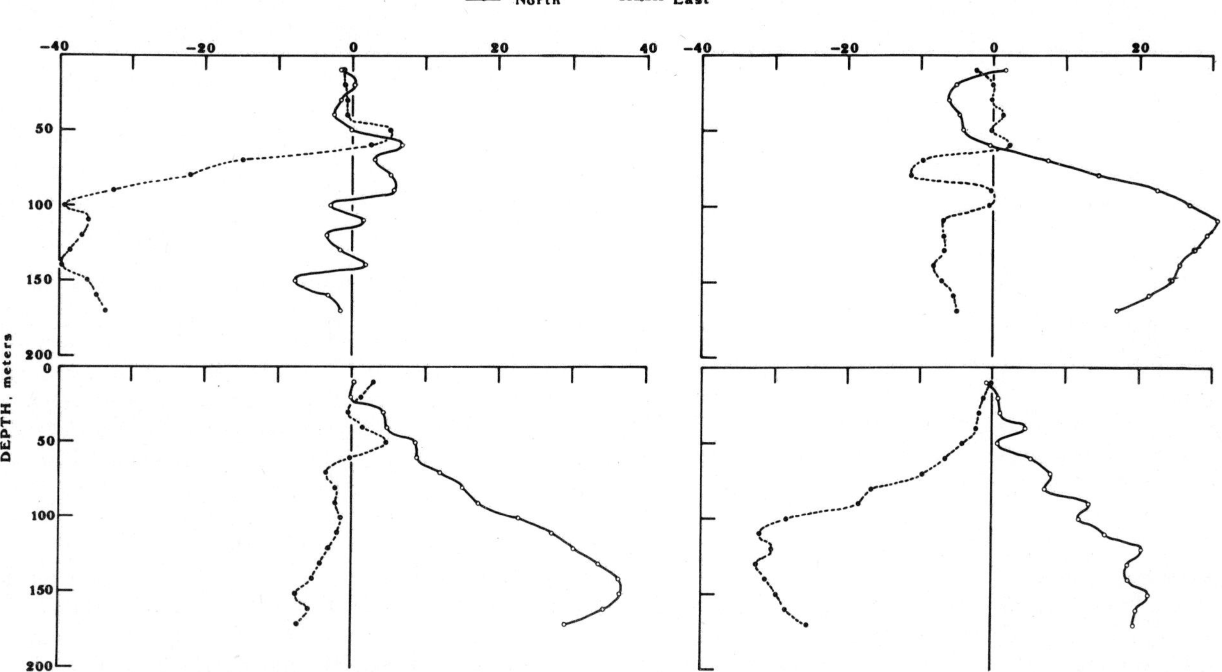

FIG. 5. Vertical profiles of subsurface current maximum from AIDJEX main camp (1972). Observation times are:
UL—0050 Mar. 16, UR—0120 Mar. 17, LL—1900 Mar. 30, LR—0610 Apr. 1.

recrossing of the March 30–April 1 feature. The density surfaces are distorted upward or downward by as much as 18 m. In the two larger eddies there is a general upwarping of the density surfaces above the current maximum and a downwarping below the maximum. This corresponds to a high pressure or anticyclonic

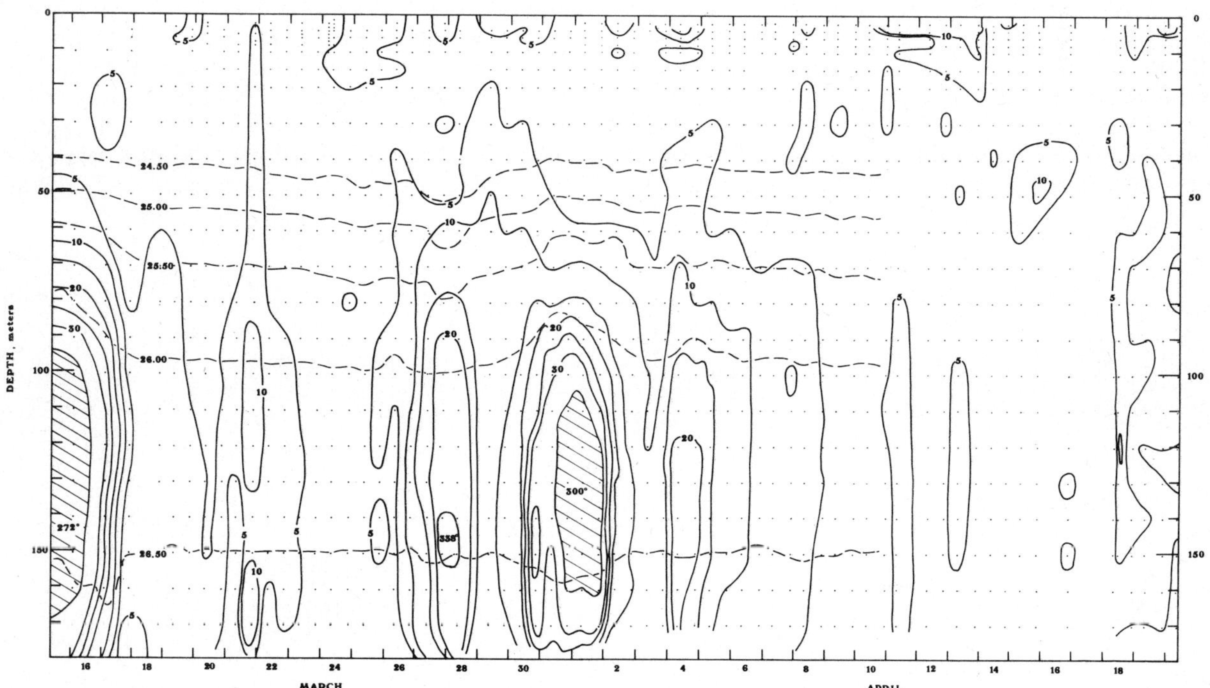

FIG. 6. Current speed and sigma-t as a function of time at the AIDJEX main camp. Solid lines are contours of current speed at intervals of 5 cm/sec. Dashed lines are density surfaces at intervals of 0.5 sigma-t units based on hydrographic stations. Dots represent individual current measurements. Hatched areas indicate current speeds in excess of 35 cm/sec.

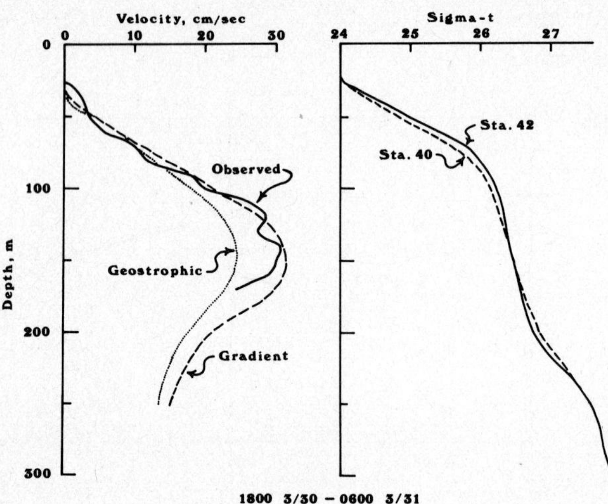

FIG. 7. Comparison of observed currents with calculated geostrophic and gradient currents and comparison of density profiles at center of and outside eddy.

subsurface system. The density surfaces in the vicinity of the March 27–28 eddy are displaced in the opposite sense indicating a cyclonic system.

Geostrophic currents calculated from pairs of hydrographic stations, one station near the center and one near the edge of the eddy, show agreement with directly measured currents. Satellite navigation provided positioning accuracy of ± 0.01 km, making possible sufficiently accurate distance determination despite the small spacing between hydrographic stations of 3.22 km. The profile shape, level and speed agree fairly well with the geostrophic profile although the observed speeds are slightly higher (Fig. 7). For anticyclonic flow, which characterizes this eddy, geostrophically calculated velocity will underestimate the current velocity if centrifugal force effects are significant. If a radius of 10 km is assumed better agreement in speed is achieved. The

gradient flow, which includes centrifugal force, was calculated from the relation

$$-V^2/R + fV - fV_g = 0$$

where V = gradient current velocity, V_g = geostrophic current velocity, f = Coriolis parameter, and R = radius of curvature. The time variation is neglected since the eddies seem to vary only slowly over a period of several days. The density profiles for the station pairs show greater mixing or vertical elongation between 50 and 250 m at the center of this anticyclonic feature.

The horizontal pattern of the eddies is revealed more clearly by a plot of current vectors at a fixed depth along the drift track. Five areas of swifter currents appear on the 100 m level (Fig. 8). The features are about 10 km across with spacing between them ranging from 10 to 50 km. The eddy pattern shows most clearly when the station drift is rapid in comparison with the drift of the eddies. In most cases a clear pattern does not emerge from the current vector pattern plotted on the drift track. This is apparently due to the fact that the platform is drifting irregularly over a system which is also drifting but at a different rate and direction. However, on April 17–18, the station drifted on a nearly straight path across a cyclonic counterclockwise eddy. The ice drift was rapid enough relative to advection of the eddy to effectively freeze the eddy motion in time. An enlargement from the drift track shows the currents at the 100 m level (Fig. 9). The same eddy was apparently recrossed on April 22–25 so that only four independent eddies were present. Although the Apr. 17–18 eddy was not well sampled by the scanty hand-lowered current observations of Fig. 8, fortunately continuous current measurements and closely-spaced STD stations were taken during the April 17–18 period so that considerable structural detail was obtained. The salinity surfaces are depressed above and elevated below the 150 m current core indicating a cyclonic feature (Fig.

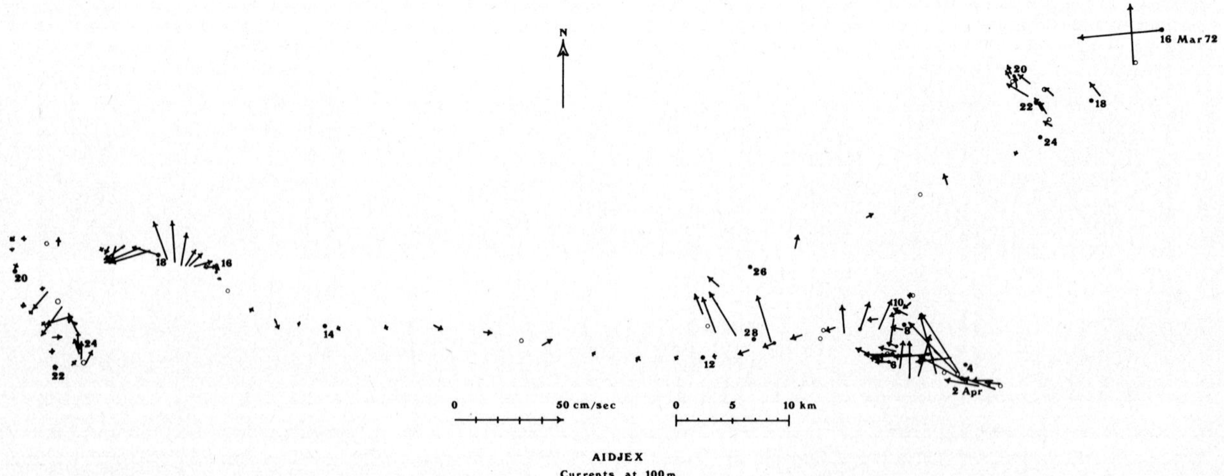

FIG. 8. Current vectors at the 100 m level along the drift track of the main camp showing locations of subsurface eddies.

10). The temperature field, with temperatures decreasing with depth between 75 and 170 m shows behavior similar to that of the salinity field (Fig. 11). Of especial interest in the temperature plot is the presence of anomalously warm water (-1.0 C) at the 75 m level near the eddy center. The wind speeds plotted on the temperature and salinity diagrams show no simple relationship with the presence or absence of subsurface eddies.

A comparison of the density surfaces between the three different camps provides further evidence of the small horizontal scales of the eddies. In the absence of complete current data at all three camps, the density anomalies provide an indication of the presence of eddies since there is a direct relationship between the velocity and mass fields. There is little correlation between perturbations of the sigma-t surfaces at the three camps. Since the camps are spaced 100 km apart, this is to be expected for eddies which are only about 10 km in diameter. The array spacing was chosen to monitor synoptic scale ice motion rather than subsurface eddies.

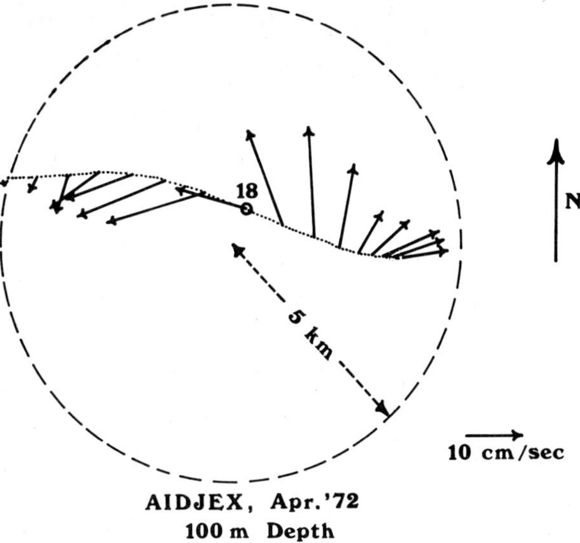

FIG. 9. Cyclonic eddy of April 17–18. Current vectors at the 100 m level plotted at 2-hour intervals along the drift track.

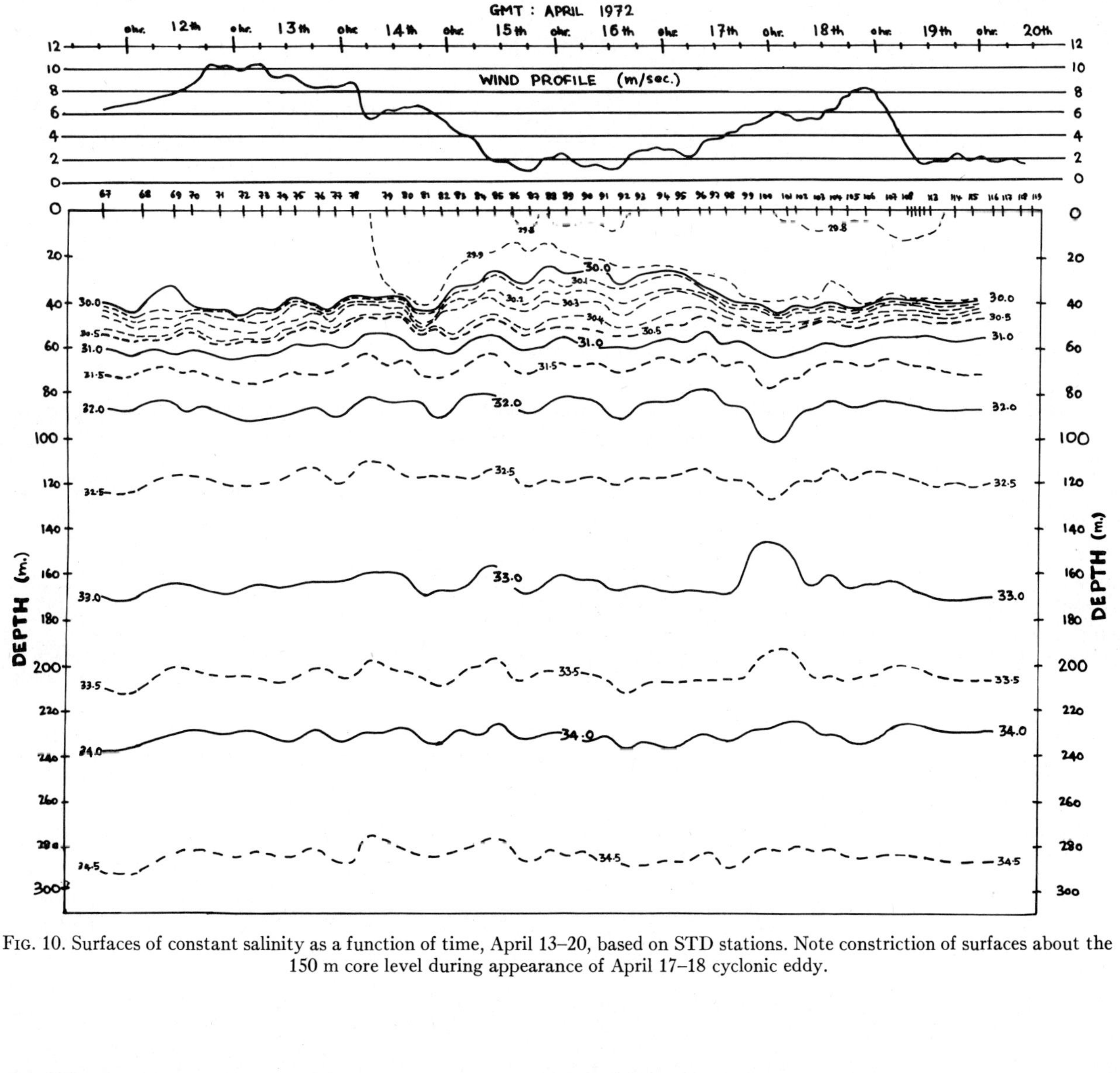

FIG. 10. Surfaces of constant salinity as a function of time, April 13–20, based on STD stations. Note constriction of surfaces about the 150 m core level during appearance of April 17–18 cyclonic eddy.

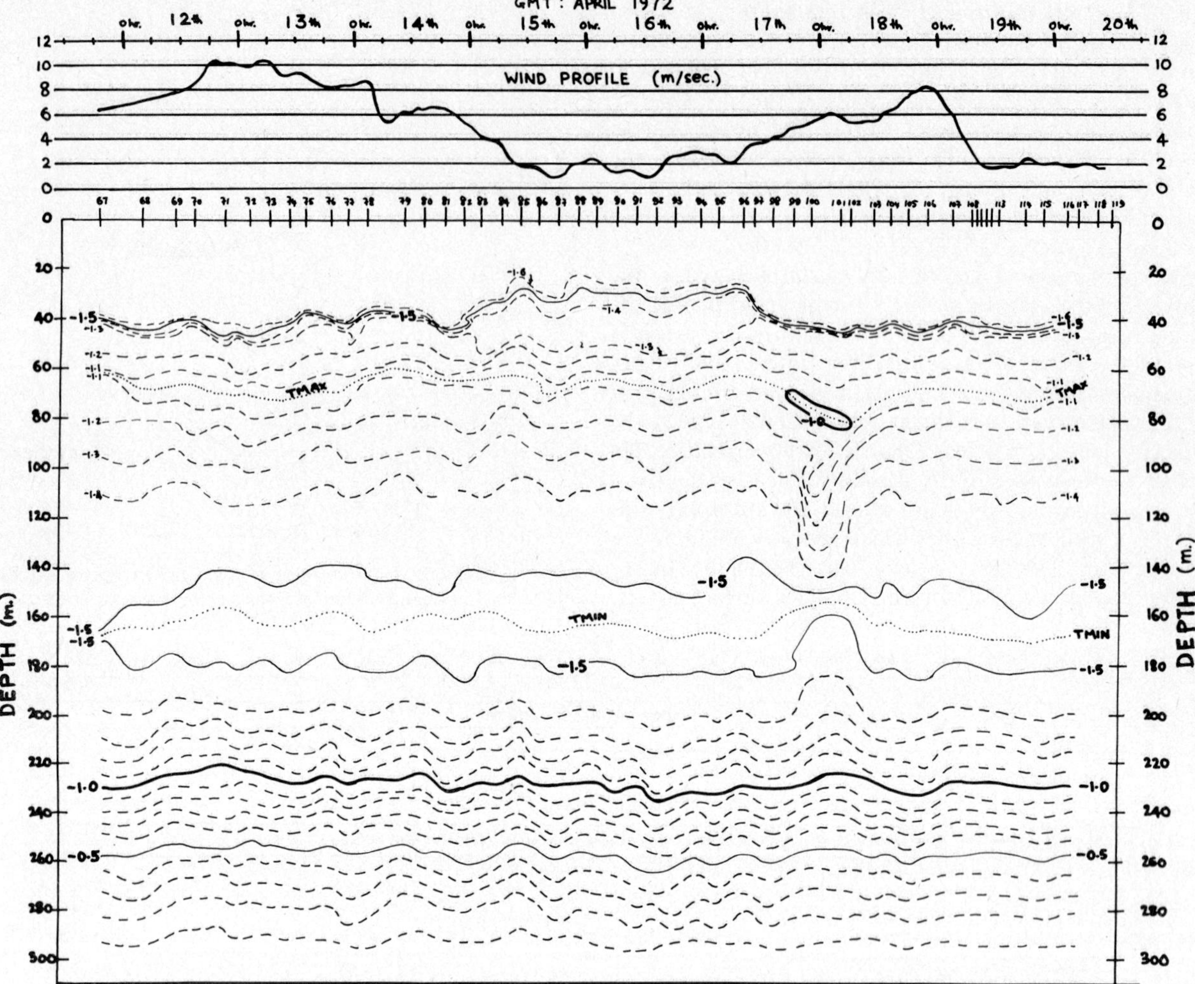

FIG. 11. Surfaces of constant temperature as a function of time, April 13–20, based on STD stations.

4. The origin of subsurface eddies

The existence of these eddies raises questions about their origins and development. There are several sources of energy which might possibly lead to eddy motions.

Winds drive the ice which in turn drives surface currents. The generation of surface currents in the mixed layer is an obvious result. Winds might also provide energy for deeper currents. Wind and pack ice vorticity would lead to divergences in the mixed layer and consequent vertical velocities at its base. Distortion of the density surfaces and a compensating flow at depth would follow. Explanations by Browne and Crary, (1958) and by Shirshov (as discussed in Belyakov, 1972) of early observations of arctic undercurrents were based on wind-driven effects. These authors referred to the eddies as "counter-currents" and considered them to be a secondary flow induced by Ekman divergence in the mixed layer.

Experience at the AIDJEX 1972 site does not support a wind-driven hypothesis, however. There was little apparent relation between wind or ice drift and the presence of eddies which were noted both during strong winds and during calms. The observed small size of the eddies is a further argument against a wind source. The synoptic scale of wind systems is on the order of 1000 km. Ice drift closely follows the wind and has the same horizontal scale. Wind-driven eddies would presumably have the same horizontal scale as the winds but the observed eddies are, in fact, two orders of magnitude smaller in size.

The freezing process is another possible energy source. During the winter the pack ice frequently cracks exposing areas of open water which freeze over quickly under the prevailing low air temperatures. The freezing releases salt. The heavy brine sinks to reestablish equilibrium. The sinking brine must disturb the base of the mixed layer and lead to some distortion of the density field. The release would occur over local areas of open water which are generally meters to tens of meters in scale. In this case the source scale appears to be smaller than the eddy scale. It is not clear whether anomalies of the magnitude seen will be produced by this mechanism. The freezing occurs only in winter and could not operate in summer, yet strong eddies have been observed in the summer. If they have indeed been produced by freezing they must have persisted for many months.

The observed dimensions of 10 km are in the neighborhood of the internal Rossby radius of deformation for the Arctic Ocean. The deformation radius is the ratio of the speed of long gravity waves to the inertial frequency. For nearly geostrophic flow under conditions of hydrostatic equilibrium and conservation of potential vorticity, the radius of deformation is the natural horizontal scale. The simplest model for the Arctic Ocean density structure is a layer of depth h, and density ρ_1, overlying a much thicker layer of density ρ_2. In this case the internal deformation radius is

$$R_D = (g'h)^{\frac{1}{2}}/f,$$

where

$$g' = [(\rho_2 - \rho_1)/(\rho_2 + \rho_1)]g.$$

Selecting typical values for the Arctic Ocean,

$$h = 100 \text{ m}$$
$$\rho_1 = 1.024 \text{ g} \cdot \text{cm}^{-3}$$
$$\rho_2 = 1.028 \text{ g} \cdot \text{cm}^{-3}$$
$$g = 10^3 \text{ cm} \cdot \text{sec}^{-2}$$
$$f = 1.4 \times 10^{-4} \text{ sec}^{-1},$$

we have,

$$R_D = 10.0 \text{ km}$$

For a continuously stratified model, the radius of deformation takes the form

$$R_D = ND/f$$

where the Väisälä frequency is

$$N = [(-g/\rho_0)\partial\rho/\partial Z]^{\frac{1}{2}},$$

and D is depth of the stratified layer. Applying this to the baroclinic layer between 50 and 300 m depth, $D = 250$ m and for $N = 0.01$ sec, we have $R_D = 17.9$ km. Both of these values are in approximate agreement with the observed sizes of the eddies. For eddies induced by Ekman divergence or by freezing processes, there will not be selective amplification for wavelengths in the vicinity of R_D. The eddy size will be determined by the dimensions of the source in these cases.

The field results do not permit a conclusive determination of the origin of these eddies but instability theories seem to present the most attractive mechanism for their generation. Instability theories predict that a basic baroclinic flow such as exists in the Arctic Ocean is not stable. Small disturbances tend to grow spontaneously, extracting potential energy from the horizontal density gradient and converting it into the kinetic energy of eddies. The theories show that disturbances with wavelengths shorter than R_D are stable, but longer wavelengths tend to amplify. The rate of growth is most rapid for certain intermediate wavelengths a few times larger than R_D. These fastest growing waves will eventually dominate the flow to the exclusion of shorter and longer wavelengths. Theories of small perturbations cannot predict subsequent development. However, experience with actual atmospheric situations, with numerical computer models, and with rotating tank experiments shows that the preferred wavelengths continue to dominate during later development, eventually being cut off to form closed systems which then are advected with the mean flow. The fact that arctic subsurface eddies have dimensions on the order of R_D is in general agreement with instability theories.

One of the simplest instability models is that developed by Eady (1949) for the atmosphere. The model assumes a linear basic velocity gradient, constant Väisälä frequency and rigid boundaries at top and bottom. No variation of coriolis parameter with latitude is assumed. This model is probably the simplest one which incorporates the basic features of baroclinic instability. Although the Eady theory only crudely approximates the actual situation in this case, it is useful for certain comparisons. The rate of growth for the fastest growing waves is predicted to be proportional to the mean vertical shear. At the AIDJEX site the mean shear was low, only about 1 cm sec^{-1} (100 m)$^{-1}$. Application of the theory indicates that a time period of about one month will be required for the disturbances to double in amplitude. This slow growth rate does not appear especially favorable for development at the experimental site. In the mean current axis south of the AIDJEX array, however, there is a frontal zone with higher shear which would be more favorable to growth. The mean shear in that region is about 10 cm sec^{-1} (100 m)$^{-1}$ which would produce a doubling time of two or three days. It may be that the arctic eddies are spawned principally near the current axis north of Barrow and are then advected to other areas such as the AIDJEX site.

A tilting of the phase lines with depth is a further prediction of instability theories. In the case of mean westward currents which decrease with depth, as at the observational site, the phase lines would slope to the west with depth. There is some indication in Figs. 10 and 11 for a slope in the proper direction, but the tilt is small. The arctic eddies are apparently in a mature stage of development, having been completely cut off, so that steep tilting might not be expected and the lack of it does not seriously detract from a baroclinic instability hypothesis.

The water at the center of an eddy formed by instability would have distinctly different properties from the surrounding water, whereas for wind-generated eddies the water within the eddy would be derived locally and would have the same properties as that without. For the event of April 17–18 (Fig. 11) there is clear evidence of a different water mass at the center. At 75 m there was water with a temperature of -1.0 C. which was not found at that level at any other time during the observation period shown in this figure. This water must have been introduced when the eddy was formed along a front separating two distinct water masses. Water with this relatively warm temperature is found in the Chukchi Sea area south of the experimental site, and the eddy may have been formed in the frontal area mentioned earlier.

One of the unique aspects of the arctic eddies, their sub-surface velocity maximum, still remains to be interpreted. This peak amplitude within the pycnocline is not predicted by results of simple instability theories, which show exponential behavior in depth. The actual profiles of mean shear and Väisälä frequency are more complex than assumed in simple theories, and it may be that the changing ratio of these quantities, the Richardson number, is responsible for the maximum at depth. Friction is another factor in the real ocean not included in simple theories. Energy would be extracted from the eddies by friction against the base of the ice, resulting in kinetic energy and velocity maxima at depth.

The subsurface eddies contain a major portion of the kinetic energy in this area of the Arctic Ocean. They must be a significant factor in the exchange of momentum, salt and heat between the Arctic Ocean and bordering areas under the influence of the Atlantic and Pacific Oceans. On the basis of their potential importance to global transfer processes, they deserve continued investigation.

Acknowledgments. This investigation was made possible by the continued support of the Office of Naval Research under contract N00014-67-A-0108 0016. Logistic support was provided by the AIDJEX Project Office funded by the National Science Foundation and by the Naval Arctic Research Laboratory. Barry Allen and Allan Gill assisted with the Lamont current meter program on AIDJEX '72. The Lamont STD program was operated by Anthony Amos with the assistance of Roy Wilkins. Myron Fliegel wrote the computer programs for reducing the digital current results and carried out the data reduction.

REFERENCES

AIDJEX, 1972: AIDJEX pilot study. *AIDJEX Bulletin* 14, July. University of Washington, Seattle.

Belyakov, L. N., 1972: Triggering mechanism of deep episodic currents in the Arctic Basin. *Probs. Arctic and Antarctic*, **39**, 22–32 (in Russian).

Bernstein, R., 1971: Observations of currents in the Arctic Ocean. Unpublished doctoral dissertation, Columbia University, 78 pp.

Browne, A. M., and A. P. Crary, 1958: The movement of ice in the Arctic Ocean, *in* Arctic Sea Ice. Publ. 598, Nat. Acad. Sci., Wash., C. D., 191–207.

Eady, E. T., 1949: Long waves and cyclone waves. *Tellus*, **1**, 33–52.

Galt, J., 1967: Current measurements in the Canadian Basin of the Arctic Ocean. Summer, 1965. Tech. Rpt. No. 184, Univ. of Wash., Dept. of Oceanography, March, 17 pp.

Kusunoki, K., 1962: Hydrography of the Arctic Ocean with special reference to the Beaufort Sea. Contr. from the Instit. of Low Temp. Sci., Ser. A, No. 17, Hokkaido Univ., Sapporo, Japan, 74 pp.

Newton, J. L., 1973: The Canada Basin: mean circulation and intermediate scale flow features. Unpublished doctoral dissertation, Univ. of Wash. 158 pp.

Newton, J. L., and L. K. Coachman, 1973: '72 AIDJEX interior Flow Field Study. Preliminary report and comparison with previous results. *AIDJEX Bulletin* 19, March, pp. 19–42.

Microwave Maps of the Polar Ice of the Earth

P. Gloersen, T. T. Wilheit, T. C. Chang and W. Nordberg

Goddard Space Flight Center, Greenbelt, Maryland

AND

W. J. Campbell

Ice Dynamics Project, U. S. G. S.

Abstract

Synoptic views of the entire polar regions of Earth have been obtained free of the usual persistent cloud cover using a scanning microwave radiometer operating at a wavelength of 1.55 cm on board the Nimbus-5 satellite. Three different views at each pole are presented utilizing data obtained at approximately one-month intervals during the winter of 1972–1973. The major discoveries resulting from an analysis of these data are as follows: 1) Large discrepancies exist between the climatic norm ice cover depicted in various atlases and the actual extent of the canopies. 2) The distribution of multiyear ice in the north polar region is markedly different from that predicted by existing ice dynamics models. 3) Irregularities in the edge of the Antarctic sea ice pack occur that have neither been observed previously nor anticipated. 4) The brightness temperatures of the Greenland and Antarctica glaciers show interesting contours probably related to the ice and snow morphologic structure.

---

1. Background

The Electronically-Scanned Microwave Radiometer (ESMR) used for obtaining the measurements to be described here has been discussed in detail elsewhere (Wilheit, 1972). It consists of a Dicke-type radiometer (Dicke, 1946) with a temperature sensitivity of 2 K fed by a phased-array antenna which step-scans across the subsatellite track in 78 beam positions by means of ferrite phase shifters contained in the antenna elements. The total swath covered is $\pm 50°$ from nadir. The radiometric data are telemetered orbit-by-orbit, along with internal calibration data, and are computer-processed into the format presented in this paper. Approximately one day's worth of data are accumulated for one polar projection; redundant data in a given map cell, resulting from orbit swath overlap, are averaged for that time period. Brightness temperatures, which are directly proportional to the received radiometric power since the Rayleigh-Jeans approximation applies, are assigned various colors so as to produce a false-color image. The resolution cell size in the processed image is 32 Km.

The brightness temperatures observed with the ESMR in general depend on the physical temperature and emissivity of the surface and the opacity and temperature profile of the intervening atmosphere. However, the atmospheric contributions in the polar regions are generally negligible due to the low humidity and near absence of liquid water droplets in these regions (Wilheit *et al.*, 1972). The cloud cover generally consists of low-altitude stratus clouds, whose liquid water content is too small to affect the microwave emission. The ice crystals contained in cirrus clouds are quite transparent to the 1.55 cm radiation.

The surface emissivity accounts for the largest signal contrast observed in the polar regions; however, variations in the physical temperature of the surface are observed also. At 1.55 cm, the emissivity of sea water is about 0.4, for first-year sea ice it is about 0.95, and for multiyear ice it is about 0.8 (Wilheit *et al.*, 1972; Gloersen *et al.*, 1973). Thus, in the presence of first-year ice only, the fraction of F of unresolved open water in a given resolution cell may be determined from the following expression:

$$F = (T_B - 0.95\, T_S)/(T_W - 0.95\, T_S)$$

where T_B is the brightness temperature observed at 1.55 cm, T_S is the thermodynamic temperature of the ice surface, and T_W is the brightness temperature of smooth open water. T_S may be assumed to be the seasonal average ± 10 K and T_W is 131 ± 5 K (Wilheit *et al.*, 1972). If T_B is measured to within 2 K, the uncertainties in T_S and T_W lead to an accuracy of the determination of the fractional open water, F, to within 6 percentage points.

It has been suggested that the assumed emissivity for first-year ice (0.95) may not be correct for temperatures within 10 K of the melting point of the

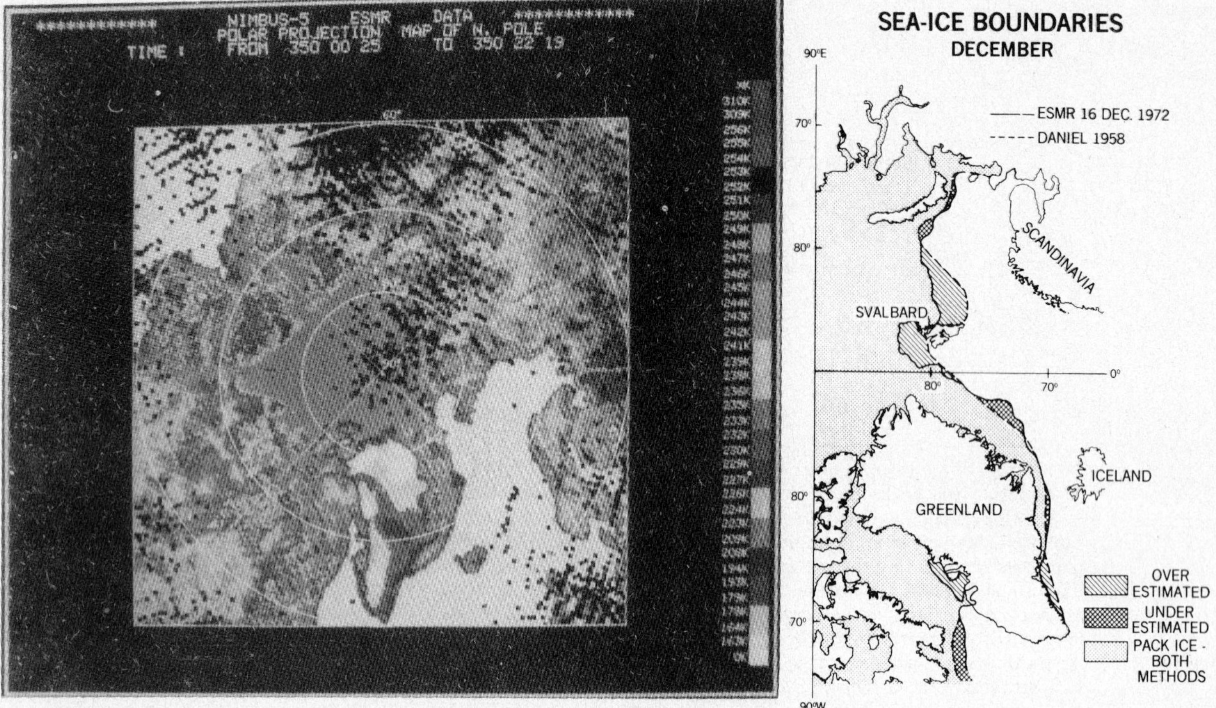

PLATE 1. Black and white plate of false-color polar projection map of 1.55-cm microwave radiometer data obtained on December 16, 1972 from the Nimbus-5 satellite in the vicinity of the North Pole. Greenland appears in the lower center of the image.

FIG. 1. Comparison of part of the data in Plate 1 (ESMR) with predictions based on data from the same month in the USN Polar Atlas (Daniel). The indicated edge of the ice pack was used in both cases.

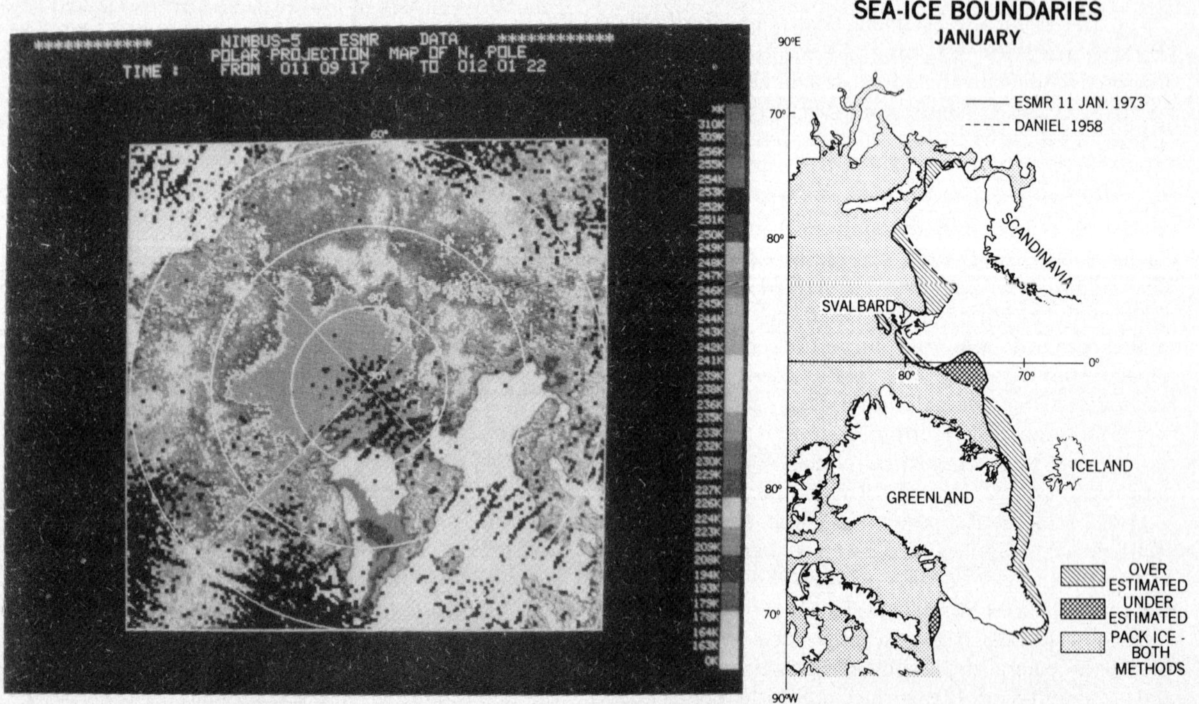

PLATE 2. Black and white plate of false-color polar projection map of 1.55-cm microwave radiometer data obtained on January 11, 1973 from the Nimbus-5 satellite in the vicinity of the North Pole. Greenland appears in the lower center of the image.

FIG. 2. Comparison of part of the data in Plate 2 (ESMR) with predictions based on data from the same month in the USN Polar Atlas (Daniel). The indicated edge of the ice pack was used in both cases.

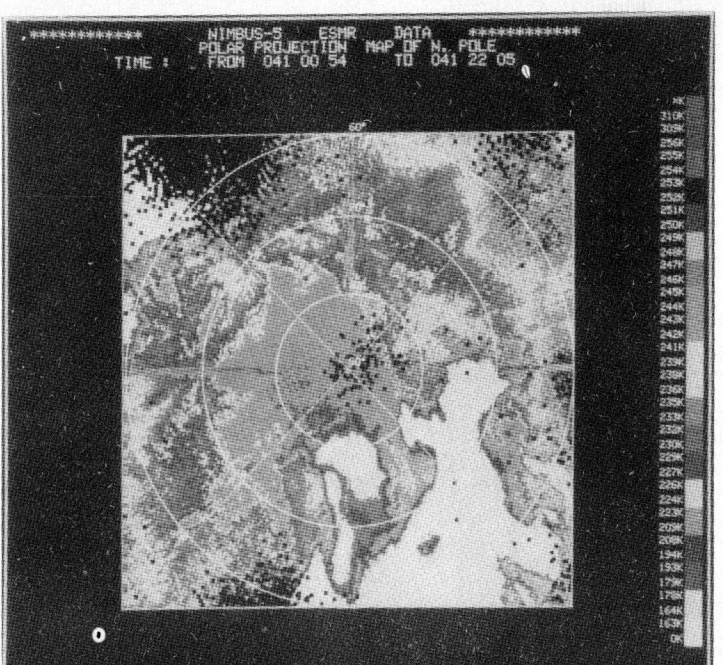

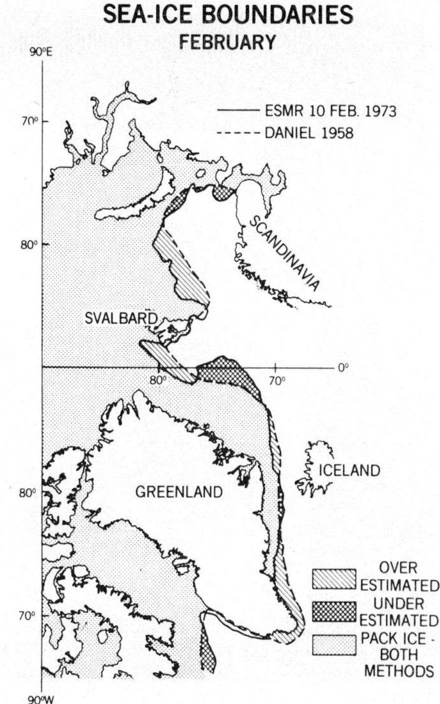

PLATE 3. Black and white plate of false-color polar projection map of 1.55-cm microwave radiometer data obtained on February 10, 1973 from the Nimbus-5 satellite in the vicinity of the North Pole. Greenland appears in the lower center of the image.

FIG. 3. Comparison of part of the data in Plate 3 (ESMR) with predictions based on data from the same month in the USN Polar Atlas (Daniel). The indicated edge of the ice pack was used in both cases.

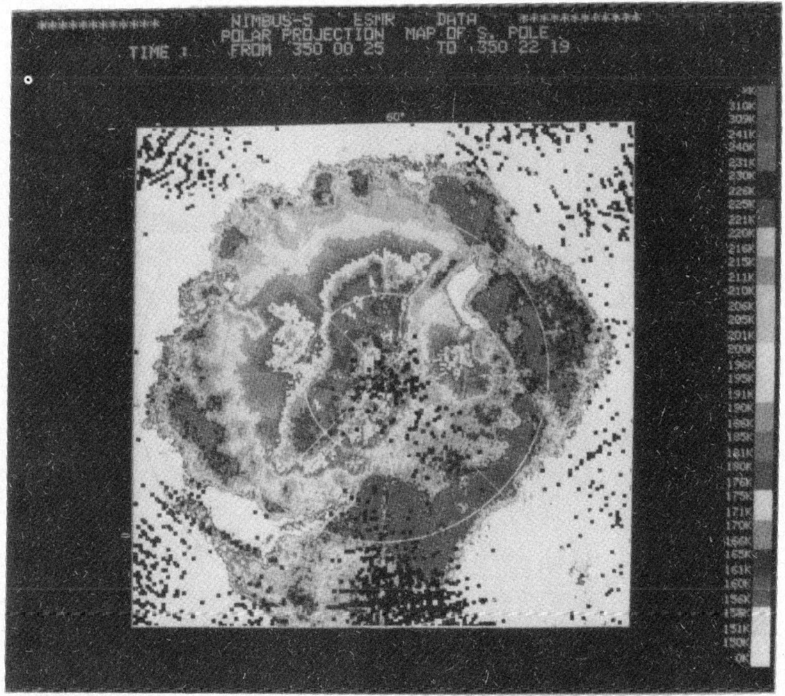

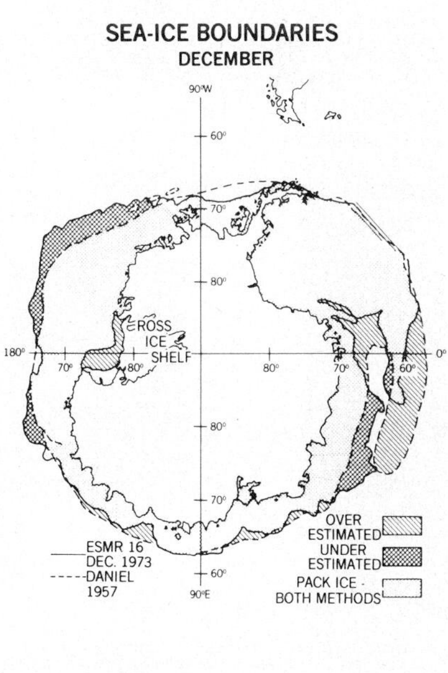

PLATE 4. Black and white plate of false-color polar projection map of 1.55-cm microwave radiometer data obtained on December 16, 1972 from the Nimbus-5 satellite in the vicinity of the South Pole. The white area enclosed in the upper right corner of Antarctica is open water in the Ross Sea between the Ross Ice Shelf and the sea ice pack.

FIG. 4. Comparison of part of the data in Plate 4 (ESMR) with predictions based on data from the same month in the USN Polar Atlas (Daniel). The indicated edge of the ice pack was used in both cases.

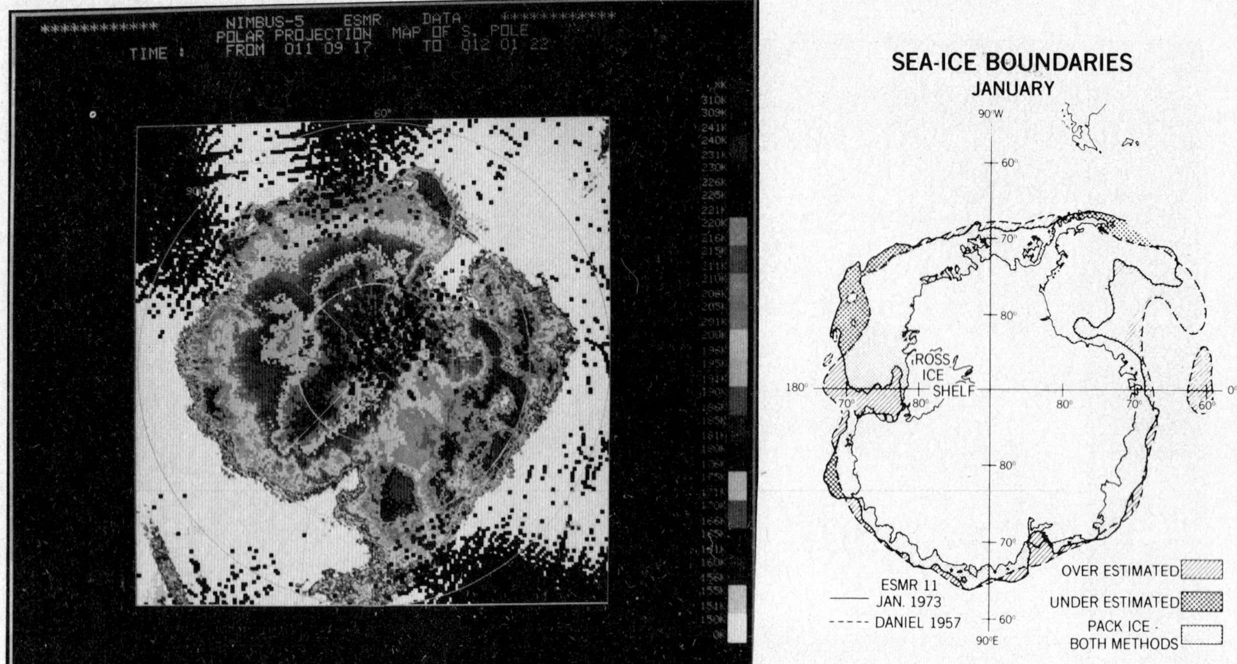

PLATE 5. Black and white plate of false-color polar projection map of 1.55-cm microwave radiometer data obtained on January 11, 1973 from the Nimbus-5 satellite in the vicinity of the South Pole. The white area enclosed in the upper right corner of Antarctica is open water in the Ross Sea between the Ross Ice Shelf and the sea ice pack.

FIG. 5. Comparison of part of the data in Plate 5 (ESMR) with predictions based on data from the same month in the USN Polar Atlas (Daniel). The indicated edge of the ice pack was used in both cases.

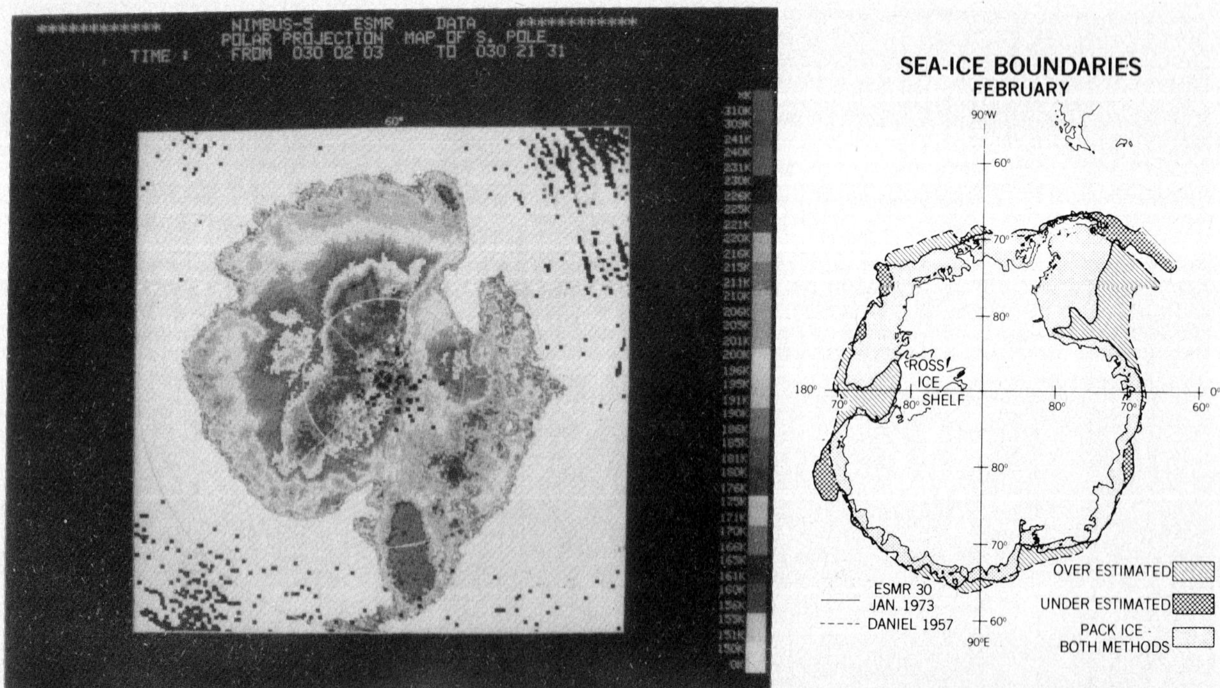

PLATE 6. Black and white plate of false-color polar projection map of 1.55-cm microwave radiometer data obtained on January 30, 1973 from the Nimbus-5 satellite in the vicinity of the South Pole. The white area enclosed in the upper right corner of Antarctica is open water in the Ross Sea between the Ross Ice Shelf and the sea ice pack.

FIG. 6. Comparison of part of the data in Plate 6 (ESMR) with predictions based on data from February in the USN Polar Atlas (Daniel). The indicated edge of the ice pack was used in both cases.

GREENLAND

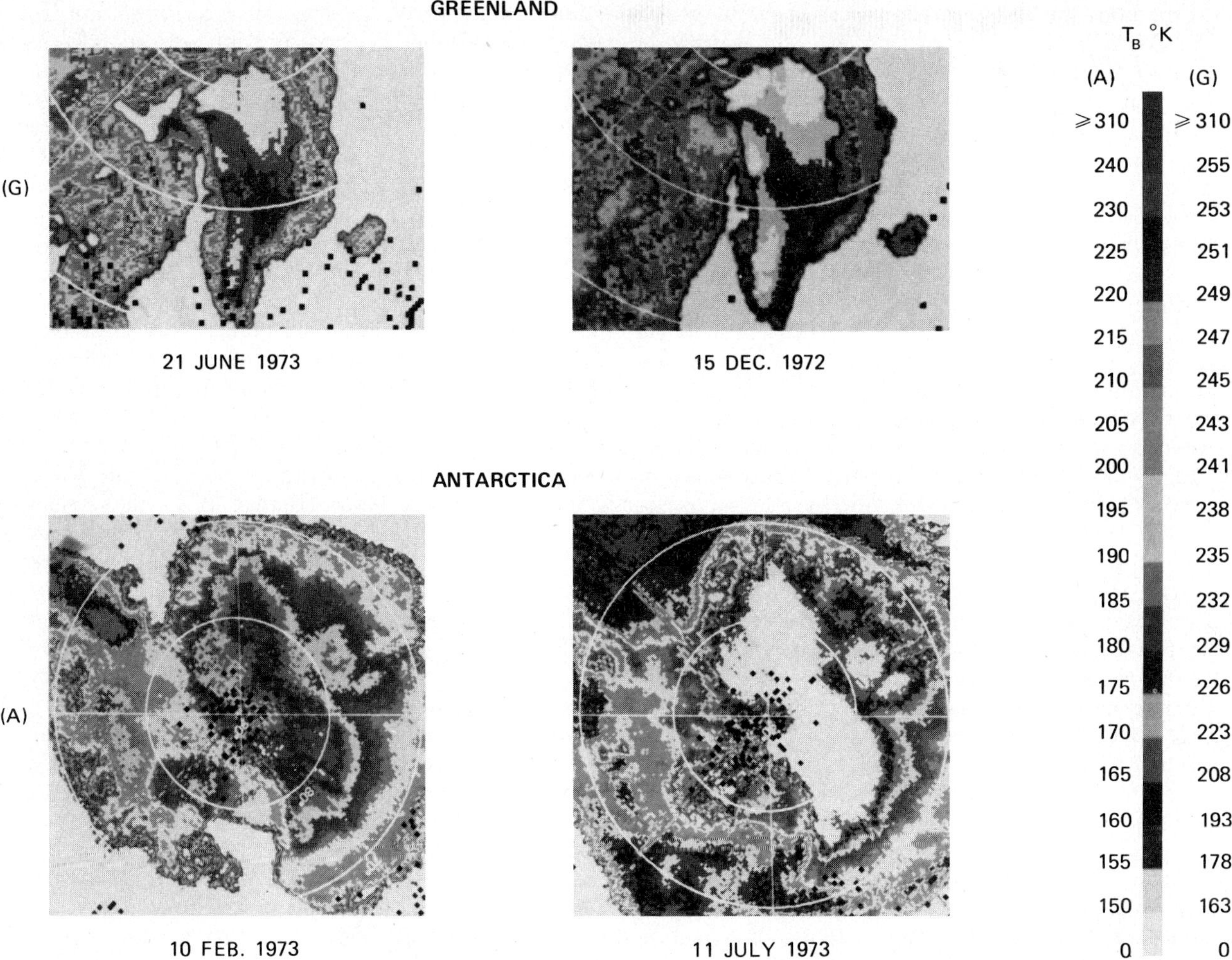

PLATE 7. Seasonal variations of the brightness temperatures over the continental ice sheets in Greenland and Antarctica.

first-year sea ice (Edgerton *et al.*, 1971). However, radiometric data obtained from aircraft flights over Arctic sea ice in the summer (Wilheit *et al.*, 1972) are consistent with an emissivity of 0.95 for first-year ice, based on encounters with surface temperatures within 2 K of the melting point as determined with an onboard infrared radiometer.

2. Ice pack boundary measurements

A comparison between the predicted and actual boundaries of the polar ice packs for three different time periods is given in Plates 1–6 and opposing Figs. 1–6. The predictions were based (Daniel, 1957 and 1958) on available ship and aircraft reports; for Antarctica, the information is substantially the same in several atlases, published both in the Soviet Union and in the U. S. A. In comparing our actual measurements of the ice boundaries with the predictions it is of course recognized that there are trends in the state of the ice cover that cannot be covered in the atlases and that the predictions are based upon long past

seasons. The purpose of the comparison is to illustrate that large differences exist between the actual ice edge and the climatic norm.

In the Arctic, probably the most striking observation is that during the 1972–3 season much more ice cover was observed in the East Greenland Sea than is estimated in the atlas. Off northern Greenland, the ice extends more than 4° longitude further eastward than expected for two of the three time periods illustrated. On the other hand, the seas north of Svalbard and southeast of Greenland are shown as ice-covered in the atlases but are actually open, as shown in the microwave images. Finally, freezing of the waters in the Northern Baffin Bay, the White Sea, the Chukchi sea, Bering Strait, and the Bering Sea occurred later during the 1972–3 winter than is predicted by the atlases.

The differences noted in the Antarctic between climatic data and the 1972–3 observations are even more striking, particularly in the Ross and Weddell Seas where the observed ice cover is consistently less solid than shown in the atlas. For instance, according to the atlas the Ross Sea is never completely open to the South Pacific. Observations on both January 11 and 30 (Plates 5 and 6) show that the ice cover is less than 15% at the Ross Sea-Pacific boundary. In mid-December, there is considerable open water off the Ross Ice shelf, when the atlas would lead one to expect a 50–80% cover at that time. Such disparity between the synoptic observation via Nimbus-5 and the statistical prediction of the atlases aptly illustrates the need to observe sea ice distribution over large space scales at small time scales in order to develop and test dynamic rather than statistical models for more accurate forecasting. It is interesting also that the minimum ice cover that is climatically expected for the shore along Coats Land is greater than 50%, whereas it was observed to be less than 15% on January 30, 1973. Perhaps the most obvious difference between the observed and predicted ice boundaries of the Antarctic is that the observations, especially for mid-December, show large irregular perturbations around the ice edge whereas the seasonal averages in the atlases show smooth edges. These irregularities are new knowledge, unforeseen by statistics or intuition. So far, all of these observations are, of course, just for one particular season of one year. If Nimbus-5 and the ESMR meet or exceed their design lifetimes, we will be in a position to map these changes for a complete year and perhaps much more accurate statistics can be derived from similar observations in future years.

There are also indicated uncertainties in the shoreline of Antarctica (Daniels, 1957). An overlay of the atlas data on the ESMR image indicates discrepancies of several resolution elements at various places along the coastline. A judicious combination of ESMR maps and surface information may faciliate improvement of the accuracy of the coastline determination.

3. Ice pack density and ice dynamics observations

In Antarctica, there are two features of particular interest. First, the long finger of ice, less than 50% cover, that stretches out from the Palmer Peninsula and almost closes off the Weddell Sea on December 16, 1973 drifted about 8° due north by January 11, and was out of the field of view by January 30. The second interesting feature is the nature of the opening of the Ross Sea and the shoreline along Marie Byrd Land and the Ellsworth Highland. A distinct impression of a tearing away of the ice pack from the continent is given as the amount of open water progressively increases along the shoreline in the series of three scenes (Plates 4–6). In the case of the Ross Sea ice pack, the displacement of the jigsaw puzzle-like edge of the pack from the shoreline is suggestive of a shearing induced by a prevailing local wind. Although surface wind observations on the Ross Ice Shelf are not available for this period, suffcient studies have been

made (Rubin, 1959) to reveal a close correlation between the katabatic winds draining seaward off the shelf and the observed winds at McMurdo Station. These katabatic winds can be strong, with average wind velocities of about 25 knots for periods as long as several days to a week. During December 1972 and January 1973, the surface isobaric charts and wind records indicate that several periods of intense katabatic activity occurred on the Ross Ice Shelf. It appears that the katabatic winds strip the ice away from the shelf edge and transport it northward. The ambient surface wind flow on the Ross Sea during December 1972 was from the east. Thus, the ice distribution in the Ross Sea shown in Plate 4 results apparently from a combination of the southerly katabatic winds flowing off the Shelf and the ambient eastward winds acting on the ice north of the Shelf.

The U. S. Navy Atlas (Daniel, 1957) shows such a prevailing wind for November, but data were not available for December or January. The prevailing wind for February is shown as reversed, consistent with the apparent tearing away of the remaining pack ice from the shoreline of Marie Byrd Land.

The Arctic ice canopy, especially in the shear zones, is subject to large variations in the density in the pack. This will probably become more evident later when more than three synoptic views become available, but even in the views shown here (Plates 1–3) there is evidence of the pack in the East Laptev Sea becoming less dense as winter progresses, and as the ice in the Beaufort Sea becomes more consolidated. Changes in the consolidation of the pack ice in the Bering Sea are easily discerned in these three views, also, but since the ambient temperature is steadily decreasing, the observation may be related simply to the *in situ* freezing of the ice pack. The gradual decrease in the consolidation of the pack with distance off the eastern shore of Greenland is readily seen in the original color plates, but can also be observed on the black and white plates; the ice is 100% consolidated along the shoreline, has some patches of less than 20% open throughout, is largely 20% open for most of the area, has some fringed areas of about 35% open near the edge, and at the very edge has some areas of 50% open water. The accuracy of the determinations directly from the false-color images is approximately ±6% points based on the assumption that the bulk of the ice is first-year. Multiyear ice in this area injected by the Trans-Polar Drift Stream could affect these estimates, but the amount of multiyear ice so injected is unknown and assumed to be small. A large number of changes in this distribution are evident in the series of three plates.

4. Distribution of multiyear ice in the Arctic

The similarity of the average brightness temperature for multiyear ice and first-year ice with 20% open water on Plates 1–3 makes it difficult to determine the extent of multiyear ice coverage on a *prima facie* basis. Ultimately, when a full year's data become available, this task will become easier, since the ice that persists through a summer is by definition multiyear ice, and initial boundaries can be established which can be traced forwards or backwards into time. For the time being, we must be content to speculate on the basis of some very limited aircraft (Gloersen *et al.*, 1973; Campbell *et al.*, 1973) and surface data (Hibler *et al.*, 1973) accumulated over the Beaufort Sea and some qualitative knowledge of the ice dynamics in the Beaufort Sea. Perhaps the most surprising result is the finger of multiyear ice that apparently extends south to about 72°N in the Eastern Beaufort Sea. Such a southward extension of the multiyear ice was not expected on the basis of most current ice dynamics models (Rothrock, 1975). Support for these observations has been obtained recently also from ERTS-1 imagery (Campbell *et al.*, 1973).

5. Continental ice

Brightness temperatures measured over Greenland and Antarctica are lower than over any surface on Earth except for open water. They range from 130 to 160°K over the interior of Antarctica and from 155 to 200°K over Greenland.

In Antarctica, the brightness temperature patterns are related strongly, although not entirely, to the horizontal distribution of physical temperatures in the upper layer of the continental ice sheet, as determined from climatic records. This is not the case for Greenland, however, where the lowest brightness temperatures (155°K) are measured over the northern and southwestern portions. In those regions, the elevation of the ice sheet is lower (and the surface temperature is therefore probably higher) than the center of the ice plateau where about 40°K higher brightness temperatures are observed.

The emissivities inferred from these measurements over Greenland and Antarctica and from climatic records of upper layer temperatures range from 0.65 to 0.75, except for some Antarctic glaciers, especially the Lambert Glacier, and the Amery, Ross, and Filchner Ice Shelves which have an emissivity of about 0.8. Generally higher emissivities, namely 0.75, 0.85, and 0.95 obtained over the South Cascade Glacier in the North Cascade Mountains, Washington (Schmugge *et al.*, 1974), over multiyear sea ice (Wilheit *et al.*, 1973, Gloersen *et al.*, 1973), and over first-year sea ice (*ibid.*), respectively. These latter emissivities were derived from airborne radiometer measurements at 1.55 cm and 11 micrometers during the winters of 1971/72 and 1970/71. We believe that these differing emissivities must be attributed to varying crystaline forms, amounts of entrapped air, depth and frequency of fissures, and, at least in the case of sea ice, amounts of entrapped brine in the freeboard layer.

A preliminary analysis of the Antarctic and Greenland ice sheet emissivities derived from the ESMR measurements shows that they are practically constant for the period from December 1972 to July 1973. We conclude, therefore, that this invariance of emissivities with seasons is a further indication that they are correlated primarily with structural rather than with temperature variations in the ice.

6. Conclusions

We have shown here some of the early results from the data acquired by the ESMR on board the Nimbus-5 satellite. It is clear that imaging thermally emitted microwaves with satellites is a powerful tool for studying sea ice coverage, type, and distribution in the polar areas of Earth. The independence of this technique from cloud cover in the polar regions will permit a detailed study of the sea ice characteristics as a function of time. The ESMR images are already being used operationally as an aid to navigation in polar waters (Ellinghausen, 1973). More analysis will be done when a larger data base has been acquired. Work in progress includes a more precise determination of the actual extent of the multiyear ice pack in the Arctic, observations of the ice pack motion on a longer time scale using smaller time intervals, a study of the open water distribution as a function of time, and finally a test of the consequences of utilizing the open water distribution information in a global weather model study. It is hoped that the early results presented here will inspire others to conceive still other applications of these data.

REFERENCES

Campbell, W. J., P. Gloersen, W. Nordberg, and T. T. Wilheit, Dynamics and morphology of Beaufort Sea ice determined from satellites, aircraft, and drifting stations, Paper No. A.5.6, Proc. of the Symp. on Approaches to Earth Sciences through the Use of Space Technology, COSPAR WG6 (1973).

Daniel, H. C., Oceanographic atlas of the polar seas, U. S. Navy Hydrographic Office Publication No. 705; Part I Antarctic (1957), Part II Arctic (1958).

Dicke, R. H., The measurement of thermal radiation at microwave frequencies, *Rev. Sci. Inst.* **17**, 280 (1946).

Edgerton, A. T., A. Stogryn, D. P. Williams, and G. Poe, A study of the microwave emission characteristics of sea ice, Summary Report 1741R-2, NOAA/NESS Contract No. 1-35139 (1971).

Ellinghausen, W. A., Priv. comm. (1973) (U. S. Navy Fleet Facility Service.)

Gloersen, P., W. Nordberg, T. J. Schmugge, T. T. Wilheit, and W. J. Campbell, Microwave signatures of first-year and multiyear sea ice, *J. Geoph. Res.* **78**, 3564 (1973).

Hibler, W., W. Weeks, S. Ackley, A. Kovacs, and W. Campbell, Mesoscale strain measurements on the Beaufort Sea pack ice, *J. Glaciol.* **12**, 65, 187–206 (1973).

Rothrock, D., The steady drift of an incompressible ice cover in the Arctic Ocean, Proc. of Climate of the Arctic, 24th Alaska Science Conference (1975).

Rubin, M. J., Advection across the Antarctic boundary, Proceedings of the Antarctic Meteorology Symposium held in Melbourne (1959).

Schmugge, T., T. T. Wilheit, P. Gloersen, M. F. Meier, D. Frank, and I. Dirnhirm, Microwave signatures of snow and fresh water ice, Paper No. 5.12, Proc. of the Interdisciplinary Symp. on Adv. Concepts and Techniques in the Study of Snow and Ice Resources, Asilomar, 551–562 (1974).

Wilheit, T. T., The electronically scanning microwave radiometer (ESMR), pp. 59–104, The Nimbus-5 User's Guide, U. S. Government Printing Office 1972–735–963/259 (1972).

Wilheit, T. T., W. Nordberg, J. Blinn, W. Campbell, and A. Edgerton, Aircraft measurements of microwave emission from Arctic sea ice, *Remote Sensing of Environment* **2**, 129 (1973).

Environmental Research and Applications Using the Very High Resolution Radiometer (VHRR) on the NOAA-2 Satellite— A Pilot Project in Alaska

E. Paul McClain

National Oceanic and Atmospheric Administration, Washington, D. C.

Abstract

The VHRR is a new experimental scanning radiometer carried on NOAA's most recent operational environmental satellite. It detects reflected solar radiation in the visible range and emitted terrestrial radiation in the thermal infrared band. Ground resolution of both types of data is one kilometer at nadir. Although the VHRR is primarily a direct-readout device, a single pass transmitted to NOAA's command and data acquisition (CDA) station near Fairbanks, Alaska is over 2000 km wide and covers an area from northwest Greenland westward across the Arctic Ocean to as far as the East Siberian Sea. Since the launch of the NOAA-2 satellite in October 1972, rather complete VHRR coverage of Alaska and neighboring seas has been obtained through a full ice season.

The National Environmental Satellite Service of NOAA has contracted with the Geophysical Institute, University of Alaska, to manage and operate an Alaska VHRR Pilot Project. Commencing September 1, 1973, the pilot project has as its goal the development and testing of operational techniques for applying VHRR data to environmental problems in Alaska. The VHRR observations are to be analyzed by an interdisciplinary research team experienced in meteorology, hydrology, and oceanology. Operational analyses of VHRR data will be conducted on a daily, nearly real time basis, by an interdisciplinary team of specialists stationed part-time at the CDA station near Fairbanks. The development or improvement of analysis techniques and the evaluation of their feasibility and effectiveness will be carried out by the research team at the University of Alaska.

If enough of the objectives of the pilot project are successfully met, it could well evolve into a regular service for many of the numerous environmental data users, both research and operational, in the Alaska area. The project is also expected to provide support to such efforts as the Arctic Ice Dynamics Joint Experiment (AIDJEX) and the Polar Experiment (POLEX).

---

1. Introduction

The Alaska area abounds in environmental variety, contrasts, and extremes. It possesses an enormous coastline that ranges from the relatively mild and ice-free perimeter of the Gulf of Alaska to the seasonally ice-bound borders of the Bering, Chukchi, and Beaufort Seas. Major mountain ranges rim the Gulf of Alaska to the south and another sprawls along the Arctic Circle to the north. The mighty Yukon and numerous other rivers drain the plains or the North Slope. Many of man's activities are vulnerable to the environmental vagaries of this large and diverse land, operations as varied as the Bristol Bay fisheries or the exploitation of petroleum reserves on the North Slope. Conventional ground-based or ship-based environmental observations are few and far between in this sparsely-inhabited region of climatic extremes.

Although weather forecasting services and, to a lesser extent, sea ice surveillance, have benefited from the availability of environmental satellite pictures for at least five years now, the resolving power of the satellite sensors was too gross for some meteorological, and nearly all oceanographic and hydrological, usage. The addition of the Very High Resolution Radiometer (VHRR) on the NOAA-2 operational satellite in October 1972 has opened up the possiblity for more varied and more effective application of satellite data to supplement and complement the sparse networks of land and ship stations in and around Alaska.

The National Environmental Satellite Service of NOAA near Washington, D. C. has contracted with the Geophysical Institute, University of Alaska, to manage and operate an Alaska VHRR Pilot Project commencing Sept. 1, 1973. The pilot project has as its goal the development and testing of operational techniques for applying VHRR data to environmental problems in Alaska. The VHRR observations are to be analyzed by an interdisciplinary research team experienced in meteorology, hydrology, and oceanography. Operational analyses will be conducted on a daily, nearly real time basis, by an inter-disciplinary team of specialists stationed part-time at NOAA's satellite command and data acquisition (CDA) station at Gilmore Creek near Fairbanks. The development or improvement of analy-

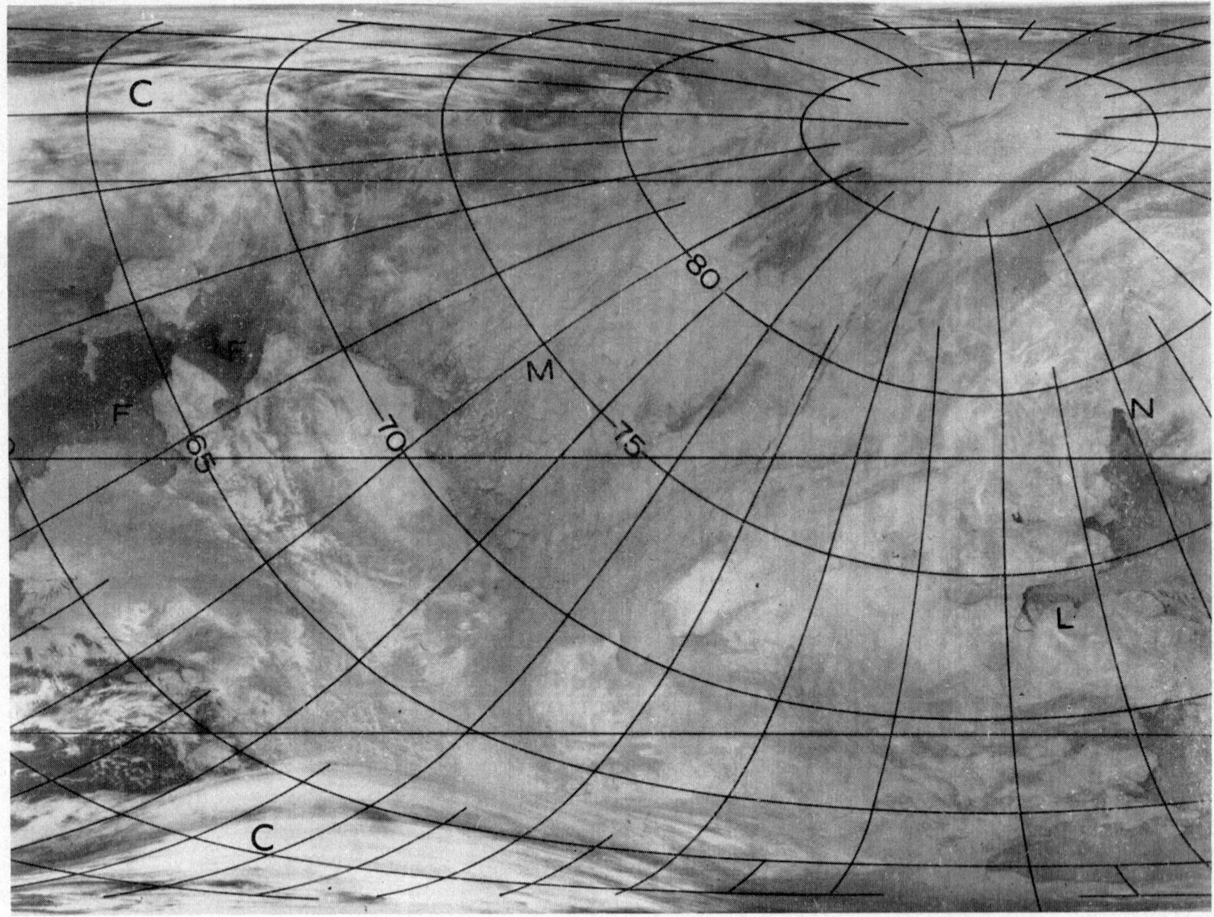

FIG. 1. VHRR-IR image, 12-15-72. Satellite thermal infrared images are conventionally displayed such that the warmer the radiating surface, the darker the tone. Open water appears the darkest and thick clouds or snow-covered land the brightest. North Water (N); Lancaster Sound (L); multiyear ice in Beaufort Sea (M); first-year ice in Norton and Kotzebue Sounds (F); thick cloud layers (C).

sis techniques and evaluation of their feasibility will be carried out by the research team at the University of Alaska.

2. The NOAA-2 satellite and the VHRR

The first experimental TIROS weather satellite was placed in orbit about the Earth in April 1960. The TIROS R&D satellites evolved five years later into the TIROS Operational Satellite (TOS) system, which provided daily cloud cover on a global basis by means of the Advanced Vidicon Camera System (AVCS) on board the ESSA-1, 3, ..., 9 satellites. Local direct readout of cloud pictures to an ever-growing number of simple ground stations the world over was provided by the APT (Automatic Picture Transmission) system on the ESSA-2, 4,..., 8 satellites.

The next generation, called Improved TIROS Operational Satellites (ITOS), which like the ESSA series were in near-polar, sun-synchronous, circular orbits at a nominal altitude of 1500 km, began with ITOS-1 early in 1970. ITOS-1 combined the AVCS and APT functions in a single spacecraft, and it also carried the first dual-channel (visible and thermal infrared) Scanning Radiometer (SR) for global and local direct readout coverage. ITOS-1 was followed by NOAA-1 about a year later, NOAA-2 being placed in orbit in October of 1972. A significant change in sensor complement took place with NOAA-2: no vidicon cameras were included and their global and local readout functions were assumed by the SR; and a dual-channel Very High Resolution Radiometer (VHRR) was added (Schwalb, 1972).

The SR is a two-channel scanning instrument sensitive to reflected solar energy in the 0.5–0.7 μm visible spectrum and to emitted thermal energy in that part of the water vapor "window" region from 10.5–12.5 μm. The visible data have a nominal ground resolution at nadir of 3.5 km, whereas the thermal infrared measurements can resolve details to no better than about 8 km.

The VHRR is very similar to the SR in many respects. The visible band pass is somewhat narrower, being 0.6–0.7 μm, but that of the thermal energy detector is identical. The main differences are that the VHRR's scanning mirror must rotate much faster than that of the SR, and the infrared detectors are rather different on the two radiometers. A thermistor bolometer on the SR is replaced by a mercury-cadmium-telluride detector, which must be cooled to an operating temperature near 105 K, on the VHRR. The designed instantaneous field-of-view of each channel is 0.6 milliradians, yielding a ground resolution at nadir of about one kilometer. Although the SR and VHRR were designed primarily as imagers, provision was made for onboard calibration of both channels.

The Very High Resolution Radiometer (VHRR) is designed primarily for direct readout use, but the required ground station is considerably more costly than that needed for local readout of SR data. NOAA presently is able to read out VHRR data at its two CDA stations, one at Wallops Island, Virginia and the other near Fairbanks, Alaska. A third NOAA VHRR data acquisition station will go into operation early in 1974 near San Francisco. The area that can be covered in the direct readout mode is rather large, viz. a strip of about 2200 km wide and more than 5000 km long for the satellite pass most nearly overhead. The VHRR also has a stored-data mode, but its capacity is very limited, viz. eight minutes (about 8%) per orbit. This yields an image about 2200 km wide and 2200 km long.

3. The Alaska VHRR pilot project

The operational analysis objectives of the pilot project are the use of VHRR data, together with the often sparse conventional observations, to detect, interpret, analyze, and monitor important meteorological, hydrological, or oceanic features, phenomena, or events. These will include fronts, cloud types, sea ice cover and temperature, sea surface temperatures and gradients, river and lake ice conditions, snow cover, flood conditions, and other environmental conditions. The images themselves and information derived from their analysis will be transmitted to NOAA offices in Fairbanks and

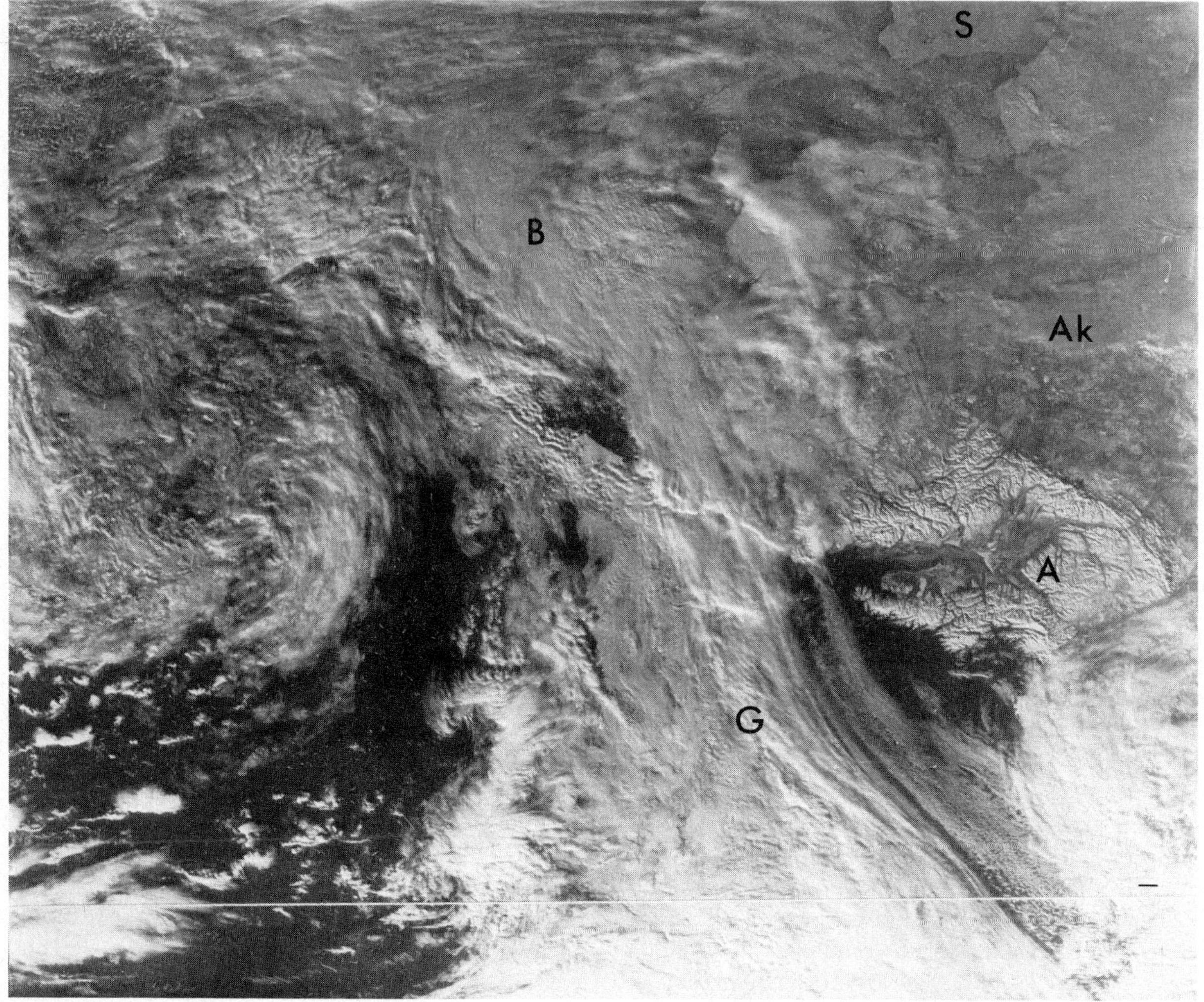

Fig. 2. VHRR-VIS, 2-18-73. Western Alaska (Ak), Bering Sea (B), and northern Gulf of Alaska (G). Cloud layers cover much of the area, but the eastern tip of Siberia (S) and the Bering Strait are dimly seen under a low sun, and the Cook Inlet and Anchorage area (A) are free of cloud.

FIG. 3. VHRR-VIS, 2-18-73. Enlargement of that portion of Fig. 2 in and around Anchorage, Alaska (A). Ice is present in the northern and eastern portions of Cook Inlet (C), and Tustumena Lake (T) is frozen and snow-covered.

Anchorage via special image-transmission devices for further distribution on an experimental basis to other federal, State, or local agencies or private groups in Anchorage and elsewhere in Alaska.

Objectives in the development of data interpretation techniques will be to use the VHRR data in the identification of selected environmental features of special importance to Alaska and to study their interrelationships. In the field of meteorology this analysis will include: development of thunderstorms, including their spatial and temporal distributions and relations to forest fires; sea water temperature as an indicator of impending coastal fogs; extent of fog over ocean areas; feasibility of identifying strong wind conditions on mountain passes, especially in S.E. Alaska; determination of cloud type and probable ceiling; the effects of mountain ranges in cloud development; and feasibility of distinguishing the frost line.

The oceanographic analyses will include determination of sea ice cover and surface temperature and water surface temperature. The information will be related to oceanic circulation features, such as upwelling and currents, and temperature distribution pertaining to regional climatology.

The hydrologic analyses will include determination of snow cover and temperature, land freeze-up conditions, lake and river ice and temperature, beginning of run-off, flood extent, and ice jams. This information will be related to forecasting activities such as flood prediction, break-up extent and ice conditions.

Delays in obtaining suitable equipment for real time display of VHRR imager from the signals received and taped at the Gilmore Creek CDA station dictate that the first four months or so of the pilot project be confined to training and research based chiefly on VHRR data acquired between November 1972 and November

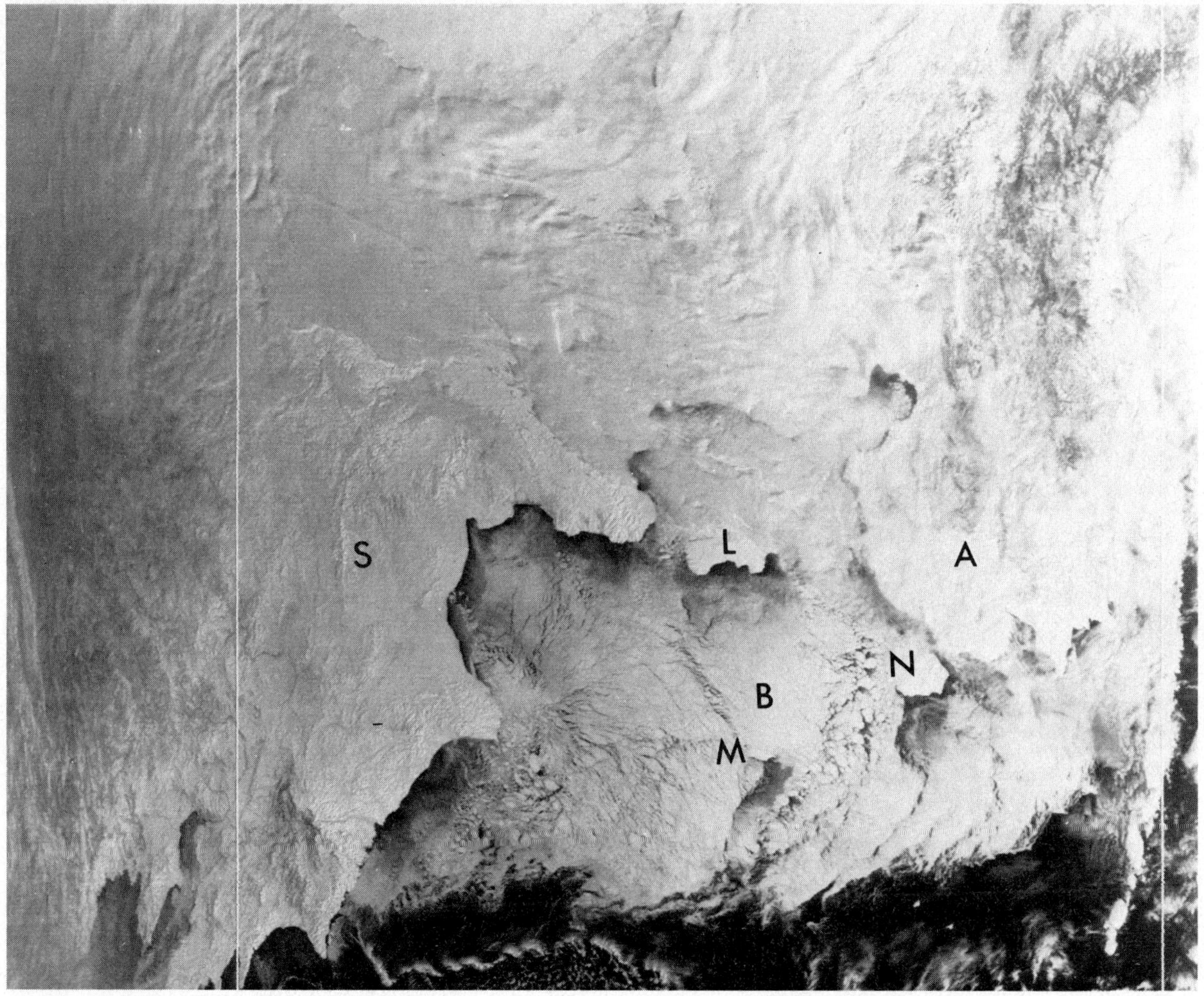

FIG. 4. VHRR-VIS, 3-31-73. This scene exhibits a variety of ice features and structure in the Bering Sea (B). Snow-covered Siberia (S) and interior Alaska (A) are virtually cloudfree. Newer, thinner and less-reflective ice appears just south or east of the Siberian coast, St. Lawrence Island (L), St. Mathew Island (M) and Nunivak Island (N) where refreezing of the inshore waters is taking place as the pack moves offshore.

of this year.* These data have been acquired and displayed in two rather different ways. Some have been acquired by direct readout to the Alaska CDA station, the analog tapes being mailed to the NOAA/NESS central facility outside Washington, D. C. The VHRR images are then generated on the prototype model of a specialized laser-exposure display device with self-contained, dry-type, photo-processor, called the VHRRFAX, which produces a film positive or negative. Fairly complete VHRR coverage of the North American side of the Arctic from Greenland westward across the Beaufort, Chukchi, and Bering Seas to areas deep into the East Siberian Sea was obtained from December 1972 until the present.* The 1-km resolution infrared data enabled useful imagery of sea ice, clouds, and other features even during the months of polar darkness (Fig. 1).

* Editor's note: 1973.

Other VHRR data have been acquired for the Alaska area via the stored-data mode (called VREC) and subsequently transmitted from the satellite to the Virginia CDA station. From here the data are relayed by landline to the NOAA/NESS central facility, and then fed into a digital picture terminal (DPT) for generation of the image. The DPT output is an exposed negative, which requires conventional darkroom processing to produce a developed negative, prints, etc. The VREC data mode has been used for over the past six months to obtain coverage of the Beaufort and Bering Seas, resp., on alternate days.

Although the VIIRRFAX device was originally intended to be the display device used at the Alaska CDA station for the VHRR pilot project, technical and manufacturing problems led to a change in plans. Now it is planned to employ a modified version of the sectorizer display equipment being built for use with the

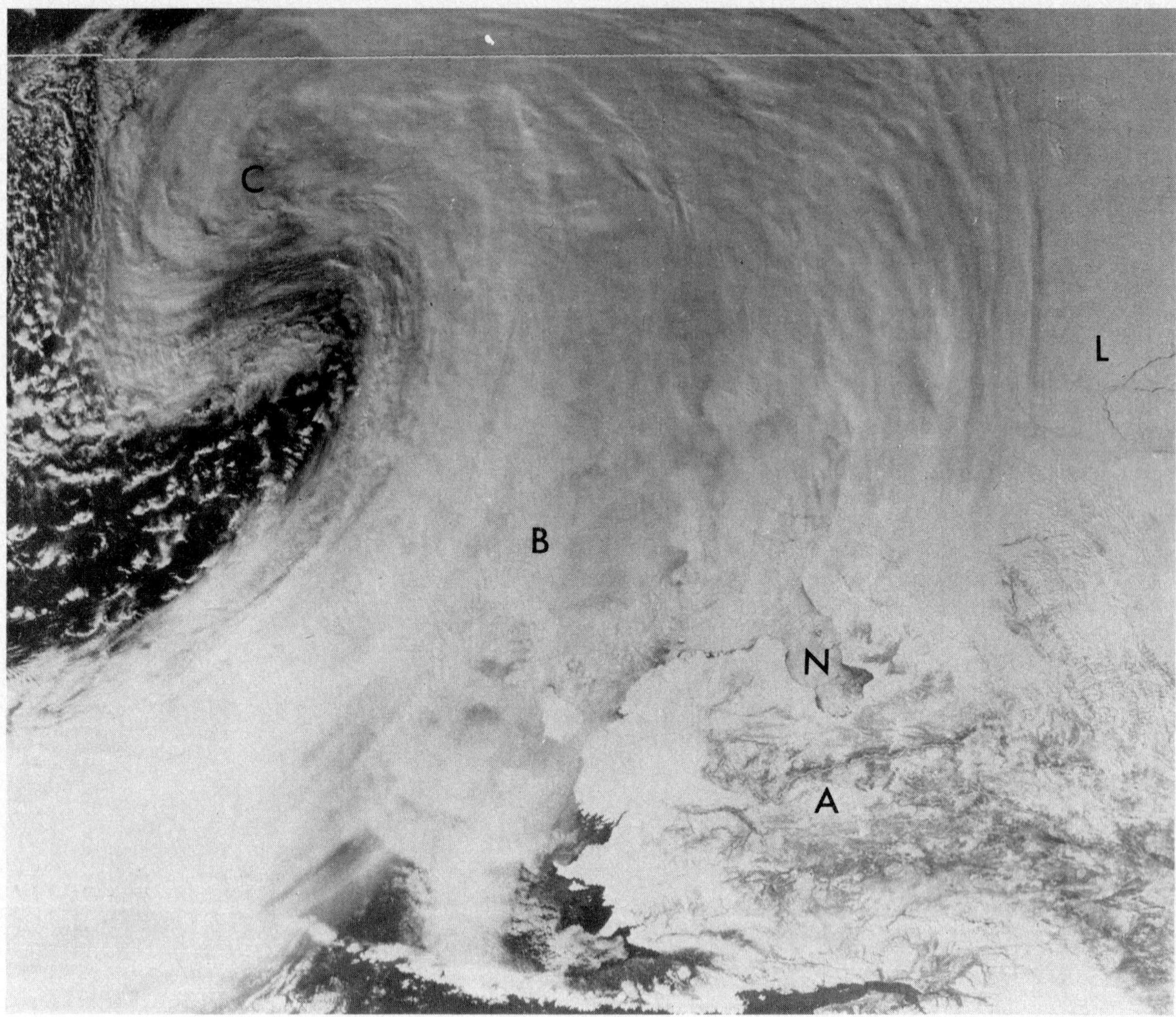

FIG. 5. VHRR-VIS, 4-4-73. Although nearly all of central and western Alaska (A) are cloudfree, the deep clouds of a strong cyclone (C) cover the Bering Sea (B). Norton Sound (N) is filled with ice, but some rather large leads (L) are visible in the pack ice just off the North Slope.

operational geostationary satellite to be launched in 1974. This device, called the VHRR Sectorizer Display (VSD), employs a minicomputer, and at one stage in the processing the analog data are digitized. This provides much more flexibility for image enhancement and for quantitative manipulation of the VHRR data than is the case with the VHRRFAX. Furthermore, the VSD can be used to transmit VHRR data over conditioned phone lines for purposes of remote display on commercially available digital picture terminals.

Present plans call for installation of VSD systems at the Alaska and Virginia CDA stations and at the VHRR data acquisition station near San Francisco early in 1974. The VSD at Wallops Station, Virginia will transmit to a DPT in the NOAA/NESS central facility in Suitland, Maryland. The VSD systems near Fairbanks and San Francisco will have co-located picture terminals. The Fairbanks VSD, however, will transmit its VHRR images experimentally to NOAA's National Weather Service (NWS) regional office in Anchorage. Two experiment modes are envisioned: one involves an image scanner at Gilmore Creek, transmission over an ordinary telephone line to Anchorage, and regeneration of a somewhat degraded image by a display device there. The second would require a suitable DPT in Anchorage and a conditioned (C5) telephone line, but there would be no loss in picture quality in transmission.

The number of personnel available to the Alaska VHRR Pilot Project permit the equivalent of only a single-shift, five days per week, type of operation, and it was felt to be desirable also that the pilot project staff be somewhat removed from the pressures of a real time operational posture. The VHRR data will be read out at the CDA station at Gilmore Creek on the average of six to eight times daily and the images,

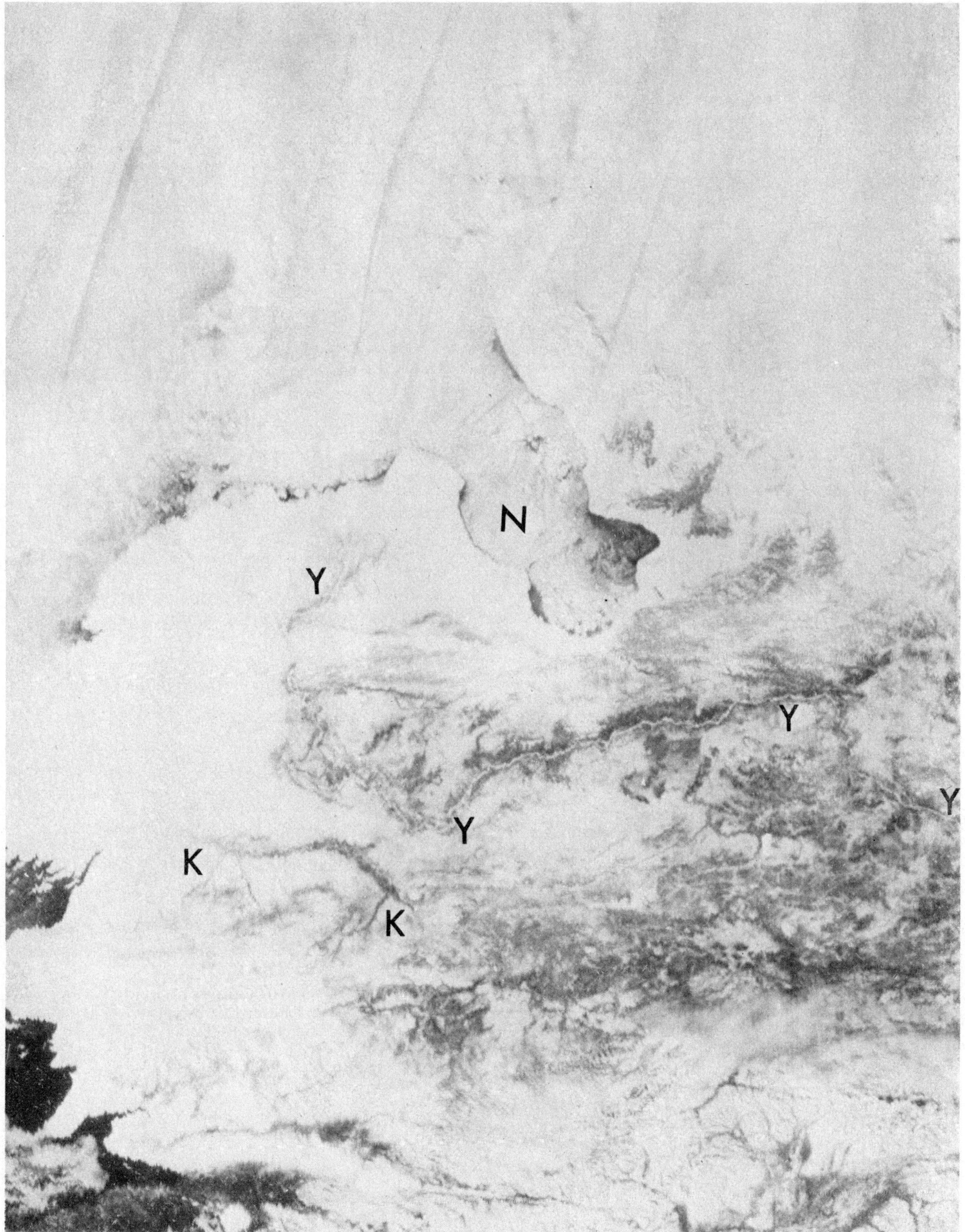

FIG. 6. VHRR-VIS, 4-4-73. This is an enlargement of a portion of Fig. 5. Ice-choked Norton Sound (N) has some areas of new ice formation in the inner part of the sound. The frozen and snow-covered Yukon River (Y) and Kuskokwin River (K) stand out clearly where snow-covered but darker-toned forest areas exist in the river bottoms. Non-forested snow-covered areas, such as in the coastal regions, appear uniformly very bright.

FIG. 7. VHRR-VIS, 6-7-73. A variety of ice conditions and floe sizes are in evidence around Banks Island (B), which is in the process of rapidly losing its snow cover. A very large polynya has opened up west of Banks Island, and the thawing and less reflective ice in Amundsen Gulf (A) to the south is starting to break up and move out into the mostly cloud-obscured Beaufort Sea (S). A bit of the North Slope coastline near Harrison Bay (H) is visible.

FIG. 8. VHRR-VIS, 6-13-73. Same area as Fig. 7 but almost one week later. Banks Island (B) is almost completely free of snow, but remains essentially locked in thawing fast ice or pack ice, especially in McClure Strait (M) to the north. The break-up and westward movement of ice from Amundsen Gulf (A) continues. Wrangell Island (W) in the East Siberian Sea is visible, although cloud covers much of the rest of the Chukchi and Beaufort Seas.

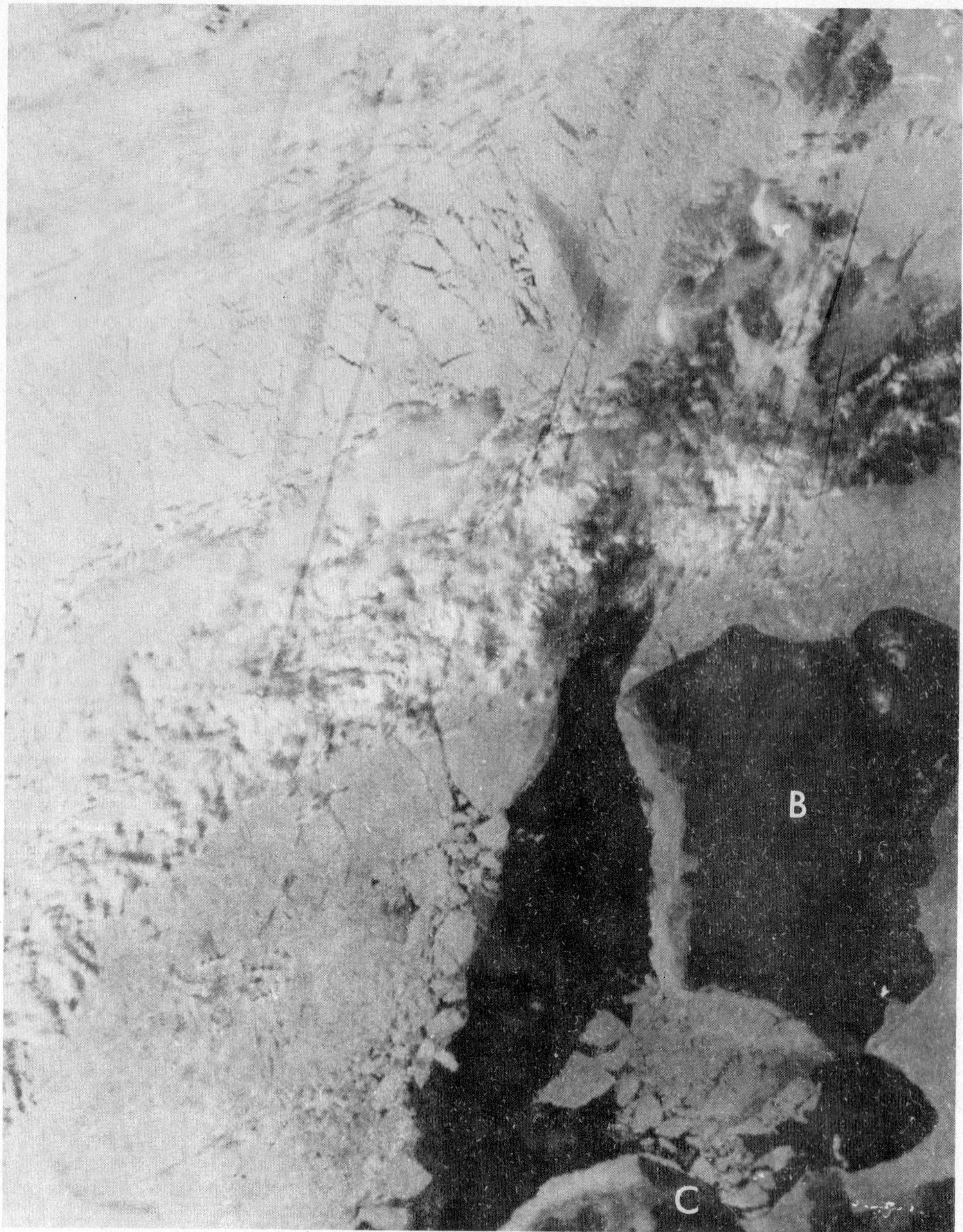

FIG. 9. VHRR-VIS, 6-13-73. This scene is an enlargement of part of Fig. 8. Note the fast ice structure along the west shore of Banks Island (B) and around Cape Bathurst (C), where the darkest portions of the ice appear to be flooded by river outflows.

FIG. 10. VHRR-VIS, 6-19-73. Same area as Figs. 7 and 8, but twelve and six days later, resp. Note the further breakup and drift of ice out of Amundsen Gulf just south of Banks Island (B). A sizable polynya has opened up north of Wrangel Island (W) also.

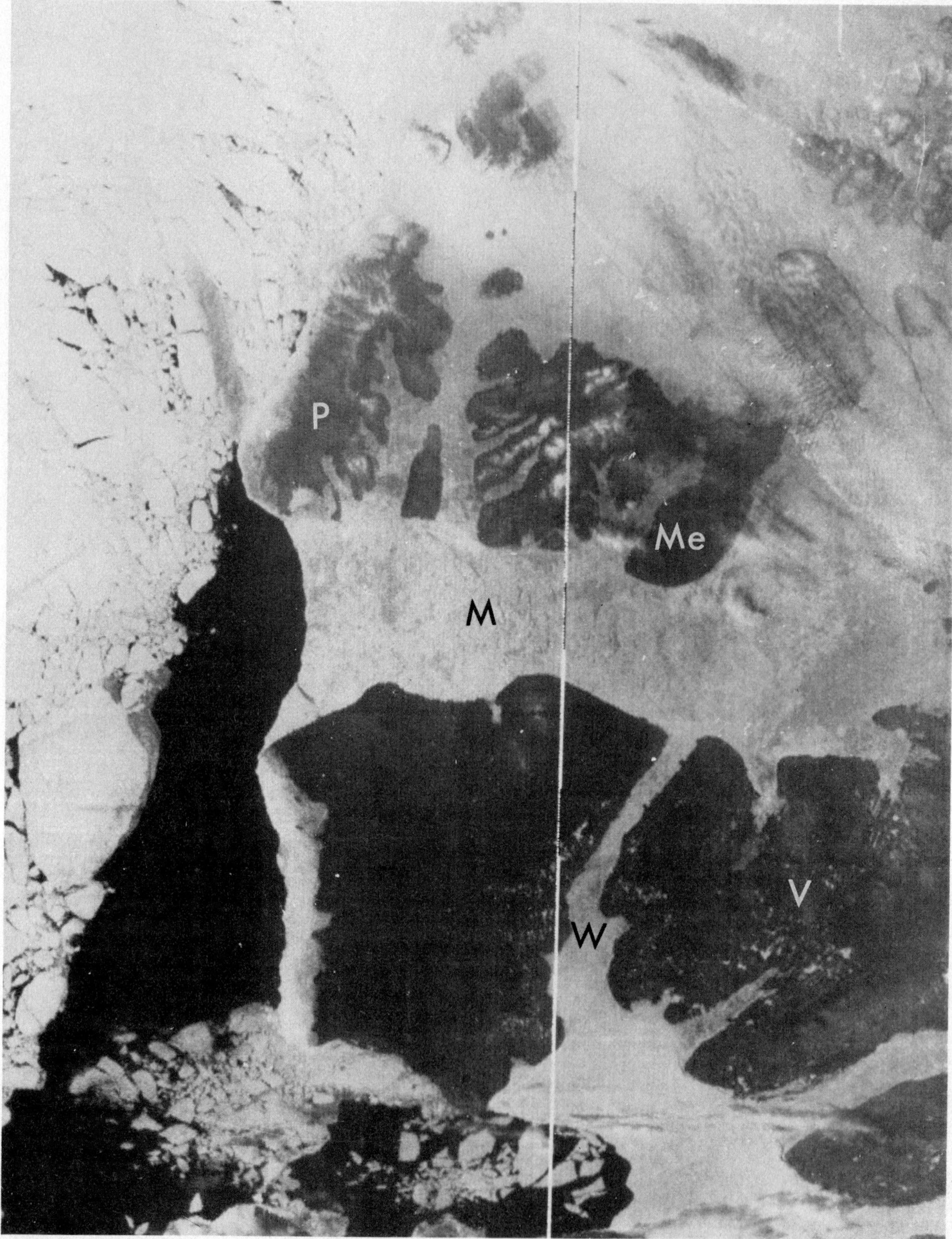

FIG. 11. VHRR-VIS, 6-19-73. An enlargement of a part of Fig. 10. Thawing ice still chokes McClure Strait (M), Prince of Wales Strait (W) and the sounds of Prince Patrick Island (P), Melville Island (Me) and Victoria Island (V), with snow still present at the higher elevations on Prince Patrick and Melville.

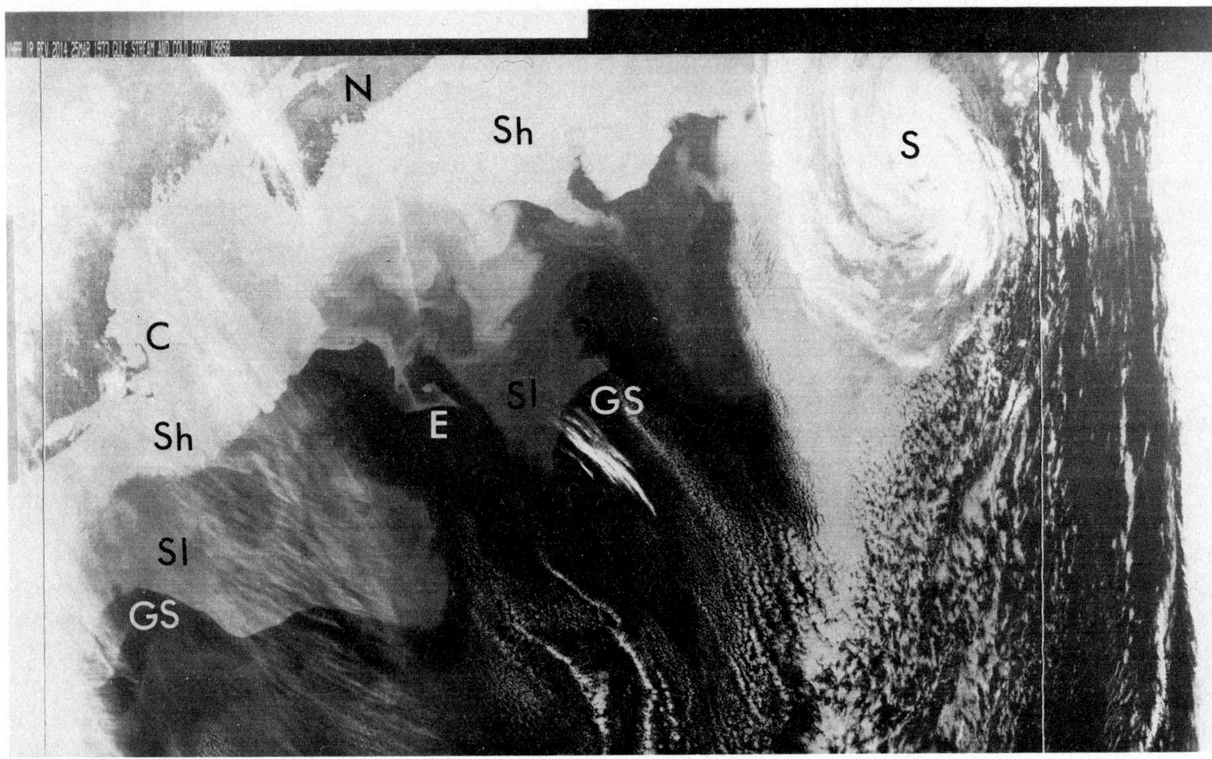

FIG. 12. VHRR-IR, 3-25-73. This thermal infrared image illustrates the type of enhancement that is possible after VHRR data are digitized. The cold cloud tops of a strong storm (S) are seen northeast of Nova Scotia (N) and Cape Cod (C). The various thermal fronts defined by the ocean surface temperature contrasts between warm Gulf Stream (GS) water, cool slope water (SI), and colder shelf water (Sh) have been greatly deformed by the passage of this storm through the area. Even a mesoscale eddy (E) has been generated.

visible and infrared, displayed by means of the VSD. Many of the images will be displayed more than once so that special enhancement for oceanographic or hydrologic purposes can be accomplished. Darkroom equipment will enable production of working and archival prints, transparencies, duplicate negatives, etc. for the operational specialists and researchers of the project and for an archive to be maintained at the NOAA/NESS central facility in Suitland. Location will be achieved by fitting of universal grid overlays to landmarks or rectification of the image by means of an optical device and landmarks.

Near real time analysis of the VHRR images will be performed by the operational specialists in the several disciplines with the aid of high quality optical devices for image magnification, rotation, stretching, and transfer. After the analyzed information is transcribed to base charts or other form of line graphics, it can be transmitted to Anchorage readily via line scanner or telecopier devices and an ordinary telephone line. For comparative and backup purposes, VHRR prints or transparencies may also be forwarded to Anchorage daily via scheduled airlines. Figs. 2 through 11 represent VHRR images and enlargements covering a variety of Alaska area scenes from which meteorological, oceano-

graphic (McClain, 1973a, b), or hydrological information (Wiesnet and McGinnis, 1973; Wiesnet, 1973) can be obtained. Fig. 12 is an example of a VHRR image that has been specially enhanced for displaying ocean thermal features (Stumpf et al., 1973; Strong and DeRycke, 1973).

4. Concluding remarks

Although the VHRR was designed primarily as an analog *imager*, and some calibration problems were revealed during pre-launch thermal-vacuum tests, a small amount of IR data has been digitized and preliminary analyses made. These would indicate that, in spite of some increase in signal-to-noise ratio due to condensation of out-gassing products on the detector surface, the data appear to be stable and with a surprisingly low noise level. It is anticipated that with some dependence upon cross calibration with simultaneous SR temperatures and external calibration against known Earth targets, it may be possible to achieve better than 2 C absolute values and near 1 C relative values of effective blackbody temperatures of the sea surface, water or ice, and continuous snow surfaces.

TABLE 1.

Federal Agency	Some types of environmental data needed
NOAA/National Marine Fisheries Service	Upwelling water temp., sea ice, coastal currents, weather.
NOAA/National Weather Service	Clouds, weather, winds, land and water temps., sea ice.
NOAA/National Ocean Survey	Currents, water temp., coastline mapping, sea ice.
Coast Guard	Currents, water temp., sea ice.
Environmental Protection Agency	Sediment discharge into coastal areas, thermal maps of rivers and lakes.
Forest Service	Lightning strikes, smoke, thunderstorms, floods, snow cover.
Soil Conservation Service	Water level, snow cover, floods, soil moisture and temperature.
Geological Survey	Floods, water-level, geologic structure, sediment, permafrost, ice, geothermal studies.
Department of Defense	Weather, ice, permafrost, lakes and river ice and temps., soil moisture, coastal and ocean temps and currents.
Alaska Power Administration	Snowmelt and snow pack and glacier conditions, water level, floods.
Bureau Land Management	Climatal and land use, thermal land maps, thunderstorms, forest fires.

TABLE 2.

State Agencies	Some types of environmental data needed
Health and Welfare	Floods, extreme weather, forest fires.
Natural Resources	Forest fires, coastal sediment, surface water, land use.
Fish and Game	Forest fires, land and water temp., ice on lakes and rivers.
Highways and Public Works	Weather, snow cover, ice on lakes and rivers, permafrost.
University of Alaska	
Agricultural Experiment Station	Snow and ice cover, floods, soil moisture and temperature.
Water Resources Institute	Snow and ice, lake and river freeze/thaw.
Geophysical Institute	Geothermal mapping, volcanic eruptions. Meteorological and hydrological research.
Institute of Marine Science	Oceanographic research
Dept. Land Resources and Agricultural Sciences	Land use, snow cover, soil moisture and temperature.
Dept. of Geology	Geothermal mapping, glaciers, volcanic eruptions, geomorphology.
Dept. of Geography	Land forms, coastal ice, climatic factors.
Sea Grant Program	Oceanographic research.

TABLE 3.

Private Industry	Some types of environmental data needed
Commercial aviation and private aviation	Clouds, weather, freeze conditions on lakes.
Construction industry	Weather, permafrost, snow cover, lake and river ice, coastal currents and temps, soil moisture, flooding, thaw conditions.
Agricultural interests	Freeze/thaw conditions, weather, flooding, soil moisture.
Mineral exploration	Thermal maps for geologic structure and reconnaissance mapping.
Petroleum industry	Coastal ice maps, coastal currents, winds, thermal maps for geologic structure.
Commercial fisheries	Coastal temp. and currents, weather, sea ice.

A secondary aspect of the pilot project will be the development of contacts with the various federal, state, and local agencies, and nonpublic organizations, who could possibly make use of VHRR information in their areas of activity. Many of these groups are located in the Anchorage or Fairbanks areas where a VHRR service could be provided most easily. The organizations in Tables 1–3 are likely to be included among such groups.

If enough of the objectives of the pilot project are successfully met, it could well evolve into a regular service for many of the numerous environmental data users, research and operational, in the Alaska area. This could take the form of a Satellite Field Serivce Station (SFSS) being established, probably in Anchorage, and staffed by NOAA/NESS. The Alaska VHRR Pilot Project, and later perhaps a SFSS, is also expected to provide useful support to such large-scale research efforts as the Arctic Ice Dynamics Experiment (AIDJEX) and the Polar Experiment (POLEX) associated with the Global Atmospheric Research Program (GARP).

REFERENCES

McClain, E. P., 1973a: Earth satellite measurements as applied to sea ice measurements. Proceed. of Symposium on Approaches to Earth Sciences through the Use of Space Technology, COSPAR Working Group 6, Konstanz, Germany, May 1973.

McClain, E. P., 1973b: Some new satellite measurements and their application to sea ice analysis in the Arctic and Antarctic. Proceed. of IHD Interdisciplinary Symposium on Advanced Concepts and Techniques in Study of Snow and Ice Resources, Monterey, Calif., Dec. 1973.

Schwalb, A., 1972: Modified version of the improved TIROS operational satellite (ITOS D-G). NOAA Technical Memorandum NESS-35. Washington, D. C. 48 p.

Strong, A. E., and R. J. DeRycke, 1973: Ocean current monitoring employing a new satellite sensing technique. *Science* **182**, 482–484.

Stumpf, H. G., A. E. Strong and J. Pritchard, 1973: Large cyclonic eddies of the Sargasso Sea. *Mariners Weather Log,* **17**, 208–210.

Wiesnet, D. R., and D. F. McGinnis, 1973: Hydrologic applications of the NOAA-2 very high resolution radiometer. *Remote Sensing and Water Resources Management* (Edited by K. P. B. Thompson, R. K. Lane and S. C. Csallany). American Water Resources Association, Urbana, Illinois, p. 179–190.

Wiesnet, D. R., 1973: The role of satellites in snow and ice measurements. IHD Interdisciplinary Symposium on Advanced Concepts and Techniques in Study of Snow and Ice Resources, Monterey, Calif., Dec. 1973.

Some Elements of a Scientific Plan for POLEX

N. Untersteiner

AIDJEX, University of Washington

Abstract

It is suggested that, as a contribution to POLEX, theoretical models and field experiments be pursued with particular emphasis on the factors influencing the position of the outer boundaries of sea ice. While the theory should be applicable to both arctic and antarctic sea ice, the initial emphasis of field work should be in the North Atlantic. Other recommended studies concern the shear zone (land boundary of arctic sea ice) and the expansion of the numerical ice model being developed under AIDJEX to cover the entire Arctic Basin. In addition, it is proposed to numerically model the lateral boundaries of an ice-covered region, allowing for both dynamic and thermodynamic effects. A time plan is given of recommended theoretical and experimental work between the present and about 1980.

NOTE

At a meeting in June 1973, the Joint Panel for POLEX of the National Academy of Sciences undertook the development of a scientific plan for the U. S. contribution to POLEX. The following article is one of several contributions that have been prepared by different members of the Panel, and it reflects personal views of the author only. A comprehensive report by the Joint Panel, including scientific background and recommended new research activities, was completed in December 1973 and has been published by the National Academy of Sciences (NAS, 1974).

1. Introduction

The POLAR EXPERIMENT (POLEX), as originally proposed by Soviet scientists (Borisenkov and Treshnikov, 1971), aims at an understanding of the mass and energy exchange between the atmosphere and the oceans at high latitudes. It seems uncertain whether the extensive observational systems envisioned in the general POLEX objectives can become a reality within the next few years. We therefore propose to concentrate primarily on improving our understanding of the physical processes controlling the boundaries of drift and pack ice in the world oceans, with an initial emphasis on the Northern Hemisphere. If suitable theoretical concepts can be established and supported by field observations, it should be possible to include sea ice variations in the calculations of world climate. Such concepts should be applicable to both the Northern and the Southern Hemisphere.

POLEX has now acquired the status of a recognized subprogram of the Global Atmospheric Research Programme (GARP) (Fig. 1) [1973]. For purposes of the first GARP objective (improvement of de-terministic weather forecasting) it is sufficient to introduce the position of the edge of the pack ice as an external parameter. Free ice drift velocities range up to 100 km per day. In extreme cases, the addition of ice drift and local formation of new ice may displace the ice boundary one or two points (400–800 km) in the proposed basic GARP modeling grid, but the rarity of such events obviates the inclusion of time-dependent ice boundaries in deterministic models of the atmosphere.

On time scales of years to millennia, variation in sea ice cover produces perhaps the most drastic changes that occur in the surface properties of a given area, particularly in the Southern Hemisphere. The next section attempts to identify the problem in the general context of the second GARP objective, the development of a theory of climate.

2. Objectives

Those aspects of POLEX which relate to the circulation of the global fluid system lie clearly within the accepted scientific and technological rationale of GARP and need not be elaborated in this report. What concerns us here is the stated POLEX aim to study, in greater physical and regional detail, the role of sea ice in affecting these global fluid systems.

It has been speculated that world climate and ice distribution have more than one quasi-steady state. Donn and Shaw (1966) and Budyko (1972) argue, along different lines, that an ice-free Arctic Ocean would remain free of ice once the condition had been established by, say, a climatic anomaly. The only global model calculations which have been performed assuming an ice-free Arctic Ocean [at the RAND Corporation (Fletcher *et al.*, 1971; Warshaw and Rapp,

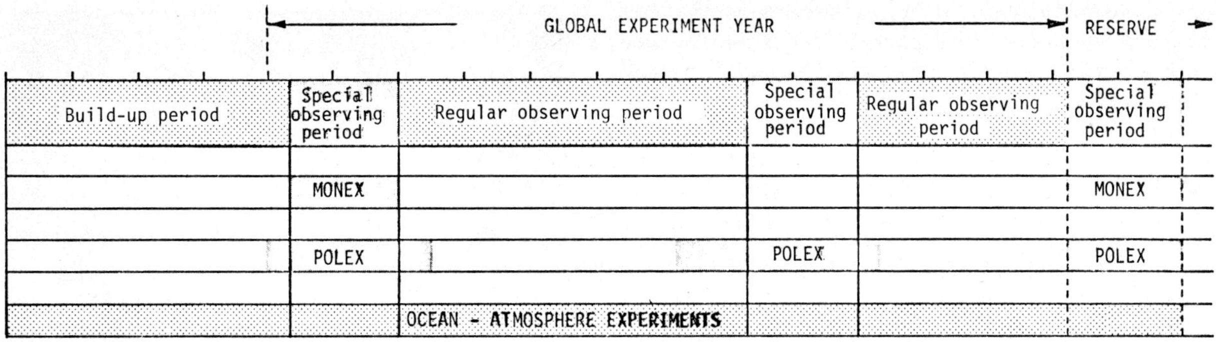

FIG. 1. Preliminary time schedule for the First GARP Global Experiment (from GARP Joint Organizing Committee, 1973).

1973)] yielded statistically significant differences between the ice-in and ice-out conditions at high latitudes; but during the 60-day time span of this numerical experiment, there was no discernible effect on the hemispheric circulation patterns.

Neither in recorded history nor in the interpretation of sedimentary records is there undisputed evidence that the Arctic Ocean was ever free of ice during the past 10^5 years. On the other hand, there is considerable evidence that the boundaries of drift ice have shifted in both hemispheres. The cause and effect of such variations in relation to atmosphere and ocean circulation patterns is not quantitatively understood.

Numerous studies during the past decades have suggested that statistical relationships exist between ice extent and circulation pattern over the North Atlantic (e.g., Brennecke, 1904; Strübing, 1967) and that fluctuations of the ice boundary in the North Atlantic are associated with fluctuations of the general circulation of the atmosphere (e.g., Scherhag, 1936). More recently it has been shown that temperature anomalies at the surface of the subtropical Pacific Ocean can cause anomalous conditions in the North Atlantic (Namias, 1972; Bjerknes, 1969). To understand and predict these complex interactive phenomena, the behavior of the ice itself must be understood.

There is also an immediate and practical reason to study these phenomena. Sea ice is at present a severe obstacle to all marine operations. It poses many specific problems to transportation, resource development, and environmental protection. Resource development in the northern regions, as exemplified in the "technology forecast" (Arctic Institute of North America, 1973) summarizing the opinions of experts in the field (Fig. 2), needs a broad base of scientific environmental knowledge to serve the planning of human activities in the high latitudes.

3. Questions

In reaching, through POLEX, an understanding of the physical processes in the atmosphere and at the boundary, the scientific plan should address itself to three broad questions:

What is the evidence for variations of the outer sea ice boundaries?

The answer to this question should be pursued along three lines.

1. It will be necessary to compile and make accessible the great wealth of historical data (e.g., in Fletcher, 1969) at a few central depositories. These data are now widely scattered and only partially accessible.

Ice records go back a thousand years to the first Icelandic accounts (Bergthórsson, 1969) and include such sporadic inferential information as that connected with the Norse colony in Greenland from the 10th to the 15th century. In modern times, various government services have maintained ice records, notably in the Soviet Union, Canada, Denmark, Norway, Great Britain, the United States, Iceland, and Japan. A considerable effort will be needed to compile these data and transform them to a form admitting of objective analysis. The primary emphasis here should be on seasonal and annual variations and trends during the past century.

Ice charts and surveys such as those regularly published by the British Meteorological Office usually define the ice edge by a percentage area of ice coverage. Better definitions should be found which convey some information about the physical conditions of the ice edge, such as its ability to transmit internal stresses.

2. Arrangements should be made for well-considered, uniform, and uninterrupted evaluation of the satellite images of the polar regions that are currently being acquired. The most useful types of images should be processed and stored as part of an overall polar record.

3. Every encouragement and support should be given to the efforts by several investigators under the CLIMAP program to unravel the paleoclimatic record. Fig. 3 is an example of this work, by Ruddiman and McIntyre (1973). They identify "polar water" by the presence of certain cold-water species in the faunal

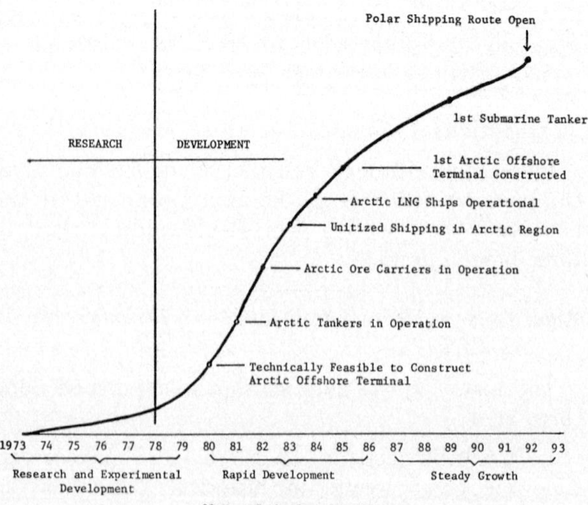

Fig. 2. Projection of marine activities in Arctic waters (from AINA, 1973).

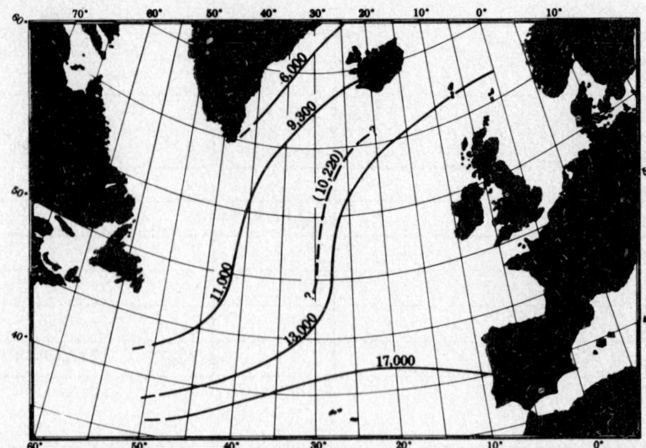

Fig. 3. Map of retreat positions of "polar water" in the North Atlantic from 17,000 to 6000 years B.P. (from Ruddiman and McIntyre, 1973).

sedimentary record. The isolines shown in Fig. 3 delineate water masses with a winter temperature no higher than 0.5 C. This does not imply a record of sea ice retreat after the peak of the Wisconsin Ice Age, but it stands to reason that the range of sea ice in the North Atlantic has undergone variations comparable to those shown for "polar water."

What are the processes controlling the position of the outer sea margin?

As an intermediate step, it is useful to treat the physical processes at the edge of the ice as phenomena in which air, ice, and water interact only locally while the large-scale advective effects are external. This step will include suitable formulations of the state of stress and the thickness distribution in the ice, ice compactness and heat balance, and the small-scale modification of the boundary layers in air and water near the ice edge. It will also include the displacement of that edge as a result of freezing/thawing, and drift caused by water and air stresses.

Of particular interest will be an assessment of the relative importance of thermodynamic and dynamic effects. Among the dynamic effects, a further distinction may be made between those originating from air and water drag at the ice edge and those transmitted from within the interior of the ice sheet.

Physical processes at solid (land) boundaries also fall into this category. The difference between a confined (Arctic) and an unconfined (Antarctic) ice sheet should be given special attention.

What are the feedback mechanisms coupling sea ice with the circulations in the atmosphere and the ocean?

Although it has not been convincingly demonstrated that sea ice variations of the magnitude experienced in recorded history have a feedback effect on large-scale circulation systems, it is difficult to image that the expanses of sea ice that existed during the Wisconsin glaciation did not profoundly alter the radiation balance of the earth and hence its climate. Perhaps the question of ice feedback is primarily one of scale and possible instabilities or self-enhancing effects.

The general question of the interaction between water, ice, and air on a large scale can be solved only by a global, or at least a hemispheric, model which includes realistic sub-models and parameters describing the ice.

4. Approach

Theory

Sea ice research during the past century has encompassed a wide range of geophysical subjects, but stages which emphasize certain topics can be distinguished.

The first stage, naturally, was characterized by geographical discovery and accumulation of some fundamental meteorological and oceanographic facts and the first data on the kinematics of sea ice. Once it had been proved (Soviet North Pole-1) that research camps could be established safely on drifting ice in the Arctic Ocean, the emphasis, in the second stage, shifted to thermodynamic studies. In the third and present stage we are attempting to elucidate the dynamics of sea ice in the interior of large ice sheets. The fourth stage will concentrate on the boundaries of these ice sheets, both where they border on land and where the ice ends at a free boundary in the open ocean.

The Arctic Ice Dynamics Joint Experiment (AIDJEX) is directed primarily at solving the problem of ice dynamics without regard to ice boundaries in the horizontal dimension. The solution of the whole problem, however, will require suitable methods to model the behavior of the boundaries as well. We suggest that this should be identified as one of the most important steps toward meeting POLEX objectives. It will also be necessary to extend the model calculations of the relatively small (800 km diameter) AIDJEX station array to cover the whole central Arctic Basin. As will be shown below, these requirements follow a sequence which is logical in itself and which fits easily into other international projects now under way.

SHEAR ZONE (SOLID BOUNDARY)

In the coastal waters of northern Alaska, Siberia, and northern Europe, the ice frequently vanishes during the summer so that a temporary free boundary exists in these areas. However, even in winter occasional extensive leads form that decouple the immovable nearshore ice from the drifting pack. Between northern Greenland and Prince Patrick Island, the ice almost always abuts the coast, sometimes under great onshore pressure. In addition, there are five major groups of

islands located in the Arctic Basin, whose role in large-scale ice dynamics cannot be adequately represented in the models.

The problem of modeling the behavior of the ice in a zone adjacent to the coast has been encountered by several investigators. No-slip, or free-drift, conditions (and the absence of any velocity across the coast) are applicable during certain parts of the year and in certain regions, but a generally useful formulation describing the mechanical properties of the ice in the zone where it is in contact with land has not been given.

The theoretical concepts developed under AIDJEX must be extended to those regions. What few data are available on the movement of nearshore ice should be analyzed and used to design an appropriate field experiment following the main AIDJEX effort in 1975–1976.

ARCTIC BASIN MODEL

Since publication of the AIDJEX Scientific Plan (Maykut *et al.*, 1972) the area covered by the experimental array has had to be reduced to about one-fourth of the Beaufort Sea. Manned stations and buoys will be far enough from shore that boundary effects should be negligible. Model calculations based on data to be obtained in 1975–1976 are expected to provide thickness distributions and large-scale strain of the ice.

The original AIDJEX plan called for a network of buoys covering the entire central Arctic Basin (Fig. 4). A network of that extent is now being proposed under POLEX-GARP during the First GARP Global Experiment.

It seems logical to extend modeling work of AIDJEX to incorporate the data obtained during FGGE and to extend calculations and forecasts to the entire basin. Since it is improbable that realistic models of the outer ice boundaries will be available before FGGE, these calculations should concentrate on interior solutions.

Depending on the outcome of the AIDJEX model calculations, both improvements and adjustments of the computational schemes will be made to allow for the larger matrix.

FREE BOUNDARY MODEL

The greatest effort in developing theory under POLEX should be applied to modeling the free ice boundary. It is perhaps useful to recall here that the central problem of AIDJEX is the difficult task of modeling a geophysical material whose properties and behavior are essentially unknown. The free-boundary problem of POLEX, in contrast, is more complex but less difficult. The position of the edge is dominated by many individual processes, all relatively well known.

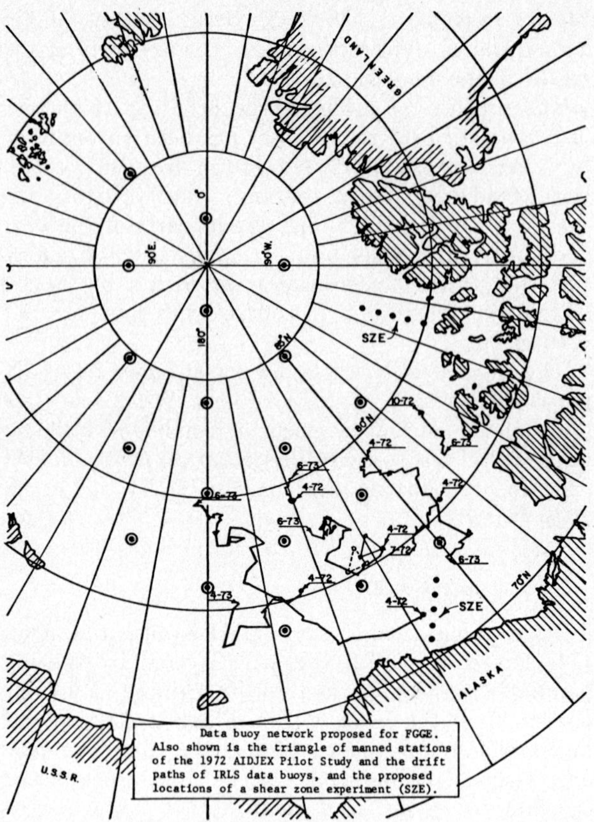

FIG. 4. Data buoy network proposed for FGGE. Also shown is the triangle of manned stations of the 1972 AIDJEX Pilot Study and the drift paths of IRLS data buoys, and the proposed locations of a shear zone experiment (SZE).

The difficulty here lies more in the complexity of their interactions than in a basic understanding.

It is proposed that a model of the kind sketched in Fig. 5 be developed under the auspices of POLEX. The box at the left of the figure contains essentially a formulation of ice drift without internal stress, at least initially. The ice velocity thus computed, together

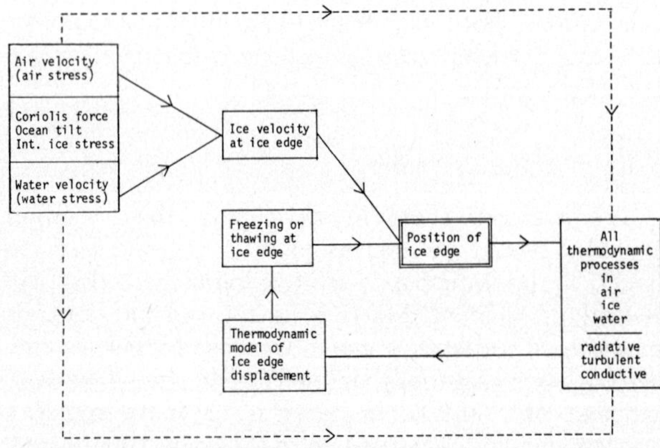

FIG. 5. Proposed structure of a free ice boundary model.

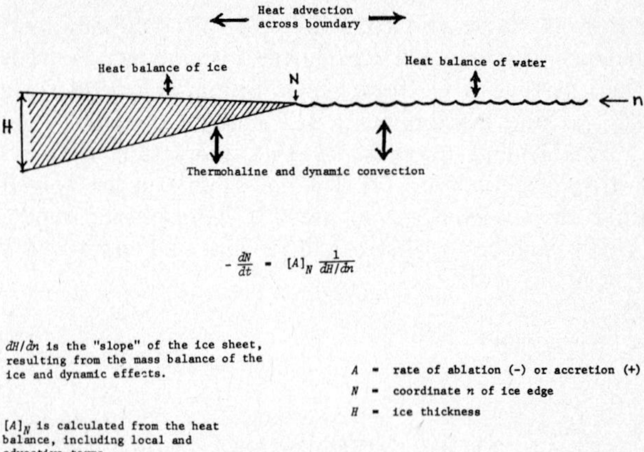

$$-\frac{dN}{dt} = [A]_N \frac{1}{dH/dn}$$

dH/dn is the "slope" of the ice sheet, resulting from the mass balance of the ice and dynamic effects.

$[A]_N$ is calculated from the heat balance, including local and advective terms.

A = rate of ablation (−) or accretion (+)

N = coordinate n of ice edge

H = ice thickness

FIG. 6. Processes affecting the position of a free ice boundary.

with freezing or thawing at the ice edge, determines its position. However, the ice position itself causes a complex feedback into the freeze/thaw condition. The box at the right contains all thermodynamic processes, including heat exchange between ice/air and ice/water. It is likely that there are also effects reaching higher into the troposphere which lead to the formations of the persistent summer stratus clouds typical of the ice-covered oceans in both the Arctic and the Antarctic. It has been speculated that these clouds are initiated by advective processes at the ice boundaries, while their further growth in thickness is enhanced by radiative cooling from the upper cloud surface. A theoretically study of this problem has been started by G. Hermann (personal communication).

A possible way to model the ice edge is shown in Fig. 6. At the outer boundaries of the pack there is often a gradual transition between open water and ice of low concentration. The concept of an ice wedge as shown in Fig. 6 may be of only limited usefulness.

The elements of this comprehensive ice boundary model should first be assembled without regard to available data or the chance to actually perform the necessary calculations. Next, all the data available and needed in the model should be assembled and the feasibility of performing actual calculations should be evaluated. After that, it should be possible to take two further steps: (1) decide which parts of the comprehensive model must be simplified in order to operate it, and (2) identify major gaps in the data upon which the plan for a major POLEX field experiment will be based.

One of the most informative experiments to be performed with an ice-edge model of any degree of sophistication is calculations of the annual cycle of ice coverage. Although not well documented, annual changes of the ice cover are large, and crude monthly means of the forcing function may suffice to produce results suitable for evaluating the efficacy of the model.

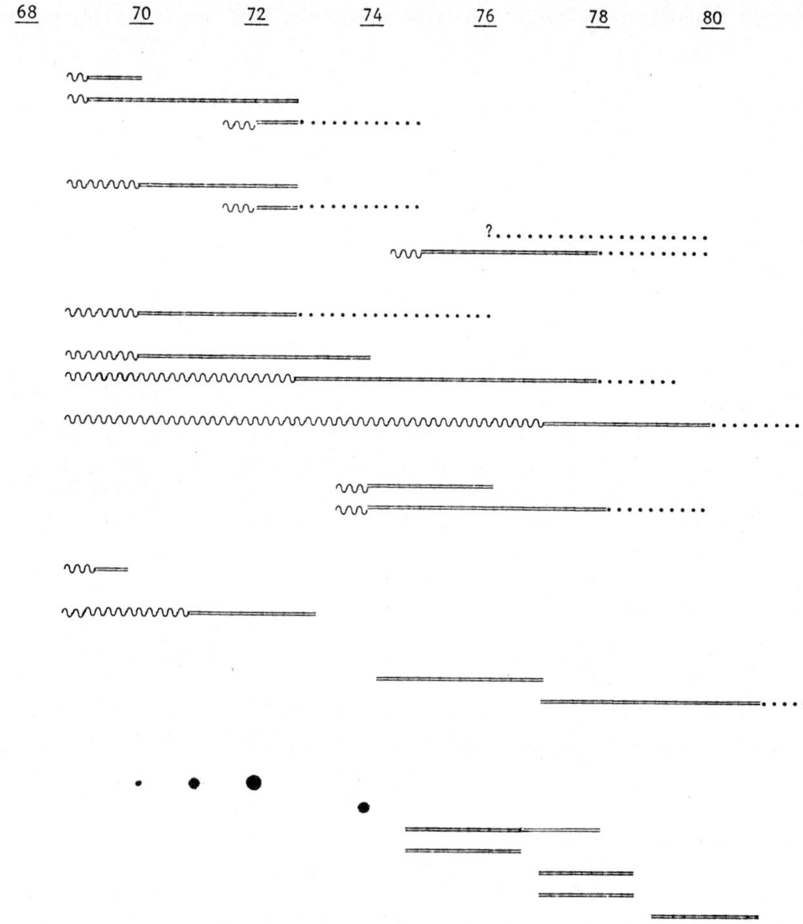

FIG. 7. Summary of current and proposed activities of AIDJEX and POLEX.

Experiments

REMOTE SENSING IMAGE ANALYSIS

In recent years, many papers have been published on remote sensing of sea ice using visual and infrared light and passive and active microwave images. These papers only demonstrate capability; no significant effort has been made to use remote sensing images to interpret the information they contain. Two-dimensional images are notoriously cumbersome to process, and the merging of their information content with other data (such as synoptic weather charts and other satellite-sensed images) would require that the data to be extracted be clearly defined and serve a specific scientific analysis.

An increased effort should be made to put past and future remote sensing data to optimal use, not only to document the existence of sea ice but also, in conjunction with other data, to analyze its dynamic behavior.

ARCTIC OCEAN HEAT BALANCE

The heat balance of the Arctic Ocean lends itself to certain experiments that need not necessarily occur simultaneously with other experiments in the atmosphere. One of the main questions concerns the magnitude and variability of the advective heat and salt exchange between the Arctic Ocean and other oceans. Suitable experiments should be planned, emphasizing the use of moored buoys (current, temperature, salinity), satellite images (ice export), and occasional detailed surveys by oceanographic research vessels.

SHEAR ZONE EXPERIMENT

This experiment, originally proposed as part of the main AIDJEX effort in 1975–1976, had to be postponed. We recommend that this experiment be carried out during FGGE (1977). At that time, the technical and scientific experience gained in AIDJEX can be brough to bear on the POLEX design, and data buoys are expected to be operating in the Arctic Basin (see below). The use of remote sensing images in analyzing the behavior of the ice in the shear zone should be given special attention. At present it appears most likely that the shear zone experiment will involve a combination of airborne or satellite-borne imaging devices, data buoys deployed in the ice, and radar targets.

FGGE DATA BUOY NETWORK

It is recommended that during FGGE (1977) a network of data buoys be deployed, as shown in Fig. 4, with a spacing of about 400 km. These buoys will be position-located by satellite to an accuracy of about 5 km. They will telemeter surface pressure, temperature, and possibly a few other parameters.

FREE BOUNDARY EXPERIMENT

Based on the outcome of the model development outlined above a free ice-boundary experiment should be planned for 1979–1980. Extrapolating the rapid development of satellite and unmanned buoy technology of the past ten years, such an experiment might well consist primarily of the deployment of automatic devices, possibly augmented by observations from aircraft or other airborne platforms.

5. Summary

Fig. 7 is an attempt to summarize the development of crucial scientific concepts (first four items), previous and planned comprehensive model calculations, and field experiments. *Undulating lines* indicate previous activities, many of them reaching well into the past. *Double lines* indicate activities presently under way, firmly planned as part of AIDJEX, or proposed for POLEX. *Dotted lines* indicate possible future activities.

REFERENCES

Arctic Institute of North America, 1973: *Arctic Marine Commerce: Airlie House Workshop, Warrenton, Virginia, February 26–28, 1973*. Washington, D. C., Arctic Institute of North America.

Bergthórsson, Páll, 1969: An estimate of drift ice and temperature in Iceland in 1000 years. *Jökull 19 Ár*, 94–101.

Bjerknes, J., 1969: Atmospheric teleconnections from the equatorial Pacific. *Monthly Weather Review*, 97(3), 163–172.

Borisenkov, E. P., and A. F. Treshnikov, 1971: The Polar experiment. (Translated by S. M. Olenicoff.) *AIDJEX Bulletin No. 11*, 1–10. Division of Marine Resources, University of Washington.

Brennecke, Wilhelm, 1904: Beziehungen zwischen der Luftdruckverteilung und den Eisverhältnissen des Ostgrönländischen Meeres. *Annalen der Hydrographie und Maritimen Meteorologie*, 32(II), 49–62.

Budyko, M. I., 1972: The future climate. $E \oplus S$, *Transactions, American Geophysical Union*, 53(10), 868–874.

Donn, W. L., and D. M. Shaw, 1966: The stability of an ice-free Arctic Ocean. *Journal of Geophysical Research*, 71(4), 1087–1095.

Fletcher, J. O., 1969: Ice extent on the Southern Ocean and its relation to world climate. RAND Memorandum RM-5793-NSF. Prepared for the National Science Foundation by the RAND Corporation, Santa Monica, California.

Fletcher, J. O., Y. Mintz, A. Arakawa and T. Fox, 1971: Numerical simulation of the influence of arctic sea ice on climate. In *Energy Fluxes Over Polar Surfaces*, Proceedings of the IAMAP/IAPSO/SCAR/WMO Symposium, Moscow, 3–5 August 1971. World Meteorological Organization Technical Note No. 129, 181–218.

GARP Joint Organizing Committee, 1973: *The First GARP Global Experiment—Objectives and Plans*. GARP Publications Series, No. 11, 9–50. International Council of Scientific Unions, World Meteorological Organization.

Maykut, G. A., A. S. Thorndike and N. Untersteiner, 1972: AIDJEX scientific plan. *AIDJEX Bulletin No. 15*. Division of Marine Resources, University of Washington.

Namias, Jerome, 1972: Large-scale and long-term fluctuations in some atmospheric and oceanic variables. In *Nobel Symposium 20*. Stockholm: Almqvist and Wiksell, 27–48.

NAS, 1974: U. S. contribution to the Polar Experiment (POLEX) Part 1, POLEX-GARP (North). National Academy of Sciences, Washington, D. C., 119 pp.

Ruddiman, W. F., and A. McIntyre, 1973: Time-transgressive deglacial retreat of polar waters from the North Atlantic. *Quaternary Research*, 3(1), 117–130.

Scherhag, R., 1936: Eine bemerkenswerte Klimaänderung über Nordeuropa. *Annalen der Hydrographie und Maritimen Meteorologie*, 64, 96–100.

Strubing, Klaus, 1967: Über Zusammenhänge zwischen der Eisführung des Ostgrönlandstroms und der atmosphärischen Zirkulation über dem Nordpolarmeer. *Deutsche Hydrographische Zeitschrift*, 20(6), 257–265.

Warshaw, M., and R. R. Rapp, 1973: An experiment on the sensitivity of a global circulation model. *Journal of Applied Meteorology*, 12, 43–49.